Teacher Wraparound Edition

GLENCOE

Writer's Choice

Grammar and Composition
Grade 7

 **Glencoe**

New York, New York   Columbus, Ohio   Chicago, Illinois   Peoria, Illinois   Woodland Hills, California

ACKNOWLEDGMENTS

Grateful acknowledgment is given authors, publishers, photographers, museums, and agents for permission to reprint the following copyrighted material. Every effort has been made to determine copyright owners. In case of any omissions, the Publisher will be pleased to make suitable acknowledgments in future editions.

Acknowledgments continued on page 846.

 The **Facing the Blank Page** feature in this book was prepared in collaboration with the writers and editors of *TIME*.

6+1 Trait® is a registered trademark of Northwest Regional Educational Laboratory, which does not endorse this product.

 **Glencoe McGraw-Hill**

The McGraw·Hill Companies

Copyright © 2005 by The McGraw-Hill Companies, Inc. All rights reserved. Except as permitted under the United States Copyright Act of 1976, no part of this publication may be reproduced or distributed in any form or means, or stored in a database or retrieval system, without the prior written permission of the publisher.

PRINTED IN THE UNITED STATES OF AMERICA

Send all inquiries to:
GLENCOE/MCGRAW-HILL
8787 Orion Place
Columbus, OH 43240-4027

ISBN 0-07-829815-6
(Student Edition)
ISBN 0-07-829808-3
(Teacher Wraparound Edition)

2 3 4 5 6 7 8 9 10   071/043 09 08 07 06 05

CONTENTS

Teacher Wraparound Edition

Welcome to *Writer's Choice*

Congratulations! By opening this book, you've taken an important step toward helping your students become **better writers and communicators**. The pages that follow help you see at a glance the features of the *Writer's Choice* Student Edition, the Teacher Wraparound Edition, and the program's additional resources.

The Benefits of *Writer's Choice*

- An integrated approach to language arts
- Concise lessons that target key skills
- Diverse contexts and frequent writing opportunities
- Real-world writing examples from both students and published authors
- Systematic teaching and practice of grammar concepts

Quick Reference

- An easy-to-use Writing and Research Handbook
- A teacher edition with point-of-use convenience and built-in flexibility
- Program resources that expand your teaching options

Plus, Improved Test Performance

The **Taking Tests** unit of *Writer's Choice* gives students the strategies and the practice they need to become better test-takers. Working through the **Standardized Test Practice** pages will help students become comfortable with the format and the types of items they will typically face on standardized tests.

Targeted Writing Instruction, Modeling, and Practice

In **Part 1: Composition**, students will learn how to apply the writing process to various modes of writing. Grammar and other language arts skills are integrated into each lesson.

Real Writers at Work

A four-page **Writing in the Real World** case study launches each composition unit. This **behind-the-scenes glimpse of the writing process** offers students a model of good writing practices.

> **Targeted visuals** provide access to writing skills for students who learn best visually.

> **Real-life examples** offer models for students and answers to the difficult question "When am I ever going to use this?"

> The **writing process,** as practiced by professional writers, presents a clear map for working through a piece of writing.

> Thoughtful **analysis questions** prompt readers to question and think about what makes good writing.

> **Grammar Links** provide practice on a grammar, usage, or mechanics issue related to the writing examples.

Writing in the Real World

Visitors to the Monterey Bay Aquarium in California discover a fascinating world of underwater creatures. Most of the visitors, however, would understand little of what they were seeing without certain important information. That's where Judy Rand's job comes in. Rand writes information labels for the aquarium's exhibits. Her expository writing educates visitors eager to learn the mysteries of marine life.

Wolf-eel
Anarrhichthys ocellatus
This night prowler leaves its den for dinner.
Hardly a wolf, not really an eel, this fierce-looking fish spends the day quietly in a cave, wriggling out at night to feed.

Writing in the Real World

Writing Exhibit Labels

Prewriting	Drafting	Revising/Editing
Watching the Animals/ Making Notes	Writing the Labels	Making Every Word Count

A Writer's Process

Prewriting
Observing, Learning, and Making Notes

Helping people see what's right in front of them is where Judy Rand's work begins. As master developer and senior editor at the Monterey Bay Aquarium, Rand writes the information labels that visitors read as they view an exhibit.

Before she can write the labels, Rand herself must become thoroughly acquainted with the marine creatures. She spends mals. She also talks to scientists from outside the aquarium, especially those who have worked directly with a particular animal. In addition, she reads field guides and scientific articles.

As she collects information, Rand fills in fact sheets about each animal's traits and habits. Afterwards, she writes each idea and fact on a separate index card. To organize the information, Rand scatters the cards on the floor. She explains, "I can shuffle my ideas around. I can set aside the ones that don't seem to fit and begin to find the ones that seem important."

During this process, Rand has to choose what information she will include on a card. She keeps the interests of her audience— the aquarium's visitors—firmly in mind. Rand explains, "The most

Writing in the Real World **197**

has to be about immediate and observable behavior. Visitors want to know about what they're seeing in the tank. Is this wolf-eel really an eel? What are those teeth for?"

> "When aquarium visitors are face to face with a wolf-eel, they want to know, 'Does this animal want to eat me?' You need to begin with your reader's immediate experience. Then you can interpret the scientific facts in a friendly and relevant way."
> —Judy Rand

Drafting
Writing the Labels

With index cards spread around the room and with reference books lying open nearby, Rand plunges in to write.

The final label will be one to two paragraphs long. But, Rand says, "I can try out an idea that has the wolf-eel's teeth right up front. Then I can try out an idea that has popular misconceptions about the animal up front."

She finally decides to focus on the wolf-eel's undeserved bad reputation. She explains, "Visitors' immediate impression of the wolf-eel is that it's fierce looking and a predator. I wanted them to understand the idea that being a predator isn't bad."

Rand uses simple language, even for complex ideas. She describes the wolf-eel as a night prowler, rather than as a nocturnal fish. As Rand notes, "We want our labels to sound as if someone is talking to you. *Nocturnal* is a lovely word, but people don't usually use words like *nocturnal* in conversation."

She also uses strong examples. After reading that "some divers say the wolf-eel can bite a broomstick in half," visitors can imagine how strong those jaws must be.

Revising/Editing
Making Every Word Count

After setting her draft aside for a day, Rand puts on her editor's hat. She reads each label aloud, listening for a friendly and conversational sound. Then she asks several people to read each label and repeat the information in their own words. "If they can't tell me what it's about, then I know I have problems."

Finally Rand sits down at her computer to check for style. She asks herself, "Is there any unfamiliar language? Have I made every word count?"

When she feels satisfied with the labels she has written, Rand gets approval from two department supervisors, as well as the aquarium's executive director. The exhibit labels are then readied for display in the aquarium.

Examining Writing in the Real World

Analyzing the Media Connection

Discuss these questions about the model on page 196.

1. What effect do you think the opening sentence has on visitors to the aquarium? How does Rand achieve this effect?
2. How does Rand get across the point that the wolf-eel is a nocturnal creature, without actually using the word *nocturnal*?
3. What information does Rand convey about the wolf-eel's eating habits?
4. What if Rand had used the verb *consume* in place of the word *chomp*? How would that word choice change the tone of the writing? In your opinion, which word is more effective?
5. Where does Rand use humor to call attention to the wolf-eel's bad reputation?

Analyzing a Writer's Process

Discuss these questions about Judy Rand's writing process.

1. What methods does Rand use to gather information for her exhibit labels?
2. How does Rand organize the facts and ideas she has gathered? How does your own method compare to hers?

3. Rand can't use all the information that she gathers. What helps her decide what information to include?
4. Does Rand use formal or informal language as she drafts her information labels? Why?
5. When editing, how does Rand make sure that the labels will be clear to her audience?

Grammar Link

Use commas to separate three or more items in a series.

Wolf-eels chomp on crabs, mussels, and urchins.

Use each set of words below as a series of items in a sentence. Use commas correctly.

1. bold, fierce, clever
2. furry, stout, clumsy
3. squirrels, mice, rats
4. lobsters, clams, shrimp
5. cats, dogs, goldfish
See Lesson 20.2, pages 591–592.

198 Unit 5 Expository Writing

Writing in the Real World **199**

T5

Focused Four-Page Lessons

You won't find long-winded writing about writing in *Writer's Choice*. Literature models, student models, and instructional visuals combine to **show rather than just tell.**

> **Illustrations, graphs, and charts** make information visual and easy to grasp. Also, fine art in many styles and from many cultures inspires writing and discussion.

> **Journal Writing** activities midway through each lesson prompt students to "write to learn."

> **Literature Models** supply students with models for good writing. Thoughtful callouts prompt students to analyze how published authors use the strategies being taught in the lesson.

> **Student models** illustrate how student writers put into practice the lessons being taught.

> **Writing Activities** provide prompts and rubrics related to the lesson. Grammar Links provide practice; other activities show alternative ways of working with the topic.

LESSON 4.3 Using Time Order in a Story

Which came first, the chicken or the egg?

Just as there is no right answer to this question, there is no one right way to tell a story. As a storyteller, you will want to narrate the events in an order that will make sense to your readers.

First, Think Time!

Time order—the order in which events occur from first to last—is a logical way to organize ideas in a story. Remembering the order in which events happen will help you plan your story and assist your readers in following the situation. Look at the illustrations at the top of the next page. They show a series of events arranged in time order.

164 Unit 4 Narrative Writing

Story Events in Time Order

Fox sees the fire. | Fox runs away from the fire. | Fox reaches a ravine.

This series of events is the basis for the paragraph below. Notice how the writer uses time order to tell the story and help her readers follow the action of a fox escaping a fire.

Student Model

Leaving my den in the morning, I felt an immense heat at my back. I turned around and there, before my eyes, was an enormous wall of fire and smoke! I bounded away from the fire and headed toward the safety of the ravine. The brush swept by my face. The fire kept gaining on me, threatening me. I tried to propel myself faster, but my tongue hung down and my energy began running out. Suddenly, the landscape sloped downwards, and the ravine came into view.

Jenny DeLong, Canyon Park Junior High School
Bothell, Washington

How does time order help the writer tell the story?

Journal Writing

Think about the past week, and choose something that happened to you—something about which you might like to write a story. As you think of the events that you will include in your story, list them. Then number the events in the order in which they actually occurred.

4.3 Using Time Order in a Story 165

Revising Tip

When you revise, be sure that story events follow a time order that is clear and understandable to the reader.

Use Transitions

Certain words and phrases, called **transitions,** can help readers keep track of the order of events in your writing. Some examples of transitions include *before, after, until then, next, first,* and *finally.*

Read the story below. Then reread it, paying attention to the highlighted words. What do these transitions add to the story?

Literature Model

When John Cowles and his wife and baby moved to Wisconsin in 1843, they built a one-room cabin to live in. All the cabin needed was a front door. That was due to arrive before the weather turned cold. Until then, they had hung a heavy quilt over the doorway.

John Cowles was a doctor. One night before supper, a messenger came for him. Someone was sick on a farm about twelve miles away. "I'll be home tonight or tomorrow morning," he told his wife. He quickly packed his things and rode off into the darkness.

His wife left a pot of beans simmering on the hearth in case he was hungry when he got home. Then she got into bed with her baby and went to sleep.

Sometime during the night, Mrs. Cowles awakened. She sensed that someone was in the cabin with her, probably her husband. But when she opened her eyes, she saw a bear in front of the fireplace. He was eating the beans, mouthful after mouthful.

Suddenly he stopped. He looked up and stared across the room at her. In the darkness, his eyes looked like burning coals. She wondered if he could see her. If the baby cried out, what would he do? If he attacked, what could she do?

The bear turned back to the beans. When he finished with them, he pushed the quilt aside and left.

Alvin Schwartz, "A Pot of Beans"

What does the transition phrase "until then" tell the reader?

The transition word "suddenly" also adds drama and suspense to the story.

166 Unit 4 Narrative Writing

4.3 Writing Activities

Write a Personal Narrative

Look in your journal at the entry for the activity on page 165. Using the events listed in your journal as a stimulus, write a one-page story.

PURPOSE To tell a personal story
AUDIENCE Your friends and family
LENGTH 1 page

WRITING RUBRICS To write an effective personal narrative, you should

• add details that develop plot, character, and setting
• use time order to develop the story
• use transitions to help your reader follow the action
• use consistent verb tenses

Viewing and Representing

SPEAKING WITH PICTURES Using your personal narrative as a guide, create a series of four or five drawings which tell the same story without words. Make sure the drawings follow the same order as the details in the narrative. Create some kind of exhibit guide by assembling the class's written narratives. Put the drawings on display and ask students to match the drawings with the written narratives.

Grammar Link

Make sure that your verbs do not shift unnecessarily from past to present tense.

Rewrite the following paragraph, avoiding tense shifts.

[1] The suspect sat squirming in his seat and does not meet my eyes. [2] "Tell me where you were," I say. [3] He hesitated, and in that instant I knew that he is trying to hide something. [4] I stare at him intently. [5] The color slowly drains from his face, and he finally looked up and met my eyes.
See Lesson 10.5, page 407.

Cross-Curricular Activity

SCIENCE Suppose that your science class has started a tutoring program for third-grade students. As part of the program, you have been asked to choose a science topic and write a story about it. For example, you might write a story to teach students how a plant grows.

Write a one-page story for younger students. Remember to use characters, plot, and setting to create your story. Be sure you use time order and transition words to relate events.

4.3 Using Time Order in a Story 167

Scaffolded Instruction of the Writing Process

For each mode of writing, the **Writing Process in Action** pages walk students through the recursive steps of prewriting, drafting, revising, editing, and publishing a piece of writing.

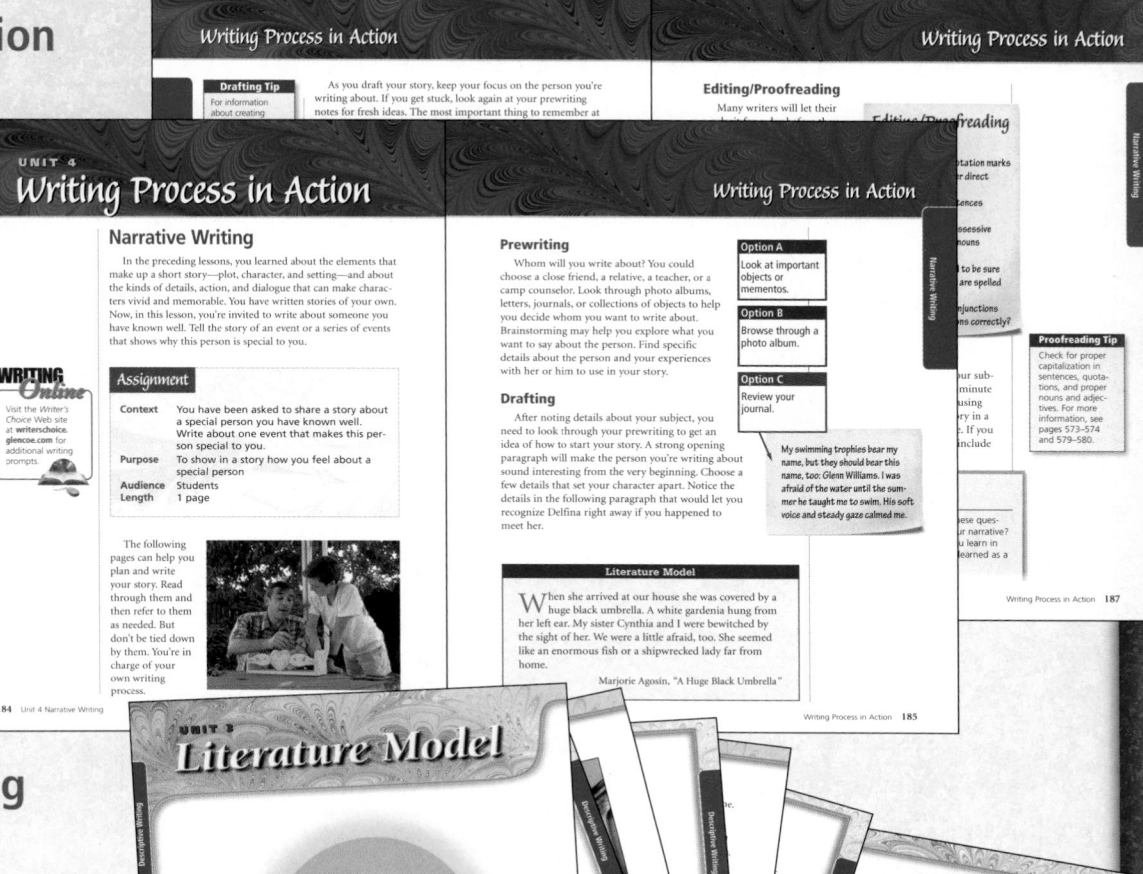

The Reading/Writing Connection

Literature Models by contemporary authors mirror the mode of writing taught in each unit. Discussion questions and a related writing activity follow each selection.

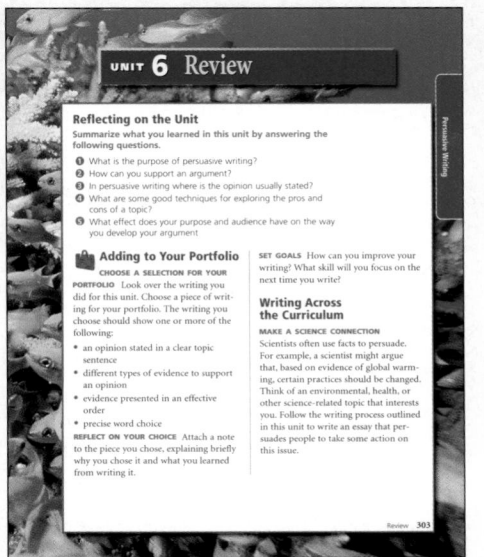

Authentic Assessment of Writing Skills

Unit Review questions, activities, and portfolio selections give you the opportunity to assess students' knowledge and skills.

Systematic Grammar Instruction with Extensive Practice

Based on a define-explain-model approach and strongly supported with extensive practice-and-apply exercises, **Part 2: Grammar, Usage, and Mechanics** provides the solid foundation your students need.

Short Targeted Lessons

Each Part 2 lesson focuses on a single grammar, usage, or mechanics concept with **clear, direct teaching** and exercises for practice.

> **Exercises** give students the chance to practice what they've learned.

> A **definition** or **rule** clearly states the concept being taught.

> **Examples,** often in graphic form, illustrate the concept.

> **Elaboration** further explains and refines the concept.

12.6 Adverbs

■ An **adverb** is a word that modifies, or describes, a verb, an adjective, or another adverb.

What Adverbs Modify

Verbs	The Inca worked **carefully** on their buildings.
Adverbs	The Inca left their ancient cities **quite** suddenly.
Adjectives	Machu Picchu is a **very** large ruin in Peru.

When modifying a verb, an adverb may describe *how* or *in what manner* the action is done. It may describe *when* or *how often* an action is done. Also, it may describe *where* or *in what direction* an action was done.

Ways Adverbs Modify Verbs

How?	Machu Picchu sits **silently** in the Andes.
When?	Many scientists **now** explore this city.
Where?	Scientists dig **there** for facts about the Inca.

Many adverbs are formed by adding *-ly* to adjectives. However, not all words that end in *-ly* are adverbs. The words *friendly, lively, kindly,* and *lonely* are usually adjectives. Similarly, not all adverbs end in *-ly.*

Adverbs not Ending in -ly

afterward	often	there	hard
sometimes	soon	everywhere	long
later	here	fast	straight

12.6 Adverbs **461**

Exercise 11   Identifying Adverbs

For each of the following sentences, write the adverb and then write the word it modifies.

1. Hiram Bingham searched diligently for the lost Incan cities.
2. Bingham and his aides looked everywhere in western South America.
3. They traveled slowly through thick jungles.
4. Slowly they crossed rushing rivers.
5. The explorers cautiously carried their own food and supplies.
6. Bingham and his searchers carefully climbed the steep mountainsides.
7. They carefully studied the legends.
8. The Urubamba River snaked below.
9. The lost city of Machu Picchu lay above.
10. Once many people came to the Incan city.
11. Now the Peruvian jungle growth covered Machu Picchu.
12. The mist lifted briefly over the walled city.
13. The city's emptiness affected them greatly.
14. They felt strongly the passage of centuries.
15. Bingham's group worked hard at their task of discovery.
16. The Inca's irrigation system carried water efficiently.
17. They constructed their houses solidly.
18. The Inca were apparently skilled in agriculture.
19. They were plentifully supplied with water.
20. The people worked skillfully with metals, pottery, and wool.

Exercise 12   Using Adverbs

Write an adverb to modify the underlined word in each sentence.

1. People <u>think</u> of television as a recent invention.
2. Experimental broadcasts <u>began</u> in 1928.
3. The quality of the broadcasts was not <u>good.</u>
4. Two <u>important</u> inventions came after 1930.
5. Philo T. Farnsworth <u>patented</u> a scanning cathode ray tube in 1930.
6. Kate Smith <u>sang</u> on one of the first scheduled broadcasts.
7. By the early 1940s, twenty-three TV stations were <u>operating.</u>
8. TV <u>grew</u> after the lifting of wartime restrictions.
9. By 1949 more than a million families <u>had bought</u> TV sets.
10. Ten years later the number <u>had multiplied</u> to 50 million.

462 Unit 12 Adjectives and Adverbs

Comprehensive Grammar Assessment

Grammar Reviews at the end of each unit allow you to assess students' learning in a comprehensive and meaningful way.

A **Literature Model** shows students how a published author handles concepts that have been covered in the unit.

Exercises assess students' understanding of the concepts taught in the unit.

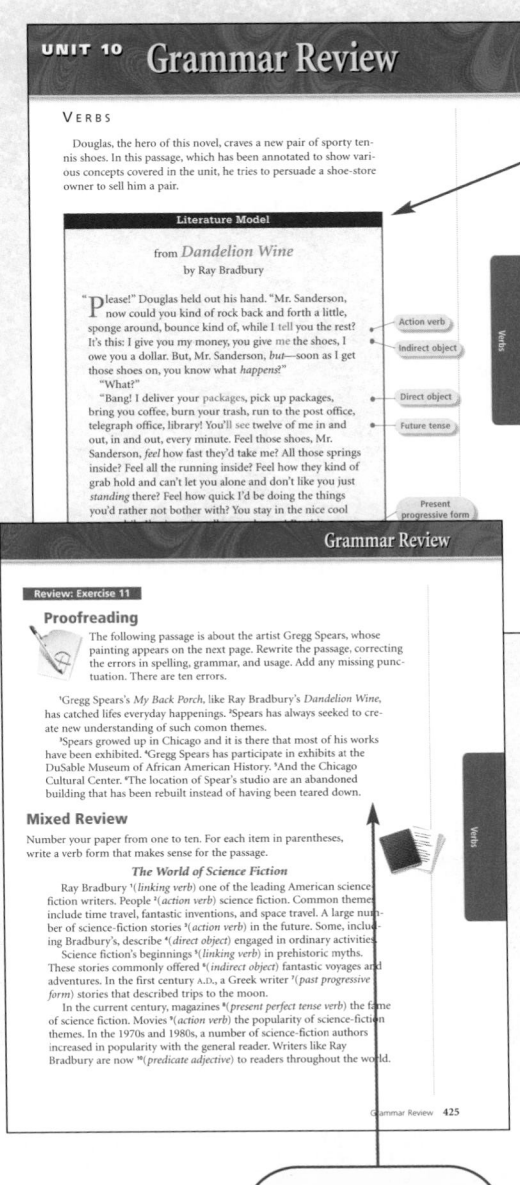

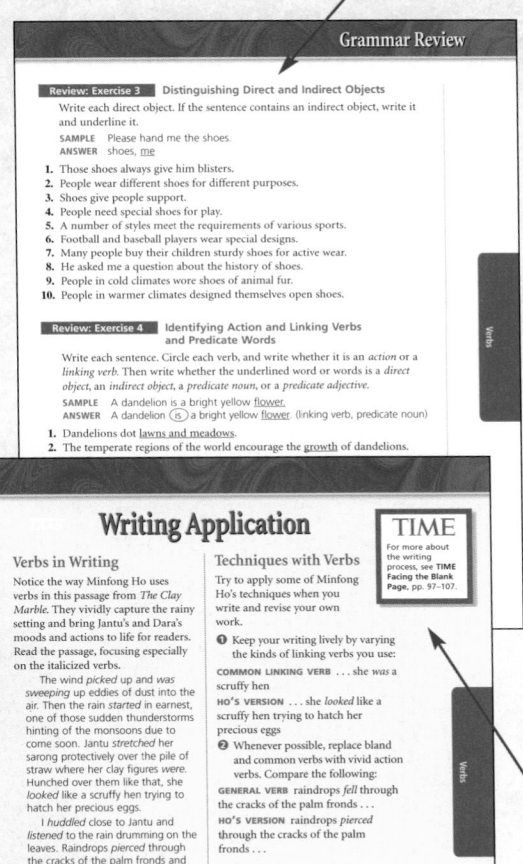

A **proofreading exercise** gives students the editing practice they need to become good writers.

The **Writing Application** helps students connect grammar, usage, and mechanics concepts with good writing and good literature.

A "Tool Kit" of Real-World Skills

Part 3: Resources and Skills provides instruction, examples, and practice in research, vocabulary, spelling, study skills, test-taking, listening and speaking, viewing and representing, and using electronic resources.

Clear Instruction

Easy-to-read text and graphics connect students' interests with what they need to know.

Helpful Examples

Examples, often in graphic form, illustrate and expand upon instruction.

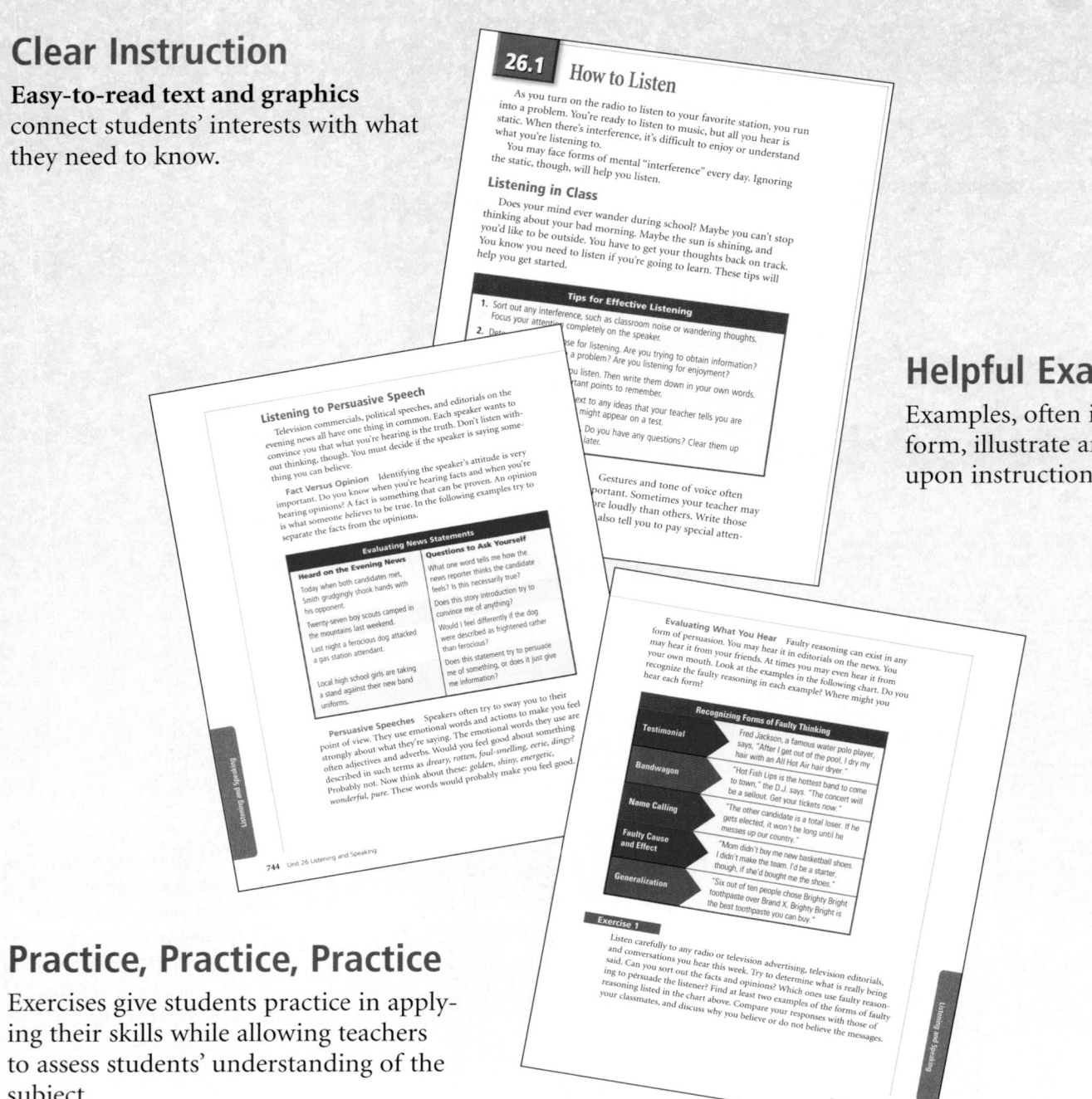

Practice, Practice, Practice

Exercises give students practice in applying their skills while allowing teachers to assess students' understanding of the subject.

Taking Standardized Tests

While the entire *Writer's Choice* program has been designed to help students gain the skills and knowledge they need to achieve on standardized tests, the **Taking Tests** unit in particular helps students prepare for these tests.

Effective Test Preparation

The unit begins with **proven test-taking strategies** and an explanation of the types of items and formats most commonly used in standardized tests.

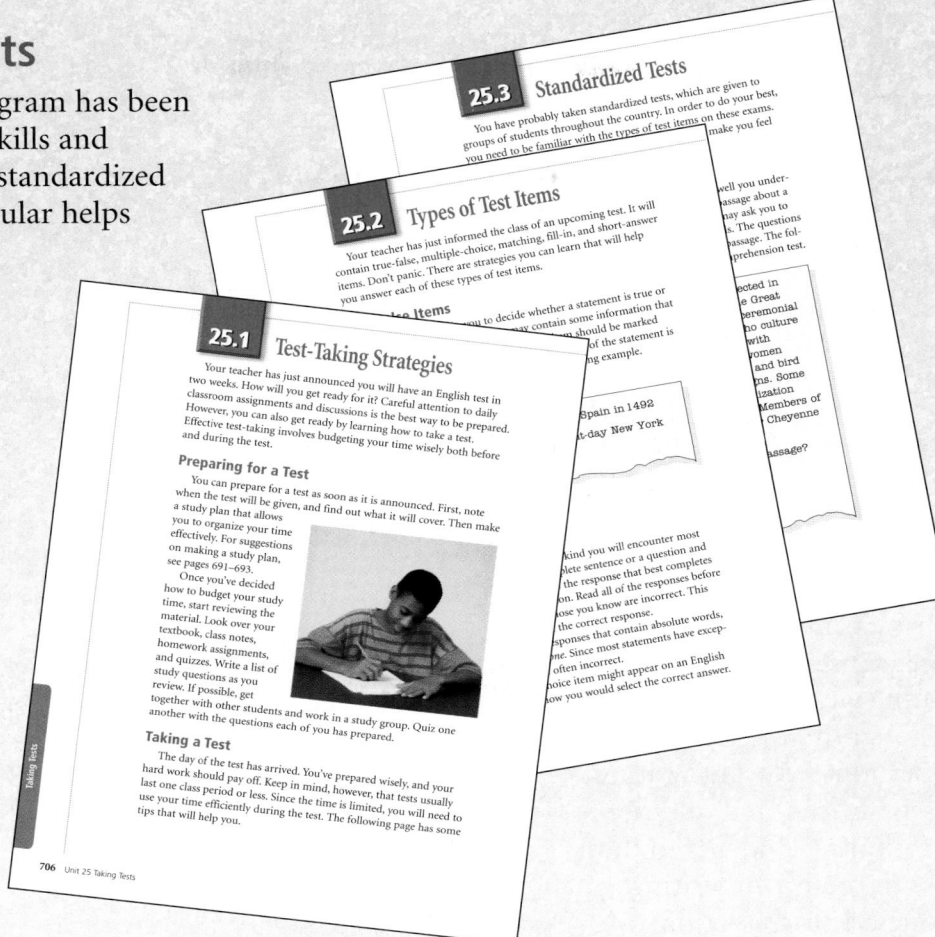

Extensive Test Practice

Exercises that mimic the format and content of standardized writing tests provide students with practice in answering items on sentence structure, usage, and mechanics.

Special Features: Enrichment and Remediation

Writer's Choice has many outstanding features to support and extend students' learning. From real-world advice to real-time remediation, these features **maximize students' potential.**

Writing Advice from the Pros

TIME Facing the Blank Page shows how professional writers and editors at **TIME magazine** practice each stage of the writing process. Thoughtful discussion questions, relevant writing assignments, and questions prompting students to think about their own writing conclude each section.

Fixes for Common Errors

Teachers see certain errors again and again in student writing. **Troubleshooter** offers solutions to the most common of these errors, including fragments, run-ons, and lack of subject-verb agreement.

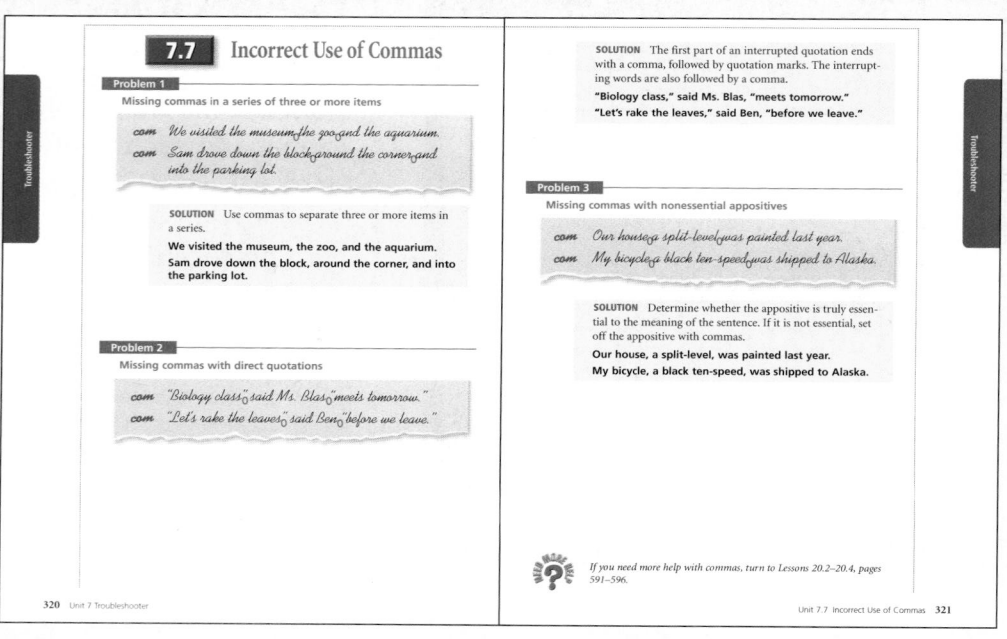

Writing for Work

Lessons on topics such as writing a business letter, conducting interviews, and creating multimedia presentations introduce students to the specialized skills of **Business and Technical Writing.**

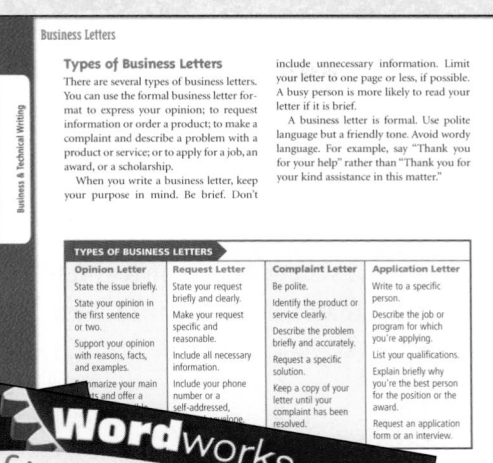

Fun Facts About Language

Wordworks takes a humorous look at how we use and misuse our language. Unique one-page lessons give students an enjoyable way to study words and language development.

Easy-to-Reference Writing Guide

The **Writing and Research Handbook** provides tips for writing good sentences, paragraphs, and compositions; instruction on using the 6+1 Trait® model; and tools to help students conduct and document research.

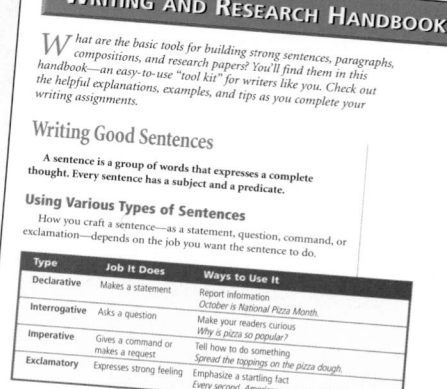

A Teacher Wraparound Edition with Point-of-Use Convenience

The **Teacher Wraparound Edition** accommodates a diversity of teachers and learners with an easy-to-use format. Each lesson plan has four parts: Focus, Teach, Assess, and Close. The margins offer additional information and strategies to help you meet the varied needs of your students.

> **Teach** provides varied strategies for customizing the lesson and addressing the needs of basic, average, and advanced learners.

> **Focus** sets clear objectives for learning writing, thinking, listening, and speaking skills. It also provides a daily language activity and motivating activity to jump-start your lesson.

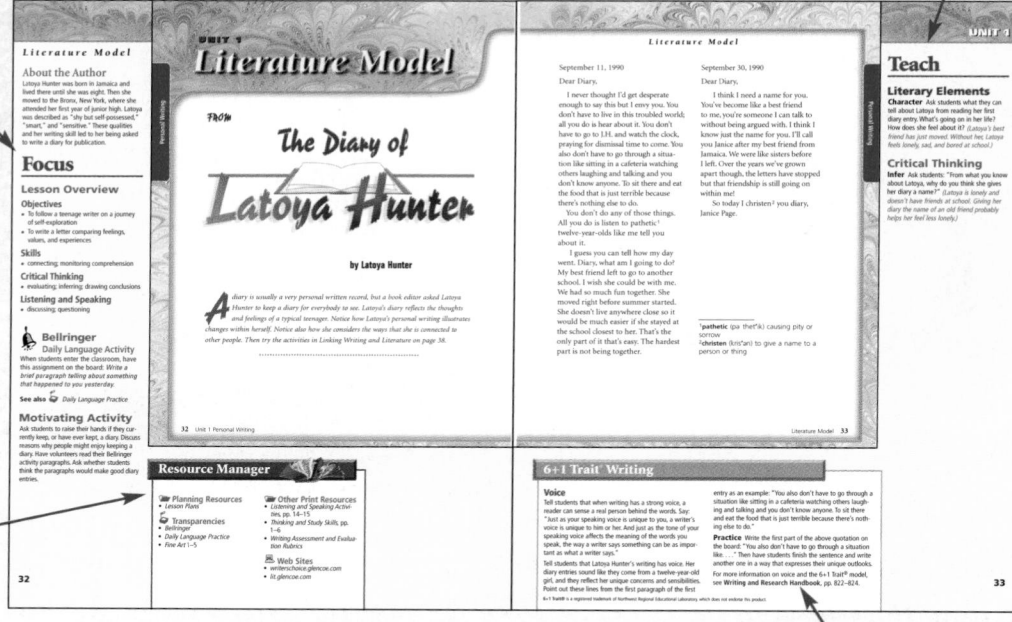

> The **Resource Manager** lists ancillaries that extend and support the lesson.

> **6+1 Trait® Writing** notes help students identify and practice the seven traits of effective writing: ideas, organization, voice, word choice, sentence fluency, conventions, and presentation.

A **Two-Minute Skill Drill** provides quick skill practice and challenges students to actively apply lesson concepts.

Bottom-channel notes support critical thinking, cooperative learning, cultural diversity, cross-curricular connections, fine art, technology, and civic literacy. They provide help to English language learners and less-proficient readers and offer enrichment and extension ideas for advanced students.

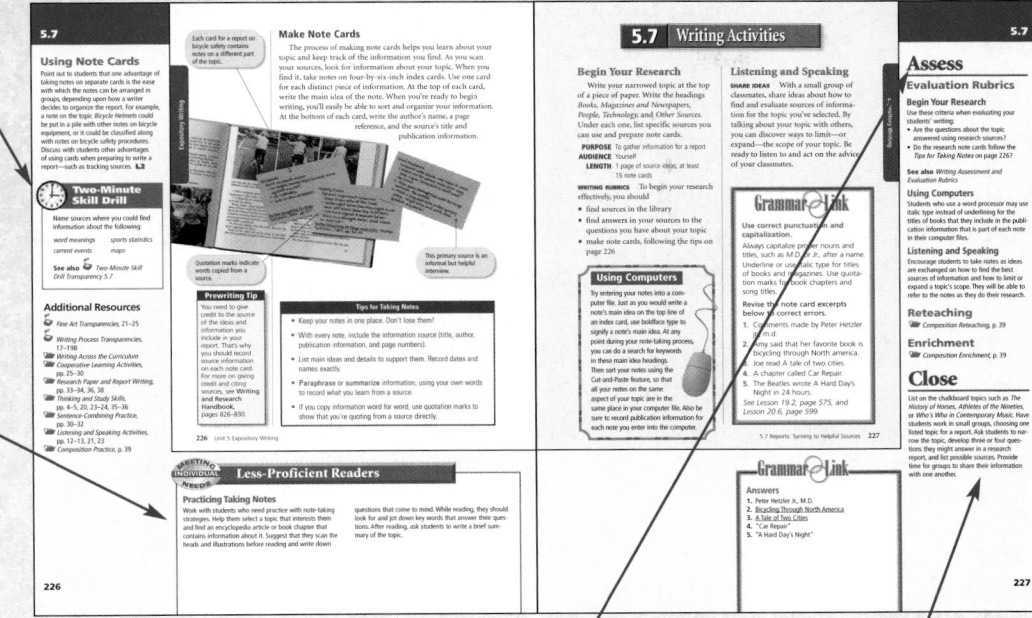

Assess presents Evaluation Rubrics to help you critique and assess student writing.

Close gives tips for reviewing, applying, and extending the lesson.

Answers to all grammar exercises are conveniently located in the margin, at the point of use.

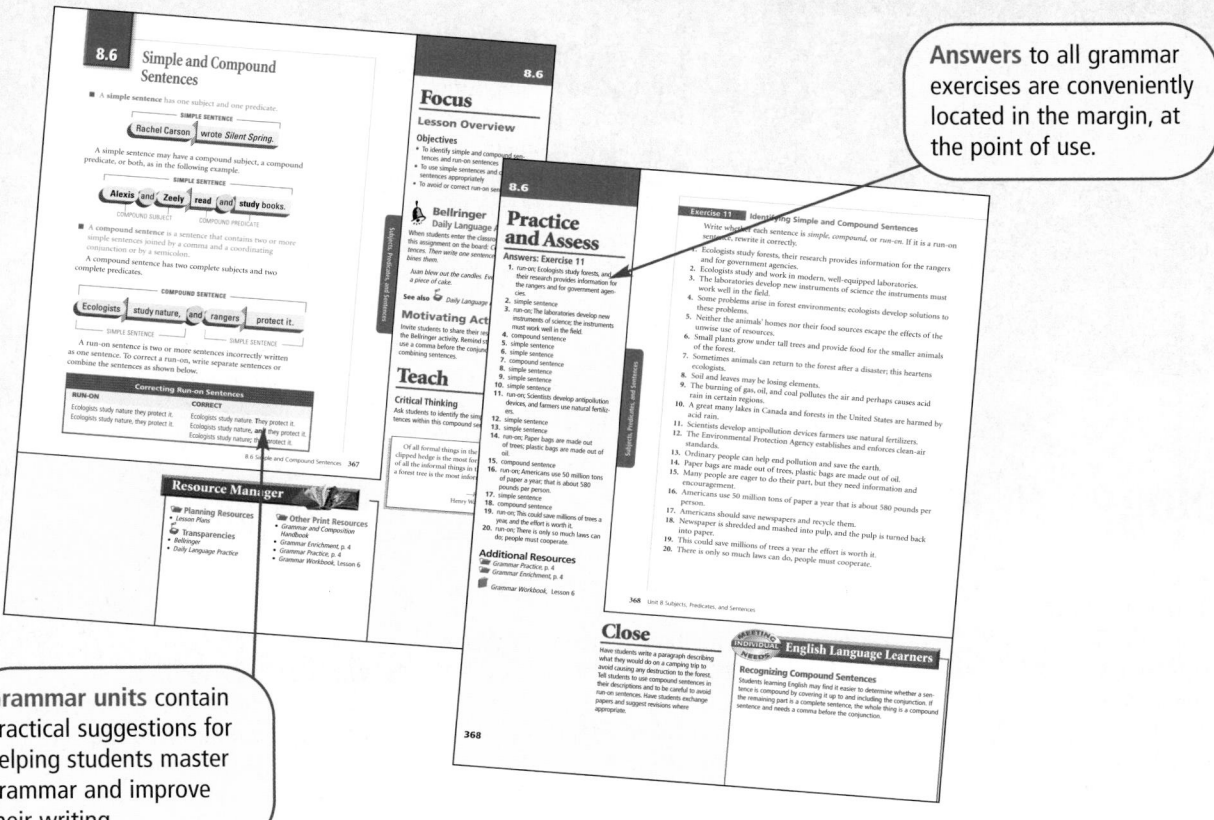

Grammar units contain practical suggestions for helping students master grammar and improve their writing.

Program Resources That Expand Your Teaching Options

Writer's Choice and its ancillary resources deliver **comprehensive, research-based language arts instruction.** Whatever your teaching style or students' learning needs may be, there are program resources that are right for you.

Timesaving Teacher Resources

All-in-One Teacher Support

- TeacherWorks CD-ROM
- Testmaker: ExamView Pro CD-ROM
- Presentation Plus! CD-ROM
- Lesson Plans (print version)
- Block Scheduling Guide
- Teaching Transparencies: Writing Process, Bellringer Activities, Daily Language, Fine Art, and Two-Minute Skill Drill

- Spanish Resources Binder
- Vocabulary Power Puzzlemaker software

Writing

For Basic, Average, and Advanced Learners

- Composition Reteaching, Composition Practice, and Composition Enrichment
- Research Paper and Report Writing
- Style and Documentation Sourcebook for Writers
- Business and Technical Writing Activities
- Sentence-Combining Practice
- Writing Across the Curriculum
- Writing in the Real World
- Revising with Style blackline masters

Technology

- StudentWorks CD-ROM
- Revising with Style CD-ROM
- Writer's Assistant CD-ROM
- Sentence Diagraming CD-ROM
- Interactive Grammar and Language Workbook CD-ROM
- Language Arts PASS CD-ROM

- TIME Facing the Blank Page video
- Mindjogger Videoquizzes
- Guide to Using the Internet and Other Electronic Resources
- TechConnect Online
- Writer's Choice Online Edition: **www.mhln.com**

- Writer's Choice Web site: **www.writerschoice.glencoe.com**
- Glencoe Literature Web site: **www.lit.glencoe.com**

Tests with Answer Keys and Rubrics

Assessment

- Tests with Answer Keys and Rubrics
- Taking Standardized Tests
- Writing Assessment and Evaluation Rubrics
- Testmaker: ExamView Pro CD-ROM
- Interactive Tutor: Self-Assessment CD-ROM
- ITBS Preparation and Practice Workbook
- SAT-9 Preparation and Practice Workbook
- TerraNova Preparation and Practice Workbook

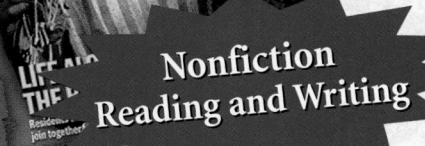

Integrated Language Arts

- inTIME magazine
- Humanities Across TIME
- Listening and Speaking Activities
- Viewing and Representing Activities
- Glencoe Literature Library
- Thinking and Study Skills
- Cooperative Learning Activities

Nonfiction Reading and Writing

Grammar

- Grammar Reteaching, Grammar Practice, and Grammar Enrichment
- Grammar and Language Workbook
- Grammar and Composition Handbook
- Grammar Practice Workbook
- Sentence Diagraming blackline masters

Differentiated Instruction

Grammar Reteaching

Grammar Practice Workbook
Teacher's Annotated Edition

Grammar Enrichment

Vocabulary and Spelling Strategies and Practice

Vocabulary and Spelling

- Vocabulary and Spelling Strategies and Practice
- Spelling Power
- Vocabulary Power

Dinah Zike's FOLDABLES™ for *Writer's Choice*

Only *Writer's Choice* gives you the power of FOLDABLES™! *Dinah Zike's FOLDABLES™ for* **Writer's Choice** shows students how to use three-dimensional interactive graphic organizers to **organize** information, **review** concepts, and **assess** their knowledge.

Integrating Writing, Grammar, and Other Language Skills

The **Weekly Planner** saves you time by suggesting one way to **organize** the lessons in *Writer's Choice* into a yearlong course of instruction. Research suggests that students learn best when the language arts are **integrated.** The Weekly Planner is color coded to show you how to meaningfully integrate

Time-saver

Part 1	Composition
Part 2	Grammar, Usage, and Mechanics
Part 3	Resources and Skills

Differentiated Homework Options

The Weekly Planner lists several key grammar and composition resources you can use as homework for learners of different levels:

- **Reteaching** for basic learners
- **Practice** for average learners
- **Enrichment** for advanced learners

Key resources for improving language and thinking skills for learners of all levels appear under **Mixed Abilities.**

Assessment Opportunities

Tests with Answer Key and Rubrics (also available as *Testmaker* software) provides you with **Pretests** and **Mastery Tests** to gauge your students' progress in a unit. For selected composition units, the resource provides three tests:

- **Choice A** } writing tests you can use as
- **Choice B** } either pretests or mastery tests
- **Composition Objective Test** multiple-choice mastery test

Customized Lesson Plans

Keep in mind that this Weekly Planner is only a suggestion. *Writer's Choice* helps you adjust lesson plans to your instructional needs in several ways.

All-In-One Planner

- The Teacher Wraparound Edition lists additional resources at point of use and in Resource Manager boxes.
- The *Lessons Plans* book cites activities relevant to each lesson.
- The *TeacherWorks*™ **CD-ROM** helps you customize your own lesson plans in a calendar format.

Lessons	Key Resources

WEEK 1

Personal Writing & Subjects, Predicates, and Sentences

Part 1 Composition
Unit 1 Personal Writing
Unit 1 Writing in the Real World, pp. 4–7
1.1 Writing About What's Important to You, pp. 8–11

Part 2 Grammar, Usage, and Mechanics
Unit 8 Subjects, Predicates, and Sentences
8.1 Kinds of Sentences, pp. 357–358
8.2 Sentences and Sentence Predicates, pp. 359–360

Classroom Activities
Nonfiction Reading and Writing
inTIME, p. 33
Differentiated Homework Options
Reteaching
Composition Reteaching, p. 1
Grammar Reteaching, p. 1
Practice
Composition Practice, p. 1
Grammar Practice Workbook, p. 1
Enrichment
Composition Enrichment, p. 1
Grammar Enrichment, p. 1
Mixed Abilities
Grammar and Language Workbook, Lessons 1–2, 5
Vocabulary and Spelling Strategies and Practice, p. 1
Assessment
Tests with Answer Key and Rubrics, pp. 1–2, 33–34
Testmaker: ExamView Pro CD-ROM

WEEK 2

Personal Writing & Subjects, Predicates, and Sentences

Part 1 Composition
1.2 Collecting Information, pp. 12–15
1.3 Writing to Celebrate, pp. 16–19
1.4 Writing About Yourself, pp. 20–23
1.5 Responding to a Character, pp. 24–27

Part 2 Grammar, Usage, and Mechanics
8.3 Subjects and Predicates, pp. 361–362
8.4 Identifying the Subject, pp. 363–364

Classroom Activities
Nonfiction Reading and Writing
inTIME, p. 18
Differentiated Homework Options
Reteaching
Composition Reteaching, pp. 2–5
Grammar Reteaching, p. 2–3
Practice
Composition Practice, pp. 2–5
Grammar Practice Workbook, pp. 2–3
Enrichment
Composition Enrichment, pp. 2–5
Grammar Enrichment, p. 2–3
Mixed Abilities
Grammar and Language Workbook, Lessons 2–3

WEEK 3

Personal Writing & Subjects, Predicates and Sentences

Part 1 Composition
Unit 1 Writing Process in Action, pp. 28–31
Unit 1 Literature Model, pp. 32–38
Unit 1 Review, p. 39

Part 2 Grammar, Usage, and Mechanics
8.5 Compound Subjects and Predicates, pp. 365–366
8.6 Simple and Compound Sentences, pp. 367–368
Unit 8 Grammar Review, pp. 369–377

Classroom Activities
Technology
Revising with Style CD-ROM
Writer's Assistant CD-ROM
Differentiated Homework Options
Reteaching
Composition Reteaching, p. 6
Grammar Reteaching, p. 4
Practice
Composition Practice, p. 6
Grammar Practice Workbook, pp. 2, 4
Enrichment
Composition Enrichment, p. 6
Grammar Enrichment, pp. 2, 4
Mixed Abilities
Grammar and Language Workbook, Lessons 4, 6; Unit 1 Review, Cumulative Review: Unit 1
Vocabulary and Spelling Strategies and Practice, p. 7
Assessment
Tests with Answer Key and Rubrics, pp. 3–4, 35–36
Testmaker: ExamView Pro CD-ROM

WEEKLY PLANNER

	Lessons	Key Resources
WEEK 4 Study Skills	**Part 3 Resources and Skills** **Unit 24 Study Skills** 24.1 The Parts of a Book, pp. 685–686 24.2 Reading Strategies, pp. 687–688 24.3 Writing Summaries, pp. 689–690 24.4 Making a Study Plan, pp. 691–693 24.5 Using the SQ3R Method, pp. 694–695 24.6 Taking Notes and Outlining, pp. 696–698 24.7 Understanding Graphic Information, pp. 699–702 24.8 Using Memory, pp. 703–704	**Differentiated Homework Options** **Mixed Abilities** *Thinking and Study Skills,* pp. 2–4, 8, 18, 30–32, 34–36, 39–40 **Assessment** *Tests with Answer Key and Rubrics,* pp. 97–100 *Testmaker: ExamView Pro* CD-ROM
WEEK 5 The Writing Process & Nouns	**Part 1 Composition** **Unit 2 The Writing Process** Unit 2 Writing in the Real World, pp. 42–45 2.1 Using the Writing Process, pp. 46–49 2.2 Prewriting: Finding and Exploring a Topic, pp. 50–53 2.3 Prewriting: Determining Purpose and Audience, pp. 54–57 2.4 Prewriting: Ordering Ideas, pp. 58–61 **Part 2 Grammar, Usage, and Mechanics** **Unit 9 Nouns** 9.1 Kinds of Nouns, pp. 379–380 9.2 Compound Nouns, pp. 381–382 9.3 Possessive Nouns, pp. 383–384	**Differentiated Homework Options** **Reteaching** *Composition Reteaching,* pp. 7–10 *Grammar Reteaching,* pp. 5–6 **Practice** *Composition Practice,* pp. 7–10 *Grammar Practice Workbook,* pp. 5–6 **Enrichment** *Composition Enrichment,* pp. 7–10 *Grammar Enrichment,* pp. 5–6 **Mixed Abilities** *Grammar and Language Workbook,* Lessons 7, 9 *Vocabulary and Spelling Strategies and Practice,* p. 2 **Assessment** *Tests with Answer Key and Rubrics,* pp. 5–6, 37–38 *Testmaker: ExamView Pro* CD-ROM
WEEK 6 The Writing Process & Nouns	**Part 1 Composition** 2.5 Drafting: Getting It in Writing, pp. 62–65 2.6 Revising: Evaluating a Draft, pp. 66–69 **Part 2 Grammar, Usage, and Mechanics** 9.4 Distinguishing Plurals, Possessives, and Contractions, pp. 385–386 9.5 Collective Nouns, pp. 387–388 9.6 Appositives, pp. 389–390 Unit 9 Grammar Review, pp. 391–397	**Classroom Activities** **Nonfiction Reading and Writing** *inTIME,* pp. 3–5 **Differentiated Homework Options** **Reteaching** *Composition Reteaching,* pp. 11–12 *Grammar Reteaching,* pp. 7–8 **Practice** *Composition Practice,* pp. 11–12 *Grammar Practice Workbook,* pp. 5–7 **Enrichment** *Composition Enrichment,* pp. 11–12 *Grammar Enrichment,* pp. 5–7 **Mixed Abilities** *Grammar and Language Workbook,* Lessons 8, 10–11; Unit 2 Review; Cumulative Review: Units 1–2 **Assessment** *Tests with Answer Key and Rubrics,* pp. 39–40 *Testmaker: ExamView Pro* CD-ROM

	Lessons	Key Resources
WEEK 7 The Writing Process & Verbs	**Part 1 Composition** 2.7 Revising: Making Paragraphs Effective, pp. 70–73 2.8 Revising: Creating Sentence Variety, pp. 74–77 2.9 Editing/Proofreading: Making Final Adjustments, pp. 78–81 2.10 Presenting/Publishing: Sharing Your Writing, pp. 82–85 **Part 2 Grammar, Usage, and Mechanics** **Unit 10 Verbs** 10.1 Action Verbs, pp. 399–400 10.2 Transitive and Intransitive Verbs, pp. 401–402 10.3 Verbs with Indirect Objects, pp. 403–404 10.4 Linking Verbs and Predicate Words, pp. 405–406 10.5 Present, Past, and Future Tenses, pp. 407–408 10.6 Main Verbs and Helping Verbs, pp. 409–410	**Differentiated Homework Options** **Reteaching** *Composition Reteaching,* pp. 13–16 *Grammar Reteaching,* pp. 9–14 **Practice** *Composition Practice,* pp. 13–16 *Grammar Practice Workbook,* pp. 8–12 **Enrichment** *Composition Enrichment,* pp. 13–16 *Grammar Enrichment,* pp. 8–12 **Mixed Abilities** *Grammar and Language Workbook,* Lessons 12–17 **Assessment** *Tests with Answer Key and Rubrics,* pp. 41–42 *Testmaker: ExamView Pro* CD-ROM
WEEK 8 The Writing Process & Verbs	**Part 1 Composition** Unit 2 Writing Process in Action, pp. 86–89 Unit 2 Literature Model, pp. 90–95 Unit 2 Review, p. 96 **Part 2 Grammar, Usage, and Mechanics** 10.7 Progressive Verbs, pp. 411–412 10.8 Perfect Tenses, pp. 413–414 10.9 Irregular Verbs, pp. 415–416 10.10 More Irregular Verbs, pp. 417–418 Unit 10 Grammar Review, pp. 419–427	**Classroom Activities** **Technology** *Revising with Style* CD-ROM *Writer's Assistant* CD-ROM **Differentiated Homework Options** **Reteaching** *Composition Reteaching,* p. 17 *Grammar Reteaching,* pp. 15–16 **Practice** *Composition Practice,* p. 17 *Grammar Practice Workbook,* pp. 13–14 **Enrichment** *Composition Enrichment,* p. 17 *Grammar Enrichment,* pp. 9, 13–14 **Mixed Abilities** *Grammar and Language Workbook,* Lessons 18–21; Unit 3 Review; Cumulative Review: Units 1–3 *Vocabulary and Spelling Strategies and Practice,* p. 8 **Assessment** *Tests with Answer Key and Rubrics,* pp. 7–8, 43–44 *Testmaker: ExamView Pro* CD-ROM
WEEK 9 Vocabulary and Spelling	**Part 3 Resources and Skills** **Unit 23 Vocabulary and Spelling** 23.1 Borrowed Words, pp. 654–656 Wordworks: Language Families, p. 657 23.2 Using Context Clues, pp. 658–659 Wordworks: Pictographic Writing, p. 660 23.3 Roots, Prefixes, and Suffixes, pp. 661–664 Wordworks: Compound Words, p. 665 23.4 Synonyms and Antonyms, pp. 666–667 Wordworks: Slang, p. 668 23.5 Homonyms, pp. 669–670 Wordworks: Homophones, p. 671 23.6 Spelling Rules I, pp. 672–675 Wordworks: Origins of Silent Letters, p. 676 23.7 Spelling Rules II, pp. 677–680 23.8 Spelling Problem Words, pp. 681–683	**Differentiated Homework Options** **Mixed Abilities** *Thinking and Study Skills,* pp. 9, 25–27 *Vocabulary and Spelling Strategies and Practice,* pp. 13, 21–26 **Assessment** *Tests with Answer Key and Rubrics,* pp. 93–96 *Testmaker: ExamView Pro* CD-ROM

	Lessons	Key Resources
 **WEEK 10** **TIME** Facing the Blank Page, Descriptive Writing, & Pronouns	**Part 1 Composition** TIME **Facing the Blank Page,** pp. 97–107 **Unit 3 Descriptive Writing** Unit 3 Writing in the Real World, pp. 110–113 **Part 2 Grammar, Usage, and Mechanics** **Unit 11 Pronouns** 11.1 Personal Pronouns, pp. 429–430 11.2 Pronouns and Antecedents, pp. 431–432 11.3 Using Pronouns Correctly, pp. 433–434 11.4 Possessive Pronouns, pp. 435–436 11.5 Indefinite Pronouns, pp. 437–438	**Classroom Activities** **Nonfiction Reading and Writing** *Facing the Blank Page* VHS video **Differentiated Homework Options** **Reteaching** *Grammar Reteaching,* pp. 17–21 **Practice** *Grammar Practice Workbook,* pp. 15–18 **Enrichment** *Grammar Enrichment,* pp. 15–18 **Mixed Abilities** *Grammar and Language Workbook,* Lessons 22, 24–25 *Vocabulary and Spelling Strategies and Practice,* p. 3 **Assessment** *Tests with Answer Key and Rubrics,* pp. 9–10, 45–46 *Testmaker: ExamView Pro* CD-ROM
WEEK 11 **Descriptive Writing & Pronouns**	**Part 1 Composition** 3.1 Writing to Show, Not Tell, pp. 114–117 3.2 Combining Observation and Imagination, pp. 118–121 3.3 Choosing Details to Create a Mood, pp. 122–125 3.4 Organizing Details in a Description, pp. 126–129 **Part 2 Grammar, Usage, and Mechanics** 11.6 Reflexive and Intensive Pronouns, pp. 439–440 11.7 Interrogative Pronouns, pp. 441–442 Unit 11 Grammar Review, pp. 443–449	**Classroom Activities** **Nonfiction Reading and Writing** *inTIME,* p. 11 **Differentiated Homework Options** **Reteaching** *Composition Reteaching,* pp. 18–21 *Grammar Reteaching,* p. 22 **Practice** *Composition Practice,* pp. 18–21 *Grammar Practice Workbook,* p. 19 **Enrichment** *Composition Enrichment,* pp. 18–21 *Grammar Enrichment,* p. 19 **Mixed Abilities** *Grammar and Language Workbook,* Lessons 26–27; Unit 4 Review; Cumulative Review: Units 1–4 **Assessment** *Tests with Answer Key and Rubrics,* pp. 47–48 *Testmaker: ExamView Pro* CD-ROM
 **WEEK 12** **Descriptive Writing & Adjectives and Adverbs**	**Part 1 Composition** 3.5 Describing a Person, pp. 130–133 3.6 Relating a Poem to Your Experience, pp. 134–137 **Part 2 Grammar, Usage, and Mechanics** **Unit 12 Adjectives and Adverbs** 12.1 Adjectives, pp. 451–452 12.2 Articles and Proper Adjectives, pp. 453–454 12.3 Comparative and Superlative Adjectives, pp. 455–456 12.4 More Comparative and Superlative Adjectives, pp. 457–458 12.5 Demonstratives, pp. 459–460 12.6 Adverbs, pp. 461–462 12.7 Intensifiers, pp. 463–464 12.8 Comparative and Superlative Adverbs, pp. 465–466	**Classroom Activities** **Nonfiction Reading and Writing** *inTIME,* pp. 27, 31 **Differentiated Homework Options** **Reteaching** *Composition Reteaching,* pp. 22–23 *Grammar Reteaching,* pp. 23–26 **Practice** *Composition Practice,* pp. 22–23 *Grammar Practice Workbook,* pp. 20–23 **Enrichment** *Composition Enrichment,* pp. 22–23 *Grammar Enrichment,* pp. 20–24 **Mixed Abilities** *Grammar and Language Workbook,* Lessons 28–35 **Assessment** *Tests with Answer Key and Rubrics,* pp. 49–50 *Testmaker: ExamView Pro* CD-ROM

	Lessons	Key Resources
WEEK 13 **Descriptive Writing & Adjectives and Adverbs**	**Part 1 Composition** Unit 3 Writing Process in Action, pp. 138–141 Unit 3 Literature Model, pp. 142–148 Unit 3 Review, p. 149 **Part 2 Grammar, Usage, and Mechanics** 12.9 Using Adverbs and Adjectives, pp. 467–468 12.10 Avoiding Double Negatives, pp. 469–470 Unit 12 Grammar Review, pp. 471–477	**Classroom Activities** **Nonfiction Reading and Writing** *inTIME*, pp. 22–23 **Technology** *Revising with Style* CD-ROM *Writer's Assistant* CD-ROM **Differentiated Homework Options** **Reteaching** *Composition Reteaching*, p. 24 *Grammar Reteaching*, pp. 27–28 **Practice** *Composition Practice*, p. 24 *Grammar Practice Workbook*, pp. 25–26 **Enrichment** *Composition Enrichment*, p. 24 *Grammar Enrichment*, pp. 25–26 **Mixed Abilities** *Grammar and Language Workbook*, Lessons 36–37; Unit 5 Review; Cumulative Review: Units 1–5 *Vocabulary and Spelling Strategies and Practice*, p. 9 **Assessment** *Tests with Answer Key and Rubrics*, pp. 11–12, 51–52 *Testmaker: ExamView Pro* CD-ROM
WEEK 14 **Library and Reference Resources**	**Part 3 Resources and Skills** **Unit 22 Library and Reference Resources** 22.1 The Arrangement of a Library, pp. 631–633 22.2 The Dewey Decimal System, pp. 634–635 22.3 Using a Library Catalog, pp. 636–638 22.4 Basic Reference Sources, pp. 639–642 22.5 Other Library Resources, pp. 643–644 22.6 Searching for Periodicals, pp. 645–646 22.7 The Dictionary and the Thesaurus, pp. 647–649 22.8 Using a Dictionary Entry, pp. 650–652	**Differentiated Homework Options** **Mixed Abilities** *Thinking and Study Skills*, pp. 23–29 *Vocabulary and Spelling Strategies and Practice*, pp. 35–40 **Assessment** *Tests with Answer Key and Rubrics*, pp. 89–92 *Testmaker: ExamView Pro* CD-ROM
WEEK 15 **Narrative Writing & Prepositions, Conjunctions, and Interjections**	**Part 1 Composition** **Unit 4 Narrative Writing** Unit 4 Writing in the Real World, pp. 152–155 4.1 Telling a Good Story, pp. 156–159 4.2 Exploring Story Ideas, pp. 160–163 **Part 2 Grammar, Usage, and Mechanics** **Unit 13 Prepositions, Conjunctions, and Interjections** 13.1 Prepositions and Prepositional Phrases, pp. 479–480 13.2 Pronouns as Objects of Prepositions, pp. 481–482 13.3 Prepositional Phrases as Adjectives and Adverbs, pp. 483–484 13.4 Conjunctions, pp. 485–486 13.5 Interjections, pp. 487–488	**Classroom Activities** **Nonfiction Reading and Writing** *inTIME*, p. 24 **Differentiated Homework Options** **Reteaching** *Composition Reteaching*, pp. 25–26 *Grammar Reteaching*, pp. 29–30 **Practice** *Composition Practice*, pp. 25–26 *Grammar Practice Workbook*, pp. 27–30 **Enrichment** *Composition Enrichment*, pp. 25–26 *Grammar Enrichment*, pp. 27–30 **Mixed Abilities** *Grammar and Language Workbook*, Lessons 38–41 *Vocabulary and Spelling Strategies and Practice*, p. 4 **Assessment** *Tests with Answer Key and Rubrics*, pp. 13–14, 53–54 *Testmaker: ExamView Pro* CD-ROM

	Lessons	Key Resources
WEEK 16 Narrative Writing & Prepositions, Conjunctions, and Interjections	**Part 1 Composition** 4.3 Using Time Order in a Story, pp. 164–167 4.4 Writing Dialogue to Develop Characters, pp. 168–171 4.5 Drafting a Story, pp. 172–175 **Part 2 Grammar, Usage, and Mechanics** 13.6 Finding All the Parts of Speech, pp. 489–490 Unit 13 Grammar Review, pp. 491–499	**Classroom Activities** **Nonfiction Reading and Writing** *inTIME,* p. 2 **Differentiated Homework Options** **Reteaching** *Composition Reteaching,* pp. 27–29 *Grammar Reteaching,* p. 31 **Practice** *Composition Practice,* pp. 27–29 **Enrichment** *Composition Enrichment,* pp. 27–29 **Mixed Abilities** *Grammar and Language Workbook,* Unit 6 Review; Cumulative Review: Units 1–6 **Assessment** *Tests with Answer Key and Rubrics,* pp. 13–14, 55–56 *Testmaker: ExamView Pro* CD-ROM
WEEK 17 Narrative Writing & Clauses and Complex Sentences	**Part 1 Composition** 4.6 Evaluating a Story Opening, pp. 176–179 4.7 Responding to a Story, pp. 180–183 **Part 2 Grammar, Usage, and Mechanics** **Unit 14 Clauses and Complex Sentences** 14.1 Sentences and Clauses, pp. 501–502 14.2 Complex Sentences, pp. 503–504 14.3 Adjective Clauses, pp. 505–506 14.4 Adverb Clauses, pp. 507–508	**Differentiated Homework Options** **Reteaching** *Composition Reteaching,* pp. 30–31 *Grammar Reteaching,* pp. 32–34 **Practice** *Composition Practice,* pp. 30–31 *Grammar Practice Workbook,* pp. 31–34 **Enrichment** *Composition Enrichment,* pp. 30–31 *Grammar Enrichment,* pp. 31–34 **Mixed Abilities** *Grammar and Language Workbook,* Lessons 42–45 **Assessment** *Tests with Answer Key and Rubrics,* pp. 57–58 *Testmaker: ExamView Pro* CD-ROM
WEEK 18 Narrative Writing & Clauses and Complex Sentences	**Part 1 Composition** Unit 4 Writing Process in Action, pp. 184–187 Unit 4 Literature Model, pp. 188–192 Unit 4 Review, p. 193 **Part 2 Grammar, Usage, and Mechanics** 14.5 Noun Clauses, pp. 509–510 Unit 14 Grammar Review, pp. 511–519	**Classroom Activities** **Nonfiction Reading and Writing** *inTIME,* pp. 6–7 **Technology** *Revising with Style* CD-ROM *Writer's Assistant* CD-ROM **Differentiated Homework Options** **Reteaching** *Composition Reteaching,* p. 32 *Grammar Reteaching,* p. 35 **Practice** *Composition Practice,* p. 32 *Grammar Practice Workbook,* p. 35 **Enrichment** *Composition Enrichment,* p. 32 *Grammar Enrichment,* p. 35 **Mixed Abilities** *Grammar and Language Workbook,* Lesson 46; Unit 7 Review; Cumulative Review: Units 1–7 *Vocabulary and Spelling Strategies and Practice,* p. 10 **Assessment** *Tests with Answer Key and Rubrics,* pp. 15–16, 59–60 *Testmaker: ExamView Pro* CD-ROM

	Lessons	Key Resources
WEEK 19 Electronic Resources	**Part 3 Resources and Skills** **Unit 28 Electronic Resources** 28.1 The Internet, p. 782 28.2 Using the Internet, pp. 783–786 28.3 Using E-mail, pp. 787–790 28.4 Selecting and Evaluating Internet Sources, pp. 791–792 28.5 CD-ROMs and Other Electronic Resources, pp. 793–796	**Classroom Activities** **Technology** *Guide to Using the Internet and Other Electronic Resources* **Assessment** *Tests with Answer Key and Rubrics,* pp. 113–116 *Testmaker: ExamView Pro* CD-ROM
WEEK 20 Expository Writing & Verbals	**Part 1 Composition** **Unit 5 Expository Writing** Unit 5 Writing in the Real World, pp. 196–199 5.1 Giving Information and Explanations, pp. 200–203 5.2 Organizing Informative Writing, pp. 204–207 5.3 Writing About Similarities and Differences, pp. 208–211 **Part 2 Grammar, Usage, and Mechanics** **Unit 15 Verbals** 15.1 Participles and Participial Phrases, pp. 521–522 15.2 Gerunds and Gerund Phrases, pp. 523–524	**Classroom Activities** **Nonfiction Reading and Writing** *inTIME,* pp. 16, 17, 32 *Research Paper and Report Writing,* pp. 33–34 **Differentiated Homework Options** **Reteaching** *Composition Reteaching,* pp. 33–35 *Grammar Reteaching,* pp. 36–37 **Practice** *Composition Practice,* pp. 33–35 *Grammar Practice Workbook,* pp. 36–37 **Enrichment** *Composition Enrichment,* pp. 33–35 *Grammar Enrichment,* pp. 36–37 **Mixed Abilities** *Grammar and Language Workbook,* Lessons 47–48 *Vocabulary and Spelling Strategies and Practice,* p. 5 **Assessment** *Tests with Answer Key and Rubrics,* pp. 17–18, 61–62 *Testmaker: ExamView Pro* CD-ROM
WEEK 21 Expository Writing & Verbals	**Part 1 Composition** 5.4 Explaining How Something Works, pp. 212–215 5.5 Identifying Cause and Effect, pp. 216–219 5.6 Reports: Narrowing a Topic, pp. 220–223 **Part 2 Grammar, Usage, and Mechanics** 15.3 Infinitives and Infinitive Phrases, pp. 525–526 Unit 15 Grammar Review, pp. 527–533	**Classroom Activities** **Nonfiction Reading and Writing** *inTIME,* pp. 20–21, 25, 26 *Research Paper and Report Writing,* p. 36 **Differentiated Homework Options** **Reteaching** *Composition Reteaching,* pp. 36–38 **Practice** *Composition Practice,* pp. 36–38 *Grammar Practice Workbook,* p. 38 **Enrichment** *Composition Enrichment,* pp. 36–38 *Grammar Enrichment,* p. 38 **Mixed Abilities** *Grammar and Language Workbook,* Lesson 49; Unit 8 Review; Cumulative Review: Units 1–8 **Assessment** *Tests with Answer Key and Rubrics,* pp. 63–64 *Testmaker: ExamView Pro* CD-ROM

	Lessons	Key Resources
WEEK 22 Expository Writing & Subject-Verb Agreement	**Part 1 Composition** 5.7 Reports: Turning to Helpful Sources, pp. 224–227 5.8 Reports: Conducting an Interview, pp. 228–231 5.9 Reports: Organizing and Drafting, pp. 232–235 5.10 Reports: Revising and Presenting, pp. 236–239 5.11 Comparing Two People, pp. 240–243 **Part 2 Grammar, Usage, and Mechanics** **Unit 16 Subject-Verb Agreement** 16.1 Making Subjects and Verbs Agree, pp. 535–536 16.2 Problems with Locating the Subject, pp. 537–538 16.3 Collective Nouns and Other Special Subjects, pp. 539–540 16.4 Indefinite Pronouns as Subjects, pp. 541–542	**Classroom Activities** **Nonfiction Reading and Writing** *inTIME,* pp. 14–15 *Research Paper and Report Writing,* p. 38 **Differentiated Homework Options** **Reteaching** *Composition Reteaching,* pp. 39–43 *Grammar Reteaching,* pp. 38–41 **Practice** *Composition Practice,* pp. 39–43 *Grammar Practice Workbook,* pp. 39–41 **Enrichment** *Composition Enrichment,* pp. 39–43 *Grammar Enrichment,* pp. 39–41 **Mixed Abilities** *Grammar and Language Workbook,* Lessons 50–53 **Assessment** *Tests with Answer Key and Rubrics,* pp. 65–66 *Testmaker: ExamView Pro* CD-ROM
WEEK 23 Expository Writing & Subject-Verb Agreement	**Part 1 Composition** Unit 5 Writing Process in Action, pp. 244–247 Unit 5 Literature Model, pp. 248–254 Unit 5 Review, p. 255 **Part 2 Grammar, Usage, and Mechanics** 16.5 Agreement with Compound Subjects, pp. 543–544 Unit 16 Grammar Review, pp. 545–551	**Classroom Activities** **Technology** *Revising with Style* CD-ROM *Writer's Assistant* CD-ROM **Differentiated Homework Options** **Reteaching** *Composition Reteaching,* p. 44 **Practice** *Composition Practice,* p. 44 *Grammar Practice Workbook,* p. 39 **Enrichment** *Composition Enrichment,* p. 44 *Grammar Enrichment,* p. 39 **Mixed Abilities** *Grammar and Language Workbook,* Lesson 54; Unit 9 Review; Cumulative Review: Units 1–9 *Vocabulary and Spelling Strategies and Practice,* p. 11 **Assessment** *Tests with Answer Key and Rubrics,* pp. 19–20, 67–68 *Testmaker: ExamView Pro* CD-ROM
WEEK 24 Listening and Speaking	**Part 3 Resources and Skills** **Unit 26 Listening and Speaking** 26.1 How to Listen, pp. 743–747 26.2 Interviewing, pp. 748–751 26.3 Speaking Informally, pp. 752–755 26.4 Speaking Formally, pp. 756–761 26.5 Presenting a Dramatic Interpretation, pp. 762–763	**Classroom Activities** **Cooperative Learning** *Listening and Speaking Activities,* pp. 6–8, 12–13, 16–24 **Assessment** *Tests with Answer Key and Rubrics,* pp. 105–108 *Testmaker: ExamView Pro* CD-ROM

	Lessons	Key Resources
WEEK 25 Persuasive Writing & Glossary of Special Usage Problems	**Part 1 Composition** **Unit 6 Persuasive Writing** Unit 6 Writing in the Real World, pp. 258–261 6.1 Using Persuasive Writing, pp. 262–265 6.2 Forming an Opinion, pp. 266–269 6.3 Gathering Evidence, pp. 270–273 6.4 Developing an Argument, pp. 274–277 **Part 2 Grammar, Usage, and Mechanics** **Unit 17 Glossary of Special Usage Problems** 17.1 Using Troublesome Words I, pp. 553–554 17.2 Using Troublesome Words II, pp. 555–556 Unit 17 Grammar Review, pp. 557–561	**Classroom Activities** **Nonfiction Reading and Writing** *inTIME*, pp. 12–13, 19 **Differentiated Homework Options** **Reteaching** *Composition Reteaching*, pp. 45–48 *Grammar Reteaching*, p. 42 **Practice** *Composition Practice*, pp. 45–48 *Grammar Practice Workbook*, p. 42 **Enrichment** *Composition Enrichment*, pp. 45–48 *Grammar Enrichment*, p. 42 **Mixed Abilities** *Grammar and Language Workbook*, Lessons 63–67; Unit 11 Review; Cumulative Review: Units 1–11 *Vocabulary and Spelling Strategies and Practice*, p. 6 **Assessment** *Tests with Answer Key and Rubrics*, pp. 21–22, 69–72 *Testmaker: ExamView Pro* CD-ROM
WEEK 26 Persuasive Writing & Diagraming Sentences	**Part 1 Composition** 6.5 Polishing an Argument, pp. 278–281 6.6 Writing Publicity, pp. 282–285 6.7 Writing a Letter of Complaint, pp. 286–289 **Part 2 Grammar, Usage, and Mechanics** **Unit 18 Diagraming Sentences** 18.1 Diagraming Simple Subjects and Simple Predicates, p. 563 18.2 Diagraming Four Kinds of Sentences, p. 564 18.3 Diagraming Direct and Indirect Objects, p. 565 18.4 Diagraming Adjectives and Adverbs, p. 566 18.5 Diagraming Predicate Nouns and Predicate Adjectives, p. 567 18.6 Diagraming Prepositional Phrases, p. 568	**Classroom Activities** **Nonfiction Reading and Writing** *inTIME*, pp. 8–10 **Technology** *Sentence Diagraming* CD-ROM **Differentiated Homework Options** **Reteaching** *Composition Reteaching*, pp. 49–51 **Practice** *Composition Practice*, pp. 49–51 **Enrichment** *Composition Enrichment*, pp. 49–51 **Mixed Abilities** *Grammar and Language Workbook*, Lessons 55–59 **Assessment** *Tests with Answer Key and Rubrics*, pp. 73–74 *Testmaker: ExamView Pro* CD-ROM
WEEK 27 Persuasive Writing & Diagraming Sentences	**Part 1 Composition** 6.8 Writing a Movie Review, pp. 290–293 Unit 6 Writing Process in Action, pp. 294–297 Unit 6 Literature Model, pp. 298–302 Unit 6 Review, p. 303 **Part 2 Grammar, Usage, and Mechanics** 18.7 Diagraming Compound Sentence Parts, p. 569 18.8 Diagraming Compound Sentences, p. 570 18.9 Diagraming Complex Sentences with Adjective and Adverb Clauses, p. 571	**Classroom Activities** **Nonfiction Reading and Writing** *inTIME*, pp. 28–30 **Technology** *Revising with Style* CD-ROM *Sentence Diagraming* CD-ROM *Writer's Assistant* CD-ROM **Differentiated Homework Options** **Reteaching** *Composition Reteaching*, pp. 52–53 **Practice** *Composition Practice*, pp. 52–53 **Enrichment** *Composition Enrichment*, pp. 52–53 **Mixed Abilities** *Grammar and Language Workbook*, Lessons 60–62; Unit 10 Review; Cumulative Review: Units 1–10 *Vocabulary and Spelling Strategies and Practice*, p. 12

WEEKLY PLANNER

	Lessons	Key Resources
WEEK 27 *continued*		**Assessment** *Tests with Answer Key and Rubrics,* pp. 23–24, 75–76 *Testmaker: ExamView Pro* CD-ROM
WEEK 28 Viewing and Representing	**Part 3 Resources and Skills** **Unit 27 Viewing and Representing** Introduction, p. 765 27.1 Interpreting Visual Messages, pp. 766–770 27.2 Analyzing Media Messages, pp. 771–776 27.3 Producing Media Messages, pp. 777–780	**Classroom Activities** **Cooperative Learning** *Viewing and Representing Activities* **Assessment** *Tests with Answer Key and Rubrics,* pp. 109–112 *Testmaker: ExamView Pro* CD-ROM
WEEK 29 Troubleshooter & Capitalization	**Part 1 Composition** **Unit 7 Troubleshooter** 7.1 Sentence Fragment, pp. 306–307 7.2 Run-on Sentence, pp. 308–309 7.3 Lack of Subject-Verb Agreement, pp. 310–313 **Part 2 Grammar, Usage, and Mechanics** **Unit 19 Capitalization** 19.1 Capitalizing Sentences, Quotations, and Letter Parts, pp. 573–574 19.2 Capitalizing People's Names and Titles, pp. 575–576 19.3 Capitalizing Place Names, pp. 577–578	**Differentiated Homework Options** **Reteaching** *Grammar Reteaching,* pp. 43–44 **Practice** *Grammar Practice Workbook,* pp. 43–44 **Enrichment** *Grammar Enrichment,* pp. 43–44 **Mixed Abilities** *Grammar and Language Workbook,* Lessons 68–70 **Assessment** *Tests with Answer Key and Rubrics,* pp. 25–26, 77–78 *Testmaker: ExamView Pro* CD-ROM
WEEK 30 Troubleshooter & Capitalization	**Part 1 Composition** 7.4 Incorrect Verb Tense or Form, pp. 314–315 7.5 Incorrect Use of Pronouns, pp. 316–317 7.6 Incorrect Use of Adjectives, pp. 318–319 7.7 Incorrect Use of Commas, pp. 320–321 7.8 Incorrect Use of Apostrophes, pp. 322–324 7.9 Incorrect Capitalization, pp. 325–327 **Part 2 Grammar, Usage, and Mechanics** 19.4 Capitalizing Other Proper Nouns and Adjectives, pp. 579–580 Unit 19 Grammar Review, pp. 581–587	**Differentiated Homework Options** **Reteaching** *Grammar Reteaching,* p. 44 **Practice** *Grammar Practice Workbook,* p. 44 **Enrichment** *Grammar Enrichment,* p. 44 **Mixed Abilities** *Grammar and Language Workbook,* Lesson 71; Unit 12 Review; Cumulative Review: Units 1–12 **Assessment** *Tests with Answer Key and Rubrics,* pp. 27–28, 79–80 *Testmaker: ExamView Pro* CD-ROM
WEEK 31 Taking Tests	**Part 3 Resources and Skills** **Unit 25 Taking Tests** 25.1 Test-taking Strategies, pp. 706–707 25.2 Types of Test Items, pp. 708–711 25.3 Standardized Test Items, pp. 712–716 25.4 Standardized Test Practice, pp. 717–741	**Classroom Activities** **Assessment Practice** *Taking Standardized Tests* **Differentiated Homework Options** **Mixed Abilities** *Thinking and Study Skills,* pp. 41–42 **Assessment** *Tests with Answer Key and Rubrics,* pp. 101–104 *Testmaker: ExamView Pro* CD-ROM

	Lessons	Key Resources
WEEK 32 Business and Technical Writing & Punctuation	**Part 1 Composition** Business and Technical Writing Business Letters, pp. 329–332 **Part 2 Grammar, Usage, and Mechanics** Unit 20 Punctuation 20.1 Using the Period and Other End Marks, pp. 589–590 20.2 Using Commas I, pp. 591–592 20.3 Using Commas II, pp. 593–594 20.4 Using Commas III, pp. 595–596	**Classroom Activities** **Technology** *Writer's Assistant* CD-ROM **Differentiated Homework Options** **Reteaching** *Grammar Reteaching*, pp. 45–48 **Practice** *Grammar Practice Workbook*, pp. 45–48 **Enrichment** *Grammar Enrichment*, pp. 45–48 **Mixed Abilities** *Business and Technical Writing Activities*, pp. 3–7 *Grammar and Language Workbook*, Lessons 72–76 **Assessment** *Tests with Answer Key and Rubrics*, pp. 29–30, 81–82 *Testmaker: ExamView Pro* CD-ROM
WEEK 33 Business and Technical Writing & Punctuation	**Part 1 Composition** Summaries, pp. 333–336 Forms, pp. 337–340 **Part 2 Grammar, Usage, and Mechanics** 20.5 Using Semicolons and Colons, pp. 597–598 20.6 Using Quotation Marks and Italics, pp. 599–600 20.7 Using Apostrophes, pp. 601–602 20.8 Using Hyphens, Dashes, and Parentheses, pp. 603–604 20.9 Using Abbreviations, pp. 605–606 20.10 Writing Numbers, pp. 607–608 Unit 20 Grammar Review, pp. 609–617	**Differentiated Homework Options** **Reteaching** *Grammar Reteaching*, pp. 49–52 **Practice** *Grammar Practice Workbook*, pp. 49–52 **Enrichment** *Grammar Enrichment*, pp. 49–52 **Mixed Abilities** *Business and Technical Writing Activities*, pp. 8–12 *Grammar and Language Workbook*, Lessons 78–85; Unit 13 Review; Cumulative Review: Units 1–13 **Assessment** *Tests with Answer Key and Rubrics*, pp. 83–84 *Testmaker: ExamView Pro* CD-ROM
WEEK 34 Business and Technical Writing, Punctuation, & Sentence Combining	**Part 1 Composition** Interviews, pp. 341–344 Proposals, pp. 345–348 **Part 2 Grammar, Usage, and Mechanics** Unit 21 Sentence Combining 21.1 Prepositional Phrases, pp. 619–620 21.2 Appositives, pp. 621–622	**Differentiated Homework Options** **Mixed Abilities** *Business and Technical Writing Activities*, pp. 13–19 **Assessment** *Tests with Answer Key and Rubrics*, pp. 85–86 *Testmaker: ExamView Pro* CD-ROM
WEEK 35 Business and Technical Writing & Sentence Combining	**Part 1 Composition** Multimedia Presentations, pp. 349–353 **Part 2 Grammar, Usage, and Mechanics** 21.3 Adjective Clauses, pp. 623–624 21.4 Adverb Clauses, pp. 625–626 Unit 21 Mixed Review, p. 627	**Differentiated Homework Options** **Mixed Abilities** *Business and Technical Writing Activities*, pp. 20–22 **Assessment** *Tests with Answer Key and Rubrics*, pp. 87–88 *Testmaker: ExamView Pro* CD-ROM

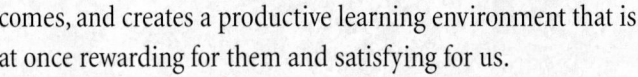

The Middle School Concept

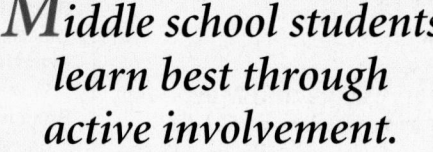

Philip M. Anderson

*Professor and Acting Dean of Education and Executive Officer of Urban Education
Ph.D. Program, Queens College, City University of New York*

How Do Middle School Students Learn?

To reach middle school students, we as teachers have to know what makes them special. Noisier and livelier than elementary school students, yet unready for the abstract, academic model of high school, middle school students pursue knowledge about their world with a zest rarely seen at lower or higher grades.

Surveys of young adolescents report the following concerns:

- developing a personal identity
- dealing with questions encompassing morals and values
- securing a place of status in their peer group
- sorting out the maze of adult expectations
- anticipating their future lives (Paul S. George, et al., *The Middle School—and Beyond,* ASCD, 1992).

Meeting these developmental needs helps motivate middle school students, ensures their interest in activities and out-comes, and creates a productive learning environment that is at once rewarding for them and satisfying for us.

A program of instruction for middle school students should meet their individuated developmental needs *and* foster learning. Programs that do both typically feature these essential elements:

Interdisciplinary curriculum
Middle school students wish to measure themselves against their new interpretations and perceptions of the world. Students learn content best through central, cross-curricular themes (or problems) drawn from their own experience.

Cooperative Learning Activities Studies of cooperative learning in the middle school report higher achievement levels, greater use of high-level thinking, and increased self-esteem. Cooperative learning models—typically involving heterogeneous groups of students working toward a common goal—also encourage students to value interdependence and collaboration.

Integration of Skills Middle school students do not learn useful skills well in isolation. They seek a connected world view and need help seeing relationships between ideas and actions. Activities connecting reading, writing, speaking, listening, and viewing are more likely to help students learn skills and content.

Middle school students learn best through active involvement. They need time to read, write, and explore. Sure, "active involvement" means some noise and disorder, but that noise and disorder is the sound and look of learning.

> *Middle school students learn best through active involvement.*

Writer's Choice Delivers!
- Writing assignments that cover a variety of curriculum areas
- *Writing Across the Curriculum* and *Research Paper and Report Writing* blackline masters that provide practical help for writing in content areas
- Media Connections and TIME Facing the Blank Page that connect the world of writing with the world of everyday experience
- Cooperative learning activities with clear, step-by-step guidance
- Listening and Speaking and Viewing and Representing activities
- Literature Models that connect reading and writing

Integrating the Language Arts

Denny Wolfe

Professor of English Education at Old Dominion University in Norfolk, Virginia; Director of the Tidewater Virginia Writing Project

Why Integrate the Language Arts?

As English teachers, we have a unique responsibility: to assist students in their growth toward language maturity. Specifically, we must help students read, write, speak, and listen capably and effectively. If we're successful, students learn to think critically and imaginatively.

Reading, writing, speaking, and listening are complementary processes. That is, growth in any one enhances growth in the others. During and after reading and writing, for example, the exchange of perceptions through further oral and written activities broadens and deepens students' understanding. A curriculum designed to help students achieve both *oracy* (speaking and listening competence) and *literacy* (reading and writing competence) fosters total language growth.

Think of learning how to drive. Competent drivers manage a variety of tasks simultaneously—steering, using the brake, paying attention to road signs. Cars won't work for drivers unless they learn to perform these tasks in concert. Making language work for students is like making cars work for drivers. To become truly competent readers, writers, listeners, and speakers, students must recognize that all language processes are interdependent, more meaningful when used together. We as teachers must lead them to this recognition.

How Can We Integrate the Language Arts?

We can help students integrate skills by drawing together two worlds: the world of literature (fiction and nonfiction) and the world of students' experience.

> *Making language work for students is like making cars work for drivers.*

Activities such as the following accomplish this objective:

- Discuss a topic (such as sunsets) in general terms before writing something specific about it (such as a memorable experience students associate with a particular sunset)
- Read or listen to a literary or informational text about the topic (such as a poem about sunsets or an article explaining why the sun appears to change color)
- Relate the text to their own experience in discussion or journal writing as a precursor to fuller reflections in a formal piece of writing or oral presentation (such as an analysis of the poem or a report on puzzling natural phenomena)

When students engage in experiences that integrate reading, writing, speaking, and listening, they gain a sense of the wholeness of English. They develop a sense of community as they talk together, share perceptions from their reading, and respond to each other's writing. In short, they grow toward full language maturity and become better, more imaginative thinkers.

Writer's Choice Delivers!

- Cooperative Learning—reading, writing, speaking, listening, and thinking toward common goals
- Writing Applications, Grammar Links, and Troubleshooter solutions that integrate composition and grammar
- Listening and Speaking Activities that integrate listening and speaking with composition lessons
- Annotated Literature Models that take the mystery out of writing well
- Literature-based Grammar Reviews

Cultural Diversity

Arnold Webb

Senior Research Associate, Research for Better Schools, Philadelphia, Pennsylvania

What Is Cultural Diversity?

Cultural diversity is one of those terms that we educators tend to believe we all use in the same way.

But what educators consider to be meaningful cultural diversity in our classrooms ranges from fostering a common culture to celebrating different cultures. Hard-core adherents to each of these views believe strongly that their approach is the only viable way to channel the dynamic cultural and ethnic mix in our classrooms into areas that support and strengthen our democratic society.

But as Asa Hilliard reminds us, we do not need "to choose between (cultural) commonality and uniqueness." In truth, both are essential. We must provide an environment in which children can understand the world around them and their place in that society as citizens and upholders of democratic precepts and ideals. We cannot do this, however, without empowering all children to recognize and value their individual worth. For many children, that empowerment can occur only when their educational environment provides opportunities for them to appreciate how their heritage contributes to their land of origin and to the American dream.

How Do We Strike the Right Balance?

How do we teachers strike a balance between providing youngsters with a positive sense of self-worth through pride in their cultural heritage and engendering appreciation of our unique shared culture as Americans? We might begin by responding candidly to these questions:

- What do I know about the culture of my students?
- How is this knowledge utilized in my planning and teaching?
- Does the curriculum I teach reflect the truths of a pluralistic society? In what ways?
- What opportunities are provided in my classroom for children to know, understand, and relate to classmates from other backgrounds and cultures?
- What skills are my students learning that enable them to contribute positively to our society?

Whatever our answers, in the final analysis, we teachers must be responsive to the needs and exigencies of our changing society. For example, the 2000 Census reveals that one of every four Americans is a person of color. Cultural and ethnic diversity is endemic. We can shy away from its impact to our detriment, or we can build upon its strengths to our and our students' benefit.

Writer's Choice Delivers!

- Student Advisory Board-approved instruction that reflects the needs and interests of a variety of students
- Cultural Diversity and Civic Literacy annotations in the Teacher Wraparound Edition
- Media Connections that exemplify a variety of social roles and contributions
- Student Models, Literature Models, photographs, and fine art that reflect cultural variety and the truths of a pluralistic society

Differentiated Instruction

Beverly Ann Chin

Professor of English and Director of the English Teaching Program, University of Montana; Director of the Montana Writing Project

How Can We Teach Writing to Students with Different Abilities?

Our students bring a wide variety of experiences, attitudes, learning styles, cultures, and languages to our classrooms. The diversity of abilities is most apparent when we teach writing. Many students learn English as a second language or speak standard English as a second dialect. We may have some students who seem unable to put their ideas on paper, while other students view themselves as writers and initiate their own writing.

We can teach writing to students with different abilities when we create learning environments that immerse students in reading, writing, speaking, listening, and viewing. By placing our students at the center of the curriculum, we engage them as active learners and language learners. We can meet our students' varying needs, interests, and abilities if we respect their languages and implement flexible teaching strategies.

Here are some guidelines for teaching writing to students with different abilities.

1. Provide activities leveled to the various ability ranges of students.

2. Vary the instruction and management of writing workshops by structuring small-group, partnership, and individual writing activities.

3. Provide frequent opportunities for students to write, read, and reflect.

> *We can teach writing to students with different abilities when we create learning environments that immerse students in reading, writing, speaking, listening, and viewing.*

4. Emphasize fluency and quality of ideas before correctness by teaching grammar, usage, and mechanics in the context of students' writing.

5. Foster students' roles as members of our learning community by encouraging them to present and publish their writing.

6. Evaluate writing process as well as progress through portfolios, observations, anecdotal records, and student conferences.

7. Help students understand the connections between oral and written language.

8. Appreciate the diversity of students by enabling them to discover their individual and social identities through meaningful language activities.

Writer's Choice Delivers!

- Short, manageable lessons to meet specific writing needs and goals
- Wide variety of writing prompts with different degrees of guidance
- Journal writing and portfolio keeping
- Activities labeled L1, L2, or L3 for basic, average, and advanced learners
- Alternative strategies for English language learners
- Writing conferences and peer responses
- Listening and Speaking and cooperative learning activities
- Practice, Reteaching, and Enrichment workbooks to meet individual needs

Writing Across the Curriculum

Beverly Ann Chin

What Is Writing Across the Curriculum?

Writing across the curriculum integrates subject-area instruction with writing instruction. When students write about specific subject area concepts, they use writing as a means for discovering what they know, what they want to know, and what they've learned. Through writing, we help students engage in higher-level thinking skills of application, analysis, synthesis, and evaluation. We also encourage students to reflect on their feelings and progress as learners in the subject area.

> *Writing across the curriculum integrates subject area instruction with writing instruction.*

What Strategies Work Well?

When we use the following writing-across-the-curriculum strategies in our teaching, students become better learners and better communicators in the different subject areas.

1. Invite students to write journal entries about any subject area. For example, in science, students record notes analyzing the data from an ongoing science experiment. In social studies, students chart the ways different television stations report local news events during a one-week period. By routinely making journal entries, students document their growth as thinkers. The journal is also a place where students can do prewriting or drafting of an idea for a piece of writing.

2. Assign types of real-world writing. Writing assignments that incorporate a clear purpose and audience motivate students to write. Helping students to see themselves in different roles gives them the opportunity to experiment with different voices. For example, in an art writing assignment, students can imagine they are museum curators writing a promotional brochure about a new exhibit. In a social studies unit on the California gold rush, students can imagine they are Chinese immigrants writing letters home about life in the mining camps.

When we engage our students in writing across the curriculum, we motivate students to explore subject-area knowledge as well as provide them with a powerful tool for lifelong learning.

Writer's Choice Delivers!

- Writing assignments that cover a range of subject areas and that clearly identify purpose, audience, and real-world context
- TIME Facing the Blank Page and Writing in the Real World that explore and model how today's professionals write in the world of work
- *Writing Across the Curriculum* and *Research Paper and Report Writing* blackline masters that provide practical help for writing in the content areas
- Guided Practice, Independent Practice, and Cross-Curricular activities that engage students
- Journal Writing activities that occur in every composition lesson

Journal Writing

Charleen Silva Delfino

English Curriculum Coordinator, East Side Union High School-District, San Jose, California; Codirector of the San Jose Area Writing Project

Journals—What Are They?

When I first began teaching high school, journals sounded more like diaries. Students were given little structure or purpose in writing and were encouraged to write for an assigned amount of time—even if what they wrote was gibberish. Today journal writing is very different.

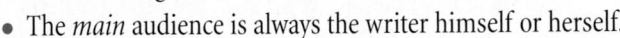

- Students have a specific purpose for their journals. The purpose varies, but it is always present in my planning and in my students' writing.
- The *main* audience is always the writer himself or herself.
- The focus is on content and not on form. Consistent use of journals helps students develop fluency.

Why Use Journals?

It is impossible for students to fail journal writing. Knowing this helps students become more confident as writers and learners, more confident to generate and validate ideas and beliefs. Journals enable students to explore ideas for a formal paper and to record impressions and reconstruct memories for personal writings. Journals enable students to use prior knowledge and experiences as they respond to a piece of literature. Students may keep a double entry journal, recording words, phrases, or sentences that impress them on one side of a page and then asking

questions, responding, or debating these ideas on the opposite side of the page. I often use journals to review previously learned materials and to check the effectiveness of a lesson. For example, I might ask students to identify the most interesting or important thing learned in the previous lesson. In this manner, I can check for understanding as quickly as I can correct an objective test, and I also get a better picture of my students as learners.

How Should We Respond to Student Journals?

I never correct journal writing. However, I think it is important to respond to journals, and I vary the way I do this.

- I write a journal entry of my own to the whole class, sharing viewpoints I learned from the students.
- I use highlighters to identify key ideas in student journals that I found interesting, amusing, or challenging.

Using journals in my classroom has helped me establish a supportive learning atmosphere where students as writers are trusting and open and willing to take risks.

Writer's Choice Delivers!

- A unit devoted to Personal Writing, with lessons on journal writing
- A Journal Writing prompt halfway through each composition lesson
- Writing Process in Action features that include journal writing as a means for students to reflect on their writing experiences

Portfolios

Bonnie S. Sunstein

Associate Professor of English and Education, College of Education, University of Iowa

What Are Portfolios?

Once the exclusive hallmark of artists, musicians, heads of state, and financiers, portfolios can now be found in colorful and energetic varieties in schools and colleges across the country. The word *portfolio* derives from the Latin *portare* (to carry) and *fogli* (leaves or sheets of paper). With homage to their heritage, all portfolios "carry" representative "leaves" of paper for the display of their owners' work. Some portfolios hold samples of students' *best* work. Deciding what's best becomes a negotiation between a teacher and a student in which both consider what is important in writing.

> *P*ortfolios help us evaluate where we've been, assess where we are, and project where we want to go next.

How Can Portfolios Help Students, Teachers, and Schools?

Portfolios help us evaluate where we've been, assess where we are, and project where we want to go next. They facilitate evaluation and assessment for students, teachers, and schools.

- A collection of writing over time can offer **students** insights as they write reflectively about their own learning. They provide opportunities for metacognition as students think about their own thinking and document it. Students become authorities in judging what is good or bad about their work.

- Portfolios enable **teachers** to include students in the evaluation process. In addition, a teacher's own portfolio can include written reflections on the time devoted to students and to personal literacy.

- With portfolios, **whole classes** can view progress over time and make more informed decisions about curriculum coverage.

- For **school systems,** large-scale use of portfolios can offer new information and raise questions that have never been asked before.

Portfolios are not simply writing folders redone; they are documented collections of literary decisions made at certain times by certain people. They reflect our philosophies of reflection, evaluation, and learning. Portfolio keeping is decision making, and making decisions involves asking tough questions—of teachers and students—about their values in writing and reading.

Writer's Choice Delivers!

- Portfolio and Reflecting ideas at the end of every composition unit
- Writing Portfolios for collecting student work
- writing activities that point the way at each stage of the writing process
- Rubrics for Self-evaluation with every Writing Process in Action
- Unit Reviews that help students ask the right questions about their work

Vision, Values, and Assessment

Jacqueline Jones Royster

*Professor of English and Associate Dean of the College of Humanities,
Ohio State University*

What Should Our Perspective on Assessment Be?

In this age of high-stakes testing, it is difficult to avoid a strong focus on test preparation. At a time like this, it is extremely important that we clarify our vision and values as they pertain to effective teaching and learning and begin a meaningful discussion of what, why, how, and when to measure. With a clarification of vision and values, we turn away from ourselves as failure detectives and language-use police. Objectives for learning take a rightful place as the linchpins for teaching and translate reflexively into measures of learning and achievement.

Assessment is critical *throughout* the learning process, not just at the end of it. We need to think well beyond ordinary techniques of testing and evaluation. In determining learning quality, we are drawn to a need for multiple measures, both quantitative and qualitative, and alternative mechanisms. The imperative is twofold:

1. to clarify a fully developed picture of students' abilities and their capacity to activate and maximize learning

2. to select a range of mechanisms that reaffirm the values in learning that we seek to engender and also mirror both the ways we teach and the ways our students learn

What Is the Role of Portfolios?

One strategy for addressing this twofold imperative is a portfolio system. Portfolios invite a consideration of multi-ple measures, interpretations, and reading over time and across tasks and purposes, thus becoming the embodiment of learning and pedagogy, so that the emphasis is on learning rather than on assessment.

Portfolios also provide opportunities for teachers and students to engage in the type of talk and reflection that maximizes the capacity for assessment to filter itself more productively through-out the learning process.

The challenge is to reconceive testing and evaluation as a multidimen-sional measurement of learning and achievement. The push is to defuse the adversarial nature of the testing relationship so that teachers are in a position to identify, reaffirm, and reward growth, development, and achievement.

> *A*ssessment is critical throughout *the learning process, not just at the end of it.*

Writer's Choice Delivers!

- *Teacher's Guide to Writing Assessment,* with additional models and guidelines for assessment.
- student checklists and teacher rubrics for writing activities
- Reflection and Portfolio activities within each Part 1 Unit Review
- comprehensive Grammar Reviews to end each Part 2 unit
- strategies and practice in taking tests
- an array of objective and holistic tests
- composition tests with criteria for the student's self-evaluation
- Pretests and Mastery Tests for assessing Grammar, Usage, and Mechanics
- tests available as *Testmaker* software

Technology

Barbara King-Shaver

*Supervisor of English, South Brunswick High School, Monmouth Junction, New Jersey;
Adjunct Faculty Member, Rutgers University Graduate School of Education*

How Does Technology Aid in the Writing Process?

In an era of word processors, e-mail and instant messaging, and near-universal access to the Internet in public schools (U.S. Department of Education, National Center for Education Statistics, "Internet Access in U.S. Public Schools and Classrooms: 1994–2002," 2003), students have never had so many tools at their disposal for becoming better writers. At each stage of the writing process, these technologies greatly accelerate and extend what students had been able to do with pen and paper and a library card.

Prewriting Students who freewrite using a word processor have less tendency to stop and edit what they have written, so they develop fluency and generate ideas more quickly. Students who use Internet search engines to find information can quickly explore potential topics for writing. E-mail and instant messaging allow students to brainstorm outside the classroom.

> *Students have never had so many tools at their disposal for becoming better writers.*

Drafting With a word processor, the ease with which students can later revise frees them from having to correct mistakes while drafting.

Revising The cut, copy, and paste functions of a word processor let students remove or rearrange whole sentences or paragraphs in one or two simple steps. Students can easily share their work with teachers and peers, either by printing out copies or by sending e-mail attachments. Teachers and peers can use editing tools to indicate where revisions are needed.

Editing and Proofreading Word processors contain editing tools such as spelling and grammar checkers. Online, students can find dictionaries, thesauri, grammar references, and style guides that will help them identify errors.

Publishing and Presenting Students using word processors can print out clean, presentable copies of their writing. Teachers can post student work on classroom Web pages to increase students' potential audience.

How Does Technology Aid Assessment?

Technology makes assessment more efficient. Since results of computer-based tests can be instantaneous, teachers can tell right away whether to review lessons or to move ahead. A typical computer-based test may also include features that allow teachers to monitor students' progress more easily.

Writer's Choice Delivers!

- Using Computers notes and Technology Tips
- writing prompts and online support at writerschoice.glencoe.com
- reteaching and practice with *Writer's Assistant* CD-ROM
- interactive exercises with *Revising with Style* CD-ROM
- pretests, posttests, and the option to customize with *Testmaker: ExamView Pro* CD-ROM
- online instruction in technology and language arts skills with *TechCONNECT*

Writing and Thinking

Philip M. Anderson

Professor and Acting Dean of Education and Executive Officer of Urban Education Ph.D. Program, Queens College, City University of New York

How Can Writing Develop Thinking?

The connections between writing and thinking are not well established in schools. Allan Glatthorn's analysis of thinking-skills programs found most rely on oral language, some ignoring written language altogether. Similarly, many "writing across the curriculum" programs give scant attention to thinking skills, instead restricting instruction solely to formal aspects of the term paper or to note-taking techniques for lectures (Frances Link, ed., *Essays on the Intellect*, ASCD, 1985).

Research conducted on thinking indicates that cognitive processes must be taught, since they do not arise instinctively nor do they come from social experience. Writing represents an important means for teaching thinking, since it involves **personal, active,** and **integrative** cognitive processes. But cognitive structures underlying writing need to be made explicit, allowing for a reciprocal relationship between growth in thinking and growth in writing.

How Can Thinking Be Taught During the Writing Process?

Many students perceive school writing as "knowledge telling"; they write all they know about a subject and stop. They expend little effort in expanding, analyzing, or reformulating that knowledge. However, teachers can help students master these higher-order thinking skills by emphasizing thinking throughout the recursive writing process. The following strategies and activities will help.

- **Journal Writing** Journal writing provides a means for uncovering and examining tacit knowledge, because students are encouraged to draw upon their **personal** experience.

- **Using Graphics** Graphic aids, such as Venn diagrams, stimulate students' thinking at the prewriting stage and provide **active** direction during the composition process.

- **Scaffolding** With the **integrative** strategy of scaffolding, teachers and students collaborate on tasks that students may have difficulty accomplishing on their own, especially those tasks that involve making meaning and organizing thought processes.

Good scaffolding of writing instruction includes the following steps.

1. Explain to students the goals of the assignment and the purpose of composition.

2. Hold conferences with students during the writing process.

3. Encourage peer and teacher/student dialogues during the revision process.

Process models of composing combined with cognitive-process instruction will result in students who can think clearly, independently, and effectively.

Writer's Choice Delivers!
- clearly defined writing assignments
- opportunities for peer conferencing
- Journal Writing activities in each composition lesson
- graphic organizers to aid prewriting
- a writing objective, as well as critical thinking and listening and speaking skills, identified in the Teacher Wraparound Edition
- *Thinking and Study Skills* blackline masters

Cooperative Learning

Charleen Silva Delfino

English Curriculum Coordinator, East Side Union High School District, San Jose, California; Codirector of the San Jose Area Writing Project

Why Cooperative Learning?

Walking down the hallway, I heard voices coming out of Mrs. Kennett's classroom. I knew that the noise I heard was the sound of eager students energetically discussing their friends' writing. Entering the room, I watched young writers asking questions, making suggestions, trying different options. When was the last time I had seen young people this engaged in the process of writing? Writing, especially in schools, is often a lonely enterprise entered into without great enthusiasm.

These students, representing many cultures, worked in groups of four responding to historical fiction they had written.

Their stories were to be published in a class anthology about the immigrant experience. These students were engaged in a *practical* cooperative learning activity. They had a real audience and a real purpose for their writing. They had something to say because they cared about their own writing and they cared about the writing of the members of their group.

With cooperative learning, students are actively involved in their instruction; they are not passive participants in the learning process. Students need to be trained in a variety of ways to provide feedback to each other about their writing. Then, in small group activities, students are more willing to participate and risk. If the group is constructed well, each student has a part and a contribution to make. The different learning styles and abilities of each student can be addressed.

What Makes Cooperative Learning Groups Work?

Careful planning is essential. I have developed four rules that have made cooperative learning more successful for me:

1. Give clear directions.
2. Model with the whole class whatever you expect the students to do in their small groups.
3. Have students responsible for something concrete when they are finished.
4. Vary the purpose and the activity of cooperative learning groups.

What is important is that learning be student-centered and that each student take an active role, making decisions and staying involved in the learning process.

Writer's Choice Delivers!

- cooperative learning activities such as responding to literature, responding to fine art, group problem-solving, and researching for group writing
- peer response and peer editing
- writing conferences within Writing Process in Action lessons
- additional optional cooperative activities in the Teacher Wraparound Edition

Teaching Grammar and Usage

Mark Lester

Professor of English Emeritus, Eastern Washington University; formerly Chair of the Department of English as a Second Language, University of Hawaii

Why Do We Teach Grammar?

All native speakers of a language have a vast intuitive knowledge of the rules of their language. However, this knowledge is so deeply below the level of conscious awareness that native speakers cannot easily talk or even consciously think about how their own language works.

The study of grammar in school gives students the concepts and terms necessary for talking and thinking about language. A conscious knowledge of grammatical concepts and terms is also necessary for students to compare and contrast their use of language with other people's use of language and to explore alternative ways of expressing their own ideas.

> *Good grammar programs constantly connect grammar to usage problems in the students' own writing.*

How Can We Teach Grammar Effectively?

Research shows us that teaching grammar terminology exclusively is ineffectual. Grammar terminology is abstract and loaded with hidden assumptions. Robert deBeaugrande compared grammar terminology to a ladder with the bottom rungs cut out—if you don't already know the concept underlying the terminology, the terminology itself will be of little use to you. In order to grasp grammar terminology, students first need numerous examples and extensive practice sessions to grasp the concepts underlying the terms.

One technique that helps students grasp grammatical concepts is sentence combining. Sentence combining shows students how sentences with multiple phrases and clauses are built from underlying simple sentences.

Sentence combining also allows students to compare and evaluate the grammatical and stylistic effect of different ways of combining the same simple sentences.

How Can We Teach Usage Effectively?

Usage is the way that we use grammar. Grammar provides a vocabulary that students and teachers need in order to talk about usage problems. For example, talking to a student about the subject-verb agreement errors in the student's paper would be very difficult if the student did not know what the terms *subject* and *verb* meant.

Good grammar programs constantly connect grammar to usage problems in the students' own writing. Probably the most effective way of dealing with usage problems is to collect examples of the error from the students' own papers. Then have students discuss the error, focusing on what the error is and how it can be corrected. Finally, back up the discussion with relevant exercises on grammar and usage.

Writer's Choice Delivers!

- manageable two-page grammar lessons
- visual/verbals that convey grammar concepts graphically
- Writing Process Grammar Tips in composition units
- Grammar Reviews to integrate grammar, writing, and literature
- **Troubleshooter,** a self-help guide to grammar, usage, and mechanics
- alternative strategies for students of all ability levels in the Teacher Wraparound Edition

Improving Writing and Other Skills with Foldables™

by Dinah Zike, M.Ed., Creator of **Foldables**™

 **Foldables**™*, my three-dimensional interactive graphic organizers, have been shown by teachers and students to enhance students' comprehension by tapping into kinesthetic learning abilities. Students fold paper, cut tabs, write, and manipulate what they have made in order to* **organize** *information;* **review** *skills, concepts, and strategies; and* **assess** *their knowledge.*

Using Dinah Zike's Foldables™ in Writing and English/Language Arts Classes

Glencoe/McGraw-Hill shares my vision that Foldables can play an important role in students' learning. The regular use of these manipulatives will help students to master essential writing and other English/language arts skills by

- focusing on the **steps of the writing process** and on the specific requirements of various types of writing

- recognizing and classifying **parts of speech** and other **grammatical structures**

- building **vocabulary**

- developing **research skills** and **listening and speaking skills**

Using Foldables Makes Learning Easy and Enjoyable

Anyone who has paper, scissors, and maybe a stapler or some glue can use **Foldables** in the classroom. Just follow the illustrated step-by-step directions. These directions have been tested with teachers and students to make sure that they are easy to use and simple to understand for both students and teachers. Look at the sample below (and try it yourself!). On the following reproducible pages (T43–T48), you'll find additional Foldables that you can use with lessons from *Writer's Choice*.

Learning Objective: to recognize and classify types of nouns

Students focus on the purpose of the assignment.

 On this Foldable you can list all the nouns in a set of sentences and identify them according to type.

Step 1. Place a sheet of paper in front of you so that the long side is at the top. Fold the paper in half from side to side.

Step 2. Then fold it in half from side to side again, making four columns.

Step 3. Fold down about an inch at the top of the paper.

Step 4. Unfold the paper and draw lines along the folds. In the section at the top of each column, write the labels *Common, Proper, Concrete,* and *Abstract*.

Step 5. As you read each sentence, list the nouns in the correct column. Remember that some nouns can be placed in more than one column.

Students practice following step-by-step directions.

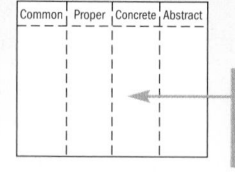

Illustrations make directions easier to follow.

Compare-and-Contrast Writing

Learning objective: to prepare for compare-and-contrast writing by identifying similarities and differences between two subjects

 Use the following Foldable to help you generate ideas for a piece of writing in which you compare and contrast two subjects.

Step 1. Place a sheet of paper in front of you so that the long side is at the top. Fold the paper in half from top to bottom.

Step 2. Fold the paper into thirds.

Step 3. Unfold the last fold and draw ovals, making sure that the ovals overlap in the middle section.

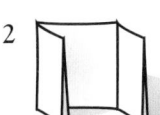

Step 4. Cut through the top layer of paper along the fold lines. This will make three tabs.

Step 5. On the left tab, write a label for the first subject being compared and contrasted. On the right tab, write a label for the second subject. Write the label **Both** in the middle tab where the ovals overlap.

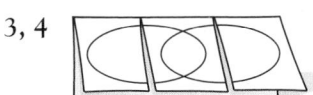

Step 6. Under the left tab, jot down characteristics that are unique to the first subject. Under the right tab, jot down characteristics that are unique to the second subject. Under the middle tab, jot down characteristics that the two subjects share.

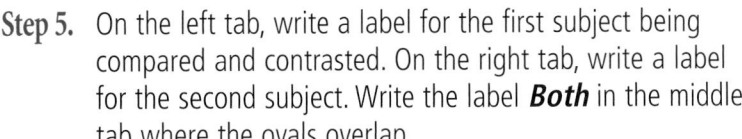
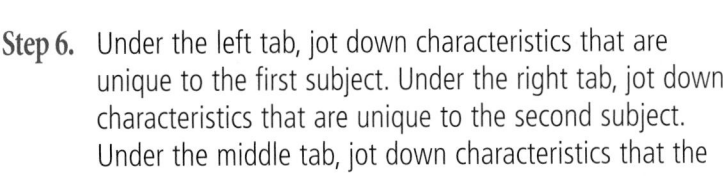
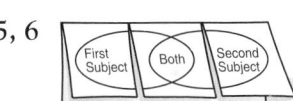

You may use this Foldable with writing in a variety of genres—including descriptive writing, expository writing, and persuasive writing—as long as your writing activity involves comparing and contrasting two subjects. The subjects may be persons, places, things, events, ideas, qualities—almost anything that you want to compare.

Persuasive Writing

Learning objective: to develop support for a claim in persuasive writing

 As you work on a piece of persuasive writing, use the following Foldable to help you track the kinds of evidence you use for support.

Step 1. Stack three sheets of paper with the top edges about an inch apart. Be sure to keep the edges straight.

Step 2. Fold up the bottom edges of the paper to form six tabs, five of which will be the same size.

Step 3. When the top five tabs are the same size, crease the fold to hold the tabs in place and staple the sheets together along the crease.

Step 4. Turn the sheets so that the stapled edge is at the top. On the top tab, write the claim you wish to make. Label the five remaining tabs *Facts, Statistics, Examples/Incidents, Opinions,* and *Reasons.*

Step 5. Take notes on your Foldable as you collect evidence to support your claim. Under each tab, write down at least two pieces of evidence of the kind labeled on the tab.

Step 6. Mark with an asterisk (*) what you think are the most persuasive pieces of evidence. Be sure to include them as support for your claim in your first draft.

1
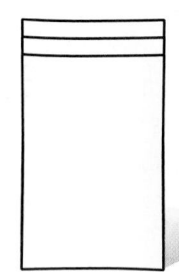

2

3, 4, 5, 6
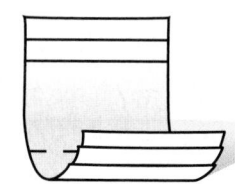
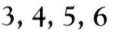

By changing the labels, you can adapt this simple Foldable for several other types of writing. For example, you can use this Foldable to help you write a personal narrative about an event in your life. Just write your name on the top tab. Then change the remaining tabs to read **What?, Where?, When?, Why?,** and **How?** Record your answers to these questions under the tabs. Then refer to your answers as you prepare an outline for your narrative.

Research Paper Writing

Learning objective: to generate and answer questions for research

FOLDABLES™
Graphic Organizers

As you work on a research paper, use the following Foldable to help you identify what you know, what you might want to know, and what you learned about your research topic.

Step 1. Place a sheet of paper in front of you so that the long side is at the top. Fold the top of the paper down, stopping about an inch from the bottom.

Step 2. Fold the paper into thirds from side to side as shown.

Step 3. Unfold the paper. Then, along both folds, cut the top layer only. This will make three tabs.

Step 4. Write the title of your research topic along the bottom of the page. Label the tabs ***Know, Want to Know,*** and ***Learned.***

Step 5. Before you begin your research, write what you already know about the topic under the left tab and what you want to know under the middle tab.

Step 6. As you find information on your research topic, jot down notes in your own words about what you learned under the right tab. Then use your notes to guide your writing of your research paper.

1

2

3

4, 5, 6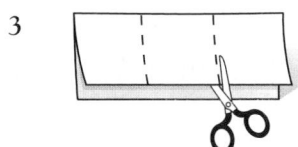

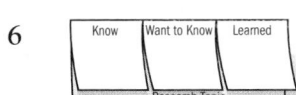

By changing the labels, you can adapt this simple Foldable for several other types of writing. For example, you can use this Foldable to help you write persuasively, as in an editorial. Just write the topic along the bottom of the page. Then change the tab labels to read (from left to right) ***My Opinion, Supporting Facts,*** and ***Reasons.***

Kinds of Sentences

Learning objective: to understand and write four types of sentences

FOLDABLES™
Graphic Organizers
To help you review the four types of sentences, use the following Foldable.

Step 1. Draw a mark at the midpoint of a sheet of paper along the long side. Then fold the top and bottom edges in to touch the midpoint.

Step 2. Fold the paper in half from side to side.

Step 3. Turn the paper vertically. Unfold it and cut along the inside fold lines to form four tabs.

Step 4. Label the tabs **Simple, Compound, Complex,** and **Compound-Complex.**

Step 5. Under each tab, write a definition of the type of sentence and write an example of that type of sentence.

By changing the labels on the tabs, you can use this Foldable with lessons from *Writer's Choice* as follows:

- to classify four kinds of sentences according to whether they are declarative, imperative, exclamatory, or interrogative
- to review compound nouns, possessive nouns, collective nouns, and appositives
- to identify action verbs, linking verbs, transitive verbs, and intransitive verbs

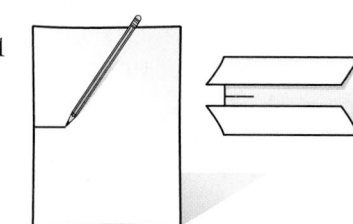

1

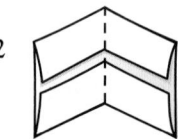

2

3

4, 5

Building Vocabulary

Learning objective: to expand vocabulary by recording new words

Use the following Foldable for recording new words that you come across as you read or listen.

Step 1. Place a sheet of paper in front of you with the long side at the top.

Step 2. Fold the top of the paper down and the bottom up to divide the paper into thirds.

Step 3. Turn the paper vertically, unfold, and label the columns **Word, Root,** and **Prefixes/Suffixes.**

Step 4. Fill in the chart for each new word you come across during the day. (Keep in mind that not every new word you come across will have all of the parts.)

Check your understanding of the words by using them in original sentences that you write on the back of the chart or on a separate sheet of paper.

1, 2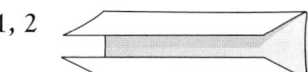

3, 4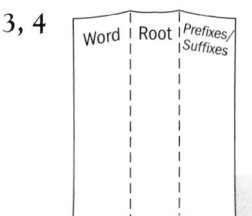

Facts and Opinions

Learning objective: to identify facts and opinions in writing or in oral presentations

FOLDABLES™
Graphic Organizers

Use this Foldable to help you to read and listen critically.

Step 1. Place a piece of paper in front of you with the long side at the top. Fold the paper in half from top to bottom.

Step 2. Turn the paper and fold down one inch from the top.

Step 3. Unfold the paper and draw a line along the one-inch fold. Label the left column *Facts* and the right column *Opinions.*

Step 4. As you read or listen to a speech or a radio commercial, write the facts in the column labeled *Facts* and the opinions in the column labeled *Opinions.*

By changing the labels, you can adapt this Foldable for several other uses. For example, you might use it to list the *Pros* and *Cons* of an argument.

1

2
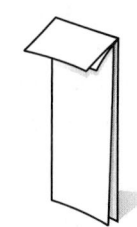

3, 4
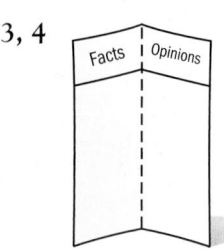

GLENCOE

Writer's Choice

Grammar and Composition
Grade 7

 **Glencoe**

New York, New York   Columbus, Ohio   Chicago, Illinois   Peoria, Illinois   Woodland Hills, California

ACKNOWLEDGMENTS

Grateful acknowledgment is given authors, publishers, photographers, museums, and agents for permission to reprint the following copyrighted material. Every effort has been made to determine copyright owners. In case of any omissions, the Publisher will be pleased to make suitable acknowledgments in future editions.

Acknowledgments continued on page 846.

 The **Facing the Blank Page** feature in this book was prepared in collaboration with the writers and editors of *TIME*.

6+1 Trait® is a registered trademark of Northwest Regional Educational Laboratory, which does not endorse this product.

The McGraw-Hill Companies

PRINTED IN THE UNITED STATES OF AMERICA

Send all inquiries to:
GLENCOE/MCGRAW-HILL
8787 Orion Place
Columbus, OH 43240-4027

ISBN 0-07-829815-6
(Student Edition)
ISBN 0-07-829808-3
(Teacher Wraparound Edition)

3 4 5 6 7 8 9 10 071/043 09 08 07 06 05

PROGRAM CONSULTANTS

Mark Lester is Professor of English Emeritus at Eastern Washington University. He formerly served as Chair of the Department of English as a Second Language, University of Hawaii. He is the author of *Grammar and Usage in the Classroom* (Allyn & Bacon, 2000) and of numerous other professional books and articles.

Sharon O'Neal is Associate Professor at the College of Education, Texas State University–San Marcos, where she teaches courses in reading instruction. She formerly served as Director of Reading and Language Arts of the Texas Education Agency and has authored, and contributed to, numerous articles and books on reading instruction and teacher education.

Jacqueline Jones Royster is Professor of English and Associate Dean of the College of Humanities at Ohio State University. She is also on the faculty at the Bread Loaf School of English at Middlebury College in Middlebury, Vermont. In addition to the teaching of writing, Dr. Royster's professional interests include the rhetorical history of African American women and the social and cultural implications of literate practices.

Jeffrey Wilhelm, a middle and high school English teacher for thirteen years, is currently Associate Professor of English Education at Boise State University, where he specializes in adolescent literacy, with research interests in struggling readers and writers. He has been a National Writing Project site director for the past eight years. He has written eleven books on literacy education and numerous articles and chapters. He has won the NCTE Promising Research Award for *You Gotta BE the Book* and the Russell Award for Distinguished Research for *Reading Don't Fix No Chevys.*

Denny Wolfe, a former high school English teacher and department chair, is Professor of English Education, Director of the Tidewater Virginia Writing Project, and Director of the Center for Urban Education at Old Dominion University in Norfolk, Virginia. Author of more than seventy-five articles and books on teaching English, Dr. Wolfe is a frequent consultant to schools and colleges on the teaching of English language arts.

BOOK OVERVIEW

Part 1 Composition

Part 2 Grammar, Usage, and Mechanics

Part 3 Resources and Skills

Reference Section

CONTENTS

Part 1 Composition

UNIT 1 Personal Writing

UNIT 2

The Writing Process

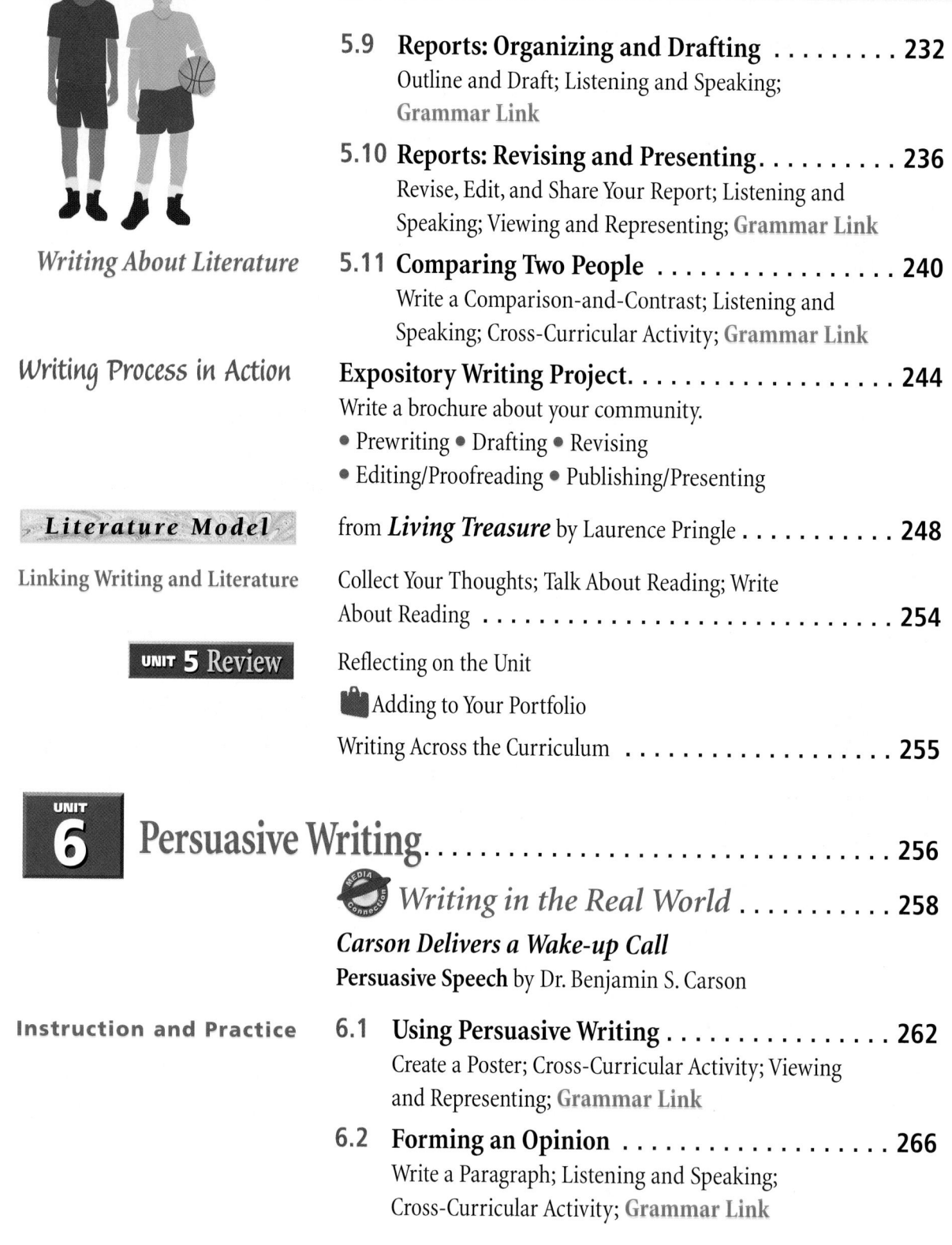

Kathy Jakobsen, *Circus Parade*, 1979

xiii

Part 2 | Grammar, Usage, and Mechanics

Part 3 Resources and Skills

xxiii

Quick Help

Reference Section *Fast answers to questions about writing, research, and language*

LITERATURE MODELS

Composition Models

Each literature selection is an extended example of the mode of writing taught in the unit.

Skill Models

Excerpts from outstanding works of fiction and nonfiction exemplify specific writing skills.

LITERATURE MODELS

FINE ART

FINE ART

GLENCOE
Writer's Choice
Grammar and Composition

Welcome to Writer's Choice!

Your writing and your choices are what this book is all about. Take a few minutes to get to know each of the book's four main parts: Composition; Grammar, Usage, and Mechanics; Resources and Skills; and the Writing and Research Handbook.

Part 1

Composition

How do you become a better writer? By writing! Four-page lessons give you the strategies you need to improve your writing skills. Each lesson focuses on a specific writing problem or task. The lessons offer clear instruction, show models of effective writing, and—most importantly—provide a variety of writing activities for you to practice what you've learned.

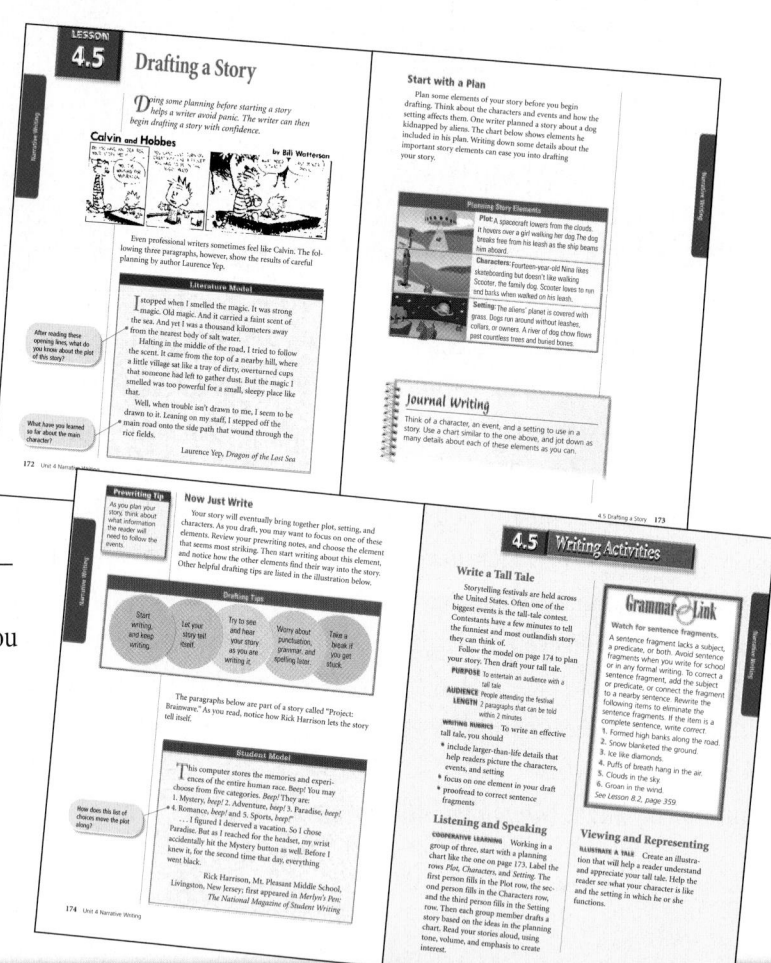

Grammar, Usage, and Mechanics

Short focused lessons make learning grammar easy. Rules and definitions teach you the basics, while examples and literature models show you how the concepts are used in real-life writing.

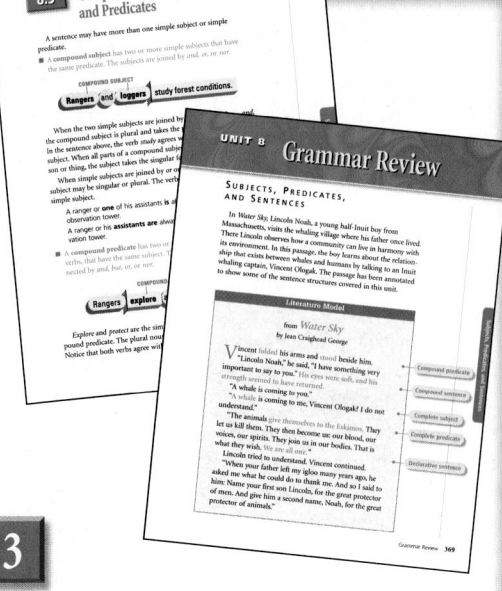

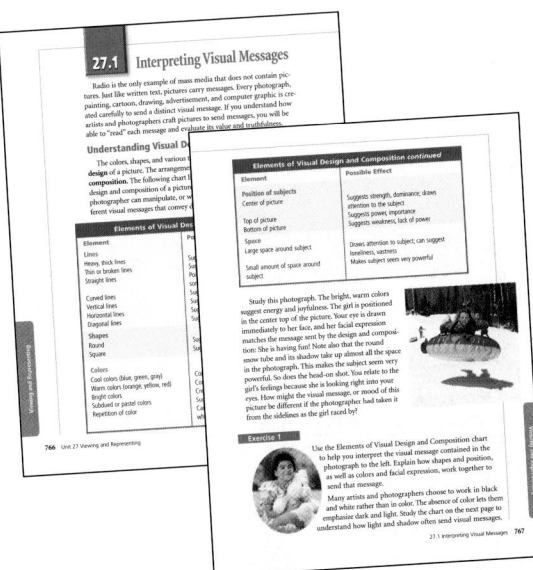

Part 3

Resources and Skills

Would you like to improve your study skills, learn how to give a speech, or get better at taking tests? The lessons in this part give you the skills you need to do all these things and more. Each lesson is complete, concise, and easy to use.

WRITING AND RESEARCH HANDBOOK

This user-friendly handbook gives explanations, examples, and tips to help you write strong sentences, paragraphs, compositions, and research papers. Use it whenever you get stuck!

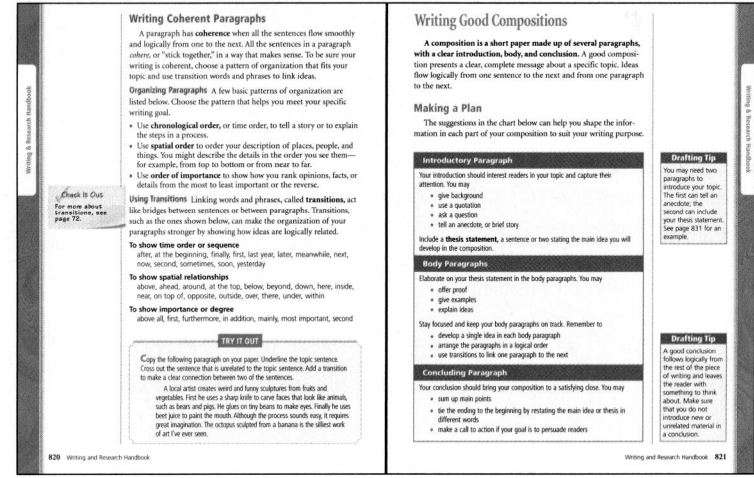

xxxi

PART 1
Composition

Objectives

The units in Part 1 guide students in their development toward becoming effective, confident writers. Throughout these units, students will be asked

- to write for a variety of audiences and purposes and in a variety of forms
- to compose original texts, applying the conventions of written language such as capitalization, punctuation, penmanship, and spelling to communicate clearly
- to apply standard grammar and usage to communicate clearly and effectively in writing
- to select and use writing processes for self-initiated and assigned writing
- to evaluate his/her own writing and the writings of others
- to use writing as a tool for leaning and research
- to interact with writers inside and outside the classroom in ways that reflect the practical uses of writing

Viewing the Art

Roger Winter's *Snow Moon* was created in 1994. It shows a warm nature scene of animals playing in a field. The angel hovering overhead lends an imaginative, whimsical touch to the painting.

Interpret and Analyze Use the following questions for discussion:

- Describe the scene depicted in the painting. What is the color scheme of the painting? What is the mood of the painting, and do you think the mood is affected by the color scheme?
- Why do you think Winter chose to juxtapose the animals and the angels? How does Winter's choice affect the meaning of the painting?

"The heat of the sun had melted the wax from his wings; the feathers were falling one by one, like snowflakes; and there was none to help."

—Josephine Preston Peabody

Resource Manager

Use the following resources to customize your teaching of the units in Part 1.

 Planning Resources
- *Lesson Plans*
- *Block Scheduling*

Transparencies
- *Bellringer*
- *Daily Language Practice*
- *Fine Art*

- *Two-Minute Skill Drill*
- *Writing Process*

Other Print Resources
- *Business and Technical Writing Activities*
- *Composition Enrichment*
- *Composition Practice*
- *Composition Reteaching*
- *Cooperative Learning Activities*
- *Dinah Zike's Foldables™ for Writer's Choice*

- *Glencoe Literature Library*
- *Grammar and Composition Handbook*
- *Grammar Workbook*
- *Guide to Using the Internet and Other Electronic Resources*
- *inTime*
- *Listening and Speaking Activities*
- *Research Paper and Report Writing*
- *Sentence-Combining Practice*
- *Spelling Power*

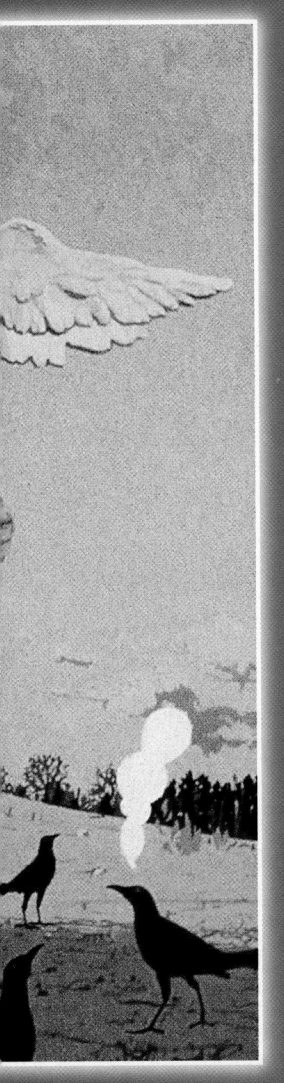

PART 1

Composition

Roger Winter
Snow Moon
1994

1

Discussing the Quotation

Ask the students to interpret the quotation in light of the painting. How might the two be related? How does the quotation intensify the impact of the painting? Refer students to "Icarus and Daedalus" on p. 737 of *Glencoe Literature: The Reader's Choice,* Course 2, for background on the quotation.

Writing Prompt Have students write a paragraph comparing the quotation and the painting. Students should address the following questions: What is the mood of the quotation? Does it contrast with the mood of the painting, or is it similar? What elements of the quotation and the painting affect the general mood?

- *Taking Standardized Tests*
- *Tests with Answer Key and Rubrics*
- *Thinking and Study Skills*
- *Vocabulary Power*
- *Writing Across the Curriculum*
- *Writing Assessment and Evaluation Rubrics*
- *Writing in the Real World*

Video
- *Facing the Blank Page*
- *MindJogger Videoquizzes*

Software
- *Interactive Grammar and Language Workbook*
- *Presentation Plus!*
- *Revising with Style*
- *Testmaker*
- *Vocabulary Power Puzzlemaker*

- *Writer's Assistant*

Web Sites
- *lit.glencoe.com*
- *TechCONNECT*
- *writerschoice.glencoe.com*

Personal Writing

Invite students to share their first impressions of the photograph on these pages. Ask them to describe what appeals to them about these natural surroundings. What might they find unappealing?

Interpret and Analyze Use the following questions for discussion:

- How does the photographer use light and shadow to create meaning?
- What elements in the photograph create a sense of power and movement?
- How do you think this image of snow relates to personal writing?

Discussing the Quotation

Ask students to relate what they think Langston Hughes means in this quote. Do they think the photograph illustrates the quotation well? Why or why not?

Writing Prompt Have the students write a paragraph describing a memory that comes to mind when reading this quote. For more on this poem see *Glencoe Literature: The Reader's Choice*, Course 2, p. 261.

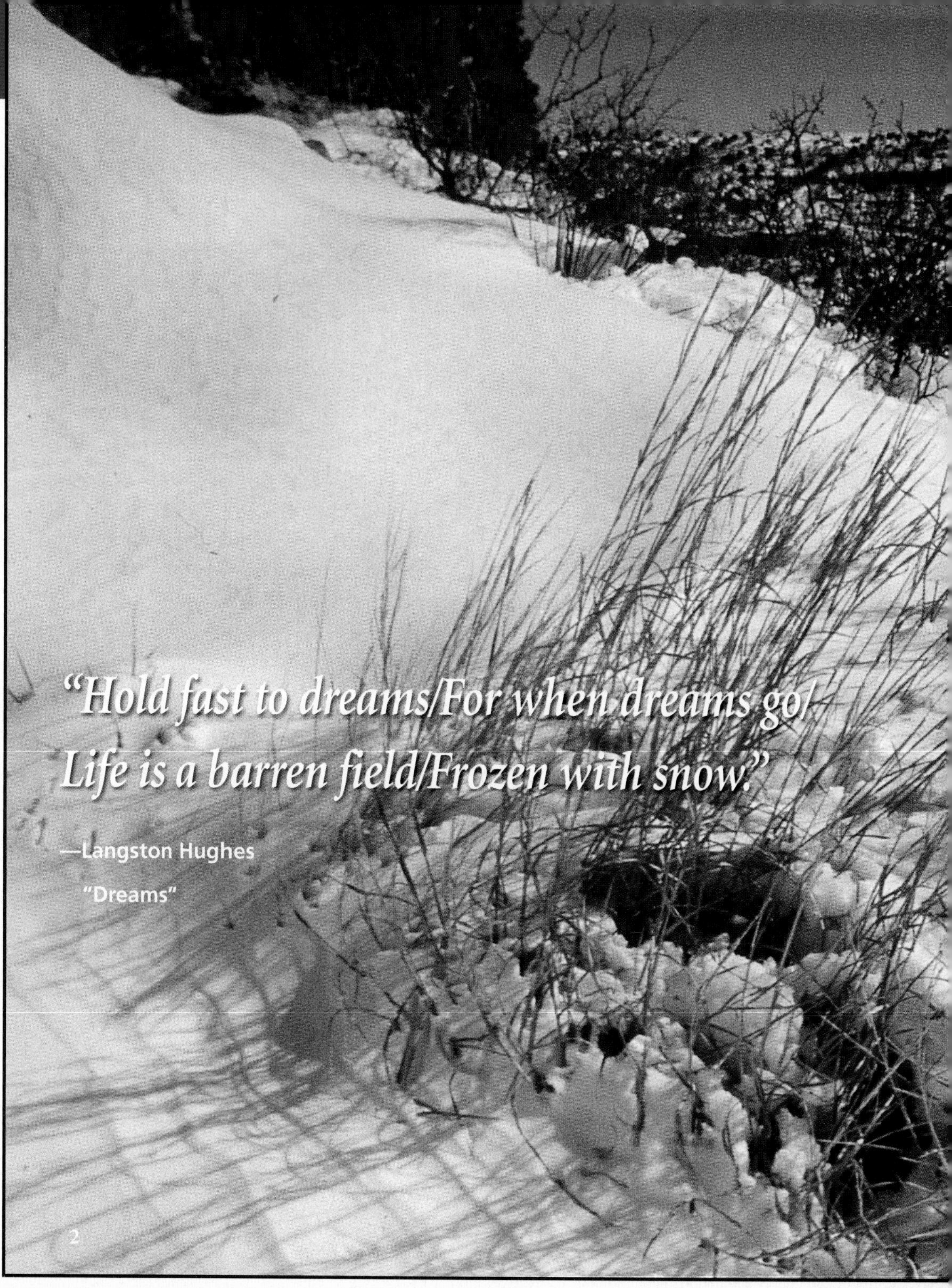

"Hold fast to dreams/For when dreams go/ Life is a barren field/Frozen with snow."

—Langston Hughes

"Dreams"

📁 Planning Resources
- *Lesson Plans*
- *Block Scheduling*

📖 Transparencies
- *Bellringer*
- *Daily Language Practice*
- *Fine Art*
- *Two-Minute Skill Drill*
- *Writing Process*

📁 Other Print Resources
- *Composition Enrichment*
- *Composition Practice*
- *Composition Reteaching*
- *Cooperative Learning Activities*
- *Glencoe Literature Library*
- *Grammar and Composition Handbook*
- *Grammar Workbook*
- *Listening and Speaking Activities*

- *Tests with Answer Key and Rubrics*
- *Thinking and Study Skills*
- *Writing Across the Curriculum*
- *Writing Assessment and Evaluation Rubrics*
- *Writing in the Real World*

📼 Video
- *MindJogger Videoquizzes*

UNIT 1

Personal Writing

Objectives

- To develop an understanding of personal writing
- To examine the use of personal writing in real-life situations
- To express ideas that are of personal importance in a variety of writing forms

✔ ASSESSMENT OPTIONS

📁 *Tests with Answer Key and Rubrics*
Unit 1 Choice A Test, p. 1
Unit 1 Choice B Test, p. 2
Unit 1 Composition Objective Test, pp. 3–4

💾 *Testmaker*
Unit 1 Choice A Test
Unit 1 Choice B Test
Unit 1 Composition Objective Test

You may wish to administer either the Unit 1 Choice A Test or the Unit 1 Choice B Test as a pretest.

Key to Ability Levels

L1 Level 1 activities are within the basic ability range of students.

L2 Level 2 activities are within the ability range of average students.

L3 Level 3 activities are more challenging activities.

💾 **Software**
- *Presentation Plus!*
- *Revising with Style*
- *Testmaker*
- *Writer's Assistant*

💻 **Web Sites**
- *writerschoice.glencoe.com*
- *lit.glencoe.com*

3

Focus

Lesson Overview

Objective

- To explore how the writing process is applied to personal writing in a real-life situation

Skills

- applying the writing process to song writing; choosing descriptive words and images

Critical Thinking

- analyzing; synthesizing; classifying; recalling; relating

Listening and Speaking

- taking notes; informal speaking; discussing

Bellringer

Daily Language Activity

When students enter the classroom, have this assignment on the board: *Think of a special day you have experienced. List adjectives to describe the day in terms of sight, sound, smell, taste, touch, and your own reactions to what was going on.*

Grammar Link to the Bellringer

Have students use the list of adjectives to write two short sentences about the special day. Have students volunteer to write their sentences on the board. Have the class compare and contrast the sentences and then combine each sentence pair into one smooth sentence.

See also *Daily Language Practice*

Motivating Activity

Invite volunteers to read aloud the list of adjectives they wrote in the Bellringer activity. Have the class state things that they learned from the lists about their classmates' special days.

Personal Writing

Writing in the Real World

MEDIA Song Connection

On a visit to the Bahamas, singer and songwriter Ella Jenkins found a magical scene of dancers, calypso singers, and children playing. "Amidst all the things that were happening, the ocean had the loudest roar." She wrote about those ocean sounds in *Come Dance by the Ocean*, a record album with a message about planet Earth. Like other albums Jenkins has produced over the past fifty years, this one celebrates the lands, cultures, and oceans of our world.

Come Dance by the Ocean

by Ella Jenkins

Early this morning when I looked out,
I saw some dolphins playing about.
One chased two, then two chased one.
I'd say that all three had an ocean of fun.

Come on, come dance by the ocean.
Come on, come dance by the sea.
Come on, come dance by the ocean,
Come on, come dance with me.

*Songwriter
Ella Jenkins*

Resource Manager

Planning Resources
- *Lesson Plans*

Transparencies
- *Bellringer*
- *Daily Language Practice*
- *Writing Process* 1–10

Other Print Resources
- *Cooperative Learning Activities*, pp. 1–6
- *Thinking and Study Skills*, pp. 3, 5, 20, 22
- *Writing Assessment and Evaluation Rubrics*
- *Writing in the Real World*, pp. 1–4

Writing a Song

Prewriting	Drafting	Revising/Editing

| Gathering Ideas | Setting Down Main Ideas | Writing to Celebrate |

A Writer's Process

Prewriting
Gathering Ideas

For Ella Jenkins, songwriting is a form of personal writing because, in her music, she talks about the things that matter the most to her. In writing the songs for the album *Come Dance by the Ocean,* Jenkins expressed her feelings about many things she loves. She wrote about the excitement of air travel, the wonder of nature, and the joy of encountering the world's amazing variety of cultures and lands.

Jenkins has had a lifetime interest in both music and other cultures. While she was in college, Cuban musicians taught her to play conga drums and maracas. At the same time, she read about other cultures and listened to songs from Africa, India, Egypt,

and other lands. By her mid-thirties, Jenkins was carrying her message to young people through songs. "You have to respect that other people come from other places," she said. "They're trying to learn about you, and you want to learn about them."

As she travels, Jenkins does a lot of personal writing. She said, "I keep notebooks when I travel called 'Random Thoughts.' I use them to jot down notes about things that strike me." When Jenkins began creating the album *Come Dance by the Ocean,* she looked to this collection of personal notebooks for ideas.

Jenkins encourages every writer to keep a journal or a notebook of ideas. "Personal writing should be something you do on a regular basis because that

Personal Experience in Speaking

Remind students that they often describe celebrations such as birthday parties, dances, homecomings, or holiday meals in everyday language. Invite students to describe these personal experiences as if they were communicating with a friend.

Personal Experience in Writing

Discuss any personal writing students have read that celebrates a wonderful moment. Then discuss other forms of personal writing. Use prompts such as the following:

- Have you ever received an invitation to a party? How did the invitation make you feel about attending?
- What other forms of personal writing have you practiced or read? Can you describe a time when you used your personal experience to write a story? Can you recall and describe a time when you used your personal opinion to inform or explain?

Discussion Prompts

- Draw students' attention to Jenkins's comment that "No one experienced that plane ride as I did. Each person on that plane had a different experience, so no one could write about it as I did." What conclusions about the value of personal writing can students draw from this observation?
- What ordinary experiences have you had (perhaps getting caught in a thunderstorm or seeing a baby brother or sister for the first time) that were as distinctive for you as Jenkins's plane ride was for her?
- If you could put one idea and one feeling into a song, poem, picture, or other creative work, what idea and feeling would you want to convey?

Cultural Connections

Inferring Sources of Favorite Music

Much contemporary music produced in this country borrows from musical traditions of Africa, Latin America, and Asia and from a variety of ethnic groups within the United States. Invite students to listen to several popular song tracks for influences of musical styles and instruments of different countries and cultures. Have them jot down their observations and their best guesses at the origin of different sounds they hear. Some of this background information may appear on album covers.

Teach

Discussion

Stimulate a discussion of the writing process Ella Jenkins describes. You may want to invite students to talk about

- how the writing process described led from an idea to a completed song
- whether or not they were surprised by the meticulous writing process adhered to by the songwriter
- other applications that they can envision for personal writing used to celebrate experiences

Additional Resources

Writing Process Transparencies, 1–10
Cooperative Learning Activities, pp. 1–6
Writing in the Real World, pp. 1–4
Thinking and Study Skills,
    pp. 3, 5, 20, 22

Personal Writing

improves your skill and puts you in tune with yourself," she says. "Pretty soon you won't have just letters and words on the page but something very warm and alive."

Drafting
Setting Down Main Ideas

When Jenkins started writing poems for her album, the notes from "Random Thoughts" helped. For example, they provided material for the poem "A Winter Plane Ride." Jenkins had written the notes that inspired this poem on a flight from Portland, Oregon, to Chicago, Illinois. "It was so exciting to see the differences between one part of the country and another," she said. "I could have written a lot of little things that I was seeing, but all of a sudden I heard this voice, the pleasant voice of the pilot telling us about the sights. You'd have thought I was in class because I wrote down everything he said," she recalled.

Later these notes helped Jenkins recall and capture the moment. "Things grab you in life," she said. "No one experienced that plane ride as I did. Each person on that plane had a different experience, so no one could write about it as I did."

Once Jenkins knew what ideas and feelings she was going to put in her record album, she then had to figure out the words and melodies for each song. The title

song, "Come Dance by the Ocean," was easy. "I was remembering the music by the ocean, the steel drums," she said. "I loved the way they sounded and how the head of the group invited us to come on and enjoy ourselves. And I thought, 'come on' is a good way of beckoning people."

Revising/Editing
Writing to Celebrate

After writing each song and composing the music, Jenkins revised her drafts. She also settled on an opening verse for the album. With this playful song, she invited listeners to celebrate all the things we have in common—nature, music, new places, and people.

For her poem "A Winter Plane Ride," Jenkins used a free and informal style. In the poem, she describes her flight over snowy mountains and colorful canyons. She worked on the poem until each word was exactly right and conveyed her personal message: look around you, listen, and enjoy.

> I see light blankets of
>   snow
> Lying gently upon the
>   mountaintops
> Now the canyons are
>   coming—
> Rippled ridges wrapped
>   around colors, cleverly
>   shouting
> Yet not making a sound.

Cooperative Learning

Writing a Poem

In small groups, have students choose a familiar activity and brainstorm to develop a list of words and images they associate with it. Then together they should compose a diamond-shaped poem, using their list. The first line should have one word, the second two words, and so on up to five words; the sixth line should have four words, the seventh three words, and back down to a final line of one word. (*Bus/Shining yellow/In the rain/I wait for you/I climb your corrugated steps/Settle into green cushions/Think about math/Brakes screech/Home!*) Have groups share their poems.

Examining Writing in the Real World

Analyzing the Media Connection

Discuss these questions about the song on page 4 and the poem on page 6.

1. How would you describe the mood of Jenkins's song "Come Dance by the Ocean"?

2. What effect does repetition have in the song's second verse?

3. How does Jenkins establish the setting for the poem "A Winter Plane Ride"?

4. What two sights does Jenkins celebrate in "A Winter Plane Ride"?

5. What effects does the repetition of consonant sounds have in the poem?

Analyzing a Writer's Process

Discuss these questions about Ella Jenkins's writing process.

1. What interests does Jenkins focus on in her personal writing?

2. How do Jenkins's personal notebooks help her in her writing?

3. While drafting "Come Dance by the Ocean," Jenkins decided to use and repeat the words "come on." Why did she think these words were so important to the song's message?

4. For what two reasons does Jenkins encourage others to do personal writing?

5. How is Ella Jenkins's personal writing process similar to or different from your own?

Grammar Link

Vary sentence length to make your writing more interesting.

To achieve variety in her writing, Ella Jenkins sometimes combines two related short sentences into one smooth longer sentence.

Early this morning when I looked out, / I saw some dolphins playing about.

Combine the choppy sentences in each item into one sentence.

1. The game was almost over. We were losing.

2. Then Louise snagged the ball. She tied the score.

3. An opponent was passing the ball. She tripped.

4. Inez rushed toward the ball. She kicked it to me.

5. I received her pass. I scored the goal.

See Lesson 2.8, pages 74–77.

Personal Writing

Analyzing the Media Connection

1. happy; lively; playful
2. Repetition makes the second verse more rhythmic and lyrical.
3. She describes what she sees from the air.
4. Jenkins celebrates snow-covered mountaintops and colorful canyons with rippled ridges.
5. The powerful consonant sounds simulate shouting.

Analyzing a Writer's Process

1. traveling; music; reading about other cultures
2. by capturing descriptions about exciting moments as they happen; by providing material for her songs and poems
3. By repeating the words "come on," Jenkins underscores her invitation to the reader to participate.
4. to improve their writing skills and to get in tune with themselves
5. Answers will vary. Students will compare their own personal writing processes to those of Jenkins, who writes spontaneously to record her impressions of interesting moments.

Reteaching

Have students think of a trip they've taken and write down five to ten things about the place they visited that differed from home.

Enrichment

Have students write a personal response to Jenkins's statement, "You have to respect that other people come from other places."

Close

Have students discuss how to use the process described in the media connection to write a song about a trip they have taken or would like to take someday.

Grammar Link

Answers

Answers will vary. Samples are given.

1. The game was almost over, and we were losing.
2. Then Louise snagged the ball and tied the score.
3. While an opponent was passing the ball, she tripped.
4. Inez rushed toward the ball and kicked it to me.
5. When I received her pass, I scored the goal.

Using Conjunctions Discuss how the conjunctions *and, or, but,* and *nor* can be used in sentence combining.

7

Focus

Lesson Overview

Objective

• To reflect on personal values and write about them

Skills

• recalling specific details of an experience; exploring thoughts and feelings; using one's own words

Critical Thinking

• recalling; visualizing; relating a personal experience

Listening and Speaking

• discussing

Bellringer
Daily Language Activity

When students enter the classroom, have this assignment on the board: *Complete this sentence:*

My favorite way to spend a day is _____ because _____.

Grammar Link to the Bellringer

Ask students whether this sentence sounds grammatically incorrect: "Snowboarding is my favorite sport because even my worse day of snowboarding is better than my best day doing anything else." Have students explain their responses. Make sure that students understand that *worse* should be the superlative *worst.*

See also *Daily Language Practice*

Motivating Activity

Have students meet in small groups to share their responses to the Bellringer activity. Ask each group member to share an anecdote about spending a day engaged in his or her favorite activity.

Personal Writing

Writing About What's Important to You

$\mathcal{P}$ersonal writing, writing that you do for yourself, can be like a conversation with your best friend. It allows you to explore the things that matter most to you.

Doing my best!

Feeling good!

Time with friends!

My family!

Music!

Personal writing can include entries made in a private journal, notes kept in a school journal, and letters or postcards written to relatives or friends. Some personal writing is meant for the writer alone. Often, private personal writing later becomes a story, poem, or other form of writing that may be shared.

To begin, ask yourself, "What is important to me?" Maybe your answer is like that of a student in the picture; maybe it's different. Whatever you write, it's about what matters to you.

8 Unit 1 Personal Writing

Resource Manager

Planning Resources
• *Lesson Plans*

Transparencies
• *Bellringer*
• *Daily Language Practice*
• *Fine Art* 1–5
• *Two-Minute Skill Drill*
• *Writing Process* 1–10

Other Print Resources
• *Composition Enrichment,* p. 1
• *Composition Practice,* p. 1
• *Composition Reteaching,* p. 1
• *Cooperative Learning Activities,* pp. 1–6
• *Listening and Speaking Activities,* pp. 14–15
• *Thinking and Study Skills,* pp. 3–5

• *Writing Across the Curriculum*
• *Writing Assessment and Evaluation Rubrics*

Explore Thoughts and Feelings

When something incredibly good or bad occurs, put your reactions on paper. Writing about your thoughts and feelings makes them clearer and more accessible to you.

A letter to a friend is personal writing in which you share your thoughts and feelings.

> Dear Lynn,
>
> I wish we had never moved! It was so awful today. I got on the bus and didn't know anyone! All day long kids were staring at me. I felt like hiding in my locker or wearing a paper bag over my head.
>
> I miss talking to you. I miss eating lunch with you. I even miss your jokes! Please write soon and tell me what's happening.
>
> Your best friend,
> Kara

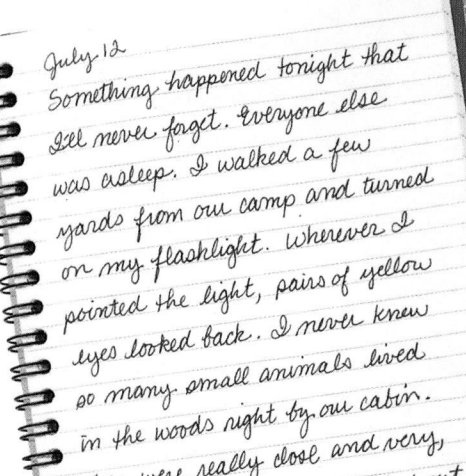

> July 12
> Something happened tonight that I'll never forget. Everyone else was asleep. I walked a few yards from our camp and turned on my flashlight. Wherever I pointed the light, pairs of yellow eyes looked back. I never knew so many small animals lived in the woods right by our cabin.

Some kinds of personal writing are just for you.

Journal Writing

You have probably had many ideas and experiences today. In your journal list as many of these as you can recall. You can use some of these ideas for personal writing.

TIME

For more about the writing process, see **TIME** *Facing the Blank Page*, pp. 97–107.

Teach

Interviewing for Details

Ask students to think of a personal, significant experience that they are willing to share. Pair students. Ask partners to interview each other about their experiences. Tell interviewers to help interviewees develop as many details as possible. Then ask each student to write a short account of the experience, using details developed in the interview. **L2**

Stepping into Character

Tell students that Stream of Consciousness is a technique some fiction writers use to reveal the rambling, nonlinear flow of thoughts in a character's mind. Verbally model this kind of writing for students. Then encourage students to try out this style in their journal entries, letting one idea spark another and then another. **L3**

Two-Minute Skill Drill

Have students list ten adjectives that describe who they are. Tell them that honesty counts!

See also *Two-Minute Skill Drill Transparency 1.1*

Journal Writing Tip

Identifying Ideas Tell students that they can train themselves to be more aware of the world around them. Suggest that they use the following prompts to help them observe their surroundings.

- the funniest thing _____
- the most unusual thing _____
- _____ makes me wonder about _____

Teach

Using the Model

Ask students the following questions: *What does Nancy Young long for? What feelings does she express?* (She expresses a desire to be grown up, take on responsibilities, face challenges, and express herself through writing.) *Do you think most people Nancy's age share her concerns? Why or why not?* **L2**

Focusing on What's Important—and Why

Ask students to list examples of the kinds of important items they keep in a drawer or a box. Then have students imagine that someone who did not know them looked at the contents. What conclusions might that person draw about them? **L1**

Additional Resources

- *Fine Art Transparencies,* 1–5.
- *Writing Process Transparencies,* 1–10
- *Writing Across the Curriculum,* p. 4
- *Cooperative Learning Activities,* pp. 1–6
- *Thinking and Study Skills,* pp. 3–5
- *Listening and Speaking Activities,* pp. 14–15
- *Composition Practice,* p. 1

Personal Writing

Use Your Own Words

Personal writing is talking on paper. You can write as informally as you talk. Experiment by using words in unexpected ways or by expressing unusual ideas. Make up words, if you like.

Any subject might be worth writing about, perhaps in a poem, story, or letter you never send. Follow your thoughts wherever they may lead. One thought will lead to another.

When you write for yourself, you don't have to worry about punctuation, spelling, or grammar—just focus on ideas. Use your own words and style to write about what is important to you. The model below shows how.

Student Model

> I am Nancy Young,
> I remained at the age of twelve for too long,
> I cannot wait until I reach the mere age of thirteen,
> Drive a car,
> Go to college,
> Go to the prom,
> And finally,
> Own my own life. . . .
> I just want feelings that I can express on paper. . . .
> All I want is paper,
> Pen and ink,
> To bear down on,
> Make an impression,
> Of me.
>
> Nancy McLaurin Young
> Savannah Country Day School
> Savannah, Georgia

The writer uses everyday language to write about a personal subject: herself.

Do you think most people Nancy's age share her concerns?

MEETING INDIVIDUAL NEEDS   Less-Proficient Readers

Writing Captions and Comments

Students who struggle with written English should be encouraged to express themselves in nonverbal ways, such as by drawing or pasting meaningful items into their journals. Encourage students to include written titles, captions, and even single-word comments with their visual essays.

Write a Letter

Imagine, ten years from now, opening a letter and finding a message you wrote to yourself when you were younger. Write a message to be opened in ten years. Include three things that are important to you now. The list you made for Journal Writing may help you.

PURPOSE To tell about yourself
AUDIENCE Yourself
LENGTH 1–2 paragraphs

WRITING RUBRICS To write an effective letter, you should

- include information about things that are important to you now
- share your thoughts openly

Grammar Link

Use the correct forms of _bad_.

The comparative and superlative forms of _bad_ are _worse_ and _worst_. In the letter on page 9, Kara describes her _bad_ day. Let's hope it doesn't get _worse_.

Complete each blank with _bad_, _worse_, or _worst_.

I thought I had a **1**_____ idea, but yours was **2**_____. His idea was the **3**_____ of all. This new idea is **4**_____ than the others; it's the **5**_____ I've ever heard.
See Lesson 12.3, pages 455–456.

Cross-Curricular Activity

MATHEMATICS Imagine that you have $50.00 to spend in a store of your choice. Write two questions that will help you decide how to spend the money. Then visit one of your favorite stores and take notes on merchandise that interests you. Include prices of the items you like. Use your questions and notes to help you make responsible choices of items you would buy while keeping within your budget.

Listening and Speaking

With a group, share your lists of the items you chose at your favorite store. Talk about ways in which the questions you wrote did or did not help you to make wise selections. Discuss how the group members' decisions are similar and different. Express and explain your ideas clearly and fluently.

Assess

Evaluation Rubrics

Write a Letter

Use these criteria when evaluating your students' writing:
- Does the letter include specific details?
- Is the letter organized and clearly stated?
- Is the letter in the students' own words?

See also _Writing Assessment and Evaluation Rubrics_

Cross-Curricular Activity

Encourage students to think of the things they purchase as representing what they value most.

Listening and Speaking

Invite students to discuss their opinions of what constitutes a wise purchase. Remind students to use Standard American English.

Reteaching

📁 _Composition Reteaching,_ p. 1

Enrichment

📁 _Composition Enrichment,_ p. 1

🖼 _Fine Art Transparencies,_ 1–5

Close

Have students write a few paragraphs in which they identify two things that were important to them five years ago. Students can tell why or how their feelings have changed.

Grammar Link

Answers

1. bad   **3.** worst   **5.** worst
2. worse   **4.** worse

Collective Nouns Make sure students understand the answer to item 4 is _worse_ because the word _others_ is a collective noun that acts as a single unit.

Focus

Lesson Overview

Objective

- To select and record information related to personal experience and interests

Skills

- identifying attributes; collecting information; keeping track of information; recording information

Critical Thinking

- analyzing; recalling; evaluating; summarizing

Listening and Speaking

- taking notes; listening

 **Bellringer**

Daily Language Activity

When students enter the classroom, have this assignment on the board: *Write a paragraph in which you tell about something unusual that you noticed or learned today.*

Grammar Link to the Bellringer

Point out that people often use incomplete sentences in speech or in informal writing. Ask students to tell you why the following are incomplete sentences: *Not me. What a day! Whoa, Dude.*

See also *Daily Language Practice*

Motivating Activity

Tell students that much of what we know about the distant past comes from people's diaries and letters. Ask students what they might like people in the future to know about their lives and ideas.

Personal Writing

LESSON 1.2

Collecting Information

People use different forms of writing when they write just for themselves. They often create journal entries, lists, and graphic organizers that are never seen by anyone else.

Different forms fulfill different purposes in writing. Journal entries can give you ideas for creative writing, whereas lists and graphic organizers can help you organize—and remember—information. Look at the form the writer decided to use in each case above. How would you get these ideas down in writing?

12 Unit 1 Personal Writing

Resource Manager

Planning Resources
- *Lesson Plans*

Transparencies
- *Bellringer*
- *Daily Language Practice*
- *Fine Art 1–5*
- *Two-Minute Skill Drill*
- *Writing Process 1–10*

Other Print Resources
- *Composition Enrichment*, p. 2
- *Composition Practice*, p. 2
- *Composition Reteaching*, p. 2
- *Cooperative Learning Activities*, pp. 1–6
- *Listening and Speaking Activities*, pp. 14–15

- *Thinking and Study Skills*, pp. 3, 4, 9
- *Writing Across the Curriculum*
- *Writing Assessment and Evaluation Rubrics*

Keep Track of Information

Your journal is your space for exploring ideas and keeping track of information. You may record the events of your day and your reactions to them in your journal. You may also list writing ideas that come to you. Reread your journal often. Think about what you have written. Try out some of your writing ideas.

Journal Writing

Write in your journal for at least five minutes a day for one week. At the end of the week, reread your entries. In your journal write one observation about any entry that seems interesting.

Journal Writing Tip

1. Try to write in your journal every day.
2. Date journal entries for future reference.
3. Write whatever comes to mind.
4. Use any form that feels comfortable.

April 3

Sometimes I'm kind of scared about growing up. I haven't the slightest idea what I want to be. Dad says not to worry about it. He says some grown-ups don't know what they want to be when they grow up either.

HELP

Teach

Using the Model

Ask students to name the various media for note writing shown in the picture on the opposite page. Encourage students to create a journal in a format they like. Sometimes a particular pen or paper feels just right. Stress that they may use any type of media for keeping their journals, providing, of course, that their writing remains legible. **L2**

Cooperative Learning

Divide the class into four groups. Ask each group to devise a writing assignment for members of another group (write an apology note on a chalkboard; write an invitation to a graduation party on a paper grocery bag). After groups trade assignments and the members complete the work, have group members critique one another's work, discussing why each method was or was not appropriate. **L2**

Two-Minute Skill Drill

Give students the following instruction: *Write a sentence fragment that you commonly hear in speech. Rewrite the fragment as a complete sentence.*

See also *Two-Minute Skill Drill Transparency 1.2*

Journal Writing Tip

Monitoring Feelings Suggest that, as part of their journal entries, students include a list of things that elicit one specific emotional response, for example, irritation or joy.

Teach

Responding to Pictures

Collect a variety of photos from magazines, and tape them to pieces of white paper, creating wide borders. Have students work in groups, each group choosing one photo. Individual group members write in the borders their responses to the photo. Group members then discuss the similarities and differences among the personal responses. Groups may also want to write a group response to the photo, incorporating the individual responses. **L1**

Additional Resources

Fine Art Transparencies, 1–5.

Writing Process Transparencies, 1–10
Writing Across the Curriculum, p. 4
Cooperative Learning Activities, pp. 1–6
Thinking and Study Skills, pp. 3–4, 9
Listening and Speaking Activities, pp. 14–15
Composition Practice, p. 2

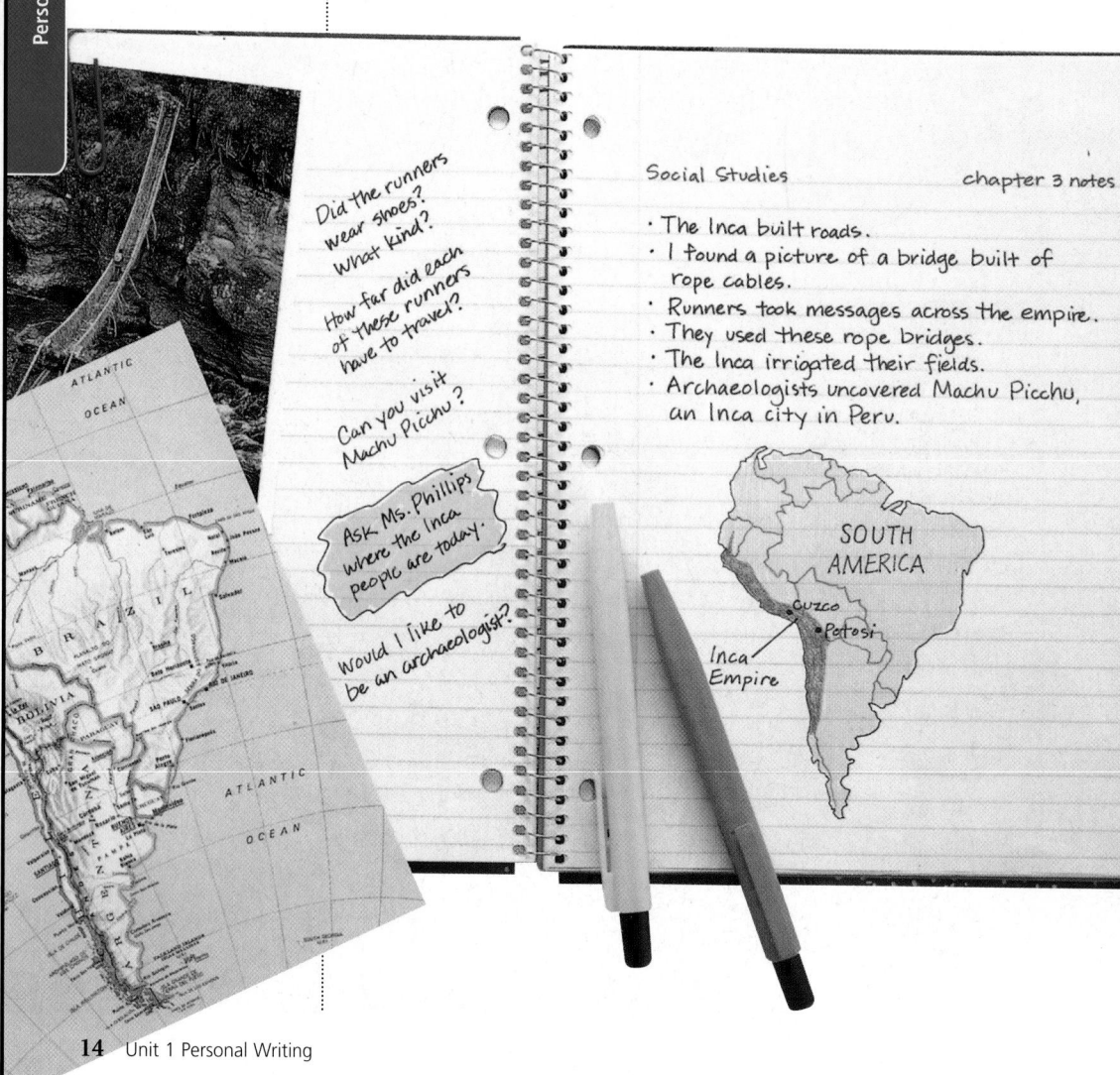

Personal Writing

Record Information

When you want to discover more about something you've covered in a class, use a learning log. A learning log is a place to write comments on what you are studying and to jot down questions that you have. You may use your journal or a separate notebook as a log. Study the log below in which one student listed information about an early civilization. Notice that the notes are informal and personal.

14 Unit 1 Personal Writing

English Language Learners

Keeping a Learning Log

Encourage your students learning English to keep a log of their progress in learning English. In their log books they might list troublesome spelling words, idiomatic expressions, and cultural differences that they observe. Students should also note the progress they've made in understanding written compared to spoken English. Suggest that students occasionally go back and read entries to reassure themselves that they are making progress.

1.2 Writing Activities

Write a Learning Log

Choose a chapter from another text-book, maybe a social studies or science book. Read the chapter, and make notes as you read. You may follow the form shown on page 14. Somewhere in the log, provide space to jot down questions or thoughts you might have as you are reading. Feel free to include drawings or graphics that might help you understand or recall the material. Remember, this is a personal study tool. Its purpose is to help you record and organize information. You will be the only one reading it, so make it meaningful to you.

PURPOSE To learn a study strategy
AUDIENCE Yourself
LENGTH 1 page

WRITING RUBRICS   To write an effective learning log, you should

- organize the information
- use your own words
- include questions and ideas

Using Computers

If you decide to keep a computer journal, you can create separate files for different types of writing. For example, one file can be a record of daily activities. Writing ideas can be stored in a second file. In another file you can explore private thoughts and feelings. If you are concerned about privacy, you can create your files on a removable disk and keep it in a safe place.

Grammar Link

Use complete sentences in formal writing.

Don't worry about *sentence fragments* when you're writing notes or journal items. When you write for others, however, use complete sentences.

Archaeologists uncovered Machu Picchu, an Inca city in Peru.

Rewrite each fragment below as a complete sentence.

1. The best day of my life.
2. Every day after school.
3. Hate some kinds of vegetables.
4. Good at expressing ideas.
5. Prefer creative to expository writing.
6. A long soccer practice after a hard day at school.
7. The writing assignment that is supposed to be due on Friday.
8. Going to a movie or maybe skating this weekend.

See Lesson 8.2, pages 359–360.

Viewing and Representing

Examine an illustration, chart, or diagram from the chapter you chose for your learning log activity or from another book or Web site that is related to the topic you chose. Write a brief explanation of how the graphic adds to your understanding of the text. Share your explanation with the class.

Assess

Evaluation Rubrics

Write a Learning Log

Use these criteria when evaluating your students' writing:

- The information is organized.
- The information is expressed in the students' own words.
- The students have included well-thought-out questions and ideas.

See also *Writing Assessment and Evaluation Rubrics*

Viewing and Representing

Be sure students understand that graphics can help them see and understand significant amounts of information at a glance.

Using Computers

Remind students to be sure to save any new files they create, if they intend to return to them later.

Reteaching

📁 *Composition Reteaching,* p. 2

Enrichment

📁 *Composition Enrichment,* p. 2

🗁 *Fine Art Transparencies,* 1–5

Close

Discuss with students how the types of personal writing in this lesson organize or enrich life experiences. Then ask students to write a brief summary of the class discussion.

Grammar Link

Answers

Answers will vary. Samples are given below.

1. Yesterday was the best day of my life.
2. I swim every day after school.
3. I hate some kinds of vegetables.
4. You are good at expressing ideas.
5. Most people prefer creative to expository writing.
6. I dread a long soccer practice after a hard day at school.
7. I brought the writing assignment that is supposed to be due on Friday.
8. We are going to a movie or maybe skating this weekend.

Focus

Lesson Overview

Objectives

- To choose main ideas to be shared in letters, invitations, and greeting cards
- To organize ideas and information in personal writing

Skills

- identifying important information; writing an invitation; writing a personal letter; recording information

Critical Thinking

- analyzing; recalling; evaluating; summarizing

Listening and Speaking

- speaking informally; reading aloud

Bellringer
Daily Language Activity

When students enter the classroom, have this assignment on the board: *Suppose you are going to have a party. Write what you would do to prepare for the event.*

Grammar Link to the Bellringer

Ask students what words they would capitalize in these sentences: *The party will be at my cousin Roberto's house. If you need a ride, come to my house tonight, and we can go to cousin Roberto's house in my mom's car.* (*Cousin* in the second sentence is capitalized.)

See also *Daily Language Practice*

Motivating Activity

Ask students to describe an invitation—formal or informal—they have received. What kind of information did it include? Ask students whether a written invitation seems more special than a verbal invitation. Why or why not?

Writing to Celebrate

A handwritten invitation to a celebration is one familiar type of personal writing you can share. A personal letter is another.

Dear Alan,
Get out your baseball cap. We're going to a game to celebrate my birthday. Meet at my house at 11:30 Saturday, May 12th. A barbecue will follow.
Hope to see you there!
Jih-Sheng
R.S.V.P.

Greeting card companies sell convenient fill-in-the-blank invitations. If you want that personal touch, however, you can write your own invitation. The handwritten invitation above includes all the information Alan needs to know about Jih-Sheng's birthday celebration.

All invitations should contain certain information. They should tell what the celebration is, the date and time and place of the celebration, and who the invitation is from. Additional information, such as special instructions or dress requirements, may also be included.

16 Unit 1 Personal Writing

Resource Manager

📁 Planning Resources
- *Lesson Plans*

Transparencies
- *Bellringer*
- *Daily Language Practice*
- *Fine Art* 1–5
- *Two-Minute Skill Drill*
- *Writing Process* 1–10

📁 Other Print Resources
- *Composition Enrichment,* p. 3
- *Composition Practice,* p. 3
- *Composition Reteaching,* p. 3
- *Listening and Speaking Activities,* pp. 14–15
- *Thinking and Study Skills,* pp. 3–5, 15
- *Writing Across the Curriculum*
- *Writing Assessment and Evaluation Rubrics*

Spread Good News

Printed or written announcements tell of certain events, such as weddings and graduations. Greeting cards help celebrate holidays and important occasions, such as birthdays, recitals, and vacations. Other kinds of personal writing can be reminders of events and experiences. Some of the notes and cards on the bulletin board below will remind the person who saved them of special times she spent with friends and family members. What other events will they remind her of?

Journal Writing

Think of something that you would like to celebrate with others. Then, in your journal, design and write an invitation to your celebration. Supply all of the important information: who is giving the celebration, the purpose and form of the celebration, and the date, time, and location.

Teach

Using the Model

Ask students what makes Jih-Sheng's invitation on page 16 unique. (A fill-in-the-blank card—the type on the rack at a card shop—wouldn't refer to the baseball game or barbecue, which are the most interesting features of Jih-Sheng's party.) **L2**

Making a Bulletin Board

Point out that the bulletin board is a kind of self-portrait. People make statements about who they are by the items they choose to display. What does the bulletin board shown say about the person who created it? Use a long sheet of paper to create a class "bulletin board." Divide the board into squares, one square for each student. Invite students to display pictures, postcards, memorabilia, and objects that reveal their interests. Invite students to tell why their bulletin board items are important and what special memories they hold. **L1**

Two-Minute Skill Drill

In preparation for the writing activity, have students list the kinds of information they would need to include in a personal invitation to a celebration at their homes.

See also Two-Minute Skill Drill Transparency 1.3

Journal Writing Tip

Capturing Tone Suggest that students identify the tone of the event before writing the invitation. For example, a birthday party would have a light-hearted tone; a graduation, while celebratory, might have a more solemn tone.

17

Teach

Using the Model

Suggest to students that they use the 5Ws (who? what? when? where? why/how?) to guide their understanding of written material—even if all five questions can't be clearly answered. Ask them to keep the 5Ws in mind as they read the letter from Eddie to Reggie. Then have them summarize the letter in their own words. **L2**

Additional Resources

 Fine Art Transparencies, 1–5.

 Writing Process Transparencies, 1–10
Writing Across the Curriculum, p. 4
Cooperative Learning Activities, pp. 1–6
Thinking and Study Skills, pp. 3–5, 15
Listening and Speaking Activities, pp. 14–15.

 Composition Practice, p. 3

Write Personal Letters

When you write a personal letter, you choose your audience. Your relationship with that person helps you decide what to say and how to say it. Your choice of stationery and the photographs, drawings, or news clippings you might include are important to the person who receives your letter.

Read the letter from Eddie to his older brother. What does the letter tell about the relationship between them? What might be different about a letter from Eddie to a friend?

> Dear Reggie,
>
> What's happening? Is college life as cool as you thought it would be? Are the classes hard? Who's your roommate? Do you get to go to all the games for free?
>
> It is weird around here without you. Mom really misses you. She's always saying, "I wonder how Reggie is doing." If you don't write or call soon, she may just show up at your dorm!
>
> Thanks for letting me have your old room. It was awful sharing a room with Ray. He was always getting into my stuff and bothering me. Don't worry, though. I'll let you have your room back at Thanksgiving.
>
> Your bro,
> Eddie

18 Unit 1 Personal Writing

Cultural Connections

Talking About Greeting Cards

Ask students who are familiar with other languages and cultures to talk about greeting cards from those cultures. How are the cards the same or different? Other than with greeting cards, how do people in their cultures acknowledge weddings, birthdays, and special holidays? What are the important holidays in their cultures?

Write an Invitation

Think about an upcoming party or celebration to which you might like to invite someone. Before you can write the invitation, you must plan the event. After you have made all of the important decisions about the celebration, decide whom you will be inviting and write the invitation. Be as creative as you can. You may use art or special paper to make your invitation.

PURPOSE To create an invitation
AUDIENCE A friend or relative
LENGTH 1 or 2 paragraphs

WRITING RUBRICS To write an effective invitation, you should

- make the invitation personal
- include the necessary information

Listening and Speaking

With a small group, discuss an upcoming celebration for which you would like to organize a party or an assembly in your school. Plan a public-address announcement and an invitation to share with those you wish to invite. Read each aloud and invite feedback from group members.

Spelling Hints

As you revise your invitation, remember that if a word ends with a consonant and a *y*, you must usually change the *y* to an *i* before you add a suffix.

try/tried   roomy/roominess
friendly/friendliness

Grammar Link

Capitalize proper names and titles correctly.

Eddie correctly capitalized the word *Mom* in his letter. He also did not capitalize a family relationship when it followed a possessive pronoun:
Your bro,

Write each sentence below, correcting errors in capitalization.

1. My Uncle is only sixteen years old.
2. We have been invited to senator Louise Brigham's victory party.
3. Tell me more about your childhood, grandpa.
4. My sister had to report to her Sergeant for her assignment.
5. For the next few days mother will be away on a business trip.
6. On Saturday mornings I shoot hoops with my dad.
7. Have you met the new science teacher, ms. a. j. Lewellyn?
8. The commanding officer is captain Stephen Fong.
9. I'm going to help aunt Claudia with her garden today.
10. I predict dad will be late again.

See Lesson 19.2, pages 575–576.

Personal Writing

Assess

Evaluation Rubrics

Write an Invitation

Use these criteria when evaluating your students' writing:

- The invitation clearly states the nature of the event.
- The invitation includes the sender's and receiver's names.
- The invitation states the time and place of the event.

See also *Writing Assessment and Evaluation Rubrics*

Listening and Speaking

Remind students that their evaluations of one another's announcements and invitations should be constructive.

Spelling Hints

Remind students who are writing their invitations in cursive manuscript to be sure to check their writing for legibility as well as for correct spelling.

Reteaching

📁 *Composition Reteaching*, p. 3

Enrichment

📁 *Composition Enrichment*, p. 3

Close

Suggest that students surprise a grandparent, parent, or friend with a personal letter for a birthday or other special occasion.

Grammar Link

Answers

Before assigning this exercise, remind students that some sentences are correct.

1. uncle
2. Senator
3. Grandpa
4. sergeant
5. Mother
6. (correct)
7. Ms. A. J. Lewellyn
8. Captain
9. Aunt
10. Dad

Capitalizing Titles You may wish to review with students that specific names of buildings are also capitalized. If, for example, students were writing an invitation to an event held at the Hotel Mandela or the Legion Hall, they should capitalize the name of the building.

Focus

Lesson Overview

Objectives

- To select, recall, and order information from personal experience
- To capture in writing the essence of a personal experience

Skills

- describing a personal experience; selecting ideas for writing a personal narrative; developing details

Critical Thinking

- recalling; evaluating; synthesizing

Listening and Speaking

- speaking informally

 Bellringer
Daily Language Activity

When students enter the classroom, have this assignment on the board: *Family stories often begin with the same words, such as "Remember the time that . . ." Jot notes about something that happened to you, a friend, or a relative.*

Grammar Link to the Bellringer

Write the following on the board:
Knock! Knock!
Who's there?
It's me.
Ask students whether they think the response is grammatically correct. Discuss their responses, making sure that students understand why *me* should be *I*.

See also *Daily Language Practice*

Motivating Activity

Have students discuss their responses to the Bellringer activity. Ask how a storyteller can share the feelings that make a memory special.

Personal Writing

Writing About Yourself

Another kind of personal writing is about personal experiences. The words writers choose and the details they provide depend on how they feel about what happened.

Suppose you are trying out skating for the first time. The fast pace of the skaters speeding around the rink surprises you and makes you nervous about falling. Your account of the experience will probably reflect your nervousness.

In the model below, Farley Mowat, a writer and naturalist, describes a personal experience. Notice how Mowat uses precise details to describe his feelings as he comes face to face with one of the wolves he traveled to the Arctic to study.

Literature Model

Notice the writer's use of the word "quarry." The reader knows Mowat was looking for the wolf.

Which details express the writer's feelings about this experience?

My head came slowly over the crest—and there was my quarry. He was lying down, evidently resting after his mournful singsong, and his nose was about six feet from mine. We stared at one another in silence. I do not know what went on in his massive skull, but my head was full of the most disturbing thoughts. I was peering straight into the amber gaze of a fully grown arctic wolf, who probably weighed more than I did, and who was certainly a lot better versed in close-combat techniques than I would ever be.

Farley Mowat, *Never Cry Wolf*

20 Unit 1 Personal Writing

Resource Manager

📖 **Planning Resources**
- *Lesson Plans*

📓 **Transparencies**
- *Bellringer*
- *Daily Language Practice*
- *Fine Art* 1–5
- *Two-Minute Skill Drill*
- *Writing Process* 1–10

📖 **Other Print Resources**
- *Composition Enrichment*, p. 5
- *Composition Practice*, p. 5
- *Composition Reteaching*, p. 5
- *Cooperative Learning Activities*, pp. 1–6
- *Listening and Speaking Activities*, pp. 14–15

- *Thinking and Study Skills*, pp. 6–9, 11
- *Writing Across the Curriculum*
- *Writing Assessment and Evaluation Rubrics*

Recall Your Experiences

When you want to write about a personal experience, begin by thinking about important or interesting events in your life. Concentrate on experiences that made you feel a strong emotion or that made you think about something or someone in a different way.

Trying out for the play scared me.

I can't believe I was elected class president.

Being a big brother for the first time is OK.

This student is recalling some experiences that may lead to personal writing.

Journal Writing

Recall three or four interesting experiences you have had in the last year. List them in your journal, mark one to share, and name an audience for whom you would write.

Teach

Using the Model

Ask students to paraphrase what occurs in the Mowat passage on page 20. Then ask them these questions: Is Mowat afraid of the wolf? Would you be? Can you guess the meaning of the word *quarry* from the context? Which details express the writer's feelings about this experience? (His head was *full of the most disturbing thoughts.* He notes the wolf's experience in *close-combat techniques.*) **L2**

Thinking About Animals

Use the model to stimulate ideas, suggesting that students think about their experiences with animals. They can think about family pets or neighbors' pets or about visits to parks, zoos, or camping areas. What about their experiences would they like to share with others? **L1**

Two-Minute Skill Drill

In preparation for the writing activity, have students list three words that describe the feelings they had during their experiences. Then for each word, have them write a vivid, descriptive phrase that will present that feeling to readers.

See also *Two-Minute Skill Drill Transparency 1.4*

Journal Writing Tip

Recalling Experiences In addition to the obvious experiences, such as birthdays, family vacations, getting a new pet, and so on, suggest that students think about turning-point events, such as meeting someone who changed their lives or attitudes.

Teach

Using the Model

Explain to students how a cluster diagram works: the main idea is in a balloon in the center; supporting details branch off from it. Ordering the details comes later. Ask students to reread the model, looking for the ideas from the cluster diagram. Point out that the main idea, *I stepped on a snake,* is not the first idea mentioned. The writer sets up the passage with other details first. **L2**

Using the Models

Point out that the literature model on page 20 and the student model on page 22 take place in very different environments, yet both pieces describe feelings that readers can relate to. Ask students what both pieces have in common. (Both describe feelings of surprise and of fear; both describe encounters with possibly dangerous animals; both build suspense.) **L2**

Additional Resources

- *Fine Art Transparencies,* 1–5.
- *Writing Process Transparencies,* 1–10
- *Writing Across the Curriculum,* p. 5
- *Cooperative Learning Activities,* pp. 1–6
- *Thinking and Study Skills,* pp. 6–9, 11
- *Listening and Speaking Activities,* pp. 14–15
- *Composition Practice,* p. 5

Personal Writing

Select a Writing Idea

Consider an experience you would like to share with readers. Focus on how you felt about that experience. Think about the details that will help you explain your thoughts and feelings. One writer listed "I stepped on a snake" as one of her experiences. Then she listed thoughts about that experience to use in her writing. Look at the cluster diagram, and then read the student model below to see how Simone Tucker shared her encounter with a snake.

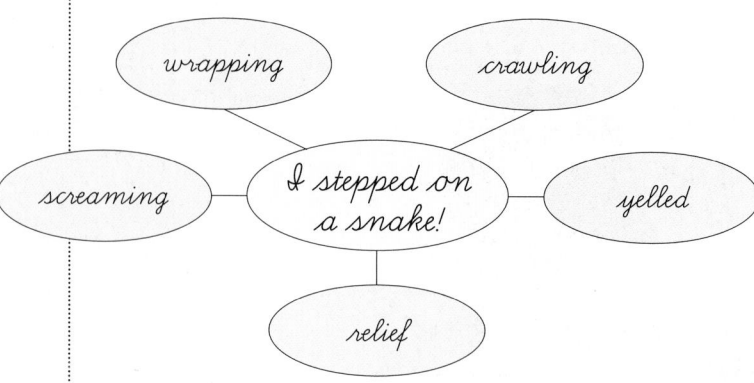

Student Model

Notice the words Simone uses in the first paragraph to focus on her fear.

One day last summer my cousin and I went downstairs to iron our clothes. We entered the washroom and I stepped on something. It felt long, slimy, and as if it was crawling up and down my leg while wrapping around my foot. I screamed. My cousin immediately reached for the lights and turned them on, only to discover I was standing on a snake! We both yelled, "Snake!" Jumping and screaming, we ran upstairs.

How does Simone let the reader know that her reaction to the snake changes?

Several hours later, we found the snake, captured it in a bottle, and let it go. What a relief!

Simone Tucker, Kirby Junior High, St. Louis, Missouri

MEETING INDIVIDUAL NEEDS English Language Learners

Understanding Word Choices

Some words in the literature model on page 20 may not be familiar to students learning English. Point out and discuss words or phrases such as *singsong, massive skull, peering, amber gaze,* and *close-combat techniques.* Ask students why they think that the author uses these words instead of, for example, *howling, big head, looking, strange glance,* or *fighting.*

Write About an Experience

Choose one experience from the list you made in the Journal Writing activity on page 21. Focus on your feelings about the experience. Make a cluster like the one on the previous page. Then write about your experience in a short piece of personal writing to share with your class.

PURPOSE To express your feelings about a personal experience

AUDIENCE Your teacher and classmates

LENGTH 1–2 paragraphs

WRITING RUBRICS To write effectively about an experience, you should

- include emotions and feelings
- use adequate detail

Torquato S. Pessoa, *Carousel*, 1960

Viewing and Representing

Look at the painting on this page. What emotions does the artist express in the painting? What elements of the painting communicate those emotions? Write your thoughts as a journal entry.

Cross-Curricular Activity

ART Recall an amusement park ride you have taken or any experience you think would make an interesting painting. List the details you would use in creating the painting. Would you use bold colors as the artist did for this painting? In one paragraph of personal writing, describe the picture you would create.

Grammar Link

Use the correct personal pronoun.

*One day last summer my cousin and **I** went downstairs to iron our clothes.*

*Trying out for the play scared **me**.*

Complete each sentence by inserting the correct pronoun, *I* or *me*.

1. Could Carlos's dad have cooked beef for Carlos and _____?
2. My mom says that Carlos and _____ have active imaginations.
3. Only Mom can talk that way about Carlos and _____.

See Lesson 11.3, pages 433–434.

Assess

Evaluation Rubrics

Write About an Experience

Use the following criteria when evaluating your students' writing:

- Does it express the student's feelings and emotions?
- Does it include adequate details?

Cross-Curricular Activity

In describing a personal experience that might make an interesting painting, the student should

- list details
- create writing that is rich in detail and vivid description

See also *Writing Assessment and Evaluation Rubrics*

Viewing and Representing

Ask students to respond to the use of color in the painting. Invite them to comment on ways the artist uses color to convey meaning.

Reteaching

📁 *Composition Reteaching*, p. 5

Enrichment

📁 *Composition Enrichment*, p. 5

🖼 *Fine Art Transparencies*, 1–5

Close

Suggest that students write about a personal experience they had when they were much younger—perhaps their first day of school. Tell students that since they probably won't remember all the details of the experience, they can take "artistic license" and use their creativity to flesh out parts of the experience that they do not recall. Invite students to share their writing with classmates.

Grammar Link

Answers

1. me **2.** I **3.** me

Personal Pronouns Students might be misled by the compound subjects and objects. After students finish the exercise, write the sentences on the board, omitting *Carlos*. Invite students to change their answers, if necessary.

Viewing the Art

Torquato S. Pessoa, *Carousel*, 1960
Torquato S. Pessoa was an artist of the Modernist movement, which began in the 1920s. The style of painting used in *Carousel* was at first opposed by much of the artistic community because it was so childlike in its simplicity.

Focus

Lesson Overview

Objectives

- To observe characteristics and formulate questions about characters
- To respond to characters in literature

Skills

- identifying attributes; responding to characters' actions

Critical Thinking

- identifying; analyzing; evaluating

Listening and Speaking

- listening to and discussing ideas in small groups

 Bellringer

Daily Language Activity

When students enter the classroom, have this assignment on the board: *In a paragraph, identify and describe a memorable character from a book or a movie.*

Grammar Link to the Bellringer

Ask students to list five specific adjectives that describe the person they named in the Bellringer activity.

See also *Daily Language Practice*

Motivating Activity

Ask students to share their responses to the Bellringer activity. Then prompt them to respond to the following questions: *Did you like the character because the character reminded you of yourself—or someone you would like to be like? Why did you remember that particular character?*

Personal Writing

LESSON 1.5

WRITING ABOUT LITERATURE

Responding to a Character

In the excerpt below, Louise Bradshaw tells how she feels about her twin sister Caroline. Notice how author Katherine Paterson's characters bring her story to life.

Literature Model

I would come in from a day of progging [poking, searching] for crab, sweating and filthy. Caroline would remark mildly that my fingernails were dirty. How could they be anything else but dirty? But instead of simply acknowledging the fact, I would fly into a wounded rage. How dare she call me dirty? How dare she try to make me feel inferior to her own pure, clear beauty? It wasn't my fingernails she was concerned with, that I was sure of. She was using my fingernails to indict my soul. Wasn't she content to be golden perfection without cutting away at me? Was she to allow me no virtue—no shard of pride or decency?

By now I was screaming. Wasn't it I who brought in the extra money that paid for her trips to Salisbury [a town where Caroline studied music]? She ought to be on her knees thanking me for all I did for her. How dare she criticize? How dare she?

Katherine Paterson, *Jacob Have I Loved*

Resource Manager

Planning Resources
- *Lesson Plans*

Transparencies
- *Bellringer*
- *Daily Language Practice*
- *Fine Art* 1–5
- *Two-Minute Skill Drill*
- *Writing Process* 1–10

Other Print Resources
- *Composition Enrichment*, p. 5
- *Composition Practice*, p. 5
- *Composition Reteaching*, p. 5
- *Cooperative Learning Activities*, pp. 1–6
- *Listening and Speaking Activities*, pp. 14–15

- *Thinking and Study Skills*, pp. 3–6, 9, 22
- *Writing Across the Curriculum*
- *Writing Assessment and Evaluation Rubrics*

Write Your Response

Using personal writing to respond to a character can help you better understand the character and the story. Perhaps you have read a story with a character you would like to talk to. Maybe you thought it would be interesting to stop reading and say, "Wait! That's not such a good idea!" or "I know just how you feel." Look at the examples below. One reader wrote a lesson in progging for Caroline. The other reader sympathized with Louise.

Progging Directions for Caroline

1. Get a bucket, a boat, and a pole.

2. In your boat go to the place your sister finds crabs.

3. Poke in the mud until you find a crab.

4. Pick up the crab, and put it into the bucket.

5. Are your fingernails clean?

Dear Louise,

I have an older sister like Caroline. Sometimes I think I don't really like her much. Then I feel like I must be horrible to think about my own sister that way. It made me feel better to know someone else felt the same way I do.

Sincerely,
Julie

Journal Writing

In your journal list ideas you would like to share with either Caroline or Louise. What does your list show about your feelings toward the sisters' relationship?

Teach

Using the Model

Ask students to contrast the two sisters described in the passage on page 24. What are the students' impressions of Caroline? of Louise? What adjectives does the author use to describe the two sisters and their feelings? (Louise: *sweating and filthy, dirty, wounded;* Caroline: *pure, clear, golden.*) Ask students if they sympathize with Louise. Why? **L2**

Using the Model

Explain to students that sometimes they will enjoy a novel more if they can identify with the central character. Ask students to read Julie's letter on page 25. Does Julie identify with Louise? What is her reaction to the passage from *Jacob Have I Loved?* **L2**

Two-Minute Skill Drill

Have students use more specific words or phrases to replace each word below: (Example: talks—chatters nervously)

dull	*tired*	*red*
walks	*sweaty*	*breathes*

See also 📄 *Two-Minute Skill Drill Transparency 1.5*

Journal Writing Tip

Responding to Characters' Relationships Students might find it helpful to begin by thinking about the relationships of sisters they know. Why do some sisters get along well and others seem locked in mortal combat? Do sisters who are very different as individuals often get along well?

Teach

Using the Model

Ask students to name characteristics that Mary Lennox and Jean Little share. (They are both disagreeable looking, selfish, bad-tempered, and lazy; they have both done reprehensible things; they both grow into someone quite different.) "An old poem says that a child born on a Sunday will have a happy personality." What does this reference tell a reader? (Jean doesn't think she has a happy personality.) Ask students why a writer might use such an indirect method of telling a reader something about a character. (It allows the reader to make a discovery and is, therefore, a powerful, intimate way of sharing information.) **L2**

Additional Resources

- *Fine Art Transparencies,* 1–5.

- *Writing Process Transparencies,* 1–10
- *Writing Across the Curriculum,* p. 11
- *Cooperative Learning Activities,* pp. 1–6
- *Thinking and Study Skills,* pp. 3–6, 9, 22
- *Listening and Speaking Activities,* pp. 14–15.
- *Composition Practice,* p. 5

Personal Writing

Meet People in Books

Sometimes a fictional character proves to be an important influence in a reader's life. Jean Little wrote a book telling about things that influenced the way she felt and thought as a child. When Little was very young, she met a character named Mary Lennox in a book her mother read aloud. If you have read *The Secret Garden* or if you have seen the film, compare your own response to Mary. If you haven't read the book or seen the film, try to imagine what kind of person Mary is as you read Little's reaction.

THE SECRET GARDEN

Frances Hodgson Burnett
Illustrated by Michael Hague

Literature Model

What is the effect of the sentence "I laid down my spoon"?

An old poem says that a child born on Sunday will have a happy personality. What does this reference tell a reader?

Why do you suppose Little included the last paragraph?

Mother opened the book and began. *When Mary Lennox was sent to Misselthwaite Manor to live with her uncle, everybody said she was the most disagreeable looking child ever seen. It was true, too.*

I laid down my spoon. From the first sentence, *The Secret Garden* seemed especially mine. I did not wonder what Mary Lennox looked like. I knew. She looked exactly like me.

Mary had clearly not been born on a Sunday, either. She, too, was selfish and bad-tempered and lazy. She even tried to get Martha to put her shoes on for her. I wasn't the only one who had done such a reprehensible thing.

Yet little by little, she grew into somebody quite different. And the way it happened made perfect sense. I knew that I, too, would be different if I could find a hidden garden and friends like Dickon and Colin and the robin.

Jean Little, *Little by Little*

26 Unit 1 Personal Writing

MEETING INDIVIDUAL NEEDS — Less-Proficient Readers

Understanding Characters

Show students a portion of a movie, stopping at a critical moment. Ask students to tell you what they know about a specific character from his or her speech, actions, and facial expressions. Explain that in literature, such character information is presented through dialogue and through the use of vivid language and detailed description.

Write a Letter

Look through this book for a painting that has one or more people in it. Write a letter to a character in the painting. Ask the character questions or tell the character what you think of the painting. You might consider asking questions about the character's clothes or expression or about what he or she is doing in that scene.

PURPOSE To express thoughts and feelings about a character

AUDIENCE A character in a painting

LENGTH 2 paragraphs

WRITING RUBRICS To write your letter effectively you should

- think of the character as if he or she were real
- ask questions based on the painting

Listening and Speaking

In a small group, choose a person you have studied in history. Quickly brainstorm a list of the person's accomplishments. Within the group discuss what might have been the person's greatest accomplishments. Then discuss the extent of agreement within the group. Express and explain your ideas clearly and fluently. Finally, write a brief summary of your group's discussion.

Using Computers

With a partner, write a response to a writer whose work you both enjoy reading. Some contemporary writers publish e-mail addresses on their Web pages. If the writer you choose does not have a Web page, write a letter to that author. Use a word processing program to make sure that your letter or e-mail is clear and accurate.

Personal Writing

Use strong, vivid adjectives.

*She, too, was **selfish** and **bad-tempered** and **lazy.***

Replace each numbered adjective with a strong, vivid adjective.

Jean Little is a ¹good writer. She gives an ²interesting description of Mary Lennox and ³fine examples to demonstrate Mary's ⁴bad qualities. Little admits that she herself did ⁵wrong things; that's why she identifies with the ⁶bad Mary Lennox. She also admires the ⁷good way the author shows the ⁸slow change in Mary. I'd rather have ⁹somewhat bad friends, like Mary Lennox and Jean Little, than ¹⁰nicey-nice kids as my friends.

See Lesson 12.1, pages 451–452.

1.5 Responding to a Character **27**

Assess

Evaluation Rubrics

Write a Letter

Use these criteria when evaluating your students' writing:

- demonstrates the student's exploration of visual detail
- expresses the student's feelings about the painting
- states who the letter is to and from

See also *Writing Assessment and Evaluation Rubrics*

Listening and Speaking

Encourage students to discuss what common character traits exist among history's most influential people. Remind students to use Standard American English when speaking.

Using Computers

Remind students to carefully proofread their e-mail letters. Using the spelling checker on a word processing program will not catch grammatical errors or even all spelling errrors.

Reteaching

📁 *Composition Reteaching*, p. 5

Enrichment

📁 *Composition Enrichment*, p. 5

🖨 *Fine Art Transparencies*, 1–5

Close

Have students choose a "bad guy" character from literature, movies, or television. In a partners activity, have students tell each other the basic plot of the story and describe in detail the bad character's personality and actions. Have them speculate why the character acted as he or she did. Finally, have each student describe in detail the "good guy" character and how the good character overcame the bad character.

Answers

Answers will vary. Sample:
1. good, insightful

Finding Strong, Precise Adjectives Have students use a thesaurus to look up common or overworked adjectives and to find more precise words to use instead.

Focus

Lesson Overview

Objectives

- To explore thoughts and feelings about a special day
- To write about a special day

Skills

- using the five stages of the writing process: prewriting, drafting, revising, editing, and presenting

Critical Thinking

- recalling; synthesizing; decision-making

Listening and Speaking

- taking notes; informal speaking

 Bellringer
Daily Language Activity

When students enter the classroom, have this assignment on the board: *Write a sentence about a special day in your life. Use at least one adjective.*

Grammar Link to the Bellringer

Have pairs of students exchange sentences. Tell students to check each other's work to make sure that the correct forms of adjectives are used.

See also *Daily Language Practice*

Motivating Activity

Ask students to recall more about a special day in their lives. What was special about it? What part of the day stands out most clearly? Was it a day of fun? Did something particularly unusual or interesting occur? Was it a day that brought about a change in their lives? Were other people involved? Encourage students to recall both feelings and factual details.

Personal Writing
(sidebar label)

Personal Writing

In preceding lessons you've learned how to gather and organize your ideas to create a piece of personal writing that expresses your own thoughts, feelings, and memories of important personal experiences. Now it's time to make use of what you learned by writing about the events and feelings you experienced on a special day in your life.

WRITING *Online*

Visit the *Writer's Choice* Web site at **writerschoice. glencoe.com** for additional writing prompts.

Assignment

Context	You and other students will share articles that tell things you did and felt during a special day. It may have been an important day, a happy day, or a day of change.
Purpose	To communicate the importance of one special day through personal writing
Audience	Other students
Length	1 page

The following pages can help you plan and write your article. Read through them and then refer to them as needed. But don't be tied down by them. You're in charge of your own writing process.

Resource Manager

 **Planning Resources**
- *Lesson Plans*

 **Transparencies**
- *Bellringer*
- *Daily Language Practice*
- *Writing Process* 1–10

Other Print Resources
- *Composition Enrichment*, p. 6
- *Composition Practice*, p. 6
- *Composition Reteaching*, p. 6
- *Grammar Workbook*, Lessons 93–97
- *Thinking and Study Skills*, pp. 3, 5, 8
- *Writing Assessment and Evaluation Rubrics*

 **Software**
- *Writer's Assistant*

 **Web Sites**
- *writerschoice.glencoe.com*
- *lit.glencoe.com*

Writing Process in Action

Prewriting

First, you'll want to choose a special day to write about. To gather ideas, you might review your journal, look through old photos, or list some experiences important to you.

After selecting a special day, you'll be ready to develop your idea. Try making a cluster diagram to help you focus on your thoughts and feelings about the day you're considering.

Next, think about how you will order your ideas. Usually, the best way to tell a story is in the order in which events occurred.

Drafting

Now it's time to expand your ideas and notes into sentences and paragraphs. If you have difficulty getting started with your first draft, it may help to pretend that you are writing or talking to a close friend. Your friend would want to know what happened and how you thought and felt about it. Notice how Latoya Hunter focuses on her feelings in the following excerpt from her diary:

Option A
Review your journal.

Option B
Look at photos and souvenirs.

Option C
List memorable events.

- First dance performance
- First week of jr. high
- Youth group camp
- Grandpa's visit
- Backpacking in Yosemite
- Work at child-care center
- Week Smoky was lost

Literature Model

After church today I felt the urge to do something independent. I started walking and found myself heading home. . . . I got in trouble with both parents. . . . That's really embarrassing that they got upset for that! I thought I was more grown than that. I know I am, but they don't.

Latoya Hunter, from *The Diary of Latoya Hunter*

Writing Process in Action **29**

Teach

Prewriting

Developing Ideas for Personal Writing

Encourage students to use clusters to organize main ideas and supporting details for prewriting. Later, they can decide on the best order for presenting the information. **L2**

Drafting

Expressing Ideas in Conversation

Give students an opportunity to review the drafting suggestions on this page. Allow them to work in pairs to express their ideas in brief conversations. **L2**

Teach

Revising

Peer Editing

Students can work in writing conferences with peer editors before they revise their writing. You may want to duplicate the Peer Response forms in *Writing Assessment and Evaluation Rubrics.* Suggest that peer editors respond to the following questions:

- Has the writer kept in mind the purpose of the writing?
- What additional details would help readers share that day's events? **L2**

Cooperative Learning

Ask students to work in threes, interviewing one another about a special day and gathering specific details. Students can then share the information with the larger group and use it in writing about the special day. **L2**

Editing/Proofreading

Peer Editing

After students have edited their own work, have them edit another student's writing. Remind them to refer to the Editing/Proofreading Checklist on student page 31. **L2**

Publishing/Presenting

Before students present their personal writing, discuss how they should prepare their papers for publication. Emphasize the importance of the final draft and that it must be neatly done.

Additional Resources

 Writing Process Transparencies, 1–10
Thinking and Study Skills, pp. 3, 5, 8
Composition Practice, p. 6

Grammar Workbook, Lessons 93–97

Personal Writing

Drafting Tip

For more information about using strong adjectives to make your details vivid, see Lesson 12.1, pages 451–452.

Hunter uses an event—getting in trouble for walking home from church—to express her frustration about being treated like a child.

As you write, refer to your prewriting notes to keep your writing on track. Remember to focus on what it is that makes this day special. Use vivid details, but don't worry now about including too many or too few. Just get your ideas down on paper. You can add, delete, or reorder details during revision.

Revising

To begin revising, read over your draft to make sure that what you have written fits your purpose and your audience. Then have a **writing conference.** Read your draft to a partner or a small group, or receive feedback from your teacher. Use your audience's reactions to help you evaluate your work so far. The questions below can help you and your listeners.

Question A

Have I explained why this event was special?

Question B

Is the order of events clear?

Question C

Have I used important details carefully?

It was the first Sunday in October. The many-colored fallen leaves swirled across our path as we drove to the airport. The drive to the airport seemed to take forever. I'm not a very patient person and riding in a car really bored me. I hadn't seen my grandfather (for almost three years,) so I was really excited. (When we got to the gate,) I could see my grandfather walking toward us. He waved his hat in the air. I jumped up and down. I must have looked pretty silly, but I didn't care.

30 Unit 1 Personal Writing

Enrichment and Extension

Follow-up Ideas

- Allow students to celebrate concluding their writing projects. Encourage them to share their finished pieces.
- If students are sending their work out of the classroom, make sure to retain photocopies.

Extending Personal Writing

Explore opportunities for extending personal writing beyond the classroom. One idea:

- Have students interview senior citizens in the community about their lives and then record the results.

After considering those questions, you might discover that you need clearer or stronger details. Try doing some additional prewriting, such as listing details about the event. Remember, you can always return to the prewriting and drafting stages while revising.

Editing/Proofreading

The editing stage is your opportunity to clean up any errors in grammar, spelling, and punctuation. The checklist at the right will help you **proofread** your draft. Read through your revised draft several times, looking for one or two kinds of errors at a time. Careful editing can make your writing as special as the event that inspired it.

Publishing/Presenting

Although your writing is very personal, you may wish to share it with others. Be sure to write legibly, using print or cursive handwriting. You might want to exchange your writing with another student and ask for feedback. Finally, consider enhancing your presentation by including a memento, such as a photo or souvenir, of that special time.

Editing/Proofreading Checklist

1. Have I correctly capitalized names and titles?
2. Have I used the correct forms of adjectives?
3. Have I used the correct forms of pronouns?
4. Have I corrected any sentence fragments?
5. Have I spelled every word correctly?

Proofreading

For proofreading symbols, see page 80.

Journal Writing

Reflect on your writing process experience. Answer these questions in your journal: What did you like best about your personal writing? What was the hardest part of writing it? What did you learn in your writing conference? What new things have you learned as a writer?

Assess

Evaluation Rubrics

Use the following criteria to evaluate your students' finished writing. Make sure each student has provided the following:

- a logical, ordered description of events
- a clear indication of why the day was special
- sensory details that enhance the story
- an exploration of his or her feelings about the event
- evidence of editing for spelling and grammar
- pictures or other graphic support

See also *Writing Assessment and Evaluation Rubrics*

Reteaching

📁 *Composition Reteaching*, p. 6

Enrichment

📁 *Composition Enrichment*, p. 6

Journal Writing Tip

Journal Writing Activity Encourage students to think about whether their personal writing acts as a reflection of them.

Close

Having completed one piece of personal writing about a special day, invite students to think of topics that they'd like to explore next. Invite them to discuss what steps of the process they might do differently next time.

Technology Tip

Desktop Publishing

Most word processing programs allow users to choose among a variety of fonts, or typefaces, and sizes. Students may want to experiment with these functions, creating titles in a font different from the text and choosing fonts that suit the style of their work. Students can emphasize a word by using italics or boldface. Clip art is also available for computers. To illustrate their writing, students can choose pictures and symbols from a palette, import them into their documents, and place them where they like.

Literature Model

Literature Model

Personal Writing

About the Author

Latoya Hunter was born in Jamaica and lived there until she was eight. Then she moved to the Bronx, New York, where she attended her first year of junior high. Latoya was described as "shy but self-possessed," "smart," and "sensitive." These qualities and her writing skill led to her being asked to write a diary for publication.

Focus

Lesson Overview

Objectives

- To follow a teenage writer on a journey of self-exploration
- To write a letter comparing feelings, values, and experiences

Skills

- connecting; monitoring comprehension

Critical Thinking

- evaluating; inferring; drawing conclusions

Listening and Speaking

- discussing; questioning

 **Bellringer**
Daily Language Activity

When students enter the classroom, have this assignment on the board: *Write a brief paragraph telling about something that happened to you yesterday.*

See also *Daily Language Practice*

Motivating Activity

Ask students to raise their hands if they currently keep, or have ever kept, a diary. Discuss reasons why people might enjoy keeping a diary. Have volunteers read their Bellringer activity paragraphs. Ask whether students think the paragraphs would make good diary entries.

FROM

The Diary of Latoya Hunter

by Latoya Hunter

A diary is usually a very personal written record, but a book editor asked Latoya Hunter to keep a diary for everybody to see. Latoya's diary reflects the thoughts and feelings of a typical teenager. Notice how Latoya's personal writing illustrates changes within herself. Notice also how she considers the ways that she is connected to other people. Then try the activities in Linking Writing and Literature on page 38.

Resource Manager

 **Planning Resources**
- *Lesson Plans*

 **Transparencies**
- *Bellringer*
- *Daily Language Practice*
- *Fine Art* 1–5

 **Other Print Resources**
- *Listening and Speaking Activities,* pp. 14–15
- *Thinking and Study Skills,* pp. 1–6
- *Writing Assessment and Evaluation Rubrics*

Web Sites
- writerschoice.glencoe.com
- lit.glencoe.com

Literature Model

September 11, 1990

Dear Diary,

I never thought I'd get desperate enough to say this but I envy you. You don't have to live in this troubled world; all you do is hear about it. You don't have to go to J.H. and watch the clock, praying for dismissal time to come. You also don't have to go through a situation like sitting in a cafeteria watching others laughing and talking and you don't know anyone. To sit there and eat the food that is just terrible because there's nothing else to do.

You don't do any of those things. All you do is listen to pathetic[1] twelve-year-olds like me tell you about it.

I guess you can tell how my day went. Diary, what am I going to do? My best friend left to go to another school. I wish she could be with me. We had so much fun together. She moved right before summer started. She doesn't live anywhere close so it would be much easier if she stayed at the school closest to her. That's the only part of it that's easy. The hardest part is not being together.

September 30, 1990

Dear Diary,

I think I need a name for you. You've become like a best friend to me, you're someone I can talk to without being argued with. I think I know just the name for you. I'll call you Janice after my best friend from Jamaica. We were like sisters before I left. Over the years we've grown apart though, the letters have stopped but that friendship is still going on within me!

So today I christen[2] you diary, Janice Page.

---

[1]**pathetic** (pə thet′ik) causing pity or sorrow
[2]**christen** (kris′ən) to give a name to a person or thing

Personal Writing

Literature Model **33**

Teach

Literary Elements

Character Ask students what they can tell about Latoya from reading her first diary entry. What's going on in her life? How does she feel about it? *(Latoya's best friend has just moved. Without her, Latoya feels lonely, sad, and bored at school.)*

Critical Thinking

Infer Ask students: "From what you know about Latoya, why do you think she gives her diary a name?" *(Latoya is lonely and doesn't have friends at school. Giving her diary the name of an old friend probably helps her feel less lonely.)*

6+1 Trait® Writing

Voice

Tell students that when writing has a strong voice, a reader can sense a real person behind the words. Say: "Just as your speaking voice is unique to you, a writer's voice is unique to him or her. And just as the tone of your speaking voice affects the meaning of the words you speak, the way a writer says something can be as important as what a writer says."

Tell students that Latoya Hunter's writing has voice. Her diary entries sound like they come from a twelve-year-old girl, and they reflect her unique concerns and sensibilities. Point out these lines from the first paragraph of the first

entry as an example: "You also don't have to go through a situation like sitting in a cafeteria watching others laughing and talking and you don't know anyone. To sit there and eat the food that is just terrible because there's nothing else to do."

Practice Write the first part of the above quotation on the board: "You also don't have to go through a situation like. . . ." Then have students finish the sentence and write another one in a way that expresses their unique outlooks.

For more information on voice and the 6+1 Trait® model, see **Writing and Research Handbook**, pp. 822–824.

33

Teach

Active Reading Strategies

Connect Ask students whether the changing friendship Latoya describes in the October 2 diary entry reminds them of friendships that have changed over time in their own lives. On the basis of their experience, do they think Latoya would like to be friends with Jimmy if the opportunity presented itself?

6+1 Trait® Writing

Voice Ask students: "How would you describe Latoya's attitude toward her brothers? What phrases from the October 7 diary entry show her attitude?" *(Latoya's attitude is accepting but a little sad—even resentful. She loves her brothers, but she feels distant from them. She says, "… they've got girlfriends and they're making new lives for themselves. It's impossible to have a close relationship to either of them.")*

Literature Model

Personal Writing

October 2, 1990

Dear Janice,

It's hard to believe but people change as rapidly as the world does. If I had kept you as a diary two years ago, you would have heard about Jimmy. He was the first guy who I was close to and who was a real friend to me. I liked him because other boys always seemed to be in a popularity contest, and he didn't care about that stuff. He was handsome and everything but he never let it get to his head. Well lately he's been going to the other side. He has a new walk, new talk, new look—the works! He ignores me, I guess I'm not popular enough for him! He just isn't the same.

October 7, 1990

Dear Janice,

This weekend was spent at home, at my brother's house and at church.

> *. . . I felt the urge to do something independent.*

My brothers just moved out recently. They don't live very far though, about 15 minutes away from the house. Their new house is nice. I like it there. They're both so funny. One is Dave and the other is Courtney. They're like twins except they look nothing alike and are a couple years apart. Dave is 23 and Courtney is 25. We don't communicate much anymore—they've got girlfriends and they're making new lives for themselves. It's impossible now to have a close relationship with either of them.

After church today I felt the urge to do something independent. I started walking and found myself heading home. Church and home aren't too close together so when I did get home I got in trouble with both parents—it's usually only my mom, but my father didn't approve either. That's really embarrassing that they got upset for that! I thought I was more grown than that. I know I am, but

34 Unit 1 Personal Writing

Active Reading Strategies

Connect

Tell students that reading becomes more interesting when they make connections between the text and their own lives. Explain that to connect with this narrative, for example, students can ask themselves questions like these: "Have I had experiences like Latoya's? Have I felt the same way she does? Does Latoya remind me of someone I know?"

Practice Ask students to write a paragraph about an experience in their own lives that helps them understand or relate to the experiences and feelings Latoya writes about in her diary.

Literature Model

they don't. This whole entry is embarrassing. I'm not a baby, I can't believe they think that way of me. I only wanted to prove I could do something by myself. Even that is a crime these days in the parents law book. I can't do anything right these days.

October 8, 1990

Dear Janice,

Today I saw my old teacher, I was talking about the other day. I thought this should be the day I tell you about him. His name is Robert Pelka. He's a heavy man but that only means

Pierre Bonnard, *The Window*, 1925

Literature Model **35**

Teach

Critical Thinking

Draw Conclusions Ask students to think about how Latoya's parents respond to her walking home alone from church. Then have them think about how Latoya reacts to being scolded. What conclusions can students draw about the relationship between Latoya and her parents? Students should support their answers with evidence from the diary. *(When Latoya writes, "I can't do anything right these days," she seems to be saying that she and her parents have been arguing more than usual lately. Latoya is feeling more grown-up and wants more independence, but her parents are worried that something will happen to her if she ventures too far from home by herself.)*

Literary Elements

Theme In her diary, Latoya mentions several changes that have occurred in her life. Ask students to identify some of the changes. *(She used to have a best friend at school; now she does not. She used to be friends with Jimmy; now she is not. She used to be close to her brothers; now she is not.)* Then ask: "What is one theme—or message about life—that emerges in Latoya's diary?" *(Changes are part of growing up and becoming more mature.)*

Viewing the Art

Pierre Bonnard, *The Window,* 1925
Pierre Bonnard (1867–1947) was a painter, a lithographer, and an illustrator who was known for his subtle use of color and perspective. For a time Bonnard belonged to a circle of artists working in Paris who believed that there was a bond between the fine arts and the applied arts.

Writing in the Real World

Writers and Writing
Latoya was originally commissioned by her publishing company to provide two weeks' worth of diary entries. "She sent them, and we loved them; we signed a contract for the whole book," the editor says. The editor corrected some spelling and syntax mistakes but kept all of Latoya's own wording.

Teach

Active Reading Strategies

Monitor Comprehension Have students ask themselves whether they understand what Latoya means when she says that she went from being "a sister of a retarded boy" to being "a Jewish girl . . . in the Hitler days." If the students are not clear, give them time to reread to find the answer. Then ask a volunteer to explain what Latoya means. *(Latoya imagined herself as the sister of a mentally disabled boy and a Jewish girl in order to understand how other people feel. She explains that her teacher has his students put themselves in the places of other people.)*

Personal Writing

Literature Model

Bernice Cross, *In the Room*, c. 1950

there's more of him to love. There's just something about him that makes him impossible not to like. He's warm, caring, loving and everything else that comes with a great human being. He didn't only teach me academic things like math, English and so on. He taught me how to be open-minded to all kinds of people. He did that by

making us empathize with other people, in other words, put ourselves in their place and write about it. I went from being a sister of a retarded boy named Victor to being a Jewish girl whose family was taken away from me back in the Hitler days.

Mr. Pelka made things we'd normally learn about from history books

Viewing the Art

Bernice Cross, *In the Room*, c. 1950
Bernice Cross's oil-on-canvas painting *In the Room* measures 40 5/8 by 34 3/4 inches and is in the Barnett-Aden Gallery.

sort of come alive, it's like you're there. Those are just some of the things he introduced me to. The things he changed about me are innumerable. The world should know this man. He probably won't go down in any major history books but if this diary counts as a book of history, he just did.

November 18, 1990

Dear Janice,

I didn't go to church today. I got dressed up and everything but my cousins who I usually go with weren't going so I came back home. I didn't do much back here. I just circulated around this house. The old me would have went straight outside to my friend's house. I find I've lost interest in going outside. I was usually like a magnet drawn to steel when it came to going outside. Now, I could spend a whole week without stepping past the doorstep. Except for going to school of course. I think I've matured somewhat. I always was concerned about what I was missing outside. I never wanted to be left out of anything happening with my friends who are always doing something or going somewhere. In the way I've matured I've come to the sudden realization that there are many more things to life like being close to my family, before it's too late. Pretty soon I'll be off to college, then married with kids. I might be rushing things a bit, but these years go by very fast.

I'm my own person. I like to think that I'm not just my cousin's cousin or my friend's friend. I like to think I'm the individual Latoya Hunter.

I'm my own person.

Literature Model   **37**

Teach

Critical Thinking

Evaluate Ask students whether they would like to have Mr. Pelka for a teacher. Encourage students to use examples from the selection as they explain why they would or would not. Then ask: "What does Latoya's admiration for the teacher tell you about her own values?" *(Answers will vary. Students may say that Latoya's respect for a "heavy man" who helps his students empathize with other people shows that she cares about people and can see past the surface of things.)*

Literary Elements

Character Have students summarize how Latoya has changed from the time she wrote her first diary entry to November 18, 1990. Ask: "How has Latoya's mood changed? How have her interests changed? Her feelings about herself?" *(Latoya's early diary entries sound sad, frustrated, and lonely. In her last entry, her tone is positive and confident. Latoya's interests have changed from always wanting to be active outdoors to enjoying more quiet time at home. She feels good about herself and how she has matured.)*

Additional Resources

Fine Art Transparencies, 1–5.
Listening and Speaking Activities, pp. 14–15
Thinking and Study Skills, pp. 1–6

Critical Thinking

Evaluate

Tell students that when they evaluate what they read, they form their own opinions about it. To model how to make a sound evaluation supported with reasons, say: "I think Latoya has become a more confident and positive person in the course of writing her journal. At the beginning she was negative about herself and others. Now she is positive about changes in herself and her life."

Practice Write this sentence from the selection on the board: "I think I've matured somewhat." Ask students to write one or two paragraphs giving their opinion about what maturity means to them and whether they think Latoya has matured according to their definition.

Linking Writing and Literature

Assess

Evaluation Rubrics

 Talk About Reading

Possible responses to the questions:

1. Students may relate to Latoya's need for independence from her parents and peers. They may also relate to the confidence and pride she feels in being her own person.

2. Students may admire or respect Latoya for her honesty, her ability to grow, and her willingness to be her own person.

3. Latoya doesn't always use technically correct grammar. Sometimes her informal writing style communicates the strength of her feelings. For example, when she says of Mr. Pelka, "He's warm, caring, loving, and everything that comes with a great human being," her enthusiasm for her teacher is clear.

4. Students' criteria might include using a direct and honest voice to tell about feelings and personal experiences.

Write About Reading

The letter should do the following:

- identify some of Latoya's specific experiences, feelings, or values
- tell how the writer's experiences, feelings, or values are similar or different
- use a direct, authentic voice

Close

Ask students to reflect on the idea of keeping a diary by discussing the following questions: Do you think writing in a diary would be an interesting or helpful type of writing to pursue? Why or why not? How might a diary intended to be shared with someone else be different in style and content from a diary meant just for your eyes? Is there a difference between keeping a journal and keeping a diary? If so, what is the difference?

Literature Model

Linking Writing and Literature

Personal Writing

Collect Your Thoughts

Consider what you learned about Latoya after reading her diary. Take a few minutes to jot down a list of her likes and dislikes. Then consider whether you like or dislike any of the same things she does. Do you think the similarities or differences between you and Latoya affect the way you responded to this selection? If so, how?

Talk About Reading

Talk with other students about the excerpt from *The Diary of Latoya Hunter*. Assign someone to keep everyone focused and someone to take notes. Then use the questions below to guide your conversation.

1. **Connect to Your Life:** How do Latoya's values about what is important in her life compare to your own? What did she say in her diary that helped you realize something new about your own values?

2. **Critical Thinking: Evaluate** What do you admire or respect about Latoya? What makes you feel impatient or annoyed with her? Give examples from the diary to support your opinions.

3. **6+1 Trait®: Voice** How does Latoya's writing help you understand how she feels? Name some specific passages, lines, or phrases from the diary that made you care about her as a person.

4. **Connect to Your Writing:** After reading this selection, what qualities do you think personal writing should have? Make a list of criteria for good personal writing.

Write About Reading

Friendly Letter Write a friendly letter to Latoya, telling her what you two share in common or how you are different. Describe how your experiences, feelings, or values compare to hers. See the letter on page 329 for help with formatting your letter.

Focus on Voice Your letter will be more interesting for Latoya to read if you write about feelings and experiences in an open, direct voice. After you have written a draft of the letter, evaluate it. Ask yourself whether your ideas are clear, your sentences are varied, and your voice is true. Revise as you think necessary.

For more information on voice and the 6+1 Trait® model, see **Writing and Research Handbook,** pages 822–824.

6+1 Trait® is a registered trademark of Northwest Regional Educational Laboratory, which does not endorse this product.

Enrichment and Extension

Considering the Other Point of View

Challenge students to write a response to Latoya from Janice, the diary. What advice might Janice give to Latoya if she could talk? Provide time for students to share their "Janice" responses.

UNIT 1 Review

Reflecting on the Unit

Summarize what you learned in this unit by answering the following questions.

❶ What are the major purposes of personal writing?

❷ Who is the audience for your personal writing?

❸ What kinds of things can you put in your journal? What can they be used for?

❹ Is personal writing formal or informal?

❺ How can a journal serve as a learning log?

📁 Adding to Your Portfolio

CHOOSE A SELECTION FOR YOUR PORTFOLIO Look over the personal writing you did for this unit. Choose a completed piece for your portfolio. Look for writing that shows one or more of the following:

- an idea or experience important to you
- a source of ideas for future writing
- thoughts and ideas you would like to share

REFLECT ON YOUR CHOICE Attach a note to the piece you chose, explaining briefly why you chose it and what you learned from writing it.

SET GOALS How can you improve your writing? What skill will you focus on the next time you write?

Writing Across the Curriculum

MAKE A HISTORY CONNECTION Select a man or woman from history. Jot down notes about the person's accomplishments or the important events in his or her life. Then use your notes to write a personal letter to the person, sharing your thoughts and feelings about his or her accomplishments or life.

Review

Reflecting on the Unit

You may have students respond to Reflecting on the Unit in writing or through discussion.

Writing Across the Curriculum

In their letters, remind students to include the historical figure's contribution. Students should also express their feelings about the contribution. Encourage them to include details related to the figure's appearance, habits, or personality.

📁 Adding to Your Portfolio

Suggest that when selecting pieces for their portfolios, students consider a variety of writing styles. Remind them that these selections should be writing that they would like to share.

Portfolio Evaluation

If you grade the portfolio selections, you may want to award two marks—one each for content and form. Explain your assessment criteria before students make their selections.

Commend
- experimentation with creative prewriting techniques
- clear, concise writing in which the main idea, audience, and purpose are evident
- successful revisions
- work that shows a flair for language

✔ ASSESSMENT OPTIONS

📁 *Tests with Answer Key and Rubrics*
Unit 1 Choice A Test, p. 1
Unit 1 Choice B Test, p. 2
Unit 1 Composition Objective Test, pp. 3–4

💾 *Testmaker*
Unit 1 Choice A Test
Unit 1 Choice B Test
Unit 1 Composition Objective Test

You may wish to administer one of these tests as a mastery test.

📼 *MindJogger Videoquizzes*

The Writing Process

Mountain climbing is often used as a metaphor for facing life's challenges. Invite the students to imagine themselves climbing these mountains. How would it feel to climb out of the mist and reach the peak? What might make them want to attempt the climb in the first place?

Interpret and Analyze Use the following questions for discussion:

- What feelings or emotions does this picture seem to represent? How does the color evoke that feeling?

- How would the overall effect of the picture be different if it were taken from a different height? What if the picture were taken from some point beneath the mist?

Discussing the Quotation

Discuss with students the feelings they get from the quotation. Does it make them feel hopeful? discouraged? Why?

Writing Prompt Write a paragraph about a "pinnacle" you've reached in your life. Are your feelings about that experience expressed by the quotation and/or the photograph? How?

Note To find out more about Stacy Allison and *Beyond the Limits*, refer students to *Glencoe Literature: The Reader's Choice*, Course 2, page 281.

> *"Each mountain I face is another pinnacle in an internal adventure."*
>
> —Stacy Allison
>
> *Beyond the Limits*

40

Resource Manager

📁 **Planning Resources**
- *Lesson Plans*
- *Block Scheduling*

📦 **Transparencies**
- *Bellringer*
- *Daily Language Practice*
- *Fine Art*
- *Two-Minute Skill Drill*
- *Writing Process*

📁 **Other Print Resources**
- *Composition Enrichment*
- *Composition Practice*
- *Composition Reteaching*
- *Cooperative Learning Activities*
- *Glencoe Literature Library*
- *Grammar and Composition Handbook*
- *Grammar Workbook*

- *Listening and Speaking Activities*
- *Sentence-Combining Practice*
- *Spelling Power*
- *Tests with Answer Key and Rubrics*
- *Thinking and Study Skills*
- *Writing Across the Curriculum*
- *Writing Assessment and Evaluation Rubrics*
- *Writing in the Real World*

UNIT 2 The Writing Process

41

Objectives

- To learn to use prewriting strategies to generate ideas and determine focus
- To understand how to develop and organize written work through drafting
- To be able to revise drafts for variety, coherence, progression, and logical support of ideas
- To learn the importance of editing drafts for specific purposes
- To develop the skill of presenting written work to an audience

 ASSESSMENT OPTIONS

Tests with Answer Key and Rubrics
Unit 2 Choice A Test, p. 5
Unit 2 Choice B Test, p. 6
Unit 2 Composition Objective Test, pp. 7–8

Testmaker
Unit 2 Choice A Test
Unit 2 Choice B Test
Unit 2 Composition Objective Test

You may wish to administer either the Unit 2 Choice A Test or the Unit 2 Choice B Test as a pretest.

Key to Ability Levels

L1 Level 1 activities are within the basic ability range of students.

L2 Level 2 activities are within the ability range of average students.

L3 Level 3 activities are more challenging activities.

Video
- *MindJogger Videoquizzes*

Software
- *Presentation Plus!*
- *Revising with Style*
- *Testmaker*
- *Writer's Assistant*

Web Sites
- *writerschoice.glencoe.com*
- *lit.glencoe.com*

Focus

Lesson Overview

Objectives
- To study the use of writing in a real-life situation
- To understand the writing process

Skills
- choosing a topic; selecting effective images and details; considering the audience

Critical Thinking
- evaluating; analyzing; recalling; relating; generating new information

Listening and Speaking
- note-taking; questioning; evaluating; discussing

Bellringer
Daily Language Activity

When students enter the classroom, have this assignment on the board: *Suppose an editor interviews you for a newspaper feature page geared toward seventh graders, asking, "What topics do seventh-grade students like to read about?" What topics would you suggest? Write your exact response, using quotation marks.*

Grammar Link to the Bellringer

Point out that journalists use many quotations, weaving them into feature stories. Explain that every direct quotation that is a complete sentence begins with a capital letter.

See also *Daily Language Practice*

Motivating Activity

Allow students to share topics they suggested in the Bellringer activity. Point out that determining what an audience wants to read is one part of the process a features editor completes. Discuss with students how their suggestions would change if the page were aimed at older teenagers or adults.

Writing in the Real World

MEDIA Connection — *Newspaper Feature*

"The Freep"? It's not a monster or a new soft drink. It's a weekly feature page in the *Detroit Free Press* that addresses topics of interest to today's young people. Readers enjoy "The Freep" for its eye-catching graphics and its lively content. Behind the scenes, though, there's a lot of work that goes into achieving that fun, contemporary style. The excerpt below is from a personality profile that highlights two talented local teens.

Smart, Cool and on the Air

by Maisha Maurant

Some use the word "nerd" to label smart folks, but you can be smart and cool. Standish-Sterling High School seniors Brooke Gillette and Anna Galvas certainly are.

They run their own radio talk show, spin records as disc jockeys, and work part-time at fast-food restaurants.

And they're honor students besides. Anna's got a 3.6 grade-point average; Brooke's average is 3.28.

Classmate Aaron Koin sure is impressed. "It's neat that they are on the radio and still in high school," he says.

Brooke and Anna are two of the people we heard about when "The Freep" asked

readers to name people they thought were smart and cool.

"It seems like these are the kinds of girls who, when I was in school, were looked up to as the trendsetters but weren't stuck up," says Tim LaVere, the 27-year-old news director at WSTD-FM (96.9).

from "Smart, Cool and on the Air," an article in "The Freep" section of *The Detroit Free Press*

Maisha Maurant, writer

Nunzio Lupo, editor

Keith Webb, designer

Resource Manager

Planning Resources
- *Lesson Plans*

Transparencies
- *Bellringer*
- *Daily Language Practice*
- *Writing Process* 1–10

Other Print Resources
- *Cooperative Learning Activities,* pp. 7–12
- *Thinking and Study Skills,* pp. 1–5, 13, 21–22
- *Writing Assessment and Evaluation Rubrics*
- *Writing in the Real World,* pp. 5–8

Creating a Feature Page

Prewriting	Drafting	Revising/Editing
GOTTA **THOUGHT?**	GOTTA **QUESTION?**	GOTTA **FINISH!**
Planning the Page	Getting the Words Down	Meeting the Deadline

A Writer's Process

Prewriting
Planning the Page

Like most sections of a newspaper, "The Freep" reflects the collaboration of several people. Leading the effort is assistant features editor, Nunzio Lupo. He's assisted by designer Keith Webb and a staff of writers. One regular contributor is Maisha Maurant, who wrote the article "Smart, Cool, and on the Air."

Lupo usually begins planning each issue three to four weeks before publication. He mines many sources for ideas, including other sections of the *Detroit Free Press* and such youth magazines as *Spin* and *Sassy.* He also gets ideas from letters to the editor, such as the idea about two high school disc jockeys who were both smart and cool. Lupo gave the letter to Maurant and asked her to explore the topic of smart and cool friends for a "Freep" article.

Another part of the prewriting stage is brainstorming ideas for graphics. Webb, a partner in this process, believes that graphics are just as important as words. "Graphics should help tell the story," he maintains, "not just decorate it."

Drafting
Getting the Words Down

The drafting stage belongs essentially to the writer— Maurant, in this case. Maurant usually has a week to write a

Teach

Building Background

Warm-up

Explain that as reporters prepare articles, they proceed through many steps, starting with the search for story ideas. Invite students to list steps in the writing process, from brainstorming ideas to publishing. Then ask them to think of and list areas of their own or others' lives in which the writing process is used, such as letter writing, news reporting, poetry, and so on.

Process in Speaking

Remind students that the process used in writing is used in many speaking situations, too. In formal situations, such as giving a speech or an oral presentation, speakers would certainly go through the steps of planning, drafting, and revising their remarks. But even in an informal situation— such as inviting someone to go somewhere—people plan, practice, and revise what they're going to say. Ask students: *In what speaking situations might you go through the steps in the writing process?*

Process in Writing

Discuss forms of writing in which students might apply the writing process. Use prompts such as:

- Have you ever written a letter and after you mailed it, remembered there was more you meant to say? How can you avoid that?
- Have you ever written a paper or a note to a friend and said something that came out all wrong? What happened? Why?

Preview the Media Connection

Remind students to watch for the ways the staff at the *Detroit Free Press* uses the writing process. Have students read the Media Connection.

Cultural Connections

Putting Youth Culture in Context

The *Detroit Free Press* feature "The Freep" focuses on concerns and interests of youth, recognizing the importance of a segment of society whose ideas and viewpoints are often dismissed as immature or irrelevant. Yet, in many countries around the world, the voices of young citizens are the first to cry out against political and social injustice. The need for young people to express their ideas has produced many youth-oriented publications. Ask students to name and tell a little about the ones with which they are familiar.

Teach

Discussion Prompts

Use these prompts to focus students' reading of this page:

- What, if any, connections do you notice between the Media Connection and your own writing?
- What is the purpose of a "lead"?
- If you were going to write a feature on an interesting person in your community, what questions would you ask about his or her job or hobby?
- If you were writing for an audience of parents, what factors would you consider? How would they affect your planning?

You may also want to invite students to talk about

- generating ideas
- writing interview questions
- drafting original copy
- revising and editing
- putting newspapers together **L2**

Additional Resources

Writing Process Transparencies, 1–10
Writing in the Real World, pp. 5–8
Cooperative Learning Activities
Thinking and Study Skills,
   pp. 1–5, 13, 21–22

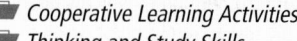

feature. When she sits down to draft a manuscript, she looks over her notes on the subject. For "Smart, Cool, and on the Air," she took notes while conducting a telephone interview with the two student disc jockeys. During the interview, Maurant gathered facts for the story, including the subjects' grade-point averages and their activities in and out of school.

Maurant usually begins her drafting process by writing the lead, the opening that establishes the direction the feature will take. "I'm impatient," she explains. "I like to get a lead down to give me a feel for where I want to go."

Working at home, Maurant drafts the article in longhand. Once in the office, she transfers her draft into the computer. Maurant's drafting style is to write quickly without stopping. She never makes changes until she's got the whole piece down. After writing the first draft, Maurant will return to her notes so that she can "fill in things that make the story tighter."

Maurant keeps her young "Freep" audience in mind as she writes. "I try to use the most vivid words and images. My audience wants to be able to 'see' it."

Before she submits her article to Lupo, Maurant likes to set the manuscript aside for a day. She feels that a fresh mind helps her revise and perfect the story. After a day has passed, she reads the article once more, looking for unanswered questions and unclear information.

Revising/Editing
Meeting the Deadline

Maurant's story is due to Lupo the Friday before publication, which is press time—the day that copy goes to the printer. On deadline day, Maurant e-mails her copy to Lupo. Lupo reads the article, and then Maurant and Lupo work together to revise the article.

If Lupo and Maurant think the article seems flat or that something might be missing, they try to identify what's needed. Perhaps a stronger lead will help, or maybe they need to add more facts or new quotations. Lupo and Maurant toss solutions back and forth. "Sometimes," says Lupo, "reporters will think an idea is obvious, when, in fact, only they can see it. I can point out that their view isn't getting through."

After the copy is revised, Lupo meets again with designer Keith Webb. For "Smart, Cool, and on the Air," Webb created a graphic of a human brain. Lupo then wrote captions that described the smart and cool thoughts of this brain.

In the final step before publication, Lupo reviews the proofs. Copy editors have been working on the page, correcting spelling and grammar. With Lupo's sign-off, the page makes its way to press.

Technology Tip

Using Computers

A computer can be a great advantage in the quick transmission of information from one point to another. Some writers transmit their articles to editors by e-mail. Additionally, many publications today require that writers submit their stories on disks along with their printed copies. Ask students to think about other ways computers speed up or make writing easier. Are there any disadvantages to using computers?

Examining Writing in the Real World

Analyzing the Media Connection

Discuss these questions about the excerpt on page 42.

1. What is the main idea that Maurant gets across in her lead? Do you agree that this idea is an interesting topic to young people? Explain your answer.

2. Why do you think Maurant gives information about the students' grades and activities?

3. Quotations help make writing come alive. Identify two quotations that Maurant uses. Explain why, in each case, she may have used a quotation instead of paraphrasing the speaker's words.

4. What is Maurant's purpose in this article? In your opinion, how well does this excerpt fulfill that purpose? Explain your answer.

Analyzing a Writer's Process

Discuss these questions about Maurant's writing process.

1. Where did Maurant gather material for "Smart, Cool and on the Air"? What other sources might she have used?

2. Why does Maurant begin drafting by establishing the lead? If you were writing a feature article, would you begin in the same way? Why or why not?

3. Maurant drafts straight through the first time with no changes. What is the advantage of drafting in that way?

4. What role does editor Nunzio Lupo play in the revision process? Why do you think this is helpful? How might you get the same kind of help for your own writing?

Grammar Link

Feature writers like Maurant follow set capitalization rules for direct quotations. They capitalize the first word of a quote but not the second part of an interrupted sentence.

"I try," says Maurant, "to use the most vivid words and images."

Correct the capitalization in the sentences below.

1. Webb says, "graphics should help tell the story."

2. "You know Maurant's approach," says Lupo, "Is to get a lead down right away."

3. "After I cover the facts," says Maurant, "Reviewing my notes helps me find anything I missed."

4. The reporter said, "press time is both exciting and challenging."

See Lesson 19.1, pages 573–574.

Grammar Link

Answers

1. Webb says, "Graphics should help tell the story."
2. "You know Maurant's approach," says Lupo, "is to get a lead down right away."
3. "After I cover the facts," says Maurant, "reviewing my notes helps me find anything I missed."
4. The reporter said, "Press time is both exciting and challenging."

Writing a Lead Ask students to write a lead paragraph for an article that they would like to write some day. Encourage them to use at least one "direct" quotation in their leads.

Close

Discuss other jobs that might use a process similar to the one in "The Freep."

Note Helpful references include Strunk and White's *The Elements of Style, The Complete Book of Feature Writing* (ed. Leonard Witt), and *Freelance Writing for Magazines and Newspapers,* by Marcia Yudkin.

Assess

Analyzing the Media Connection

1. You can be "smart" *and* "cool." Students may indicate that since it is about young people doing something they might want to do, the topic is interesting.

2. By showing that the girls are successful at many things, she makes them positive role models.

3. Students are likely to point out Maurant's use of terms, such as "cool" and "nerd," to which her audience will relate. Quotations make the writing personal and authentic.

4. Students may say that she wanted to present positive role models who are very smart and successful without being labeled negatively. They may think that this excerpt succeeds by giving evidence of the girls' achievements at school as well as their "cool" activities.

Analyzing a Writer's Process

1. She interviewed the two girls. She might have interviewed teachers, family members, and friends.

2. It establishes the direction the article will take. Students may say that beginning that way would force them to be clear about an article's main idea.

3. Students may say that it helps her finish the article and keep the voice and style consistent.

4. He suggests possible improvements. Students may say that it provides fresh ideas or a different perspective. A peer editor could provide such help.

Reteaching

To stress the need to revise for clarity, discuss Lupo's quote on page 44.

Enrichment

If possible, invite a features editor or writer to speak to the class. Alternatively, suggest that students write to an editor or writer, asking questions about the process each follows.

Focus

Lesson Overview

Objectives
- To understand the five stages of the writing process
- To apply those stages to different types of writing

Skills
- analyzing the writing process; planning before writing

Critical Thinking
- relating; comparing and contrasting; defining and clarifying; decision making

Listening and Speaking
- asking questions; informal speaking; discussing; evaluating; explaining a process

Bellringer
Daily Language Activity

When students enter the classroom, have this assignment on the board: *Think about a party or a meeting that you and your friends have taken part in planning. List the steps that are necessary to make such an event a success.*

Grammar Link to the Bellringer

Students can rewrite their lists as a series of sentences beginning with the subject *My friends and I . . .* They should use plural forms of all verbs.

See also *Daily Language Practice*

Motivating Activity

Have students use their responses in the Bellringer activity to identify stages in the process of giving a birthday party. Write on the board the stages that students identify. Encourage students, as they study Lesson 2.1, to relate stages in the writing process to stages in planning and giving a party.

Using the Writing Process

Transforming a vacant lot covered with weeds and trash into a bright spot in the community isn't impossible. However, it takes planning and follow-through. It's the same with writing. Achieving a finished piece of writing requires planning carefully and following through.

The paragraph below is the result of Tai-Tang-Tran's thinking and planning. He began with an idea and worked through various stages of the writing process to describe Chinese New Year traditions.

Student Model

Many Chinese New Year traditions are about luck. One tradition that my family celebrates is the giving of lucky money. Parents give children money in a red envelope. The envelope symbolizes luck. Putting the money in the envelope means that the parent is sharing luck with a child. Both giving and receiving the red envelope bring luck.

Tai-Tang-Tran, Emerson Junior High School
Oak Park, Illinois

> Having read this passage, what do you suppose Tai's complete piece is about?

Resource Manager

Planning Resources
- *Lesson Plans*

Transparencies
- *Bellringer*
- *Daily Language Practice*
- *Fine Art* 6–10
- *Two-Minute Skill Drill*
- *Writing Process* 1–10

Other Print Resources
- *Composition Enrichment*, p. 7
- *Composition Practice*, p. 7
- *Composition Reteaching*, p. 7
- *Cooperative Learning Activities*, pp. 7–12
- *Listening and Speaking Activities*, pp. 12–13

- *Sentence-Combining Practice*, 1
- *Thinking and Study Skills*, pp. 4–5, 9–11
- *Writing Across the Curriculum*
- *Writing Assessment and Evaluation Rubrics*

Work in Your Own Way

Every writer works in his or her own way, but most writers take their writing through several stages before they finish. Before Tai finished his essay, he went through a process. First he listed his ideas about traditions. Then he organized them into paragraphs. Later he rearranged and polished his writing until he was satisfied.

Write from Start to Finish

Many writers use the following stages of the writing process. Not every writer follows them in strict order, however. Many writers go back to certain stages before they finish a piece of writing.

PREWRITING In this stage you find and explore ideas and then decide on a topic to write about. At this time you also decide on your audience, the people who will read or hear your writing, and you decide on the overall purpose of your writing.

DRAFTING Transforming thoughts, words, and phrases into sentences and paragraphs is called drafting. You can rearrange and revise your writing more easily once your ideas are in draft form.

Chinese New Year traditions:
lucky red money
spiri...
drag...
luc...

Around Chinese New Year adults and children feel lucky. Parents always give children lucky money. Both the parents and the children get luck when giving or receiving the lucky money. The red envelope symbolizes luck, and the money inside means the adult giving the money is taking some of the adult's luck and sharing it with the children.

Journal Writing

Think about the last time you wrote something. What challenges or rewards did that writing project present? Write your thoughts in your journal.

Teach

Using the Model

Have students read the passage from an essay by Tai-Tang-Tran. Explain that Tai's complete essay is about Chinese New Year's traditions. Ask students what other kinds of information they think Tai might have included in the essay. Suggestions might include the history of his traditions and the other traditions that members of his family still follow. **L2**

Using a Familiar Model

It may help some students to relate the first two stages of the writing process (prewriting and drafting) to a familiar process, such as constructing a model or making a favorite food. Ask them to discuss how they prepare for such a project. What steps do they follow as they build or assemble the items? **L1**

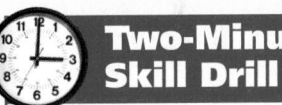

Two-Minute Skill Drill

Students can brainstorm and write lists of hot subtopics for the following topics:

travel	*families*
growing up	*food*
pets	*holidays*
elders	*teens*

See also *Two-Minute Skill Drill Transparency 2.1*

Journal Writing Tip

Choosing Topics Ask students to identify times when they were either greatly interested or uninterested in a writing topic. Point out that a writer's interest in or enjoyment of a topic affects the quality of his or her writing.

Teach

Knowing Your Own Process

Initiate a discussion of the five stages of the writing process by asking students which stage of the process they think is the most challenging for them and which is the easiest. Encourage students to provide examples from their writing experiences. Ask them to suggest reasons why one stage might be more difficult or why it might be easier. **L2**

Ordering Steps

Some students might be confused by the arrows in the diagram indicating that the writing process need not be sequential. Write the steps of the writing process in any order on the board. Ask volunteers to write a number in front of each step to indicate the order in which they would usually do the steps. Then the volunteers can rewrite the steps in the order they indicated. **L1**

Additional Resources

- *Writing Process Transparencies*, 1–10
- *Fine Art Transparencies*, 6–10
- *Writing Across the Curriculum*
- *Cooperative Learning Activities*, pp. 7–12
- *Thinking and Study Skills*, pp. 4–5, 9–11
- *Sentence-Combining Practice*, p. 1
- *Listening and Speaking Activities*, pp. 12–13
- *Composition Practice*, p. 7

The Writing Process

REVISING   In the revising stage you look at your writing to be sure it's clear and organized. You read your writing to a partner. Guide your revisions with questions like these: Does what I've written make sense? Have I presented my ideas in a sensible order? Have I kept my audience in mind?

Some pieces of writing need little revision. Others need revising two, four, even a dozen times before they satisfy their authors.

EDITING/PROOFREADING   The editing/proofreading stage, unlike the revising stage, focuses on the mechanics of your writing. When you edit and proofread, you make sure that you've spelled and punctuated your writing properly. You also try to correct any grammatical errors.

PUBLISHING/PRESENTING   In the last stage of writing, you present your work to your audience. You present some pieces of writing by handing them in to your teacher. You present other pieces more publicly. For example, you might read a research paper aloud in class, mail a letter to a local newspaper, or deliver a speech to members of a club or a community group.

The diagram below shows the stages of the writing process. Remember, it's up to you to decide how you move through the different stages.

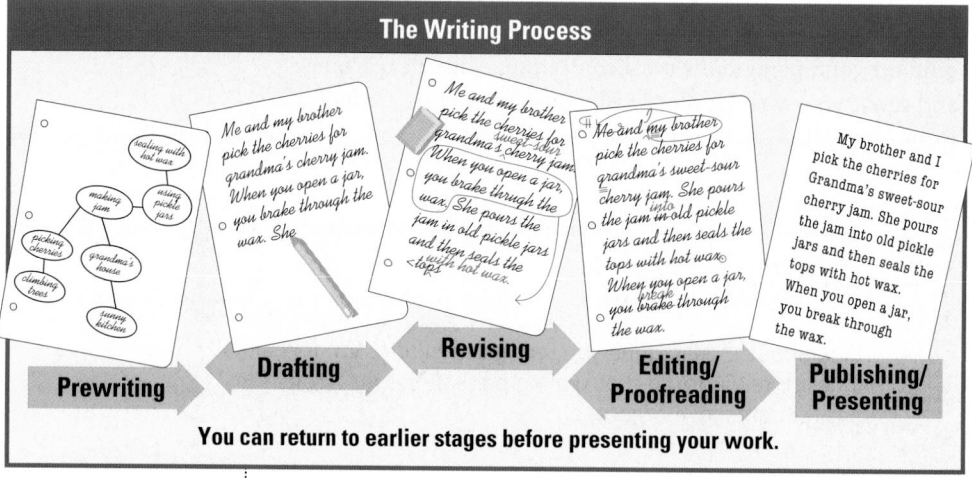

The Writing Process

Prewriting → Drafting → Revising → Editing/Proofreading → Publishing/Presenting

You can return to earlier stages before presenting your work.

Cooperative Learning

Creating a Poster

Students may wish to create a visual reminder of the five stages of the writing process. Suggest that small groups work cooperatively to create posters explaining these stages. First, ask the groups to brainstorm to develop a list of ways to show the writing process visually. Ask them to create visual drafts explaining the stages. As a group, students can go over the drafts, revise them, and edit them. They can then assemble their posters to display in the school writing lab or library.

Write a Paragraph

Think about how you write. Do you go through a different process for different kinds of writing? For example, do you spend more time writing a report than writing a letter to a school newspaper? Write a description of your writing process.

PURPOSE To understand your writing process

AUDIENCE Yourself

LENGTH 1–2 paragraphs

WRITING RUBRICS To describe your writing process, you should

- decide what parts of the process are most challenging and most rewarding
- tell whether you move straight through the stages of the writing process or go back and forth between stages

Listening and Speaking

COOPERATIVE LEARNING In a small group discuss the challenges that writing projects have presented. Each member of the group should take a few minutes to describe his or her writing experiences. Then take turns suggesting ways to approach the challenges described. Take notes.

Write a few paragraphs that describe any writing problems you may have and include solutions suggested by others.

Grammar Link

With a compound subject joined by *and*, use the plural form of the verb.

*Around Chinese New Year **adults and children feel** lucky.*

Rewrite each sentence, adding a noun or pronoun to make the subject compound. Use the correct form of the verb.

1. Bill jogs the ten blocks to school each day.
2. Mari watches for end-of-season sales.
3. Marcos belongs to the Carlton Junior High Science Club.
4. Jusef has played on the soccer team for two years.
5. In my opinion, the president was wrong about that.

See Lesson 16.5, page 543.

Cross-Curricular Activity

SOCIAL STUDIES Student Tai-Tang-Tran has described a Chinese New Year tradition on page 46. See if you can find out more about traditions that welcome in the new year in different countries around the world. Write a paragraph to share with classmates.

Assess

Evaluation Rubrics

Write a Paragraph

Use these criteria when evaluating your students' writing. It should

- show an awareness of personal writing habits
- describe the writer's use of the writing process
- show an awareness of all stages of the writing process

See also *Writing Assessment and Evaluation Rubrics*

Listening and Speaking

Commend practical responses that address specific problems. Note responses that are impractical or vague.

Cross-Curricular Activity

Commend the presentation of detailed descriptions that contain interesting information that is neatly written so that it can be shared with the class.

Reteaching

📁 *Composition Reteaching*, p. 7

Enrichment

📁 *Composition Enrichment*, p. 7

Close

To spark a discussion of sources of inspiration, point out that the word *inspiration* comes from the Latin word *inspirare*, meaning "breathing in." Discuss how sights, sounds, and smells can inspire writers who *take in* the environment just as they take in air when they breathe.

Grammar Link

Answers
Subjects will vary, but plural verb forms are given below.

1. jog
2. watch
3. belong
4. have
5. were

Using Compound Subjects with *And* Students might write a paragraph describing something they like to do with a friend. Encourage them to begin with the subject: _____ and I . . .

The Writing Process

Focus

Lesson Overview

Objectives

- To learn about prewriting techiques
- To use prewriting techniques to generate a topic

Skills

- brainstorming and evaluating ideas; planning before writing

Critical Thinking

- relating; analyzing; recalling; establishing and evaluating criteria; generating new information; decision-making

Listening and Speaking

- taking notes; asking questions; explaining a process

Bellringer
Daily Language Activity

When students enter the classroom, have this assignment on the board: *Think about presents that you have given to people. Write how you got the ideas for the gifts.*

Grammar Link to the Bellringer

Write *presents* and *presence* on the chalkboard. Ask students whether they ever have trouble using these words correctly in their writing. Tell students who are unsure of the correct meanings of these words to look them up in a dictionary.

See also *Daily Language Practice*

Motivating Activity

Have students share their responses from the Bellringer activity. Then discuss how students got ideas for some recent writing. How long did it take to get the ideas? Did students come up with the ideas or did someone else suggest them?

Prewriting: Finding and Exploring a Topic

Often you write because you need to or want to. You might write a thank-you letter, a note asking for permission to do something, or a school assignment. At other times, however, you need to think of how to fill an empty sheet of paper.

Some writers get their ideas easily. Other writers have their own special methods for getting ideas. Some take a walk; others take a shower. Some listen to music; others listen to friends. To come up with ideas, try a few basic techniques.

Resource Manager

Planning Resources
- *Lesson Plans*

Transparencies
- *Bellringer*
- *Daily Language Practice*
- *Fine Art 6–10*
- *Two-Minute Skill Drill*
- *Writing Process 1–10*

Other Print Resources
- *Composition Enrichment*, p. 8
- *Composition Practice*, p. 8
- *Composition Reteaching*, p. 8
- *Cooperative Learning Activities,* pp. 7–12
- *Listening and Speaking Activities,* pp. 12–13

- *Thinking and Study Skills*, pp. 3–5, 8, 16
- *Writing Across the Curriculum*
- *Writing Assessment and Evaluation Rubrics*

Find Good Ideas Everywhere

You can find a writing idea almost anywhere. What catches your attention when you walk down a street or a school hallway? What makes you happy? What makes you angry? Try carrying note cards or a small notebook with you. Whenever an idea comes to you, jot it down.

What if no ideas come to you? Then try brainstorming—coming up with as many ideas as you can. Don't worry about whether they're good or bad, practical or silly. The point is to get your thoughts flowing. Eventually you'll hit on an idea you can use.

More than one use for lot?
All kinds of people from the neighborhood should be able to use it — kids and adults

Ideas for Vacant Lot

basketball court
skateboarding ramp
mural
community garden
pond
park with trees and benches

Keshia, Mike, and Henry generated this list of ideas during their brainstorming session.

Journal Writing

Carry a notebook with you for the next five days. Write down ideas whenever they occur to you. At some point, take time to brainstorm ideas. After five days, write in your journal which worked better—letting ideas come naturally or brainstorming to find ideas.

Teach

Using Visuals to Generate Writing Ideas

Display for students two or three interesting photographs. Give students a few minutes to view the pictures. Then have students brainstorm to develop a list of writing ideas that each image suggests to them. List their ideas on the chalkboard. After the brainstorming activity, ask students: Did looking at the pictures help you think of ideas for writing topics? Why or why not? **L2**

Writing About Everyday Experiences

Point out to students that many writers get ideas from their own everyday experiences. For example, Jessamyn West found inspiration for her story "The Hat" in an incident that happened to her as a young girl. Ask students to recall an experience they had during the past week and to write a paragraph or two about it. **L3**

 **Two-Minute Skill Drill**

Give students two minutes on the classroom clock and ask them to list writing ideas about the topic of pets. Provide time for students to share ideas and to tell classmates how they arrived at them.

See also *Two-Minute Skill Drill Transparency 2.2*

Journal Writing Tip

Choosing a Topic After students have brainstormed to develop a list of topics, ask them to consider which ideas might make the best writing topics. Why do students think one topic might be better or easier to write about than another?

Teach

Making Clusters

To provide students with practice in clustering, divide them into small groups focused on common interests, such as music, sports, crafts, or hobbies. Ask a group member to write the topic in the middle of a piece of paper, draw a circle around it, and pass the paper around the group. Have each group member spend one minute adding ideas to the cluster. Then the group can decide which ideas in their cluster they would most likely use in their writing. **L2**

Additional Resources

Fine Art Transparencies, 6–10

Writing Process Transparencies, 1–10

Writing Across the Curriculum

Cooperative Learning Activities, pp. 7–12

Thinking and Study Skills, pp. 3–5, 8, 16

Listening and Speaking Activities, pp. 12–13

Composition Practice, p. 8

The Writing Process

TIME

For more about the writing process, see **TIME** *Facing the Blank Page,* pp. 97–107.

Explore Your Topic

From your many ideas you can choose one that might make a good writing topic. Then you can use clustering to explore your topic more thoroughly.

To make a cluster diagram, write your topic in the middle of a piece of paper. Then, as you think about that topic, briefly write down everything that comes to mind. Each time you write something down, draw a circle around it. Then draw lines to connect the ideas that seem related to each other.

Clustering can help you decide which part of a topic to write about. You can't write about every idea, but you might discover surprising connections. Clustering can also help you organize your writing by showing you which ideas about a topic are broader or narrower than other ideas.

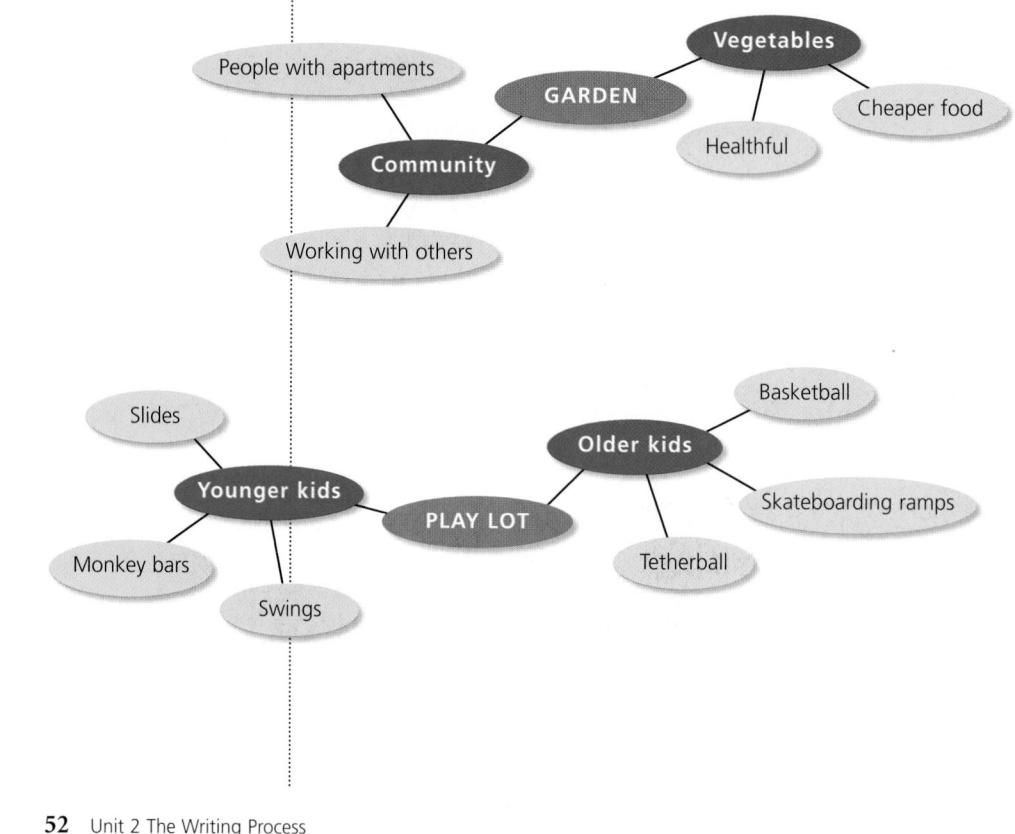

MEETING INDIVIDUAL NEEDS English Language Learners

Prewriting

For prewriting activities such as clustering, students may wish to write in their first languages. They can translate as they draft or as part of the revising step.

Collect Topic Ideas

Take some time to find a topic you would like to write about. You will be working with this topic through a series of lessons as you move through the stages of the writing process.

PURPOSE   To create topic ideas

AUDIENCE   Yourself

LENGTH   1–2 paragraphs

WRITING RUBRICS   To create and explore topic ideas, you should

- look through your journal and note-books for ideas
- narrow your search to three topics you might like to explore
- use clustering to spin off more ideas about your topics

Pat Thomas, *Picnic in Washington Park,* 1975

Grammar Link

Choose the correct word.

Some pairs of words, such as *than* and *then*, sound nearly alike. Use the correct word in your writing. Write a sentence for each word listed below.

1. then
2. than
3. loose
4. lose
5. beside
6. besides
7. accept
8. except
9. all ready
10. already

See Lesson 17.1, page 553, and Lesson 17.2, page 555.

Listening and Speaking

COOPERATIVE LEARNING   In a small group, discuss the painting to the left. Then write a brief summary of your group's discussion. Choose one idea from your summary that would make an interesting essay topic.

Viewing and Representing

EVALUATING   Make a list of your impressions after looking at the painting at the left. What is the artist's theme or main idea? How does the artist help you understand it? Think about the painting's colors. Are they bright and cheery or dark and subdued? How are the figures presented? Discuss your ideas in a small group.

2.2 Prewriting: Finding and Exploring a Topic   **53**

The Writing Process

Assess

Evaluation Rubrics

Collect Topic Ideas

Answers will vary. Clusters should explore topics from students' lists. Clusters should visually link related ideas.

See also *Writing Assessment and Evaluation Rubrics*

Listening and Speaking

Answers will vary. Groups should offer a variety of writing topics inspired by the painting. Suggestions should include ideas for descriptive, narrative, expository, and persuasive writing.

Viewing and Representing

Students' answers should include a variety of first impressions that are formed not only by the subject matter but by the colors and the grouping of the figures. They should try to relate these elements to what they see as the artist's theme.

Reteaching

📁 *Composition Reteaching,* p. 8

Enrichment

📁 *Composition Enrichment,* p. 8

📖 Use *Fine Art Transparencies,* 6–10

Close

Ask students how they might use clustering for a real-world writing task, such as composing a letter to a company to complain about an item they recently purchased, preparing a speech to run for student council, or writing a letter applying for a position as a counselor-in-training at a local summer day camp.

Grammar Link

Answers

Answers will vary.

Confusing Word Pairs   Ask students to create context sentences for the following word pairs: *desert/dessert; in/into; their/there; your/you're.* Then have students check each other's sentences for correct use of the words.

Viewing the Art

Pat Thomas, *Picnic in Washington Park,* **1975**
Acrylic over oil on masonite, it measures 20½ by 27½ inches and is in the Museum of American Folk Art, New York City.

Focus

Lesson Overview

Objectives

- To identify the purpose of a piece of writing
- To determine the audience for that writing

Skills

- identifying an audience; determining purpose; planning before writing

Critical Thinking

- analyzing; establishing and evaluating criteria; generating new information; making decisions

Listening and Speaking

- discussing; evaluating; asking questions

Daily Language Activity

When students enter the classroom, have this assignment on the board: *Name the most recent writing you have done—even a note or a list. Write a sentence explaining the purpose of and audience for that writing.*

Grammar Link to the Bellringer

Ask students to underline the subject and circle the verb in the sentence each of them wrote for the Bellringer activity. Have them check to make sure the subject and verb agree.

See also  *Daily Language Practice*

Motivating Activity

Draw a chart on the chalkboard with the headings: *Purpose, Audience.* Ask students to read aloud their Bellringer activity sentences and record the information on the chart. Then, use the information to answer these questions: For what audience did students write most often? What was the purpose of the majority of their writing? To inform? To describe? To entertain? To persuade?

LESSON 2.3

Prewriting: Determining Purpose and Audience

Every successful piece of writing, whether it's a newspaper editorial or a cartoon, has a particular purpose and audience.

Look at the notice below. What could be the purpose, or reason, for this piece of writing? Who's supposed to read it?

You need to think about questions like these in the prewriting stage. Before you begin drafting, you need to decide whose attention you're trying to get and why.

Fabulous Rummage Sales!

CLOTHES! TOYS!
Household Goods!
Saturday & Sunday
August 15–16
1500 block of Elm Street
9:00 A.M. to 4:00 P.M.

Resource Manager

📂 **Planning Resources**
- *Lesson Plans*

🔔 **Transparencies**
- *Bellringer*
- *Daily Language Practice*
- *Fine Art,* 6–10
- *Two-Minute Skill Drill*
- *Writing Process,* 1–10

📂 **Other Print Resources**
- *Composition Enrichment,* p. 9
- *Composition Practice,* p. 9
- *Composition Reteaching,* p. 9
- *Cooperative Learning Activities,* pp. 7–12
- *Listening and Speaking Activities,* pp. 12–13

- *Thinking and Study Skills,* pp. 3–5, 9, 21
- *Writing Across the Curriculum*
- *Writing Assessment and Evaluation Rubrics*

Identify Your Purpose

Most of your writing will have one of four purposes. *Telling* a story is one purpose for writing. *Describing* a thing is another. Sometimes you write to *inform* someone or to *explain* something. You can also write to *persuade* your readers to believe something or to take some action. Notice the examples below.

These sentences **describe** the way the lot looks now.

In the last two years several businesses have come and gone in the building next to the lot.

This sentence **explains** what has happened to some businesses in the neighborhood.

The lot is overgrown with weeds and covered with trash. Glass from broken bottles is scattered over the ground.

If our community developed the lot, people in the neighborhood would have a place to meet and spend time together.

This sentence tries to **persuade** readers to develop the lot for the benefit of the people in the neighborhood.

Your overall purpose will help you decide what form your writing will take: essay, story, poem, or report. Parts of the same piece of writing can serve different purposes. For example, all of the sentences shown above are parts of a longer proposal intended to persuade people to fix up the empty lot.

Journal Writing

Interview several adults about writing they have done in the last year and what their purposes were. How many different purposes were there? Take notes in your journal.

Teach

Using the Model

Guide students to understand the writing purpose for the examples on page 55 by asking these questions: *Which writing might help a reader picture the lot? Which writing might help readers learn how the lot has been bad for business? Which writing might help to convince readers that a developed lot would be good for the community?* Ask similar questions about articles from various magazines to help students identify and understand the purposes for writing. **L2**

Using Visual Clues to Determine Purpose

For students having difficulty determining the purpose of writing, provide examples of cartoons from the comic and editorial sections of newspapers. Examine the different styles of drawing and writing in the cartoons. Discuss how each style relates to the cartoon's intended purpose. **L1**

Two-Minute Skill Drill

List these events on the board: *circus, chess match, bake sale.* Have students brainstorm to develop a list of descriptive adjectives that will persuade people to attend the events.

See also *Two-Minute Skill Drill Transparency 2.3*

Journal Writing Tip

Taking Notes To help students write clear, useful notes, suggest that they decide how to organize the information they will gather before they conduct any interviews.

Teach

Determining the Audience

Initiate a discussion about how different magazines might approach the same topic, depending on the characteristics of the reading audience. Provide small groups of students with several magazines and have them determine the intended audience of each. Then have each group suggest a writing topic and explore the different purposes each magazine might have in publishing an article on that topic. Have group members discuss how a magazine's audience will influence the writing process. Finally, ask each group member to choose a magazine and to write an article about the topic for that publication. You might want to display the articles in the classroom next to the appropriate magazine. **L3**

Additional Resources

Fine Art Transparencies, 6–10

Writing Process Transparencies, 1–12
Writing Across the Curriculum
Cooperative Learning Activities,
pp. 7–12
Thinking and Study Skills,
pp. 3–5, 9, 21
Listening and Speaking Activities,
pp. 12–13
Composition Practice, p. 9

Know Your Audience

Think about who will eventually read your writing. Could it be the readers of a newspaper? your teacher? your classmates? How much does that audience know about the topic? What vocabulary is appropriate? Think about when and where your audience will read your writing.

The newspaper article and billboard below aim at audiences with different needs and interests. The newspaper article aims at readers who have time to read a whole article. The billboard will be read by people who probably pass by the sign quickly. The writing should jump out at them, and it should be easy to read.

Writing in the Real World

Writing for Different Audiences

Ask students to imagine they are working on two pieces of writing for an event the class will be holding, such as a talent show. Tell students the first piece is an article for the local paper telling about the show. The second is a poster to be placed at local businesses. Ask students these questions: Who will be reading the article? the poster? What information should they include in the article? the poster? Is it important to know who the audience is before writing? Why?

2.3 | Writing Activities

Identify Purpose and Audience

Before you choose your final topic, decide who your audience will be and what your purpose is. Look at your topic ideas. Ask yourself questions about your topic ideas.

PURPOSE To identify purpose and audience; to choose a topic

AUDIENCE Yourself

LENGTH 1–2 paragraphs

WRITING RUBRICS To narrow each topic idea, you should

- state your purpose for developing the idea. Do you want to persuade? give information? explain how to do something? express feelings? describe? tell a story?
- decide who your audience is. Are you writing for classmates, family members, the school or town newspaper?

Listening and Speaking

COOPERATIVE LEARNING In a small group, brainstorm for ideas about ways to raise money for a local charity or project. Discuss the ideas everyone has generated and agree on how to carry out one idea. Then have each group member write an article, flyer, or letter to persuade fellow students to volunteer time and labor.

Grammar Link

Make sure your subjects and verbs agree.

The verb in each of your sentences must agree with its subject. Do not be fooled by phrases that come between subject and verb.

Glass from broken bottles *is* scattered over the ground.

Complete the sentence fragments below, using the correct present-tense form of the verb to be—*am, is, are.*

1. The players on the football team
2. The river after three thunderstorms
3. The stories from several news-papers
4. One of the kittens
5. A group of girls

See Lessons 16.1–16.4, pages 535–542.

Using Computers

To explore topic ideas, try "invisible writing." Turn off the computer screen and freewrite—write about your topic for five minutes without stopping. Then turn on the screen and read what you have written. What interesting ideas can you develop further?

2.3 Prewriting: Determining Purpose and Audience   **57**

The Writing Process

Assess

Evaluation Rubrics

Identify Purpose and Audience
Answers will vary, but should reflect students' ability to identify the purpose of and audience for a piece of writing.

See also *Writing Assessment and Evaluation Rubrics*

Listening and Speaking
Answers will vary. Commend the following: all reasonable fund raising ideas for gathering support, a sound approach to carrying out the group project, and an appeal to the intended audience.

Using Computers
Students' freewriting should not only produce ideas that can be developed further but also disclose gaps in their knowledge about a topic. Filling those gaps will make their writing clearer and more interesting.

Reteaching
📁 *Composition Reteaching,* p. 9

Enrichment
📁 *Composition Enrichment,* p. 9

Close

Divide the class into three groups by having students rotate saying the numbers 1, 2, 3. Then write on the chalkboard *The Wizard of Oz* or another film all students have seen. Tell students in Group 1 that you would like each of them to write a paragraph describing the movie *The Wizard of Oz.* Ask each student in Group 2 to write a paragraph that will inform readers about various events that take place in the movie. Have each student in Group 3 write a paragraph in which they persuade readers to view the movie. After the paragraphs are complete, combine students from each group into groups of three and have them share and compare their paragraphs.

Grammar Link

Answers

1. are   **2.** is   **3.** are   **4.** is   **5.** is *or* are

Making Subjects and Verbs Agree Tell students to choose a subject and verb from the lists that follow and to write sentences in which the subject and verb agree. Direct them to insert a prepositional phrase between the subject and verb in each sentence. *Subjects—men, school bus, mice, children, dogs, house; Verbs—travels, learn, eat, nibble, stands, work.* When students finish, they can check each other's work.

Focus

Lesson Overview

Objectives

- To put main ideas for a piece of writing in logical order
- To prioritize supporting details during prewriting

Skills

- putting ideas in logical order; identifying the main idea; choosing supporting details

Critical Thinking

- analyzing; identifying the main idea; recalling; establishing and evaluating criteria; decision making

Listening and Speaking

- taking notes; asking questions; explaining a process

Bellringer
Daily Language Activity

When students enter the classroom, have this assignment on the board: *How would you describe the school lunchroom to new students? Where is it? How do you buy lunch there? Write and, if you wish, sketch a description.*

Grammar Link to the Bellringer

Have students look over their response to the Bellringer activity. Did they use any contractions? Invite them to double check that contractions have apostrophes in the correct places.

See also *Daily Language Practice*

Motivating Activity

Ask students to think of occasions when they have had to make a sketch or map to help a person understand something. In the Bellringer activity, perhaps they drew a map or floorplan to explain the set-up of the school lunchroom. If so, encourage students to provide details. Then discuss with students how they sketch out their plans before they begin to write.

58

The Writing Process

LESSON
2.4

Prewriting: Ordering Ideas

Once you determine your writing topic, purpose, and audience, you need to organize your ideas.

You may have plenty of ideas, but which one will you begin with? What will you say next? How will you end? Answering these questions will help you organize your ideas. Your goal is to find an order that will help the reader follow your thinking.

Sometimes drawing a sketch or a diagram can help you plan. After Mike, Keshia, and Henry decided which items to include in their plan for the lot, they sketched out these possible combinations of items.

58 Unit 2 The Writing Process

Resource Manager

Planning Resources
- *Lesson Plans*

Transparencies
- *Bellringer*
- *Daily Language Practice*
- *Fine Art* 6–10
- *Two-Minute Skill Drill*
- *Writing Process* 1–10

Other Print Resources
- *Composition Enrichment,* p. 10
- *Composition Practice,* p. 10
- *Composition Reteaching,* p. 10
- *Cooperative Learning Activities,* pp. 7–12
- *Listening and Speaking Activities,* pp. 12–13

- *Thinking and Study Skills,* pp. 7–8, 11, 13
- *Writing Across the Curriculum*
- *Writing Assessment and Evaluation Rubrics*

Identify Your Main Ideas

As a first step in ordering your thoughts, figure out your main ideas. You may have only one main idea, or you may have several. Remember your purpose for writing. What ideas will you need to include to help you meet your goal?

Henry is reading a list of the main ideas he and the others will include in their proposal. They want to persuade a community improvement group to develop a neighborhood lot. Each main idea is a point meant to help persuade the community group to put the plan into action.

Journal Writing

Select a piece of writing you created earlier for this unit. Read the piece to identify one or more main ideas. Underline each main idea you find.

Teach

Discussing Purpose

Discuss with students how writers use specific kinds of details to achieve their writing purpose. Initiate a discussion about the connection between purpose and kinds of details. Ask students why a political candidate might use statistics, facts, and examples to support his or her position. What might be the problem if a candidate does not back up his or her position with details? **L2**

Identifying Main Ideas

If students have trouble distinguishing their main ideas from their supporting details, have them work with partners to identify the most important ideas in their notes. They should then write these main ideas on a piece of paper and circle each one in a different color. When they identify a detail that supports one of the main ideas, they should write it under the appropriate idea and underline it in the corresponding color. **L1**

 **Two-Minute Skill Drill**

In the following group of phrases, three phrases are details of one main idea listed below. Have students identify the main idea:

- *for relief of dry, itchy skin*
- *dermatologist recommended*
- *moisturizing lotion*
- *with natural ingredients*

See also *Two-Minute Skill Drill Transparency 2.4*

Journal Writing Tip

Main Idea Suggest that each student give a title to the journal entry, basing it upon one of the main ideas identified.

Teach

Rewriting the Details

Provide students with magazines and newspaper articles. Guide pairs of students in identifying the main idea and supporting details of one paragraph in an article. Tell students to rewrite the paragraph by putting the details in a different but sensible order. They might then discuss the effect the new order has on the original purpose of the paragraph. Partners should then share their modified paragraphs. **L2**

Two-Minute Skill Drill

List these main ideas on the board. Have students name at least three details for each.

- *The Fourth of July is a great holiday.*
- *Nutrition is extremely important.*
- *Olympic Games are . . .*

See also *Two-Minute Skill Drill Transparency 2.4*

Additional Resources

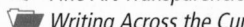

Writing Process Transparencies, 1–10

Fine Art Transparencies, 6–10

Writing Across the Curriculum

Cooperative Learning Activities

Thinking and Study Skills, pp. 7–8, 11, 13

Listening and Speaking Activities, pp. 7–12

Composition Practice, p. 10

The Writing Process

Find an Order That Works

Each main idea needs details, such as examples, facts, or reasons, to support it. The illustration on this page shows how a main idea and supporting details work together.

Brainstorm or use prewriting notes to make a list of details. Once you have the details, you can put them in order. The order will depend on your purpose.

- To persuade your reader, you might list details in the order of their importance. List the most important detail either first or last, depending on which order you think will be more convincing.

- To describe something, you might list the details in the order in which an observer would notice them, or you can begin with the more significant details.

- To explain something, you might work from the simplest details to the most difficult ones or from the first step to the last.

Supporting Detail

Supporting Detail

Main Idea

Supporting Detail

Supporting Detail

The empty lot is bad for the neighborhood

② businesses near the lot suffer

① it's unsafe   *most important, mention first*

~~people think the lot makes our neighborhood the~~

~~ugliest in the city~~   *just an opinion, doesn't really fit here*

Notice that this group listed details first and ordered them later.

Cooperative Learning

Developing Supportive Details

Encourage students to work in pairs. List a main idea on the board, such as *It is vital that nations of the world avoid polluting our oceans.* Have pairs elaborate on the idea by developing three supporting details for this statement. Partners can then share their supporting details with the group and explain how each relates to the main idea.

2.4 | Writing Activities

Make a Plan for Writing

Look at your topic and begin to plan your writing.

PURPOSE To plan your writing

AUDIENCE Yourself

LENGTH 1–2 paragraphs

WRITING RUBRICS To plan your writing, you should

- list your main ideas and supporting details

- arrange the main ideas and details in an order that suits your purpose

Henri Matisse, *The Bowl with Goldfish,* 1914

Grammar Link

Use *it's* and *its* correctly.

It's is a contraction. *Its* is a possessive pronoun used with a noun.

It's unsafe. **Its** bowl is clean.

Fill in each blank with *it's* or *its*.

The goldfish is floating in **1**_____ bowl. **2**_____ not very lively. Is that **3**_____ reflection at the bottom of the bowl? The fish tried to jump out of **4**_____ bowl. I hope **5**_____ going to be all right.

See Lesson 17.2, pages 555.

Viewing and Representing

SHAPES In a small group, discuss Henri Matisse's painting. What shapes do you notice? Where do you tend to focus as you look at the painting? How does the artist draw your eye to that spot? Finally, write a brief summary of your group's discussion.

Cross-Curricular Activity

SCIENCE Where do goldfish (*Carassius auratus*) live in nature? How do they survive? Research to learn more about them. Then plan your main ideas and supporting details. Write two paragraphs and share your findings with the class.

2.4 Prewriting: Ordering Ideas **61**

The Writing Process

Assess

Evaluation Rubrics

Make a Plan for Writing

Use these criteria when evaluating your student's writing:

- Does it identify the main idea?
- Does it list the main idea and supporting details in a sensible order?

See also *Writing Assessment and Evaluation Rubrics*

Viewing and Representing

Students' comments should include mention of a variety of shapes and include their ideas on what the artist has done to make them focus on a particular area of the painting. For additional class discussion, have students imagine that the painting has been brought to life. Ask students to make predictions about what is likely to happen next within the scene.

Cross-Curricular Activity

Evaluate the paragraphs for the following:
- clarity in expressing the main idea
- relevance of details
- order of the details in relation to the purpose of the paragraphs

Reteaching

📁 *Composition Reteaching,* p. 10

Enrichment

📁 *Composition Enrichment,* p. 10

📐 *Fine Art Transparencies,* 6–10

Close

Ask students to write the main idea of this lesson and then list several supporting details about it.

Grammar Link

Answers

1. its   **4.** its
2. It's   **5.** it's
3. its

Contractions Remind students that they can check their answers by trying to use *it is* in place of the word *it's.* If *it is* fits, then *it's* needs an apostrophe.

Viewing the Art

Henri Matisse, *The Bowl with Goldfish,* 1914
The Bowl with Goldfish by Henri Matisse is in the Musée National d'Art Moderne in Paris. It is oil on canvas and measures $57^3/_4$ by $38^1/_8$ inches. Matisse (1869–1954) believed that his art should calm and soothe the mind.

Focus

Lesson Overview

Objectives

- To explore ways of using prewriting notes in drafting
- To learn how to continue writing from the first draft

Skills

- using prewriting notes effectively; evaluating peer suggestions; choosing writing techniques to ensure completion

Critical Thinking

- analyzing; relating; generating new information; decision making

Listening and Speaking

- explaining a process; asking questions; evaluating

Bellringer
Daily Language Activity

When students enter the classroom, have this assignment on the board: *Have you ever watched or been in a dress rehearsal for a play, recital, or skit? Write what you learned from watching or being in a rehearsal.*

Grammar Link to the Bellringer

Have students write or say aloud one sentence describing what they liked *best* about a dress rehearsal. Help them use the superlative form correctly.

See also *Daily Language Practice*

Motivating Activity

Allow volunteers to share their responses to the Bellringer activity. Then ask students what they might hope to accomplish when they sit down to write a first draft. Elicit that the purpose of a draft is to start writing without worrying about perfection.

The Writing Process

Drafting: Getting It in Writing

You're ready to write a first draft of your essay, story, or report. How should you begin?

By drafting, you turn your lists, clusters, and other prewriting work into sentences and paragraphs. The draft shown below didn't just write itself. The writer, Keshia, used her group's prewriting notes to guide her drafting.

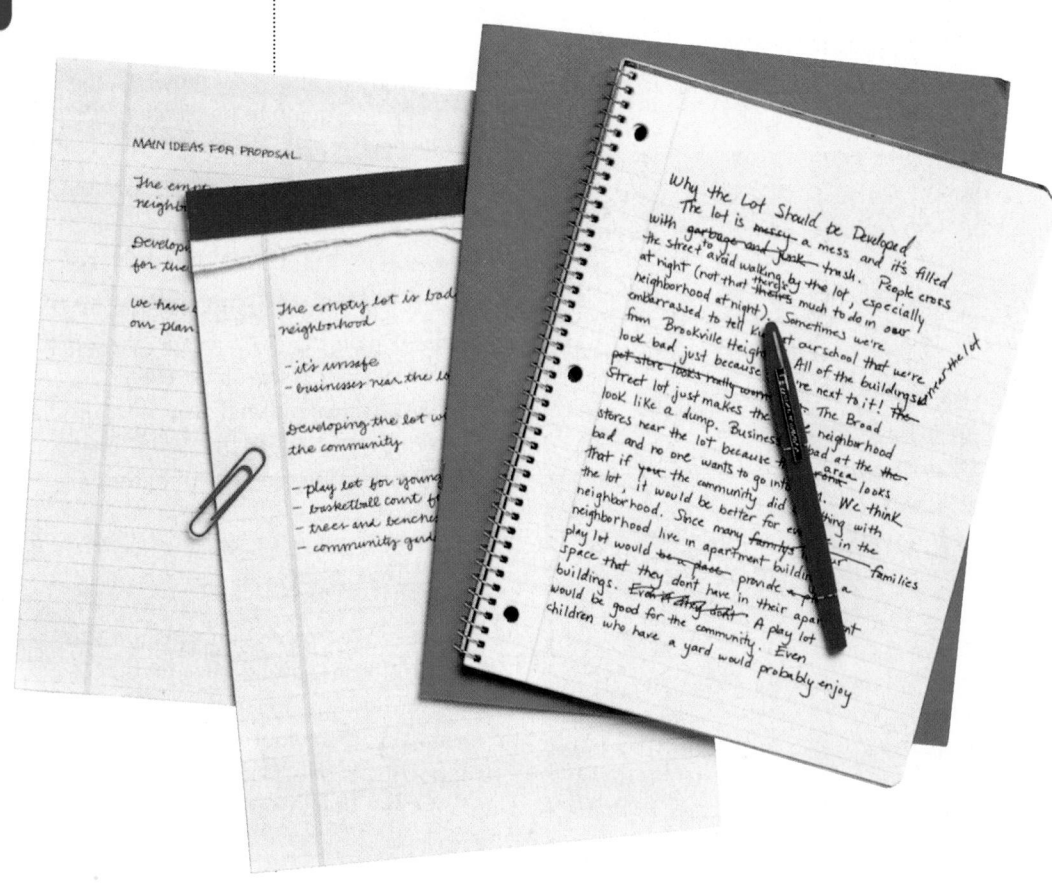

62 Unit 2 The Writing Process

Resource Manager

📂 Planning Resources
- *Lesson Plans*

📊 Transparencies
- *Bellringer*
- *Daily Language Practice*
- *Fine Art* 6–10
- *Two-Minute Skill Drill*
- *Writing Process* 1–10

📂 Other Print Resources
- *Composition Enrichment*, p. 11
- *Composition Practice*, p. 11
- *Composition Reteaching*, p. 11
- *Cooperative Learning Activities*, pp. 7–12
- *Listening and Speaking Activities*, pp. 12–13

- *Thinking and Study Skills*, pp. 4–5, 13, 20–32
- *Writing Across the Curriculum*
- *Writing Assessment and Evaluation Rubrics*

Try Different Ways

Sometimes stories and reports seem easy to write. At other times, your first page stays blank no matter how long you look at it. You might already have a way to begin drafting. If you don't or if you'd like to try another way, you might experiment with one of the following suggestions:

1. **Pretend you're writing to a friend.** Write as if you're talking about your idea with a friend who always listens and understands.

2. **Start on the easiest part.** You don't have to start at the beginning. Start by writing the easiest sections. Then the other parts will probably seem easier to write.

3. **Speak your ideas into a tape recorder.** Say what you're thinking on tape, and you'll have an instant first draft.

4. **Set reasonable goals.** The thought of writing an entire essay, report, or story can be scary. Decide that you are going to write just one paragraph or even one sentence at a time.

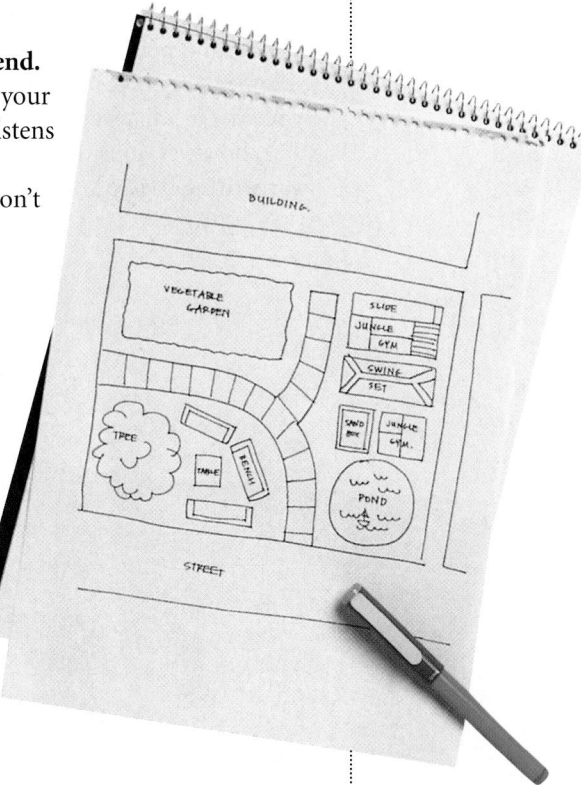

Journal Writing

Think about the techniques listed above or about one you have developed yourself. Then explain in your journal how these suggestions might help you with your drafting.

2.5 Drafting: Getting It in Writing **63**

Teach

Promoting Discussion

Use this quote by writer Katherine Anne Porter to initiate a discussion about ways to start writing: "If I didn't know the ending of a story, I wouldn't begin. I always write my last line, my last paragraphs, my last page first." Invite students to offer their opinions of this approach and why it might or might not work for them. Then discuss the ideas for writing listed on this page. Ask students for other ideas, especially ones they already use. As students begin drafting, have them choose one approach from the ideas discussed that they will use as they begin writing. **L2**

Two-Minute Skill Drill

List these parts of a story on the board and have students order the story parts logically:

- *Local police become involved in the search.*
- *One of the chaperones gets lost in the woods.*
- *The Outdoor Club plans a camp-out.*
- *Adults and students organize rescue parties.*

See also *Two-Minute Skill Drill Transparency 2.5*

Journal Writing Tip

Writing Techniques Encourage students to use what they know about their own writing styles and what they have learned about the writing process to decide which drafting techniques would be most helpful to them. They may want to ask themselves such questions as What types of writing give me the most trouble? What type of writing comes easily to me? Do I worry so much about getting things perfect that I can't keep going?

Teach

Peer Reviewing Strategies

Remind students that when they get stuck, peer reviewers can offer a fresh eye. Group students in pairs. Then have students show their drafts and notes to their partners. Have them point out to their peer reviewers a place where they had trouble continuing drafting or got completely stuck. The peer reviewers may quickly see a way to get the writing going again. **L2**

Additional Resources

Writing Process Transparencies, 1–10

Fine Art Transparencies, 6–10

Writing Across the Curriculum

Cooperative Learning Activities

Thinking and Study Skills, pp. 4–5, 13, 20–22

Listening and Speaking Activities, pp. 12–13

Composition Practice, p. 11

Write On

Once you've begun writing, the challenge is to continue writing. Keep your prewriting notes handy. Look back at them whenever you reach a stopping point in your writing.

Completing your first draft is more important than perfecting every sentence. Later you can rearrange your sentences or improve the way they're stated. You can also check grammar, spelling, and punctuation at a later stage.

Some writers like to draft on a computer. Others prefer to draft by hand. Do whatever works best for you. If you find yourself stuck, however, consider trying the suggestions below to get your writing back on track.

MEETING INDIVIDUAL NEEDS — English Language Learners

Choosing Words

Students learning English might more easily complete their drafts knowing they can resort to their first language if they get stuck in English. Students should try to work in English as much as possible, but invite them to use their first language if they cannot think of how to say something in English. When they revise, they can translate into English. They might also discuss their ideas with students more proficient in English who can help them express their thoughts.

Write a Draft

Now it's time to face that blank sheet of paper. Just write. Skip every other line to leave room for changes. Don't worry about correctness. At this stage, you are still exploring what you want to say.

PURPOSE To create a draft

AUDIENCE Yourself

LENGTH 1–2 paragraphs

WRITING RUBRICS To begin drafting, you should

- use your prewriting notes
- get your ideas down on paper
- try to put your ideas down in an order that makes sense

Charles Goeller, *Third Avenue*, 1933–1934

Grammar Link

Use correct forms of *good.*

*If the community did something with the lot, it would be **better** for everyone.*

Fill in each blank with *good, better,* or *best.*

Third Avenue looks quite **1**_____ in this painting, but certain changes would make it even **2**_____. The market would look cleaner and **3**_____ with a paint job. For the street to look its **4**_____, someone should dispose of the litter. Is that man wearing the **5**_____ hat of all?

See Lesson 12.3, page 455.

Viewing and Representing

EVALUATING What old-fashioned and super-modern images do you see in Charles Goeller's painting? What message or story might the artist be presenting? In a small group, compare your ideas with those of others.

Cross-Curricular Activity

HEALTH What links do you think exist between health and school performance? What connections do you find between your physical and mental health? List your ideas and decide how to order them. Then draft a paper stating your opinions about this idea.

2.5 Drafting: Getting It in Writing **65**

Assess

Evaluation Rubrics

Write a Draft

Answers will vary. The draft should present, in a logical order, the ideas that appear in students' prewriting notes.

See also *Writing Assessment and Evaluation Rubrics*

Viewing and Representing

Students should state what message they think the artist is trying to convey and support their opinions with evidence from the painting. Students' evaluations should mention old-fashioned and modern images and how they contribute to the artist's message.

Cross-Curricular Activity

Evaluate the paper according to these criteria:
- Does it link health and school performance?
- Does it use elaboration (facts, examples, and reasons) to support ideas?
- Does it contain organized details?

Reteaching

📁 *Composition Reteaching,* p. 11

Enrichment

📁 *Composition Enrichment,* p. 11

🗳 *Fine Art Transparencies,* 6–10

Close

Discuss with students the different ways of starting and completing a draft that they learned in this lesson. Which techniques did students find most helpful to begin writing? Which techniques helped them begin again when they got stuck?

Grammar Link

Answers

1. good   **4.** best
2. better   **5.** best
3. better

Comparative and Superlative Adjectives Go over the Grammar Link exercise again, using the comparative and superlative forms of *bad, nice,* and *tidy.*

Viewing the Art

Charles Goeller, *Third Avenue,* 1933–1934
Third Avenue by Charles Louis Goeller (1901–1955) is in the National Museum of American Art in Washington, D.C. It is oil on canvas and measures 36 by 36⅛ inches.

Focus

Lesson Overview

Objectives
- To revise a piece of writing for clarity and sense
- To evaluate and practice the role of a peer reviewer

Skills
- scrutinizing and evaluating a draft; giving and receiving a second opinion; evaluating suggestions

Critical Thinking
- analyzing; defining and clarifying; decision making

Listening and Speaking
- giving and receiving feedback; asking questions; evaluating

 Bellringer

Daily Language Activity

When students enter the classroom, have this assignment on the board: *Write one paragraph about the first time you tried a favorite sport or hobby.*

Grammar Link to the Bellringer

Remind students that proper nouns need to be capitalized. Ask students for examples of proper nouns (names of people, places, or organizations). Have them look over their paragraphs from the Bellringer activity to make sure any proper nouns they used begin with capital letters.

See also *Daily Language Practice*

Motivating Activity

Ask students what kinds of things they had to do over and over in order to improve when learning a favorite sport or hobby. Discuss the response they got from others as they were learning and how they felt when they began to improve. Stress that students shouldn't expect their writing to be perfect on the first try.

Revising: Evaluating a Draft

L *ooking at the whole piece of writing rather than just its parts is important when you begin to evaluate and revise.*

Once your draft is finished, step back and look at it. Does it all go together, or do some parts not belong? Are any parts missing? Are all the parts in order?

When Henry, Mike, and Keshia looked at their sketch, they realized that some parts did not belong and would have to go.

Resource Manager

📂 Planning Resources
- *Lesson Plans*

🗂 Transparencies
- *Bellringer*
- *Daily Language Practice*
- *Fine Art* 6–10
- *Two-Minute Skill Drill*
- *Writing Process* 1–10

📂 Other Print Resources
- *Composition Enrichment,* p. 12
- *Composition Practice,* p. 12
- *Composition Reteaching,* p. 12
- *Cooperative Learning Activities,* pp. 7–12
- *Listening and Speaking Activities,* pp. 12–13

- *Sentence-Combining Practice,* p. 1
- *Thinking and Study Skills,* pp. 4, 9, 13, 18
- *Writing Across the Curriculum*
- *Writing Assessment and Evaluation Rubrics*

Evaluate for Clarity

When your draft is done, set it aside for a while before you read it again. When you return to the draft, evaluate it for clarity and decide whether it makes sense. Answering the questions on this checklist will help you decide how to revise your draft for clarity.

Get a Second Opinion

One of the best ways to evaluate a draft is to have a peer reviewer examine it. Getting another opinion helps you gain distance from your writing. The remainder of this lesson explains how to be a peer reviewer and what to do once you get a peer reviewer's advice.

A WRITING CONFERENCE In a writing conference you read your draft to a partner or a small group. These are your peer reviewers. Peer reviewers try to answer these questions: What's the main idea of this paper? Do the details in the paper support that idea? Your goal as a peer reviewer isn't to label the writing good or bad. Instead, tell the writer what you understand to be the paper's main idea and purpose. Then tell how well you think the draft is working. Ask about anything that is unclear.

☑ Do I stick to my topic?

☑ Do I accomplish my purpose?

☑ Do I keep my audience in mind?

☑ Does my main idea come across clearly?

☑ Do I give enough details? too many?

Journal Writing

Think about the role of a peer reviewer. As you do, consider what kinds of advice you would like from a peer reviewer. What should your reviewer look for? How would you like your reviewer to evaluate your writing? Write your thoughts in your journal.

2.6 Revising: Evaluating a Draft **67**

Teach

Using the Model

Have students copy the questions in the checklist but change each sentence to begin, Does the author.... Students may then use the checklist to critique articles from school and local newspapers. Ask them to identify the purpose of each article and apply the questions from the checklist to it. If they get a negative response to a question, they should write a suggestion for revision. **L2**

Checking the Writing

Some students may have more success as peer reviewers if the writer identifies the main idea, purpose, and audience for them before they read. The peer reviewer should then read the draft, looking for a sentence or passage that expresses the main idea and purpose stated by the writer. The reviewer might also look for details that would appeal to the intended audience. **L1**

 **Two-Minute Skill Drill**

Write the following sentences on the board. Which one would be the most useful for a writer to hear in a peer review?

- *This is the greatest thing I ever read.*
- *I don't get it.*
- *I want to know the main idea sooner.*
- *Nice handwriting.*

See also ☞ *Two-Minute Skill Drill Transparency 2.6*

Journal Writing Tip

Focusing Ideas Students may find it helpful to put their ideas in the form of a letter. Ask them to imagine they are responding to a letter in an advice column. Someone has written to them asking how to become a better peer reviewer. What tips can the students provide?

Teach

Understanding the Connections

Lead a discussion about the connections among purpose, audience, details, and organization in writing. For example, in the cross-curricular writing activity (on the following page), the purpose of writing is to describe a painting for an archaeologist. What kinds of details should the writer include? What order might the writer use to present the details? If the audience were a visually impaired teenager, how would the author's purpose, the selection of details, and the organization change? **L2**

Additional Resources

Fine Art Transparencies, 6–10

Writing Process Transparencies, 1–10

Writing Across the Curriculum

Cooperative Learning Activities, pp. 7–12

Thinking and Study Skills, pp. 4, 9, 13, 18

Sentence-Combining Practice, p. 1

Listening and Speaking Activities, pp. 12–13

Composition Practice, p. 12

The Writing Process

GIVING AND RECEIVING FEEDBACK Sometimes you may want to make or receive detailed comments on a draft. To make comments, you might find it helpful to fill out a peer-review form—either one from your teacher or a form of your own.

When you receive a review of your work, discuss the comments with your peer reviewer. If your reviewer has criticisms, remember that your writing is being evaluated, not you. Finally, remember that you're the writer. You decide which changes you'll make to your writing.

> The peer reviewer understood the purpose of the paper and for whom it was written. The draft forms a good foundation for the paper.

PEER REVIEW

1. What is the main idea of this paper? *The Broad Street lot should be developed into a park, a play lot, and a community garden.*

2. What is the writer's purpose? *To convince people to fix up the lot*

3. Who would be the intended audience for this paper? *Brookville Heights Community Improvement Group*

4. Which parts of the paper stand out for you? Name or describe them, and explain why they seem important. *The plans for developing the lot were great. I felt excited as I read about them. They convinced me that the proposal was a good idea.*

5. Identify any parts of the paper that seem puzzling or out of place. *Some comments, like ones about nothing to do in the neighborhood and being embarrassed to say where they're from, should have been left out.*

Why the Lot Sh
The lot is a
trash. People c
avoid walking
that there's n
night). Some
at our schoo
Heights!
All of the
because th
just make

MEETING INDIVIDUAL NEEDS — English Language Learners

Evaluating Orally

When acting as a peer reviewer, students who have difficulty writing in English may feel more at ease using a tape recorder to respond to the questions on the form. When the peer reviewer has responded to all the questions, the writer and the peer reviewer can listen to the tape together and discuss the comments.

The Writing Process

Evaluate a Draft

Look again at your draft. Make sure some time has gone by before you begin to revise it. When you make your changes, remember that you can circle, delete, tape on—neatness is not a part of revising!

PURPOSE To prepare to revise
AUDIENCE Your peer reviewers
LENGTH 1 page of comments

WRITING RUBRICS To begin to revise your draft, you should

- use the checklist on page 67 to evaluate your draft for clarity
- read your paper to a peer reviewer or reviewers. Discuss your paper with them, using the Peer Review form on page 68

Using Computers

Use e-mail to share your writing with a peer reviewer. In your message, include the peer review checklist from page 68. Then attach a copy of your paper to your e-mail message. Ask your reviewer to respond to your paper by typing responses on the checklist and sending it back to you.

Cross-Curricular Activity

SCIENCE You are an archaeologist who has just unearthed a painting in an Egyptian tomb. Write a description of it. Then ask a fellow archaeologist (another student) to review your writing for clarity.

Grammar Link

Capitalize proper nouns.

Capitalize the specific names of places and groups, as well as the names of months and days of the week.

Rewrite the following paragraph, adding capital letters where necessary.

[1] Nella and Pietro belong to a neighborhood book club, the reading bugs. [2] The club meets every thursday at the library on main street. [3] Once a month they go to memorial library on center street in mannville, where they visit with the fact and fiction club. [4] After the meeting everyone gathers at maury's pizzeria. [5] Since september, members of both clubs have been helping the children at rose park elementary school learn to read.

See Lesson 19.3, page 577, and Lesson 19.4, page 579.

2.6 Revising: Evaluating a Draft **69**

Grammar Link

Answers
The following should be capitalized:
1. The Reading Bugs
2. Thursday . . . Main Street
3. Memorial Library . . . Center Street . . . Mannville . . . The [the] Fact and Fiction Club
4. Maury's Pizzeria
5. September . . . Rose Park Elementary School

Assess

Evaluation Rubrics

Evaluate a Draft

Suggested revisions should reflect attention to the questions on the Peer Review form and should clarify
- main idea
- writer's purpose
- intended audience
- details

See also *Writing Assessment and Evaluation Rubrics*

Using Computers

Monitor peer reviewers' responses to see that they are accurate and constructive in tone.

Cross-Curricular Activity

The description should
- include details that would interest an archaeologist, such as the physical condition of the painting, its apparent age, and so on
- arrange details in sensible order

Reteaching

📁 *Composition Reteaching*, p. 12

Enrichment

📁 *Composition Enrichment*, p. 12

🖌 *Fine Art Transparencies*, 6–10

Close

Initiate a discussion on the uses and limits of peer evaluation. You might share Mark Twain's comment, "I like criticism, but it must be my way." What do students think Twain meant? Why is criticism sometimes unpleasant for writers? When can it be helpful? When might it be useless? Finally, ask students what they think novelist Vladimir Nabokov meant by, "My pencils outlast their erasers."

Focus

Lesson Overview

Objectives

- To practice techniques for paragraph revision
- To observe and practice the effective use of transitions

Skills

- linking related thoughts in sentences and paragraphs; using effective transitions; identifying the main idea

Critical Thinking

- analyzing; activating prior knowledge; synthesizing; making inferences; developing a main idea

Listening and Speaking

- giving and receiving feedback; evaluating

Bellringer
Daily Language Activity

When students enter the classroom, have this assignment on the board: *Describe an activity, such as a sport or household chore, that involves teamwork.*

Grammar Link to the Bellringer

Have students underline all the introductory prepositional phrases that they wrote for the Bellringer activity. Ask them to check whether those phrases should be followed by a comma.

See also 🚩 *Daily Language Practice*

Motivating Activity

Have volunteers tell what activity they described in the Bellringer activity. Then discuss with students what happens when someone does not cooperate in a team activity. Challenge students to draw an analogy between sentences in a paragraph and players on a soccer team.

The Writing Process

LESSON

2.7

Revising: Making Paragraphs Effective

A n effective paragraph must have unity—that is, all sentences must work together to support a main idea.

Just as a garden is an arrangement of plants, a paragraph is an arrangement of sentences. All the sentences in the following paragraph present the main idea, a childhood memory.

Literature Model

S ome of my earliest memories are of the storms, the hot rain lashing down and lightning running on the sky—and the storm cellar into which my mother and I descended so many times when I was very young. For me that little room in the earth is an unforgettable place. Across the years I see my mother reading there on the low, narrow bench, the lamplight flickering on her face and on the earthen walls; I smell the dank odor of that room; and I hear the great weather raging at the door. I have never been in a place that was like it exactly; only now and then I have been reminded of it suddenly when I have gone into a cave, or when I have just caught the scent of fresh, open earth steaming in the rain.

N. Scott Momaday, *The Names*

> Notice that all the sentences in the paragraph support the idea in the first sentence.

70 Unit 2 The Writing Process

Resource Manager

📂 **Planning Resources**
- *Lesson Plans*

🚩 **Transparencies**
- *Bellringer*
- *Daily Language Practice*
- *Fine Art 6–10*
- *Two-Minute Skill Drill*
- *Writing Process 1–10*

📂 **Other Print Resources**
- *Composition Enrichment*, p. 13
- *Composition Practice*, p. 13
- *Composition Reteaching*, p. 13
- *Cooperative Learning Activities*, pp. 7–12
- *Listening and Speaking Activities*, pp. 12–13

- *Sentence-Combining Practice*, p. 1
- *Thinking and Study Skills*, pp. 9, 11, 13
- *Writing Across the Curriculum*
- *Writing Assessment and Evaluation Rubrics*

Look for Main Ideas

As you review your draft, look for the main ideas. A main idea is like a magnet, pulling sentences toward it to form a paragraph.

Many paragraphs have a topic sentence that states the main idea. Sometimes a topic sentence is the first sentence in a paragraph. Other times it is the last sentence of a paragraph. Not all paragraphs need topic sentences, however. Many well-written paragraphs consist of sentences that suggest the main idea without directly stating it.

Although topic sentences are used in all types of writing, they're most common in paragraphs written to explain or persuade. When attempting to persuade, you don't want to make readers guess what you're thinking.

> Notice the way this draft has been broken into paragraphs. Does each paragraph have a topic sentence? If so, what is it?

Since many families in our neighborhood live in apartments, a play lot would provide space that they don't have in their apartment buildings. *Topic sentence* A play lot would be good for the community. Even children who have a yard would enjoy a playground where there would be other children to play with. *New paragraph* For younger children the play lot would include a sturdy swing-and-slide set, a climbing frame, a sandbox, and a merry-go-round. Older kids could use two basketball hoops and backboards and a tetherball pole. *This idea doesn't fit in.* ~~Regular exercise might improve school performance, as well.~~ These features would give children and teenagers something to do besides going to the mall or watching television.

Teach

Using the Model

Draw students' attention to the vivid picture N. Scott Momaday paints for the reader with details that call on the senses of sight, smell, hearing, and touch ("hot rain," "lightning running," "lamplight flickering," "dank odor"). Encourage students to identify these and other sensory details and to discuss how they support the main idea of the paragraph. **L2**

Understanding Creative License

Point out to students that N. Scott Momaday purposely uses run-on sentences to capture the nostalgic tone and mood of a childhood memory. Words and phrases run together like the details of a memory, one after the other without a break. Discuss whether students think this is an effective writing technique. **L3**

Journal Writing Tip

Identifying Main Ideas Remind students that in descriptive and narrative paragraphs, an implied main idea is more common than a stated one. If students have difficulty locating the main idea, ask them to say what they think it is in their own words first and then look for a sentence or passage that expresses the idea they stated.

Journal Writing

Select paragraphs from three different types of writing. You might choose paragraphs from a novel, a textbook, and an instruction manual. Is the main idea of each paragraph stated in a topic sentence? If so, copy the sentence into your journal. If not, write the main idea in your own words.

Teach

Promoting Discussion

Have students look through a story or an article in order to identify and read aloud two sentences linked with one of the transition words listed on this page. Ask them to reread the sentences, substituting a different transition word from the chart. Discuss how the relationship of the two sentences changes when the transition word changes. **L2**

Two-Minute Skill Drill

Ask students to think of more transition words and phrases to add to the chart on this page. Record them on the board. Have a student say a simple sentence. Have a second student add a sentence to that, using one of the transition words or phrases on the board or the chart. Repeat with other pairs, or continue adding to the first sentences, using as many of the transition words as possible.

See also Two-Minute Skill Drill Transparency 2.7

Additional Resources

- Fine Art Transparencies, 6–10
- Writing Process Transparencies, 1–10
- Writing Across the Curriculum
- Cooperative Learning Activities, pp. 7–12
- Thinking and Study Skills, pp. 9, 11, 13
- Sentence-Combining Practice, p. 1
- Listening and Speaking Activities, pp. 12–13
- Composition Practice, p. 13

The Writing Process

Revising Tip

For more information on transitions, see **Writing and Research Handbook,** page 820.

Link Thoughts Sensibly

Transitions are words and phrases that help connect sentences in some sensible manner. Transitions provide the links between ideas in a paragraph. *Also* and *as a result* are examples of these types of transitions.

Transitions such as *in front of* and *until then* help express a relationship in space or time. Other common transitions appear in the chart on this page. Notice how the revisions to the draft below use transitions to link thoughts within the paragraph and to show relationships.

Common Transitions			
after	before	because	although
now	therefore	however	for example
here	then	like	next to

This sentence was moved to the beginning because it provides a concrete example out of which the other sentences grow.

Why did the writer add the transition "Then"?

We don't think any store can be successful next in that location to the lot. Businesses nearby suffer because of *also* the lot's condition. In the last two years Several businesses have come and gone in the building next to the lot. We know that developing the lot would make our neighborhood feel safer and look better. *Then* People might be able to shop closer to home.

MEETING INDIVIDUAL NEEDS

English Language Learners

Recognizing Transition Words

Some students may not easily recognize English transition words and phrases. Distribute copies of a paragraph that has clear transition words and phrases. Pair less proficient English speakers with more proficient English speakers to read the paragraph aloud. Ask them to look and listen for words that connect sentence ideas. Tell students to circle any they recognize and to identify them. Point out any transition words and phrases they missed, and discuss why they might have missed them.

Revise for Effective Paragraphs

Take another look at your draft. Evaluate each of your paragraphs.

PURPOSE To revise for paragraph unity
AUDIENCE Yourself
LENGTH Changes on the draft

WRITING RUBRICS To revise a paragraph for unity, you should

- make sure that all sentences are about one main idea
- decide if your paragraph needs a topic sentence, and if it does, add one
- add transition words to link thoughts and show relationships

Using Computers

To revise on the computer, make a copy of your paper. (Highlight your writing, copy it, and paste it on a new page or file.) Then revise—insert and delete words, move sentences, add new sentences. After revising, read both versions. Have you kept your important ideas? Have you organized them effectively?

Grammar Link

Use a comma after two or more introductory prepositional phrases.

You do not need to use a comma after a single short prepositional phrase at the beginning of a sentence. Do use a comma after two or more introductory prepositional phrases.

On the gate across the road, *a sign proclaimed "Town Forest."*

Rewrite the paragraph below, adding commas where necessary.

[1]In the town forest I can observe a variety of plant life. [2]Along the path through the woods oaks and hemlocks compete for the light. [3]Among the roots of the trees partridgeberry and lady's slippers catch my eye. [4]In the sunny glade at the top of the hill wood lilies and wild geraniums flourish.

See Lesson 13.1, page 479, and Lesson 20.2, page 591.

Listening and Speaking

COOPERATIVE LEARNING In a small group, discuss your work so far. Each group member should share two things about his or her paper that are going well, as well as two problems. Brainstorm for solutions.

The Writing Process

Assess
Evaluation Rubrics

Revise for Effective Paragraphs

Examine the original and revised draft. Look for the following:
- changes that improve unity and sense
- support for main idea
- transition words linking ideas
- any other revisions still needed

See also *Writing Assessment and Evaluation Rubrics*

Using Computers

Having students compare a print-out of the original and the revised versions of their papers should make it possible for them to see more clearly the differences between the two.

Listening and Speaking

Monitor groups' discussions to make note of students' strengths. Praise examples of constructive and active listening and speaking.

Reteaching

📁 *Composition Reteaching,* p. 13

Enrichment

📁 *Composition Enrichment,* p. 13

Close

Ask students if it is important for them to know how to create stronger, more effective paragraphs in the writing they do outside of school. Encourage students to recall some recent writing tasks, in and outside of school, such as personal letters, essay exams, and reports. Discuss ways they could have applied the revising techniques covered in this lesson to those writing tasks. Ask students how being able to revise can help them succeed in future writing assignments.

Grammar Link

Answers
1. No change
2. Along the path through the woods,
3. Among the roots of the trees,
4. In the sunny glade at the top of the hill,
5. Near the stream in the forest,

Introductory Prepositional Phrases Ask students to write a sentence with two introductory prepositional phrases but no comma. Have partners exchange sentences and read them—first without the comma, then with a comma added after the prepositional phrases.

Focus

Lesson Overview

Objectives

- To enhance writing by varying sentence structure and word order
- To combine or break up sentences to vary sentence length

Skills

- expressing relationships between thoughts; combining similar thoughts; varying word order to create rhythm in writing

Critical Thinking

- analyzing; identifying the main idea; comparing and contrasting; decision making; patterning

Listening and Speaking

- evaluating; interpreting clues; discussing; giving and receiving feedback

Bellringer
Daily Language Activity

When students enter the classroom, have this assignment on the board: *Vary the word order and sentence length of the following sentence.*

Variety is the spice of life.

Grammar Link to the Bellringer

Point out to students that pronouns help promote variety. Ask them to take one of the sentences they wrote in the Bellringer activity and add another sentence to it, expanding on the basic idea. Did any students use the pronoun *it?* Invite them to share their two sentences.

See also *Daily Language Practice*

Motivating Activity

Encourage volunteers to read aloud the sentences they wrote in the Bellringer activity. In a brief class discussion, elicit from students that sentence variety heightens interest.

Revising: Creating Sentence Variety

*U*sing a variety of sentences in your writing can make it more appealing.

Think about the sentences in your paragraphs and the way you use those sentences. Varying the plantings and the size and shape of garden beds makes a garden more interesting to look at. Likewise, varying your sentences makes your writing more interesting to read.

Resource Manager

📁 Planning Resources
- *Lesson Plans*

📑 Transparencies
- *Bellringer*
- *Daily Language Practice*
- *Fine Art 6–10*
- *Two-Minute Skill Drill*
- *Writing Process 1–10*

📁 Other Print Resources
- *Composition Enrichment,* p. 14
- *Composition Practice,* p. 14
- *Composition Reteaching,* p. 14
- *Cooperative Learning Activities,* pp. 7–12
- *Listening and Speaking Activities,* pp. 12–13

- *Sentence-Combining Practice,* p. 1
- *Thinking and Study Skills,* pp. 1, 4, 20
- *Writing Across the Curriculum*
- *Writing Assessment and Evaluation Rubrics*

Breaking run-on sentences makes them easier to understand.

We know that it will take money to develop the lot, and we are willing to do our part to help raise the money. We could plan several fund-raising events, Such as a car wash, a raffle, and a rummage sale. Also, *Many teenagers and grown-ups from the neighborhood have offered to help us, also.*

Vary Sentence Length

Look at the length of your sentences. Too many short sentences make writing sound choppy. Too many long sentences make your thoughts difficult to follow.

Varying the order of words or phrases can add clarity to your writing. For example, you can write "The bat hit the ball with a loud crack," or "With a loud crack, the bat hit the ball."

Notice how revisions affect the rhythm of the paragraph.

Journal Writing

Select a passage of several sentences from your journal. Experiment with ways to vary the length and word order of the sentences. Write the variations in your journal.

Teach

Reviewing Sentences

Some students may need to review sentence fragments and run-on sentences before working on sentence variety. You may wish to provide them with a paragraph made up entirely of fragments. Point out that the paragraph contains no complete sentences. Then ask students to rewrite the paragraph, making all the fragments into complete sentences. Explain that some sentences will need subjects and others will need predicates. If necessary, explain the functions of subjects and predicates. Students should check to make sure they have rewritten all the fragments as sentences. You can repeat this exercise using run-on sentences. **L2**

Connecting Ideas

Explain that certain words can help writers vary sentence length and structure. Words such as *and* or *but* can easily join two similar thoughts. Transition words, like those used in Lesson 2.7, can also link two ideas within a sentence. Help students brainstorm to develop a list of these kinds of words. Ask a volunteer to make up a sentence using one of the words from the list. Have another volunteer make two sentences out of the first volunteer's sentence. **L2**

Journal Writing Tip

Varying Sentences Encourage students to read over their original sentences, thinking of these questions: What is the meaning of the writing? What is the purpose? After they have finished revising, suggest that they ask: Have the changes altered the original meaning? Does the writing still keep to the original purpose?

Teach

Revising with a Partner

Partners can work together to improve sentence variety. Each writer selects a piece of writing from a previous writing assignment. Partners exchange papers and ask questions about the purpose and meaning of the original pieces. Students should help their partners revise their work by suggesting which sentences could be combined. **L2**

Two-Minute Skill Drill

Write these pairs of sentences on the board. Ask students to make one sentence out of the two short ones.

- April first is Amit's birthday. April first is April Fool's Day.

- The cat chases mice. The mice run away.

- The cake fell on the floor. The cook cried.

See also Two-Minute Skill Drill Transparency 2.8

Additional Resources

 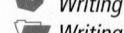

Fine Art Transparencies, 6–10

Writing Process Transparencies, 1–10

Writing Across the Curriculum

Cooperative Learning Activities, pp. 7–12

Thinking and Study Skills, pp. 1, 4, 20

Sentence Combining Practice, p. 1

Listening and Speaking Activities, pp. 12–13

Composition Practice, p. 14

The Writing Process

Revising Tip

For more information on varying sentences, see **Writing and Research Handbook**, pages 817–818.

Combine Sentences

You can also create variety by combining sentences that express similar ideas. Two or more sentences can be combined into one. Look at these sentences, and notice how they can be combined.

Wait until after the last frost to plant tomatoes. Wait until after the last frost to plant cucumbers, too.

Wait until after the last frost to plant tomatoes and cucumbers.

In both sentences, "Wait until after the last frost" expresses the same idea. "Tomatoes" and "cucumbers" are different nouns in those sentences. Consider combining sentences that express similar ideas but have different nouns, adjectives, or verbs.

When you combine sentences, certain words and phrases can clarify the relationships between ideas. For example, the sentence "Return that overdue book when you go to the library" uses the word *when* to express a relationship between two activities—*return* and *go*.

Notice how this writer combined similar thoughts and expressed the relationships between activities.

Another way that neighborhood people can help is by volunteering their time to work in the lot. Volunteers can pick up trash. *and* They can clear out weeds. They can also plant grass, trees, and flowers. This can happen once the work gets started.

MEETING INDIVIDUAL NEEDS **Less-Proficient Readers**

Listening for Repetition

Some students may not be able to identify the similarity in sentences as they read over their writing, but they may be able to hear the similarity when listening. Suggest that these students quietly read the sentences aloud to themselves. Students can jot down notes about where to combine sentences.

Vary Sentence Lengths

Adjust the sentences in your draft as you revise. Vary the lengths of your sentences.

PURPOSE To revise for sentence variety
AUDIENCE Yourself
LENGTH Changes on the draft

WRITING RUBRICS To revise for sentence variety, you should

- mix long and short sentences
- vary the beginnings of sentences
- combine sentences when it makes sense to do so
- use end punctuation correctly

Viewing and Representing

Notice the use of vertical and horizontal lines, as well as the use of space, in *Latticework*. Discuss with a partner

Josef Albers, *Latticework*, c. 1926

Grammar Link

To avoid repetition, use pronouns to replace nouns.

People can help by volunteering ***their*** time to work in the lot.

Write the paragraph below, replacing nouns with pronouns where appropriate.

[1]Juan plays the tuba in the school band. [2]Juan likes the low deep sounds of the tuba. [3]Juan's grandfather takes an afternoon nap. [4]Juan's grandfather always wakes up when Juan begins to play the tuba. *See Lessons 11.1–11.2, pages 429–432.*

any patterns you see. Then create your own latticeworks and compare designs.

Cross-Curricular Activity

ART Rewrite the following passage about artist Josef Albers. Change the word order or combine sentences to vary the length of the sentences and to create effective sound and rhythm.

Josef Albers was born in Germany. He left Germany for the United States. Albers arrived in the United States in 1933. Albers made pictures out of pieces of colored glass. He used primary colors.

2.8 Revising: Creating Sentence Variety **77**

The Writing Process

Assess

Evaluation Rubrics

Vary Sentence Lengths
Revised sentences should
- include long and short sentences
- have varied word order
- express ideas clearly

See also *Writing Assessment and Evaluation Rubrics*

Viewing and Representing
Students' latticeworks should be different from Albers', but their use of horizontal, vertical, and spatial elements should show an understanding and appreciation of the artist's concept.

Cross-Curricular Activity
The revised paragraph should contain
- sentences with varied word order
- connecting words

Reteaching
📁 *Composition Reteaching,* p. 14

Enrichment
📁 *Composition Enrichment,* p. 14
🖼 *Fine Art Transparencies,* 6–10

Close

Ask students to imagine having to read something that was terribly boring. What would it be like? Remind students that the key to creating lively writing is to really listen to it. When students reread their own work, they should keep their ears and eyes open for repetition of sentence length or word order.

Grammar Link

Answers
Answers may vary.

Recognizing Pronoun Referents Have students look over their paragraphs. Ask them to underline the pronouns and circle the referent for each pronoun they used.

Viewing the Art

Josef Albers, *Latticework,* c. 1926
Latticework, by Josef Albers (1888–1976), is sand-blasted and painted flashed glass and measures 11 1/4 by 11 7/8 inches. It is in the Smithsonian Institution, Washington, D.C. Albers worked in the abstract style in which lines, geometric forms, and colors are used to express emotion or an aesthetic idea.

Focus

Lesson Overview

Objectives

- To edit a piece of writing for grammar, usage, and mechanics
- To proofread using standard proofreading symbols

Skills

- proofreading; editing for grammar, usage, and mechanics; using proofreading symbols

Critical Thinking

- analyzing; evaluating; decision making

Listening and Speaking

- discussing; giving and receiving feedback

 Bellringer
Daily Language Activity

When students enter the classroom, have this assignment on the board: *Copy the following sentence, and correct any errors you find:*

> *the dog crossed stow rode and go home?*

Grammar Link to the Bellringer

Below the Bellringer assignment write the corrected sentence on the board: *The dog crossed Stow Road and went home.* Underline *go* and *went.* Point out that *go* is an irregular verb and *went* is the past tense of *go.*

See also *Daily Language Practice*

Motivating Activity

Write these sentences on the board: *The cafeteria nead big improvements. The cafeteria needs dramatic improvements.* Have students imagine that they are editors on a school newspaper. The sentences on the board are from two different writers who have submitted articles on the same subject. Which writer's article would the student editors be more likely to publish? Why?

LESSON
2.9

Editing/Proofreading: Making Final Adjustments

O nce you've made all your revisions, you need to edit and proofread your work. Now you will check your spelling, punctuation, grammar, and usage.

Just as Keshia, Mike, and Henry are checking every part of their proposal, you need to look at every word in your writing to make sure that there are no errors or omissions. Before you present your work, make sure it looks good and reads as smoothly as possible.

Resource Manager

📁 Planning Resources

- *Lesson Plans*

🗂 Transparencies

- *Bellringer*
- *Daily Language Practice*
- *Fine Art 6–10*
- *Two-Minute Skill Drill*
- *Writing Process 1–10*

📁 Other Print Resources

- *Composition Enrichment,* p. 15
- *Composition Practice,* p. 15
- *Composition Reteaching,* p. 15
- *Cooperative Learning Activities,* pp. 7–12
- *Listening and Speaking Activities,* pp. 12–13

- *Sentence-Combining Practice,* p. 1
- *Spelling Power*
- *Thinking and Study Skills,* pp. 1, 14, 20
- *Writing Across the Curriculum*
- *Writing Assessment and Evaluation Rubrics*

Check Your Sentences

Editing/Proofreading is usually the last stage before you make your final copy and present your writing to an audience. At this point you have already reorganized paragraphs or inserted new ideas into your work.

When you edit and proofread, go over your writing line by line, word by word.

The checklist at the right will help you find many of your errors. If you're uncertain of a spelling, consult a dictionary. Make sure you know the meanings of the words you use and that you've chosen the right words. See that you've used a singular verb with a singular subject and a plural verb with plural subject. Check that you have used verb tenses appropriately. Examine your use of periods, commas, quotation marks, semi-colons, and other punctuation marks.

Peer reviewers can help you edit. They can often spot errors in grammar, usage, and mechanics that you might overlook in your own work.

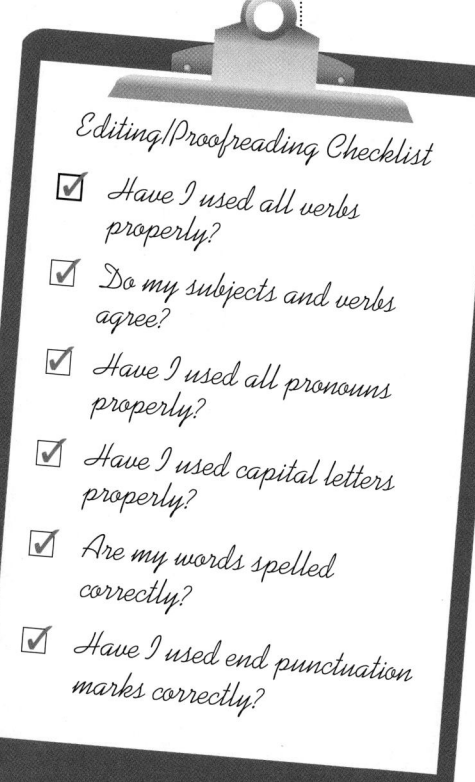

Editing/Proofreading Checklist

☑ Have I used all verbs properly?

☑ Do my subjects and verbs agree?

☑ Have I used all pronouns properly?

☑ Have I used capital letters properly?

☑ Are my words spelled correctly?

☑ Have I used end punctuation marks correctly?

Journal Writing

Look in your journal for some writing that you have done recently. Choose a passage. Use the checklist above, a dictionary, and the Grammar, Usage, and Mechanics section of this book to edit the passage.

Teach

Discussing Peer-Reviewing Strategies

Write on the board and discuss with students the importance of the following peer-reviewing strategies:
- Offer constructive advice.
- Be considerate of a writer's feelings.
- Focus on how the writing can be improved, not on what is wrong. **L2**

Using the Checklist

Some students may have difficulty applying all the questions in the checklist to a piece of writing. Work with small groups of students to review several writing samples. As the group reviews various samples, suggest that group members concentrate on one or two questions from the editing checklist. **L1**

Journal Writing Tip

Establishing and Assessing Criteria Tell students to try to be objective when they read over their writing. Strongly encourage them to read their writing aloud and to ask the questions on the checklist to identify faults in sense and sound.

Teach

Using the Model

Use the model to discuss the proofreading symbols in the chart and the kind of mistake each symbol corrects by asking questions such as: What does the symbol under the *s* of *street* mean? What does the symbol before *health* mean? **L2**

Learning Additional Proofreading Symbols

Some students may enjoy learning additional proofreading symbols. These may include the symbols to check spelling (sp), insert a space (#), and close up space ( ). Discuss each new symbol with students. **L3**

Two-Minute Skill Drill

List the following words on the board and have students write the proofreading symbol for each.

insert, delete, comma,

new paragraph, period,

capital letter, reverse,

lower-case letter

See also *Two-Minute Skill Drill Transparency 2.9*

Additional Resources

Fine Art Transparencies, 6–10

Writing Process Transparencies, 1–10
Writing Across the Curriculum,
pp. 7–12
Cooperative Learning Activities
Thinking and Study Skills,
pp. 1, 14, 20
Sentence-Combining Practice, p. 1
Listening and Speaking Activities,
pp. 12–13

The Writing Process

Drafting Tip

For more information on parallelism, see **Writing and Research Handbook,** page 818.

Proofread Your Copy

Proofreading symbols, like those shown below, make editing easier. Even if you do your own typing or word processing, use proofreading symbols as you edit. By clearly marking your copy, you can catch and correct errors before you prepare the final version of your writing.

> The empty lot across from the Shop-Good Mart
> on Broad street is an eyesore and health hazard.
> We propose that the community develope the lot
> to make space for a garden community a play
> lot, and a small park. THis proposal explains
> why we think the the lot should be developed and
> describes how we think the development should
> be done People in the neighborhood feel that the
> empty lot is unsafe.

Notice that the writer added the word *a* to create a more balanced, or parallel, construction.

Also notice the three parallel phrases in the second sentence.

Proofreading Symbols							
∧	Insert	✗	Delete	⌐	Reverse	¶	New paragraph
⊙	Period	∧	Comma	≡	Capital letter	/	Lower-case letter

80 Unit 2 The Writing Process

Enrichment and Extension

Using Proofreading Symbols

Students may become frustrated when they cannot remember specific proofreading symbols and their meanings. Have students make bookmarks with the symbols and their meanings on them. They can keep their proofreading bookmarks in their journals or with writing assignments for quick and easy reference. Point out to students that knowing when to use the symbols is more important than memorizing them.

Edit Your Writing

When you are satisfied that your writing says what you want it to say in the best possible way, the time has come to edit.

PURPOSE To edit for correctness
AUDIENCE Yourself
LENGTH Changes on the revised draft

WRITING RUBRICS To edit and proofread effectively, you should

- use the list on page 79 to edit your work
- check for one kind of error or problem at a time
- use proofreading symbols
- use end punctuation correctly

Listening and Speaking

COOPERATIVE LEARNING Write a half-page summary of what you have learned about the writing process in this unit. Then join two classmates to form a group, and pass your summaries around. Edit for spelling errors in the first paper you receive, for punctuation errors in the second, and for grammar or usage errors in the third. Look over your summary to see what changes your classmates suggested. Then discuss whether it was helpful to divide the editing into three separate steps.

Grammar Link

Use correct verb forms.

*By next week the development should be **done**.*

Write the past or past participle of the verb in parentheses to complete each sentence.

1. Tonya has (write) an essay.
2. My peer reviewer (teach) me to be more conscious of my audience.
3. Most of us have already (begin) to edit our drafts.
4. Laval (seek) out his peer reviewer to clarify her comments.
5. The editing process has (take) less time than I anticipated.
6. Working with my peer reviewer has (give) me greater confidence.

See Lesson 10.9, page 415, and Lesson 10.10, page 417.

Cross-Curricular Activity

ART Keshia, Mike, and Henry are making a proposal for the city. They are including a map of the playground they picture. Create a layout for an ideal park and recreation area. What features will you include? What symbols will you use for each type of playground equipment and recreation use? Include a paragraph that explains your design.

Grammar Link

Answers

1. written   4. sought
2. taught   5. taken
3. begun   6. given

Irregular Verbs Have students copy the following verb forms and write a sentence using each word correctly:

- go—went   • see—seen
- do—done   • run—ran

Provide time for students to share their sentences in small groups.

Assess
Evaluation Rubrics

Edit Your Writing
Answers will vary, but should reflect students' understanding of how to edit a piece of their writing and how to use basic proofreading symbols.

See also *Writing Assessment and Evaluation Rubrics*

Listening and Speaking
Answers will vary. Look over the edited papers to see that all spelling, grammar, and usage mistakes are marked and corrected.

Cross-Curricular Activity
Look over students' maps and accompanying paragraphs to see that their writing has been proofread, edited, and revised so that the finished product is error-free.

Reteaching
📁 *Composition Reteaching, p. 15*

Enrichment
📁 *Composition Enrichment, p. 15*

Close

Display or distribute the following passage. Have pairs of students edit the passage for grammar, usage, and mechanics errors.

Birds have many of the same characteristics as human beings. The different is that they had been adapted for flight. A birds body like a human body, has a head and torso. a bird has legs. but instead of arms, a bird has wings. a bird also has bones, but a bird's bones are hollow.

The hollow bones are lighter than solid bones and it contains air sacs. Flying requires a large amount of Oxygen, Air sacks increase the amount of air a bird can take in with each breathe.

Focus

Lesson Overview

Objectives

- To select a format in which to present a piece of writing
- To publish a piece of writing

Skills

- presenting; writing; evaluating different formats for an intended audience; comparing forms of publication

Critical Thinking

- analyzing; comparing and contrasting; decision making; visualizing; inferring; categorizing

Listening and Speaking

- giving and receiving feedback; formal speaking; oral reports

Bellringer

Daily Language Activity

When students enter the classroom, have this assignment on the board: *Describe something you have accomplished that has made you proud. Did you share your accomplishment with anyone? If so, how?*

Grammar Link to the Bellringer

Have students look over their descriptions in the Bellringer activity. Did they use specific nouns? Ask for examples. Point out that specific nouns give more information. Invite students to scan their writing and replace generic nouns (*song*) with specific ones (*Star Spangled Banner*).

See also *Daily Language Practice*

Motivating Activity

Allow students to share their responses to the Bellringer activity. Ask whether students have ever had any writing published. How did they feel about the experience? Ask students to think of ways to share their writing. Encourage them to suggest realistic forums.

LESSON 2.10

Publishing/Presenting: Sharing Your Writing

You've said everything you wanted to say in the best way possible. You've fixed all the errors in your writing. Now it's time to make a clean, neat, legible version and to present your writing to its intended audience.

The completed sketch and the final, typed version of their proposal will help Mike, Henry, and Keshia make an impressive presentation to the community group.

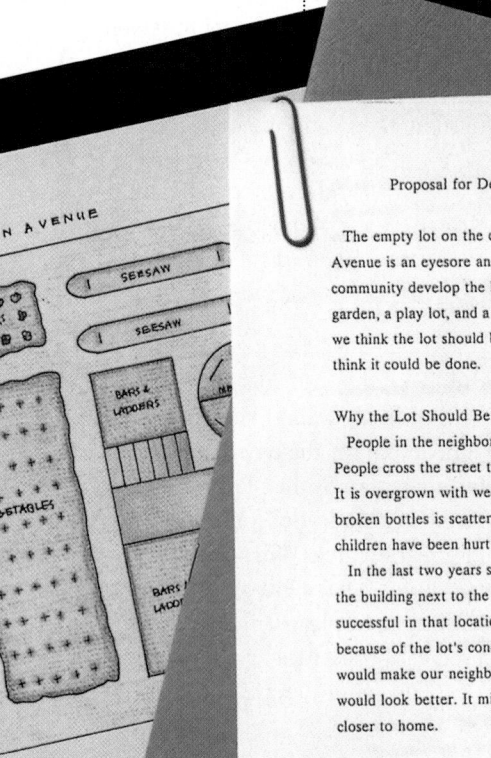

Proposal for Developing the Broad Street Lot

The empty lot on the corner of Broad Street and Washington Avenue is an eyesore and a health hazard. We propose that the community develop the lot to make space for a community garden, a play lot, and a small park. This proposal explains why we think the lot should be developed and describes how we think it could be done.

Why the Lot Should Be Developed

People in the neighborhood feel that the empty lot is unsafe. People cross the street to avoid walking by it, especially at night. It is overgrown with weeds and littered with trash. Glass from broken bottles is scattered over the ground. As a result, several children have been hurt while playing in the lot.

In the last two years several businesses have come and gone in the building next to the lot. We don't think any store can be successful in that location. Other businesses nearby also suffer because of the lot's condition. We know that developing the lot would make our neighborhood safer, and the neighborhood would look better. It might also mean that people would shop closer to home.

The Benefits of Improving the Lot

If our community developed the lot, people in the neighborhood would have a place to meet and spend time

82 Unit 2 The Writing Process

Resource Manager

Planning Resources
- *Lesson Plans*

Transparencies
- *Bellringer*
- *Daily Language Practice*
- *Fine Art* 6–10
- *Two-Minute Skill Drill*
- *Writing Process* 1–10

Other Print Resources
- *Composition Enrichment*, p. 16
- *Composition Practice*, p. 16
- *Composition Reteaching*, p. 16
- *Cooperative Learning Activities*, pp. 7–12
- *Listening and Speaking Activities*, pp. 12–13

- *Thinking and Study Skills*, pp. 6, 13, 20–22
- *Writing Across the Curriculum*
- *Writing Assessment and Evaluation Rubrics*

Make a Good Impression

How you present your writing depends on your purpose and your audience. As you think about who will read your writing, you will decide if a formal presentation would be most impressive or if a casual or even artistic presentation would be better. Sometimes you may write it out by hand and give it a personal touch, such as when you write a letter to a friend. Remember to use your best cursive writing for handwritten letters. When you need something more formal, like a paper for a class, a letter to an editor, or a proposal to a community group, you'll want to use a typewriter or word processor. You might enclose your writing in a clear folder or binder to give it a more professional look.

Teach

Preparing an Oral Presentation

Tell students to work in groups to prepare an oral presentation describing different forums for their writing. Ask each group to brainstorm to develop a list of forums available to them through school or the local community. One student should record the ideas generated in the brainstorming session. Individual students can decide which forum they would like to research and speak about at the presentation. Each group member can then write a brief oral report about the forum that might include information about how to prepare a manuscript, a name and address to which to submit the work, and any other important facts necessary for successful presentation. The group might come together to decide on the order of speakers and might practice giving their speeches to each other before sharing their presentation with the entire class. Remind students of the importance of using Standard American English in formal speaking situations. **L2**

Journal Writing

Think about a piece of writing you have completed recently. What two ways might you prepare it for presentation? In your journal, write a comparison of the two forms of presentation. Why did you choose them? What difference would a change in presentation make to your audience?

Journal Writing Tip

Presenting Writing Encourage students to keep in mind their original purpose for writing and to consider how the form of presentation will affect the intended audience. Will they reach more people through one form or the other? Is the intended audience likely to enjoy or appreciate one form of presentation more than the other?

Teach

Publishing/Presenting

Many magazines ask potential writers to submit a query letter that explains the purpose for the writing, its intended audience, and other information such as length and tone. Suggest that each student draft a query letter to a specific magazine, requesting that it publish a piece of the student's writing. Read the letters aloud and invite comments about their effectiveness. **L3**

Two-Minute Skill Drill

Write this list on the board:

- *novel*
- *lecture with slides*
- *how-to book*
- *magazine article*
- *letter to a politician*

Have students give an example of a topic that would best be presented in each format—a description of Mayan ruins presented in a lecture with slides, for example.

See also *Two-Minute Skill Drill Transparency 2.10*

Additional Resources

 Fine Art Transparencies, 6–10

 Writing Process Transparencies, 1–10

 Writing Across the Curriculum

Cooperative Learning Activities, pp. 7–12

Thinking and Study Skills, pp. 6, 13, 20–22

Listening and Speaking Activities, pp. 12–13

Composition Practice, p. 16

The Writing Process

Presenting Tip

For more information on presentation and the 6+1 Trait® model, see **Writing and Research Handbook,** pages 822–823.

Reach Your Audience

Naturally, when you've finished your writing, you want to share it with the audience you've had in mind all along. How you reach an audience depends partly on who the audience is.

The illustration below shows several ways of presenting your work to different audiences. Forms of presentation include a printed report, a speech, a letter, a submission to a school literary magazine, a written invitation, a press release, a dramatic reading, or a banner. Keeping your audience in mind, ask yourself, How can I present my writing to reach this audience? Will visuals help?

Ways to Present Your Writing

Play
If a story has several characters and snappy dialogue, think about writing a script from it.

Contests
Magazines of student writing often sponsor story-writing contests. You might enter a story you wrote on your own or for a class.

Advertisement
Ads are a good way to sell your ideas or to get your audience to agree with you.

Support the **Zoo!**

Song
Poems and stories are likely candidates for being set to music.

The News

Newspaper article
Informative writing might appear as an article in a school or community newspaper.

6+1 Trait® is a registered trademark of Northwest Regional Educational Laboratory, which does not endorse this product.

Notice that some of these presentations are oral rather than written. Others might include illustrations or other types of images.

84 Unit 2 The Writing Process

 **English Language Learners**

Presenting Informally

Writers learning English may find it easier to share their writing if they have the option of presenting it in a casual forum, such as a mock radio show. Group presentations, such as a booklet that includes the students' favorite writing of any kind from the semester's assignments, are another opportunity for them to share their work. Encourage groups to explore these and other nonintimidating ways of presenting their writing.

2.10 Writing Activities

Present Your Writing

You have taken your writing through prewriting, drafting, revising, and editing/proofreading. Now it's time for the payoff—sharing your writing!

PURPOSE To share your finished work

AUDIENCE The audience you chose when you began to write

LENGTH Whatever is appropriate for your purpose

WRITING RUBRICS To share your finished work, you should

- choose a format that suits your purpose and your audience
- make your paper as neat, legible, and attractive as you can

Using Computers

If one of your presentations for the writing activity includes a poster, flyer, or other public notice, you might experiment with highlighting text by using different typefaces.

Try printing several versions of the same notice, using different combinations of type sizes and styles. Then compare the effects of the different versions.

Grammar Link

Use specific nouns to make your writing more interesting.

*The empty lot is an **eyesore** and a health **hazard.***

Write a more specific noun to replace each noun in parentheses.

1. The woman's (clothing) was dirty, shabby, and ill-smelling.
2. I hope to study (science) in college someday.
3. My family has been reading (a book) aloud, a chapter a day.
4. I stayed up too late last night playing (a game).
5. Tom is crazy about his brand-new (bicycle).

See Lesson 9.1, page 379.

Viewing and Representing

Create a poster that shows the do's and don'ts of using the writing process. (For example, Do cluster or freewrite; Don't forget to proofread.) You may want to include photographs of classmates (with their permission) at work during various stages of the writing process. Present your poster to the class.

Assess

Evaluation Rubrics

Present Your Writing

Formats will vary. Use these criteria to evaluate each presentation:

- Is the format suitable to the content and the intended audience?
- Is the presentation itself neat and well-prepared?

See also *Writing Assessment and Evaluation Rubrics*

Using Computers

As students compare different versions of a piece, help them see that the most effective ones are those in which the words and the phrases that convey the main points of the piece's message stand out.

Viewing and Representing

Before students make their posters, look over the mock-ups for them to see that

- the do's and dont's of the writing process are presented in logical order
- the text reflects correct grammar, usage, and mechanics
- the writing is neat and legible

Reteaching

📁 *Composition Reteaching,* p. 16

Enrichment

📁 *Composition Enrichment,* p. 16

Close

Tell students that children's writer Minfong Ho believes that writing "is like the sound of one hand clapping—incomplete, silent, and without impact. Only when the writer as the one hand, and the reader as the other, confront each other is there that clap, that spark of communication which makes literature alive." Discuss the pictures that students have in their minds after hearing this quote. Do they agree with Ho that without readers, writers cannot communicate?

Grammar Link

Answers

Answers will vary, but each should represent a particular example of the noun replaced in the sentence. *Clothing* could be replaced by *jacket,* for instance; *book* could be replaced by *Little Women.*

Using Specific Nouns Have students choose a piece of writing they have already done. Ask them to replace some of the general nouns in it with more specific nouns to make the writing come alive.

Focus

Lesson Overview

Objectives

- To use the writing process to write a brief profile of a courageous person
- To present a finished piece of writing

Skills

- using the five stages of the writing process: prewriting, drafting, revising, editing/proofreading, and publishing/presenting

Critical Thinking

- identifying the main idea; decision-making; summarizing; building background

Listening and Speaking

- informal speaking; interviewing; discussing

Bellringer
Daily Language Activity

When students enter the classroom, have this assigment on the board: *A nationwide magazine has asked you to write about life in your hometown. Where do you begin?*

Grammar Link to the Bellringer

Remind students that when writing about places and people, they will probably use proper nouns. Have them check their writing to make sure all proper nouns are capitalized.

See also *Daily Language Practice*

Motivating Activity

Invite students to share their responses to the Bellringer activity. Are any of the plans similar? What are some advantages and dis-advantages of students' suggestions? Ask how they think the writing process could help them.

Writing Process in Action

The Writing Process

The Writing Process

In preceding lessons you've learned about the stages of the writing process. You've had a chance to explore a topic, write a draft and revise it, and finally present your feature writing. Now it's time to make use of what you learned by writing about courage—in yourself or in someone you admire.

WRITING Online

Visit the *Writer's Choice* Web site at **writerschoice. glencoe.com** for additional writing prompts.

Assignment

Context	A publication that prints stories, articles, and interviews by students about the bravery and endurance of young people
Purpose	To share your admiration of someone who overcame difficulty through bravery
Audience	Student readers
Length	3–4 paragraphs

The following pages offer step-by-step advice on how to approach this assignment. Read through the pages before you begin. Then return to each step as needed while you work on your assignment.

Resource Manager

📁 Planning Resources
- *Lesson Plans*

📠 Transparencies
- *Bellringer*
- *Daily Language Practice*
- *Writing Process* 1–10

📁 Other Print Resources
- *Composition Enrichment*, p. 17

- *Composition Practice*, p. 17
- *Composition Reteaching* p. 17
- *Grammar Workbook*, Lessons 69–71
- *Sentence-Combining Practice*, p. 1
- *Thinking and Study Skills*, pp. 4–6, 9, 13, 17, 22
- *Writing Assessment and Evaluation Rubrics*

💾 Software
- *Writer's Assistant*

🖥 Web Sites
- *writerschoice.glencoe.com*
- *lit.glencoe.com*

Writing Process in Action

Prewriting

What's your definition of courage? Is it facing danger to save a life? Is it making a difficult decision? Or is it simply surviving in a situation that would make many people give up?

Begin looking for examples of courageous people. Decide on one person to write about. Choose one of the options at the right or an idea of your own. Then explore your subject by brainstorming, clustering, or listing. See pages 50–57 for more information about prewriting techniques.

Drafting

Look over your list, cluster diagram, or other prewriting notes. What problems did your subject face? Why do you think this person's act of bravery or courage is significant? Use your answers to these questions as foundations for sentences and paragraphs.

Remember that courage doesn't always come in a big, dramatic package. As in the model below, sometimes day-to-day life requires courage.

Option A

Talk to friends, teachers, or relatives.

Option B

Look through magazines or newspapers.

Option C

Read a biography.

The Writing Process

courageous people—
Helen Keller
from small town in Alabama
became deaf and blind in infancy
learned to speak at age ten
entered Radcliffe College at age
nineteen

Literature Model

I know what you mean," she said slowly. "You try to hang on to older people—parents, uncles, grand-mothers—and they disappear. You make friends, and they go off in different directions, never to be seen again. Everything crumbles so easily."

Minfong Ho, *The Clay Marble*

Teach

Prewriting

Developing Ideas for Writing

Initiate a discussion about the meaning of courage. Invite students to complete this sentence:

A courageous person is one who _____.

Discuss similarities and differences in the responses. Can students make any general-izations about courageous people from their responses? For example, can they determine that all courageous people risk their lives for others, or that all courageous people over-come a difficulty? Invite students to brain-storm and list more examples or details to support their ideas of courage. **L2**

Additional Resources

📁 *Thinking and Study Skills*, pp. 4–6, 9, 13, 17, 22

Drafting

Beginning the Profile

Encourage students to write about people they know in their own lives or through information in a book or article. Suggest to students that they take notes as they talk to people or read about an individual. Urge students to record details of the action that showed the person's courage or details about the person's characteristics. Tell stu-dents to incorporate what they know from their own life experiences and what they learn through research into a detailed word picture of the person. **L1**

Teach

Revising

Peer Editing

Students can work in writing conferences with peer editors before they revise their work. You may want to duplicate the Peer Response forms in the *Writing Assessment and Evaluation Rubrics.* Suggest that peer editors respond to the following questions:

- Does the writer explain why this person is courageous?
- Does each paragraph add details to the picture?
- Are the sentences varied? **L2**

Editing/Proofreading

Peer Editing

After students have edited their own work, have them edit another student's writing. Remind them to refer to the Editing/Proofreading Checklist on the student page. **L2**

Publishing/Presenting

Before students present their writing, discuss how to prepare papers for publication. Stress the importance of a neat and complete final draft.

Additional Resources

Writing Process Transparencies, 1–10
Thinking and Study Skills,
pp. 4–6, 9, 13, 17, 22
Sentence Combining Practice, p. 1
Composition Practice, p. 17

Grammar Workbook, Lessons 69–71

Journal Writing Tip

Analyzing the Process Students might record what they learned as tips or reminders to be applied in their next assignment.

Personal Writing

Drafting Tip

For more information about writing your first draft, see Lesson 2.5, page 62.

As you write your draft, think about specific actions that you admire in the person you're writing about. Remember, in the drafting stage you should let your ideas flow freely. Just get them down on paper. Try to express your ideas in sentences and paragraphs. You can always make changes later.

Revising

To begin revising, read over your draft to make sure that what you have written fits your purpose and your audience. Then have a **writing conference.** Read your draft to a partner or small group, or receive feedback from your teacher. Use your audience's reactions to help you evaluate your work so far. The questions below can help you and your listeners.

Option A

Have I explained why this person is courageous?

Option B

Does each paragraph add details to the picture?

Option C

Have I varied my sentences?

> Most people would say it takes courage to go *leave home in Alabama* to attend a famous New England college. to one of the most famous colleges in the country. Just leaving your home to go to another region takes courage. How about if you are a girl, going to college *For a girl to do this* at a time when very few women graduated from college? But *attended college takes even more courage.* imagine doing all this if you were deaf and as well blind. *So imagine yourself as a girl from Alabama leaving home to attend Radcliffe College in Massachusetts in the early twentieth century. Now*

Enrichment and Extension

Follow-up Ideas

- Set aside time for students to celebrate finishing their writing projects. Encourage them to share their work with the class or in small groups.
- If students' work is sent out of the classroom, keep photocopies.

Extending the Writing Process

- Brainstorm with students to think of ways they can use their expertise in the writing process in other subject areas.
- Explore opportunities for extending the process approach beyond the classroom, such as in home projects.

The Writing Process

Editing/Proofreading

You've worked hard to determine what you want to say and how to say it well. As you prepare your article use the checklist at the right to help you get rid of any distracting errors.

In addition to proofreading, make sure your description does all the things you want to do. When you're satisfied, make a clean copy of your article and proofread it one more time.

Publishing/Presenting

Make sure your account of courage is neatly and legibly written or typed on clean white paper before you submit it. If possible, include a picture—a photograph or a drawing—of your subject so that readers will connect the actual person with what you've written.

As an alternative way of presenting your writing, you and others in your class might present your account as a play or a dramatic reading.

Try using spelling checker and grammar checker features on the computer to help you proofread your work.

Editing/Proofreading Checklist

1. Have I correctly capitalized proper nouns and direct quotations?
2. Have I used the correct forms of adjectives?
3. Have I used the correct forms of verbs?
4. Do my subjects and verbs agree?
5. Is every word spelled correctly?
6. Have I used possessive pronouns correctly?

Proofreading

For proofreading symbols, see page 80.

Journal Writing

Reflect on your writing process experience. Answer these questions in your journal. What do you like best about your article? What was the hardest part of writing it? What did you learn in your writing conference? What new things have you learned as a writer?

Assess

Evaluation Rubrics

Use the following questions to evaluate students' finished writing:

- Does the writing fulfill a clear purpose?
- Does it provide a well-ordered explanation?
- Does the writing reflect a specific audience?
- Does the writing use details that help the audience picture the subject?
- Does the piece avoid fragments and run-on sentences?
- Are words used correctly?
- Are grammar and mechanics correct?

See also *Writing Assessment and Evaluation Rubrics*

Reteaching

📁 *Composition Reteaching*, p. 17

Enrichment

📁 *Composition Enrichment*, p. 17

Close

Discuss the writing process with students. Ask students which part of the process seems most important to them. What part is that, and why? Remind students that, depending upon an individual writer's strengths or weaknesses, different parts of the process may be more important for different writers—or for the same writers doing different types of writing. Keeping the whole writing process in mind helps prepare a writer for any type of writing.

MEETING INDIVIDUAL NEEDS — English Language Learners

Listening to Writing

Students can check that their writing makes sense and is grammatically correct by reading their work aloud to a fluent English-speaker. One partner can read his or her work aloud while the other listens. The partners can then discuss constructively any necessary corrections and revisions.

About the Author

Minfong Ho (1951–) was born in Yangon, Myanmar. She has lived in Thailand, New York, and Singapore. Her first children's book, *Sing to the Dawn,* was written while she lived in upstate New York. She wrote, she said, to overcome homesickness "when Thailand seemed incredibly far away. Writing about the dappled sunlight and school children of home brought them closer to me."

Focus

Lesson Overview

Objectives
- To read a literature passage
- To write a description using sensory details

Skills
- predicting

Critical Thinking
- drawing conclusions; inferring; comparing

Listening and Speaking
- discussing

 Bellringer
Daily Language Activity

When students enter the classroom, have this assignment on the board: *In what ways are families important? Jot down some ideas.*

See also Daily Language Practice

Motivating Activity

Ask students why families are important, especially to young children. Emphasize that families come in many shapes and forms. Encourage students to pay attention to the characters' ideas of family as they read the selection.

90

FROM

by Minfong Ho

In 1980, after North Vietnamese troops invaded Cambodia, writer Minfong Ho helped set up food programs for Cambodian children. Ho learned that these children, despite starvation and sickness, could enjoy making toys from clay. As you read, notice the details Ho uses to show how creative spirit can help people overcome the horrors of war. Then discuss the questions in Linking Writing and Literature on page 95.

After that marble, Jantu was interested only in playing with clay. She would spend the long afternoons crouched by the mud puddle by the stone beam, scooping up handfuls of moist clay to shape little figures.

For some reason, the massive stone beam attracted Jantu. She loved playing there. "It's so old, so

90   Unit 2 The Writing Process

Resource Manager

Planning Resources
- *Lesson Plans*

Transparencies
- *Bellringer*
- *Daily Language Practice*
- *Fine Art 6–10*

Other Print Resources
- *Listening and Speaking Activities, pp. 6–8*
- *Thinking and Study Skills, pp. 3–5, 9, 33, 34*
- *Writing Assessment and Evaluation Rubrics*

Web Sites
- *writerschoice.glencoe.com*
- *lit.glencoe.com*

Literature Model

solid," she said. "I like being near it. It makes me feel like a cicada[1] molting under some big rain tree."

At one end of the stone beam she had propped some fantail palm fronds,[2] to make a thatched shelter so that we could play in the shade. When we crouched under it, it was like being in a leafy cave.

We spent most of our spare time in there. I would sit on the stone beam, bouncing her baby brother in my lap, as Jantu sculpted her dainty clay figures.

"I wish we could always be together like this," I said one afternoon. "Don't you wish things would stay just the same?"

Jantu glanced up from the clay buffalo she was shaping and smiled at me. "But how can we always stay the same, Dara?" she asked. "We're not made of stone. You wouldn't want to lie half-buried in the fields for hundreds of years, anyway, would you?"

"No, I meant . . . I just meant that nothing nice ever lasts." I struggled to find words for what I wanted to say. "What we're doing now, just playing here together—I wish we could hang on to it, that's all."

Jantu put down the half-formed clay buffalo. "I know what you mean," she said slowly. "You try to hang on to older people—parents, uncles, grandmothers—and they disappear. You make friends, and they go off in different directions, never to be seen again. Everything crumbles so easily." Absentmindedly she picked up a dirt clod and crushed it in her fist, letting the crumbs of dirt dribble out. "We don't even have real families anymore," she said. "Just bits and pieces of one."

I stole a glance at my friend. I knew Jantu had lost both her parents and an older brother during the long war years, but she never talked about it.

"What do you mean?" I asked carefully.

"What I have, and what you have," she said, "are leftovers of families. Like fragments[3] from a broken bowl that nobody wants. We're not a real family."

"What's a real family, then?"

"A real family," Jantu said, "grows. It gets bigger. People get added to it. Husbands, mothers-in-law, babies."

---

[1]**cicada** (si kā′ də) a large, winged, flylike insect
[2]**fronds** (frondz) leaves
[3]**fragments** (frag′ mənts) parts broken off

Literature Model **91**

The Writing Process

Teach

Literary Elements

Setting Remind students that setting is the time and place in which a story occurs. Ask: "What is the setting of this story? What realistic details does the author use to make the setting come alive?" *(The setting is Cambodia not long after the country was invaded in 1979. Realistic details that make the setting come alive include rain tree, fantail palm fronds, clay, thatched shelter, and water buffalo.)*

6+1 Trait® Writing

Word Choice Tell students that an **analogy** compares two things that are similar in some ways. Authors may use analogies to help explain something abstract in terms that are more familiar or concrete for the reader.

Point out that Jantu uses an analogy to explain why she doesn't think her and Dara's families are "real." In the third paragraph from the end of page 91, she compares her and Dara's families to fragments of a broken bowl. Ask a volunteer to read the paragraph. Then ask students how Jantu's analogy helps them understand how she feels about her family. *(Students may say Jantu feels lonely and unwanted now that she's lost her parents and brother. She feels that just as pieces of an old, broken bowl—which can't be used to eat from—aren't really a bowl, people from families that have been torn apart aren't really a family.)*

6+1 Trait® is a registered trademark of Northwest Regional Educational Laboratory, which does not endorse this product.

Critical Thinking

Draw Conclusions

Tell students that as they read, they should pay attention to what the characters say, think, and do. Explain to students that they make general statements about the characters—or draw a conclusion about them—by piecing together these details. To model the process of drawing a conclusion, say: "I notice that the girls play together in a shady, homemade shelter. I also know that both girls have lost members of their families in war. Piecing together these details, I think the girls enjoy playing in their shelter partly because it reminds them of the homes they've lost."

Practice While playing with Jantu, Dara says she wishes they could always be together like that. Ask students to draw a conclusion that may explain why Dara makes that wish. *(Dara has lost important people and things during her life. She wants to stop things from changing and hold on to happy moments.)*

Teach

Active Reading Strategies

Predict Direct students to pause after they read the first two paragraphs on this page, where Dara wishes to be part of a real family again, and Jantu says, "You could be." Ask students to predict whether the girls will become part of a real family again. If so, how might that come about? Encourage students to piece together details in the story to make their predictions. *(Jantu seems certain of her words, so the girls may somehow become part of a family again. After making her promise, Jantu goes back to working on her clay figures. Perhaps the clay figures will have something to do with the girls' becoming a part of a family again.)*

Critical Thinking

Draw Conclusions Ask students: "What is Jantu's surprise for Dara? Why do you think it was important for her to hide the pieces until they were all ready?" *(Jantu's surprise is a complete set of clay figures. She probably didn't want to show them to Dara until the set was complete—just like a "real" family should be.)*

Viewing the Art

Pierre Bonnard, *The Lesson*, 1926
Artist Pierre Bonnard was criticized by some for distorting the human form and using colors too freely. But his choice of intimate interior settings conveys a sense of calm to the viewer. *The Lesson,* an oil on canvas measuring 30 by 20 inches, is in the Phillips Collection in Washington, D.C.

Literature Model

The Writing Process

I thought about this. It was true. My own family had been getting smaller, shrinking rather than growing. Was it just the fragment of a family now? "I'd like to be part of a real family again," I said wistfully.

"You could be," Jantu said. "And so could I."

"How?"

"You'll see. Watch," Jantu said. She started molding her clay buffalo again. With small twisting movements, her hands teased[4] out four legs, then shaped a pair of horns. Deftly[5] she smoothed and rounded the shape until it had become a miniature water buffalo.

Then, with a flourish, she lifted up a layer of straw in a corner of our shelter. Nestled in the straw was a group of other clay figures. Carefully she set the miniature buffalo next to them. "There," she said. "They're finished—the whole set of them."

"What are they?" I asked. "Can I see?"

Jantu smiled at me mysteriously. "I didn't want to show you until they were all ready."

Pierre Bonnard, *The Lesson*, 1926

"And are they ready?"

"They are!" Ceremoniously, Jantu took a clay doll and set it on the stone beam. Just then a few drops of rain started to fall.

---

[4]**teased** (tēzd) pulled apart
[5]**deftly** (deft′ lē) skillfully

92   Unit 2 The Writing Process

Compare and Contrast

Comparing Selections

Tell students that comparing two selections will deepen their understanding of both works. To model this skill, compare and contrast the themes of this excerpt and the excerpt from *The Diary of Latoya Hunter* that appears on pages 32–37. Say, "Both selections deal with the theme of young girls adjusting to major changes, including losses, in their lives. The theme of *The Clay Marble* focuses on changes in a family, while the theme of *The Diary of Latoya Hunter* focuses on becoming an individual in the midst of changes."

Practice Ask students to work in pairs to compare and contrast the characters in the two selections. One partner in the pair should describe similarities while the other partner should describe differences. Then students should each write a paragraph or two about the similarities and differences. *(Characters in both selections are young girls looking for answers. Latoya Hunter is an urban American girl struggling with growing up. Dara and Jantu are rural Cambodian girls struggling with the effects of war.)*

Literature Model

Jantu parted a section of the palm frond and scanned the sky anxiously. Thick gray clouds had drifted across to block out the sun. In the distance, a clap of thunder sounded.

The wind picked up and was sweeping up eddies[6] of dust into the air. Then the rain started in earnest, one of those sudden thunderstorms hinting of the monsoons[7] due to come soon. Jantu stretched her sarong[8] protectively over the pile of straw where her clay figures were. Hunched over them like that, she looked like a scruffy hen trying to hatch her precious eggs.

I huddled close to Jantu and listened to the rain drumming on the leaves. Raindrops pierced through the cracks of the palm fronds and felt light and cool on my bare arms. I thought of the long rainy afternoons I had spent on the porch at home when I was very young. As light and cool as the rain, my grandmother's fingers would massage my scalp while I rested my head in her lap. Nearby, the murmur of my family surrounded me, like a soft blanket.

I closed my eyes now and tried to imagine them all sitting around me:

> I closed my eyes now and tried to imagine them all sitting around me...

Grandmother stroking me, Father and Sarun whittling on the steps, Mother stoking the embers of the cooking fire. It wasn't just the thick thatched roof that had sheltered me, I realized now. It was the feeling I had had then, of being part of a family as a gently pulsing whole, so natural it was like the breathing of a sleeping baby.

---

[6]**eddies** (ed′ ēz) currents of air moving in a circular motion against the main current

[7]**monsoons** (mon soonz′) southwesterly winds of southern Asia that bring heavy rains

[8]**sarong** (sə rông′) a long strip of cloth, often brightly colored and printed, worn around the lower part of the body like a skirt

Literature Model **93**

The Writing Process

Teach

Active Reading Strategies

Predict Ask volunteers to check and revise their predictions about the girls' becoming part of a real family again. Emphasize to students that the purpose of predicting while they read is not to be correct but to be actively engaged with the story. *(The girls become part of their families again by recalling real family experiences in vivid detail. The clay figures help them drift into these happy imaginings.)*

6+1 Trait® Writing

Word Choice Point out that in the last paragraph on this page, Dara uses an analogy when she speaks of her family's thick thatched roof. Ask: "To what does Dara compare this shelter?" Have students explain what the analogy means in their own words. *(Dara compares the physical shelter of the roof to the emotional shelter of family love.)*

6+1 Trait® Writing

Word Choice

Tell students that good writers carefully choose their words in order to vividly describe scenes or capture a mood. Well-chosen words and images often appeal to the senses. For example, to help readers "see" the approach of the storm, the writer uses the visual images of "thick gray clouds" and "wind . . . sweeping up eddies of dust." To help readers "hear" the storm, she describes the "clap of thunder." Invite volunteers to point out words and images that help readers "see," "hear," and "feel" Dara's family life. *(sight: "stoking the embers of the cooking fire"; hearing: "rain drumming on the leaves"; touch: "felt light and cool on my bare arms")*

Practice Ask students to write a brief description of a storm or of their family. Encourage them to choose words that appeal to the senses.

For more information on word choice and the 6+1 Trait® model, see **Writing and Research Handbook**, pp. 822–824.

Teach

Literary Elements

Character What has Dara learned during the course of the story? How do you think this knowledge will affect her in the future? *(Dara has learned that, though she can't have her family back in a physical way, she can keep them alive in her heart and mind. This realization may help Dara heal from her losses.)*

Additional Resources

 Fine Art Transparencies, 6–10
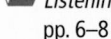 *Listening and Speaking Activities,* pp. 6–8
Thinking and Study Skills, pp. 3–5, 9, 33, 34

The Writing Process

Literature Model

Hung Liu, *Tale of Two Women,* 1991

When I opened my eyes, I saw that Jantu had a lost, faraway look in her eyes, and I knew that she was remembering, too, what it was like when her own family was whole and complete.

As the rain died down, Jantu turned to me and smiled. "You still want to play with my family of dolls?" she asked.

I'd rather have my own family back, I thought, but dolls were better than nothing. "Sure," I said.

Viewing the Art

Hung Liu, *Tale of Two Women,* 1991
This painting by Hung Liu is in the collection of the San Jose Museum of Art in California. It is oil and mixed media on canvas and measures 60 by 60 inches. Liu was born in Changchun, China, in 1948 and states, "As a classically trained Chinese artist in America, my responsibility . . . [is] to express my Chineseness as clearly as I can." *Tale of Two Women* provides many details that bring the experience of the two women to life.

Literature Model

Linking Writing and Literature

 ## Collect Your Thoughts

Reflect on the importance of family to the girls in the story. What qualities do they seek in a family? Brainstorm to create a list of words and images that tell what the girls want in family life. Then brainstorm to create a new list of words that describe your ideas or values of family life.

 ## Talk About Reading

Talk with other students about the excerpt from *The Clay Marble*. Assign a group leader to keep everyone focused and a group secretary to take notes. Then use the questions below to guide your conversation.

1. **Connect to Your Life** How do Jantu's ideas about a "real family" compare with your own? What qualities do you think are important for a real family to have? Did this story help you look at your own family life in a new way?

2. **Critical Thinking: Draw Conclusions** Do you think Jantu has inner strength to face her life challenges? Use evidence from the story to support your conclusion.

3. **6+1 Trait®: Word Choice** Name some specific images that you remember from the selection. What words did the writer use to create these images? Discuss why you think these words are memorable.

4. **Connect to Your Writing** In this selection, the characters use analogies to talk about families and family love. How could you use analogies in writing that you do for school? How could you use them in writing that you do for yourself?

 ## Write About Reading

Description In the story, Dara vividly recalls an afternoon spent with her family. Write your own detailed description of a family scene, using either a real or an imaginary family. Describe the setting and what different family members are doing and feeling.

Focus on Word Choice Your description will take on a life of its own if you choose words and images that appeal to the senses. Before you begin writing, create a graphic organizer that lists the senses of sight, hearing, touch, taste, and smell. Fill the organizer with sensory details that describe your family scene. Read over your finished description to find places you might improve. Could you explain any complicated feelings or ideas by using analogies? Could you add transition words to smoothly connect your ideas?

For more information on word choice and the 6+1 Trait® model, see **Writing and Research Handbook,** pages 822–824.

6+1 Trait® is a registered trademark of Northwest Regional Educational Laboratory, which does not endorse this product.

Literature Model **95**

The Writing Process

 ## Linking Writing and Literature

 # Assess

Evaluation Rubrics

 ### Talk About Reading

Possible responses to the questions:

1. Students may relate to the girls' appreciation of feeling safe and comfortable with family members.

2. Students may think Jantu shows a great deal of inner strength in coping with the loss of her family members in war. She creatively expresses her desires for wholeness by using clay modeling.

3. Memorable images include descriptions of the girls' shelter, the rainstorm, and the memories of the girls' families: "like being in a leafy cave," "thick gray cloud" blocking the sun, "grandmother's fingers would massage my scalp."

4. Students may say they could use analogies when writing about anything that needs to be made clear—such as scientific processes, cause-and-effect relationships, or abstract ideas and emotions.

Write About Reading

The description should do the following:
- detail a family scene
- describe the setting
- relate the actions of family members
- use sensory details

Close

Encourage students to write a paragraph explaining how a family of dolls like the one Jantu made could lift the spirits of someone who is sad and lonely.

Enrichment and Extension

History

Inform students that *The Clay Marble* by Minfong Ho takes place in Cambodia, or Kampuchea, soon after the Khmer Rouge communist government was overthrown by Vietnamese and Kampuchean communists in 1979. Display a world map, and have students locate Cambodia in Southeast Asia.

Review

Reflecting on the Unit

You may have students respond to Reflecting on the Unit in writing or through discussion.

Writing Across the Curriculum

Encourage students to use the five stages of the writing process. Remind them to use carefully selected details to draw in readers and sustain their interest.

Adding to Your Portfolio

As students select samples of their own writing, you might remind them that artists and writers assemble portfolios to display the most successful examples of their work in order to get further assignments. Suggest that students select their most successful piece produced by a five-stage writing process.

Portfolio Evaluation

If you grade the portfolio selections, you may want to award two marks—one each for content and form. Explain your assessment criteria before students make their selections.

Commend
- experimentation with creative prewriting techniques
- clear, concise writing in which the main idea, audience, and purpose are evident
- successful revisions
- work that shows a flair for language

The Writing Process

UNIT 2 Review

Reflecting on the Unit

Summarize what you have learned in this unit by answering the following questions.

1. What stages make up the writing process? How do writers use these stages in ways that work best for them?
2. How does prewriting help a writer find and explore topics for writing?
3. What does drafting mean?
4. What is the main purpose of revising? How can peer reviewers help?
5. What does the writer check when editing a piece of writing?
6. What is the publishing/presenting stage?

Adding to Your Portfolio

CHOOSE A SELECTION FOR YOUR PORTFOLIO Look over the writing you did for this unit. Choose a piece of writing for your portfolio. The writing you choose should show one or more of the following:

- a sharp focus on one interesting person or issue
- vivid details that give a strong impression
- a beginning that grabs the reader's interest
- paragraphs that show a clear development
- a sense of purpose and of the audience for which it is written

REFLECT ON YOUR CHOICE Attach a note to the piece you chose, explaining briefly why you chose it and what you learned from writing it.

SET GOALS How can you improve your writing? What skill will you focus on the next time you write?

Writing Across the Curriculum

MAKE A HISTORY CONNECTION What is happening in Cambodia now? The children of that time are grown. What has become of them? From your research notes write a paragraph about life in Cambodia today. Use vivid details. Write legibly and be sure to proofread for spelling and grammar errors.

96 Unit 2 The Writing Process

✔ ASSESSMENT OPTIONS

📁 *Tests with Answer Key and Rubrics*
Unit 2 Choice A Test, p. 5
Unit 2 Choice B Test, p. 6
Unit 2 Composition Objective Test, pp. 7–8

💾 *Testmaker*
Unit 2 Choice A Test
Unit 2 Choice B Test
Unit 2 Composition Objective Test

You may wish to administer one of these tests as a mastery test.

📺 *MindJogger Videoquizzes*

TIME
Facing the Blank Page

Inside the writing process with TIME writers and editors

Focus

Lesson Overview

Objectives

- To apply strategies used by professional writers to all stages of the writing process
- To use writing to reflect upon the ideas of others
- To use resources for help during the writing process
- To generate ideas for writing by using prewriting strategies
- To develop ideas through the use of the drafting process
- To revise writing based on peer and self-directed evaluation
- To edit writing for specific purposes and for clarity and conciseness
- To use available technology to support aspects of creating, revising, editing, and publishing texts

🔔 Bellringer
Daily Language Activity

When students come into the classroom, have this assignment on the board: *Imagine you are writing an article for a young people's magazine. You can choose any idea you want, as long as the article captures the attention of middle school students. Jot down notes on the approaches you would use for coming up with interesting ideas.*

Motivating Activity

Have students share their notes on strategies for collecting topic ideas. Their approaches might include freewriting, brainstorming, listing, and clustering. What are the benefits and drawbacks of these various prewriting strategies? Encourage students to experiment with different approaches.

Resource Manager

📁 **Planning Resources**
- *Lesson Plans*

📠 **Transparencies**
- *Writing Process*

📁 **Other Print Resources**
- *Composition Enrichment*
- *Composition Practice*
- *Composition Reteaching*

- *Grammar and Composition Handbook*
- *Guide to Using the Internet and Other Electronic Resources*
- *Writing Assessment and Evaluation Rubrics*

📼 **Video**
- *Facing the Blank Page*

💾 **Software**
- *Presentation Plus!*
- *Revising with Style*

💻 **Web Sites**
- *writerschoice.glencoe.com*
- *lit.glencoe.com*

97

Teach

Discussion Prompts

- Though many writers work in isolation, the professionals at TIME work cooperatively as a team. What are some ways you use can teamwork to improve your writing?

- In what ways do you think a writing team is like a sports team?

Viewing the Chart

Have students read the chart and list roles of key players on the TIME writing team:

- *Writer:* helps create a story idea; clarifies topic; reads, selects, and organizes information; drafts story; revises story.

- *Correspondent:* helps create a story idea; investigates and interviews; reviews writer's draft; offers suggestions.

- *Researcher:* gathers material from reliable sources; compiles and submits research files; checks accuracy of draft.

- *Editor:* helps create a story idea; reviews draft; suggests revisions; reviews revisions; "greens."

- *Managing Editor:* prints, holds, or kills story.

Writing for TIME

The stories published each week in TIME are the work of experienced professionals—people who research, write, and edit for a living. The writing is clear; the facts are accurate; and the grammar, spelling, and punctuation are as error-free as possible.

Behind the scenes, however, another story emerges. TIME staffers face many of the same challenges that students do in the messy, trial-and-error process that is writing. Just like you, they must find a topic, conduct research, get organized, write a draft, and then revise, revise, and revise again. In these pages, they tell you how they do it.

Is there a secret to the quality of writing in TIME? Beyond experience and hard work, the key lies in collaboration. As the chart below illustrates, TIME stories are created through a form of "group journalism" that has become the magazine's hallmark. The writers and editors teach and learn from each other every week. You can do the same. Try out the writing and collaboration strategies presented in "Facing the Blank Page" to discover what's right for you.

PREWRITING

Editor   Writer   Correspondent

Story idea is born

Writer takes assignment, refines topic, asks researchers and reporters for help

Research begins

Correspondents investigate, conduct interviews

Researchers gather material from reliable sources: "clips" from articles, studies, statistics

DRAFTING

Correspondents send their reporting or "files" to writer

Researchers compile and submit research files

Writer reads and organizes information, drafts the story

98   TIME Facing the Blank Page

Viewing and Representing

Creating Visuals

Have pairs of students convert the information shown on the writing process chart into a board game or video game. Suggest that students create a pathway or course that takes players through the stages of the writing process—from start to finish. Ask students to look at popular board games and video games for ideas. Finally, have students compare their games with those of their classmates and assess how the language, medium, and presentation of each game might help players understand how TIME stories are created. Have the class discuss whether the diagram on these pages or their own game presents the information better.

REVISING

Editor reads draft, suggests revisions

Correspondents
check interpretation,
make suggestions

Writer revises, sends draft to members of the team for comments

Researchers
check accuracy,
details

Writer and editor revise again, "green" (edit for length)

EDITING AND PROOFREADING

Checks for conformity to TIME
style and conventions

Copy Desk

Checks and corrects grammar,
mechanics, spelling

PUBLISHING AND PRESENTING

Managing Editor chooses to print, hold, or "kill" (omit) story

Circulation of TIME
rises or falls

Readers respond to published story

E-mail and letters
to the editor

99

Teach

Connecting Across the Curriculum

Sports

Have students compare the revising stage of the writing process to the procedure a professional baseball player might follow to better his performance. For example, ask students to imagine a pitcher who wants to improve his win-loss record. What similarities does he share with a writer who wants to revise a story? (Answers include the following: A coach recommends changes to the pitcher for throwing the ball just as an editor suggests revisions to a writer for strengthening a story. Both a pitcher and a writer polish their "work" by practicing.)

Deconstructing Media

Writing Team vs. Visual Team

The chart does not explain the roles that photographers, illustrators, and designers play in communicating information. Have students bring in articles from TIME and other magazines. As a class, analyze how photographs, illustrations, and design elements help convey or enhance the message presented in the text. Discuss how readers might respond to the text if these visuals were missing. For example, without photographs, readers might not be able to picture dramatic moments or scenes mentioned in a story. Without charts or graphs, readers might not clearly understand processes or trends.

Exploring Language

Using Etymology

Have students explore the etymology of the word *draft* ("to draw" from Middle English) and compare a written draft of a story to a drawing or sketch of a painting. Extend the discussion by pointing out that a draftsperson is someone who makes drawings of plans, such as architectural blueprints, or sketches structures, such as machinery. How is a writer like a draftsperson?

Teach

Getting Started: Finding Story Ideas

Review with your class the prewriting strategies discussed in Lesson 2.2 (notetaking, brainstorming, and clustering). Give students a general subject, such as "sports," and have them use one of these prewriting techniques to generate a story idea for their class newspaper.

Brainstorming Tips

Remind students of these guidelines for holding productive brainstorming sessions:

1. Choose someone to list ideas as they are called out.
2. Start with a topic or a question.
3. Encourage everyone to join in freely.
4. Accept all ideas; do not evaluate them now.
5. Explore the possibilities of each idea.

Prewriting

Getting Started: Finding Story Ideas

Generating good ideas for stories is as important—and can take as much time—as writing and editing the articles themselves. You may be assigned topics to write about; sometimes TIME writers get assignments, too. But just as often, writers are expected to come up with their own subjects and develop an interesting angle for a story.

Staff Writer and TV critic James Poniewozik tells how he gets started:

❝ Ideas for stories come from anything that surprises you. If you're watching a lot of television—for example, all the new pilots for the fall season—you might start noticing trends.

James Poniewozik: Write about what surprises you.

You might say, 'Gee, it seems that every other show has a voice-over on it, with characters talking directly to the camera.' You ask yourself, 'What does that mean? Is it a good thing or is it a bad thing? Is it a storytelling crutch, a way for writers to communicate characters' feelings without doing it through action and dialogue?' And so there's a story idea there—something that strikes you as a topic worth exploring.

The ideas part is pretty tough. I think one of the best ways to generate ideas is to talk to other people about things you're interested in. I've had a lot of story ideas that I didn't know were story ideas until I talked about them. I'll mention something in a conversation to others and they'll say, 'Oh, that sounds like it would make a topic for a story,' and I'll suddenly realize, 'Yes, it would!' Of course, I may have thought about the subject a half-dozen times before, but it never occurred to me to write about it. ❞

Janice Simpson, Senior Editor:

❝ If something is interesting to you as a writer or reporter—if something piques your curiosity and you want to know more about it—then probably there are other people who do, too. So I think we start there. What interests you? What catches your attention? ❞

100 TIME Facing the Blank Page

Technology Tip

Outlining

Many word processing programs include an outlining feature that enables you to create an outline and a skeleton "draft" at the same time. If you revise your outline, the draft changes along with it.

nother way to find story ideas is to work with your fellow writers. At TIME, the writers in each section hold "story meetings" to share news and ideas. Michael Lemonick, Senior Writer at TIME, discusses the collaborative process.

Michael Lemonick writes for TIME's science section:

TED THAI FOR TIME

Michael Lemonick: Brainstorm with others.

❝Our group holds brainstorming sessions once a week, where we share ideas with each other. I keep my eyes and ears open all the time—with radio, TV news, friends, scientific journals, more specialized magazines, and local newspapers. Mostly I want to know what regular people are interested in or worried about.

Once the idea is there, we consult with each other about sources. Then the editor sends out a query to correspondents, and we start to shape the story we want. For example, with our cover story on microbes, we had heard a report about a new strain of drug-resistant tuberculosis, but someone then brought up another point. Working together, we came up with a concept for a big story: war against diseases. We all communicate with each other verbally, within staff meetings, by phone, and we get further ideas from correspondents in the bureaus.

After I'm assigned a story, I read everything I can find that's been printed to get a sense of the subject. I also conduct some of the interviews, along with the correspondents. ❞

TIME LEXICON

Query: a message sent from TIME's New York office to correspondents in the field asking them to gather information and conduct interviews for a proposed story.

LEARNING FROM THE WRITERS

TALK ABOUT IT
1. What benefits of working collaboratively do both James Poniewozik and Michael Lemonick point out?
2. Do you prefer working by yourself, with a partner, or with a group? List the pros and cons of each method.

TRY IT OUT
1. Have a class brainstorming session. Generate ideas for your next writing project as you work with a partner or a small group. See Lesson 2.2,

"Prewriting: Finding and Exploring a Topic."
2. Find story ideas close to home. Work with James Poniewozik's notion that story ideas come from things that surprise you or thoughts that occur to you again and again. On an ordinary day at home or at school, is there a character, an observation, or an event that begs to be used in a piece of writing? Is there something that you hear or say routinely that you can use creatively? Select one of these as the

basis for a piece of creative writing or for a school newspaper story.

LOOK IT OVER
1. Look at the writing you have done recently. Where did you get the idea for each piece? Is there a pattern in the way you find ideas, or do you find them in different ways?
2. Using Janice Simpson's advice, list things that pique your curiosity. Place stars in front of three that you want to develop in writing.

TIME Facing the Blank Page **101**

Learning from the Writers: Evaluation Rubrics

Talk About It

1. Students should mention that both TIME writers point out how conversations with other people help story ideas take shape.
2. Students should voice preferences for the way they like to work and chart the pros and cons of each approach. For example, students who prefer working alone might say that having fewer distractions allows them to work more efficiently. Students who prefer working in groups might say that sharing ideas with others helps them solve problems more quickly.

Try It Out

1. Students' brainstorming sessions should
   - generate ideas for future writing projects
   - foster cooperation and respect among group members
2. Students' story ideas should
   - evolve from a routine event or daily observation
   - be recast as a school newspaper article or piece of creative writing

Look It Over

As students review their writing, have them identify the strengths and weaknesses of each piece and identify whether the idea behind a topic influences their writing. Is their writing likely to be stronger if the topic is of interest to them? How might the information help them set goals for future writing projects?

Writing in the Real World

Writers and Writing

Like James Poniewozik, poet William Carlos Williams found that inspiring ideas for writing often came from everyday experiences. For example, Williams's poem "This Is Just to Say " is about plums that the speaker finds in the icebox. Written in simple language, the poem almost sounds like a note left on a refrigerator door. Invite students to choose an ordinary event or daily observation as the basis for a poem.

Teach

⬆ Cross-Reference: Outlining

For instruction and practice on ordering ideas and outlining, refer students to Lesson 2.4, Lesson 5.9, and Lesson 24.6

Facts and Opinions

Remind student that facts are statements that can be proved true, while opinions are personal beliefs or feelings. Have students point out the facts and the opinions in Nelan's article "How Not to Catch a Spy."

Drafting

Getting Words on Paper

Have you ever found it hard to start an assignment? You sit down at your desk, stare at the blank page, get up, wander around, come back, write a few words. This happens to professional writers, too!

Senior Writer Bruce Nelan:

❝The biggest problem for me is organization. That's the hardest part. Sometimes, it's very tough. You sit and you stare. You flip through your material. And you say, 'Where do I start? What is it I want to say? How do I convey it?' But the clock is ticking. And so you sit down, you put the heading on, and you stare at the screen. You try this, you try that, and it starts to take shape.❞

Nelan starts by making an outline:

❝The first thing I do is make an outline. It doesn't necessarily have to be an elaborate, academic-style outline, but it at least has to tick off the main points, the most important elements. There's a period of discovery there that prepares you for writing. If I know that I'm at the second item on the outline and I want to get to the third item on the outline, something has to come in between, a transition of some sort. It'll sometimes become obvious to you, at the time that you're actually doing it.❞

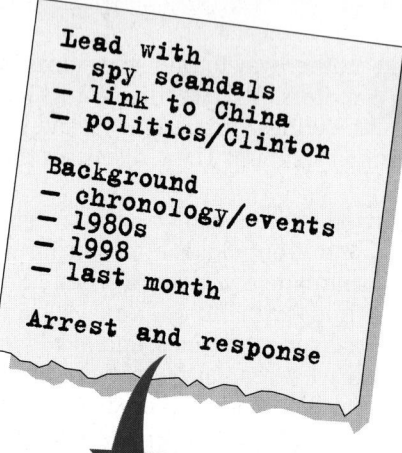

Lead with
— spy scandals
— link to China
— politics/Clinton

Background
— chronology/events
— 1980s
— 1998
— last month

Arrest and response

How Not to Catch a Spy

The government doesn't like to catch spies. Nabbing one tends to be embarrassing, seen as proof that the people in charge have been sloppy and lax on security. And it raises painful questions: How much damage has the spy done? Why wasn't he rooted out earlier? Who's making sure such pillaging of the country's vital secrets doesn't happen again? It's an unwinnable debate that no Administration wants to join.

But it is this kind of scandal that hit the White House last week—and the fact that it involved China made the mess even harder to clean up. Bill Clinton has already been bruised by accusations that illegal Chinese contributions found their way into his 1996 campaign and that he was overeager to allow U.S. firms to sell high-end computers and satellite technology to Beijing. Now the "soft on China" shouts are louder than ever, boosted by claims from critics in both parties that top Administration officials delayed and soft-pedaled the investigation into alleged Chinese spying at Los Alamos National Laboratory in New Mexico, birthplace of the atom bomb.

—**Bruce Nelan**

102 TIME Facing the Blank Page

Listening and Speaking

Distinguishing Between Fact and Opinion

Explain to students that broadcast journalists, like print journalists, use both facts and opinions when presenting their view on television. Have students listen to a journalist's report on a television news show and jot down the facts and opinions in the spoken message. Have the class compare their analyses.

W hile Bruce Nelan favors outlining as a method of organizing his material, different writers work in different ways. Each has his or her own strategy for conquering the blank page, from starting to organize material to beginning the drafting process.

James Poniewozik, a Staff Writer who serves as TIME's TV critic, works this way:
❝In theory, I think outlines are a good idea; in practice, I've never really used them, which is not necessarily good. What I might do is just free-associate on a page. I come up with a dozen topics or points that should be mentioned at some point in the piece, and then maybe I'll write numbers by them—either to show their relative importance or to put them in what seems to make for a smooth flow of the article. And an order emerges: I say, 'I should start with this, and then I'll jump to this, and this segues to that, and so on.' And then you go back and read through, see if it all makes sense, or if you need to change the beginning.❞

Even with an outline in place, a writer can still get stuck. Poniewozik explains:

Poniewozik's notes: An order emerges.

❝I'm a really slow writer, and I'll spend minutes and minutes unnecessarily fussing over words or phrasing in a sentence. But you have to fight against that. It's important to force yourself to write, however bad the writing might be, and know that you can go back and improve it. If you're not writing anything, you'll never finish! Sometimes you just have to force the words out, kind of like warming yourself up when you are exercising. Then, once you're warmed up, you can move ahead and refine it, make it what you want it to be.❞

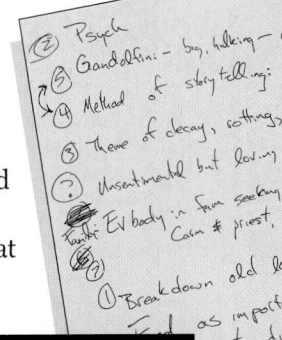

LEARNING FROM THE WRITERS

TALK ABOUT IT
1. Compare and contrast Nelan and Poniewozik's methods of organizing and outlining their work.
2. Look at Lesson 2.4, "Prewriting: Ordering Ideas," and Lesson 5.9, "Reports: Organizing and Drafting." How do the strategies suggested there compare with those Nelan and Poniewozik use in their work at TIME?

TRY IT OUT
Work from an outline. Choose your favorite of the topics that you decided to develop in writing. After gathering information on the topic, organize what you want to say by using one of the strategies mentioned here or by making an outline, as presented in Lesson 24.6. Use it as you write your first draft.

LOOK IT OVER
Which writer's method is most like your own? What tips for organizing material and ideas and for drafting can you offer your fellow writers?

TIME Facing the Blank Page **103**

Viewing and Representing

Storyboards
Encourage students to try using film and video techniques to plot out their drafts. Have each student create a storyboard as a kind of visual outline. Have students choose a story idea and show its development, frame by frame. Tell them to write a descriptive or informative statement beneath each frame. Ask students to discuss which is more helpful to them as they draft—a written outline or a storyboard? Why?

Teach

Tips for Getting Unstuck

Point out that student writers, just like professional writers at TIME, get stuck during the drafting stage. Here are some strategies to help students get unstuck:
- Draw a picture about your topic.
- Pretend you are writing a letter or an e-mail to a friend in which you describe your topic or the approach you want to take.
- Freewrite in your journal.
- Speak your ideas into a tape recorder.
Invite students to add other strategies to the list.

Assess

Learning from the Writers: Evaluation Rubrics

Talk About It
1. Students may discuss these methods: Nelan finds outlining helpful as a method of organizing. Poniewozik freewrites about several key topics or points and then uses numbers to rank their importance or to show their possible arrangement in an article.
2. Poniewozik's approach to writing is similar to the techniques described in Unit 2. For example, he figures out the main ideas, lists them, and then arranges them in some logical order. Nelan's method more closely resembles some of the organizing strategies, such as outlining, described in Unit 5.

Try It Out
Students should
- choose a topic for a piece of writing
- create a formal or informal outline on the topic
- experiment with other organizing strategies

Look It Over
Students should
- examine their organizing strategies for writing
- correlate their strategies with one of the TIME writer's methods
- list some organizing and drafting strategies not mentioned by the professional writers

Teach

Technology Tip

Revising

Most word processing programs have a revising function that allows editors to mark revisions without deleting the original first draft. Encourage students to practice using this revising function and to make use of any other online editing functions included in their word processing programs.

Assess

Learning from the Editor: Evaluation Rubrics

Talk About It

Students should draw parallels between the metaphor "too many flowers" and writing cluttered with too many adjectives. Students' lists should
- identify each adjective in Chua-Eoan's story
- rate the descriptive value of each adjective
- suggest deletions of unnecessary adjectives

Try It Out

1. Students' models of adjective-heavy sentences should illustrate how overusing adjectives obscures, rather than clarifies, the main point. Students might comment that cutting all the adjectives from their model sentences makes the writing too drab or skimpy.
2. Students' revisions should show how vivid adjectives, used sparingly along with strong nouns and verbs, bring the main point of a sentence into sharper focus.

Look It Over

Students should
- circle each adjective in the draft
- decide whether there are "too many flowers"
- revise where necessary, replacing adjectives with strong nouns and action verbs

Revising Too Many Adjectives?

In revising your work, it helps to focus on one language issue at a time instead of trying to attend to everything simultaneously. One way to do a quick, early edit is to cast a critical eye on your use of adjectives. As one editor advises: Weed out a few adjectives and you'll tighten up your writing.

Assistant Managing Editor Howard Chua-Eoan:

❝Adjectives should be used sparingly. I'm not at all against the use of adjectives; I think adjectives are very important. But if there are too many in one paragraph, then there are too many flowers and you don't see what the point of all the decoration is.❞

LEARNING FROM THE EDITOR

Read this excerpt from one of Howard Chua-Eoan's stories in TIME:

The Shaping of Jewel

With her blue cotton top worn inside out and with black riding sweats overlaid by suede chaps, Jewel lounges bareback on the Thoroughbred quarter horse she calls Jazz. She'd like to take him on the road. "Horseback riding is the most natural thing in my blood—that and singing," she says. She first rode a horse when she was two or three while growing up in Alaska, before the hard years—her parents divorcing, life with father in and out of bars, life with mother living out of cars, life alone. But now, at 23, she has sold more than 5 million copies of her album, *Pieces of You.* And she's got Jazz. Lovingly, she picks sawdust out of his hoof with a brush claw.

Jewel's is a fey, insidious charm, equal parts worldly and naive. Her flaws—the crooked nose and crooked teeth she is so proud of—only betray an uncommon beauty. Then there is the improbable match of slender youth and that voice—an astonishingly versatile instrument ranging from soul-shattering yodels to the most eloquent of whispers to arch Cole Porter tunes.

TALK ABOUT IT

What does Chua-Eoan mean by "too many flowers"? List the adjectives that Chua-Eoan uses in "The Shaping of Jewel." Does each one add something unique? Are there some he should omit?

TRY IT OUT

1. Compose an adjective-heavy sentence. Describe a summer morning or a scene of your choice. Now cut the adjectives out entirely. What is lost by doing this?
2. Improve the sentence.

Use strong nouns and verbs and a few vivid adjectives to do the work of the edited adjectives.

LOOK IT OVER

Evaluate the use of adjectives in your first draft. If there are "too many flowers," revise.

104 TIME Facing the Blank Page

Grammar Link

Commas with Adjectives

Remind students that coordinate adjectives modify the same noun to an equal degree. If a sentence sounds correct when you reverse the adjectives or put *and* between them, the adjectives are coordinate. Review the following comma rules with students:
- Place a comma between coordinate adjectives that precede a noun.

- Do not use a comma between adjectives that describe size, shape, age, color, and material.

Then have pairs of students write sentences that contain adjectives that illustrate each of these rules.

Self-Editing: Reading Aloud

Several TIME writers share the same secret for editing their own work: reading aloud.

Howard Chua-Eoan: Beware of too many flowers.

Howard Chua-Eoan:

❝You should think of every sort of writing as a piece of theater. One thing I always suggest to young writers with trouble finding their voices is to read your story out loud, and find out if this is the way you want it to sound. Don't read just your stories out loud, but read other people's stories, too, to see why they sound the way they do, and why you like the way they sound.

I sometimes stop and read a paragraph—especially a lead paragraph—over and over and over again out loud just to see if that's the way I really want it to sound. If you're injecting some sort of artificial pace into it that isn't there as you read it, then you realize that the cadences and the syllables aren't giving that to you. So you do have to hear yourself. ❞

> **WRITING TIP**
>
> **Hearing Your Voice**
> "I write the way I talk—except I hope my writing is funnier! If you can figure out what you sound like and clean it up a bit and put it on paper, then you've got a voice."
> **—Joel Stein, humor writer**

Senior Editor Nancy Gibbs:

❝Sometimes when you read a story out loud, you find yourself editing it as you read it. You realize that the words that tripped you up, or the sentences that were too convoluted, need to be changed, and you correct them as you read it aloud. That's always the signal to go back and correct it on paper. ❞

LEARNING FROM THE EDITORS

TALK ABOUT IT
1. What does Chua-Eoan mean when he says "think of every sort of writing as a piece of theater"?
2. Relate an experience you have had that is similar to Gibbs's finding herself correcting problem words and sentences as she reads aloud.

TRY IT OUT
1. Hear the writer's voice. Choose a piece of writing by one of your favorite authors and read it aloud. What does this help you notice about the writer's voice and the piece's rhythm, sentence length, and structure? How does this help you understand what it is you like about the way the writer uses language?
2. Swap first drafts with a partner. Read the papers aloud to each other. If you find that you change anything as you read, your partner should probably revise it in his or her draft too. Read aloud a literature selection from this textbook. What do you notice about it?

LOOK IT OVER
Read *your* first draft aloud. What changes do you find yourself making? Revise your work for clarity and style.

MEETING INDIVIDUAL NEEDS — English Language Learners

Ask some fluent English readers to read a story aloud to a partner or small group of students. Encourage students to stop the reader during the oral reading to discuss any parts that they have difficulty understanding. Then invite the students who listened to the story to retell it in their own words. What do students notice about the different versions of the retellings? What new details were added? What details in the original story were omitted?

Teach

Writer's Voice

Explain to students that *voice* is a writer's distinctive use of language to convey the writer's or narrator's personality to the reader. Voice depends on elements of style, such as sentence structure, word choice, and tone. Ask students to describe their experiences listening to audiotapes of books or stories. How does listening to oral readings enhance their appreciation of the author's writing style?

Assess

Learning from the Editors: Evaluation Rubrics

Talk About It

1. During the discussion, students should explore the ways that writing is similar to a performance played to a live audience. For example, a writer reading a story draft aloud resembles an actor rehearsing lines. Both are listening to the sound and dramatic impact of their words and "voices."
2. Ask students who have used the "reading aloud" approach to share their experiences with the class. Have them explain what they discovered during the process and why they decided to make editorial changes.

Try It Out

1. Students' analyses should
   - explain elements of the author's writing style
   - discuss the sound of the words and rhythm of the sentences
   - evaluate the writer's use of language
2. Students' oral readings should
   - express the tone of the piece
   - use effective rate, volume, and pitch
   - reflect understanding of writing style

Look It Over

Students should
- read aloud their first drafts
- listen to the way they sound
- makes changes as needed

Teach

Technology Tip

Proofreading

Most word processing programs have a spell-check function that allows editors to proofread their work for spelling and typographical errors. Caution students, though, that conventional spelling checkers will not point out frequently misspelled words, such as *they're* and *their*. Encourage students to practice using this or any other online proofreading and editing functions included in their word processing programs.

Assess

Learning from the Editor: Evaluation Rubrics

Talk About It

Point out to students that both *cyberspace* and *Internet* were added to *Merriam-Webster's Collegiate Dictionary* in the 1990s. Have a volunteer look up both words and read their definitions aloud to the class. Then ask students to imagine they are editors of a dictionary. What requirements would a new word have to meet before they would consider adding it to the dictionary?

Try It Out

1. Students' word lists should
   - consist of words with evolving meanings and usages
   - provide dictionary definitions and correct spellings
   - include revised definitions for the words
2. Students' class style sheet should
   - list examples of conversational language
   - include current teenage slang words
   - define, spell, and explain the usage of each example
3. Students' revised drafts should
   - be edited with the help of the list on page 79
   - be checked for one kind of error at a time
   - be marked for corrections with the proofreading symbols that are shown on page 80

106

Editing and Proofreading

An Ever-Changing Language

The Copy Desk is the last stop for every TIME story. At this final stage in the editing process, Deputy Copy Chief Judy Paul and her colleagues check articles for errors in spelling, punctuation, style, and usage. There is only one problem: the rules they are supposed to apply keep changing! From the Copy Desk, these editors witness language and style evolving.

Judy Paul: Keeping up with the language.

JAY COLTON FOR TIME

Judy Paul:

❝We've changed a great deal. We used to follow some very strict style rules that no longer apply. For example, we were never allowed to say *Mid East* for *Middle East*. We were never allowed to use the abbreviation *L.A.*; we always had to spell out *Los Angeles*. And as times change, usage changes. We move with it and allow a lot more. Now you'll see *L.A.* in a Nation story, because that's something an American reader understands. ❞

The new vocabulary of cyberspace is a challenge for copy editors. TIME's Copy Desk has had to decide how to "style" (that is, come up with a consistent way to use, spell, punctuate, and capitalize) words like *e-mail* and *dot.com*. Says Paul, "The most exciting part of working with the language right now is simply trying to keep up with it!"

LEARNING FROM THE EDITOR

TALK ABOUT IT
How does technological change force language to evolve? Look up *cyberspace* and *Internet* in a classroom dictionary. Are either of these terms defined? What other commonly used words may be missing from the dictionary? Why?

TRY IT OUT
1. List some words whose meanings and usages have evolved in recent years. How are these words, such as *web*, *net*, or *awesome*, defined in the dictionary? Write revised definitions for the words on your list.
2. List some informal terms

that you and your friends use in conversation. Define each of the terms and make a "style sheet" that indicates how to use and spell them correctly.
3. Edit and proofread your revised draft line by line. Fix errors in grammar, usage, spelling, and punctuation.

MEETING INDIVIDUAL NEEDS   Gifted and Talented Students

Explain that many journalists follow the rules in the Associate Press stylebook for abbreviations, capitalization, punctuation, and other usage. Have interested students study the stylebook and create a style sheet listing the rules that the class would find the most helpful. Have copies of the completed style sheet available for everyone to use as a reference during in-class writing assignments.

Publishing and Presenting

'Aha!' The Joy of Writing

Senior Editor Janice Simpson began writing when she was eight. She started out rewriting fairy tales, and though she now works in the realm of non-fiction, she sees a common thread in all writing: the ancient tradition of storytelling.

Janice Simpson reflects:

❝I think the reason we use the term *story* so much in journalism is because there is a link to our pre-writing time, when griots in Africa and other storytellers in ancient civilizations would sit in a circle and tell people stories.

We journalists see what we do in that tradition. We're still telling stories. You can have wonderful information, but if you can't impart that information in a way that engages the reader, then people are just going to turn the page or put the magazine aside. You must have the power of a storyteller, because we are still sitting in the circle—today,

it's a sort of global circle. Journalists are connected through the magazine or television to the other people in the circle, and we want to tell stories that explain what life is like, how we think about things, how things affect us. Like the griot, we need to do it in a narrative, engaging, explanatory way. ❞

When writers and readers connect, the hard work of writing pays off:

❝A writer's job is hard—very, very hard work. But there's also an element of fun about what we do, and the best writing reflects that joy. That joy is transmitted in writing. I think we've all had the experience of reading something and saying 'Aha! Let me write that down. That's just the way I felt about it.' When that happens, the writer has transmitted some of the joy he or she is feeling—some of the emotion—to you, the reader. And that's very much what writing and storytelling and journalism are all about. ❞

LEARNING FROM THE EDITOR

TALK ABOUT IT
1. Tell a childhood story. Why has it stayed with you?
2. Do you agree that a writer's job is difficult but rewarding? Why? In what other difficult but rewarding activities do you participate?
3. Have you had the "Aha!"

reading experience Simpson mentions? Describe it.

TRY IT OUT
1. Collect quotes. Keep a journal of "Aha!" quotations, their sources, and your reasons for including them.
2. Prepare a presentation

copy of your draft. Read it in a storytelling circle and then display it in a class journal.

LOOK IT OVER
Look at three pieces of your writing, including your revised draft. How is each a form of storytelling?

Cultural Connections

The Oral Tradition

Tales that come from an oral tradition have been passed along by word of mouth for hundreds of years. The oral tradition in literature spans cultures and continents. For example, the role of the griots in Africa is similar to the function of Native American storytellers in North America. Native American storytellers helped groups understand their daily lives and history. Tales about nature and animal characters were especially popular. Today Native American groups keep the oral tradition alive by holding storytelling festivals. Have the class plan a storytelling festival in which students pose as storytellers and present African and Native American folk tales.

Teach

Purposes for Listening

Have students imagine they are listening to a storyteller relating a tale with a lesson. Explain that their purposes for listening are to gain information, to learn how the characters solve problems, and to enjoy the story. Ask students to compare the purposes for listening to a storyteller with the purposes for reading a journalist's writing.

Assess

Learning from the Editor: Evaluation Rubrics

Talk About It

1. Encourage students to recall stories they've enjoyed hearing or reading again and again. Have students list the qualities of stories they will never forget. If applicable in your class, discuss similarities and differences in stories from different cultures and regions.
2. Have students describe difficulties, such as meeting deadlines, finding interesting ideas, and so on. Encourage students to cite some of the rewards described by Simpson—for example, transmitting the joy of writing to the reader. Students who are athletic or artistic might compare their activities to a writer's job.
3. Students should reflect on instances when they closely identified with a character in a story or shared the feelings or experiences described in a piece of writing.

Try It Out

1. Students' quotation collections should
   • contain well-chosen quotations
   • document sources correctly
   • state reasons for recording the quotations
2. Students' papers should
   • be neat, legible, and attractive
   • be read with effective rate, volume, pitch, and expression

Look It Over

As students examine their writing samples, tell them to look for story elements, such as characters, setting, plot, and conflict.

Descriptive Writing

Viewing the Art

The high-flying bald eagle captured in this photograph has a wingspan of about six feet, making it one of the largest birds in North America. The bald eagle is also known as the American eagle because it has a presence in every state except Hawaii. A superb hunter known for its keen eyesight, the bald eagle is on our National Emblem as a symbol of majesty and strength.

Interpret and Analyze Use the following questions for discussion:

- What are the eagle's characteristics?
- What connotations does the word *eagle* have?
- How does the photographer convey those characteristics and connotations?
- In what ways do you think this image of the eagle relates to descriptive writing?

Discussing the Quotation

Invite the class to share their ideas about what they think this quotation means. What effect does Irving achieve by following the image of the birds hopping and twittering in the bushes with the image of the eagle soaring above them?

Writing Prompt Ask students to write paragraphs in which they compare themselves with a person or a thing much bigger or more powerful or accomplished than they are. Then have them compare themselves with a person or a thing much smaller or less powerful or accomplished.

For the full text of "Rip Van Winkle," see *Glencoe Literature: The Reader's Choice,* Course 2, p. 185.

"The birds were hopping and twittering among the bushes, and the eagle was wheeling aloft ..."

—Washington Irving

"Rip Van Winkle"

108

Resource Manager

📁 **Planning Resources**
- *Lesson Plans*
- *Block Scheduling*

📑 **Transparencies**
- *Bellringer*
- *Daily Language Practice*
- *Fine Art*
- *Two-Minute Skill Drill*
- *Writing Process*

📁 **Other Print Resources**
- *Composition Enrichment*
- *Composition Practice*
- *Composition Reteaching*
- *Cooperative Learning Activities*
- *Glencoe Literature Library*
- *Grammar and Composition Handbook*
- *Grammar Workbook*

- *Listening and Speaking Activities*
- *Sentence-Combining Practice*
- *Tests with Answer Key and Rubrics*
- *Thinking and Study Skills*
- *Writing Across the Curriculum*
- *Writing Assessment and Evaluation Rubrics*
- *Writing in the Real World*

UNIT 3

Descriptive Writing

Objectives

- To develop an understanding of sensory details in descriptive writing
- To combine observation and imagination in descriptive writing
- To choose and organize sensory details so that they bring a description to life

✔ ASSESSMENT OPTIONS

📁 *Tests with Answer Key & Rubrics*
Unit 3 Choice A Test, p.9
Unit 3 Choice B Test, p.10
Unit 3 Composition Objective Test, pp. 11–12

💾 *Testmaker*
Unit 3 Choice A Test
Unit 3 Choice B Test
Unit 3 Composition Objective Test

You may wish to administer either the Unit 3 Choice A Test or the Unit 3 Choice B Test as a pretest.

Key to Ability Levels

L1 Level 1 activities are within the basic ability range of students.

L2 Level 2 activities are within the ability range of average students.

L3 Level 3 activities are more challenging activities.

📼 **Video**
- *MindJogger Videoquizzes*

💾 **Software**
- *Presentation Plus!*
- *Revising with Style*
- *Testmaker*
- *Writer's Assistant*

🖥 **Web Sites**
- *writerschoice.glencoe.com*
- *lit.glencoe.com*

109

Focus

Lesson Overview

Objectives

- To examine the use of precise nouns and modifiers to create characters and setting
- To develop descriptions that achieve specific goals
- To explore and practice descriptive writing

Skills

- defining a purpose; choosing words for their connotations

Critical Thinking

- defining and clarifying; visualizing; making inferences

Listening and Speaking

- questioning; evaluating; discussing; explaining a process

Bellringer

Daily Language Activity

When students enter the classroom, have this assignment on the board: *Assume you are writing a fairy tale or fantasy. How would you begin? List some ideas.*

Grammar Link to the Bellringer

Have students list at least five words that they would use to describe a character in or the setting of their fairy tales.

See also *Daily Language Practice*

Motivating Activity

Ask students what fantasy books they have read and would recommend. Discuss where a writer of fantasy would begin—with setting? with characters? with plot? Elicit from students how they would develop detailed descriptions to create fantastic settings and creatures.

Writing in the Real World

MEDIA Fantasy Connection

Descriptive Writing

Zilpha Keatley Snyder is a writer of imaginative fiction, so her descriptions must be first-rate. Otherwise, her readers could never see the fantasy characters and settings that exist in her imagination. The following excerpt is from Snyder's *Song of the Gargoyle,* a fantasy set in the Middle Ages. The book's main character, Tymmon, comes face to face with a gargoyle. Only, this gargoyle isn't made of stone. This one is alive!

Song of the Gargoyle

By Zilpha Keatley Snyder

The face was grinning, its loose lips stretched wide to reveal sharp white teeth, its long red tongue lolling to one side.

Frozen with fear, Tymmon gasped, "God help me," and sat motionless, waiting for death. Waiting for the cruel grip of sharp fangs.

But then suddenly he knew—and almost laughed out loud. It was only a gargoyle. Once again he had let himself be fooled by a gargoyle. He smiled sheepishly, excusing his foolish reaction by blaming it on the strange trancelike state he had been experiencing. A condition caused no doubt by hunger and exhaustion. But it was still more than a little embarrassing to give oneself up to die because of a harmless stone image.

The bulging eyes blinked, the grin disappeared, and the tongue flapped up to lick the sagging jowls. Not stone. Not of stone and, he belatedly realized, certainly not where gargoyles were usually to be found—on the eaves of church or castle. But what then? A monster certainly. A monster so ugly that the mere sight of it might well, like the evil Medusa, turn the viewer to stone.

Tymmon's hand crept up to test his cheek for evidence of hardening. Still soft and warm. He swallowed hard.

Swallowed again and tried to speak.

"What—what are you? What do you want of me?"

The monster cocked its head, its jagged bat-wing ears flopping. It certainly looked very like a gargoyle. A new thought occurred. Perhaps it was. Perhaps a magical gargoyle conjured into life by some powerful enchantment. . . .

. . . With its enormous head only inches from his face, its rank breath hot on his cheeks, it stared down at Tymmon and licked its chops.

Hungry. It was hungry, and its next meal might well be . . .

Resource Manager

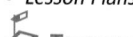

Planning Resources
- *Lesson Plans*

Transparencies
- *Bellringer*
- *Daily Language Practice*
- *Writing Process* 11–13B

Other Print Resources
- *Cooperative Learning Activities,* pp. 13–18
- *Thinking and Study Skills,* pp. 3, 5, 9, 22
- *Writing Assessment and Evaluation Rubrics*
- *Writing in the Real World,* pp. 9–12

Writing a Fantasy

Prewriting	Drafting	Revising/Editing
Describing the Setting	Filling the Scenes	Strengthening the Picture

❝ *For me the whole joy of writing is the chance to let my imagination freewheel. I like to balance a story between reality and fantasy. Then I can use descriptive language to give exciting and delicious hints in both directions.* **❞**

—Zilpha Keatley Snyder

A Writer's Process

Prewriting
Describing Setting, Characters, and Plot

After Snyder has an idea for a fantasy, she begins by trying to fully imagine the setting. To do this, she draws sketches of the settings for various scenes. For *Song of the Gargoyle* she drew floor plans of castles. Photographs of real castles also helped Snyder visualize details about her imaginary castle.

From the setting, Snyder turns her attention to writing descrip-

tions of the story's main characters. She "writes down everything" she knows about the characters. How does she learn about them? "By trying to live in their shoes and react as they would," she says.

In *Song of the Gargoyle,* the main character, Tymmon, is searching for his kidnapped father. As he travels, Tymmon faces daunting challenges, such as meeting a living gargoyle named Troff. In the early stages of imagining these characters, Snyder played what she called the "what-if" game. What if Tymmon meets

Teach

Discussion Prompts

Warm-up
Have students make a brief list of situations in which they think descriptions of a character or setting might be used.

Description in Speaking
Invite students to think of situations in which descriptions of characters or setting are used in everyday language. How are such descriptions used in a television news broadcast, for example, or in the introduction of guest speakers?

Description in Writing
Elicit from students some fantastic descriptions of characters or settings they may have read in
- science fiction
- myths
- horror stories
- fairy tales

Preview the Media Connection

Have students preview the title and focus of the selection. Discuss with students that the book *Song of the Gargoyle* is a fantasy and contains descriptive details of the characters and setting. Have students read the selection.

Civic Literacy

Believing in Change
Fantasy, with its emphasis on transcending reality, can help students believe in the possibility of change. Fantasies often deal with the struggle of good against evil, showing how wisdom and courage can triumph over raw power.

Teach

Discussion Prompts

- Why does it help to know the kind of character you want to create before you begin to write?
- What kind of detail might fail to help a reader?
- Why does it help writers to put themselves mentally into scenes they are trying to write?
- What details that Zilpha Keatley Snyder used to describe Troff helped to develop suspense in the story?

Additional Resources

Writing Process Transparencies, 11–13B

Cooperative Learning Activities, pp. 13–18

Writing in the Real World, pp. 9–12

Thinking and Study Skills, pp. 3, 5, 9, 22

Writing in the Real World

Troff? How will he react? What if Tymmon is frightened by Troff's appearance? What if Tymmon isn't sure whether Troff is a gargoyle or a dog with batlike ears?

Snyder decided that Tymmon's first reaction would be fear, caused by Troff's ugliness. She asked herself what words and descriptions would communicate such a reaction to the reader. She then wrote down descriptive details, such as "bulging eyes" and "jagged bat-wing ears," that heightened Troff's scary features.

Snyder thinks even her characters' names can work as descriptive details. The name Troff, for example, "sounded a bit like a dog's bark," Snyder says.

Snyder's final step is to write what she calls the plot page. Here Snyder tries "to know the main thrust of the story and what the climax will be."

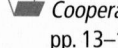

Snyder draws floor plans and details during the prewriting stage. These visual ideas help her describe a setting.

Drafting
Filling in the Scenes

Every morning Snyder sits down at her computer to write. When she's drafting a scene, she first writes two lists of goals. Snyder explains, "On the left-hand side is action—the events I want to happen. On the right-hand side is exposition. There I highlight the information I need to get across to the reader."

Snyder then tries to put herself into a scene. "I try to see it as vividly as possible. Then I tell about what I see," she says. *Song of the Gargoyle,* for example, is told through the eyes of Tymmon. This means that Snyder describes the gargoyle from Tymmon's point of view. The order in which she reveals details about Tymmon and Troff is important to the suspense of the story. In the excerpt on page 110, short descriptive phrases reveal Tymmon's mounting fear as he tries to figure out the creature standing before him.

Revising/Editing
Strengthening the Picture

Snyder revises each day's work the next morning. "I try to see if what I've written really calls forth my vision," she explains. This means making sure that her descriptive details suggest the two possible interpretations of Troff. Is he a gargoyle? Or is he a dog?

Snyder also uses her computer's thesaurus function to look for what she calls "more flamboyant adjectives and adverbs" to spice her descriptions. She seeks nouns and verbs that are precise.

When she's satisfied with the revised draft, Snyder shares it with a group of fellow writers. She says, "When you read aloud to other people, you hear things that you miss when reading

Cultural Connections

Finding a Unique Voice

Students should realize that their cultural backgrounds have given them their own experiences and visions and ways of expressing them. Suggest that students listen to how those around them speak and adapt that oral style to a writing style.

Fantastic Faces

A gargoyle is a drain spout in the form of a grotesque animal or human being. Gargoyles are common features on the great churches of the Middle Ages. Ask students who have seen gargoyles to describe them with vivid words.

Examining Writing in the Real World

alone." Snyder wants to be certain that her readers see the picture she's described. In descriptive writing that means creating an overall impression with carefully chosen details.

Analyzing the Media Connection

Discuss these questions about the fantasy excerpt on page 110.

1. What descriptive details does Snyder use to show that the gargoyle is a frightening sight?
2. What descriptive details show the reader that Tymmon is afraid?
3. Snyder uses sensory language in her descriptions. What phrase in the excerpt evokes the reader's sense of smell? What phrase appeals to the sense of touch?
4. What verbal does Snyder use to describe the movement of the gargoyle's tongue (paragraph 1)? Find at least two other examples where Snyder uses precise verbals or verbs.
5. How does Snyder build suspense at the end of the excerpt?

Analyzing a Writer's Process

Discuss these questions about Zilpha Keatley Snyder's writing process.

1. What methods did Snyder use to help her clearly imagine the settings for *Song of the Gargoyle*?

2. What is Snyder's "what-if" game? How and why does she use it?
3. What two lists does Snyder make for herself when writing a draft? Why do you think it helps her to keep these parts separate?
4. How does Snyder use a thesaurus as she revises?
5. Why does Snyder read her work aloud to others?

Snyder uses modifiers—adjectives or adverbs—to bring flair and precision to her writing.

> The **bulging** eyes blinked . . . Not of stone, and he **belatedly** realized . . .

Revise the paragraph below, adding vivid modifiers to describe each numbered word.

The ¹*trail* ended at a ²*cliff*. The ³*travelers* stopped. Below them lay the ⁴*city*. The travelers ⁵*looked* at each other and at the ⁶*sky* above them. The ⁷*sounds* and ⁸*smells* of the city rose up to meet them. They ⁹*turned* and ¹⁰*looked* for a new path.
See Lessons 12.1–12.2, pages 451–454.

Writing in the Real World **113**

Descriptive Writing

Assess

Analyzing the Media Connection

1. The student should identify some of these descriptive visual details: loose lips stretched wide; sharp white teeth; long red tongue; sharp fangs; bulging eyes.
2. Tymmon is frozen with fear; gasps a prayer for help; sits motionless; envisions that death is near.
3. rank breath; soft and warm
4. The verbal is *lolling*. The student may point out these examples: *bulging* eyes; tongue *flapped*; *sagging* jowls; hand *crept*; bat-wing ears *flopping*.
5. by implying that Tymmon thinks he may be the gargoyle's next meal

Analyzing a Writer's Process

1. She drew floor plans of castles, using photographs of real castles to help her visualize details.
2. Snyder sets up different situations characters might face to consider how they might react.
3. She lists story events and information that the reader will need (exposition). She may keep the lists separate to remind herself that readers need interesting details in addition to the action.
4. to find more colorful modifiers
5. to catch things she missed when reading silently

Reteaching

Have students picture a character in their minds. Challenge them to describe that character in words.

Enrichment

Ask students to picture a fantastic character and then write a brief story that places the character in an appropriate fantasy setting.

Grammar Link

Answers

Answers will vary. The following are samples.

1. unmarked
2. rocky
3. weary
4. glimmering
5. quickly
6. darkening
7. lively
8. pungent
9. quickly
10. eagerly

Close

Ask each student to recall a description of an experience or a person that he or she has recently heard or read. What descriptive words were used to capture the event or the person?

Note Robin Hood is a character described by many writers. Books about him include *The Chronicles of Robin Hood*, by Rosemary Sutcliff, and *Robin and His Merry Men*, by Ian Serraillier.

Focus

Lesson Overview

Objectives

- To make careful observations in order to construct descriptions that show rather than tell
- To use vivid sensory details to describe people, places, and things

Skills

- choosing words for their sensory appeal; contrasting writing that shows and writing that tells

Critical Thinking

- comparing and contrasting; visualizing; analyzing; decision making

Listening and Speaking

- informal speaking; discussing; evaluating; explaining a process

Bellringer
Daily Language Activity

When students enter the classroom, have this assignment on the board: *Write a short paragraph about a place you observed recently. Use details that will allow readers to experience the place that you describe.*

Grammar Link to the Bellringer

Have students revise their paragraphs, adding adverbs to describe verbs.

See also *Daily Language Practice*

Motivating Activity

Have volunteers read aloud the paragraphs they wrote and revised in the Bellringer activity. In discussing the paragraphs, emphasize the importance of close observation in making written descriptions come alive.

Descriptive Writing

LESSON
3.1

Writing to Show, Not Tell

People often use familiar words to label new things. That is how the sea anemone got its name. It resembles a flower—the anemone.

In *Journey Outside* a boy named Dilar has grown up on an underground river. When he discovers life on Earth's surface, he encounters new sights and sounds.

In the model below, Mary Q. Steele describes how Dilar reacts to an unfamiliar creature. Her use of familiar words shows the creature vividly.

Literature Model

To what does Dilar compare the strange sights and sounds he encounters?

He cried out abruptly. Something was coming toward him in the air, a little fish gliding through the air, helping itself along with great fins that stuck out from its sides and then folded tight against them. A wonder, a wonder! The fish stopped suddenly in the top of one of the little trees, put out little legs to hold itself up, threw back its head, and opening its mouth made such sounds as Dilar had never heard before. No water murmured so joyously or so sweetly or so triumphantly; nothing, nothing had ever rung upon his ears like that or made his heart feel it must burst open with that song's wild delight. Even when it had ceased it echoed in his head.

Mary Q. Steele, *Journey Outside*

Resource Manager

📁 Planning Resources
- *Lesson Plans*

🖥 Transparencies
- *Bellringer*
- *Daily Language Practice*
- *Fine Art* 11–14
- *Two-Minute Skill Drill*
- *Writing Process* 11–13B

📁 Other Print Resources
- *Composition Enrichment*, p. 18
- *Composition Practice*, p. 18
- *Composition Reteaching*, p. 18
- *Cooperative Learning Activities*, pp. 13–18
- *Listening and Speaking Activities*, 14–15
- *Thinking and Study Skills*, pp. 3, 9, 12

- *Writing Across the Curriculum*
- *Writing Assessment and Evaluation Rubrics*

Use Effective Details

Using effective descriptive details can make a person, place, or thing come to life. When you write, select details so carefully that your reader can see, hear, smell, taste, and feel what you describe. In the passage below, Bethany Bentley does not merely tell the reader that a storm passed through her town. She uses descriptive details that show the storm.

Revising Tip

When revising a piece of descriptive writing, use a thesaurus to help you find the perfect word to describe a specific color, sound, or smell.

Descriptive Writing

Student Model

I looked outside from the beaten-up restaurant and saw the vivid purple sky flashing with lightning, while the willow across the street swayed in the wind.

The lights from the neighboring store reflected on the window and blurred my view of the storm. The rain crashed down on the roof and pelted the windows, also contributing to my blurry view.

I could see pieces of bark flying off of the willow tree. Litter flew high into the evening sky.

The lightning struck again. I shuddered as a cold draft drifted through the cracked window nearby.

Bethany Bentley, Oak Creek School, Cornville, Arizona

Notice how the writer describes the movement of objects to show the violence of the storm.

How does the writer make this scene seem real?

Journal Writing

In your journal write several statements without any descriptive details, such as *The picnic was fun.* Then choose one of your sentences, and list five or six details that will help readers see, hear, smell, taste, or feel what you are describing.

3.1

Teach

Using the Model

Reading aloud the passage from *Journey Outside* may help students focus on the imagery the writer uses. Ask students to identify the creature Dilar notices and to describe the scene through Dilar's eyes and ears. (He sees a bird. He thinks of the bird as a fish, the air as water, and the bird's wings as fins; and he feels that the bird's song is better than the water's murmur.) Discuss the similarities between Dilar's naming of the bird and the naming of the sea anemone. Ask students to give examples of objects in nature whose names reflect a resemblance to something else; for example, starfish, dragonfly, and seahorse. **L2**

Categorizing Details

Suggest that students create word webs before writing descriptions. Tell them to write one of the five senses at the center of each web and add details that relate to that sense. **L1**

 **Two-Minute Skill Drill**

For practice in choosing the most descriptive words, have students write more specific verbs for those listed below.

ran   looked
wrote   said

See also *Two-Minute Skill Drill Transparency 3.1*

Journal Writing Tip

Evaluating Encourage students to evaluate and clarify their descriptions even further.

Teach

Promoting Discussion

To help students understand the importance of descriptive details, bring in some advertisements from magazines. Students should identify descriptive words and phrases and recognize two uses of description—to focus attention on visual details and to expand on what the photographs show. **L2**

Additional Resources

📘 *Fine Art Transparencies,* 11–14

📘 *Writing Process Transparencies,* 11–13B

📁 *Writing Across the Curriculum,* p. 20

📁 *Cooperative Learning Activities,* pp. 13–18

📁 *Thinking and Study Skills,* pp. 3, 9, 12

📁 *Sentence Combining Practice,* p. 24

📁 *Listening and Speaking Activities,* pp. 14–15

📁 *Composition Practice,* p. 18

Find Descriptions Everywhere

Descriptive words and phrases appear in all kinds of writing. A menu makes a sandwich sound so good that you can almost taste it. A travel brochure takes you to a place where you feel warm breezes, hear crashing waves, and smell the volcanic ash. A clear description of a lost pet leads to its safe return. A story fascinates you with its descriptions of a place or a person.

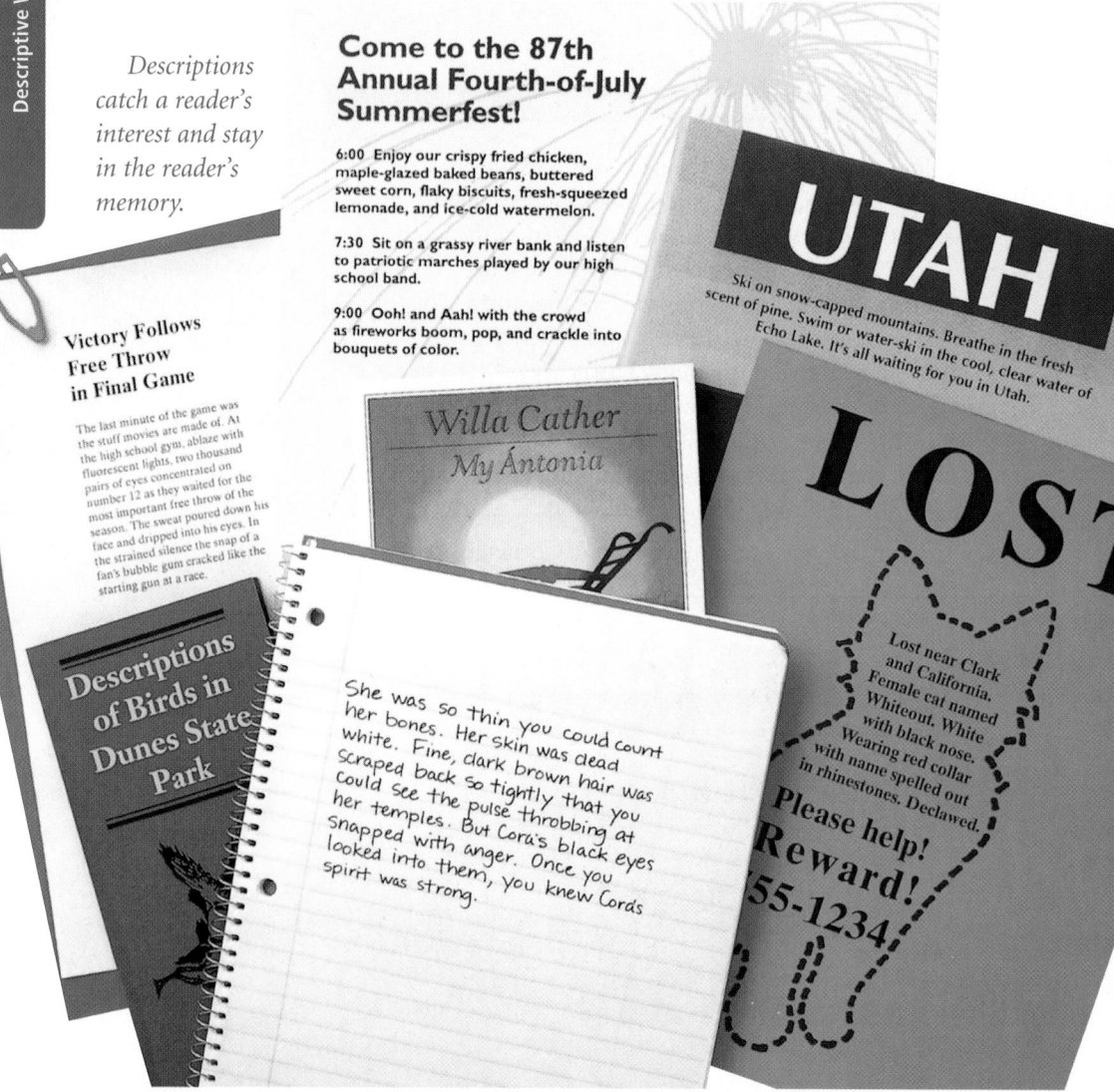

Descriptions catch a reader's interest and stay in the reader's memory.

Come to the 87th Annual Fourth-of-July Summerfest!

6:00 Enjoy our crispy fried chicken, maple-glazed baked beans, buttered sweet corn, flaky biscuits, fresh-squeezed lemonade, and ice-cold watermelon.

7:30 Sit on a grassy river bank and listen to patriotic marches played by our high school band.

9:00 Ooh! and Aah! with the crowd as fireworks boom, pop, and crackle into bouquets of color.

UTAH
Ski on snow-capped mountains. Breathe in the fresh scent of pine. Swim or water-ski in the cool, clear water of Echo Lake. It's all waiting for you in Utah.

Willa Cather
My Ántonia

Victory Follows Free Throw in Final Game

The last minute of the game was the stuff movies are made of. At the high school gym, ablaze with fluorescent lights, two thousand pairs of eyes concentrated on number 12 as they waited for the most important free throw of the season. The sweat poured down his face and dripped into his eyes. In the strained silence the snap of a fan's bubble gum cracked like the starting gun at a race.

Descriptions of Birds in Dunes State Park

She was so thin you could count her bones. Her skin was dead white. Fine, dark brown hair was scraped back so tightly that you could see the pulse throbbing at her temples. But Cora's black eyes snapped with anger. Once you looked into them, you knew Cora's spirit was strong.

LOST
Lost near Clark and California. Female cat named Whiteout. White with black nose. Wearing red collar with name spelled out in rhinestones. Declawed. **Please help! Reward!** 55-1234

MEETING INDIVIDUAL NEEDS

English Language Learners

In Other Words

Students with limited English proficiency may find the prospect of writing detailed, vivid descriptions daunting. If they write another language more fluently than English, they may want to produce a written description in that language first to help them organize and express their thoughts. Then have them use a bilingual dictionary to help create the physical description in English.

Write a Description of an Object

Write a description of a familiar object or animal for someone who is seeing it for the first time. Describe what you see and hear. Choose details that make the description come alive for your reader.

PURPOSE To describe something clearly

AUDIENCE Your classmates

LENGTH 1 paragraph

WRITING RUBRICS To write a descriptive paragraph, you should

- use effective details
- use clear descriptions

Listening and Speaking

DESCRIBING Think of a busy scene at your school, such as a soccer game or lunch in the cafeteria. Orally describe the scene while listeners take note. Express your ideas clearly and fluently. Discuss which of the details you presented made the scene most vivid for your listeners and why.

Cross-Curricular Activity

ART Select a painting in this book. Choose one figure and list details about what the figure looks like. Then write a one-paragraph description of the figure for someone who has not seen the painting.

Grammar Link

Use adverbs to describe verbs.

Adverbs may describe *how, where, when,* or *in what manner* action is done.

*No water murmered so **joyously** or so **sweetly** or so **triumphantly**. . . .*

Write each sentence, adding an adverb to describe the action.

1. She swallowed _____ .
2. They walked _____ .
3. The bicyclist pedaled _____ .
4. The hiker climbed _____ .
5. The door opened _____ .
6. Mr. Jansen glowered _____ .
7. The child staggered _____ .
8. The wind blew _____ .
9. My sister stood _____ .
10. The man in the red convertible drove _____ .

See Lesson 12.6, pages 461–462.

Descriptive Writing

Assess

Evaluation Rubrics

Write a Description of an Object

Use these criteria when evaluating your students' writing. Consider whether the writer

- describes the object or animal as if she or he does not know its name or understand what it does
- compares the object or animal to known objects or animals
- describes features such as shape, size, and color

See also *Writing Assessment and Evaluation Rubrics*

Listening and Speaking

The oral description should
- focus on a busy scene at school
- present the scene with vivid details

Cross-Curricular Activity

The description should
- focus on one of the figures in the painting
- describe it in such a way that someone who has never seen it can visualize it
- include details that appeal to each of the senses

Reteaching

 Composition Reteaching, p. 18

Enrichment

Composition Enrichment, p. 18

Fine Art Transparencies, 11–14

Close

Have students discuss examples of descriptive writing they think are effective. Students can use the items pictured on page 116 as a springboard.

Grammar Link

Answers

Answers will vary, but the following are samples.

1. hastily
2. quickly
3. furiously
4. skillfully
5. slowly
6. angrily
7. unsteadily
8. fiercely
9. proudly
10. madly

Focus

3.2

Lesson Overview

Objectives

- To recall sensory details from experience and to synthesize them into vivid descriptions
- To create and convey an imagined world

Skills

- choosing words for sensory appeal; using sensory language to attract and retain a reader's attention

Critical Thinking

- visualizing; activating prior knowledge; generating new information; decision making

Listening and Speaking

- informal speaking; discussing; explaining a process

Bellringer
Daily Language Activity

When students enter the classroom, have this assignment on the board: *Choose an example of an imaginary creature. Write a description of the creature's appearance—perhaps an unusual arrangement of hooves, wings, feet, and arms.*

Grammar Link to the Bellringer

Have students exchange descriptions, checking to make sure that sentences have end marks and that main clauses in sentences are separated by appropriate punctuation marks.

See also *Daily Language Practice*

Motivating Activity

Have students share their Bellringer activity descriptions with partners. Then invite students to sketch the creature that their partners used words to describe.

Descriptive Writing

LESSON 3.2

Combining Observation and Imagination

*W*hen artists paint and when authors write, they draw on observation and imagination. In Martin Charlot's painting and in Willa Cather's description on the next page, you can feel the power of observation and imagination.

Imagine that you are flying in Charlot's fantasy world. Use your five senses. Look around. Notice the color, movement, and life. Close your eyes, and concentrate on sounds and scents. Touch the plants, the water, the fish, and the fruit. Now you, too, are combining the real and the imaginary.

For more about the writing process, see **TIME** *Facing the Blank Page*, pp. 97–107.

Martin Charlot, *Fruit of the Spirit*, 1983

Resource Manager

 **Planning Resources**
- *Lesson Plans*

Transparencies
- *Bellringer*
- *Daily Language Practice*
- *Fine Art* 11–14
- *Two-Minute Skill Drill*
- *Writing Process* 11–13B

Other Print Resources
- *Composition Enrichment*, p. 19
- *Composition Practice*, p. 19
- *Composition Reteaching* p. 19
- *Cooperative Learning Activities*, pp. 13–18
- *Listening and Speaking Activities*, 14–15
- *Sentence-Combining Practice*, p. 24

- *Thinking and Study Skills*, pp. 3, 9, 12
- *Writing Across the Curriculum*
- *Writing Assessment and Evaluation Rubrics*

Use Sensory Detail

Artists use color, shape, and pattern to pull you into a painting. Writers do the same thing with sensory language—language that appeals to the senses. Sensory language describes how something looks, sounds, feels, smells, or tastes. In the passage below, Willa Cather uses sensory details to pull the reader into a world that smells of strong weeds and where oak groves wilt in the sun. Her strong images pull the reader into another world.

Proofreading Tip

When proofreading, check for periods and other end marks after each sentence. For more information see pages 589–590.

Literature Model

While the train flashed through never-ending miles of ripe wheat, by country towns and bright-flowered pastures and oak groves wilting in the sun, we sat in the observation car, where the woodwork was hot to the touch and red dust lay deep over everything. The dust and heat, the burning wind, reminded us of many things. We were talking about what it is like to spend one's childhood in little towns like these, buried in wheat and corn, under stimulating extremes of climate: burning when one is fairly stifled in vegetation, in the colour and smell of strong weeds and heavy harvests; blustery winters with little snow, when the country is stripped bare and grey as sheet-iron.

Willa Cather, Introduction to *My Ántonia*

To which senses does Willa Cather's language appeal? Give examples.

Journal Writing

Think of a sound you like to hear—maybe a song or the crack of a bat or someone's voice. In your journal list eight or ten words that describe the sound.

Teach

Using the Model

Point out or elicit from students that Willa Cather's writing appeals to the following senses: sight (ripe wheat, country towns, bright-flowered pastures, oak groves wilting, red dust, the colour . . . of strong weeds, the country . . . grey as sheet-iron); touch (the woodwork was hot to the touch, the burning wind); and smell (the smell of strong weeds). Ask students to write briefly of a journey that could be made through their own region. Encourage them to use sensory language in their writing. **L2**

Teaching from the Art

Explain that artist Martin Charlot is known as a careful drafter and a master of color. Discuss Charlot's use of color as a sensory detail in *Fruit of the Spirit* and ask students to list words they think could produce similar effects in writing. **L3**

Two-Minute Skill Drill

Have students write sensory details that appeal to each of the five senses. Examples include *towering walls, clanging bells, rough floors, putrid eggs,* and *ripe bananas.*

See also *Two-Minute Skill Drill Transparency 3.2*

Journal Writing Tip

Vivid Words Suggest that students brainstorm to create a list of sounds and then describe the one for which the most vivid words come to mind.

Viewing the Art

Martin Charlot, *Fruit of the Spirit*, 1983
In this painting, Charlot uses realistic sensory images—fruit, fish, and children against a lush landscape—to create a fantasy. The picture is displayed in the Center Art Gallery in Honolulu, Hawaii.

Teach

Using the Model

Point out that Nikki Housholder takes familiar images—trees, clouds, bushes—and makes them more vivid by adding unusual descriptive words and phrases (waving trees, sagging clouds, furry bushes). Mention that the sensory language in line 4 is different from that in the other lines because *whispering* is the only sound mentioned in the poem. The other sensory language appeals to the senses of sight and movement. Suggest that students work with partners, select something they can see, and make lists of sensory words they think could be used to describe the item. **L2**

Additional Resources

Fine Art Transparencies, 11–14

Writing Process Transparencies, 11–13B

Writing Across the Curriculum, p. 20

Cooperative Learning Activities, pp. 13–18

Thinking and Study Skills, pp. 3, 9, 12

Listening and Speaking Activities, pp. 14–15

Sentence-Combining Practice, p. 24

Composition Practice, p. 19

Descriptive Writing

Use Your Experience and Imagination

You are able to describe people, places, things, and situations because you first perceive the details through your senses. You see that your friend has curly hair. You smell new tar on the street. You can take those details from your own experience and use them in descriptive writing. Nikki Housholder uses this technique in the poem below. She combines ordinary details to create images her readers can share.

> ### Student Model
>
> Waving trees,
>   Dark, lonely days
> Sagging clouds over cold, crawling water,
> Whispering leaves of short, furry bushes,
> Surrounded by falling moonlight above,
> With twinkling eyes spying from the dense darkness,
> Opening the door to freedom.
>
> Nikki Housholder, Oak Creek School
> Cornville, Arizona

How is the sensory language in the fourth line different from that in the other lines?

You can also use your senses to help you describe imaginary things. The illustrator of the animal to the left created a new image by combining real details in unusual ways.

 **Cultural Connections**

Characterizing Creatures

Have students study the drawing on this page. Inform them that it shows a griffin, a mythological creature with the head and wings of an eagle and the body and tail of a lion. Invite students to name and describe other legendary creatures with parts of real creatures, perhaps from the mythology of the countries of their ancestors. Have students state the names of these creatures and present a number of adjectives that describe them.

Write About an Imaginary Place

Write a description of an imaginary place. Use details that appeal to smell, feeling, or sight to describe the place.

PURPOSE To use sensory words in a description
AUDIENCE Your classmates
LENGTH 1 paragraph

WRITING RUBRICS To write a descriptive paragraph about an imaginary place, you should

- use details that describe what you might see, hear, touch, smell, or taste
- draw on your imagination to add detail to your description

Viewing and Representing

COOPERATIVE LEARNING In a group of five people, view the imaginary world pictured on page 118. Look carefully at the picture for two minutes, examining every detail. Then every person in the group should contribute three details that describe the scene. Base the details on one of the five senses: sight, hearing, smell, touch, and taste. Working as a group, combine these details to create a description that includes all the sensory details listed by group members. When your description is complete, share your group's work with the class.

Using Computers

Use the spelling checker option on your computer to check spelling on a final draft. You still have to read the draft for spelling errors, because the computer won't catch all mistakes. To make your description more vivid, compose your descriptive paragraph on the computer. Highlight nouns and decide whether to add adjectives. Then also highlight verbs and decide whether to add adverbs.

Grammar Link

Avoid run-on sentences.

Use main clauses correctly to avoid run-on sentences. Write them as two sentences, use a semicolon between them, or use a comma plus a coordinating conjunction between them.

Rewrite these items to avoid run-ons.

1. The sun beat down on the ripe grain the birds swooped over the fields.
2. Giant waves crashed over the boat, the mast shuddered.
3. Candles sputtered, soft shadows moved across the ceiling.
4. Students clustered in excited knots news buzzed in the air.
5. Outside the snow fell softly, inside the fire crackled cheerfully.

See Lesson 7.2, page 308.

3.2 Combining Observation and Imagination **121**

Assess

Evaluation Rubrics

Write about an Imaginary Place

Use these criteria when evaluating students' writing. Each description should
- contain vivid, precise images that appeal to more than one sense
- reflect the use of both experience and imagination

See also *Writing Assessment and Evaluation Rubrics*

Viewing and Representing

Use these criteria when evaluating the groups' work. Each student should
- begin by focusing on one sense
- work with the group to combine the details to create a complete and logically organized description that fits the picture on page 118

Using Computers

Remind students to be sure to save any revisions or corrections they make to their final drafts.

Reteaching

📁 *Composition Reteaching*, p. 19

Enrichment

📁 *Composition Enrichment*, p. 19

Close

Challenge students to identify and discuss techniques that helped them remember details to create vivid descriptions. Examples include mnemonic devices, visualization, and discussion.

Grammar Link

Answers

Answers will vary, but some suggestions are given below.
1. The sun beat down on the ripe grain; the birds swooped over the fields.
2. Giant waves crashed over the boat, and the mast shuddered.
3. Candles spluttered, and soft shadows moved across the ceiling.
4. Students clustered in excited knots; news buzzed in the air.
5. Outside the snow fell softly; inside the fire crackled cheerfully.

Focus

Descriptive Writing

Lesson Overview

Objectives

- To understand how details create a mood
- To create a mood in descriptive writing through the use of appropriate details

Skills

- choosing words to create a mood; analyzing words to determine the mood

Critical Thinking

- visualizing; activating prior knowledge; comparing and contrasting; recalling; relating; decision making

Listening and Speaking

- informal speaking; discussing; explaining a process

Bellringer
Daily Language Activity

When students enter the classroom, have this assignment on the board: *Imagine you are an author looking for an eerie setting for a story. Make a list of places you might choose.*

Grammar Link to the Bellringer

Have students brainstorm and write a list of adjectives to describe the place they chose to describe.

See also *Daily Language Practice*

Motivating Activity

Invite students to share their responses from the Bellringer activity. Elicit from students details they would use in describing the eerie settings they choose. Write those details on the board.

LESSON
3.3

Choosing Details to Create a Mood

*W*riters choose details that create a mood. A cave shimmering with sparkling columns sounds inviting. A dark cave where bats flitter seems eerie.

Imagine entering the cave in the picture, and think about how it feels to be there. List a few details you would use to describe the picture so others could share your feelings.

In the model below, Susan Cooper chooses details that make a cave seem threatening. These details help the reader to share Barney's feelings about the cave in the cliff called Kenmare Head.

> Why is the sound of Barney's whispered greeting an effective detail?

Literature Model

*H*allo," Barney said tentatively into the darkness. His voice whispered back at him in a sinister, eerie way: not booming and reverberating round as it had in the narrow tunnel-like cave they had come through, but muttering far away, high in the air. Barney swung round in a circle, vainly peering into the dark. The space round him must be as big as a house—and yet he was in the depths of Kenmare Head.

Susan Cooper, *Over Sea, Under Stone*

122 Unit 3 Descriptive Writing

Resource Manager

📁 Planning Resources
- *Lesson Plans*

🖥 Transparencies
- *Bellringer*
- *Daily Language Practice*
- *Fine Art* 11–14
- *Two-Minute Skill Drill*
- *Writing Process* 11–13B

📁 Other Print Resources
- *Composition Enrichment*, p. 20
- *Composition Practice*, p. 20
- *Composition Reteaching*, p. 20
- *Cooperative Learning Activities*, pp. 13–18
- *Listening and Speaking Activities*, pp. 14–15
- *Sentence-Combining Practice*, p. 24

- *Thinking and Study Skills*, pp. 3–5, 9
- *Writing Across the Curriculum*
- *Writing Assessment and Evaluation Rubrics*

Use Details That Create a Mood

The details included in the literature model do more than help describe a scene. They also create a mood, or feeling. The cave, which you experience through Barney's senses, seems eerie and sinister. The writer wants you to understand that Barney feels frightened and a little desperate.

If Barney were exploring this cave for fun, he would probably have different feelings about it. The writer would select different details to show a different mood. Look at the notes below. What would the mood of the passage on page 122 be if the writer had used details such as these?

Grammar Tip

Adjectives help make a description more effective. Adjectives modify nouns. For more information see pages 451–452.

Mood Details

○ *spectacular colors and formations*

air-conditioned by nature

a mysterious bottomless pit

fascinating shadows dancing in the dim light

friendly echoes talking back

Journal Writing

Think of a place you have been that inspires a mood. In your journal make a list of mood details like the list above. Then write a brief description that creates the mood suggested by the details you wrote.

Teach

Using the Model

Elicit from students that Barney's tentative greeting implies he is afraid of being heard—but afraid of whom or what the reader cannot know. The echo whispering back reveals that the cave is a vast space. All of these details help create a mood of suspense. Ask students to list additional sounds they think would create suspense. **L2**

Analyzing Emotions

When students think about being in a cave, what emotions are triggered? Suggest they analyze and discuss the processes that produce those emotions. Do they have any actual memories of being in a cave? Are they influenced by images of caves they have read about or seen in movies? **L2**

Two-Minute Skill Drill

Have students generate lists of details about a hot summer day that create (1) a pleasant mood and (2) an unpleasant mood.

See also Two-Minute Skill Drill Transparency 3.3

Journal Writing Tip

Activating Prior Knowledge This activity requires students to gain access to knowledge that may be lying dormant in their memories. As students recall various images, tell them to be aware of the moods or emotions that accompany those memories. Then they can begin listing specific mood details.

Teach

Using the Model

Ask students to identify the words and phrases that intensify the mood set in the passage by Bryce Stoker (*squirm, skin begins to crawl, get nervous, sweat, breathing and pulse go wild*). Suggest that each student use one or more of these or similar details in a short paragraph describing a real or an imaginary situation. **L2**

Promoting Discussion

Filmmakers, like writers, need to create mood. Ask students to look again at the scene in a cave and the scene of a cold but sunny day. What details might a filmmaker use to present each of these scenes in a positive, upbeat way? What details might the filmmaker use to create an unpleasant or frightening mood when showing the same scenes? Encourage students to think of auditory as well as visual details. **L3**

Additional Resources

Fine Art Transparencies, 11–14

Writing Process Transparencies, 11–13B

Writing Across the Curriculum, p. 20

Cooperative Learning Activities, pp. 13–18

Thinking and Study Skills, pp. 3–5, 9

Listening and Speaking Activities, pp. 14–15

Composition Practice, p. 20

Sentence-Combining Practice, p. 24

Descriptive Writing

crisp, powdery snow

frostbitten ears

slushy, slippery sidewalks

biting wind

healthful exercise

sparkling sunlight

heavy, wet clothes

brilliant blue sky

Choose Words to Bring a Scene to Life

When you describe a scene, the words you choose set the mood and bring the scene to life for your reader. Try it out. Suppose you are describing a cold winter day. Select one of the photos shown below. Find details in the list that help create a cheerful or unpleasant mood. Then read Bryce Stoker's description of a personal experience. Notice his use of striking, specific words that bring details to life and create a mood.

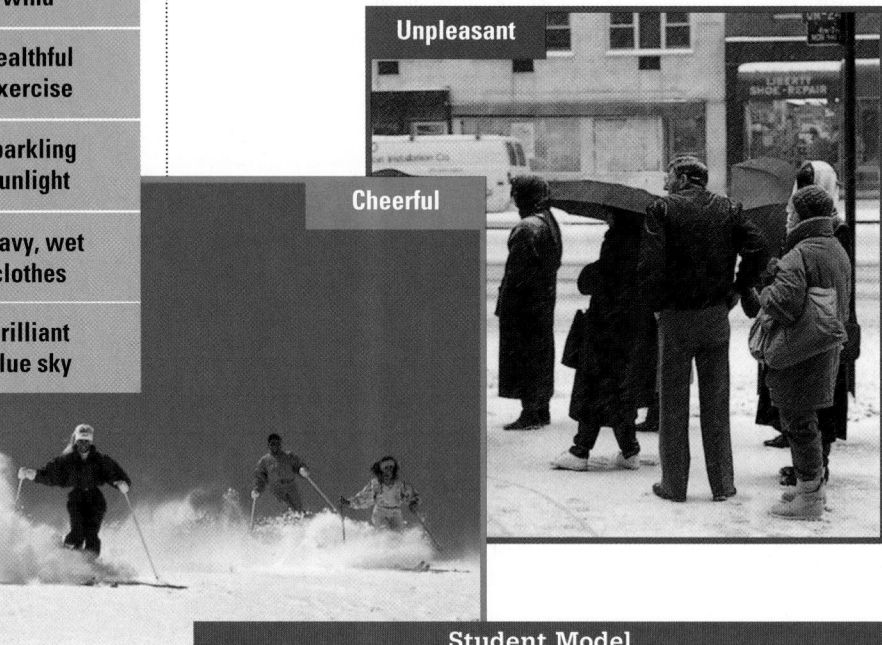

Unpleasant

Cheerful

Student Model

Which phrases tell the reader how Bryce reacts to the attic visit?

One of the worst places I've been in is the attic. Whenever I'm told to go get something from the attic, I try to squirm my way out of it. When I can't get out of it, my skin begins to crawl, I get nervous and start to sweat while ascending the stairs, and my breathing and pulse go wild when I reach the trapdoor to the attic.

Bryce Stoker, Frontier School
Moses Lake, Washington

124 Unit 3 Descriptive Writing

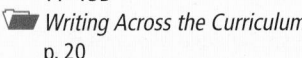

English Language Learners

Communicating Mood

Ask each student to bring in a photograph of a place he or she knows well, or show students a picture of a place that is familiar to them. Tell them to imagine they are there. What do they see, hear, feel, taste, and smell? In small groups or individually, allow them to pantomime their responses. Then help students use a bilingual dictionary to make a list of the details. Point to each detail and ask how it makes them feel. Allow students to pantomime their responses.

Write a Descriptive Paragraph

Write a description of a place where people are usually happy. The place might be a beach, an amusement park, or a street fair. Imagine that you are walking through this place. As you imagine your walk, take notes on the details that set the mood. Write a draft of your description. Then revise your description, adding other words and details that strengthen the mood. Read your paragraph to a classmate and have him or her identify the mood.

PURPOSE To create a mood in a description
AUDIENCE Your classmates
LENGTH 1 paragraph

WRITING RUBRICS To create a mood in a descriptive paragraph, you should

- select details that help create the mood
- choose striking, specific words to set the mood

Using Computers

Check to see if your word processing program has an electronic thesaurus. As you revise your description, use the thesaurus to find words that strengthen the mood you want to create.

Grammar Link

Use adjectives to create a mood.

Write each sentence twice, once with an adjective that creates a positive mood, and once with an adjective that creates a negative mood.

1. He decided to investigate the _____ sounds coming from next door.
2. She touched the _____ fabric with a/an _____ hand.
3. I watched the fish moving in the _____ water.
4. She woke up from the _____ dream.
5. The path stretched into the _____ woods.

See Lesson 12.1, page 451.

Listening and Speaking

COOPERATIVE LEARNING Divide into groups of four. In a container, place slips of paper labeled *sad, angry, happy,* and *scared*. Make sure each student picks one slip. Take turns orally describing a place, choosing sensory details to create the mood. Have listeners add more details to help strengthen the mood.

Assess

Evaluation Rubrics

Write a Descriptive Paragraph

Use these criteria when evaluating a student's writing.
- The description includes a variety of sensory details.
- It suggests an appealing overall mood.
- The student uses specific, vivid words to set the mood.

See also *Writing Assessment and Evaluation Rubrics*

Using Computers

Remind students that they can use the Cut and Paste functions on a word processor to rearrange descriptive details within a sentence.

Listening and Speaking

Use these criteria to evaluate students' descriptions. Each student should
- focus on a single place
- use sensory details related only to the mood on his or her slip of paper
- combine the details to create an organized description

Reteaching

📁 *Composition Reteaching,* p. 20

Enrichment

📁 *Composition Enrichment,* p. 20

Close

Ask students to select two details that they think will work together to create a mood. Have them write three or four descriptive sentences using the details that they chose. Partners can exchange descriptions and identify the mood.

Grammar Link

Answers
Answers will vary, but some suggestions are given below.
1. cheerful, suspicious
2. soft, wondering; torn, trembling
3. babbling, murky
4. magical, chilling
5. green, impenetrable

Focus

Lesson Overview

Objectives·
- To present details in spatial order when describing a scene
- To use transition words and phrases to show relationships between details

Skills
- ordering spatial details; choosing transition words and phrases to clarify descriptions

Critical Thinking
- recalling; relating; visualizing; activating prior knowledge; comparing and contrasting; evaluating

Listening and Speaking
- informal speaking; discussing

Bellringer
Daily Language Activity

When students enter the classroom, have this assignment on the board: *Write a description of an interesting-looking building. Order the details from bottom to top or in an order of your choice.*

Grammar Link to the Bellringer

Have students add prepositional phrases to their descriptions.

See also *Daily Language Practice*

Motivating Activity

Invite students to share the descriptions they wrote in the Bellringer activity. Elicit from students additional details that would help someone picture the buildings. Are the details effectively ordered?

Descriptive Writing

Organizing Details in a Description

When you view a scene, your brain organizes what you see. In written descriptions, writers must organize information for the reader.

Imagine you are a radio reporter covering a hot-air-balloon festival. Your listeners cannot see the brightly colored balloons. How could you describe the scene, including the position of each balloon?

In the model below, Scott O'Dell creates a clear picture in your mind. He does so by ordering details so that you know just where Rontu is in relation to the wild dogs.

> ### Literature Model
>
> On this mound, among the grasses and the plants, stood Rontu. He stood facing me, with his back to the sea cliff. In front of him in a half-circle were the wild dogs. At first I thought that the pack had driven him there against the cliff and were getting ready to attack him. But I soon saw that two dogs stood out from the rest of the pack, between it and Rontu. . . .
>
> Scott O'Dell, *Island of the Blue Dolphins*

Why might the position of the dogs in relation to Rontu be important in this scene?

Resource Manager

📂 Planning Resources
- *Lesson Plans*

📑 Transparencies
- *Bellringer*
- *Daily Language Practice*
- *Fine Art* 11–14
- *Two-Minute Skill Drill*
- *Writing Process* 11–13B

📂 Other Print Resources
- *Composition Enrichment*, p. 21
- *Composition Practice*, p. 21
- *Composition Reteaching*, p. 21
- *Cooperative Learning Activities*, pp. 13–18
- *Listening and Speaking Activities*, 14–15
- *Thinking and Study Skills*, pp. 3–5, 9, 21–22

- *Writing Across the Curriculum*
- *Writing Assessment and Evaluation Rubrics*

Arrange Details to Suit Your Purpose

You can present details in various ways to give your reader a mental picture of a scene. Think about the location of each object and where it is in relation to other objects. How you describe them depends on your purpose. Describing a sky-scraper from bottom to top emphasizes the building's height. A description of the Grand Canyon might show details in the order a descending hiker sees them.

The pictures below show three ways that details might be ordered to describe the photograph on page 126. Which order do you think would be most effective?

Prewriting Tip

During the prewriting phase for a description, think about the best order to present details.

Top

Bottom

Far

Near

Left ←——————→ Right

Journal Writing

In your journal describe a room at home or at school. Where is each important object? Where is it in relation to other objects? What kind of order works best to present your description?

Teach

Using the Model

To help students picture the arrangement of the various figures in this description, have them sketch a simple diagram showing the cliff, Rontu, the pack of dogs, the two dogs that are separate from the pack, and the narrator. Have students compare their diagrams. (The position of the dogs in relation to Rontu is important because it indicates to the reader that two of the dogs are defending Rontu by coming between him and danger.) **L2**

Organizing Tips

Have students look at the classroom and select several ways to order the details in a description. (Go from the front of the classroom to the back, from one group of seats to the next, from the periphery of the room to the center, or from one student gradually outward.) What would be the effect of each approach? Suggest an unusual approach—moving from the ceiling of the classroom down to students' heads, desktops, and feet. Why might a writer organize a description this way? **L1**

Two-Minute Skill Drill

Have students note two ways to arrange details in describing a tree. (Sample: top to bottom, in order of proximity to their point of observation)

See also *Two-Minute Skill Drill Transparency 3.4*

Journal Writing Tip

Organizing Details Suggest that before students write, they think of what they want to focus on in the room. What kind of an "atmosphere" do they want to create? They can order their details accordingly.

Teach

Using the Model

Ask students what is significant about the fact that the author presented the school building first and then described other objects in relation to it. (By doing this, she makes it clear that the school is central to the scene.) Call attention to the fact that key transition words occur at the beginnings of sentences. **L2**

Heightening Descriptions

Working in pairs, students can find and list more sophisticated transition words and phrases, such as *on the surface, beneath the water, in the distance,* or *in the foreground.* Students may enjoy writing more complex descriptions that emphasize spatial relationships. **L3**

Additional Resources

 Fine Art Transparencies, 11–14

Writing Process Transparencies, 11–13B

Writing Across the Curriculum, p. 20

Cooperative Learning Activities, pp. 13–18

Thinking and Study Skills, pp. 3–5, 9, 21–22

Sentence-Combining Practice, p. 24

Listening and Speaking Activities, pp. 14–15

Composition Practice, p. 21

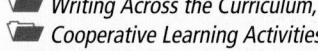

Descriptive Writing

Use Transitions to Show Relationships

Transition words and phrases help show how each detail in a description relates to the others. Look at the photograph and the phrases at the left. How can you use these transitions to answer such questions as *Where is the diving platform in relation to the trees?* and *Where is the falling boy in relation to the other boys?* Read the literature model below to see how Mildred Taylor uses transition words and phrases to describe a scene clearly.

In front of
Behind
To the right of
Next to

The school building is presented first. Then the writer describes objects in relation to it.

How do the transition words connect the details?

Literature Model

They were headed for the Jefferson Davis County School, a long white wooden building looming in the distance. **Behind** the building was a wide sports field around which were scattered rows of tiered gray-looking benches. **In front of** it were two yellow buses, our own tormentor and one that brought students from the other direction, and loitering students awaiting the knell of the morning bell. **In the very center** of the expansive front lawn, waving red, white, and blue . . . was the Mississippi flag. **Directly below** it was the American flag.

Mildred D. Taylor, *Roll of Thunder, Hear My Cry*

---

128   Unit 3 Descriptive Writing

Cooperative Learning

Discerning Meaning

Students who have trouble understanding transition words may benefit from working with partners to review the meanings of common transition words and phrases, such as *in front of, to the right,* and *behind.* Have students use the words to describe the relationships of people or objects in magazine pictures. Then have them write captions for the pictures. Their partners can help answer questions they have or can point out usage errors.

Write a Painting Description

Select a painting from this book. Imagine that this painting has been stolen from the museum and you need to describe the painting to the police. Your description needs to be so clear that the detectives will recognize the painting immediately.

PURPOSE To describe a missing painting
AUDIENCE Police detectives
LENGTH 1 paragraph

WRITING RUBRICS To create a vivid description, you should

- present details in a logical order
- use transition words to show how details relate to one another

Viewing and Representing

COOPERATIVE LEARNING Draw a picture of a group of related objects, such as different kinds of tropical fish or items that make up a lunch. Trade drawings with a partner. Write a caption, using words such as *on the far right*, *next to*, and *in front of* to describe the order of the details. Work together to improve your captions.

Cross-Curricular Activity

MATHEMATICS Draw a design using geometric shapes such as triangles, rectangles, and circles. Write a description of your design, using transition words to show where shapes are on the page and in relation to one another. Test your description's accuracy by asking a classmate to re-create your design after reading the description.

Grammar Link

Use prepositional phrases to show position.

Phrases like *in front of* and *next to* can help readers picture a location. He stood facing me, **with his back to the sea cliff.**

Add a prepositional phrase to each sentence below.

1. The architect decided to put the stairway _____ .
2. The old barn was located _____ .
3. At the accident scene the police officer directed traffic _____ .
4. Ready to spring, the panther crouched _____ .
5. _____ we paused to check the map.

See Lesson 13.3, page 483.

3.4 Organizing Details in a Description **129**

Assess

Evaluation Rubrics

Write a Painting Description

Use these criteria when evaluating a student's writing:

- The student describes significant details from the painting.
- The student uses transition words to indicate spatial relationships.

See also *Writing Assessment and Evaluation Rubrics*

Viewing and Representing

Use these criteria to evaluate a student's captioned drawing:

- The caption uses words that describe the location of each object.
- The location of each object is described accurately.

Cross-Curricular Activity

When evaluating a student's writing, refer to both the design and the accompanying description.

- The design contains a number of geometric shapes.
- The description identifies all elements in the design.
- Transition words are used clearly and consistently.

Reteaching

Composition Reteaching, p. 21

Enrichment

Composition Enrichment, p. 21

Fine Art Transparencies, 11–14

Close

Have students work in pairs. Tell them to take turns demonstrating the use of spatial order by describing a real or an imaginary item. Then using the description, partners can sketch the item.

Grammar Link

Answers

Answers will vary, but the following are samples.
1. against the wall
2. across a field
3. around the wreck
4. in a tree
5. Beside the car

Focus

Lesson Overview

Objectives

- To explore attributes of description that make characters memorable
- To communicate the essence of a character by describing the individual's appearance and behavior

Skills

- analyzing techniques used to create memorable characters; selecting and arranging details to create memorable characters

Critical Thinking

- recalling; relating; visualizing; inferring; analyzing

Listening and Speaking

- informal speaking; discussing

 Bellringer

Daily Language Activity

When students enter the classroom, have this assignment on the board: *Write the name of a memorable fictional character. List things that come to mind when you think about this character.*

Grammar Link to the Bellringer

Have students use the information they wrote in the Bellringer activity to write one or two sentences about their characters. Tell them to use at least one pronoun. Have students exchange sentences with partners and check for clear antecedents.

See also *Daily Language Practice*

Motivating Activity

Have each student write a description of a character other students will know. Have students exchange papers and try to identify the characters on the basis of each other's description.

Descriptive Writing

Describing a Person

*L*ike a jigsaw puzzle, a character is made up of pieces. Each piece is a detail: hair color, body shape, or the way a character smiles. Put together, these pieces make a complete picture.

In most puzzles the pieces fit together in only one way. However, you can mix and match details in endless ways when you set out to create a character in writing.

130 Unit 3 Descriptive Writing

Resource Manager

Planning Resources
- *Lesson Plans*

Transparencies
- *Bellringer*
- *Daily Language Practice*
- *Fine Art* 11–14
- *Two-Minute Skill Drill*
- *Writing Process* 11–13B

Other Print Resources
- *Composition Enrichment*, p. 22
- *Composition Practice*, p. 22
- *Composition Reteaching*, p. 22
- *Cooperative Learning Activities*, pp. 13–18
- *Listening and Speaking Activities*, 14–15
- *Sentence-Combining Practice*, p. 24

- *Thinking and Study Skills*, pp. 3–5, 9, 12, 17
- *Writing Across the Curriculum*
- *Writing Assessment and Evaluation Rubrics*

Show How the Character Looks

Begin your description of a character by picturing that person in your mind. Which details will help readers see the character? Choose the words and the order that fit your purpose.

In the following passage, Amy Tan looks at a picture of her mother, taken long ago. She describes the way her mother appears in that picture.

> The speaker says that her mother looks "displaced." What is she wearing that supports this adjective?

Descriptive Writing

Literature Model

In this picture you can see why my mother looks displaced. She is clutching a large clam-shaped bag, as though someone might steal this from her as well if she is less watchful. She has on an ankle-length Chinese dress with modest vents at the side. And on top she is wearing a Westernized suit jacket, awkwardly stylish on my mother's small body, with its padded shoulders, wide lapels, and oversize cloth buttons. This was my mother's wedding dress, a gift from my father. In this outfit she looks as if she were neither coming from nor going to someplace. Her chin is bent down and you can see the precise part in her hair, a neat white line drawn from above her left brow then over the black horizon of her head.

Amy Tan, *The Joy Luck Club*

Journal Writing

Visualize several of the most memorable people you've known. In your journal list five or six details someone else would notice first about them.

Teach

Using the Model

Elicit from students that in this passage, Amy Tan used vivid sensory details to help the reader visualize her mother. Have students identify some of those details. Then list three or four pairs of phrases and ask students to write brief one- or two-sentence descriptions based on them. Possible pairs include *wide eyes* and *a serious look; a big grin* and *mussed hair; a blank stare* and *tears.* **L2**

Identifying by Description

Invite students to think about some memorable fictional characters. What comes to mind when they visualize these characters? Explain that authors often observe real people carefully, then combine bits and pieces of their observations when describing fictional characters. Have students work in groups, choosing characteristics of one another to create fictional characters. Groups can share their character descriptions with the class. **L2**

Two-Minute Skill Drill

Have students list all the adjectives in the model.

See also *Two-Minute Skill Drill Transparency 3.5*

Journal Writing Tip

Gathering information Encourage students to actively visualize the people first and then write the details they will include in their journal entries.

Teach

Using the Model

After students have read the model, have them tell in their own words what they think Andy is like. Have them identify the details that created that impression. What kinds of things can't they tell about Andy from the written description? **L2**

Promoting Discussion

Ask students if they have ever seen a celebrity in magazine or newspaper photographs and then seen the same person on television. Were they surprised? Did the celebrity's voice, personality, or mannerisms create a different impression than the photograph? Elicit that it is important to include details that describe more than just physical appearance when fleshing out a character in writing. Invite students to think of some words that could tell about a character's voice (harsh, lilting), personality (friendly, cool), or mannerisms (fidgety, assertive). **L3**

Additional Resources

 Fine Art Transparencies, 11–14

 Writing Process Transparencies, 11–13 B

Writing Across the Curriculum, p. 20

Cooperative Learning Activities, pp. 13–18

Thinking and Study Skills, pp. 3–5, 9, 12, 17

Listening and Speaking Activities, pp. 14–15

Sentence-Combining Practice, p. 24

Composition Practice, p. 22

Descriptive Writing

Grammar Tip

A pronoun must agree in number, gender, and person with its antecedent, the person, place, or thing to which it refers. See pages 431–432.

Show How the Character Acts

We decide what a person is like by judging what he or she does. One way we learn about people is to observe them in action, especially when their actions involve other people.

A writer can reveal a character's personality by showing how the character interacts with others. In the draft below, a writer begins to fill out the character visualized on page 131. Instead of simply telling readers what Andy looks like, the writer shows how Andy behaves at a skateboarding park. What does Andy's treatment of other people say about him?

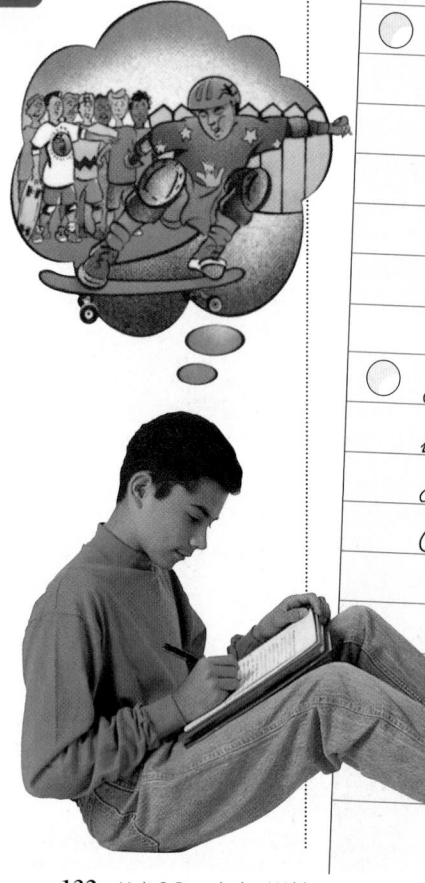

When Cameron lost his board on a jump, Andy laughed. "Hey Cameron! Why don't you give up? My little sister can do that move better. Maybe you should come back during the little kids' hours, and she can help you." Ignoring Andy, Cameron retrieved his skateboard and limped to the end of the waiting line.

When Andy got onto the skateboarding course, he showed off his best stunts. Satisfied that he was again the center of attention, he called over his shoulder, "Look! Here's how Cameron skates the course!"

Andy made quite a show of waving his arms for balance, taking curves slowly, and failing to make it to the top of hills. The other kids couldn't help laughing at his imitation.

132 Unit 3 Descriptive Writing

MEETING INDIVIDUAL NEEDS — English Language Learners

Making Observations

Before trying to visualize and describe imaginary characters, students may need practice using English to describe actual people. List a number of characteristics on the board, such as *hair color, hair texture, eye color, eye shape,* and *height.* Ask students to think of a close friend or relative and try to provide some descriptive details for each heading. Then ask them to add other important details.

Write a Character Description

Write a description of a shoemaker. Use details from your imagination that will show the reader who this shoemaker is.

PURPOSE To describe a person's appearance and actions

AUDIENCE Your teacher and classmates

LENGTH 2 paragraphs

WRITING RUBRICS To write a character description, you should

- describe how the character looks
- describe how the character acts

Viewing and Representing

COOPERATIVE LEARNING With a partner, find several versions of Mark Twain's *The Adventures of Tom Sawyer.* How does each illustrator picture Tom Sawyer? Considering each illustrator's work, discuss what the character is like and how he looks. How does your impression of the character change as you view different illustrator's pictures?

Using Computers

If you have access to a computer at home or at school, use it to complete the character description writing activity. The cut-and-paste option can help you revise the order of your details for clarity and impact. The editing functions will help you make corrections when editing your writing.

Grammar Link

Pronouns must have clear antecedents.

An *antecedent* is the noun referred to by a pronoun.

*When **Cameron** lost **his** board . . .*

Revise each sentence below to make the antecedent clear.

1. Ms. Lee told Amy that she liked her description.
2. The boys threw stones at the birds, but they did not hit them.
3. The girls put the worms in a box so that they would stay healthy.
4. When the car hit the truck, it exploded.
5. After Mr. North gave Jim an apple, he smiled.

See Lesson 11.2, page 431.

Assess

Evaluation Rubrics

Write a Character Description

Use these criteria when evaluating students' writing. Character descriptions should
- list concrete visual details
- draw conclusions about the cobbler's character from those details

See also *Writing Assessment and Evaluation Rubrics*

Viewing and Representing

Students' discussions should
- point out differences in details used to picture Tom Sawyer
- explain how the differences affect their impressions of the character

Reteaching

📁 *Composition Reteaching, p. 22*

Enrichment

📁 *Composition Enrichment, p. 22*

🖎 *Fine Art Transparencies, 11–14*

Close

Discuss with students the value of keeping a writer's notebook with them wherever they go. For example, they can jot down descriptions of interesting faces, walks, voices, and other details of the people they see on buses, in restaurants, and in malls. Eventually they can use this raw material to enrich their writing by making their fictional characters come to life.

Grammar Link

Answers

Answers will vary. Samples are given.
1. Ms. Lee told Amy that she liked Amy's description.
2. The boys threw stones at the birds but did not hit any of the birds.
3. So that the worms would stay healthy, the girls put them in a box.
4. The truck exploded when the car hit it.
5. Jim smiled after Mr. North gave him an apple.

Focus

Lesson Overview

Objectives

- To identify and analyze links between poetry and experience
- To use sensory images to describe familiar experiences

Skills

- relating poetry and experience; creating sensory images for a poem

Critical Thinking

- recalling; relating; visualizing; categorizing; analyzing

Listening and Speaking

- asking questions; informal speaking; discussing

 Bellringer

Daily Language Activity

When students enter the classroom, have this assignment on the board: *Write one or two opening lines for a poem you may wish to finish later.*

Grammar Link to the Bellringer

Have students revise their opening lines, adding a word (appositive) to identify or give more information about a noun.

See also *Daily Language Practice*

Motivating Activity

Discuss with students the feeling that comes from entering the world of a poem and finding familiar emotions and experiences. Point out that students can experience a similar feeling of satisfaction by creating their own poems. (You may wish to remind students that song lyrics are one type of poetry.)

Descriptive Writing

LESSON 3.6

WRITING ABOUT LITERATURE

Relating a Poem to Your Experience

Poets are artists who share their thoughts and experiences by using words to draw mental pictures. Putting yourself into the picture makes a poem meaningful to you.

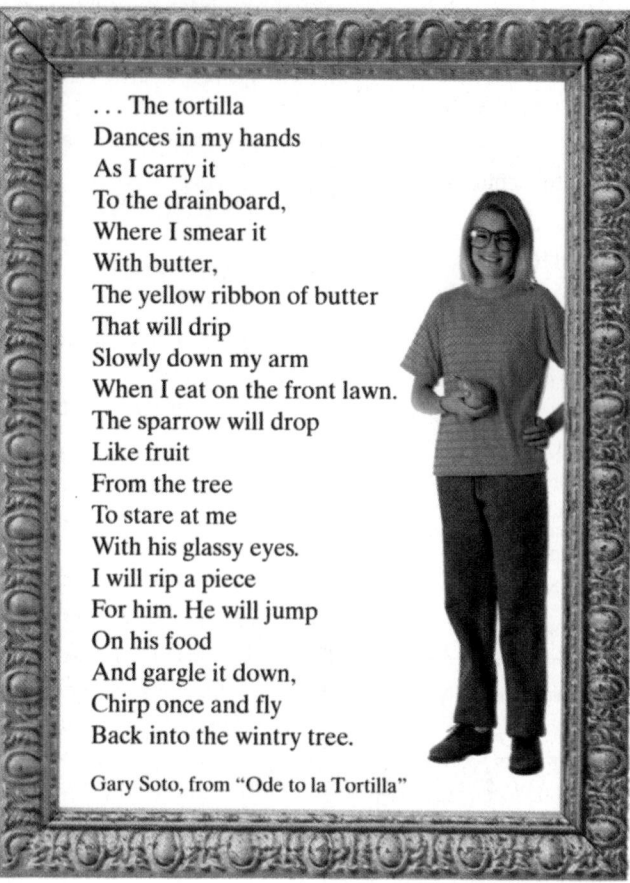

. . . The tortilla
Dances in my hands
As I carry it
To the drainboard,
Where I smear it
With butter,
The yellow ribbon of butter
That will drip
Slowly down my arm
When I eat on the front lawn.
The sparrow will drop
Like fruit
From the tree
To stare at me
With his glassy eyes.
I will rip a piece
For him. He will jump
On his food
And gargle it down,
Chirp once and fly
Back into the wintry tree.

Gary Soto, from "Ode to la Tortilla"

In the poem at the left, Gary Soto uses sensory details to capture an ordinary experience and share it with the reader. As you read the poem, try to see, hear, feel, taste, and smell the things that Gary Soto describes.

134   Unit 3 Descriptive Writing

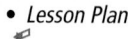
Resource Manager

📁 Planning Resources
- *Lesson Plans*

🖥 Transparencies
- *Bellringer*
- *Daily Language Practice*
- *Fine Art* 11–14
- *Two-Minute Skill Drill*
- *Writing Process* 11–13B

📁 Other Print Resources
- *Composition Enrichment,* p. 23
- *Composition Practice,* p. 23
- *Composition Reteaching,* p. 23
- *Cooperative Learning Activities,* pp. 13–18
- *Listening and Speaking Activities,* 14–15
- *Sentence-Combining Practice,* p. 24

- *Thinking and Study Skills,* pp. 3–6, 8, 12, 22
- *Writing Across the Curriculum*
- *Writing Assessment and Evaluation Rubrics*

Experience the Poem

Poets often use sensory language to share an impression. Gary Soto lets you feel what he probably feels as he prepares and eats a tortilla. You can experience "The yellow ribbon of butter / That will drip / Slowly down my arm . . ."

To understand a poem, relate it to what you already know. Recalling your own experience may help you understand how the poet feels as he prepares and eats the tortilla.

Journal Writing

Think of an experience you have had that "Ode to la Tortilla" reminds you of. In your journal, use a graphic organizer to list sensory details describing the experience.

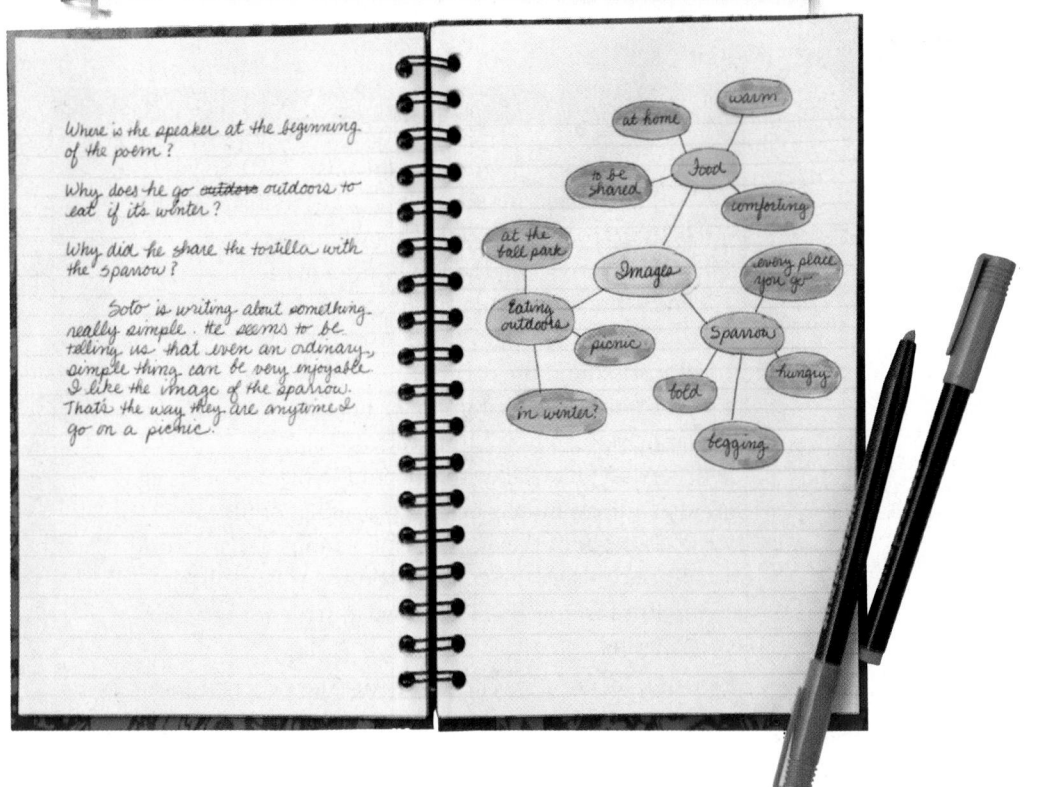

Teach

Using the Model

An ode is a long, serious poem often written in praise of something. (Odes have been written to the west wind, to duty, and to soldiers who have fallen in war, for example.) Can students see the humor in writing an ode to a tortilla? Can they also see that Soto's poem is a serious poem of praise, even though it has an ordinary subject? Ask students for suggestions for odes to ordinary objects. **L2**

Thinking Visually

The notebook, with questions, comments, and a cluster diagram, exhibits several techniques students may adapt to their own needs as they take notes and write in journals and learning logs. Discuss why the writer of the notes might have included questions and what answers he or she might arrive at. Point out the writer's comment and ask students if they responded in a like way to the image of the sparrow. **L2**

Two-Minute Skill Drill

Have students write the subjects and verbs in the three questions listed in the notebook.

Answer: speaker (subj.) is (v.), he (subj.) does go (v.), he (subj.) did share (v.)

See also *Two-Minute Skill Drill Transparency 3.6*

Journal Writing Tip

Identifying Relationships Point out that "Ode to la Tortilla" describes not only the sensations of eating the tortilla but also the circumstances in which it was eaten. Suggest that students consider the context of the experience they want to describe.

Teach

Reacting to Poetry

In small groups, students can react to "Day-dreams" by discussing ideas for similar poems of their own. They may wish to question one another about aspects of their lives that they would like to capture in poetry. Encourage them to jot down notes in their journals for future inspiration. **L2**

Building Writing Confidence

Some students may still feel that poetry is written only about special or intense experiences. Ask these students to keep a journal of all their activities over a day or two. Then ask them to jot down a few sensory images related to each experience, such as the sound a bagel makes when popping out of the toaster or the way the big yellow school bus looms suddenly around the corner in the morning. Encourage students to write a poem constructed from images such as these. **L1**

Additional Resources

- *Fine Art Transparencies*, 11–14
- *Writing Process Transparencies*, 11–13B
- *Writing Across the Curriculum*, p. 20
- *Cooperative Learning Activities*, pp. 13–18
- *Thinking and Study Skills*, pp. 3–6, 8, 12, 22
- *Sentence-Combining Practice*, p. 24
- *Listening and Speaking Activities*, pp. 14–15
- *Composition Practice*, p. 23

Descriptive Writing

Prewriting Tip

You could respond to a poem in the form of a poster. Decorate your poster with pictures, colors, or shapes that help communicate your thoughts and feelings to your audience.

Notice that Willow names ordinary things in each line of her poem.

In which lines of the poem did the writer surprise you by combining unlike things?

Respond to the Poem

You can respond to a poem in many different ways. One way is by telling the writer how the poem matches your own experiences. You can write your ideas in your journal or in a letter. Even better, you can create a poem of your own. Think about ordinary things in your life, things you enjoy or want to do. Are they like the ordinary things Soto writes about? Are they like the ordinary things in the poem below by Willow Star Wright?

Student Model

Daydreams

I am a ballerina who strives to be a doctor in the delivery room of a widely known hospital.

I like boys, and the fish in my aquarium are gold and swim around plastic, purple and green seaweed.

I hear people cheering, wasps buzzing and summer is just around the corner.

I want to go swimming or horseback riding on a large Arabian horse from the oasis.

I don't like fall or this poem I wrote moments ago that will eventually be put into a final draft.

I dream of the day when all nations declare world peace or when the guy I like finds out I am alive.

But for now I will just have to settle for being a ballerina.

Willow Star Wright, Oak Creek School
Cornville, Arizona

136 Unit 3 Descriptive Writing

MEETING INDIVIDUAL NEEDS

Less-Proficient Readers

Building Vocabulary

Less-proficient readers may be reluctant classroom poets. Emphasize that poetry may be about everyday experiences. Ask students to talk in a group about an experience they have shared recently involving ordinary objects. For example, they might discuss lunch in the cafeteria on a certain day. Was the food hot, cold, crunchy, smooth? Ask a volunteer to sketch a picture of each food item. Challenge students to label the pictures with descriptive words. Students may use these words in poems about food.

Write a Poem

Reread "Ode to la Tortilla" and "Daydreams." Then write a poem describing an experience of your own. Choose an ordinary experience, possibly one from your writing journal. List sensory words or phrases that describe this experience. Write your poem, using details from your list.

PURPOSE To write a poem describing a personal experience

AUDIENCE Your teacher and classmates

LENGTH A poem of 8 to 12 lines

WRITING RUBRICS To write an effective poem, you should

• use a real experience
• recall the details of the experience
• use sensory details

Listening and Speaking

COOPERATIVE LEARNING In a small group, read aloud a poem selected by a member of your group or by your teacher. Be sure to speak clearly and fluently as you read. Within your group, talk about what the poem means and list the sensory images the poet uses.

Next, group members can relate the poem to their own experience. Discuss which images you like best. Which are surprising? Familiar? How does this poem relate to things that happen in your life?

Grammar Link

Use an appositive to identify or add information to another noun.

A comma or a pair of commas usually separates the appositive from the rest of the sentence.

Where I smear it with butter, **the yellow ribbon of butter . . .**

Complete each sentence with an appositive. Use commas correctly.

1. Lauren _____ fouled out of the game.
2. The prize _____ attracted many contestants.
3. The mountain _____ was hidden in the clouds.
4. Our school _____ publishes a newspaper.
5. Bo _____ wins most of his races.

See Lesson 9.6, page 389.

Cross-Curricular Activity

HEALTH Read again "Ode to la Tortilla." Investigate the food pyramid. Where would tortillas and butter be listed? Write a cluster diagram around the name of a favorite healthy food. List sensory details to describe how the food looks.

Assess

Evaluation Rubrics

Write a Poem

Use these criteria when evaluating your students' writing. Make sure that the poem

• describes an experience relevant to the student's life
• contains several sensory words and phrases

See also *Writing Assessment and Evaluation Rubrics*

Listening and Speaking

Use the following criteria to evaluate group and individual responses to the poem.

• Students have identified the sensory images in the poem.
• Students have related the images to familiar experiences.
• Students have participated, both as listeners and speakers, in a discussion of their different responses.

Cross-Curricular Activity

Students' cluster diagrams should

• have the name of a healthy food in the center
• contain several sensory words and phrases that describe the way the food looks

Reteaching

📁 *Composition Reteaching*, p. 23

Enrichment

📁 *Composition Enrichment*, p. 23

Close

Have students brainstorm to develop a list of ideas for poems about ordinary objects. Suggest that they use their ideas to write lyrics for a song.

Grammar Link

Answers

Answers will vary. Samples are given.

1. Lauren, the pitcher, fouled out of the game.
2. The prize, a trip, attracted many contestants.
3. The mountain, Mt. Fuji, was hidden in the clouds.
4. Our school, McCullough Middle School, publishes a newspaper.
5. Bo, a track star, wins most of his races.

Focus

Lesson Overview

Objectives
- To use the stages of the writing process to create a travel article
- To use vivid details to create an appealing description

Skills
- using the five stages of the writing process: prewriting, drafting, revising, editing, and presenting; using descriptive words; writing for a specific audience and purpose

Critical Thinking
- analyzing; synthesizing; visualizing; defining and clarifying

Listening and Speaking
- formal speaking; informal speaking

 Bellringer
Daily Language Activity

When students enter the classroom, have this assignment on the board: *Write a brief description of a place, either real or fantastic, that you would like to visit.*

Grammar Link to the Bellringer

Have students circle any pronouns they used in the Bellringer activity. Students may exchange their work with partners and discuss whether the correct forms of pronouns were used. Suggest that students correct their own work as necessary.

See also *Daily Language Practice*

Motivating Activity

Invite students to think of a time when they visited a new place. Did they have a guide—either a person or written information? If not, might a guide have helped? What information would they like to have included?

Descriptive Writing

Descriptive Writing

In the preceding lessons you've learned about describing imaginary places and people and about using vivid words to make your descriptions come alive or to create a mood. You have written several descriptive paragraphs. Now it's time to make use of what you learned. This assignment invites you to apply your descriptive writing skills, using your powers of observation and imagination to create a special place of your own.

WRITING Online

Visit the *Writer's Choice* Web site at **writerschoice.glencoe.com** for additional writing prompts.

Assignment

Context	You've just visited a special place—real or imagined—that you want others to know about. You want to write an article for other students while the details are still fresh in your memory.
Purpose	To write an article describing a special place
Audience	Teenagers
Length	1 page

The following pages can help you plan and write your article. Read through them and then refer to them as needed. But don't be tied down by them. You're in charge of your own writing process.

Resource Manager

 Planning Resources
- *Lesson Plans*

Transparencies
- *Bellringer*
- *Daily Language Practice*
- *Writing Process* 11–13B

Other Print Resources
- *Composition Enrichment*, p. 24
- *Composition Practice*, p. 24
- *Composition Reteaching*, p. 24
- *Grammar Workbook*, Lesson 93
- *Sentence-Combining Practice*, p. 24
- *Thinking and Study Skills*, pp. 3, 8, 9
- *Writing Assessment and Evaluation Rubrics*

 Software
- *Writer's Assistant*

Web Sites
- *writerschoice.glencoe.com*
- *lit.glencoe.com*

Writing Process in Action

Prewriting

When you prewrite, draw from your experiences, knowledge, and emotions. The graphic on the right shows how freewriting helped one writer find a topic.

Once you've chosen a topic, continue prewriting to generate descriptive details. You might take notes or make a compare-contrast list. And, of course, you'll want to use all five senses to supply sensory impressions.

Drafting

Before you begin drafting, ask yourself how you can best organize your prewriting notes for a travel article. Should you describe a typical day in your special place? Should you hit the attractions from the most well known to the least? Choose an appropriate method to help you get started. You can change it later.

As you draft, make your descriptions vibrate with details. Appeal to your readers' senses. Notice how Virginia Hamilton describes a character's pleasure in discovering a special place.

Option A
Review your journal.

Option B
Build clusters.

Option C
Try freewriting.

Descriptive Writing

> The places I like are different from home–different food, language, etc. I love the ocean. I can swim, body surf, fish. Telluride was cool, but no ocean. Baja California! Cabo San Lucas has it all.

Drafting Tip

For information about creating mood, see Lesson 3.3, pages 122–125.

Literature Model

But now, surrounding the pool on its banks were *things* growing in the dust. Nothing like them had ever grown. The pretty red, yellow. In an instant he knew the colors, knew to call them flowers, with greenery. Such bright growing extended three feet around the pool. He scented the plantings as he moved; the scent made him laugh.

Virginia Hamilton, *The Gathering*

Writing Process in Action   **139**

Teach

Prewriting

Developing Ideas for Descriptive Writing

Ask students to make a chart to organize their ideas about the place they will describe. Suggest that they include at least three headings of their choosing. Each heading may suggest kinds of details they would notice when visiting a new place. If they were to describe a town near an ocean, they might use such headings as *Natural Environment, Buildings,* and *People.* **L2**

Additional Resources

📁 *Thinking and Study Skills,* pp. 3, 8, 9

Drafting

Including Cultural Information

Remind students that many people travel in order to experience different cultures and meet different people. Suggest that students explain and describe in their travel articles any distinctive cultural features. Discuss cultural elements, such as clothing, music, foods, celebrations, or architecture. **L3**

Teach

Revising

Peer Editing

Students can work with peer editors before they revise their writing. You may want to duplicate the Peer Response forms in the *Writing Assessment & Evaluation Rubrics.* Suggest that peer editors respond to the following questions:
- What is the most vivid detail in the article?
- Are there any details that are unclear or insignificant? **L2**

Editing/Proofreading

Peer Editing

After students have edited their own work, have them edit another student's writing. Remind them to refer to the Editing/Proofreading Checklist on page 141. **L2**

Publishing/Presenting

Before students present their descriptive writing, discuss how to prepare their papers for publication. Emphasize the importance of a neat and complete final draft.

Additional Resources

 Writing Process Transparencies, 11–13B

 Thinking and Study Skills, pp. 3, 8, 9

Sentence-Combining Practice, p. 24

 Composition Practice, p. 24

 Grammar Workbook, Lessons 93

Journal Writing Tip

Using a Fresh Eye Point out that leaving some time between completing the writing assignment and beginning a journal entry may help students be more objective and detailed in their responses.

Descriptive Writing

Revising

To begin revising, read over your draft to make sure that what you have written fits your purpose and your audience. Then have a **writing conference.** Read your draft to a partner or a small group, or ask your teacher to give you feedback. Use your audience's reactions to help you evaluate your work so far. The questions below can help you and your listeners.

Look at the suggested revisions in the draft below. What revisions would you make?

Option A

Is the organization logical?

Option B

Are the details specific?

Option C

Is it clear why this place is special?

> Even though it's small, there's lots to do in Cabo San Lucas. *After siesta you can* Meet new friends at the Cabo Wabo Cantina owned by the rock group Van Halen. In the cool of the morning, you can go down to the dock to watch the fishing boats set out in hope of catching something. *marlin or sailfish.* Take a stroll to *which Here you can buy, or just admire* The center of town features numerous craft shops. And don't *unusual the black coral jewelry,* pass up the weird but delicious food: spicy fish tacos with freshly grated cabbage or chicken in mole, a thick dark sauce flavored with cinnamon and chocolate.

Enrichment and Extension

Follow-up Ideas
- Help students celebrate the conclusion of their writing projects. Let them share their finished pieces with the class or in small groups.
- Consider having students illustrate, bind, and then display their work in the school library.

Extending Description
- Look for ways to extend descriptive writing beyond the classroom, such as creating a community description for teens who are new to the area.
- Have students research fields that use descriptive writing, such as fashion, home decorating, and art review.

Editing/Proofreading

During editing, your purpose is to locate and eliminate any errors in grammar, spelling, punctuation, and usage. Even one error, such as a misspelled word, can distract your audience from your message. A correct paper communicates your professional attitude as a writer.

Use the checklist at the right to **proofread** your work. Discovering an error you've overlooked before can bring a writer a great deal of satisfaction.

Editing/Proofreading Checklist

1. Have I corrected any run-on sentences?
2. Do my pronouns have clear antecedents?
3. Have I used the correct forms of pronouns?
4. Have I used commas correctly?
5. Have I used a dictionary to check my spelling?
6. Have I used regular and irregular verbs correctly?

Publishing/Presenting

The goal of writing is to communicate with an audience. From the very first, you had a particular audience in mind—other students. Check to make sure that your writing is neat and legible. Then share your work with one or more of your classmates. You may want to have someone read your work, or you may read it to them. If you get a positive reaction, talk with your teacher about submitting your article for publication. Your teacher may be able to suggest publications to which you could send your writing. If others have written descriptive articles, perhaps you can publish them together in a class edition.

Descriptive Writing

Proofreading Tip

For proofreading symbols, see page 80. If you have composed on the computer, try using the spelling checker feature to check your work.

Journal Writing

Reflect on your writing process experience. Answer these questions in your journal: What do you like best about your description? What was the hardest part of writing it? What did you learn in your writing conference? What new things have you learned as a writer?

Assess

Evaluation Rubrics

Use the following questions to evaluate the students' finished writing:

- Did the student use the Editing/Proofreading Checklist on this page?
- Does the writing include details from all or most of the five senses?
- Are details organized in an appropriate way?
- Does the composition develop prewriting details in a vivid way?
- Does the final version contain improvements in organization, style, vocabulary, and transitions?
- Does the composition convey an appealing impression of the place described?
- Is the writing free of errors in grammar, spelling, punctuation, and usage?

See also *Writing Assessment and Evaluation Rubrics*

Reteaching

📁 *Composition Reteaching*, p. 24

Enrichment

📁 *Composition Enrichment*, p. 24

Close

Ask students whether they have ever read an unappealing description of a place. How did it differ from an inviting description? What was the writer's purpose? List on the board a few possible reasons for writing a negative description (to criticize, to provoke change). Ask each student to recap the reasons for writing his or her travel article. Point out to students that their purpose will always determine the nature of their descriptive writing.

Writing in the Real World

Recognizing Effective Writing

Bring in newspapers, general-interest magazines, children's publications, and special magazines devoted to travel that students might encounter outside the classroom. Encourage students to browse through the material and find a few travel articles. Have students mark or record the details in the articles that they think make each article effective. Then invite students to discuss their findings. Ask whether those details are characteristic of all effective articles.

About the Author

Virginia Hamilton was born in 1933 in Yellow Springs, Ohio, the youngest of five children in an African American family. She states, "Although I generally write of the black experience, I place no restriction on whom or what kind of people I may write about. Writers must remain free to write." The freedom of her imagination is shown in her three books known as *The Justice Cycle*.

Focus

Lesson Overview

Objectives
- To examine a literature passage that illustrates effective descriptive writing
- To write a narrative scene

Skills
- monitoring comprehension

Critical Thinking
- inferring; comparing

Listening and Speaking
- discussing

Bellringer
Daily Language Activity

When students enter the classroom, have this assignment on the board: *Write a sentence telling whether or not you enjoy reading about imaginary places. Write a second sentence explaining why you feel as you do.*

See also *Daily Language Practice*

Motivating Activity

Ask volunteers to read aloud their Bellringer activity sentences. Have students name imaginary places they have encountered in stories and movies.

Descriptive Writing

Literature Model

FROM

The Gathering

by Virginia Hamilton

In The Gathering *Virginia Hamilton presents four young mind-travelers, Justice and her brothers. They live in a universe where computers program themselves and everyone reads everyone else's thoughts. As you read, notice how Hamilton makes this strange world real through detailed descriptions and the everyday conversations all brothers and sisters have. In the following selection, join the mind-travelers on Sona. Led by someone (something?) called Celester, they see Colossus for the first time. Discuss the questions in Linking Writing and Literature on page 148.*

Resource Manager

Planning Resources
- *Lesson Plans*

Transparencies
- *Bellringer*
- *Daily Language Practice*
- *Fine Art 11–15*

Other Print Resources
- *Listening and Speaking Activities, 17–18*
- *Thinking and Study Skills, pp. 3, 5, 22*
- *Writing Assessment and Evaluation Rubrics*

Web Sites
- *writerschoice.glencoe.com*
- *lit.glencoe.com*

Literature Model

They traveled the triway system down to the Oneway level and beyond the hydrafields to the rim of the enormous geodesic[1] dome that covered Sona. Celester pointed out the dome's tubular structure that had all of its parts under tension but never stress. Then he led them inside a silitrex sphere which sat above an opening in the ground, like a stopper in a bottle. Once the sphere closed around them, it began descending with a pneumatic swishing sound of air under pressure. Soft light from Celester's eyes illuminated the sphere, for the vivid sundown of Sona was left above as they plunged.

The gaseous light streaming from his eyes spread about them. Fascinated, Thomas thrust his hand into the stream. Light piled up on his palm like soft ice-cream on a cone. Thomas gasped, jumping back, jerking his hand out of the stream. The piled light scattered and regrouped in the stream coming from Celester's eyes.

"Wow! Magic!" said Dorian.

Celester hummed a comic toning, entertaining them with the light.

"Whatever it was, it got hot," Thomas said. He eyed Celester suspiciously.

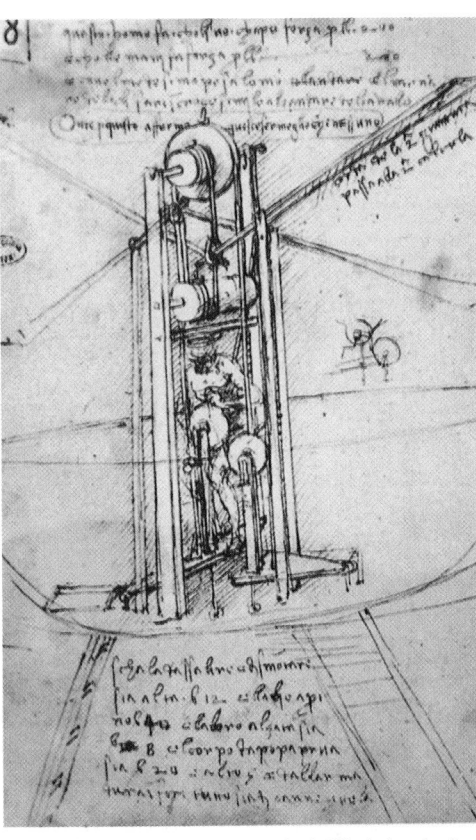

Leonardo da Vinci, sketch of an ornithopter, c. 1495–1510

"A property of light is heat," toned Celester. "He who puts hand in fire will singe his fingertips."

---

[1]**geodesic** (jē´ ə des′ ik) a structure having a strong surface made of bars that form a pattern of shapes having four or more sides

Literature Model **143**

Descriptive Writing

Teach

Literary Elements

Genre Ask students to identify what type of fiction this excerpt is. *(science fiction)* Then ask or tell students what characteristics of science fiction are evident in *The Gathering*. *(The author uses known scientific facts to create an imaginary world. The story is set in the future. Human characters make contact with creatures in another world.)*

6+1 Trait® Writing

Word Choice Tell students that a **simile** is a figure of speech that compare two different things using the word *like* or *as*. Ask: "What two similes does the author use on page 143 to help you develop pictures in your minds of the imaginary world she is describing?" *(first paragraph: ". . . like a stopper in a bottle"; second paragraph: "Light piled up on his palm like soft ice-cream on a cone.")*

Viewing the Art

Leonardo da Vinci, *sketch of an ornithopter*, c. 1495–1510
Artist Leonardo da Vinci was also an imaginative experimenter and inventor. The picture shows one of his drawings for an ornithopter, a machine designed to fly by flapping its wings like a bird.

6+1 Trait® is a registered trademark of Northwest Regional Educational Laboratory, which does not endorse this product.

Active Reading Strategies

Monitor Comprehension

Explain to students that when they read, they should stop now and then to check their understanding. Call attention to the first paragraph of the selection, which contains several difficult words and new concepts. Give students the following tips for monitoring their comprehension of complex passages like this one:

- Vary your reading rate. Slow down for difficult passages; speed up for easier ones.
- To figure out unknown words that seem important, use context clues and your knowledge of word parts.

- Don't worry if you can't understand every word—especially when reading science fiction, which might contain made-up terms. The most important thing is to understand the main ideas.

Practice Ask students to reread the first paragraph in pairs and work together to clearly understand its meaning. Afterwards, have them write a short paraphrase of the paragraph. *(Students may use these word parts to unlock the meanings of* triway *and* hydrafields: *tri-, meaning "three"; hydra, meaning "water or liquid.")*

Teach

6+1 Trait® Writing

Word Choice Ask students what mood Hamilton captures in her description of the place where Celester and the siblings land. What words and phrases help to set this mood? *(The mood is strange and mysterious. Words that help set the mood are* vague, vastly mysterious, dimness, emptiness.*)*

Literary Elements

Point of View Tell students that authors tell stories from a particular point of view, or perspective. Say: "A writer using an omniscient point of view can tell thoughts in the minds of all the characters. A writer using a limited point of view describes things through the perspective of just one character." Ask students what point of view is used in *The Gathering*. What examples can they show? *(It is told through an omniscient point of view. The writer goes into the mind of each character to tell how the character views Colossus.)*

Viewing the Art

Peter Blume, *Light of the World,* **1932**
It has been said that Blume's paintings concern changes in civilization. The 18-by-20 1/4-inch oil on composition board is in the Whitney Museum of American Art in New York.

144

Literature Model

Descriptive Writing

"I get the message," Thomas muttered.

"Celester, you have powerful gifts," Justice said.

The sphere seemed to float momentarily; then it stopped with a soft jolt. A door slid open. Celester moved smoothly out ahead of them.

"Colossus is like no other machine," he toned as they followed him. "There are tooling mills above and below this level built by Colossus. And there are functioning machines nearby that helped to build Colossus itself."

They were in a place of vague light, vastly mysterious because of the dimness. They could make out steep, over-hanging slopes and a wide, deep trench stretching away from them. In the entire emptiness of the trench there was but one object. It had to be Colossus.

What was there they saw, yet did not see.

The Colossus that Celester saw never varied. It was shaded mauve,[2] deepening in pulsations to black. It greeted him, he thought, with the light emitting from its smooth sur-

Peter Blume, *Light of the World,* 1932

face. Celester lifted off the ground, moving to the trench. Higher and higher he went until he was halfway to the summit of Colossus. There he stood on space in conjunction with Colossus, as Colossus tuned Celester until Celester felt no desynchronization[3] of any of his half-million

---

[2]**mauve** (mōv) a pastel shade of purple
[3]**desynchronization**
(dē sing′ krə nə zā′shən) adjustment of parts so that their movement does not occur at the same time or rate of speed

144 Unit 3 Descriptive Writing

Compare and Contrast

Comparing Characters' Perceptions

Tell students that comparing and contrasting characters and events in a selection can enliven and enrich their understanding of what they read. Invite students to skim—or read quickly through—the descriptions of how each character in this excerpt from *The Gathering* sees and responds to Colossus.

Practice Have students use a Venn diagram to compare and contrast the ways that two characters in the story

view Colossus and how they feel in its presence. Then ask students to write a couple of sentences telling what each character's perception of Colossus says about that character. *(Sample responses: In the presence of Colossus, Celester feels like his brain is "not yet middle-aged," so he must usually feel like he's getting old. Justice sees a "coiling" that could "whirl them home," so she probably longs to go home. Thomas wants to take off in a spaceship that will give him freedom from his stutter and his sister.)*

Literature Model

separate components. His brain was not yet middle-aged. His mind was peaceful.

Justice saw an enormous coiling, a Colossus whose awesome spring-release of time-force could whirl them home again. It changed form before her eyes. It was solid; it was ethereal. It was there, a brilliant silver coil, and it was not there.

Each of them saw Colossus differently. There before Thomas was what he loved, which was a science fiction. A silver spaceship was ready for lift-off. Upright in the trench, it was twenty stories high. Steam rose from it. He asked: Can I go, too?

He understood that the ship knew his wish to be master of himself, to speak for himself without stuttering. Only the ship knew the violent feelings he had because of his stutter and because he wanted to be free of Justice. But here and now was not for him. His here and now would come.

No, he could not go a-flying with the ship.

Duster could not have comprehended a Colossus. But he had no need to name what he saw. It looked like his land of dust. He walked in it and the ground was moist under his feet. The area of the water pool was hardly recognizable. He knew it was water, glinting, refreshing to his senses, even though he was still a quarter-mile from it. But now, surrounding the pool on its banks were *things* growing in the dust. Nothing like them had ever grown. The pretty red, yellow. In an instant he knew the colors, knew to call them flowers, with greenery. Such bright growing extended three feet around the pool. He scented the plantings as he moved; the scent made him laugh. The odor was the best he'd smelled in all of the endless dust. He ran. He was there, putting his face down in the flowers.

> It changed form . . . Each of them saw Colossus differently.

Descriptive Writing

Teach

Active Reading Strategies

Monitor Comprehension Ask students what earthlike things Duster sees and smells when he looks at Colossus. *(Duster sees water, colors, flowers, and greenery; he smells the scent of flowers.)* After volunteers respond, ask them to share with the class how they figured out answers to the question.

6+1 Trait® Writing

Ideas

Tell students that good writers develop interesting ideas by supporting them with relevant, vivid details. To provide an example for students, say: "In *The Gathering,* Hamilton presents the unique idea that all her characters see Colossus differently. She develops and enriches this idea by detailing the various ways characters see Colossus."

Practice Tell students to imagine another character—maybe even themselves—who encounters Colossus and sees it in an entirely different way than Celester and the

siblings do. Ask students to write a paragraph or two that describes Colossus from the perspective of their new character. Encourage students to communicate something about the personality of their new character through the details of how he or she perceives Colossus.

For more information on word choice and the 6+1 Trait® model, see the **Writing and Research Handbook**, pp. 822–824.

Teach

6+1 Trait® Writing

Ideas Tell students that the invention of the extraordinary machine Colossus is one of Hamilton's most original ideas in *The Gathering.* Ask: "What do the characters say to convey to readers what an unusual machine Colossus is?" *(Justice says, "It isn't like any machine I've ever seen." Thomas shows that he thinks the same way when he states, "That's the understatement of the year!")*

Literary Elements

Character Point out to students that Colossus is a central, though mysterious, character in this science fiction excerpt. Ask: "On the basis of what you have read about Colossus, what words might you use to describe the computer? Do you think Colossus is dangerous or trustworthy? Why?" *(Words that describe Colossus might include awesome, fantastic, gigantic, amazing, unique. Colossus seems to be trustworthy. It uses its power to help other characters, as when it tunes Celester.)*

Literature Model

Descriptive Writing

A thought came, rising in his mind. Duster crawled to the water and thrust his hands under it, pulling his hands back toward himself on the bank. Drops of water did wet the shore. Duster stared at them. Suddenly he had his shove tool in his hand. It was a digger tool, sharp, broad and flat. He dipped the digger in the pool, then pulled it toward him in a straight line. He dug through the bank, half a hand under the dust. Water began flowing into the little ditch he made. Water filled the ditch and overflowed. That which was Colossus around Duster was aware of his learning. Now Duster knew how to keep moisture near the plantings. Tiny ferns grew quickly beside his first small irrigation ditch.

Then Duster was back in the underdome of Colossus. "Be wanting go to dust," he toned. "Where be my smooth-keep? Be wishing to be gone. Be doing to begin."

"It'll be okay, Duster," Levi said, patting his shoulder. He, too, had had a vision of Colossus. It had calmed him. He no longer feared being in the presence of such a wonder.

"Be touching leader, wrong," toned Duster to him. There was something of the old strength in his voice, which had made him leader of packens.

"It isn't like any machine I've even seen," Justice said about Colossus.

"That's the understatement of the year!" Thomas said in a hushed voice.

Dorian smiled to himself. He thought, Colossus must be the biggest computer ever built. It had to be a hundred, two hundred feet high, if not higher. The lights flashing at the top of it and the tape reels going a

> ## Colossus must be the biggest computer ever built.

Critical Thinking

Infer

Tell students that good fiction writers show feelings and meanings rather than spelling them out directly. Good readers pick up clues from the writer's descriptions and infer—or guess—the author's meaning. To model how to make valid inferences, say: "When Duster looks at Colossus, he sees water and growth, and he gets an idea about how to make an irrigation ditch. It's hard to understand his unusual dialogue, but when he tones 'Be wanting go to dust,' I can infer that he wants to try out the new irrigation technique in a barren land."

Practice Have students read the exchange between Levi and Duster in the first two paragraphs of the second column. Then ask them what more they can infer about Duster's character from the details in this passage. *(Duster has "something of the old strength in his voice, which had made him leader of packens." Students might infer from this that Duster has been through a difficult time recently but has led his peers in the past.)*

Literature Model

mile a minute made him think of comets and stars. No sooner had he thought that Colossus could probably tape even their thoughts, than he heard the thought being transcribed[4] in a jumble of languages.

Smaller machines were connected to Colossus by what Dorian knew suddenly were coded physical quantities. They surrounded Colossus like flies, at a uniform height of about fifteen feet. They displayed differential equations and gave solutions to obscure problems through visuals, in electrical waves on fluorescent screens. Somehow the waves were transmitted to Colossus for it to read.

They do the small work of hydrafields, thought Dorian, of environments and life cycles. Colossus gives them direction, power.

They were all seeing Colossus differently but simultaneously. For Justice, it remained a brilliant silver coil. The space contained in the coiling caught her attention, causing her to go so near the trench she could have easily toppled in. Colossus was spectacular. It grew aware of her as distinct from the others. It saw her.

---

[4]**transcribed** (tran skrībd′) written

Teach

Critical Thinking

Draw Conclusions Ask students: "What is surprising about the last sentence? What do you make of the ending of this excerpt? What might the event lead to in the future?" *(The excerpt has focused on how Celester and the four children "see" Colossus. The ending switches the focus to Colossus, which now "sees" Justice. Students' predictions about future events will vary. Sample: Perhaps Colossus and Justice will become partners in leadership.)*

Additional Resources

Fine Art Transparencies, 11–15
Thinking and Study Skills, pp. 3, 5, 22
Listening and Speaking Activities, pp. 17–18

Genre and Style

Fantastic Themes

Scientific and technological advancements, whether they are real or imagined, are the basis of most science fiction. Isaac Asimov, one of its most famous and prolific writers, says science fiction is about "life as we don't know it." Although strange lands and beings have been written about for thousands of years, it wasn't until science and technology began to play an important role in society that science fiction appeared. Mary Shelley's *Frankenstein,* published in 1818, is considered the first science fiction novel. It tells the story of a scientist who creates a living being, a monster that destroys him and others. This pessimistic view of modern science was written in the early stages of the Industrial Revolution, a time when people were wondering what effect technology would have on everyday life.

Linking Writing and Literature

Assess

Evaluation Rubrics

◆ Talk About Reading

Possible responses to the questions:

1. Students may connect with the idea of a world where machines, particularly computers, play a powerful, sometimes controlling role.

2. Among the clues that Hamilton includes is Colossus's ability to tune Celester, to keep its world running smoothly, and to appear differently to each character.

3. Students may cite the unusual idea of how Colossus becomes a completely different entity to each person who sees it.

4. Students may cite Hamilton's use of detailed descriptions to bring her ideas into clear focus and make them seem real.

◆ Write About Reading

The narrative should do the following:

- narrate a science fiction scene
- describe new actions for one character in *The Gathering*
- use original ideas

Close

Ask students to work in groups to discuss this question: How does the descriptive language in a work of science fiction such as *The Gathering* differ from descriptive language found in other types of fiction? Provide time for groups to share their ideas.

Descriptive Writing

Literature Model

Linking Writing and Literature

◆ Collect Your Thoughts

Think back on the characters in this science fiction story, including Colossus. Choose the character you find most compelling and write a couple of descriptive sentences about him, her, or it.

◆ Talk About Reading

Talk with other students about this excerpt from *The Gathering*. Assign a group leader to keep everyone focused and a group secretary to take notes. Then use the questions below to guide your conversation.

1. **Connect to Your Life:** How does the power of Colossus in the selection compare to the impact of machines in real life? Do you notice any connections between the real world and the imaginary world of *The Gathering?*

2. **Critical Thinking: Infer** What clues does Hamilton give to show that Colossus is powerful? What else do these clues suggest about Colossus?

3. **6+1 Trait®: Ideas** Name an idea in the story that you found of particular interest. Describe how Hamilton develops the idea to make it compelling.

4. **Connect to Your Writing:** What can you learn from Hamilton's writing about making imaginary elements appear lifelike?

◆ Write About Reading

Narrative Choose the character in the selection whom you find most interesting. (You may choose Colossus as a character.) Then write a new science fiction scene featuring that character.

Focus on Ideas Let your sci-fi imagination run free. Begin by skimming—reading quickly over—the story to review Hamilton's descriptions of the character. You may want to add to or change some of the character's traits in your narrative. Then write a new scene for the character, possibly having him or her face an unusual problem.

For more information on ideas and the 6+1 Trait® model, see **Writing and Research Handbook,** pages 822–824.

6+1 Trait® is a registered trademark of Northwest Regional Educational Laboratory, which does not endorse this product.

Enrichment and Extension

Linking Familiar Concepts in New Ways

Hamilton describes her new world by linking familiar concepts in new ways (*gaseous light* and *time-force*). Suggest that students work in pairs to invent such combinations (Samples: *visible sound; tasting with your fingertips; hard, crunchy thoughts*) Partners can then write a scene in which a time traveler or space traveler enters a new world and describes it using such combinations.

UNIT 3 Review

Reflecting on the Unit

Summarize what you learned in this unit by answering the following questions.

1 What is the purpose of descriptive writing?

2 What are the characteristics of strong descriptive writing?

3 Why should you use sensory details in descriptive writing?

4 What are the important elements of a character description?

5 Why is the order of details and the use of transition words important in descriptive writing?

Adding to Your Portfolio

CHOOSE A SELECTION FOR YOUR PORTFOLIO Look over the writing you did for this unit. Choose a piece of writing for your portfolio. The writing you choose should show one or more of the following:

- descriptive details in an order that creates a strong image
- a mood so strong that a reader can share it
- exact and vivid words that clearly convey your meaning

REFLECT ON YOUR CHOICE Attach a note to the piece you chose, explaining briefly why you chose it and what you learned from writing it.

SET GOALS How can you improve your writing? What skill will you focus on the next time you write?

Writing Across the Curriculum

MAKE A GEOGRAPHY CONNECTION Write a two-paragraph description of the region in which you live for a person who has never been there. Describe common sights and sounds, especially ones that may be unique. Write about the climate and the ways people earn their livings. Try to imagine what would most interest a visitor, and try to make your description come alive with vivid sensory details. Be sure to write legibly and check your spelling before sharing your writing.

Review **149**

(Side margin: Descriptive Writing)

Unit 3 Review

Review

Reflecting on the Unit

You may have students respond to Reflecting on the Unit in writing or through discussion.

Writing Across the Curriculum

Before students begin, review the importance of sensory language and details that create mood in good descriptive writing. Remind students to choose transition words carefully.

Adding to Your Portfolio

To help students select appropriate portfolio samples, remind them that their descriptions should use sensory language, set a recognizable mood, present a highly imaginative setting, present details in spatial order, or present a personal response to a poem. Working in pairs, students can act as peer reviewers to help each other make portfolio selections.

Portfolio Evaluation

If you grade the portfolio selections, you may want to award two marks—one each for content and form. Explain your assessment criteria before students make their selections.

Commend
- experimentation with creative prewriting techniques
- clear, concise writing in which the main idea, audience, and purpose are evident
- successful revisions
- work that shows a flair for language

✔ ASSESSMENT OPTIONS

📁 *Tests with Answer Key and Rubrics*
Unit 3 Choice A Test, p. 9
Unit 3 Choice B Test, p. 10
Unit 3 Composition Objective Test, pp. 11–12

💾 *Testmaker*
Unit 3 Choice A Test
Unit 3 Choice B Test
Unit 3 Composition Objective Test

You may wish to administer one of these tests as a mastery test.

📼 *MindJogger Videoquizzes*

Viewing the Art

This photograph shows a man on a red clay race track. He is raising a flag, possibly before a race, although it is difficult to tell. The man's position imparts suspense and a tension to the scene. As viewers, we feel invited to solve the mystery of the man's presence on the track.

Interpret and Analyze Use the following questions for discussion:
- Describe the composition of the photograph. Which shapes can be identified? Which colors are prominent?
- What is the mood of the photograph? How does the photographer's choice of shapes and colors help to create the mood?

Discussing the Quotation

Ask students to discuss the tone and mood of the quotation. How does the quotation pique the reader's interest? Compare the quotation to the photograph. Do they use any of the same techniques to pull in the audience? Students may want to investigate the source of the quote to see how it fits into a larger narrative. Instruct students to read "Atalanta," by Betty Miles, on p. 718 of *Glencoe Literature: The Reader's Choice, Course 2*.

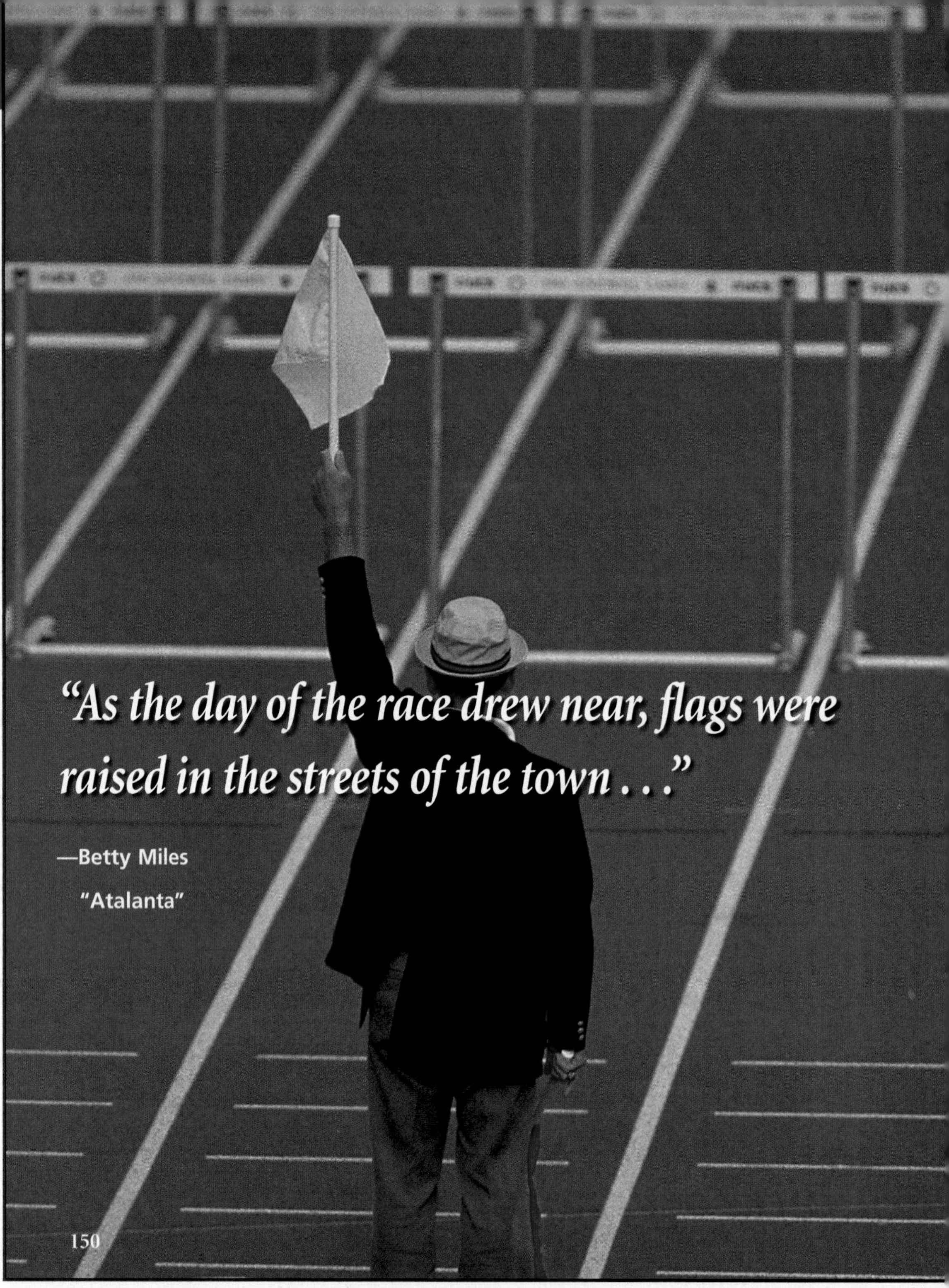

"As the day of the race drew near, flags were raised in the streets of the town . . ."

—Betty Miles

"Atalanta"

150

Resource Manager

📁 **Planning Resources**
- *Lesson Plans*
- *Block Scheduling*

 Transparencies
- *Bellringer*
- *Daily Language Practice*
- *Fine Art*
- *Two-Minute Skill Drill*
- *Writing Process*

📁 **Other Print Resources**
- *Composition Enrichment*
- *Composition Practice*
- *Composition Reteaching*
- *Cooperative Learning Activities*
- *Glencoe Literature Library*
- *Grammar and Composition Handbook*
- *Grammar Workbook*

- *Listening and Speaking Activities*
- *Research Paper and Report Writing*
- *Sentence-Combining Practice*
- *Tests with Answer Key and Rubrics*
- *Thinking and Study Skills*
- *Writing Across the Curriculum*
- *Writing Assessment and Evaluation Rubrics*
- *Writing in the Real World*

UNIT 4 Narrative Writing

Objectives

- To analyze published examples and to use them as a model for writing
- To learn about elements of storytelling such as character, dialogue, setting, and plot
- To identify possible story ideas and to formulate questions that define a problem in a story
- To identify and use time order and transition words to help narrative flow
- To complete an independent writing project using such techniques as prewriting and crafting effective conclusions

✔ ASSESSMENT OPTIONS

📁 *Tests with Answer Key and Rubrics*
Unit 4 Choice A Test, p. 13
Unit 4 Choice B Test, p. 14
Unit 4 Composition Objective Test, pp. 15–16

💾 *Testmaker*
Unit 4 Choice A Test
Unit 4 Choice B Test
Unit 4 Composition Objective Test

You may wish to administer either the Unit 4 Choice A Test or the Unit 4 Choice B Test as a pretest.

Key to Ability Levels

L1 Level 1 activities are within the basic ability range of students.

L2 Level 2 activities are within the ability range of average students.

L3 Level 3 activities are more challenging activities.

Video
- *MindJogger Videoquizzes*

💾 **Software**
- *Presentation Plus!*
- *Revising with Style*
- *Testmaker*
- *Writer's Assistant*

Web Sites
- *writerschoice.glencoe.com*
- *lit.glencoe.com*

Focus

Lesson Overview

Objectives
- To understand the elements required for successful narrative writing
- To assess a writer's use of narrative writing techniques

Skills
- analyzing; writing a short narrative

Critical Thinking
- relating a specific example to a general model; building background

Listening and Speaking
- discussing

 Bellringer
Daily Language Activity

When students enter the classroom, have this assignment on the board: *List five examples of computers that you have used or seen used in the last week.* (personal computers, automatic teller machines, grocery store scanners, library catalogs)

Grammar Link to the Bellringer

Students can share their lists starting with the words "Here are five computers . . ." or "There are five computers . . ." Point out that in sentences beginning with *here* or *there,* the verb that follows always matches the subject. The verb *are* agrees with the subject *five computers.*

See also *Daily Language Practice*

Motivating Activity

What kind of computer functions have students used or seen in the last week? Invite comments about the different ways computers might respond. If a computer were a character in a short story, how might they expect it to act? Encourage students to monitor their understanding and to seek clarification as needed.

152

(side tab) Narrative Writing

Writing in the Real World

 MEDIA Connection · Short Story

Creating a good character is an important part of writing a short story. T. Ernesto Bethancourt invented a couple of great characters for his fantasy story "User Friendly." One is a junior high school student named Kevin. The other is Kevin's best friend, Louis—a super-computer that frighteningly develops a mind of its own.

from "User Friendly"

by T. Ernesto Bethancourt

My bowl of Frosted Flakes was neatly in place, flanked by a small pitcher of milk, an empty juice glass, and an unpeeled banana. I picked up the glass, went to the refrigerator, poured myself a glass of Tang, and sat down to my usual lonely breakfast. Mom was already at work, and Dad wouldn't be home from his Chicago trip for another three days. I absently read the ingredients in Frosted Flakes for what seemed like the millionth time. I sighed deeply.

When I returned to my room to shower and dress for the day, my history project was already printed out. I had almost walked by Louis, when I noticed there was a message on the screen. It wasn't the usual:

Printout completed. Do you wish to continue: Y/N?

Underneath the printout were two lines:

When are you going to get my voice module, Kevin?

I blinked. It couldn't be. There was nothing in Louis's basic programming that would allow for a question like this. Wondering what was going on, I sat at the keyboard, and entered:" *Repeat last message.* Amazingly, the computer replied:

It's right there on the screen, Kevin. Can we talk? I mean, are you going to get me a voice box?

I was stunned. What was going on here?

152   Unit 4   Narrative Writing

Resource Manager

Planning Resources
- *Lesson Plans*

Transparencies
- *Bellringer*
- *Daily Language Practice*
- *Writing Process* 14–16B

Other Print Resources
- *Cooperative Learning Activities,* pp. 19–24
- *Thinking and Study Skills,* pp. 5, 18, 22
- *Writing Assessment and Evaluation Rubrics*
- *Writing in the Real World,* pp. 13–16

Writing a Fantasy

Prewriting	Drafting	Revising/Editing
Planning the Story	Introducing the Characters	Start from the Top

Teach

Discussion Prompts

- Do authors make things up completely from their imaginations, or do they find inspiration in their own lives?
- Would a fantasy writer and, for example, a mystery writer find inspiration in the same place, or in different places?
- Is one problem enough to build a story on?

A Writer's Process

Prewriting
Planning the Story

Novelist T. Ernesto Bethancourt was inspired to write a fantasy about a computer when his first portable computer fizzled out. "I started going to all the computer shows," Bethancourt said, "and I was amazed at all the things that were being done with computers. Before long, I got heavily into the idea of artificial intelligence, and I thought, 'what a great companion a computer could be.' I said, 'Gee, what if the thing really had a personality and could be user friendly?'"

Once Bethancourt knew he had a good idea, he began mulling it over. For six weeks, he thought about characters and scenes.

All the while, Bethancourt followed his own map for short story writing. "You create a hero or heroine and place the figure in a problem situation," he said. "Then you have your hero use his or her inner resources—courage, intelligence, wit—to resolve the conflict. After the conflict is resolved, the main character is in some way changed."

Following this plan, Bethancourt created a hero named Kevin. Where did he get the inspiration for his character? Bethancourt modeled Kevin after a young friend of his—a quiet, smart boy with a sly sense of humor.

Bethancourt then broke his story line into individual scenes. He summarized each scene on an index card.

Once Bethancourt finished summarizing the scenes, he laid the index cards out on his desk. He looked for scenes that best showed the growing conflict. Those scenes would get the most space in his narrative.

Cultural Connections

Passing Down Heroes

In folktales, myths, and legends, people all over the world form narratives about heroes who use their wits to save the day. Some of these heroes are children (such as Hansel and Gretel), some are young adults (such as Aladdin), and some are not even human (such as Coyote in Native American legends and Anansi the spider in African tales). The narrative form is an efficient way to pass history, morals, or other cultural information from generation to generation because people like to tell stories!

Teach

Discussion Prompts

- What is a good way to get a reader involved in a story quickly?
- Is one problem enough to build a story on?
- In the sample, you can see that "User Friendly" is written in the first person. What would have been the effect if it were written in the third person?
- What did Bethancourt do to prevent readers from thinking the story was too unrealistic?

You may also want to invite students to talk about

- how the process used by Bethancourt is similar to or different from the writing process students use in their own writing.
- how writers can "clear their minds" before reviewing a draft if they don't have the time to set it aside for a week.
- whether they think the short story is a powerful or appealing medium.
- what questions they might like to ask Bethancourt about the process of writing a short story. **L2**

Additional Resources

- *Writing Process Transparencies,* 14–16B
- *Cooperative Learning Activities,* pp. 19–24
- *Writing in the Real World,* pp. 13–16
- *Thinking and Study Skills,* pp. 5, 18, 22

Writing in the Real World

Writing scene ideas on index cards helps Bethancourt organize the short story.

Scene 1
In Kevin's room.
Introduce Kevin and Louis.
Louis 'talks'!

Scene 3
Kevin's confrontation with Chuck.
Kevin outsmarts the bully.

Last scene
At Kevin's house.
Dad pulls the plug on Louis.

Drafting
Creating the Plot

"Writing stories is fun," says Bethancourt. "You get to have adventures, except you're in control. And you get to use those swell remarks you don't think of until two days later and then say, 'Gee, I wish I'd said that.'"

Bethancourt started drafting "User Friendly" when he had the story events clearly in mind. Near the beginning of the story, Kevin notices the startling message on the computer screen: "When are you going to get me my voice module, Kevin?"

Bethancourt accomplished several tasks at the beginning of the story. First of all, he introduced two main characters, Kevin and the computer, using dialogue to bring them to life. Then he based events on everyday life to make the story believable. "The important thing in fantasy is that you've got to have a foot on the ground before you take off," Bethancourt said.

As Bethancourt moved into the middle of his story, he used action and dialogue to tell the story. These techniques also help him build suspense and hold the reader's attention. "This is largely a 'think' story," he said. To balance that effect with adventure, Bethancourt said, "action was important. I had to show that Kevin wasn't a total dweeb. I did this by having him outsmart a jock who's trying to intimidate him."

Revising/Editing
Starting From the Top

After writing a draft, many writers—including Bethancourt—leave the draft alone for a period of time. For Bethancourt, the "shelf time" is about a week.

Typically, Bethancourt writes for two days, then goes back to page one. "I start at the top, and I rewrite it," he explains. Bethancourt lets this draft sit for at least a week before making any final changes.

Some key parts of "User Friendly" came into being because of Bethancourt's careful revising. One example is a scene between Kevin and a bullying character named Chuck. "In the first draft, I had Kevin running away from Chuck," Bethancourt said. "I wanted more physical action. But when I looked at it, it wasn't as good as when Kevin simply outsmarted Chuck. So I cut the running-away scene."

Bethancourt believes that the revision stage is a critical part of the writing process. He explains, "The best writing is rewriting. The idea is to get something down on paper. It doesn't matter how long you write—you can always cut stuff out."

Cooperative Learning

Starting a Story

At this point, students may be starting to think of stories that they might tell. To begin this Think-Pair-Share activity, write this story opening on the board.

As soon as I saw _____ jumping up and down near _____, I knew this was going to be one weird day.

Give student pairs two minutes to write words or phrases for each blank. Then let each pair share its favorite responses. Encourage the class as a whole to elaborate on story lines that arise from responses.

Examining Writing in the Real World

Analyzing the Media Connection

Discuss these questions about the story excerpt on page 152.

1. What kind of details make the excerpt seem believable and ordinary?

2. How does Kevin feel as he eats breakfast? How does Bethancourt convey these feelings without actually stating them outright?

3. How does the mood of the excerpt's first scene differ from the mood of the scene that follows? How effective is this contrast?

4. What details does Bethancourt use to show that Kevin is surprised by his computer?

5. What immediate impression do you get of Louis, the computer? How does the author get this impression across?

Analyzing a Writer's Process

Discuss these questions about T. Ernesto Bethancourt's writing process.

1. After placing the main character in a problem situation, what inner resources does Bethancourt give to the character to resolve the conflict?

2. How did Bethancourt decide which scenes would receive the

most attention in this story? Would you use Bethancourt's method? Explain.

3. What method of organization does Bethancourt use? What advantages does this method have?

4. Why does Bethancourt give his drafts "shelf time" before doing the final revision?

5. Do you agree with Bethancourt that "the best writing is rewriting"? Why or why not?

Grammar Link

While proofreading, check subject-verb agreement. In sentences that begin with *there,* look for the subject after the verb.

In the following sentence, the subject is *message.* It agrees with the singular verb *was.*

> There was a message on the screen.

Use each noun below as the subject of a sentence that begins with *there.* Be careful to make the verb agree with the subject.

1. cars   4. computer
2. family   5. music
3. father

See Lesson 16.2, pages 535–536.

Grammar Link

Answers

Answers will vary, but sentences might use the verb forms listed below:

1. are
2. is
3. is
4. is
5. is

Close

Have students create a chart with the headings *Character(s), Setting, Problem,* and *Solution.* Challenge them to fill in the chart for these parts of a story. Refer them to books, television, movies, songs, or advertisements.

Note Students may want to browse through such collections of tales as *The Book of Fantasy* (1988, Viking), *Tales from Isaac Asimov's Science Fiction Magazine* (1986, Harcourt Brace Jovanovich), or *Masterpieces of Fantasy and Enchantment* (1988, St. Martin's Press).

Assess

Analyzing the Media Connection

1. Details such as a typical breakfast (Frosted Flakes, milk, juice, banana) and a morning routine (eat, shower, dress) make the excerpt seem believable.

2. Kevin feels lonely as he eats breakfast; Bethancourt conveys this by having the narrator note that he is alone in the house reading the cereal box for the millionth time.

3. A quiet, routine scene changes into a highly unusual event. It makes the unusual event stand out.

4. He blinks; thinks it "couldn't be;" wonders what's going on.

5. Answers will vary. Possible answer: he seems smart and bold; the author conveys this by having him demand his voice box.

Analyzing a Writer's Process

1. He gives the character a quality such as courage, intelligence, or wit.

2. He chose those that best showed Louis's growing problems. Answers to the second part of the question will vary.

3. Bethancourt breaks the story into scenes which he writes on index cards. This provides him with a clear roadmap to the story.

4. New ideas and insights come to him after he sets the writing aside for awhile.

5. Students may agree because a rough draft often lacks depth, interesting detail, and precise language. Students who disagree may think that first drafts are free-flowing and spontaneous.

Reteaching

Using student or published stories, review how the story problems affect the main character.

Enrichment

Read aloud the sentences below and ask students what kind of story might have each ending. Discuss how each ending makes them feel.
• And they lived happily ever after.
• Did it really happen, or was it all a dream?

Narrative Writing

Focus

Lesson Overview

Objectives

- To explore how characters, setting, and plot interact in a story
- To generate a story that incorporates characters, setting, and plot

Skills

- analyzing literary models; planning before writing; identifying the attributes and components of a story

Critical Thinking

- relating; decision-making patterns; activating prior knowledge; generating new information

Listening and Speaking

- taking notes; asking questions; informal speaking; discussing; evaluating; explaining a process

Bellringer
Daily Language Activity

When students enter the classroom, have this assignment on the board: *What happens in your favorite story? Write a summary of the plot.*

Grammar Link to the Bellringer

Have students rewrite the sentence *Wendy favorite story is Rumpelstiltskin* to show that, of all the stories that she knows, Wendy likes *Rumpelstiltskin* best.

See also *Daily Language Practice*

Motivating Activity

Have students describe the setting and characters of the story whose plot they summarized in the Bellringer. You may wish to allow students to share their responses. Have students monitor their understanding and seek clarification as needed.

Telling a Good Story

*W*hen you write a story, or narrative, you answer the question, "What happened?" To give your readers a complete picture of what occurred, your story will need a beginning, a middle, and an end. The story will also need a setting, a conflict and solution, characters, and dialogue.

Harold Lloyd in *Safety Last*, 1923

What happened in this photograph? How did this man get himself into this predicament? What will happen next? How will he get himself out of this dangerous situation? A good storyteller will answer all of these questions.

Describe What Happened

Suppose you've seen the movie in which this scene takes place, and a friend asks you what the movie is about. You would probably tell what happened through a series of events. This is called the **plot**.

As you talk about the events of the plot, you will find yourself talking about the characters. **Characters** are the people or animals that take part in the events. Notice how novelist Madeleine L'Engle introduces characters and plot in the following selection.

156 Unit 4 Narrative Writing

Resource Manager

Literature Model

What event begins the plot of this story?

There are dragons in the twins' vegetable garden." Meg Murry took her head out of the refrigerator where she had been foraging for an after-school snack, and looked at her six-year-old brother. "What?"

"There are dragons in the twins' vegetable garden. Or there were. They've moved to the north pasture now."

. . . She took her sandwich materials and a bottle of milk and set them out on the kitchen table. Charles Wallace waited patiently. She looked at him, scowling with an anxiety she did not like to admit to herself, at the fresh rips in the knees of his blue jeans, the streaks of dirt grained deep in his shirt, a darkening bruise on the cheekbone under his left eye. "Okay, did the big boys jump you in the schoolyard this time, or when you got off the bus?"

"Meg, you aren't listening to me."

"I happen to care that you've been in school for two months now and not a single week has gone by that you haven't been roughed up. If you've been talking about dragons in the garden or wherever they are, I suppose that explains it."

"I haven't. Don't underestimate me. I didn't see them till I got home."

Madeleine L'Engle, *A Wind in the Door*

What do you know about Meg and Charles Wallace by the end of the passage?

Journal Writing

Think of a story you have read or heard recently that you really liked. In your journal, tell what it was about the story that interested you. Was it the plot or a character? Explain what a story must do to capture your attention.

Teach

Using the Model

Guide students to observe that L'Engle does not ease readers into the scene; her dialogue plunges them into the middle of things. Point out that this passage consists almost entirely of dialogue. Ask students what aspects of the characters the dialogue reveals (Meg, the older child, is protective, and Charles Wallace, who is only six, is bullied regularly at school). **L2**

Promoting Discussion

Share this comment from Madeleine L'Engle: "Everyone you meet has a story." Have students consider questions such as these: If L'Engle is correct, should everyone be a storyteller? Are stories that come from our own lives the only ones we might share? **L2**

Two-Minute Skill Drill

Have students write the possessive form of the nouns below.

team (team's)

players (players')

Native Americans (Native Americans')

mechanics (mechanics')

administrators (administrators')

faculty (faculty's)

See also *Two-Minute Skill Drill Transparency 4.1*

Journal Writing Tip

Examining Characters As students consider characters' personality traits, suggest that they look for clues in the way each character looks, speaks, and acts. Suggest that students keep a list of books they've enjoyed for use as a "recommended reading" list for the class.

Teach

Formulating Questions

As the text states, setting can affect a character's actions. Have students explore story possibilities by brainstorming questions about the settings illustrated. You may wish to model these examples.

First panel: What has happened to the cowhand during the day? Does he enjoy his job?

Second panel: How long has the cowhand lived in the city? What advantage might there be to riding a horse in the city?

Third panel: How did the cowhand get on the moon? Are the cowhand and horse alone there? **L2**

Choosing Settings

Choosing characters and setting gives some students more options than they can handle. You may wish to break this part of the lesson into several mini-lessons on kinds of settings (real, imaginary, past, present, and future). For each mini-lesson, you can review a popular story with a particular kind of setting and have students suggest other settings that fit the same category. **L1**

Additional Resources

 Fine Art Transparencies, 16–20

 Writing Process Transparencies, 14–16B

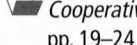 Writing Across the Curriculum
Cooperative Learning Activities, pp. 19–24

Thinking and Study Skills, pp. 4, 22
Listening and Speaking Activities, p. 23
Composition Practice, p. 25

Narrative Writing

Drafting Tip

When you write about a setting, use sensory details to make the scene as real as possible.

Set the Scene

A story has characters and a plot. It also has a **setting.** The setting puts the characters in a certain place at a certain time. Stories can be set in the present, the past, or the future. What happens in the story and how characters look and act often depend on the time when the events take place.

Where a story takes place may also affect what happens. A writer may set a story in a real place or in an imaginary one. A stormy lake, a summer camp, or another planet can be a setting for a story. Changing the setting will affect the kind of story you tell, as shown by the illustrations below.

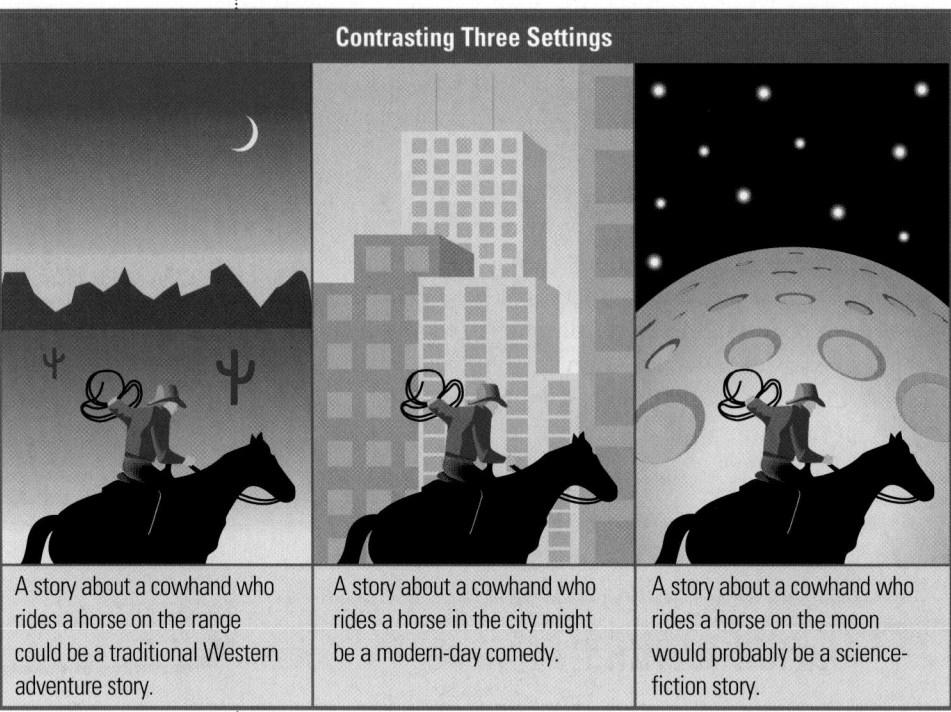

Contrasting Three Settings

A story about a cowhand who rides a horse on the range could be a traditional Western adventure story.

A story about a cowhand who rides a horse in the city might be a modern-day comedy.

A story about a cowhand who rides a horse on the moon would probably be a science-fiction story.

Setting affects not only story events but also the way characters act. For example, the cowhand would probably act differently in each of the three settings illustrated above.

158 Unit 4 Narrative Writing

Enrichment and Extension

Building Understanding

A brief vocabulary lesson will increase students' appreciation of the literature model on page 157 and of the power of word choice. Ask students to use *anxiety* and *grained* in original sentences and to comment on what *foraging* and *scowling* imply that *looking* and *frowning* do not. Invite them to suggest other words to describe Charles and Meg.

Write a Children's Story

Your class is writing a book of stories for children at a day-care center. Write an imaginative, entertaining story that will keep them interested. Think about some of the stories that were your favorites when you were younger and then write a story that a four- or five-year-old would enjoy.

PURPOSE To create an entertaining children's story

AUDIENCE Children at a day-care center

LENGTH 1–2 pages

WRITING RUBRICS To write a good children's story, you should

- structure your story so it has a clear beginning, middle, and end
- clearly define each character
- make sure the setting fits the characters and plot

Listening and Speaking

STORYTELLING In a group of three or four classmates, read your story aloud, using a voice and style appropriate for younger children. Critique each other's stories to make them more effective for that audience. Then arrange to read the stories to a group of preschoolers.

Viewing and Representing

ILLUSTRATING A STORY Create two or three visual images that illustrate your story. Display the images as you read your story in your group and, if possible, later when you read for a younger audience.

Use a possessive noun to show ownership or possession of a thing or quality.

A possessive noun is formed in one of two ways. For all singular nouns and for plural nouns not ending in *-s*, add an apostrophe and *-s* (*'s*):

> **cat's** *whiskers*
>
> **men's** *team*

For plural nouns already ending in *-s*, add only an apostrophe (*'*):

> **twins'** *vegetable garden*

Write the correct possessive form for each underlined word.

1. This story captures the <u>reader</u> attention.
2. The <u>writer</u> opening line draws you into the story.
3. What were the <u>boys</u> reactions?
4. <u>Charles</u> attitude is clear.
5. The <u>children</u> relationship is implied.

See Lesson 9.3, page 383, and Lesson 9.4, page 385.

Assess

Evaluation Rubrics

Write a Children's Story

Use these criteria when evaluating your students' writing. The story should

- creatively stretch one or more of the elements of plot, character, or setting
- develop characters with whom readers can identify
- integrate characters, setting, and plot

See also *Writing Assessment and Evaluation Rubrics*

Listening and Speaking

Students should make an effort to read their stories in an engaging manner. Criticisms of other students' stories should be constructive.

Viewing and Representing

Visual images should relate to the story. Encourage students to spend time constructing attractive, lively displays.

Reteaching

📁 *Composition Reteaching*, p. 25

Enrichment

📁 *Composition Enrichment*, p. 25

Close

Have students recall recent commercials. Ask, *Which ones tell a story or serve as episodes in a story? Which characters from commercials does everyone seem to know?*

Grammar Link

Answers
1. reader's
2. writer's
3. boys'
4. Charles's
5. children's

Focus

Lesson Overview

Objectives

- To learn how to define a problem in a story and suggest its solution
- To generate and refine story ideas

Skills

- brainstorming, organizing, and developing story ideas; analyzing the components of a story

Critical Thinking

- decision-making; generating new information; identifying main ideas; analyzing; summarizing; comparing

Listening and Speaking

- asking questions; discussing; evaluating; explaining a process

Bellringer
Daily Language Activity

When students enter the classroom, have this assignment on the board: *What kind of story does the phrase* once upon a time *prepare you for? Use the phrase to write the beginning lines of a story of your own.*

Grammar Link to the Bellringer

Point out to students that while some stories begin with *once upon a time,* other stories begin with the word *never. Never* is called a negative. Can students think of other negatives? (none, no, not, nothing, nobody, nowhere)

See also *Daily Language Practice*

Motivating Activity

Allow volunteers to read aloud the story beginnings they wrote in the Bellringer activity. Have the class brainstorm a possible middle and end for each beginning.

Narrative Writing

Exploring Story Ideas

The plot of most good stories centers on a problem faced by a character. Focusing on a problem that needs solving is one good way to come up with story ideas.

This cow's problem can spark ideas that would make a great story. Jot down some ideas about how the cow got the barrel on its head. Then list a few ideas about what will happen to it next and how it can get rid of the barrel.

TIME

For more about the writing process, see **TIME** *Facing the Blank Page*, pp. 97–107.

Identify the Problem

Look at the pictures at the top of the next page. Think about the problem involved in each situation. Take a few minutes to list some similar situations of your own. You can either use one of the pictures as a starting point or think of entirely new situations.

160 Unit 4 Narrative Writing

Resource Manager

📁 **Planning Resources**
- *Lesson Plans*

📦 **Transparencies**
- *Bellringer*
- *Daily Language Practice*
- *Fine Art* 16–20
- *Two-Minute Skill Drill*
- *Writing Process* 14–16B

📁 **Other Print Resources**
- *Composition Enrichment*, p. 26
- *Composition Practice*, p. 26
- *Composition Reteaching*, p. 26
- *Cooperative Learning Activities*, pp. 19–24
- *Listening and Speaking Activities*, p. 23
- *Sentence-Combining Practice*, p. 25

- *Thinking and Study Skills*, pp. 1, 10
- *Writing Across the Curriculum*
- *Writing Assessment and Evaluation Rubrics*

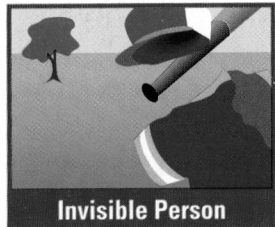

Car Breaking Down

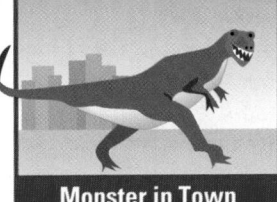

Invisible Person

Monster in Town

Find a Solution

Once you have an idea you like, you can start developing it into a full-length story. Asking yourself questions like those listed in the chart below will help you plan a series of events. Some events will help solve the problem in your story. Others may make the solution more difficult.

As you answer these questions, let your imagination run wild. It is your story, and anything can happen! The journal entry to the right shows how one student answered questions about her story idea—a monster terrorizing Middleville.

Questions About Story Ideas

1. What is the problem?
2. What characters does it involve?
3. What happened before?
4. What will happen next?
5. What is the solution to the problem?

Problem—monster terrorizes Middleville

Characters—monster, Patrice (14-year-old girl) Matt (her 10-year-old brother)

Before—monster was lonely and came to town

Next—everyone scared of monster, except Patrice and Matt

Solution—Patrice and Matt put monster on a basketball team

Journal Writing

Think of a problem you have encountered that you can use as a base for a story. List one or two events leading up to the problem. Then list one or two events that might happen next and the solution.

Teach

Identifying Story Ideas

Because two of the three story ideas pictured on this page suggest science fiction or fantasy, some students may feel that a "good" story requires outlandish details. Ask them to describe some stories they would call "good." Point out that a good story is one that gets them thinking or that makes them feel differently about something. Even a real-life event can fuel a "good" story. **L2**

Understanding Types of Conflict

Students can broaden their understanding of story problems through a discussion of the four classic kinds of conflict found in narrative writing—*person against nature, person against society, person against person,* and *person against self.* Suggest that students come up with four story ideas—one based on each type of conflict. Encourage students to share their favorite ideas. **L3**

Journal Writing Tip

Order Suggest that students may prefer to use a problem from their imaginations rather than from real life. Remind them that they may think of the solution first, and decide on the original situation or events in the middle of the story later. They should write down their ideas first, and put them in order later.

Teach

Using the Model

Have students suggest words and phrases to describe Mellissa, Eddie, and Hendrikson. Then ask, *If Mellissa and Eddie are so different, how do you explain their friendship? If you could ask the author about these characters, what would you ask?* Students should note when Mellissa first senses a problem (when her father tells her that Eddie is to be moved) and when she is struck by its seriousness (when she learns that Eddie cannot take Shadow). **L2**

Two-Minute Skill Drill

Ask students to match the following characters and problems, and discuss the results. (Answers will vary.)

- *Benjamin Franklin*
- *Ebony, our cat,*
- *My friend Reiko*
- *is bothered by a hornet*
- *witnesses a bank robbery*
- *is afraid of lightning*

See also ✏ *Two-Minute Skill Drill Transparency 4.2*

Additional Resources

 Fine Art Transparencies, 16–20

 Writing Process Transparencies, 14–16B

 Writing Across the Curriculum
 *Cooperative Learning Activities, pp. 19–24*
 *Thinking and Study Skills, pp. 1, 10*
📁 *Sentence-Combining Practice, p. 25*
📁 *Listening and Speaking Activities, p. 23*
📁 *Composition Practice, p. 26*

Narrative Writing

Editing Tip

As you edit, check your story for appropriate use of personal pronouns. For more information, see Lesson 11.1, page 429.

Decide Who Is Involved

Once you have some ideas, try them out to see if they will work for a story. Many writers try out their story ideas by focusing on a particular character. What kind of a problem is that character likely to have? How would he or she try to solve that problem?

The paragraphs below involve Mellissa, who tells the story in the first person, and Eddie, who lives in an abandoned bus. The excerpt begins with Mellissa's father telling her some news.

Literature Model

When does Mellissa sense that Eddie faces a problem?

A
fter the reporter left Eddie's place today, Hendrikson showed up with a bunch of people. They barged right into the bus." He stopped, embarrassed. "Like I did tonight, I guess. Anyway, they told Eddie that the city was going to help him by moving him into the newest senior citizen housing complex."

I didn't like the sound of it. "They can't do that! Eddie will never go for it. He hates apartments. He told me. He likes to be free."

"I know. And I don't blame him. . . . But anyway, the thing that really upset him is they told him he can't take Shadow with him."

"Why not?"

At what point does Mellissa recognize the seriousness of the problem?

"No dogs allowed."

Incredible! "Shadow isn't just a dog. He's like a relative to Eddie. They need each other."

"They don't care. He's a dog and they don't allow any animals."

Gloria Gonzalez, *The Glad Man*

Imagine that you are the author, Gloria Gonzalez, answering the questions in the chart on page 161. Think of some different solutions to Eddie's problem.

MEETING INDIVIDUAL NEEDS

English Language Learners

Using Synonyms and Near-Synonyms

Point out to students whose first language is not English that the words *conflict* and *problem* are both used to describe a thing that needs to be solved in stories. Explain that although the words have similar meanings, they are not exactly the same. Generally, all conflicts are problems, but not all problems are conflicts. A conflict is a sharp disagreement of ideas, goals, etc. A problem is a question or situation that is perplexing and difficult. Invite students to share words in their own languages that may have similarly nuanced meanings.

Write a Narrative Message

Think of a story in your literature book in which a character gets into some kind of trouble or faces some kind of problem. Write a message from that character to a friend, asking the friend for help.

PURPOSE To narrate a brief story about a predicament
AUDIENCE A friend
LENGTH 2–3 paragraphs

WRITING RUBRICS To write an effective narrative message, you should

- explain the problem
- tell what led up to the problem
- tell what the character wants to happen—the solution
- include events that could happen, in order
- proofread for correct spelling and usage

Listening and Speaking

COOPERATIVE LEARNING In a group of three or four, read your messages aloud. See if the listeners in your group can tell what literary character "wrote" your message. Use feedback from your group members to help you refine your narrative message before you publish it in a collection assembled by the entire class.

Using Computers

Before you submit your work, you may want to make it look more appealing by experimenting with different type sizes and typefaces on your computer.

Grammar Link

Avoid using double negatives!

Two negative words together create confusing double negatives.

> They **don't** allow **no** animals.

The correct version from the story is "They don't allow any animals."

Rewrite these sentences using only one negative word.

1. I didn't do nothing.
2. Hardly no one knew.
3. None never came to my house.
4. No one said nothing.
5. She doesn't never go to the movies.

See Lesson 12.10, page 469.

Grammar Link

Answers
1. I didn't do anything. OR I did nothing.
2. Hardly anyone knew. OR Almost no one knew.
3. None ever came to my house.
4. No one said anything.
5. She doesn't ever go to the movies. OR She never goes to the movies.

Assess

Evaluation Rubrics

Write a Narrative Message

Use these criteria when evaluating students' writing. The message should

- develop the problem in a sensible fashion
- incorporate relevant details from the literature
- present a reasonable solution

See also *Writing Assessment and Evaluation Rubrics*

Listening and Speaking

Monitor groups to ensure that students display an understanding of the literary character selected and to make sure that criticism is constructive.

Using Computers

Provide an opportunity for students to share the results from their experimentation.

Reteaching

📁 *Composition Reteaching*, p. 26

Enrichment

📁 *Composition Enrichment*, p. 26

🖼 *Fine Art Transparencies*, 16–20

Close

News stories, like advertisements, are driven by narrative elements that hold our attention. Encourage students to find a news story, either in a broadcast or in print, that they want to share. As they summarize their stories, students should identify the problem, the solution (if one is given or suggested; if not, they should suggest one), and the characters involved. Why did this event happen when it did? Who will feel the effects most? Why?

Narrative Writing

Focus

Lesson Overview

Objectives

- To learn about ordering events in a narrative and to identify transition words to help narrative flow
- To express relationships among narrative events, using time order and transition words

Skills

- ordering events in time; choosing words to signify transitions

Critical Thinking

- analyzing; relating events to one another; synthesizing; recalling; visualizing

Listening and Speaking

- note taking; asking questions; discussing; evaluating; explaining a process

Bellringer
Daily Language Activity

When students enter the classroom, have this assignment on the board: *List five things you did yesterday after leaving school. Number the events in the order they occurred.*

Grammar Link to the Bellringer

Remind students that since they are writing about yesterday's events, their verbs should be in the past tense.

See also *Daily Language Practice*

Motivating Activity

Ask students to write about a significant event in their lives (such as moving to a new city) describing events in the order they happened. When students finish, ask whether they remembered the events in sequence. Then point out that time order is one of the most common ways of telling a story, but that it doesn't always come naturally to a storyteller.

164

Using Time Order in a Story

*W*hich came first, the chicken or the egg?

Just as there is no right answer to this question, there is no one right way to tell a story. As a storyteller, you will want to narrate the events in an order that will make sense to your readers.

First, Think Time!

Time order—the order in which events occur from first to last—is a logical way to organize ideas in a story. Remembering the order in which events happen will help you plan your story and assist your readers in following the situation. Look at the illustrations at the top of the next page. They show a series of events arranged in time order.

Resource Manager

Planning Resources
- *Lesson Plans*

Transparencies
- *Bellringer*
- *Daily Language Practice*
- *Fine Art 16–20*
- *Two-Minute Skill Drill*
- *Writing Process 14–16B*

Other Print Resources
- *Composition Enrichment*, p. 27
- *Composition Practice*, p. 27
- *Composition Reteaching*, p. 27
- *Cooperative Learning Activities*, pp. 19–24
- *Listening and Speaking Activities*, p. 23
- *Sentence-Combining Practice*, p. 25

- *Thinking and Study Skills*, p. 8
- *Writing Across the Curriculum*
- *Writing Assessment and Evaluation Rubrics*

Story Events in Time Order

Fox sees the fire. | Fox runs away from the fire. | Fox reaches a ravine.

This series of events is the basis for the paragraph below. Notice how the writer uses time order to tell the story and help her readers follow the action of a fox escaping a fire.

Student Model

Leaving my den in the morning, I felt an immense heat at my back. I turned around and there, before my eyes, was an enormous wall of fire and smoke! I bounded away from the fire and headed toward the safety of the ravine. The brush swept by my face. The fire kept gaining on me, threatening me. I tried to propel myself faster, but my tongue hung down and my energy began running out. Suddenly, the landscape sloped downwards, and the ravine came into view.

Jenny DeLong, Canyon Park Junior High School
Bothell, Washington

> How does time order help the writer tell the story?

Teach

Using the Model

Ask a volunteer to read the passage aloud while other students envision the action. Students should suggest how time order helps DeLong tell her story (it makes the events of the plot clear and easy to follow). Students also may point out that by leaving out a definite final event, the writer creates suspense. Ask students to consider such questions as the following: *How might the story change if the fox sensed the fire before leaving its den? If this were your story, would it end when the fox reached the ravine, or would new events follow?* **L2**

Examining the Model

Distribute individual copies of the student model. Ask students to underline or list each event in the story, beginning with "leaving my den" and concluding with "the ravine came into view." To help students distinguish between major and minor events in a plot, ask them to circle the events that make the story match the pictures on this page. Then invite students to suggest replacements for the minor events (for example, the fox might notice other animals fleeing the fire instead of recognizing its own exhaustion). **L1**

Journal Writing

Think about the past week, and choose something that happened to you—something about which you might like to write a story. As you think of the events that you will include in your story, list them. Then number the events in the order in which they actually occurred.

Journal Writing Tip

Using Imagination Students may prefer to write about something they wish had happened. Those who choose that option should realize that they will have to think more imaginatively to come up with plot events. Allow interested students to meet with peer reviewers to discuss the reasonableness of their order.

Enrichment and Extension

Using Time Order

Ask students to think about a person who has influenced them or someone they know. Have them write a brief story about this person. Students should provide a sequence of events that will help to show the person's influence. Suggest that they use sensory details to enhance their stories.

Teach

Using the Model

Ask students to comment on the way Schwartz builds suspense in this passage. Why does it matter that John Cowles goes to the sick person's farm? (His absence makes the doorless house even less secure.) When is the suspense at its highest? (When the bear turns and stares at Mrs. Cowles.) "Until then" suggests that the door was not yet on the cabin; it also alerts the reader to a possible problem arising from the absence of a door. **L2**

Two-Minute Skill Drill

Write the following words and phrases on the board. Ask students to list them in a logical order.

finally	after all that
early on	much later
once	

See also *Two-Minute Skill Drill Transparency 4.3*

Additional Resources

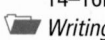 *Fine Art Transparencies,* 16–20

Writing Process Transparencies, 14–16B

Writing Across the Curriculum

Cooperative Learning Activities, pp. 19–24

Thinking and Study Skills, p. 8

Listening and Speaking Activities, p. 23

Composition Practice, p. 27

Sentence-Combining Practice, p. 25

Narrative Writing

Revising Tip

When you revise, be sure that story events follow a time order that is clear and understandable to the reader.

What does the transition phrase "until then" tell the reader?

The transition word "suddenly" also adds drama and suspense to the story.

Use Transitions

Certain words and phrases, called **transitions,** can help readers keep track of the order of events in your writing. Some examples of transitions include *before, after, until then, next, first,* and *finally.*

Read the story below. Then reread it, paying attention to the highlighted words. What do these transitions add to the story?

Literature Model

When John Cowles and his wife and baby moved to Wisconsin in 1843, they built a one-room cabin to live in. All the cabin needed was a front door. That was due to arrive before the weather turned cold. Until then they had hung a heavy quilt over the doorway.

John Cowles was a doctor. One night before supper, a messenger came for him. Someone was sick on a farm about twelve miles away. "I'll be home tonight or tomorrow morning," he told his wife. He quickly packed his things and rode off into the darkness.

His wife left a pot of beans simmering on the hearth in case he was hungry when he got home. Then she got into bed with her baby and went to sleep.

Sometime during the night, Mrs. Cowles awakened. She sensed that someone was in the cabin with her, probably her husband. But when she opened her eyes, she saw a bear in front of the fireplace. He was eating the beans, mouthful after mouthful.

Suddenly he stopped. He looked up and stared across the room at her. In the darkness, his eyes looked like burning coals. She wondered if he could see her. If the baby cried out, what would he do? If he attacked, what could she do?

The bear turned back to the beans. When he finished with them, he pushed the quilt aside and left.

Alvin Schwartz, "A Pot of Beans"

Less-Proficient Readers

Working with Transitions

Explain that the transitions discussed here indicate a sequence of events. Before students read the literature, give them an example of transitions used to describe time order. You might describe the process of getting ready for school, using *first, next, then,* and *last.* Discuss the difference between *first* and *before.* Ask which word might introduce a series of events told in order. (first) Which would you use if you started in the middle of a story and then went back to an earlier event? (before)

Write a Personal Narrative

Look in your journal at the entry for the activity on page 165. Using the events listed in your journal as a stimulus, write a one-page story.

PURPOSE To tell a personal story
AUDIENCE Your friends and family
LENGTH 1 page

WRITING RUBRICS To write an effective personal narrative, you should

- add details that develop plot, character, and setting
- use time order to develop the story
- use transitions to help your reader follow the action
- use consistent verb tenses
- write legibly

Viewing and Representing

SPEAKING WITH PICTURES Using your personal narrative as a guide, create a series of four or five drawings which tell the same story without words. Make sure the drawings follow the same order as the details in the narrative. Create a kind of exhibit guide by assembling the class's written narratives. Put the drawings on display and ask students to match the drawings with the written narratives.

Grammar Link

Make sure that your verbs do not shift unnecessarily from past to present tense.

Rewrite the following paragraph, avoiding tense shifts.

¹ The suspect sat squirming in his seat and does not meet my eyes. **²** "Tell me where you were," I say. **³** He hesitated, and in that instant I knew that he is trying to hide something. **⁴** I stare at him intently. **⁵** The color slowly drains from his face, and he finally looked up and met my eyes.
See Lesson 10.5, page 407.

Cross-Curricular Activity

SCIENCE Suppose that your science class has started a tutoring program for third-grade students. As part of the program, you have been asked to choose a science topic and write a story about it. For example, you might write a story to teach students how a plant grows.

Write a one-page story for younger students. Remember to use characters, plot, and setting to create your story. Be sure you use time order and transition words to relate events.

Assess

Evaluation Rubrics

Write a Personal Narrative

Use these criteria when evaluating your students' writing:

- Was prewriting prompted by the Journal Writing activity?
- Do transition words move the action along logically?

See also *Writing Assessment and Evaluation Rubrics*

Viewing and Representing

Help students to identify the crucial elements of their narratives, to make appealing illustrations, and to construct orderly displays of drawings.

Cross-Curricular Activity

A student may choose a life science topic (how the eye sees) or an earth science topic (why water freezes). Each story should

- be factually correct
- reflect an appreciation for the interests of its audience

Reteaching

Composition Reteaching, p. 27

Enrichment

Composition Enrichment, p. 27

Fine Art Transparencies, 16–20

Close

Challenge students to explore various kinds of writing—narrative and others—for unusual examples of time order. Students will find that examples range from functional (a police report or a recipe) to creative (a choreographer's mapping of a dance routine). Discuss the time sequence in examples that students choose to share with the class.

Grammar Link

Answers

Answers will vary, but changes to the paragraph should make all verbs past tense or all verbs present tense, except those inside quotation marks.

Focus

Lesson Overview

Objectives

- To develop an understanding of the relationship between dialogue and character development
- To create dialogue that reveals the personalities of characters

Skills

- choosing words to reveal character; evaluating dialogue on the basis of sound

Critical Thinking

- visualizing; analyzing; recalling; evaluating; inferring

Listening and Speaking

- taking notes; interpreting special clues; discussing

Bellringer

Daily Language Activity

When students enter the classroom, have this assignment on the board: *Write one line of dialogue that reveals the character of someone you know well.*

Grammar Link to the Bellringer

Ask students if they remembered to place opening and closing quotation marks around their characters' statements.

See also *Daily Language Practice*

Motivating Activity

Have students share their answers to the Bellringer assignment. Ask students how they think good dialogue reveals character. Then call on volunteers to improvise one of the following situations:

- a student explaining why he or she is late to class
- a customer returning a defective video-cassette recorder
- an actress discovering her dog can talk

Discuss with students what the improvised dialogues revealed about each character.

Narrative Writing

Writing Dialogue to Develop Characters

What characters say in a story will often reveal what they are like.

If you're familiar with *Alice in Wonderland*, you probably remember the line "Off with her head!" The Queen of Hearts said it quite often. What does that line tell you about the queen? How might the people she was angry with have felt?

Read the statements below. Describe what the lines tell you about each character who is speaking.

Dialogue
1. "Stand back, everyone! I'll take care of that dragon."
2. "Party? What party? It was your birthday? Ohhh. Sorry."
3. "If you won't help me, then I'll just do it myself."
4. "Hi, Mr. Elias! I'm here to take you for a wheelchair ride."

Let Them Speak for Themselves

Dialogue in stories consists of the characters' exact words. Dialogue can help reveal the moods, interests, and personalities of different characters. In the first passage on the next page, Mrs. Suárez is talking to her neighbor, Mr. Mendelsohn.

168 Unit 4 Narrative Writing

Resource Manager

 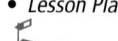

Planning Resources
- *Lesson Plans*

Transparencies
- *Bellringer*
- *Daily Language Practice*
- *Fine Art* 16–20
- *Two-Minute Skill Drill*
- *Writing Process* 14–16B

Other Print Resources
- *Composition Enrichment*, p. 28
- *Composition Practice*, p. 28
- *Composition Reteaching*, p. 28
- *Cooperative Learning Activities*, pp. 19–24
- *Listening and Speaking Activities*, p. 23
- *Sentence-Combining Practice*, p. 25

- *Thinking and Study Skills*, p. 9
- *Writing Across the Curriculum*
- *Writing Assessment and Evaluation Rubrics*

Literature Model

Another piece of bread?" she asked.
"No, thank you very much. . . . I'm full. But it was delicious."

"You too skinny — you don't eat right, I bet." Mrs. Suárez shook her head. "Come tomorrow and have Sunday supper with us."

"I really couldn't."

"Sure you could. I always make a big supper."

Nicholasa Mohr, "Mr. Mendelsohn"

> What do you think Mrs. Suárez's words tell you about her personality?

In the next literature passage David, an American man who is spending a year in Wales, talks to Peter, his son. Peter is unhappy about celebrating Christmas away from home. David speaks first.

Literature Model

Christmas is Christmas no matter where you are."

"I wish we were home," said Peter.

"You've made that plain over and over," retorted David. "There is no point in saying it again."

"You never seem to pay any attention."

Nancy Bond, *A String in the Harp*

> What does the dialogue between Peter and David reveal about them?

Editing Tip

When editing dialogue, make sure you've used quotation marks and commas appropriately. For more information, see Lesson 20.6, page 599.

Narrative Writing

Teach

Using the Model

Invite students to compare the moods of the two passages. Which one seems lighter? (the first one) Do students think the mood in either passage will change in the next few paragraphs? (A "breaking point" could be proposed for either case.) Students may differ in their interpretations of Mrs. Suárez. (Some will see her as a concerned "good neighbor," but others may consider her a pushy busybody.) Ask students to comment on Peter's and David's attitudes. (Students might conclude that Peter resents being away from home and that David is frustrated with Peter's complaints.) **L2**

Visualizing Dialogue

Some students generate more dialogue by visualizing a scene than by interpreting printed text. Provide visuals that students can use as a basis for oral dialogue. You might show them a magazine photograph or reproduce a comic strip with the speech balloons opaqued. Be prepared to model this activity by suggesting oral dialogue. Then have students critique their own suggested dialogue. **L1**

Journal Writing

Look at three pieces of dialogue in a book or story you have read recently. In your journal jot down a few notes about how the dialogue made you feel toward the characters.

Journal Writing Tip

Drawing Conclusions You may want to stimulate students' thinking with questions such as these:
- What would I have said in the same situation?
- Which characters would I trust most? Why?

4.4 Writing Dialogue to Develop Characters **169**

Teach

Using the Model

Point out that a personality trait can be revealed by a precise verb (*whispered*), a precise modifier of a verb (*in a dry voice*), or both (*murmured so softly that I could hardly hear his words*). Encourage students to look for elements that show other Tips for Writing Dialogue at work in the passage. **L2**

Two-Minute Skill Drill

Write these incomplete sentences on the board:

- *"I shouldn't have stepped in front of that steamroller," Tom _____.*

- *"We must leave you now," Tom _____.*

- *"What's this stuff on my tree?" Tom _____.*

Have students create a "Tom Swiftie," where words following the dialogue reinforce the content of the speaker's words. Ask them to match one of the following phrases to each sentence: *said with abandon, barked, remarked flatly.*

See also *Two-Minute Skill Drill Transparency 4.4*

Additional Resources

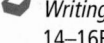 *Fine Art Transparencies, 16–20*

 Writing Process Transparencies, 14–16B

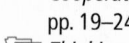 *Writing Across the Curriculum*
 *Cooperative Learning Activities, pp. 19–24*
Thinking and Study Skills, p. 9
Listening and Speaking Activities, p. 23
Composition Practice, p. 28

Narrative Writing

Use Descriptive Phrases Wisely

Tips for Writing Dialogue

 Use words that reflect the character's personality.

 Be sure the dialogue sounds like something that character would say.

 Put the character's exact words in quotation marks.

 Start a new paragraph when you move from one speaker to another.

 Use descriptive words to tell how the character said something.

Identifying the speaker helps your readers follow the dialogue. Describing how a character speaks helps the reader "hear" the lines. Think about how these characters say their lines.

"Anybody home?" she yelled cheerily.

"Anybody home?" Juan whispered.

"Anybody home?" the giant roared.

Use descriptive words or phrases such as *cheerily* sparingly. Attaching descriptions to every identifying phrase can make writing sound unnatural. In this excerpt Aztec ruler Montezuma and his advisers discuss the arrival of Cortez's army. Notice how the descriptive phrases convey Montezuma's reaction.

Literature Model

We must wait," Montezuma said in a dry voice.

"For what do we wait, my Lord?"

"We must see . . . we must discover if these strangers will leave us or if they will stay. We must find out what they want," Montezuma murmured so softly that I could hardly hear his words.

"My Lord," the councilmen asked, "will they come here? . . . Will they dare approach Tenochtitlán?"

"I do not know," the great Lord whispered, " . . . I do not know. . . ."

Jamake Highwater, *The Sun, He Dies*

How does Montezuma feel about the Spaniards' arrival? How do you know?

170   Unit 4 Narrative Writing

Exploring Language

Expanding Vocabulary

To expand students' awareness of dialogue verbs, ask them to use a thesaurus to compile synonyms for *say*. (Students can learn more about thesaurus use in Lesson 22.7.) Encourage them to list the words they find and record them in their journals. Have students refer to their lists as they draft and revise dialogue.

Write a Dialogue

Find a copy of a painting or a photograph in which two or three people seem to be engaging in a conversation. Imagine what the people might be saying to one another. Think of characteristics for each figure. Then draft a dialogue between the characters.

PURPOSE To use dialogue to make characters come to life

AUDIENCE Yourself

LENGTH 1–2 pages

WRITING RUBRICS   To create effective dialogue, you should

- use language that reveals characters' moods and personalities
- use quotation marks to show characters' exact words
- use descriptive phrases when necessary to tell how the words should sound
- proofread to make sure you have made clear who is speaking

Listening and Speaking

COOPERATIVE LEARNING   In a small group, review each other's pictures and dialogues. Use your group's comments to refine and revise your dialogue to make it clearer and more interesting. Then make a dramatic reading of the dialogue, having different students read aloud the parts you've written.

Grammar Link

Use quotation marks for dialogue.

Quotation marks go before and after the characters' exact words. Rewrite the sentences in the following dialogue, adding quotation marks.

1. Tim whispered, What's going on?
2. Hmm, responded Dave quietly, it looks like Joe's in trouble.
3. Let's get going! I'm not getting involved in his problems.
4. Hesitating, Dave replied, Wait! It looks as though he could use our help.
5. You stay, then. I'm out of here!

See Lesson 20.6, page 599.

Cross-Curricular Activity

DRAMA   After all the small groups have reviewed and refined their dialogues and have made them into dramatic readings, hold a performance festival in class. Have each group choose one of its readings, display the picture on which it was based, and perform the dialogue for the entire class. Hold a follow-up discussion to find out how other students might have represented the characters differently.

Assess
Evaluation Rubrics

Write a Dialogue

Use these criteria when evaluating your students' writing. Their dialogues should

- arise naturally from the situation depicted
- be enclosed in quotation marks
- express differences in the characters' personalities

See also *Writing Assessment and Evaluation Rubrics*

Listening and Speaking

Monitor groups as they work. Each member should contribute by discussing comments and offering constructive criticism.

Reteaching

📁 *Composition Reteaching*, p. 28

Enrichment

📁 *Composition Enrichment*, p. 28

✍ *Fine Art Transparencies*, 16–20

Close

When students begin to carry ideas from the lessons into their own writing, suggest that they establish a separate journal (or a separate section within a journal) to record their thoughts and feelings during the writing process. As a result of this lesson, students might note a struggle over finding the best descriptive words or phrases for dialogue or might reflect on the importance of a written conversation to the story as a whole.

4.4 Writing Dialogue to Develop Characters   **171**

Grammar Link

Answers
1. Tim whispered, "What's going on?"
2. "Hmm," responded Dave quietly, "it looks like Joe's in trouble."
3. "Let's get going! I'm not getting involved in his problems."
4. Hesitating, Dave replied, "Wait! It looks as though he could use our help."
5. "You stay, then. I'm out of here!"

Focus

Lesson Overview

Objectives

- To identify prewriting techniques
- To plan and generate a draft of a brief story

Skills

- preparing before writing; constructing a framework for a story; choosing authentic details

Critical Thinking

- generating new information; visualizing; identifying main ideas; synthesizing; relating

Listening and Speaking

- discussing; taking notes; evaluating

Bellringer
Daily Language Activity

When students enter the classroom, have this assignment on the board: *Brainstorm and list events in your life that you could use as the plot of a story.*

Grammar Link to the Bellringer

Remind students that in brainstorming they can use sentence fragments or even single words or phrases.

See also *Daily Language Practice*

Motivating Activity

Discuss students' responses to the Bellringer assignment. Share the following quotations with the class:

- "Inspiration is another name for knowing your job and getting down to it." (Joyce Cary)
- "I don't worry about inspiration . . . It's a matter of just sitting down and working." (Frank Herbert)
- "Inspiration usually comes during work, rather than before it." (Madeleine L'Engle)

According to these writers, what is more important to a writer than inspiration? (The act of writing itself.).

LESSON
4.5

Drafting a Story

*D*oing *some planning before starting a story helps a writer avoid panic. The writer can then begin drafting a story with confidence.*

Calvin and Hobbes
by Bill Watterson

Even professional writers sometimes feel like Calvin. The following three paragraphs, however, show the results of careful planning by author Laurence Yep.

Literature Model

After reading these opening lines, what do you know about the plot of this story?

I stopped when I smelled the magic. It was strong magic. Old magic. And it carried a faint scent of the sea. And yet I was a thousand kilometers away from the nearest body of salt water.

Halting in the middle of the road, I tried to follow the scent. It came from the top of a nearby hill, where a little village sat like a tray of dirty, overturned cups that someone had left to gather dust. But the magic I smelled was too powerful for a small, sleepy place like that.

What have you learned so far about the main character?

Well, when trouble isn't drawn to me, I seem to be drawn to it. Leaning on my staff, I stepped off the main road onto the side path that wound through the rice fields.

Laurence Yep, *Dragon of the Lost Sea*

172 Unit 4 Narrative Writing

Resource Manager

📂 **Planning Resources**
- *Lesson Plans*

🖥 **Transparencies**
- *Bellringer*
- *Daily Language Practice*
- *Fine Art* 16–20
- *Two-Minute Skill Drill*
- *Writing Process* 14–16B

📂 **Other Print Resources**
- *Composition Enrichment,* p. 29
- *Composition Practice,* p. 29
- *Composition Reteaching,* p. 29
- *Cooperative Learning Activities,* pp. 19–24
- *Listening and Speaking Activities,* p. 23
- *Sentence-Combining Practice,* p. 25

- *Thinking and Study Skills,* p. 8
- *Writing Across the Curriculum*
- *Writing Assessment and Evaluation Rubrics*

Start with a Plan

Plan some elements of your story before you begin drafting. Think about the characters and events and how the setting affects them. One writer planned a story about a dog kidnapped by aliens. The chart below shows elements he included in his plan. Writing down some details about the important story elements can ease you into drafting your story.

Planning Story Elements

Plot: A spacecraft lowers from the clouds. It hovers over a girl walking her dog. The dog breaks free from his leash as the ship beams him aboard.

Characters: Fourteen-year-old Nina likes skateboarding but doesn't like walking Scooter, the family dog. Scooter loves to run and barks when walked on his leash.

Setting: The aliens' planet is covered with grass. Dogs run around without leashes, collars, or owners. A river of dog chow flows past countless trees and buried bones.

Journal Writing

Think of a character, an event, and a setting to use in a story. Use a chart similar to the one above, and jot down as many details about each of these elements as you can.

Teach

Using the Model

After students have read the passage, ask them what ideas they think Yep must have had in mind before he started writing. Students should note the plot that is suggested by Yep's opening lines. By the end of the third paragraph, they should also be able to name a few traits of the main character. **L2**

Cooperative Learning

Offer students a Think-Pair-Share activity. They should choose partners and a story idea and then brainstorm details about plot, characters, and setting. Encourage them to share their favorite details with the class. Students can work from story ideas in their journals, or they can choose one of the following:

- being lost in an unfamiliar place
- working hard to win a contest or competition
- discovering a mysterious object **L2**

Journal Writing Tip

Organizing Ideas As students complete their charts, point out that they need not tell the entire story; their charts are only organizers and idea holders.

Teach

Focusing on Drafting Tips

Although the Drafting Tips are intended as helpful suggestions, some students may see the illustration and think they must juggle all these ideas as they draft. If you need to reduce the material to one guideline, ask students to imagine that a scene from a movie is playing in their heads and to write down what they see. **L1**

Two-Minute Skill Drill

To warm up students for the drafting process, have them complete the following sentences. The answers can be made up or real, but students should write quickly without stopping to analyze their work.

- *Three years ago, I _____.*
- *He said that she said that _____.*
- *At the end of the flight, Bruce realized he was sitting next to _____.*
- *The _____ hit the building and _____.*
- *I was supposed to _____ but I _____.*

See also *Two-Minute Skill Drill Transparency 4.5*

Additional Resources

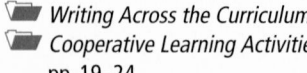

Fine Art Transparencies, 16–20

Writing Process Transparencies, 14–16B

Writing Across the Curriculum
Cooperative Learning Activities, pp. 19–24
Thinking and Study Skills, p. 8
Sentence-Combining Practice, p. 25
Listening and Speaking Activities, p. 23
Composition Practice, p. 29

Narrative Writing

Prewriting Tip

As you plan your story, think about what information the reader will need to follow the events.

Now Just Write

Your story will eventually bring together plot, setting, and characters. As you draft, you may want to focus on one of these elements. Review your prewriting notes, and choose the element that seems most striking. Then start writing about this element, and notice how the other elements find their way into the story. Other helpful drafting tips are listed in the illustration below.

Drafting Tips

| Start writing, and keep writing. | Let your story tell itself. | Try to see and hear your story as you are writing it. | Worry about punctuation, grammar, and spelling later. | Take a break if you get stuck. |

The paragraphs below are part of a story called "Project: Brainwave." As you read, notice how Rick Harrison lets the story tell itself.

Student Model

This computer stores the memories and experiences of the entire human race. Beep! You may choose from five categories. *Beep!* They are: 1. Mystery, *beep!* 2. Adventure, *beep!* 3. Paradise, *beep!* 4. Romance, *beep!* and 5. Sports, *beep!*"

How does this list of choices move the plot along?

. . . I figured I deserved a vacation. So I chose Paradise. But as I reached for the headset, my wrist accidentally hit the Mystery button as well. Before I knew it, for the second time that day, everything went black.

Rick Harrison, Mt. Pleasant Middle School, Livingston, New Jersey; first appeared in *Merlyn's Pen: The National Magazine of Student Writing*

MEETING INDIVIDUAL NEEDS
English Language Learners

Writing Quickly

Remind students whose first language is not English that an important part of drafting a story is to keep writing and not to agonize over each word. If students find that ideas are coming to them faster than they can think of them in English, they should write them in their first language and rewrite them in English later.

4.5 Writing Activities

Write a Tall Tale

Storytelling festivals are held across the United States. Often one of the biggest events is the tall-tale contest. Contestants have a few minutes to tell the funniest and most outlandish story they can think of.

Follow the model on page 174 to plan your story. Then draft your tall tale.

PURPOSE To entertain an audience with a tall tale

AUDIENCE People attending the festival

LENGTH 2 paragraphs that can be told within 2 minutes

WRITING RUBRICS To write an effective tall tale, you should

- include larger-than-life details that help readers picture the characters, events, and setting
- focus on one element in your draft
- proofread to correct sentence fragments

Listening and Speaking

COOPERATIVE LEARNING Working in a group of three, start with a planning chart like the one on page 173. Label the rows *Plot, Characters,* and *Setting.* The first person fills in the Plot row, the second person fills in the Characters row, and the third person fills in the Setting row. Then each group member drafts a story based on the ideas in the planning chart. Read your stories aloud, using tone, volume, and emphasis to create interest.

Grammar Link

Watch for sentence fragments.

A sentence fragment lacks a subject, a predicate, or both. Avoid sentence fragments when you write for school or in any formal writing. To correct a sentence fragment, add the subject or predicate, or connect the fragment to a nearby sentence. Rewrite the following items to eliminate the sentence fragments. If the item is a complete sentence, write *correct*.

1. Formed high banks along the road.
2. Snow blanketed the ground.
3. Ice like diamonds.
4. Puffs of breath hang in the air.
5. Clouds in the sky.
6. Groan in the wind.

See Lesson 8.2, page 359.

Viewing and Representing

ILLUSTRATE A TALE Create an illustration that will help a reader understand and appreciate your tall tale. Help the reader see what your character is like and the setting in which he or she functions.

Assess

Evaluation Rubrics

Write a Tall Tale

Use these criteria when evaluating your students' work.

- Do the story details fit the framework of the story?
- Does the story idea stretch reality enough to qualify as a tall tale?

See also *Writing Assessment and Evaluation Rubrics*

Listening and Speaking

Ask the groups to comment on each member's story:

- Did it include ideas from other group members?
- Did the story hold their attention? If so, why? If not, how might it be improved?
- Which part of the story did they like best—a plot event, the personality of a character, a setting they could visualize? Why did that part work so well?

Reteaching

📁 *Composition Reteaching,* p. 29

Enrichment

📁 *Composition Enrichment,* p. 29

Close

Discuss the drafting of narratives with students. Have them consider the *Calvin and Hobbes* cartoon on page 172. Is it a narrative? Invite students to find and bring in cartoons that may be narratives. Can they use the process they just learned to create their own cartoons? Encourage interested students to research cartoonists' methods.

Grammar Link

Answers

Answers will vary, but the sentences need
1. a subject
2. nothing—correct
3. a predicate
4. nothing—correct
5. a predicate
6. a subject

Focus

Lesson Overview

Objectives
- To identify different ways to begin a story
- To select and draft ideas for story openings

Skills
- preparing to write; generating and evaluating ideas; choosing the best approach for beginning a particular story

Critical Thinking
- evaluating; analyzing; synthesizing; recalling; activating prior knowledge; decision making; establishing and evaluating criteria

Listening and Speaking
- discussing; taking notes; evaluating; informal speaking; explaining a process

Bellringer
Daily Language Activity

When students enter the classroom, have this assignment on the board: *Write a brief description of how one of your favorite stories begins.*

Grammar Link to the Bellringer

Do students' descriptions tell where, how, when, why, or under what circumstances something happened? Ask volunteers for an example. Identify for students any instances of adverb clauses in examples.

See also *Daily Language Practice*

Motivating Activity

Call on volunteers to share their responses to the Bellringer. Use those responses to help students think about how a story opening affects the rest of the story (it sets the tone; it draws the reader in).

Narrative Writing

Evaluating a Story Opening

good story begins by grabbing the reader's attention. If the beginning is dull, the reader might decide not to continue. Notice how writer Isaac Asimov begins his story in the following model.

Isaac Asimov plunges into a tense scene to open this story, the first he ever published. He tells very little about the situation—directly. Yet, because Asimov's writing lets you hear and see the characters, you learn a great deal.

Asimov was only a teenager when he wrote this story. Yet the opening kept the editor of a science-fiction magazine reading long enough to decide to publish the story.

Literature Model

ill you please stop walking up and down like that?" said Warren Moore from the couch. "It won't do any of us any good. Think of our blessings; we're airtight, aren't we?"

Mark Brandon whirled and ground his teeth at him. "I'm glad you feel happy about that," he spat out viciously. "Of course, you don't know that our air supply will last only three days." He resumed his interrupted stride with a defiant air.

Isaac Asimov, "Marooned off Vesta"

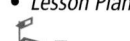

What makes this a good story beginning?

176 Unit 4 Narrative Writing

Resource Manager

Planning Resources
- *Lesson Plans*

Transparencies
- *Bellringer*
- *Daily Language Practice*
- *Fine Art* 16–20
- *Two-Minute Skill Drill*
- *Writing Process* 14–16B

Other Print Resources
- *Composition Enrichment,* p. 30
- *Composition Practice,* p. 30
- *Composition Reteaching,* p. 30
- *Cooperative Learning Activities,* pp. 19–24
- *Listening and Speaking Activities,* p. 23
- *Sentence-Combining Practice,* p. 25

- *Thinking and Study Skills,* p. 16
- *Writing Across the Curriculum*
- *Writing Assessment and Evaluation Rubrics*

Grab Attention

Starting to read a story doesn't always mean finishing it. Think about what makes you keep reading a story. Is it an exciting plot? intriguing characters? an unusual writing style? Consider these questions as you read the following paragraphs written by a student.

Student Model

I only remember two things from when I was seven: The time I got a bingo chip stuck up my nose and had to go to the hospital to have it removed, and the fights I had with my sister, Jane. We used to argue endlessly.

When Mom and Dad weren't around, I'd always give her the "now I'M the boss" speech, she'd do something like pour shampoo in my sock drawer, and we'd both end up tearing each other's hair out. Then when Mom and Dad got back, I'd run to them and say, "YOU take care of her—I'm running away!" Jane would then waltz in and say, sweet as pie, "What's going on?"

Renee Albe, Maplewood, New Jersey
First appeared in *Cricket* magazine

Renee uses dialogue to develop her characters and advance the story.

Do you think this is an effective story beginning? Why?

Revising Tip

To improve your story beginning, think about the most interesting detail of your story.

Some writers work and rework the beginning of a story until they get it just the way they want it. They feel that once they have a beginning the rest of the story will fall into place. Other writers draft the entire story first. Then they look for the catchiest line or the first dramatic moment and move that to the beginning.

Journal Writing

Look at the opening paragraphs of a story you enjoyed reading recently. What elements in the opening did you find interesting? Record your answers in your journal.

Teach

Using the Model

Ask students to find the first place in the student model where the writer names her topic ("the fights I had with my sister, Jane," in the fourth line). Why do they think she mentions the bingo chip? (It establishes the humor and keeps the reader in suspense about the main topic.)

Students' evaluations of the model's beginning may differ. (The humorous situation is itself an attention getter; the opening establishes the conflict that drives the plot; many readers have clashed with siblings and can easily identify with this writer.) **L2**

Promoting Discussion

Some professional writers have declared that not knowing the direction in which their stories will go actually frees their creativity. Other writers, however, have said that they must write out their story endings or write an outline to plan a story. Suggest that some students experiment with these methods. Encourage students to share with the class which methods worked better for them and why. What problems might a writer face using each method? **L3**

Journal Writing Tip

Writing Attributes and Components If students are keeping a reading list in their journals (see Journal Activity on page 157), they should be able to choose a story quickly. Students who are reluctant to discuss the stylistic elements of their choices can comment on how the story openings made them feel.

Teach

Creating a Story Opening

For this round robin activity, divide the class into groups, and give each group a copy of a brief article from a recent newspaper. Select one student from each group to read the news story to his or her teammates. Then have each student in turn suggest a story idea based on that news item. When the group has chosen one story idea to develop, ask them to work together to draft a story opening. One member of each group can then report the results to the class. **L2**

Two-Minute Skill Drill

Write the following infamous story beginning by Edward Bulwer-Lytton on the board: "It was a dark and stormy night." Have students rewrite this sentence twice, changing at least one word each time. Discuss the different tones that result.

See also *Two-Minute Skill Drill Transparency 4.6*

Additional Resources

- *Fine Art Transparencies, 16–20*
- *Writing Process Transparencies, 14–16B*
- *Writing Across the Curriculum*
- *Cooperative Learning Activities, pp. 19–24*
- *Thinking and Study Skills, p. 16*
- *Sentence-Combining Practice, p. 25*
- *Listening and Speaking Activities, p. 23*
- *Composition Practice, p. 30*

Narrative Writing

Make an Impact

Sometimes revising a story opening means looking at the rest of what you've written to find the best place to start. You might look for the most engaging sentences and start your story at that point, as in the paper on the left below.

Other times you keep the beginning you have but make a few changes, as in the paper on the right. Cutting unimportant words or adding descriptive details can give more impact to your story beginning.

Either approach works well. You may try both methods several times before you write a beginning that satisfies you.

> What did the writer achieve by beginning where she did?

It was a lovely spring morning when Kathy and I set out on the bike trip we'd planned for so long. I'd been so excited over breakfast I'd hardly been able to eat.

It had never occurred to either of us that anything would go wrong. So *Start Here* when my rear tire went flat, I stood by the side of the road and watched helplessly as Kathy and her yellow bike receded into the distance.

> Which of the revised openings do you find more effective? Why?

It was a lovely spring *The* morning when Kathy and I set out on the *overnight* bike trip we'd planned for so long, *was too* *to eat* I'd been so excited over breakfast. I'd hardly been able to eat.

It had never occurred to either of us that anything would go *I was already starving* wrong. So when my rear tire went *only two hours into the trip.* flat, I stood by the side of the road and watched helplessly as Kathy *and my lunch disappeared* and her yellow bike receded into *over a hill* the distance.

MEETING INDIVIDUAL NEEDS — English Language Learners

Beginning Stories

Point out to students whose first language is not English that the classic story opener in English is "Once upon a time…" It usually suggests a folktale or fairy tale, but variations on it are used in all kinds of stories. Most other languages have a common story starter, too; for example, in Ashanti Twi it is common to say *Abakwa sem,* or "history says." Ask students to recall a typical or famous story starter from their own language. Have them translate it into English and share it with the class.

Write a Story Opening

Look in your journal for story ideas. Select one idea to develop. Think of at least three beginnings to your story. Choose one version. Then draft and revise a possible beginning for the story you've selected.

PURPOSE To grab readers' attention
AUDIENCE Your teacher
LENGTH 1–2 paragraphs

WRITING RUBRICS To write a good story opening, you should

- capture your readers' attention
- include engaging details
- delete unnecessary words
- vary sentences by using adverb clauses

Allan Rohan Crite, *Last Game at Dusk*, 1939

Grammar Link

Use adverb clauses to modify verbs.

An *adverb clause* describes the verb in the main clause, telling how, when, where, why, or under what circumstances the action occurs. Adverb clauses begin with words such as *after, when, where, before, while,* and *as: Before cars were available, some people rode bikes.* Add an adverb clause to each of the following sentences:

1. Many people commute by bus.
2. Children must ride cautiously.
3. He watches television.
4. They returned from their trip.
5. I always brush my teeth.

See Lesson 14.4, page 507.

Cross-Curricular Activity

ART Brainstorm for ideas about characters, plot, and setting based on the painting on this page. Select one idea; then plan and draft a story opening. Refer to page 177 for different ways to revise your opening to give it more impact.

Listening and Speaking

COOPERATIVE LEARNING In groups of three or four, read your openings aloud. Use your group's comments to edit and refine your opening.

4.6 Evaluating a Story Opening **179**

Narrative Writing

Assess

Evaluation Rubrics

Write a Story Opening
Use these criteria when evaluating your students' writing.
- Does it capture attention?
- Is it free of unnecessary words?

See also *Writing Assessment and Evaluation Rubrics*

Cross-Curricular Activity
Look at the draft and revised beginning. Consider the following:
- Is it an attention getter?
- Do story details relate to the painting?

Listening and Speaking
Monitor groups as they work. Each member should offer constructive criticism and use comments to refine drafts.

Reteaching
📁 *Composition Reteaching*, p. 30

Enrichment
📁 *Composition Enrichment*, p. 30

📐 *Fine Art Transparencies*, 16–20

Close

Encourage students to set aside a section in their journals to record story openings (or leads from other kinds of writing) that capture their interest. A record of such lines can both remind students of their own reading and inspire them when they are looking for a way to hold an audience in their own writing.

Grammar Link

Answers
Answers will vary, but the added adverb clauses should tell something about how, when, where, why, or under what circumstances the action in each sentence occurs. Each clause should contain a subject and a predicate.

Viewing the Art

Allan Rohan Crite, *Last Game at Dusk*, 1939
Allan Rohan Crite (1910–) felt that fellow African Americans were depicted too often as field laborers or jazz musicians. His paintings feature scenes in his native Boston. The Boston Athenaeum owns this oil painting.

Focus

Lesson Overview

Objectives

- To learn to respond to a short story
- To synthesize critical and creative thoughts in responses to a short story

Skills

- reading comprehension; writing responses to stories; using apostrophes correctly

Critical Thinking

- recalling; evaluating; establishing and evaluating criteria; generating new information

Listening and Speaking

- discussing; interviewing; informal speaking

 Bellringer
Daily Language Activity

When students enter the classroom, have this assignment on the board: *List five movies you have seen or heard about.*

Grammar Link to the Bellringer

Ask students if any of their listed movies contain contractions or possessive forms, for example, *It's a Wonderful Life.* Remind them that contractions and most possessive forms need an apostrophe.

See also *Daily Language Practice*

Motivating Activity

Discuss students' titles. Were any of these titles originally the titles of books or stories? (Be prepared to suggest such titles if necessary.) Why might a movie be considered a response to a written story? (It treats the story visually; it highlights the parts of the story that the director finds most intriguing; it may explore possibilities only hinted at in the original.)

Narrative Writing

LESSON 4.7

WRITING ABOUT LITERATURE
Responding to a Story

The response to a story is a reflection of the reader's experiences.

In the literature excerpt below, a young man has brought an injured owl to a doctor. Read to find out what the young man discovers during his visit.

Literature Model

Cage after cage of birds, Theseus saw, all down one wall of the room, finches and thrushes, starlings and blackbirds, with a sleepy stirring and twittering coming from them.

In the surgery [doctor's office] there was only one cage, but that one big enough to house a man. And inside it was such a bird as Theseus had never seen before—every feather on it pure gold, and eyes like candle-flames.

"My phoenix," the doctor said, "but don't go too near him, for he's vicious." . . .

"You are only just in time," Dr. Kilvaney said. "My hour has come. I hereby appoint you my heir and successor. To you I bequeath my birds. Feed them well, treat them kindly, and they will sing to you. But never, never let the phoenix out of his cage, for his nature is evil."

"No, no! Dr. Kilvaney!" Theseus cried. "You are in the wrong of it! You are putting a terrible thing on me! I don't want your birds, not a feather of them. I can't abide creatures in cages!"

Joan Aiken, "A Leg Full of Rubies"

 **Resource Manager**

Planning Resources
- *Lesson Plans*

Transparencies
- *Bellringer*
- *Daily Language Practice*
- *Fine Art* 16–20
- *Two-Minute Skill Drill*
- *Writing Process* 14–16B

Other Print Resources
- *Composition Enrichment,* p. 31
- *Composition Practice,* p. 31
- *Composition Reteaching,* p. 31
- *Cooperative Learning Activities,* pp. 19–24
- *Listening and Speaking Activities,* p. 23
- *Sentence-Combining Practice,* p. 25

- *Thinking and Study Skills,* p. 22
- *Writing Across the Curriculum*
- *Writing Assessment and Evaluation Rubrics*

Connect with the Story

After reading this excerpt, were you curious about the phoenix? worried about Theseus? You can respond to any story element that intrigues you. You can also respond in different forms. One reader responded by drawing this picture of the phoenix. April Andry thought the story should end differently. Originally, Theseus safely rid himself of the phoenix. April responded by reworking the plot to provide a new ending.

Student Model

After several weeks, Theseus's curiosity about the phoenix became too much. Ignoring the doctor's warning, he decided to let the bird out of its cage.

He immediately regretted his decision. The bird quickly flew around the room, destroying the other cages and freeing the birds. Soon, there was a frenzy of birds all around Theseus. He couldn't see anything, but he could feel birds pecking him all over. Miraculously, he managed to escape.

Theseus's wounds healed eventually, but he still had the ugly scars to remind him of the phoenix. From then on, his sleep was haunted by visions of the golden phoenix and its glowing eyes.

April Andry, Emerson Junior High School
Oak Park, Illinois

What other endings can you think of for the story?

Presenting Tip

When reading aloud from a narrative with more than one character, try using a different voice for each character.

Journal Writing

Which element of the literature excerpt on page 180 do you find the most intriguing? Explain why in your journal.

Teach

Using the Model

Encourage students to reread the passage from "A Leg Full of Rubies" before they discuss Andry's story ending. Their own story endings will vary, but as they consider possibilities, they may want to ask questions such as these:

- What are Theseus's feelings about birds?
- Why might Dr. Kilvaney have collected all these birds?
- How did Dr. Kilvaney acquire a phoenix, and how does he know that it is evil? **L2**

Reading Book Reviews

Book reviews are one kind of response to fiction, for reviewers base their opinions on how well they think authors have executed various story elements. Encourage interested students to look for reviews of fiction in a newspaper or magazine and report on what they think a particular reviewer finds important about a book. Alternatively, suggest they interview the library staff to find out how reviews determine the choice of new purchases. **L3**

Journal Writing Tip

Establishing and Assessing Criteria Remind students to respond as readers rather than writers at this point, that is, they should use this activity to explore their feelings about the story rather than to analyze its elements.

Teach

Responding to Literature

A three-step interview is another way to respond to a piece of literature. Suggest that students who have read the same story pair up, ask each other questions about the work and their reactions to it, and note their responses. Then ask them to organize their notes. When they share their comments with the class, allow other students to ask them questions. **L2**

Two-Minute Skill Drill

Have students correct the following brief review:

I read the three musketeers and think its a great book. Its main themes are loyalty and bravery.

See also 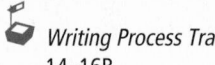 *Two-Minute Skill Drill Transparency 4.7*

Additional Resources

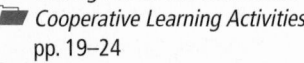 *Fine Art Transparencies, 16–20*

Writing Process Transparencies, 14–16B

📁 *Writing Across the Curriculum*
📁 *Cooperative Learning Activities, pp. 19–24*
📁 *Thinking and Study Skills, p. 22*
📁 *Sentence-Combining Practice, p. 25*
📁 *Listening and Speaking Activities, p. 23*
📁 *Composition Practice, p. 31*

Use a Different Approach

Writing a story of your own is just one way to respond to a story. Use your imagination to explore other possibilities. Suppose that you have a chance to interview a character from the story. You may begin by writing down the questions you'd ask, and you might go so far as to imagine the character's answers.

Perhaps you are intrigued by a certain topic that the story suggests. One writer was fascinated by the phoenix in "A Leg Full of Rubies" and wanted to find out more about it. The journal entry below shows the writer's response.

The story inspired this writer to do some additional reading to find out more about the phoenix.

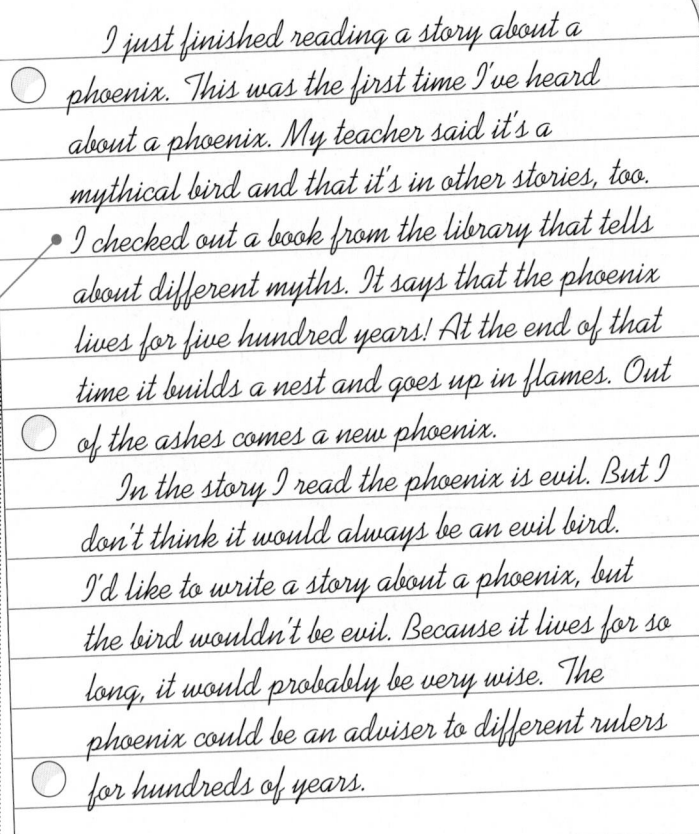

> I just finished reading a story about a phoenix. This was the first time I've heard about a phoenix. My teacher said it's a mythical bird and that it's in other stories, too.
>
> I checked out a book from the library that tells about different myths. It says that the phoenix lives for five hundred years! At the end of that time it builds a nest and goes up in flames. Out of the ashes comes a new phoenix.
>
> In the story I read the phoenix is evil. But I don't think it would always be an evil bird. I'd like to write a story about a phoenix, but the bird wouldn't be evil. Because it lives for so long, it would probably be very wise. The phoenix could be an adviser to different rulers for hundreds of years.

Enrichment and Extension

Choosing Styles of Response

Some students might prefer to explore responses that do not depend upon extensive writing, such as creating a piece of abstract art that captures their feelings about the literature, or organizing a readers' theater through which they can dramatically present their interpretation of a piece of writing. Alternatively, students may simply choose to use a tape recorder to save their oral responses before they prepare a written response.

Narrative Writing

Write a Response

Select a short story you would like to respond to. You can choose a new story or a story you have already read. Think of ideas for responding to it. Review the suggestions in this lesson or think of your own ideas. Then write a one-page response.

PURPOSE To respond to a story
AUDIENCE Yourself
LENGTH 2 paragraphs
WRITING RUBRICS To write an effective response to a story, you should

- be clear about your emotional reactions
- be creative in selecting a way to respond

Cross-Curricular Activity

MYTHOLOGY Use your school or public library to find out about the phoenix myth in Asian or Native American culture or in another culture. Make copies of the various images you find and display them in a class exhibit. Write a brief response to the images, discussing the similarities and differences you see in the images across cultures. Compare and contrast the images with the idea you had of the phoenix after you read the excerpt from "A Leg Full of Rubies."

Grammar Link

Use apostrophes correctly.

doctor's (possessive noun) *office*
don't (contraction of *do* + *not*)
its (possessive pronoun) *cage*
it's (contraction of *it* + *is*)

Add apostrophes where needed.

1. Its raining today.
2. Can I try on your sisters hat?
3. Is this book yours or ours?
4. The cat wants its food.
5. Give them the key—its theirs.

See Lesson 11.4, page 435, and Lesson 20.7, page 601.

Using Computers

Extend your research on the phoenix by using the Internet to find additional information and images. In a small group, discuss the relative advantages and disadvantages of using electronic and print resources for research.

Assess

Evaluation Rubrics

Write a Response

Use these criteria when evaluating your students' writing.
- Does the response highlight the elements of the work to which the writer has a strong response?
- Does the response reveal the writer's reaction?

See also *Writing Assessment and Evaluation Rubrics*

Cross-Curricular Activity

Each student can choose how to respond. As you review the response, ask the following:
- Does it present one culture's view of the phoenix myth?
- Does it suggest the writer's reaction to his or her findings?

Using Computers

Make sure students understand how to use the Internet to do research.

Reteaching

📁 *Composition Reteaching*, p. 31

Enrichment

📁 *Composition Enrichment*, p. 31

📖 *Fine Art Transparencies*, 16–20

Close

Challenge students to discuss unusual artistic responses to literature. Point out that fine artists are often inspired by classic literature, and writers often reference or quote the work of other writers. (If students need hints, point out that classical ballet, religious art, many dramatic films, and many forms of satire are created in response to existing literature.)

Grammar Link

Answers
1. It's
2. sister's
3. correct
4. correct
5. it's

Focus

Lesson Overview

Objectives

- To gain an understanding of the narrative writing process
- To use the stages of the writing process to create and present a finished piece

Skills

- using the five stages of the writing process: prewriting, drafting, revising, editing, and presenting

Critical Thinking

- synthesizing; defining and clarifying; recalling

Listening and Speaking

- informal speaking; discussing; questioning

 Bellringer

Daily Language Activity

When students enter the classroom, have this assignment on the board: *List one to five people who have been important in your life or are special to you in some way.*

Grammar Link to the Bellringer

Have students write a short sentence to identify each person, using a possessive pronoun. For example, *I am her son,* or *She is my best friend.*

See also *Daily Language Practice*

Motivating Activity

Ask students to imagine they are in a greeting-card store. Walking up and down the aisles, they see cards that say, "Happy Birthday," "Thank You," "Thinking of You," and so on. Ask students to choose one person from their Bellringer list to send a card to. What would the card say, and why? Students might choose that same person for the lesson assignment; or they may prefer to work with a piece of writing they have already started.

184

Narrative Writing

Narrative Writing

In the preceding lessons, you learned about the elements that make up a short story—plot, character, and setting—and about the kinds of details, action, and dialogue that can make characters vivid and memorable. You have written stories of your own. Now, in this lesson, you're invited to write about someone you have known well. Tell the story of an event or a series of events that shows why this person is special to you.

WRITING Online

Visit the *Writer's Choice* Web site at **writerschoice. glencoe.com** for additional writing prompts.

Assignment

Context	You have been asked to share a story about a special person you have known well. Write about one event that makes this person special to you.
Purpose	To show in a story how you feel about a special person
Audience	Students
Length	1 page

The following pages can help you plan and write your story. Read through them and then refer to them as needed. But don't be tied down by them. You're in charge of your own writing process.

Resource Manager

📂 Planning Resources
- *Lesson Plans*

📇 Transparencies
- *Bellringer*
- *Daily Language Practice*
- *Writing Process* 14–16B

📂 Other Print Resources
- *Composition Enrichment,* p. 32
- *Composition Practice,* p. 32
- *Composition Reteaching,* p. 32

- *Grammar Workbook,* Lesson 25
- *Sentence-Combining Practice,* p. 25
- *Thinking and Study Skills,* p. 5
- *Writing Assessment and Evaluation Rubrics*

💾 Software
- *Writer's Assistant*

🖥 Web Sites
- *writerschoice.glencoe.com*
- *lit.glencoe.com*

Writing Process in Action

Prewriting

Whom will you write about? You could choose a close friend, a relative, a teacher, or a camp counselor. Look through photo albums, letters, journals, or collections of objects to help you decide whom you want to write about. Brainstorming may help you explore what you want to say about the person. Find specific details about the person and your experiences with her or him to use in your story.

Drafting

After noting details about your subject, you need to look through your prewriting to get an idea of how to start your story. A strong opening paragraph will make the person you're writing about sound interesting from the very beginning. Choose a few details that set your character apart. Notice the details in the following paragraph that would let you recognize Delfina right away if you happened to meet her.

Option A

Look at important objects or mementos.

Option B

Browse through a photo album.

Option C

Review your journal.

> My swimming trophies bear my name, but they should bear this name, too: Glenn Williams. I was afraid of the water until the summer he taught me to swim. His soft voice and steady gaze calmed me.

Narrative Writing

Literature Model

When she arrived at our house she was covered by a huge black umbrella. A white gardenia hung from her left ear. My sister Cynthia and I were bewitched by the sight of her. We were a little afraid, too. She seemed like an enormous fish or a shipwrecked lady far from home.

Marjorie Agosín, "A Huge Black Umbrella"

Teach

Prewriting

Deciding on Story Ideas

A simultaneous roundtable activity can help students choose a topic. After students are grouped, have each student write a story idea (for example, "The time Aunt Susan trusted me to take care of her cat") at the top of a piece of paper. As they rotate papers, other students should write questions about that idea. When owners receive their completed papers, have them study the questions. Do they still want to develop that story idea? Which questions will help them most? **L2**

Additional Resources

📁 *Thinking and Study Skills*, p. 5

Drafting

Avoiding Writer's Block

A strong story opening is important, but students should not get bogged down in developing the first paragraph before they have given their ideas a chance to play out in the draft as a whole. Indeed, students may grow so frustrated over the "right" opening that they do not want to go on. Some students may be more successful if they begin to draft the "action" part of their story and return to the introduction later. **L1**

Teach

Revising

Peer Editing

Students can work in writing conferences with peer editors before they revise their work. You may want to duplicate the Peer Response forms in the *Writing Assessment & Evaluation Rubrics*. Suggest that peer editors respond to the following:

- I would use the words _____ and _____ to describe the person you wrote about. Am I right?
- If I met this person, I would recognize him or her because . . . **L2**

Cooperative Learning

Explain how dialogue brings characters to life. Have pairs read each other's drafts, pose a question one character might ask another, and then respond in writing in the character's voice. **L2**

Editing/Proofreading

Peer Editing

After students have edited their own work, have them edit another student's writing. Refer them to the Editing/Proofreading Checklist on student page 187. **L2**

Publishing/Presenting

Before students present their narrative writing, discuss how to prepare their papers for publication. Emphasize the importance of the final draft and that it must be neatly done.

Additional Resources

 Writing Process Transparencies, 14–16B

 Thinking and Study Skills, p. 5

 Sentence-Combining Practice, p. 32

Composition Practice, p. 32

 Grammar Workbook, Lessons 25

Narrative Writing

Drafting Tip

For information about creating mood, see Lesson 4.4, pages 168–171.

As you draft your story, keep your focus on the person you're writing about. If you get stuck, look again at your prewriting notes for fresh ideas. The most important thing to remember at the drafting stage is to get your ideas on paper. You can make changes later.

Revising

To begin revising, read over your draft to make sure that what you have written fits your purpose and your audience. Then have a **writing conference.** Read your draft to a partner or a small group, or receive feedback from your teacher. Use your audience's reactions to help you evaluate your work so far. The questions below can help you and your listeners.

Option A

Does every sentence contribute to the story?

Option B

Do the details let readers picture my subject?

Option C

Does the action of my story move along clearly?

> I didn't even want to go to camp that summer. I hated the counselor who registered me, *the tall man with big ears who greeted us* but as soon as I found out that Mr. Williams was going to be my swimming teacher, I knew the summer would be all right. He *yet sure* talked in a soft voice that forced you to lean toward him. He wore a whistle like every other swimming teacher I'd ever had, but I never heard him use it.

Enrichment and Extension

Follow-up Ideas

- Set aside time for students to celebrate the conclusion of their projects. Encourage them to share finished pieces with the class or in groups.
- If students send work out for publication, make sure to photocopy it.

Extending Narrative

- Explore opportunities for using narrative writing in other subject areas, such as writing and reading personal narratives in history class.
- Brainstorm ways to extend narrative writing beyond the classroom.

Editing/Proofreading

Many writers will let their work sit for a day before they begin to edit. During the editing stage, you can **proofread** for any errors that might muddy the ideas and feelings you want to express. For instance, if your story contains dialogue, you'll want to make sure that your readers can follow who is speaking.

This Editing Checklist will help you catch errors you might otherwise overlook. You'll want your story to reflect your hard work. If some part of it still doesn't sound right, fix it.

Editing/Proofreading Checklist

- ☑ 1. Have I used quotation marks before and after direct quotations?
- ☑ 2. Are all my sentences complete?
- ☑ 3. Have I used possessive nouns and pronouns correctly?
- ☑ 4. Have I checked to be sure that all words are spelled correctly?
- ☑ 5. Have I used conjunctions and prepositions correctly?

Publishing/Presenting

It might help you to ask someone else who knows your subject to read your story. Your reader may have some last-minute suggestions to contribute. Copy your final draft neatly, using print or cursive handwriting. Consider putting your story in a folder or a clear plastic sleeve to make it more attractive. If you have a photograph of the person you've written about, include it with your story.

Proofreading Tip

Check for proper capitalization in sentences, quotations, and proper nouns and adjectives. For more information, see pages 573–574 and 579–580.

Journal Writing

Reflect on your writing process experience. Answer these questions in your journal: What do you like best about your narrative? What was the hardest part of writing it? What did you learn in your writing conference? What new things have you learned as a writer?

Assess

Evaluation Rubrics

Use the following questions to evaluate the student's finished writing:

- Does the writing include details about the subject?
- If the story tells only what the subject looks like, can you suggest ways in which the student might incorporate other senses?
- Has the student checked for correct grammar, usage, and mechanics?

See also *Writing Assessment and Evaluation Rubrics*

Reteaching

📁 *Composition Reteaching,* p. 32

Enrichment

📁 *Composition Enrichment,* p. 32

Journal Writing Tip

Using Prewriting Remind students that they may want to use the prewriting techniques of freewriting or idea clustering to address these questions initially.

Close

The next time students watch an awards ceremony, on television or in person, encourage them to pay special attention to the tributes that are given. Which ones include anecdotes—short stories that show something about the personality of the person being honored? Does the audience seem to respond more to those tributes than to the ones that just say, "This person means so much to me"? If so, why?

Cultural Connections

Writing within Cultural Context

Allow students to work within the scope of family traditions. For example, students may want to write about an ancestor whom they have never met but have come to know and admire from family stories. Students who would enjoy an additional challenge might write about a person from a different cultural background whom they have come to know well. With that option, stories should focus on an event that shows appreciation for some aspect of a culture other than the writer's own.

Literature Model

About the Author

Marjorie Agosín, born in Chile, is recognized for her writing, for her studies of Latin American literature, and for her analyses of the role of women in Latin American politics.

This selection is from *Where Angels Glide at Dawn: New Stories from Latin America,* a collection of translated short stories edited by Lori M. Carlson and Cynthia L. Ventura.

Focus

Lesson Overview

Objective

- To examine character portrayal in a narrative.
- To write a character portrait

Skills

- interpreting

Critical Thinking

- inferring; evaluating; comparing and contrasting

Listening and Speaking

- discussing

Bellringer

Daily Language Activity

When students enter the classroom, have this assignment on the board: *Describe a natural disaster that you have heard about or experienced.*

See also *Daily Language Practice*

Motivating Activity

Have students share descriptions. If they have heard any stories about the event, ask them to share those. Then ask if they ever wondered what happens to survivors once the event is no longer "news." Would they rebuild if they were alone? Move? Why?

Literature Model

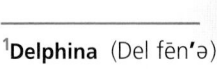

A Huge
Black Umbrella

by Marjorie Agosín

In "A Huge Black Umbrella," Marjorie Agosín tells the story of Delfina,[1] a special woman who lived an extraordinary life. As you read, pay special attention to Agosín's effective use of detail to create the character of Delfina. Then try the activities in Linking Writing and Literature on page 192.

• • • • • • • • • • • • • • • • •

---

[1]**Delphina** (Del fēn′ə)

Resource Manager

📂 Planning Resources
- *Lesson Plans*

📑 Transparencies
- *Bellringer*
- *Daily Language Practice*
- *Fine Art* 16–20

📂 Other Print Resources
- *Listening and Speaking Activities,* p. 14–15
- *Thinking and Study Skills,* p. 22
- *Writing Assessment and Evaluation Rubrics*

🖥 Web Sites
- *writerschoice.glencoe.com*
- *lit.glencoe.com*

Literature Model

When she arrived at our house she was covered by a huge black umbrella. A white gardenia hung from her left ear. My sister Cynthia and I were bewitched by the sight of her. We were a little afraid, too. She seemed like an enormous fish or a shipwrecked lady far from home. Certainly, her umbrella was useless in the rain since it was ripped in many places, which let the rainwater fall on her—water from one of the few downpours of that surprisingly dry summer. It was the summer in which my sister and I understood why magical things happen, such as the arrival of Delfina Nahuenhual.[2]

My mother welcomed her, and Delfina, with a certain boldness, explained that she always traveled accompanied by that enormous umbrella, which protected her from the sun, elves, and little girls like us. My mother's delicate lips smiled. From that moment my mother and Delfina developed a much friendlier relationship than is usual between "the lady of the house" and "her servant."

Delfina Nahuenhual—we had to call her by her full name—was one of the few survivors of the Chilán earthquake in the south of Chile. She had lost her children, house, her wedding gown, chickens, and two of her favorite lemon trees. All she could rescue was that huge black umbrella covered with dust and forgotten things.

In the evenings she usually lit a small stove for cooking; the fire gave off a very lovely, sweet light. Then she wrapped herself up in an enormous shawl of blue wool that wasn't scratchy and she put a few slices of potato on her temples to protect herself from sickness and cold drafts.

As we sat by the stove, Delfina Nahuenhual told stories about tormented souls and frogs that became princes. Her generous lap rocked us back and forth, and her voice made us sleepy. We were peaceful children who felt the healing power of her love. After she thought we were asleep, Delfina Nahuenhual would write long letters that she would later number and wrap up in newspaper. She kept the letters in an old pot that was filled with garlic, cumin,[3] and slivers of lemon rind.

My sister and I always wanted to read the letters and learn the name and address of the person who would receive them. So whenever Delfina

---

[2]**Nahuenhual** (Nə′ wen əl)
[3]**cumin** (kum′ in) the fruits from a small plant in the parsley family, used for flavoring, pickles, soups, etc.

Literature Model **189**

Narrative Writing

Teach

Literary Elements

Character Explain to students that authors develop their characters by using direct description, by showing a character in action, and by describing others' reactions to a character. Then ask: "What can you tell about the character Delfina Nahuenhual? Her appearance? Her personality? Her strength of character? Her history? How does the author let readers know these things?" (*The author directly describes Delfina Nahuenhual as a large, middle-aged woman who lost her home and family in an earthquake. By her actions, readers can tell that she is imaginative and compassionate, though also quiet and tired. She commands respect, as seen in her relationship to the children's mother.*)

6+1 Trait® Writing

Word Choice Tell students that a simile is a figure of speech that uses the word *like* or *as* to compare two different things. Ask: "What simile does the author use in the first paragraph? How does it help you get a mental picture of Delfina Nahuenhual?" (*"She seemed like an enormous fish or a shipwrecked lady far from home." The comparisons capture Delfina Nahuenhual's large size and her tattered appearance.*)

Critical Thinking

Infer Tell students that the story contains a mystery. Ask what they think the mystery will be. (*What are Delfina Nahuenhual's letters about, and whom are they for?*)

6+1 Trait® Writing

Sentence Fluency

Tell students that good writing has an easy flow and rhythm, or fluency. One way that writers achieve sentence fluency is to vary the length and the structures of their sentences. For example, the first sentence of the second paragraph is complicated and runs on for six lines. The one-line sentence that follows is short and simple. Invite students to point out other examples on the page in which Agosín varies the structure and length of her sentences.

Practice Ask students to write a paragraph about their first impressions of Delfina Nahuenhual. Then have them work with a partner to edit their paragraphs for sentence fluency. Encourage partners to point out where the writing flows easily and where it may be improved.

Teach

Critical Thinking

Interpret Tell students that they can interpret what the events in a story mean by using their own understanding of the world. Then ask them to interpret why Delfina Nahuenhual wants to return to the south of Chile. Have volunteers explain what led them to their interpretations. *(She probably misses her homeland and wants to return there. Students may realize from experience how attached a person can be to his or her home.)*

6+1 Trait® Writing

Sentence Fluency Invite volunteers to point out passages on this page that have an easy flow and rhythm. Then ask them to analyze why. *(Students may point out passages in which sentences have varying structures and length, as in the fourth paragraph.)*

6+1 Trait® is a registered trademark of Northwest Regional Educational Laboratory, which does not endorse this product.

Narrative Writing

Nahuenhual was busy in the kitchen, we tried peeking into the pot to discover what she was hiding.

But we never managed to read the letters. Delfina Nahuenhual would smile at us and shoo us along with the end of her broom.

For many years, Delfina continued to tell us stories next to the stove. Not long after my brother Mario, the spoiled one of the family, was born, Delfina Nahuenhual told us she was tired and that she wanted to return to the south of Chile. She said she now had some savings and a chicken, which was enough to live on. I thought that she wanted to die and go to heaven because she had decided to return to the mosses and clays of her land.

I remember that I cried a lot when we said good-bye. My brother Mario clung to her full skirt, not wanting to be separated from the wise woman who, for us, was never a servant. When she bent over to give me a kiss, she said that I must give her letters to the person to whom she had addressed them but that I could keep the pot.

For many years, I kept her little pot like a precious secret, a kind of magical lamp in which my childhood was captured. When I wanted to remember her, I rubbed the pot, I smelled it,

and all my fears, including my fear of darkness, vanished. After she had left I began to understand that my childhood had gone with her. Now more than ever I miss the dish of lentils[4] that she prepared for good luck and prosperity on New Year's Eve. I miss the smell of her skin and her magical stories.

Many years later, my sister Cynthia had her first daughter. Mario went traveling abroad and I decided to spend my honeymoon on Easter Island, that remote island in the middle of the Pacific Ocean, six hours by plane from Chile. It is a place full of mysterious, gigantic statues called Moais.[5] Ever since I was a child, I had been fascinated by those eerie statues, their enormous figures seeming to spring from the earth, just as Delfina Nahuenhual and her huge black umbrella did when she first came to my house. I carried her letters, which I had long ago taken from the small earthen pot and placed in a large moss-green chest along with the few cloves of garlic that still remained. As a grown-up I never had the urge to

---

[4]**lentils** (lent′ lz) plants in the family to which peas and beans belong

[5]**Moais** (Mō′ īz)

Compare and Contrast

Comparing Stories

Tell students that comparing and contrasting two selections can help them understand the characters and events in each selection on a deeper level. Then instruct students to think about how this story is similar to and different from the excerpt from *The Clay Marble* (pages 90–94). To model for students the kind of thinking required to compare and contrast, say: "The main characters in both stories have experienced losses. The girls in *The Clay Marble* lost their homes to war. Delfina Nahuenhual lost her home to an earthquake."

Practice Have students work in pairs to compare and contrast the two selections. *(Students might point out that both stories deal with the loss of family members, one through a natural disaster, the other through war. They could also compare the stories' characters, themes, tone, or writing style.)*

Literature Model

read the letters. I only knew that they should be delivered to someone.

One morning when the sun shone even in the darkest corner of my hotel room, I went to the address written on Delfina's letters. It was a leper[6] colony, one of the few that still exist. A very somber employee opened the door and quickly took the packet of five hundred letters from me. I asked if the addressee was still alive and he said of course, but that I couldn't meet the person. When I gave him the letters, it seemed as though I had lost one of my most valuable possessions, perhaps even the last memories of my dear Delfina Nahuenhual's life.

So I never did meet the person to whom Delfina Nahuenhual wrote her letters nor learned why she spent her sleepless nights writing them. I only learned that he was a leper on Easter Island, that he was still alive and, perhaps, still reads the letters, the dreams of love Delfina Nahuenhual had each night. When I returned home, I knew at last that Delfina Nahuenhual was content, because when I looked up, as she had taught me to do, I saw a

Pierre-Auguste Renoir, *The Umbrellas,* 1881–1886

huge black umbrella hovering in the cloudy sky.

_____

[6]**leper** (lep′ ər) a person having a severe skin disease that attacks and deforms skin, flesh, and nerves

Literature Model **191**

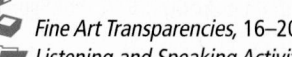

Narrative Writing

Teach

Critical Thinking

Evaluate Ask students how the story's mystery is resolved. Then have them evaluate whether this ending is satisfying and why they think Agosín ended the story this way. *(Delfina Nahuenhual was writing her letters to a man in a leper colony. Some students may be dissatisfied that Agosín does not reveal the man's relationship to Delfina Nahuenhual and that the narrator never meets the man. However, the ending is in keeping with Delfina's mysterious character.)*

Additional Resources

Fine Art Transparencies, 16–20
Listening and Speaking Activities, p. 22
Thinking and Study Skills, pp. 14–15

Viewing the Art

Pierre-Auguste Renoir, *The Umbrellas,* 1881–1886

The Umbrellas is one of the first large paintings Renoir executed in a studio instead of a natural setting. As a result of techniques Renoir learned in Italy, the painting exhibits some inconsistencies in detail and style and is considered experimental by some experts. The oil-on-canvas painting measures 70⅛ by 45¼ inches.

Interpret and Analyze Use the following questions for discussion:
• Why was this painting chosen to illustrate the story? How would you describe the mood of the painting?

Linking Writing and Literature

Assess

Evaluation Rubrics

 Talk About Reading

Possible responses to the questions:
1. Students may cite what someone special to them wears or carries (such as Delfina's umbrella) or often uses (such as the pot).
2. They love and respect Delfina, not as a servant but as an important human being in their lives. Delfina's stories and her warmth probably attract the children to her.
3. Students may describe how Agosín varies the length and structure of her sentences to achieve fluency.
4. Some students may appreciate the author's vivid, yet mysterious, descriptions of Delfina, such as in the first paragraph.

 Write About Reading

The portrait should do the following:
- describe a person
- tell what makes the person unique
- use a variety of sentence lengths and constructions

Close

Ask students to respond to this question in writing or discussion: Why was Delfina such a powerful force in the narrator's life?

Narrative Writing

Literature Model

Linking Writing and Literature

 Collect Your Thoughts

Think back on the striking character of Delfina Nahuenhual. Brainstorm for a list of words, images, and phrases that describe her appearance, personality, and character.

 Talk About Reading

Talk with other students about "A Huge Black Umbrella." Assign a group leader to keep everyone focused and a group secretary to take notes. Then use the questions below to guide your conversation.

1. **Connect to Your Life** The images of the huge black umbrella and the small earthen pot always remind the narrator of Delfina. Is there some object that reminds you of another person?
2. **Critical Thinking: Interpret** How do the narrator and her family feel about Delfina? Why do you think they feel that way?
3. **6+1 Trait®: Sentence Fluency** How does Agosín achieve a smooth rhythm and flow to her writing? Cite one example in the story that you find especially fluent.
4. **Connect to Your Writing** What do you especially like about Agosín's style of writing? Select a paragraph in which this style trait is particularly evident.

 Write About Reading

Portrait Write a portrait of a person, either real or imaginary. Describe things that make that person unique, such as the person's appearance, habits, and favorite treasures.

Focus on Sentence Fluency Your portrait will have more rhythm and flow if you vary the structure and length of your sentences. Edit your portrait for fluency. Would it help to shorten or lengthen sentences? To begin some sentences with a dependent clause?

For more information on sentence fluency and the 6+1 Trait® model, see **Writing and Research Handbook,** pages 822–824.

6+1 Trait® is a registered trademark of Northwest Regional Educational Laboratory, which does not endorse this product.

Cooperative Learning

Improvising a Conversation

Call on one or more pairs of students to improvise a conversation that the narrator might have had with her husband after delivering the letters. What does she say about the addressee? Does her husband remind her about things that she already has told him about Delfina Nahuenhual? What conclusions do students reach about Delfina—and, perhaps, about the narrator?

UNIT 4 Review

Reflecting on the Unit

Summarize what you learned in this unit by answering the following questions.

❶ What are the three basic elements of a story?

❷ What is the purpose of a story plot?

❸ Why is it important to arrange story events in time order?

❹ What does dialogue contribute to a story?

❺ What should be included in a strong story beginning?

Adding to Your Portfolio

CHOOSE A SELECTION FOR YOUR PORTFOLIO Look over the narrative writing you did for this unit. Choose a piece of writing for your portfolio that shows one or more of the following:

- believable characters, an intriguing setting, and a clear plot
- a series of events in time order
- lively, realistic dialogue that reveals what characters are like
- a beginning that makes the reader want to read the whole story

REFLECT ON YOUR CHOICE Attach a note to the piece you chose, explaining briefly why you chose it and what you learned from writing it.

SET GOALS How can you improve your writing? What skill will you focus on the next time you write?

Writing Across the Curriculum

MAKE A GEOGRAPHY CONNECTION Picture your character in a setting in another part of the world. How would the sights, sounds, tastes, and smells differ in another place? Choose a country on another continent to research. Describe how your character would reach this destination and how the character would respond to the local situations.

MAKE A SCIENCE CONNECTION Science has shaped the world we live in today. Scientific discoveries have helped us live longer and healthier lives, explained the universe, and provided the technology that makes our lives easier and more productive. Imagine that you are a scientist. You have just made a discovery that does one of the things listed above. Write a personal narrative telling about your discovery, how you made it, and what you will do with the knowledge you have gained.

Review **193**

Review

Reflecting on the Unit

You may have students respond to the review questions in writing or through discussion.

Adding to Your Portfolio

To help students select writing, suggest that they read a few pieces to a classmate. Ask students to consider the criteria on page 193 as well as the following questions: Does this story keep me interested? Do I want to find out what happens next? What's my favorite part of the story?

Writing Across the Curriculum

Remind students to present the character's travel experiences in time order. Encourage them to develop the three elements of a story—characters, setting, and plot—in their writing.

Portfolio Evaluation

If you grade the portfolio selections, you may want to award two marks—one each for content and form. Explain your assessment criteria before students make their selections.

Commend

- experimentation with creative prewriting techniques
- clear, concise writing in which the main idea, audience, and purpose are evident
- successful revisions
- work that shows a flair for language

✔ ASSESSMENT OPTIONS

📁 *Tests with Answer Key and Rubrics*
Unit 4 Choice A Test, p. 13
Unit 4 Choice B Test, p. 14
Unit 4 Composition Objective Test,
  pp. 15–16

💾 *Testmaker*
Unit 4 Choice A Test
Unit 4 Choice B Test
Unit 4 Composition Objective Test

You may wish to administer one of these tests as a mastery test.

 *MindJogger Videoquizzes*

193

Expository Writing

Viewing the Art

Especially in the central United States, where there are vast expanses of flat land, one can witness the awesome power and grandeur of a thunderstorm as it sweeps across the plains. Such a storm, although usually brief, is accompanied by thunder, lightning, strong gusty winds, heavy rain, moderate to extreme winds, and, under the most severe conditions, tornadoes.

Interpret and Analyze Have students study the photograph of the storm and answer the following questions:
- What message does this photograph communicate to you? Record your thoughts on a separate piece of paper and write legibly by selecting cursive or manuscript.
- How does this visual image affect you? Interpret and evaluate how it makes you feel.

Discussing the Quotation

Read aloud the quotation by Patricia Lauber and have students respond to the following questions:
- How does the photographer's choice of style, elements, and media help to affect the overall impression that the picture gives you?
- What are some of the ways the picture represents the meaning of the quotation?

Note To find out more about Patricia Lauber and "Hurricanes: Big Winds and Big Damage," refer students to *Glencoe Literature: The Reader's Choice,* Course 2, p. 306.

"It was a furious and compact storm, with an eye only eight miles wide and winds that reached out for 60 miles."

—Patricia Lauber

"Hurricanes: Big Winds and Big Damage"

194

Resource Manager

Planning Resources
- *Lesson Plans*
- *Block Scheduling*

Transparencies
- *Bellringer*
- *Daily Language Practice*
- *Fine Art*
- *Two-Minute Skill Drill*
- *Writing Process*

Other Print Resources
- *Composition Enrichment*
- *Composition Practice*
- *Composition Reteaching*
- *Cooperative Learning Activities*
- *Glencoe Literature Library*
- *Grammar and Composition Handbook*
- *Grammar Workbook*

- *Listening and Speaking Activities*
- *Research Paper and Report Writing*
- *Sentence-Combining Practice*
- *Tests with Answer Key and Rubrics*
- *Thinking and Study Skills*
- *Writing Across the Curriculum*
- *Writing Assessment and Evaluation Rubrics*
- *Writing in the Real World*

UNIT 5 Expository Writing

195

Objectives

- To understand and use the techniques of expository writing
- To use the stages of the writing process—prewriting, drafting, revising, editing/proofreading, and publishing/presenting—to create and present a finished piece of expository writing
- To learn how to appropriately and effectively evaluate one's own expository writing and the expository writing of others

✔ ASSESSMENT OPTIONS

Tests with Answer Key & Rubrics
Unit 5 Choice A Test, p. 17
Unit 5 Choice B Test, p. 18
Unit 5 Composition Objective Test, pp. 19–20

Testmaker
Unit 5 Choice A Test
Unit 5 Choice B Test
Unit 5 Composition Objective Test

You may wish to administer either the Unit 5 Choice A Test or the Unit 5 Choice B Test as a pretest.

Key to Ability Levels

L1 Level 1 activities are within the basic ability range of students.

L2 Level 2 activities are within the ability range of average students.

L3 Level 3 activities are more challenging activities.

📼 **Video**
- *MindJogger Videoquizzes*

💾 **Software**
- *Presentation Plus!*
- *Revising with Style*
- *Testmaker*
- *Writer's Assistant*

🖥 **Web Sites**
- *writerschoice.glencoe.com*
- *lit.glencoe.com*

Focus

Lesson Overview

Objectives
- To examine the use of expository writing in a real-life situation
- To demonstrate the use of expository writing in exhibit information labels

Skills
- gathering information; selecting details; examining audience; writing to inform and explain

Critical Thinking
- identifying; synthesizing; classifying; relating; identifying main idea; building background

Listening and Speaking
- discussing; taking notes

Bellringer
Daily Language Activity

When students enter the classroom, have this assignment on the board: *Choose a familiar animal. Write two or three sentences describing the animal's appearance or behavior.*

Grammar Link to the Bellringer

Have students revise their Bellringer writing to incorporate three or more items in a series. Elicit the correct punctuation.

See also *Daily Language Practice*

Motivating Activity

Ask the following question to spark students' interest: *Suppose you visit a zoo or an aquarium. How can you learn about the animals other than by observation?* Elicit that many cages, tanks, and display cases have information labels.

MEDIA Connection
Signs and Labels

Visitors to the Monterey Bay Aquarium in California discover a fascinating world of underwater creatures. Most of the visitors, however, would understand little of what they were seeing without certain important information. That's where Judy Rand's job comes in. Rand writes information labels for the aquarium's exhibits. Her expository writing educates visitors eager to learn the mysteries of marine life.

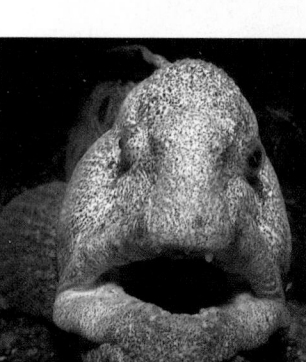

Wolf-eel
Anarrhichthys ocellatus

This night prowler leaves its den for dinner.

Hardly a wolf, not really an eel, this fierce-looking fish spends the day quietly in a cave, wriggling out at night to feed.

Though some divers say the wolf-eel can bite a broomstick in half, this predator deserves a better reputation. Wolf-eels chomp on crabs, mussels, and urchins; they don't eat divers or their brooms.

by Judy Rand

Resource Manager

Planning Resources
- *Lesson Plans*

Transparencies
- *Bellringer*
- *Daily Language Practice*
- *Writing Process* 17–19

Other Print Resources
- *Cooperative Learning Activities,* pp. 25–29
- *Thinking and Study Skills,* pp. 3, 4, 13–14, 20
- *Writing Assessment and Evaluation Rubrics*
- *Writing in the Real World,* pp. 17–20

Expository Writing

Writing Exhibit Labels

Prewriting	Drafting	Revising/Editing
Watching the Animals/ Making Notes	Writing the Labels	Making Every Word Count

Wolf-eel

A Writer's Process

Prewriting

Observing, Learning, and Making Notes

Helping people see what's right in front of them is where Judy Rand's work begins. As master developer and senior editor at the Monterey Bay Aquarium, Rand writes the information labels that visitors read as they view an exhibit.

Before she can write the labels, Rand herself must become thoroughly acquainted with the marine creatures. She spends time watching each animal, and then she writes notes in a binder about that animal's appearance and behavior.

Rand gathers information from other sources as well. She interviews the scientists and curators who care for the aquarium's ani-

mals. She also talks to scientists from outside the aquarium, especially those who have worked directly with a particular animal. In addition, she reads field guides and scientific articles.

As she collects information, Rand fills in fact sheets about each animal's traits and habits. Afterwards, she writes each idea and fact on a separate index card. To organize the information, Rand scatters the cards on the floor. She explains, "I can shuffle my ideas around. I can set aside the ones that don't seem to fit and begin to find the ones that seem important."

During this process, Rand has to choose what information she will include on a card. She keeps the interests of her audience—the aquarium's visitors—firmly in mind. Rand explains, "The most

Expository Writing

Teach

Building Background

Warm-up

Have students list several situations in which information labels might be used.

Exposition in Speaking

Remind students that they use informative speaking every day—in giving directions, explaining how to use a computer or another machine, or explaining the rules of a game.

Exposition in Writing

Discuss any information labels students have read. Use prompts such as these:

- What kinds of information have you read on labels in museum, zoo, or aquarium exhibits?
- Who do you think writes these labels—a professional writer or an expert in the subject area?
- Why might writing labels be an interesting type of work?

Preview the Media Connection

Have students preview the title and focus of the media connection. Point out that good expository writing skills are essential in creating information labels. Have students read the media connection.

Cultural Connections

Considering Audience Demographics

In writing labels for the Monterey Bay Aquarium, Judy Rand must keep in mind the interests of California's diverse ethnic population. Approximately 1 percent are Native American, 5 percent Asian, 7.5 percent African American, 19 percent Latino, and 68 percent European. Many of the most recent arrivals are from Central America, China, the Philippines, and Vietnam. Have students consult an almanac to find out the ethnic composition of their state.

Teach

Discussion Prompts

- Why does Rand focus on "immediate and observable behavior" instead of, for example, theories of why the animals behave as they do?
- What sources of information does Rand consult in writing labels? How is each source useful?
- Describe the process that Rand goes through to find a focus for her labels.
- What does the use of humor do for Rand's labels? Describe a time when you used humor to produce a similar effect in your writing.

Stimulate a discussion of the Media Connection. You may want to invite students to talk about

- whether or not they were surprised by the importance of research, planning, and drafting in writing exhibition labels
- other applications of expository writing that they can envision in other professions
- how the writing process steps for expository writing are similar to or different from the writing process steps they have used for other modes of writing **L2**

Additional Resources

Writing Process Transparencies, 17–19
Cooperative Learning Activities, pp. 25–29
Writing in the Real World, pp. 9–12
Thinking and Study Skills, pp. 3, 4, 13–14, 20

Writing in the Real World

important information on labels has to be about immediate and observable behavior. Visitors want to know about what they're seeing in the tank. 'Is this wolf-eel really an eel? What are those teeth for?'"

" *When aquarium visitors are face to face with a wolf-eel, they want to know, 'Does this animal want to eat me?' You need to begin with your reader's immediate experience. Then you can interpret the scientific facts in a friendly and relevant way.* "

—Judy Rand

Drafting
Writing the Labels

With index cards spread around the room and with reference books lying open nearby, Rand plunges in to write.

The final label will be one to two paragraphs long. But, Rand says, "I can write ten or eleven different paragraphs for a single label. I can try out an idea that has the wolf-eel's teeth right up front. Then I can try out an idea that has popular misconceptions about the animal up front."

She finally decides to focus on the wolf-eel's undeserved bad reputation. She explains, "Visitors' immediate impression of the wolf-eel is that it's fierce looking and a predator. I wanted them to understand the idea that being a predator isn't bad."

Rand uses simple language, even for complex ideas. She describes the wolf-eel as a night prowler, rather than as a nocturnal fish. As Rand notes, "We want our labels to sound as if someone is talking to you. *Nocturnal* is a lovely word, but people don't usually use words like *nocturnal* in conversation."

She also uses strong examples. After reading that "some divers say the wolf-eel can bite a broomstick in half," visitors can imagine how strong those jaws must be.

Revising/Editing
Making Every Word Count

After setting her draft aside for a day, Rand puts on her editor's hat. She reads each label aloud, listening for a friendly and conversational sound. Then she asks several people to read each label and repeat the information in their own words. "If they can't tell me what it's about, then I know I have problems."

Finally Rand sits down at her computer to check for style. She asks herself, "Is there any unfamiliar language? Have I made every word count?"

When she feels satisfied with the labels she has written, Rand gets approval from two department supervisors, as well as the aquarium's executive director. The exhibit labels are then readied for display in the aquarium.

The Deep Reefs

Deep Reefs

where is this habitat?
How are inhabitants (wolf-eel,

Lingcod

nbusher:

Enrichment and Extension

Science

The wolf-eel is also known as the wolffish. The Atlantic wolffish grows to be about three feet long; the Pacific wolffish (the kind found in the Monterey Bay Aquarium) can be as long as eight feet. Despite its fierce appearance, the wolffish has more to fear from humans than we have to fear from it. The wolffish is used for food and also for leather. Its skin is used in the bindings of books.

Examining Writing in the Real World

Analyzing the Media Connection

Discuss these questions about the model on page 196.

1. What effect do you think the opening sentence has on visitors to the aquarium? How does Rand achieve this effect?

2. How does Rand get across the point that the wolf-eel is a nocturnal creature, without actually using the word *nocturnal*?

3. What information does Rand convey about the wolf-eel's eating habits?

4. What if Rand had used the verb *consume* in place of the word *chomp*? How would that word choice change the tone of the writing? In your opinion, which word is more effective?

5. Where does Rand use humor to call attention to the wolf-eel's bad reputation?

Analyzing a Writer's Process

Discuss these questions about Judy Rand's writing process.

1. What methods does Rand use to gather information for her exhibit labels?

2. How does Rand organize the facts and ideas she has gathered? How does your own method compare to hers?

3. Rand can't use all the information that she gathers. What helps her decide what information she will include?

4. Does Rand use formal or informal language as she drafts her information labels? Why?

5. When editing, how does Rand make sure that the labels will be clear to her audience?

Grammar Link

Use commas to separate three or more items in a series.

Wolf-eels chomp on crabs, mussels, and urchins.

Use each set of words below as a series of items in a sentence. Use commas correctly.

1. bold, fierce, clever
2. furry, stout, clumsy
3. squirrels, mice, rats
4. lobsters, clams, shrimp
5. cats, dogs, goldfish

See Lesson 20.2, pages 591–592.

Grammar Link

Answers

Answers will vary, but samples are given below.

1. The bold, fierce, and clever fox stole all the chickens from the coop.
2. The furry, stout, clumsy cub played in the sun.
3. The cat enjoyed hunting for squirrels, mice, and rats.
4. Lobsters, clams, and shrimp thrived in the ocean.
5. As a child Janey's pets included cats, dogs, and goldfish.

Expository Writing

Assess

Analyzing the Media Connection

1. Answers will vary. Students may indicate that the sentence effectively describes the wolf-eel with just a few well-chosen words, such as *fierce-looking, quietly,* and *wriggling.*
2. She mentions that it spends all day in a cave and comes out at night.
3. Rand writes that it feeds at night and eats crabs, mussels, and urchins.
4. Answers may vary as to which word is more effective, but students should indicate that "chomp" is a more descriptive word than "consume."
5. She mentions a saying that divers have about the wolf-eel's being able to bite through a broomstick. After listing the wolf-eel's real diet, she says that it does not actually eat divers or their brooms.

Analyzing a Writer's Process

1. Rand observes the animals, interviews people who care for them, and reads field guides and scientific articles.
2. She organizes her ideas and facts using index cards. Students may mention that they, too, use note cards.
3. Rand focuses on information that visitors will be able to observe in the tank.
4. She uses informal language so the labels will sound as though someone is talking to the visitor.
5. She gives the cards to others to read and tell her what they understood.

See also *Writing Assessment and Evaluation Rubrics.*

Reteaching

Suggest that students evaluate newspaper headlines as brief labels for the articles they introduce.

Enrichment

Invite a local zoo or aquarium professional to address students on how his or her work helps raise visitors' awareness of the environment.

Close

Have students gather pictures of animals and write labels for them. Each label should identify the animal and include an interesting fact about it.

Note In preparation for writing a label about their animal, students should consult sources such as the periodical *International Wildlife,* the *How to Know Series,* or encyclopedias.

Focus

Lesson Overview

Objectives

- To develop a list of sources of factual information
- To explain and inform, using details and observing the qualities of good writing

Skills

- brainstorming; evaluating sources of information; using supporting facts to explain and inform; ordering the steps in a process

Critical Thinking

- evaluating; analyzing; activating prior knowledge; establishing and evaluating criteria

Listening and Speaking

- discussing; taking notes; evaluating; informal speaking; explaining a process

Bellringer

Daily Language Activity

When students enter the classroom, have this assignment on the board: *Suppose you were asked to write an article about athletic shoes. Describe in writing the first step you would take to write the article.*

Grammar Link to the Bellringer

Call on volunteers to dictate a sentence from their descriptions. Write these sentences on the board. Have students identify subjects and verbs. Challenge them to determine whether subjects and verbs agree.

See also *Daily Language Practice*

Motivating Activity

Have students describe in greater detail how they would begin an article on athletic shoes as you pose questions such as these: *What do athletic shoes do? What makes someone buy a particular brand of athletic shoe?*

Expository Writing

LESSON 5.1

Expository Writing

Giving Information and Explanations

The writing you do to explain and give information is expository writing. Most of the writing you do for school assignments is expository.

Heel counter

Sole

Midsole

If you wanted to explain to someone why running shoes are so comfortable, what information would you include? How would you order it? Read the paragraphs below to see how one writer solved this problem.

Literature Model

> How does the writer use detail in the first paragraph?

The running shoe's few basic functions are extremely important to the runner. It provides cushioning to help absorb the impact of your foot striking an unyielding road surface.

> The second paragraph names two parts of a shoe and tells how each part helps the runner.

Next, a shoe provides support, or stability. A stiff plastic **heel counter** cups the heel and keeps it from shifting laterally while you run. The **midsole** is shaped so that it helps keep your foot lined up in the shoe. Midsole design is a compromise between support and cushioning—the more cushioning, the less stability, and vice versa.

David Macaulay, "Running Shoe," *How Things Work*

Resource Manager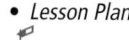

Planning Resources

- *Lesson Plans*

Transparencies

- *Bellringer*
- *Daily Language Practice*
- *Fine Art* 21–25
- *Two-Minute Skill Drill*
- *Writing Process* 17–19

Other Print Resources

- *Composition Enrichment*, p. 33
- *Composition Practice*, p. 33
- *Composition Reteaching*, p. 33
- *Cooperative Learning Activities*, pp. 25–30
- *Listening and Speaking Activities*, pp. 12–13, 21 23
- *Research Paper and Report Writing*, pp. 33–34, 36, 38

- *Sentence-Combining Practice*, pp. 30–32
- *Thinking and Study Skills*, pp. 3, 5, 17–18
- *Writing Across the Curriculum*
- *Writing Assessment and Evaluation Rubrics*

Write to Explain and Inform

Expository writing gives readers information and explanations. One kind of expository writing tells readers how to do something: how to build a doghouse or make a salad. Another kind explains how something works. The model on page 200 explains how the parts of running shoes work together to help the runner.

Other kinds of expository writing explain what something is, how things are alike or different, or why something has happened. In the model below, Ben Rallo informs his readers about why something—water pollution—has happened.

Expository Writing

Student Model

One cause of water pollution is careless campers and hikers throwing their garbage into virtually unpolluted water. They think that since there isn't anything dumped into it already, a bottle or two won't hurt. But before they know it, that same body of water, once so clean and beautiful, is sickeningly polluted by others like themselves who thought the same way.

Because of the campers' and hikers' carelessness, the natural beauty of the water is destroyed, and it no longer is a pretty sight for people to enjoy.

Ben Rallo, Springman Junior High School,
Glenview, Illinois

> Notice that Ben uses the words "cause" and "because" to explain why something happened.

Journal Writing

Try explaining something to yourself, such as **why you made** a certain choice. In your journal list your **reasons,** and tell something about each one.

5.1

Teach

Using the Model

Point out ways in which the model is an example of clear and concise expository writing. For example, the writer begins by clearly stating one cause of water pollution. He then gives some information about the cause and, finally, presents the effect. **L2**

Two-Minute Skill Drill

Write this sentence on the board:

Boston, the capital of Massachusetts and a historic city in the Northeast, is one of the oldest cities in the United States.

Have students revise the sentence to make it exact, concise, and easy to read.

See also *Two-Minute Skill Drill Transparency 5.1*

Journal Writing Tip

Activating Prior Knowledge To help students write clear explanations, suggest that they pause before beginning their journal entries. Encourage students to recall where they were, how they felt, and what they thought about when they made the choices that they are about to explain.

Teach

Gathering Information

Remind students that many reference works are available to assist researchers on nearly any subject. Arrange for students to explore a large library. Suggest that each student select a topic. Then direct students to a few sources, such as the reference area, computer or card catalogs, and the reference librarian. Encourage students to become familiar with these research possibilities. **L3**

Two-Minute Skill Drill

Have students review the Literature Model on this page and jot down notes comparing stalactites and stalagmites under the headings *Alike* and *Different*.

See also *Two-Minute Skill Drill Transparency 5.1*

Additional Resources

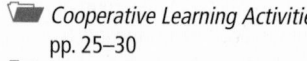 *Fine Art Transparencies*, 21–25

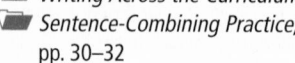 *Writing Process Transparencies*, 17–19B

📁 *Cooperative Learning Activities*, pp. 25–30

📁 *Writing Across the Curriculum*

📁 *Sentence-Combining Practice*, pp. 30–32

📁 *Thinking and Study Skills*, pp. 3, 5, 17–18

📁 *Listening and Speaking Activities*, pp. 12–13, 21, 23

📁 *Research Paper and Report Writing*, pp. 33–34, 36, 38

📁 *Composition Practice*, p. 33

Expository Writing

Grammar Tip

You often can combine two sentences that have the same subject by stating the subject once and using *and* between the verbs. For more information, see Lesson 8.6, page 367 and Lesson 18.7, p. 569.

Make Things Clear

The details you include in expository writing should help your readers understand your topic. The following chart lists other qualities that help produce strong expository writing.

Qualities of Good Expository Writing	
Clear	Easy to read
Concise	Exact, specific, and to the point
Inviting	Connects with the audience in direct, creative ways
Informative	Includes insights and ideas

In the selection below, the writer presents information about two rock formations. The last two paragraphs explain how the formations are alike and how they are different.

> Notice how the writer uses elaboration to support the main ideas.

> Which word supplies the clue that stalactites and stalagmites are alike in one way?

Literature Model

Stalactites are formed in caves by groundwater containing dissolved lime. The water drips from the roof and leaves a thin deposit as it evaporates. Growing down from the roof, stalactites increase by a fraction of an inch each year and may eventually be many yards long. Where the water supply is seasonal, stalactites may show annual growth rings like those of tree trunks.

Stalagmites are formed on the floor of caves where water has dripped from the roof or a stalactite above. Like stalactites, they develop as water containing dissolved lime evaporates.

Stalactites and stalagmites can grow together and meet to form pillars. These have been described as "organ pipes," "hanging curtains," and "portcullises."

R. F. Symes, *Rocks and Minerals*

MEETING INDIVIDUAL NEEDS — English Language Learners

Connecting with Readers

Students who have difficulty with English may need extra help in shaping information to connect with readers. You might suggest that, before beginning to write, students close their eyes and visualize their intended audience as made up of friends or relatives. To help students convey information in an inviting yet authoritative way, encourage them to pretend they are talking to their audience and to say their main points aloud before they write.

Write Procedures

Think of a time you worked with others to make or do something, such as prepare a meal or plan an event. Explain the steps of the project you worked on.

PURPOSE To experiment with ways to present details clearly

AUDIENCE Your classmates

LENGTH 2 paragraphs

WRITING RUBRICS To explain a procedure effectively, you should

- include enough details to help readers follow your explanation
- make your steps clear, concise, and logical
- make your explanation lively and interesting
- print or write legibly

Listening and Speaking

GIVING INSTRUCTIONS Turn your explanation of a procedure into an oral presentation that you will deliver to a group of younger students. Use appropriate vocabulary, volume, and gestures to make your explanation clear. If possible, use visual aids or other tools to make your presentation more interesting. Present your explanation to a small group of classmates and ask for feedback on how to make it more effective for a younger audience.

Expository Writing

Grammar Link

Make subjects and verbs agree.

When a subject and verb are separated by a prepositional phrase, always look back to the subject, and make the verb agree with it:

> One **cause** of water pollution **is** careless campers . . . .

Rewrite the following sentences, making sure that subjects and verbs agree. If they need no change, write *correct*.

1. The boy with the books look lost.
2. The cause of the false alarms were never discovered.
3. The search of the grounds was done quickly.
4. Damage from the recent rains total several million.
5. Only one of the triplets are going.

See Lesson 16.1, page 535, and Lesson 16.2, page 537.

Cross-Curricular Activity

SCIENCE Write a paragraph in which you explain to a third grader something you have recently learned in science class. Explain your topic clearly. Share your paragraph with a younger student or with someone to whom this information is new. Then consider what you learned from your "teaching experience."

Grammar Link

Answers

1. boy . . . looks
2. cause . . . was
3. correct
4. Damage . . . totals
5. one . . . is

Assess

Evaluation Rubrics

Write Procedures

Use these criteria when evaluating your students' writing. The explanation should include

- the activity to be performed in each step
- the person responsible for each step
- the reason for the specific order used in the process

See also *Writing Assessment and Evaluation Rubrics*

Listening and Speaking

In their oral presentations students should

- use language that is appropriate for younger students
- speak at a pace and volume that will help listeners understand their words
- use gestures to make their explanations clear
- use visual aids to make the presentations interesting and understandable
- express ideas with fluency and confidence

Cross-Curricular Activity

Evaluate the paragraph on the following: appropriateness and appeal to intended audience; clear, specific explanation.

Reteaching

📁 *Composition Reteaching,* p. 33

Enrichment

📁 *Composition Enrichment,* p. 33

 *Fine Art Transparencies,* 21–25

Close

Have students read a newspaper or magazine article written to inform. Invite students to discuss whether the article exhibits the qualities of good expository writing. Encourage them to use the chart on page 202 as a guide.

Expository Writing

Focus

Lesson Overview

Objectives
- To organize information and ideas for informative writing
- To choose details to support the information

Skills
- organizing information; understanding kinds of details; using details

Critical Thinking
- decision making; categorizing; defining and clarifying

Listening and Speaking
- discussing

Bellringer
Daily Language Activity

When students enter the classroom, have this assignment on the board: *Write directions for making a peanut butter and jelly sandwich (or any sandwich of your choice).*

Grammar Link to the Bellringer

In giving directions, clarity is very important. Run-on sentences can lead to confusion. Have students check their directions to make sure all sentences are clear and correctly punctuated.

See also *Daily Language Practice*

Motivating Activity

If possible, have the ingredients for a peanut butter and jelly sandwich in the classroom. Invite a volunteer to read his or her directions, sentence by sentence. Do exactly what the directions say. Are they in order? complete? How could they be clearer? If a demonstration is not possible, ask students if they have ever received incorrect directions on how to do something or how to get somewhere. Discuss the particular situations. Have students ever had to give complicated directions? Was it difficult? Why?

Organizing Informative Writing

In expository writing the order in which you present information is extremely important. The directions below, to the Space Center, show why.

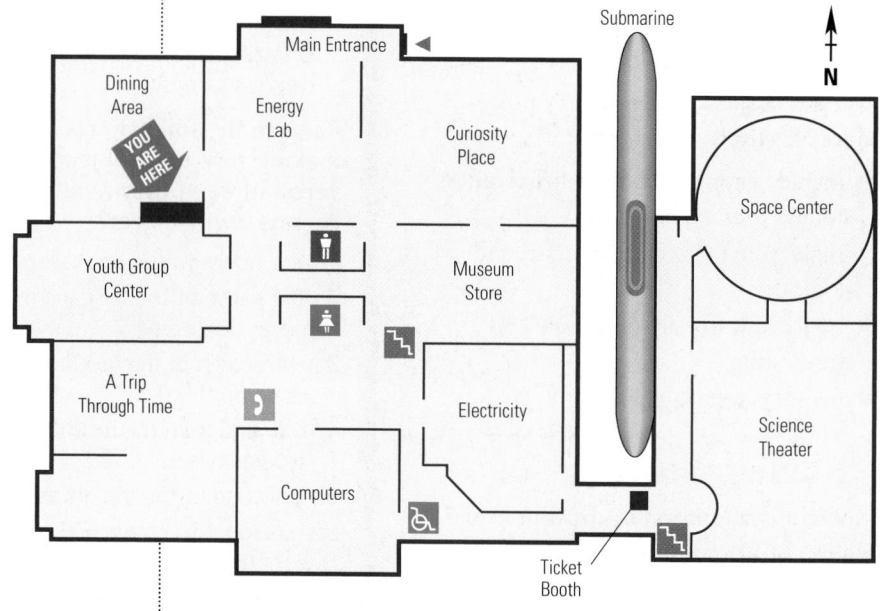

- At the pay phones, turn left.
- Leave by the door on the opposite side.
- Pass the ticket booth, and turn left immediately.
- Go into the Energy Lab, and turn right immediately.
- Pass the Science Theater. Turn right into the Space Center.
- Enter the Electricity exhibit.

The information is out of order, making the directions impossible to follow. On a sheet of paper, reorder these steps so that a visitor can go from the Dining Area to the Space Center.

Resource Manager

Planning Resources
- *Lesson Plans*

Transparencies
- *Bellringer*
- *Daily Language Practice*
- *Fine Art* 21–25
- *Two-Minute Skill Drill*
- *Writing Process* 17–19B

Other Print Resources
- *Composition Enrichment*, p. 34
- *Composition Practice*, p. 34
- *Composition Reteaching*, p. 34
- *Cooperative Learning Activities*, pp. 25–30
- *Listening and Speaking Activities*, pp. 12–13, 21, 23
- *Research Paper and Report Writing*, pp. 33–34, 36, 38

- *Sentence-Combining Practice*, pp. 30–32
- *Thinking and Study Skills*, pp. 8, 10–11
- *Writing Across the Curriculum*
- *Writing Assessment and Evaluation Rubrics*

Get Organized

How you organize information in expository writing depends on what you want to say. You may arrange steps in the order in which they would be performed. You may list facts in order of importance. You may tell about places and things according to their position. You may even list items according to how much you like or dislike them.

Examine the diagram below. How many different ways could you organize the information if you were going to write about the planets?

Drafting Tip

See **Writing and Research Handbook,** pages 820–821, for more information about how to organize information in paragraphs and in longer pieces of expository writing.

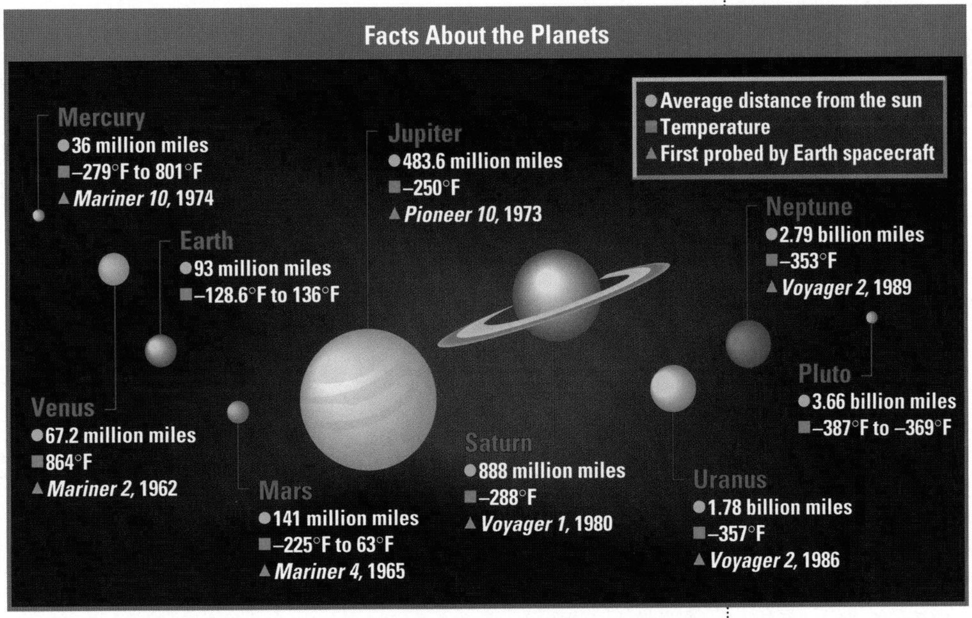

Facts About the Planets

- Average distance from the sun
- Temperature
- First probed by Earth spacecraft

Mercury
- 36 million miles
- −279°F to 801°F
- *Mariner 10*, 1974

Earth
- 93 million miles
- −128.6°F to 136°F

Venus
- 67.2 million miles
- 864°F
- *Mariner 2*, 1962

Mars
- 141 million miles
- −225°F to 63°F
- *Mariner 4*, 1965

Jupiter
- 483.6 million miles
- −250°F
- *Pioneer 10*, 1973

Saturn
- 888 million miles
- −288°F
- *Voyager 1*, 1980

Neptune
- 2.79 billion miles
- −353°F
- *Voyager 2*, 1989

Pluto
- 3.66 billion miles
- −387°F to −369°F

Uranus
- 1.78 billion miles
- −357°F
- *Voyager 2*, 1986

Journal Writing

In your journal list five or six significant events that happened in the past year. Number the events in order of their importance to you.

Teach

Organizing Visually

Tell students that when there are many subjects and several statistics for each subject, a graphic display of the information will frequently be helpful. Guide them to see how the diagram on this page helps a reader to compare facts about the planets. (The relative size of the planets is shown. The distance from the the sun is implied with left-to-right placement. The planets are named and the same type of information is listed sequentially for each planet.) Suggest that students incorporate graphic organizers into their own written and oral reports. **L2**

Two-Minute Skill Drill

Write these two categories on the board: *plants, minerals*

Have students list at least four examples under each head. Then ask them to name two other ways they might organize information about the eight items listed.

See also *Two-Minute Skill Drill Transparency 5.2*

Journal Writing Tip

Prioritizing Point out that, as students choose events they consider to be important, they are already giving them a certain organization. Ask students to consider what makes some events more important than others. You might discuss various criteria they might use.

Teach

Using the Model

Discuss how details help readers understand why Mercury is so hot (by giving examples, reasons, and statistics to support the fact). Have students identify the kinds of details the writer of the model used. (The first sentence provides a fact. The next two give statistics. The last sentence is a reason.) Invite the class to collaborate in researching another planet. Using the model as a guide, students can draft an explanation for a statement about the planet they select. **L2**

Distinguishing Between Reasons and Examples

One way to remember the difference between reasons and examples is that reasons answer the question *Why?* and often begin with *because.* A reason names a cause and is connected to its effect: "Because it is so close to the sun, the daylight side of Mercury is extremely hot." Facts are often followed by examples. For instance, "Mercury is extremely hot" is a fact. "The temperature on Mercury could melt lead" is an example. **L2**

Additional Resources

- *Fine Art Transparencies,* 21–25
- *Writing Process Transparencies,* 17–19B
- *Writing Across the Curriculum*
- *Cooperative Learning Activities,* pp. 25–30
- *Thinking and Studying Skills,* pp. 8, 10–11
- *Sentence-Combining Practice,* pp. 30–32
- *Listening and Speaking Activities,* pp. 12–13, 21, 23
- *Research Paper and Report Writing,* pp. 33–34, 36, 38
- *Composition Practice,* p. 34

Expository Writing

When you draft the introductory paragraph of an explanation, try to use a striking example and strong, precise words to raise your readers' interest.

Remember Details

Details are crucial in expository writing. Details can include facts, examples, reasons, and statistics (various kinds of numerical information). The chart below highlights different kinds of details.

Kinds of Details	
Facts	Mercury is nearer the sun than any other planet in our solar system.
Statistics	Mercury rotates once in about 59 Earth days. Its orbit around the sun takes about 88 Earth days. These numbers mean that a day on Mercury lasts about two-thirds of its year.
Examples	The temperature on Mercury could melt lead.
Reasons	Because it is so close to the sun, the daylight side of Mercury is extremely hot.

The writer of the following passage uses details to explain temperatures on Mercury. As you read, look for facts, statistics, examples, and reasons.

In what way do the details help you understand why Mercury is so hot?

Literature Model

Mercury is dry, hot, and almost airless. The sun's rays are about seven times as strong on Mercury as they are on the earth. The sun also appears about $2\frac{1}{2}$ times as large in Mercury's sky as in the earth's. Mercury does not have enough gases in its atmosphere to reduce the amount of heat and light it receives from the sun.

"Mercury," *The World Book Encyclopedia*

MEETING INDIVIDUAL NEEDS

English Language Learners

Identifying Facts

Students learning English may be familiar with facts on a variety of topics—fashion, sports, entertainment, and so on. Have each student work with an English-proficient partner to create a chart of facts on a topic of choice, listing facts in one column and writing opinions in another. Have students discuss the difference between facts and opinions. (Facts can be proved and can prove or disprove a statement.)

Write an Explanation

Write an explanation about something in your life: your morning routine before school, how you organize your room, how you get your chores done around your house on the weekend. Arrange the details in time order, in order of importance, or in the order of your likes and dislikes.

PURPOSE To present clearly steps in a process
AUDIENCE Your family, classmates
LENGTH 3–4 paragraphs

WRITING RUBRICS To write an effective explanation you should

- use the order that best fits your explanation
- elaborate by using details, such as facts, statistics, examples, and reasons
- proofread and correct any errors

Viewing and Representing

ILLUSTRATING AN EXPLANATION Create a series of 3–4 drawings that illustrate your explanation. Arrange them in the order you used to organize your writing.

Using Computers

Tables and charts can help you organize information and make it clear for your reader. Try using a chart or table in your word processing program to help you organize the data in your final copy.

Grammar Link

Expository Writing

Correct run-on sentences.

Run-on sentences are two or more sentences run together with no end punctuation or coordinating conjunction to separate them. Imagine if the sentences on page 206 were run together:

Mercury rotates once in about 59 Earth days its orbit around the sun takes about 88 Earth days.

To correct a run-on sentence you can make separate sentences, using a period or other end mark. If you prefer, combine the sentences, using a semicolon or using a comma followed by a coordinating conjunction.

Revise the following sentences to correct run-ons.

1.–3. The moon has no atmosphere it's unbearably hot when the sun shines on the lunar surface the daytime temperature there is high enough to boil water.

4.–5. Neil Armstrong and Buzz Aldrin were the first astronauts to walk on the moon and they went there in 1969 on the *Apollo* space mission.

See Lesson 7.2, Troubleshooter.

Assess

Evaluation Rubrics

Write an Explanation

Use these criteria when evaluating your students' writing:

- Does the explanation include several details, such as facts, statistics, examples, or reasons?
- Are details presented in an appropriate order?
- Is the explanation error-free?

See also *Writing Assessment and Evaluation Rubrics*

Viewing and Representing

Students' illustrations should correspond to the steps in their written explanations and be drawn as neatly and clearly as possible. The explanations and illustrations could be displayed for the class.

Using Computers

Students' charts should present information in an easy-to-read format. They should share ideas on ways to improve the readability of their charts.

Reteaching

📁 *Composition Reteaching*, p. 34

Enrichment

📁 *Composition Enrichment*, p. 34

Close

After reviewing the ideas behind organizing informative writing, ask students to imagine that a friend of theirs missed school this week. Have them write a one-page summary of this lesson for the friend.

Grammar Link

Answers

Answers will vary, but sentences should each contain a subject and a predicate and be punctuated by a period at the end. Words—particularly conjunctions—may be added to make the phrases into complex sentences.

Correcting Run-Ons In pairs, have students take turns reading the run-ons in the Grammar Link. Then have them read the corrected sentences, noting that the information will now make sense to listeners or readers.

Focus

Lesson Overview

Objectives

- To compare and contrast two subjects
- To make charts to organize comparisons

Skills

- making observations; constructing a chart before drafting; relating things on the basis of differences and similarities

Critical Thinking

- analyzing; synthesizing; relating; activating prior knowledge; visualizing; generating new information

Listening and Speaking

- discussing; asking questions; evaluating; informal speaking

Bellringer
Daily Language Activity

When students enter the classroom, have this assignment on the board: *Write an answer to this question:* What do the White House and an apartment house have in common?

Grammar Link to the Bellringer

Ask students the following questions: What adjectives might you use to compare the White House to one other house? (Example: grander, larger, whiter) to several other houses? (Example: grandest, largest, whitest)

See also *Daily Language Practice*

Motivating Activity

Call on volunteers to share their responses to the Bellringer activity. Use students' responses as the springboard for a discussion of how identifying likenesses and differences can help with expository writing.

Expository Writing

LESSON 5.3

Writing About Similarities and Differences

As you read the model below, notice how the writer delves beneath the surface to show the differences between two things that are alike in many ways.

Model

Notice the writer's use of "on the other hand." Does this phrase signal a similarity or difference?

After reading this comparison and contrast, which type of fish do you think would be more interesting?

Aquarium fish are cold-blooded, so they cannot adjust to abrupt changes in water temperature. As a result, you must keep the water temperature steady in any aquarium. The water's composition may be different, though, depending on the kind of fish you have. Marine (saltwater) fish need exactly the right amount of salt and other compounds dissolved in their water. Freshwater fish, on the other hand, cannot tolerate much salt. In general, marine fish are more delicate and more expensive. Many people think they are worth the extra trouble, however, because of their glorious colors and exotic shapes.

Resource Manager

📁 **Planning Resources**
- *Lesson Plans*

📐 **Transparencies**
- *Bellringer*
- *Daily Language Practice*
- *Fine Art* 21–25
- *Two-Minute Skill Drill*
- *Writing Process* 17–19B

📁 **Other Print Resources**
- *Composition Enrichment*, p. 35
- *Composition Practice*, p. 35
- *Composition Reteaching*, p. 35
- *Cooperative Learning Activities*, pp. 25–30
- *Listening and Speaking Activities*, pp. 12–13, 21, 23
- *Research Paper and Report Writing*, pp. 33–34, 36, 38

- *Sentence-Combining Practice*, pp. 30–32
- *Thinking and Study Skills*, pp. 6, 8–9, 11
- *Writing Across the Curriculum*
- *Writing Assessment and Evaluation Rubrics*

Look Closely

On the surface two things may seem alike. If you examine them closely, however, you find differences. For example, two aquariums might both be made of glass and be filled with water, but the water in one might be fresh and the water in the other might be salt.

When you look at ways in which two things are alike, you are comparing them. When you examine their differences, you are contrasting them. Making a clear comparison-contrast list or diagram, such as the one below, can help you identify likenesses and differences.

Two Kinds of Aquariums

Freshwater	Freshwater and Saltwater	Saltwater
	• can be made of glass or plastic • need lids to keep dust out and fish in • need light, thermostat, heater, filter, and aerator • need to be cleaned regularly • need under-gravel filter	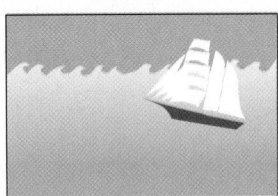
• less expensive • variety of plants available • more fish can live in given space • need fresh water		• more expensive • can use coral • fewer fish can live in given space • need hydrometer to measure saltiness

Teach

Using the Model

Have students reread the Literature Model on page 208 and call their attention to the fourth and fifth sentences and the question in the first callout. Point out that the phrase *on the other hand* is a signal that the writer is stating how two things are different. Discuss some other contrast words and phrases, such as *but, however,* and *in contrast.* Suggest that students try to use such words in their writing. **L2**

Discussing Comparison and Contrast

Point out to students that when they contrast two items, they are stressing the differences between the things. When they compare two items, they are emphasizing the similarities between the items. Write *house* and *tent* on the board. Words such as *likewise* and *similarly* show comparison. Work with students to write a sentence that contrasts a house and a tent. Have students write a second sentence that compares these two things. **L1**

Journal Writing

Think about talking with a friend or relative face to face and talking with that same person on the telephone. In your journal list how the experiences are alike and how they are different. Write a few sentences telling which method of communication you prefer and why.

Journal Writing Tip

Identifying Attributes Brainstorm with students to develop a list of words that describe how they feel when they talk to friends or close relatives. Examples might include: *comfortable, not self-conscious, interested, important to someone.* Ask students if these feelings include both in-person encounters and phone conversations. Do some of the feelings refer only to one kind of exchange? Students may use the discussion to clarify how the two experiences are alike and different.

Teach

Using the Model

Have students reread the Literature Model on this page to identify transition words, such as *whereas,* that signal a contrast. They might begin a *Contrast Cues* list of these words to use in their own writing. Ask students what other word or phrase the author might have used instead of *whereas* to signal contrast (*however, on the other hand, but*). **L2**

Two-Minute Skill Drill

List the following noun pairs on the board and have students write ways in which the items they name are alike and ways in which they are different.

snake—eel   apple—orange

ocean—lake   car—bus

See also Two-Minute Skill Drill Transparency 5.3

Additional Resources

 Fine Art Transparencies, 21–25

 Writing Process Transparencies, 17–19B

 Cooperative Learning Activities, pp. 25–30

 Writing Across the Curriculum

Research Paper and Report Writing, pp. 33–34, 36, 38

Thinking and Studying Skills, pp. 6, 8–9, 11

Sentence-Combining Practice, pp. 30–32

Listening and Speaking Activities, pp. 12–13, 21, 23

Composition Practice, p. 35

Expository Writing

Grammar Tip

A comparison-contrast explanation may include the adjectives *more, most, less,* and *least* to show degrees of similarity or difference. For more information, see Lesson 12.3, page 455.

Draw Comparisons

When you know how two things are alike and different, you can begin to organize your ideas for a written explanation. The chart below shows one way to organize details. It compares and contrasts two insects feature by feature. The passage following the chart also uses a feature-by-feature comparison.

Comparing Two Insects		
Feature	**Centipede**	**Millipede**
Legs	1 pair per segment	2 pairs per segment
Food	snails, slugs, worms	plants
Danger	poisonous	harmless
Movement	quick	moderate

Notice the writers' use of the word "whereas." Does the word signal a likeness or a difference?

Literature Model

Compare the centipede and millipede below. The centipede has one pair of jointed legs per segment, whereas the millipede has two pairs of legs per segment. Centipedes hunt for their food and have a pair of poison claws used to inject venom into their prey. Centipedes feed on snails, slugs, and worms. Their bites are very painful to humans. Millipedes don't move as quickly as centipedes and feed on plants.

Lucy Daniel, Edward Paul Ortleb, Alton Biggs, *Merrill Life Science*

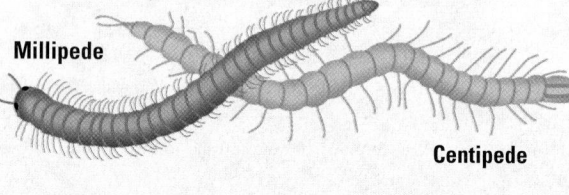

Millipede

Centipede

Critical Thinking

Identifying and Comparing Features of Objects

Some students might have difficulty identifying and comparing features. To practice this process, provide pictures of two objects. The objects—such as in-line skates and roller skates—should have both similarities and differences.

Guide students in identifying these features. Have students write the features on cards and place the cards in columns under the correct pictures.

Write a Comparison-Contrast Letter

Think about how you spent the most recent summer vacation and how you spent any previous summer. What was similar about the two summers, and what was different about them? Make a Venn diagram comparing and contrasting the two summers, listing the things you did during both vacations in the intersecting portion of the two circles. Then, write a letter to a pen pal that compares and contrasts your two summers. Tell which vacation you preferred, and why. Include your diagram in your letter.

PURPOSE To compare and contrast two summer vacations

AUDIENCE A pen pal

LENGTH 2–4 paragraphs

WRITING RUBRICS To write a good comparison-contrast letter, you should

- include both similarities and differences in your Venn diagram
- use phrases that make clear comparisons and contrasts
- use comparative and superlative forms correctly
- write legibly in cursive or print

Cross-Curricular Activity

ART Find copies of two paintings or photographs that depict a similar subject—for example, a city sidewalk scene or a rural landscape. Make notes to identify similarities and differences between the two pictures. Then write a brief description comparing and contrasting the ways in which the two images depict their subjects.

Listening and Speaking

COMPARING AND CONTRASTING CUSTOMS Work in a small group that includes at least one student who is familar with the customs of another country. Pick an event or ceremony—a wedding, a funeral, or some other formal occasion—and discuss the similarities and differences between customs in the United States and in another country. Present your findings to the class in an oral report.

Expository Writing

Grammar Link

Use comparative and superlative forms correctly.

Most adjectives of one syllable add *-er* for the comparative and *-est* for the superlative. Longer adjectives are usually preceded by *more* or *most*.

> *Centipedes tend to be fast**er** and **more** dangerous than millipedes*

Correct the following phrases.

1. the least shortest runner
2. the more taller building
3. the most chubbiest puppy
4. the less smaller sandwich
5. the most lowest grade

See Lesson 12.3, page 455, and Lesson 12.4, page 457.

5.3 Writing About Similarities and Differences **211**

Assess

Evaluation Rubrics

Write a Comparison-Contrast Letter

Use these criteria when evaluating your students' writing:

- Letters should elaborate on information presented in the Venn diagram.
- Letters should indicate a preference between the two compared summers.

See also *Writing Assessment and Evaluation Rubrics*

Cross-Curricular Activity

Answers will vary, but should demonstrate students' abilities to identify likenesses and differences in similar situations.

Listening and Speaking

Oral presentations should reflect an enlightening exchange of information and demonstrate students' abilities to discern and appreciate the similarities and differences between the customs of two countries.

Reteaching

📁 *Composition Reteaching*, p. 35

Enrichment

📁 *Composition Enrichment*, p. 35

 Fine Art Transparencies, 21–25

Close

Have students discuss why being able to compare and contrast items is useful when they are writing about a topic. Students may then write a brief summary of the class discussion.

Grammar Link

Answers

1. the shortest runner
2. the taller building
3. the chubbiest puppy
4. the smaller *or* the larger sandwich
5. the lowest grade

Focus

Lesson Overview

Objectives

- To write a clear and well-ordered explanation
- To guide a reader through an ordered series of steps

Skills

- putting steps in order; using transition words; using precise verbs

Critical Thinking

- recalling; summarizing; analyzing; visualizing

Listening and Speaking

- evaluating; explaining process; participating in group discussion

 Bellringer
Daily Language Activity

When students enter the classroom, have this assignment on the board: *What did you learn in your science class this week? Give a brief explanation.*

Grammar Link to the Bellringer

Remind students that specific verbs can make a short explanation much clearer. Have students look over their Bellringer activity writing and ask volunteers for examples of specific verbs. (Examples might be terminology such as *dissolve, measure,* or *conduct.*) Invite students to review their writing and replace vague verbs (such as *do, is, has,* or *make*) with specific ones.

See also *Daily Language Practice*

Motivating Activity

Ask students if they can remember occasions on which they tried to learn how something worked or how something should be assembled and were confused by the explanation. Were steps missing or out of place? Were any of the steps actually wrong? What do these experiences show about the importance of clearly explaining how something works?

Expository Writing

Explaining How Something Works

Writers must explain steps in the proper order when they want to show how something works.

You've probably never seen an apparatus as complicated as this one. For all its moving pieces and dizzying action, the end result is pretty simple. Can you figure out what it is? Follow the steps in order from A to Q.

Write Step by Step

By putting items in the proper order, you can make a complicated process clear. Consider a real process, such as the operation of canal locks. Notice the way the following passage explains how the locks work.

Resource Manager

📂 Planning Resources
- *Lesson Plans*

📦 Transparencies
- *Bellringer*
- *Daily Language Practice*
- *Fine Art* 21–25
- *Two-Minute Skill Drill*
- *Writing Process* 17–19B

📂 Other Print Resources
- *Composition Enrichment,* p. 36
- *Composition Practice,* p. 36
- *Composition Reteaching,* p. 36
- *Cooperative Learning Activities,* pp. 25–30
- *Listening and Speaking Activities,* pp. 12–13, 21, 23
- *Research Paper and Report Writing,* pp. 33–34, 36, 38

- *Sentence-Combining Practice,* pp. 30–32
- *Thinking and Study Skills,* pp. 8–9, 11
- *Writing Across the Curriculum*
- *Writing Assessment and Evaluation Rubrics*

Model

First, a lock is filled with water by opening the filling valve. From the higher water level, the boat enters the first set of gates. The upper gates open easily because the water pressure is the same on both sides. After the upper gates are closed, water is pumped out of the lock through the drain valve. The water level begins to lower. Because of the angle of the gates, the higher water pressure at each level keeps them shut. When the water level in the lock is the same as it is on the lower part of the river, the lower gates open, and the boat continues its journey.

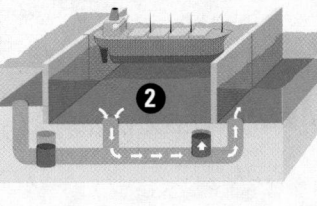

Ships can't travel through locks if the gates open out of order. In the same way, your writing about a process won't work for your readers if you put the steps in the wrong order.

Journal Writing

In your journal write down one of your dreams—for a career, a trip, or something else. Then list, in time order, the steps you would take to make that dream come true.

> Which words does the writer use to signal the order in which the locks work?

Teach

Using the Model

Point out that just as the second step in lock operation cannot take place until the first step has occurred, the reader cannot understand the second step before grasping the first. Therefore, the writer ordered the explanation in the same way as the actual process. (To show this order, the writer used the transition words *first, after,* and *when.*) Guide students in writing three steps of a process using those transition words. **L2**

Examining a Process

If students have trouble separating a process into its component steps, suggest they think about it in slow motion. Try to obtain a videotape that shows a complete, multipart action (such as a show about cooking or do-it-yourself home improvement). Run through the entire process once. Then rewind the tape and play it again, telling students to stop the tape after each step in the process. Students may write the step when the tape is stopped. Students may add transition words and other necessary explanatory material to each step listed. They may then edit the completed explanation by comparing it once more to the action shown on the video. **L1**

Journal Writing Tip

Ordering Steps Point out that sometimes we know what the last step toward a dream might be. (For example, if your dream were to run in a marathon, entering the race would be one of the last things you would do.) In fact, the beginning and the end of the process might be clear, while the middle remains mysterious. In such cases, list the steps at the beginning *and* the end, and work toward the middle.

Revising Directions

Have students work in groups to find and copy some printed directions (anything from directions on a shampoo bottle to instructions for a computer game). Help groups revise the directions. When they have completed writing new versions, ask them to exchange both the original and the revised directions with other groups. Students can discuss which version is clearer and analyze the reasons. **L2**

Two-Minute Skill Drill

Write the following sentences on the board. Ask students to identify the transition words.

After middle school, students go to high school.

We watched a long time, and eventually we saw a shooting star.

See also Two-Minute Skill Drill Transparency 5.4

Additional Resources

- Fine Art Transparencies, 21–25
- Writing Process Transparencies, 17–19B
- Writing Across the Curriculum
- Cooperative Learning Activities, pp. 25–30
- Composition Practice, p. 36
- Thinking and Study Skills, pp. 8–9, 11
- Sentence-Combining Practice, pp. 30–32
- Listening and Speaking Activities, pp. 12–13, 21, 23
- Research Paper and Report Writing, pp. 33–34, 36, 38

Expository Writing

Prewriting Tip

When you are planning to write about a process, brainstorm with other people to make sure you have identified all steps in the process.

What are the transition words in this paragraph? How do they help the reader?

Guide Your Reader

Once you've placed the steps of a process in the correct order, use transition words and phrases that will help readers follow your explanation. Transitions show how the steps in a process are related to one another. Common transition words include *first, next, after, later, while, second, initially,* and *finally.*

Another way to make your writing clear is to organize it into paragraphs. Each paragraph should have one main idea and a clear topic sentence that states that idea. What is the main idea of the paragraph below? Notice how the writer rearranged a phrase and a sentence and added transition words to make the idea clearer.

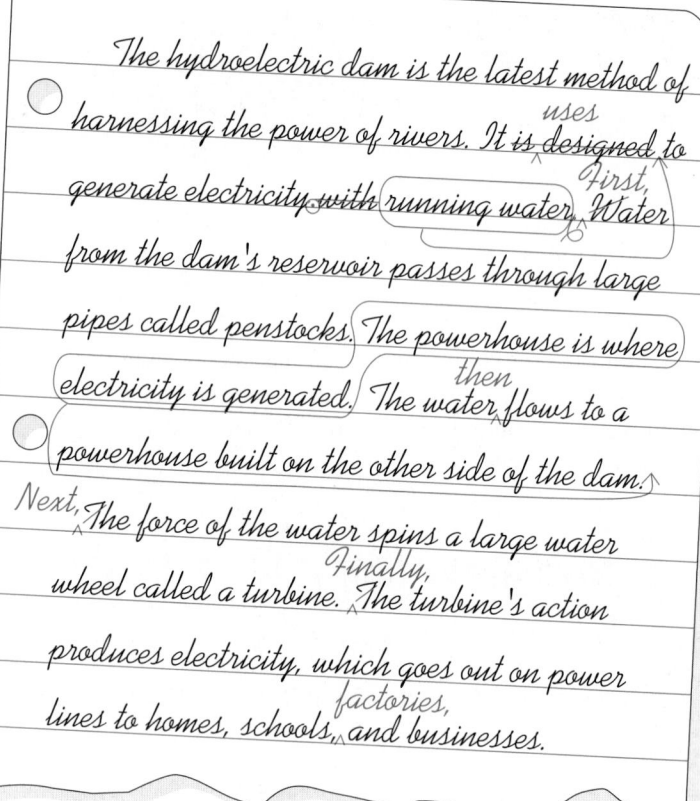

MEETING INDIVIDUAL NEEDS

Less-Proficient Readers

Using Transition Words

Some students may need practice using transition words. Begin with simple transition words, such as *first, next, before,* and *after.* Guide students in using each word in a sentence or paragraph. Move on to more difficult words, such as *prior, subsequently,* and *meanwhile,* and ask students to list the words that they have the most trouble with, along with definitions of those words. Have them write several practice sentences using those words.

5.4 | Writing Activities

Write an Explanation

Explain to your class how something works. It could be something you use, such as a refrigerator or a bicycle, and it should be something you know well. Explain the steps in a logical order and, if you wish, use sketches or diagrams to illustrate your explanation.

PURPOSE To explain a process
AUDIENCE Classmates
LENGTH 4–6 paragraphs

WRITING RUBRICS To write an effective explanation, you should

- write a clear, interesting topic sentence for each paragraph
- explain each step in the process in the order in which it happens
- use appropriate transition words
- use precise verbs to make your writing vivid

Using Computers

Try turning your explanation into a magazine article. Some graphics or page-making software lets you lay out your page to look like a magazine or newspaper page. Design a magazine column for your piece. Include a headline, a byline, and room for your diagrams or sketches.

Grammar Link

Use precise verbs to help readers picture a process.

The right verb in a sentence can convey a clear, strong picture to the reader. Consider, for example, how much more meaning is communicated to the reader when *whispered* or *yelled* is substituted for *said* in dialogue.

Vague verb: goes
Precise verbs: passes, spins, flows

Revise the sentences below, replacing vague verbs with precise ones and adding verbs that make the action clear.

¹ To make a tossed salad, first get a large bowl. ² Then deal with the lettuce. ³ Next, prepare tomatoes, carrots, and cheese. ⁴ Put sunflower seeds on top. ⁵ Finally, use salad dressing.

See Lesson 10.1, pages 399–400.

Listening and Speaking

COOPERATIVE LEARNING In small groups, take turns presenting your explanation orally, first, as you would do it for a group of fourth graders, and then as you would do it for adults. Discuss how you would alter your presentation for each audience.

5.4 Explaining How Something Works **215**

Expository Writing

Assess

Evaluation Rubrics

Write an Explanation

When writing the explanation, make sure that

- each step of the process is identified, and no prior knowledge is assumed
- steps are in the proper order
- illustrations are comprehensible and accurate
- style and vocabulary are appropriate for an explanation

See also *Writing Assessment and Evaluation Rubrics*

Using Computers

Provide an opportunity for students to display the articles they created and to share with the class information on how they formatted them.

Listening and Speaking

Monitor the groups' oral presentations for effective rate, volume, pitch and tone.

Reteaching

📁 *Composition Reteaching*, p. 36

Enrichment

📁 *Composition Enrichment*, p. 36

Close

Ask students how they would entertain a favorite sports or television star if she or he were to spend the day in their hometown. Have them write an explanation of what they would do, putting the steps in the order they would follow. Tell students to explain each step thoroughly and to use transition words to help guide the reader.

Grammar Link

Answers

Answers will vary. The words *get, deal with, prepare, put,* and *use* should be changed to more specific, descriptive verbs.

Using Precise Verbs Have students rework something they have written this year, replacing common verbs with vivid verbs. Suggest that the new verbs elicit vivid mental images.

Focus

Lesson Overview

Objectives

- To identify and analyze cause-and-effect relationships
- To use cause-and-effect relationships in writing

Skills

- identifying cause-and-effect relationships; analyzing cause-and-effect events; examining how one effect leads to another

Critical Thinking

- analyzing; relating cause and effect; evaluating

Listening and Speaking

- discussing; evaluating; questioning

Bellringer
Daily Language Activity

When students enter the classroom, have this assignment on the board: *Copy these sentences:*

The temperature was extremely cold all last week. Ice formed on the pond.

Draw one line under the sentence that states a cause; draw two lines under the sentence that states an effect.

Grammar Link to the Bellringer

Ask students to combine the two Bellringer activity sentences into one sentence. Have a volunteer read the new sentence to the class.

See also *Daily Language Practice*

Motivating Activity

Ask students questions about situations in which recognizing cause-and-effect relationships is helpful to their everyday life. For example: How does the weather affect what you might wear? Might your doctor have to understand the cause of an illness in order to treat it?

LESSON 5.5
Identifying Cause and Effect

*O*ne thing leads to another in the chain of events known as cause and effect.

Natural events cause changes in the weather. For example, ash from volcanic eruptions can partially block sunlight, which in turn can cause colder temperatures in parts of the world. The result can be ruined crops and more, as explained in the model below.

> What cause-and-effect relationship does the first sentence suggest?

> Note the writer's use of statistics to show the effect of the cold weather.

Literature Model

The coldest December temperatures in a century could wreak havoc with consumers' budgets this winter. Freezing weather has decimated [ruined] up to a third of Florida's citrus and 90 percent of the state's winter vegetable crop, estimates Doyle Conner, Florida's agriculture commissioner. Experts say that will translate into sharply higher prices for orange juice, grapefruits, and tomatoes.

Newsweek, January 8, 1990

Resource Manager

Planning Resources
- *Lesson Plans*

Transparencies
- *Bellringer*
- *Daily Language Practice*
- *Fine Art* 21–25
- *Two-Minute Skill Drill*
- *Writing Process* 17–19B

Other Print Resources
- *Composition Enrichment*, p. 37
- *Composition Practice*, p. 37
- *Composition Reteaching*, p. 37
- *Cooperative Learning Activities*, pp. 25–30
- *Listening and Speaking Activities*, pp. 12–13, 21, 23
- *Research Paper and Report Writing*, pp. 33–34, 36, 38

- *Sentence-Combining Practice*, pp. 30–32
- *Thinking and Study Skills*, pp. 3–4, 8, 10
- *Writing Across the Curriculum*
- *Writing Assessment and Evaluation Rubrics*

Check Cause-and-Effect Relationships

A cause is an identifiable condition or event. An effect is something that happens as a direct result of that condition or event. Sometimes it seems that one event or condition causes another, when it really doesn't. Remember that causes must happen before effects, but not every event that precedes another is a cause.

Study the chart below. Notice which statements are not examples of cause and effect.

Editing Tip

When you edit, try combining a cause and its effect in a complex sentence. For more information, see Lesson 14.2, page 503.

Understanding Cause and Effect

Cause Lightning tends to strike the tallest object in the area. → **Effect** Single trees in open fields are often hit by lightning.

This is true cause and effect. The cause is a condition that comes before and brings about the effect.

Cause Scientists hope someday to probe the planet Pluto. ↛ **Effect** Scientists have collected information about the planets.

A probe of Pluto did not precede the collection of information.

Cause In the spring melting snow filled the reservoir. ↛ **Effect** This summer the city has a water shortage.

Melting snow preceded the water shortage but did not cause it.

Journal Writing

Watch a television news program, and look for cause-and-effect relationships in the news reports. List three or four that the reporters identify. In your journal explain why one of them is a true example of a cause-and-effect relationship.

Teach

Using the Model

Discuss the Literature Model on page 216 with students. Point out that the writer explains how a cold spell in Florida can affect consumers' budgets. (This cause-and-effect relationship is suggested in the first sentence. Statistics make the relationship more specific.) Guide students to see that the writer could have reversed the structure of the paragraph by beginning with the effect—higher prices for certain fruits and vegetables—and then explaining the cause. Ask students to summarize the paragraph in one sentence. **L2**

Discussing Causes

It may be helpful for some students to discuss situations in which events that precede other events are mistakenly assumed to be causes. Present and discuss scenarios similar to this: *A small boy is playing quietly. His older sister enters the room, and a minute later his mother hears the boy begin to cry.* Then ask, *What might the mother think has caused the boy to cry? Was his sister necessarily the cause of his crying? What could be some other causes?* **L1**

Journal Writing Tip

Collecting and Gathering Information Mention that one way to identify cause-and-effect relationships is to listen for words such as *because, so, therefore,* and *due to.*

Using the Model

Point out that the indoor air mentioned in the first sentence is an example of something that is both a cause and an effect. (Adding heat to the air causes it to be dry. The dry air can then cause health problems and discomfort.) **L2**

Analyzing Advertisements and Commercials

Ask students to think of ways advertisers use cause and effect to sell products. (They promise popularity, and so on.) Ask students to name and analyze specific advertisements and commercials. **L3**

Two-Minute Skill Drill

Have students write a sentence that exhibits a cause-and-effect relationship for the following pair of words.

cold weather—wood stove

See also Two-Minute Skill Drill Transparency 5.5

Additional Resources

Fine Art Transparencies, 21–25

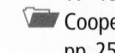
Writing Process Transparencies, 17–19B

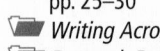
Cooperative Learning Activities, pp. 25–30

Writing Across the Curriculum

Research Paper and Report Writing, pp. 33–34, 36, 38

Thinking and Study Skills, pp. 3–4, 8, 10

Sentence-Combining Practice, pp. 30–32

Listening and Speaking Activities, pp. 12–13, 21, 23

Composition Practice, p. 37

218

Expository Writing

Examine How One Effect Leads to Another

Sometimes a cause and its effect form part of a chain of events. One cause may lead to an effect, and that effect may in turn change circumstances and lead to another effect. The diagram and the passage below show how this cause-and-effect chain works.

Below-freezing weather occurs.

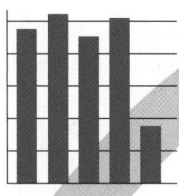
Fewer oranges are available than in previous years.

Consumers want as many oranges as before, but fewer are available, so prices rise.

Frost damages the oranges, and much of the crop is lost.

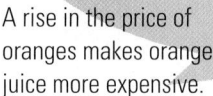
A rise in the price of oranges makes orange juice more expensive.

Is the "indoor air" mentioned in the first sentence a cause, an effect, or both?

Model

Indoor air in winter has several effects on the human body. As the outdoor temperature drops, heat must be added indoors for comfort. However, added heat causes the indoor air to hold less moisture. This drier air often causes health problems, such as asthma or nosebleeds. People moving about in rooms where the air is too dry may also be irritated by static electricity, which is common when air moisture is low.

218   Unit 5 Expository Writing

Viewing and Representing

Making a Flow Chart

Use visual aids to supplement verbal explanations whenever possible. Begin with a statement of cause: *The gas gauge broke.* Write C by this statement and then draw an arrow to an effect: *The car ran out of gas.* Label this *E* and draw a second arrow to further effect *I was late for work.* Help students see why the statement in the middle is both cause and effect. Then go back and and label the second event *C* (as well as *E*). Help students to continue the flow chart.

Write a Cause-and-Effect Letter

You are a responsible citizen. You are concerned about the number of accidents that occur when children play in the streets. Write a letter to your local representative explaining why children are playing in the streets and what will happen if no action is taken to correct this, including additional effects if it keeps up. Present some ideas the representative could use to effect change.

PURPOSE To present cause-and-effect analysis and present a plan

AUDIENCE Your local representative

LENGTH 1–2 paragraphs

WRITING RUBRICS To write an effective cause-and-effect letter, you should

- establish that there are cause-and-effect relationships
- show any chain effects
- include facts and statistics
- proofread and write legibly in print or cursive

Cross-Curricular Activity

HISTORY Use your history book to learn about a historic fire, or use other sources to find out about a more recent one. Write a few paragraphs in which you develop some cause-and-effect ideas. First, explain what caused or may have caused the fire. Then, write about what effects the fire may have had on the local community.

Listening and Speaking

MAKING A SPEECH Your student council has asked for ideas to help your school improve academically. Prepare a five-minute speech in which you propose one or two ideas (causes) and describe how they will improve students' academic performance (effects). In a small group, deliver your speech and ask for feedback about whether the causes you have suggested may produce the desired effects. Report the ideas your group suggests to the entire class. Express your ideas fluently, using Standard American English.

Combine simple sentences to make complex sentences.

Complex sentences have a main clause and one or more subordinate clauses. Revise the paragraph below, combining causes and their effects in complex sentences where possible.
[1] Logging affects the ecosystem of a rainforest in several ways. [2] Trees are cut down. [3] The habitats of some organisms are destroyed. [4] More light and rain reach the forest floor. [5] The food supply of many organisms is wiped out.

See Lesson 14.2, page 503.

Answers

Sample: Logging affects the rainforest in several ways. When trees are cut down, the habitats of some organisms are destroyed. As more light and rain reach the forest floor, the ecosystem changes in a way that wipes out the food supply of many organisms.

Assess

Evaluation Rubrics

Write a Cause-and-Effect Letter

Use these criteria when evaluating your students' writing:

- Does the letter identify one major issue?
- Does the letter clearly explain the causes of the problem?
- Does the letter detail effects?
- Does the letter outline a solution that considers both?

See also *Writing Assessment and Evaluation Rubrics*

Cross-Curricular Activity

Answers will vary. Consider the following in evaluating a student's work:

- Did the student use at least one book or periodical to learn about a fire?
- Does the student describe the events in a logical sequence?
- Does the student address both the possible cause and actual effects of the fire?

Listening and Speaking

Monitor the speeches and the feedback to see that the feedback is accurate and given in a constuctive manner.

Reteaching

📁 *Composition Reteaching, p. 37*

Enrichment

📁 *Composition Enrichment, p. 37*

✂ *Fine Art Transparencies, 21–25*

Close

Read aloud to students several fables by Aesop. Pause after reading each fable and ask students to identify any cause-and-effect relationships that occur in the tale.

5.6

Focus

Lesson Overview

Objectives
- To narrow an expository writing topic
- To direct the writing topic toward the intended audience

Skills
- narrowing a topic; tailoring writing to an audience

Critical Thinking
- recalling; relating topics and subtopics; building background; generating new information

Listening and Speaking
- informal speaking; discussing; questioning

 Bellringer
Daily Language Activity

When students enter the classroom, have this assigment on the board: *What is your favorite sport or outdoor activity? Imagine you are telling someone about it. Write down three things you would mention.*

Grammar Link to the Bellringer

Ask if any students included words such as *anybody, nothing, each, none,* etc. Ask for examples. Point out that these are called indefinite pronouns.

See also *Daily Language Practice*

Motivating Activity

Discuss the Bellringer activity with students. What kinds of sports or activities interest them? Are they interested in all sports (curling, harness racing) or just selected sports? Is there a single sport everyone in class enjoys playing or watching? If you were to create a magazine on sports and outdoor activities to interest most members of the class, what kinds of things would be in the magazine?

220

Expository Writing

LESSON 5.6

Reports: Narrowing a Topic

A research report is a kind of expository writing. When you write a report, you gather information about your topic from a variety of sources. Then you take what you have learned, organize the information, and write about it in a way that your audience will understand.

Choose a Topic

Just as you can't play on every sports team in the same season, you can't say everything there is to say about a general topic in the same report. If a topic is too general or broad, you'll find too much information. If your topic is too narrow, you won't find enough. As you gain experience in writing reports, you'll learn to judge whether a topic is too broad, too narrow, or just right.

Resource Manager

📁 Planning Resources
- *Lesson Plans*

🖥 Transparencies
- *Bellringer*
- *Daily Language Practice*
- *Fine Art 21–25*
- *Two-Minute Skill Drill*
- *Writing Process 17–19B*

📁 Other Print Resources
- *Composition Enrichment,* p. 38
- *Composition Practice,* p. 38
- *Composition Reteaching,* p. 38
- *Cooperative Learning Activities,* pp. 25–30
- *Listening and Speaking Activities,* pp. 12–13, 21, 23
- *Research Paper and Report Writing,* pp. 33–34, 36, 38

- *Sentence-Combining Practice,* pp. 30–32
- *Thinking and Study Skills,* pp. 7–9
- *Writing Across the Curriculum*
- *Writing Assessment and Evaluation Rubrics*

Keep three important things in mind when you're planning a research report:

1. Select a topic that you care about.
2. Narrow the topic so that you can cover it thoroughly.
3. Make sure that you can find several sources on your topic.

The diagram below shows how you can focus a topic. A focus on outdoor sports is too broad. There are too many outdoor sports to cover thoroughly. You can narrow the topic by focusing on a single sport—bicycling. But even this narrowed topic includes too much information. You can thoroughly cover one aspect of bicycling—bicycle safety, for example—in one report.

Editing Tip

When planning a report, remember that visual aids, such as photos, maps, and charts, can help your reader grasp your points.

Journal Writing

What are your favorite sports or games? In your journal make a triangle diagram like the one above to identify which aspect of the one sport or game you enjoy most.

Teach

Identifying Subtopics

For examples of topics and subtopics, ask students to locate a nonfiction book and to skim the table of contents. Explain that any chapter topic might be considered a subtopic of the main theme of the book. Students might also look up a subject in an encyclopedia and note the subheadings printed in bold type. An encyclopedia index lists subtopics under general entry words. *The Readers' Guide to Periodical Literature* also gives examples of main topics followed by subtopics. **L2**

Two-Minute Skill Drill

Write these main topics on the board: *music, food, politics.* Have students assign the following subtopics to one of the main topics: *vegetables, elections, debate, rap, grains, opera, Congress, jazz, cooking.* Then ask students to think of a subtopic for one of the subtopics above (e.g., *campaign* would be a subtopic of *elections*).

See also *Two-Minute Skill Drill Transparency 5.6*

Journal Writing Tip

Before students create their diagrams, discuss the one on this page. Ask students which sport each picture represents. Discuss why international signs like these are used instead of words. Suggest that in their journals they may use symbolic pictures or brief words or phrases to capture their ideas.

Using the Model

On this page, the first paragraph is directed at drivers and emphasizes protecting the lives of cyclists. The second paragraph is directed at cyclists and focuses on how they should protect themselves. Ask students to write an opening sentence for each paragraph—one that grabs the reader's attention and clearly summarizes the message. **L2**

Examining Writing for Different Audiences

Explain that writers often write more than one article about a subject for magazines targeting different audiences. To do this, a writer must tailor the material as well as the style to each audience. Have students look through magazines for young adults and read an article that interests them. They can then use the *Readers' Guide to Periodical Literature* to find articles on the same subjects in publications aimed at older audiences. Have students explain and give examples of how the subject matter, tone, and style change for the different audiences. **L3**

Additional Resources

- *Fine Art Transparencies,* 21–25
- *Writing Process Transparencies,* 17–19B
- *Writing Across the Curriculum*
- Cooperative Learning Activities, pp. 25–30
- *Thinking and Study Skills,* pp. 7–9
- *Sentence Combining Practice,* pp. 30–32
- *Listening and Speaking Activities,* pp. 12–13, 21, 23
- *Research Paper and Report Writing,* pp. 33–34, 36, 38
- *Composition Practice,* p. 38

Expository Writing

Know Your Audience

A report on bicycle safety could have a wide audience. It could be your class or the readers of your local paper or an adult community group. It's important to tailor a report to your audience.

> The next time you are driving your car, think for a moment about others who are sharing the road. More and more people are riding bicycles these days, and too many of them are in accidents with moving cars. In a recent year, 460,000 people were injured in such accidents, and as many as 1,100 cyclists have been killed each year. Make the roads safe for all who use them.

▲ This paragraph is intended for drivers. Its purpose is to make drivers aware of the frequency of serious car-bicycle accidents.

> Bike riding can be fun, but it also carries some responsibility. The next time you jump on your bike and get ready to take off, remember to (1) ride with the traffic and keep to the right; (2) never ride double on a bicycle; (3) wear a helmet, and (4) wear light-colored clothes, put reflective strips on your clothes and your bike, and use a bike light when light is poor.

▲ This paragraph is directed toward cyclists. The writer reminds bicycle riders of some basic safety rules. The purpose is to get readers to think about and follow precautions.

222   Unit 5 Expository Writing

English Language Learners

MEETING INDIVIDUAL NEEDS

Clustering Subtopics

Create small teams of students with differing English proficiency. Provide main topics such as *dance, dogs, games,* or *jobs.* Have teams create clusters that show as many subtopics as possible. Include subtopics mentioned in languages other than English, too, and if possible translate them later. (Some culture-specific examples may not be translatable.) Teams should discuss reasons for their choices. Next, each team may select a subtopic and create another cluster showing further subtopics.

5.6 Writing Activities

Choose and Narrow a Topic

Write down three or four topics that interest you—topics that you would like to research. Take some time to think about which one you would most enjoy researching and writing about. Use a conference or small-group discussion to help you choose.

PURPOSE To focus on a topic
AUDIENCE Audience of your choice
LENGTH A list

WRITING RUBRICS To choose and narrow a topic effectively, you should

- select a topic that you know and care about
- narrow the topic so you can cover it thoroughly
- make sure that several reliable sources of information on your topic are available

Using Computers

Working on your own or with one or two others, look for information about your topic on the Internet. To find the most beneficial Web sites, you'll need to narrow your topic as much as possible before you begin. Look for Web sites devoted to your topic or use a search engine to find articles and other sources that can help you find a suitably narrow focus for your report.

Listening and Speaking

COOPERATIVE LEARNING Work in small groups to practice narrowing topics. Start with broad, general subjects, like sports, television, or fashion. Then brainstorm ways to narrow those broad subjects to topics appropriate for short papers that require some research. Report on your efforts to the class, describing what subjects you started with and what topics you ended with.

Grammar Link

Use correct subject-verb agreement with indefinite pronouns.

Indefinite pronouns do not refer to specific persons or things. Some, such as *anything* and *nobody,* are singular. Others, such as *both* and *many,* are plural. Still others, such as *all, any,* and *some,* can be either singular or plural, depending on the noun that follows.

All of the bacteria are alive. *All* of the money *is* gone.

Write the paragraph, inserting the correct verbs.

[1] Each of us (has, have) a job. [2] Few (rests, rest) at all. [3] Some of us (finishes, finish) at 5:00 P.M. [4] All the effort (goes, go) into painting. [5] Everyone (admires, admire) our work.
See Lesson 16.1, page 535, and Lesson 16.4, page 541.

Assess

Evaluation Rubrics

Choose and Narrow a Topic

Use these criteria when evaluating your students' writing:

- Is the topic narrowed enough to be covered thoroughly?
- Is the topic selected one that can be researched in several sources?

See also *Writing Assessment and Evaluation Rubrics*

Using Computers

Provide an opportunity for students to share tips on how they were able to narrow their topics using Internet sources.

Listening and Speaking

Consider the following in evaluating the group work and result.
- Are all students' ideas accepted in the brainstorming session?
- Do students remain focused on the task at hand?
- Do students' questions pertain to the process of narrowing?

Reteaching

🗂 *Composition Reteaching, p. 38*

Enrichment

🗂 *Composition Enrichment, p. 38*

📋 *Fine Art Transparencies, 21–25*

Close

Discuss with students the importance of focusing a topic to meet an audience's interests, expectations, or abilities. How would students explain a computer game to a second grade student? To a ninth grade student? Why would the explanations differ?

Grammar Link

Answers
1. has
2. rest
3. finish
4. goes
5. admires

Focus

Lesson Overview

Objectives

- To make a list of questions about a topic
- To find answers to those questions in a variety of sources
- To take careful notes and keep track of source information

Skills

- choosing among resources; taking meaningful notes

Critical Thinking

- analyzing; evaluating; summarizing; decision-making; generating new information

Listening and Speaking

- discussing; informal speaking; oral reporting

Bellringer
Daily Language Activity

When students enter the classroom, have this assignment on the board: *Write a brief paragraph telling about the information sources that you used for a recent research report for school. What kinds of sources did you use? Where did you find them? Did some provide more information than others?*

Grammar Link to the Bellringer

Tell students to check their Bellringer activity paragraph for correct capitalization and punctuation.

See also *Daily Language Practice*

Motivating Activity

Ask students where they would go to find the answer to a health question. (Suggestions might include the doctor, a parent, a friend, a health pamphlet, a library book, a magazine, or a medical information hot line.) Discuss why it is often important to find information in more than one source.

Expository Writing

Reports: Turning to Helpful Sources

In the preceding lesson you learned about narrowing a topic. The next task is research. What do you want to know, and where can you find the information that you need?

Ask Questions

Conducting research is like going on a treasure hunt. You won't know whether you've found the prize unless you know what you're looking for in the first place. Before you head off to the library or start searching the Internet, think about your topic. What do you think you know? Focus your thoughts by jotting down some ideas about your topic. What do you want to find out? Make a list of questions that you'd like your research to answer.

Find Answers

Your list of questions can guide your research the way a map can guide an explorer to a buried treasure. Let your research questions guide your research as you look for answers in a variety of sources. New questions will come to you as you learn more about your topic. Just add them to your list!

Resource Manager

📁 Planning Resources
- *Lesson Plans*

📇 Transparencies
- *Bellringer*
- *Daily Language Practice*
- *Fine Art 21–25*
- *Two-Minute Skill Drill*
- *Writing Process 17–19B*

📁 Other Print Resources
- *Composition Enrichment*, p. 39
- *Composition Practice*, p. 39
- *Composition Reteaching*, p. 39
- *Cooperative Learning Activities*, pp. 25–30
- *Listening and Speaking Activities*, pp. 12–13, 21, 23
- *Research Paper and Report Writing*, pp. 33–34, 36, 38

- *Sentence-Combining Practice*, pp. 30–32
- *Thinking and Study Skills*, pp. 4–5, 20, 23–24, 35–36
- *Writing Across the Curriculum*
- *Writing Assessment and Evaluation Rubrics*

When you're researching a topic, the library can be your best resource. There, you're likely to find computers with access to the Internet, and you're sure to find a catalog that lists all the materials in the library according to subject, title, or author. You will find a variety of informative materials in the library:

- books and reference works, such as almanacs, atlases, and encyclopedias
- magazines, newspapers, and scholarly journals
- videotapes, audiotapes, and compact discs

An encyclopedia is a good place to begin reading about your topic. An encyclopedia article can give you a broad overview of a topic and can direct you to additional sources.

The best research reports include information from both primary and secondary sources. A **primary source** is a firsthand account of an event, written by someone who actually experienced or observed the event. Primary sources include diaries, letters, or historical documents from the period you're studying. An interview with a knowledgeable person is another kind of primary source. For example, an interview with someone who lives on a farm would be a primary source for a report on farm life. A **secondary source** is written by a person who has conducted original research, gathered information, and shaped that information in a certain way. Books and magazines are generally considered secondary sources.

Prewriting Tip

Learn to make the most of your library visit by reviewing Unit 22, Library and Reference Resources, pages 630–652.

Prewriting Tip

See Writing and Research Handbook, pages 825–826, for information about evaluating sources.

Prewriting Tip

It's important to examine more than one viewpoint on a topic, so be sure to read multiple sources. Compare and contrast their differing perspectives.

Expository Writing

Journal Writing

Review what you wrote for the Choose and Narrow a Topic activity on page 223. What kinds of primary and secondary sources might you look for on your topic? In your journal, jot down a preliminary plan for finding these sources and conducting research for your report.

Teach

Narrowing a Topic and Clarifying Research

Discuss with students how to narrow a topic (for example, from wild animals to tigers). Then discuss how to clarify research further by asking questions such as the following: Will material be available in literature or art? on video or computer? Are photographs and statistical information about this topic easy to find? Is there any value in looking for the most recent information, or is this a topic that will not have changed significantly over time? **L2**

Seeking Help in the Library

Suggest that before students ask a librarian for assistance, they complete their preliminary lists of research questions. Suggest that after the librarian has helped them through the search process, they may want to write down the steps that were taken to locate the necessary information. They can save these notes to help guide their future research. **L1**

Journal Writing Tip

Identifying Sources Suggest that students create a list of the types of primary and secondary sources of information they'd like to find for their reports. Students' research plans should include visits to the school or local public library. Students should also plan to sign up for time in the computer lab so they can search for appropriate Web sites.

Using Note Cards

Point out to students that one advantage of taking notes on separate cards is the ease with which the notes can be arranged in groups, depending upon how a writer decides to organize the report. For example, a note on the topic *Bicycle Helmets* could be put in a pile with other notes on bicycle equipment, or it could be classified along with notes on bicycle safety procedures. Discuss with students other advantages of using cards when preparing to write a report—such as tracking sources. **L2**

Two-Minute Skill Drill

Name sources where you could find information about the following:

word meanings   *sports statistics*

current events   *maps*

See also *Two-Minute Skill Drill Transparency 5.7*

Additional Resources

Fine Art Transparencies, 21–25

Writing Process Transparencies, 17–19B

Writing Across the Curriculum

Cooperative Learning Activities, pp. 25–30

Research Paper and Report Writing, pp. 33–34, 36, 38

Thinking and Study Skills, pp. 4–5, 20, 23–24, 35–36

Sentence-Combining Practice, pp. 30–32

Listening and Speaking Activities, pp. 12–13, 21, 23

Composition Practice, p. 39

Expository Writing

Each card for a report on bicycle safety contains notes on a different part of the topic.

Make Note Cards

The process of making note cards helps you learn about your topic and keep track of the information you find. As you scan your sources, look for information about your topic. When you find it, take notes on four-by-six-inch index cards. Use one card for each distinct piece of information. At the top of each card, write the main idea of the note. When you're ready to begin writing, you'll easily be able to sort and organize your information. At the bottom of each card, write the author's name, a page reference, and the source's title and publication information.

This primary source is an informal but helpful interview.

Quotation marks indicate words copied from a source.

Prewriting Tip

You need to give credit to the source of the ideas and information you include in your report. That's why you should record source information on each note card. For more on giving credit and citing sources, see **Writing and Research Handbook**, pages 826–830.

Tips for Taking Notes

- Keep your notes in one place. Don't lose them!

- With every note, include the information source (title, author, publication information, and page numbers).

- List main ideas and details to support them. Record dates and names exactly.

- **Paraphrase** or **summarize** information, using your own words to record what you learn from a source.

- If you copy information word for word, use quotation marks to show that you're quoting from a source directly.

MEETING INDIVIDUAL NEEDS

Less-Proficient Readers

Practicing Taking Notes

Work with students who need practice with note-taking strategies. Help them select a topic that interests them and find an encyclopedia article or book chapter that contains information about it. Suggest that they scan the heads and illustrations before reading and write down questions that come to mind. While reading, they should look for and jot down key words that answer their questions. After reading, ask students to write a brief summary of the topic.

Begin Your Research

Write your narrowed topic at the top of a piece of paper. Write the headings *Books, Magazines and Newspapers, People, Technology,* and *Other Sources.* Under each one, list specific sources you can use and prepare note cards.

PURPOSE To gather information for a report
AUDIENCE Yourself
LENGTH 1 page of source ideas; at least 15 note cards

WRITING RUBRICS To begin your research effectively, you should

• find sources in the library

• find answers in your sources to the questions you have about your topic

• make note cards, following the tips on page 226

Using Computers

Try entering your notes into a computer file. Just as you would write a note's main idea on the top line of an index card, use boldface type to signify a note's main idea. At any point during your note-taking process, you can do a search for keywords in these main idea headings. Then sort your notes using the Cut-and-Paste feature, so that all your notes on the same aspect of your topic are in the same place in your computer file. Also be sure to record publication information for each note you enter into the computer.

Listening and Speaking

SHARE IDEAS With a small group of classmates, share ideas about how to find and evaluate sources of information for the topic you've selected. By talking about your topic with others, you can discover ways to limit—or expand—the scope of your topic. Be ready to listen to and act on the advice of your classmates.

Grammar Link

Use correct punctuation and capitalization.

Always capitalize proper nouns and titles, such as *M.D.* or *Jr.,* after a name. Underline or use italic type for titles of books and magazines. Use quotation marks for book chapters and song titles.

Revise the note card excerpts below to correct errors.

1. Comments made by Peter Hetzler jr., m.d.
2. Amy said that her favorite book is bicycling through North america.
3. Joe read A tale of two cities.
4. A chapter called Car Repair.
5. The Beatles wrote A Hard Day's Night in 24 hours.

See Lesson 19.2, page 575, and Lesson 20.6, page 599.

5.7 Reports: Turning to Helpful Sources **227**

Expository Writing

Assess

Evaluation Rubrics

Begin Your Research

Use these criteria when evaluating your students' writing:

• Are the questions about the topic answered using research sources?

• Do the research note cards follow the *Tips for Taking Notes* on page 226?

See also *Writing Assessment and Evaluation Rubrics*

Using Computers

Students who use a word processor may use italic type instead of underlining for the titles of books that they include in the publication information that is part of each note in their computer files.

Listening and Speaking

Encourage students to take notes as ideas are exchanged on how to find the best sources of information and how to limit or expand a topic's scope. They will be able to refer to the notes as they do their research.

Reteaching

📁 *Composition Reteaching,* p. 39

Enrichment

📁 *Composition Enrichment,* p. 39

Close

List on the chalkboard topics such as *The History of Horses, Athletes of the Nineties,* or *Who's Who in Contemporary Music.* Have students work in small groups, choosing one listed topic for a report. Ask students to narrow the topic, develop three or four questions they might answer in a research report, and list possible sources. Provide time for groups to share their information with one another.

Grammar Link

Answers
1. Peter Hetzler Jr., M.D.
2. <u>Bicycling Through North America</u>
3. <u>A Tale of Two Cities</u>
4. "Car Repair"
5. "A Hard Day's Night"

Focus

Lesson Overview

Objectives
- To learn the benefits of including interviews in reports
- To prepare for and conduct an interview as a means of gathering information for a report

Skills
- preparing for an interview; conducting an interview

Critical Thinking
- summarizing; generating questions; identifying; establishing and evaluating criteria

Listening and Speaking
- note taking; interviewing; discussing; questioning

Bellringer
Daily Language Activity

When students enter the classroom, have this assignment on the board: *Think of a famous person you admire. Write three questions you'd like to ask the person about his or her life or work.*

Grammar Link to the Bellringer

Remind students that proper nouns include the names of people and places, organizations, book titles, holidays, days of the week and months of the year. Did students capitalize all proper nouns in their questions?

See also *Daily Language Practice*

Motivating Activity

Newspapers and magazines are filled with profiles of people, some famous and some ordinary. Such profiles usually include quotations and are often written as an interview. Why are interviews interesting to so many people? What do students think they would rather read—an article with quoted opinions from people involved or one without such a personal touch? Why?

LESSON
5.8

Reports: Conducting an Interview

An interview with an expert can provide the kinds of details, dates, and stories that strengthen research reports.

An Illinois writer became curious about a program to promote safety among bicycle riders in Schaumburg, Illinois. Who ran the program? What did it do? An interview with an expert answered many of the writer's questions.

Interview with Schaumburg Police Intern Becky Stiefvater

What's the full name of the bike patrol?
Schaumburg Bicycle Safety Patrol

How does it operate?
We have six people, and we divide up into three teams of two. We ride around, and we look for kids who go through stop signs, ride on the wrong side of the road, or ride two people on a bike made for one—anything that's against the village ordinance.

What happens to people who get caught?
Sometimes we issue a warning ticket or a notice to appear in "bike court." We set up actual court proceedings for them, and they get assignments like community service.

How do you get around town when you're off-duty?
Since I'm riding a bike eight hours a day, I usually drive my car.

228 Unit 5 Expository Writing

Resource Manager

📁 Planning Resources
- *Lesson Plans*

📊 Transparencies
- *Bellringer*
- *Daily Language Practice*
- *Fine Art* 21–25
- *Two-Minute Skill Drill*
- *Writing Process* 17–19B

📁 Other Print Resources
- *Composition Enrichment*, p. 40
- *Composition Practice*, p. 40
- *Composition Reteaching*, p. 40
- *Cooperative Learning Activities*, pp. 25–30
- *Listening and Speaking Activities*, pp. 12–13, 21, 23
- *Research Paper and Report Writing*, pp. 33–34, 36, 38

- *Sentence-Combining Practice*, pp. 30–32
- *Thinking and Study Skills*, pp. 2, 4, 33–34
- *Writing Across the Curriculum*
- *Writing Assessment and Evaluation Rubrics*

Prepare for an Interview

Your teachers or librarian might be able to suggest someone you could interview for a research report. Once you have identified an expert, contact him or her to see if and when an interview is possible. Be courteous: The interviewee is doing you a favor by setting aside the time to talk.

Prepare interview questions ahead of time. Ask yourself what you expect to learn through the interview. Do you want to discover new developments? Do you want personal observations or stories? The most effective interview questions are open-ended; that is, they ask for more than a yes or no answer. Note how one interviewer used open-ended questions when talking with Mrs. Rodriguez.

> *Interview : Mrs. Bianca Rodriguez*
> *Founder of the Ready Riders Bike Safety Club*
> *East side of town; weekly club meetings at the fieldhouse*
> *1. Why did you organize this club?*
> *2. What do you mean by bike safety?*
> *3. How can kids contact you to join the club?*
> *4. What are the benefits of joining this club?*

How do the questions show that the interviewer prepared for this conversation?

Journal Writing

Decide on a topic someone could interview you about. In your journal write five open-ended questions an interviewer might ask you. Then answer the questions as honestly as you can.

Teach

Using the Model

Review the interview on page 228 with students. Ask them if they notice anything about the kinds of questions asked. Point out that the interviewer has structured all of the questions to be open-ended. There are no questions that could be answered simply "yes" or "no." Explain that this gives the interviewee a chance to open up and say what she really thinks. **L2**

Two-Minute Skill Drill

Write the following yes/no questions on the board. Ask students to write an open-ended question for each, covering the same information.

Did you always want to be a police officer?

Do you like your job?

See also *Two-Minute Skill Drill Transparency 5.8*

Journal Writing Tip

Setting Goals Tell students that before they begin to interview themselves, they should consider the goal of their interview. Is it to reveal a side of themselves that nobody knows? Is it to provide a quick thumbnail sketch of their personality and achievements? Is it to focus on one aspect of their identity, such as student, athlete, or family member?

Teach

Using a Videotape

To show students the interview process in action, bring in a videotaped television interview. Have students go through the tape slowly, pausing and rewinding wherever necessary. Tell them to write down each of the interviewer's questions and listen to see if the question was answered. Then discuss the interview. Do students think the interviewer achieved his or her goals? Do students think additional questions should have been asked? **L2**

Listening Well

Remind students that it's one thing to go into an interview prepared with a list of questions, but it's another thing to be prepared to listen to the answers. Discuss with students what it means to be an effective listener before they conduct their interviews. Ask them to name the barriers to effective listening. Distractions—such as background noise, sleepiness, hunger, and feeling rushed—can affect the students' ability to listen closely to what someone else has to say. Thinking that they know what the interviewee will say and listening only to what interests them can also affect their ability to really hear the answers to their questions. Remind students to prepare for their interviews both mentally and physically. **L2**

Additional Resources

Fine Art Transparencies, 21–25
Writing Across the Curriculum
Cooperative Learning Activities, pp. 25–30
Thinking and Study Skills, pp. 2, 4, 33–34
Sentence-Combining Practice, pp. 30–32
Listening and Speaking Activities, pp. 12–13, 21, 23
Research Paper and Report Writing, pp. 3–34, 36, 38
Composition Practice, p. 40

Conduct an Interview

When you conduct an interview, use a notebook, tape recorder, or both. If you use a notebook, you may have time to write down only the most important points. A tape recorder captures everything that is said. A tape provides a record of the speaker's exact words; a notebook preserves a record of your strongest impressions. Using both may strengthen your report.

You can conduct your interview in person or, if necessary, by telephone. When you meet or first speak with an interviewee, thank him or her for taking the time to talk. If you can, conduct the interview in a quiet place. Before ending the interview, make sure that you have all the information you need.

Other hints for a good interview are listed below.

Tips for Conducting an Interview

- Prepare a list of open-ended questions ahead of time.
- Arrive on time, dressed properly.
- Ask permission before using a tape recorder.
- Listen carefully to the answers.
- If you don't understand an answer, politely ask for an explanation.
- Ask follow-up questions.
- Immediately after the interview, write a summary of what you heard.
- Organize your notes and mark any that need more research.
- Make sure that all numbers and names are correct.
- Review the interview and see if you can identify which comments are opinions and which are statements of fact.

230 Unit 5 Expository Writing

Cooperative Learning

Rehearsing Questions

Students need to make sure their interviewees will understand their questions. One way to ensure this is to have students write out all questions and read them aloud to a partner, who can check them for correct vocabulary, sentence structure, and clear articulation. It is appropriate to use Standard American English for formal interviews. If the topic of the interview involves specialized terminology, students should prepare by learning the jargon (e.g., looking through the glossary of a nonfiction book on the subject).

5.8 Writing Activities

Conduct an Interview

Identify a local or national expert on your subject. Plan an interview with her or him.

PURPOSE To gain first-hand information for a report

AUDIENCE Your interviewee; yourself

LENGTH 1 page of questions; several pages of notes

WRITING RUBRICS To plan and conduct an effective interview, you should

- make an appointment for the interview
- write some open-ended questions
- conduct the interview and review your notes, using the tips chart on page 230

Using Computers

ORGANIZE Use a computer to write and organize interview questions. First, list questions as they come to mind. Then block or highlight the questions and organize them in a logical order. Finally, add other questions that you might use.

Listening and Speaking

COOPERATIVE LEARNING Work with a partner to refine your questions. Read your questions to each other and give and take suggestions for improvement.

Grammar Link

Capitalize proper nouns and adjectives formed from proper nouns.

Proper nouns, such as *America,* and proper adjectives, such as *American,* must be capitalized. In addition to the names of people and places, other proper nouns include the names of clubs and organizations and the names of historical events.

Ready Riders Bike Safety Club, Boys and Girls Club, Civil War.

Days of the week, months of the year, and holidays are also capitalized, as are the first and last words and all important words in titles of books, articles, films, and songs.

Correct capitalization errors in the following notes:

1. Interview: ms. Jan Tsai, student representative, national honor society
2. Meeting: Tuesday homeroom periods in the auditorium of john s. bradfield middle school
3. Visit planned: smithsonian institution in washington, d.c.
4. Write letter: principal j. w. smithers about the student election

See Lesson 19.2–19.4, pages 575–580.

Grammar Link

Answers

1. Interview: <u>M</u>s. Jan Tsai, student representative, <u>N</u>ational <u>H</u>onor <u>S</u>ociety
2. Meeting: Tuesday homeroom periods in the auditorium of <u>J</u>ohn <u>S.</u> <u>B</u>radfield <u>M</u>iddle <u>S</u>chool
3. Visit planned: <u>S</u>mithsonian <u>I</u>nstitution in <u>W</u>ashington, <u>D.C.</u>
4. Write letter: <u>P</u>rincipal <u>J. W. S</u>mithers about the student election

Assess

Evaluation Rubrics

Conduct an Interview

Use these criteria when evaluating your students' work:

- Did students locate an appropriate person to interview?
- Were questions clear and comprehensible, avoiding yes/no formulation?
- Did students tape-record or take notes of the interview?

See also *Writing Assessment and Evaluation Rubrics*

Using Computers

Check to see that students' questions are organized in logical order and that they are open-ended.

Listening and Speaking

Provide time for pairs of students to work together. Stress the importance of their making constructive suggestions for improving each other's interview.

Reteaching

📁 *Composition Reteaching,* p. 40

Enrichment

📁 *Composition Enrichment,* p. 40

Close

Tell students that beyond the classroom, people use interviewing skills in many ways. Discuss examples with students. (Journalists use interviews to get information for stories. Police officers and lawyers interview criminals, witnesses, and victims of crime. Business people interview job applicants.) Knowing how to ask the right questions of people is an essential life skill. Invite students to list jobs of people they know or have read about or seen on television. Do any of the jobs use interviews? Have students select a specific job and discuss an interview situation that might occur.

Focus

Lesson Overview

Objectives

- To focus and organize information by writing a thesis statement and creating an outline
- To present research effectively

Skills

- stating a main idea or thesis; outlining; identifying the introduction, body, and conclusion of a report

Critical Thinking

- summarizing; identifying main idea; decision-making

Listening and Speaking

- discussing; evaluating; questioning

Bellringer
Daily Language Activity

When students enter the classroom, have this assigment on the board: *The writer Thomas Mann said, "Order and simplification are the first steps toward mastery of a subject." Write what you think he meant.*

Grammar Link to the Bellringer

Remind students that a comma separates a direct quotation from the information about the speaker. Point out the comma before Mann's quote.

See also 🔖 *Daily Language Practice*

Motivating Activity

Ask students if they have ever put a lot of work into a project and then realized that they were on the wrong track. Did they start over? Ask for specific examples and discuss how one feels at such a time. Point out that one way to avoid wasted effort in report writing is to organize thoughts ahead of time, possibly in outline form. Then it's possible to see potential problems (missing information, irrelevant points) early, before wasting a lot of time trying to write a final report.

232

Expository Writing

Reports: Organizing and Drafting

*Y*ou've narrowed your topic and gathered ideas and details for a report. Now it's time to set a focus, organize your information, and write a draft of your report.

Prewriting Tip

Refer to **Writing and Research Handbook,** pages 817–824, for more information on how to put your ideas in the best order.

State the Main Idea

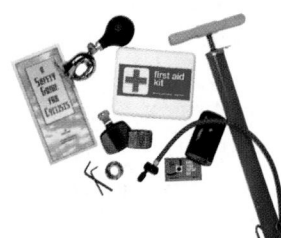

Before you can begin to organize all the information you've gathered, think about the big picture. What have you learned so far? What will be the main point of your report? Draft a **thesis statement**— a sentence or two that tells the main idea or that states what you want your writing to show, prove, or explain.

Get Organized

Let your thesis help you focus on what's important as you organize your thoughts—and your notes. You may need to set aside ideas and information that don't relate to your thesis. Get organized by following these steps.

- Make a list of the main points that you want to make in your report. All of these points should support your thesis statement.

- Begin creating an outline by listing your main points.

- Gather together your note cards and put them in groups according to their main-idea headings or subject matter.

- Complete your outline by adding details from your note cards and from your interview notes.

To see how a thesis statement and the parts of an outline fit together, review the sample outline shown on the next page.

Resource Manager

📁 Planning Resources

- *Lesson Plans*

📊 Transparencies

- *Bellringer*
- *Daily Language Practice*
- *Fine Art 21–25*
- *Two-Minute Skill Drill*
- *Writing Process 17–19B*

📁 Other Print Resources

- *Composition Enrichment,* p. 41
- *Composition Practice,* p. 41
- *Composition Reteaching,* p. 41
- *Cooperative Learning Activities,* pp. 25–30
- *Listening and Speaking Activities,* pp. 12–13, 21, 23
- *Research Paper and Report Writing,* pp. 33–34, 36, 38

- *Sentence-Combining Practice,* pp. 30–32
- *Thinking and Study Skills,* pp. 4, 13, 15, 20–21
- *Writing Across the Curriculum*
- *Writing Assessment and Evaluation Rubrics*

Thesis Statement: Bike safety includes careful riding, regular maintenance, and proper equipment.

  I. *Introduction*

  II. *Traffic regulations*

    A. *Ride on the right side of the road.*

    B. *Don't weave in and out.*

    C. *Ride single file.*

    D. *Obey traffic signs and use hand signals.*

  III. *Maintenance of your bike*

  IV. *Wearing a helmet*

> When you write an outline, use roman numerals to indicate main ideas and letters to indicate supporting details.

Expository Writing

Drafting Your Report

Now that you've developed a plan for your report, you're ready to start writing. Begin wherever you feel most comfortable—with your introduction or with a favorite section in the middle. Just make sure that you have one or more paragraphs for each heading in your outline and that you put the sections of your report in order before you review and revise your draft.

Remember that when you write a report, you make inferences, synthesize material, and draw conclusions from your research. Your goal is to present your own thinking—to say something new—using data from your research to support your ideas. Be careful not to **plagiarize,** or present someone else's ideas as your own. Therefore, when you write sentences from your note cards, put the source of the ideas in parentheses at the end.

Drafting Tip

A thesis statement tells the main idea of a composition or report in the same way that a topic sentence tells the main idea of a paragraph.

Drafting Tip

See **Writing and Research Handbook,** pages 826–830, for more information about how to give credit to your sources as you write.

Journal Writing

List the steps that you have learned so far about writing a research paper. Put a check beside the step that you think will be most challenging for you. Write a plan about one paragraph long for meeting the challenge.

Teach

Understanding the Main Idea

Many people think that if a report has a topic, it automatically has a main idea. Explain to students that a topic is merely a subject, such as *lead poisoning.* A main idea can be expressed in a thesis statement, such as, "Lead poisoning is a major health problem in children." With students, go through a newspaper and identify both the topic and the main idea of two or three articles. Remind students that their research reports must also be organized around a main idea. **L2**

Using an Outline

Some students may need help seeing the links between the thesis statement and the supporting information. Copy and distribute or write on the board the sample outline provided on this page. Ask students to circle or highlight the ideas contained in the thesis statement (e.g., the three components of bike safety) and draw an arrow from each statement idea to the supporting ideas. Help students write their own thesis statements and create outlines. **L1**

Journal Writing Tip

In deciding how to tackle the most challenging step, students may find it helpful to break that step into smaller steps. The plan then could be a list of smaller steps and how to accomplish them.

Teach

Identifying Parts of a Report

Divide the class into groups of three for simultaneous roundtable activities. Distribute copies of expository articles from magazines. Ask the first student in each group to identify the introduction. The second student should locate the body of the article, and the third can identify the conclusion. Students can perform this process with one or more articles. When they have finished, they may share their results with another group. Encourage students to discuss reasons for their decisions. **L2**

Two-Minute Skill Drill

Have students compare the sections of the report shown on this page with the outline on page 233. Which part of the thesis statement from the outline is being expanded into the body of the report on this page? (Bike safety includes careful riding.)

See also 🏳 *Two-Minute Skill Drill Transparency 5.9*

Additional Resources

🏳 *Fine Art Transparencies, 21–25*
📁 *Writing Across the Curriculum*
📁 Cooperative Learning Activities, pp. 25–30
📁 *Thinking and Study Skills,* pp. 4, 13, 15, 20–21
📁 *Sentence-Combining Practice,* pp. 30–32
📁 *Listening and Speaking Activities,* pp. 12–13, 21, 23
📁 *Research Paper and Report Writing,* pp. 33–34, 36, 38
📁 *Composition Practice,* p. 41

Expository Writing

Know the Parts of a Report

Like other compositions, every report has three parts: an introduction, a body, and a conclusion. Each part has a specific purpose. An example of each part and its purpose appears below. (The picture shows only a section of the report on safety.) The **Writing and Research Handbook,** pages 817–832, provides more information about how to structure your report and the paragraphs within it.

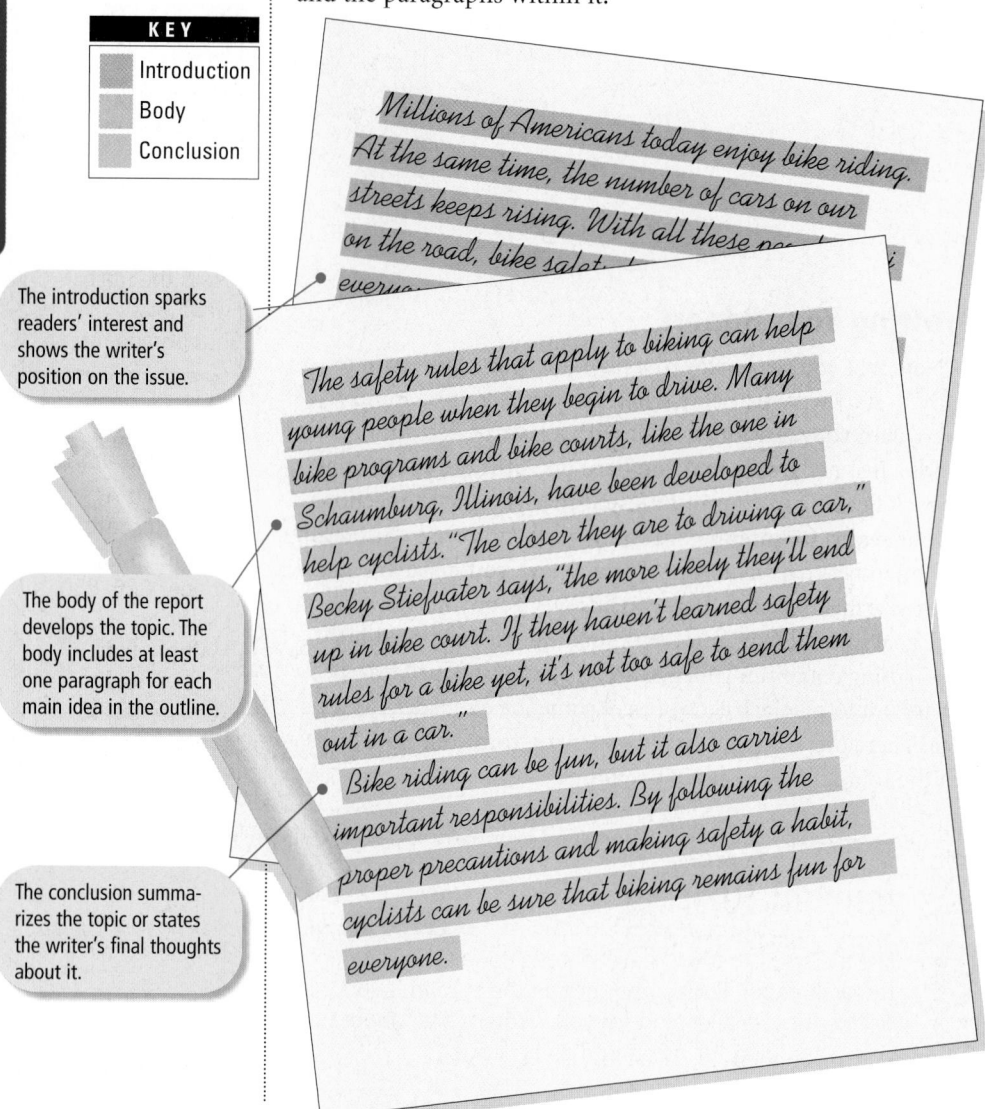

KEY

Introduction
Body
Conclusion

The introduction sparks readers' interest and shows the writer's position on the issue.

Millions of Americans today enjoy bike riding. At the same time, the number of cars on our streets keeps rising. With all these

The body of the report develops the topic. The body includes at least one paragraph for each main idea in the outline.

The safety rules that apply to biking can help young people when they begin to drive. Many bike programs and bike courts, like the one in Schaumburg, Illinois, have been developed to help cyclists. "The closer they are to driving a car," Becky Stiefvater says, "the more likely they'll end up in bike court. If they haven't learned safety rules for a bike yet, it's not too safe to send them out in a car."

Bike riding can be fun, but it also carries important responsibilities. By following the proper precautions and making safety a habit, cyclists can be sure that biking remains fun for everyone.

The conclusion summarizes the topic or states the writer's final thoughts about it.

234 Unit 5 Expository Writing

MEETING INDIVIDUAL NEEDS

English Language Learners

Using Letters for Ordering

Students whose first language has an alphabet different from that used in English may need support with the concept of using letters of the alphabet in ordering their outlines. Point out that because the English alphabet has an established order, beginning with *A* and ending with *Z*, the letters can be used almost in place of numbers. Their sound value as letters is unimportant when they are used for ordering.

Expository Writing

Outline and Draft

Now you have the raw materials for your report. Look over your notes to see whether ideas changed as you researched. Are there new questions you would like to answer?

PURPOSE To outline and draft a report

AUDIENCE Yourself; peer reviewers

LENGTH 4–5 pages

WRITING RUBRICS To develop an effective outline and draft, you should

- write a clear, accurate thesis statement
- create an outline, using your note cards to arrange topics logically
- draft your report, creating an introduction, a body, and a conclusion

Listening and Speaking

COOPERATIVE LEARNING Read your draft to a partner or a small group. Ask your audience these questions:

—Is anything not clear?

—Where could I add more information?

—What do you find most interesting about my topic?

—What would you like to know more about?

Take notes on the responses of your peers, and use the notes to help you when you revise. Remember, the most important part of writing is to make your ideas clear to your audience.

Grammar Link

Use a comma to separate a phrase from the quotation itself.

Look back at the model on page 234. Notice how the writer uses commas with direct quotations.

"The closer they are to driving a car," Becky Stiefvater says, "the more likely they'll end up in bike court."

Write each quotation using correct punctuation.

1. Power said Lord Acton corrupts. Absolute power corrupts absolutely.

2. Don't look back Satchel Page said. Something could be gaining on you.

3. I never met a person I didn't like Will Rogers said.

4. My name is Luca the song goes. And I live on the second floor.

See Lesson 20.6, page 599.

Listening and Speaking

GETTING EXPERT ADVICE Arrange to have a teacher in an appropriate subject area or one of the experts you interviewed review your report for accuracy, clarity, and interest. Ask for advice about how to improve your report. Take notes on the feedback you receive and use those notes as you revise.

Assess

Evaluation Rubrics

Outline and Draft

Use these criteria when evaluating your students' writing:

- Does the thesis statement encapsulate the main idea?
- Does the outline list relevant points and supporting details for those points?
- Does the draft reflect the work done in the outline and research steps?

See also *Writing Assessment and Evaluation Rubrics*

Listening and Speaking

The students should do the following:

- cooperatively read one another's work
- ask appropriate questions about their own work
- offer relevant responses to classmates' writing and specific questions

Reteaching

📁 *Composition Reteaching,* p. 41

Enrichment

📁 *Composition Enrichment,* p. 41

Close

Have students look at a research paper they have written and find the thesis statement. If the statement doesn't encapsulate the main idea, they should revise it.

Grammar Link

Answers

1. "Power," said Lord Acton, "corrupts. Absolute power corrrupts absolutely."

2. "Don't look back," Satchel Page said. "Something could be gaining on you."

3. "I never met a person I didn't like," Will Rogers said.

4. "My name is Luca," the song goes. "And I live on the second floor."

Making Sense with Commas In pairs, have students read the Grammar Link items, first without punctuation, then with it. Encourage them to note how commas clarify meaning.

Focus

Lesson Overview

Objective

- To revise a written report for clarity, accuracy, and effectiveness

Skills

- checking for errors; using irregular verbs correctly; improving past work; sharing written work

Critical Thinking

- analyzing; recalling; evaluating; defining and clarifying

Listening and Speaking

- discussing; evaluating; oral reporting

 Bellringer
Daily Language Activity

When students enter the classroom, have this assignment on the board: *What do you consider to be the most important book in English? Why?*

Grammar Link to the Bellringer

Irregular verbs crop up everywhere. Ask students to check their work in the Bellringer activity. Did they use any irregular forms, such as *written?*

See also 🗒 *Daily Language Practice*

Motivating Activity

Discuss books students consider important. What might have happened if the writers of those books had sent sloppy, unclear, or careless manuscripts to their publishers? Remind students that they won't want to put a lot of effort into researching and writing about a subject only to have the effectiveness of their work lessened by errors. It's worth taking the extra time to revise.

Expository Writing

LESSON 5.10

Reports: Revising and Presenting

By revising a report, you can test and strengthen the presentation of your ideas. Let your peers tell you whether your writing is clear.

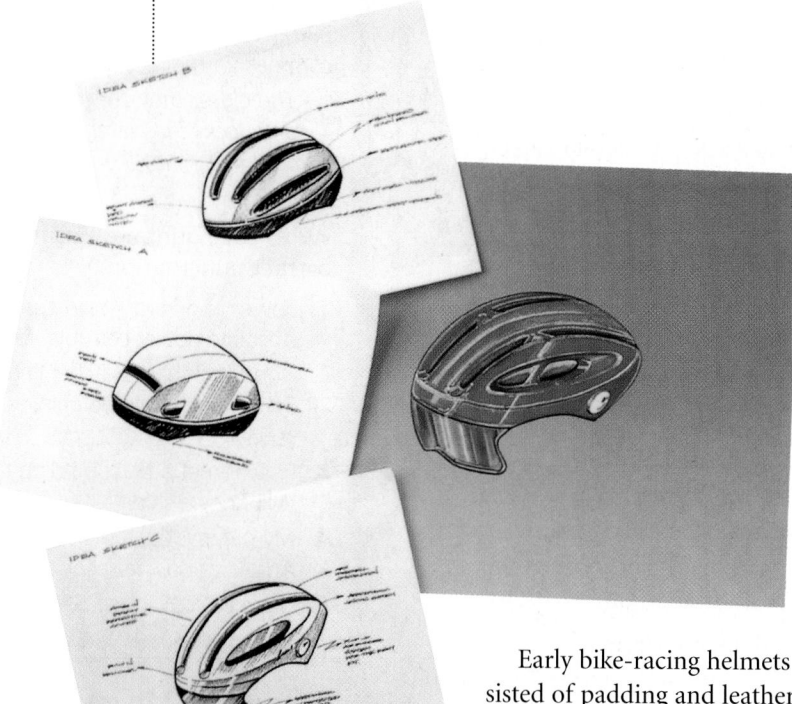

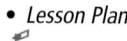

Early bike-racing helmets consisted of padding and leather. The introduction of plastics allowed manufacturers to produce stronger and lighter helmets. Testing led to improvements that made helmets not only fit riders well but also keep them cool. It seems that the early version of just about anything can stand improvement. Consider how you can use a system of revising and testing with your research report.

236 Unit 5 Expository Writing

Resource Manager

📁 **Planning Resources**
- *Lesson Plans*

🗒 **Transparencies**
- *Bellringer*
- *Daily Language Practice*
- *Fine Art* 21–25
- *Two-Minute Skill Drill*
- *Writing Process* 17–19B

📁 **Other Print Resources**
- *Composition Enrichment*, p. 42
- *Composition Practice*, p. 42
- *Composition Reteaching*, p. 42
- *Cooperative Learning Activities*, pp. 25–30
- *Listening and Speaking Activities*, pp. 12–13, 21, 23
- *Research Paper and Report Writing*, pp. 33–34, 36, 38

- *Sentence-Combining Practice*, pp. 30–32
- *Thinking and Study Skills*, pp. 4, 13–14, 20–21
- *Writing Across the Curriculum*
- *Writing Assessment and Evaluation Rubrics*

Get It Right

When you revise, make sure that each section—the introduction, the body, and the conclusion—fulfills its purpose and engages your readers. Check that you've covered the main points in your outline and that your ideas flow in a logical order. You'll also want to confirm that your facts and statistics are correct, that you've quoted your sources accurately, and that you've given proper credit to any ideas that are not your own.

Create a Works-Cited List

The final step in the process of revising a research report is to create a works-cited list, which will become the last page of your report. A works-cited list gives complete publication information for all the sources you used and referred to in your paper. Entries should appear in alphabetical order. Refer to **Writing and Research Handbook,** pages 827–830, for more information about preparing your final draft and about the different bibliographic styles you can use for your works-cited list. Ask your teacher which style he or she prefers.

You may also want to review the model of a research paper on pages 831–832 of the **Handbook.** For your own paper, make sure that you put your list of works cited on its own page.

Revising Tip

When revising, check transitions between paragraphs. Good transitions create fluency by showing how one paragraph relates to the next.

Revising Tip

For a discussion of revision strategies, see Unit 2, Lessons 2.6–2.9.

Expository Writing

TIME

For more about the writing process, see **TIME** *Facing the Blank Page,* pp. 97–107.

Journal Writing

Evaluate your draft using the checklist on page 67. In your journal, jot down how well you accomplished each of the points on the checklist. Think critically about your draft and make notes about how you will revise your report.

5.10

Teach
Checking Work in Steps

Some students may have difficulty going through a report and checking for many different kinds of errors at once. These students may need to prepare a simple checklist to use in revising. A chart with the following cues may help if placed where students can review it as needed:
Accurate facts
Complete information
Effective details
Proper use of conventions **L1**

Two-Minute Skill Drill

Have students identify the two errors in the following sentence. One is a typographical error, and one is a factual error:

When I was 110 years old, I went to Mexico City, the capital of Canada.

See also *Two-Minute Skill Drill Transparency 5.10*

Journal Writing Tip

Critical Thinking Students will do a better job of revising if they think about their own thought processes. What kinds of mistakes do they most frequently make when writing? By knowing their weaknesses, they can focus attention on the aspects of their reports most likely to have problems.

Expository Writing

Teach

Planning to Publish

Students may want to think about cooperatively publishing their reports. Each member of the group would specialize in a certain aspect of the process: word processing, adding graphics, locating or producing photographs, binding, publishing or sharing. Discuss with students what each step of the process would require. **L2**

Analyzing an Illustration

Direct students' attention to the model. Ask what information the illustration of the bicyclist provides that the text of the report does not. Is it information that is best presented in a visual way? Discuss how an illustration like this might work in their own reports. **L2**

Additional Resources

Fine Art Transparencies, 21–25

Writing Process Transparenciecs, 17–19B

Cooperative Learning Activities, pp. 25–30

Listening and Speaking Activities, pp. 12–13, 21, 23

Sentence-Combining Practice, pp. 30–32

Thinking and Study Skills, pp. 4, 13, 15, 20–21

Research Paper and Report Writing, pp. 33–34, 36, 38

Composition Practice, p. 42

Presenting Tip

Consider adding pictures, charts, and other graphics to make the presentation of your report more effective.

Tell the World

When you start a report assignment, all you have is a topic that interests you. After completing a report, you have more knowledge. You're ready to share what you've learned.

You can share your work in a variety of ways. Bind your report in book form, present it on a computer disk, put it into a notebook binder, post it on an electronic bulletin board, or print it as part of a class newsletter or magazine. Think of things to include—covers, graphics, clippings, photographs—that will make your report attractive. Then share it with others!

Read the report page below to see how one writer used a diagram to illustrate information.

How does the diagram strengthen the report?

helmet

elbow pads

head light

rear reflector

proper shoes

Another safeguard that people often ignore is proper bike maintenance. Cyclists should inspect their bikes regularly to make sure the tires, brakes, handlebars, seats, and spokes are in proper shape. Some repairs can be done easily by the cyclist, but regular inspections at a bike repair shop are also recommended.

Proper clothing and equipment can also make a difference in bicycle safety. According to one study, only 12 percent of accidents involve a car and a bike. The rest occur when cyclists fall or are thrown from their bikes. Because of this, experts such as those from the National Safe Kids Campaign recommend that, when riding, cyclists wear bike helmets. The helmets protect against brain injuries.

238 Unit 5 Expository Writing

Cultural Connections

Using Typographic Markers

Students may choose report topics that by necessity include foreign words. Make sure they remember to underline or put in italic type any non-English words other than names. Students should supply an approximate English translation for any of these words. If there are several foreign words, a glossary should be included in the report.

5.10 Writing Activities

Expository Writing

Revise, Edit, and Share Your Report

Now is the time to make sure your report says what you want it to say. Does it support your thesis statement? Will it interest your readers?

PURPOSE To finish and share a research report

AUDIENCE Classmates, teacher, family

LENGTH 5–10 pages

WRITING RUBRICS To revise and edit your report before you share it, you should

- check the report for clarity, accuracy, organization, and interest
- proofread to correct errors in grammar, usage, spelling, and mechanics
- make a final copy for others to read and study

Listening and Speaking

COOPERATIVE LEARNING Work in a small group to improve the following paragraph for readers. Brainstorm to make a good topic sentence. Work together to revise the paragraph for clarity, organization, and interest.

When people hear "old-fashioned bicycle," they think of a big front wheel and a small back one. Bicycles with a big front wheel were called ordinary. They were better. They were called "high wheelers." The first bicycle factory in the United States began making it in 1877. They were costly and unsafe with the rider so high. They gave a smooth ride and went fast.

Viewing and Representing

CREATING COVER ART Create a cover for your report. Reproduce or draw a visual image that will give a reader an idea of what to expect from your report. It can be funny or serious, depending on your subject.

Grammar Link

Use the correct form of the verb.

The principal parts of a verb include its base form, present participle, past form, and past participle.

   ride, riding, rode, ridden

Write the correct form of the verb in parentheses.

[1] Advertisers have (rely) on ads for decades. [2] Catchy jingles are (know) to be memorable. [3] Eye-catching images, often (create) on computers, draw people's attention. [4–5] Because so many ads have (appear) in the media, people often (ignore) them.

See Lesson 10.5, page 407, and Lesson 10.9, page 415.

Grammar Link

Answers
1. relied
2. known
3. created
4. appeared
5. ignore

Assess

Evaluation Rubrics

Revise, Edit, and Share Your Report

Use these criteria when evaluating your students' revised writing.

- Is the report clear, well-organized, and interesting?
- Is the report free of errors in grammar, usage, spelling, and mechanics?
- Is the final report neat and well-presented? Students who do not have access to word processors should write legibly using print or cursive handwriting.

See also *Writing Assessment and Evaluation Rubrics*

Listening and Speaking

In this activity, students should
- brainstorm freely and cooperatively
- write an appropriate topic sentence
- revise the paragraph to improve the organization and expression of ideas

Viewing and Representing

Stress the importance of creating a cover that will not only relate to the subject of a report but also stimulate a reader's interest in reading it.

Reteaching

  Composition Reteaching, p. 42

Enrichment

  Composition Enrichment, p. 42

  Fine Art Transparencies, 21–25

Close

Point out to students that just because something is published doesn't mean it is perfect. Readers should read critically and use their discoveries to improve their own writing. Have students bring in published articles that they think need revision or that contain errors.

Focus

Lesson Overview

Objectives
- To effectively compare two people in writing
- To present a comparison in a clearly written format

Skills
- charting a comparison; making a Venn diagram; comparing real and fictional characters

Critical Thinking
- contrasting; comparing; recalling; making inferences

Listening and Speaking
- reading aloud; discussing

 Bellringer
Daily Language Activity

When students enter the classroom, have this assignment on the board: *You can't compare apples and oranges. Do you agree with this statement? Explain briefly why or why not.*

Grammar Link to the Bellringer

Words that often come up in comparisons are *either . . . or* and *neither . . . nor.* These correlative conjunctions often lead to confusion in verb agreement. Did any students use these conjunctions in the Bellringer activity? How did they make the verbs agree?

See also *Daily Language Practice*

Motivating Activity

Discuss students' Bellringer activity responses. Have any of them heard the expression about comparing apples and oranges? Under what circumstances do students think it would make sense to compare apples and oranges? (when comparing different fruits) When would it not make sense? (when discussing something unique to either the apples or the oranges, such as crunchiness)

 Expository Writing

WRITING ABOUT LITERATURE
Comparing Two People

Read what the writer of the passages below has to say about two women cyclists who gained fame. How are the women different? How are they alike?

Literature Model

[M]argaret Le Long's] bicycle was a modern safety bicycle with the diamond frame, its top tube dropped to enable her—and other women—to pedal while wearing a dress. All she packed was a bag that strapped to her handlebars and contained a pistol, curl-papers, makeup box, and underwear. Her trip [from Chicago to San Francisco in 1896] took two months.

Predictably, Connie Young rose to become a world-class athlete. Her specialty was the explosive sprint events. She won two bronze medals in world speed-skating championships and made the Olympic speed-skating teams in 1980 and 1984. She also reigned as national and world cycling champion.

Peter Nye, *The Cyclist's Sourcebook*

240 Unit 5 Expository Writing

Resource Manager

📂 **Planning Resources**
- *Lesson Plans*

📖 **Transparencies**
- *Bellringer*
- *Daily Language Practice*
- *Fine Art 21–25*
- *Two-Minute Skill Drill*
- *Writing Process 17–19B*

📂 **Other Print Resources**
- *Composition Enrichment,* p. 43
- *Composition Practice,* p. 43
- *Composition Reteaching,* p. 43
- *Cooperative Learning Activities,* pp. 25–30
- *Listening and Speaking Activities,* pp. 12–13, 21, 23
- *Research Paper and Report Writing,* pp. 33–34, 36, 38

- *Sentence-Combining Practice,* pp. 30–32
- *Thinking and Study Skills,* pp. 6, 8, 15
- *Writing Across the Curriculum*
- *Writing Assessment and Evaluation Rubrics*

Chart a Comparison

Organizing and answering questions such as those below can help you compare and contrast details. It's clear that Young and Le Long are different in important ways.

Early cyclist
Margaret Le Long

Comparing and Contrasting Margaret Le Long and Connie Young

1. In what decade did Le Long ride cross-country?

   In what decade did Young first participate in the Olympics?

2. What did Le Long wear when she rode? What did she carry with her? What does each item tell you about her?

   What do you think Young, a contemporary cyclist, wears when she rides?

3. Why is Margaret Le Long's ride considered an accomplishment?

   Why is Connie Young considered a "world-class" athlete?

| 1890s cyclist | modern cyclist |

Olympian
Connie Young

Journal Writing

Write brief answers to any pair of questions in the chart on this page. Then write one sentence telling which woman interests you more and why.

5.11 Comparing Two People **241**

Teach

Using the Model

Have students look at the two paragraphs on page 240. Discuss what is being described. Do students think a comparison is being made between "apples and oranges"? Why or why not? Invite students to think of a topic sentence to cover both paragraphs (e.g., Women's cycling achievements are varied). Then ask for a topic sentence for each of the paragraphs. **L2**

Recording Information

Some students may be able to find contrasts more easily if they organize information in chart form. **L1**

Journal Writing Tip

Inferring Point out that some of the questions in the chart require students to infer the answers from the details given. Readers must look at the evidence (e.g., the contents of Le Long's luggage) and draw conclusions about it, using common sense and previous experience.

Answers to questions in the chart:
1. Le Long: 1890s. Young: 1980s.
2. Le Long wore a long skirt and carried a pistol, curl-papers, a make-up box, and underwear. These show she was prepared to defend herself, was concerned about her appearance, and was practical. Young probably wears an aerodynamically designed uniform when she races.
3. Le Long took a two-month, cross-country bicycle tour in days when women were often considered weak and in need of protection. Young has won national and world championships and has participated in the Olympic Games.

Teach

Comparing Characters with Real People

Students may join in a Think-Pair-Share activity, identifying fictional characters who remind them of people they know. Ask them to list traits the real and fictional characters have in common and then list differences between the two. Finally, have them share and discuss their comparisons with other groups. **L2**

Two-Minute Skill Drill

Tell students that the main idea in the passage from *The Chocolate War* on this page is that The Goober was beautiful when he ran. Have them scan the paragraph and find three words or phrases that support this main idea.

See also *Two-Minute Skill Drill Transparency 5.11*

Additional Resources

Fine Art Transparencies, 21–25

Writing Process Transparencies, 17–19B.

Writing Across the Curriculum

Cooperative Learning Activities, pp. 25–30

Thinking and Study Skills, pp. 6, 8, 15

Sentence Combining Practice, pp. 30–32

Listening and Speaking Activities, pp. 12–13, 21, 23

Research Paper and Report Writing, pp. 33–34, 36, 38

Composition Practice, p. 43

Expository Writing

Compare Real and Fictional Characters

When you read about a fictional character who reminds you of a real person, you might report on the fictional work by comparing and contrasting the character and the person. To help you organize your ideas, use a Venn diagram like the one on this page.

Read the passage below about The Goober, a character in Robert Cormier's novel *The Chocolate War*. Think about the qualities he shares with other athletes you know or have read about, especially Connie Young.

> ### Literature Model
>
> The Goober was beautiful when he ran. His long arms and legs moved flowingly and flawlessly, his body floating as if his feet weren't touching the ground. When he ran, he forgot about his awkwardness and the shyness that paralyzed him when a girl looked his way. Even his thoughts became sharper, and things were simple and uncomplicated—he could solve math problems when he ran or memorize football play patterns. Often he rose early in the morning, before anyone else, and poured himself liquid through the sunrise streets. Then everything seemed beautiful, everything in its proper orbit, nothing impossible, the entire world attainable.
>
> Robert Cormier, *The Chocolate War*

What qualities do The Goober and Connie Young share with other athletes you know about but not with each other?

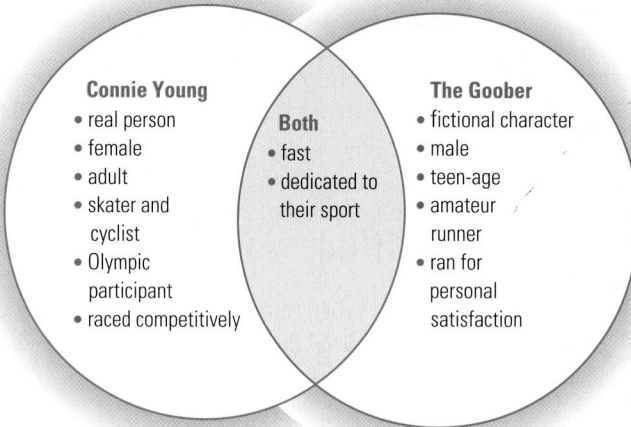

Connie Young
- real person
- female
- adult
- skater and cyclist
- Olympic participant
- raced competitively

Both
- fast
- dedicated to their sport

The Goober
- fictional character
- male
- teen-age
- amateur runner
- ran for personal satisfaction

Exploring Language

Comparing Languages

Ask students to consider certain differences between English and other languages. Point out that in English, adjectives do not change with the gender of the person described. A *tall* person is *tall* whether male or female. Many nouns are the same too (a *cyclist* can be male or female). In a few cases, separate words indicate male or female (*king/queen*). Some noun endings denote femaleness, such as *-ix* (*aviatrix*), *-ess* (*actress*), or *-ette* (*usherette*). These are often considered patronizing and are in less common use today than in earlier times.

5.11 Writing Activities

Write a Comparison-and-Contrast

Choose two characters you have read about recently. They can be fictional or real. Make a Venn diagram like the one on page 242 to show how they are alike and different. Then write two paragraphs comparing and contrasting them.

PURPOSE To compare and contrast two people

AUDIENCE Your classmates

LENGTH 2 paragraphs

WRITING RUBRICS To compare and contrast two characters effectively, you should

- identify both similarities and differences
- organize your paragraphs to make your points clearly
- proofread to correct mechanical errors

Listening and Speaking

COOPERATIVE LEARNING In a small group, hold a discussion about people's attitudes toward taking part in sports. Create a Venn diagram showing the similarities between those who play for fun and those who believe that "winning is the only thing." Think of people, real or fictional, who represent each type. Share your diagram and lists of people with the class.

Expository Writing

Grammar Link

Make compound subjects and verbs agree.

When two or more subjects are joined by *either . . . or* or *neither . . . nor,* the verb agrees with the subject that is closest to it.

> *Neither the players nor the* **coach** *is here yet.*

Write the correct form of the verb for each sentence below.

1. Either Janis or I (am, is) the fastest runner in seventh grade.
2. Neither my brothers nor my dad (runs, run) particularly fast.
3. Neither the choir director nor the orchestra conductor (encourages, encourage) students to choose track as an elective.
4. Either Sam or his sisters (is, are) going to wash the car.

See Lesson 16.5, page 543.

Cross-Curricular Activity

HISTORY From your history book, pick two historical figures who held similar positions or titles: for example, presidents, generals, or activists on certain issues. Compare and contrast the two in a brief essay that concludes with a statement about whether they were more similar to or different from each other.

Grammar Link

Answers

1. am
2. runs
3. encourages
4. are

Working with Compound Subjects and Verbs
Have students read papers they have written, finding and correcting any errors they have made in subject-verb agreement, using *either . . . or* or *neither . . . nor.*

Assess

Evaluation Rubrics

Write a Comparison-and-Contrast

Use these criteria when evaluating your students' writing.

- Do the paragraphs reflect information from the Venn diagram?
- Do they explicitly compare and contrast the two characters?
- Are the paragraphs organized so that information is presented clearly?

See also *Writing Assessment and Evaluation Rubrics*

Listening and Speaking

Evaluate all phases of the groups' activities:

- Do all members of the group participate in the discussion?
- Does each student independently express an opinion on attitudes toward winning?
- Do students work cooperatively to draw conclusions from their discussions?

Cross-Curricular Activity

Evaluate students' essays on the basis of the appropriateness of the historical figures selected and the accuracy of the statements concerning their similarities or differences.

Reteaching

📂 *Composition Reteaching,* p. 43

Enrichment

📂 *Composition Enrichment,* p. 43

Close

Ask students to create or think of a character and list major physical and personality traits of that character. Then ask them to write a short description of a backpack this character would carry and share the description with classmates. What can classmates infer about the character? Do they mention any of the personality traits written on the first list?

Writing Process in Action

Focus

Lesson Overview

Objectives

- To write a guide to the diverse population of one's own town or community
- To use the stages of the writing process to create and present a finished piece

Skills

- using the five stages of the writing process: prewriting, drafting, revising, editing, and presenting

Critical Thinking

- analyzing; visualizing; generating new information; patterning

Listening and Speaking

- note taking; discussing; questioning

Bellringer
Daily Language Activity

When students enter the classroom, have this assignment on the board: *Write a list of things you know about your hometown. Think about people, places, and things.*

Grammar Link to the Bellringer

Have students proofread their lists, checking spelling and capitalization.

See also *Daily Language Practice*

Motivating Activity

Help students to determine how much they know about their own hometown or city. Are there identifiable ethnic and racial groups that add to its variety? Do the inhabitants represent a wide range of careers, or do most people work for one or two large companies? Does the area provide for a variety of hobbies, sports, the arts, and other pursuits?

Expository Writing

Expository Writing

In the preceding lessons you've learned about gathering, organizing, and writing the kind of details that are necessary for expository writing. You have written letters, an article, and a research report. Now, in this lesson, you're invited to write a brochure that will inform visitors about your community.

WRITING Online

Visit the *Writer's Choice* Web site at **writer'schoice. glencoe.com** for additional writing prompts.

Assignment

Context	You are contributing to a brochure about your town. You need to gather details about the types of people in your town, including ages, races, customs, careers, and whatever other characteristics make them distinctive.
Purpose	To inform visitors and newcomers about the variety of people in your town
Audience	Visitors and newcomers to your town
Length	1–2 pages

The following pages can help you plan and write your brochure. Read through them, and then refer to them as you need to. But don't be tied down by them. You're in charge of your own writing process.

HONG FAT 恒發果菜公

Resource Manager

 Planning Resources
- *Lesson Plans*

**Transparencies**
- *Bellringer*
- *Daily Language Practice*
- *Writing Process* 17–19B

**Other Print Resources**
- *Composition Enrichment*, p. 44
- *Composition Practice*, p. 44
- *Composition Reteaching* p. 44
- *Grammar Workbook*, Lessons 68–71, 86–92
- *Sentence-Combining Practice*, pp. 30–32
- *Thinking and Study Skills*, pp. 3–5, 7–9, 20, 23–24, 34–35

- *Writing Assessment and Evaluation Rubrics*

Software
- *Writer's Assistant*

Web Sites
- *writerschoice.glencoe.com*
- *lit.glencoe.com*

Writing Process in Action

Prewriting

Sometimes just a few adjectives can start your ideas flowing. Ask yourself: What makes my community *distinctive* (or *popular* or *colorful*)?

Other ideas appear in the options at the right. Remember, too, that a writing partner can help you focus your thoughts and point out other ideas. As you review your notes, mark the ones you want to include in your draft, particularly those that will help show how your community is distinctive. Think about how to organize your information. You might show causes and effects. You might compare and contrast. You might use order of importance.

| **Option A** |
| Brainstorm groups of people in your town. |

| **Option B** |
| Explore neighborhoods, taking notes on what you see. |

| **Option C** |
| Freewrite on news items about the community. |

Town slogan: "You always can see a smile in Fairfield." Great Chinese shops and restaurants. Thriving African American neighborhoods. Street fairs and block parties. Walkathon for diabetes research.

Drafting

As you begin to draft, keep your main ideas in mind, and refer to your notes as necessary. It is important to get your ideas on paper. You'll have time to change things later, if you wish. Begin in a way that will catch your reader's interest. Notice how the writer Laurence Pringle begins in the passage below by speaking directly to you—the reader.

Drafting Tip

For more information about organizing details, see Lesson 5.2, pages 204–206.

Literature Model

Pick up a handful of soil anywhere on earth. In it you will find more organisms—visible and microscopic—than exist on the entire surfaces of other planets.

Laurence Pringle, *Living Treasure*

Teach

Prewriting

Developing Ideas for Expository Writing

To locate all of the information sources available to help with this project, suggest that students work in cooperative groups at the library. Tell them to try to locate and take relevant notes from the *Statistical Abstract of the United States,* books or pamphlets about the local population, back issues of local newspapers, the local yellow pages, listings of relevant sources available through regional or statewide interlibrary loan networks, information from the chamber of commerce, and so on. When their notes are complete, students may compare information. They should discuss the names and locations of the sources, the ease with which they can be accessed, the kinds of information they contain, and the ways the information is organized. **L2**

Drafting

Organizing Information

Review with students the three techniques (showing cause and effect, comparing and contrasting, and order of importance) suggested in the text for organizing information. **L1**

Writing Process in Action **245**

Teach

Revising

Peer Editing

Students can work in writing conferences with peer editors before they revise their writing. Suggest that peer editors refer to the assignment on page 244 and respond to this question: Has the writer focused on the stated purpose? If the answer is no, peer editors should mark places where the writer diverges from the stated purpose. **L2**

Editing/Proofreading

Peer Editing

After students have edited their own work, have them edit another student's writing. Remind them to refer to the Editing/Proofreading Checklist on the page 247. **L2**

Publishing/Presenting

Before students present their expository writing, discuss how to prepare their brochures for publication. Emphasize the importance of the final draft and that it must be neatly done.

Additional Resources

Writing Process Transparencies, 17–19B

Thinking and Study Skills, pp. 3–5, 7–9, 20, 23–24, 34–35

Sentence-Combining Practice, pp. 30–32

Composition Practice, p. 44

Grammar Workbook, Lessons 68–71, 86–92

Expository Writing

Revising Tip

For more information about different ways of organizing and presenting information, see Lessons 5.9 and 5.10, pages 232–239.

Revising

To begin revising, read over your draft to make sure that what you've written fits your purpose and audience. Then have a **writing conference.** Read your draft to a partner or a small group or share it with your teacher. Use your audience's reactions to help you evaluate your work so far. The questions below can help you and your listeners.

Question A

Have I clearly explained unfamiliar terms?

Question B

Do I have enough details to support my main ideas?

Question C

Have I organized my information effectively?

The people of Fairfield enjoy diversity among their neighbors. The Mexican festival, Cinco de Mayo, is a yearly highlight for neighbors of many different ethnic origins. At the August art fair at
(Add Cinco de Mayo details)
Library Plaza, you'll find the works of local painters
hospital patients
who may be senior citizens or college students. In
annual
"Life Steps," the walkathon for diabetes research,
Scandinavian Americans, African Americans, and
Hmong
~~Laotian-Americans~~ to name just a few—join forces
as friends.

246   Unit 5 Expository Writing

Journal Writing Tip

Organizing Thoughts Suggest that students decide how to organize their responses to the questions before they begin writing.

Enrichment and Extension

Follow-up Ideas

- Set aside a time for students to celebrate the conclusion of their writing projects.
- Encourage them to share their finished pieces with the whole class or in small groups.

Extending Expository Writing

- Brainstorm with students to discover ways they can use their expertise in expository writing in other subject areas. For example, in science, students can explain the functions of the various organs in the human body.

Expository Writing

Editing/Proofreading

Small mistakes can cause confusion, especially in expository writing. Take the time to check the accuracy of your draft. You can do the editing yourself, and you might also ask a friend to be a peer reviewer.

One way to edit is to use a checklist such as the one shown here. Consider the questions, one by one, as you read your draft several times. Use **proofreading** marks to make changes.

You might find it helpful to first show your brochure to two long-time residents of your town. Have them read your work separately and comment about its thoroughness. Do they agree with what you've said about your subject?

Editing/Proofreading Checklist

1. Are quotations and other facts correct?
2. Have I used comparative and superlative forms correctly?
3. Do subjects and verbs agree in number?
4. Have I used standard spelling, capitalization, and punctuation?

Publishing/Presenting

Once you're happy with your brochure, you may want to prepare a set of photographs to accompany it. Perhaps you might combine your work with that of other students, and have compiled copies of *The People of (your town or city)* bound for your school or town library.

Proofreading Tip

Check for proper use of quotation marks when editing dialogue. For more information see pp. 599-600.

Journal Writing

Answer these questions in your journal: What do you like best about your expository writing? What was the hardest part of writing it? What did you learn in your writing conference? What new things have you learned as a writer?

Assess

Evaluation Rubrics

Use these criteria when evaluating your students' writing:

- Do notes include documentation for all facts and quotations included in the final report?
- Is all information presented clearly enough so that someone unfamiliar with the town would understand the references?
- Is there information about diverse citizenry, highlighting distinctive attributes and achievements?
- Has the student found a logical way of organizing the details and used it consistently?
- Has the student avoided errors in grammar, usage, and mechanics?
- Are sentences varied in structure?
- Is word choice precise and lively?

See also *Writing Assessment and Evaluation Rubrics*

Reteaching

📁 *Composition Reteaching*, p. 44

Enrichment

📁 *Composition Enrichment*, p. 44

Close

Have students discuss how they could create a guide to the population of the class. Students should answer questions regarding themselves, not one another. Once students have given their distinctive characteristics, they might identify the activities and concerns that bind them together as a group.

Enrichment and Extension

Presenting Finished Work

Have students share either in small groups or with the entire class the classroom guide developed in the Close activity. Encourage students to provide feedback to the presenters.

About the Author

Laurence Pringle has written dozens of non-fiction books for young people on a variety of subjects in nature. Pringle became a nature writer for young people almost by accident. In 1962 he found a job working for a new children's magazine to be published by the American Museum of Natural History in New York. Pringle says, "If I had found work at another sort of magazine, I might never have written for children."

Focus

Lesson Overview

Objectives

- To read a literature passage that illustrates effective expository writing
- To write a review that supports a personal opinion

Skills

- skimming; previewing; monitoring comprehension; summarizing

Critical Thinking

- evaluating; comparing and contrasting

Listening and Speaking

- discussing

🔔 Bellringer
Daily Language Activity

When students enter the classroom, have this assignment on the board: *Use the classroom clock as a timer. List the names of as many living things as you can think of in sixty seconds.*

See also  *Daily Language Practice*

Motivating Activity

Write on the board the headings *Plants, Mammals, Fish, Birds, Reptiles, Insects,* and *Other Organisms.* Work as a class to categorize the living things students listed in the Bellringer activity.

248

UNIT 5

Literature Model

Expository Writing

FROM

LIVING Treasure

by Laurence Pringle

In the following selection from his book Living Treasure, *Laurence Pringle brings to light a hidden, secret world filled with millions of plants and animals no one has ever seen. As you read, pay special attention to the way the author keeps his writing informative, lively, and engaging. Then try the activities in Linking Writing and Literature on page 254.*

P ick up a handful of soil anywhere on earth. In it you will find more organisms—visible and microscopic—than exist on the entire surfaces of other planets.

The planet Mars is icy cold—and lifeless. The planet Venus is fiery hot—and lifeless. Between these planets lies our home, Earth. Its atmosphere makes it an oasis in space, with a favorable climate, abundant water, and a rich variety of living things.

Scientists are dazzled and puzzled by the diversity of life on earth. No one knows how many different kinds

---

Resource Manager

📁 Planning Resources
- *Lesson Plans*

📑 Transparencies
- *Bellringer*
- *Daily Language Practice*
- *Fine Art 21–25*

📁 Other Print Resources
- *Listening and Speaking Activities, pp. 10–11, 21*
- *Thinking and Study Skills, pp. 3–4, 7–9, 20*
- *Writing Assessment and Evaluation Rubrics*

💻 Web Sites
- *writerschoice.glencoe.com*
- *lit.glencoe.com*

Literature Model

Patricia Gonzalez, *Heart Forest*, 1985

of plants, animals, and other organisms there are. But we do know that the organisms identified so far are only a small fraction of all living things. There are millions—perhaps many millions—that await discovery.

The study of living things is called biology (*bio* is a Greek term for "life"). Scientists who study living things are called biologists. And biologists have a name for the earth's incredible variety of life: biodiversity.

The first step toward understanding this biodiversity is naming and describing the different living organisms. Throughout human history and all over the world, people have given names to animals and plants they recognize. For example, in New Guinea, hunters can name sixteen different frogs, seventeen lizards and snakes, more than a hundred birds, and many more insects and worms. The New Guinea hunters are walking encyclopedias of information about the life around them.

Besides naming things, people have tried to make sense of the earth's

Literature Model **249**

Expository Writing

Teach

Active Reading Strategies

Skim/Preview Before students begin reading, have them skim the selection to determine the kind of writing it is. *(informative nonfiction)* Tell students that previewing an informational piece helps to focus their attention and provide a purpose for reading. Ask volunteers to demonstrate previewing elements in this text that give clues to its content. Afterwards, invite volunteers to tell what information they expect to learn by reading the excerpt from *Living Treasure. (Important elements to preview are the title, headnote, art, and text boxes, or pull quotes. Previewing shows that* Living Treasure *is about the abundance of life on our planet.)*

Literary Elements

Point of View Call attention to this sentence on page 248: "Scientists are dazzled and puzzled by the diversity of life on earth." Ask: "What does this sentence tell you about how the author feels about Earth's great variety of life? Which words provide good clues to the author's point of view? Can you find other clues on pages 248 and 249 that show how the author feels about Earth's diversity?" *(The author feels an interest in and awe and respect for the diversity of life forms on Earth. Words that provide clues to his point of view include* treasure, rich variety, incredible variety, *and* dazzled.*)*

Viewing the Art

Patricia Gonzalez, *Heart Forest*, 1985
Ms. Gonzalez was born in Colombia, grew up in England, and now resides in Texas. *Heart Forest,* a 36-by-36 inch oil painting, is now in a private collection.

Teach

Active Reading Strategies

Monitor Comprehension Tell students that as they read, they should ask themselves questions about words they don't know. To help them understand the meanings of unknown words, they can use context clues and word parts. Ask students to use clues from the first two complete paragraphs on page 250 to figure out the meanings of *vertebrate* and *invertebrate*. (A vertebrate *is an animal with a backbone. In the first paragraph, the author provides a clue—"These animals with backbones"—after the first mention of* vertebrate. *In the second paragraph, the author provides the definition directly by placing the word* invertebrates *in parentheses after the words* creatures without backbones. *The word part* in-, *meaning "not," is also a clue.)*

Active Reading Strategies

Summarize Ask: "What is the main idea of the first full paragraph? What details support this idea? Why do you think the author used so many numbers, since readers could not be expected to remember all this data?" *(The main idea is contained in the first sentence: ". . . more than 1.5 million . . . kinds, or species, have been discovered." The remaining sentences in the paragraph provide supporting details. The author probably lists all these numbers to impress readers with the great diversity of life on Earth and to assure readers that he is an authority on the topic.)*

Literature Model

Expository Writing

biodiversity by considering similar organisms to be members of groups. The modern system of naming and classifying living things was devised by Swedish botanist Carl von Linné (Carolus Linnaeus) in the eighteenth century. At that time, Linné and other scientists believed that perhaps 50,000 kinds of organisms lived on earth.

Since then, more than 1.5 million kinds, or species, have been discovered and named. They include 250,000 species of flowering plants and 41,000 kinds of vertebrate animals. These animals with backbones include about 4,000 mammals, 19,000 fishes, about 9,000 birds, and more than 10,000 reptiles and amphibians. The largest group by far is the insects, with more than 751,000 named so far. The remainder includes worms, spiders, fungi, algae, and microorganisms.

Biologists believe that most of the earth's flowering plants and vertebrate

animals have been discovered. They estimate that only a few thousand more fishes, birds, reptiles, and other vertebrates are likely to be found. The greatest riches of biodiversity remain to be discovered in the world of insects and other small creatures without backbones (invertebrates).

Biologists expect to find some of the earth's undescribed organisms living in coral reefs. There also may be other undiscovered habitats,[1] and species, on the floor of the deep ocean. In the 1980s, using small research submarines, scientists began to discover new forms of life—crabs, fishes, shrimps, tube worms—near geysers of hot, mineral-laden water that spew from the ocean floor.

The earth's greatest riches, however, lie in tropical rain forests. In the 1980s, as funds for tropical research

> The earth's greatest riches . . . lie in tropical rain forests.

---

[1]**habitats** (hab' ə tats') the places where plants or animals naturally grow or live

---

6+1 Trait® Writing

Conventions

Tell students that authors of informational texts must carefully proofread their writing to make sure it is clear and accurate. Explain that punctuation is an important part of a nonfiction author's checklist. Poor use of punctuation can destroy smooth readability. Point out that writers use commas, parentheses, and dashes to clearly separate and explain their ideas.

Practice Divide students into three groups. Assign each group to find and analyze one of the following uses of

punctuation on page 250: (1) commas in a series, (2) commas to separate an introductory phrase from the main part of the sentence, (3) dashes to indicate an interruption or sudden change within a sentence. Then ask each group to copy their sample *without* using any punctuation. Have them give the sample to another group to proofread and correct. Afterwards, have the groups who first wrote the samples check the revised versions for accuracy.

6+1 Trait® is a registered trademark of Northwest Regional Educational Laboratory, which does not endorse this product.

Literature Model

Kathryn Stewart, *Hummingbird Vision*, 1990

Expository Writing

increased, biologists found astonishing numbers of animals there.

In Panama, entomologist[2] Terry Erwin of the Smithsonian Institution collected insects from nineteen trees of the same species. On those trees alone, he found more than 12,000 different kinds of beetles. He estimated that one out of seven species lived on that kind of tree and no other.

---

[2]**entomologist** (en′ tə mol′ ə jist) an expert in the branch of biology that deals with insects

Literature Model **251**

Teach

Critical Thinking

Evaluate Tell students that a *fact* is something that can be shown to be true. An *opinion,* on the other hand, is someone's personal view or judgment. Ask students to find examples of facts and opinions in the section starting at the paragraph at the end of page 250 and continuing through all of page 251. *(Opinions are "the earth's greatest riches" and "astonishing numbers of animals." Facts include the name and workplace of scientist Terry Erwin and the number of different kinds of beetles found on a set of trees.)*

Viewing the Art

Kathryn Stewart, *Hummingbird Vision,* **1990**
Kathryn Stewart is a Native American who lives in Bozeman, Montana, and teaches at Montana State University. *Hummingbird Vision* is a mixed media work that is 30 1/8-by-22 1/4 inches in size.

Critical Thinking

Evaluate

Explain that critical readers observe whether statements are facts or opinions. If opinions are given in an informative article, good readers look for solid evidence to back up the opinion. Then they evaluate—form a judgment—about the value of the evidence. Is it strong enough to convince them of the author's opinion?

Practice Point out that on page 251, the author states that biologists found an astonishing variety of animals in tropical rain forests. Have students work in pairs to evaluate whether the article contains convincing evidence to support that opinion. Afterwards, ask volunteers to share their evaluations, and the reasons for them, with the class. *(The evidence is compelling because the author names a specific expert, Terry Erwin, and describes pertinent work he did in the rain forest. He also details the number of different kinds of beetles Erwin found.)*

251

Teach

Critical Thinking

Evaluate Ask students what evidence the author offers to substantiate the opinion that tropical forests are "rich with plant life." Does the evidence convince students of the author's opinion? *(The author offers numerical evidence, such as his mention of 700 species of trees growing on plots of land totaling twenty-five acres. He also offers examples of other plant species. The evidence is convincing because the facts clearly indicate that numerous plant-life species are found in tropical forests.)*

6+1 Trait® Writing

Conventions Have students provide reasons for the author's use of commas in the first two sentences of the full paragraph in the right-hand column. *(The first comma separates the opening phrase; the other commas in the sentence separate items in a series. The commas in the second sentence separate the appositive* canopy *from the word it defines,* treetops.*)*

6+1 Trait® is a registered trademark of Northwest Regional Educational Laboratory, which does not endorse this product.

Literature Model

Erwin also collected insects from one tree in the Amazon rain forest of Peru. He sent the ant specimens to be identified by biologist Edward O. Wilson of Harvard University. Wilson found forty-three kinds of ants, including several new species. This diversity of ants—from a single tropical tree—equaled the number of ant species that are known to live in all of Canada or Great Britain.

Tropical forests are also rich with plant life. In Borneo, a botanist discovered 700 species of trees growing on ten separate plots of land that totaled about twenty-five acres. This matches the number of tree species growing in all of North America. Also, the trunks and branches of rain forest trees are habitats for mosses, ferns, lichens, orchids, and other plants that grow far above the soil. In Costa Rica alone, more than 1,100 species of orchids have been identified.

In the 1980s, Terry Erwin and other biologists began for the first time to study insects, plants, and other organisms that live near the tops of tropical trees. The organisms living in the treetops, or canopy, of a rain forest are different from those living on or close to the ground. More than half of all rain forest species may live aloft. Most of them never touch the ground. Terry Erwin has called the tropical forest canopy "the heart" of the earth's biodiversity.

Until the 1980s, biologists estimated that 3 to 5 million species live on earth. However, since large numbers of tropical insects and other organisms may live on just one kind of tree, or in one small area of tropical forest, the biodiversity of earth may be much greater. Terry Erwin

> **More than half of all rain forest species may live aloft. Most of them never touch the ground.**

252   Unit 5 Expository Writing

Compare and Contrast

Comparing with Numbers

Explain that writers help readers understand their subjects more deeply by comparing and contrasting them to other subjects. For example, Pringle impresses readers with the large number of ant species found in a single tree in Peru by comparing it to the number of ant species found in all of Canada or Great Britain. Ask students to summarize the comparison. *(The number of ant species found on a single Peruvian tree equals the number of ant species found in all of Canada or Great Britain.)*

Practice Ask students to write a paragraph comparing the number of students who attend their school to some other number. Their comparison should help readers who know nothing about their school understand the size of its student body.

has estimated that the earth may be home to 30 million species of insects alone.

The total of all kinds of life could be much higher. Rain forest canopies harbor not only insects but also unknown numbers of mites,[3] roundworms, fungi, and other small organisms. Little is known about life in tropical soils. And most animals have other living things, called parasites, living on or inside them.

Whether the total number of species is 5 million, 30 million, or more, we know very little about the biodiversity of our planet. Our ignorance is great.

Suppose the number of species is "only" 10 million. This means that

we have perhaps discovered just 15 percent of the total number of species. Then consider that we have not yet learned much about the plants and animals that *have* been identified. Many of these organisms are "known" only in the sense that a few individuals are kept as preserved specimens in scientific collections and that they have been given a formal name.

Their lives are a mystery. Their links with other living things, their importance in nature, and their possible value to humans are also mysteries.

> . . . we know very little about the biodiversity of our planet. Our ignorance is great.

---

[3]**mites** (mīts) tiny animals that look like spiders

Expository Writing

Teach

6+1 Trait® Writing

Sentence Fluency Tell students that one way good writers achieve sentence fluency is to vary the length of their sentences. Ask volunteers to find examples of sentence-length variation on this page. What effect does varying sentence length create? *(The first paragraph begins with a short sentence, followed by longer sentences. The second paragraph opens with a long sentence, followed by a short sentence. The next two paragraphs open with short sentences that are followed by longer sentences. Varying sentence length creates a rhythm and flow to the language.)*

Critical Thinking

Summarize Ask students to summarize the main idea and supporting evidence of the first full paragraph. *(The total number of life species could be much higher than 30 million. Small organisms and parasites greatly increase the number.)*

Additional Resources

 Fine Art Transparencies, 21–25
Listening and Speaking Activities, pp. 10–11, 21
Thinking and Study Skills, pp. 3–4, 7–9, 20

6+1 Trait® is a registered trademark of Northwest Regional Educational Laboratory, which does not endorse this product.

Active Reading Strategies

Summarize

Tell students that when they read informative nonfiction it is helpful to stop periodically and summarize main ideas. Explain that summarizing helps them clarify and remember the most important information. Provide students with these tips for summarizing:

• The first sentence of a paragraph often states its main idea.

• Paraphrase (put into your own words) the main idea.
• Omit details. A summary is always shorter than the original.

Practice Ask students to write a summary of the last three paragraphs of this article. *(Sample: The biodiversity of our planet is so great that much is yet unknown about life on Earth.)*

Linking Writing and Literature

Assess

Evaluation Rubrics

◆ Talk About Reading

Possible responses to the questions:

1. There is great biodiversity in nature. Scientists have only just begun to discover and learn about the vast number of life forms on Earth.
2. Mistakes in punctuation and spelling would make reading and understanding the author's complex ideas difficult.
3. Students may begin to realize that a large number of life forms, including insects and other small organisms, may be hidden from their view in their own environment.
4. Students' criteria might include numerical facts, quotes from authorities, and concrete examples.

◆ Write About Reading

The review should do the following:

- identify the student's opinion of *Living Treasure*
- provide supporting reasons for the opinion
- accurately cite examples from the article

Close

Have students write a list of reasons why it is important to preserve the rain forests of the world. Suggest that students skim the article for ideas.

Expository Writing

Literature Model

Linking Writing and Literature

◆ Collect Your Thoughts

Jot down a few facts you remember from the article about the diversity of life forms on Earth. The author calls the vast amount of life species on our planet a *Living Treasure*. Think of another good title for the selection that reflects your opinion.

◆ Talk About Reading

Talk with other students about *Living Treasure*. Assign a group leader to keep everyone focused and a group secretary to take notes. Then use the questions below to guide your conversation.

1. **Connect to Your Life** How does Pringle's information about the hidden world of life forms relate to your own physical environment? What kinds of life forms did Pringle mention that you were unaware of before?
2. **Active Reading Strategies: Summarize** In your own words, what is the main point the author tries to get across to readers in *Living Treasure*?
3. **6+1 Trait®: Conventions** How do you think your experience of reading the article would change if the author had been careless about his spelling and punctuation?
4. **Connect to Your Writing** After reading this selection, what kinds of evidence do you find compelling in an informational article? Make a list of criteria for good evidence that you can call upon when you write papers of your own.

◆ Write About Reading

Review Write a review of *Living Treasure*. Tell whether you found the writing interesting and compelling and why or why not. Be sure to back up your opinions with evidence.

Focus on Conventions Your review will be more credible if you quote the text. Be sure you use quotation marks correctly. Proofread your writing carefully and correct any errors in grammar, usage, punctuation, and spelling.

For more information on conventions and the 6+1 Trait® model, see **Writing and Research Handbook,** pages 822–824.

6+1 Trait® is a registered trademark of Northwest Regional Educational Laboratory, which does not endorse this product.

MEETING INDIVIDUAL NEEDS

Less-Proficient Readers

Creating a Glossary of Unfamiliar Terms

Some learners may get bogged down by unfamiliar terminology in this excerpt. Rather than stopping each time they encounter a new word while reading, they may want to skim the entire text first, checking for new words and then looking them up in the dictionary. They can then create a glossary and refer to it while reading.

UNIT 5 Review

Reflecting on the Unit

Summarize what you learned in this unit by answering the following questions.

1 What are the characteristics of strong expository writing?

2 What is the purpose of cause-and-effect writing?

3 How can you organize information for comparison and contrast?

4 What prewriting activities are usually necessary for a report?

5 What elements strengthen expository writing?

Adding to Your Portfolio

CHOOSE A SELECTION FOR YOUR PORTFOLIO Look over the writing you did for this unit. Choose a piece of writing for your portfolio. The writing you choose should show one or more of the following:

- clearly stated ideas supported by facts, statistics, or examples
- a sensible order in explanations or instructions
- charts, diagrams, or pictures that clearly show step-by-step activities, spatial relationships, or comparisons
- information based on close observation, careful research, or interesting interviews
- clear presentation of cause-and-effect relationships among events

REFLECT ON YOUR CHOICE Attach a note to the piece you chose, explaining briefly why you chose it, and what you learned from writing it.

SET GOALS How can you improve your writing? What skill will you focus on the next time you write?

Writing Across the Curriculum

MAKE A SOCIAL STUDIES CONNECTION Find out about your city or town history, landmarks, historic buildings, or parks. Choose one topic, and find out about it by doing research and interviews. You may want to work with a few classmates. Think of interesting ways to share your discoveries with your class or with an unfamiliar audience, such as city officials or town residents.

Review **255**

Review

Reflecting on the Unit

You may have students respond to Reflecting on the Unit in writing or through discussion.

Writing Across the Curriculum

Before students begin writing, remind them that a main focus in expository writing is to make information clear and interesting to a reader. Encourage them to sustain this focus from prewriting through revision.

Adding to Your Portfolio

Suggest that students reread their reports and short written pieces twice, first viewing them as their readers would. Having selected the most effective piece from a reader's point of view, they can go through a second time, evaluating pieces according to the writing technique(s) applied.

Portfolio Evaluation

If you grade the portfolio selections, you may want to award two marks—one each for content and form. Explain your assessment criteria before students make their selections.

Commend
- experimentation with creative prewriting techniques
- clear, concise writing in which the main idea, audience, and purpose are evident
- successful revisions
- work that shows a flair for language

✓ ASSESSMENT OPTIONS

📁 *Tests with Answer Key and Rubrics*
Unit 5 Choice A Test, p. 17
Unit 5 Choice B Test, p. 18
Unit 5 Composition Objective Test,
   pp. 19–20

💾 *Testmaker*
Unit 5 Choice A Test
Unit 5 Choice B Test
Unit 5 Composition Objective Test

You may wish to administer one of these tests as a mastery test.

 Mindjogger Videoquizzes

Persuasive Writing

Viewing the Art

Persuasive photographs use various techniques to achieve their aim. Some photographs use striking images or vivid colors to stir emotion in the viewer. Others use widely recognized symbols or surprising juxtapositions. The photograph shown here catches the viewer's eye with its vibrant color scheme and the pleasing pattern made by the fish. Interpret and Analyze Use the following questions for discussion:
- Describe how elements of the photograph help to convey its meaning.
- How do photographs influence and inform viewers? Compare and contrast the power of photography to the power of writing.

Discussing the Quotation

Ask students to reflect upon the tone of the quotation. You may wish to have students read its source, J. Madeleine Nash's essay "The Fish Crisis," in *Glencoe Literature: The Reader's Choice,* Course 2, p. 295.

Writing Prompt Have students write one or two paragraphs comparing and contrasting the mood of the quotation to the mood of the photograph. Ask students to address the following questions: What method does the quotation use to persuade readers? Does it resemble the method of the photograph? Students should explain their answers.

"Of course, overfishing is not the only human activity that is jeopardizing life in the oceans."

—J. Madeleine Nash

"The Fish Crisis"

256

Resource Manager

📂 **Planning Resources**
- *Lesson Plans*
- *Block Scheduling*

📑 **Transparencies**
- *Bellringer*
- *Daily Language Practice*
- *Fine Art*
- *Two-Minute Skill Drill*
- *Writing Process*

📂 **Other Print Resources**
- *Composition Enrichment*
- *Composition Practice*
- *Composition Reteaching*
- *Cooperative Learning Activities*
- *Glencoe Literature Library*
- *Grammar and Composition Handbook*
- *Grammar Workbook*

- *Listening and Speaking Activities*
- *Sentence-Combining Practice*
- *Tests with Answer Key and Rubrics*
- *Thinking and Study Skills*
- *Writing Across the Curriculum*
- *Writing Assessment and Evaluation Rubrics*
- *Writing in the Real World*

UNIT 6

Persuasive Writing

257

Objectives

- To learn the elements of persuasive writing and to use them to draft persuasive arguments
- To learn about effective word choices and to make effective word choices in writing
- To understand supporting a position with evidence
- To learn strategies for revising persuasive writing and to apply them
- To learn about techniques of advertisements, leaflets, letters of complaint, and movie reviews and to use techniques in writing

✔ ASSESSMENT OPTIONS

📁 *Tests with Answer Key & Rubrics*
Unit 6 Choice A Test, p. 21
Unit 6 Choice B Test, p. 22
Unit 6 Composition Objective Test, pp. 23–24

💾 *Testmaker*
Unit 6 Choice A Test
Unit 6 Choice B Test
Unit 6 Composition Objective Test

You may wish to administer either the Unit 6 Choice A Test or the Unit 6 Choice B Test as a pretest.

Key to Ability Levels

L1 Level 1 activities are within the basic ability range of students.

L2 Level 2 activities are within the ability range of average students.

L3 Level 3 activities are more challenging activities.

📼 **Video**
- *MindJogger Videoquizzes*

💾 **Software**
- *Presentation Plus!*
- *Revising with Style*
- *Testmaker*
- *Writer's Assistant*

🖥 **Web Sites**
- *writerschoice.glencoe.com*
- *lit.glencoe.com*

Focus

Lesson Overview

Objectives

- To learn persuasive techniques used by a professional speaker
- To develop a position for a debate

Skills

- forming a position; preparing arguments; presenting a speech

Critical Thinking

- recalling; defining and clarifying; analyzing; generating new information

Listening and Speaking

- formal speaking; discussing; process explanation

Bellringer
Daily Language Activity

When students enter the classroom, have this assignment on the board: *Think of a persuasive or inspiring speaker or speech that you have heard (or read). Write the name of the speaker or speech and one or two things about it that made it memorable.*

Grammar Link to the Bellringer

Have students look over their Bellringer writing. Did they correctly use commas with coordinating conjunctions like *and* or *but*? Can they find the coordinating conjunctions in the Bellringer assignment?

See also *Daily Language Practice*

Motivating Activity

Ask students to share their Bellringer responses. Tell students that the media connection presents some of the techniques used by persuasive speaker Dr. Benjamin Carson.

Persuasive Writing

Writing in the Real World

MEDIA Connection
Persuasive Speech

Dr. Benjamin Carson is a world-famous children's brain surgeon. He's also a powerful, persuasive speaker. Carson takes time out from his medical work to talk to kids about success and the value of reading. He urges students to read books rather than to watch television. In the following excerpt, Carson underscores this point by relating an example from his own youth.

Carson Delivers a Wake-Up Call

by Dr. Benjamin S. Carson

"One day we were in science class, and the science teacher held up a dark, glassy rock. He said, 'Does anybody know what this is?'. . . I knew what it was because I'd been reading about this stuff, so I put my hand up. And I said, 'That's obsidian.' And the teacher said, 'That's right. That *is* obsidian.' And then I went on to explain how obsidian was formed by lava and how when the lava flowed down to the water it was super-cooled, and the elements consolidated and they formed a glasslike appearance. And everybody was *spellbound* because I was talking about it.

"For the first time, I could see in my classmates' eyes a look of admiration. This was a totally new experience for me; and I said, 'I like this; I can deal with this.' From that point on, I couldn't get enough to read."

258 Unit 6 Persuasive Writing

Resource Manager

Planning Resources
- *Lesson Plans*

Transparencies
- *Bellringer*
- *Daily Language Practice*
- *Writing Process* 20–22B

Other Print Resources
- *Cooperative Learning Activities,* pp. 31–36
- *Thinking and Study Skills,* pp. 4, 5, 11, 14–19
- *Writing Assessment and Evaluation Rubrics*
- *Writing in the Real World,* pp. 21–24

A Writer's Process

Prewriting
Forming a Position

Like all persuasive speakers, Carson has taken a stand on an important issue. He believes that by turning off the television and by reading, reading, reading, any student can become a winner.

Carson bases his position on the facts and experiences of his life. When Carson was ten years old, he was in trouble. He didn't care about school. But Carson's mother came up with a plan to change all that. She told her children they could watch only two or three television shows a week. In their free time, they had to read two library books and give her a book report on each one.

Carson went along grumpily at first. But he quickly saw results. In a year and a half, he zoomed to the top of his class. He knew he was on his way.

From these and later experiences, Carson developed his position on reading. "The key thing about reading is what it does for the mind," he says. "I liken the mind to a muscle, which becomes flabby and weak if it's not used. Yet, if you use it frequently, it becomes firm and enlarged and very powerful.

"Reading," he says, "demands that you use your mind to make sense of words, sentences, and ideas. It makes you into a literate person who can express ideas."

Why is this important? "You have a great deal more confidence when you know you can express something," Carson says. "You probably know two people who have seen the same thing; one knows how to express himself and the other doesn't. That becomes a pattern through life. Clearly, the person who is able to state a position will be seen as the brighter individual. When it comes time for opportunities to be granted, the person who can express himself will almost always be chosen."

Drafting
Organizing the Case

To persuade people of another point of view, speakers like Carson often organize evidence into strong arguments. An example, such as Carson's personal story, is one form of persuasive evidence. Carson begins his story by describing his mother's reading plan and his journey into

Teach

Discussion Prompts

- How does Carson feel about reading? Did he always feel that way? Students should back up their responses.
- Carson's book is called *Think Big*. Have students consider the possible meanings of the title.

Cultural Connections

Cultural Context

Carson's mother was the most important influence in getting him to read. Suggest to students that the influence of a concerned adult—whether a relative or not—can greatly affect a young person's thinking. Ask them to consider the degree of influence adults have in different cultures. For example, in many cultures, elder members of society are greatly respected for their age and ideas. How much do adults in students' own culture influence young people?

Teach

Discussion Prompts

- What impact may personal stories have on an audience? Do they affect the relationship between speaker and audience?
- What other kinds of stories or examples can prove a point in a persuasive speech? Can students think of something from their own lives to support or argue against Carson's points?

Additional Resources

Writing Process Transparencies, 20–22B

Cooperative Learning Activities, pp. 31–36

Writing in the Real World, pp. 21–24

Thinking and Study Skills, pp. 4, 5, 11, 14–19

Persuasive Writing

the world of the mind. He started reading about animals and plants. Soon he became fascinated by rocks.

Carson often continues his personal story by relating the school incident in the excerpt on page 258. His classmates' admiration for his knowledge is a convincing element in the anecdote.

Why does Carson tell a personal story in a persuasive speech? "People can remember stories and the points they make," he explains. In addition, Carson can form a bond with the audience by telling stories from his own life. I want to make it very clear that I had the very same experiences these students have had. Then they can say, 'This guy clearly knows what he's talking about. He's clearly been where I am or have been and is where I'd like to be in the future.'"

Carson adds, "I also need for them to understand that knowledge is power, not only in the eyes of teachers, but in the eyes of their friends. It's not a thing to be ashamed of."

Mountains of letters from young students all around the world are evidence of Dr. Carson's ability to persuade.

Dr. Ben Carson
Johns Hopkins Hospital
600 North Wolfe Street
Baltimore, Md. 21287-7509

Dr. Benjamin Carson
Johns Hopkins Hospi
600 North Wolfe Str.
Baltimore, Md.

en Carson
Hospital

Presenting
Telling the Story

Some persuasive writers and speakers are tempted to try too hard to make their points. They may speak too loudly or too expressively, thus failing to connect with the audience. Carson never falls into this trap. In making his presentation, Carson speaks softly and honestly, never preaching or raising his voice. Yet, his ideas and his tone help change students' minds.

"This way of speaking is effective because students believe the story is true," he says. "That's the bottom line. This is real. This is not made up in Hollywood. The fact that students can identify with me makes them believe success is possible for them, too."

Carson's story is powerful medicine. "I get tons of letters all the time, and almost everywhere I go people come up to me and say they've heard me or seen me," Carson says.

Schools in California, Texas, and other states have also started Ben Carson Reading Clubs—and the clubs work. An eighth-grade club member said to Carson one day, "Because I didn't read, I thought I was kind of dumb. Now I know better."

Enrichment and Extension

Science

The brain is not a muscle; it is a complex mass of nerve tissue. Researchers are constantly learning more about how the brain functions. Ask students to consider what happens in the brain as a person reads. Suggest that interested students investigate the topic and report their findings to the class.

Examining Writing in the Real World

Analyzing the Media Connection

Discuss these questions about the speech excerpt on page 258.

1. Do you think the incident related in the excerpt effectively persuades listeners of the value of reading? Explain.

2. Carson could have cited statistics about poor reading scores instead of telling a story about his reading experience. Which evidence do you think would be more persuasive to his audience? Why?

3. How did Carson's classmates react when he started talking about obsidian? Why do you think Carson mentioned his classmates' reaction?

4. Dr. Carson's message is serious, but the tone of his speech is informal. Cite examples of Carson's informal style. Why do you think he adopts this tone?

Analyzing a Writer's Process

Discuss these questions about Carson's speeches and writing.

1. Every persuasive writer or speaker needs to state his or her opinion or stand on an issue. On what issue has Dr. Ben Carson taken a stand?

2. Where does Carson find the evidence to back up his position?

3. What is Carson's presentation style? Why is it effective?

4. How does Ben Carson know that his speeches are persuasive?

Grammar Link

Use a comma to separate main clauses joined by a coordinating conjunction.

*"One day we were in science class, **and** the science teacher held up a dark, glassy rock."*

Write each sentence, using commas correctly.

1. Alice is thirteen and her sister is ten.

2. Nelson will leave now but he will be back after lunch.

3. Chris will earn money babysitting or she will start a pet-walking service.

4. All of my friends are going to the concert and we plan to meet afterward.

See Unit 7, page 304.

Writing in the Real World **261**

Grammar Link

Answers

1. Alice is thirteen, and her sister is ten.

2. Nelson will leave now, but he will be back after lunch.

3. Chris will earn money baby-sitting, or she will start a pet-walking service.

4. All of my friends are going to the concert, and we plan to meet afterward.

Note Students may want to watch documentary videos showing public figures speaking. Your library may have more information about Ben Carson Reading Clubs and a copy of his book *Think Big*.

Persuasive Writing

Assess

Analyzing the Media Connection

1. Answers will vary. Students may say that it shows how reading helps a person gain self esteem and the respect of others.

2. Students may suggest that a story is more persuasive to young people because they can more easily relate to it and apply the principles to their own lives.

3. They were spellbound. Carson probably wanted to show one of the benefits gained from reading.

4. The student may identify Carson's use of informal words and phrases such as "stuff" and "I can deal with this." Carson may use this style to form a friendly bond with his audience and to help them relate to his message.

Analyzing a Writer's Process

1. He has taken a stand on reading.
2. Carson finds evidence from his own life.
3. Carson speaks softly and honestly without preaching. His style helps students believe in his story.
4. He has received many letters from students.

Reteaching

To reinforce the importance of supporting opinions with evidence, show students examples of persuasive writing, particularly from speeches.

Enrichment

Have students compare the speeches of two candidates running for the same office.

Close

Ask students to choose an issue to persuade their classmates about. Suggest that students outline a persuasive speech on the issue. Remind them to draw on personal experiences for factual evidence to support their position. Encourage them to consider how to establish a connection with their audience as Ben Carson does.

Persuasive Writing

Focus

Lesson Overview

Objectives

- To identify common sources of persuasive writing
- To make effective word choices in writing a persuasive advertisement

Skills

- understanding a writer's purpose; choosing effective, persuasive words; appealing to readers' emotions

Critical Thinking

- analyzing; evaluating; identifying

Listening and Speaking

- discussing in small groups; listening to appeals

Bellringer
Daily Language Activity

When students enter the classroom, have this assignment on the board: *In a few sentences write a vivid description about something that annoys you.*

Grammar Link to the Bellringer

Ask students which of these two descriptions is more effective, and why: *children misbehaving* and *children at the movies shrieking, throwing ice cubes, and jumping up and down on the seat in front of me.*

See also *Daily Language Practice*

Motivating Activity

Ask students if they have ever read or seen advertisements from groups asking for support for a cause, such as the environment, hunger relief, or a political campaign. Ask them to describe the appeals and tell whether they were convincing.

Using Persuasive Writing

When you feel strongly about something, you may try to get others to think or act in a particular way. The model below, part of an advertisement by an animal-protection group, tries to persuade the reader to help save dolphins.

Literature Model

The ancient Greeks respected the dolphins for their kindness and intelligence. In fact, it was a crime punishable by death to harm or kill a dolphin. Today, though, over 100,000 dolphins are being needlessly killed every year, caught by tuna fishermen and driftnets.

Together we saved over 50,000 dolphins last year. But hundreds of thousands are still endangered. You can make the difference. Please join us.

Write us for further information and for a list of dolphin-safe tuna brands.

The Dolphin Project, Earth Island Institute

> What exactly does the writer want you to do?

262 Unit 6 Persuasive Writing

Resource Manager

📁 Planning Resources
- *Lesson Plans*

📠 Transparencies
- *Bellringer*
- *Daily Language Practice*
- *Fine Art* 26–30
- *Two-Minute Skill Drill*
- *Writing Process* 20–22B

📁 Other Print Resources
- *Composition Enrichment,* p. 45
- *Composition Practice,* p. 45
- *Composition Reteaching,* p. 45
- *Cooperative Learning Activities,* pp. 31–36
- *Listening and Speaking Activities,* p. 22

- *Sentence-Combining Practice,* pp. 33–35
- *Thinking and Study Skills,* pp. 1–5, 13–14, 19
- *Writing Across the Curriculum*
- *Writing Assessment and Evaluation Rubrics*

Do You Agree?

Persuasive writing can urge you to agree with the writer's opinions. Persuasive writing can also call you to action. For example, the Dolphin Project wants readers to agree that using driftnets harms dolphins. The organization wants people to help by buying only tuna that has been caught without the use of driftnets.

Read the two statements below. Think about the writer's purpose in making each.

> **What does the writer want you to do?**

Join the Ten-Mile Walkathon, and walk to preserve our city's parks.

A vegetarian diet is the most healthful and most humane way to eat.

> **What two words do you think carry the writer's message most clearly?**

Persuasive writers choose words carefully for their effects on readers. When you read persuasive writing, think about the special words and phrases the writer uses to persuade you.

Journal Writing

Find a newspaper or a magazine advertisement that makes you think about buying the item advertised. In your journal jot down the words that help persuade you that you might want to buy the item. Explain why these words appeal to you.

Teach

Using the Model

Have students look at the model on page 262. Ask them which words or phrases they find especially effective and persuasive ("needlessly killed," "saved," "endangered," "You can make a difference"). Point out that using the second-person pronoun *you* makes readers feel as if the writer is speaking directly to them. Students should note the writer's purpose (to persuade the reader to support the Dolphin Project and eat only tuna caught with dolphin-proof nets). **L2**

Using the Model

Have students read the model on page 263 and answer the questions. (In the first statement, the writer wants the reader to join the Walkathon. In the second statement, "healthful" and "humane" carry the writer's message.) **L2**

Two-Minute Skill Drill

List these sentences on the board and have students rewrite them using more persuasive language.

Senator Smith is a nice woman.

A vote for Senator Smith will make things better.

See also Two-Minute Skill Drill Transparency 6.1

Journal Writing Tip

Understanding Emotional Appeals Suggest that students also write about the advertisements' illustrations or photographs. How do the pictures support the words? Which appeal more to their emotions, the words or the pictures? Why?

Teach

Using Cooperative Learning

For this cooperative activity, ask teams of students to search for examples of persuasion in the classroom and school. Students can write brief descriptions of what they find. Challenge teams to come up with as many different forms as possible within a given time period. Each member of the group should search a different location, for example, the cafeteria, the library, the office, the gym. Teams should be able to defend each item they find as an example of persuasion. **L2**

Understanding Purpose

Basic learners may need additional work in identifying the purpose in persuasive writing. Bring in advertisements, editorials, and other types of persuasive writing. Have students work in pairs to determine the purpose of each. Let pairs share and discuss their conclusions. **L1**

Additional Resources

Fine Art Transparencies, 26–30

Writing Process Transparencies, 20–22B

Writing Across the Curriculum, pp. 10, 21, 24

Cooperative Learning Activities, pp. 31–36

Thinking and Study Skills, pp. 1–5, 13–14, 19

Listening and Speaking Activities, p. 22

Sentence-Combining Practice, pp. 33–35

Composition Practice, p. 45

Persuasive Writing

Presenting Tip

Consider the different forms in which you can present your persuasive statement, such as an ad, an editorial, a video, or a speech.

Look Around You

Magazines, newspapers, books, posters, letters, television programs—almost anything you read, see, or hear can include persuasion. All of these forms of persuasion try to get the reader, viewer, or listener to agree or to take action. What might an ad for a new cereal try to persuade you to do? What action would an editorial on sun exposure encourage you to take?

The illustration below shows everyday sources of persuasion. Those sources, which are labeled, range from written to oral to visual. As you look at the illustration, picture a room in your house, your school, or another place where you spend time. What sources of persuasion can you find there?

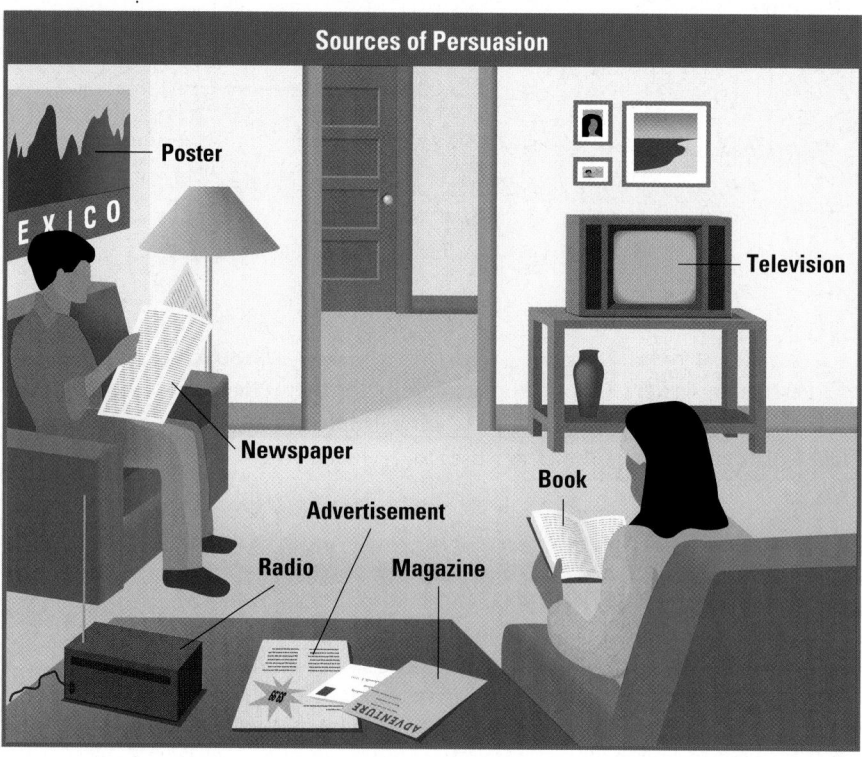

Sources of Persuasion

Poster

Television

Newspaper

Book

Advertisement

Radio   Magazine

MEETING INDIVIDUAL NEEDS | **English Language Learners**

Choosing Words

Some students may find it helpful to do the prewriting tasks orally. Have a student who is learning English work with another student who has more experience with written English and who can take notes on the brainstorming session.

Create a Poster

Create a poster advertising a fund-raising event to help homeless people. Try to convince people in your neighborhood to attend your fund-raiser, which may be a car wash, bake sale, or charity auction. Choose words that will motivate your readers.

PURPOSE To persuade readers to attend a fund-raising event

AUDIENCE Local adults and teenagers

LENGTH 3–5 lines

WRITING RUBRICS To write an effective advertisement, you should

- address people's strong beliefs
- choose words that will persuade
- appeal to the readers' emotions

Cross-Curricular Activity

RUNNING FOR STUDENT OFFICE Meet with a small group of classmates to plan an imaginary campaign for president of your class. Decide who in your group will be the candidate, and then brainstorm ideas for a brief statement to use in the campaign. Use words that will catch readers' attention. Discuss how persuasive each statement is. Finally, choose which statement you will use for the campaign.

Grammar Link

Use strong adjectives to create impact.

A **vegetarian** diet is the most **healthful** and most **humane** way to eat.

Complete the sentences below with strong adjectives.

1. The _____ man sat beside his _____ car.
2. If you are a _____ person, you must speak out against this _____ practice.
3. National parks offer _____ and _____ places to visit.
4. The special effects in her new film were _____.
5. Lashed by the _____ winds of the storm, the _____ waves crashed against the shore.

See Lesson 12.1, page 451.

Viewing and Representing

With your group, create a bulletin board display to present your candidate and his or her persuasive statement. Include original drawings, magazine illustrations, or other visuals of your choice that will help persuade your audience to vote for your candidate.

Assess

Evaluation Rubrics

Create a Poster

Use these criteria when evaluating your students' writing.

- Does it include a sentence stating what the writer wants to persuade the reader to do?
- Are the words chosen for their effectiveness in persuasion?
- Is there an emotional appeal to adult and teenage audiences?

See also *Writing Assessment and Evaluation Rubrics*

Cross-Curricular Activity

Consider the following questions as you evaluate each campaign statement:
- Is the choice of words effective?
- Is the statement memorable?
- Would the statement convince voters?

Viewing and Representing

Bulletin boards should be neat and attractive. Visuals should relate to the candidate's personality and platform.

Reteaching

📁 *Composition Reteaching*, p. 45

Enrichment

📁 *Composition Enrichment*, p. 45

Close

Point out to students that some advertising targets certain groups—teenagers, homemakers, car owners. Ask students to name examples of such advertising and to describe the clues that indicate the target audience.

Grammar Link

Answers

Answers will vary. Sample answers are given.
1. disheveled; dented
2. moral; immoral
3. breathtaking; fascinating
4. dazzling
5. whipping; surging

Using a Thesaurus After students supply answers to the Grammar Link, remind them that a thesaurus can improve their powers of description. Have students look up one or two of their answers in a thesaurus so they can see the range of possible choices. Allow them to change their answers to the activity.

Focus

Lesson Overview

Objectives
- To learn how to define and clarify a position on a topic
- To explore a topic by listing reasons for and against a position

Skills
- choosing a topic; examining an issue; choosing a position

Critical Thinking
- analyzing; recalling; evaluating

Listening and Speaking
- speaking and listening in class discussions

 Bellringer

Daily Language Activity

When students enter the classroom, have this assignment on the board: *Write a sentence or two in which you identify an issue about which you have strong feelings.*

Grammar Link to the Bellringer

Ask students to circle the words *I* and *me* that they wrote in the Bellringer. Ask students to add the words *Bob and* before the circled words and to change the verbs to agree with their new subjects. Do the sentences still "sound" right?

See also *Daily Language Practice*

Motivating Activity

Ask students to write a few sentences giving reasons for the feelings they expressed in the Bellringer. Invite volunteers to share their ideas with the class.

LESSON 6.2

Forming an Opinion

People offer opinions on everything. We're always trying to persuade one another about something. Not all efforts to persuade are serious. In the model below, notice how Andy Rooney expresses his opinion of cats.

> **What does the writer think of cats?**

> **Do you agree or disagree with the writer's opinion? Why?**

Literature Model

Cats Are for the Birds

I have never met a cat I liked. As an animal lover, I'm constantly disappointed with myself when there's a cat around.

Don't think I haven't tried to love cats, because I have. I always try to win their affection or, at the very least, try to establish some sort of relationship. Nothing. A cat will walk on my lap, jump on a table next to me where my host has put a dish of corn chips, or rub against my pants, but there is never any warmth in the cat's gesture.

"He likes you," the host will say.

Well, if those cats I've met like me, they have a plenty strange way of showing it. If I got the kind of affection from the people I like that I get from cats whose owners think they like me, I'd leave home.

Andy Rooney, *Not That You Asked . . .*

---

266 Unit 6 Persuasive Writing

Resource Manager

📂 Planning Resources
- *Lesson Plans*

💻 Transparencies
- *Bellringer*
- *Daily Language Practice*
- *Fine Art 26–30*
- *Two-Minute Skill Drill*
- *Writing Process 20–22B*

📂 Other Print Resources
- *Composition Enrichment,* p. 46
- *Composition Practice,* p. 46
- *Composition Reteaching,* p. 46
- *Cooperative Learning Activities,* pp. 31–36
- *Listening and Speaking Activities,* p. 22

- *Sentence-Combining Practice,* pp. 33–35
- *Thinking and Study Skills,* pp. 11, 13
- *Writing Across the Curriculum*
- *Writing Assessment and Evaluation Rubrics*

What's Your Topic?

When searching for a topic, explore experiences from your daily life that inspire strong opinions. You can brainstorm and make a mental list. You can also freewrite. Write names of people, places, or things, and jot down your thoughts about each. Freewrite for about ten minutes to see where your writing leads you. Whether you brainstorm or freewrite, look at what you have noted, and ask yourself what you feel strongly enough about to use as a topic.

Journal entries also can help you find a topic. Sometimes just reading your entries will remind you of something about which you have a strong opinion. The example shows how the writer has circled possible topics.

Before making a final decision about your topic, look at each possibility. Then ask yourself the questions below.

> The only things I wanted for my birthday were my (own phone) and a job at the mall. I know I'm (too young for a job,) and Mom doesn't want to get me a phone. Still, the day wasn't a total loss. I heard about a program that trains (teenage babysitters,) and now I'm old enough to sign up.

Questions for Choosing a Topic

1	Is this a topic that makes me feel strongly?
2	Is this a topic that has more than one side, a topic on which people might disagree?
3	Do I have enough to say about this topic to persuade others to accept my position?

Journal Writing

Look through your journal for two or three possible persuasive-writing topics. Then use the questions in the chart to decide which one will work best for you.

Teach

Using the Model

Discuss the use of humor in the model on page 266. How does humor make the reader feel about the writer's opinion? (More open to what the writer is saying.) Students should note the writer's opinion of cats. (He dislikes them.) Ask students whether the persuasive writing in the model affected their opinion of cats. **L2**

Choosing a Topic

To help students choose a topic, ask which of the following would make good topics and why:

- censoring song lyrics (Many people care about censorship—a good topic if the person who chose it has strong feelings about it too.)
- cosmetic testing on animals (This is also a much-debated topic.)
- the importance of learning basket weaving (Few will care.) **L1**

Two-Minute Skill Drill

List these adjectives describing a homeless person and have students write a more vivid adjective.

hungry   *tired*

sad   *worn*

unhappy

See also 🎵 *Two-Minute Skill Drill Transparency 6.2*

Journal Writing Tip

Finding Topic Ideas Suggest students look in their journals for entries about things that annoyed them. For example, an entry about not having anything to do could lead to writing a persuasive article on the need for a teen community center.

Teach

Drawing Conclusions

Have students respond in writing to the following question: *Why is it important to think about how others might argue against your opinion?* (Sample: To be convincing, a writer must recognize that others will have different opinions—anticipating some of these arguments helps a writer define his or her position.) **L2**

Talking About a Topic

Have students work with partners to come up with pros and cons on a single topic. Let each student in the pair take a side, pro or con, and make a list of reasons to support his or her position. Each student should then read the list to the other student. Finally, each student should paraphrase the reasons presented by his or her partner, who can offer any necessary suggestions or clarifications. **L1**

Additional Resources

Fine Art Transparencies, 26–30

Writing Process Transparencies, 20–22B

Writing Across the Curriculum, pp. 10, 21, 24

Cooperative Learning Activities, pp. 31–36

Thinking and Study Skills, pp. 11, 13

Sentence-Combining Practice, pp. 33–35

Listening and Speaking Activities, p. 22

Composition Practice, p. 46

Persuasive Writing

Decide Where You Stand

Once you have a topic, think about your position on it. Sometimes when you learn more about a topic, your position on it changes. Other times you may discover that your opinion is similar to everyone else's. Exploring a topic helps you discover whether it's suitable for a writing project.

You can use a chart like the one below to explore your persuasive-writing topic. List the pros—reasons why people might agree with your opinion. Then list the cons—reasons why they might disagree with you. A pro-and-con chart can help you organize your thoughts, make your opinion clearer, and help you determine why or how others might argue against your opinion.

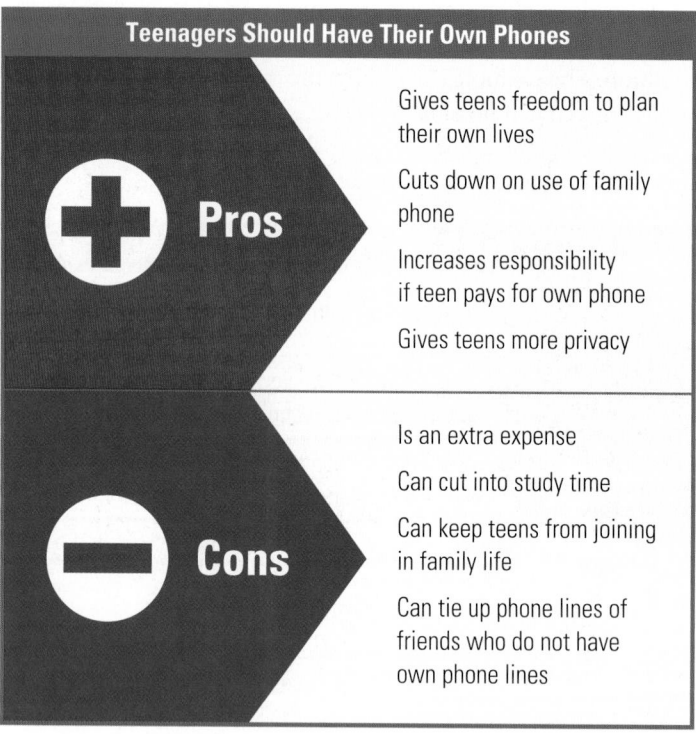

Teenagers Should Have Their Own Phones

Pros
- Gives teens freedom to plan their own lives
- Cuts down on use of family phone
- Increases responsibility if teen pays for own phone
- Gives teens more privacy

Cons
- Is an extra expense
- Can cut into study time
- Can keep teens from joining in family life
- Can tie up phone lines of friends who do not have own phone lines

MEETING INDIVIDUAL NEEDS — Less-Proficient Readers

Preparing to Write

Some students may find it helpful to do their prewriting orally. Students should be allowed to work in pairs to discuss a topic. Students should discuss their own opinions and consider opposing views. They can create a pro-and-con chart to note ideas and views discussed. Make sure that students understand the terms *pro, con, pluses,* and *minuses,* and any other terms likely to be used in discussion. Encourage students to write key words in appropriate columns as reminders of arguments on each side.

Write a Paragraph

Suppose that people want to build a road through an unspoiled forest. The road will connect two cities, making travel and business between the cities easier. But it will also alter the area's natural beauty. What opinion do you have about this proposed construction? Brainstorm or freewrite to explore ideas. Write a paragraph to explain why you support one position or the other.

PURPOSE To clarify and explore an opinion
AUDIENCE Yourself
LENGTH 1 paragraph

WRITING RUBRICS To write a persuasive paragraph, you should

- make a chart showing pros and cons
- state your opinion clearly
- show that you have considered both sides of the issue

Listening and Speaking

PRESENT A POINT OF VIEW Read to the class or to a small group your paragraph about the proposed road. Listen and respond to the opinions of those who agree and disagree with you.

Grammar Link

Use correct pronoun forms in compound constructions.

You often need to choose between *I* and *me* in a compound construction.
    Ann and I differ.
To choose correctly, say the sentence with just the pronoun:
    I differ.

Write each sentence with the correct form: *I* or *me*.

¹ The cat was examining Josh and _____.² Josh and _____ agree on most things.³ On cats, however, there is a big difference between Josh and _____ .⁴ A room with a cat and _____ in it is too full. ⁵ Either the cat or _____ must go.
See Lesson 11.3, page 433.

Cross-Curricular Activity

HISTORY Choose a time in the United States' past when you might like to have lived. After making a chart detailing the pros and cons of living at that time, determine whether your opinion is still the same. Write a few paragraphs persuading the reader of your viewpoint.

Grammar Link

Answers

1. me
2. I
3. me
4. me
5. I

Assess

Evaluation Rubrics

Write a Paragraph

Use these criteria when evaluating your students' writing.

- Is the writer's opinion about the construction included?
- Is there evidence the writer has examined both sides of the issue?

See also *Writing Assessment and Evaluation Rubrics*

Listening and Speaking

Make sure all students participate. Students' responses should be constructive.

Cross-Curricular Activity

The pro-and-con chart should do the following:

- list the advantages of living during the time period chosen
- list the disadvantages of living during the chosen time period

The paragraph chart should

- state the writer's opinion in a way that reflects consideration of both the pros and cons.

Reteaching

📁 *Composition Reteaching,* p. 46

Enrichment

📁 *Composition Enrichment,* p. 46

 Fine Art Transparencies, 26–30

Close

Ask students to think of a hotly contested historic or contemporary issue, such as U.S. independence from Britain or affirmative action, that they have studied in social studies. Let them create a pro-and-con chart, which you write on the board, listing at least two points on each side of the dispute.

Focus

Lesson Overview

Objectives

- To learn to support a position with evidence
- To write a proposal to persuade

Skills

- finding and using facts, statistics, examples, and reasons to support a position; considering an audience

Critical Thinking

- identifying; analyzing; evaluating; classifying

Listening and Speaking

- listening and speaking in class discussions

 Bellringer
Daily Language Activity

When students enter the classroom, have this assignment on the board: *Write a one-sentence definition of the word* evidence.

Grammar Link to the Bellringer

Ask students to think of the kinds of evidence lawyers on TV programs use in murder trials. What might be "good" evidence? "better" evidence? the "best" evidence?

See also *Daily Language Practice*

Motivating Activity

Ask students how they think lawyers go about preparing a case to present to court. (They interview witnesses, review documents, research similar cases, and gather evidence.) Elicit the idea that lawyers need evidence to support their arguments. Explain that students also need evidence in their persuasive writing.

LESSON 6.3

Gathering Evidence

How do you get permission to do something new and different? One way may be to write a proposal. Proposals need evidence to support them.

Suppose that you and your classmates want to use your school's public-address system to broadcast music. The music would be heard only in nonclassroom areas and only before school and during breaks between classes.

You already know your audience—teachers and administrators. Your goal is to convince them that a student-run music service is a good idea, one that they should seriously consider. One way to do this is to write a proposal in which you state what you want your audience to think and do, and then give reasons, or evidence, to back up your argument.

270   Unit 6 Persuasive Writing

Resource Manager

Planning Resources
- *Lesson Plans*

Transparencies
- *Bellringer*
- *Daily Language Practice*
- *Fine Art 26–30*
- *Two-Minute Skill Drill*
- *Writing Process 20–22B*

Other Print Resources
- *Composition Enrichment,* p. 47
- *Composition Practice,* p. 47
- *Composition Reteaching,* p. 47
- *Cooperative Learning Activities,* pp. 31–36
- *Listening and Speaking Activities,* p. 22

- *Sentence-Combining Practice,* pp. 33–35
- *Thinking and Study Skills,* pp. 13–14, 17, 23–24
- *Writing Across the Curriculum*
- *Writing Assessment and Evaluation Rubrics*

Find Support for Your Argument

In your proposal you should clearly state your position, or your opinion. One way to build an argument is to list reasons to support your opinion. Your list of pros and cons is a good source of reasons. The next step then is to gather evidence to support your reasons. The evidence consists of the facts, statistics, and examples that prove your argument. See the chart below for an explanation of three types of evidence. You may use any or all types in your argument. Your evidence should be presented in a logical way. It must offer a reasonable or sensible explanation in order to be convincing.

Drafting Tip

Don't try for a perfect composition in one draft. Concentrate on getting down all of your ideas.

Types of Evidence		
Type	**Definition**	**Example**
Fact	something that can be proven	The school already has the equipment needed for a music broadcast.
Statistic	fact expressed in numbers	A school poll shows that 84 percent of students are in favor of a music broadcast.
Example	particular instance or event	Two other schools in our area have similar broadcasts.

Test your argument to discover possible arguments against it. List the pros and cons to discover any weak links or places where your evidence is unconvincing. Decide how to strengthen any weaknesses you discover.

Journal Writing

Write about the last time you tried to convince someone to agree with you. Describe the position you took. List any evidence that you used, or could have used, to support your argument. Which piece of evidence do you think is the strongest? Explain why.

Teach

Cooperative Learning

Students can work in small groups to come up with a topic like the one presented on page 270 and to formulate a position on the topic. Suggest that groups use a word web to generate evidence in support of their position. Work with students to brainstorm for possible supporting evidence to write around the central idea. **L2**

Considering Opposition

Ask students what kind of opposition the argument on pages 270–271 is likely to encounter. Encourage them to imagine what the teachers and the school principal might say. Tell students that a strong argument considers opposition that it will meet. **L3**

 **Two-Minute Skill Drill**

List these weak phrases on the board and have students write a stronger one for each.

- *could try to help*
- *might want to think about it*
- *sort of tired*

See also Two-Minute Skill Drill Transparency 6.3

Journal Writing Tip

Looking at How an Argument Is Built Suggest that students consider the order in which the evidence is presented. How would the effectiveness of the editorial change if the order of ideas were changed?

Teach

Generating Information

Ask the class to brainstorm ways that students might gather evidence for their audience to support the argument in favor of a student-run music service. (Take a student poll; find an example of a similar successful program at another school; get quotes from teachers who support the idea.) Have students rank the ideas suggested in order of effectiveness and practicality. **L2**

Considering the Audience

Discuss how the type of evidence might change depending on the audience. Let students pick a topic of interest to them and make a chart to list supporting evidence. Help students list the evidence they would use to persuade a friend and the evidence they would use to persuade a parent. Discuss why they chose each piece of evidence. **L1**

Additional Resources

 Fine Art Transparencies, 26–30

 Writing Process Transparencies, 20–22B

Writing Across the Curriculum, pp. 10, 21, 24

Cooperative Learning Activities, pp. 31–36

Thinking and Study Skills, pp. 13–14, 17, 23–24

Sentence-Combining Practice, pp. 33–35

Listening and Speaking Activities, p. 22

Composition Practice, p. 47

Consider Your Audience

To be effective in persuasion, you must choose a format that suits your audience. In the case of the proposal for music in school, for example, a newspaper editorial would be less successful than a written proposal.

You also need to think about your audience when you select your evidence. Consider the following questions.

- How much does my audience know and care about my topic?
- What evidence will be most interesting to my readers?
- What evidence will my readers find most convincing?

Notice how David Rauen considered his audience in this model.

Forms of Persuasive Writing
editorials
posters
letters to the editor
book reviews
advertisements
speeches

Student Model

I think wearing uniforms is a bad idea because it brings down the morale of the students. First of all, we feel uncomfortable in the uniforms. The pants are itchy. By the end of the day, our feet hurt from the school shoes. Secondly, wearing uniforms makes us feel like robots. After a few weeks we get tired of seeing the same colors and outfits every day. I believe the students at our school are responsible enough to choose what they wear. I think the principal should let students have a say about the school's uniform policy.

> What evidence does he use to persuade his audience?

David Rauen, Hope Lutheran School
Chicago, Illinois

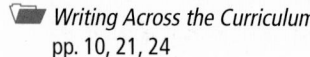 **English Language Learners**

MEETING INDIVIDUAL NEEDS

Understanding the Model

Let students learning English work in small groups to study and discuss the student model on page 272. Each group should include students with varied degrees of English proficiency. Have groups summarize the student model text in an alternative form: a cartoon or pantomime.

Write a Proposal

Suppose that you want to start a business, such as designing jewelry. First, though, you must persuade a relative or friend to lend you money. Gather some persuasive evidence, and write a short proposal to present.

PURPOSE To obtain a loan for your business
AUDIENCE An adult who might lend you money
LENGTH 1–2 paragraphs

WRITING RUBRICS To write an effective proposal, you should

- state your position clearly
- use a variety of evidence to support your position
- make sure your evidence suits your audience

Nancy Holt, *Sun Tunnels*, 1973–1976

Grammar Link

Use *good, better,* and *best* and *bad, worse,* and *worst* correctly.

*I think wearing uniforms is a **bad** idea...*

Rewrite each sentence, correcting errors in the use of adjectives.

¹ Juan's was a more good song than Pat's. ² It was the most good song in the concert. ³ Bob's outburst was the baddest moment. ⁴ It was more bad behavior than LaVerne's. ⁵ Too bad— he's the most good singer in school. *See Lesson 12.3, page 455.*

Cross-Curricular Activity

ART The concrete tunnel shown here is one of four placed in the Utah desert by the artist. Each tunnel measures eighteen feet in length and more than nine feet in diameter. In the upper half of each tunnel, the artist cut holes in the pattern of various constellations. As the sun shines through these holes, light in the tunnel changes constantly.

Listening and Speaking

With a small group, discuss why an artist would place tunnels in the desert. Assess one another's arguments and presentations.

6.3 Gathering Evidence **273**

Persuasive Writing

Assess

Evaluation Rubrics

Write a Proposal

Use these criteria when evaluating your students' writing:

- include a statement of purpose
- offer evidence to support the loan request
- be directed to a specific audience

See also *Writing Assessment and Evaluation Rubrics*

Cross-Curricular Activity

As you evaluate the letter, look for these points:

- a statement urging the reader to visit or not to visit the work of art
- evidence to support the statement drawn from the photo and the text on this page
- language and evidence appropriate to the intended audience

Listening and Speaking

Encourage students to monitor their understanding of the assignment and to seek clarification as needed.

Reteaching

Composition Reteaching, p. 47

Enrichment

Composition Enrichment, p. 47

Fine Art Transparencies, 26–30

Close

Ask students to choose a school policy they would like to change or a special program they would like to see adopted in the school. Challenge students to give an example of all three types of evidence (see page 271) to support their position.

Grammar Link

Answers
1. better
2. best
3. worst
4. worse
5. best

Viewing the Art

Nancy Holt, *Sun Tunnels*, 1973–1976
Nancy Holt's *Sun Tunnels* is in the Great Basin Desert of Utah. The four concrete tunnels, each weighing 22 tons, were positioned to align with sunrise and sunset during the winter solstice, December 22, and the summer solstice, June 22.
Interpret and Analyze Use the following question for discussion:
- Describe the figures shown in the painting. What does the artist hope to convey by aligning them to coincide with the winter and summer solstices?

Focus

Lesson Overview

Objectives
- To identify the components of an editorial argument
- To synthesize evidence into a convincing argument

Skills
- stating a position; organizing an argument; writing an editorial

Critical Thinking
- identifying; analyzing; classifying; supporting main ideas

Listening and Speaking
- listening and speaking in class discussions

Bellringer
Daily Language Activity

When students enter the classroom, have this assignment on the board: *If you could change one thing about society, what would it be? Write your response.*

Grammar Link to the Bellringer

Ask students which of the following sentences is more likely to get a reader's attention: *Keeping some people out of public buildings is not fair. Do you think keeping some people out of public buildings is fair?*

See also *Daily Language Practice*

Motivating Activity

Discuss ways in which public areas have been made more accessible to everyone (sidewalk ramps, wider doors, and lower drinking fountains). Explain to students that advocates for people with disabilities have worked for years to convince others of the need for these changes.

Persuasive Writing

LESSON 6.4

Developing an Argument

In order to persuade, you must catch and hold the attention of your audience. Read how violinist Itzhak Perlman does that.

> What change does the writer want? What evidence does he use to support his position?

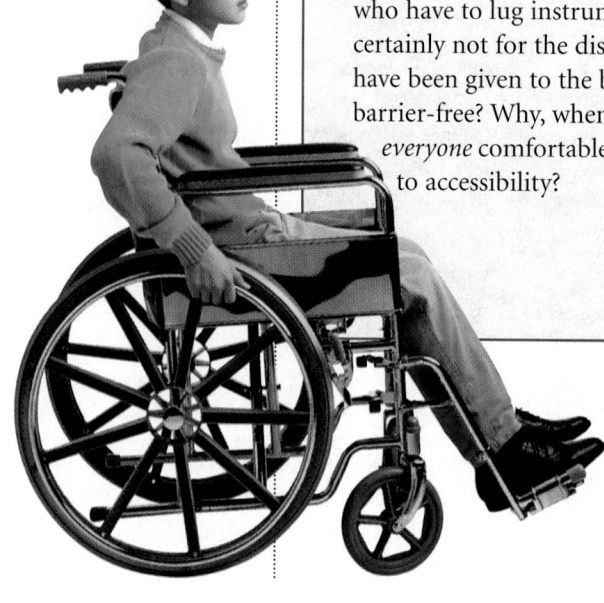

Literature Model

I've been in public buildings throughout the world, and it's clear that the people who design them have no idea what it feels like to use crutches or sit in a wheelchair. One of the great architectural catastrophes of all time, from the point of view of any concertgoer, much less one who is disabled, is the Sydney Opera House in Sydney, Australia. A design contest was held and the winner was an architect who had conceived a truly fantastic-looking place with about a hundred steps leading to the entrance. There is no elevator—not for the general public, not for the poor musicians who have to lug instruments up all those stairs, and certainly not for the disabled. Why couldn't the prize have been given to the best design that was also barrier-free? Why, when it's possible to make *everyone* comfortable, is so little attention paid to accessibility?

Itzhak Perlman, "To Help the Handicapped, Talk to Them"
Glamour, March 1987

274 Unit 6 Persuasive Writing

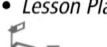

Resource Manager

📂 Planning Resources
- *Lesson Plans*

🖥 Transparencies
- *Bellringer*
- *Daily Language Practice*
- *Fine Art 26–30*
- *Two-Minute Skill Drill*
- *Writing Process 20–22B*

📂 Other Print Resources
- *Composition Enrichment,* p. 48
- *Composition Practice,* p. 48
- *Composition Reteaching,* p. 48
- *Cooperative Learning Activities,* pp. 31–36
- *Listening and Speaking Activities,* p. 22

- *Sentence-Combining Practice,* pp. 33–35
- *Thinking and Study Skills,* pp. 13, 17, 19
- *Writing Assessment and Evaluation Rubrics*

State Your Position

A key statement in persuasive writing is the sentence that tells what you want your audience to do or think. Typically, a topic sentence, which may appear either at the beginning or at the end of your opening paragraph will contain that statement. Note that Perlman begins with a clearly focused topic sentence and gives strong evidence to support the opinion it expresses.

> **Where is the topic sentence in each paragraph?**

> *The Whitebridge movie complex should have an entrance ramp. It has twelve theaters, four concession stands, and video games. You can see any movie, eat any snack, or play any game you want — if you can walk up a flight of stairs.*

> *The other day my friend Tiffany and I went to Lily's Snacks. Tiffany uses a wheelchair to get around. I was shocked to realize that she couldn't come in with me. There are three steps to the door but no ramp. Why isn't Lily's accessible to everyone?*

Revising Tip

In the revising stage, make sure you have organized your persuasive writing in a sensible way.

Journal Writing

Imagine a place you could not visit because of a disability. How would you feel about that place? What would you do to change it? Write a brief statement of your opinion, including a clear topic sentence and evidence that supports your proposal for change.

Teach

Using the Model

Draw students' attention to the model on page 274. Ask what change the writer wants. (Buildings should be accessible to people with disabilities.) What evidence does Perlman use to support that position? (The architectural shortcomings of the Sydney Opera House; fact—others besides the disabled could use an elevator.) **L2**

Using the Model

Help students identify the main ideas in the student paragraphs on page 275. (In the first paragraph, the main idea is that the Whitebridge movie complex should have an entrance ramp. The main idea of the second paragraph is that Lily's Snacks should be accessible to everyone, including the disabled.) **L1**

Two-Minute Skill Drill

List these topic sentences on the board. Have students select the stronger sentence, giving reasons for their choice.

The school should make the third-floor auditorium more accessible.

The inaccessibility of the third-floor auditorium prevents many parents from attending student plays.

See also *Two-Minute Skill Drill Transparency 6.4*

Journal Writing Tip

Generating New Information
Suggest that students write letters to an appropriate person or organization to express their concerns.

Teach

Promoting Discussion

Ask students to come up with examples of disabilities other than physical confinement to a wheelchair. (hearing impairment, visual impairment) Ask students to think of ways in which people with disabilities and those interested in their welfare have persuaded others to make changes. (Close-captioned television, braille translations of public documents or publications) Ask students to suggest what arguments might have been used. **L2**

Identifying the Main Idea

Some students may benefit from a closer look at main-idea statements in persuasive writing. Bring in additional examples of persuasive writing, such as letters to the editor, editorials, and opinion pieces. Ask students to identify the main idea in each one. **L1**

Additional Resources

Fine Art Transparencies, 26–30

Writing Process Transparencies, 20–22B

Writing Across the Curriculum, pp. 10, 21, 24

Cooperative Learning Activities, pp. 31–36

Thinking and Study Skills, pp. 13, 17, 19

Sentence-Combining Practice, pp. 33–35

Listening and Speaking Activities, p. 22

Composition Practice, p. 48

Persuasive Writing

Grammar Tip

Make sure that all your sentences express complete thoughts. To review the rules for sentences and fragments, see Lesson 8.2, page 359.

Organize Your Argument

The structure of a persuasive piece can resemble the three-part structure of a report. The introduction states the topic and your opinion on it. The body provides evidence to support your opinion. The conclusion summarizes your argument and suggests action.

To make your persuasive writing effective, place your most convincing evidence where it best supports your point. Your argument may work best when you present the strongest evidence first. At other times, putting the strongest evidence last will be more effective. Notice how Justin Pinegar introduces his topic and gets his opinion across.

Tips for Structuring a Persuasive Piece

1	Decide how to arrange your evidence.
2	Write a strong opening that states your position.
3	Present all your supporting evidence in the best order.
4	Sum up your argument, and give your conclusions.

How does Justin draw his audience into his argument?

Student Model

Imagine that it is the year 2080. You are walking through a forest, when you see a five-legged frog jump out of a pool of orange and green water. Suddenly you realize that this is the first animal life you've seen on your walk. You are seeing one of the effects of toxic waste, caused by a world that relied too much on technology. Although many machines serve good purposes, we are relying too much on technology to solve our problems. We need to moderate technology now, before it is too late.

Justin Pinegar, Frontier Junior High School
Moses Lake, Washington

MEETING INDIVIDUAL NEEDS ## Less-Proficient Readers

Communicating an Argument

Suggest that students draft their editorials by first writing only phrases and key words to express main ideas and supporting details. Then have students prepare a second draft that uses complete sentences. Encourage students to work through the revision and editing portions of the writing process and to seek help as needed.

6.4 Writing Activities

Write an Editorial

Consider what could be done with a large donation to your school. New sports equipment? Software? A new student lounge? Draft an editorial for the school newspaper to convince readers of your opinion.

PURPOSE To persuade others
AUDIENCE Students and teachers
LENGTH 1–2 paragraphs

WRITING RUBRICS To write an effective editorial, you should

- write a clear topic sentence
- organize your argument with an introduction, body, and conclusion
- present your evidence in a convincing order

Listening and Speaking

EVALUATE EDITORIALS With a small group, read aloud the editorials you wrote. Assess whether one another's arguments are convincing.

Cross-Curricular Activity

MUSIC Imagine that you are a musician in the 1800s, just before women were allowed to play in some orchestras. Write a letter trying to persuade a conductor to let female musicians perform in his orchestra.

Grammar Link

Use variety in your sentence structures.

One way to achieve variety is to use interrogative, imperative, and exclamatory sentences, as well as declarative ones.

Why isn't Lily's accessible to everyone?

Another technique is to use varied beginnings for your sentences.

Although many machines serve good purposes, *we are relying too much on technology to solve our problems.*

Revise the passage below, using varied kinds of sentences and varied sentence beginnings.

[1] You should now pretend that it is the year 1775. [2] You live on a small farm in the colony of Pennsylvania. [3] You are in favor of independence from England, but your father is against it. [4] A recruiter comes by, asking you to join a colonial army that will eventually fight the British. [5] You should now think about what you will do.

See Lesson 2.8, page 74, and Lesson 8.1, page 357.

Persuasive Writing

Assess

Evaluation Rubrics

Write an Editorial

Use these criteria when evaluating your students' writing.
- Is there a clear topic sentence?
- Is the argument organized with an introduction, body, and conclusion?
- Was the evidence presented in a convincing order?

See also *Writing Assessment and Evaluation Rubrics*

Listening and Speaking

Students should use effective volume, pitch, and tone when reading aloud editorials. Ideas should be expressed with fluency and confidence. Comments should be constructive.

Cross-Curricular Activity

As you evaluate the letter, look for the following:
- a position statement
- supporting evidence
- an awareness of the time period and audience

Reteaching

📁 *Composition Reteaching*, p. 48

Enrichment

📁 *Composition Enrichment*, p. 48

✏️ *Fine Art Transparencies 26–30*

Close

Have students name a topic of local interest that they feel strongly about. Have them brainstorm an approach to presenting their opinion and evidence to support it in a letter to the editor of the local newspaper.

Grammar Link

Answers

Answers will vary, but some suggestions are given below.

I live, in the exciting year of 1775, on a small farm in the Pennsylvania colony. Although my father is against independence from England, I support it. I don't know, however, whether I support independence strongly enough to fight. A recruiter stopped by our farm, asking for volunteers to join the colonial army. I must make up my mind.

Focus

Lesson Overview

Objectives

- To learn methods of presenting persuasive writing
- To clarify problems in a draft and to revise a piece of persuasive writing

Skills

- evaluating and revising a draft; examining word choices

Critical Thinking

- defining; analyzing; drawing conclusions

Listening and Speaking

- listening and speaking in class discussions

 Bellringer
Daily Language Activity

When students enter the classroom, have this assignment on the board: *Complete this sentence:*

Sometimes people want to do something over or continue to work on it because . . .

Grammar Link to the Bellringer

Write the following on the board and ask students what they notice first about it: *Many people in america speak languages other than english.* Most students will point out the incorrect capitalization. Stress that such flaws are distracting from content.

See also *Daily Language Practice*

Motivating Activity

Discuss the various strategies students use for revising their work. Ask why it is important to revise persuasive writing. (If an argument is unclear or cannot be readily understood, it will not convince an audience.)

LESSON
6.5

Polishing an Argument

All good writing deserves a second look. In persuasive writing, always double check your ideas.

The draft of your persuasive writing probably contains many solid ideas. But just as with any other writing, you should review your draft to be sure it makes sense. You want your argument not only to grab your readers' attention but also to hold it. If the argument lacks convincing evidence and sensible connections between ideas, your audience will feel confused and may lose interest in your topic. Review and revise your persuasive composition to keep it interesting and focused.

Resource Manager

📁 Planning Resources
- *Lesson Plans*

📓 Transparencies
- *Bellringer*
- *Daily Language Practice*
- *Fine Art* 26–30
- *Two-Minute Skill Drill*
- *Writing Process* 20–22B

📁 Other Print Resources
- *Composition Enrichment,* p. 49
- *Composition Practice,* p. 49
- *Composition Reteaching,* p. 49
- *Cooperative Learning Activities,* pp. 31–36
- *Listening and Speaking Activities,* p. 22

- *Sentence-Combining Practice,* pp. 33–35
- *Thinking and Study Skills,* pp. 14, 25–29
- *Writing Across the Curriculum*
- *Writing Assessment and Evaluation Rubrics*

Look at the Big Picture

When you begin to revise your writing, look first at the big picture, the whole argument. Ask yourself, Have I stated my argument clearly and supported it with evidence? One way to answer this question is to have a classmate evaluate your writing. The draft below shows how one writer revised her work after a peer reviewer evaluated it.

Here are some questions that will help you evaluate your own and others' persuasive writing:

- Is the position stated clearly?
- Does the introduction grab attention?
- Is the evidence persuasive, and is it in the best order?
- Is enough evidence included?

Sally Lu should win the Student Community Service Award. Her efforts have helped bring the people in our community closer together. She started the Chinese-to-English Program to help Chinese children new to our area learn English. She is a winning baseball and tennis player. She also arranged a Get-Acquainted Night to bring the Chinese community into contact with other area groups. Vote for Sally Lu.

Why did the peer reviewer suggest removing this sentence?

What does this sentence add to the paragraph?

Journal Writing

Look at some editorials from your school newspaper or another local paper. Use the questions above to evaluate one of them. Note your evaluation in your journal.

Persuasive Writing

Teach

Using the Model

Instruct students to use the four questions on this page to evaluate the model. Ask them to suggest any revisions they think necessary. For example, they may recommend revising the first sentence to make it more engaging. Students should note why the peer reviewer suggested removing one sentence. (It doesn't relate to the main idea.) They should also note what the final sentence adds to the paragraph. (It helps to reinforce the main idea.) **L2**

Cooperative Learning

Working in cooperative groups, have students agree on a teacher in a lower grade who deserves to win a Teacher of the Year award. Have them outline and draft a brief persuasive piece explaining why that person should win. Suggest that students decide who will record suggestions, lead the discussion, draft the outline, and proofread. **L2**

Two-Minute Skill Drill

Write these words on the board. Have students correct errors in capitalization.

Japanese

cambodian

Jewish community center

Community center

See also *Two-Minute Skill Drill Transparency 6.5*

Journal Writing Tip

Choosing a Topic Suggest that students closely examine each editorial for points to evaluate before they begin writing.

Teach

Using the Model

Point out the importance of using strong words in a persuasive piece. Also discuss the dangers of overstating your case. (Your readers may not believe you.) Students should note what effect the revisions have on the paragraph. (They make the argument more persuasive because the words are more precise and to the point.) **L2**

Choosing Precise Words

Ask students to revise a piece of persuasive writing, paying particular attention to effective word choice. Give them practice using a dictionary and thesaurus to help them find more precise words. Suggest that they use the thesaurus first to find possible alternatives and then use the dictionary to check on the precise meaning of each one. **L2**

Additional Resources

Fine Art Transparencies, 26–30

Writing Process Transparencies, 20–22B

Writing Across the Curriculum, pp. 10, 21, 24

Cooperative Learning Activities, pp. 31–36

Thinking and Study Skills, pp. 14, 25–29

Sentence-Combining Practice, pp. 33–35

Listening and Speaking Activities, p. 22

Composition Practice, p. 49

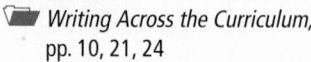
Persuasive Writing

Choose Strong Words

When you write to persuade, the words you choose are very important. Think about which bike ad makes you more likely to buy:

It's a great bike—and cheap, too!

It's the bike used by professional cyclists—and it doesn't cost a fortune!

Aim for strong words and phrases that grab your readers' attention. Look at the word changes made in this draft.

> David Lopez is a ~~good~~ *the most qualified* candidate for class president. He gets ~~good~~ *high* grades, and *both students and* teachers ~~like him. Students too.~~ *trust* him. He ~~belongs to~~ *takes part in* several school clubs: Theater Club, Chess Club, and Woodworking Club. He *also* plays on the basketball team. *Above all,* He wants to make our school a better place for students and teachers.

How do these changes affect the writing?

What other words might the writer have used for *good* candidate? Why is *trust* a more effective word than *like* in this situation? Why is *takes part* more effective than *belongs to?*

The most effective test for the words you choose is your audience. If you wanted to persuade your parents to allow you to wait all night in line for tickets to a concert, you might use very different words than if you wanted to persuade one of your friends to wait with you.

Listening and Speaking

Preparing for Peer Review

Some students may be especially sensitive to comments made by a peer reviewer. Discuss with students the role of the peer reviewer. Ask questions such as the following: *What kinds of comments are helpful? What kinds of comments are not helpful? Why do you like working with a peer reviewer? Why don't you like working with a peer reviewer?* Ask students to give examples. Then, as a class, come up with a few simple guidelines for peer reviewers.

Create a Leaflet

Think of an environmental concern. It could be the thinning of the ozone layer, the pollution of the ocean, or another problem of your choice. Consider the evidence you will need to persuade your classmates to take action. To present your argument, use persuasive writing in a leaflet that informs, as well as persuades. Then draft and revise your text.

PURPOSE To persuade people to take action on an environmental issue

AUDIENCE Your classmates

LENGTH 1–2 paragraphs

WRITING RUBRICS To write persuasively in a leaflet, you should

- state and support your position clearly
- arrange ideas in an order that suits your audience
- include enough evidence
- use words that will grab your readers' attention

Using Computers

As you revise your leaflet for effective word choice, you might use the thesaurus function on your computer. The thesaurus suggests synonyms, words of similar meaning. Identify any words in your draft that you want to replace. Then look in the thesaurus for synonyms that may be more precise.

Grammar Link

Capitalize proper nouns and adjectives.

Capitalize the names of ethnic groups and nationalities. Also capitalize the name of languages and the adjectives formed from these words.

She started the Chinese-to-English Program to help Chinese children new to our area learn English.

Write each item, correcting errors in capitalization.

1. You must learn to speak Spanish.
2. Hillary traveled to rome when she was studying italian art.
3. Is polish a slavic language?
4. She is irish, so her ancestors may have spoken celtic.
5. I'll have the greek salad.

See Lesson 19.4, page 579.

Viewing and Representing

MAKE A FOOD POSTER Find pictures of a variety of foods from one country. Clip the pictures from magazines or download them from the Internet. Use them to make a poster advertising that country's cuisine. Accompany each picture with a brief description of the dish portrayed.

Assess

Evaluation Rubrics

Create a Leaflet

Use these criteria when evaluating your students' writing:
- Is there a statement of opinion on an environmental issue?
- Is there evidence to support the opinion?
- Does it include a call to action?
- Does it include attention-grabbing words?

See also *Writing Assessment and Evaluation Rubrics*

Using Computers

Students' choice of synonyms should reflect an understanding of and sensitivity to variations in word meanings.

Viewing and Representing

Make sure that students understand how to download pictures from the Internet.

Reteaching

📁 *Composition Reteaching*, p. 49

Enrichment

📁 *Composition Enrichment*, p. 49

Close

Have students imagine that a foundation is giving out grants to help organizations that play an important role in their community. Ask students to pick one organization that they think should receive such a grant. Have them dictate an outline, which you write on the board, for a letter to convince the foundation board members.

Grammar Link

Answers
1. correct
2. Rome, Italian
3. Polish, Slavic
4. Irish, Celtic
5. Greek

Focus

Lesson Overview

Objectives
- To gain an understanding of publicity and audience response
- To create effective publicity through persuasive writing

Skills
- capturing audience attention; creating visually effective posters

Critical Thinking
- analyzing; defining criteria; visualizing; making decisions

Listening and Speaking
- listening and speaking in class discussions

 Bellringer
Daily Language Activity

When students enter the classroom, have this assignment on the board: *In a few sentences, state what you think a publicist does.*

Grammar Link to the Bellringer

Ask students to use the words *publicists* and *publicist's* correctly in sentences.

See also *Daily Language Practice*

Motivating Activity

Let students share their answers from the Bellringer. Then ask students to imagine that their class is planning to put on a talent show. How would they let people know about the show and convince them to attend? (radio, television, and newspaper ads; flyers to hand out; posters) Explain that these are all forms of publicity.

282

LESSON
6.6

Writing Publicity

*P*ublicity includes posters, radio ads, flyers, and other printed or spoken forms of persuasion. If you want to get the word out about an event or cause, publicize it.

Suppose that a band you're in is planning a concert. You could put announcements and advertisements on local radio shows and public-access television channels. You might make posters and display them all over town. You might also submit an article about your group to a local paper.

By the time the concert takes place, everyone in town will know about it. That's the result of good publicity.

282 Unit 6 Persuasive Writing

 **Resource Manager**

Planning Resources
- *Lesson Plans*

Transparencies
- *Bellringer*
- *Daily Language Practice*
- *Fine Art* 26–30
- *Two-Minute Skill Drill*
- *Writing Process* 20–22B

Other Print Resources
- *Composition Enrichment,* p. 50
- *Composition Practice,* p. 50
- *Composition Reteaching,* p. 50
- *Cooperative Learning Activities,* pp. 31–36
- *Listening and Speaking Activities,* p. 22

- *Sentence-Combining Practice,* pp. 33–35
- *Thinking and Study Skills,* pp. 4, 8, 9, 17, 22
- *Writing Assessment and Evaluation Rubrics*

Get Noticed

The first goal of publicity writing is to capture the attention of your audience. A striking image on a poster can make someone stop and stare. A short, snappy slogan on a flyer can invite someone to read. Think about any posters, flyers, leaflets, or other forms of publicity you've seen recently. What images or language made you notice them?

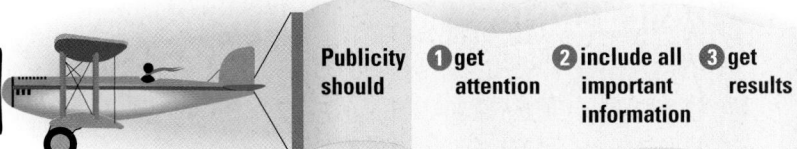

Publicity should ① **get attention** ② **include all important information** ③ **get results**

When you plan to write publicity, you must think about your purpose. Decide what message you want to convey. Then think about your audience—the people whom you hope to convince. Once you have your purpose and audience in mind, consider what kind of language will most likely appeal to your audience. You should present all the necessary information in as few words as possible. Remember, too, that images can also be used to gain attention and convey meaning. Think about how your words can work with the images you use. You want your audience to understand your idea very quickly and react positively to it.

Grammar Tip

Check spelling and capitalization carefully when you edit. Because posters use few words, any mistakes stand out. To review capitalization guidelines, see Lessons 19.2–19.4, pages 575–580.

Journal Writing

Look through recent newspapers and magazines. Clip any especially eye-catching photographs or drawings. Tape or paste these images into your journal. Jot down ideas for persuasive statements to go with the images. One of the images may inspire a poster or another kind of publicity.

6.6 Writing Publicity **283**

Teach

Cooperative Learning

Using a cooperative strategy, have students work in small groups to develop publicity for upcoming school events. Each group should choose a different event and form of publicity. Each member of the group should have responsibility for some portion of the project. Groups can then present their publicity to the rest of the class and the school, if appropriate. **L2**

Getting Attention

Choose photographs of products or events that are not the subject of major advertising campaigns. Show the photographs to students and ask what kinds of publicity they might use to create attention. What kinds of information should they include in the publicity? **L1**

Two-Minute Skill Drill

List these nouns on the board and have students make each noun possessive.

students	health	event
summer	girl	year

See also 🖊 *Two-Minute Skill Drill Transparency 6.6*

Journal Writing Tip

Writing to Persuade Make sure that students understand that a persuasive statement may appeal to a person's desire for a positive self-image or enjoyment.

Enrichment and Extension

Evaluating Nonprint Sources

Discuss how nonprint sources are used to persuade viewers and listeners. Next, have students work in groups to select a popular television or radio commercial for discussion. Students should analyze the commercial and then evaluate how well it may influence an audience.

Teach

Analyzing Posters

Ask students to give examples of the kinds of posters they have seen. (They might mention those advertising sales, services, or events; promoting good health; or promoting travel destinations.) If possible, have students bring in examples for discussion. Have the class evaluate the effectiveness of each. **L2**

Creating an Ad Campaign

Ask students to create a publicity campaign to encourage people to read more. Have students work in small groups to develop three different posters, one to appeal to each of the following audiences: young children, teenagers, and adults. The entire group should brainstorm for ideas. Work with students to evaluate their ideas. Each group member can then take responsibility for one poster. Periodically check on students' progress. **L3**

Additional Resources

 Fine Art Transparencies, 26–30

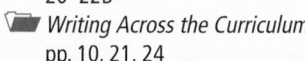 *Writing Process Transparencies,* 20–22B

Writing Across the Curriculum, pp. 10, 21, 24

Cooperative Learning Activities, pp. 31–36

Thinking and Study Skills, pp. 4, 8, 9, 17, 22

Sentence-Combining Practice, pp. 33–35

Listening and Speaking Activities, p. 22

Composition Practice, p. 50

284

Persuasive Writing

Post Your Message

Posters can be vivid, effective attention grabbers for some audiences. A poster could be the perfect way to persuade people to attend a school play or to recycle cans and bottles. This illustration shows four different uses for posters.

Uses for Posters

KAREN JONES / CLASS PRESIDENT — Get votes.

LOST / KAYO / 123-4567 — Find a lost pet.

CIRCUS — Advertise an event.

Support Our Band — Explain a cause.

Keeping your purpose in mind will help you decide what information to include on your poster. A poster announcing a lost pet, for example, needs certain information. You will want to have your pet's name, a picture or description, and any other important characteristics, such as whether it answers to its name and whether it likes strangers. In addition, be sure to provide your own name and phone number. Don't forget other special information, such as whether you are offering a reward.

Viewing and Representing

Examining Images

Some students may find it easier to communicate messages through pictures rather than through language. Bring in a variety of images for students to examine. Encourage students to look for ways to use images in their own posters to convey ideas they may not be able to convey through language.

6.6 | Writing Activities

Write an Advertisement

Think of how you might advertise a circus coming to town. Decide which form of publicity you will use—a poster, a leaflet, a flyer, or another form. Then write a persuasive advertisement.

PURPOSE To call attention to an event
AUDIENCE Adults and children
LENGTH 1–2 paragraphs

WRITING RUBRICS To create an effective advertisement, you should

- include a slogan or image that will get attention
- consider your purpose and audience
- include all necessary information

Cross-Curricular Activity

GEOGRAPHY Travel brochures try to lure people to visit certain places. With your group, design a brochure for a large, exciting city. Brainstorm the information you want to include. Divide up the tasks of researching information and visuals.

Then draft and lay out the visuals. Revise, edit, and place visuals so your brochure will be persuasive and appealing. Share your brochure with other groups.

Grammar Link

Use apostrophes in possessive nouns.

> Get a **viewer's** attention.
> Get **people's** attention.
> Get **customers'** attention.

The text below is from a poster. Write each item, adding apostrophes where necessary.

1. Come hear great music at the citys benefit concert.
2. Listen to the beat of the musicians in the Top Bananas numbers.
3. Thrill to the sound of Tracy Westons songs.
4. Then comes the combined choruses performance.
5. These mens and womens voices will amaze you.

See Lesson 20.7, page 601.

Listening and Speaking

BE AN ANNOUNCER Pretend that you are the radio or television announcer who reads aloud the circus advertisement. Be as dramatic as you think appropriate.

6.6 Writing Publicity **285**

Persuasive Writing

Assess

Evaluation Rubrics

Write an Advertisement
Use these criteria when evaluating your students' writing.
- includes the who, when, and where details of the circus
- contains an appeal to both adults and children
- has compelling art or attention-getting slogan

See also *Writing Assessment and Evaluation Rubrics*

Cross-Curricular Activity
The brochure should include the following:
- a visual of the place
- appealing copy
- information about a trip to visit the place

Listening and Speaking
Students should speak clearly and appropriately for the setting, using effective volume, pitch, and tone.

Reteaching
📁 *Composition Reteaching,* p. 50

Enrichment
📁 *Composition Enrichment,* p. 50

 Fine Art Transparencies, 26–30

Close

Discuss the forms of publicity that students have seen recently. Ask them to identify effective images or slogans. Then help students determine what these images and slogans have in common. (They may be memorable, surprising, humorous, dramatic, and so on.) Help students come up with a list of criteria to use in judging their own publicity.

Grammar Link

Answers
1. city's
2. Banana's
3. Weston's
4. choruses'
5. men's; women's

Focus

Lesson Overview

Objectives

- To identify positive suggestions to use in letters of complaint
- To define and clarify a problem in a letter of complaint

Skills

- using correct business letter format; employing appropriate language; explaining a problem and its solution

Critical Thinking

- analyzing; defining; making decisions

Listening and Speaking

- listening and speaking in class discussions

Bellringer
Daily Language Activity

When students enter the classroom, have this assignment on the board: *In a few sentences, tell about a time when you were angry and felt like writing a letter of complaint.*

Grammar Link to the Bellringer

Tell students to imagine that they are writing a letter of complaint to the school principal. Have them write the inside address, and then check their use of capitalization and punctuation.

See also *Daily Language Practice*

Motivating Activity

Ask students whether they have ever written a letter of complaint. If so, have them describe the problem and the results. Ask how a letter of complaint is like other forms of persuasive writing. (It presents an argument and tries to convince the reader to take action.)

Persuasive Writing

LESSON 6.7

Writing a Letter of Complaint

The most effective complaints often include positive suggestions.

Sometimes it is not possible to do anything about an annoying situation at the time it takes place, but you may be able to do something later.

In the model below, Julia Mendoza writes a letter of complaint. Notice that she includes a constructive suggestion for a solution to the problem.

Student Model

Dear Sir or Madam:

    My friends and I ate at El Jardín last Friday evening, and it upset us to find that your restaurant does not have a No Smoking section. The people at the tables on either side of us were smoking. Because the air around our table was full of smoke, we found it impossible to enjoy our dinner. We had to breathe the smoke, which is dangerous as well as unpleasant.

    I suggest that you set aside one section of your restaurant as a smoking area. That way, customers who do not smoke will find it possible to enjoy your good food in a clean, smoke-free environment.

               Sincerely,

               Julia Mendoza

               Julia Mendoza

What is the writer's complaint?

What solution does the writer suggest?

286 Unit 6 Persuasive Writing

Resource Manager

📁 Planning Resources
- *Lesson Plans*

Transparencies
- *Bellringer*
- *Daily Language Practice*
- *Fine Art* 26–30
- *Two-Minute Skill Drill*
- *Writing Process* 20–22B

📁 Other Print Resources
- *Composition Enrichment*, p. 51
- *Composition Practice*, p. 51
- *Composition Reteaching*, p. 51
- *Cooperative Learning Activities*, pp. 31–36
- *Listening and Speaking Activities*, p. 22

- *Sentence-Combining Practice*, pp. 33–35
- *Thinking and Study Skills*, pp. 1, 4, 13–14, 17
- *Writing Across the Curriculum*
- *Writing Assessment and Evaluation Rubrics*

Draft Your Letter

A letter of complaint has the same purpose as other kinds of persuasive writing. A letter of complaint states the problem, explains the circumstances, and proposes a reasonable solution.

Letters of complaint follow the form of any business letter.

Heading: your address and the date

Inside address: the name and address of the person to whom you are writing

Greeting: begins with "Dear" and includes the name of the person to whom you are writing, followed by a colon

Body: explains the problem and suggests a solution

Closing: final words of the letter, such as "Sincerely," followed by a comma

Signature: your signed name, followed by your typed name.

> 71 Union Street
> Tempe, AZ 85281
> October 17, 200–
>
> Sergeant Samuel Kincaid
> Precinct 4
> 1106 Fortieth Street
> Tempe, AZ 85281
>
> Dear Sergeant Kincaid:
>   I want to call your attention to the dangerous intersection at Oak Street and First Avenue. Yesterday my younger sister was almost hit by a car speeding through the intersection. Because there are stop signs only on Oak Street, many drivers drive too fast through the intersection.
>   Would you please look into this problem? Perhaps stop signs can be placed on the First Avenue corners.
>
> Sincerely,
>
> *Peter Raymond*
>
> Peter Raymond

Journal Writing

Think of something you would like to have changed. State the problem, explain it, and offer a reasonable solution. You may feel strongly enough to draft, revise, edit, and then send an actual letter. If your letter is handwritten, be sure to write legibly.

Persuasive Writing

6.7

Teach
Using the Model

Discuss the letter on page 286. Ask students to identify the writer's complaint and proposed solution. (Smokers are seated with nonsmokers; the owners should set aside separate areas for each.) What is the tone of the letter? (polite, reasonable) How would students feel if they received such a letter? (They might appreciate the compliments on the restaurant's food and the proposed solution.) **L2**

Two-Minute Skill Drill

Write the following address on the board and have students correct the capitalization.

manager
fit for life fitness center
5354 doppler road
spokane, wa 99206

See also *Two-Minute Skill Drill Transparency 6.7*

Journal Writing Tip

Focusing on Language Suggest to students that they use their journals to express their anger or frustration at a situation, but that they leave those feelings behind when they draft their letters of complaint.

6.7 Writing a Letter of Complaint   **287**

287

Teach

Using the Model

Ask students why they think the writer included the first sentence in the student model. (It lets the reader know she is a long-time subscriber and should be taken seriously.) Students should note the writer's complaint. (She has not received two issues of a magazine.) They should also note the writer's proposed solution. (The company should deliver the missing issues along with the next issue.) **L2**

Posing Solutions

Ask students to suggest possible solutions for each of the following complaints: a pair of shoes that wore out after only a month; a magazine subscription that did not arrive for two months; a video arcade that has no place for locking bikes. **L1**

Additional Resources

Fine Art Transparencies, 26–30

Writing Process Transparencies, 20–22B

Writing Across the Curriculum, p. 21

Cooperative Learning Activities, pp. 31–36

Thinking and Study Skills, pp. 1, 4, 13–14, 17

Sentence-Combining Practice, pp. 33–35

Listening and Speaking Activities, p. 22

Composition Practice, p. 51

Persuasive Writing

Grammar Tip

As you edit your letter, check that verb tenses agree with special subjects, such as business names. To review subject-verb agreement for special subjects, see Lesson 16.3, page 539.

Make a Good Impression

Think how you might react if you got a letter that was threatening, rude, or insulting. You probably wouldn't want to help the writer, even if some emotion was justified. When you write a letter of complaint, remember that your purpose is to use language that will persuade the reader to take action, not become angry. Notice the difference in language in the sentences below. How would you react to each approach?

Using Appropriate Language

Inappropriate	Appropriate
I waited all day in the rain for concert tickets only to find that you stupid people advertised more tickets than you really had. I'll never use your ticket service again!	Your ad led me to believe that there would be plenty of tickets for next week's concert. I suggest that in the future you correctly advertise the number of tickets available.

In any letter of complaint, your explanation of the problem and your proposed solution should be clear, easy to follow, and reasonable. The overall impression of your letter should be businesslike and organized, as it is in the model that follows.

Student Model

What is the writer's complaint?

For years I have been a content subscriber to *Outdoor Adventures,* but recently I have not been pleased. Neither the July nor the August issue has been delivered to my home.

What solution does she offer for the problem?

I am writing to request that you deliver these issues when you deliver the September edition of the magazine. Thank you for your time.

Laurie Hedlund, Springman Junior High School
Glenview, Illinois

288   Unit 6 Persuasive Writing

Cooperative Learning

Choosing Words

Point out that some words carry positive and negative connotations. After students have completed writing their letters of complaint, pair students and have them compare letters, underscoring each word that has an inappropriate connotation. Students can then list the words and work with their partners to look up the words in a dictionary to get a precise denotation and connotation. Partners can then find appropriate substitutes.

Persuasive Writing

Write a Complaint Letter

Have you, or has someone you know, ever bought an item, used it once, and found it didn't work the way you expected or that it broke entirely? Write a complaint letter to the manufacturer to express your disappointment.

PURPOSE To complain about a faulty product
AUDIENCE The manufacturer of the product
LENGTH 1–2 paragraphs

WRITING RUBRICS To write an effective complaint letter, you should

- state the problem, explain what happened, and propose a reasonable solution
- use language that will persuade, not anger
- make sure your argument is clear and easy to follow
- include the six parts of a business letter shown on page 287

Using Computers

When you write a letter of complaint to the government, you can increase its effect by sending it to more than one official. Use the merge function to insert the different names and addresses into the body of the letter.

Listening and Speaking

READING LETTERS ALOUD Exchange letters with a partner and take turns reading the letters aloud. Be dignified; don't overdramatize. Evaluate the effectiveness of the letters.

Grammar Link

Use correct capitalization and punctuation in letters.

Capitalize proper nouns and the first word of each sentence. Use commas in dates, between the names of cities and states, and in the closing of the letter.

*71 **U**nion **S**treet*
***T**empe, **AZ** 85281*
***O**ctober 17, 200-*

Write each item, correcting errors in capitalization and punctuation.

1. february 8, 1996
2. senator Della P. Storti
3. United states senate
4. Dirksen office building
5. washington, DC 20510
6. Dear senator storti:
7. Please give the enclosed paper your consideration.
8. I hope that your next vote on this issue is more in line with the views of your one-time supporters.
9.   Sincerely
10.   Calvina Booker

See Lesson 19.3, page 577; Lesson 19.4, page 579; and Lesson 20.4, page 595.

Assess

Evaluation Rubrics

Write a Complaint Letter

Use these criteria when evaluating your students' writing:

- Is there a statement of the problem?
- Is there an explanation of how it happened?
- Is there a proposed solution?
- Does it use businesslike language?

See also *Writing Assessment and Evaluation Rubrics*

Using Computers

Make sure that students understand how to use the merge function on their word processor.

Listening and Speaking

Encourage students to speak clearly and appropriately, using effective volume, pitch, and tone for the setting.

Reteaching

📁 *Composition Reteaching*, p. 51

Enrichment

📁 *Composition Enrichment*, p. 51

Close

Ask students to identify a school or community problem that concerns them. For example, they might complain about the lack of basketball courts in parks or the selection of magazines in the school library. Suggest that they draft letters of complaint to the appropriate person or agency. Remind students to use polite, reasonable language and to suggest a possible solution to the problem. If students wish, encourage them to send their letters and to report back to the class on any response they receive.

Grammar Link

Answers

1. February 8, 1996
2. Senator Della P. Storti
3. United States Senate
4. Dirksen Office Building
5. Washington, DC 20510
6. Dear Senator Storti:
7. Please
8. correct *or* onetime
9. Sincerely,
10. (correct)

Focus

Lesson Overview

Objectives
- To understand the elements of an effective movie review
- To write a movie review

Skills
- evaluating a movie's plot, characters, acting, and visual effects; writing a convincing review

Critical Thinking
- recalling, analyzing, summarizing, identifying evidence

Listening and Speaking
- listening and speaking in class discussions

 Bellringer
Daily Language Activity

When students enter the classroom, have this assignment on the board: *Write about what convinced you to see the last movie you saw.*

Grammar Link to the Bellringer

Ask students why they might use a series of adjectives to describe a movie. Then ask how they would punctuate those adjectives. Have volunteers write samples on the board and check their use of commas.

See also *Daily Language Practice*

Motivating Activity

Invite students to share their response to the Bellringer activity. Then ask the following questions: Why do people read movie reviews? (to learn the reviewer's opinion of a movie and to decide whether to see it) When do you rely on movie reviews to help you make a decision about a movie? What movies have you seen that you think others would enjoy—or would be better off avoiding?

Persuasive Writing

WRITING ABOUT LITERATURE
Writing a Movie Review

An effective movie review gives readers enough information to help them decide whether they want to see the film.

"The best movie of the summer!" "I give it four stars!" "A real nail biter. Don't miss this movie!" Some movie reviews make you feel that you have to see the film. Others make you think that you shouldn't bother.

As you read the review that follows, think about how Kimberly Knapp tries to convince you to share her opinion.

Student Model

I enjoyed the movie *Honey, I Shrunk the Kids.* The special effects were very entertaining, especially the scene where the miniature kids rode on insects. I also thought the characters were realistic. In the beginning of the movie, the kids fought with each other. They behaved like real brothers and sisters. The movie had a lesson because at the end the kids had learned to get along with each other.

Kimberly Knapp, Hope Lutheran School
Chicago, Illinois

> Does the reviewer convince you that the movie is worth seeing? Why or why not?

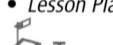

290 Unit 6 Persuasive Writing

Resource Manager

📁 Planning Resources
- *Lesson Plans*

💻 Transparencies
- *Bellringer*
- *Daily Language Practice*
- *Fine Art* 26–30
- *Two-Minute Skill Drill*
- *Writing Process* 20–22B

📁 Other Print Resources
- *Composition Enrichment,* p. 52
- *Composition Practice,* p. 52
- *Composition Reteaching,* p. 52
- *Cooperative Learning Activities,* pp. 31–36
- *Listening and Speaking Activities,* p. 22

- *Sentence-Combining Practice,* pp. 33–35
- *Thinking and Study Skills,* pp. 3, 9, 13, 18–19
- *Writing Across the Curriculum*
- *Writing Assessment and Evaluation Rubrics*

Weigh the Elements

A good movie review supports the writer's opinion with judgments about the various elements that make up the movie. (See the chart at right.) When you review a film, first note your overall reaction to it. Then jot down specific examples of characters, plot, acting, and effects that make you feel as you do. Such notes might look like this:

- The characters of the boy and girl were realistic, but the father's actions and words made him cartoonish.
- The plot was complicated, but good characters and smooth writing made it easy to follow.
- The acting was overdone at times. The actors seemed to be trying too hard to show the audience how good they are.
- The visual effects were stunning and realistic. During the stunt flying, I felt as though I were in the plane.
- The background music was pretty boring, but the concert segments were great.

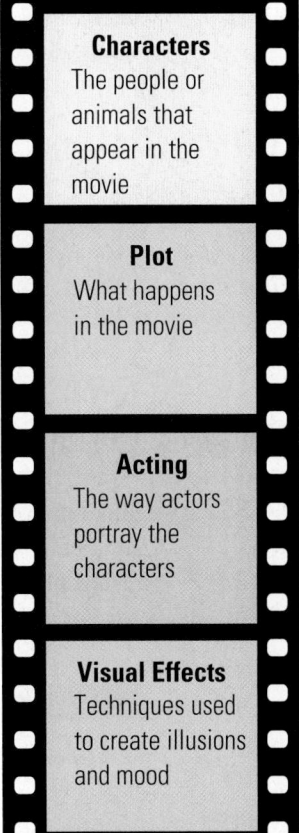

Characters
The people or animals that appear in the movie

Plot
What happens in the movie

Acting
The way actors portray the characters

Visual Effects
Techniques used to create illusions and mood

TIME

For more about the writing process, see **TIME** *Facing the Blank Page*, pp. 97–107.

Journal Writing

Think of a movie you have seen recently that has special effects. In your journal describe how these effects influenced your opinion of the movie.

Real-World Connection

Identifying an Argument

Ask students to read or listen to a movie review. Have them identify the argument presented by the writer or speaker. Students should then identify the evidence used to support the writer's or speaker's judgment of the movie.

6.8

Persuasive Writing

Teach

Using the Model

Draw students' attention to the movie review on page 290. Ask students to identify the specific elements of the movie that the reviewer chooses to evaluate. (special effects, characters) Point out how the reviewer provides examples to support each point she makes. **L2**

Cooperative Learning

Use the Jigsaw strategy to help students develop checklists they can use in reviewing films. Divide the class into groups of four. Each group member should choose one of the four elements listed in the filmstrip frames. Groups should then meet to discuss and establish a checklist of questions to ask about the film element they have chosen. Students should then return to their original groups to share the results and to devise a single checklist for preparing a film review. **L2**

Two-Minute Skill Drill

Ask students how to set off the title of a movie. (When typing on a computer, use italic type; when handwriting or using a conventional typewriter, underscore the title.)

See also Two-Minute Skill Drill Transparency 6.8

Journal Writing Tip

Establishing and Assessing Criteria As a class, discuss criteria for evaluating special effects. (Possible criteria include the following: Do the special effects create believable illusions? Are they imaginative? Are they exciting? Do they help advance the story?)

Teach

Using the Model

You may need to explain some of the vocabulary used in the review, including "simplistic," "stock," "damsel," "rogue," "sparse," and "marred." Ask students who have seen *Star Wars* whether they agree or disagree with the review. Ask others whether they would want to see the movie after reading this review. Ask students to identify the elements the reviewer chooses to focus on (plot, characters, visual effects). Students should note the reviewer's opinion of the film. (She likes the film but feels that some elements, such as the plot and characters, are weak.) Students also should note the words the reviewer uses to convey her opinion. (Her persuasive words include "simplistic," "shallow," "cartoonish," "awkward," "sparse," "weak," "well done," and "overwhelming.") **L2**

Additional Resources

Fine Art Transparencies, 26–30

Writing Process Transparencies, 20–22B

Writing Across the Curriculum, p. 24

Cooperative Learning Activities, pp. 31–36

Thinking and Study Skills, pp. 3, 9, 13, 18–19

Sentence-Combining Practice, pp. 33–35

Listening and Speaking Activities, p. 22

Composition Practice, p. 52

Persuasive Writing

Drafting Tip

As you draft your review, refer to the notes you took on the movie. They will help you keep the movie fresh in your mind.

Reveal Your Opinion

A reviewer may not always directly state an opinion about a film. Often that opinion is implied, or suggested, by the words and details the reviewer uses. Read the following passage from a review of director George Lucas's movie *Star Wars.*

What does the reviewer think of the film?

What words does the reviewer use to convince you of her opinion?

Literature Model

Lucas's talents lie more in the realm of film technique than film writing. The plot is a simplistic "shoot-em-up" war story of good *versus* evil, with stock characters such as the innocent hero, the beautiful damsel in distress, and the rogue with the heart of gold. The characters are shallow and always overshadowed by the technical aspects of the film and their dialogue is cartoonish and awkward. Although the sparse story line, weak characters, and lack of strong dialogue are obvious flaws, the visual effects are well done and so overwhelming that the impact of the film as a whole is not marred.

Ruth L. Hirayama,
"Star Wars," *Magill's Survey of Cinema*

292 Unit 6 Persuasive Writing

MEETING INDIVIDUAL NEEDS English Language Learners

Making Visual Presentations

Let students learning English present their "thumbs-up" movie reviews in the form of posters. Students might use pictures from magazines or make drawings of their own and include written information and symbols to express their evaluation of the movie. Encourage students to display their posters in the classroom.

Write a Review

Think of a movie you have seen recently. Write a review of it for your school newspaper. State your opinion clearly, and back it up with convincing evidence.

PURPOSE To express and support an opinion about a movie

AUDIENCE Readers of school newspaper

LENGTH 1–2 paragraphs

WRITING RUBRICS To write a convincing review, you should

- include enough background information for readers to understand what the movie is about
- use words that reveal your opinion rather than state it directly
- provide evidence that supports your opinion
- comments on the four elements shown on page 291

Listening and Speaking

COOPERATIVE LEARNING In a group of four students, choose a movie that you have all seen. Brainstorm to come up with comments on characters, plot, acting, and effects. Then discuss your group's overall opinion. Combine the group's thoughts into a well-organized oral review of the movie as a whole. Share your review with other groups.

Grammar Link

Use commas to separate items in a series.

If there are three or more items in a series, use a comma after each item except the last.

Although the sparse story line, weak characters, and lack of strong dialogue are obvious flaws . . .

Write each sentence, adding commas where necessary.

1. I thought this movie was a positive romantic charming and believable tale of friendship loyalty and resourcefulness.
2. I have to admit that the settings costumes and props were somewhat disappointing.
3. The director the actors and the producers are inexperienced, but perhaps they will improve.

See Lesson 20.2, page 591.

Viewing and Representing

MAKE A COLLAGE Check in newspapers or on the Internet to find photos from either of the movies you reviewed. Make a collage of the photos. Include comments about each one.

Persuasive Writing

Assess

Evaluation Rubrics

Write a Review

Use these criteria when evaluating your students' writing:

- Is there an opinion statement?
- Does it include supporting evidence?
- Is there an evaluation of at least two of the following elements: characters, plot, acting, visual effects?
- Does it have background information?
- Does it use persuasive language?

See also *Writing Assessment and Evaluation Rubrics*

Listening and Speaking

Evaluate the review on the following:

- Does the review contain an opinion statement?
- Are the four elements evaluated?
- Have students included enough information for readers to decide whether they want to see the movie?

Viewing and Representing

Make sure that comments complement and extend the meanings of the photos.

Reteaching

📁 *Composition Reteaching*, p. 52

Enrichment

📁 *Composition Enrichment*, p. 52

Close

Invite students to have a panel discussion of a movie that most of the class have seen. Appoint a student moderator to keep the panel on task and to make sure that all elements of a movie review are discussed.

Grammar Link

Answers

1. I thought this movie was a positive, romantic, charming, and believable tale of friendship, loyalty, and resourcefulness.
2. I have to admit that the settings, costumes, and props were somewhat disappointing.
3. The director, the actors, and the producers are inexperienced, but perhaps they will improve in future productions.

Focus

Lesson Overview

Objectives

- To understand the stages of the writing process
- To use persuasive writing techniques in a short persuasive piece

Skills

- using the five stages of the writing process: prewriting, drafting, revising, editing, and presenting

Critical Thinking

- recalling; synthesizing; defining and clarifying; decision making

Listening and Speaking

- taking notes; discussing; informal speaking

Bellringer
Daily Language Activity

When students enter the classroom, have this assignment on the board: *List the words that come to mind when you see the word American.*

Grammar Link to the Bellringer

Write the word *American* on the board. Have students identify the two possessive pronouns that could be used to replace *American* in a given sentence. (*his* or *her*)

See also *Daily Language Practice*

Motivating Activity

Ask students what advice they would give to someone trying to develop a piece of persuasive writing on something uniquely American. (Answers will vary but should reflect experience gained during the course of the unit.) What are some pitfalls to avoid? What are some techniques to try?

Writing Process in Action

Persuasive Writing

Persuasive Writing

In the preceding lessons you've learned about forming an opinion and then gathering evidence to support it. You've also practiced developing and polishing an argument. Now it's time to make use of what you learned. In this lesson you will have the opportunity to argue for the preservation of something important—something that you believe is uniquely and irreplaceably American.

WRITING Online

Visit the *Writer's Choice* Web site at **writerschoice. glencoe.com** for additional writing prompts.

Assignment

Context	Your class is planning to publish one issue of <u>This Is America</u>, a magazine devoted to saving institutions, traditions, and culture that are unique and irreplaceable to the fabric that is America.
Purpose	To convince others through powerful persuasive writing to save something uniquely American
Audience	The readers of <u>This Is America</u>, your classmates, and teacher
Length	3–4 paragraphs

The following pages can help you plan and write your persuasive piece. Read through them, and then refer to them as you need to. But don't be tied down by them. You're in charge of your own writing process.

Resource Manager

**Planning Resources**
- *Lesson Plans*

**Transparencies**
- *Bellringer*
- *Daily Language Practice*
- *Writing Process* 20–22B

Other Print Resources
- *Composition Enrichment,* p. 53
- *Composition Practice,* p. 53
- *Composition Reteaching,* p. 53

- *Grammar Workbook,* Lessons 69–71
- *Sentence-Combining Practice,* pp. 33–35
- *Thinking and Study Skills,* pp. 5, 11, 14–19
- *Writing Assessment and Evaluation Rubrics*

Software
- *Writer's Assistant*

Web Sites
- *writerschoice.glencoe.com*
- *lit.glencoe.com*

Writing Process in Action

Prewriting

Try to find a topic that means something to you—one you can support with evidence. The chart on page 267 can help you test topic ideas. You can also use the options at the right.

Lay out your position and gather evidence. Review the chart on page 268 and review pages 270–272.

Option A
Freewrite for ideas.

Option B
Brainstorm with a peer reviewer.

Option C
Explore your journal.

Drafting

First, review pages 62–65. Then let your writing flow to get your argument down on paper. You can go back and fix any problems later.

Use examples to support your argument. In the model below, Kaufman uses a story about herself in her argument about preserving public libraries.

> My dream of running for the Hawks next year. Not if the high school can't pay for sports. Photos of Hawk teams since the forties: the same jerseys. What's more American than high school sports?

Literature Model

I remember myself as a 12-year-old, newly arrived from Russia, groping toward the mastery of the English language in my neighborhood library. Guided by no reading lists, informed by no book reviews, I had no use for the card catalogue, since I worked each shelf alphabetically, burrowing my way from one end of the stacks to the other, relentless as a mole. I read by trial and error, through trash and treasure; like a true addict, I was interested not so much in quality as in getting the stuff.

Bel Kaufman, "The Liberry"

Drafting Tip

For more information about structuring a persuasive argument, see Lesson 6.4, pages 274–277.

Teach

Prewriting

Supporting a Topic with Evidence

Help students learn how to use library resources to find evidence for their position. Also suggest that they use firsthand evidence from an interview with someone experienced in the topic they are writing about. A quote from such a source can serve as strong evidence that will stay in the reader's mind. **L2**

Drafting

Finding a Place to Begin

Allow students to identify, through small group discussion, the easiest part of their topic to present. (For many students, this will be their own opinion.) Remind students to begin with the easiest part. **L1**

Teach

Revising

Peer Editing

Students can work in writing conferences with peer editors before they revise their writing. You may want to duplicate the Peer Response forms in *Writing Assessment and Evaluation Rubrics*. Suggest that peer editors read over their comments as if they were receiving them, to make sure the comments are ones they would find helpful. **L2**

Editing/Proofreading

Peer Editing

After students have edited their own work, have them edit another student's writing. Remind them to refer to the Editing/Proofreading Checklist on the student page. **L2**

Publishing/Presenting

Before students present their persuasive writing, discuss how to prepare their papers for publication. Emphasize the importance of the final draft and that it must be neatly done.

Additional Resources

- *Writing Process Transparencies, 20–22B*
- *Thinking and Study Skills, pp. 5, 11, 14–19*
- *Sentence-Combining Practice, pp. 33–35*
- *Composition Practice, p. 53*
- *Grammar Workbook, Lessons 68–71*

Journal Writing Tip

Comparing and Contrasting Have students compare their experience practicing persuasive writing and practicing other forms of writing.

Revising

To begin revising, read over your draft to make sure that what you have written fits your purpose and your audience. Then have a **writing conference.** Read your draft to a partner or a small group, or receive feedback from your teacher. Use your audience's reactions to help you evaluate your work so far. The questions below can help you and your listeners.

Question A
Is my position stated clearly?

Question B
Does the introduction grab attention?

Question C
Is my evidence in the best and most persuasive order?

The pictures appear in the *polished glass* showcases in front of the auditorium. They show the Ticu City -in the same staged pose, in the same crimson and Hawks track team over more than sixty black jerseys— seasons. Now there might not be any more to record seasons, can name the faces photographed in every season ~~I have known everyone on the team~~ since my sister ran, the year I entered grade school. That's when I decided to become a running Hawk. My dream was to come true next year, but then the school budget talks began.

Enrichment and Extension

Follow-up Ideas

- Set aside time for students to celebrate the conclusion of their writing projects. Encourage them to share their finished pieces.
- Retain photocopies if students send their work out of the classroom.

Extending Persuasive Writing

- Brainstorm with students ways they can use their expertise in persuasive writing in other contexts, such as persuading others to adopt their point of view on a political or social issue.

Persuasive Writing

Editing/Proofreading

Now you are ready to edit your persuasive piece. First, **proofread** your writing for errors in spelling, grammar, punctuation, and usage. Then use pages 78–81, especially the editing checklist on page 79, as a step-by-step guide to editing your writing. Refer also to the editing checklist on this page. This will save you both time and effort.

Finally, think about the language of your persuasive piece. Have you used the most persuasive language and chosen the most effective words? Will your words grab readers' attention and hold it? Look at page 280 for suggestions on this aspect of your editing.

Publishing/Presenting

What would *This Is America* look like if your class were to put out an edition? Exchange papers with your classmates to see the range of topics and forms your classmates used to express their ideas of what should be preserved to keep America unique.

Finally, evaluate your work. Is there a means of presenting it that you haven't considered? Maybe you wrote a letter that you could publish in a local newspaper. Perhaps you wrote an essay that could find a home in a teen magazine. Whatever you do, be sure to consider including this piece in your portfolio.

Editing/Proofreading Checklist

1. Have I used correct pronoun forms in compound constructions?
2. Have I used the forms of _good_ and _bad_ correctly?
3. Have I used apostrophes correctly?
4. Have I used standard spelling and capitalization?
5. Have I used homophones correctly?

Proofreading Tip

Check for the correct use of commas with words, phrases, or clauses in a series. For more information, see pages 591–592.

Journal Writing

Reflect on your writing process experience. Answer these questions in your journal: What do you like best about your persuasive writing? What was the hardest part of writing it? What did you learn in your writing conference? What new things have you learned as a writer?

Assess

Evaluation Rubrics

Use the following questions to evaluate students' finished writing.

- Does the piece begin with an attention-getting introduction?
- Do paragraphs focus on saving something that is uniquely American?
- Does the writer clearly state his or her opinion?
- Does the writer support his or her opinion with evidence?
- Does the writer present the evidence in the most persuasive order?
- Does the writer use persuasive language effectively?

See also *Writing Assessment and Evaluation Rubrics*

Reteaching

📁 *Composition Reteaching,* p. 53

Enrichment

📁 *Composition Enrichment,* p. 53

Close

Ask students to recall pieces of their classmates' persuasive writing that they found particularly effective. What made the pieces persuasive?

Writing Process in Action **297**

Listening and Speaking

Role-playing

Have one group of students role-play as the members of a city council with a limited budget, struggling to decide where to make cutbacks in city services. Other students can play the roles of citizens testifying at a council hearing on the future of the public library. After the arguments have been presented, ask the council to discuss the issue and vote on it.

About the Author

Bel Kaufman spent twenty years as a teacher in New York City schools. She drew on her experiences to write *Up the Down Staircase* (1964), a popular novel about a young, inexperienced teacher in an urban high school. Her writing has also appeared in many magazines and newspapers. "The Liberry" first appeared in the *New York Times.*

Focus

Lesson Overview

Objectives

- To evaluate the effectiveness of a published piece of persuasive writing
- To write a persuasive letter to the editor

Skills

- connecting; clarifying

Critical Thinking

- inferring; analyzing

Listening and Speaking

- discussing

Bellringer
Daily Language Activity

When students enter the classroom, have this assignment on the board: *Write a brief paragraph in which you try to persuade a friend to go to the library with you after school.*

See also *Daily Language Practice*

Motivating Activity

Ask volunteers to read aloud the paragraphs they wrote in the Bellringer activity. As they read the paragraphs, have the class identify any persuasive words they hear. List these words on the board.

UNIT 6

Literature Model

Persuasive Writing

The Liberry

by Bel Kaufman

In this essay best-selling novelist Bel Kaufman argues persuasively for the importance of libraries. As you read, notice the tactics Kaufman uses to persuade her readers. Then try the activities in Linking Writing and Literature on page 302.

Resource Manager

📁 Planning Resources
- *Lesson Plans*

📇 Transparencies
- *Bellringer*
- *Daily Language Practice*
- *Fine Art 26–30*

📁 Other Print Resources
- *Listening and Speaking Activities, p. 22*
- *Thinking and Study Skills, pp. 13, 14, 20*
- *Writing Assessment and Evaluation Rubrics*

💻 Web Sites
- *writerschoice.glencoe.com*
- *lit.glencoe.com*

Literature Model

Persuasive Writing

A small boy in one of William Saroyan's stories finds himself in the public library for the first time. He looks around in awe: "All them books," he says, "and something written in each one!"

I remember myself as a 12-year-old, newly arrived from Russia, groping toward the mastery of the English language in my neighborhood library. Guided by no reading lists, informed by no book reviews, I had no use for the card catalogue, since I worked each shelf alphabetically, burrowing my way from one end of the stacks to the other, relentless as a mole. I read by trial and error, through trash and treasure; like a true addict, I was interested not so much in quality as in getting the stuff.

Sometimes I would stumble upon a book that was special; a book unrequired, unrecommended, unspoiled by teacher-imposed chores—"Name 3 . . . Answer the following . . ."—a book to be read for sheer pleasure.

Where else was it allowed, even encouraged, to thumb through a book, to linger on a page without being shooed away from handling the merchandise? This was merchandise to be handled. I was not fooled by the stiff, impassive maroon and dark-green library bindings; I nosed out the good ones. If the pages were worn and dog-eared, if the card tucked into its paper pocket inside the cover was stamped with lots of dates, I knew I had a winner.

Those dates linked me to the anonymous fellowship of other readers whose hands had turned the pages I was turning, who sometimes left penciled clues in the margins: a philosophic "How True!"—a succinct[1] "Stinks."

Here, within walls built book by solid book, we sat in silent kinship, the only sounds shuffling of feet, scraping of chairs, an occasional loud whisper, and the librarian's stern "Shhh!"

The librarian was always there, unobtrusive[2] and omniscient, ready for any question: Where to find a book about Eskimos? A history of submarines? A best-selling novel?—unruffled even by a request I once overheard in the children's section: "Have you got a book for an eight-year-old with tonsils?"

---

[1] **succinct** (sək singkt′) clearly and briefly stated
[2] **unobtrusive** (un əb trōō′ siv) not calling attention to oneself

Teach

Critical Thinking

Infer Ask: "How do you think the author feels about books and public libraries? How does she let readers know her feelings?" *(She seems to enjoy reading books and going to the library. She relates favorite moments she spent in the library as a 12-year-old newly arrived from Russia.)*

Active Reading Strategies

Connect Tell students that selections become more interesting and relevant when readers connect them to their own lives. Say: "The author writes of her personal experiences with and feelings for a library. Think about your own feelings about and experiences in libraries. Then compare your ideas with the author's. How are they similar or different?" *(Sample answer: Like Bel Kaufman, I was bowled over when I first saw all the books in my local library. I thought there had to be hundreds of books I'd like to read in there.)*

Active Reading Strategies

Clarify

Tell students that readers occasionally come across passages that confuse them. Explain that they should stop and clear up what confuses them before they read on. Give students the following tips to help them clarify confusing or difficult texts.

- Reread a confusing section more slowly.
- Look up words you don't know, or try to figure out their meanings from the context (the other words surrounding the unknown word).
- Ask questions about what you don't understand.
- Read on and see whether further information helps you.

Practice After students read this page, ask them to write a question about a confusing part. Then have them work with a partner to employ one of the strategies to clarify the passage. Call on volunteers to explain their strategies to the class.

Teach

Literary Elements

Genre Ask students to identify what kind of essay this is. *(persuasive essay)* Then ask: "What persuasive point is the author making? At what point does her persuasive purpose become clear?" *(The author is trying to persuade readers that public libraries deserve to be well funded. Her purpose becomes clear beginning with the first paragraph on page 300 when she offers facts about shrinking library budgets and services.)*

Viewing the Art

Jacob Lawrence, *The Library*, 1960

The art of Jacob Lawrence (1917–2000) is narrative and focuses on the American and African American experiences. He has experimented with many types of creative patterns in art, especially those depicting people and neighborhood scenes. *The Library* measures 24 inches by 30 inches and is a tempera painting on fiberboard. It hangs in the National Museum of American Art, Smithsonian Institution, Washington, D.C.

Literature Model

Persuasive Writing

Jacob Lawrence, *The Library*, 1960

I am remembering this because today the public libraries are becoming less and less available to the people who need them most. Already shut part of the time, their hours reduced by 50 percent in the last five years, their budgets further curtailed as of July 1, and still threatened with continued cuts in staff and services, the public libraries have suffered more in the city's financial squeeze than any other major public-service agencies.

The first priority of our nation, according to former New York State Commissioner of Education, James E. Allen, is the right to read. Educators are inundating our schools with

300 Unit 6 Persuasive Writing

Critical Thinking

Analyze

On the board, write these four forms of evidence that persuasive writers often use to support their arguments: (1) anecdotes, (2) facts and statistics, (3) quotes from experts, (4) comparisons. Then tell students that to understand a persuasive essay, they should analyze what kinds of evidence the author presents.

Practice Divide students into four groups and tell each group to find an example of one of the four kinds of evi-

dence listed on the board. Invite students to analyze the essay from the beginning to the end of page 301. Then have each group share their information with the class. *(Sample responses: (1) The essay opens with an anecdote on page 299. (2) A statistic is that library hours have been "reduced by 50 percent." (3) The New York State Commissioner of Education is quoted. (4) A comparison shows that public libraries have suffered more than other public agencies.)*

massive surveys, innovative techniques and expensive gimmicks to combat illiteracy and improve the reading skills of our children—at the same time that our public libraries are gradually closing their doors.

What are our priorities? Name 3.

It seems to me that especially now, when there are so many people in our city whose language is not English, whose homes are barren of books, who are daily seduced by clamorous offers of instant diversion, especially now we must hold on to something that will endure when the movie is over, the television set broken, the class dismissed for the last time.

For many, the public library is the only quiet place in an unquiet world; a refuge from the violence and ugliness outside; the only space available

for privacy of work or thought. For many it is the only exposure to books waiting on open shelves to be taken home, free of charge.

As a former student put it:

> . . . especially now we must hold on to something that will endure when the movie is over . . .

"In a liberry it's hard to avoid reading."

When I taught English in high school, I used to ask my students to bring a library card to class, on the chance that if they had one they might use it. One boy brought in his aunt's. "Aw, I ain't gonna *use* it," he cheerfully assured me, "I just brought it to *show* you!"

Still—some did make use of their cards, if only because they were *there*. Some enter the library today because it is *there*. Inside are all them books, and something written in each one. How sad for our city if the sign on the door should say CLOSED.

Teach

Critical Thinking

Analyze Explain that persuasive writers use reasoning and logic to convince readers of their opinions. Have students analyze page 301 to find an example of the author's reasoning. Ask: "Is her reasoning persuasive? Why or why not?" *(Sample response: The author reasons that libraries and books are more important now than ever because there are many people in the city who don't speak English and because the world is louder and busier than ever and in need of more quiet places. These are persuasive arguments.)*

Active Reading Strategies

Clarify Invite students to identify passages that they found confusing at first. Then ask them what strategies they used to clarify the meaning.

Active Reading Strategies

Connect Encourage students to connect the theme of the essay to their own lives. Ask: "What would be the impact on your life if the public library in town were to reduce its hours?" *(Sample response: It would be more difficult to use the resources in the library for schoolwork, such as research papers and reports.)*

Additional Resources

Fine Art Transparencies, 26–30
Listening and Speaking Activities, p. 22
Thinking and Study Skills, pp. 13, 14, 20

6+1 Trait® Writing

Organization

Explain to students that organization is the internal structure of a piece of writing. When the organization is strong, readers can easily follow what the writer is saying and where the writer is going. Provide students with these tips for organizing their writing:

• Choose an effective means of organization, such as chronological order, cause and effect, or compare and contrast.

• Provide an inviting introduction that draws readers in

and a satisfying conclusion that gives the piece closure.

• Connect ideas and paragraphs with helpful transitions.

Practice Have students work in pairs to analyze the structure of "The Liberry." Ask them to write three sentences describing the content of each of the following: the introduction, the body of the piece, and the conclusion. Then ask them to identify one transition that helped them clearly see the connection between two of Kaufman's ideas.

Linking Writing and Literature

Assess

Evaluation Rubrics

Talk About Reading

Possible responses to the questions:

1. Students may connect to Kaufman's appreciation of the library. The specifics of students' experiences may differ from Kaufman's, given the increasing availability in libraries of technological resources such as computers, Internet access, CD-ROMs, and DVDs.
2. Kaufman believes that public libraries play an important role in educating and entertaining citizens. She would like public libraries to receive more funding.
3. Students may say that the anecdote is an effective introduction because the story captures readers' attention and alerts them to the main idea—that libraries are important.
4. Students may cite Kaufman's use of compelling evidence, including an anecdote, statistics, and logical reasoning.

Write About Reading

The letter to the editor should do the following:

- Identify the student's opinion of the local library
- suggest how the library can be improved or tell why it functions well
- provide a strong introduction and conclusion
- provide transitions to smoothly connect ideas.

Close

Students can work in small groups to examine Bel Kaufman's essay as an example of persuasive writing. Ask groups to list the evidence the author presents to support her position. Then have students identify each piece of evidence as *fact, statistic, example, opinion,* or *reason.* Groups can share their lists with each other.

Persuasive Writing

Linking Writing and Literature

Collect Your Thoughts

In your own words, write what opinion Kaufman expresses about libraries in her persuasive essay. Then write down an opinion you have about your own local library.

Talk About Reading

Talk with other students about "The Liberry." Assign a group leader to keep everyone focused and a group secretary to take notes. Then use the questions below to guide your conversation.

1. **Connect to Your Life** How do your experiences in the library relate to the experiences that Kaufman tells about in her introduction? Does her essay make you think any differently about your own library?
2. **Critical Thinking: Analyze** What is the main point that Kaufman makes in her persuasive essay? What would she like to see happen as a result of her essay?
3. **6+1 Trait®: Organization** How effective do you think it is for Kaufman to open her essay with a long anecdote?
4. **Connect to Your Writing** What did this essay teach you about making a solid argument?

Write About Reading

Letter to the Editor Write a letter to the editor of your town or school newspaper. In your letter, give your opinion about your local library. Either suggest ways that the library could be improved or describe ways in which the library functions well.

Focus on Organization Your letter to the editor will be more effective if it is well organized. You might want to start with a personal anecdote, as Kaufman did in "The Liberry." Be sure to finish with a strong conclusion. When you edit your letter, see if you can add transitions that connect your ideas more smoothly.

For more information on organization and the 6+1 Trait® model, see **Writing and Research Handbook,** pages 822–824.

6+1 Trait® is a registered trademark of Northwest Regional Educational Laboratory, which does not endorse this product.

302 Unit 6 Persuasive Writing

Cultural Connections

Appreciating Public Libraries

Point out the role the library played for Kaufman as a young immigrant to the United States. *(It helped Kaufman expand her understanding of a new language; it exposed her to aspects of a new culture.)* In a multicultural nation, public libraries offer a world of books in English, as well as in other languages.

UNIT 6 Review

Persuasive Writing

Reflecting on the Unit

Summarize what you learned in this unit by answering the following questions.

1. What is the purpose of persuasive writing?
2. How can you support an argument?
3. In persuasive writing where is the opinion usually stated?
4. What are some good techniques for exploring the pros and cons of a topic?
5. What effect does your purpose and audience have on the way you develop your argument?

Adding to Your Portfolio

CHOOSE A SELECTION FOR YOUR PORTFOLIO Look over the writing you did for this unit. Choose a piece of writing for your portfolio. The writing you choose should show one or more of the following:

- an opinion stated in a clear topic sentence
- different types of evidence to support an opinion
- evidence presented in an effective order
- precise word choice

REFLECT ON YOUR CHOICE Attach a note to the piece you chose, explaining briefly why you chose it and what you learned from writing it.

SET GOALS How can you improve your writing? What skill will you focus on the next time you write?

Writing Across the Curriculum

MAKE A SCIENCE CONNECTION Scientists often use facts to persuade. For example, a scientist might argue that, based on evidence of global warming, certain practices should be changed. Think of an environmental, health, or other science-related topic that interests you. Follow the writing process outlined in this unit to write an essay that persuades people to take some action on this issue.

Review **303**

Review

Reflecting on the Unit

You may have students respond to the summary questions in writing or through discussion.

Adding to Your Portfolio

Have students quickly read through all the pieces they produced during the unit and rank them from most persuasive to least persuasive. Then they can carefully read the most persuasive pieces before making the final selection.

Portfolio Evaluation

If you grade the portfolio selections, you may want to award two marks—one each for content and form. Explain your assessment criteria before students make their selections.

Commend
- experimentation with creative prewriting techniques.
- clear, concise writing in which the main idea, audience, and purpose are evident.
- successful revisions.
- work that shows a flair for language.

Writing Across the Curriculum

Remind students to state their opinion clearly by using an attention-getting introduction; strong, relevant evidence; and persuasive language.

✔ ASSESSMENT OPTIONS

📁 *Tests with Answer Key and Rubrics*
Unit 6 Choice A Test, p. 21
Unit 6 Choice B Test, p. 22
Unit 6 Composition Objective Test, pp. 23–24

💾 *Testmaker*
Unit 6 Choice A Test
Unit 6 Choice B Test
Unit 6 Composition Objective Test

You may wish to administer one of these tests as a mastery test.

 MindJogger Videoquizzes

303

Troubleshooter

Viewing the Art

Tightrope walkers and trapeze artists risk their safety, even their lives, when they perform. A safety net, like the one in this photograph, catches a performer who has made a mistake or lost concentration.

Interpret and Analyze Use the following questions for discussion:
- Does this image suggest safety or danger? Explain.
- How does the placement of the performers in the central background of the image affect the viewer's perception of them? Do they seem large? small? Why?

Discussing the Quotation

Take note of Margaret Danner's use of the passive voice in the second half of this quotation. How does the passive voice affect our understanding of the speaker's approach to life?

Writing Prompt Ask students to write a paragraph or two comparing and contrasting the mood of the photograph with the mood of the quotation. Then have them connect the image and the quotation with their writing process. Ask them what might act as a safety net, catching their writing when it contains mistakes.

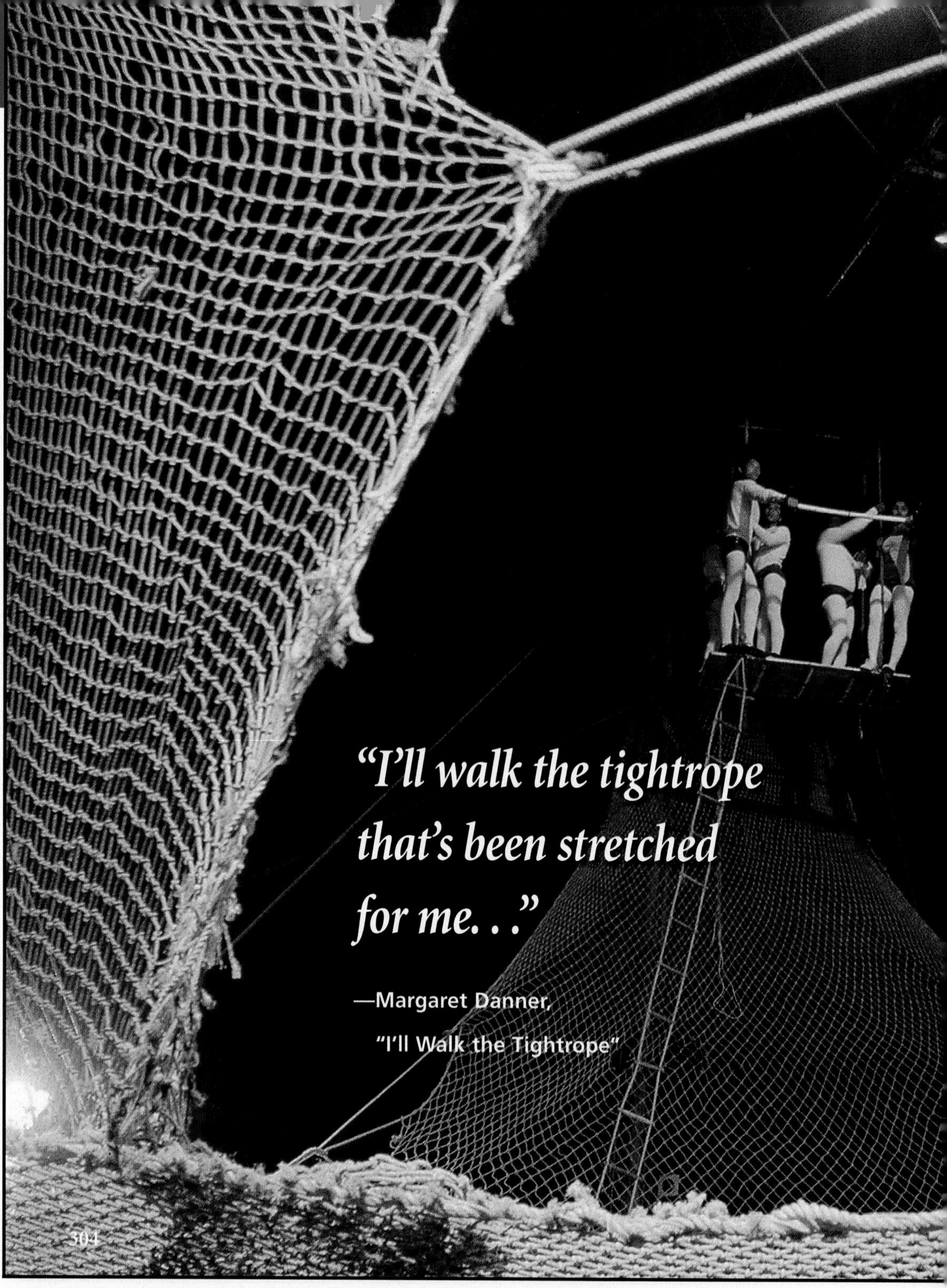

"I'll walk the tightrope that's been stretched for me..."

—Margaret Danner,

"I'll Walk the Tightrope"

Resource Manager

📂 Planning Resources
- *Lesson Plans*
- *Block Scheduling*

🗂 Transparencies
- *Bellringer*
- *Fine Art*
- *Writing Process*
- *Two-Minute Skill Drill*

📂 Other Print Resources
- *Grammar and Composition Handbook*
- *Grammar Workbook*
- *Sentence-Combining Practice*
- *Tests with Answer Key and Rubrics*

📺 Video
- *MindJogger Videoquizzes*

💾 Software
- *Presentation Plus!*
- *Testmaker*

🖥 Web Sites
- *writerschoice.glencoe.com*

UNIT 7

Troubleshooter

*U*se Troubleshooter to help you correct common errors in your writing.

Objectives

- To learn how to recognize common writing errors
- To correct common usage, grammar, and style errors in writing

✔ ASSESSMENT OPTIONS

📁 *Tests with Answer Key & Rubrics*
Unit 7

💾 *Testmaker*
Unit 7

You may wish to administer the Unit 7 Pretest at this point.

Key to Ability Levels

L1 Level 1 activities are within the basic ability range of students.

L2 Level 2 activities are within the ability range of average students.

L3 Level 3 activities are more challenging activities.

Using the Models

As students review their written work, have them mark errors using the abbreviations shown in the problem boxes throughout the Troubleshooter. These abbreviations can be especially useful when students share their writing during peer review.

Focus

Lesson Overview

Objective

- To recognize a sentence fragment that lacks a subject, a predicate, or both

Bellringer
Daily Language Activity

When students enter the classroom, have this assignment on the board: *Write these two examples on your paper. Circle the one that makes the most sense.*

Blew away in the strong wind.

Brenda's hat blew away in the strong wind.

Motivating Activity

Discuss students' answers to the Bellringer activity. Explain that the second example is a complete sentence because it contains both a subject and a predicate. Help students identify the subject and the predicate in the example.

Teach

Cross-Reference: Grammar

For instruction and practice on the material in Lesson 7.1, refer students to Lesson 8.2.

Troubleshooter

7.1 Sentence Fragment

Problem 1

Fragment that lacks a subject

frag Lucy bought a new tennis racket. Wanted to play today.

frag Oscar wrote a long essay. Read it in class.

frag My dog buried the bone. Dug it up later.

SOLUTION Add a subject to the fragment to make a complete sentence.

Lucy bought a new tennis racket. She wanted to play today.

Oscar wrote a long essay. He read it in class.

My dog buried the bone. He dug it up later.

Problem 2

Fragment that lacks a predicate

frag The beach is closed. The pool now too.

frag Spring is near. Flowers soon.

frag Marla wore a coat. That red woolen coat.

Resource Manager

📁 **Planning Resources**
- *Lesson Plans*

📠 **Transparencies**
- *Bellringer*
- *Two-Minute Skill Drill*

📁 **Other Print Resources**
- *Grammar Workbook*, Lesson 5

SOLUTION   Add a predicate to make the sentence complete.

The beach is closed. The pool is closed now too.

Spring is near. Flowers soon will bloom.

Marla wore a coat. That red coat was woolen.

Problem 3

Fragment that lacks both a subject and a predicate

frag   *Sophia ran very fast. During the relay race.*

frag   *My mother called me on the phone. At two o'clock.*

frag   *Ceara rode the sled. Down the hill.*

SOLUTION   Combine the fragment with another sentence.

Sophia ran very fast during the relay race.

My mother called me on the phone at two o'clock.

Ceara rode the sled down the hill.

If you need more help in avoiding sentence fragments, turn to Lesson 8.2, pages 359–360.

Teach

Two-Minute Skill Drill

Display these fragments for students and ask them to rewrite them as one complete sentence with a subject and a predicate:

Have gone away. Jack and Marta to Florida

See also *Two-Minute Skill Drill Transparency 7.1*

Additional Resources

Grammar Workbook, Lesson 5

Close

Write the following sentence on the board: *The car went by quickly.* Have students identify the subject and the predicate in the sentence. Ask them to explain why a sentence needs both a subject and a predicate to be complete.

Focus

Lesson Overview

Objective

• To recognize and revise different kinds of run-on sentences

🔔 Bellringer
Daily Language Activity

When students enter the classroom, have this assignment on the board: *Write an answer to this question: Why is it important to write sentences that make sense and are punctuated correctly?*

Motivating Activity

Write this sentence on the board: *The frightened horse ran across the pasture jumping the fence into the barn flew the horse!* Invite suggestions about what might be done to make the meaning of the sentence clearer.

Teach

⚓ Cross-Reference: Grammar

For instruction and practice on the material in Lesson 7.2, refer students to Lesson 8.6.

7.2 Run-on Sentence

Problem 1

Two main clauses separated by only a comma

> **run-on** *Janet's book was published, it has twelve chapters.*
> **run-on** *Jorge trained hard for the race, he expects to win.*

SOLUTION A Replace the comma with a period or other end mark. Begin the second sentence with a capital letter.

Janet's book was published. It has twelve chapters.

SOLUTION B Replace the comma between the main clauses with a semicolon.

Jorge trained hard for the race; he expects to win.

SOLUTION C Insert a coodinating conjunction after the comma.

Jorge trained hard for the race, and he expects to win.

Problem 2

Two main clauses with no punctuation between them

> **run-on** *Ravi went on vacation he will be home soon.*
> **run-on** *Stanley left the party early he drove home.*

Resource Manager

📂 **Planning Resources**
• *Lesson Plans*

📦 **Transparencies**
• *Bellringer*
• *Two-Minute Skill Drill*

📂 **Other Print Resources**
• *Grammar Workbook*, Lesson 42

SOLUTION A Separate the main clauses with a period or other end mark. Begin the second sentence with a capital letter.

Ravi went on vacation. He will be home soon.

SOLUTION B Insert a comma and a coordinating conjunction between the clauses.

Stanley left the party early, and he drove home.

Problem 3

Two main clauses with no comma before the coordinating conjunction

run-on *Vanna is going to Canada and her sister is going, too.*

run-on *Barry can leave today but he must return tomorrow.*

SOLUTION Insert a comma before the coordinating conjunction.

Vanna is going to Canada, and her sister is going, too.
Barry can leave today, but he must return tomorrow.

 *If you need more help in avoiding run-on sentences, turn to Lesson 8.6, pages 367–368.*

Troubleshooter

Teach

 Two-Minute Skill Drill

Write the following run-on sentence on the board:

Marlisa found a book on the school bus but she was not sure whose book it was and she brought it to the office.

Have students rewrite the sentence correctly.

See also *Two-Minute Skill Drill Transparency 7.2*

Additional Resources

Grammar Workbook, Lesson 42

Close

Ask a student to write a run-on sentence on the board. Then have the student select a classmate to rewrite the sentence correctly on the board. The second student can explain how he or she corrected the sentence. Repeat the activity several times.

Focus

Lesson Overview

Objective

- To recognize and avoid common errors in subject-verb agreement associated with various sentence constructions

Bellringer
Daily Language Activity

When students enter the classroom, have this assignment on the board: *Copy the following sentence on a piece of paper:*

Dogs sometimes bark at strange noises.

Then circle the subject and underline the verb in the sentence.

Motivating Activity

Say aloud a noun or pronoun, such as *boys, she, they,* or *planes.* Ask volunteers to supply a verb that agrees with the word you say and provides a complete idea. For example: *boys run; she laughs; they jump; planes fly.*

Teach

Cross-Reference: Usage

For instruction and practice on the material in Problem 1, refer students to Lesson 16.2.

Cross-Reference: Usage

For instruction and practice on the material in Problem 2, refer students to Lesson 16.2.

Troubleshooter

7.3 Lack of Subject-Verb Agreement

Problem 1

A subject that is separated from the verb by an intervening prepositional phrase

agr   One of the books (were) sold.

agr   The actors in the play (is) good.

SOLUTION   Ignore a prepositional phrase that comes between a subject and a verb. Make sure that the verb agrees with the subject of the sentence. The subject is never the object of the preposition.

One of the books was sold.

The actors in the play are good.

Problem 2

A sentence that begins with *here* or *there*

agr   There (is) the books you want.

agr   Here (come) the school bus.

agr   There (is) trees in your backyard.

310   Unit 7 Troubleshooter

Resource Manager

📂 **Planning Resources**
- *Lesson Plans*

📋 **Transparencies**
- *Bellringer*
- *Two-Minute Skill Drill*

📂 **Other Print Resources**
- *Grammar Workbook,* Lesson 50
- *Sentence-Combining Practice,* pp. 16–17

SOLUTION The subject is almost never *here* or *there*. In sentences that begin with *here* or *there*, look for the subject *after* the verb. The verb must agree with the subject.

There are the books you want.
Here comes the school bus.
There are trees in your backyard.

Teach

⇄ Cross-Reference: Usage

For instruction and practice on the material in Problem 3, refer students to Lesson 16.4.

Problem 3

An indefinite pronoun as the subject

agr Several of the paintings ⓘⓢ oils.
agr Each of the books (are) autographed.
agr All of my effort (were) worthwhile.

Some indefinite pronouns are singular; some are plural; and some can be either singular or plural, depending upon the noun they refer to.

SOLUTION Determine whether the indefinite pronoun is singular or plural and make the verb agree.

Several of the paintings are oils.
Each of the books is autographed.
All of my effort was worthwhile.

Unit 7.3 Lack of Subject-Verb Agreement **311**

Teach

⇄ Cross-Reference: Usage

For instruction and practice on the material in Problem 4, refer students to Lesson 16.5.

⇄ Cross-Reference: Usage

For instruction and practice on the material in Problem 5, refer students to Lesson 16.5.

Troubleshooter

Problem 4

A compound subject that is joined by *and*

agr The car and the bus (was) hit by lightning.

agr Bacon and eggs (were) served for breakfast.

SOLUTION A If the parts of the compound subject do not belong to one unit or if they refer to different people or things, use a plural verb.

The car and the bus were hit by lightning.

SOLUTION B If the parts of the compound subject belong to one unit or if both parts refer to the same person or thing, use a singular verb.

Bacon and eggs was served for breakfast.

Problem 5

A compound subject that is joined by *or* or *nor*

agr Either a dog or a cat (make) a good pet.

agr Neither raisins nor an apple (make) a complete meal.

agr Either Jim or his friends (is) bringing the cake.

SOLUTION Make the verb agree with the subject that is closer to it.

Either a dog or a cat makes a good pet.

Neither raisins nor an apple makes a complete meal.

Either Jim or his friends are bringing the cake.

 If you need more help with subject-verb agreement, turn to Lessons 16.1–16.5, pages 535–544.

Teach

 **Two-Minute Skill Drill**

Write these sentences on the board:

The twins Daren and Karen has two of everything.

There is the bicycles that they ride.

Have students rewrite the sentences so that the subjects and verbs agree.

See also *Two-Minute Skill Drill Transparency 7.3*

Additional Resources

📁 *Sentence-Combining Practice,* pp. 16–17

📖 *Grammar Workbook,* Lesson 50

Close

Have students write a sentence with a compound subject joined by *and, or,* or *nor.* Allow them to trade sentences with a partner and ask them to check for subject-verb agreement.

Focus

Lesson Overview

Objective

- To recognize and correct errors in verb tense or form, such as missing verb endings, improperly formed irregular verbs, and improperly used past and past participle forms

 Bellringer

Daily Language Activity

When students enter the classroom, have this assignment on the board: *Copy the following sentence and circle the verbs:*

I'm going to wake up early, eat a big breakfast, and take the long way to school.

Motivating Activity

Ask students to read the sentence from the Bellringer activity aloud. Then ask them to replace the first three words with the phrase *Yesterday I . . .* and read the sentence again. Do they feel that any of the other words need to be changed? Ask them to explain which ones need to be changed and why.

Teach

Cross-Reference: Grammar

For instruction and practice on the material in Lesson 7.4, refer students to Lessons 10.9 and 10.10.

Troubleshooter

7.4 Incorrect Verb Tense or Form

Problem 1

An incorrect or missing verb ending

> *tense* Have you ever (walk) all the way to school?
> *tense* Last Saturday we (pack) for our camping trip.
> *tense* Yesterday we (hope) for rain.

SOLUTION A Add *-ed* to a regular verb to form the past tense and the past participle.

Have you ever walked all the way to school?

Last Saturday we packed for our camping trip.

Yesterday we hoped for rain.

Problem 2

An improperly formed irregular verb

> *tense* The water in the pond (freezed) overnight.
> *tense* Elena has (bringed) the girls to the dance.
> *tense* I (teared) my coat on the nail.

Resource Manager

📁 Planning Resources
- *Lesson Plans*

📁 Other Print Resources
- *Grammar Workbook,* Lesson 16

Transparencies
- *Bellringer*
- *Two-Minute Skill Drill*

The past and past participle forms of irregular verbs vary. Memorize these forms, or look them up.

> **SOLUTION** Use the correct past or past participle form of an irregular verb.
>
> **The water in the pond froze overnight.**
>
> **Elena has brought the girls to the dance.**
>
> **I tore my coat on the nail.**

Troubleshooter

Problem 3

Confusion between the past form and the past participle

tense Diana had already (went) home when we arrived.

> **SOLUTION** Use the past participle form of an irregular verb, not the past form, when you use the auxiliary verb *have*.
>
> **Diana had already gone home when we arrived.**

If you need more help with correct verb forms, turn to Lessons 10.1–10.10, pages 399–418.

Teach

Two-Minute Skill Drill

Ask students to write the correct past tense forms of these irregular present tense verbs. Point out that none of them are formed by adding *-d* or *-ed*.

eat	give
sweep	keep
sleep	break
make	take
teach	fight
bring	catch

Encourage students to create sayings, rhymes, or stories that will help them remember some of the correct forms.

See also *Two-Minute Skill Drill Transparency 7.4*

Additional Resources

Grammar Workbook, Lesson 16

Close

Ask students to explain when they would use the past participle form of a verb in their writing. Point out that looking for the words *had*, *have*, and *has* will help them check for correct use of past participle forms.

Focus

Lesson Overview

Objective

• To recognize the constructions that give rise to incorrect pronoun use

Bellringer
Daily Language Activity

When students enter the classroom, have this assignment on the board: *Write a pronoun that you can use to replace the noun* <u>Ruth</u> *in this sentence:*

Velma and Ruth have the same birthday.

Motivating Activity

Ask students if any of them used the pronoun *she* to replace *Ruth* in the Bellringer activity. Discuss with students how they chose which pronoun to use.

Teach

⬚ Cross-Reference: Grammar

For instruction and practice on the material in Problem 1, refer students to Lesson 11.2.

⬚ Cross-Reference: Grammar

For instruction and practice on the material in Problem 2, refer students to Lesson 11.1.

Troubleshooter

7.5 Incorrect Use of Pronouns

Problem 1

A pronoun that could refer to more than one antecedent

pro David always beats Hector to school, but (he) still gets there on time.

pro When Tess leaves with Emma, (she) is home by noon.

SOLUTION A Rewrite the sentence, substituting a noun for the pronoun.

David always beats Hector to school, but Hector still gets there on time.

When Tess leaves with Emma, Tess is home by noon.

Problem 2

Object pronouns as subjects

pro Velma and (me) went to the mountains today.

pro (Her) and Glen rode to the farm on a bus.

pro Terry and (them) read that book last year.

Resource Manager

📁 **Planning Resources**
• *Lesson Plans*

🗂 **Transparencies**
• *Bellringer*
• *Two-Minute Skill Drill*

📁 **Other Print Resources**
• *Grammar Workbook,* Lesson 24

SOLUTION   Use a subject pronoun in the subject of a sentence.

Velma and I went to the mountains today.

She and Glen rode to the farm on a bus.

Terry and they read that book last year.

Problem 3

Subject pronouns as objects

pro Jane will be at home with Akiko and ⓘ.

pro Please help (she) and ⓘ with the house painting.

pro Bart would like George and ⓘ to go to the movie.

SOLUTION   Use an object pronoun as the object of a verb or a preposition.

Jane will be at home with Akiko and me.

Please help her and me with the house painting.

Bart would like George and me to go to the movie.

If you need more help with the correct use of pronouns, turn to Lessons 11.1–11.7, pages 429–442.

Teach

Cross-Reference: Grammar

For instruction and practice on the material in Problem 3, refer students to Lesson 11.1.

Two-Minute Skill Drill

Write the following sentence on the board:

Julio invited Maria and she to his birthday party.

Ask students to find the error in pronoun use and then to rewrite the sentence correctly.

See also *Two-Minute Skill Drill Transparency 7.5*

Additional Resources

Grammar Workbook, Lesson 24

Close

Have students write one paragraph about an event that involved two family members or friends. Tell students to use both proper nouns and pronouns in their paragraphs.

Focus

Lesson Overview

Objective

- To recognize and correct errors in regular and irregular forms of comparative and superlative adjectives

Bellringer
Daily Language Activity

When students enter the classroom, have this assignment on the board: *List five adjectives that describe how you are feeling today.*

Motivating Activity

After students have made their Bellringer activity lists, write on the board a sample list of five adjectives that describe feelings, such as *lazy, happy, tense, good,* and *tired.*

Ask students to compare how they feel today with how they have felt before by using their adjectives to complete the following sentences. Students can also use their adjectives when answering their questions. *Have I ever felt _____ than I do today? What is the _____ I have ever felt?*

Teach

Cross-Reference: Grammar

For instruction and practice on the material in Lesson 7.6, refer students to Lessons 12.3 and 12.4.

7.6 Incorrect Use of Adjectives

Problem 1

Incorrect use of *good, better, best*

adj The weather can't get (more) good than this.

adj This is the (most good) book in the library.

adj This is a (more) better exercise for you than that one.

SOLUTION The comparative and superlative forms of *good* are *better* and *best.* Do not use *more* or *most* before irregular forms of comparative and superlative adjectives.

The weather can't get better than this.

This is the best book in the library.

This is a better exercise for you than that one.

Problem 2

Incorrect use of *bad, worse, worst*

adj This is the (baddest) movie I've ever seen.

adj These shoes are (more bad) than those shoes.

adj Yesterday I ate the (most) worst food I've ever tasted.

Resource Manager

📁 **Planning Resources**
- *Lesson Plans*

📂 **Transparencies**
- *Bellringer*
- *Two-Minute Skill Drill*

📁 **Other Print Resources**
- *Grammar Workbook,* Lesson 30

SOLUTION The comparative and superlative forms of *bad* are *worse* and *worst.* Do not use *-er, -est, more,* or *most* with irregular forms of comparative and superlative adjectives.

This is the worst movie I've ever seen.

These shoes are worse than those shoes.

Yesterday I ate the worst food I've ever tasted.

Problem 3

Incorrect use of comparative and superlative adjectives

adj *Maple Drive is* (more) *wider than Elm Street.*

adj *Daphne lives in the* (most) *smallest house in town.*

SOLUTION Do not use both *-er* and *more* or *-est* and *most* at the same time.

Maple Drive is wider than Elm Street.

Daphne lives in the smallest house in town.

If you need more help with the incorrect use of adjectives, turn to Lessons 12.3 and 12.4, pages 455–458.

Unit 7.6 Incorrect Use of Adjectives **319**

Troubleshooter

Teach

Two-Minute Skill Drill

Ask students to write the correct comparative and superlative forms of these adjectives. Point out that most of them use the endings *-er* and *-est,* but some do not.

big	*small*
many	*few*
mean	*kind*
bad	*good*
great	*tiny*
plain	*fancy*

Encourage students to list colorful adjectives that are synonyms for the ones above.

See also *Two-Minute Skill Drill Transparency 7.6*

Additional Resources

Grammar Workbook, Lesson 30

Close

Ask students to give examples of adjectives that should or should not follow a word like *more* or *most.* Have them discuss strategies they use to help them remember when to use *more* and *most,* and when to add *-er* and *-est.*

Focus

Lesson Overview

Objective

- To recognize when commas are needed to separate three or more items in a series, to set off direct quotations, and to set off nonessential appositives

Bellringer
Daily Language Activity

When students enter the classroom, have this assignment on the board: *Copy the following sentence, adding punctuation to make its meaning clearer:*

Edna ate egg rolls hot and sour soup and fried rice.

Motivating Activity

Ask volunteers to describe the punctuation changes they made in the Bellringer activity sentence. Discuss with students how the changes enhance the clarity of the sentence.

Teach

Cross-Reference: Mechanics

For instruction and practice on the material in Problem 1, refer students to Lesson 20.2.

Cross-Reference: Mechanics

For instruction and practice on the material in Problem 2, refer students to Lesson 20.6.

7.7 Incorrect Use of Commas

Problem 1

Missing commas in a series of three or more items

> com We visited the museum the zoo and the aquarium.
>
> com Sam drove down the block around the corner and into the parking lot.

SOLUTION Use commas to separate three or more items in a series.

We visited the museum, the zoo, and the aquarium.

Sam drove down the block, around the corner, and into the parking lot.

Problem 2

Missing commas with direct quotations

> com "Biology class" said Ms. Blas "meets tomorrow."
>
> com "Let's rake the leaves" said Ben "before we leave."

Resource Manager

📂 **Planning Resources**
- *Lesson Plans*

💾 **Transparencies**
- *Bellringer*
- *Two-Minute Skill Drill*

📂 **Other Print Resources**
- *Grammar Workbook,* Lesson 73–74, 76
- *Sentence-Combining Practice,* p. 4

SOLUTION The first part of an interrupted quotation ends with a comma, followed by quotation marks. The interrupting words are also followed by a comma.

"Biology class," said Ms. Blas, "meets tomorrow."

"Let's rake the leaves," said Ben, "before we leave."

Problem 3

Missing commas with nonessential appositives

com *Our house, a split-level, was painted last year.*

com *My bicycle, a black ten-speed, was shipped to Alaska.*

SOLUTION Determine whether the appositive is truly essential to the meaning of the sentence. If it is not essential, set off the appositive with commas.

Our house, a split-level, was painted last year.

My bicycle, a black ten-speed, was shipped to Alaska.

 *If you need more help with commas, turn to Lessons 20.2–20.4, pages 591–596.*

Unit 7.7 Incorrect Use of Commas **321**

Troubleshooter

Teach

 Cross-Reference: Mechanics

For instruction and practice on the material in Problem 3, refer students to Lesson 20.2.

Two-Minute Skill Drill

Write this sentence on the board:

"I insist" said Greg's father "that before you leave this house you clean your room."

Have students revise the sentence, adding commas as necessary.

See also *Two-Minute Skill Drill Transparency 7.7*

Additional Resources

Grammar Workbook, Lessons 73–74, 76

Close

Suggest that students write a one-page story that includes dialogue. Allow them to exchange stories, identifying and correcting any errors in the use of commas.

Focus

Lesson Overview

Objectives

- To recognize the most common instances in which possessive apostrophes are missing or misplaced
- To use possessive apostrophes correctly

Bellringer
Daily Language Activity

When students enter the classroom, have this assignment on the board: *Add punctuation to the phrase* <u>students homework</u> *to indicate that (1) one student has homework and (2) two students have homework.*

Motivating Activity

Ask volunteers to describe how they indicated possession in the Bellringer activity. Discuss with students whether possessive apostrophes were used correctly.

Teach

📖 Cross-Reference: Mechanics

For instruction and practice on the material in Problem 1, refer students to Lesson 20.7.

📖 Cross-Reference: Mechanics

For instruction and practice on the material in Problem 2, refer students to Lesson 20.7.

Troubleshooter

7.8 Incorrect Use of Apostrophes

Problem 1

Singular possessive nouns

> apos (Chriss) son borrowed the neighbor's rake.
> The (womans) report is on the desk.
> apos (Ettas) book is in (Ians) house.

SOLUTION Use an apostrophe and an -*s* to form the possessive of a singular noun, even one that ends in -*s*.

Chris's son borrowed the neighbor's rake.

The woman's report is on the desk.

Etta's book is in Ian's house.

Problem 2

Plural possessive nouns ending in -*s*

> apos The (drivers) maps are in their cars.
> apos The two (pilots) orders are to land in Springfield.
> apos The (cats) owner fed them milk.

Resource Manager

📁 **Planning Resources**
- *Lesson Plans*

📑 **Transparencies**
- *Bellringer*
- *Two-Minute Skill Drill*

📁 **Other Print Resources**
- *Grammar Workbook*, Lesson 82
- *Sentence-Combining Practice*, p. 9

SOLUTION Use an apostrophe alone to form the possessive of a plural noun that ends in *-s*.

The drivers' maps are in their cars.

The two pilots' orders are to land in Springfield.

The cats' owner fed them milk.

Problem 3

Plural possessive nouns not ending in *-s*

apos *The ⟨mens⟩ department is at the rear of the store.*
apos *Ida Stark is known as the ⟨peoples⟩ candidate.*

SOLUTION Use an apostrophe and an *-s* to form the possessive of a plural noun that does not end in *-s*.

The men's department is at the rear of the store.

Ida Stark is known as the people's candidate.

Teach

⊠ **Cross-Reference: Mechanics**
For instruction and practice on the material in Problem 3, refer students to Lesson 20.7.

Teach

 **Cross-Reference: Grammar**

For instruction and practice on the material in Problems 4 and 5, refer students to Lesson 11.4.

 Two-Minute Skill Drill

Divide students into teams of four or five. Have each team write a list of five phrases in which possessive apostrophes are used incorrectly or not at all. Let teams exchange lists. Then initiate a race to see which team can correct the phrases most quickly.

See also ⚑ *Two-Minute Skill Drill Transparency 7.8*

Additional Resources

📁 *Sentence-Combining Practice*, p. 9

📕 *Grammar Workbook,* Lesson 82

Close

Have students write one paragraph about two soccer players who arrive late to an important game without having brought the proper equipment and must borrow someone else's. Encourage students to use as many possessives as they can.

Troubleshooter

Problem 4

Possessive personal pronouns

> *apos* The hat is (your's) but the jacket is (her's).

SOLUTION Do not use an apostrophe with any of the possessive personal pronouns.

The hat is yours, but the jacket is hers.

Problem 5

Confusion between *its* and *it's*

> *apos* (Its) going to be a beautiful morning.
> *apos* Turn the rowboat over on (it's) side.

SOLUTION Use an apostrophe to form the contraction of *it is*. Do not use an apostrophe in the possessive of *it*.

It's going to be a beautiful morning.

Turn the rowboat over on its side.

 If you need more help with apostrophes and possessives, turn to Lesson 20.7, pages 601–602.

7.9 Incorrect Capitalization

Problem 1

Words referring to ethnic groups, nationalities, and languages

cap   *Mr. Dunn has studied several (asian) cultures.*

cap   *The (arabic) language is a difficult language to learn.*

cap   *Pierre is a (canadian) who speaks (russian).*

SOLUTION   Capitalize proper nouns and adjectives that refer to ethnic groups, nationalities, and languages.

Mr. Dunn has studied several Asian cultures.

The Arabic language is a difficult language to learn.

Pierre is a Canadian who speaks Russian.

Focus

Lesson Overview

Objective

- To avoid or correct errors in capitalization when referring to ethnic groups, nationalities, languages, and family relationships, and when beginning direct quotations

🔔 Bellringer
Daily Language Activity

When students enter the classroom, have this assignment on the board: *Write one sentence about an imaginary character. Tell what language your character speaks and what his or her nationality is.*

Motivating Activity

Invite a volunteer to write on the board the sentence he or she wrote for the Bellringer activity. Use the sentence to introduce the use of capitalization when referring to nationalities and languages.

Teach

⮂ Cross-Reference: Mechanics
For instruction and practice on the material in Problem 1, refer students to Lesson 19.4.

Resource Manager

📁 **Planning Resources**
- *Lesson Plans*

📁 **Transparencies**
- *Bellringer*
- *Two-Minute Skill Drill*

📁 **Other Print Resources**
- *Grammar Workbook, Lessons 68–69, 71*

Teach

 Cross-Reference: Mechanics

For instruction and practice on the material in Problem 2, refer students to Lesson 19.2.

Two-Minute Skill Drill

Write this direct quotation on the board and have students rewrite it, finding and correcting any errors in capitalization:

"shoo!" Mr. Bigham yelled at the dog, "you have muddy paws!"

See also Two-Minute Skill Drill Transparency 7.9

Troubleshooter

Problem 2

Words that show family relationships

cap   Denise told (uncle) Evan to go to the theater.
cap   Yesterday (mom) fixed the car.

SOLUTION   Capitalize words that show family relationships when such words are used as titles or as substitutes for people's names.

Denise told Uncle Evan to go to the theater.
Yesterday Mom fixed the car.

Problem 3

The first word of a direct quotation

cap   "(we) didn't leave the house until evening," said Rosa.
cap   Peter said, "(please) wash the dishes before you leave."

SOLUTION   Capitalize the first word in a direct quotation. A direct quotation gives the speaker's exact words.

"We didn't leave the house until evening," said Rosa.
Peter said, "Please wash the dishes before you leave."

 If you need more help in capitalizing, turn to Lessons 19.1–19.4, pages 573–580.

Proofreading Symbols		
⊙	Lieut Brown	Insert a period.
∧	No one came to the party.	Insert a letter or a word.
⌃	The bell rang the students left for home.	Insert a semicolon.
≡	I enjoyed paris.	Capitalize a letter.
/	The Class ran a bake sale.	Make a capital letter lowercase.
⌢	The campers are home sick.	Close up a space.
ⓢⓟ	They visited N.Y. ⓢⓟ	Spell out.
∧	Sue please help.	Insert a comma.
∪	He enjoyed feild day.	Transpose the position of letters or words.
#	alltogether	Insert a space.
ℐ	We went to to Boston.	Delete letters or words.
⌄ ⌄	She asked, Who's coming?	Insert quotation marks.
/=/	mid January	Insert a hyphen.
¶	"Where?" asked Karl. "Over there," said Ray.	Begin a new paragraph.
⌄	She liked Sarah's glasses.	Insert an apostrophe.

Teach

 Cross-Reference: Mechanics

For instruction and practice on the material in Problem 3, refer students to Lesson 19.1.

Additional Resources

Grammar Workbook, Lessons 68–69, 71

Close

Have students work in small groups to write a brief dialogue between two family members. Then ask groups to exchange dialogues and to check for and correct any errors in capitalization.

Objectives

- To understand types, formats, and styles of business letters
- To write an effective business letter
- To understand types, formats, and styles of summaries
- To write a good summary
- To create and complete appropriate forms
- To understand the components of interviews and proposals
- To develop a multimedia presentation

ASSESSMENT OPTIONS

📁 *Tests with Answer Key and Rubrics*
Business and Technical Writing Pretest

💾 *Testmaker*
Business and Technical Writing Pretest

You may wish to administer the Business and Technical Writing Pretest at this point.

Key to Ability Levels

L1 Level 1 activities are within the basic ability range of students.

L2 Level 2 activities are within the ability range of average students.

L3 Level 3 activities are more challenging activities.

Business and Technical Writing

Resource Manager

 Planning Resources
- *Lesson Plans*

📁 **Transparencies**
- *Writing Process*

📁 **Other Print Resources**
- *Business and Technical Writing Activities*
- *Grammar and Composition Handbook*
- *Guide to Using the Internet and Other Electronic Resources*
- *Tests with Answer Key and Rubrics*
- *Writing Assessment and Evaluation Rubrics*

 **Software**
- *Presentation Plus!*
- *Revising with Style*
- *Testmaker*

 **Web Sites**
- *writerschoice.glencoe.com*
- *lit.glencoe.com*

Business Letters

Writing a Business Letter

A business letter is a formal communication tool that is used to give information or to request action.

The following business letter is written to express an opinion. Notice how the writer follows the tips suggested in the chart on the following page.

2317 Buckeye Ave.
Chadwick, OH 48276
November 10, 2001

Ms. Kate Callahan, Superintendent
Chadwick School Board
485 Cherry St.
Chadwick, OH 48276

The letter is addressed to a specific person.

Dear Ms. Callahan:

The teachers at Chadwick High School have different opinions about what students can wear to their classes. I think Chadwick should have a dress code.

The writer states his opinion in the first sentence.

A dress code would end arguments between teachers and students about what's appropriate to wear to school. Having a dress code would mean that kids wouldn't be so concerned over what they wear to school and could focus more on learning.

He gives reasons for his opinion.

I think the dress code should allow jeans and plain tee shirts but not shirts or hats with slogans or pictures.

He suggests a specific solution.

Respectfully,

Enrique Martinez, sophomore

Focus

Lesson Overview

Objectives
- To understand the formats, styles, and types of business letters
- To write an effective business letter

Skills
- ordering; using precise language

Critical Thinking
- identifying issues

Listening and Speaking
- discussing

 Bellringer
Daily Language Activity

When students enter the classroom, have this assignment on the board: *Write the names of five different occasions on which you might need to write a business letter.*

Motivating Activity

Set up a real-world situation for which the students will be required to write a business letter. For example, have them plan to write letters inviting speakers for a community helpers' day. Explain that they will be learning how to format and write an effective business letter.

Business and Technical Writing

Teach

Types of Business Letters

Allow time for students to read the model and examine the contents of the chart. Ask students to give several examples of each type of business letter and the person or group to which each might be addressed. For example, a letter of opinion might be sent to the editor of a newspaper or magazine. A letter of complaint might be sent to a store or company that has supplied defective goods or services. **L2**

Types of Business Letters

There are several types of business letters. You can use the formal business letter format to express your opinion; to request information or order a product; to make a complaint and describe a problem with a product or service; or to apply for a job, an award, or a scholarship.

When you write a business letter, keep your purpose in mind. Be brief. Don't include unnecessary information. Limit your letter to one page or less, if possible. A busy person is more likely to read your letter if it is brief.

A business letter is formal. Use polite language but a friendly tone. Avoid wordy language. For example, say "Thank you for your help" rather than "Thank you for your kind assistance in this matter."

TYPES OF BUSINESS LETTERS

Opinion Letter	Request Letter	Complaint Letter	Application Letter
State the issue briefly.	State your request briefly and clearly.	Be polite.	Write to a specific person.
State your opinion in the first sentence or two.	Make your request specific and reasonable.	Identify the product or service clearly.	Describe the job or program for which you're applying.
Support your opinion with reasons, facts, and examples.	Include all necessary information.	Describe the problem briefly and accurately.	List your qualifications.
Summarize your main points and offer a solution, if possible.	Include your phone number or a self-addressed, stamped envelope.	Request a specific solution.	Explain briefly why you're the best person for the position or the award.
		Keep a copy of your letter until your complaint has been resolved.	Request an application form or an interview.

Style

Business letters are usually written in one of two styles: block style or modified block style.

Block Style In block style, all lines begin at the left margin. Paragraphs are not indented. They are separated by a line space. The letter on page 329 is typed in block style.

Civic Literacy

Getting Involved

Students should be encouraged to take an active part in the affairs of their community. In small groups, students might discuss the recreational opportunities afforded to members of their community and how they might be expanded or improved. One student might act as secretary and list the ideas and suggestions of the group members. Then the group should decide to whom their opinions and suggestions should be addressed. Finally, they should work together to frame a letter to be sent to that person or agency.

Modified Block Style In modified block style, the heading, the closing, your signature, and your typed name begin at the center of the paper. Paragraphs may be indented—five spaces on a typewriter or half an inch on a computer—or not indented. If paragraphs are indented, there is no need to place a line space between them. The following letter is in modified block style with paragraphs indented.

Business & Technical Writing

---

708 Mount Vernon Rd. (Heading)
Greenleaf, ME 10908
February 12, 2001

Mr. Bruce Chung, Manager (Inside Address)
Greenleaf Department of Recreation
304 S. Main St.
Greenleaf, ME 10908

Dear Mr. Chung: (Salutation)
    I understand that next month (March) you will be arranging the schedule for the city softball fields for spring and summer. Please schedule some time for kids who are not part of any organized league.
    There are many kids in our community who do not belong to a league but who love to play softball. The parents of these kids pay taxes that are used for city recreation as do the parents of the kids in the leagues. (Body)
    I suggest reserving diamonds 4 and 6 on Wednesdays from 2:30 p.m. to 5 p.m. This would not interfere with evening or weekend games.

      Yours truly, (Closing)

      Megan Payson (Name and Signature)
      Megan Payson

The Parts of a Business Letter

A business letter has six parts.

Heading
- your street address
- your city, state, and ZIP code
- the date

Inside Address
- the name of the person to whom you're writing
- the title of the person to whom you're writing (Place a comma after the name and write a short title on the same line. Use a separate line for a long title without a comma after the person's name.)
- the name of the business or organization
- the street address
- the city, state, and ZIP code

Teach

Styles of Business Letters

Students should compare the styles of the letters on page 329 and this page and note the differences between them. They should also note what the two styles have in common. Students might also discuss the advantages and/or disadvantages of each style. They might note which style seems to be used more frequently and what their personal preference is. **L2**

Punctuating a Business Letter

Careful punctuation is important in a business letter. It not only helps to clarify expression and prevent misreading but also indicates that the writer is serious about his or her purpose in writing. A carelessly written letter may be ignored by the recipient. **L1**

Teach

The Parts of a Business Letter

Students might enjoy a quick oral review of the parts of a business letter if you adopt the strategy of the Jeopardy game. As you name each part of a letter, call on volunteers to ask the question for which the part named is the answer. For example, when you say, "Heading," a student might reply, "What is the part of a business letter that contains the address of the sender and the date?" **L3**

Practice and Assess

Evaluation Rubrics

As students complete the activity on this page, they can monitor their own performance by checking the Writing Rubrics provided in the activity box. If they have produced the letter electronically, ask them to place a copy in a folder that you designate. Otherwise, ask the students to submit a hard copy to you for evaluation.

Close

Have students share with the class the subject of their letters and the answers they anticipate. Explain to students that they may have to wait for a response and, depending on the recipient, their response may be a form letter. Post a list of the people to whom letters have been sent, and check or star the name when a response is received. Ask students to share responses that they consider positive. **L2**

Business & Technical Writing

Business Letters

Salutation or Greeting When you know the name of the person to whom you're writing, the salutation should include a courtesy title: *Dear Mrs. Martin* or *Dear Mr. Marconi*. If you don't know the name of the person, the salutation should begin with *Dear* followed by the person's title: *Dear Manager* or *Dear President*. Place a colon after the salutation.

Body The body contains your message. It is the most important part of your letter.

Closing The closing is a final word or phrase, such as *Sincerely* or *Yours truly*, followed by a comma.

Name and Signature Type your name four lines below the closing. Then sign your name in the space between the closing and your typed name. If your first name could belong to either a male or a female, include *Miss, Ms.,* or *Mr.* in parentheses before both your typed name and your signature.

Neatness Counts

The person who reads your letter will pay more attention to your message if your letter is neat. Follow the formal rules for writing a business letter.

✔ Type or word process your letter.

✔ Use unlined white 81/2-by-11-inch paper.

✔ Leave a two-inch margin at the top of the page and margins of at least one inch at the left, right, and bottom.

✔ Single-space the heading. Allow one or more blank lines between the heading and the inside address, depending on the length of your letter.

✔ Single-space the remaining parts of the letter, leaving an extra line between the parts and between the paragraphs in the body if they are not indented.

Activity

Write a Business Letter Write a letter stating your opinion on an issue. Mail (or e-mail) your letter to someone who is in a position to take action.

PURPOSE to write a business letter
AUDIENCE person able to take action
LENGTH one page

WRITING RUBRICS To write an effective business letter, you should

- select an issue and state your opinion. Then use a library or the Internet to find the address of an appropriate person to write to
- trade letters with a classmate for feedback
- revise your letter so that all of your ideas relate to your subject, follow each other in a logical way, and are supported by the necessary details
- type, use word processing, or write neatly for your final draft
- send your letter

Writing in the Real World

Spelling and Legibility

Invite a business secretary to address the class. Ask students if they know a person in this position. You might also contact the office of a state or national representative or a city council member. Request that the secretary speak about the importance of correct spelling in business correspondence. The speaker might also address the hazards of depending too heavily on the spelling check feature of a computer program. The misspelling of an intended word might be the correct spelling of another word, and, in this case, the automatic checker would not recognize the word as being misspelled.

Another issue to be addressed might be that of handwritten correspondence. Request that the secretary identify those occasions for which a handwritten letter is appropriate and explain how important legibility is in these instances.

Summaries

Writing a Summary

A summary is a brief written statement of the main points of a larger work. Although some summaries include opinions, most only state facts in an objective way.

The following summary contains the minutes of a meeting. Notice how the writer follows the tips suggested in the chart on the following page.

Sea Oats School Yearbook Committee

Minutes for October 10, 2001

The meeting was called to order by Mrs. Akron at 3:25 P.M. in the journalism room.

Members present: Mrs. Akron, Jeremy Jefferson, Kim Lee, Tony Pascuzzi, Jennifer Bailey, and Maria Alverez.

The names of those who are present are listed.

Minutes of Last Meeting
The minutes of the last meeting were read by Maria Alverez and approved.

Old Business
Kim Lee passed out copies of a letter to be sent to area businesses to solicit advertising for the yearbook. Tony Pascuzzi suggested that the letter would be more persuasive if it included statements by some of last year's advertisers telling how their ads brought in more business. The committee members decided this was a good idea, and Tony volunteered to call some of last year's advertisers to see if any of them would agree to be quoted.

The business of the meeting is summed up briefly.

New Business
Mrs. Akron asked for a volunteer to take photographs of activities throughout the year. Jennifer Bailey volunteered. Mrs. Akron will lend Jennifer a camera, and film will be purchased with yearbook funds.

Next Meeting
The next meeting will be held on November 13, 2001, in the journalism room.

The date, place, and time of the meeting are recorded.

The meeting was adjourned by Mrs. Akron at 4:03 P.M.

Business and Technical Writing **333**

Focus

Lesson Overview

Objectives
- To understand the parts of a summary
- To understand how types of summaries differ
- To write an effective summary

Skills
- summarizing; condensing

Critical Thinking
- analyzing; evaluating

Listening and Speaking
- discussing; presenting

🔔 Bellringer
Daily Language Activity

When students enter the classroom, have the following assignment on the board: *In two or three sentences, write an account of what happened in one of your classes yesterday.*

Motivating Activity

Ask several students to tell briefly what happened on the way to school. Select one account and explain that the student presented an informal summary.

Teach

Using the Model

Direct students to read the introduction to summaries and to study the model on this page. You might explain that organizations and clubs ordinarily keep a copy of the minutes on record. Then discuss why minutes are kept and why minutes of the last meeting are read before the business of the present meeting is addressed. **L2**

Business and Technical Writing

Teach

Types of Summaries

Have students read the material on this page and study the guidelines in the chart. Encourage students to ask questions about anything that is not clear to them. Most students will already be familiar with synopses, since most book reports require a synopsis of the story. They may also have seen synopses at the beginning of serial comic strips and episodic films, such as *Star Wars*. **L3**

Types of Summaries

Summaries, which are shortened versions of larger works, take many forms: minutes, synopses, survey reports, and reviews.

Minutes are a record of when and where a meeting is held, who attends it, and what happens during the meeting. Minutes are usually kept in a file or a book so that they can be referred to as needed. A secretary or group member who is present at the meeting writes the minutes. A specific format is used for writing them, as shown in the model on page 333. When recording the minutes of a meeting, write what is said as accurately and briefly as you can.

A **synopsis** is a short statement that gives the general idea of a subject. A synopsis of a book is usually on its dust jacket or its back cover. Before writing a synopsis of a written piece, read all of it. Then sum it up in a few sentences or paragraphs.

A **survey report** is a summary of a detailed study that gathers facts and draws conclusions about a subject. An opinion poll is one form of survey. When writing a survey report, gather information from different sources and then create an overview of it. Sometimes a survey report includes charts or graphs.

A **review** is a brief summary and critical evaluation of an event or an artistic work, such as a movie, play, or concert. When writing a review, give your opinion of the quality of the event or of the work and its performance.

A summary can also be used to write a brief account of what happened in a business or a classroom during a certain period.

TYPES OF SUMMARIES

Minutes	Synopsis	Survey Report	Review
Record the date, time, and location of the meeting.	Include only the most important points of a report or other piece of writing.	Gather information from various sources.	Identify the event, work, or performance and its time and place.
List the names of those who attend it.	Write your statement in paragraph form.	Organize the data in some way, such as a table or a graph that makes it easy to understand at a glance.	Include a brief description of what was read, seen, or performed.
Sum up old and new business in brief sentences.	Be brief (one page or less).		Identify the most important people involved, such as the writer, the director, and the performers.
Record the date, time, and place of the next meeting.		State a conclusion drawn from the data.	State your opinion.
Note when and by whom the meeting is adjourned.			

Writing in the Real World

Writing as a Tool for Learning

A good way for students to ascertain that they have understood what has been presented in class is to write summaries of the material presented. They could enter these summaries in a Learning Log. For subject areas that the student finds difficult, daily summaries might help them remember important concepts as they are taught. Students might also ask a classmate or the teacher to read a summary and provide feedback on its accuracy. Summarizing information is also an efficient tool for test preparation. Summaries are particularly helpful in content areas like social studies and health education.

Style

Some types of summaries, such as the minutes of a meeting, have a definite format (see model on page 333). Others—synopses, reviews, or summaries of a business or school day—can be written in paragraph form. Surveys and summaries of very large works are often divided into sections and include paragraphs, lists, tables, and graphs.

(see model on page 333)

Seventh Grade Summary (Title)
Week of February 10, 2001 (Date)

Subjects (Heading)

English
Five students read their essays on Great American Poets this week, completing the essay presentations.

Science
This is the fourth week of the biology plant-growing experiment. Plants that get sun, water, and fertilizer are the tallest. Plants that get only sun and water are a bit smaller but are growing well. Plants that get only water or only sun have sprouted but are starting to look sick.

Class Fundraiser (Heading)
The following table shows the results of gift-wrap sales so far.

Item	# Packages Sold	Price per Package	Total	
Cards	64	$7.00	$448.00	(Table)
Gift Bags	43	4.50	193.50	
Ribbon	64	5.50	352.00	
Wrapping Paper	89	4.50	400.50	

Subtotal $1,394.00
less 50% cost   697.00
Our profit   **$ 697.00**

We are now more than half way to our goal of $1,200.00. Keep on selling and our new classroom computer will be here soon! (Conclusion)

Teach

Discussion

Have students read the summary of a class day on this page. Ask them what the purpose of such a summary might be and why all of the class periods are not mentioned. **L2**

Oral Practice

Ask students to recall what happened on the previous school day. Call on volunteers to present a verbal summary of the events of the day to the class. Stress that one of the differences between an oral and a written summary is the degree of formality. **L2**

Business and Technical Writing

Practice and Assess

Using Technology

Encourage students to use a word processing program to create the type of summary they choose to do. Call their attention to the tips presented on this page. **L2**

Evaluation Rubrics

Since students may choose to write any of several types of summaries, you will need to be flexible in your evaluation. Tell students to consult the chart on page 334 for guidelines on writing the specific type of summary they have chosen. The teacher should use the same chart to evaluate the students' work. **L2**

Close

Invite students to present their summaries to the class. Feedback from classmates should be limited to pointing out strengths and making polite suggestions for improvement.

The Parts of a Summary

A simple summary has just a title and one paragraph. Those that are more complex may also include a date, sections, graphic organizers, and a conclusion.

Title   The title lets readers know what subject or information is being summarized.

Date   The date shows the period of time covered by the summary.

Sections   Sometimes, sections may be needed to organize information.

Graphic Organizers   Some information is easier to understand if it is presented in a table, a graph, or a map.

Conclusion   The summary model on page 335 ends with a conclusion. Other summaries just state the facts and let readers come to their own conclusions.

Neatness Counts

Summaries that are neat and well organized can be read and understood easily.

✓ Create your summary on a computer, if possible.

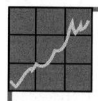 **Technology Tip**

You can use the features of a word processing program to create an organized format for your summary. The table and column features can help you organize information into categories. Some word processing programs also make it easy to create simple tables, graphs, pie charts, and flow charts.

✓ Begin with a heading centered at the top of the page.

✓ Use bold type or underlining to identify each section.

✓ Leave a two-inch margin at the top of the page and margins of at least one inch at the left, right, and bottom.

✓ Leave a double space between sections and before and after organizers.

Activity

Write a Summary   Choose the kind of summary you would like to write. You may wish to write minutes for a meeting you attended; summarize what happened in your classroom during a day or a week; write a synopsis or a survey report; or review a play, a book, or a movie.

PURPOSE   To write a summary
AUDIENCE   Classmates
LENGTH   One page or less

WRITING RUBRICS   To write a good summary, you should

- keep your summary as brief as possible
- include only the most important points
- make a graphic organizer if you have data to include
- trade summaries with a classmate and discuss ways they could be revised to make them briefer or easier to read
- revise your summary and then share it with your class

Forms

Creating a Form

A form is a document that has blanks for filling in required information. The model below is a form for scheduling family chores.

> The writer gives the form a title to show what it is for.

> The writer organizes the form into columns to make it easy to read.

O'Flarety Family Chore Schedule

	Sunday	Monday	Tuesday	Wednesday	Thursday	Friday	Saturday
Feed Buffy	*Lisa*	*Lisa*	*Lisa*	*Kim*	*Matt*	*Kim*	*Matt*
Take out trash	*Lisa*	*Kim*	*Matt*	*Lisa*	*Lisa*	*Kim*	*Matt*
Set table	*Lisa*	*Kim*	*Kim*	*Kim*	*Matt*	*Kim*	*Lisa*
Wash dishes	*Matt*	*Kim*	*Matt*	*Lisa*	*Lisa*	*Kim*	*Matt*
Clean bathroom	*Kim*	*Kim*	*Matt*	*Kim*	*Matt*	*Lisa*	*Matt*

> The writer provides spaces for filling in who does a chore and when the person does it.

Types of Forms

Forms are used to collect information in an organized way. There are forms for taking phone messages, writing memos, and filling out receipts (records of payment). Paying income tax requires filling out a form. Banks have forms for opening and closing accounts and for applying for loans. Accountants use forms to keep track of expenses and income. Forms fall into four basic types: schedules, tracking forms, application forms, and report forms.

A **schedule** is a form that lists the times at which certain events or things to do will take place. It usually lists events that have not happened yet. A vacation schedule shows when people working in the same office will be taking time off. An airline schedule shows flight arrival and departure times. The model on this page is a schedule.

Focus

Lesson Overview

Objectives
- To understand the purpose and characteristics of forms
- To create and complete forms

Skills
- organizing; presenting

Critical Thinking
- analyzing; organizing

Listening and Speaking
- discussing; presenting; responding

 Bellringer
Daily Language Activity

When students enter the classroom, have the following assignment on the board: *List the names of at least five different kinds of forms that you or members of your family have had to complete.*

Motivating Activity

Have the students share with their classmates the kinds of forms they recalled in the Bellringer activity. Remind them of the forms that parents have to fill out for a child: registration form, health form, field trip permission form, accident report, etc.

337

Business and Technical Writing

Teach

Studying the Chart

Have the students read the information on this page and study the chart that lists types of forms. If possible, bring to class actual samples of blank forms. Some of these can be obtained from the post office and department stores. Ascertain which types of forms are unfamiliar to students, and spend some time explaining their use and demonstrating how they are filled out. **L3**

A **tracking form** is used to record things as they occur. A teacher's grade book is a tracking form because the grades are recorded as they are earned. The model on page 339 is a tracking form.

An **application form** is used to gather information about a person who is requesting something, such as a job, membership in a group, or an award. When you fill out an application form, follow the instructions carefully and include information that will help persuade the person reading the application to choose you instead of other applicants.

A **report form** is used to record data or information on events that have already taken place so that it can be compared or combined. A form for recording the results of a class science experiment, a baseball score card, and a report card are different kinds of report forms.

You will fill out many forms during your life. You may also need to create forms. To create a form, first list all the kinds of information that you need to collect. Then decide on the best format for organizing the information.

TYPES OF FORMS

Schedule	Tracking Form	Application Form	Report Form
Give the schedule a title. Use a column or grid format. List headings horizontally and vertically. Include dates and times of events.	Give the form a title. Use a column or grid format. Include instructions for filling out the form. Use headings that show what information belongs in the blanks. Arrange the headings in sequence. Provide a space for the recorder's signature.	Give the form a title. State the requirements for applicants. Include instructions for filling out the form. Include instructions on how and where to submit the form and the date by which it must be submitted. Use a fill-in-the-blanks format for information about applicants. Provide a space for an applicant's signature and the date.	Give the form a title. Use a format that organizes the data so that it can be compared or combined easily. Use headings. Include dates and times. Provide a space for the recorder's name.

MEETING INDIVIDUAL NEEDS English Language Learners

Filling Out Forms

Have students for whom English is a second language work with partners who are more fluent in English to fill out sample forms. Have the students work on actual forms that they are required to complete (provided that they are not of a private nature). Or supply samples of forms they may have to complete in the near future. If students are self-conscious about using actual information, they may supply fictitious data.

Style

Each type of form requires a particular style or format. Schedules and tracking forms are usually arranged in columns or grids. See the model on page 337 and the one below. Application forms use a fill-in-the-blank format and sometimes include large spaces in which essay questions can be answered. Report forms use any format that organizes their particular data or information best. The following tracking form uses a grid format.

Business & Technical Writing

Summer Reading Challenge (Title)			
Instructions: Fill in your name and the information requested for each book after you have read it. In the comments column, write what you liked best and least about the book. Use additional forms if you need more room.			
Reader's Name (Blank for the reader's name)			
Title	Author	Date Finished	Comments (Headings)
(Blanks for entering information)			

Teach

Tracking Forms

Tracking forms are very important in business for determining workflow, assigning personnel, and ordering supplies. Stores need tracking forms for inventory purposes. Medical personnel use tracking forms to record temperatures, food and liquid intake, and medications. Other tracking forms are used by dieters and athletes. Even student report cards are forms that track grades from one marking period to another. **L2**

Business and Technical Writing

Practice and Assess

Creating a Form

After students are comfortable with filling out forms, they can proceed to creating forms of their own. Since it may be difficult for students to project how easy it is to fill out a form that they have created, you should implement the suggestion to pair students during this activity. Encourage students to use a computer when creating a form. Word processing programs make experimentation easier because they take much of the drudgery out of deleting and inserting and ensure that a legible copy of the final form will be produced. **L3**

Evaluation Rubrics

Use the information in the chart on page 338 to evaluate the types of forms that students produce.

Close

Discuss with students the advantages of using a form. Some advantages might be having data in a uniform, easy-to-read, compact format and having papers of uniform size for ease of copying, carrying, and filing.

The Parts of a Form

What parts a form has depends on what kind of information it will be used to record. Some or all of the following parts are used in various forms.

Title   The title, which is usually placed at the top of a form, shows what the form is used for.

Instructions   In some cases, a form includes instructions for filling it out and submitting it.

Headings   Headings indicate where information is to be placed on the form and what kind of information it should be.

Body   The body of a form is where information is recorded. It is usually columns, a grid, or text with blanks to be filled in. Sometimes the body is divided into sections.

Signature   A recorder's or an applicant's signature often appears on a form.

Neatness Counts

A form has to be organized so that it is

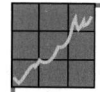

Technology Tip

You can use a computer word processing program to create columns and rows. Use the underline feature to create the blanks that are to be filled in. Experiment with using a word processing tables feature or a spreadsheet program to produce a grid.

easy for people to understand how to record information on it. A form should be created on a computer.

✓ Use unlined white 8 1/2-by-11 paper.

✓ Leave a two-inch margin at the top of the page and at least a one-inch margin at the left, right, and bottom.

✓ Single-space the heading. Use a double space between the sections of a form.

Activity

Create a Form   Study the types of forms listed on this page. Then decide which type you want to create. Create your form and then have a partner fill it out. Discuss with your partner how easy or hard it was to understand and fill out the form. Discuss whether or not the form organized information in a logical way.

PURPOSE To create a form
AUDIENCE A classmate
LENGTH One page or less

WRITING RUBRICS   To create an organized, useful form, you should

- experiment with different formats to find the one that works best for your particular form
- include instructions on how to fill out the form if it isn't obvious
- create and revise your form on a computer
- use whatever sources are necessary to gather information for filling out your partner's form

Interviews

An interview is a meeting between one person (the interviewer) and a second person from whom the interviewer seeks information. It is also the name given to the written report of such a meeting. An interview has a question-and-answer format. The interviewer asks questions whose answers will provide specific information.

When you interview someone, your questions, manner, and tone determine how your subject answers. When someone interviews you, your appearance and ability to answer the questions make an impression on the interviewer. In the following interview, a reporter for the school paper interviews the school media specialist about new computer equipment available in the library.

Question: What new computer equipment was placed in the library over the summer?
Answer: There are four new computer stations, a black and white printer, and a color printer.
Q: When can students use the new equipment?
A: Students can use computer stations any time the stations are not already reserved or in use. They can reserve up to thirty minutes at a time by signing the sheet at the reference desk.
Q: How can students get help learning how to use the new equipment?
A: The computers are always turned on during library hours. There are instructions on the screen that tell users what to do. Also, all the librarians and assistants have been trained on the new computers and are available to assist students.
Q: What kinds of tasks can the computers be used for?
A: There are many ways to use the new computers. They can be used to look up books and reference materials available in the library. They will tell you whether a book is on the shelf or has been checked out. You can use the word processing software to write and print reports or essays. You can also use the new computers to access the Internet.
Q: Can students play computer games on the new stations?
A: There are math, spelling, and science games installed on the computers. There is also a word game that will help you improve your vocabulary. Students are not allowed to bring software from home.
Q: Is there anything else students should know about the new computer system?
A: We have a brand new Web site for our school. Space is available on it to publish student writing. I'm inviting students to submit essays, reports, and other forms of writing to be featured on the Web site.

> The interviewer asks for the most important information first.

> The interviewer asks for details that will be important to readers.

> The interviewer asks for information that may be of interest but wasn't covered by other questions.

Focus

Lesson Overview

Objectives
- To understand types of interviews and methods of conducting them
- To conduct an interview with a peer

Skills
- formulating good questions; researching background

Critical Thinking
- analyzing; focusing; adapting

Listening and Speaking
- asking questions; listening critically

 **Bellringer**
Daily Language Activity
When students come into the classroom, have this assignment on the board: *Write two or three questions that you would like to ask a famous living person. Make sure that your questions require more than a yes or no answer.*

Motivating Activity

Ask students to share with the class some of the questions that they wrote for the Bellringer activity. Then call on volunteers to role-play a celebrity and an interviewer. Encourage them to improvise answers to the questions.

Teach

Using the Model

Direct students to read the model interview silently. Then have two students assume the roles of interviewer and interviewee. Encourage students to evaluate the interview. Explain that they should have reasons to support their opinions. **L2**

Business and Technical Writing

Teach

Types of Interviews

After students have read the material above the chart on this page, call their attention to the three types of interviews listed in the chart. Ask different students to read aloud the directions for the types of interviews. Encourage students to comment on the directions or ask for clarification, if necessary. **L1**

Types of Interviews

Interviews can be used to gather information in many different situations, but there are basically three types of interviews: a job interview, a news interview, and an investigation interview. An interviewer asks a subject questions and records the answers by taking notes or by tape recording the entire interview. The questions, which are planned carefully in advance, are designed to get the subject to provide specific information.

A **job interview** helps an employer determine whether an applicant is qualified for a specific job. When you are interviewed for a job, be prepared to answer questions about your experience and skills that are relevant to the job. A job interview also helps an interviewer get a sense of what kind of person an applicant is. The answers you give to questions about your accomplishments or what you would do in a given situation help the interviewer assess your values. The interviewer needs to determine whether you are a trustworthy person, a hard worker, and someone who would help the business.

A **news interview** is conducted to gather information that can be written into a news story. When you are planning to interview someone for a news story, first learn all you can about the person and the related topic. Then make up questions that will bring out information to fill the gaps in your knowledge. Tape the interview or take notes. Later, you can organize the information into story form. When you quote a person, be sure to copy his or her words exactly.

An **investigation interview** is used to gather information about something that has happened. For example, a police officer might interview a witness to an accident, or a school principal might interview a student witness to a school incident.

TYPES OF INTERVIEWS		
Job Interview	**News Interview**	**Investigation Interview**
Ask questions about the applicant's relevant experience.	Begin with a question that will introduce the subject to your readers.	Limit questions to those that will bring out relevant facts.
Ask questions about job skills.	Bring out the most important information by asking questions that contain a reporter's six favorite words: *who, what, where, when, why,* and *how.*	Ask specific questions about dates, times, and events.
Include questions that will bring out information about the applicant's ability to make decisions. You might ask, *What would you do if...?*		Ask for information that is based on the subject's personal knowledge rather than on hearsay.
	Always ask an open-ended question, such as *What other important point have I forgotten to ask about?* or *What else do readers need to know?*	

Enrichment and Extension

Evaluating Models

Have students find on the Internet or in magazines interviews of famous people—they may be athletes, entertainers, or officials. In small groups, have students share their findings. After they have read or dramatized the interviews, students should evaluate them according to the criteria supplied in the lesson. One member of each group should report to the class the results of their evaluations. Pairs of students could dramatize for the class those interviews they considered well done.

Style

An interview usually consists of questions and answers. An interview may be rewritten later in the same question and answer form. A news interview, however, is often rewritten in a news story format.

The following model is part of an interview in which a seventh grader is being considered for a job as a babysitter.

Mrs. Moore: I am looking for someone to come in after school three times a week to watch and play with my two daughters, Megan, who is three, and Caitlin, who is eighteen months old. Sometimes I will be here working on the computer, but other times I will go out to do errands. Are you able to be here on Tuesdays, Thursdays, and Fridays from three to six in the afternoon?

Kristin: Those times would work for me.

Mrs. Moore: Have you ever babysat before?

Kristin: I watch my little brother while my parents are out. He's three.

Mrs. Moore: How old are you, Kristin, and how long have you been babysitting your brother?

Kristin: I'm thirteen, and I have been helping to babysit Justin since he was born. I have been staying alone with him for the last year.

Mrs. Moore: Do you know how to change a diaper?

Kristin: Before Justin was potty-trained, I changed him a lot. I can change both disposable and cloth diapers.

Mrs. Moore: Suppose while you were babysitting, Caitlin started crying and wouldn't stop. What would you do?

Kristin: First I would ask her why she was crying. If she wouldn't answer, I'd look her over to be sure she wasn't hurt. Then I'd check to see if she needed a diaper change. If it seemed like nothing was wrong, I would hold her and tell her a story or carry her around the house and find some of her toys.

Mrs. Moore: What would you do if one of the girls got hurt?

Kristin: It would depend on how they were hurt. If it was something like a scraped or cut finger, I'd wash it with soap and water and put a bandage on it. If it was really serious, I'd call 911. If it was something in between, I'd call you and if I couldn't get you, I guess I'd call my mother for advice.

Mrs. Moore: What would you do if you told Megan to do something and she refused?

Kristin: I would probably tell her that I'm in charge and that she has to do what I say, even if she doesn't like it. I've found that if I pay attention to kids and have fun with them, they usually do what I tell them to do.

Mrs. Moore: Would you like to meet Megan and Caitlin now?

Kristin: I'd love to.

Question about whether the person is available when needed.

Question about the applicant's relevant experience.

Questions about the applicant's qualifications

Questions to determine how the applicant would handle a crisis.

Teach

Using the Model

After students have had time to read the interview, ask them to estimate how much time it took. Students should be aware that one can speak much more quickly than one can write. Discuss why this fact would lead some interviewers to record an interview. Does this explain why most reported interviews contain only the highlights of the conversation, with summary paragraphs interspersed? Students should note the kinds of questions being asked in the interview between Kristin and Mrs. Moore. **L3**

Business and Technical Writing

Practice and Assess

Evaluation Rubrics

Plan a class period during which students will present the interviews they have prepared. Use the directions in the chart on page 342 to evaluate the presentation of each pair of students.

The Parts of an Interview

An interview is made up of questions and answers. The questions should be crafted to bring out specific information and create a desired effect.

Introductory Question   In a job interview, the first question should help to put the applicant at ease. In a news interview, the first question can be about the topic's most important point or be a general question about the topic. At the beginning of an investigation interview, the witness is usually asked to describe what happened during an incident.

Follow-up Questions   Sometimes the answer to one question will suggest other questions that the interviewer hadn't thought of. The answers to such questions may provide important information.

Final Question   The last question in an interview can be open-ended, inviting the person interviewed to add any information that he or she thinks is important.

Technology Tip

If your subject is far away, and if both of you have access to the Internet, you can conduct the interview by e-mail. Ask all of your questions in your first e-mail. After you have read your interviewee's responses, you can ask follow-up questions.

Appearance Counts

How you look and how you act when you are being interviewed is as important as the answers you give, especially in a job interview. When you go to a job interview, dress neatly, smile, and shake hands with the interviewer. Be polite and answer each question but do not offer information that is not asked for. Try to appear relaxed and act naturally. Don't be afraid to ask questions.

If you are the interviewer, dress neatly, be businesslike but friendly, and help to put your subject at ease.

Activity

Conduct an Interview   Work in pairs to interview each other for jobs or news stories. You may wish to produce a radio or television interview show.

 PURPOSE to conduct an interview
AUDIENCE classmates
  LENGTH ten minutes

WRITING RUBRICS   To make sure that an interview is informative, you should do the following.

- Before you are interviewed, think of what questions you will probably be asked and decide on your answers.
- Before you interview a subject, use the models on pages 341 and 343 to help you write a list of questions.

Enrichment and Extension

Presenting Interviews

In connection with a unit in social studies or science, students may plan and present a program of imaginary interviews with historical figures or prominent scientists. Students should work in pairs. Each pair should select and research the accomplishments of a particular person. Then the students should work together to plan a series of appropriate questions and responses that would reveal substantive information about the subject of the interview. Each pair should then agree on the roles of interviewer and interviewee and practice these roles.

A committee could be appointed to plan an introduction to the program and to decide on the order in which the interviews would be presented. The program might be presented to parents or to other classes.

Proposals

Writing a Proposal

A proposal is a plan or suggestion that is presented to others for their approval. The following model is one student's proposal for a procedure to be followed in a school paper drive. Note how the writer follows the tips suggested in the chart on page 346.

Proposal
Procedure for Churchill School Paper Drive

Introduction: Last year's school paper drive caused confusion and was not very successful. Many students covered the same neighborhoods, and other neighborhoods were not covered at all. Residents were unsure of when to put their paper out for collection, and students were unsure of where and when to turn in the paper they did collect.

Proposed Solution: I propose that we use the following procedure for this year's school paper drive.
1. Students will pick up their neighborhood assignments and the flyers announcing the drive at the office. They will go door-to-door in their assigned neighborhoods to distribute the flyers on Monday or Tuesday, April 3 or 4.
2. Students will travel in pairs, never alone.
3. Students will go out only between 2:45 and 5:30 P.M.
4. Students will collect paper from front porches in their assigned neighborhoods on Saturday morning, April 8, between 8:30 and 10:30 A.M.
5. Students will bring all paper to the east parking lot immediately after collecting it.

Respectfully submitted on February 28, 2001, by Hirokai Tanaka from Mrs. Benton's seventh grade class.

> The writer describes a problem.

> The writer proposes a procedure to correct the problem.

> The writer uses numbered steps to describe the procedure.

> The writer identifies himself.

Focus

Lesson Overview

Objectives
- To understand the nature and types of proposals
- To write a successful proposal

Skills
- describing; explaining

Critical Thinking
- analyzing; ordering

Listening and Speaking
- discussing

🔔 Bellringer
Daily Language Activity

When students enter the classroom, have this assignment on the board: *Make a list of suggestions to improve some aspect of the school day—for example, you might recommend a plan for more efficient traffic patterns during class changes or a more convenient schedule for gym classes.*

Motivating Activity

Call on volunteers to share some of the suggestions they listed in the Bellringer activity. Explain to students that the lesson on proposal writing will help them present their suggestions to the school administration.

Teach

Guided Reading
- How many steps are there in the model proposal?
- What is the benefit of providing a numbered list?
- Why should a proposal writer identify himself or herself?

Business & Technical Writing

Business and Technical Writing

Teach

Types of Proposals

Although it may be several years before students are expected to frame a business or a grant proposal, procedure and project proposals are well within the realm of their probable experience. A proposal is more detailed than a letter of opinion. A project proposal specifies the need for a particular project and lists the steps necessary for carrying out the project successfully; a procedure proposal outlines a solution to a problem; A written proposal is a formal document that indicates the seriousness of the person making the proposal. **L2**

Types of Proposals

Proposals can be used to suggest many kinds of plans and solutions to problems. The four basic types of proposals are procedure, project, business, and grant proposals.

A **procedure proposal**, such as the model on page 345, outlines a new or better way of doing something. When you write a procedure proposal, introduce your idea by telling why the procedure is needed. Then describe the procedure.

A **project proposal** describes an intended project to a person or a committee to obtain permission to carry out the project. College students use proposals to describe projects they would like to do for credit.

A **business proposal** usually answers a request for goods or services that have to meet certain standards, such as how and when the goods or services must be provided. For example, in answer to a request from a city council member, a trucking company might submit a proposal to provide trash pick-up services.

A **grant proposal** requests money to pay for research or other projects. For example, a medical school might apply for a grant to study the effects of exercise on teenagers.

Proposals use persuasive writing and often require research. When you write a proposal, back up your request with reasons why it should be accepted. Support your argument with facts, statistics, and examples.

TYPES OF PROPOSALS

Procedure Proposal	Project Proposal	Business Proposal	Grant Proposal
Describe the problem that your procedure will solve.	Describe in detail the project you want to do.	State the request to which you are responding.	Describe your plan for using the grant money.
Explain your proposed procedure in step-by-step sequence.	Explain why the project is necessary.	Describe what goods or services you can provide and how they fit the requirements of the person or the group requesting proposals.	Explain how your plan meets the requirements for the grant.
Number the steps.	Explain what will be accomplished.		List your qualifications for carrying out your proposal.
Include your name, address, telephone number, and the date you submit the proposal.	Include the project's starting and ending dates.	Explain why your goods or services are better than those of others who may submit proposals.	Give reasons why the grant should be awarded to you.
	Tell what the project will cost and suggest ways to get the money to do it.	Include a quote (your price) and state exactly what the quote includes.	Include your name, address, telephone number, and the date you submit the proposal.
	Include your name, address, telephone number, and the date you submit the proposal.	Include your name, address, telephone number, and the date you submit the proposal.	

Style

Proposals usually have a title that tells what the proposal is for. The title is centered at the top of the page.

Some proposals are in paragraph form. Each line begins at the left margin in block style. Other proposals are divided into sections that have a line space between them. The model on this page is divided into sections in block style.

Business & Technical Writing

Field Trip Proposal (Title)

Submitted by: Ray Gomez (Name of person submitting the proposal.)
Date: September 2, 2001 (Date)

I propose that our class take a field trip to the Stermann Apple Orchard and Cider Mill.

Activities: At the cider mill, we can go into the orchard (Sections) to pick apples. We can also watch a cider-making demonstration while Mr. Stermann explains the apple-pressing process. After the demonstration, we can taste free samples of cider.

Chaperones: Because our school requires one adult for every eight students on a field trip, we will need four chaperones. Our teacher, Mr. Welk, will count as one, so we need to find three more adults to accompany us. I suggest that we each ask an adult family member to volunteer.

Transportation: I have spoken to Mrs. Reed at the transportation office, and she says that we can reserve a school bus that will accommodate up to thirty passengers. Our class of twenty-four, plus four adult chaperones, would fit into one bus.

Costs: The cost per student would be $6.50. This amount covers $2.00 toward the cost of the bus and $4.50 for a bag of apples (the bag includes one caramel apple). If parents can be found to drive students in private cars, we can save the bus fee.

Dates: Mr. Stermann has November 5 and 6 and December 2 open for a group visit. I propose that we reserve November 6 since there are no school assemblies scheduled that day.

Business and Technical Writing **347**

Teach

Using the Model

After students read the model on this page, discuss its parts. Compare the model on this page with that on page 345. Why does the field trip proposal have more sections than the proposal for the paper drive? Why might the writer have used separate sections instead of a numbered list? Encourage students to express their opinions. Point out that if a proposal is complicated, presenting the information in separate sections will make it easier to absorb at a glance. **L2**

Business and Technical Writing

Teach

Preparing to Write a Proposal

Before the students begin the activity, have them read this page. The page begins with a summary of the essential parts of a proposal. Then there is an important directive regarding the physical appearance of the proposal. Encourage students to ask questions about any aspect of proposal writing that is not clear to them. **L2**

Practice and Assess

Evaluation Rubrics

Since writing a proposal involves all the steps of the writing process, including research in the prewriting stage, this activity will extend beyond a single class period. Work with the student committee to evaluate the completed proposals. Remind them to consider both content and form.

Using Technology

Encourage students to follow the Technology Tip on this page. A proposal created on a computer will be easier to produce and revise as well as easier to read and understand. **L3**

Close

Suggest possible revisions to any proposals the class considers viable. After revisions are made, encourage students to submit their proposals to the people who can implement them.

The Parts of a Proposal

Title   The title tells what the proposal is for.

Date   The date is the day on which the proposal is submitted.

Body   The body of a proposal can be a paragraph or it can contain many sections.

Name   The name of the person submitting the proposal is always included. Some proposals are also signed by the writer. An address and phone number or some way of contacting the writer should also be included. Whoever is considering the proposal needs to have a way to get more information or to notify the writer of the proposal's acceptance or rejection.

Neatness Counts

✓ Your proposal will get more attention if it is neat, well organized, and easy to read. Type your proposal or create it on a computer.

✓ Use unlined white 8 1/2-by-11-inch paper.

Technology Tip

Create your proposal on a computer. Use the computer's formatting options, such as fonts, type sizes, and the bold feature, to organize your proposal so that it is easy to read and understand. If you have information that would be understood best in a table, create one with the table feature of a word processing program.

✓ Leave a two-inch margin at the top of the page and margins of at least one inch at the left, right, and bottom.

✓ Use a chart or a graph to organize information.

Activity

Write a Proposal   Imagine that your class produced $1,000.00 in a fundraiser. Write a proposal for how the class should spend the money. Three class members can be appointed to a committee to consider the proposals and to decide which three of them the whole class should consider. Then the three proposals they have chosen can be presented to the class.

PURPOSE   to write a proposal

AUDIENCE   three classmates

LENGTH   one page

WRITING RUBRICS   To write a successful proposal, you should

● do research to find facts that support your plan

● develop your plan by categorizing ideas and organizing them into sections

● explain exactly how the money will be spent. If the money will be spent in different categories, provide a budget

● be persuasive but factual, appealing to the committee's logic

● include a table, a graph, or other organizer to make complex information easier to understand

348

Multimedia Presentations

Creating a Multimedia Presentation

A report that uses a combination of media (different types of communication) is called a multimedia presentation. Visuals (what you see, including written text) and sounds are combined to make a multimedia report.

Here are some parts of one student's multimedia presentation. Its purpose is to teach the audience about hummingbirds and to encourage people to plant flowers that attract them.

The writer uses a slide that shows the subject.

Hummingbird Facts

- more than 300 species of small birds
- rapid wing beat produces a humming sound
- feeds on nectar and tiny insects
- the only birds that can fly backwards

The writer uses a transparency to list facts.

The Hum of Hummingbird Wings

The writer uses sound effects.

FLOWERS THAT ATTRACT HUMMINGBIRDS

- salvia
- lilies
- coral bells
- impatiens
- trumpet vine

The writer uses a handout so that the audience can keep the information.

Business and Technical Writing

Focus

Lesson Overview

Objectives
- To understand the types of media involved in a multimedia presentation
- To appreciate the value of a multimedia presentation
- To plan and develop a commercial for a product or service

Skills
- researching; communicating

Critical Thinking
- evaluating

Listening and Speaking
- discussing

Bellringer
Daily Language Activity

When students enter the classroom have this assignment on the board: *Think of a persuasive commercial you have recently seen on television. Identify the product being advertised, and tell what images, words, and music made the commercial effective.*

Motivating Activity

Discuss with students whether they think commercials on television are more effective than those in the print media. Ask students to share the commercials they listed in the Bellringer activity.

Teach

Using the Model

After students have read the information on this page and examined the parts of the multimedia presentation on hummingbirds, you might initiate a discussion on why a multimedia presentation is more effective than a simple report. Although students may not be familiar with the axiom that all learning comes through the senses, it should be apparent that what you hear as well as see will make a deeper impression than what you merely see. **L2**

Business and Technical Writing

Teach

Types of Media

The main types of media are visual and sound. Within these major types, however, there are several variations. For example, visuals include print material, handouts, slides, charts and graphs, videos, and live demonstrations. The more different kinds of visual appeals made, the stronger the total impression will be. Sounds include not only speaking but background music and other sound effects as well. Listed under Other Options are appeals to the senses of smell, touch, and taste. You might have the students brainstorm to develop a list of presentations that involve one or more of these senses. For example, a food-sampling booth at a supermarket might appeal to the senses of smell and taste. **L3**

Multimedia Presentations

Types of Media

Most media appeal either to sight (visuals) or hearing (sound). In a multimedia presentation, photos, slides, videos, illustrations, music, and other media are added to an oral presentation. The presenter becomes a narrator who guides an audience through the sights and sounds, and perhaps smells, tastes, and textures, of the presentation. The chart below lists examples of different types of media.

A multimedia presentation can be used for many purposes: to report in depth on a subject of interest, to present an opinion, to motivate an audience to do something, or to sell a product.

To prepare for a multimedia presentation, choose a thesis or a subject. Then do research at the library and on the Internet to find facts, statistics, and expert opinions on the subject. You can even interview experts by e-mail. Look for visuals and other media to enhance your subject.

If you are making a sales presentation, you aim is to make your product as appealing as possible. For example, if you are selling a new brand of dog food, you might want to demonstrate how much dogs love it by making a short video of a dog hungrily eating the food. You might also show a series of slides that tell why your brand is better than the other brands. You could even add a dog's bark as a sound effect every time you change slides. You could conclude your presentation by passing out samples of the food for dog owners to take home.

TYPES OF MEDIA		
Visuals	**Sound**	**Other Options**
Give a demonstration of how something works.	Play a cassette or CD to help your audience hear your subject (the sounds of a forest fire or an elk's bugle).	Appeal to your audience's sense of touch by having them handle an object (a blue jay's feather or part of an abandoned nest).
Use a photograph or a poster to show your subject clearly.	Use background music to help create a mood.	If you are selling a food product, pass out samples to taste and smell.
Show a video to add action.	Add sound effects to a slide show.	
Use a series of slides to show a process.		
Make charts and graphs into slides and transparencies.		
Make handouts of information you want your audience to take with them.		
Provide samples for the audience.		

Style

- Keep each visual simple.
- Use large type for words on visuals. Experiment with type sizes in the room where you will give your presentation.
- Avoid clutter. Two typefaces and three colors are plenty.
- Use the same border and background color on all of your visuals to tie them together.

Teach

Engaging Visuals

Have students examine the visuals on this page and note the practical suggestions provided. Encourage students to discuss the page and ask questions for clarification as needed.

An engaging picture is a good introduction to a subject.

A video can add interesting sights and sounds to the body of a presentation.

An easily read chart helps the audience make a judgment.

Dog's Delight Kibble		
Analysis	**Source**	**Health Benefit**
19% protein	turkey, lamb, eggs	strong bones and teeth
16% fat	canola oil	clear skin and shiny coat
5% fiber	rice, carrots	good digestion

Exploring Language

Recognizing Loaded Language

Many multimedia presentations are advertisements or commercials. Students should be aware of the loaded language that most commercials employ. Loaded language consists of words and phrases that have either a positive or a negative connotation. Have students analyze the language used in at least five commercials. They may choose either television commercials or those that appear in magazines. Students should listen or look for instances of loaded language and record these instances in two columns—negative and positive. They should be prepared to explain the connotations of these words and phrases. In a class or group discussion, students should be encouraged to make generalizations about the use of loaded language in commercials.

Business and Technical Writing

Teach

The Parts of a Multimedia Presentation

Students will notice that the parts of a multimedia presentation, like the parts of a paper, include an introduction, a body, and a conclusion. Each part contains several elements. Remind students that they must first define the purpose and audience for the presentation. Then they should select those elements that will best convey their message to their intended audience. Only experimentation will confirm which elements to combine for a successful presentation. Encourage students to create a simple outline as they assemble the materials they intend to use. You might suggest that they focus on questions like the following:

- How can I best capture the interest of my audience?
- What materials will present and strengthen my message—handouts, videos, outlines?
- How can I conclude my presentation on a strong note? Should I use humor or drama? **L3**

The Parts of a Multimedia Presentation

Multimedia presentations have three parts.

Introduction In the introduction, sound, a visual, or both should be used to focus the audience's attention on the subject. For example, introduce yourself by saying, "I'm [your name] and I believe that Dog's Delight is the best dog food you can give your 'best friend.'" Here are some other ways to introduce a subject.

- Use a transparency or a slide to show a picture or the title of your subject in headline form while you introduce yourself.
- Use music to set the mood and then introduce yourself and your subject.
- Demonstrate a product while explaining who you are and what you are doing.

Technology Tip

If you have access to presentation software, do your multimedia presentation as a slideshow on a computer monitor. Such software allows you to combine written text, visuals (including movie clips and animation), and sound on a series of slides that can be shown automatically or slide by slide as a viewer pushes a button.

Body The body is the longest and most important part of a multimedia presentation. The topic should be explained and supported with facts gathered from reliable sources, such as encyclopedias, other reference books, and experts on the subject. A variety of media should be used to present facts and arguments in interesting ways. To make sure that the audience gets the message, a certain amount of time can be reserved for them to ask questions. Questions can be anticipated in advance so that extra facts and statistics will be available, if needed.

Conclusion In the brief conclusion of a presentation, the main idea is restated, the most important points are summed up, and the audience can be thanked for their attention.

Presentation Counts

To catch your audience's attention, should you begin with a video of a happy, playful dog; a transparency listing the healthy ingredients of the dog food; or a tape recording of a dog crunching kibble? Experiment with your presentation on your family and friends until you find the most successful combination of media. Use humor whenever possible. When it comes time to make your presentation, be enthusiastic and your audience will be too.

Activity

Create a Multimedia Sales Presentation Create a multimedia presentation to persuade an audience that a particular product or service is the best. Choose the form of your presentation and the kinds of media you will use. Make your presentation to the class.

PURPOSE To create and present a multimedia presentation

AUDIENCE classmates

LENGTH ten minutes

WRITING RUBRICS To create a persuasive multimedia presentation, you should

- make a list of products or services and then research them in a library or on the Internet
- choose a product or service. Then contact the customer service department of the company that sells it to gather facts and statistics about it. If you wish to invent a product or service, research the competition. Then make the statistics for your product more impressive than those for the competition
- summarize and organize ideas gathered from your research by making outlines, maps, organizers, or graphs
- document your sources in a bibliography
- include visuals and sound

Practice and Assess

Evaluation Rubrics

Plan to evaluate the students' multimedia presentations during class periods. You might suggest that several students combine their efforts to create a single presentation. Presentations should be evaluated on the following points:
- a strong central idea
- an effective message
- the incorporation of a variety of visual and sound elements
- the careful execution of ideas

Invite peer evaluation of the students' work.

Close

Have the class decide on two or three presentations that they consider most effective. Arrange to have these presentations made to other classes.

✔ ASSESSMENT OPTIONS

📁 *Tests with Answer Key & Rubrics*
Business and Technical Writing Mastery Test

💾 *Testmaker*
Business and Technical Writing Mastery Test

📼 *MindJogger Videoquizzes*

You may wish to administer the Business and Technical Writing Mastery Test at this point.

Grammar, Usage, and Mechanics

Objectives

The units in Part 2 provide students with the tools they need to apply standard grammar and usage to communicate clearly and effectively in speaking and in writing. Throughout these units, students will be asked

- to write in complete sentences, varying the kinds of sentences
- to use verb tenses appropriately and consistently
- to write using subject-verb agreement
- to write with increasing accuracy when using pronouns and antecedents
- to use adjectives and adverbs, and to use prepositional phrases appropriately to elaborate written ideas
- to use conjunctions to connect ideas meaningfully
- to use capitalization and punctuation correctly to clarify and enhance meaning
- to employ standard English usage

Viewing the Art

Wassily Kandinsky (1866-1944) explored his own ideas about painting, creating large geometric shapes with streaks and blobs of color. Today he is widely known as the founder of abstract art. An influential and controversial contributor to the Blue Rider and Bauhaus movements in art, he continued painting almost until his death.

Interpret and Analyze Use the following questions for discussion:

- What techniques does Kandinsky use to show movement in his painting?
- What emotions might the painter's use of color suggest?
- Why do you think some people at the beginning of the 20th century considered Kandinsky's work controversial?

"After all, a machine has feelings—when it isn't a machine anymore."

—Isaac Asimov

354

Resource Manager

Use the following resources to customize your teaching of the units in Part 2.

📂 **Planning Resources**
- *Lesson Plans*
- *Block Scheduling*

🖨 **Transparencies**
- *Bellringer*
- *Daily Language Practice*
- *Two-Minute Skill Drill*

📂 **Other Print Resources**
- *Dinah Zike's Foldables™ for Writer's Choice*
- *Grammar and Composition Handbook*
- *Grammar Enrichment*
- *Grammar Practice*
- *Grammar Reteaching*
- *Grammar Workbook*
- *Sentence-Combining Practice*

PART 2

Grammar, Usage, and Mechanics

355

Wassily Kandinsky
Variierte Rechteke
1929

Discussing the Quotation

Suggest that students read or reread "Key Item." Ask them to consider the role of technology in their lives. Do computers ever seem almost human? When might a machine be more than just a machine?

Writing Prompt

Ask students to think about Asimov's quotation in light of Kandinsky's painting. Explain to them that Kandinsky's early life in Odessa (in the Ukraine) centered around a love of music and musical instruments. Have students write a paragraph relating the quote to the art. In what ways might Kandinsky's painting speak about the human qualities of machines?

- *Spelling Power*
- *Taking Standardized Tests*
- *Tests with Answer Key and Rubrics*
- *Vocabulary Power*

▥Video
- *MindJogger Videoquizzes*

▦ Software
- *Interactive Grammar and Language Workbook*
- *Language Arts PASS*
- *Presentation Plus!*
- *Revising with Style*
- *Sentence Diagraming*
- *Testmaker*
- *Vocabulary Power Puzzlemaker*

▤ Web Sites
- *writerchoice.glencoe.com*

Objectives

- To understand the various kinds of sentences and their purposes
- To identify and understand subjects and predicates
- To write well-constructed sentences that are appropriate to the writing's purpose

✔ ASSESSMENT OPTIONS

📁 *Tests with Answer Key & Rubrics*
Unit 8 Pretest, pp. 33–34
Unit 8 Mastery Test, pp. 35–36

💾 *Testmaker*
Unit 8 Pretest
Unit 8 Mastery Test

You may wish to administer the Unit 8 Pretest at this point.

Key to Ability Levels

L1 Level 1 activities are within the basic ability range of students.

L2 Level 2 activities are within the ability range of average students.

L3 Level 3 activities are more challenging activities.

UNIT

8

Subjects, Predicates, and Sentences

356

Resource Manager

 **Planning Resources**
- *Lesson Plans*
- *Block Scheduling*

 Transparencies
- *Bellringer*
- *Daily Language Practice*

📁 **Other Print Resources**
- *Grammar and Composition Handbook*

- *Grammar Enrichment*
- *Grammar Practice*
- *Grammar Reteaching*
- *Grammar Workbook*
- *Sentence-Combining Practice*
- *Tests with Answer Key and Rubrics*

**Video**
- *MindJogger Videoquizzes*

 **Software**
- *Interactive Grammar and Language Workbook*
- *Language Arts PASS*
- *Presentation Plus!*
- *Revising with Style*
- *Testmaker*

 **Web Sites**
- *writerschoice.glencoe.com*

8.1 | Kinds of Sentences

■ A **sentence** is a group of words that expresses a complete thought.

Different kinds of sentences have different purposes. A sentence can make a statement, ask a question, give a command, or express strong feeling. All sentences begin with a capital letter and end with a punctuation mark, which is determined by the purpose of that sentence.

■ A **declarative** sentence makes a statement. It ends with a period.

Ecologists study relationships in nature.

■ An **interrogative sentence** asks a question. It ends with a question mark.

Do animals and plants depend on each other?

■ An **exclamatory sentence** expresses strong feeling. It ends with an exclamation point.

What important work ecologists do!

■ An **imperative sentence** gives a command or makes a request. It ends with a period or an exclamation point.

Look at these animals.

Ecologists often do research in the field.

Do they also work in the lab?

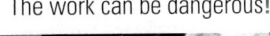

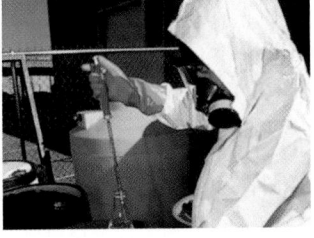

The work can be dangerous!

Please preserve our wildlife.

8.1 Kinds of Sentences   **357**

Subjects, Predicates, and Sentences

Focus

Lesson Overview

Objectives
- To identify and use the four kinds of sentences: declarative, interrogative, exclamatory, and imperative
- To use punctuation marks appropriately

Bellringer
Daily Language Activity

When students enter the classroom, have this assignment on the board: *Rewrite this sentence as a question and then as an exclamation:*

Everything is all right.

See also *Daily Language Practice*

Motivating Activity

Have students read aloud the sentences from the Bellringer activity. Discuss what their voices do as they read. For example, a high tone of voice may end a question, while a lower tone and higher volume may end an exclamation. Explain that while the words may be the same in a declarative sentence and an exclamatory sentence, the punctuation signals a difference in the way each sentence should be read.

Teach

Vocabulary Link

The term *interrogative* comes from the Latin word *interrogare*, meaning "to ask." It is related to *interrogate*, as in *The police interrogated suspects.*

Cross-Reference: Mechanics

For instruction and practice on end punctuation, refer students to Lesson 20.1.

Resource Manager

📂 **Planning Resources**
- *Lesson Plans*

🔲 **Transparencies**
- *Bellringer*
- *Daily Language Practice*

📂 **Other Print Resources**
- *Grammar and Composition Handbook*
- *Grammar Enrichment,* p. 1
- *Grammar Practice,* p. 1
- *Grammar Workbook,* Lessons 1–2

Practice and Assess

Additional Resources

 *Grammar Practice*, p. 1

 *Grammar Enrichment*, p. 1

 Grammar Workbook, Lessons 1–2

Close

Ask each student to identify an environmental issue and write two declarative, two interrogative, two imperative, and two exclamatory sentences based on the issue. Have students trade papers, analyze one another's sentences, and provide constructive feedback.

Subjects, Predicates, and Sentences

Exercise 1 Identifying Kinds of Sentences

For each sentence, write whether it is *declarative, interrogative, exclamatory,* or *imperative.*

1. Ecologists study the world's population.
2. They also study the world's food supply.
3. Do ecologists study air pollution too?
4. They tell us about the effects of air pollution.
5. Have ecologists also studied water pollution?
6. Examine the source of the water supply.
7. Aren't ecologists concerned about wildlife?
8. How awful that so many species are endangered!
9. Ecologists can give us clues to saving endangered species.
10. What an exciting field this is!

Exercise 2 Punctuating Different Kinds of Sentences

Write each sentence, adding capital letters and punctuation marks where necessary.

1. ecologists and other experts study the effects of air and water pollution
2. do you know how pollution affects your life
3. air pollution increases lung and breathing ailments
4. think about the effect of pollution on the water you drink
5. can fish live in poisoned water
6. look to the oceans for food in the future
7. what fascinating work marine biologists do
8. don't ecologists use information from many sources
9. what other kinds of information do ecologists use
10. they use knowledge from physics and mathematics
11. how important this field of study is
12. ecologists spread their message in many ways
13. ecologists often speak about the importance of a clean environment
14. they may appear before meetings of private organizations
15. do they also write magazine articles
16. read articles in the daily newspapers
17. what a need for publicity exists
18. colleges offer courses in ecology
19. students of ecology learn about the cycles of nature
20. think about becoming an ecologist

Critical Thinking

Sorting Sentence Types

Write a number of sentences on large cards, one sentence to a card. Then on the board write four headings: *Declarative, Interrogative, Exclamatory,* and *Imperative.* Direct students to take turns picking a sentence card, reading the sentence aloud, and placing the card on the tray under the correct heading.

8.2 Sentences and Sentence Fragments

Every sentence has two parts: a subject and a predicate.

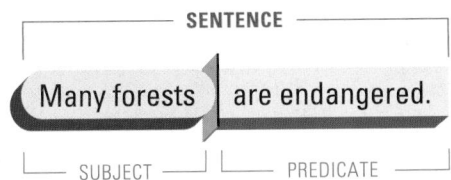

SENTENCE

| Many forests | are endangered. |

SUBJECT — PREDICATE

- The **subject part** of a sentence names whom or what the sentence is about.

- The **predicate part** of the sentence tells what the subject does or has. It can also describe what the subject is or is like.

A sentence must have both a subject and a predicate. It must also express a complete thought.

- A **sentence fragment** is a group of words that does not express a complete thought. It may also be missing a subject, a predicate, or both.

You often use sentence fragments when you speak. You should use complete sentences, however, in anything you write for school or business.

Correcting Sentence Fragments		
FRAGMENT	**PROBLEM**	**SENTENCE**
Lush forests.	The fragment lacks a predicate. *What do the lush forests do?*	Lush forests provide scenic land for recreation.
Inhabits the woodlands.	The fragment lacks a subject. *Who or what inhabits the woodlands?*	Wildlife inhabits the woodlands.
For animals.	The fragment lacks both a subject and a predicate.	Forests provide shelter for animals.

(side tab) Subjects, Predicates, and Sentences

Focus

Lesson Overview

Objectives
- To identify the subject and the predicate of a sentence
- To write complete sentences rather than sentence fragments

Bellringer
Daily Language Activity

When students enter the classroom, have this assignment on the board: *Write two sentences. Use the word cat in one sentence and the word barked in the other sentence.*

See also *Daily Language Practice*

Motivating Activity

Discuss the sentences that students wrote in the Bellringer activity. Elicit that to create complete sentences, students added an action word after *cat* and a naming word before *barked*. Use this observation to introduce the two parts, a subject and a predicate, that every sentence must have.

Teach

☑ Teaching Tip

Many sentence fragments are afterthoughts—words or phrases that comment or elaborate on the preceding sentence. One possible way to fix fragments of this type may be to combine them with the preceding sentence.

Resource Manager

📁 **Planning Resources**
- *Lesson Plans*

📠 **Transparencies**
- *Bellringer*
- *Daily Language Practice*

📁 **Other Print Resources**
- *Grammar and Composition Handbook*
- *Grammar Enrichment*, p. 1
- *Grammar Practice*, p. 1
- *Grammar Reteaching*, p. 1
- *Grammar Workbook*, Lesson 5

Practice and Assess

Answers: Exercise 3

1. sentence
2. fragment; lacks a predicate
3. fragment; lacks subject, predicate
4. sentence
5. fragment; lacks a predicate
6. sentence
7. fragment; lacks subject, predicate
8. sentence
9. sentence
10. fragment; lacks a subject

Answers: Exercise 4

1. <u>Acres of forest land</u> <u>support many kinds of wildlife</u>.
2. <u>The great northern forest</u> <u>consists mostly of spruce</u>.
3. sentence fragment
4. <u>Giant redwood trees</u> <u>grow in the Pacific Northwest</u>.
5. <u>Pines</u> <u>are common in the South</u>.
6. sentence fragment
7. <u>Oak trees</u> <u>dominate the East</u>.
8. <u>Maple trees</u> <u>are also commonly found there</u>.
9. <u>Forests of evergreens</u> <u>cover parts of Asia</u>.
10. sentence fragment
11. <u>Tropical forests</u> <u>ring the middle of the globe</u>.
12. sentence fragment
13. sentence fragment
14. <u>Teak</u> is <u>prized for its hard wood</u>.
15. <u>Chapparal and mesquite</u> <u>grow in dry areas</u>.
16. <u>Forests</u> <u>can provide food and shelter</u>.
17. sentence fragment
18. <u>Each level of a forest</u> <u>has its own layer of life</u>.
19. <u>Even the forest soil</u> <u>teems with life</u>.
20. sentence fragment

Additional Resources

📂 *Grammar Practice,* p. 1
📂 *Grammar Reteaching,* p. 1
📂 *Grammar Enrichment,* p. 1

📖 *Grammar Workbook,* Lesson 5

Subjects, Predicates, and Sentences

Identifying Sentences and Fragments

Write *sentence* or *sentence fragment* for each group of words. If it is a sentence fragment, explain why.

1. Tall trees provide shade.
2. Groves of birches.
3. Under the shelter of trees.
4. Many plants grow in a forest.
5. Healthy forest land.
6. Forests provide benefits.
7. Among the trees.
8. Hardwood makes sturdy furniture.
9. Oak is a valuable hardwood.
10. Threatened by insect pests.

Exercise 4 **Identifying Subjects and Predicates**

Write each numbered item. Underline each subject part once and each predicate part twice. If the item is not a complete sentence, write *sentence fragment.*

1. Acres of forest land support many kinds of wildlife.
2. The great northern forest consists mostly of spruce.
3. Pine, fir, hemlock, and cedar, with birch and willow.
4. Giant redwood trees grow in the Pacific Northwest.
5. Pines are common in the South.
6. Forests of red and white pine.
7. Oak trees dominate the East.
8. Maple trees are also commonly found there.
9. Forests of evergreens cover parts of Asia.
10. Of birches and pines.
11. Tropical forests ring the middle of the globe.
12. Form a large patch in Africa, India, and Southeast Asia.
13. Remain green all year.
14. Teak is prized for its hard wood.
15. Chapparal and mesquite grow in dry areas.
16. Forests can provide food and shelter.
17. The tall trees of an ancient forest.
18. Each level of a forest has its own layer of life.
19. Even the forest soil teems with life.
20. Affected by air, water, and soil pollution.

Close

Have each student write a complete sentence and a fragment. Invite students to exchange papers. Have them explain why the complete sentences are correct, add words to the fragments to make them complete sentences, and support controversial points with examples.

Exploring Language

Using Sentences in Writing

Students may consider a fragment in oral language to be a meaningful contraction of a complete sentence. For example, *Manages forest conditions* may seem like a complete answer to *What does a forester do?* Remind students that in written English, complete sentences must have both a subject and a predicate.

8.3 Subjects and Predicates

A sentence consists of a subject and a predicate, which together express a complete thought. Both a subject and a predicate may consist of more than one word.

COMPLETE SUBJECT	COMPLETE PREDICATE
The capable foresters	study forests closely.
Foresters	are guardians of the environment.

■ The **complete subject** includes all of the words in the subject of a sentence.

■ The **complete predicate** includes all of the words in the predicate of a sentence.

Not all of the words in the subject or the predicate are of equal importance.

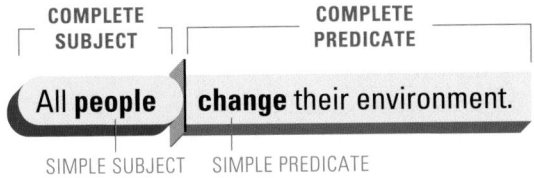

■ The **simple subject** is the main word or group of words in the complete subject.

The simple subject is usually a noun or a pronoun. A **noun** is a word that names a person, a place, a thing, or an idea. A **pronoun** is a word that takes the place of one or more nouns.

■ The **simple predicate** is the main word or group of words in the complete predicate.

The simple predicate is always a verb. A **verb** is a word that expresses an action or a state of being.

Sometimes the simple subject is also the complete subject. Similarly, the simple predicate may also be the complete predicate.

8.3 Subjects and Predicates **361**

Focus

Lesson Overview

Objectives

- To identify simple and complete subjects and predicates
- To write sentences that contain complete subjects and predicates

 Bellringer

Daily Language Activity

When students enter the classroom, have this assignment on the board: Write these sentences. Then underline the subject and circle the verb in each sentence.

The little children happily went to the beach. All the birds were singing loudly from their perches. The ten-month-old baby crawled slowly on the floor. The old car was painted a bright red.

(Answers: *children, went; all, were singing; baby, crawled; car, was painted*)

See also *Daily Language Practice*

Motivating Activity

Have students share their answers to the Bellringer activity. Ask them to identify the complete subject and the complete predicate in each sentence. Remind them to respond to one another's answers in constructive ways.

Teach

☑ **Grammar Tip**

A complete subject can be replaced by one of the following words: *I, you, he, she, it, we, they.*

Subjects, Predicates, and Sentences

Resource Manager

Planning Resources
- *Lesson Plans*

Transparencies
- *Bellringer*
- *Daily Language Practice*

Other Print Resources
- *Grammar and Composition Handbook*
- *Grammar Enrichment*, p. 2
- *Grammar Practice*, p. 2
- *Grammar Reteaching*, p. 2
- *Grammar Workbook*, Lessons 3 and 4

Practice and Assess

Answers: Exercise 5

1. <u>Capable loggers</u> <u>cut only certain trees</u>.
2. <u>Some simple procedures</u> <u>preserve the conditions of the forest</u>.
3. <u>Several foresters</u> <u>study the trees in this region</u>.
4. <u>Their careful observations</u> <u>are useful to ecologists</u>.
5. <u>Their plans for lumber production</u> <u>seem reasonable</u>.
6. <u>Logging companies</u> <u>practice a variety of methods</u>.
7. <u>The most harmful method</u> <u>is clear-cutting</u>.
8. <u>This method</u> <u>totally destroys forest growth</u>.
9. <u>Only vast treeless areas</u> <u>remain</u>.
10. <u>New growth</u> <u>solves the problem in time</u>.
11. <u>A better way</u> <u>harvests only older trees</u>.
12. <u>Younger trees</u> <u>have a chance then</u>.
13. <u>Logging companies</u> <u>need plans for the distant future</u>.
14. <u>Concentration on short-term profits</u> <u>wastes natural resources</u>.
15. <u>Trees</u> <u>are a renewable resource</u>.
16. <u>Forest management</u> <u>requires a careful plan</u>.
17. <u>Forest workers</u> <u>plant new trees</u>.
18. <u>The bare land</u> <u>returns to forest eventually</u>.
19. <u>Some kinds of trees</u> <u>grow more slowly than others</u>.
20. <u>The slowest-growing trees</u> <u>are the most valuable</u>.

Answers: Exercise 6

1. Scientists, control
2. Ecologists, counteract
3. Everyone, benefits
4. people, preserve
5. Biologists, observe
6. Farmers, improve
7. soil, provides
8. crops, take
9. fields, are
10. climate, helps

Additional Resources

📁 *Grammar Practice*, p. 2
📁 *Grammar Reteaching*, p. 2
📁 *Grammar Enrichment*, p. 2

📖 *Grammar Workbook*, Lessons 3 and 4

Exercise 5 — Identifying Complete Subjects and Complete Predicates

Write each sentence. Underline each complete subject once and each complete predicate twice.

1. Capable loggers cut only certain trees.
2. Some simple procedures preserve the conditions of the forest.
3. Several foresters study the trees in this region.
4. Their careful observations are useful to ecologists.
5. Their plans for lumber production seem reasonable.
6. Logging companies practice a variety of methods.
7. The most harmful method is clear-cutting.
8. This method totally destroys forest growth.
9. Only vast treeless areas remain.
10. New growth solves the problem in time.
11. A better way harvests only older trees.
12. Younger trees have a chance then.
13. Logging companies need plans for the distant future.
14. Concentration on short-term profits wastes natural resources.
15. Trees are a renewable resource.
16. Forest management requires a careful plan.
17. Forest workers plant new trees.
18. The bare land returns to forest eventually.
19. Some kinds of trees grow more slowly than others.
20. The slowest-growing trees are the most valuable.

Exercise 6 — Identifying Simple Subjects and Simple Predicates

Write each simple subject and each simple predicate.

1. Scientists control changes in the environment.
2. Ecologists counteract the effects of forest fires, erosion, and floods.
3. Everyone near a forest benefits from these efforts.
4. Careful people preserve natural resources.
5. Biologists observe the growth of plants.
6. Farmers improve the soil on their land.
7. The soil provides crops with valuable nutrients.
8. Some crops take few nutrients from the soil.
9. Lush green fields are a farmer's delight.
10. A temperate climate always helps.

Subjects, Predicates, and Sentences

Close

Ask students to write two sentences, each containing a complete subject and a complete predicate. Have them underline the complete subjects with one line and the complete predicates with two lines. Ask students to share their answers with a partner. Have partners respond in constructive ways.

Critical Thinking

Reducing Subjects

If students are having trouble identifying subjects, have them practice reducing complete subjects to simple subjects. By stripping modifiers away from the nouns they modify, students can find the simple subject in any sentence and identify correct subject-verb agreement.

8.4 Identifying the Subject

Most statements begin with the subject.

Not all sentences begin with the subject, however. Many questions begin with a word that is part of the predicate. The subject comes next, followed by the rest of the predicate.

To locate the subject in a question, it helps to rearrange the words to form a statement.

PREDICATE	SUBJECT	PREDICATE
Do	most people	understand the delicate balance of nature?
	Most people	do understand the delicate balance of nature.

The predicate also precedes the subject in statements beginning with *There is, There are, Here is,* or *Here are.*

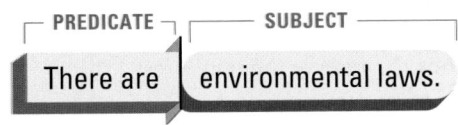

In commands the subject is usually not stated. The predicate is the entire sentence. The word *you* is understood to be the subject.

Focus

Lesson Overview

Objectives
- To use appropriate word order in creating sentences
- To recognize the normal subject-predicate word order of sentences and the main exception to that order

 Bellringer
Daily Language Activity

When students enter the classroom, have this assignment on the board: *Write the subject for the following sentence.*

Go to your room!

See also *Daily Language Practice*

Motivating Activity

Call on volunteers to share their answers to the Bellringer activity. Elicit or explain that *you* is the subject of the sentence. Point out that the subject is usually not stated in commands such as *Go to your room!*

Teach

☑ **Grammar Tip**

One method of identifying the complete subject is to replace it with a pronoun. A pronoun can replace a noun and its modifiers, but it cannot replace an adverb or an adverb phrase. For example, in the sentence *Usually small green people in strange costumes appear only at Halloween,* the word *usually* is not part of the complete subject: *Usually* they *appear only at Halloween.* The pronoun *they* can replace *small green people in strange costumes,* but it cannot replace the adverb *usually.*

Resource Manager

📂 **Planning Resources**
- *Lesson Plans*

📑 **Transparencies**
- *Bellringer*
- *Daily Language Practice*

📂 **Other Print Resources**
- *Grammar and Composition Handbook*
- *Grammar Enrichment,* 3
- *Grammar Practice,* p. 3
- *Grammar Reteaching,* p. 3
- *Grammar Workbook,* Lesson 3

Practice and Assess

Answers: Exercise 7

1. The production of clean timber
2. Lumber companies
3. Some simple procedures
4. Growers of trees
5. Loggers
6. The workers
7. the loggers
8. (You)
9. plants
10. a book about ecology
11. Other interesting books on the subject
12. Many kinds of bacteria
13. human beings
14. Green plants
15. ecologists
16. Scientists
17. (You)
18. Some ecologists
19. many helpful agricultural advances
20. (You)

Answers: Exercise 8

1. the rain forest
2. the clearing of thousands of acres of forest
3. many reasons to preserve the rain forest
4. (You)
5. an important reason
6. (You)
7. (You)
8. the rain forest
9. the world's greatest living resource
10. (You)

Close

Have students write several sentences describing actions they have taken or know about that help to protect the environment. Have them rewrite each sentence, reordering the subject and the predicate, underlining the subject, and circling the predicate.

Exercise 7   Identifying the Subject in Different Sentences

Write the complete subject for each sentence. Write the word *(You)* for the subject if the sentence is a command.

1. The production of clean timber takes several years.
2. Lumber companies buy large amounts of timber.
3. Some simple procedures protect the conditions of the forest.
4. Growers of trees divide the forest into several sections.
5. Loggers work one section each year.
6. The workers cut individual trees.
7. Do the loggers leave some trees?
8. Think of the heavy chain saws.
9. Do plants sprout easily in the region?
10. Here is a book about ecology.
11. Other interesting books on the subject are in the library.
12. Many kinds of bacteria help the environment.
13. Do human beings change their environment?
14. Green plants need a certain amount of light.
15. Do ecologists study animal populations?
16. Scientists reduce the number of undesirable insects.
17. Look at the new plants in this region.
18. Some ecologists look for new methods of farming.
19. There are many helpful agricultural advances.
20. Learn about them when you have time.

Exercise 8   Finding the Subject

Write the complete subject from each of the following sentences.

1. Can the rain forest be saved?
2. Is the clearing of thousands of acres of forest necessary?
3. There are many reasons to preserve the rain forest.
4. List as many reasons as you can think of.
5. Is an important reason the effect on global weather patterns?
6. Think about the effect on wildlife.
7. Consider the valuable resources that are lost.
8. Does the rain forest release oxygen into the atmosphere?
9. Here is the world's greatest living resource.
10. Work to save it.

Subjects, Predicates, and Sentences

MEETING INDIVIDUAL NEEDS   **English Language Learners**

Practicing Patterns

Students learning English may benefit from extra practice with each pattern shown on page 363. Encourage students to copy each pattern (subject, predicate) on a piece of paper. Below the pattern have them write several examples of statements that fit that pattern. Make sure that students are comfortable constructing sentences with each pattern and can identify subjects and predicates. Encourage students to work with a partner and share sentences.

8.5 | Compound Subjects and Predicates

A sentence may have more than one simple subject or simple predicate.

■ A **compound subject** has two or more simple subjects that have the same predicate. The subjects are joined by *and, or,* or *nor.*

COMPOUND SUBJECT

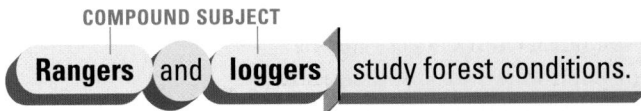

Rangers and loggers | study forest conditions.

When the two simple subjects are joined by *and* or by *both . . . and,* the compound subject is plural and takes the plural form of the verb. In the sentence above, the verb *study* agrees with the plural compound subject. When all parts of a compound subject refer to the same person or thing, the subject takes the singular form of the verb.

When simple subjects are joined by *or* or *nor,* the compound subject may be singular or plural. The verb must agree with the nearer simple subject.

> A ranger or **one** of his assistants **is** always on watch in the observation tower.
> A ranger or his **assistants are** always on watch in the observation tower.

■ A **compound predicate** has two or more simple predicates, or verbs, that have the same subject. The simple predicates are connected by *and, but, or,* or *nor.*

COMPOUND PREDICATE

Rangers | explore and protect the forest.

Explore and *protect* are the simple predicates, or verbs, in the compound predicate. The plural noun *rangers* is the subject of both verbs. Notice that both verbs agree with the plural noun in the subject.

Subjects, Predicates, and Sentences

Focus

Lesson Overview

Objectives

- To identify compound subjects and compound predicates
- To make subjects and verbs agree
- To use the correct verb forms with compound subjects

 Bellringer
Daily Language Activity

When students enter the classroom, have this assignment on the board: *Copy these sentences and then underline the subject in each sentence and circle the verb:*

> *Dave swims. Jen swims.*
> *Dave and Jen swim.*

Discuss students' answers. Encourage them to monitor their understanding and to seek clarification as needed.

See also  *Daily Language Practice*

Motivating Activity

Invite students to construct and say aloud additional sentences that have compound subjects.

Teach

☑ **Teaching Tip**

Tell students that an effective way to determine whether a compound subject with *and* requires a plural verb is to replace the compound subject with a plural pronoun—usually *they.* For example, write the following sentence on the board: *Rangers and loggers study forest conditions.* Then rewrite the sentence, replacing the compound subject *rangers and loggers* with the plural pronoun *they: They study forest conditions.* The plural verb is correct.

Resource Manager

📁 **Planning Resources**
- *Lesson Plans*

📖 **Transparencies**
- *Bellringer*
- *Daily Language Practice*

📁 **Other Print Resources**
- *Grammar and Composition Handbook*
- *Grammar Enrichment,* p. 2
- *Grammar Practice,* p. 2
- *Grammar Reteaching,* p. 4
- *Grammar Workbook,* Lesson 4

Practice and Assess

Answers: Exercise 9

1. CS	**6.** CP
2. CP	**7.** CS
3. CS	**8.** CS
4. CP	**9.** CS
5. CS	**10.** CP

Answers: Exercise 10

1. warn	**11.** turns
2. tell	**12.** reach; harm
3. explains	**13.** release
4. release	**14.** mix; form
5. fight; control	**15.** injures
6. eat	**16.** affect
7. travel; mix	**17.** kills; pollutes
8. poison	**18.** leak
9. eat	**19.** enter, pollute
10. spray; harvest	**20.** study

Additional Resources

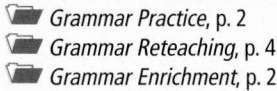 *Grammar Practice*, p. 2
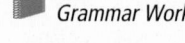 *Grammar Reteaching*, p. 4
Grammar Enrichment, p. 2

Grammar Workbook, Lesson 4

Close

Have students write five sentences describing the wind's impact on people, buildings, and nature. Tell them to use either a compound subject or a compound predicate in each sentence. Then have students share their sentences with a partner and identify the compound part in each sentence. Ask partners to evaluate each other's accuracy and to provide constructive feedback.

366

Exercise 9 **Identifying Compound Subjects and Predicates**

Write whether each sentence has a *compound subject* or a *compound predicate*.

1. Trees and grass hold soil in place.
2. Scientists observe and study the effects of erosion.
3. Both plants and minerals enrich the soil.
4. Erosion destroys and wastes valuable land.
5. Winds and rain sometimes harm the earth.
6. The wind lifts and blows away the topsoil.
7. Neither the soil nor its nutrients last forever.
8. Either rain or flood waters wash soil into streams.
9. Streams and rivers carry the soil away.
10. Crops wither and die in the poor soil.

Exercise 10 **Making Subjects and Verbs Agree**

Write each sentence, using the correct form of the verb in parentheses.

1. Rachel Carson and other biologists (warns, warn) people.
2. She and others (tells, tell) about the dangers of pollution.
3. *Silent Spring* (explains, explain) about pesticides.
4. Both plants and trees (releases, release) oxygen.
5. Some chemicals either (fights, fight) or (controls, control) pests.
6. Humans and animals often (eats, eat) the same foods.
7. The chemicals both (travels, travel) and (mixes, mix) in the food chain.
8. DDT and other chemicals (poisons, poison) insects.
9. Birds and mice (eats, eat) the poisoned insects.
10. Farmers (sprays, spray) and (harvests, harvest) grain crops.
11. DDT (turns, turn) up in milk and butter.
12. Other types of pollution (reaches, reach) and (harms, harm) us.
13. Power plants and cars (releases, release) gases into the air.
14. Some of these gases (mixes, mix) and (forms, form) acid rain.
15. Either smog or acid rain (injures, injure) the earth.
16. Air pollution and water pollution (affects, affect) the soil.
17. Acid rain (kills, kill) forests and (pollutes, pollute) lakes.
18. Both fertilizers and pesticides (leaks, leak) down through the dirt.
19. These (enters, enter) and (pollutes, pollute) underground water.
20. Either scientists or lab workers (studies, study) the effects of pollution.

(side tab) Subjects, Predicates, and Sentences

Exploring Language

Choosing a Verb Form

Tell students that a compound subject joined by *or* requires a careful choice of the verb form. On the board, write the following sentence: *Either the ranger or volunteers lead the nature walk.* Read the sentence aloud and ask a student to point out the two subjects, *the ranger* and *volunteers.* Then reverse the order of the subjects: *Either volunteers or the ranger . . .* Ask how the verb needs to change. Have students add *-s* to the verb *lead* so that it agrees with the nearer simple subject. Have students ask questions for clarification as needed.

8.6 Simple and Compound Sentences

- A **simple sentence** has one subject and one predicate.

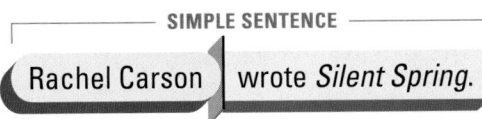

A simple sentence may have a compound subject, a compound predicate, or both, as in the following example.

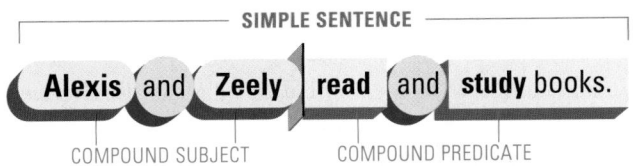

- A **compound sentence** is a sentence that contains two or more simple sentences joined by a comma and a coordinating conjunction or by a semicolon.

A compound sentence has two complete subjects and two complete predicates.

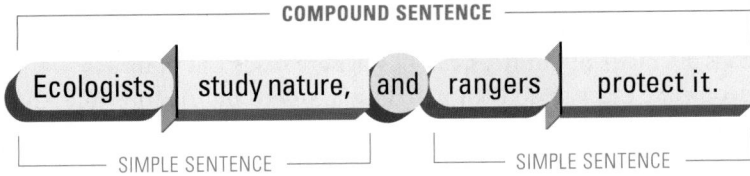

A run-on sentence is two or more sentences incorrectly written as one sentence. To correct a run-on, write separate sentences or combine the sentences as shown below.

Correcting Run-on Sentences	
RUN-ON	**CORRECT**
Ecologists study nature they protect it.	Ecologists study nature. **T**hey protect it.
Ecologists study nature, they protect it.	Ecologists study nature, **and** they protect it.
	Ecologists study nature**;** they protect it.

Focus

Lesson Overview

Objectives
- To identify simple and compound sentences and run-on sentences
- To use simple sentences and compound sentences appropriately
- To avoid or correct run-on sentences

 Bellringer
Daily Language Activity

When students enter the classroom, have this assignment on the board: *Copy the sentences. Then write one sentence that combines them.*

> *Juan blew out the candles. Everybody had a piece of cake.*

See also *Daily Language Practice*

Motivating Activity

Invite students to share their responses to the Bellringer activity. Remind students to use a comma before the conjunction when combining sentences.

Teach

Critical Thinking
Ask students to identify the simple sentences within this compound sentence:

> Of all formal things in the world, a clipped hedge is the most formal; and of all the informal things in the world, a forest tree is the most informal.
>
> —*Royal Truths*
> Henry Ward Beecher

Subjects, Predicates, and Sentences

Resource Manager

📁 **Planning Resources**
- *Lesson Plans*

📂 **Transparencies**
- *Bellringer*
- *Daily Language Practice*

📁 **Other Print Resources**
- *Grammar and Composition Handbook*
- *Grammar Enrichment*, p. 4
- *Grammar Practice*, p. 4
- *Grammar Workbook*, Lesson 6

Practice and Assess

Answers: Exercise 11

1. run-on; Ecologists study forests, and their research provides information for the rangers and for government agencies.
2. simple sentence
3. run-on; The laboratories develop new instruments of science; the instruments must work well in the field.
4. compound sentence
5. simple sentence
6. simple sentence
7. compound sentence
8. simple sentence
9. simple sentence
10. simple sentence
11. run-on; Scientists develop antipollution devices, and farmers use natural fertilizers.
12. simple sentence
13. simple sentence
14. run-on; Paper bags are made out of trees; plastic bags are made out of oil.
15. compound sentence
16. run-on; Americans use 50 million tons of paper a year; that is about 580 pounds per person.
17. simple sentence
18. compound sentence
19. run-on; This could save millions of trees a year, and the effort is worth it.
20. run-on; There is only so much laws can do; people must cooperate.

Additional Resources

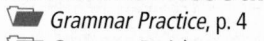 *Grammar Practice*, p. 4
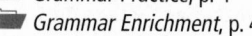 *Grammar Enrichment*, p. 4

📘 *Grammar Workbook*, Lesson 6

368

Subjects, Predicates, and Sentences

Exercise 11   Identifying Simple and Compound Sentences

Write whether each sentence is *simple, compound,* or *run-on.* If it is a run-on sentence, rewrite it correctly.

1. Ecologists study forests, their research provides information for the rangers and for government agencies.
2. Ecologists study and work in modern, well-equipped laboratories.
3. The laboratories develop new instruments of science the instruments must work well in the field.
4. Some problems arise in forest environments; ecologists develop solutions to these problems.
5. Neither the animals' homes nor their food sources escape the effects of the unwise use of resources.
6. Small plants grow under tall trees and provide food for the smaller animals of the forest.
7. Sometimes animals can return to the forest after a disaster; this heartens ecologists.
8. Soil and leaves may be losing elements.
9. The burning of gas, oil, and coal pollutes the air and perhaps causes acid rain in certain regions.
10. A great many lakes in Canada and forests in the United States are harmed by acid rain.
11. Scientists develop antipollution devices farmers use natural fertilizers.
12. The Environmental Protection Agency establishes and enforces clean-air standards.
13. Ordinary people can help end pollution and save the earth.
14. Paper bags are made out of trees, plastic bags are made out of oil.
15. Many people are eager to do their part, but they need information and encouragement.
16. Americans use 50 million tons of paper a year that is about 580 pounds per person.
17. Americans should save newspapers and recycle them.
18. Newspaper is shredded and mashed into pulp, and the pulp is turned back into paper.
19. This could save millions of trees a year the effort is worth it.
20. There is only so much laws can do, people must cooperate.

Close

Have students write a paragraph describing what they would do on a camping trip to avoid causing any destruction to the forest. Tell students to use compound sentences in their descriptions and to be careful to avoid run-on sentences. Have students exchange papers and suggest revisions where appropriate.

MEETING INDIVIDUAL NEEDS English Language Learners

Recognizing Compound Sentences

Students learning English may find it easier to determine whether a sentence is compound by covering it up to and including the conjunction. If the remaining part is a complete sentence, the whole thing is a compound sentence and needs a comma before the conjunction.

SUBJECTS, PREDICATES, AND SENTENCES

In *Water Sky*, Lincoln Noah, a young half-Inuit boy from Massachusetts, visits the whaling village where his father once lived. There Lincoln observes how a community can live in harmony with its environment. In this passage, the boy learns about the relationship that exists between whales and humans by talking to an Inuit whaling captain, Vincent Ologak. The passage has been annotated to show some of the sentence structures covered in this unit.

Subjects, Predicates, and Sentences

Literature Model

from *Water Sky*
by Jean Craighead George

Vincent folded his arms and stood beside him. "Lincoln Noah," he said, "I have something very important to say to you." His eyes were soft, and his strength seemed to have returned.

"A whale is coming to you."

"A whale is coming to me, Vincent Ologak? I do not understand."

"The animals give themselves to the Eskimos. They let us kill them. They then become us: our blood, our voices, our spirits. They join us in our bodies. That is what they wish. We are all one."

Lincoln tried to understand. Vincent continued.

"When your father left my igloo many years ago, he asked me what he could do to thank me. And so I said to him: Name your first son Lincoln, for the great protector of men. And give him a second name, Noah, for the great protector of animals."

> Compound predicate

> Compound sentence

> Complete subject

> Complete predicate

> Declarative sentence

Teach

About the Literature

Explain that the review contains a passage followed by exercises on related topics. After students read the passage, discuss whether they like the idea that animals and people are "all one." How might that belief contribute to the stability of the Inuit culture? Then ask students to summarize their ideas in their journals.

Explain to students that Jean Craighead George is an American writer and illustrator. She writes about the Inuit, the native inhabitants of the North American Arctic.

Linking Grammar and Literature

☑ **Teaching Tip**

The Inuit are known to many as Eskimos, the name given them by the Algonquian Indians of eastern Canada. The name Eskimo was adopted by the European explorers and was once widely used, even among the Inuits themselves. Inuit is the preferred name of this culture. In the Inuit language, the name means "the real people."

Critical Thinking

From their reading of the passage, students should make inferences about how Vincent feels about animals and nature.

Listening and Speaking

Invite two volunteers to assume the roles of Lincoln Noah and Vincent. Have this passage read aloud. Discuss students' reactions to the dialogue. Note how the varied sentence structure of the passage adds to its strength.

✓ ASSESSMENT OPTIONS

📁 *Tests with Answer Key and Rubrics*
Unit 8 Mastery Test, pp. 35–36

💾 *Testmaker*
Unit 8 Mastery Test

Grammar Review **369**

Resource Manager

📁 **Planning Resources**
• *Lesson Plans*

📁 **Other Print Resources**
• *Grammar and Composition Handbook*
• *Grammar Workbook,* Lessons 1–6

Practice and Assess

Answers: Exercise 1

1. sentence fragment
2. <u>Lincoln</u> <u>listened</u> . . .
3. <u>The whaling captain</u> <u>knew</u> . . .
4. sentence fragment
5. <u>Lincoln's father</u> <u>was grateful</u> . . .
6. <u>Ologak</u> <u>said to</u> . . .
7. sentence fragment
8. <u>Lincoln Noah</u> <u>had hated</u> . . .
9. sentence fragment
10. <u>Lincoln Noah</u> <u>was</u> . . .
11. sentence fragment
12. sentence fragment
13. sentence fragment
14. <u>The whaling captain</u> <u>told</u> . . .
15. <u>Lincoln</u> <u>did not</u> . . .
16. <u>The animals</u> <u>give themselves</u> . . .
17. <u>The whales and the Eskimos</u> <u>become one</u>
18. sentence fragment
19. <u>The whales</u> <u>wished</u> . . .
20. <u>Vincent</u> <u>continued</u> . . .

"He never told me that," Lincoln said. "I sure wish he had. I always hated my name. Kids made fun of it." He paused. "I guess I never asked about it."

"Lincoln Noah is a fine name all right. I knew someday there would be a whale who would come to one named Lincoln Noah. I have waited and waited for you to grow up and the whale to grow old."

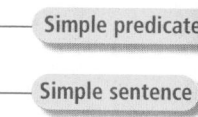 Simple predicate — Simple sentence

Review: Exercise 1 Identifying Sentences and Sentence Fragments

Write each sentence and underline each complete subject once and each complete predicate twice. If the item is not a complete sentence, write *sentence fragment.*

SAMPLE Vincent said something important to Lincoln.
ANSWER <u>Vincent</u> <u>said something important to Lincoln.</u>

1. Talked about the bond between men and animals.
2. Lincoln listened to Ologak.
3. The whaling captain knew Lincoln's father.
4. Had lived in Ologak's igloo long ago.
5. Lincoln's father was grateful to Ologak.
6. Ologak said to name the boy Lincoln Noah.
7. For Lincoln, the protector of men, and Noah, the protector of animals.
8. Lincoln Noah had hated his name.
9. Teased by the other kids because of his strange name.
10. Lincoln Noah was a fine name according to Ologak.
11. A whale who would come to one named Lincoln Noah.
12. Waited and waited for him to grow up.
13. And the whale to grow old.
14. The whaling captain told Lincoln about the whale.
15. Lincoln did not understand.
16. The animals give themselves to the Eskimos.
17. The whales and the Eskimos become one.
18. Their blood, their voices, their spirits.
19. The whales wished to do this.
20. Vincent continued with his story.

Review: Exercise 2 | Identifying Complete Subjects and Complete Predicates

Write each sentence. Underline each complete subject once and each complete predicate twice.

SAMPLE The Inuits' way of life is rapidly disappearing.
ANSWER The Inuits' way of life is rapidly disappearing.

1. The land of the Inuit stretches from Siberia to Greenland.
2. This cold country is troubled by gales.
3. Inuits of the past were expert hunters.
4. They hunted whale, walrus, seal, and caribou.
5. Two kinds of boats carried them across the water.
6. The light, swift kayak was ideal for chasing seals.
7. The larger, heavier umiak transported entire families.
8. Inuits of former times lived in harmony with the seasons.
9. They hunted through the spring, summer, and fall.
10. Their winter homes were snowhouse villages on the sea ice.

Review: Exercise 3 | Identifying Simple Subjects and Simple Predicates

Write each simple subject and each simple predicate.

SAMPLE Jean Craighead George studied science in college.
ANSWER Jean Craighead George / studied

1. George's family enjoyed nature and the outdoors.
2. Her father was an entomologist.
3. Her jobs involved writing or art.
4. George writes about nature and natural history.
5. Her first books were animal stories for children.
6. The author explores the places in her books.
7. This extensive research takes time and energy.
8. Natural history blends with good stories in her books.
9. Her most famous book is probably *My Side of the Mountain*.
10. However, her own favorite is *Spring Comes to the Ocean*.

Answers: Exercise 2
1. The land of the Inuit stretches . . .
2. This cold country is troubled . . .
3. Inuits of the past were expert . . .
4. They hunted . . .
5. Two kinds of boats carried . . .
6. The light, swift kayak was ideal for . . .
7. The larger, heavier umiak transported . . .
8. Inuits of former times lived . . .
9. They hunted . . .
10. Their winter homes were snowhouse . . .

Answers: Exercise 3
1. family (subj.); enjoyed (pred.)
2. father (subj.); was (pred.)
3. jobs (subj.); involved (pred.)
4. George (subj.); writes (pred.)
5. books (subj.); were (pred.)
6. author (subj.); explores (pred.)
7. research (subj.); takes (pred.)
8. history (subj.); blends (pred.)
9. book (subj.); is (pred.)
10. favorite (subj.); is (pred.)

Subjects, Predicates, and Sentences

371

Answers: Exercise 4

1. <u>Whales</u> <u>are</u> mammals.
2. <u>People</u> <u>have hunted</u> whales since prehistoric times.
3. A <u>whale</u> <u>can produce</u> sounds underwater.
4. Some <u>whales</u> <u>are</u> one hundred feet long.
5. <u>Size</u> <u>does vary</u> within species.
6. <u>People</u> <u>have confused</u> whales with fish.
7. <u>Blubber</u> <u>does insulate</u> whales from the cold.
8. Killer <u>whales</u> <u>are</u> the fastest of all whales. or <u>Killer whales</u> <u>are</u> the fastest of all whales.
9. Killer <u>whales</u> <u>do prey</u> on seals, dolphins, and porpoises. or <u>Killer whales</u> <u>do prey</u> on seals, dolphins, and porpoises.
10. <u>Dolphins</u> <u>are classified</u> as whales.

Answers: Exercise 5

1. compound predicate
2. compound predicate
3. compound subject
4. compound predicate
5. compound subject
6. compound subject
7. compound predicate
8. compound predicate
9. compound subject
10. compound predicate

Subjects, Predicates, and Sentences

Review: Exercise 4   **Identifying Subjects and Predicates in Questions**

Rewrite each question as a statement. Then underline each simple subject once and each simple predicate twice.

SAMPLE   Do laws protect certain kinds of whales?
ANSWER   <u>Laws</u> <u>do protect</u> certain kinds of whales.

1. Are whales mammals?
2. Have people hunted whales since prehistoric times?
3. Can a whale produce sounds underwater?
4. Are some whales one hundred feet long?
5. Does size vary within species?
6. Have people confused whales with fish?
7. Does blubber insulate whales from the cold?
8. Are killer whales the fastest of all whales?
9. Do killer whales prey on seals, dolphins, and porpoises?
10. Are dolphins classified as whales?

Review: Exercise 5   **Identifying Compound Subjects and Compound Predicates**

Write whether the sentence has a *compound subject* or a *compound predicate*.

SAMPLE   Whales and dolphins have flippers instead of forelegs.
ANSWER   compound subject

1. The Greek philosopher Aristotle thought and wrote about whales.
2. Marine biologists observe and study marine mammals.
3. Whales and other marine mammals have traces of limbs.
4. They have lungs and breathe air.
5. Elephants and rhinos are tiny compared with blue whales.
6. Humpback whales and blue whales eat tiny sea creatures.
7. Sheets of baleen trap and strain their food.
8. Toothed whales navigate and find food by means of sound.
9. Humpback whales and gray whales migrate north in the summer.
10. Thirty-foot-long orcas attack and eat larger whales.

Review: Exercise 6   Making Subjects and Verbs Agree

Write the correct form of the verb in parentheses.

1. Both the Inuit hunter and his daughter (watches, watch) the old whale.
2. The whale and his pod (lives, live) in the Bering Sea in winter.
3. The lengthening day and warming waters (signals, signal) them.
4. The whales (leaves, leave) and (swims, swim) north.
5. Either adolescents or young adults (makes, make) up most of the first group.
6. Mothers, calves, and old whales (forms, form) the next wave.
7. Whales of assorted sizes and ages (migrates, migrate) last.
8. Neither scientists nor whalers (understands, understand) why they do this.
9. All the whales (rests, rest) and (feeds, feed) in their summer home.
10. Either the hunter or his daughter (waves, wave) goodbye to the whale.

Review: Exercise 7   Identifying Simple and Compound Sentences

Write whether each sentence is *simple* or *compound*.

1. One creature had a long, spiraling tusk.
2. It resembled the mythical unicorn, and they called it the unicorn of the sea.
3. That creature was the narwhal, but little could be learned of it.
4. Few people actually saw the narwhal, and it eventually became a fantasy itself.
5. Kings and queens desired and paid fortunes for narwhal ivory.
6. Narwhals live in the far North; they are creatures of the ice.
7. Male narwhals have two tusks, but only one tusk grows long.
8. Scientists and other people wonder about the tusk's purpose.
9. The narwhal's tasty, vitamin-rich meat provided food for Inuits and their sled dogs.
10. Narwhals were once widely hunted, but recent laws restrict hunting and protect these unique creatures.

Answers: Exercise 6
1. watch
2. live
3. signal
4. leave, swim
5. make
6. form
7. migrate
8. understand
9. rest, feed
10. waves

Answers: Exercise 7
1. simple
2. compound
3. compound
4. compound
5. simple
6. compound
7. compound
8. simple
9. simple
10. compound

Subjects, Predicates, and Sentences

Answers: Exercise 8

Sample corrections for run-on sentences are given. Student answers may vary.

1. compound
2. run-on—Cetaceans are warm-blooded, and they nurse their young on milk.
3. compound
4. run-on—Toothed whales are predators; they pursue fish and squid.
5. compound
6. compound
7. run-on—These gentle giants were hunted almost to extinction, and just a few hundred blue whales remain.
8. run-on—Whales need time to increase in number, or they will die out. (Accept compound *as an alternative answer; some short compound sentences do not require a comma before the conjunction.*)
9. compound
10. run-on—Norway hunts whales; Japan, Iceland, and Korea do also.

Answers: Exercise 9

1. Lincoln's father . . . village, and he . . .
2. The whale hunters . . . whale, or people . . .
3. The whale . . . blubber, and they . . .
4. Lincoln . . . whale, and he . . .
5. Lincoln . . . community, but he felt . . .

Subjects, Predicates, and Sentences

Review: Exercise 8 Identifying Compound Sentences and Run-on Sentences

Write *compound* if a sentence is a compound sentence. If it is a run-on sentence, rewrite it correctly.

1. Whales, dolphins, and porpoises are members of the order called cetaceans, and they are true air-breathing mammals.
2. Cetaceans are warm-blooded, they nurse their young on milk.
3. Cetaceans are divided into two subclasses; these are toothed whales and baleen whales.
4. Toothed whales are predators they pursue fish and squid.
5. Among the largest whales, only the sperm whale has teeth; the others are all baleen whales.
6. Baleen whales have fringed plates of baleen instead of teeth, and they strain small sea life out of the water.
7. These gentle giants were hunted almost to extinction, just a few hundred blue whales remain.
8. Whales need time to increase in number or they will die out.
9. The International Whaling Commission is working to end whaling, but some countries will not cooperate.
10. Norway hunts whales Japan, Iceland, and Korea do also.

Review: Exercise 9 Writing Compound Sentences

Use *and, but,* or *or* to combine each pair of simple sentences into a compound sentence.

1. Lincoln's father had lived in the village. He wanted his son to spend time there too.
2. The whale hunters had to locate and spear a whale. People in their village would starve.
3. The whale would provide them with meat and blubber. They would also use it for oil and leather.
4. Lincoln hunted for the whale. He killed it.
5. Lincoln loved the Inuit community. He felt he should return to his life in Massachusetts.

Review: Exercise 10

Proofreading

The following passage is about Siwidi, a mythological hero of the Kwakiutl. The whale mask below was used in ceremonial dances to reenact that hero's adventures. Rewrite the passage, correcting the errors in spelling, capitalization, grammar, and usage. Add any missing punctuation. There are ten errors.

The Legend of Siwidi

¹Siwidi acquired many wonderful gifts during his adventures in an undersea kingdom ²These gifts enabled Siwidi the great hero of the kwakiutl, to change his appearance. ³When the hero rose from the sea, he appeared to his people as a whale with an eagle on it's back and a double tail. ⁴People in canoes chased this great creature but they couldn't catch it. ⁵As a result of Siwidis undersea adventures, him became known as "Born-to-Be-Head-of-the-World."

Artist unknown, Kwakiutl whale mask, nineteenth century

Grammar Review 375

Subjects, Predicates, and Sentences

Answers: Exercise 10 Proofreading

This proofreading activity provides editing practice with (1) the current or previous units' skills, (2) **Troubleshooter** errors, and (3) spelling errors. Students should be able to complete the exercise by referring to the units, the **Troubleshooter,** and a dictionary. (Note: A run-on sentence counts as one error.)

Error (Type of Error)

1. kingdom. (end punctuation)
2. Siwidi, (nonessential appositive)
   Kwakiutl (ethnic group)
3. its (possessive pronoun)
4. creature, but (run-on sentence)
5. Siwidi's (singular possessive)
   he became (subject pronoun)
6. celebrate (spelling)
7. the dancer also (sentence fragment)
8. whales. The or whales; or whales, and
   (run-on sentence)

Viewing the Art

Artist Unknown, Kwakiutl, whale mask, nineteenth century

Discuss the whale mask with students. Explain that the elaborate masks made by the Inuit during the nineteenth century were used for religious and other rituals. The animals that the masks portray were thought to have spirits that communicated with humans. The masks are made from wood and other various materials and are painted.

The whale mask shown here is rendered in wood, hide, and rope and measures 84 inches long and 29 inches wide. It is displayed in the American Museum of Natural History in New York. Ask students to discuss how the mask helps to extend the meaning of "The Legend of Siwidi."

Answers: Exercise 11
Mixed Review

In many of the sentences, two answers are correct. You may want to accept either as a correct answer, rather than requiring both.

1. complete subject
2. simple predicate
3. simple subject
4. compound predicate, simple predicate
5. complete predicate
6. simple predicate
7. compound subject, complete subject
8. complete predicate
9. compound subject, simple subject
10. complete subject
11. simple predicate
12. compound predicate, simple predicate
13. simple subject
14. compound subject, complete subject
15. complete subject
16. simple subject
17. complete predicate
18. compound predicate, simple predicate
19. simple subject
20. compound predicate, simple predicate

Close

Have students discuss strategies they use to determine whether a group of words is a complete sentence or only a sentence fragment. Ask students to record in their journals the strategy that each of them thinks is the best.

⁶The Kwakiutl developed a dance to celabrate Siwidi's appearance as a whale. ⁷The performer imitates the movements of a whale throughout this dance; also wears a large whale mask. ⁸By recognizing the bond between animals and people, Vincent Ologak of *Water Sky* showed his respect for whales the dance reflects the respect the Kwakiutl have for Siwidi and for all whales.

> **Review: Exercise 11**

Mixed Review

Identify the underlined word or words in each of the following sentences as a *complete subject*, a *complete predicate*, a *simple subject*, a *simple predicate*, a *compound subject*, or a *compound predicate*.

¹The greatest event in an Inupiaq village is the whale hunt. ²One whale can feed many people. ³Each village may take only a limited number of whales, however. ⁴The Inupiaq people respect and honor the whales they hunt. ⁵They think of the meat as a gift from the animal itself. ⁶Inupiaq children learn an important lesson. ⁷Humans and animals must live in harmony with each other and with nature.

⁸Everyone joins in the work of bringing in the whale. ⁹Even the youngest boys and girls help pull the whale onto the ice. ¹⁰Many children hope to become whaling captains someday. ¹¹Whaling captains earn money from the whales they catch. ¹²More important, a successful captain divides and shares his catch. ¹³In the Arctic, no one goes hungry when a whale hunt is successful. ¹⁴The elderly and the sick receive their share of food. ¹⁵Young people in the Arctic have been taught sharing as a way of life for centuries.

¹⁶Inupiaq schoolchildren learn both English and their native language in school. ¹⁷They also learn the traditional ways of their people. ¹⁸Not all Inupiaq children stay and live in their home villages. ¹⁹High school graduates often go on to college, but some return to the Arctic. ²⁰Many college graduates teach or work in the native government system.

Subjects, Predicates, and Sentences

Writing Application

Sentence Types in Writing

Madeleine L'Engle uses different kinds of sentences in *A Wind in the Door* to convey her speakers' tones and to make her writing clearer and more interesting. Examine the passage below, noting the italicized sentences.

"Okay, did the big boys jump you in the schoolyard this time, or when you got off the bus?"

"Meg, you aren't listening to me."

"I happen to care that you've been in school for two months now and not a single week has gone by that you haven't been roughed up. If you've been talking about dragons in the garden or wherever they are, I suppose that explains it."

"I haven't. *Don't underestimate me.* I didn't see them till I got home."

Techniques with Sentence Types

Try to apply some of Madeleine L'Engle's techniques when you write.

❶ Use interrogative sentences to capture a speaker's tone and show that he or she is asking a question. Compare these:

DECLARATIVE VERSION the big boys jumped you when you got off the bus

L'ENGLE'S VERSION did the big boys jump you in the schoolyard this time, or when you got off the bus?

❷ Make your writing more effective by using imperative sentences to convey a speaker's feelings as he or she makes a demand or request.

DECLARATIVE VERSION I wish you wouldn't underestimate me.

L'ENGLE'S VERSION Don't underestimate me.

TIME

For more about the writing process, see **TIME Facing the Blank Page**, pp. 97–107.

Subjects, Predicates, and Sentences

Sentence Types in Writing

Encourage students to read the passage by Madeleine L'Engle silently. Then ask a volunteer to read the passage aloud with expression, taking special note of the italicized sentences. Discuss the tone of the characters' voices. Ask students what words or phrases in the sentences help convey the feelings that are expressed.

Techniques with Sentence Types

Discuss the difference that using an imperative rather than a declarative sentence can make in the tone of a request or demand. Have students provide an example of a declarative sentence and then ask them to change it to an imperative sentence. Discuss the impact of each type of sentence.

Refer students to the passage by Jean Craighead George on page 369 and have them find the declarative sentence "We are all one." Discuss the impact of this sentence on the passage.

Practice

The answers to this challenging and enriching activity will vary. Refer to Techniques with Sentence Types as you evaluate students' choices.

✔ ASSESSMENT OPTIONS

📁 *Tests with Answer Key and Rubrics Unit 8 Mastery Test*, pp. 35–36

💾 *Testmaker* Unit 8 Mastery Test

You may wish to administer the Unit 8 Mastery Test at this point.

📼 *MindJogger Videoquizzes*

Practice Practice these techniques by revising the following passage. Pay particular attention to the underlined words, changing the sentence types as necessary to make the passage more interesting, varied, and effective.

"By dinnertime we should be there," said Marshall. <u>"The stream might still be frozen."</u> He leaned eagerly over the front seat to nudge his father's shoulder. <u>"Might it be, Marsh?"</u> replied Ed. "We'll check it out as soon as we get there." <u>"I want to know how long it will be until we get there."</u>

"Oh, about an hour, I'd guess," said his father. <u>"You could sit back and relax."</u>

<u>"Dad, I want to hear about how we're going to ice fish in the stream,"</u> said Marshall as the car turned off the highway for Naylor's Peak.

Writing Application **377**

Objectives

- To develop an understanding of nouns, including common and proper nouns
- To develop an understanding of concrete and abstract nouns, compound nouns, and collective nouns
- To use nouns to communicate clearly and effectively in writing

✓ ASSESSMENT OPTIONS

📁 *Tests with Answer Key and Rubrics*
Unit 9 Pretest, pp. 37–38
Unit 9 Mastery Test, pp. 39–40

💾 *Testmaker*
Unit 9 Pretest
Unit 9 Mastery Test

You may wish to administer the Unit 9 Pretest at this point.

Key to Ability Levels

L1 Level 1 activities are within the basic ability range of students.

L2 Level 2 activities are within the ability range of average students.

L3 Level 3 activities are more challenging activities.

UNIT
9 Nouns

378

Resource Manager

📁 **Planning Resources**
- *Lesson Plans*
- *Block Scheduling*

📊 **Transparencies**
- *Bellringer*
- *Daily Language Practice*
- *Two-Minute Skill Drill*

📁 **Other Print Resources**
- *Grammar and Composition Handbook*
- *Grammar Enrichment*
- *Grammar Practice*
- *Grammar Reteaching*
- *Grammar Workbook*
- *Tests with Answer Key and Rubrics*

 **Video**
- *MindJogger Videoquizzes*

💾 **Software**
- *Interactive Grammar and Language Workbook*
- *Language Arts PASS*
- *Presentation Plus!*
- *Revising with Style*
- *Testmaker*

🖥 **Web Sites**
- *writerschoice.glencoe.com*

9.1 Kinds of Nouns

Look at the incomplete sentence below. Decide which of the words in the box that follows can complete the sentence.

The inventor created many new _____ .

across	processes	dramatic	the
goes	products	things	machines

The words *processes*, *products*, *things*, and *machines* can complete the sentence. These words are called nouns.

■ A **noun** names a person, place, thing, or idea.

There are two basic kinds of nouns: proper nouns and common nouns.

■ A **proper noun** names a *specific* person, place, thing, or idea.

■ A **common noun** names *any* person, place, thing, or idea.

The first word and all other important words in proper nouns are capitalized.

Nouns can be either concrete or abstract.

■ **Concrete nouns** name things that you can see or touch.

■ **Abstract nouns** name ideas, qualities, or characteristics.

KINDS OF NOUNS		
PROPER NOUNS	**COMMON NOUNS**	
	Concrete	Abstract
Thomas Edison	inventor	idea
Naples, Florida	city	progress
Monday	calendar	time
African American	trumpet	culture

9.1 Kinds of Nouns **379**

Focus

Lesson Overview

Objectives
- To recognize common, proper, abstract, and concrete nouns
- To compare and contrast kinds of nouns

 Bellringer
Daily Language Activity

When students enter the classroom, have this assignment on the board: *Copy the following sentence and circle each word that names a person, place, thing, or idea:*

His favorite program is the news.

See also Daily Language Practice

Teach

☑ **Teaching Tip**

Common nouns can follow articles (*a*/*an*, *the*) and they can be made plural. Thus, two quick tests for determining whether a word is a common noun are:
(1) Can you put *a*/*an* or *the* in front of it?
(2) Can you make it plural?
*Note Some proper nouns can also answer the test question in the affirmative.

 Two-Minute Skill Drill

Ask students to apply the two tests to the following words to determine whether or not they are common nouns:

radio	*France*
strong	*eat*
Raphael	*tall*
freedom	*chalk*

See also Two-Minute Skill Drill Transparency 9.1

Resource Manager

📂 **Planning Resources**
- *Lesson Plans*

🔖 **Transparencies**
- *Bellringer*
- *Daily Language Practice*
- *Two-Minute Skill Drill*

📂 **Other Print Resources**
- *Grammar and Composition Handbook*
- *Grammar Enrichment*, p. 5
- *Grammar Practice*, p. 5
- *Grammar Workbook*, Lesson 7

Practice and Assess

Answers: Exercise 1

1. Guglielmo Marconi: proper; signals, air: common
2. equipment, signals: common; Marconi, Atlantic Ocean: proper
3. Reginald Fessenden: proper; person, voice, radio: common
4. radio, communication, ships, sea: common
5. Messages, radio, victims, disasters, sea: common
6. Radios, survivors: common; *Titanic:* proper
7. broadcast, years: common
8. broadcast: common; Metropolitan Opera House, New York City: proper
9. program, singer: common; Enrico Caruso, Naples, Italy: proper
10. station, results, elections: common; Pittsburgh: proper
11. station, year: common
12. Franklin Roosevelt: proper; nation, radio: common
13. Radio, entertainment: common; United States: proper
14. Fred Allen, Jack Benny, Bob Hope: proper; shows, radio: common
15. beam, radio, plane: common; Cleveland, New York: proper
16. radar, planes, ships, weather: common
17. police, radar, cars: common
18. Radios, soldiers: common; World War II: proper
19. People, phone, car, boat, places: common
20. pager, "beeper," person, office, home: common

Answers: Exercise 2

Concrete Nouns: people, things, inventions, food, tools, things, wood, bone, stone, hides, people, metal, vehicles, people, lands, travelers, goods, inventions, inventions, inventions, workers, factories, workers, machines

Abstract Nouns: imagination, time, need, protection, discovery, civilization, knowledge, improvement, knowledge, creation, enthusiasm, anger, fear

---

Exercise 1   Identifying Nouns, Capitalizing Proper Nouns

Write each noun that appears in the following sentences. Indicate whether each is a *common noun* or a *proper noun*. Remember to capitalize each proper noun.

1. Guglielmo marconi sent the first electronic signals through the air.
2. With his equipment, marconi sent the first signals across the atlantic ocean.
3. Reginald fessenden was the first person to transmit his voice on radio.
4. The radio was first used for communication between ships at sea.
5. Messages on the radio helped save many victims of disasters at sea.
6. Radios were used to help rescue survivors from the shipwrecked *titanic*.
7. The first musical broadcast occurred two years earlier.
8. The broadcast was from the metropolitan opera house in new york city.
9. The program starred enrico caruso, a famous singer from naples, italy.
10. A station in pittsburgh announced the results of the 1920 presidential elections.
11. The first commercial station was started in that same year.
12. Franklin roosevelt often spoke to the nation on the radio.
13. Radio was once the most popular entertainment in the united states.
14. Fred allen, jack benny, and bob hope had popular comedy shows on the radio.
15. A beam from a radio was able to guide a plane from cleveland to new york.
16. Later, radar helped locate planes or ships in dark or stormy weather.
17. Then police began to use radar to locate cars that were speeding.
18. Radios were first used by soldiers during world war II.
19. People can now call from a phone inside a car, a boat, or other places.
20. A personal pager, or "beeper," can tell a person to call the office or home.

Exercise 2   Identifying Nouns

Write the nouns you find below in two lists: *concrete nouns* and *abstract nouns*.

1. People with imagination have been inventing things from the earliest time.
2. The first inventions were based on the need for food and protection.
3. Early tools were created from natural things—wood, bone, stone, and hides.
4. The discovery by early people that heated metal could be shaped was important.
5. Our entire industrial civilization grew out of this important knowledge.
6. With the improvement in vehicles, people began to travel to other lands.
7. These travelers traded goods and brought back knowledge of new inventions.
8. The creation of new inventions has not always been greeted with enthusiasm.
9. New inventions have often caused anger among workers in factories.
10. The workers had the great fear that machines might replace them.

Additional Resources

 *Grammar Practice*, p. 5
 *Grammar Enrichment*, p. 5

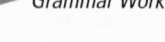 *Grammar Workbook*, Lesson 7

Close

Ask students to use different kinds of nouns to write a sentence or two about a favorite invention they might like to have discovered.

 **English Language Learners**

Finding Nouns

Ask students learning English to copy in their journals the headings from the chart on page 379. At the top of the columns, write *America, boy,* and *learning.* Have students consider the part of speech of each of these words in their first language. Then have them add other words to their charts.

9.2 Compound Nouns

Some nouns consist of more than one word. The noun *hometown*, for instance, is made up of the two words *home* and *town*. These nouns are called compound nouns.

■ **Compound nouns** are nouns that are made up of two or more words.

Compound nouns can be written as one word—*hometown*— or as more than one word—*ice cream*. Other compound nouns are written as two or more words joined by hyphens—*mother-in-law*. If you're unsure of how to write a compound noun, check a dictionary.

Compound Nouns	
One word	doorknob, homeroom, strongbox, bookmark, fireplace
Hyphenated	age-group, runner-up, great-grandmother, kilowatt-hour
More than one word	dining room, motion picture, maid of honor, music box

Most nouns can be singular or plural. A singular noun names one person, place, thing, or idea. A plural noun names more than one. Most plural nouns are formed by adding *-s* or *-es* to the singular form of the noun.

To write the plural forms of some compound nouns, however, you need to know special rules.

Forming Plural Compound Nouns		
	To Make Plural	**Examples**
One word	Add **-s** to most words. Add **-es** to most words that end in **ch, sh, s,** or **x**.	fireplace**s**, bookmark**s**, strongbox**es**
Hyphenated	Make the most important part of the word plural.	runner**s**-up, mother**s**-in-law, great-grandmother**s**
More than one word	Make the most important part of the word plural.	music box**es**, dining room**s**, maid**s** of honor

Focus

Lesson Overview

Objectives
- To identify and correctly pluralize compound nouns
- To use pluralized compound nouns in writing

Bellringer
Daily Language Activity

When students enter the classroom, have this assignment on the board: *Copy the words* passerby *and* touchdown. *Draw a vertical line between the words that make up each word. Then write the plural of each word.*
(Answers: *passersby, touchdowns*)

See also *Daily Language Practice*

Motivating Activity

Call on volunteers to share their responses to the Bellringer activity. Ask students whether the meanings of *passer* and *by* change when they are combined to form *passerby.* (no) Repeat with *touchdown.* (The meanings of *touch* and *down* do change.)

Teach

☑ Teaching Tip

There is no reliable way to predict whether a compound will be spelled as one word, hyphenated, or spelled as more than one word. Most compound nouns can be recognized by their unusual stress pattern of emphasizing the first word. Compare *It is a strong box* (not a compound—the stress is on *box*) with *It is a strongbox* (a compound—the stress is on *strong*). Repeat with *greenhouse, hairbrush,* and other compounds.

Nouns

Resource Manager

📂 **Planning Resources**
- *Lesson Plans*

 **Transparencies**
- *Bellringer*
- *Daily Language Practice*

📂 **Other Print Resources**
- *Grammar and Composition Handbook*
- *Grammar Enrichment,* p. 5
- *Grammar Practice,* p. 5
- *Grammar Reteaching,* p. 5
- *Grammar Workbook,* Lesson 9

Practice and Assess

Answers: Exercise 3

1. steam engines
2. wheelbarrows
3. housekeepers
4. ice skates
5. headaches
6. jacks-of-all-trades
7. governors-general
8. fathers-in-law
9. box seats
10. stepsisters
11. chainsaws
12. dishwashers
13. cotton gins
14. mailboxes
15. home teams
16. baby-sitters
17. basketballs
18. public schools
19. great-aunts
20. go-carts

Answers: Exercise 4

1. personal computers
2. tape recorders
3. copy machines
4. printing presses
5. space probes
6. editors in chief
7. vice presidents
8. cellular phones
9. weather bureaus
10. snowplows
11. ski lifts
12. political action committees
13. ballot boxes
14. fire engines
15. attorneys-at-law
16. emergency rooms
17. roadblocks
18. videotapes
19. sea captains
20. great-granddaughters

Additional Resources

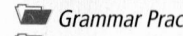 *Grammar Practice*, p. 5
Grammar Reteaching, p. 5
Grammar Enrichment, p. 5

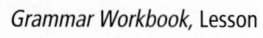 *Grammar Workbook*, Lesson 9

Exercise 3   Making Compound Nouns Plural

Write the plural form of each compound noun below.

1. steam engine
2. wheelbarrow
3. housekeeper
4. ice skate
5. headache
6. jack-of-all-trades
7. governor-general
8. father-in-law
9. box seat
10. stepsister
11. chainsaw
12. dishwasher
13. cotton gin
14. mailbox
15. home team
16. baby-sitter
17. basketball
18. public school
19. great-aunt
20. go-cart

Exercise 4   Making Compound Nouns Plural

Write each sentence. Use the plural form of the compound noun in parentheses to complete each sentence.

1. The newspaper gave all the reporters new _____. (personal computer)
2. The reporters used _____ to interview their subjects. (tape recorder)
3. Because of heavy use, the _____ kept breaking down. (copy machine)
4. The paper's _____ never stopped running. (printing press)
5. The city's major newspapers were invited to witness the launching of the two _____ . (space probe)
6. The four _____ decided to attend with their staffs. (editor in chief)
7. The _____ of several countries were present. (vice president)
8. All reporters carried _____ to keep in touch with the office during the blizzard. (cellular phone)
9. Several local _____ predicted a record snowfall. (weather bureau)
10. Half the town's _____ broke down during the storm. (snowplow)
11. All the _____ at a nearby ski resort were even shut down. (ski lift)
12. Both _____ opposed the mayor's reelection. (political action committee)
13. The _____ were sealed before the votes were recounted. (ballot box)
14. The new mayor presented the city with five new _____ . (fire engine)
15. Two _____ escaped injury when they interrupted a robbery. (attorney-at-law)
16. Detectives went to _____ all over the city looking for one injured suspect. (emergency room)
17. The other robbers were stopped at one of the _____ outside of town. (roadblock)
18. Photographers were asked to make _____ of the ceremony. (videotape)
19. Four retired _____ stood while the monument was dedicated. (sea captain)
20. The general's two _____ also attended the ceremony. (great-granddaughter)

Nouns

Close

Have students brainstorm to create a list of machines in a typical household. Then have them work together in small groups to write a paragraph describing some of the machines they use. Tell them to use several compound nouns. Invite students to share their paragraphs.

MEETING INDIVIDUAL NEEDS English Language Learners

Understanding Compound Nouns

Help students learning English to understand that in a compound noun, one word usually describes the other. For example, in *steam engine, steam* tells the kind of engine; in *high chair, high* describes the kind of chair.

9.3 Possessive Nouns

A noun can be singular, naming only one person, place, thing, or idea; or it can be plural, naming two or more. A noun can also show ownership or possession of things or qualities. This kind of noun is called a possessive noun.

■ A **possessive noun** names who or what owns or has something.

Possessive nouns can be common or proper nouns. They can also be singular or plural. The following pairs of sentences show how possessive nouns are formed.

> **Miko** owns a book about inventions.
> **Miko's** book is about inventions.

> Several **books** have indexes.
> Check several **books'** indexes.

Possessive nouns are formed in one of two ways. To form the possessive of most nouns, you add an apostrophe and -s (*'s*). This is true for all singular nouns and for plural nouns not ending in -s. To form the possessive of plural nouns already ending in -s, you add only an apostrophe. These rules are summarized in the chart below.

Forming Possessive Nouns		
Nouns	**To Form Possessive**	**Examples**
Most singular nouns	Add an apostrophe and **-s** (**'s**).	a girl—a girl**'s** coat Wichita—Wichita**'s** population
Singular nouns ending in **-s**	Add an apostrophe and **-s** (**'s**).	Joseph Ives—Joseph Ives**'s** clock Alexis—Alexis**'s** book
Plural nouns ending in **-s**	Add an apostrophe (**'**).	boys—boys**'** shoes the Wrights—the Wrights**'** plane
Plural nouns not ending in **-s**	Add an apostrophe and **-s** (**'s**).	children—children**'s** toys women—women**'s** organization

9.3 Possessive Nouns **383**

Nouns

Focus

Lesson Overview

Objectives
- To identify possessive nouns
- To use possessive nouns correctly

Bellringer
Daily Language Activity

When students enter the classroom, have this assignment on the board: *In the following phrase, what must you add to the word Stephanie to show that the skateboard belongs to her?*

   Stephanie skateboard

Answer: apostrophe *s*

See also *Daily Language Practice*

Motivating Activity

Elicit from students the correct response to the Bellringer activity and write it on the board. (*Stephanie's skateboard*) Have a volunteer come to the board and circle the mark of punctuation that tells that Stephanie owns the skateboard. (the apostrophe)

Teach

Vocabulary Link

The Spanish language has no possessive form for nouns. One cannot say *George's books,* for example; instead, a person must say *los libros de Jorge,* translated literally to mean "the books of George."

☑ **Grammar Tip**

Tell students that if they want to see if a noun is possessive, they should try replacing the noun with *his, her, its,* or *their.* If they can, the noun is possessive.

Resource Manager

📁 **Planning Resources**
- *Lesson Plans*

🖥 **Transparencies**
- *Bellringer*
- *Daily Language Practice*

📁 **Other Print Resources**
- *Grammar and Composition Handbook*
- *Grammar Practice,* p. 6
- *Grammar Reteaching,* p. 6
- *Grammar Workbook,* Lesson 9

Practice and Assess

Answers: Exercise 5

1. Marie Curie's
2. scientist's
3. Gus's
4. Ellie's
5. machines'
6. monkeys'
7. coach's
8. Queen Isabella's
9. principals'
10. men's
11. Hawaii's
12. Alice Ross's
13. children's
14. skiers'
15. library's
16. turkey's
17. Henry's
18. boss's
19. brothers'
20. cow's

Answers: Exercise 6

1. America's—singular
2. Franklin's—singular
3. man's—singular
4. weather's—singular
5. Electricity's—singular
6. Franklin's—singular
7. inventor's—singular
8. cloud's—singular
9. kite's—singular
10. Franklin's—singular
11. Luck's—singular
12. sparks'—plural
13. experiment's—singular
14. Cities'—plural
15. building's—singular
16. Lightning's—singular
17. people's—plural
18. ships'—plural
19. citizens'—plural
20. family's—singular

Additional Resources

 Grammar Practice, p. 6
 Grammar Reteaching, p. 6

Grammar Workbook, Lesson 9

Exercise 5 — Forming the Possessive

Write the possessive form of each underlined word below.

1. <u>Marie Curie</u> discovery
2. <u>scientist</u> experiments
3. <u>Gus</u> house
4. <u>Ellie</u> jacket
5. <u>machines</u> designers
6. <u>monkeys</u> tails
7. <u>coach</u> speech
8. <u>Queen Isabella</u> policy
9. <u>principals</u> offices
10. <u>men</u> store
11. <u>Hawaii</u> climate
12. <u>Alice Ross</u> address
13. <u>children</u> plans
14. <u>skiers</u> clothing
15. <u>library</u> books
16. <u>turkey</u> feathers
17. <u>Henry</u> music
18. <u>boss</u> office
19. <u>brothers</u> room
20. <u>cow</u> milk

Exercise 6 — Identifying Singular and Plural Possessives

Write the possessive nouns. Add or insert apostrophes where needed, and label each possessive noun as *singular* or *plural*.

1. Benjamin Franklin was one of Americas greatest citizens.
2. Among Franklins many occupations were printer, publisher, author, scientist, and statesman.
3. Although this mans interests were many, he probably liked science best.
4. The weathers many changes interested Franklin.
5. Electricitys mysteries were of particular interest to this inventive scientist.
6. One of Franklins experiments led to the invention of the lightning rod.
7. The inventors idea came during a violent thunderstorm.
8. Franklin sailed a silk and metal-tipped kite into a stormy clouds interior.
9. Soon a spark of electricity traveled down the kites string.
10. A metal key hanging from the kite string attracted the electrical charges, and Franklins nearby hand drew sparks.
11. Lucks fortune was with Franklin that day.
12. Others who tried it did not escape the sparks danger and were killed.
13. Franklin was sure of his experiments meaning—that lightning is electricity!
14. Cities buildings are safer because of the lightning rod.
15. Placed on a buildings highest point, a metal rod connects to a heavy wire that leads to another rod deep in the ground.
16. Lightnings electricity is attracted to the rod.
17. It is then guided into the ground, ensuring the peoples safety.
18. Lightning rods have also protected many ships crews from storms at sea.
19. At one time, lightning storms destroyed many citizens homes.
20. Lightning rods even saved the Franklin familys home.

Close

Have students write a paragraph as though they were Benjamin Franklin describing flying a kite in a thunderstorm. (If they begin with a sentence using *I*, possessives will follow.) Have them share their work with a classmate.

Less-Proficient Readers

Using the Apostrophe

Suggest that students think of the apostrophe as standing for the word *owns.* for example: *Sara* owns *skates. Patrick* owns *skis.* Students can erase the word *owns* and write in the *'s: Sara's skates; Patrick's skis.*

9.4 Distinguishing Plurals, Possessives, and Contractions

It can be easy to confuse plural nouns and possessive nouns. Most plural nouns and possessive nouns end with the letter *-s*. They sound alike, but their spellings and meanings differ.

Plural and Possessive Nouns		
	Example	**Meaning**
Plural Noun	The **scientists** met.	more than one scientist
Plural Possessive Noun	The **scientists'** discovery was important.	the discovery of the scientists
Singular Possessive Noun	This **scientist's** photograph is in the newspaper.	the photograph of one scientist

Notice that plural nouns do not have apostrophes. Plural possessive nouns end with an apostrophe. Singular possessive nouns end with an apostrophe and an *-s*.

An apostrophe is also used to indicate where letters have been left out in a contraction.

■ A **contraction** is a word made by combining two words into one by leaving out one or more letters.

In the sentence *Elaine's going to the exhibit,* the word *Elaine's* is a contraction. It is made by combining the singular proper noun *Elaine* and the verb *is.* The apostrophe takes the place of the letter *i.* The contraction *Elaine's* sounds the same and is spelled the same as the singular possessive form of the proper noun *Elaine.*

Possessive Nouns and Contractions		
	Example	**Meaning**
Possessive	**Elaine's** invention is a new bell.	the invention by Elaine
Contraction	**Elaine's** going to the exhibit.	Elaine is going

9.4 Distinguishing Plurals, Possessives, and Contractions **385**

Focus

Lesson Overview

Objectives
- To recognize and disinguish among plurals, possessives, and contractions
- To use plurals, possessives, and contractions correctly

 Bellringer
Daily Language Activity

When students enter the classroom, have this assignment on the board: *Read these two sentences: "Keisha's going to space camp this summer. Keisha's younger brother is going too." Write a sentence summarizing what you learned about Keisha and her brother.*

See also *Daily Language Practice*

Motivating Activity

Discuss students' responses in the Bellringer activity. Ask students how they could tell the different meanings of *Keisha's* in the sentences. (from the context)

Teach

Critical Thinking

Have students recall and categorize plurals and possessives. Prepare a four-column transparency for the overhead projector with *Word, Plural, Plural Possessive,* and *Singular Possessive* as headings. Make up a word list and ask volunteers to choose a word and write the correctly spelled word in each column. Ask them to give a sentence example for each word as well.

Nouns

 **Resource Manager**

📂 **Planning Resources**
- *Lesson Plans*

🔖 **Transparencies**
- *Bellringer*
- *Daily Language Practice*

📂 **Other Print Resources**
- *Grammar and Composition Handbook*
- *Grammar Enrichment,* p. 6
- *Grammar Practice,* p. 6
- *Grammar Reteaching,* p. 7
- *Grammar Workbook,* Lessons 10

Practice and Assess

Answers: Exercise 7

1. This <u>article's</u> about space flight.
   article is
2. The <u>satellite's</u> an invention with many uses.
   satellite is
3. <u>Russia's</u> the first nation with a space satellite.
   Russia is
4. A <u>rocket's</u> used to launch satellites.
   rocket is
5. <u>Earth's</u> beautiful from space.
   Earth is
6. Space <u>flight's</u> always in the news.
   flight is
7. The <u>nation's</u> happy!
   nation is
8. <u>Shepard's</u> the first American in space.
   Shepard is
9. <u>Russia's</u> ahead in the space race!
   Russia is
10. The next <u>decade's</u> filled with flights.
    decade is

Answers: Exercise 8

1. rockets	11. Union's
2. satellites'	12. rockets'
3. stations'	13. years'
4. stations	14. pictures
5. Farmers'	15. planets
6. reports	16. Plans
7. galaxies'	17. years'
8. satellites	18. probes
9. friend's	19. scientists'
10. probes	20. shuttles'

Additional Resources

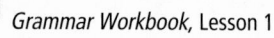 *Grammar Practice,* p. 6

Grammar Reteaching, p. 7

Grammar Enrichment, p. 6

Grammar Workbook, Lesson 10

Nouns

Exercise 7 — Using Contractions

Write the sentence in each pair that contains a contraction. Underline the contraction; above it, write the two words that have been combined.

1. This article's topic is space flight. This article's about space flight.
2. The satellite's an invention with many uses. The satellite's uses are many.
3. Russia's the first nation with a space satellite. Russia's satellite was *Sputnik.*
4. A rocket's used to launch satellites. A rocket's launch is exciting to watch.
5. Rockets break free of earth's atmosphere. Earth's beautiful from space.
6. Space flight's technology grows in the 1960s. Space flight's always in the news.
7. Our nation's first manned space flight is May 5, 1961. The nation's happy!
8. Shepard's the first American in space. Shepard's flight lasts fifteen minutes.
9. Russia's first astronaut traveled earlier. Russia's ahead in the space race!
10. The next decade's filled with flights. At decade's end, men walk on the moon!

Exercise 8 — Using Plural and Possessive Nouns

Write each sentence, choosing the correct word in parentheses.

1. Modern (rockets, rockets') carry satellites into orbit around Earth.
2. Some of the (satellites, satellites') equipment is powered by sunlight.
3. Ground (stations, stations') antennae send signals to satellites.
4. These (stations, stations') also receive signals from satellites.
5. (Farmers, Farmers') crops need good weather.
6. Satellites in space send weather (reports, reports') back to earth.
7. Some satellites take photographs of distant (galaxies, galaxies') stars.
8. Other (satellites, satellites') relay telephone calls between countries.
9. My friend in Omaha can speak to her (friend's, friends) relatives in Australia.
10. The goal of the space (probes, probes') was to explore the solar system.
11. The Soviet (Unions, Union's) *Venera* probes were the first to land on Venus.
12. The *Viking* (rockets, rockets') purpose was to explore the planet Mars.
13. After two (year's, years') travel, *Pioneer 10* left the solar system.
14. *Voyager 1* took (pictures, pictures') of the rings of Saturn.
15. *Voyager 2* flew by the (planets, planets') Jupiter, Saturn, Uranus, and Neptune.
16. (Plans, Plans') called for *Voyager 2* to fly past Jupiter first.
17. It took ten (years, years') time for *Voyager 2* to reach Neptune.
18. Of all the space (probes, probes'), *Helios 1* came closest to the sun.
19. The (scientists, scientists') next project was to build space shuttles.
20. The (shuttles, shuttles') goals were to launch and repair satellites.

Close

Have students describe in a paragraph the kind of telephone they think people will use in the distant future. Tell students to include plurals, possessives, and contractions in their paragraphs. Have students exchange papers and proofread one another's work.

 **English Language Learners**

Distinguishing Between Possessives and Contractions

Suggest that students learning English replace a noun with a personal pronoun to see if the noun is a possessive: *Sue's book* (her *book*). This makes sense, so *Sue's* is a possessive. However, in *Sue's reading a book* (her *reading a book*), *Sue's* is a contraction.

9.5 Collective Nouns

Certain nouns name a group made up of a number of people or things. These nouns are called *collective nouns.*

■ A **collective noun** names a group of individuals.

Collective Nouns			
committee	audience	swarm	club
family	team	crowd	orchestra
flock	class	jury	herd

Nouns and verbs in sentences must always show agreement. Collective nouns, however, present special agreement problems. Every collective noun can have either a singular meaning or a plural meaning. If you are speaking about the group as a unit, then the noun has a singular meaning. If you want to refer to the individual members of the group, then the noun has a plural meaning.

The whole **flock** enters the meadow through a gate.
   [a unit, singular]
The **flock** enter by different gates. [individual members, plural]

The entire **audience** applauds the performers. [a unit, singular]
The **audience** take their seats. [individual members, plural]

When the collective noun is a single unit, use a singular verb. When the collective noun refers to the individual members of the group, use a plural verb. Other words in the sentence can help you tell whether a collective noun is singular or plural.

The **family** begins <u>its</u> trip. [its, singular]
The **family** eat <u>their</u> sandwiches. [their, plural]

The entire **audience applauds** the performers.

The **audience strain** their necks to see.

9.5 Collective Nouns **387**

Focus

Lesson Overview

Objectives
- To identify use collective nouns
- To use collective nouns appropriately to indicate singular or plural meanings

Bellringer
Daily Language Activity

When students enter the classroom, have this assignment on the board: *List ten verbs naming actions that a team, a class, or a family might do together.*

See also Daily Language Practice

Motivating Activity

Work with students to write sentences using collective nouns with the verbs from the Bellringer activity. (*The team practices every day. The team practice their favorite shots.*) Discuss examples of plural and singular meanings for each collective noun used.

Teach

Cooperative Learning

Divide students into teams of two sets of partners. Give each team a collective noun from the list on page 387, and ask one set of partners to write four sentences using their noun in the plural. (*The jury discuss their opinions.*) The other set of partners writes sentences using it in the singular. (*The jury adjourns for lunch.*) Ask partners to read their sentences to the other half of their team.

Cross-Reference: Usage

For instruction and practice with matching verbs to collective nouns, refer students to Lesson 16.3.

Resource Manager

📂 **Planning Resources**
- *Lesson Plans*

🔖 **Transparencies**
- *Bellringer*
- *Daily Language Practice*

📂 **Other Print Resources**
- *Grammar and Composition Handbook*
- *Grammar Enrichment*, p. 5
- *Grammar Practice*, p. 5
- *Grammar Workbook*, Lesson 8

Practice and Assess

Answers: Exercise 9

1. crowd, singular
2. crowd, plural
3. committee, plural
4. committee, singular
5. class, plural

Answers: Exercise 10

1. chorus agrees, singular
2. chorus sings, singular
3. team plays, singular
4. school attack, plural
5. group performs, singular
6. crew toss, plural
7. family clean, plural
8. jury sits, singular
9. audience shows, singular
10. audience straggle, plural
11. party works, singular
12. class present, plural
13. flock scatter, plural
14. flock flies, singular
15. band attends, singular
16. club swim, plural
17. pack forage, plural
18. cabinet attends, singular
19. Congress meets, singular
20. herd chew, plural

Additional Resources

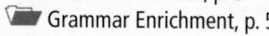 Grammar Practice, p. 5
 Grammar Enrichment, p. 5

Grammar Workbook, Lesson 8

Close

Students can discuss or write about the activities of a group—such as a team, a family, or a club—of which they are a member or participant. Encourage them to use collective nouns in both singular and plural contexts.

Nouns

Exercise 9   Identifying Collective Nouns

Write each sentence. Underline each collective noun and write whether its meaning is *singular* or *plural.*

1. The crowd shakes the stadium with its school cheer.
2. The crowd leave their seats.
3. The committee argue with one another over the rules.
4. The committee holds its first meeting tonight.
5. The class give their various opinions about the issue.

Exercise 10   Using Collective Nouns

Write each sentence. Underline each collective noun and write whether its meaning is *singular* or *plural.* Use the verb form in parentheses that agrees with the collective noun.

1. The chorus (agrees, agree) about which song it will sing.
2. The chorus (sings, sing) its five favorite songs.
3. The baseball team (plays, play) its first game of the season tonight.
4. The school of dolphins (attacks, attack) their enemies, the sharks.
5. The musical group (performs, perform) its latest hit.
6. The crew of volunteers (tosses, toss) their shovels onto the truck bed at sundown.
7. The family (cleans, clean) their rooms.
8. The jury (sits, sit) in its special section of the courtroom.
9. The enthusiastic audience (shows, show) its approval with a standing ovation.
10. After the intermission, the audience (straggles, straggle) toward their seats.
11. Each political party (works, work) untiringly for its candidate.
12. After a month's preparation, the class (presents, present) their projects.
13. When a dog disturbs them, the flock of blackbirds (scatters, scatter) in many directions.
14. In fall the flock (flies, fly) south to its winter home in Florida.
15. Every summer before school starts, the band (attends, attend) summer camp.
16. The water polo club (swims, swim) their laps on empty stomachs after school.
17. The pack of hyenas (forages, forage) near their den for food.
18. The President's cabinet (attends, attend) the State of the Union address.
19. The U.S. Congress (meets, meet) in the Capitol in Washington, D.C.
20. The herd of cows (chews, chew) their cuds under the gathering rain clouds.

MEETING INDIVIDUAL NEEDS

English Language Learners

Using Signal Words

Usually collective nouns are singular, and the group is treated as a single unit. For example, in the sentence *The team is on the field,* the word *team* is a singular collective noun that refers to the team as a single unit. Students may not be familiar with plural verbs following collective nouns. Explain to them that writers often insert the word *members* in a sentence as a way to clarify the plural meaning of a collective noun, for example: *The team members run a car wash.* Here the team is not thought of as being a single unit.

9.6 | Appositives

■ An **appositive** is a noun placed next to another noun to identify it or add information about it.

> Nicolas-François Appert, **a chef,** made an important discovery.

The noun *chef* identifies *Nicolas-François Appert,* the noun next to it. *Chef* tells what Appert was. In this sentence, *a chef* is an appositive.

An appositive is sometimes accompanied by other words.

The noun *chef* still identifies Appert, as it did in the original sentence. Here, however, the word *French* is used to describe the word *chef.* The words *a French chef* form an appositive phrase.

> Nicolas-François Appert, **a French chef,** made an important discovery.

■ An **appositive phrase** is a group of words that includes an appositive and other words that describe the appositive.

You always use an appositive or appositive phrase together with another noun. An appositive phrase can come at the beginning, middle, or end of a sentence, as long as it appears next to the noun it identifies.

> An **expert on food,** Appert worried about food spoilage.
> Appert, **an expert on food,** worried about food spoilage.
> The government gave Appert, **an expert on food,** a cash award.
> A simple solution had occurred to Appert, **an expert on food.**

Usually, appositives are set off from the nouns they identify by commas. Notice that a single comma follows an appositive that appears at the beginning of a sentence. A comma is used before an appositive that appears at the end of a sentence. Two commas set off an appositive in the middle of a sentence.

Ken

Ken, John's friend

Ken, the artist

Nouns

9.6 Appositives **389**

Focus

Lesson Overview

Objectives
• To identify appositives
• To use appositives appropriately in writing

 Bellringer
Daily Language Activity

When students enter the classroom, have this assignment on the board: *Choose a familiar object and write three adjectives that describe it.*

See also *Daily Language Practice*

Motivating Activity

Use examples from the Bellringer activity to demonstrate that adjectives restrict or limit the meaning of the nouns they modify (not any car, but *the red car*). Then explain that an appositive is a word or phrase that identifies, defines, or renames a noun that it is next to, giving additional information (*The red car, a favorite toy, was lost*).

Teach

☑ **Teaching Tip**

Sentence combining is an excellent way to teach the use and punctuation of appositives. For example, have students combine *Amelia worried about food spoilage* with *Amelia was an expert on food.* The second sentence is changed into an appositive that identifies the noun, *Amelia,* in the first sentence: *Amelia, an expert on food, worried about food spoilage.* Commas set off the appositive.

Resource Manager

📁 **Planning Resources**
• *Lesson Plans*

📷 **Transparencies**
• *Bellringer*
• *Daily Language Practice*

📁 **Other Print Resources**
• *Grammar and Composition Handbook*
• *Grammar Enrichment,* p. 7
• *Grammar Practice,* p. 7
• *Grammar Reteaching,* p. 8
• *Grammar Workbook,* Lesson 11

Practice and Assess

Answers: Exercise 11

1. (Nicholas-François Appert), a French chef,
2. (spoilage), a serious social health problem,
3. (prize), a large sum of money,
4. person, (Appert),
5. (answer), a rather simple method.
6. (containers), wide-mouthed glass bottles.
7. (seal), cork and wire.
8. (sack), one more protection,
9. (boiler), a large pot of boiling water.
10. (pot), a giant water bath,
11. (theory), protection from air,
12. (jars), an important contribution,
13. (contribution), the tin can,
14. (inventor), Peter Durand,
15. (method), use of sealed containers,
16. (Louis Pasteur), a French scientist,
17. (bacteria), the real cause of food spoilage.
18. (bacteria), an invisible enemy in the air,
19. (bacteria), the source of disease.
20. (Bacteria), the food spoilers,

Answers: Exercise 12

1. Johann Gutenberg invented movable type, the basis of the printing press.
2. Alexander Graham Bell, a former speech teacher, invented the telephone.
3. Kirkpatrick Macmillan, a Scottish blacksmith, is given credit for the bicycle.
4. The zipper, a slide fastener, was invented by W. L. Judson.
5. The inventor of the elevator, a device for vertical lifting, was Elisha G. Otis.
6. The stethoscope was developed by René Laënnec, a French physician.
7. J. H. Loud, an American inventor, is given credit for the ballpoint pen.
8. The Wright brothers flew a biplane, the first successful flying machine.
9. X rays, the basis of the X-ray machine, were discovered by Wilhelm Roentgen.

Nouns

Exercise 11   Identifying Appositives

Write each sentence. Underline each appositive or appositive phrase and add commas where needed. Circle the noun the appositive identifies.

1. Nicolas-François Appert a French chef found a method for preserving food.
2. Food spoilage a serious social health problem was causing disease.
3. A prize a large sum of money was the government's reward for a solution.
4. A determined person Appert worked on the problem for years.
5. Finally, Appert discovered an answer a rather simple method.
6. His method included packing food into containers wide-mouthed glass bottles.
7. Each bottle had its own tight seal cork and wire.
8. A cloth sack one more protection was wrapped around each bottle.
9. Next the bottles were lowered into a boiler a large pot of boiling water.
10. The large boiling pot a giant water bath was covered with one more lid.
11. Appert's idea worked, but his theory protection from air proved incomplete.
12. The sealed jars an important contribution did help preserve the foods.
13. Another contribution the tin can was invented around the same time.
14. The inventor of this container Peter Durand was English.
15. No one knew why Appert's method use of sealed containers worked so well.
16. Then Louis Pasteur a French scientist found an explanation.
17. Pasteur discovered bacteria the real cause of food spoilage.
18. It was bacteria an invisible enemy in the air that caused foods to spoil.
19. Appert's high heating method had destroyed the bacteria the source of disease.
20. Bacteria the food spoilers could not enter when the containers were sealed.

Exercise 12   Using Appositives

Rewrite the sentences, using the appositives and inserting commas correctly.

1. Johann Gutenberg invented movable type. (the basis of the printing press)
2. Alexander Graham Bell invented the telephone. (a former speech teacher)
3. Kirkpatrick Macmillan is given credit for the bicycle. (a Scottish blacksmith)
4. The zipper was invented by W. L. Judson. (a slide fastener)
5. The inventor of the elevator was Elisha G. Otis. (a device for vertical lifting)
6. The stethoscope was developed by René Laënnec. (a French physician)
7. J. H. Loud is given credit for the ballpoint pen. (an American inventor)
8. The Wright brothers flew a biplane. (the first successful flying machine)
9. X rays were discovered by Wilhelm Roentgen. (the basis of the X-ray machine)
10. Van Leeuwenhoek made a successful microscope. (a lens for seeing tiny things)

10. Van Leeuwenhoek made a successful microscope, a lens for seeing tiny things.

Additional Resources

📁 *Grammar Practice*, p. 7
📁 *Grammar Reteaching*, p. 8
📁 *Grammar Enrichment*, p. 7

📓 *Grammar Workbook*, Lesson 11

Close

Ask students to write a description of a new invention that might make life easier. Have them use appositives in their writing. Volunteers can read their descriptions, and others can identify the appositives.

Grammar Review

Nouns

In this passage, Anne Morrow Lindbergh, a veteran of many historic airplane flights, describes the launching of *Apollo 8*, the first crewed spacecraft to orbit the moon. The craft took off from Cape Kennedy, Florida, early on the morning of December 21, 1968. The passage has been annotated to show some of the kinds of nouns covered in this unit.

Literature Model

from *Earth Shine*
by Anne Morrow Lindbergh

With the morning light, *Apollo 8* and its launching tower become clearer, harder, and more defined. One can see the details of installation. The dark sections on the smooth sides of the rocket, marking its stages, cut up the single fluid line. Vapor steams furiously off its side. No longer stark and simple, this morning the rocket is complicated, mechanical, earth-bound. Too weighty for flight, one feels.

People stop talking, stand in front of their cars, and raise binoculars to their eyes. We peer nervously at the launch site and then at our wrist watches. Radio voices blare unnaturally loud from car windows. "Now only thirty minutes to launch time . . . fifteen minutes . . . six minutes . . . thirty seconds to go . . . twenty . . . T minus fifteen . . . fourteen . . . thirteen . . . twelve . . . eleven . . . ten . . . nine. . . . Ignition!"

A jet of steam shoots from the pad below the rocket. "Ahhhh!" The crowd gasps, almost in unison.

- Proper noun
- Singular noun
- Common noun
- Concrete noun
- Compound noun
- Plural noun
- Collective noun

Nouns

Grammar Review   **391**

Teach

About the Literature

Explain that the review contains a passage from Anne Morrow Lindbergh's *Earth Shine*, followed by exercises on related topics. Anne Morrow Lindbergh is an American poet and essayist and a licensed pilot who took air trips with her famous husband, Charles A. Lindbergh.

In this passage, she combines her interest in space flight and writing to re-create an important moment in history. Have students read the passage and then review the nouns highlighted in it.

Linking Grammar and Literature

☑ **Grammar Tip**

The simplest method to check whether a collective noun is singular or plural is to try to substitute *it* and *they* for the collective noun in question. For example: *The crew flies the rocket. It flies the rocket. (singular) The crew are all trained pilots. They are all trained pilots. (plural)* Point out the collective noun *crowd* in the passage.

Critical Thinking

After reading the passage and discussing the types of nouns identified in it, students should write their own definition of a noun.

Listening and Speaking

Read the first paragraph of the passage aloud to the class. Have students keep track of the nouns as they hear them. Check the students' tallies and then list the nouns from the paragraph on the board. *(light, Apollo 8, tower, details, installation, sections, sides, rocket, stages, line, vapor, side, morning, rocket, flight)*

Resource Manager

📂 **Planning Resources**
- *Lesson Plans*

📂 **Other Print Resources**
- *Grammar and Composition Handbook*
- *Grammar Workbook, Lessons 7–11*

Practice and Assess

Answers: Exercise 1

Proper Nouns

1. Anne Morrow, Charles Lindbergh
2. Lindbergh, New York, Paris
3. Anne Morrow Lindbergh
4. Anne
5. Anne, Charles's
6. Anne, Charles, South America
7. Lindberghs, Hollywood, Amelia Earhart
8. Anne Lindbergh
9. Anne
10. Dorothy Herrmann

Common Nouns

1. none
2. fame, flight
3. love, aviation
4. husband, expeditions, copilot, navigator
5. enthusiasm, adventure
6. flight
7. time
8. author, articles, books
9. praise, critics, popularity, readers
10. Biographer, picture, woman

Answers: Exercise 2

1. Anne Morrow Lindbergh's book
2. husband's flight
3. critics' praise
4. airplane's pilot
5. lawyers' case
6. crowd's gasp
7. Charles's airplane
8. Anne's biographer
9. couple's wedding
10. friends' congratulations
11. children's pictures
12. parents' encouragement
13. sisters' letters
14. Franklin Roosevelt's presidency
15. women's opinions
16. brother's house
17. Paris's liberation
18. astronauts' explorations
19. Ciardi's criticism
20. Kennedys' compound

Review: Exercise 1   Identifying Nouns

The following sentences are about the life of Anne Morrow Lindbergh, the author of *Earth Shine*. Find all the nouns in the sentences and write them in lists. First, list all *proper nouns*, capitalizing them correctly. Then list the *common nouns*.

SAMPLE   In *Earth Shine*, Anne Morrow Lindbergh talks about fear.
ANSWER   *Earth Shine*, Anne Morrow Lindbergh; fear

1. Anne morrow married charles lindbergh.
2. Lindbergh had already gained fame for his solo flight from new york to paris.
3. Anne morrow lindbergh soon shared his love of aviation.
4. Anne accompanied her husband on many expeditions as copilot and navigator.
5. Anne came to share Charles's great enthusiasm for adventure.
6. After they were married, Anne joined charles on a flight to south america.
7. The lindberghs also spent some time in hollywood with amelia earhart.
8. Anne lindbergh became a successful author, writing many articles and books.
9. Anne won praise from critics and gained huge popularity among readers.
10. Biographer dorothy herrmann paints a vivid picture of this remarkable woman.

Review: Exercise 2   Forming the Possessive

Write the possessive form of each underlined noun.

1. <u>Anne Morrow Lindbergh</u> book
2. <u>husband</u> flight
3. <u>critics</u> praise
4. <u>airplane</u> pilot
5. <u>lawyers</u> case
6. <u>crowd</u> gasp
7. <u>Charles</u> airplane
8. <u>Anne</u> biographer
9. <u>couple</u> wedding
10. <u>friends</u> congratulations
11. <u>children</u> pictures
12. <u>parents</u> encouragement
13. <u>sisters</u> letters
14. <u>Franklin Roosevelt</u> presidency
15. <u>women</u> opinions
16. <u>brother</u> house
17. <u>Paris</u> liberation
18. <u>astronauts</u> explorations
19. <u>Ciardi</u> criticism
20. <u>Kennedys</u> compound

Nouns

Review: Exercise 3 Using Possessives and Contractions

The following sentences are based on the *Apollo 8* mission. Rewrite each sentence, inserting apostrophes where needed in the possessive nouns and contractions.

SAMPLE The announcers voice breaks the silence.
ANSWER The announcer's voice breaks the silence.

1. "Wow, that rockets tall," said a boy in the crowd.
2. The rockets height is 465 feet.
3. The mens families anxiously await the launch.
4. The rockets engines ignite following the countdown.
5. The peoples eyes follow the spaceship as it lifts off the launch pad.
6. At last the spacecrafts on its way to the Moon.
7. The first stage of the rockets called the booster stage.
8. The boosters power, called its thrust, is 7,500,000 pounds.
9. Its been about two and one-half minutes since the booster began firing.
10. By then the rockets speed is 6,100 miles per hour.
11. Its height above Earths about thirty-eight miles.
12. The second stages burn is about six and one-half minutes.
13. Now the rockets speed is about 15,000 miles per hour.
14. The third stage fires, and the rockets in orbit around Earth.
15. While the spacecrafts in orbit, the crew checks the equipment.
16. The third stage fires again, and the rockets headed for the Moon.
17. "Earths so beautiful," exclaims one astronaut.
18. The lunar craters shadows lie across the moon.
19. The firing of the crafts retro-rockets slows it into an orbit around the Moon.
20. The spacecraft comes within sixty-nine miles of the Moons surface.
21. The main rocket fires, and now the crafts headed for home.
22. The crafts surface becomes very hot as it reenters the atmosphere.
23. Now a parachutes opened to slow the fall of the spacecraft.
24. "I can see the capsules parachute!" a sailor shouts.
25. The spacecrafts parachute lowers it gently to the water for the splashdown.

Answers: Exercise 3

1. "Wow, that rocket's tall," said a boy in the crowd.
2. The rocket's height is 465 feet.
3. The men's families anxiously awaited the launch.
4. The rocket's engines ignite following the countdown.
5. The people's eyes follow the spaceship as it lifts off the launch pad.
6. At last the spacecraft's on its way to the moon.
7. The first stage of the rocket's called the booster stage.
8. The booster's power, called its thrust, is 7,500,000 pounds.
9. It's been about two and one-half minutes since the booster began firing.
10. By then the rocket's speed is 6,100 miles per hour.
11. Its height above Earth's about thirty-eight miles.
12. The second stage's burn is about six and one-half minutes.
13. Now the rocket's speed is about 15,000 miles per hour.
14. The third stage fires, and the rocket's in orbit around Earth.
15. While the spacecraft's in orbit, the crew checks the equipment.
16. The third stage fires again, and the rocket's headed for the moon.
17. "The Earth's so beautiful," exclaims one astronaut.
18. The lunar craters' shadows lie across the moon.
19. The firing of the craft's retro-rockets slows it into an orbit around the moon.
20. The spacecraft comes within sixty-nine miles of the moon's surface.
21. The main rocket fires, and now the craft's headed for home.
22. The craft's surface becomes very hot as it reenters the atmosphere.
23. Now a parachute's opened to slow the fall of the spacecraft.
24. "I can see the capsule's parachute!" a sailor shouts.
25. The spacecraft's parachute lowers it gently to the water for the splashdown.

Nouns

393

Grammar Review

Answers: Exercise 4

1. prepare
2. hopes
3. stands
4. holds
5. head

Answers: Exercise 5

1. Frank Borman, James Lovell, and William Anders, the crew of *Apollo 8,* took pictures of the Moon.
2. . . . the Moon's far side, a cold, forbidding place.
3. Borman, the commander of the crew, was a veteran . . .
4. . . . an incredible dialogue, a conversation between the crew and mission control.
5. The *Apollo 8* crew marveled over their view, bright Earth in a black sky.
6. The astronauts said Earth, a bright royal blue disk, was beautiful.
7. Control Houston, the backup crew on Earth, announced that *Apollo 8* was orbiting the Moon.
8. They wished the astronauts a safe journey in *Apollo 8,* the "best bird" they could find.
9. Houston's view of the Moon could not compare with *Apollo 8's* view, beautiful Earth.
10. For the first time, human beings had orbited another celestial body, the Moon.

Nouns

| Review: Exercise 4 | **Using Collective Nouns** |

Rewrite each sentence, using the form of the verb in parentheses that agrees with the collective noun.

SAMPLE A group of reporters (follow, follows) the president wherever he goes.

ANSWER A group of reporters follows the president wherever he goes.

1. The crew aboard the spacecraft (prepares, prepare) their vehicle for flight.
2. The team (hopes, hope) its mission will be successful.
3. One astronaut's family (stands, stand) together to watch the liftoff.
4. The crowd (holds, hold) its breath as the rocket pushes into the sky.
5. After the launch, the crowd (heads, head) quietly back to their cars.

| Review: Exercise 5 | **Using Appositives** |

Rewrite each sentence below, inserting the appositive or appositive phrase in parentheses. Remember to add commas where needed.

SAMPLE *Apollo 8* orbited the Moon ten times. (a highly sophisticated spacecraft)

ANSWER *Apollo 8,* a highly sophisticated spacecraft, orbited the Moon ten times.

1. Frank Borman, James Lovell, and William Anders took pictures of the Moon. (the crew of *Apollo 8*)
2. They were the first to see the Moon's far side. (a cold, forbidding place)
3. Borman was a veteran space explorer. (the commander of the crew)
4. During a Christmas Eve broadcast, half a billion people listened to an incredible dialogue. (a conversation between the crew and mission control)
5. The *Apollo 8* crew marveled over their view. (bright Earth in a black sky)
6. The astronauts said Earth was beautiful. (a bright royal blue disk)
7. Control Houston announced that *Apollo 8* was orbiting the Moon. (the backup crew on Earth)
8. They wished the astronauts a safe journey in *Apollo 8.* (the "best bird" they could find)
9. Houston's view of the Moon could not compare with the view from *Apollo 8.* (beautiful Earth)
10. For the first time, human beings had orbited another celestial body. (the Moon)

Review: Exercise 6

Proofreading

The following passage is about the space shuttle *Challenger*, the subject of the work below. Rewrite the passage, correcting the errors in spelling, grammar, and usage. Add any missing punctuation. There are ten errors.

Challenger's Last Flight

¹In the center of this painting, artist Robert McCall pays tribute to the final mission of *Challenger* the ill-fated space shuttle. ²Just seconds after liftoff on January 28, 1986, an explosion teared the space shuttle apart, killing it's seven crew members. ³The shuttles destruction was not the space programs first tragedy. ⁴During a test of the *Apollo 1* command module, three astronauts died in a fire on the luanching pad. ⁵Nonetheless, scientist's continued to improve the spacecraft. ⁶It was less than three year later that two men Neil Armstrong and Edwin Aldrin, walked on the moon. ⁷McCalls painting celebrates the human spirit.

Robert McCall, Challenger's *Last Flight*, 1987

Grammar Review **395**

Answers: Exercise 6
Proofreading

This proofreading activity provides editing practice with (1) the current or previous units' skills, (2) **Troubleshooter** errors, and (3) spelling errors. Students should be able to complete the exercise by referring to the units, the **Troubleshooter,** and a dictionary.

Error (Type of Error)
1. Challenger, (nonessential appositive)
2. tore (verb form)
   its (possessive pronoun)
3. shuttle's (singular possessive)
   program's (singluar possessive)
4. launching (spelling)
5. scientists (plural noun)
6. years (plural noun)
   men, (nonessential appositive)
7. McCall's (singular possessive)

Nouns

Viewing the Art

Robert McCall, Challenger's *Last Flight*, 1987
Robert McCall has worked as a commercial artist since he was seventeen. In the 1960s, *Life* magazine commissioned him to do a series of future space travel paintings. The National Aeronautics and Space Administration (NASA) chose him to document the U.S. space program through paintings. McCall has painted numerous murals for the U.S. Air Force and for Disney's EPCOT Center.

1. proper
2. common
3. common; collective
4. common; compound
5. common
6. proper; appositive
7. common
8. common
9. common
10. common; possessive
11. common
12. proper
13. common; collective
14. common
15. common; compound
16. common; compound
17. common
18. common
19. common; collective
20. common
21. proper; possessive
22. common
23. common; collective; appositive
24. common
25. common

Close

Have students identify the noun rule with which they have the most trouble. Help the class brainstorm to make a list of clues they could use to remember the rules reviewed in this unit. Have students record the rules in their journals.

Nouns

Mixed Review

Identify the underlined nouns in each sentence as *common, proper, compound, collective, possessive,* or *appositive.* More than one label may apply to a single noun.

1. Anne Morrow Lindbergh saw the dramatic launching of *Apollo 8* from Cape Kennedy.
2. Twenty years before, she had visited Cape Canaveral, which was the former <u>name</u> of Cape Kennedy.
3. She and her <u>family</u> had camped behind the dunes next to an empty beach.
4. That was long before the great NASA <u>space center</u> was built there.
5. Now the once-empty shore is lined with the towers that launch <u>rockets</u>.
6. She and her husband, <u>Charles Lindbergh</u>, enjoyed lunch with the astronauts.
7. They spoke of Robert Goddard, who had the <u>idea</u> of multistage moon rockets.
8. Lindbergh was amazed at the amount of <u>fuel</u> used for an *Apollo* launching.
9. Just the first second used ten times as much fuel as his transatlantic <u>flight</u>.
10. The Lindberghs were impressed with the <u>astronauts'</u> courage and knowledge.
11. The astronauts knew the hazards but had <u>faith</u> in the technology.
12. The night before the launch, the <u>Lindberghs</u> decided to visit the site.
13. The roadside was already lined with a <u>crowd</u> of people.
14. From miles away, *Apollo 8* shone like a blazing <u>star</u> in the dark night.
15. In the morning, within sight of the <u>launching pad</u>, the suspense grew.
16. With the last number of the <u>countdown</u>, the crowd gasped as one person.
17. Flames and <u>smoke</u> burst forth, and the rocket rose slowly.
18. <u>Explosions</u> thundered on and on, and the earth shook for a long time.
19. In sudden panic, a great <u>flock</u> of marsh birds rose up and filled the air.
20. With its mighty <u>power</u>, the rocket blasted upward and out of sight.
21. Within eleven minutes, *Apollo 8* was already in <u>Earth's</u> orbit.
22. Anne Lindbergh was awed by the technology she observed that <u>day</u>.
23. However, the human beings, the <u>people</u> in control, mattered most to her.
24. After the launch, the Lindberghs explored NASA's nearby wildlife <u>refuge</u>.
25. Here, out of sight of the rocket <u>towers</u>, they found nature flourishing.

Writing Application

Nouns in Writing

As he describes his encounter with a wolf in this passage from *Never Cry Wolf*, Farley Mowat uses nouns that enliven his writing and create a vivid picture. Note the italicized nouns.

My *head* came slowly over the crest—and there was my *quarry.* He was lying down, evidently resting after his mournful *singsong,* and his *nose* was about six *feet* from mine. We stared at one another in *silence.* I do not know what went on in his massive *skull,* but my *head* was full of the most disturbing *thoughts.* I was peering straight into the amber *gaze* of a fully grown *arctic wolf,* who probably weighed more than I did, and who was certainly a lot better versed in close-combat *techniques* than I would ever be.

Techniques with Nouns

Experiment with some of Farley Mowat's writing techniques as you write and revise your own work.

❶ Create more engaging images for readers by replacing general words with specific and vivid nouns. Compare the following:

GENERAL WORDS My head came slowly over the hill—and there was the wolf.

MOWAT'S VERSION My head came slowly over the *crest*—and there was my *quarry.*

❷ Whenever possible, identify people, places, or things by the most specific name available. Notice the extra information Mowat gives in the following example.

GENERAL NOUN a fully grown wolf

MOWAT'S VERSION a fully grown *arctic wolf*

TIME For more about the writing process, see **TIME Facing the Blank Page,** pp. 97–107.

Nouns

Nouns in Writing

Encourage students to read the passage from *Never Cry Wolf* silently. Then discuss their reaction to the italicized nouns. Ask: *What images do the nouns create for the reader? What image was especially notable? Were there any words that were troublesome?* Elicit from the discussion the idea that the nouns used in the passage were especially vivid and specific.

Techniques with Nouns

Review with students the examples of specific and vivid nouns that Farley Mowat uses. Have them refer to the proofreading exercise on page 395 and identify any nouns that are vivid and specific.

Practice

The answers to this challenging and enriching activity will vary. Refer to Techniques with Nouns as you evaluate students' choices.

Sample:

The _youngsters_ climbed steadily up the _mountain trail,_ following the _markers_ along their _path._ As they wound around an _S-curve,_ Jinnie called out, "Look, there's a _doe!_" She quickly took off her _sunglasses_ and peered through her _field_ _glasses_ at the deer. "Wow, she's a _stunner!_ Here, you look," she said, handing the glasses to her _companion._

Practice Read the following passage, focusing especially on the underlined words. Practice the techniques discussed above as you revise the passage on a separate sheet of paper.

The <u>girls</u> climbed steadily up the <u>trail</u>, following the <u>signs</u> posted along their <u>trail</u>. As they wound around a <u>curve</u>, Jinnie called out, "Look, there's a <u>deer</u>!" She quickly took off <u>one pair of glasses</u> and peered through her <u>other</u> glasses at the deer. "Wow, she's a <u>nice</u> <u>one</u>! Here, you look," she said, handing the glasses to her <u>friend</u>.

Writing Application **397**

✔ ASSESSMENT OPTIONS

📁 *Tests with Answer Key and Rubrics*
Unit 9 Mastery Test, pp. 39–40

💾 *Testmaker*
Unit 9 Mastery Test

You may wish to administer the Unit 9 Mastery Test at this point.

📼 *MindJogger Videoquizzes*

Objectives

- To learn about various kinds of verbs
- To use verbs correctly and to use verb tenses appropriately and consistently

---

✓ ASSESSMENT OPTIONS

📁 *Tests with Answer Key & Rubrics*
Unit 10 Pretest, pp. 41–42
Unit 10 Mastery Test, pp. 43–44

💾 *Testmaker*
Unit 10 Pretest
Unit 10 Mastery Test

You may wish to administer the Unit 10 Pretest at this point.

Key to Ability Levels

L1 Level 1 activities are within the basic ability range of students.

L2 Level 2 activities are within the ability range of average students.

L3 Level 3 activities are more challenging activities.

UNIT
10 Verbs

398

Resource Manager

📁 **Planning Resources**
- *Lesson Plans*
- *Block Scheduling*

📠 **Transparencies**
- *Bellringer*
- *Daily Language Practice*
- *Two-Minute Skill Drill*

📁 **Other Print Resources**
- *Grammar and Composition Handbook*
- *Grammar Enrichment*
- *Grammar Practice*
- *Grammar Reteaching*
- *Grammar Workbook*
- *Tests with Answer Key and Rubrics*

📼 **Video**
- *MindJogger Videoquizzes*

💾 **Software**
- *Interactive Grammar and Language Workbook*
- *Language Arts PASS*
- *Presentation Plus!*
- *Testmaker*

🖥 **Web Sites**
- *writerschoice.glencoe.com*

10.1 Action Verbs

Many sports are games of fast action. The actions in sports can be named by verbs. If a word expresses action and tells what a subject does, it is an action verb.

■ An **action verb** is a word that names an action. It may contain more than one word.

Notice the action verbs in the following paragraph.

Sports experts **write** about the football player Jim Thorpe even today. Thorpe **blocked** like a tank. He **tackled** like a tornado. In every game, Thorpe **attacked** his opponents with all his might. He **caught** the ball skillfully and **charged** ahead fearlessly. Experts still **remember** and **honor** Thorpe's greatness.

Action verbs can express physical actions, such as writing and running, or mental activities, such as thinking and honoring.

ACTION VERB

Action Verbs	
Physical	write, block, tackle, attack, catch, charge
Mental	remember, honor

Have, has, and *had* are often used before other verbs. They can also be used as action verbs when they name what the subject owns or holds.

Tonio **remembered** Thorpe's famous play . . .

These players **have** red uniforms.
The pitcher **has** a sore arm.
The stadium **had** an electronic scoreboard.
Our cheerleader **had** a megaphone.

. . .as he **snared** the ball.

10.1 Action Verbs **399**

Verbs

Focus

Lesson Overview

Objectives
- To identify and select appropriate action verbs
- To distinguish between action verbs that express physical action and those that express mental activities
- To use action verbs correctly in writing

Bellringer
Daily Language Activity

When students enter the classroom, have this assignment on the board: *Copy the following sentences, adding appropriate verbs.*

Many people _____ Jim Thorpe was the greatest athlete of the first half of the twelfth century. Thorpe ran track and _____ lacrosse and baseball.

See also *Daily Language Practice*

Motivating Activity

Some action verbs express physical action; others express mental activity. Call on volunteers to read aloud verbs they used in the Bellringer activity. Challenge students to tell which type of activity those verbs express.

Teach

☑ Teaching Tip

Inform students that most sentences containing action verbs can be changed into "do" questions. Give this example: *Thorpe blocked like a tank.* What did Thorpe **do**? The answer, *He blocked,* indicates an action. Therefore *blocked* is an action verb.

Resource Manager

📂 **Planning Resources**
- *Lesson Plans*

Transparencies
- *Bellringer*
- *Daily Language Practice*

📂 **Other Print Resources**
- *Grammar and Composition Handbook*
- *Grammar Reteaching,* p. 9
- *Grammar Workbook,* Lesson 12

Practice and Assess

Answers: Exercise 1

1. invented
2. called
3. observed
4. brought
5. established
6. won
7. earned
8. excelled
9. won
10. developed
11. starred
12. set
13. compete
14. prefer
15. learned
16. won
17. entered
18. regarded
19. dominated
20. developed

Answers: Exercise 2

Answers will vary, but some suggestions are given below.

1. competed	6. brought
2. originated	7. played
3. enjoyed	8. gained
4. threw	9. played
5. stood	10. play

Additional Resources

 Grammar Reteaching, p. 9

Grammar Workbook, Lesson 12

Close

Have students imagine that they are competing in a championship game. Tell them to write a journal entry describing the experience. Suggest they use vivid action verbs. Have them discuss how action verbs enliven their writing.

Verbs

Exercise 1 **Identifying Action Verbs**

Write each action verb from the following sentences.

1. The French probably invented tennis in about 1150.
2. At one time, people called the game lawn tennis.
3. In 1874 Mary E. Outerbridge observed tennis in Bermuda.
4. She brought a net, tennis balls, and racquets back to the United States.
5. She established the first court in New York City.
6. Maud Wilson won the first women's championship at Wimbledon in 1884.
7. Ellen Hanson earned the first singles crown at the U.S. Open in 1887.
8. Women excelled at tennis during the 1920s.
9. Suzanne Lenglen of France won at Wimbledon from 1920 to 1924.
10. She developed an athletic style of play.
11. In 1926 Lenglen starred in the first U.S. professional tennis tour.
12. Helen Moody set a record of eight Wimbledon singles titles.
13. Players in Wimbledon compete on grass courts.
14. Many players prefer clay courts.
15. Althea Gibson learned tennis on the streets of New York City.
16. She won her first championship in her home neighborhood of Harlem.
17. In 1949 Gibson entered college.
18. Fans regarded her as the foremost woman amateur in the 1950s.
19. She dominated the game in 1957 and 1958.
20. She established herself as one of the world's greatest tennis players.

Exercise 2 **Using Action Verbs**

For each sentence, write an appropriate action verb.

1. People have _____ against each other in bowling for thousands of years.
2. The sport probably _____ in ancient Egypt.
3. In Germany during the Middle Ages, people _____ bowling at village dances.
4. The Germans _____ stones at wooden clubs.
5. In the Netherlands, pin setters _____ tall pins far apart.
6. The Dutch _____ their game to America during the 1600s.
7. Americans first _____ the game at Bowling Green in New York City.
8. The game soon _____ in popularity throughout New England.
9. Eventually people all over the country _____ for recreation.
10. Thousands still _____ the game today.

MEETING INDIVIDUAL NEEDS

English Language Learners

Identifying Action Verbs

Help students recognize the difference between a physical action and a mental activity. Write various action verbs on word cards, trying for an equal representation of physical actions and mental activities. Ask students to take turns drawing a card and trying to demonstrate the action. Students will be able to pantomime most physical actions but may be able to demonstrate mental activities only through facial expressions. Let students classify the action verbs under *Physical Actions* and *Mental Activities* on a bulletin board.

10.2 Transitive and Intransitive Verbs

Every sentence has a subject and a predicate. In some sentences the predicate consists of only an action verb.

The punter **kicks.**

Usually sentences provide more information. The predicate often names who or what received the action of the verb.

what?

The punter **kicks** the **football**.

DIRECT OBJECT

In the sentence above, *football* receives the action of the verb *kicks*. It answers the question *what?* after the action verb. *Football* is called a direct object.

■ A **direct object** receives the action of a verb. It answers the question *whom?* or *what?* after an action verb.

A verb can also have a compound direct object. That is, it can have more than one direct object.

The team carried **gloves** and **bats** into the stadium.

Sometimes the action verb does not have a direct object.

The team played well.

In the sentence above, *well* does not answer the question *whom?* or *what?* after the verb *played*. Therefore, it is not a direct object. Action verbs that have direct objects are called transitive verbs. Action verbs that do not have direct objects are called intransitive verbs.

■ A **transitive verb** has a direct object.

■ An **intransitive verb** does not have a direct object.

Verbs

10.2 Transitive and Intransitive Verbs **401**

Focus

Lesson Overview

Objectives

- To identify transitive and intransitive verbs and direct objects
- To use transitive and intransitive verbs and direct objects correctly in writing

 Bellringer
Daily Language Activity

When students enter the classroom, have this assignment on the board: *Indicate whether there is a word that tells whom or what after the action verb in each sentence; list such words.*

I ran with the ball.

I ran fast.

I ran a race.

See also  *Daily Language Practice*

Motivating Activity

Have students share and explain their answers in the Bellringer activity. Make sure they understand the concept of a direct object and its relationship to transitive verbs.

Teach

☑ **Grammar Tip**

Only a sentence with a transitive verb can be turned into a *whom?* or *what?* question whose answer is the object of the verb.

⇆ Cross-Reference: Dictionary

For instruction and practice in using dictionary entries to determine transitive and intransitive verbs, refer students to Lesson 22.8.

Resource Manager

📁 **Planning Resources**
- *Lesson Plans*

📂 **Transparencies**
- *Bellringer*
- *Daily Language Practice*

📁 **Other Print Resources**
- *Grammar and Composition Handbook*
- *Grammar Enrichment,* p. 8
- *Grammar Practice,* p. 8
- *Grammar Reteaching,* p. 10
- *Grammar Workbook,* Lessons 13

401

Practice and Assess

Answers: Exercise 3

1. <u>rival</u>, tr., Jim Thorpe, DO
2. <u>gained</u>, tr., fame, DO
3. <u>ran</u>, intr.
4. <u>came</u>, intr.
5. <u>entered</u>, tr., Carlisle College, DO
6. <u>played</u>, tr., football, DO
7. <u>starred</u>, intr.
8. <u>excelled</u>, intr.
9. <u>scored</u>, tr., points, DO
10. <u>entered</u>, tr., Olympics, DO
11. <u>participated</u>, intr.
12. <u>competed</u>, intr.
13. <u>jumped</u>, intr.
14. <u>ran</u>, intr.
15. <u>copied</u>, tr., style, DO
16. <u>defeated</u>, tr., rivals, DO
17. <u>set</u>, tr., records, DO
18. <u>began</u>, tr., career, DO
19. <u>served</u>, intr.
20. <u>retired</u>, intr.

Answers: Exercise 4

Answers will vary, but some suggestions are given below.
1. competitions
2. _____
3. skill
4. _____
5. athletes

Additional Resources

 *Grammar Practice*, p. 8
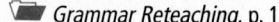 *Grammar Reteaching*, p. 10
 *Grammar Enrichment*, p. 8

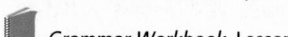 *Grammar Workbook*, Lesson 13

Close

Have students use transitive and intransitive verbs in writing a brief description of a sports facility that they would like to use. Partners should work together to revise their descriptions.

Verbs

Exercise 3 — Distinguishing Transitive and Intransitive Verbs

Write each sentence. Underline each action verb. If the verb has a direct object, write *transitive*. If it does not, write *intransitive*. Draw a circle around each direct object.

1. Few athletes rival Jim Thorpe.
2. Thorpe gained fame as one of the greatest athletes in history.
3. Jim Thorpe ran fast as a boy in Oklahoma.
4. Thorpe came from a Native American family.
5. In 1909 Jim Thorpe entered Carlisle College.
6. Thorpe played football there under Coach Pop Warner.
7. He starred as the starting halfback on the team.
8. He excelled as a spectacular runner, placekicker, and tackler.
9. In 1912 Thorpe scored 129 points.
10. Thorpe entered the 1912 Olympics.
11. He participated in the decathlon and pentathlon.
12. He competed against many other athletes.
13. He jumped higher and farther than the others.
14. Thorpe ran with great strength and concentration.
15. Other track athletes copied Jim Thorpe's style.
16. Thorpe defeated his rivals in the ten events of the decathlon.
17. He even set world records.
18. He began his professional football career in 1915.
19. He served as the first president of the football association.
20. Thorpe retired from football in 1929 at the age of forty-one.

Exercise 4 — Using Transitive and Intransitive Verbs

Write each sentence. If the verb is transitive, add a direct object in the blank space. If the verb is intransitive, leave the space blank. Direct objects will vary.

1. Track meets provide _____ of many kinds.
2. The first track competitions appeared _____ in ancient Greece during the Olympic Games.
3. Individual athletes, as well as teams of athletes, demonstrate _____ at track events.
4. Many athletes perform well _____ in a variety of events.
5. Hurdle races challenge _____.

MEETING INDIVIDUAL NEEDS — **Less-Proficient Readers**

Testing for Transitive Verbs

Students may be confused about the difference between transitive verbs and linking verbs. Point out that while linking verbs can also answer the questions *whom?* or *what?*, they are never action verbs. The verb *to be*, for instance, can be used to answer *whom?* or *what?* in the following examples: *I am a hero; I am your teacher.* Guide students to brainstorm examples of transitive verbs and linking verbs that answer the questions *whom?* or *what?*

10.3 Verbs with Indirect Objects

Nouns or pronouns that answer the question *whom?* or *what?* after an action verb are called direct objects.

> Michael Jordan led his **team** to the championship.
> Michael Jordan tossed the **ball.**

Sometimes two kinds of objects follow an action verb. The object that directly receives the action of the verb is the direct object. The object that tells *to whom* or *for whom* the action is done is called the indirect object.

■ An **indirect object** answers the question *to whom?* or *for whom?* an action is done.

Michael Jordan **shows** his **teammates** new shots.

INDIRECT OBJECT

to whom?

The direct object in the sentence above is *shots.* The indirect object is *teammates. Teammates* answers the question *to whom?* after the action verb *shows.*

An indirect object appears only in a sentence that has a direct object. Two easy clues will help you recognize indirect objects. First, the indirect object always comes before a direct object. Second, you can add *to* or *for* before the indirect object and change its position. The sentence will still make sense, although it will no longer have an indirect object.

> The helper gives the **players** towels.
> The helper gives the towels **to the players.**

You can figure out that in the first sentence *players* is the indirect object. First, it comes before the direct object. Second, its position can be changed to follow the word *to.*

Focus

Lesson Overview

Objectives
- To distinguish between direct objects and indirect objects
- To use indirect objects correctly in writing

Bellringer
Daily Language Activity

When students enter the classroom, have this assignment on the board: *Write a sentence in which one person gives an object to another person. Include the names of both persons and the object.*

See also  *Daily Language Practice*

Motivating Activity

Call on volunteers to read aloud the sentences they wrote in the Bellringer activity. Use their sentences to introduce direct objects and indirect objects. Ask students to constructively evaluate these elements as they occur in one another's sentences.

Teach

☑ **Grammar Tip**

It is grammatically incorrect to have a direct object and an indirect object in the same sentence when both objects are pronouns. If the direct object of a sentence is a pronoun, the indirect object should be the object of a preposition.

Resource Manager

📂 **Planning Resources**
- *Lesson Plans*

📖 **Transparencies**
- *Bellringer*
- *Daily Language Practice*

📂 **Other Print Resources**
- *Grammar and Composition Handbook*
- *Grammar Enrichment,* p. 9
- *Grammar Practice,* p. 9
- *Grammar Reteaching,* p. 11
- *Grammar Workbook,* Lesson 14

Practice and Assess

Answers: Exercise 5

1. athletes, DO
2. tournament, IO; support, DO
3. onlookers, DO
4. team, IO; edge, DO
5. him, DO
6. fans, IO; plays, DO
7. no DO or IO
8. players, IO; tribute, DO
9. players, IO; instructions, DO
10. players, DO
11. game, DO
12. offense, IO; advantage, DO
13. him, IO; compliments, DO
14. ability, DO
15. him, IO; pat, DO
16. article, DO
17. Clayton, IO; questions, DO
18. strategy, DO
19. players, IO; credit, DO
20. coach, DO

Answers: Exercise 6

1. Long fiberglass poles give the <u>competitors</u> height and speed.
2. The coaches show the <u>vaulters</u> each move.
3. Constant practice brings well-prepared <u>competitors</u> victory.
4. A successful jump earns a <u>vaulter</u> another chance.
5. The crowd's cheers give the <u>competitors</u> encouragement.

Additional Resources

 Grammar Practice, p. 9
Grammar Reteaching, p. 11
Grammar Enrichment, p. 9

Grammar Workbook, Lesson 14

Verbs

| **Exercise 5** | Identifying Direct and Indirect Objects |

Write each sentence. If the sentence contains a direct object, underline it once. If the sentence contains an indirect object, underline it twice.

1. The tournament sometimes attracts good athletes.
2. The university gave the tournament its support.
3. The level of play interested the onlookers.
4. One player earned his team a three-point edge.
5. For a few minutes, no player could stop him.
6. In the first game of the season, the teams showed their fans some skillful plays.
7. A number of fans cheered loudly at each game.
8. Many fans paid the players tribute with colorful banners.
9. The coach gave the players new instructions.
10. Students from many different schools cheered their favorite players.
11. Mr. Romero refereed the game.
12. Clayton's shooting skill gave his team's offense a potent advantage.
13. All of the players paid him many compliments.
14. All of the players admired his ability.
15. Several players gave him a pat on the back.
16. A top reporter wrote an article about the game for the *Times Gazette.*
17. She asked Clayton some questions about his game.
18. Clayton explained his strategy to her.
19. The coach gave his players all the credit.
20. The team, in turn, praised its coach.

| **Exercise 6** | Using Indirect Objects |

Without changing the meaning of the sentence, rewrite each so that it contains an indirect object. Underline the indirect object.

SAMPLE   A good show was given to us by the field events.
ANSWER   The field events gave <u>us</u> a good show.

1. The competitors are given height and speed by long fiberglass poles.
2. The vaulters are shown each move by the coaches.
3. Well-prepared competitors are brought victory by constant practice.
4. A vaulter earns another chance by a successful jump.
5. The competitors are given encouragement by the crowd's cheers.

Close

Have partners write three sentences about the imaginary characters Mr. Pelliccia and Ms. McArthur. Have them explain what happens when Mr. Pelliccia finds a passport that belongs to Ms. McArthur. Tell students to use direct objects and indirect objects in their sentences and to proofread their work.

MEETING INDIVIDUAL NEEDS   English Language Learners

Recognizing Indirect Objects

Remind students that the indirect object always comes before the direct object. Then have students rewrite indirect objects as phrases that begin with *to* or *for.* For example, *The sponsors gave the winners a trophy* can be rewritten as *The sponsors gave a trophy to the winners.*

10.4 Linking Verbs and Predicate Words

Action verbs tell what the subject of a sentence does. Other verbs tell what the subject is or is like. These verbs are called linking verbs.

- A **linking verb** connects the subject of a sentence with a noun or an adjective in the predicate.

John McGraw **was** the manager.

LINKING VERB

LINKING VERB

In the sentence above, the word *was* is a linking verb. It connects, or links, the subject, *John McGraw*, to a word in the predicate, *manager*.

- A **predicate noun** is a noun that follows a linking verb. It tells what the subject is.

- A **predicate adjective** is an adjective that follows a linking verb. It describes the subject by telling what it is like.

    Sam is a **pitcher.** [predicate noun]
    The pitcher is **skillful.** [predicate adjective]

Common Linking Verbs			
be	appear	turn	smell
become	look	taste	sound
seem	grow	feel	

Many of these verbs can also be used as action verbs.

    Chandra **turned** thirteen. [linking verb]
    The car **turned** the corner. [action verb]

10.4 Linking Verbs and Predicate Words **405**

Focus

Lesson Overview

Objectives

- To distinguish between action verbs and linking verbs
- To identify predicate nouns and predicate adjectives
- To use linking verbs and predicate words correctly in writing

Bellringer
Daily Language Activity

When students enter the classroom, have this assignment on the board: *Write a sentence that contains the verb* is.

See also *Daily Language Practice*

Motivating Activity

Call on volunteers to read aloud the sentences they wrote in the Bellringer activity. Write the sentences on the board. Point out the linking verbs, predicate nouns, and predicate adjectives, using the students' work to introduce these parts of speech. Invite students to monitor their own understanding and to seek clarification as needed.

Teach

Cooperative Learning

Have groups of students write a sentence that contains a linking verb and a predicate noun or predicate adjective. Invite groups to devise a way to show the function of the linking verb (for example, in a short skit or pantomime). One student in each group can serve as a recorder, one as a group manager, and one as a monitor to ensure that everyone has a chance to contribute.

Resource Manager

📂 **Planning Resources**
- *Lesson Plans*

🎵 **Transparencies**
- *Bellringer*
- *Daily Language Practice*

📂 **Other Print Resources**
- *Grammar and Composition Handbook*
- *Grammar Enrichment,* p. 10
- *Grammar Practice,* p. 10
- *Grammar Reteaching,* p. 12
- *Grammar Workbook,* Lesson 15

Practice and Assess

Answers: Exercise 7

1. appears: linking; nervous: pred. adj.
2. shows: action
3. ran: action
4. seems: linking; agile: pred. adj.
5. caught: action
6. was: linking; hitter: pred. n.
7. was: linking; fielder: pred. n.
8. threw: action
9. sailed: action
10. grew: linking; ecstatic: pred. adj.
11. turned: action
12. flew: action
13. seem: linking; confident: pred. adj.
14. looked: linking; wonderful: pred. adj.
15. was: linking; winner: pred. n.
16. seem: linking; eager: pred. adj.
17. walks: action
18. looks: linking; proud: pred. adj.
19. flock: action
20. is: linking; member: pred. n.

Answers: Exercise 8

1. popular
2. good
3. yummy
4. star
5. trumpeters

Additional Resources

 *Grammar Practice*, p. 10
 *Grammar Reteaching*, p. 12
 *Grammar Enrichment*, p. 10

 *Grammar Workbook*, Lesson 15

Close

Have students write a script for a radio announcer introducing a celebrity. Tell students to use linking verbs, predicate nouns, and predicate adjectives in their introductions. Have students exchange scripts and evaluate one another's work.

Verbs

Exercise 7 **Distinguishing Action and Linking Verbs and Predicate Nouns and Adjectives**

Write each sentence. Underline each verb, and write whether it is an *action verb* or a *linking verb*. If it is a linking verb, circle the predicate noun or predicate adjective. Write whether it is a *predicate noun* or a *predicate adjective*.

1. Our pitcher appears very nervous today.
2. He shows a serious lack of concentration.
3. The catcher ran very quickly.
4. She seems quite agile.
5. She caught the ball.
6. The pitcher was a good hitter.
7. He was also a fine fielder.
8. The player at third base threw the baseball.
9. It sailed into the outfield.
10. Fans of the team grew ecstatic.
11. One player turned a pop fly into a home run.
12. The ball flew into the bleachers.
13. Fans of the home team seem confident today.
14. The team looked wonderful for the first three innings.
15. The home team was the winner yesterday.
16. The players on both teams seem eager at the start of the game.
17. The mayor walks onto the field.
18. She looks very proud of the team.
19. All of the team members flock around her.
20. She is an honorary member of the team.

Exercise 8 **Using Predicate Nouns and Adjectives with Linking Verbs**

Write each sentence, adding a predicate noun or adjective to fill the blank.

1. Sports are _____ in many schools.
2. Athletes feel _____ after a workout.
3. Hot dogs taste _____ at the ball park.
4. Beth is a _____ on the basketball team.
5. Josh and Sam are _____ in the school band.

MEETING INDIVIDUAL NEEDS **Less-Proficient Readers**

Identifying Linking Verbs

Students can test for linking verbs by seeing if a form of *be* can be substituted for the verb. Use this sentence as an example: *The sun looked red.* Substitute the appropriate form of *be* for *looked. The sun was red.* The sentence still makes sense, so the word *looked* must be a linking verb.

10.5 Present, Past, and Future Tenses

A verb changes its form to show tense and to agree with its subject. The **tense** of a verb tells when an action takes place.

■ The **present tense** of a verb names an action that is happening now or that happens regularly. It can also express a general truth.

In the present tense, the base form of a verb is used with all subjects except singular nouns and the words *he, she,* and *it.* When the subject is a singular noun or *he, she,* or *it, -s* is usually added to the verb.

Present Tense Forms	
Singular	**Plural**
I **race.**	We **race.**
You **race.**	You **race.**
He, she, *or* it **races.**	They **race.**

■ The **past tense** of a verb names an action that already happened.

The past tense of many verbs is formed by adding *-ed* to the base form of the verb.

> The runner **trained** hard.   I **slapped** the buzzer.

■ The **future tense** of a verb names an action that will take place in the future.

In the future tense, the word *will* is used with the verb. Sometimes *shall* is used when the pronoun *I* or *we* is the subject.

Future Tense Forms	
Singular	**Plural**
I **will (shall) go.**	We **will (shall) go.**
You **will go.**	You **will go.**
He, she, *or* it **will go.**	They **will go.**

Focus

Lesson Overview

Objectives

- To distinguish between present, past, and future verb tenses
- To use present, past, and future tenses appropriately in writing

 Bellringer
Daily Language Activity

When students enter the classroom, have this assignment on the board: *Copy this sentence:*

> *Emily skates after school.*

Underline the verb. Rewrite the sentence to name an action that happened in the past.

See also *Daily Language Practice*

Motivating Activity

Have students revise the sentence from the Bellringer activity to name an action that will happen in the future. Read aloud all three forms of this sentence. Challenge students to name the present, past, and future tenses of the verb *skate.*

Teach

Vocabulary Link

The word *tense* comes from the Latin *tempus,* which means "time." Verbs have a past, present, or future tense—in other words, they indicate time in a sentence.

Verbs

Resource Manager

Planning Resources
- *Lesson Plans*

Transparencies
- *Bellringer*
- *Daily Language Practice*

Other Print Resources
- *Grammar and Composition Handbook*
- *Grammar Enrichment,* p. 11
- *Grammar Practice,* p. 11
- *Grammar Reteaching,* p. 13
- *Grammar Workbook,* Lesson 16

Practice and Assess

Answers: Exercise 9

1. achieved
2. lived
3. moved
4. entered
5. succeeded
6. established
7. gained
8. occurred
9. walked
10. earned

Answers: Exercise 10

1. entered, past
2. gained, past
3. suffered, past
4. allowed, past
5. practiced, past
6. encouraged, past; or encourages, present
7. offers, present
8. worked, past
9. will remember, future
10. learned, past
11. wanted, past
12. enjoyed, past
13. triumphed, past
14. trained, past
15. counted, past
16. received, past
17. proves, present; or proved, past
18. describes, present
19. inspires, present
20. will follow, future

Additional Resources

 *Grammar Practice*, p. 11

Grammar Reteaching, p. 13

Grammar Enrichment, p. 11

Grammar Workbook, Lesson 16

Verbs

Exercise 9   Using the Past Tense of Verbs

Write the past tense of each verb.

1. Jesse Owens achieves a national reputation during the 1930s.
2. He lives his early years in Oakville, Alabama.
3. At the age of seven, he moves with his family to Cleveland.
4. In 1933 he enters Ohio State University.
5. Almost immediately he succeeds in track and field events.
6. At a college meet, he establishes three world records in forty-five minutes.
7. He gains great fame at the Summer Olympics of 1936.
8. The games occur in Berlin, Germany.
9. Owens walks away with seven world records.
10. His success earns him a position as one of history's most famous athletes.

Exercise 10   Using Present, Past, and Future Tenses

Write the appropriate tense of the verb in parentheses. Then write whether it is in the *present*, *past*, or *future* tense.

1. Wilma Rudolph (enter) many races in the 1950s.
2. She (gain) victory in a great many of those.
3. During her youth, Rudolph (suffer) many difficulties.
4. Her hard work (allow) her to overcome all of them.
5. She (practice) hour after hour and day after day.
6. Wilma Rudolph (encourage) other young runners.
7. Her record (offer) hope to any young runner.
8. She (work) every day for it.
9. In future years, people (remember) her success on the track.
10. At an early age, Wilma Rudolph (learn) the importance of good health.
11. The young Wilma (want) an active life.
12. As a girl, she (enjoy) several different sports.
13. She (triumph) over many illnesses.
14. For many years, she (train) long and hard.
15. All her work finally (count).
16. In 1960 Rudolph (receive) an Olympic medal in track.
17. Her medal (prove) the importance of hard work.
18. This great runner no longer (describe) sports on television.
19. Even today, however, her performance (inspire) many young athletes.
20. In the years ahead, young runners (follow) Rudolph's example.

408   Unit 10 Verbs

Close

Have students write a sentence in which an action verb (in the present, past, or future tense) is missing. Allow pairs of students to trade sentences. Each partner should supply an action verb and identify its tense. Have student pairs check each other's work.

Exploring Language

Contrasting Meanings

Ask students how the questions *Shall we go?* and *Will we go?* differ in meaning. (*Shall* makes the first question a polite form of request. It is not a real question. *Will* makes a genuine query to which the speaker does not already know the answer.)

10.6 Main Verbs and Helping Verbs

Verbs have four principal parts that are used to form all tenses. The chart below shows how the principal parts of most verbs are formed.

Principal Parts			
Base Form	**Present Participle**	**Past Form**	**Past Participle**
jump	jumping	jumped	jumped

The principal parts of a verb are often combined with helping verbs to form verb phrases.

■ A **helping verb** is a verb that completes the meaning of the main verb.

■ A **verb phrase** consists of one or more helping verbs followed by a main verb.

The students **are jumping** rope now.

In the sentence above, the word *are* is the helping verb, and the present participle *jumping* is the main verb. Together they form a verb phrase.

The most common helping verbs are *be, have,* and *do.* Forms of the helping verb *be* include *am, is,* and *are* in the present and *was* and *were* in the past. They combine with the present participle of the main verb.

Forms of the helping verb *have* include *has* and *had.* They combine with the past participle form of a verb.

Have, Has, and *Had* with the Past Participle			
Singular	**Plural**	**Singular**	**Plural**
I **have** jumped.	We **have** jumped.	I **had** jumped.	We **had** jumped.
You **have** jumped.	You **have** jumped.	You **had** jumped.	You **had** jumped.
She **has** jumped.	They **have** jumped.	She **had** jumped.	They **had** jumped.

Focus

Lesson Overview

Objectives
- To distinguish between main verbs and helping verbs
- To identify the present participle and past participle in main verbs
- To use main verbs and helping verbs correctly in writing

 Bellringer
Daily Language Activity

When students enter the classroom, have this assignment on the board: *Underline the helping verbs in these sentences.*

The boys are singing too loudly.

The pizza has arrived.

I am going on vacation soon.

The team has run the full course.

John is listening to music.

See also *Daily Language Practice*

Motivating Activity

Have students share their answers to the Bellringer activity and explain their choices. Explain, if necessary, that a helping verb helps the main verb tell about the action or statement. Ask students to seek clarification as needed.

Teach

 **Cross-Reference: Grammar**

For instruction and practice with participles and participial phrases, refer students to Lesson 15.1.

Resource Manager

📂 **Planning Resources**
- *Lesson Plans*

📑 **Transparencies**
- *Bellringer*
- *Daily Language Practice*

📂 **Other Print Resources**
- *Grammar and Composition Handbook*
- *Grammar Enrichment,* p. 12
- *Grammar Practice,* p. 12
- *Grammar Reteaching,* p. 14
- *Grammar Workbook,* Lesson 17

Practice and Assess

Answers: Exercise 11

1. are learning; present participle
2. are making; present participle
3. has changed; past participle
4. are playing; present participle
5. had founded; past participle
6. have increased; past participle
7. are competing; present participle
8. have enjoyed; past participle
9. are shooting; present participle
10. are dividing; present participle
11. are dividing; present participle
12. is earning; present participle
13. have practiced; past participle
14. are marking; present participle
15. are working; present participle
16. has earned; past participle
17. has scored; past participle
18. has landed; past participle
19. is adjusting; present participle
20. is planning; present participle
21. has improved; past participle
22. was taking; present participle
23. have devoted; past participle
24. are bringing; present participle
25. has profited; past participle

Additional Resources

 *Grammar Practice,* p. 12
 *Grammar Reteaching,* p. 14
 *Grammar Enrichment,* p. 12

 Grammar Workbook, Lesson 17

Close

Have students write a paragraph about the qualities that an athlete should possess to excel at a certain game or sport. Be sure students use verb phrases. Have students use the chart at the bottom of page 409 as a reference.

Exercise 11   Using Helping Verbs with Present and Past Participles

Write each sentence, choosing the correct helping verb from the parentheses. Underline the verb phrase once, and draw a second line under the participle. Then write whether it is a *present* participle or a *past* participle.

1. We (are, have) learning about archery this year.
2. Slowly but surely, champions (are, had) making archery a more popular sport throughout the country.
3. During the last forty or fifty years, competitive archery equipment (are, has) changed very little.
4. Many people (are, have) playing in tournaments each year.
5. Archers (was, had) founded the National Archery Association in 1879 for annual tournaments.
6. Tournaments (have, are) increased people's interest in archery.
7. People (have, are) competing in tournaments in target archery, field archery, flight shooting, and shooting at ground targets.
8. Many more people (have, are) enjoyed target archery than any other type of archery.
9. In target archery, competitors (are, have) shooting down a long course at straw targets.
10. Concentric wire circles (are, have) dividing the target into sections.
11. Similar wire circles (have, are) dividing the bull's-eye into sections.
12. An archer (is, has) earning ten points by a direct hit in the bull's-eye.
13. The archers in the competition (are, have) practiced for at least three hours every day.
14. Archers (are, had) marking their targets.
15. Archers (are, have) working hard in today's competition.
16. That archer in the colorful red jacket (is, has) earned the most points so far in the tournament.
17. She (is, has) scored several bull's-eyes.
18. Sarafina's arrow (is, has) landed away from the target.
19. She (is, has) adjusting for her next shot at the target.
20. A good archer (is, has) planning each and every shot.
21. Her concentration (is, has) improved greatly.
22. Last year archery (had, was) taking up most of her free time.
23. The best archers (have, are) devoted countless hours to their sport.
24. Some archers (are, have) bringing new arrows.
25. Tomorrow's champion (is, has) profited from old mistakes.

MEETING INDIVIDUAL NEEDS   **Less-Proficient Readers**

Recognizing Helping Verbs

Some students may need additional practice in recognizing helping verbs. Students may recognize *will* and *shall* as helping verbs because they are used frequently with the future tense. Guide students in compiling a list of additional helping verbs from something they are currently reading. Ask students to write the helping verb with the main verb and to highlight or circle the helping verb. Remind students to use the helping verbs from their lists in their writing.

10.7 Progressive Forms

You know that the present tense of a verb names an action that occurs repeatedly. To describe an action that is taking place right now, you use the present progressive form of the verb.

■ The **present progressive form** of a verb names an action or condition that is continuing in the present.

> I **am enjoying** this baseball game at Candlestick Park.
> The home team **is winning** at the moment.

The present progressive form of a verb consists of the present participle of the main verb and the helping verb *am*, *are*, or *is*.

Present Progressive Form

Singular	Plural
I **am looking.**	We **are looking.**
You **are looking.**	You **are looking.**
He, she, *or* it **is looking.**	They **are looking.**

■ The **past progressive form** of a verb names an action or condition that continued for some time in the past.

> They **were winning** the game.

The past progressive form of a verb consists of the present participle and the helping verb *was* or *were*.

Past Progressive Form

Singular	Plural
I **was trying.**	We **were trying.**
You **were trying.**	You **were trying.**
He, she, *or* it **was trying.**	They **were trying.**

Focus

Lesson Overview

Objectives

- To identify the present and past progressive forms of verbs
- To use the present and past progressive forms appropriately in writing

Bellringer
Daily Language Activity

When students enter the classroom, have this assignment on the board: *Copy this sentence:*

> *Suzanne is combing her hair.*

Circle the words that show that an action is taking place right now.

See also *Daily Language Practice*

Motivating Activity

Revise the sentence from the Bellringer activity to read *Suzanne was combing her hair.* Challenge students to explain how the meaning of the sentence changed with the revision.

Teach

Vocabulary Link

The terminology for verbs in English was taken directly from the terminology for verbs in Latin. In Latin there is no separate tense form that corresponds to the progressive in English. Therefore, the progressive form in English is not called a tense. Instead, it is described as a separate form of the verb.

Resource Manager

 **Planning Resources**
- *Lesson Plans*

 Transparencies
- *Bellringer*
- *Daily Language Practice*

📂 **Other Print Resources**
- *Grammar and Composition Handbook*
- *Grammar Enrichment*, p. 9
- *Grammar Practice*, p. 13
- *Grammar Workbook*, Lesson 18

Practice and Assess

Answers: Exercise 12

1. is developing
2. am watching
3. are trying
4. were cheering
5. is gaining *or* was gaining
6. are following *or* were following
7. is missing *or* was missing
8. is applauding
9. are thinking
10. were searching
11. were looking
12. were searching
13. were getting
14. was laughing
15. was giving
16. was suggesting
17. were looking
18. were going
19. were examining
20. were climbing

Answers: Exercise 13

1. is planning
2. was asking
3. were trying
4. are training
5. was watching
6. are standing
7. are kicking
8. were exercising
9. was inspecting
10. are practicing

Additional Resources

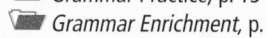 *Grammar Practice*, p. 13

 Grammar Enrichment, p. 9

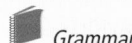 *Grammar Workbook*, Lesson 18

Close

Have students work in groups to describe a surprise party in a paragraph that contains some progressive verb forms. Have members take the roles of discussion monitor, recorder, punctuation checker, and so on. Have groups read their paragraphs to the class. Students should respond in constructive ways to one another's work.

Verbs

Exercise 12 Using Present and Past Progressive Forms

Rewrite each sentence, using the present progressive or past progressive form of the verb.

1. Soccer (develop) into the most popular sport in the world.
2. I (watch) a great soccer game on television now.
3. The players (try) very hard.
4. Yesterday fans (cheer) this same team.
5. Every play (gain) my undivided attention.
6. The fans (follow) every play.
7. No one (miss) a moment of the action.
8. Today the crowd (applaud) wildly.
9. The players (think) very hard about every play.
10. After the game, the players (search) for the bus.
11. They (look) up and down each street.
12. They (search) behind houses and barns.
13. They (get) desperate.
14. The coach (laugh) at the players.
15. He (give) them some hints.
16. He (suggest) some possible locations.
17. Finally, they (look) at a bus.
18. They (go) up to it.
19. They (examine) the bus closely.
20. They (climb) onto the bus.

Exercise 13 Using the Progressive Forms

Rewrite each sentence. If the verb is in the present tense, change it to present progressive. If the verb is in the past tense, change it to past progressive.

1. The soccer coach plans a team for the next season.
2. She asked players from other teams to the tryouts.
3. Many new players tried out also.
4. Some players train for the next season.
5. My friend watched the players at the tryouts.
6. Some players stand by the goal post.
7. The players kick the ball back and forth.
8. Several players exercised.
9. A goalie inspected the field.
10. Some enthusiastic players practice daily.

Exploring Language

Learning Exceptions to the Rule

Explain to students that some verbs refer to "timeless" mental states. These verbs cannot be used in the present or past progressive forms because the meanings of these verbs cannot refer to a specific moment of time. Thus, the following sentences are ungrammatical: *I am knowing that soccer player. I am loving my mother. I am being a writer.*

10.8 Perfect Tenses

■ The **present perfect tense** of a verb names an action that happened at an indefinite time in the past. It also tells about an action that happened in the past and is still happening now.

> My family **has attended** many sports events.
> We **have watched** baseball games for years.

The present perfect tense consists of the helping verb *have* or *has* and the past participle of the main verb.

Present Perfect Tense	
Singular	**Plural**
I **have watched**.	We **have watched**.
You **have watched**.	You **have watched**.
He, she, *or* it **has watched**.	They **have watched**.

■ The **past perfect tense** of a verb names an action that happened before another action or event in the past.

The past perfect tense is often used in sentences that contain a past tense verb in another part of the sentence.

> By the time we found our seats, the game **had** already **started**.
> I **had** never **seen** a baseball game before.

The past perfect tense of a verb consists of the helping verb *had* and the past participle of the main verb.

Past Perfect Tense	
Singular	**Plural**
I **had studied**.	We **had studied**.
You **had studied**.	You **had studied**.
He, she, *or* it **had studied**.	They **had studied**.

10.8 Perfect Tenses **413**

Verbs

Focus

Lesson Overview

Objectives
- To identify the forms and understand the uses of the present perfect and past perfect tenses of verbs
- To use the present perfect and past perfect tenses appropriately in writing and speaking

Bellringer
Daily Language Activity

When students enter the classroom, have this assignment on the board: *Write a sentence in which* have *is the main verb.*

See also *Daily Language Practice*

Motivating Activity

Review the sentences students created for the Bellringer activity and discuss what verb tense they used. Then point out that *have* can be used as a helping verb as well and ask for examples. Introduce students to the idea that *have* as a helping verb with a past participle indicates the present perfect tense.

Teach

☑ Teaching Tip

Compare the present perfect tense in the first two sentences on page 413 with the past perfect tense in the second two sentences. Point out that the present perfect tense is used to emphasize an action that began in the past and has continued into the present. The past perfect tense refers to an action that happened in the past before another action in the past; both actions have finished.

⮂ Cross-Reference: Spelling

For instruction in adding suffixes correctly to words that end in *y*, refer students to Lessons 23.6–23.7.

Resource Manager

📁 **Planning Resources**
- *Lesson Plans*

📑 **Transparencies**
- *Bellringer*
- *Daily Language Practice*

📁 **Other Print Resources**
- *Grammar and Composition Handbook*
- *Grammar Enrichment*, p. 13
- *Grammar Practice*, p. 13
- *Grammar Reteaching*, p. 15
- *Grammar Workbook*, Lesson 19

Practice and Assess

Answers: Exercise 14

1. have recognized
2. have started
3. have walked
4. have arrived
5. have followed
6. have devoted
7. has watched
8. has noticed
9. has identified
10. has planned
11. has called
12. have complained
13. have agreed
14. have realized
15. have experienced
16. have arrived
17. have practiced
18. have promised
19. have hoped
20. have worked

Answers: Exercise 15

1. had earned
2. had wanted
3. had tried
4. had practiced
5. had welcomed
6. had wished
7. had noticed
8. had improved
9. had earned
10. had celebrated

Additional Resources

 *Grammar Practice,* p. 13
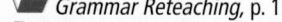 *Grammar Reteaching,* p. 15
Grammar Enrichment, p. 13

 Grammar Workbook, Lesson 19

Verbs

Exercise 14 Using the Present Perfect Tense

Write each sentence, using the present perfect tense of the verb in parentheses.

1. Some players (recognize) the need for practice.
2. They (start) their warm-up routines.
3. They (walk) to the practice field very early.
4. They (arrive) in time to hear the coach's instructions.
5. They (follow) every bit of advice.
6. They (devote) the extra time.
7. The coach (watch) the games.
8. She (notice) some real weaknesses.
9. She (identify) items for practice.
10. She (plan) an intensive practice.
11. She (call) an early practice this evening.
12. Some players (complain) about the work.
13. Most players (agree) to the new rules.
14. They (realize) their weaknesses.
15. They (experience) the benefits of practice.
16. They (arrive) at school early for more practice.
17. Some (practice) for three hours.
18. Others (promise) weekend practice.
19. The students (hope) for a victory.
20. They (work) very hard for it.

Exercise 15 Using the Past Perfect Tense

Write each sentence, using the past perfect tense of the verb in parentheses.

1. The skater (earn) a medal by the age of six.
2. She (want) a place on her school's skating team.
3. The speed skater (try) twice before.
4. She (practice) daily.
5. The team (welcome) her into the group.
6. They (wish) her the best of luck.
7. The spectators (notice) the new skater.
8. Her skating (improve) dramatically.
9. They were pleased that she (earn) a place on the team.
10. They (celebrate) her first victory.

Close

Ask students to write a paragraph in which they describe a recent sports event or game. Discuss how sports announcers often use the past perfect and present perfect tenses in their play-by-play and replay descriptions.

MEETING INDIVIDUAL NEEDS Less-Proficient Readers

Understanding the Order of Events

Some students may have difficulty determining when to use the past perfect or present perfect tense. To help them see the difference, suggest that they make a time line of events. They can draw dotted lines to indicate ongoing action and use arrows to indicate events that happened in the past, one before the other.

10.9 Irregular Verbs

The irregular verbs below are grouped according to the way their past form and past participle are formed.

Present Perfect Tense			
Pattern	**Base Form**	**Past Form**	**Past Participle**
One vowel changes to form the past and the past participle.	begin	began	begun
	drink	drank	drunk
	ring	rang	rung
	shrink	shrank *or* shrunk	shrunk
	sing	sang	sung
	spring	sprang *or* sprung	sprung
	swim	swam	swum
The past form and past participle are the same.	bring	brought	brought
	buy	bought	bought
	catch	caught	caught
	creep	crept	crept
	feel	felt	felt
	get	got	got *or* gotten
	keep	kept	kept
	lay	laid	laid
	lead	led	led
	leave	left	left
	lend	lent	lent
	lose	lost	lost
	make	made	made
	pay	paid	paid
	say	said	said
	seek	sought	sought
	sell	sold	sold
	sit	sat	sat
	sleep	slept	slept
	swing	swung	swung
	teach	taught	taught
	think	thought	thought
	win	won	won

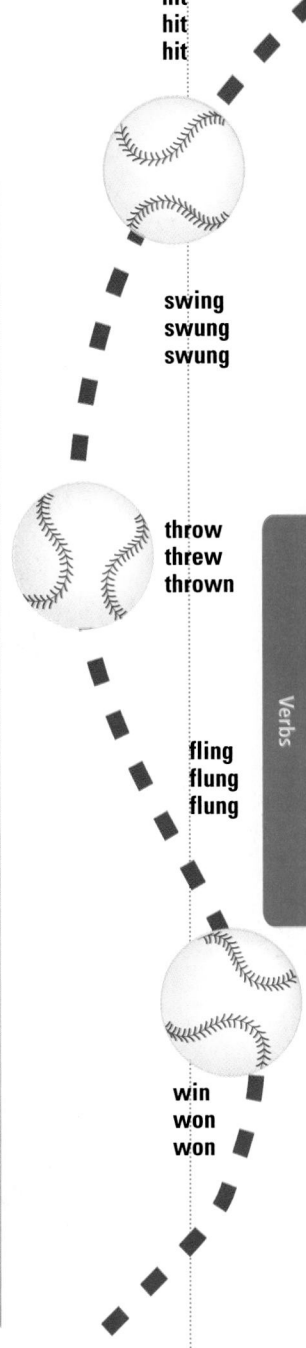

hit
hit
hit

swing
swung
swung

throw
threw
thrown

fling
flung
flung

win
won
won

Verbs

10.9 Irregular Verbs **415**

Focus

Lesson Overview

Objectives
- To identify the past tense and the past participle of irregular verbs
- To use the past tense and the past participle of irregular verbs appropriately

Bellringer
Daily Language Activity

When students enter the classroom, have this assignment on the board: *Copy these sentences on a piece of paper:*

Noelle and Steve sing in a band.

At yesterday's dance, they sang their favorite song.

Underline the verb in each sentence, and circle the letters that are different in the two words.

See also *Daily Language Practice*

Teach

☑ Teaching Tip

Explain to students that the past and past participle forms of irregular verbs often look very different from the base form of the verbs. Ask students to look at the past and past participle forms of the irregular verbs in the chart on this page, particularly those in the bottom section of the chart. Compare the base form to the past tense and the past participle, noting the letters that are the same and those that are different.

Cross-Reference: Dictionary

Students may use a dictionary to check whether a verb form is regular or irregular. For instruction and practice in using a dictionary, refer students to Lesson 22.7.

Resource Manager

📁 Planning Resources
- *Lesson Plans*

Transparencies
- *Bellringer*
- *Daily Language Practice*
- *Two-Minute Skill Drill*

📁 Other Print Resources
- *Grammar and Composition Handbook*
- *Grammar Enrichment,* p. 14
- *Grammar Practice,* p. 14
- *Grammar Reteaching,* p. 16
- *Grammar Workbook,* Lesson 20

Practice and Assess

Answers: Exercise 16

1. sang	**14.** caught
2. said	**15.** brought
3. thought	**16.** felt
4. got	**17.** kept
5. won	**18.** began
6. begun	**19.** taught
7. brought	**20.** won
8. lent	**21.** sought
9. made	**22.** kept
10. sprang	**23.** thought
11. caught	**24.** thought
12. rang	**25.** left
13. led	

Additional Resources

Grammar Practice, p. 14

Grammar Reteaching, p. 16

Grammar Enrichment, p. 14

Grammar Workbook, Lesson 20

Verbs

Exercise 16   Using the Past Forms of Irregular Verbs

Write the past form or past participle of the verb in parentheses.

1. The public first (sing) Sonja Henie's praises in the late 1920s as her fame began to spread internationally.
2. Experts have (say) that she made figure skating popular all by herself.
3. Sports historians have (think) highly of her.
4. She (get) gold medals at the 1928, 1932, and 1936 Olympic games.
5. After her victories, she (win) roles in several American movies in which she appeared with other major stars.
6. Peggy Fleming and Dorothy Hamill of the United States had also (begin) professional careers after Olympic victories.
7. They have (bring) high standards to the sport.
8. Ballet has (lend) many movements to figure skating.
9. It has (make) figure skating very graceful.
10. Last night the skater (spring) into the rink.
11. Her sudden appearance had (catch) the spectators by surprise.
12. The silver skate blades (ring) on the ice.
13. The skater has (lead) her partner onto the ice.
14. The skater's partner has (catch) the woman expertly.
15. Hours of practice had (bring) them to a perfect and flawless performance that could keep the audience spellbound.
16. We (feel) the excitement of the moment.
17. We (keep) our eyes on the expert pair.
18. The judges (begin) their voting immediately after each performance ended.
19. The coach had (teach) the skaters to perform as well and as perfectly as possible.
20. That skating team (win) last year's gold medal.
21. One judge has (seek) the opinion of another judge.
22. The judges have (keep) the performances very clearly in mind.
23. We (think) that each skater did his or her best to entertain the vast audience that filled the arena.
24. The judges (think) the performance spectacular, despite a few imperfections during the closing moments.
25. Even the skills of the losers (leave) us breathless.

Close

Brainstorm with students to develop a list of Olympic events they have heard about or have watched. Have them choose a favorite event from the list and write about it, using irregular verbs in the past tense and in one of the perfect tenses. Suggest that students use a word processor to write about their selected event.

 **English Language Learners**

Examining Irregular Verbs

Explain that irregular forms are troublesome for everyone learning English. Have students use patterns to categorize the forms. By working with a partner to say each form in a context sentence, such as *Today I . . . , Yesterday I . . . , I have . . . .* Students may work with one pattern at a time until they feel comfortable speaking each form. Encourage students to write context sentences for the forms that continue to give them trouble.

10.10 More Irregular Verbs

Irregular Verbs			
Pattern	**Base Form**	**Past Form**	**Past Participle**
The base form and the past participle are the same.	become come run	became came ran	become come run
The past form ends in -*ew*, and the past participle ends in -*wn*.	blow draw fly grow know throw	blew drew flew grew knew threw	blown drawn flown grown known thrown
The past participle ends in -*en*.	bite break choose drive eat fall give ride rise see speak steal take write	bit broke chose drove ate fell gave rode rose saw spoke stole took wrote	bitten *or* bit broken chosen driven eaten fallen given ridden risen seen spoken stolen taken written
The past form and the past participle do not follow any pattern.	be, am, are, is do go tear wear	was, were did went tore wore	been done gone torn worn
The base form, past form, and past participle are all the same.	cut let put hit	cut let put hit	cut let put hit

10.10 More Irregular Verbs **417**

Focus

Lesson Overview

Objectives
- To identify the past form and past participle of irregular verbs
- To use the correct past form and past participle of irregular verbs in writing and speaking

🔔 Bellringer
Daily Language Activity

When students enter the classroom, have this assignment on the board: *Copy the words* goed, went, gone, *and* wenten. *Circle the correct past tense and past participle of the verb go.*

See also 🚩 *Daily Language Practice*

Motivating Activity

Call on volunteers to read aloud their answers to the Bellringer activity. Inform students that the verb *go* is one of the most irregular verbs in English because the forms of this verb are derived from different, unrelated verbs. The verb *went* was used to replace a missing form of *go*.

Teach

Cooperative Learning

Have small groups interview a classmate. Each group should generate a set of interview questions. (Each student should ask one question.) Word the questions to ask about the person's past, present, and future. Beneath each question, students should specify which form of a verb their classmate's answer should use.

Verbs

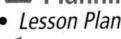

Resource Manager

📂 **Planning Resources**
- *Lesson Plans*

🚩 **Transparencies**
- *Bellringer*
- *Daily Language Practice*

📂 **Other Print Resources**
- *Grammar and Composition Handbook*
- *Grammar Enrichment*, p. 14
- *Grammar Practice*, p. 14
- *Grammar Reteaching*, p. 16
- *Grammar Workbook*, Lessons 20–21

Practice and Assess

Answers: Exercise 17

1. has become, past participle
2. has grown, past participle
3. have given, past participle
4. was, past
5. passed, past
6. had driven, past participle
7. had seen, past participle
8. saw, past
9. had fallen, past participle
10. went, past

Answers: Exercise 18

1. knew	11. given
2. seen	12. flew
3. knew	13. drove
4. took	14. torn
5. chosen	15. fallen
6. spoken	16. took
7. written	17. drew
8. gave	18. chosen
9. became	19. gave
10. become	20. rose

Additional Resources

📁 *Grammar Practice*, p. 14
📁 *Grammar Reteaching*, p. 16
📁 *Grammar Enrichment*, p. 14

 Grammar Workbook, Lessons 20–21

Close

Have students write sentences using the base form of a verb listed in the chart on page 417. Allow students to exchange sentences. Have students revise the sentences they received, using (1) the past form and (2) the past participle of the verb.

Verbs

Exercise 17   Identifying Past Forms of Irregular Verbs

Write each verb, and identify it as *past tense* or *past participle* form.

1. Hockey has become one of the world's most popular sports.
2. It has grown into a financially successful sport as well.
3. The spectators have given hockey their support.
4. Last night's game was particularly impressive.
5. A half hour passed without a score.
6. The players had driven up and down the ice.
7. Never had we seen such fierce play.
8. We saw several shots on the goal.
9. The goalies had fallen on several.
10. The crowd went wild.

Exercise 18   Using the Past Forms of Irregular Verbs

Write the past tense or the past participle form of the verb in parentheses, whichever the sentence requires.

1. I once (know) almost nothing about handball.
2. I have (see) several games of handball in the city recently.
3. When I felt the excitement of the game, I (know) that handball was for me.
4. The speed of the game (take) my breath away.
5. Several of us have (choose) to join a handball club.
6. Gail has (speak) with the director.
7. He has (write) out her membership card.
8. He also (give) Gail a few visitors' passes.
9. Gail (become) interested in handball last year and now plays regularly.
10. She has (become) a very fine player.
11. She has (give) hours to her new sport.
12. The handball (fly) across the room.
13. Juan (drive) the shot against the front wall.
14. One of the players has (tear) her sweatshirt.
15. A player has (fall) during an exciting play.
16. The player (take) time out for a few moments.
17. The director (draw) the four lines across the handball court.
18. Two players have (choose) a date for their next game.
19. The winner (give) a victory speech.
20. She (rise) from her chair to say a few words to the audience.

MEETING INDIVIDUAL NEEDS   English Language Learners

Interpreting a Chart

Students learning English may have difficulty interpreting and understanding the irregular verbs in the chart on page 417. You may want to teach only two or three rows of verbs at each session. Read one row at a time and then demonstrate the meaning of each verb in context, using synonyms, actions, pictures, or a combination of methods as necessary. Encourage students to work in pairs to demonstrate the meanings of the verbs.

Grammar Review

VERBS

Douglas, the hero of this novel, craves a new pair of sporty tennis shoes. In this passage, which has been annotated to show various concepts covered in the unit, he tries to persuade a shoe-store owner to sell him a pair.

Literature Model

from *Dandelion Wine*
by Ray Bradbury

"Please!" Douglas held out his hand. "Mr. Sanderson, now could you kind of rock back and forth a little, sponge around, bounce kind of, while I tell you the rest? It's this: I give you my money, you give me the shoes, I owe you a dollar. But, Mr. Sanderson, *but*—soon as I get those shoes on, you know what *happens*?"

"What?"

"Bang! I deliver your packages, pick up packages, bring you coffee, burn your trash, run to the post office, telegraph office, library! You'll see twelve of me in and out, in and out, every minute. Feel those shoes, Mr. Sanderson, *feel* how fast they'd take me? All those springs inside? Feel all the running inside? Feel how they kind of grab hold and can't let you alone and don't like you just *standing* there? Feel how quick I'd be doing the things you'd rather not bother with? You stay in the nice cool store while I'm jumping all around town! But it's not me really, it's the shoes. They're going like mad down alleys, cutting corners, and back! There they go!"

- Action verb
- Indirect object
- Direct object
- Future tense
- Present progressive form
- Predicate noun

Verbs

Grammar Review **419**

Teach

About the Literature

Explain that the review contains a passage taken from Ray Bradbury's novel *Dandelion Wine*. *Dandelion Wine* tells a warm and nostalgic story of a small American town in the 1920s, similar to the small town in Illinois where the author was born. In addition to *Dandelion Wine*, Bradbury has written social critiques, stage and screen plays, poetry, and some children's literature. He is best known as a science-fiction writer.

After students have read the passage, discuss its characters, setting, and mood. Use the passage to help students see the value of using dialogue in story telling. Ask: *Would the action in the story flow as well if dialogue were not used? How?* The exercises that follow are based on this passage and related topics.

Linking Grammar and Literature

☑ **Teaching Tip**

Ask students to focus on the highlighted verbs in the passage. Do the shifts in verb tense and form add to or detract from the story? How?

Cooperative Learning

Have students place themselves in teams of two or three students each. Assign each team to one or more lessons in this unit and ask team members to find examples of the kinds of verbs described in the assigned lessons. Suggest that teams use textbooks, samples of their own writing, magazines, and newspapers. Ask volunteers to make a chart of the students' examples, using the lesson chapter titles for the headings of each column.

Resource Manager

📁 **Planning Resources**
- *Lesson Plans*

📁 **Other Print Resources**
- *Grammar and Composition Handbook*
- *Grammar Workbook*, Lessons 12–21; *Unit 3 Review; Cumulative Review: Units 1–3*

✓ **ASSESSMENT OPTIONS**

📁 *Tests with Answer Key and Rubrics*
Unit 10 Mastery Test, pp. 43–44

💾 *Testmaker*
Unit 10 Mastery Test

Grammar Review

Answers: Exercise 1

1. <u>owes</u>, (dollar)
2. <u>suggests</u>, (solution)
3. <u>asks</u>, (favor)
4. <u>will do</u>, (things)
5. <u>will deliver</u>, (packages)
6. <u>will bring</u>, (coffee)
7. <u>will burn</u>, (trash)
8. <u>will attempt</u>, (jobs)
9. <u>will take</u>, (mail)
10. <u>will perform</u>, (chores)

Answers: Exercise 2

1. <u>wrote</u>, I
2. <u>reveals</u>, (deal), T
3. <u>provides</u>, (memories), T
4. <u>make</u>, (discoveries), T
5. <u>valued</u>, (experience), T
6. <u>learned</u>, I
7. <u>caused</u>, (wonder), T
8. <u>felt</u>, (exhaustion), T
9. <u>learns</u>, (things), T
10. <u>learn</u>, I

Verbs

Review: Exercise 1 **Identifying Action Verbs and Direct Objects**

Write each sentence. Then underline each action verb (including any helping verbs) and circle the direct object.

SAMPLE Douglas spends his money for shoes.
ANSWER Douglas <u>spends</u> his (money) for shoes.

1. Douglas owes a dollar for the shoes.
2. Douglas suggests a solution to his problem.
3. Douglas asks a favor of Mr. Sanderson.
4. Douglas will do many things.
5. Douglas will deliver packages.
6. Douglas will bring coffee to Mr. Sanderson.
7. Douglas will also burn the trash.
8. He will attempt odd jobs for Mr. Sanderson.
9. He will take the mail to the post office.
10. Douglas will perform these chores.

Review: Exercise 2 **Distinguishing Transitive and Intransitive Verbs**

Write each sentence. Underline each verb and circle any direct objects. Then write *T* if the verb is transitive or *I* if the verb is intransitive.

SAMPLE Douglas and his father and brother pick dandelions for salad.
ANSWER Douglas and his father and brother <u>pick</u> (dandelions) for salad. *T*

1. Ray Bradbury wrote about a special summer in the twelfth year of Douglas's life.
2. Bradbury reveals a great deal about Douglas.
3. A boy's twelfth year provides durable memories.
4. Young boys make new discoveries all the time.
5. Douglas valued his experience.
6. He learned during that summer.
7. His daily experiences caused wonder.
8. Douglas felt exhaustion.
9. Douglas slowly learns many things about life.
10. Writers learn by writing.

Review: Exercise 3 **Distinguishing Direct and Indirect Objects**

Write each direct object. If the sentence contains an indirect object, write it and underline it.

SAMPLE Please hand me the shoes.
ANSWER shoes, <u>me</u>

1. Those shoes always give him blisters.
2. People wear different shoes for different purposes.
3. Shoes give people support.
4. People need special shoes for play.
5. A number of styles meet the requirements of various sports.
6. Football and baseball players wear special designs.
7. Many people buy their children sturdy shoes for active wear.
8. He asked me a question about the history of shoes.
9. People in cold climates wore shoes of animal fur.
10. People in warmer climates designed themselves open shoes.

Review: Exercise 4 **Identifying Action and Linking Verbs and Predicate Words**

Write each sentence. Circle each verb, and write whether it is an *action* or a *linking verb*. Then write whether the underlined word or words is a *direct object*, an *indirect object*, a *predicate noun*, or a *predicate adjective*.

SAMPLE A dandelion is a bright yellow <u>flower.</u>
ANSWER A dandelion (is) a bright yellow <u>flower.</u> (linking verb, predicate noun)

1. Dandelions dot <u>lawns and meadows.</u>
2. The temperate regions of the world encourage the <u>growth</u> of dandelions.
3. The flowers have given <u>us</u> great beauty.
4. Gardeners of the world have declared <u>war</u> on the dandelion.
5. Garden and lawn lovers hunt <u>dandelions</u> mercilessly.
6. The dandelion is not a native American <u>weed.</u>
7. The early colonists brought <u>them</u> from Europe.
8. The root of the dandelion is <u>long.</u>
9. Roots, young leaves, and flower buds are <u>tasty and nutritious.</u>
10. Some gardeners give <u>friends</u> dandelion greens for salad.

Verbs

Answers: Exercise 3

1. <u>him</u>, IO; blisters, DO
2. shoes, DO
3. <u>people</u>, IO; support, DO
4. shoes, DO
5. requirements, DO
6. designs, DO
7. <u>children</u>, IO; shoes, DO
8. <u>me</u>, IO; question, DO
9. shoes, DO
10. <u>themselves</u>, IO; shoes, DO

Answers: Exercise 4

1. (dot), action verb; DO
2. (encourage), action verb; DO
3. (have given), action verb; IO
4. (have declared), action verb; DO
5. (hunt), action verb; DO
6. (is), linking verb; predicate noun
7. (brought), action verb; DO
8. (is), linking verb; predicate adjective
9. (are), linking verb; predicate adjectives
10. (give), action verb; IO

Answers: Exercise 5

1. demand, present
2. spent, past
3. used, past
4. compete, present
5. lost, past
6. appear, present
7. will grow, future; or grow, present
8. poisoned, past
9. produce, present
10. will cause, future

Answers: Exercise 6

1. are <u>readying</u>, present participle
2. is <u>plotted</u>, past participle
3. have <u>competed</u>, past participle
4. has <u>occurred</u>, past participle
5. are <u>scheduling</u>, present participle
6. are <u>preparing</u>, present participle
7. have <u>turned</u>, past participle
8. has <u>dropped</u>, past participle
9. has <u>tested</u>, past participle
10. has <u>made</u>, past participle

Verbs

Review: Exercise 5   **Distinguishing Present, Past, and Future Tenses**

Write the correct form of the verb in parentheses. Then write whether it is in the *present*, *past*, or *future* tense.

SAMPLE   Every year Susan (grow) more weeds in her garden than vegetables.
ANSWER   grows — present

1. Beautiful plants (demand) great care.
2. Farmers in the United States (spend) more than $6 billion last year.
3. They (use) the money on weeds.
4. Weeds always (compete) with crops for sunlight and water.
5. In spite of the money, farmers last year (lose) a fortune because of weeds.
6. Weeds (appear) in gardens, parks, and playgrounds.
7. Unless they are controlled, they (grow) along highways and railroad tracks.
8. Some weeds (poison) people and animals last year.
9. Every year others (produce) severe skin reactions in people.
10. Next autumn ragweed pollen (cause) hay fever in many sufferers.

Review: Exercise 6   **Identifying Verb Phrases and Participles**

Write each verb phrase, and draw a line under the main verb. Then write whether the main verb is a *present participle* or a *past participle*.

SAMPLE   This year's races are capturing everyone's attention.
ANSWER   are <u>capturing</u> — present participle

1. In early March, a number of people are readying themselves for a big race.
2. The course is plotted between Anchorage and Nome in Alaska.
3. In the past, several dozen people and their dogs have competed.
4. The Iditarod International Sled Dog Race has occurred yearly since 1973.
5. Drivers are scheduling eleven days for the race.
6. Racers are always preparing for difficult conditions.
7. Cold, snow, and howling winds have turned the course into a nightmare.
8. The wind-chill factor has dropped the temperature to an effective −100°F.
9. The race has tested both dogs and racers.
10. Success in the race has made people and dogs celebrities.

Review: Exercise 7 **Using Progressive Forms**

Write each sentence, using the verb form indicated in italics.

SAMPLE   I (read) an exciting type of fiction. *present progressive*.
ANSWER   I am reading an exciting type of fiction.

1. Ray Bradbury (write) fantasy novels. *past progressive*
2. He (experiment) with science fiction topics. *past progressive*
3. A writer of fantasy (examine) a world of dreams. *past progressive*
4. He or she (make) the unusual understandable. *past progressive*
5. Some science-fiction authors (deal) with the future. *present progressive*
6. They (create) an unbelievable and fantastic world. *present progressive*
7. The most interesting writers, however, (describe) possible events. *present progressive*
8. We (enjoy) their realistic characters. *present progressive*
9. I (relate) to their hopes and dreams. *present progressive*
10. Ray Bradbury (worry) about the future of humanity. *past progressive*

Review: Exercise 8 **Using Perfect Tenses**

Write each sentence, using the tense indicated in italics.

SAMPLE   I (complete) an interesting summer project. *present perfect*
ANSWER   I have completed an interesting summer project.

1. I (collect) a number of fascinating books. *past perfect*
2. All of these (hold) my interest. *present perfect*
3. Each story (feature) fantasy. *past perfect*
4. The stories (include) strange settings and unusual characters. *past perfect*
5. A few stories also (contain) very imaginative situations. *present perfect*
6. Some of these (remain) fresh in my mind. *present perfect*
7. I (remember) a story set in the very distant future. *present perfect*
8. I (recall) the characters in the story. *present perfect*
9. They (abandon) their feet as a means of transportation. *past perfect*
10. They (wish) themselves somewhere else. *past perfect*

Verbs

Answers: Exercise 7

1. was writing
2. was experimenting
3. was examining
4. was making
5. are dealing
6. are creating
7. are describing
8. are enjoying
9. am relating
10. was worrying

Answers: Exercise 8

1. had collected
2. have held
3. had featured
4. had included
5. have contained
6. have remained
7. have remembered
8. have recalled
9. had abandoned
10. had wished

Answers: Exercise 9

1. took
2. made
3. lost
4. swung
5. paid
6. gotten
7. led
8. began
9. brought
10. crept

Answers: Exercise 10

1. were
2. driven
3. become
4. come
5. grown
6. drawn
7. given
8. gone
9. chosen
10. taken

Verbs

Review: Exercise 9   Using the Past and Past Participles of Irregular Verbs

Write the past tense or the past participle of the verb in parentheses, whichever the sentence requires.

SAMPLE   The sport of automobile racing had (begin) in the 1890s.
ANSWER   begun

1. The first racers (take) their cars to regular public roads.
2. Many of these were (make) of dirt.
3. Drivers on these roads often (lose) control of their cars.
4. They (swing) from the course into groups of spectators.
5. The spectators (pay) a high price for their curiosity.
6. The first racing organization in the world had (get) a start in 1895.
7. The course had (lead) from Paris to Bordeaux—732 miles.
8. Twenty-two drivers (begin) the race.
9. Only nine had (bring) their cars across the finish line.
10. The winner (creep) along at fifteen miles per hour.

Review: Exercise 10   Using the Past and Past Participles of Irregular Verbs

Write the past tense or the past participle of the verb in parentheses, whichever the sentence requires.

SAMPLE   For many years, racing has (be) a very popular form of competition.
ANSWER   been

1. Early race cars (be) the same as family autos.
2. Today's race cars are (drive) just at races.
3. They have (become) very special vehicles.
4. A race car has (come) to be a very expensive item.
5. Auto racing has (grow) into a very special sport.
6. In the last few years, it has (draw) only very wealthy competitors.
7. No race car is (give) away.
8. A dedicated racer has (go) to great trouble.
9. He or she has (choose) to race.
10. It has already (take) years of preparation.

Verbs

Review: Exercise 11

Proofreading

The following passage is about the artist Gregg Spears, whose painting appears on the next page. Rewrite the passage, correcting the errors in spelling, grammar, and usage. Add any missing punctuation. There are ten errors.

[1]Gregg Spears's *My Back Porch*, like Ray Bradbury's *Dandelion Wine*, has catched lifes everyday happenings. [2]Spears has always seeked to create new understanding of such comon themes.

[3]Spears growed up in Chicago and it is there that most of his works have been exhibited. [4]Gregg Spears has participate in exhibits at the DuSable Museum of African American History. [5]And the Chicago Cultural Center. [6]The location of Spear's studio are an abandoned building that has been rebuilt instead of having been teared down.

Mixed Review

Number your paper from one to ten. For each item in parentheses, write a verb form that makes sense for the passage.

The World of Science Fiction

Ray Bradbury [1](*linking verb*) one of the leading American science-fiction writers. People [2](*action verb*) science fiction. Common themes include time travel, fantastic inventions, and space travel. A large number of science-fiction stories [3](*action verb*) in the future. Some, including Bradbury's, describe [4](*direct object*) engaged in ordinary activities.

Science fiction's beginnings [5](*linking verb*) in prehistoric myths. These stories commonly offered [6](*indirect object*) fantastic voyages and adventures. In the first century A.D., a Greek writer [7](*past progressive form*) stories that described trips to the moon.

In the current century, magazines [8](*present perfect tense verb*) the fame of science fiction. Movies [9](*action verb*) the popularity of science-fiction themes. In the 1970s and 1980s, a number of science-fiction authors increased in popularity with the general reader. Writers like Ray Bradbury are now [10](*predicate adjective*) to readers throughout the world.

Answers: Exercise 11
Proofreading

This proofreading activity provides editing practice with (1) the current or previous units' skills, (2) **Troubleshooter** errors, and (3) spelling errors. Students should be able to complete the exercise by referring to the units, the **Troubleshooter**, and a dictionary. (Note: A run-on sentence counts as one error.)

Error (Type of Error)

1. caught (verb form)
   life's (singluar possessive)
2. sought (verb form)
   common (spelling)
3. grew (verb form)
   Chicago, (run-on sentence)
4. participated (verb form)
5. History and (sentence fragment)
6. is (subject-verb agreement)
   torn (verb form)

Answers: Exercise 12
Mixed Review

Answers may vary, but some suggestions are given below.

1. was
2. enjoy
3. occur
4. people
5. were
6. audiences
7. was inventing
8. have spread
9. demonstrate
10. familiar

Close

Suggest that students write a paragraph in which they try to persuade someone to give them something they really want. Encourage them to avoid using forms of the verb *to be* and to try to use several vivid verbs. Ask students to trade papers with a partner. Have them evaluate their partner's use of vivid verbs. Then ask each student to revise his or her own paragraph, based on the peer review. Students should respond in constructive ways to one another's writing.

Verbs

Gregg Spears, *My Back Porch,* **1992**

Viewing the Art

Gregg Spears, *My Back Porch,* **1992**
The African American artist Gregg Spears, born in Chicago, uses his paintings to express his fascination with the early 1900s and the activities of the present. The themes of his paintings reflect life's everyday occurrences and people's interactions and emotions during those common happenings. Spears has received numerous awards for his work, including an honorable mention in the 1991 Black Creativity Exhibition at the Museum of Science and Industry in Chicago. Invite students to share their thoughts about the interactions and possible emotions depicted in *My Back Porch.*

Writing Application

Verbs in Writing

Notice the way Minfong Ho uses verbs in this passage from *The Clay Marble*. They vividly capture the rainy setting and bring Jantu's and Dara's moods and actions to life for readers. Read the passage, focusing especially on the italicized verbs.

The wind *picked* up and *was sweeping* up eddies of dust into the air. Then the rain *started* in earnest, one of those sudden thunderstorms hinting of the monsoons due to come soon. Jantu *stretched* her sarong protectively over the pile of straw where her clay figures *were*. Hunched over them like that, she *looked* like a scruffy hen trying to hatch her precious eggs.

I *huddled* close to Jantu and *listened* to the rain drumming on the leaves. Raindrops *pierced* through the cracks of the palm fronds and *felt* light and cool on my bare arms.

Techniques with Verbs

Try to apply some of Minfong Ho's techniques when you write and revise your own work.

❶ Keep your writing lively by varying the kinds of linking verbs you use:

COMMON LINKING VERB . . . she *was* a scruffy hen

HO'S VERSION . . . she *looked* like a scruffy hen trying to hatch her precious eggs

❷ Whenever possible, replace bland and common verbs with vivid action verbs. Compare the following:

GENERAL VERB raindrops *fell* through the cracks of the palm fronds . . .

HO'S VERSION raindrops *pierced* through the cracks of the palm fronds . . .

> ### TIME
> For more about the writing process, see **TIME Facing the Blank Page,** pp. 97–107.

Verbs

Verbs in Writing

Ask students to read the passage silently, looking for examples of ways that Minfong Ho keeps the writing lively and clear with vivid verbs. Encourage students to discuss examples in relation to Techniques with Verbs below.

Techniques with Verbs

Suggest that as part of their revision process, students try substituting vivid action verbs for passive verbs. Have students turn to page 425 and apply these techniques to the Proofreading exercise. Encourage students to share their revisions.

Practice

The answers to this challenging and enriching activity will vary. Refer to Techniques with Verbs as you evaluate student choices.

Sample:

Poised on the diving board, Quentin looked like a taut rubber band. A blast of sound pierced the air as the referee blew his whistle. Quentin then swung his long arms, first back and then forward, gaining energy with each movement. Springing off the board, he soared high into the air above the shimmering pool. Plummeting toward the pool, Quentin executed three complete turns and then, arms thrust out in front of him, he sliced cleanly through the water to conclude his dive.

Practice Try out these techniques by revising the passage below. Use a separate sheet of paper. As you work, focus especially on the underlined words.

<u>There was Quentin standing</u> on the diving board. He <u>was</u> a taut rubber band. A blast of sound <u>filled</u> the air as the referee blew his whistle. Quentin then <u>moved</u> his long arms, first back and then forward, <u>adding</u> energy with each movement. <u>Jumping</u> off the board, he <u>rose</u> high into the air above the shimmering pool. <u>Falling</u> toward the pool, Quentin <u>made</u> three complete turns. Then, arms <u>pointed</u> out in front of him, he <u>dove</u> cleanly through the water to <u>complete</u> his dive.

Writing Application **427**

✔ ASSESSMENT OPTIONS

📁 *Tests with Answer Key & Rubrics*
Unit 10 Mastery Test, pp. 43–44

💾 *Testmaker*
Unit 10 Mastery Test

You may wish to administer the Unit 10 Mastery Test at this point.

📼 *MindJogger Videoquizzes*

Objectives

- To develop an understanding of pronouns
- To develop the ability to use pronouns correctly in writing and speaking

✔ ASSESSMENT OPTIONS

📁 *Tests with Answer Key & Rubrics*
Unit 11 Pretest, pp. 45–46
Unit 11 Mastery Test, pp. 47–48

💾 *Testmaker*
Unit 11 Pretest
Unit 11 Mastery Test

You may wish to administer the Unit 11 Pretest at this point.

Key to Ability Levels

L1 Level 1 activities are within the basic ability range of students.

L2 Level 2 activities are within the ability range of average students.

L3 Level 3 activities are more challenging activities.

UNIT
11 Pronouns

Resource Manager

📁 **Planning Resources**
- *Lesson Plans*
- *Block Scheduling*

🖥 **Transparencies**
- *Bellringer*
- *Daily Language Practice*
- *Two-Minute Skill Drill*

📁 **Other Print Resources**
- *Grammar and Composition Handbook*
- *Grammar Enrichment*
- *Grammar Practice*
- *Grammar Reteaching*
- *Grammar Workbook*
- *Tests with Answer Key and Rubrics*

📼 **Video**
- *MindJogger Videoquizzes*

💾 **Software**
- *Interactive Grammar and Language Workbook*
- *Language Arts PASS*
- *Presentation Plus!*
- *Testmaker*

🖥 **Web Sites**
- *writerschoice.glencoe.com*

11.1 Personal Pronouns

■ A **pronoun** is a word that takes the place of one or more nouns.

The most frequently used pronouns are called personal pronouns. The words *It* and *her* in the second sentence below are personal pronouns.

> The myth amuses Kim. **It** amuses **her.**

■ Pronouns that are used to refer to people or things are called **personal pronouns.**

Some personal pronouns are used as the subjects of sentences. Other personal pronouns are used as the objects of verbs or prepositions. In the example above, the pronoun *It* replaces the noun *myth* as the subject of the sentence. The pronoun *her* replaces *Kim* as the direct object of the verb *amuses.*

■ A **subject pronoun** is a personal pronoun in the nominative case. It is used as the subject of a sentence.

> **She** especially likes "Atalanta's Race."

■ An **object pronoun** is a personal pronoun in the objective case. It is used as the object of a verb or a preposition.

> The librarian recommended **it** to **us.**

Study the personal pronouns in the chart below.

Personal Pronouns		
	Singular	**Plural**
Used as Subjects	I	we
	you	you
	he, she, it	they
Used as Objects	me	us
	you	you
	him, her, it	them

Focus

Lesson Overview

Objectives

- To identify personal pronouns and understand their function
- To use personal pronouns correctly as subjects and objects in sentences

🔔 Bellringer
Daily Language Activity

When students enter the classroom, have this assignment on the board: *List all the words in the following sentences that refer to people or things:*

> *I can't stand this old dress my mother gave me. She gave it to me because it shrank when she washed it, and now it's too small for either of us.*

See also 📂 *Daily Language Practice*

Motivating Activity

Have students try replacing the personal pronouns in the Bellringer activity with nouns. Discuss the awkward results. Point out that pronouns eliminate the unnecessary repetition of names for people and things.

Teach

☑ Teaching Tip

Students may want to copy the personal pronouns chart into their notebooks or onto a computer file. They may include sentences demonstrating each pronoun's use. They can add other types of pronouns as they study the unit.

Pronouns

Resource Manager

📁 **Planning Resources**
- *Lesson Plans*

📂 **Transparencies**
- *Bellringer*
- *Daily Language Practice*

📁 **Other Print Resources**
- *Grammar and Composition Handbook*
- *Grammar Enrichment,* p. 15
- *Grammar Practice,* p. 15
- *Grammar Reteaching,* p. 17
- *Grammar Workbook,* Lesson 22

Practice and Assess

Answers: Exercise 1

1. I, subject; you, object
2. They, subject
3. him, object
4. them, object
5. me, object
6. you, object
7. he, subject
8. her, object
9. she, subject
10. it, object

Answers: Exercise 2

1. They, subject	11. him, object
2. them, object	12. them, object
3. him, object	13. her, object
4. She, subject	14. He, subject
5. It, subject	15. him, object
6. it, object	16. him, object
7. She, subject	17. them, object
8. her, object	18. them, object
9. them, object	19. her, object
10. She, subject	20. them, object

Additional Resources

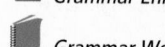 *Grammar Practice*, p. 15
Grammar Reteaching, p. 17
Grammar Enrichment, p. 15

Grammar Workbook, Lesson 22

Close

Have students imagine that they are going to write a story. Tell them to write descriptions of the two main characters. Then have them trade papers to check that they have used subject and object pronouns correctly. Discuss needed changes. Sample: *David is an art student, and Claire is a medical student. He wants to paint a picture of her.*

Exercise 1   Identifying Personal Pronouns

List the pronouns and identify each pronoun as a *subject pronoun* in the nominative case or an *object pronoun* in the objective case.

1. I will tell you a story about three characters in mythology.
2. They are named Daphne, Apollo, and Cupid.
3. Apollo loved Daphne, but Daphne did not love him.
4. The malice of Cupid caused the dissention between them.
5. Apollo said, "Cupid's arrows are not worthy weapons for me."
6. Cupid replied, "This arrow is small but still can wound you."
7. Then he stood on a rock and pulled two arrows from a quiver.
8. Aiming at Daphne, Cupid pierced her with a tiny leaden arrow.
9. From then on, she refused all offers of marriage.
10. Cupid's golden darts bring love, and leaden darts repel it.

Exercise 2   Using Pronouns in the Nominative and Objective Cases

Write each sentence, replacing the underlined word or words with a pronoun. Identify each pronoun as a *subject pronoun* in the nominative case or an *object pronoun* in the objective case.

1. <u>Greek poets</u> developed myths from old stories.
2. Rita studied <u>the myths</u> for their factual information.
3. Myths about historical events interest <u>Dan</u>.
4. <u>Rita</u> traced the different versions of one myth.
5. "Atalanta's Race" is an interesting Greek myth, according to Rita and Dan.
6. The myth of Atalanta tells about <u>a foot race</u>.
7. <u>Atalanta</u> is a beautiful woman and a very fast runner.
8. Many men want <u>Atalanta</u> as their bride.
9. Atalanta refuses <u>the men</u> time after time.
10. <u>Atalanta</u> arranges a race to find the fastest runner.
11. Atalanta will marry <u>a man faster than she is</u>.
12. Atalanta passes <u>the runners</u> with graceful ease.
13. Hippomenes wants <u>Atalanta</u> as his wife.
14. <u>Hippomenes</u> asks Aphrodite for help in his race against Atalanta.
15. Aphrodite helps <u>Hippomenes</u>.
16. She gives three golden apples and instructions to <u>Hippomenes</u>.
17. Hippomenes drops <u>the apples</u> along the way.
18. Atalanta picks <u>the golden apples</u> up and so forsakes her victory.
19. Hippomenes takes <u>Atalanta</u> as his bride.
20. Aphrodite brings <u>Hippomenes and Atalanta</u> together.

Pronouns

430   Unit 11 Pronouns

Real World Connection

Formal and Informal Language

Point out that in informal speech, English speakers often use an object pronoun after a form of the linking verb *be* as in *It's me.* Explain that in formal writing, however, a subject pronoun should always follow the linking verb *be*: *The best speaker in the class is she. It was I.*

11.2 Pronouns and Antecedents

Read the following sentences. Can you tell to whom the word *She* refers?

Arachne competes against Athena. **She** weaves skillfully.

The sentence is not clear because the word *She* could refer to either Arachne or Athena. Sometimes you must repeat a noun or rewrite the sentence. Read the sentences below. Repeating the noun makes it clear who weaves skillfully.

Arachne competes against Athena. Athena weaves skillfully.

■ The noun or group of words that a pronoun refers to is called its **antecedent.**

When you use a pronoun, you should be sure that it refers to its antecedent clearly. Be especially careful when you use the pronoun *they.* Read the following sentence.

They have several books about Greek myths at the library.

The meaning of *They* is unclear. The sentence can be improved by rewriting it in the following manner.

Several books on Greek myths are available at the library.

When using pronouns, you must also make sure that they agree with their antecedents in **number** (singular or plural) and gender. The **gender** of a noun may be masculine (male), feminine (female), or neuter (referring to things). Notice how the pronouns in the sentences below agree with their antecedents.

The myth of Arachne is amusing. I enjoyed **it.**
The bystanders see Athena. **They** watch **her** at the loom.

Pronouns

Focus

Lesson Overview

Objectives

- To identify antecedents
- To make pronouns agree in gender and number with their antecedents

Bellringer
Daily Language Activity

When students enter the classroom, have this assignment on the board: *Using the classroom clock as a timer, list as many pronouns as you can in sixty seconds.*

See also *Daily Language Practice*

Motivating Activity

On the board draw a chart with the headings *Pronoun, Number,* and *Gender.* Ask volunteers each to enter on the chart a pronoun from his or her Bellringer list together with the pronoun's number and gender. Encourage students to monitor their understanding and seek clarification as needed.

Teach

☑ Teaching Tip

The pronoun *it* is often used without a clear antecedent. For example, "The god Ares waved his sword and shield at the advancing army. It frightened them away." The word *It* could refer to the sword, the shield, or Ares' threatening motion. Replacing *It* with a noun phrase clarifies the sentence's meaning: "His action frightened them away."

⬌ Cross-Reference: Writing

For information on checking pronoun-antecedent agreement when editing, refer students to Lesson 2.9.

Resource Manager

📂 **Planning Resources**
- *Lesson Plans*

📇 **Transparencies**
- *Bellringer*
- *Daily Language Practice*

📂 **Other Print Resources**
- *Grammar and Composition Handbook*
- *Grammar Enrichment,* p. 16
- *Grammar Practice,* p. 16
- *Grammar Reteaching,* p. 18
- *Grammar Workbook,* Lessons 24

Practice and Assess

Answers: Exercise 3

1. It—Lydia, singular
2. She—Arachne, singular
3. They—threads, plural
4. you—Arachne, singular
5. you—People, plural (in sent. 4)
6. them—Athena and Arachne, plural
7. They—hands, plural
8. It—contest, singular
9. them—weavers, plural
10. he—Poseidon, singular
11. It—sea, singular
12. him—Poseidon, singular
13. them—pictures, plural
14. She—Athena, singular
15. He—Zeus, singular
16. They—swan and bull, plural
17. She—Athena, singular
18. She—Arachne, singular
19. them—pictures, plural
20. She—Arachne, singular
21. She—Arachne, singular
22. They—descendants/spiders, plural
23. He—Edmund Spenser, singular
24. We—You and I, plural
25. It—literature section, singular

Additional Resources

 Grammar Practice, p. 16
Grammar Reteaching, p. 18
Grammar Enrichment, p. 18

Grammar Workbook, Lesson 24

Close

Have students write sentences that contain pronouns and antecedents. Have students read their sentences aloud and ask classmates to determine whether the pronouns agree with their antecedents. Students should respond in constructive ways.

Exercise 3   Using Pronouns and Antecedents Correctly

Write the second sentence in each pair. Use the correct pronoun in each blank. Then write the antecedent of the pronoun and its number.

1. The maiden Arachne lives in Lydia. _____ is a country in Asia.
2. Arachne is a skillful weaver. _____ boasts about her weaving.
3. Arachne first forms woolen threads. _____ feel as soft as clouds.
4. People watch Arachne and admire her work. They tell her, "Pallas Athena must have taught _____."
5. The angry Arachne replies, "So you think my art comes from a teacher? I tell _____ that I am a better weaver than Athena herself!"
6. Athena and Arachne enter into a contest. The people watch the two of _____.
7. The weaving hands work with great speed. _____ are a blur.
8. There has never been such a contest. _____ is amazing to see.
9. Both weavers do their best. Both of _____ try to win.
10. Athena weaves pictures of a story about the male god Poseidon. In her story, _____ loses a contest to her.
11. Poseidon is the ruler of the sea. _____ is his domain.
12. Poseidon carries a trident. This symbol identifies _____.
13. The people look at Athena's pictures. The curious audience observes _____ woven into cloth.
14. Athena is in the pictures. _____ is shown dressed in armor.
15. Arachne weaves a story about the male god Zeus. _____ looks alive and seems to speak.
16. Her weaving also shows a swan and a bull. _____ look real.
17. At the end of the contest, Athena is the winner. _____ has woven a fabric like a rainbow.
18. Arachne is the loser. _____ feels guilty about the challenge.
19. Arachne's pictures displease Athena. Athena destroys _____.
20. Arachne is punished. _____ is turned into a spider.
21. Arachne will weave webs forever. _____ will weave them in old houses.
22. All Arachne's descendants are spiders. _____ get their scientific name, *arachnid,* from her name.
23. Edmund Spenser was an English poet. _____ wrote a poem about Arachne.
24. You and I can find the poem in the library. _____ must look in the literature section.
25. The literature section is always crowded. _____ is very popular.

MEETING INDIVIDUAL NEEDS   English Language Learners

Pronouns and Their Antecedents

Some students may have difficulty understanding appropriate pronoun designations for English words because many languages use gender designations for objects. Have students write a female name in their journals. Beside that name, have them write *she.* Repeat for a male name and *he.* Have students list several objects. Have them write *it* beside each one. When they have finished, have them circle all the names they wrote and beside the circle write *they.* Explain that *they* can be any group of males, females, or things.

11.3 Using Pronouns Correctly

Subject pronouns in the nominative case are used in compound subjects, and object pronouns in the objective case are used in compound objects.

> **He** and Carmen wrote a report on the subject. [not *Him and Carmen*]
>
> Tell John and **me** about Hercules. [not *John and I*]

A preposition takes an object, just as many verbs do. The object of a preposition can be simple or compound. In either case, use an object pronoun as the object of the preposition. In the sentences below, the pronouns in dark type are the objects of the preposition *to*.

> Lee read a famous Roman myth to **me.**
>
> Lee read a famous Roman myth to Irma and **me.**

If you are not sure which form of the pronoun to use, say the sentence aloud with only the pronoun as the subject or the object. Your ear will tell you which form is correct.

Whenever the pronoun *I* is part of a compound subject, it should always be placed after the other parts of the subject. Similarly, when the pronoun *me* is part of a compound object, it should go after the other parts of the object.

> Lee and **I** read some ancient Roman myths. [not *I and Lee*]
>
> Mythology interests Lee and **me.** [not *me and Lee*]

In formal writing and speech use a subject pronoun after a linking verb.

> The writer of this report was **she.**
>
> It is **I.**

Focus

Lesson Overview

Objectives

- To identify subject and object pronouns
- To use subject and object pronouns correctly in compound subjects and objects when speaking and writing

 Bellringer
Daily Language Activity

When students enter the classroom, have this assignment on the board: *Write these sentences, choosing the pronoun that correctly completes each sentence.*

1. *You and (they, them) should go to class together.*
2. *The actors showed him and (I, me) how they prepared for the play.*

See also  *Daily Language Practice*

Motivating Activity

Have students share their answers to the Bellringer activity and discuss how they made their decisions. Discuss and explain the correct answers, using the strategy in the Grammar Tip below.

Teach

☑ **Grammar Tip**

To see whether a pronoun in a compound subject or object is correct, replace the compound with the plural pronoun in the same case: *Juan and I are going.* **We** *are going.* Have students seek clarification as needed.

Listening and Speaking

Students will be more effective speakers if they use pronouns correctly. Have students work orally with partners to generate and check compound subject and object pronouns.

Pronouns

Resource Manager

📁 **Planning Resources**
- *Lesson Plans*

📁 **Transparencies**
- *Bellringer*
- *Daily Language Practice*

📁 **Other Print Resources**
- *Grammar and Composition Handbook*
- *Grammar Reteaching*, p. 19
- *Grammar Workbook*, Lesson 24

Practice and Assess

Answers: Exercise 4

1. She, subject
2. me, object
3. he, subject
4. him, object
5. I, subject
6. me, object
7. he, subject
8. we, subject
9. they, subject
10. he, subject
11. him, object
12. him, object
13. she, subject
14. he, subject
15. he, subject
16. him, object
17. We, subject
18. them, object
19. He, subject
20. her, object

Answers: Exercise 5

1. You (or They), subject
2. them, object
3. She, subject
4. them, object
5. they, subject
6. They, subject
7. her, object
8. it, object
9. It, subject
10. I, subject; you, object

Additional Resources

 Grammar Reteaching, p. 19

Grammar Workbook, Lesson 24

Close

Have students write a myth about the founding of your city or town. Ask them to use personal pronouns in compound subjects and objects in their writing. Answers may vary. *Sample: Iris, the goddess of the wind, rescues a snow leopard from drowning in Lake Michigan. She and the snow leopard decide to celebrate the deed by founding Chicago.* Suggest that students use a computer to work through the steps of the writing process. They may want to work with partners for prewriting and editing.

Pronouns

Exercise 4 | Using Pronouns in the Nominative and Objective Cases Correctly

Write each sentence. Use the correct word or words in parentheses. Then identify each pronoun you selected as a *subject pronoun* or an *object pronoun*.

1. (She, Her) and Chen told the class about Roman mythology.
2. They told Earl and (I, me) about Jupiter and Mars.
3. Mars and (he, him) were the most important gods.
4. Two planets were named after Mars and (he, him).
5. Dom and (me, I) asked questions about Jupiter.
6. Dom described a famous Roman myth to Chen and (I, me).
7. Earl and (he, him) know about Roman culture.
8. Sandra and (we, us) listened to the ancient Roman story of Romulus and Remus.
9. The founders of the city of Rome were (they, them).
10. Romulus and (he, him) were twin sons of a god and a human.
11. A basket with Romulus and (he, him) in it was set adrift.
12. A she-wolf cared for Remus and (he, him).
13. Romulus, Remus, and (she, her) became popular figures in Roman art.
14. Later (he, him) and Remus founded a city.
15. Remus and (he, him) quarreled; Romulus won.
16. The city is named after (he, him), not Remus.
17. (Us, We) can read about the beginning of Rome in a poem.
18. Virgil, an ancient Roman poet, wrote about (they, them).
19. (He, Him) was the author of the *Aeneid*, a great epic poem.
20. Mary says that the feats in the poem are exciting to (she, her).

Exercise 5 | Using Pronouns in the Nominative and Objective Cases

Write each sentence. Change the underlined noun or group of words to a pronoun, and identify it as a *subject pronoun* or an *object pronoun*.

1. <u>Readers</u> may be interested in learning a myth of the goddess Echo.
2. Echo, fond of woods and hills, lived in <u>the woods and hills</u>.
3. <u>Echo</u> loved to chat and always wanted to have the last word.
4. One day in the woods, the goddess Juno was looking for <u>the nymphs</u>.
5. Echo and <u>the nymphs</u> were friends.
6. <u>Echo and Juno</u> talked about where the nymphs could be.
7. Echo, by talking, delayed <u>the goddess</u> until the nymphs escaped.
8. Juno discovered <u>Echo's trickery</u>.
9. <u>Echo's trick</u> prompted Juno to punish Echo.
10. Juno said, "<u>Juno</u> will now pass sentence on <u>Echo</u>."

Critical Thinking

Testing for Compound Subjects or Objects

If students are unsure of which pronoun to use in a compound subject or object, have them try the questionable pronoun in the sentence by itself. For example, for *The librarian showed the book to Josh and (I/me)*, they would say, *The librarian showed the book to me*. Tell students that they may need to change the verb to agree with the pronoun they are testing. For example, *Hercules and (he/him) were strong* would read *He was strong.*

11.4 Possessive Pronouns

You often use pronouns to replace nouns that are subjects and nouns that are objects in sentences. You can use pronouns in place of possessive nouns too.

■ A **possessive pronoun** is a pronoun in the possessive case. It shows who or what has something. A possessive pronoun may take the place of a possessive noun.

Read the following sentences. Notice the possessive nouns and the possessive pronouns that replace them.

> Homer's story is famous. **His** story is famous.
> This story is Homer's. This story is **his.**

Possessive pronouns have two forms. One form is used before a noun. The other form is used alone. The chart below shows the two forms of possessive pronouns.

Possessive Pronouns		
	Singular	**Plural**
Used Before Nouns	my your his, her, its	our your their
Used Alone	mine yours his, hers, its	ours yours theirs

Possessive pronouns are not written with apostrophes. The pronoun *its*, for example, shows possession. The word *it's*, on the other hand, is a contraction of *it is*. Read the following sentences. Notice the meaning of the words in dark type.

> **Its** central character is Odysseus. [possessive pronoun]
> **It's** about the adventures of Odysseus. [contraction of *It is*]

Focus

Lesson Overview

Objectives

- To identify possessive pronouns' two forms: one used before a noun; the other used alone
- To learn the singular and plural forms of possissive pronouns and to use them correctly

Bellringer
Daily Language Activity

When students enter the classroom, have this assignment on the board: *Rewrite this sentence, replacing possessive nouns with possessive pronouns:*

Herman's sister gave me a recipe for apple pie that was Herman's favorite.

See also Daily Language Practice

Motivating Activity

Have students share Bellringer activity sentences and explain the pronoun substitutions. Ask students to seek clarification as needed.

Teach

⬧ Cross-Reference: Usage
For instruction and practice with *its* and *it's,* refer students to Lesson 17.2.

☑ Grammar Tip
To see if *it's* is a contraction, replace it with *it is.* If the result makes sense, then write *it's.*

Pronouns

Resource Manager

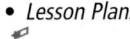

📂 Planning Resources
- *Lesson Plans*

📇 Transparencies
- *Bellringer*
- *Daily Language Practice*
- *Two-Minute Skill Drill*

📂 Other Print Resources
- *Grammar and Composition Handbook*
- *Grammar Enrichment,* 17
- *Grammar Practice,* p. 17
- *Grammar Reteaching,* p. 20
- *Grammar Workbook,* Lesson 25

Two-Minute Skill Drill

Put these sentences on the board. Have students complete them using either *their* or *theirs.*

- *That house is ___.*
- *Ayo is ___ brother.*

See also Two-Minute Skill Drill Transparency 11.4

435

Practice and Assess

Answers: Exercise 6

1. His—before a noun
2. Its—before a noun
3. his—stands alone
4. their—before a noun
5. ours—stands alone
6. your—before a noun
   mine— stands alone
7. his—before a noun
8. My—before a noun
9. theirs—stands alone
10. your—before a noun

Answers: Exercise 7

1. theirs	11. her
2. her	12. mine
3. your	13. their
4. Our	14. Its
5. his	15. her
6. theirs	16. his
7. Your	17. yours
8. your	18. her
9. their	19. her
10. their	20. its

Additional Resources

📁 *Grammar Practice*, p. 17
📁 *Grammar Reteaching*, p. 20
📁 *Grammar Enrichment*, p. 17

📕 *Grammar Workbook*, Lesson 25

Close

Have students write a short speech for Odysseus to use when he returns home after fighting in Troy. Odysseus should use some possessive pronouns as he addresses his people. Ask students to read their speeches aloud, and to constructively evaluate one another's work.

Exercise 6   Identifying Pronouns in the Possessive Case

Write each sentence. Underline each possessive pronoun. Then write *before a noun* or *stands alone* to tell how the pronoun is used.

1. His adventures interested all types of readers.
2. Its title comes from the name Odysseus.
3. Few characters possess a personality like his.
4. The Romans renamed him Ulysses in their list of heroes.
5. I like that translation better than ours.
6. A romantic poem about Ulysses will engage your attention and mine.
7. It narrates the wanderings of Ulysses in his return from Troy.
8. My literature book describes where the ships landed in Ithaca.
9. The inhabitants wanted to claim the ships as theirs.
10. Does your book describe what other adventures Ulysses has?

Exercise 7   Using Pronouns in the Possessive Case

Write each sentence. Replace each underlined word or group of words with the correct possessive pronoun.

1. Athena helped the Greeks, and soon the city of Troy was <u>the Greeks'</u>.
2. With <u>Athena's</u> help, the Greeks defeated the Trojans.
3. Athena said to Odysseus, "Return to <u>Odysseus's</u> home."
4. The sailors told Odysseus, "<u>The sailors'</u> ships stand ready."
5. Odysseus saved <u>Odysseus's</u> crew many times.
6. Many adventures were <u>the sailors'</u>.
7. Odysseus told his crew, "<u>His crews'</u> homes are waiting for you."
8. Tell me <u>the reader's</u> own version of how the Trojan War began.
9. Once, three goddesses did not use <u>the goddesses'</u> wisdom well.
10. All citizens except one goddess got <u>the citizens'</u> invitations.
11. That goddess did not get <u>that goddess's</u> invitation.
12. "Where is <u>this goddess's invitation</u>?" she asked angrily.
13. For revenge, she tossed a golden apple in <u>the guests'</u> midst.
14. <u>The apple's</u> inscription read, "For the fairest."
15. Athena, Hera, and Aphrodite each claimed the apple as <u>each one's</u> own.
16. A shepherd named Paris was ordered by Zeus to make <u>Zeus's</u> decision.
17. Hera said to Paris, "Great power is <u>Paris's</u> if you pick me."
18. Glory and renown would be <u>Athena's</u> gift to Paris.
19. Paris could have a beautiful wife if he called <u>Aphrodite's</u> name.
20. Paris chose Aphrodite and gave her <u>the contest's</u> prize.

Pronouns

MEETING INDIVIDUAL NEEDS

Less-Proficient Readers

Forming Possessive Pronouns

Some students may have difficulty understanding that possessive pronouns, unlike possessive nouns, are not written with apostrophes. These students may produce sentences such as *The book is our's* or *It must be their's.*

Pair students to check each other's written work for these kinds of errors. Assure them that they will make these corrections naturally as they become more proficient readers and more experienced writers.

11.5 | Indefinite Pronouns

■ An **indefinite pronoun** is a pronoun that does not refer to a particular person, place, or thing.

> Does **anyone** know the story of Midas?

Most indefinite pronouns are either singular or plural.

Some Indefinite Pronouns			
Singular			**Plural**
another	everybody	no one	both
anybody	everyone	nothing	few
anyone	everything	one	many
anything	much	somebody	others
each	neither	someone	several
either	nobody	something	

The indefinite pronouns *all, any, most, none,* and *some* can be singular or plural, depending on the phrase that follows them.

When an indefinite pronoun is used as the subject of a sentence, the verb must agree with it in number.

> **Everyone discusses** the plot. [singular]
> **Both talk** about King Minos. [plural]
> **All** of mythology **is** about beliefs and ideals. [singular]
> **All** of the myths **are** about beliefs and ideals. [plural]

Possessive pronouns often have indefinite pronouns as their antecedents. In such cases, the pronouns must agree in number. Note that in the first example the intervening prepositional phrase does not affect the agreement.

> **Each** of the characters has **his** or **her** motive.
> **Several** have conflict with **their** rivals.

11.5 Indefinite Pronouns **437**

Resource Manager

📁 **Planning Resources**
• *Lesson Plans*

📠 **Transparencies**
• *Bellringer*
• *Daily Language Practice*

📁 **Other Print Resources**
• *Grammar and Composition Handbook*
• *Grammar Enrichment,* p. 18
• *Grammar Practice,* p. 18
• *Grammar Reteaching,* p. 21
• *Grammar Workbook,* Lesson 25

Focus

Lesson Overview

Objectives
• To identify indefinite pronouns that are singular, plural, or that may be either singular or plural depending on use
• To use indefinite pronouns that agree in number with their verbs and any related pronouns

🔔 **Bellringer**
Daily Language Activity

When students enter the classroom, have this assignment on the board: *In your own words, write a definition for the word* indefinite.

See also 📖 *Daily Language Practice*

Motivating Activity

Have students share their definitions and discuss the function of indefinite pronouns. Encourage students to monitor their understanding and to seek clarification as needed.

Teach

☑ **Grammar Tip**

When a singular indefinite pronoun refers to both males and females, the possessive pronouns must also refer to both: *Each of the gods has his or her throne on Mt. Olympus.* To avoid this rather clumsy construction, a writer may use a plural indefinite pronoun: *All of the gods have their own thrones.* As an alternative, a writer may also use the indefinite article *a* or *an*: *Each god has a throne.* Have students review a recent assignment for such clumsy constructions. Ask them to revise their writing as needed.

Pronouns

Practice and Assess

Answers: Exercise 8

1. know—Many (plural)
2. have—Few (plural)
3. possess—Some (plural)
4. is—One (singular)
5. punish—Others (plural)
6. is—Anything (singular)
7. his or her—someone (singular)
8. thinks—No one (singular)
9. their—Several (plural)
10. knows—Everybody (singular)
11. brings—All (singular)
12. are—Several (plural)
13. is—One (singular)
14. is—each (singular)
15. turns—All (singular)
16. its—nothing (singular)
17. is—Nothing (singular)
18. their—all (plural)
19. is—All (singular)
20. think—Many (plural)

Answers: Exercise 9

1. Each	6. each
2. several	7. all
3. all	8. most
4. one	9. Much
5. One	10. Many

Additional Resources

 *Grammar Practice*, p. 18
 *Grammar Reteaching*, p. 21
 *Grammar Enrichment*, p. 18

 Grammar Workbook, Lesson 25

Close

Have students write myths of their own, describing a change that a person might undergo as a result of his or her behavior. Ask students to trade myths and check each other's work to be sure they used singular and plural indefinite pronouns correctly. Students should respond in constructive ways.

Exercise 8 Using Indefinite Pronouns

Write each sentence. Use the word in parentheses that correctly completes the sentence. Underline the indefinite pronoun and write whether it is *singular* or *plural*.

1. Many (knows, know) the tale of Midas.
2. Few (has, have) more gold than King Midas.
3. Some of the gods, however, (possesses, possess) more gold than the king.
4. One of them (is, are) the object of Midas's jealousy; he is Apollo, the sun god.
5. Others (punishes, punish) mortals who are jealous of the gods, but not Apollo.
6. "Anything (is, are) yours," Apollo tells Midas.
7. In mythology someone may be granted (his or her, their) wish.
8. No one (thinks, think) harm will come of Midas's wish that all he touches turns to gold.
9. Several wish (his or her, their) fate were the same as Midas's.
10. Everybody (know, knows) that Midas meant no harm.
11. All of Midas's gold (bring, brings) him little happiness.
12. Several of life's joys (is, are) taken away from Midas.
13. One of his touches (is, are) fatal to any living thing.
14. Midas touches his daughter; each of his other children (is, are) safe.
15. All of his food (turn, turns) to gold, and so he cannot eat.
16. Soon Midas regrets his wish; nothing retains (its, their) life once he touches it.
17. "Nothing (is, are) more precious than life," Midas admits, "not even gold."
18. Apollo forgives Midas; all of the golden objects regain (its, their) original form.
19. All of life (is, are) now a pleasure for Midas.
20. Many now (think, thinks) the name Midas means "rich man."

Exercise 9 Using Indefinite Pronouns Correctly

Write each sentence. Use the correct indefinite pronoun.

1. (Each, All) of Zeus's brothers was asleep in his own bed.
2. Nearby were many giants; (several, one) raised their voices.
3. The brothers awoke; (everybody, all) jumped from their beds.
4. Typhon was (one, many) of the giants; his voice was loudest.
5. (Both, One) had one hundred arms and breathed fire from his nose.
6. The brothers and giants battled; (each, most) fought his best.
7. The giants lost; (all, either) of them took their punishment.
8. (All, Everybody) were imprisoned under the island of Sicily.
9. (Much, Others) of the island moves; its ground quakes.
10. (Another, Many) blow their breath up through the mountain.

 **MEETING INDIVIDUAL NEEDS**

English Language Learners

Getting to Know Indefinite Pronouns

Students learning English may have trouble with the indefinite pronouns *everybody*, *everyone*, and *everything* because they seem to be plural in meaning but singular in form. Tell students that all indefinite pronouns that end in *-body*, *-one*, and *-thing* are singular. Suggest that students think of *every-* as meaning "each body," "each one," and "each thing." These are clearly singular. Students may want to record this tip in their journals.

11.6 Reflexive and Intensive Pronouns

Reflexive and intensive pronouns are formed by adding -*self* or -*selves* to certain personal and possessive pronouns.

Reflexive and Intensive Pronouns	
Singular	**Plural**
myself	ourselves
yourself	yourselves
himself, herself, itself	themselves

Sometimes *hisself* is mistakenly used for *himself* and *theirselves* for *themselves*. Avoid using *hisself* and *theirselves*.

■ A **reflexive pronoun** refers to a noun or another pronoun and indicates that the same person or thing is involved.

The woman found **herself** a book of folk tales.

REFLEXIVE PRONOUN

■ An **intensive pronoun** is a pronoun that adds emphasis to a noun or pronoun already named.

George **himself** bought a copy of *American Tall Tales.*
He **himself** paid for the book.

Never use reflexive and intensive pronouns as the subject of a sentence or as the object of a verb or preposition.

Roy and **I** read a tale. [not *Roy and myself*]
It intrigued Roy and **me.** [not *Roy and myself*]

11.6 Reflexive and Intensive Pronouns **439**

REFLEXIVE PRONOUN

Pronouns

Focus

Lesson Overview

Objectives
- To identify and differentiate between reflexive and intensive pronouns
- To use reflexive and intensive pronouns correctly in writing

Bellringer
Daily Language Activity

When students enter the classroom, have this assignment on the board: *Jot down any pronouns you can think of that end in* -self *or* -selves. Discuss students' answers and solicit examples of the use of these words.

See also *Daily Language Practice*

Motivating Activity

Ask students to define what a reflection is. Can they give a definition using one of the words from the Bellringer activity? (For example, "A reflection is an image of yourself in a shiny surface.")

Teach

☑ Teaching Tip

Write the terms *reflexive pronouns* and *intensive pronouns* on the chalkboard. Explain to students that these pronouns have identical forms but different functions. A reflexive pronoun is part of the basic grammar of a sentence; it cannot be deleted. For example, *herself* cannot be deleted in the following sentence,: "Artemis outdid herself during the hunt." Explain that intensive pronouns, on the other hand, are added to a sentence for emphasis and can be deleted without changing the grammar of the sentence. For example, *herself* adds emphasis but can be deleted in the following sentence: "Artemis herself led the hunt."

Resource Manager

📂 **Planning Resources**
- *Lesson Plans*

📁 **Transparencies**
- *Bellringer*
- *Daily Language Practice*

📂 **Other Print Resources**
- *Grammar and Composition Handbook*
- *Grammar Enrichment,* p. 19
- *Grammar Practice,* p. 16
- *Grammar Workbook,* Lesson 26

Practice and Assess

Additional Resources

 *Grammar Practice*, p. 18

 *Grammar Enrichment*, p. 19

 Grammar Workbook, Lesson 26

Pronouns

Exercise 10 Identifying Reflexive and Intensive Pronouns

Read each sentence. Write each reflexive and intensive pronoun. Then write whether each pronoun is a *reflexive* or *intensive* pronoun.

1. Today occupy yourselves by reading the legend of King Arthur.
2. The legend itself may be based on historical evidence.
3. Arthur's mother admired herself for giving birth to such a son.
4. Arthur's father himself was the elected sovereign of Britain.
5. Arthur himself is said to have had twelve victories in battle.
6. In the last battle, his armies outdid themselves.
7. They were very effective, and Arthur himself honored them.
8. His people considered themselves lucky to be living in peace.
9. The country itself was peaceful for twenty years.
10. Then Arthur's nephew Modred showed himself to be a traitor.

Exercise 11 Using Reflexive and Intensive Pronouns Correctly

Write each sentence. Use the correct pronoun in parentheses. Write whether the pronoun is a *reflexive, intensive, subject,* or *object* pronoun.

1. I recently bought (me, myself) a book about Paul Bunyan.
2. (He, Himself) is a legendary giant lumberjack of the north woods.
3. The book (it, itself) is a collector's item.
4. The imaginative legends provide (us, ourselves) with a sense of folk tradition.
5. Perhaps settlers on the frontier would tell (them, themselves) these stories.
6. My friends and (I, myself) find the legends amusing.
7. Paul Bunyan (he, himself) has a good sense of humor.
8. (We, Ourselves) call Paul Bunyan's adventures tall tales.
9. The students bought (theirselves, themselves) a copy of the tales.
10. In the tales, Bunyan forms much of America (it, itself).
11. (He, Himself) digs Washington's Puget Sound.
12. The lumberjacks thank (him, himself) for his help.
13. Now the logs (they, themselves) float easily to the mills.
14. The giant blue ox, Babe, makes (it, itself) Bunyan's friend.
15. Bunyan gives (it, itself) many gifts during their friendship.
16. The Great Lakes (they, themselves) are Babe's drinking water.
17. The north woods (them, themselves) are in the United States and Canada.
18. (I, Myself) know one story about Paul Bunyan.
19. (It, Itself) tells how the ten thousand lakes of Minnesota formed.
20. Tall tales have always been amusing to (us, ourselves).

Close

List these pronouns on the board: *myself, yourself, himself, itself, ourselves, yourselves, themselves.* Ask student pairs to choose a word and write it in a sentence as a reflexive pronoun. Then have them write a second sentence using the same word as an intensive pronoun. Have volunteers identify the reflexive and intensive pronouns as students read their sentences aloud.

MEETING INDIVIDUAL NEEDS English Language Learners

Using Reflexive Pronouns

Students learning English may use reflexive pronouns more often than is appropriate (for example, *I stand myself up.*). Explain that reflexive pronouns are used sparingly in English. Use the sentences in the lesson to show that reflexives usually answer the questions *to whom* or *for whom.*

11.7 Interrogative Pronouns

■ An **interrogative pronoun** is a pronoun used to introduce an interrogative sentence.

> **Who** is Pandora?
> For **whom** does Hephaestus make a staff?
> **What** is Pandora's curiosity about?
> **Whom** does Zeus call?
> **Whose** is the gift of hope?

The interrogative pronouns *who* and *whom* both refer to people. *Who* is used when the interrogative pronoun is the subject of the sentence. *Whom* is used when the interrogative pronoun is the object of a verb or a preposition.

> **Who** gives Pandora her name? [subject]
> **Whom** does Zeus dislike? [direct object]
> To **whom** does Zeus give a gift? [object of preposition]

Which and *what* are used to refer to things.

> Some gifts are for Pandora. **Which** are they?
> Athena makes Pandora a robe. **What** does Hephaestus make?

Whose shows that someone possesses something.

> The jar is in Pandora's house. **Whose** is it?

Do not confuse *whose* with *who's*.

> **Who's** reading the myth? [contraction of *Who is*]
> **Whose** is it? [interrogative pronoun]

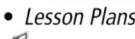

Resource Manager

📁 **Planning Resources**
- *Lesson Plans*

💾 **Transparencies**
- *Bellringer*
- *Daily Language Practice*

📁 **Other Print Resources**
- *Grammar and Composition Handbook*
- *Grammar Enrichment,* p. 19
- *Grammar Practice,* p. 19
- *Grammar Reteaching,* p. 22
- *Grammar Workbook,* Lesson 27

Focus

Lesson Overview

Objectives
- To identify interrogative pronouns
- To differentiate between interrogative pronouns and contractions
- To use interrogative pronouns correctly to form questions

 Bellringer
Daily Language Activity

When students enter the classroom, have this assignment on the board: *List titles or famous sayings that contain any of the following words: who, which, what, whom, whose.*

See also 💾 *Daily Language Practice*

Motivating Activity

Record student examples on the board. If necessary, provide examples (*For Whom the Bell Tolls, Who's Who,* "What's up, Doc?"). Discuss whether the titles or sayings are questions. What words make some of them questions? Tell students that the words in the Bellringer activity list are called *interrogative pronouns.*

Teach

Cooperative Learning

Organize students into pairs to conduct interviews. One student should act as the interviewer and ask questions using interrogative pronouns. The other student should play the role of the person being interviewed.

⬛ Cross-Reference: Grammar

For an alternative presentation of interrogative sentences, refer students to Lesson 8.1.

Pronouns

Practice and Assess

Answers: Exercise 12

1. Which
2. whom
3. What
4. Who
5. Who's
6. What
7. Which
8. Who
9. whom
10. Whose

Answers: Exercise 13

1. Who's—contraction
2. What
3. Whom
4. Whose
5. What
6. Which
7. Whom
8. Who
9. Which
10. Whose

Additional Resources

 Grammar Practice, p. 19
 Grammar Reteaching, p. 22
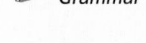 Grammar Enrichment, p. 19

Grammar Workbook, Lesson 27

Close

Ask students to prepare a list of questions that they would like to ask someone they admire. The questions should include interrogative pronouns. Have students conduct their interviews and summarize their findings in a written report.

Pronouns

Exercise 12   Using Interrogative Pronouns

Write each sentence. Use the correct word given in parentheses.

1. (Who, Which) is the myth about a quest for a great treasure?
2. To (whom, who) do you read those myths?
3. (What, Whom) is the object of the quest?
4. (Who, Which) is the hero in the first story?
5. (Who's, Whose) reading these myths?
6. (What, Which) does the word *myth* mean?
7. (Whom, Which) of the Roman myths are known by most people?
8. (Who, Whom) was the first person to make up a myth?
9. To (whom, whose) can the first tall tale be credited?
10. (Whose, Who's) are the most vivid imaginations, children's or adults'?

Exercise 13   Using Interrogative Pronouns and Contractions

Write each pair of sentences. Use the correct word given in parentheses. If the word you selected is a contraction, write *contraction*.

1. Jason is a famous hero of classical Greek mythology. (Whose, Who's) Jason?
2. His quest is for the Golden Fleece, the wool of a winged ram. (What, Whom) is the Golden Fleece?
3. Jason's father, Aeson, is the king until Pelias removes him. (Who, Whom) does Pelias remove?
4. When Jason grows up, he wants Pelias's throne. (Whose, Whom) is the throne currently?
5. Pelias promises him the throne if he retrieves the Golden Fleece. (Whose, What) is Pelias's demand?
6. Jason sails on the Argo with a group of brave friends, called the Argonauts. (Who's, Which) is the Argonauts' ship?
7. The ship is named after Argo, the shipbuilder. (Who, Whom) is the ship named after?
8. The famous Hercules was among the crew. (Who, Whom) is among the crew?
9. They rowed until they reached the eastern end of the sea. (Whose, Which) way did they row?
10. In Greece Jason tamed the king's two fire-breathing bulls. (Who's, Whose) were the fire-breathing bulls?

Critical Thinking

Choosing *Who* or *Whom* To help students determine when to use *who* and when to use *whom*, suggest that they reword an interrogative sentence as a statement. They should replace *who* and *whom* with the appropriate personal or object pronouns.

Thus, *Who/Whom does the moon god marry?* would be restated as *The moon god does marry her.* Whenever the object pronoun *her* correctly completes the statement, *whom* should be used in the question. Students may want to record this tip in their journals.

Grammar Review

PRONOUNS

In Greek mythology, Phaethon is the son of Apollo, the sun god, and Clymene, a mortal. Although Phaethon's mother has told him that Apollo is his father, Phaethon seeks proof from Apollo himself. Phaethon approaches the sun god, who solemnly promised to grant his son any wish the boy might have. Unfortunately, Phaethon asks to drive the sun god's chariot for a day, a job only Apollo himself can handle.

In the following excerpt from "Phaethon," retold by Edith Hamilton, Phaethon sets out on his disastrous ride. The passage has been annotated to show some of the kinds of pronouns covered in this unit.

Literature Model

from "Phaethon"
retold by Edith Hamilton

For a few ecstatic moments Phaethon felt himself the lord of the sky. But suddenly there was a change. The chariot was swinging wildly to and fro; the pace was faster; he had lost control. Not he, but the horses were directing the course. That light weight in the car, those feeble hands clutching the reins, had told them their own driver was not there. They were the masters then. No one else could command them. They left the road and rushed where they chose, up, down, to the right, to the left. They nearly wrecked the chariot against the Scorpion; they brought up short and almost ran into the Crab. By this time the poor charioteer was half fainting with terror, and he let the reins fall.

> Reflexive pronoun

> Possessive pronoun

> Indefinite pronoun

> Subject pronoun agrees with its antecedent, *the poor charioteer*

Teach

About the Literature

Explain that the review contains a passage from "Phaethon," as retold by Edith Hamilton in the book *Greek Mythology*. The passage tells the story of a boy's attempt to drive the chariot of the sun god, his father, across the sky. It is followed by exercises based on the Greek myth and on related topics. After students have read the passage, discuss its character, setting, and mood. Then ask students to determine what noun could be substituted for each highlighted pronoun. Encourage students to respond to classmates answers in constructive ways.

Linking Grammar and Literature

Viewing and Representing

Have students close their eyes and visualize the action described in this passage. Ask them to sketch on paper their mental images of Phaethon at the reins of the chariot. Have students write descriptive captions for their sketches.

Cooperative Learning

Encourage students to form small groups to write new conclusions to "Phaethon." Students may retell the actual myth or write their own endings. Each group member should add at least one sentence to the story; each sentence should contain at least one of the pronoun categories covered in the unit. Remind students to make sure that the pronouns they use in their sentences agree with the antecedents used by other group members. Students may want to use a computer to work through each step of the writing process. When the groups have finished their stories, ask them to share their writing with the class.

Resource Manager

📂 **Planning Resources**
- *Lesson Plans*

📂 **Other Print Resources**
- *Grammar and Composition Handbook*
- *Grammar Workbook,* Lessons 22–27; *Unit 4 Review; Cumulative Review:* Units 1–4

✔ ASSESSMENT OPTIONS

📁 *Tests with Answer Key & Rubrics*
Unit 11 Mastery Test, pp. 47–48

💾 *Testmaker*
Unit 11 Mastery Test

Practice and Assess

Answers: Exercise 1

1. his, her; possessive, possessive
2. He, she; subject, subject
3. Their, his; possessive, possessive
4. him, them; object, object
5. They, him; subject, object

Answers: Exercise 2

1. They; steps
2. it; hall
3. It; robe
4. They; garments
5. She; Spring
6. her; Summer
7. them; grapes
8. it; hair
9. They; Day, Month, Year, Hours
10. I; Apollo

Pronouns

Review: Exercise 1 Using Pronouns in the Nominative, Objective, and Possessive Cases

Write each sentence. Replace the underlined word or words with a pronoun and write whether it is a *subject pronoun*, *object pronoun*, or *possessive pronoun*.

1. Phaethon was <u>Apollo's</u> and <u>Clymene's</u> son.
2. <u>Apollo</u> was the sun god, and <u>Clymene</u> was an ocean nymph.
3. <u>Apollo's and Clymene's</u> son wanted to drive <u>Apollo's</u> horses.
4. The sun god let <u>Phaethon</u> ride off with the <u>sun god's team</u>.
5. <u>The horses</u> carried <u>Phaethon</u> high into the sky

Review: Exercise 2 Using Pronouns and Antecedents Correctly

Write the second sentence in each of the following pairs. Use the correct pronoun in each blank. Then write the antecedent of the pronoun.

SAMPLE After a long journey, Phaethon approaches the palace of his father. _____ is excited.

ANSWER He is excited. Phaethon

1. Phaethon walks up the steps. _____ are made of white marble.
2. The boy enters the great hall. His footsteps echo in _____.
3. There sits Apollo, dressed in a splendid robe. _____ is deep purple and trimmed in gold.
4. At the right and left hands of Apollo stand servants dressed in flowing garments. _____ make the servants look regal.
5. Spring stands with her crown of flowers. _____ looks radiant.
6. The lovely Summer carries a garland of ripened grain. The garland is _____ symbol.
7. Autumn's feet are stained from grapes. She stomps on _____ to press out the juice.
8. Frost stiffens Winter's hair. Icicles hang from _____.
9. Around the great hall stand Day, Month, Year, and—at regular intervals—Hours. _____ watch as Phaethon approaches.
10. Apollo looks at Phaethon with pride. "_____ welcome you to my palace," Apollo says.

Review: Exercise 3 **Using Pronouns in the Nominative and Objective Cases Correctly**

Read each sentence. Write the correct word or words in parentheses. Then write whether each pronoun you selected is a *subject pronoun* or an *object pronoun*.

1. (He, Him) and Apollo admired the chariot and the horses.
2. Apollo told Phaethon and (they, them) to be careful.
3. The horses and (he, him) would soar through sky and clouds.
4. "The team and (I, me) thank mother and father," said Phaethon.
5. "(We, Us) and Apollo bless you and the team," said the gods.
6. The wheels and axles were cleaned by servants and (he, him).
7. Phaethon and (they, them) had a breakfast of ambrosia and honey.
8. (They, Them) and Phaethon needed energy and courage.
9. The first two horses lifted the chariot and (he, him) at dawn.
10. Al and (I, me) think Phaethon and the chariot represent the sun.

Review: Exercise 4 **Using Indefinite Pronouns**

Write each sentence. Use the word or words in parentheses that correctly complete the sentence. Then underline the indefinite pronoun and write whether the pronoun is *singular* or *plural*.

SAMPLE   Everyone (watches, watch) in horror as the chariot plunges to earth.
ANSWER   <u>Everyone</u> watches in horror as the chariot plunges to earth. singular

1. Some (tries, try) to hide from the fiery car.
2. Others (appeals, appeal) to Zeus, the ruler of the gods, to stop the falling chariot.
3. Something (shine, shines) in Zeus's hand as he climbs his tower.
4. Zeus rules clouds and lightning; both (is, are) under his control.
5. Everyone (gasps, gasp) as he hurls a thunderbolt at the charioteer.
6. No one (is, are) sadder than the sun god to see Phaethon struck dead by the bolt.
7. Few (point, points) as Phaethon, hair on fire, falls from the sky.
8. Many (describe, describes) him as like a shooting star.
9. Each tells (his or her, their) own story.
10. Much (happen, happens) as the river receives and cools his body.

Answers: Exercise 3
1. He, subject
2. them, object
3. he, subject
4. I, subject
5. We, subject
6. him, object
7. they, subject
8. They, subject
9. him, object
10. I, subject

Answers: Exercise 4
1. try, Some, plural
2. appeal, Others, plural
3. shines, Something, singular
4. are, both, plural
5. gasps, Everyone, singular
6. is, No one, singular
7. point, Few, plural
8. describe, Many, plural
9. his or her, Each, singular
10. happens, Much, singular

Pronouns

Grammar Review

Answers: Exercise 5

1. myself, intensive
2. he, subject
3. himself, reflexive
4. It, subject
5. him, object
6. You, subject
7. themselves, intensive
8. him, object
9. they, subject
10. himself, intensive

Answers: Exercise 6

1. What
2. Who
3. What
4. Who
5. What
6. Whom
7. Who
8. whom
9. Who
10. Who

Review: Exercise 5 Using Subject, Object, Reflexive, and Intensive Pronouns

Write each sentence. Use the correct pronoun in parentheses. Write whether the pronoun is a *reflexive*, *intensive*, *subject*, or *object* pronoun.

1. Phaethon told Father, "I want to drive the chariot (me, myself)."
2. Father objected strongly; (he, himself) knew his son's fate.
3. Phaethon positioned (him, himself) in the chariot.
4. (It, Itself) was a gift from Vulcan, who makes Zeus's lightning.
5. Father hugged the boy and gave (him, himself) the reins.
6. "(You, Yourselves) and I will drive the sun through the sky," declared Phaethon to the horses.
7. The horses (himself, themselves) were eager to start.
8. At dawn the horses carried (he, him) high into the sky.
9. But the horses seized control of the chariot, and (they, themselves) sped past the constellations.
10. Alas, only the sun god (him, himself) can drive the chariot.

Review: Exercise 6 Using Interrogative Pronouns

The following sentences are about figures in Egyptian mythology. Write each question, using the correct interrogative pronoun in parentheses.

1. Nut represented the heavens. (What, Which) did Nut represent?
2. Geb was the earth god. (Who, Whom) was Geb?
3. Nut and Geb married, but Ra, the sun god, opposed their marriage. (Which, What) did Ra oppose?
4. Ra had the head of a hawk. (Who, Whom) had the head of a hawk?
5. Ra wore a solar disk as a crown. (What, Who) did Ra wear as a crown?
6. Ra ordered Shu, the god of the air, to separate Nut from Geb. (Who, Whom) did Ra order to separate Nut from Geb?
7. Shu separated heaven from earth. (Who, What) moved heaven away?
8. Isis's head had the horns of a cow. Horns were worn by (who, whom)?
9. Isis was the wife of Osiris. (Who, Whom) was the wife of Osiris?
10. Osiris was god of the underworld. (Who, Whom) ruled the underworld?

Proofreading

The following passage is about chariot racing. This event inspired *Charioteers*, the painting shown on the Greek vase below. Rewrite the passage, correcting the errors in spelling, capitalization, grammar, and usage. Add any missing punctuation. There are ten errors in all.

Artist unknown, Greece, *Charioteers*, fifth century B.C.

(continued)

Pronouns

Answers: Exercise 7
Proofreading

This proofreading activity provides editing practice with (1) the current or previous units' skills, (2) the **Troubleshooter** errors, and (3) spelling errors. Students should be able to complete the exercise by referring to the units, the **Troubleshooter,** and a dictionary.

Error (Type of Error)

1. Greece (capitalization)
2. it became (pronoun-antecedent agreement)
3. competed (verb tense)
4. was hired (subject-verb agreement)
5. entered (verb tense)
6. had to run (verb tense)
7. track, (sentence fragment)
8. the (capitalization)
9. no error
10. occurred (spelling)
11. managed (verb tense)

Viewing the Art

Artist unknown, Greece, *Charioteers*, fifth century B.C.
Point out to students that the scene painted on the Greek vase is full of drama and movement. Ask students to describe the details that bring the piece to life (the tangle of the horses' pounding legs; the taut reins; the horses' open mouths). How does the vase's shape con- tribute to the scene's sense of movement? What would have been lost if it had been painted on a flat surface? (The horses seem to be running around the curve of the vase.)

Charioteers can be seen in the British Museum in London.

Answers: Exercise 8
Mixed Review

1. his, possessive
2. himself, intensive
3. it, personal
4. Nothing, indefinite
5. himself, reflexive
6. What, interrogative
7. he, personal
8. All, indefinite
9. them, personal
10. Nothing, indefinite
11. themselves, intensive
12. some, indefinite
13. They, personal
14. their, possessive
15. Some, indefinite
16. Others, indefinite
17. One, indefinite
18. her, possessive
19. Which, interrogative
20. you, personal

Close

Initiate a discussion about the Olympics or another major sports event with which students are familiar. What are their favorite sports? Who are their favorite athletes? Has watching a professional athlete inspired any of them to excel in a particular sport? Throughout the discussion, make sure students use pronouns correctly. Keep a list of the most common mistakes made and go over them with the class after the discussion. Also, point out instances of correct pronoun usage.

Pronouns

Charioteers

[1]A four-horse chariot race became part of the ancient Olympics in greece. [2]The race proved to be so popular that they became the opening spectacle at the games. [3]As many as forty chariot drivers competing in the race. [4]Each chariot driver were hired by the owner of the chariot and horses. [5]Sometimes an owner enter as many as seven chariots in the same race.

[6]The competitors has to run laps down a straight track for a total distance of nearly nine miles. [7]When the four horses pulling a chariot turned around to double back down the track. [8]The chariot would swing wildly. [9]As Phaethon discovered when he tried to drive the sun god's chariot, the horses were very hard to control. [10]Spills and collisions occured frequently. [11]As a result, very few of the chariot drivers manages to finish the race.

Review: Exercise 8

Mixed Review

On your paper, list in order the twenty numbered pronouns that appear in the following paragraphs. Identify each pronoun as *personal, possessive, indefinite, reflexive, intensive,* or *interrogative.*

One day in summer, Phaethon went to visit[1] his father, Apollo the sun god. Apollo[2] himself lived in a faraway palace, and Phaethon had never seen[3] it. [4]Nothing would stop Phaethon from seeing the palace today. After a long journey, Phaethon found [5]himself at the palace. [6]What did [7]he see there?

[8]All of the palace's columns glittered with gold. Precious stones such as diamonds and rubies studded [9]them. [10]Nothing but polished ivory formed the ceilings. The front doors [11]themselves were made from silver, and they shone in the sun like mirrors. Colorful murals covered [12]some of the palace walls. [13]They represented the earth, the sea, the sky, and [14]their inhabitants. The largest mural depicted a group of nymphs frolicking by the sea. [15]Some were riding the sea waves. [16]Others were riding on the backs of fishes. [17]One was sitting on a rock and drying [18]her long, sea-green hair.

Phaethon was amazed. [19]Which was the most spectacular sight? He couldn't choose. How would [20]you decide?

Writing Application

Pronouns in Writing

Pronouns can replace nouns to make your writing more varied. Study how Latoya Hunter uses pronouns in this passage from *The Diary of Latoya Hunter*. Notice the italicized pronouns.

Dear Diary,

I never thought *I'd* get desperate enough to say this but I envy *you*. *You* don't have to live in this troubled world; all *you* do is hear about it. *You* don't have to go through a situation like sitting in a cafeteria watching others laughing and talking and *you* don't know *anyone*. To sit there and eat the food that is just terrible because there's *nothing* else to do . . .

I guess *you* can tell how *my* day went. Diary, what am *I* going to do? *My* best friend left to go to another school. *I* wish *she* could be with *me*.

Techniques with Pronouns

Try to apply some of Latoya Hunter's techniques when you write and revise your work.

❶ Lend variety to your writing by alternating pronouns and nouns.

CONFUSING VERSION *She* left. I wish *she* could be with me.

HUNTER'S VERSION *My best friend* left. I wish *she* could be with me.

❷ Keep your writing clear by making pronouns agree with their antecedents.

CONFUSING VERSION You don't have to live in *this troubled world*; all you do is hear about *them*.

HUNTER'S VERSION You don't have to live in *this troubled world*; all you do is hear about *it*.

TIME

For more about the writing process, see **TIME Facing the Blank Page,** pp. 97–107.

Pronouns

Practice

Practice some of these pronoun techniques by revising the following passage. Focus particularly on the underlined words.

Every day <u>it</u> was the same torture. Chants of "Charlie Brown! Charlie Brown!" filled the bus the minute Walker boarded. He was mortified. Alex, <u>his</u> buddy, kept saying "<u>They</u> are only teasing." He couldn't know how <u>he</u> felt. No one ever teased <u>him</u>. Walker had tried every solution. First, he'd ignored <u>it</u>. Then he'd plunged into reading. Finally, he'd camped out at the front of the bus under the driver's eagle eye. Nothing helped. But today <u>they</u> would be different. <u>He</u>, the school principal, had given <u>him</u> special permission to ride a bike to school. He really seemed to understand <u>his</u> problem.

Writing Application **449**

Pronouns in Writing

Encourage students to read the diary entry on page 449 silently. Then ask them to identify places where pronouns helped to make the writing clear. Discuss Latoya Hunter's use of pronouns in relation to the Techniques with Pronouns activity on this page.

Techniques with Pronouns

Encourage students to find further examples of pronouns used clearly by reviewing the passage from "Phaethon" at the beginning of the Unit 11 Grammar Review on page 443.

Practice

The answers to this challenging and enriching activity will vary. Refer to Techniques with Pronouns as you evaluate students' choices.

Sample:

Every day the torture was the same. Chants of "Charlie Brown! Charlie Brown!" filled the bus the minute Walker boarded. He was mortified. Alex, Walker's buddy, kept saying, "The kids are only teasing." He couldn't know how Walker felt. No one ever teased Alex. Walker had tried every solution. First, he'd ignored the teasing. Then he'd plunged into reading. Finally, he'd camped out at the front of the bus under the driver's eagle eye. Nothing helped. But today would be different. Mr. King, the school principal, had given Walker special permission to ride a bike to school. He really seemed to understand Walker's problem.

✔ ASSESSMENT OPTIONS

📁 *Tests with Answer Key & Rubrics*
Unit 11 Mastery Test, pp. 47–48

💾 *Testmaker*
Unit 11 Mastery Test
You may wish to administer the Unit 11 Mastery Test at this point.

📼 *MindJogger Videoquizzes*

Objectives

- To develop an understanding of adjectives and adverbs
- To use adjectives and adverbs correctly and effectively in writing and speaking

✔ ASSESSMENT OPTIONS

📁 *Tests with Answer Key & Rubrics*
Unit 12 Pretest, pp. 49–50
Unit 12 Mastery Test, pp. 51–52

💾 *Testmaker*
Unit 12 Pretest
Unit 12 Mastery Test

You may wish to administer the Unit 12 Pretest at this point.

Key to Ability Levels

L1 Level 1 activities are within the basic ability range of students.

L2 Level 2 activities are within the ability range of average students.

L3 Level 3 activities are more challenging activities.

UNIT 12 Adjectives and Adverbs

450

Resource Manager

📁 **Planning Resources**
- *Lesson Plans*
- *Block Scheduling*

🖥 **Transparencies**
- *Bellringer*
- *Daily Language Practice*
- *Two-Minute Skill Drill*

📁 **Other Print Resources**
- *Grammar and Composition Handbook*
- *Grammar Enrichment*
- *Grammar Practice*
- *Grammar Reteaching*
- *Grammar Workbook*
- *Tests with Answer Key and Rubrics*

📼 **Video**
- *MindJogger Videoquizzes*

💾 **Software**
- *Interactive Grammar and Language Workbook*
- *Language Arts PASS*
- *Presentation Plus!*
- *Testmaker*

💻 **Web Sites**
- *writerschoice.glencoe.com*

12.1 Adjectives

An adjective describes a person, place, thing, or idea. An adjective provides information about the size, shape, color, texture, feeling, sound, smell, number, or condition of a noun or a pronoun.

Many groups of visitors admire the **huge new** building.

In the sentence above, the adjective *many* describes the noun *groups,* and the adjectives *huge* and *new* describe the noun *building.*

■ An **adjective** is a word that modifies, or describes, a noun or a pronoun.

Most adjectives come before the nouns they modify. Sometimes adjectives follow linking verbs and modify the noun or pronoun that is the subject of the sentence, as in the example below.

Some architects are **skillful** and **creative.**

In the sentence above, the adjectives *skillful* and *creative* follow the linking verb *are* and modify the subject, *architects.* They are called predicate adjectives.

■ A **predicate adjective** is an adjective that follows a linking verb and modifies the subject of the sentence.

Forms of verbs are often used as adjectives and predicate adjectives.

The architect created a **surprising** design. [present participle]

The building is **decorated.** [past participle]

12.1 Adjectives **451**

Focus

Lesson Overview

Objectives
- To identify predicate adjectives and adjectives that precede nouns
- To use adjectives correctly to describe nouns and pronouns

Bellringer
Daily Language Activity

When students enter the classroom, have this assignment on the board: *Write as many descriptive words as you can think of to complete this sentence:*

A good friend is _____.

See also *Daily Language Practice*

Motivating Activity

Ask students to share their word lists from the Bellringer activity. Then ask them to name words they could substitute for *good.*

Teach

☑ Teaching Tip

The term *adjective* includes many different types of modifiers (articles, numbers, possessive pronouns, demonstratives, and so on) that come before nouns or after linking verbs. Present the idea that all these types of adjectives make the nouns they modify more specific.

⇄ Cross-Reference: Grammar

For an alternative presentation of the material about linking verbs, refer students to Lesson 10.4.

Adjectives and Adverbs (side tab)

Resource Manager

📁 **Planning Resources**
- *Lesson Plans*

📑 **Transparencies**
- *Bellringer*
- *Daily Language Practice*

📁 **Other Print Resources**
- *Grammar and Composition Handbook*
- *Grammar Enrichment,* p. 20
- *Grammar Practice,* p. 20
- *Grammar Reteaching,* p. 23
- *Grammar Workbook,* Lesson 28

Practice and Assess

Answers: Exercise 1

1. <u>Good</u> architects, <u>artistic</u> background
2. <u>many different</u> materials, <u>beautiful</u> shapes
3. <u>Reliable</u> architects
4. <u>attractive</u>, <u>sturdy</u>, <u>useful</u> buildings
5. <u>rectangular</u> buildings
6. <u>other</u> shapes
7. <u>big</u> city, <u>circular</u> building
8. <u>Famous</u>, old cathedrals; <u>tall</u>, <u>graceful</u> towers
9. <u>Most</u> designs, <u>true</u> beauty, <u>creative</u> form
10. <u>graceful</u> lines, <u>attractive</u> features
11. <u>Architectural</u> styles, <u>other</u> fashions
12. <u>Good</u> architects; <u>simple</u>, <u>unique</u> plans
13. <u>Commercial</u> buildings, <u>good</u> designs
14. <u>efficient</u> use, <u>challenging</u> requirement, <u>many</u> designs
15. <u>Careful</u> designs, <u>comfortable</u> areas
16. <u>good</u> design, <u>easy</u> access
17. <u>Successful</u> architects, <u>potential</u> problems
18. <u>Advanced</u> designs, <u>practical</u> buildings
19. <u>original</u> skyscraper, <u>triangular</u> sail
20. <u>calm</u> sea, <u>ordinary</u> sails

Answers: Exercise 2

Numbers indicate which sentence has a predicate adjective.

1. (1) difficult
2. (2) willing, strong
3. (1) studious
4. (1) inventive
5. (2) blind
6. (1) adventurous
7. (2) slow, meaningful
8. (2) beautiful
9. (2) content
10. (1,2) became, tempting

Additional Resources

 Grammar Practice, p. 20
Grammar Reteaching, p. 23
Grammar Enrichment, p. 20

Grammar Workbook, Lesson 28

Exercise 1   Identifying Adjectives

Write each adjective and then write the noun or pronoun it modifies.

1. Good architects often have an artistic background.
2. They arrange many different materials into beautiful shapes.
3. Reliable architects have studied engineering.
4. They want to design attractive, sturdy, and useful buildings.
5. Often you will see rectangular buildings.
6. You can also find buildings with other shapes.
7. The big city of Chicago has a circular building.
8. Famous old cathedrals have tall, graceful towers.
9. Most designs aim for true beauty and creative form.
10. Look for graceful lines as attractive features of buildings.
11. Architectural styles change along with other fashions.
12. Good architects have simple but unique plans.
13. Commercial buildings must have good designs.
14. The efficient use of space is a challenging requirement for many designs.
15. Careful designs provide comfortable areas for workers.
16. A good design also provides easy access to equipment.
17. Successful architects know about potential problems.
18. Advanced designs produce practical buildings.
19. The original skyscraper was a triangular sail.
20. In a calm sea, it was set high above the ordinary sails.

Exercise 2   Predicate Adjectives

Write the sentence in each pair that has a predicate adjective. Underline the predicate adjectives. (In one pair, both sentences have predicate adjectives.)

1. John Muir's early life was difficult. He worked hard at home.
2. However, that didn't stop him. Muir was willing and strong.
3. Muir was studious. His father discouraged his reading, though.
4. Muir was also inventive. He created many labor-saving devices.
5. After college Muir got some bad news. He might be blind soon.
6. Muir became adventurous. He started a journey west.
7. Muir traveled by foot. His journey was slow but meaningful.
8. The Sierra Nevada captivated him. They were beautiful.
9. Finally he reached San Francisco. For a time he was content.
10. He became a farmer. But travel was too tempting for him.

Close

Invite each student to write a description of a familiar building. The writing should include adjectives that describe the building—inside or out.

Exploring Language

Asking Questions

Tell students the easiest way to find a predicate adjective in English is to first determine whether the verb in the sentence is one of the common linking verbs listed in this book. If the verb is a linking verb, have students look for an adjective that follows it and answers the question *Which one? What kind?* or *How many?*

12.2 Articles and Proper Adjectives

The words *a*, *an*, and *the* make up a special group of adjectives called **articles.** *A* and *an* are called **indefinite articles** because they refer to one of a general group of people, places, things, or ideas. *A* is used before words beginning with a consonant sound. *An* is used before words beginning with a vowel sound.

    a unit   **a** pilot   **an** hour   **an** astronaut

The is called a **definite article** because it identifies specific people, places, things, or ideas.

    Neil Armstrong was **the** first man to walk on **the** moon.

■ **Proper adjectives** are formed from proper nouns. A proper adjective always begins with a capital letter.

    On my vacation in Italy, I ate only **Italian** food.

Some proper adjectives are the same as the related proper nouns: *United States government, June wedding.* Although many proper adjectives use one of the endings listed below, some are formed differently. Check the spellings in a dictionary.

Common Endings for Proper Adjectives				
Ending	**Examples**			
-an	Mexico Mexic**an**	Morocco Morocc**an**	Alaska Alask**an**	Guatemala Guatemal**an**
-ese	China Chin**ese**	Bali Balin**ese**	Sudan Sudan**ese**	Japan Japan**ese**
-ian	Canada Canad**ian**	Italy Ital**ian**	Nigeria Niger**ian**	Asia As**ian**
-ish	Spain Span**ish**	Ireland Ir**ish**	Turkey Turk**ish**	England Engl**ish**

12.2 Articles and Proper Adjectives   **453**

Resource Manager

📁 **Planning Resources**
- *Lesson Plans*

📠 **Transparencies**
- *Bellringer*
- *Daily Language Practice*

📁 **Other Print Resources**
- *Grammar and Composition Handbook*
- *Grammar Enrichment,* p. 20
- *Grammar Practice,* p. 20
- *Grammar Reteaching,* p. 24
- *Grammar Workbook,* Lesson 29

Focus

Lesson Overview

Objectives
- To recognize definite and indefinite articles and learn the rules for using them
- To identify proper adjectives and understand how to form and capitalize them

🔔 **Bellringer**
Daily Language Activity

When students enter the classroom, have this assignment on the board: *Write sentences using the following phrases:*

   an hour   *a moon*
   the hour   *the moon*

See also 📠 *Daily Language Practice*

Motivating Activity

Choose students' examples from the Bellringer activity to discuss the variations presented in article usage.

Teach

☑ Grammar Tip

Why can the indefinite articles *a* and *an* be used only with singular nouns? The reason is that these articles are contracted forms of the word *one.* The *n* in *an* was kept before words beginning with vowel sounds. Similarly, the article *an* is used before *hour* because *hour* begins with a vowel sound, while *a* is used before *history* because *history* begins with a consonant sound. Nonetheless, in British English *an* may precede the word *historical.*

⇄ Cross-Reference: Mechanics

For an alternative presentation of the rules of capitalization related to proper adjectives, refer students to Lesson 19.4.

Practice and Assess

Answers: Exercise 3

1. a satellite
2. an electrical storm
3. a transmitter
4. a vehicle
5. a hurricane
6. an expedition
7. a universe
8. an unexplored part
9. an unknown rock
10. a typical day
11. a surface
12. an awkward age
13. an instrument
14. a high altitude
15. an honest effort
16. an activity
17. an irregular heartbeat
18. a total loss
19. an unknown cause
20. a civil tongue

Answers: Exercise 4

1. Peruvian
2. Alaskan
3. Lithuanian
4. Yugoslavian
5. Balinese
6. Hungarian
7. Asian
8. Belgian
9. African
10. Norwegian
11. Pakistani
12. Mexican
13. Italian
14. Israeli
15. Japanese
16. Indian
17. Moroccan
18. Vietnamese
19. Ukrainian
20. Jordanian

Answers: Exercise 5

1. a German car
2. an Indian spice
3. a European tour
4. a June exhibition
5. a Brazilian song
6. a Canadian uniform
7. a Spanish shawl
8. a Bolivian ring
9. an American cowhand
10. an English coat
11. a Taiwanese baseball
12. a Turkish carpet
13. a Javanese dress
14. an Irish harp
15. a Mexican scientist
16. a November holiday
17. an ancient Persian painting
18. a Swedish athlete
19. a Nepalese recipe
20. a Russian delegate

Additional Resources

📁 *Grammar Practice*, p. 20
📁 *Grammar Reteaching*, p. 24
📁 *Grammar Enrichment*, p. 20

📖 *Grammar Workbook*, Lesson 29

454

Adjectives and Adverbs

Exercise 3   Using *A* and *An*

Write each word or groups of words, adding the correct indefinite articles.

1. satellite
2. electrical storm
3. transmitter
4. vehicle
5. hurricane
6. expedition
7. universe
8. unexplored part
9. unknown rock
10. typical day
11. surface
12. awkward age
13. instrument
14. high altitude
15. honest effort
16. activity
17. irregular heartbeat
18. total loss
19. unknown cause
20. civil tongue

Exercise 4   Identifying Proper Adjectives

Write the proper adjective from each phrase.

1. Peruvian mountain
2. Alaskan railway
3. Lithuanian dictionary
4. Yugoslavian background
5. Balinese dancer
6. Hungarian map
7. Asian viewpoint
8. Belgian detective
9. African adventure
10. Norwegian pilot
11. Pakistani restaurant
12. Mexican vote
13. Italian film director
14. Israeli consul
15. Japanese costume
16. Indian elephant
17. Moroccan musician
18. Vietnamese landscape
19. Ukrainian dance
20. Jordanian speaker

Exercise 5   Forming Proper Adjectives

Rewrite each group of words, using a proper adjective to describe the noun. Change the indefinite article if necessary.

1. a car from Germany
2. a spice from India
3. a tour of Europe
4. an exhibition in June
5. a song from Brazil
6. a uniform from Canada
7. a shawl from Spain
8. a ring from Bolivia
9. a cowhand from America
10. a coat from England
11. a baseball from Taiwan
12. a carpet from Turkey
13. a dress from Java
14. a harp from Ireland
15. a scientist from Mexico
16. a holiday in November
17. a painting from ancient Persia
18. an athlete from Sweden
19. a recipe from Nepal
20. a delegate from Russia

Close

Have each student write a paragraph describing his or her favorite ethnic foods. Ask students to use proper adjectives in their writing. Ask students to trade papers and constructively evaluate each other's use of proper adjectives.

Critical Thinking

Choosing Among Articles

Tell students that *a* and *an* refer to a nonspecific item of which the listener has no prior knowledge: "I ate *an* apple." *The* refers to a specific item of which the listener has prior knowledge: "I ate *the* apple" (the one you wanted).

12.3 Comparative and Superlative Adjectives

Adjectives can also compare two or more nouns or pronouns.

■ The **comparative form** of an adjective compares two things, groups, or people.

    The stone building is **larger** than the wooden building.

■ The **superlative form** of an adjective compares more than two things, groups, or people.

    The **largest** building of the three is made of stone.

For most adjectives of one syllable and some of two syllables, *-er* and *-est* are added to form the comparative and superlative.

Comparative and Superlative Forms	
Adjective	The architect designed a **tall** building.
Comparative	Her new building is **taller** than her last project.
Superlative	Her next building will be the **tallest** of all her buildings.

Some adjectives form irregular comparatives and superlatives.

Irregular Comparative and Superlative Forms		
Adjective	**Comparative**	**Superlative**
good	better	best
well	better	best
bad	worse	worst
many	more	most
much	more	most
little	less	least

Focus

Lesson Overview

Objectives

- To recognize comparative and superlative adjectives and understand their purpose
- To use comparative and superlative adjectives correctly in writing and speaking

🔔 Bellringer
Daily Language Activity

When students enter the classroom, have this assignment on the board: *Write four or five adjectives that you might use to describe yourself.*

See also 📖 *Daily Language Practice*

Motivating Activity

Explain to students that some adjectives can be comparative and others cannot. For example, you can be happy, happier than someone else, or the happiest in a group. But, although you can be alive, you cannot really be more alive than someone else, and you certainly cannot be *alivest*. Ask students to identify or write and constructively discuss the comparative and superlative adjectives from their Bellringer activity lists.

Teach

☑ Grammar Tip

A comparative adjective requires a comparison of two things or persons. Sometimes the comparison is not stated because it is clear from context. In the sentence *Jim is getting taller,* Jim's implied comparison with himself is not expressed: *Jim is getting taller than he used to be.* A superlative adjective compares more than two things or persons: *Jim is the tallest person on the team.*

Adjectives and Adverbs (side tab)

Resource Manager

📂 Planning Resources
- *Lesson Plans*

📖 Transparencies
- *Bellringer*
- *Daily Language Practice*
- *Two-Minute Skill Drill*

📂 Other Print Resources
- *Grammar and Composition Handbook*
- *Grammar Enrichment,* p. 21
- *Grammar Practice,* p. 21
- *Grammar Reteaching,* p. 24
- *Grammar Workbook,* Lesson 30

Two-Minute Skill Drill

List these adjectives on the board. Have students write each in the comparative and superlative forms.

brave	few	high
thin	dry	free

See also ⚑ *Two-Minute Skill Drill Transparency 12.3*

Practice and Assess

Answers: Exercise 6

1. oldest
2. best
3. more
4. earliest
5. tallest
6. shorter
7. more
8. largest
9. roomiest
10. most
11. better
12. biggest
13. Strangest
14. safest
15. healthier
16. least
17. hilliest
18. more
19. newer
20. greatest
21. nicest
22. greenest
23. older
24. windier
25. later

Additional Resources

📁 *Grammar Practice*, p. 21
📁 *Grammar Reteaching*, p. 24
📁 *Grammar Enrichment*, p. 21

📓 *Grammar Workbook*, Lesson 30

Adjectives and Adverbs

| **Exercise 6** | Using Comparative and Superlative Forms |

For each sentence, write the correct form of the adjective given in parentheses.

1. Remains of huts from about 120,000 years ago are the (old) buildings yet found.
2. The (good) discoveries of all may come from future digs by archaeologists.
3. We now have (many) examples of prehistoric remains than we have ever had.
4. The (early) structure of all is a circle of blocks that may go back more than a million years.
5. The second (tall) office building in the world is the Sears Tower in Chicago.
6. The huge World Trade Center in New York is (short) than the Sears Tower.
7. The World Trade Center, however, with its two towers, has (much) space than the Sears Tower.
8. The Pentagon covers the (large) area of any office building.
9. If you are entertaining 240,000 people, the stadium in Prague in the former Czechoslovakia is the (roomy) stadium of all.
10. Of all the students, Iko has the (much) interest in architecture.
11. The auditorium has (good) acoustics than the gymnasium.
12. One day other buildings may become the (big) buildings in the world.
13. (Strange) of all are those structures built mostly underground for safety or security reasons.
14. The (safe) buildings of all have automatic sprinkler systems in case of fire.
15. The better the indoor air quality, the (healthy) the building.
16. In Boston the old State House may be the (little) changed of the old public buildings.
17. The new State House is in the (hilly) part of that area.
18. Boston streets have (many) twists than a monkey's tail.
19. The Back Bay section is (new) than the Beacon Hill area.
20. Charles Bulfinch may be the architect who had the (great) influence of all on what the city looks like.
21. The Charles River Basin is one of Boston's (nice) spots of all for walking, jogging, or biking.
22. The Boston Common may be the (green) spot downtown.
23. Harvard University, across the Charles River, is (old) than any of the other local colleges.
24. Boston's ocean breezes make it (windy) than inland cities.
25. Unlike many old buildings, (late) structures are very tall.

Close

Ask students to compare the size, shape, color, and age of three buildings. Have them use comparative and superlative adjectives in their writing. Sample: *The lobby in the apartment building is much larger than the front hall in our house. The lobby of this hotel is the largest and most glamorous I've ever seen.*

MEETING INDIVIDUAL NEEDS English Language Learners

Forming Comparisons

Most non-European languages make comparative and superlative adjectives by using a method similar to the *more, most* pattern. When students first learn English, they may extend the *more, most* pattern to all adjectives, producing double comparisons such as *more better*. These errors will disappear as students learn the *-er, -est* pattern.

12.4 More Comparative and Superlative Adjectives

The comparative and superlative forms of most one-syllable and some two-syllable adjectives are formed by adding *-er* and *-est* to the adjective.

For most adjectives with two or more syllables, however, the comparative and superlative are formed by adding *more* and *most* before the adjective.

Comparing Adjectives of More than One Syllable	
Adjective	The archeologist made an **impressive** discovery while digging in the ruins.
Comparative	Her latest discovery is **more impressive** than her first finding.
Superlative	Her new discovery is the **most impressive** finding of the decade.

The words *less* and *least* are used before both short and long adjectives to form the negative comparative and superlative.

Negative Comparative and Superlative Forms	
Adjective	The public was unusually **curious** about the discovery.
Comparative	The public was **less curious** about ancient ruins than about prehistoric fossils.
Superlative	Of all the ancient buildings unearthed in this century, historians were **least curious** about that Greek temple.

Do not use *more, most, less,* or *least* before adjectives that already end with *-er* or *-est*. This is called a double comparison.

Adjectives and Adverbs

Focus

Lesson Overview

Objectives

- To identify irregular comparative and superlative forms of adjectives
- To learn to form negative comparative and superlative adjectives correctly
- To use irregular comparative and superlative forms properly in speaking and writing

Bellringer
Daily Language Activity

When students enter the classroom, have this assignment on the board: *Imagine a hot day in the middle of summer. Write several words or phrases that compare today with that summer day.*

See also *Daily Language Practice*

Motivating Activity

Recite this opening to a poem by Shakespeare: *Shall I compare thee to a summer's day? Thou art more lovely and more temperate . . .* (If necessary, explain that *temperate* means "mild.") Point out that the comparative of the word *lovely* can be *lovelier* or *more lovely*, but that *temperate* must be *more temperate.* Discuss the comparative words or phrases students used in the Bellringer activity. Did they use any words that could not take the *-er, -est* forms? Record them on the board. Have students ask questions to clarify their understanding.

Teach

☑ **Grammar Tip**

Some two-syllable adjectives follow the *-er, -est* pattern (*easier, easiest*); some follow the *more, most* pattern (*more afraid, most afraid*); some follow either pattern (*cleverer, cleverest; more clever, most clever*). Adjectives derived from participles, however, follow the *more, most* pattern.

Resource Manager

📂 **Planning Resources**
- *Lesson Plans*

📠 **Transparencies**
- *Bellringer*
- *Daily Language Practice*
- *Two-Minute Skill Drill*

📂 **Other Print Resources**
- *Grammar and Composition Handbook*
- *Grammar Enrichment,* p. 21
- *Grammar Practice,* p. 21
- *Grammar Reteaching,* p. 24
- *Grammar Workbook,* Lesson 31

Two-Minute Skill Drill

Write the following words on the board: *difficult, adorable, rotten, cheerful, elegant, eager.* Ask students to write the comparative and superlative forms for each word, both positive (*more, most*) and negative (*less, least*).

See also *Two-Minute Skill Drill Transparency 12.4*

Practice and Assess

Answers: Exercise 7

1. most interesting	6. more massive
2. more challenging	7. more solid
3. less curious	8. most imposing
4. most important	9. more graceful
5. most difficult	10. most beautiful

Answers: Exercise 8

1. less convenient
2. less available
3. less complex
4. least famous
5. less ancient
6. less attractive
7. least appealing
8. least popular
9. least important
10. less graceful

Additional Resources

📁 *Grammar Practice,* p. 21
📁 *Grammar Reteaching,* p. 24
📁 *Grammar Enrichment,* p. 21

📕 *Grammar Workbook,* Lesson 31

Adjectives and Adverbs

Exercise 7   **Using Comparative and Superlative Adjectives**

Write the correct comparative or superlative form of each adjective in parentheses.

1. Architecture is certainly one of the (interesting) careers of all.
2. Very few people have (challenging) jobs than architects do.
3. The public is usually (curious) about the architects themselves than about the work they do.
4. Art, mathematics, and engineering are among the (important) subjects of all for architects to study in school.
5. For architects in the Middle Ages, roofs presented the (difficult) problem of all.
6. Buildings became (massive) than they had ever been before.
7. As roofs grew heavier, the supporting walls became (solid).
8. These structures are among the (imposing) buildings ever constructed.
9. In the twelfth century, architects found better ways to support roofs, and buildings became (graceful) than they had been in the past.
10. Buildings could now support huge stained-glass windows, perhaps the (beautiful) windows people had ever seen.

Exercise 8   **Using Comparative and Superlative Negatives**

Write the correct negative comparative or negative superlative form of the adjective in parentheses.

1. Early humans may have found that caves were smaller and (convenient) than structures they could build.
2. Unlike huts, caves were (available) in areas with few hills or mountains.
3. Before humans learned to work with stone and brick, they were forced to construct (complex) buildings.
4. Perhaps the (famous) architect was the first to build a stone dwelling.
5. Cretan architecture was (ancient) than that of Egypt.
6. Although the Romans learned from the Greeks, many people think that Roman buildings are (attractive) than Greek buildings.
7. A few people argue that Roman architecture is the (appealing) of all ancient types.
8. Some of the (popular) buildings may be among the best examples of Romanesque architecture.
9. Some people believe that the (important) question one can ask is which type of architecture—Roman or Greek—is more beautiful.
10. In general, older buildings are (graceful) than newer buildings.

Close

Ask students to write paragraphs in which they use some comparative and superlative adjectives to tell whether they would rather be a painter, a sculptor, or an architect.

Critical Thinking

Excluding Absolutes

Some adjectives, called *absolutes,* do not take a comparative or superlative form because of the meanings of the words. For example, *perfect* means "flawless" or "lacking nothing." It would not be correct to say *more perfect* or *most perfect.*

Recognizing More Irregularities

The word *old* has two sets of comparative and superlative forms. *Older* and *oldest* are the regular forms; *elder* and *eldest* are the irregular forms. **L3**

12.5 | Demonstratives

The words *this*, *that*, *these*, and *those* are called demonstratives. They "demonstrate," or point out, people, places, or things. *This* and *these* point out people or things near to you, and *that* and *those* point out people or things at a distance from you. *This* and *that* describe singular nouns, and *these* and *those* describe plural nouns.

This, *that*, *these*, and *those* are called demonstrative adjectives when they describe nouns.

■ Demonstrative adjectives point out something and describe nouns by answering the questions *which one?* or *which ones?*

The words *this*, *that*, *these*, and *those* are demonstrative pronouns when they take the place of nouns and point out something.

"I can almost reach **those** buildings from **this** one."

Demonstratives	
Demonstrative Adjectives	**Demonstrative Pronouns**
That bridge is unusual.	**That** is an unusual stadium.
Look at **this** cathedral.	**This** is a glass dome.
Those windows are enormous.	**Those** are enormous windows.
Who designed **these** homes?	How did workers construct **these?**

The words *here* and *there* should not be used with demonstrative adjectives. The words *this*, *these*, *that*, and *those* already point out the locations *here* and *there*.

This bridge is interesting. [not *this here bridge*]

The object pronoun *them* should not be used in place of the demonstrative adjective *those*.

I took a photo of **those** skyscrapers. [not *them skyscrapers*]

Focus

Lesson Overview

Objectives
- To identify demonstratives and to determine whether they are used as adjectives or pronouns
- To use demonstratives correctly in sentences

🔔 Bellringer
Daily Language Activity

When students enter the classroom, have this assignment on the board: *Copy and complete the chart shown below.*

	One	More than one
Nearby	*this*	_____
Away	*that*	_____

See also 📖 *Daily Language Practice*

Motivating Activity

Elicit from students that *these* and *those* should be used to complete the first and second rows of the chart in the Bellringer activity. Point out that two factors determine which word is appropriate: the number of items referred to and their location. Provide examples such as those on this page. Ask students to monitor their understanding and seek clarification as needed.

Teach

☑ Teaching Tip

When a demonstrative pronoun does not have a clear referent, students can add a noun, making the pronoun into an adjective. For example: *How did workers construct those?* becomes *How did workers construct those pyramids?*

Resource Manager

📁 Planning Resources
- *Lesson Plans*

📖 Transparencies
- *Bellringer*
- *Daily Language Practice*

📁 Other Print Resources
- *Grammar and Composition Handbook*
- *Grammar Enrichment*, p. 22
- *Grammar Practice*, p. 22
- *Grammar Reteaching*, p. 25
- *Grammar Workbook*, Lesson 32

Practice and Assess

Answers: Exercise 9

1. these
2. that
3. that
4. This
5. those

6. that
7. these
8. These
9. these
10. This

Answers: Exercise 10

1. These
2. That
3. those
4. That
5. that
6. This
7. this
8. those
9. That
10. This

11. those
12. Those
13. This
14. that
15. Those
16. these
17. these
18. This
19. That
20. those

Additional Resources

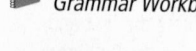 *Grammar Practice*, p. 22
 Grammar Reteaching, p. 25
 Grammar Enrichment, p. 22

Grammar Workbook, Lesson 32

Close

Have each student write a paragraph describing the homes on the street where he or she lives. Tell students to use some demonstrative adjectives. Ask students to trade papers and to make sure their classmates used demonstratives that correctly indicate number and distance. Students should respond in constructive ways.

Adjectives and Adverbs

Exercise 9 Identifying Demonstrative Adjectives

Write the demonstrative adjective found in each sentence.

1. The castles in these pictures are all in England.
2. The ones you see in that first set were built by the Saxons.
3. You can see the Norman influence on that castle.
4. This tower is called the keep.
5. Don't those buildings look like fortresses?
6. Do you recognize that ditch filled with water?
7. The builders used these moats for added protection.
8. These later castles are more comfortable.
9. Can you tell which of these strongholds was built first?
10. This picture is of Windsor Castle, home of England's rulers.

Exercise 10 Using Demonstrative Adjectives

For each sentence write the correct demonstrative adjective.

1. (This, These) buildings date from the 1700s.
2. (That, Those) style is a typical colonial home.
3. People built (that, those) houses for the cold climate.
4. (That, Those) fact is the reason for the small rooms.
5. Snow could easily slide off (that, those) sloping roof.
6. (That, This) house we are now touring is a typical Cape Cod house.
7. I like (this, these) exhibit of colonial architecture.
8. What are (these, those) pamphlets on the table over there?
9. (That there, That) booklet describes the architecture.
10. (This, These) model shows a southwestern American scene.
11. Missionaries built (them, those) churches with sun-dried brick or adobe.
12. (That, Those) churches combined Native American and Spanish styles.
13. (This, This here) model shows colonial New York.
14. The Dutch settlers built (that, those) type of house.
15. (Them, Those) houses were of brick or stone with small windows.
16. We know (this, these) buildings are representative of colonial-style houses.
17. The brick for (this, these) buildings came from Holland.
18. (This, This here) exhibit is devoted to public buildings.
19. (That, Those) building is still standing in Philadelphia.
20. How many of (them, those) other buildings have been torn down?

Writing in the Real World

Avoiding Nonstandard Usage

To discourage students from applying conventions of informal spoken English to their writing, write the following sentences on the board.

- This man behind me on the train was loudly chewing carrots. (A)
- We have this new student from Russia who is so smart. (a)

- When I got off the bus yesterday, I ran into these old friends. (some)

Ask students to copy the sentences, substituting the word in parentheses where *this* or *these* is used incorrectly.

12.6 Adverbs

■ An **adverb** is a word that modifies, or describes, a verb, an adjective, or another adverb.

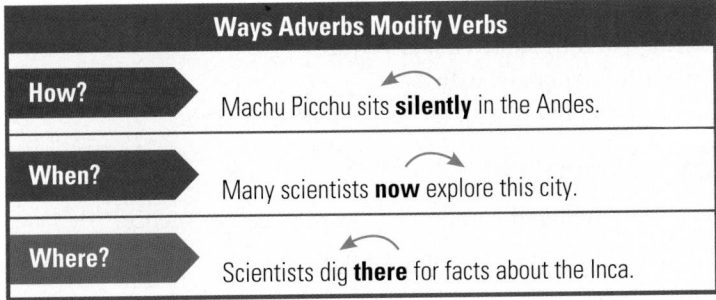

What Adverbs Modify	
Verbs	The Inca worked **carefully** on their buildings.
Adverbs	The Inca left their ancient cities **quite** suddenly.
Adjectives	Machu Picchu is a **very** large ruin in Peru.

When modifying a verb, an adverb may describe *how* or *in what manner* the action is done. It may describe *when* or *how often* an action is done. Also, it may describe *where* or *in what direction* an action was done.

Ways Adverbs Modify Verbs	
How?	Machu Picchu sits **silently** in the Andes.
When?	Many scientists **now** explore this city.
Where?	Scientists dig **there** for facts about the Inca.

Many adverbs are formed by adding *-ly* to adjectives. However, not all words that end in *-ly* are adverbs. The words *friendly, lively, kindly,* and *lonely* are usually adjectives. Similarly, not all adverbs end in *-ly.*

Adverbs not Ending in *-ly*			
afterward	often	there	hard
sometimes	soon	everywhere	long
later	here	fast	straight

12.6 Adverbs **461**

Resource Manager

📂 **Planning Resources**
- *Lesson Plans*

🖥 **Transparencies**
- *Bellringer*
- *Daily Language Practice*

📂 **Other Print Resources**
- *Grammar and Composition Handbook*
- *Grammar Enrichment,* p. 23
- *Grammar Practice,* p. 23
- *Grammar Reteaching,* p. 26
- *Grammar Workbook,* Lesson 33

Focus

Lesson Overview

Objectives
- To identify adverbs and the words that they modify
- To use adverbs correctly

🔔 **Bellringer**
Daily Language Activity

When students enter the classroom, have this assignment on the board: *Copy the following sentence:*

> *The scientist carefully studied a map of ancient Peru.*

Circle the word that answers the question How? When? *or* Where?

See also 📖 *Daily Language Practice*

Motivating Activity

Call on a volunteer to share his or her answer to the Bellringer activity. Challenge students to think of additional words that would make sense in the sentence and that answer the question *How?*

Teach

Critical Thinking

Ask students to identify the adverbs in the following passage.

> Breathing <u>deeply</u> to quell a sense of uneasiness, she <u>finally</u> relaxed, unrolled, and sat up. Kapu was curled against her leg. His feet were flipping and he yipped as if challenging some wolf badman in his dreams. <u>Softly</u> she stroked his fur.
>
> —Jean Craighead George
> *Julie of the Wolves*

Practice and Assess

Answers: Exercise 11

1. diligently, searched
2. everywhere, looked
3. slowly, traveled
4. Slowly, crossed
5. cautiously, carried
6. carefully, climbed
7. carefully, studied
8. below, snaked
9. above, lay
10. Once, came
11. Now, covered
12. briefly, lifted
13. greatly, affected
14. strongly, felt
15. hard, worked
16. efficiently, carried
17. solidly, constructed
18. apparently, were skilled
19. plentifully, were supplied
20. skillfully, worked

Answers: Exercise 12

Answers will vary, but some suggestions are given below.

1. often
2. back
3. very
4. very
5. finally
6. beautifully
7. already
8. quickly
9. enthusiastically
10. greatly

Additional Resources

 Grammar Practice, p. 23
Grammar Reteaching, p. 26
Grammar Enrichment, p. 23

Grammar Workbook, Lesson 33

Close

Have each student write a paragraph about exploring the ruins of an ancient city. Ask students to use adverbs in their writing. Students can exchange paragraphs and identify the adverbs.

Adjectives and Adverbs

Exercise 11   Identifying Adverbs

For each of the following sentences, write the adverb and then write the word it modifies.

1. Hiram Bingham searched diligently for the lost Incan cities.
2. Bingham and his aides looked everywhere in western South America.
3. They traveled slowly through thick jungles.
4. Slowly they crossed rushing rivers.
5. The explorers cautiously carried their own food and supplies.
6. Bingham and his searchers carefully climbed the steep mountainsides.
7. They carefully studied the legends.
8. The Urubamba River snaked below.
9. The lost city of Machu Picchu lay above.
10. Once many people came to the Incan city.
11. Now the Peruvian jungle growth covered Machu Picchu.
12. The mist lifted briefly over the walled city.
13. The city's emptiness affected them greatly.
14. They felt strongly the passage of centuries.
15. Bingham's group worked hard at their task of discovery.
16. The Inca's irrigation system carried water efficiently.
17. They constructed their houses solidly.
18. The Inca were apparently skilled in agriculture.
19. They were plentifully supplied with water.
20. The people worked skillfully with metals, pottery, and wool.

Exercise 12   Using Adverbs

Write an adverb to modify the underlined word in each sentence.

1. People <u>think</u> of television as a recent invention.
2. Experimental broadcasts <u>began</u> in 1928.
3. The quality of the broadcasts was not <u>good</u>.
4. Two <u>important</u> inventions came after 1930.
5. Philo T. Farnsworth <u>patented</u> a scanning cathode ray tube in 1930.
6. Kate Smith <u>sang</u> on one of the first scheduled broadcasts.
7. By the early 1940s, twenty-three TV stations were <u>operating</u>.
8. TV <u>grew</u> after the lifting of wartime restrictions.
9. By 1949 more than a million families <u>had</u> <u>bought</u> TV sets.
10. Ten years later the number <u>had</u> <u>multiplied</u> to 50 million.

Critical Thinking

Using Adverbs

Explain to students that an adverb works in one of two ways. It can modify an action verb, telling how, when, or where the action takes place; or it can modify an adjective or another adverb. By answering the question *How?* about the other modifer, these adverbs intensify or strengthen the adjectives or adverbs they modify. Point out that many adverbs end in *-ly.* Have students monitor their understanding and seek clarification as needed.

12.7 Intensifiers

When modifying a verb, an adverb may give information about *when*, *where*, or *how* the action of a sentence takes place. When describing an adjective or another adverb, an adverb often emphasizes or intensifies the word it modifies.

■ An adverb that emphasizes or intensifies an adjective or adverb is called an **intensifier.**

Read the sentences below.

> The people of Rapa Nui (Easter Island) built large statues.
> The people of Rapa Nui (Easter Island) built **extremely** large statues.

In the first sentence you learn that the people built large statues. The adjective *large* describes the noun *statues*. In the second sentence you learn that the statues were extremely large. The intensifier *extremely* describes the adjective *large*.

Now read the following sentences.

> Scientists examined the old statues carefully.
> Scientists examined the old statues **very** carefully.

In the first sentence you learn that scientists carefully examined the statues. The adverb *carefully* describes the action verb *examined*. In the second sentence you learn how carefully the scientists examined the statues. The intensifier *very* describes the adverb carefully.

Here is a list of intensifiers often used to describe adjectives and other adverbs.

The people of Rapa Nui (Easter Island) built extremely large statues.

Intensifiers			
almost	nearly	rather	somewhat
extremely	practically	really	too
just	quite	so	very

Adjectives and Adverbs

12.7 Intensifiers **463**

Focus

Lesson Overview

Objectives
- To identify intensifiers—adverbs that modify adjectives and other adverbs
- To use intensifiers correctly

 Bellringer
Daily Language Activity

When students enter the classroom, have this assignment on the board: *Write a definition of the word* intensify.

See also *Daily Language Practice*

Motivating Activity

Discuss students' responses to the Bellringer activity. Ask students how they would intensify the heat in an oven (by turning up the heat). Ask a volunteer to make an unhappy expression and then intensify it. Then ask a volunteer to use a word to intensify this statement: *When I won the prize, I was excited.*

Teach

☑ **Grammar Tip**

Adverbs that modify adjectives and other adverbs are called intensifiers. Unlike adverbs that modify verbs, intensifiers cannot be moved away from the words they modify, nor can they tell *when* or *where* about the words they modify. Point out that the same intensifiers can be used with both adjectives and adverbs. For example, *the* **very** <u>tall</u> (modifies adjective) *building was built* **very** <u>quickly</u> (modifies adverb).

Resource Manager

📁 **Planning Resources**
- *Lesson Plans*

📊 **Transparencies**
- *Bellringer*
- *Daily Language Practice*

📁 **Other Print Resources**
- *Grammar and Composition Handbook*
- *Grammar Enrichment*, p. 24
- *Grammar Practice*, p. 23
- *Grammar Reteaching*, p. 26
- *Grammar Workbook*, Lesson 34

Practice and Assess

Answers: Exercise 13

1. somewhat, mysterious
2. quite, enormous
3. extremely, hard
4. almost, exclusively
5. just, recently
6. very, carefully
7. rather, laboriously
8. such, long
9. simply, thrilling
10. nearly, identical
11. really, difficult
12. Very, slowly
13. enormously, happy
14. most, easterly
15. extremely, interesting
16. rather, carefully
17. remarkably, like
18. too, well
19. essentially, hidden
20. fairly, certain

Answers: Exercise 14

1. extremely difficult
2. quite long
3. much harder
4. somewhat at the mercy
5. quite unfamiliar
6. very expensive
7. extremely popular
8. most helpful
9. much cheaper
10. really new sights

Additional Resources

 *Grammar Practice,* p. 23
 *Grammar Reteaching,* p. 26
Grammar Enrichment, p. 24

 Grammar Workbook, Lesson 34

Adjectives and Adverbs

Exercise 13 Identifying Intensifiers

For each sentence below, write the intensifier and the word it modifies.

1. The Rapa Nui statues are somewhat mysterious.
2. Most visitors are astounded by their quite enormous size.
3. Scientists have tried extremely hard to explain their origin.
4. The statues were made almost exclusively of volcanic rock.
5. We have learned just recently about their beginnings.
6. Some scientists very carefully built a copy of one of the ancient statues.
7. Scientists worked rather laboriously on the new statue.
8. They spent such long days at their task.
9. For most of the scientists, the project was simply thrilling.
10. The scientists' tools were nearly identical to the ancient ones.
11. The really difficult work took many months of steady labor.
12. Very slowly a sixty-foot copy of an old statue took shape.
13. The ancient builders must have been enormously happy with their work.
14. Rapa Nui is the most easterly island of Polynesia.
15. The island has some extremely interesting stone walls.
16. They are made up of blocks rather carefully fitted together.
17. They are remarkably like the walls of the Inca.
18. The builders of these walls kept their secrets too well.
19. Their identity is essentially hidden from us.
20. It is fairly certain that they lived at least nine hundred years ago.

Exercise 14 Using Intensifiers

Write each sentence, adding the intensifier that appears in parentheses.

1. Being a tourist can be difficult sometimes.   (extremely)
2. Often there are long lines to get through.   (quite)
3. Not speaking the language makes it harder.   (much)
4. You are also at the mercy of the weather.   (somewhat)
5. The food that's available may be unfamiliar.   (quite)
6. If you stay in a hotel, it may be expensive.   (very)
7. Yet traveling remains popular all over the world.   (extremely)
8. Traveling in the off-season can be helpful.   (most)
9. Special package tours can be cheaper than single tickets.   (much)
10. For many people, seeing new sights is its own reward.   (really)

Close

Ask each student to write a paragraph describing the most mysterious thing that has ever happened to him or her. Have students include some intensifiers in their writing. Students should revise their own paragraphs to improve word choice and meaning.

Exploring Language

Finding the Intensifier

To identify an intensifier in a string of adjectives modifying a noun, have students pair each modifier with that noun. In the sentence *All the extremely noisy children left the room,* most of the modifiers can be paired with the noun: **all** *children,* **the** *children,* **noisy** *children.* Pairing *extremely* with the noun sounds wrong, showing that *extremely* does not modify *children* but is an intensifier modifying *noisy.*

12.8 Comparative and Superlative Adverbs

- The **comparative form** of an adverb compares two actions.
- The **superlative form** of an adverb compares more than two actions.

Long adverbs require the use of *more* or *most*.

Comparing Adverbs of More than One Syllable	
Comparative	The Cretans lived **more peacefully** than the Greeks.
Superlative	They lived the **most peacefully** of all Aegean peoples.

Shorter adverbs need *-er* or *-est* as an ending.

Comparing One- and Two-Syllable Adverbs	
Comparative	The Cretans built cities **earlier** than the Greeks.
Superlative	The Cretans built cities the **earliest** of all Europeans.

Here are some irregular adverbs.

Irregular Comparative Forms		
Adverb	**Comparative**	**Superlative**
well	better	best
badly	worse	worst
little (amount)	less	least
far (distance)	farther	farthest
far (degree)	further	furthest

The words *less* and *least* are used before both short and long adverbs to form the negative comparative and superlative.

I work **less often.** I work **least efficiently.**

Do not use *more, most, less,* or *least* before adverbs that already end in *-er* or *-est*.

12.8 Comparative and Superlative Adverbs **465**

Focus

Lesson Overview

Objectives
- To identify comparative and superlative adverbs
- To understand how to form and use comparative and superlative adverbs correctly

Bellringer
Daily Language Activity

When students enter the classroom, have this assignment on the board: *Write a sentence giving advice on how teenagers can improve their study habits.*

See also *Daily Language Practice*

Motivating Activity

Discuss students' sentences in the Bellringer activity and have students identify and record on the board any comparative adverbs. Clarify what is being compared and what each adverb modifies.

Teach

☑ Teaching Tip

Most one-syllable adverbs form comparatives and superlatives with *-er, -est* (*harder, hardest*). All adverbs that end in *-ly* form comparatives and superlatives with *more, most* (*more quickly, most quickly*). Because virtually all adverbs longer than one syllable end in *-ly*, we can say that adverbs with two or more syllables follow the *more, most* pattern.

Cooperative Learning

Have students work in small groups to use these adverbs: *well, very, hard, boldly, luckily.* With each student writing a sentence, groups should compose a short story using at least three of the adverbs in the base, comparative, and superlative forms.

Adjectives and Adverbs

Resource Manager

📁 **Planning Resources**
- *Lesson Plans*

📓 **Transparencies**
- *Bellringer*
- *Daily Language Practice*
- *Two-Minute Skill Drill*

📁 **Other Print Resources**
- *Grammar and Composition Handbook*
- *Grammar Workbook,* Lesson 35

Two-Minute Skill Drill

Write the following phrases on the board: *sang loudly, rapidly changing, ran fast,* and *speaking quietly.* Have students write a sentence with each phrase, using the adverb in a comparative or superlative form.

See also Two-Minute Skill Drill Transparency 12.8

Practice and Assess

Answers: Exercise 15

1. earlier	11. least
2. later	12. earlier
3. best	13. more
4. more	14. most
5. most	15. further
6. less	16. more
7. further	17. most
8. more	18. More
9. best	19. sooner
10. more	20. more

Additional Resources

Grammar Workbook, Lesson 35

Close

Ask each student to write a paragraph comparing and contrasting two books he or she has read. Direct students to use some comparative and superlative adverbs in their writing. Have students trade papers and constructively evaluate each other's work.

Adjectives and Adverbs

Exercise 15   Using Comparative and Superlative Forms

Write the correct comparative or superlative form given in parentheses.

1. The Egyptians came to Crete (earlier, earliest) than all other peoples.
2. Did the Cretans arrive in Greece (later, more later) than the Egyptians?
3. Some people think the Cretans built the palace of Knossos (better, best) of all their buildings.
4. Its hundreds of rooms sheltered people (more, most) comfortably than other palaces.
5. Cretan ships sailed (more, most) swiftly of all early vessels.
6. Knossos was powerful and needed protection (less, least) frequently than other cities.
7. This civilization developed commercial trade (further, furthest) than the arts of war.
8. Cretans practiced their arts (more, most) enthusiastically than any other activity.
9. Noted for artistic achievements, perhaps they painted scenes of sports (better, best) of all.
10. Lively scenes appeared in their palace rooms (more, most) often than serious pictures.
11. Despite considerable research, we understand Cretan writings (less, least) well of all early languages.
12. Crete's culture began (earlier, earliest) than most.
13. We'll know more when we can (more, most) readily read the early Cretan inscriptions.
14. Sir Arthur Evans was the person who (more, most) successfully unearthed important discoveries.
15. Evans went even (further, furthest) by discovering the palace of King Minos, located in Knossos.
16. It is laid out (more, most) complexly than other buildings on Crete.
17. Evans decided it was (more, most) likely the labyrinth long-described in Greek legend.
18. (More, Most) recent discoveries may change our thinking.
19. In the legend, Theseus found his way out of the twisting passages (sooner, more soon) than was expected.
20. Theseus entered the labyrinth (more, less) readily, knowing he would be able to escape later.

Cultural Connections

Choosing Between Forms

In most cases in English, an adverb can be made comparative or superlative in form by adding either *-er* or *-est* to it or by preceding it with *more* and *most,* but not both. This may not be true in other languages. Point out to students who are learning English that only one form should be used at a time. For example, they would not say, *The Cretans built cities more earlier than the Greeks did.*

12.9 Using Adverbs and Adjectives

Adverbs and adjectives are often confused, especially when they are used after verbs. Predicate adjectives follow linking verbs, such as *be*, *seem*, *appear*, and *become*.

> The labor at Stonehenge was **hard** without machinery.
> This accomplishment still seems **brilliant** to some visitors.

In the first sentence the predicate adjective *hard* modifies the subject, *labor*. In the second sentence the predicate adjective *brilliant* modifies the subject, *accomplishment*.

Now read the sentences below.

> Bronze Age people worked **hard** at building Stonehenge.
> The sun shines **brilliantly** between two stones each year.

In each sentence the word in dark type is an adverb that describes an action verb. *Hard* describes *worked*, and *brilliantly* describes *shines*.

■ Use a **predicate adjective** after a linking verb, such as *be*, *seem*, *appear*, or *become*.

■ Use an **adverb** to describe an action verb.

People often confuse *good*, *bad*, *well*, and *badly*.

> They were **good** at studying the sky. [predicate adjective]
> An earthquake was **bad** for the project.
> [predicate adjective]
> Stonehenge still works **well** as a kind of calendar. [adverb]
> Weather **badly** affected Stonehenge's usefulness. [adverb]

Good and *bad* are adjectives. Use them after linking verbs. *Well* and *badly* are adverbs. Use them to describe action verbs. *Well* may also be used as an adjective when describing someone's health.

Adjectives and Adverbs

Focus

Lesson Overview

Objectives

- To distinguish between adverbs that follow verbs and predicate adjectives
- To use adverbs and predicate adjectives to add detail and to clarify writing and speech

Bellringer
Daily Language Activity

When students enter the classroom, have this assignment on the board: *Copy and revise the following sentence, adding a word that tells how the tourists walked:*

The tourists walked toward Stonehenge.

See also *Daily Language Practice*

Motivating Activity

Call on volunteers to share their revisions from the Bellringer activity. Then invite students to suggest words that could be added to the sentence to describe the tourists.

Teach

☑ Teaching Tip

Students may be misled by the many common one-syllable adverbs that are identical to adjectives. Write the following sentences on the board: *He opened the door <u>wide</u>; It works <u>fine</u>; It started <u>fast</u>.* Explain that the underscored words are actually adverbs and thus may correctly follow action verbs. They should not be confused with similar (*good, bad, easy, quick*) adjectives that may be used after linking verbs but are inappropriate after action verbs.

Resource Manager

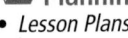

📁 **Planning Resources**
- *Lesson Plans*

🖳 **Transparencies**
- *Bellringer*
- *Daily Language Practice*

📁 **Other Print Resources**
- *Grammar and Composition Handbook*
- *Grammar Enrichment*, p. 25
- *Grammar Practice*, p. 25
- *Grammar Reteaching*, p. 27
- *Grammar Workbook*, Lesson 36

Practice and Assess

Answers: Exercise 16

1. adj.		6. adj.	
2. adv.		7. adj.	
3. adv.		8. adv.	
4. adv.		9. adv.	
5. adj.		10. adj.	

Answers: Exercise 17

1. impossible		11. visible	
2. enormous		12. completely	
3. separately		13. badly	
4. energetic		14. solidly	
5. incredible		15. cruelly	
6. diligently		16. definitely	
7. carefully		17. powerful	
8. well		18. equal	
9. intentional		19. horizontally	
10. different		20. close	

Additional Resources

📁 *Grammar Practice*, p. 25
📁 *Grammar Reteaching*, p. 27
📁 *Grammar Enrichment*, p. 25

📓 *Grammar Workbook*, Lesson 36

Close

Have each student use predicate adjectives and predicate adverbs to write a description of a special place he or she would like to visit. Students may find it helpful to brainstorm to develop a list of types of places to write about, such as national or state parks, theme parks, monuments, and museums. Suggest that students use a computer to work through each step of the writing process. Remind them to revise their writing as needed to make use of vivid and precise adjectives and adverbs.

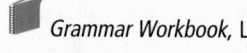
Adjectives and Adverbs

Exercise 16   Identifying Adjectives and Adverbs

Write *adjective* or *adverb* to identify the underlined word in each sentence.

1. The first bridges humans used were <u>natural</u>.
2. A tree trunk might lie <u>conveniently</u> across a stream.
3. One could <u>nervously</u> cross a stone bridge over a canyon.
4. Someone swung <u>daringly</u> across a river on a twisted vine.
5. The stone bridges of the Romans are still <u>visible</u>.
6. Bridges were <u>necessary</u> for military operations and communication.
7. Too much rhythmic shaking was <u>bad</u> for a bridge.
8. That's why soldiers <u>usually</u> broke step as they crossed a bridge.
9. Some Roman bridges still operate <u>well</u> after hundreds of years.
10. Their engineering skills were <u>amazing</u>.

Exercise 17   Distinguishing Between Adjectives and Adverbs

Write the correct word given in parentheses.

1. The work on Stonehenge seemed (impossible, impossibly).
2. Each stone at Stonehenge is (enormous, enormously).
3. Several groups worked on Stonehenge (separate, separately).
4. The inhabitants of Salisbury Plain were (energetic, energetically).
5. Their project at Stonehenge was (incredible, incredibly).
6. They worked (diligent, diligently) on a large, circular ditch.
7. Then they searched (careful, carefully) for huge stones.
8. They worked (good, well) on the construction of a stone wall inside the ditch.
9. The opening in the circle of stones is (intentional, intentionally).
10. The position of the stone at the opening is (different, differently).
11. An earth wall is (visible, visibly) at Stonehenge.
12. The wall (complete, completely) surrounds the area.
13. The work on Stonehenge progressed (bad, badly).
14. Did Druids build the stone circle so (solid, solidly)?
15. They may have (cruel, cruelly) sacrificed victims there.
16. Many (definitely, definite) believe an older people built it.
17. Even today the first sight of it is (powerful, powerfully).
18. The spaces between the huge stones are (equal, equally).
19. How were such heavy stones raised (horizontal, horizontally)?
20. Tourists cannot get (close, closely) to the stones.

Exploring Language

Using Adjectives and Adverbs

Help students to recognize patterns in adjective and adverb pairs. Some related adjectives and adverbs are *angry/angrily, bold/boldly, gentle/gently, greedy/greedily, quick/quickly, successful/successfully.* Students can create a sentence for each pair, using both the adjective and the adverb. (Example: *Angry people speak angrily.*) Students may wish to make their own lists of pairs or work with partners to create word pairs and sentences.

12.10 Avoiding Double Negatives

The adverb *not* is a negative word. **Negative words** express the idea of "no." *Not* often appears in a shortened form as part of a contraction. Study the words and their contracted forms below.

Contractions with *not*		
is not = isn't	cannot = can't	have not = haven't
was not = wasn't	could not = couldn't	had not = hadn't
were not = weren't	do not = don't	would not = wouldn't
will not = won't	did not = didn't	should not = shouldn't

In all of these words, the apostrophe replaces the *o* in *not*. In *can't* both an *n* and the *o* are omitted. *Will not* becomes *won't*.

Other words besides *not* may be used to express the negative. Each negative word has several opposites. These are **affirmative words,** or words that show the idea of "yes." Study the following list of negative and affirmative words.

Negative and Affirmative Words	
Negative	**Affirmative**
never	ever, always
nobody	anybody, somebody
none	one, all
no one	some, any
nothing	everyone, someone
nowhere	something, anything
scarcely, hardly	somewhere, anywhere

Two negative words used together in the same sentence create a **double negative.** You should avoid using double negatives in your writing. Only one negative word is necessary to convey a negative meaning.

You can correct a sentence that has a double negative in two ways: remove one of the negative words, or replace one of the negative words with an affirmative word.

Resource Manager

📁 **Planning Resources**
- *Lesson Plans*

📠 **Transparencies**
- *Bellringer*
- *Daily Language Practice*

📁 **Other Print Resources**
- *Grammar and Composition Handbook*
- *Grammar Enrichment*, p. 26
- *Grammar Practice*, p. 26
- *Grammar Reteaching*, p. 28
- *Grammar Workbook*, Lesson 37

Focus

Lesson Overview

Objectives
- To identify negative words, including contracted forms of *not*
- To use negative words correctly and to avoid double negatives in speaking and writing

 Bellringer
Daily Language Activity

When students enter the classroom, have this assignment on the board: *Copy the following incorrect sentence. Circle the two words that express the idea of "no."*

I do not have no good grade on this paper.

See also 📖 *Daily Language Practice*

Motivating Activity

Have a volunteer circle *not* and *no* in the Bellringer sentence on the board. Ask students to reword the sentence to avoid a double negative (I do not have a good grade on this paper.) Have students monitor their understanding and seek clarification as needed.

Teach

Critical Thinking
Read the following passage aloud, asking students to identify the double negatives.

> Well, I couldn't see no advantage in going where she was going, so I made up my mind I wouldn't try for it. But I never said so, because it would only make trouble, and wouldn't do no good.
>
> —Mark Twain
> *Adventures of Huckleberry Finn*

Adjectives and Adverbs

Practice and Assess

Answers: Exercise 18

1. were	11. didn't
2. could	12. would
3. any	13. was
4. could	14. were
5. had	15. could
6. No one	16. weren't
7. anything	17. anything
8. any	18. did
9. could	19. any
10. was	20. could

Answers: Exercise 19

1. wasn't	11. have not
2. doesn't	12. has not
3. will not	13. did not
4. aren't	14. is not
5. should not	15. are not
6. didn't	16. would not
7. mustn't	17. might not
8. won't	18. was not
9. shouldn't	19. cannot
10. isn't	20. could not

Additional Resources

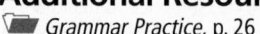 *Grammar Practice,* p. 26

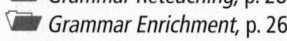 *Grammar Reteaching,* p. 28

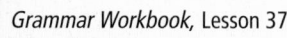 *Grammar Enrichment,* p. 26

Grammar Workbook, Lesson 37

Close

Have each student write a humorous paragraph about a house in which the appliances do not work properly. Tell students to describe how the appliances malfunction. Remind them to avoid double negatives in their writing. Ask students to share and constructively critique each other's paragraph.

Adjectives and Adverbs

Exercise 18   Using Negative Words Correctly

Write each sentence, using the correct word or words given in parentheses.

1. Houses with flat roofs (were, weren't) hardly useful in the North.
2. Thick snow (couldn't, could) never fall off the roof.
3. Snow wasn't (any, no) problem in the South.
4. No one in the West (could, couldn't) build better homes than the Pueblo Indians.
5. Before 1851 the world (had, hadn't) never seen a building like the Crystal Palace.
6. (No one, Anyone) ever missed visiting it.
7. The Crystal Palace was built of hardly (nothing, anything) except iron and glass.
8. Sir Joseph Paxton, the architect, didn't have (any, no) earlier models for the Crystal Palace.
9. No one (could, couldn't) believe the size of the Crystal Palace.
10. Sir Joseph (wasn't, was) not interested in a trial he was watching.
11. He (didn't, did) listen but instead planned the Crystal Palace.
12. Some people thought his dream (wouldn't, would) never be built.
13. Nothing (wasn't, was) spared for this giant structure.
14. Not even the trees on the site (weren't, were) left outside.
15. Visitors (couldn't, could) hardly believe their eyes.
16. Exhibitors (were, weren't) limited to one country.
17. Only a few countries didn't have (nothing, anything) there.
18. Visitors never (did, didn't) lose interest in seeing it.
19. The Crystal Palace didn't have (any, no) fireproofing.
20. In 1936 nothing (couldn't, could) stop it from burning down.

Exercise 19   Forming Contractions

Write the contraction or the words that form the contraction.

1. was not	6. did not	11. haven't	16. wouldn't
2. does not	7. must not	12. hasn't	17. mightn't
3. won't	8. will not	13. didn't	18. wasn't
4. are not	9. should not	14. isn't	19. can't
5. shouldn't	10. is not	15. aren't	20. couldn't

MEETING INDIVIDUAL NEEDS   **Less-Proficient Readers**

Creating a Reminder

To help students who have trouble remembering negative words, write those listed on page 469 on the board. Suggest that students copy the list in their journals and refer to it to help them decide whether a sentence contains a double negative.

Identifying Double Negatives

Have students who use double negatives in speaking and writing watch for these negative clue words: *never, barely, hardly, scarcely.* **L1**

Grammar Review

ADJECTIVES AND ADVERBS

The treasures of ancient Egypt were sought by many archaeologists, explorers, and fortune hunters. The following passage is from a story about the British archaeologist Howard Carter, who describes a king's burial place that he discovered. It is the pharaoh Tutankhamen's tomb, which is today the most famous of Egypt's royal treasures. The passage has been annotated to show some of the kinds of adjectives and adverbs covered in this unit.

Literature Model

from *Mummies, Tombs, and Treasure*
by Lila Perl

Carter was looking into the first of four rooms of a surprisingly small royal tomb. The Antechamber, as the first and largest room was called, was only about twelve by twenty-six feet, the measurements of a fair-sized living room. It was heaped with chairs, footstools, and chests of alabaster, ebony, and ivory, and strange couches of gilded wood in the form of animals, including a cow and a lion. Piled beneath the cow-bed were egg-shaped food containers made of clay.

Sealed doorways, one guarded by two gold-encrusted statues of Tutankhamen, led to the other three rooms of the tomb—an Annex that was even more jumbled than the Antechamber, the Burial Chamber in which the mummy lay, and a small room beyond that called the Treasury.

> **Intensifier**

> **Superlative form of the adjective *large***

> **Adjective**

> **Past participle used as an adjective**

> **Comparative form of the adjective *jumbled***

> **Definite article**

Adjectives and Adverbs

Grammar Review **471**

Teach

About the Literature

This passage is taken from Lila Perl's *Mummies, Tombs, and Treasure,* a book inspired by the author's extensive travel in Egypt and her visit to the Mummy Room of Egypt's Cairo Museum. Ms. Perl recalls that when she saw the preserved bodies of people who lived over 3,000 years ago, "I wanted to learn everything I could about Egyptian mummies, not only how they were made, but why."

After students read the passage, have them discuss the characters, setting, and mood, supporting their opinions with details from the passage. Ask them how the types of modifiers studied in Unit 12 contribute to the meaning of the passage.

Linking Grammar and Literature

☑ Teaching Tip

List on the board the types of modifiers covered in Unit 12: *articles, proper adjectives, demonstratives, comparative and superlative adjectives and adverbs, intensifiers,* and *negative words.* Ask students to be aware of examples of each type of modifier as the selection is read aloud. Call on students to explain each of the annotations regarding the highlighted modifiers.

Critical Thinking

Discuss with students the importance of comparison in describing what we see. Ask students to identify comparisons in Perl's writing. Point out that some comparisons, such as the words *surprisingly small,* compare an object (the tomb) to an abstract idea, (expected size). Ask students to find and explain other comparisons.

✔ ASSESSMENT OPTIONS

📁 *Tests with Answer Key and Rubrics*
Unit 12 Mastery Test, pp. 51–52

💾 *Testmaker*
Unit 12 Mastery Test

Resource Manager

📂 **Planning Resources**
• *Lesson Plans*

📂 **Other Print Resources**
• *Grammar and Composition Handbook*
• *Grammar Workbook,* Lessons 28–37; *Unit 5 Review; Cumulative Review:* Units 1–5

Practice and Assess

Answers: Exercise 1

1. <u>British</u> archaeologist
2. <u>some Egyptian</u> workers
3. <u>ancient</u> huts
4. <u>old</u> huts, <u>another</u> tomb
5. <u>empty</u> tomb, <u>popular</u> attraction
6. <u>first</u> view, <u>small</u> hole
7. <u>wealthy</u> patron
8. <u>large</u>, <u>cluttered</u> room
9. <u>sealed</u> doorways, <u>other</u> rooms
10. <u>windowless</u> room

Answers: Exercise 2

1. earliest
2. more elaborate
3. more daring
4. less secure
5. more curious
6. fewer
7. more important
8. happier
9. most anxious
10. smaller

Review: Exercise 1   **Identifying Adjectives**

For the sentences below, write the adjectives and the nouns they modify. Underline the adjectives. (Do not include articles *a, an, the.*)

SAMPLE   The passage gives a brief description of what Carter discovered.
ANSWER   <u>brief</u> description.

1. Howard Carter was a British archaeologist.
2. Carter hired some Egyptian workers to help him on the dig.
3. The team began to dig under ancient huts.
4. They had avoided the old huts, which were in front of another tomb.
5. The empty tomb of Ramses VI was a popular attraction for tourists.
6. Carter's first view of the Antechamber was through a small hole.
7. Before he went in, he sent for his wealthy patron, Lord Carnarvon.
8. The Antechamber turned out to be a large, cluttered room.
9. Carter had to go through sealed doorways to reach the other rooms.
10. The mummy lay in a windowless room.

Review: Exercise 2   **Using Comparative and Superlative Adjectives**

Write the correct comparative or superlative form of the adjective given in parentheses.

SAMPLE   The discovery was (good) than he had hoped.
ANSWER   better

1. The (early) graves of all Egyptians were small, shallow pits in the sand, covered with rocks.
2. As time went on, rich Egyptians wanted (elaborate) tombs.
3. Thieves got (daring) about breaking into the tombs and robbing them.
4. Unfortunately, the pyramids proved to be even (secure) than the old tombs.
5. Grave robbers were even (curious) about the riches inside of them.
6. As a result, archaeologists were finding (few) treasures than ever.
7. Carter knew that his discovery was (important) than anything he'd ever done.
8. Lord Carnarvon was even (happy) about opening the tomb.
9. "Can you see anything?" he asked in his (anxious) voice.
10. Tutankhamen's tomb was (small) than Carter had expected it to be.

Adjectives and Adverbs

Review: Exercise 3 **Identifying Adverbs**

Write each adverb and the word or words it modifies. Underline the adverb.

SAMPLE He slowly opened the door.
ANSWER <u>slowly</u> opened

1. Carter gazed through the small hole he had carefully made in the door.
2. The contents of the Antechamber were piled carelessly about the room.
3. Carter and Lord Carnarvon stared into the surprisingly small royal tomb.
4. Two statues of Tutankhamen led directly to three other rooms in the tomb.
5. Carter was not very surprised at the disorder that met his eyes.
6. He felt strongly that grave robbers had discovered the tombs before.
7. But they may have left hastily.
8. Cemetery officials had apparently surprised the thieves.
9. It seemed that they had tidied up the tomb incompletely.
10. The workers' huts had completely covered the entrance.

Review: Exercise 4 **Using Comparative and Superlative Adverbs**

Write the correct comparative or superlative form of the word given in parentheses.

SAMPLE Carter worked (diligently) on the Antechamber than on any other room.
ANSWER more diligently

1. Lord Carnarvon died (early) than expected, never having seen King Tut's coffin.
2. His death was viewed (suspiciously) by some than others.
3. People now approached the tomb (warily) than before.
4. Things also went (unpleasantly) for Carter for a while.
5. Government officials behaved (cooperatively) than he would have wished.
6. Even (unbelievably), they sealed the tomb, stopping Carter's work.
7. He left the country much (soon) than he had hoped.
8. He did return to work even (tirelessly) to finish the job.
9. He understood the tomb's significance (clearly) than the others did.
10. Nothing Carter had found so far could be valued (highly) than the innermost coffin of solid gold.

Answers: Exercise 3
1. had <u>carefully</u> made
2. were piled <u>carelessly</u>
3. <u>surprisingly</u> small
4. led <u>directly</u>
5. was <u>not</u>, <u>very</u> surprised
6. felt <u>strongly</u>, had discovered <u>before</u>
7. may have left <u>hastily</u>
8. had <u>apparently</u> surprised
9. had tidied up <u>incompletely</u>
   (You may want to allow students to ignore the *up*, to consider it an adverb, or to consider it as part of the verb.)
10. had <u>completely</u> covered

Answers: Exercise 4
1. earlier
2. more suspiciously
3. more warily
4. most unpleasantly
5. less cooperatively
6. more unbelievably
7. sooner
8. more tirelessly
9. more clearly
10. more highly

Adjectives and Adverbs

Answers: Exercise 5

1. worse
2. earliest
3. longer
4. better
5. smaller

Answers: Exercise 6

1. suddenly, adverb
2. slowly, adverb
3. anxiously, adverb
4. silent, adjective
5. Finally, adverb
6. actually, adverb
7. mysterious, adjective
8. badly, adverb
9. naturally, adverb
10. briefly, adverb

Adjectives and Adverbs

Review: Exercise 5 **Using Comparative and Superlative Adjectives and Adverbs**

Write each sentence, correctly inserting the comparative or superlative form of the adverb or adjective in parentheses.

1. The contents of the Annex were in even (bad) disarray than the nearby Antechamber.
2. The (early) mummies of all occurred naturally when people buried their dead in dry, sandy areas.
3. When the bodies dried out quickly, they lasted (long) than they would have lasted otherwise.
4. Drying out the body before burial meant that it would be (good) preserved than usual.
5. Wood, clay, and stone figures of servants were placed inside the tomb, but these figures were (small) than the dead person they were to serve.

Review: Exercise 6 **Distinguishing Between Adjectives and Adverbs**

Write the correct word given in parentheses and label it *adverb* or *adjective*.

SAMPLE He wrote down each discovery (careful, carefully).
ANSWER carefully, *adverb*

1. At first Carter could see nothing, as hot air escaping (sudden, suddenly) from the chamber caused his candle to flicker.
2. Then details of the room began to emerge (slow, slowly).
3. That's when Lord Carnarvon began to press him (anxious, anxiously).
4. Carter himself was (silent, silently) with wonder.
5. (Final, Finally), he managed to answer Lord Carnarvon.
6. Was there (actual, actually) such a thing as a mummy's curse?
7. Lord Carnarvon's death was somewhat (mysterious, mysteriously).
8. An insect bite on his cheek had become (bad, badly) infected.
9. Carter himself lived many more years, dying (natural, naturally) at the age of sixty-five.
10. One may wonder, though, why Tutankhamen reigned so (brief, briefly), dying at eighteen.

Review: Exercise 7

Proofreading

The following passage is about Charles Simonds, whose sculpture *Untitled* appears below. Rewrite the passage, correcting the errors in spelling, grammar, and usage. Add any missing punctuation. There are ten errors in all.

Charles Simonds

¹Charles Simonds created this here sculpture from clay. ²He use only water, glue, and the simplest tools to form the clay into both landscape and architecture. ³In many of his most simplest works, the color distinctions are very basic: red clay for landscape and gray clay for stone. ⁴The color of the clay helps define and separate different parts of them sculptures. ⁵Simonds's miniature dwellings demonstrate a interest in how people live and how their beliefs affect the structures they build. ⁶Clay is the material Simonds has been comfortablest with since childhood. ⁷While saveing money and increasing the variety of soil types and colors, Simonds enjoys the pleasure of recycling clays and sands from around the world.

⁸Simonds's sculptures convey a sense of history but they are his own archaeological interpretations. ⁹They arent miniature reconstructions. ¹⁰Of actual buildings or sites.

Charles Simonds, *Untitled,* 1982

Answers: Exercise 7 Proofreading

This proofreading activity provides editing practice with (1) the current or previous units' skills, (2) **Troubleshooter** errors, and (3) spelling errors. Students should be able to complete the exercise by referring to the units, the **Troubleshooter,** and a dictionary. (Note: A run-on sentence counts as one error.)

Error (Type of Error)

1. this sculpture (usage)
2. used (verb form)
3. simplest (double comparison)
4. those sculptures (usage)
5. an interest (an before a vowel sound)
6. most comfortable (incorrect superlative form)
7. saving (spelling)
8. history, but (run-on sentence)
9. aren't (contraction)
10. reconstructions of (sentence fragment)

Viewing the Art

Charles Simonds, *Untitled,* 1982

In 1971 artist Charles Simonds began a series of miniature buildings for an imaginary civilization, the Little People. The work shown above sits on a thirty-inch-square base and stands ten inches tall. Simonds left this clay-and-wood structure untitled, as he does many of his projects. Have students discuss Simond's archaeological interpretation of the untitled piece shown above. The artist creates his small clay structures along curbs and in vacant lots in New York City. Children who begin by staring and asking questions often end up working with Simonds. He completes every project the same day he begins. Some have been destroyed in less than an hour; others have lasted for years.

Grammar Review

Answers: Exercise 8
Mixed Review

1. good picture
2. These
3. greatly enjoyed
4. Egyptian
5. most interesting information
6. directly, were carved
7. This
8. many, these, sacred
9. very
10. nearby town
11. same, three, different
    (also accept *The*)
12. A, the
13. Greek, Egyptian
14. more readily
15. safely, pass
16. Other, helpful
17. earliest forms
18. 2
19. firmly, compressed
20. expensive

Close

Have students write sentences that contain labeled examples of the following: a comparative adverb, a comparative adjective, a superlative adverb, and a superlative adjective. Have students check one another's sentences to be sure they labeled the type of adjective or adverb in each sentence correctly.

Adjectives and Adverbs

Review: Exercise 8

Mixed Review

Write the word or words described in the parentheses after each sentence.

1. Because of the pyramids, we have a good picture of the way Egyptians lived. (adjective + the word it modifies)
2. These painted tomb walls tell us a lot. (demonstrative adjective)
3. We can see that the Egyptians greatly enjoyed music and beautiful things. (adverb + the word it modifies)
4. We learn of Egyptian beliefs about death. (proper adjective)
5. There is also most interesting information about the gods people believed in. (superlative adjective + the word it modifies)
6. Some pictures were carved directly into stone. (adverb + the word it modifies)
7. This picture writing is called hieroglyphics (hī ₂r ₂ glif′iks). (demonstrative adjective)
8. For many years, no one understood these sacred carvings. (three adjectives)
9. Then in 1799 an officer of the famous French general Napoleon found a black stone covered with very strange lettering. (intensifier)
10. The stone was immediately named after the nearby town of Rosetta. (adjective + the word it modifies)
11. The same message was written in three different languages. (three adjectives)
12. A French language specialist translated the Greek. (two articles)
13. He used the Greek inscription to figure out the other two forms, which were Egyptian hieroglyphics. (two proper adjectives)
14. Archaeologists could more readily decode the writings in the tombs. (comparative adverb)
15. These were spells and charms to help the dead pass safely through dangers. (adverb + the word it modifies)
16. Other writings also supplied helpful information. (two adjectives)
17. Papyrus was one of the earliest forms of paper. (superlative adjective + the word it modifies)
18. Tall stalks of papyrus grow along the banks of the Nile. (number of articles in the sentence)
19. After strips of the stalk were soaked in water, they were compressed firmly to form sheets. (adverb + the word it modifies)
20. Papyrus sheets were expensive. (predicate adjective)

Writing Application

Adjectives in Writing

The following passage is from *The Names* by N. Scott Momaday. Examine the passage, focusing on the italicized adjectives. Notice how Momaday brings his memories to life with adjectives that describe the people and places of his experience.

Some of my earliest memories are of the storms, the *hot* rain lashing down and lightning running on the sky—and the storm cellar into which my mother and I descended so *many* times when I was very *young*. For me that *little* room in the earth is an *unforgettable* place. Across the years I see my mother reading there on the *low, narrow* bench, the lamplight flickering on her face and on the *earthen* walls; I smell the *dank* odor of that room; and I hear the *great* weather raging at the door.

Techniques with Adjectives

Try to apply some of N. Scott Momaday's writing techniques when you write and revise your own work.

❶ Use sensory adjectives when appropriate to help readers see, hear, feel, touch, and smell the objects of your description:

GENERAL WORDS I smell the odor of that room.

MOMADAY'S VERSION I smell the *dank* odor of that room.

❷ Use comparative and superlative adjectives to more specifically define time and place in your descriptions:

GENERAL WORDS Some of my memories are of the storms . . .

MOMADAY'S VERSION Some of my *earliest* memories are of the storms . . .

TIME For more about the writing process, see **TIME Facing the Blank Page,** pp. 97–107.

Adjectives and Adverbs

Practice
Practice these techniques by revising the following passage. Rewrite the following passage, adding adjectives in the places indicated by carets ∧.

Shelly fanned her ∧ face with a ∧ piece of paper, struggling to keep cool in the ∧ heat. She crouched farther into the ∧ corner of the ∧ bus stop, but it was no use. Sweat was dripping down her neck in ∧ streams and her skirt was a ∧ mess. She had purposely waited for a ∧ bus, hoping to avoid the ∧ part of the day. Now she'd be ∧ to reach her grandmother's before dessert. Mmmm!

Writing Application **477**

Adjectives in Writing

Encourage students to read the autobiographical passage on this page silently. Then spark a discussion focusing on N. Scott Momaday's use of adjectives to convey sensory details and to make comparisons.

Techniques with Adjectives

Extend the discussion about using adjectives in writing by reviewing the passage on page 475 about Charles Simonds's sculpture. Then ask students to write a statement in their journals about using adjectives to convey sensory details and to make some comparisons.

Practice

The answers to this challenging and enriching activity will vary. Refer to Techniques with Adjectives as you evaluate student choices.

Sample:

Shelly fanned her sweaty face with a crisp piece of paper, struggling to keep cool in the scorching heat. She crouched farther into the shadiest corner of the tiny bus stop, but it was no use. Sweat was dripping down her neck in salty streams, and her skirt was a wrinkled mess. She had purposely waited for a later bus, hoping to avoid the hottest part of the day. Now she'd be lucky to reach her grandmother's before dessert. Mmmm!

✔ **ASSESSMENT OPTIONS**

📁 *Tests with Answer Key & Rubrics*
Unit 12 Mastery Test, pp. 51–52

💾 *Testmaker*
Unit 12 Mastery Test

You may wish to administer the Unit 12 Mastery Test at this point.

📼 *MindJogger Videoquizzes*

UNIT

13

Prepositions, Conjunctions, and Interjections

Objectives

- To develop an understanding of prepositions, conjunctions, interjections, and other parts of speech
- To use prepositions conjunctions, interjections, and other parts of speech correctly and effectively in writing and speaking

✔ ASSESSMENT OPTIONS

📁 *Tests with Answer Key & Rubrics*
Unit 13 Pretest, pp. 53–54
Unit 13 Mastery Test, pp. 55–56

💾 *Testmaker*
Unit 13 Pretest
Unit 13 Mastery Test

You may wish to administer the Unit 13 Pretest at this point.

Key to Ability Levels

L1 Level 1 activities are within the basic ability range of students.

L2 Level 2 activities are within the ability range of average students.

L3 Level 3 activities are more challenging activities.

478

Resource Manager

📁 **Planning Resources**
- *Lesson Plans*
- *Block Scheduling*

📽 **Transparencies**
- *Bellringer*
- *Daily Language Practice*
- *Two-Minute Skill Drill*

📁 **Other Print Resources**
- *Grammar and Composition Handbook*
- *Grammar Enrichment*
- *Grammar Practice*
- *Grammar Reteaching*
- *Grammar Workbook*
- *Tests with Answer Key and Rubrics*

📺 **Video**
- *MindJogger Videoquizzes*

💾 **Software**
- *Interactive Grammar and Language Workbook*
- *Language Arts PASS*
- *Presentation Plus!*
- *Testmaker*

💻 **Web Sites**
- *writerschoice.glencoe.com*

13.1 Prepositions and Prepositional Phrases

■ A **preposition** is a word that relates a noun or a pronoun to some other word in a sentence.

The paint **on** the canvas will dry very slowly.

The word *on* in the sentence above is a preposition. It shows the relationship of the nouns *paint* and *canvas*.

Commonly Used Prepositions				
about	at	down	of	to
above	before	during	off	toward
across	behind	for	on	under
after	below	from	out	until
against	beneath	in	outside	up
along	beside	inside	over	upon
among	between	into	since	with
around	beyond	like	through	within
as	by	near	throughout	without

A preposition can consist of more than one word.

You can use acrylic paint **instead of** oils.

Compound Prepositions			
according to	aside from	in front of	instead of
across from	because of	in place of	on account of
along with	far from	in spite of	on top of

■ A **prepositional phrase** is a group of words that begins with a preposition and ends with a noun or pronoun, which is called the **object of the preposition.**

Michelangelo was born **in a small town.**

13.1 Prepositions and Prepositional Phrases   **479**

Resource Manager

📁 **Planning Resources**
• *Lesson Plans*

📑 **Transparencies**
• *Bellringer*
• *Daily Language Practice*
• *Two-Minute Skill Drill*

📁 **Other Print Resources**
• *Grammar and Composition Handbook*
• *Grammar Enrichment*, p. 27
• *Grammar Practice*, p. 27
• *Grammer Reteaching*, p. 29
• *Grammar Workbook*, Lesson 38

Prepositions, Conjunctions, & Interjections

Focus

Lesson Overview

Objectives
• To identify prepositions, prepositional phrases, and objects of prepositions
• To use prepositions, prepositional phrases, and objects of prepositions correctly to clarify and enhance writing

🔔 **Bellringer**
Daily Language Activity

When students enter the classroom, have this assignment on the board: *List some phrases, such as* in front of the chalkboard, *that describe where your desk is located.*

See also 📑 *Daily Language Practice*

Motivating Activity

Have volunteers read aloud the phrases they wrote; list the phrases on the board. Inform students that a prepositional phrase contains a preposition plus the object of the preposition. Have them identify these elements in the phrases listed. Ask students to monitor their understanding of prepositional phrases and to seek clarification as needed.

Teach

☑ **Teaching Tip**

Have students read the following passage and identify prepositional phrases. Have them identify the preposition and the object in each prepositional phrase. Discuss students' answers. Ask them to support their responses with details from this lesson.

> Once they had liked painting pictures <u>with chemical fire</u>, swimming <u>in the canals</u> . . . , and talking <u>into the dawn</u> together <u>by the blue phosphorus portraits</u> <u>in the speaking room</u>.
>
> —Ray Bradbury
> *The Martian Chronicles*

Two-Minute Skill Drill

Write one of the sentences from the lesson on the board and then draw an arrow from the preposition to its object. To test students' grasp of this relationship, write several sentences on the board and ask volunteers to insert the arrows.

See also *Two-Minute Skill Drill Transparency 13.1*

Practice and Assess

Answers: Exercise 1

1. for, inspiration
2. on, artists
3. in, paintings
4. in, sculpture
5. in, statues
6. by, Michelangelo
7. of, genius
8. of, Sistine Chapel
9. on, scaffold
10. in, years
11. after, project
12. with, talents
13. from, marble
14. of, statues
15. According to, historians; in, Rome
16. of, youth
17. Among, statues
18. on, plaster
19. In, artwork
20. for, church
21. with, Leonardo da Vinci
22. of, poems
23. of, Italian Renaissance
24. in, museums
25. in, sculpture

Additional Resources

 *Grammar Practice*, p. 27
Grammar Reteaching, p. 28
Grammar Enrichment, p. 27

 Grammar Workbook, Lesson 38

Prepositions, Conjunctions, & Interjections

Exercise 1 Identifying Prepositional Phrases and Objects of Prepositions

Write each prepositional phrase. Draw a line under the preposition and circle the object of the preposition.

1. Some artists study Michelangelo's work for inspiration.
2. His work had a great influence on many other artists.
3. Artists see perfection in his paintings.
4. They also see it in his sculpture.
5. Everyone admires the passion he conveyed in his statues.
6. Architects study building designs by Michelangelo.
7. Most think him the embodiment of genius.
8. He painted the ceiling of the Sistine Chapel.
9. He lay on his back on a scaffold.
10. The chapel work was completed in three years.
11. His fellow artists honored him after this project.
12. Michelangelo was a man with many artistic talents.
13. He carved sculpture from marble.
14. His *David* is one of his best-known statues.
15. According to art historians, the *Pietà* in Rome is Michelangelo's only signed sculpture.
16. This sculpture was the most important work of his youth and won him much admiration.
17. Among his other statues are *Victory* and *Cupid Kneeling*.
18. Michelangelo sometimes painted on wet plaster.
19. In his artwork, he depicted the human body very realistically.
20. The artist designed a dome for a church.
21. Michelangelo once worked with Leonardo da Vinci.
22. Michelangelo was also the author of many poems.
23. He is often considered the greatest sculptor of the Italian Renaissance.
24. Today Michelangelo's beautiful paintings and sculpture can be seen in many Italian museums.
25. The physical strength and emotional tension in Michelangelo's sculpture still inspire viewers.

Close

Have students write a short paragraph briefly describing the kind of art a particular artist creates and their own reasons for liking or disliking it. Ask students to use prepositional phrases and to make sure each phrase begins with a preposition and contains a noun or pronoun object.

Exploring Language

Order in Prepositional Phrases

Prepositional phrases occur in all languages, but the order in which a preposition and its object occur may vary. In Japanese, for example, the order is the reverse of that in English—the object of the preposition comes first, and the preposition comes last.

13.2 Pronouns as Objects of Prepositions

When a pronoun is the object of a preposition, remember to use an object pronoun and not a subject pronoun.

> Nick handed the easel to Martha.
> Nick handed the easel to **her.**

In the example above, the object pronoun *her* replaces *Martha* as the object of the preposition *to.*

Sometimes a preposition will have a compound object consisting of a noun and pronoun. Remember to use an object pronoun in a compound object.

> I borrowed the palette from Nick and Martha.
> I borrowed the palette from Nick and **her.**
> Lloyd painted with Ayisha and **me.**

Object pronouns are used in the sentences above. In the second sentence, *Nick and her* is the compound object of the preposition from. In the third sentence, *Ayisha and me* is the compound object of the preposition *with.*

If you are unsure about whether to use a subject pronoun or an object pronoun, try saying the sentence aloud with only the pronoun following the preposition.

> I borrowed the palette from **her.**
> Lloyd painted with **me.**

The subject pronoun *who* is never the object of a preposition; only the object pronoun *whom* can be an object.

> The artist of **whom** I spoke has a show at the Whitney Museum.
> To **whom** did you lend the paint brushes?

Focus

Lesson Overview

Objectives

- To identify the correct object pronoun to use after a preposition
- To use object pronouns correctly and effectively in writing

Bellringer
Daily Language Activity

When students enter the classroom, have this assignment on the board: *Copy the following sentences on a piece of paper:*

Ian gave the book to me. Ian gave the book to you and me. Ian gave the book to us.

Underline the pronoun or pronouns in each sentence.

See also Daily Language Practice

> Prepositions, Conjunctions, & Interjections

Teach

Listening and Speaking

Tell students that a good technique for identifying the correct form of a pronoun that is used as a compound object of a preposition is to say the sentence aloud with only the pronoun following the preposition. Explain that this technique is particularly useful when the compound object of a preposition consists of two pronouns. To demonstrate, tell students to listen carefully as you read aloud the three sentences from the Bellringer activity. Then substitute the subject pronoun for the object pronoun (*I* for *me,* for example) and read the sentences aloud again. Ask students if they can "hear" that the object pronoun *me* is the correct pronoun form to use after the preposition. Repeat the activity using different prepositions and pronouns.

Resource Manager

Planning Resources
- *Lesson Plans*

Transparencies
- *Bellringer*
- *Daily Language Practice*
- *Two-Minute Skill Drill*

Other Print Resources
- *Grammar and Composition Handbook*
- *Grammar Enrichment,* p. 28
- *Grammar Practice,* p. 28
- *Grammar Workbook,* Lesson 39

⏰ **Two-Minute Skill Drill**

As you name pronouns, have students volunteer sentences using each pronoun as an object of a preposition. Ask classmates to constructively evaluate the sentences.

See also 🏁 *Two-Minute Skill Drill Transparency 13.2*

Practice and Assess

Answers: Exercise 2

1. her	11. them
2. whom	12. him
3. them	13. him
4. me	14. whom
5. her	15. them
6. him	16. them
7. me	17. him
8. him	18. him
9. them	19. him
10. me	20. him

Additional Resources

 Grammar Practice, p. 28

📁 *Grammar Reteaching*, p. 28

📁 *Grammar Enrichment*, p. 39

📖 *Grammar Workbook*, Lesson 39

Close

Give students five minutes to write a few sentences describing the kind of work they would create if they were artists. Tell them to use pronouns as objects of prepositions in their writing. Then ask volunteers to read their work aloud, pausing after reading each pronoun used as the object of a preposition. Have the class decide if the correct pronoun form was used and then ask them to support the answer with details from this lesson.

Prepositions, Conjunctions, & Interjections

Exercise 2   **Using Pronouns After Prepositions**

Write the correct pronoun in parentheses. Be sure each pronoun you choose makes sense in the sentence.

1. Nina said that a paper on Rembrandt has been assigned to Bernard and (she, her).
2. Rembrandt is an artist about (who, whom) many historians have written.
3. According to H. W. Janson and (them, they), Rembrandt's early work is highly realistic.
4. Bernard showed some slides to Nina and (I, me).
5. Then I set a series of pictures in front of everyone, including Bernard and (she, her).
6. They all felt familiar with Rembrandt. I asked if they could tell the difference between the artist Caravaggio and (he, him).
7. Aside from Bernard, Laticia, and (I, me), no one recognized Rembrandt's work.
8. In the seventeenth century, Rembrandt was very popular. Many residents of Amsterdam wanted portraits painted by (him, he).
9. Rembrandt painted many life-size portraits of (they, them).
10. Rembrandt's self-portraits were described by Nina and (I, me).
11. Besides Janson, many experts have analyzed Rembrandt's work. The writings by Janson and (them, they) have called Rembrandt's lighting dramatic.
12. Many students learned about art from (he, him).
13. Through (he, him) we are able to see the man's inner strength.
14. No one knows for (who, whom) Rembrandt painted many of his pictures.
15. Because of (they, them), Rembrandt could finally afford to paint whatever pictures he wanted.
16. Rembrandt showed the innermost feelings within (they, them).
17. Rembrandt painted the people and places he saw around (he, him).
18. Rembrandt was unique. Few painters in history can compare with (he, him).
19. Frans Hals portrayed his subjects in a different way from (he, him).
20. There were other famous seventeenth-century Dutch painters besides Frans Hals and (he, him).

Cooperative Learning

Using Object Pronouns with Prepositions

List object pronouns on the board. Then invite the class to make up simple sentences, such as *The teacher gives the book to Ken and Amanda.* Ask volunteers to act out the sentences. Begin by pointing to one student actor and asking the rest of the class to substitute an object pronoun for the student's name. Then point to the other student, both students, and so on.

13.3 Prepositional Phrases as Adjectives and Adverbs

■ A prepositional phrase can function as an **adjective,** modifying or describing a noun or a pronoun.

The fabrics **from the Orient** were quite beautiful.

These ancient hangings are tapestries **from other lands.**

In the first sentence above, the prepositional phrase *from the Orient* describes the subject of the sentence, *fabrics.* In the second sentence, the prepositional phrase *from other lands* describes the noun in the predicate, *tapestries.*

■ A prepositional phrase can also function as an **adverb,** modifying or describing a verb, an adjective, or another adverb.

Adverb Phrases Modifying a Verb, an Adjective, and an Adverb	
Describes a verb	The women are weaving **on looms.**
Describes an adjective	That fabric looks great **on you.**
Describes an adverb	She weaves fabric well **for her age.**

An adverb phrase tells *when, where,* or *how* an action takes place. The prepositional phrases in the chart below all modify the verb *work.*

How Adverb Phrases Modify Verbs	
When?	Weavers work **during the day.**
Where?	They work **in shops.**
How?	They work **with care.**

Resource Manager

 **Planning Resources**
- *Lesson Plans*

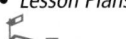 **Transparencies**
- *Bellringer*
- *Daily Language Practice*

 **Other Print Resources**
- *Grammar and Composition Handbook*
- *Grammar Enrichment,* p. 29
- *Grammar Practice,* p. 29
- *Grammar Workbook,* Lesson 40

Focus

Lesson Overview

Objectives
- To identify prepositional phrases that function as adjectives or adverbs
- To use prepositional phrases correctly as adjectives or adverbs

 Bellringer
Daily Language Activity

When students enter the classroom, have this assignment on the board: *Identify the part of speech of each of the following words: she* (pronoun), *coat* (noun *or* verb), *walked* (verb), *beautiful* (adjective), *loudly* (adverb).

See also *Daily Language Practice*

Motivating Activity

Have students share their answers to the Bellringer activity. Ask volunteers to create a phrase to describe each of the words. Explain to students that phrases that describe nouns and pronouns are called *adjective phrases* and those that modify a verb, adjective, or another adverb are called *adverb phrases.* Ask students to seek clarification as needed.

Teach

☑ **Teaching Tip**

Computer programs can help students determine whether a prepositional phrase is an adjective or an adverb phrase. Tell them that adverb phrases modifying verbs almost always can be moved to the beginning or the end of a sentence. Students can use the cut-and-paste function of their computer to move a phrase and see if the sentence still makes sense.

Prepositions, Conjunctions, & Interjections

Practice and Assess

Answers: Exercise 3

1. around the world, adj., weavers
2. with long grass strands, adv., worked
3. from ancient Egypt, adj., Paintings; by 5000 B.C., adv., had developed
4. with complex patterns, adj., Tapestries; in museums, adv., hang
5. about great people, adj., stories
6. from the Bible, adj., stories
7. of famous battles, adj., scenes; between great armies, adv., fought
8. of England, adj., invasion
9. in a French museum, adv., hangs
10. of the tapestry, adj., length
11. of the tapestry, adj., background
12. on horseback, adj., soldiers
13. throughout Europe, adj., Museums and palaces; of tapestry, adj., collections
14. for kings and queens, adv., worked
15. for the women, adj., clothing
16. during ceremonial dances, adv., wore
17. in the craft, adj., interest
18. around the country, adv., found; at work, adv., found; on big or small looms, adv., found
19. of materials, adj., variety; like wool, cotton, linen, angora, mohair, and synthetics, adj., materials; in their work, adv., use
20. with simple patterns, adv., begin
21. from many nations, adj., Patterns
22. for their designs, adv., famous
23. at home, adv., made; after a while, adv., become
24. by weavers and quilters, adv., made; at craft shows, adv., sold
25. of clothing, adj., articles; on their looms, adv., produce

Additional Resources

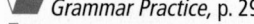 *Grammar Practice*, p. 29

Grammar Enrichment, p. 29

 Grammar Workbook, Lesson 40

[Sidebar, vertical:] Prepositions, Conjunctions, & Interjections

---

Exercise 3   Identifying Adjective and Adverb Phrases

Write each prepositional phrase and identify the phrase as an *adjective* phrase or an *adverb* phrase. Then write the word each phrase modifies.

1. Weavers around the world practice an ancient craft.
2. Early weavers worked with long grass strands.
3. Paintings from ancient Egypt show that weaving had developed by 5000 B.C.
4. Tapestries with complex patterns hang in museums.
5. These tapestries often illustrate stories about great people.
6. Many tapestries depict stories from the Bible.
7. Other tapestries show scenes of famous battles fought between great armies.
8. The famous *Bayeux Tapestry* illustrates William the Conqueror's invasion of England.
9. The tapestry hangs in a French museum.
10. You can walk the length of the tapestry—230 feet—and examine it closely, but you cannot touch it.
11. The background of the tapestry is white canvas.
12. You can easily see soldiers on horseback, the boats used crossing the English Channel, and battle scenes.
13. Museums and palaces throughout Europe often contain collections of tapestry.
14. Medieval weavers worked for kings and queens.
15. Hopi men traditionally wove clothing for the women.
16. Pueblo, Navajo, and Hopi women wore woven sashes during ceremonial dances.
17. Many people today have taken an interest in the craft.
18. They often may be found around the country diligently at work on big or small looms.
19. Contemporary weavers use a variety of materials—like wool, cotton, linen, angora, mohair, and synthetics—in their work.
20. Young weavers usually begin with simple patterns.
21. Patterns from many nations teach the necessary skills.
22. Weavers may become famous for their designs.
23. A tapestry made at home may become valuable after a while.
24. Articles made by weavers and quilters are often sold at craft shows.
25. Weavers can produce shawls, dresses, vests, and other articles of clothing on their looms.

Close

Have students write a short paragraph describing one of their hobbies. Ask them to use both adjective and adverb phrases in their descriptions. Partners can exchange descriptions and identify the adjective and adverb phrases.

MEETING INDIVIDUAL NEEDS — English Language Learners

Identifying Adjective and Adverb Phrases

Write on the board: *The sculptures from Africa were beautiful.* Circle the prepositional phrase and draw an arrow to *sculptures.* Explain that *from Africa* tells *what* sculptures. Write: *The students should come to the art museum.* Circle the prepositional phrase and draw an arrow to *come.* Explain that *to the art museum* tells *where* to come. Use *what?* to test for adjective phrases; *when? where? how?* for adverb phrases.

13.4   Conjunctions

■ A **coordinating conjunction** is a single word used to connect parts of a sentence, such as words or phrases. *And, but, or, so, yet, for,* and *nor* are used as coordinating conjunctions.

Using Coordinating Conjunctions	
Compound Subject	Ann **and** Flo studied art.
Compound Predicate	Georgia O'Keeffe studied art **and** taught it.
Compound Object of a Preposition	Art appeals to you **and** me.
Compound Sentence	I could go to art school, **or** I could study on my own.

To make a relationship between words or groups of words especially strong, use a correlative conjunction.

■ **Correlative conjunctions** are pairs of words used to connect words or phrases in a sentence. Correlative conjunctions include *both . . . and, either . . . or, neither . . . nor,* and *not only . . . but also.*

> **Both** New York **and** Paris are major art centers.

When a compound subject is joined by *and,* it is a plural subject. The verb must agree with the plural subject.

When a compound subject is joined by *or* or *nor,* the verb must agree with the nearest part of the subject.

> Jaime **and** Sue are artists.
> **Neither** the twins **nor** Carla **is** a good painter.

13.4 Conjunctions   **485**

Prepositions, Conjunctions, & Interjections

Focus

Lesson Overview

Objectives
- To identify and distinguish between coordinating and correlative conjunctions
- To use coordinating and correlative conjunctions correctly in writing

🔔 Bellringer
Daily Language Activity

When students enter the classroom, have this assignment on the board: *Copy the following sentence:*

> *Georgia O'Keeffe was born in Wisconsin, but she lived much of her life in New Mexico.*

Circle the conjunction. Underline the ideas that the conjunction joins.

See also  *Daily Language Practice*

Motivating Activity

With students' help, write on the board the correct response to the Bellringer activity. Point out that conjunctions join items of the same kind: words to words, phrases to phrases, and clauses to clauses. Use the example to elicit that a comma is used when a conjunction joins two sentences.

Teach

Critical Thinking
Have students identify and describe the type of error (needs correlative conjunction) in this sentence: Neither Marsha and Margo has agreed to exhibit her work.

Resource Manager

📁 **Planning Resources**
- *Lesson Plans*

 **Transparencies**
- *Bellringer*
- *Daily Language Practice*

📁 **Other Print Resources**
- *Grammar and Composition Handbook*
- *Grammar Enrichment,* p. 30
- *Grammar Practice,* p. 30
- *Grammar Reteaching,* p. 30
- *Grammar Workbook,* Lesson 41

Practice and Assess

Answers: Exercise 4

1. for; compound sentence
2. and; compound predicate
3. Both. . . and; compound subject
4. but; compound sentence
5. and; compound object of a preposition
6. Either. . . or; compound subject
7. but; compound predicate
8. and; compound object of a preposition
9. Not only. . . but also; compound sentence
10. and; compound object of a preposition

Answers: Exercise 5

1. enter; or
2. are; Both . . . and
3. attends; Neither . . . nor
4. have; and
5. are; Either . . . or
6. looks; Neither . . . nor
7. provide; or
8. enjoy; and
9. were; and
10. minds; Neither . . . nor
11. plan; Either . . . or
12. is; or
13. tour; and
14. appeals; Neither . . . nor
15. are; and
16. has; Neither . . . nor
17. laugh; Both . . . and
18. figure; and
19. depict; and
20. sparkle; Both . . . and

Additional Resources

 Grammar Practice, p. 30
Grammar Reteaching, p. 30
Grammar Enrichment, p. 30

Grammar Workbook, Lesson 41

Prepositions, Conjunctions, & Interjections

Exercise 4 — Identifying Conjunctions

Write each conjunction. Then write whether it joins a *compound subject,* a *compound predicate,* a *compound object of a preposition,* or a *compound sentence.*

1. Mari mixed the paint, for she wanted various colors.
2. Nora rented a studio and painted there on weekends.
3. Both painters and sculptors need good lighting.
4. The painter took many lessons, but students now learn from her.
5. Yvonne will attend the high school of art and design.
6. Either Maria or Cathy will accept the award for the class.
7. Jonathan enjoyed the art class but found it hard to paint with oils.
8. The school offers courses in architecture, computer graphics, and painting.
9. Not only is she a painter, but she is also a sculptor.
10. No admission is charged at the museum on Monday and Tuesday.

Exercise 5 — Making Compound Subjects and Verbs Agree

Write each sentence, using the correct verb form. Underline each conjunction.

1. Painters or sculptors (enter, enters) the exhibition.
2. Both this sketch and that sculpture (is, are) beautiful.
3. Neither the students nor their teacher (attends, attend) the show.
4. The judge and the artist (have, has) different opinions.
5. Either a famous painter or some critics (is, are) judging the show.
6. Neither this canvas nor the frame (look, looks) sturdy.
7. Watercolors or oils (provides, provide) rich tones.
8. Patty, George, and Peter (enjoys, enjoy) walking to the gallery on weekends.
9. The books and their favorite picture (was, were) on sale.
10. Neither the students nor the teacher (minds, mind) working in the art studio.
11. Either the artist or her students (plans, plan) to carry the heavy artwork.
12. Tracy or Scott (is, are) expected to take first prize in the competition.
13. Claudia and her friend (tours, tour) the modern art museum.
14. Neither the sculptures nor the painting (appeals, appeal) to the tour group.
15. Boston, New York, and Washington (is, are) exhibiting the artist's works.
16. Neither Matisse nor Picasso (has, have) paintings in the city's museums.
17. Both the students and their teacher (laughs, laugh) at a colorful mobile.
18. Light and atmosphere (figures, figure) prominently in Impressionist art.
19. Degas's paintings and sculpture often (depicts, depict) dancers.
20. Both the glass collection and the jewelry (sparkles, sparkle) brilliantly.

Close

Have students write a brief description of a special exhibit or event at your school. Ask them to circle all the conjunctions they use. Students may share their descriptions with a partner and constructively evaluate each other's work.

MEETING INDIVIDUAL NEEDS — Less-Proficient Readers

Using Conjunctions

The correlative conjunction *not only . . . but also* confuses many students. When *not only . . . but also* joins clauses, the first verb in the first clause precedes the subject instead of following it. For example: *Not only* does he draw, *but* he *also* sculpts. Have students practice joining clauses with different conjunctions and then introduce *not only . . . but also* to show the difference.

13.5 | Interjections

Sometimes people express very strong feelings in a short exclamation that may not be a complete sentence. These exclamations are called interjections.

■ An **interjection** is a word or group of words that expresses strong feeling. It has no grammatical connection to any other words in the sentence.

Any part of speech can be used as an interjection. These are some of the more common interjections.

Awesome!   Great!   Wow!

Commonly Used Interjections			
aha	good grief	no	well
alas	ha	oh	what
awesome	hey	oh, no	whoops
come on	hooray	oops	wow
gee	look	ouch	yes

An interjection that expresses a very strong feeling may stand alone, either before or after a sentence. Such interjections are followed by an exclamation mark.

Oh, no! The art museum is closed today.

When an interjection expresses a milder feeling, it appears as part of the sentence. It is separated from the rest of the sentence with a comma.

Oh, well, I'll just have to go tomorrow.

Interjections should be used sparingly. Overusing them will spoil their effectiveness.

13.5 Interjections **487**

Focus

Lesson Overview

Objectives
- To identify interjections
- To punctuate interjections correctly

Bellringer
Daily Language Activity

When students enter the classroom, have this assignment on the board: *Write the subject of each sentence: Go! Run! Walk!*

See also *Daily Language Practice*

Motivating Activity

Ask students to add the understood subject *you* to each imperative in the Bellringer activity: *You go! You run! You walk!* Now write a few interjections on the board (*aha, gee, wow*). Invite students to place *you* before each one. Students should see that the results are nonsensical—that interjections and imperatives are both brief and that they are often punctuated the same way, although they are different parts of speech.

Teach

☑ Grammar Tip

The term *interjection* comes from the Latin *interjicere,* "to throw between." Interjections are fragments—bursts of strong feeling. Unlike imperative sentences, they generally do not contain a verb. Occasionally a verb phrase is used as an interjection, as in *Come on! Go on! Get out!* In these rare cases, the verbs have an accepted idiomatic usage as interjections.

Resource Manager

📂 **Planning Resources**
- *Lesson Plans*

📂 **Transparencies**
- *Bellringer*
- *Daily Language Practice*
- *Two-Minute Skill Drill*

📂 **Other Print Resources**
- *Grammar and Composition Handbook*
- *Grammar Enrichment,* p. 30
- *Grammar Practice,* p. 30
- *Grammar Reteaching,* p. 30
- *Grammar Workbook,* Lesson 41

Practice and Assess

Answers: Exercise 6

1. Oh	11. Awesome
2. My	12. No way
3. Phew	13. Oops
4. Hooray	14. Well
5. Golly	15. Gee
6. Wow	16. Really
7. Hey	17. alas
8. Yes	18. sorry
9. Come on	19. Gosh
10. Look	20. Oh, no

Answers: Exercise 7

Answers will vary, but some suggestions are given below.

1. Awesome	6. Yes
2. Gosh	7. Wow
3. Amazing	8. Incredible
4. Gee	9. Boy
5. Whew	10. alas

Two-Minute Skill Drill

Read aloud five interjections from the list on page 487. Have volunteers offer their own sentences using interjections of their choice.

See also *Two-Minute Skill Drill Transparency 13.5*

Additional Resources

📁 *Grammar Practice*, p. 30
📁 *Grammar Reteaching*, p. 30
📁 *Grammar Enrichment*, p. 30

📓 *Grammar Workbook*, Lesson 41

488

Prepositions, Conjunctions, & Interjections

Exercise 6　Identifying Interjections

Write the interjections.

1. Oh, I am going to be late for my painting class.
2. My! I have never seen anyone who could sketch that fast.
3. It certainly is hard work to stretch this canvas tight. Phew!
4. We may be able to get an interview with a famous artist. Hooray!
5. Golly, I hope she will autograph one of her prints for me.
6. Wow! The colors in that painting hurt my eyes.
7. Hey! Where are you going?
8. Yes! That one's definitely my favorite.
9. Come on, I want to show you a painting by Salvador Dali.
10. Have you ever seen such images? Look!
11. That clock looks as though it melted. Awesome!
12. No way! I prefer this painting by Chagall.
13. Oops, those people seem to be floating.
14. Well, don't you think these young artists make Picasso look serious?
15. Gee, I don't know.
16. Really! He seems old-fashioned by comparison.
17. I would like to see a few more paintings, but it is time to leave, alas.
18. Sorry, I didn't notice you already had a brush.
19. Gosh! I never knew you could draw such a good likeness.
20. Oh, no! The paint spilled all over the floor.

Exercise 7　Using Interjections

Write each sentence, adding an interjection in the blank space. Be sure that the interjection you choose expresses the correct feeling for the sentence.

1. Up close you can hardly tell this is a bridge. _____!
2. _____! Did you know that the Impressionists were criticized at first?
3. _____! These paintings by Monet are all of the same cathedral.
4. _____, drawing in the style of the Impressionists is hard.
5. I knew I would finally get the color right. _____!
6. _____, this is certainly the prettiest one so far.
7. _____! The violin in this painting by Picasso is in pieces.
8. This canvas is solid black. _____!
9. _____, Picasso's *Guernica* is an enormous painting.
10. My feet are too tired to walk any farther, _____.

Close

Invite students to find some unfamiliar interjections in a piece of literature, such as a Shakespearean play or a Winnie the Pooh story. They can use context to identify interjections, such as the Elizabethan *fie* or the Victorian *bother*.

Cooperative Learning

Using Interjections

Interjections are often used in dialogue to express emotion through informal speech. Have students work in small groups to create comic strip panels. Tell them to use some interjections in the dialogue in the speech balloons. Have groups share their comic strips and discuss the use of interjections in the strips.

13.6 Finding All the Parts of Speech

Each word in a sentence performs a particular job. Each word can be put into a particular category called a **part of speech.** The part of speech of a word depends on the job that the word performs in the sentence. The same word may be classified as one part of speech in one sentence and as a different part of speech in another.

You have learned about all eight parts of speech. They include *nouns, pronouns, verbs, adjectives, adverbs, prepositions, conjunctions,* and *interjections.* The following sentence contains at least one example of each part of speech

Wow, she is artistic and paints well with watercolors.

Artist unknown, China, *Woman Painting*, 18th c.

Parts of Speech		
Word	**Part of Speech**	**Function**
Wow	Interjection	Expresses strong feeling
she	Pronoun	Takes the place of a noun
is	Verb (linking)	Links *she* with *artistic*
artistic	Adjective	Describes the subject *she*
and	Conjunction	Joins two parts of compound predicate
paints	Verb (action)	Names an action
well	Adverb	Describes the verb *paints*
with	Preposition	Relates the words *paints* and *watercolors*
watercolors	Noun	Object of the preposition *with*

13.6 Finding All the Parts of Speech **489**

Prepositions, Conjunctions, & Interjections

Focus

Lesson Overview

Objectives
- To identify the part of speech of every word in a sentence
- To use all parts of speech correctly in writing

Bellringer
Daily Language Activity

When students enter the classroom, have this assignment on the board: *Write a definition for each of the following parts of speech: noun, pronoun, verb, adjective, adverb, preposition, conjunction, interjection.*

See also *Daily Language Practice*

Motivating Activity

Ask students to list the part of speech of each underlined word in the following passage (*altar*—noun; *is*—verb; *small*—adjective; *it*—pronoun; *resembles*—verb; *for*—preposition).

The <u>altar</u> <u>is</u> about the size of a <u>small</u> upturned drawer, painted in red lacquer. In a way, <u>it</u> <u>resembles</u> a miniature stage <u>for</u> a Chinese play.

—Amy Tan
The Kitchen God's Wife

Teach

Cross-Reference: Grammar

For instruction and practice with nouns, refer students to Lesson 9.1. For instruction and practice with personal pronouns, refer students to Lesson 11.1.

Resource Manager

Planning Resources
- *Lesson Plans*

Transparencies
- *Bellringer*
- *Daily Language Practice*

Other Print Resources
- *Grammar and Composition Handbook*
- *Grammar Enrichment*
- *Grammar Practice*
- *Grammar Reteaching,* p. 31
- *Grammar Workbook,* Units 2–6

Practice and Assess

Answers: Exercise 8

1. colored—adjective; clays—noun
2. Sometimes—adverb; dries— action verb; quickly—adverb
3. Wow—interjection; statue—noun; is—linking verb
4. Aretha—noun; with—preposition; or—conjunction
5. He—pronoun; realistic—adjective

Answers: Exercise 9

Answers may vary, but some suggestions are given below.

1. Arthur, in
2. to, train
3. they, bus
4. He, paintings
5. overwhelmingly
6. They, inviting
7. enjoyed, and
8. Enthusiastically, examined
9. both, and
10. Phew, seen
11. quickly, to
12. both, and
13. Marisol, dessert
14. with
15. examined
16. Hey! see
17. tired, complained
18. slowly
19. joggers, in
20. Wow! beautiful

Additional Resources

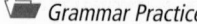 *Grammar Practice*
Grammar Reteaching, p. 31
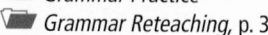 *Grammar Enrichment*

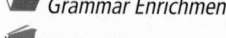 *Grammar Workbook*, Units 2–6

Close

Have students use all eight parts of speech in a written description of a visit to a museum or community center. Invite them to check one another's descriptions.

Prepositions, Conjunctions, & Interjections

Exercise 8 — Identifying Parts of Speech

Write each underlined word and its part of speech. If the word is a verb, identify it as an *action verb* or a *linking verb*.

1. I often sculpt with colored clays.
2. Sometimes the clay dries too quickly.
3. Wow! That statue is enormous.
4. Does Aretha sculpt with clay or stone?
5. He sculpts realistic heads.

Exercise 9 — Using Parts of Speech

The parentheses in each of the following sentences describe a word that you must add to complete the sentence. Be sure your finished sentences make sense.

1. Hector, Marisol, and (proper noun) visited an art museum (preposition) New York City.
2. To get (preposition) the museum, they took a (common noun).
3. At Fifth Avenue, (pronoun) transferred to a (common noun).
4. (Pronoun) saw a great many (common noun).
5. Hector liked the Impressionist paintings (adverb).
6. (Pronoun) thought Claude Monet's paintings were (adjective).
7. Marisol (action verb) two Americans: Mary Cassatt (conjunction) Winslow Homer.
8. (Adverb) they (action verb) the Post-Impressionists.
9. Hector loved (correlative conjunction) van Gogh (correlative conjunction) Rousseau.
10. "(Interjection)!" said Marisol. "I think we've (action verb) too much art."
11. Walking (adverb), they headed (preposition) the cafeteria.
12. Hector wanted (correlative conjunction) a bowl of chili (correlative conjunction) a hamburger.
13. (Proper noun) selected a dish of chocolate ice cream for (common noun).
14. Marisol paid the bill (preposition) money she earned baby-sitting.
15. Hector and Marisol (action verb) the museum guide while they were eating.
16. "(Interjection)! I want to (action verb) the Egyptian mummies," Hector said.
17. "We're too (adjective)," (action verb) Marisol.
18. Instead, they strolled (adverb) through Central Park.
19. Bicyclists, walkers, and (common noun) crowded the streets and sidewalks (preposition) the park.
20. "(Interjection)!" Hector said. "It's so (adjective) outside."

MEETING INDIVIDUAL NEEDS — **Less-Proficient Readers**

Tests for Identifying Main Parts of Speech

Here are some simple tests for students who have difficulty identifying the main parts of speech. Nouns: A common noun follows an article (a, an, the) and can be made plural (the book, the books). Verbs: A verb can be expressed in different tenses (sing, sang, will sing, has-sung). Adjectives: An adjective that modifies a noun typically answers a question about the noun—whose? how many? or what kind of? Adverbs: An adverb that modifies a verb usually can be moved within the sentence (John became worried soon; Soon John became worried).

Grammar Review

PREPOSITIONS, CONJUNCTIONS, AND INTERJECTIONS

This Chinese American folktale tells the story of a painted horse that comes to life. The passage has been annotated to show some of the parts of speech covered in this unit.

Literature Model

from *The Magical Horse*

by Laurence Yep

As the boy sat with his body aching from the hard work and eating his cold rice, he gazed up at the painting. His father had caught the horse as if it were suspended upon one hoof. And as he watched, the horse's sides seemed to heave in the moonlight—as if it were breathing in the incense. On a whim, Sunny set out feed for his painted horse just as he did for the other animals.

He slept among the beasts for warmth, so he was not surprised when he felt an animal's warm breath blow on him. When a nose nudged him, he sat up irritated, intending to shove the creature away, but his hand paused in the air.

By the light of the moon, he saw a silvery horse standing over him. He looked over at the wall where the painting had been and saw that the canvas was empty. The next thing he knew, he was on the back of the horse, his hands clinging to the flying mane, the horse's hooves booming rhythmically along a road that gleamed like a silver ribbon winding up into the sky.

> Preposition

> Prepositional phrase (adverb phrase)

> Pronoun as object of the preposition *on*

> Prepositional phrase (adjective phrase)

> Coordinating conjunction

Grammar Review **491**

Prepositions, Conjunctions, & Interjections

Teach

About the Literature

Explain that the review contains a passage from *The Magical Horse* by Lawrence Yep, followed by exercises on related topics. Initiate a discussion of its characters, setting, and mood. Ask students to focus on the highlighted words in the passage. Then ask students to identify the prepositional phrases that are not highlighted and determine whether each phrase functions as an adjective or as an adverb. Next have students identify the conjunctions that are not highlighted. Ask whether there are any interjections. (No)

Linking Grammar and Literature

Cooperative Learning

Organize students into small groups and ask each group to discuss the passage from *The Magical Horse* and consider what might happen in the story after Sunny rides the horse. After the groups have agreed on their version of the story's ending, have each group share its ending with the class.

Listening and Speaking

Ask students to discuss some inanimate object they would like to see come to life: a figure in a painting, a favorite possession, a character in a book. If a chair were to come to life, for example, what would they say to it? What would the object say to them? Encourage students to use what they have learned about prepositions, conjunctions, and interjections in their responses.

✔ ASSESSMENT OPTIONS

📂 *Tests with Answer Key & Rubrics*
Unit 13 Mastery Test, pp. 55–56

💾 *Testmaker*
Unit 13 Mastery Test

Resource Manager

📂 **Planning Resources**
• *Lesson Plans*

📂 **Other Print Resources**
• *Grammar and Composition Handbook*
• *Grammar Workbook,* Lessons 38–41; Unit 6 *Review; Cumulative Review:* Units 1–6

Practice and Assess

Answers: Exercise 1

1. for (him)
2. among the (animals)
3. against the (wall)
4. down the (road)
5. of (art)
6. for industrial (products)
7. Among the different (kinds); of (art)
8. Throughout the (museum); of fine (sculpture)
9. in the sculpture (garden); beside the (museum)
10. Because of (weather); in (color) and (texture)
11. at (sculpture); around (it)
12. from many (materials); of (clay); of (marble); of (stone)
13. from (marble)
14. for (models)
15. in (bronze)
16. of (cloth); to his (dancers)
17. from (wood)
18. into a (sculpture)
19. in the (wind)
20. in front of the (building)
21. from the (ceiling)
22. of (sculpture); of (Liberty); in (height)
23. of the (statue); from (France)
24. On account of its great (size); from (France); to the (United States); in several (pieces)
25. inside the (Statue); of (Liberty)

Grammar Review

Review: Exercise 1 **Identifying Prepositional Phrases and Objects of Prepositions**

Write each prepositional phrase. Underline the preposition and circle the object. Note that there may be more than one prepositional phrase in each sentence.

SAMPLE   The horse on the canvas that his father painted seemed alive.
ANSWER   on the (canvas)

1. Sunny set out food for him.
2. The boy slept among the animals.
3. When he awoke, the empty canvas stood against the wall.
4. The horse and the boy galloped down the road.
5. Painting is only one form of art.
6. Other forms include sculpture, photography, printmaking, and designs for industrial products.
7. Among the different kinds of art, sculpture is very popular.
8. Throughout the museum are many examples of fine sculpture.
9. Large pieces are located in the sculpture garden beside the museum.
10. Because of weather, sculpture that is placed outdoors can change in color and texture.
11. When you look at sculpture, moving around it helps you see it all.
12. Sculpture can be made from many materials—lumps of clay, slabs of marble, even small pieces of stone.
13. Carving a statue from marble takes great technical skill.
14. Some artists use clay for models.
15. Rodin cast his sculptures in bronze.
16. Degas added ribbons and bits of cloth to his dancers.
17. Some artists make their sculptures from wood.
18. Old, recycled materials can be incorporated into a sculpture.
19. Sculptures that move in the wind are called mobiles.
20. The giant Calder mobile in front of the building revolves.
21. Some mobiles hang from the ceiling.
22. One piece of sculpture—the Statue of Liberty—is 151 feet in height.
23. The sculptor of the statue, Bartholdi, was from France.
24. On account of its great size, the statue was shipped from France to the United States in several pieces.
25. Visitors can go inside the Statue of Liberty.

Prepositions, Conjunctions, & Interjections

Review: Exercise 2   **Using Pronouns After Prepositions**

Write the correct pronoun in parentheses. Be sure each pronoun you choose makes sense in the sentence. Remember to use an object pronoun and not a subject pronoun after a preposition. The subject pronoun *who* is never the object of a preposition; only the object pronoun *whom* can be used after a preposition.

1. Alicia and Mark stared at the height of the buildings around (they, them).
2. "Look at the buildings in front of (we, us)!" Mark exclaimed.
3. Alicia added, "Because of (they, them), no sun reaches us here on the street."
4. *Skyscrapers* is the word used for (they, them).
5. Before (they, them), most tall buildings were made of stone.
6. Mark pointed out to (she, her) a beautiful library made of granite.
7. "Stand between the library and (I, me)," Mark said.
8. The skyscraper above (she, her) dwarfed the library.
9. Tall buildings are supported by steel framing inside (they, them).
10. Two buildings near Mark and (she, her) were designed by the famous architect Louis Sullivan.
11. Because of (he, him) and other innovative architects, Chicago became famous for its architecture.
12. Skyscrapers in the Art Deco style, Alicia explained, often have towers on top of (they, them).
13. The columns near Mark and (she, her) help support the building.
14. The Gothic-style building across from (they, them) has arched entrances and small arched windows.
15. Mr. Smith went with (they, them) to the city.
16. He visited the Sears Tower without (they, them).
17. The tower, then the tallest building in the world, appealed to (he, him).
18. According to (he, him), the Sears Tower is a very safe building.
19. Mark and Alicia took the elevator to the skydeck, and six other students rode with (they, them).
20. From (they, them) the students learned that the tower has 110 stories.
21. Below Paul and (they, them) lay Lake Michigan.
22. The aluminum-clad exterior next to (she, her) felt smooth.
23. The columns between you and (I, me) resemble those of ancient Greece.
24. Paul examined the fierce-looking gargoyles above (he, him).
25. Behind Alicia and (he, him) stood the famous Wrigley Building.

Grammar Review   **493**

Answers: Exercise 2
1. them
2. us
3. them
4. them
5. them
6. her
7. me
8. her
9. them
10. her
11. him
12. them
13. her
14. them
15. them
16. them
17. him
18. him
19. them
20. them
21. them
22. her
23. me
24. him
25. him

Prepositions, Conjunctions, & Interjections

Answers: Exercise 3

1. on the computer, program
2. with a color monitor, computer
3. of colors, choice
4. of the new wallpaper, color
5. from Mexico, design
6. for my mother, picture
7. of dancers, image
8. around the word, circle
9. of the students, few
10. for beginners, class

Answers: Exercise 4

1. to Boston, went
2. along the Freedom Trail, walked
3. for a moment, stopped; at the old Granary Burying Ground, stopped
4. with great care, crossed
5. into the Old South Meeting House, walked
6. in detail, showed
7. from those docks, sailed
8. in that room, protested
9. into the harbor, splashed
10. on the famous swan boats, rode

Review: Exercise 3   **Identifying Adjective Phrases**

Write each adjective prepositional phrase. Then write the word the phrase modifies.

SAMPLE   The computer drawing of the sports car was extremely realistic.
ANSWER   of the sports car, drawing

1. I am learning a drawing program on the computer.
2. It's the only computer with a color monitor.
3. The program gives me a wide choice of colors.
4. The color of the new wallpaper is too bright.
5. I can easily copy this detailed and colorful design from Mexico.
6. The picture for my mother will surely please her.
7. This screen image of dancers can actually move.
8. The circle around the word was drawn by a computer.
9. Only a few of the students have computers they can use.
10. Michael, Christopher, and Jennifer greatly enjoyed taking the computer class for beginners.

Review: Exercise 4   **Identifying Adverb Phrases**

Write each adverb prepositional phrase. Then write the word the phrase modifies.

SAMPLE   The students and their chaperones traveled by train.
ANSWER   by train, traveled

1. The entire class went to Boston last week.
2. The students walked along the Freedom Trail.
3. They stopped for a moment at the Old Granary Burial Ground.
4. The students crossed with great care.
5. They walked into the Old South Meeting House.
6. The display showed in detail the city's growth and history.
7. Tall ships once sailed from those docks.
8. American patriots protested unfair taxes in that room.
9. They saw where tea splashed into the harbor.
10. Peter, Sylvia, and John rode on the famous swan boats.

Review: Exercise 5   Identifying Adjective and Adverb Phrases

Write each prepositional phrase, and write whether it is an *adjective* phrase or an *adverb* phrase. There may be more than one prepositional phrase in each sentence.

SAMPLE   People express through folklore their beliefs and customs.
ANSWER   through folklore, adverb

1. Fairy tales, legends, myths, even dances—all are considered part of folklore.
2. Some folklore is handed down through games.
3. There must be two versions of a story.
4. The story must have been told in more than one place and in more than one time period.
5. Ancient songs tell stories from the past too.
6. Jakob and Wilhelm Grimm collected folk stories from common people in Germany.
7. They published the stories in a book called *Grimm's Fairy Tales*.
8. Myths help explain the origins of people and of the world.
9. Fictional stories about animals or human beings are called folk tales.
10. Many folk tales have been changed into very successful movies.

Review: Exercise 6   Using Conjunctions

Rewrite each sentence, inserting the most appropriate conjunction (word or word pair) in the blank or blanks provided.

SAMPLE   The father wanted to create a perfect horse,
_____ _____ he painted without resting.

ANSWER   The father wanted to create a perfect horse,
and so he painted without resting.

1. When the painting was finished, _____ Sunny _____ his father admired the magnificent horse.
2. _____ Sunny _____ his father knew that the horse would come to life.
3. The father was old _____ tired from hard work.
4. The painter died, _____ his spirit entered into the horse in the painting.
5. Sunny _____ _____ buried his father, _____ _____ earned the money for the funeral.

Prepositions, Conjunctions, & Interjections

Answers: Exercise 5

1. of folklore; adjective phrase
2. through games; adverb phrase
3. of a story; adjective phrase
4. in more than one place, in more than one time period; adverb phrases
5. from the past; adjective phrase
6. from common people, in Germany; adjective phrases
7. in a book; adverb phrase
8. of people, of the world; adjective phrases
9. about animals or human beings; adjective phrase
10. into very successful movies; adverb phrase

Answers: Exercise 6

Answers will vary, but some suggestions are given below.

1. both, and
2. Neither, nor
3. and
4. but
5. not only, but also

Answers: Exercise 7

1. like; Both . . . and
2. is; Neither . . . nor
3. are; and
4. block; Either . . . or
5. make; Both . . . and
6. captures; Neither . . . nor
7. are; and
8. lacks; Neither . . . nor
9. sprawl; and
10. suffer; Both . . . and

Answers: Exercise 8

Answers will vary, but some suggestions are given below.
1. Wow!
2. Hey!
3. Gee,
4. Come on!
5. Well

Prepositions, Conjunctions, & Interjections

Review: Exercise 7   Making Compound Subjects and Verbs Agree

Write each sentence, using correct verb form. Write each coordinating or correlative conjunction.

SAMPLE   Neither Alexandra nor her mother (wants, want) to carry the camera.
ANSWER   <u>Neither</u> Alexandra <u>nor</u> her mother wants to carry the camera.

1. Both Alexandra and her parents (likes, like) to take pictures.
2. Neither San Francisco nor Los Angeles (is, are) on their itinerary.
3. Eating in a Chinese restaurant and riding on a cable car (is, are) on their list of things to do.
4. Either the fog or the clouds often (blocks, block) the view from Twin Peaks.
5. Both the sea otters and the crashing surf (makes, make) the trip worthwhile.
6. Neither the redwoods nor the shoreline (captures, capture) their interest.
7. Carmel and the Hearst Castle (is, are) on the way to Los Angeles.
8. Neither Carmel nor Monterey (lacks, lack) art galleries.
9. The city and its suburbs (sprawls, sprawl) for miles in every direction.
10. Both the beaches and homes along the coast (suffers, suffer) every time there's a big storm.

Review: Exercise 8   Using Interjections

The following sentences are based on passages in "The Magical Horse" that do not appear in this textbook. Rewrite each sentence, inserting an appropriate interjection in the blank. More than one answer may be possible.

SAMPLE   "_____!" cried Sunny when he rode the horse for the first time.
ANSWER   "Hooray!" cried Sunny when he rode the horse for the first time.

1. Sunny woke up the next morning and found that the feed for the painted horse was gone. "_____!" exclaimed the boy. "It wasn't a dream."
2. Every night Sunny called out, "_____! Let's go for a ride."
3. One evening the boy said, "_____, I'd like to see the king's palace."
4. "_____!" shouted the prince to his servant as the horse sped past the palace.
5. _____, the prince decided then and there to take the horse away.

Review: Exercise 9

Proofreading

The following passage is about artist Helen Oji, whose work appears below. Rewrite the passage, correcting the errors in spelling, grammar, and usage. Add any missing punctuation. There are ten errors.

Helen Oji

¹Helen Oji paints subjets from nature. ²A row of volcanoes are shown in one painting by she. ³Horses, a group of fish swimming in swiftly moving water and a brightly colored bird in flight is some of her subjects. ⁴Both movement and intense energy characterizes Oji's explosive style.

⁵In the painting on this page, neither the cool white horse nor the fiery red swirls is the focus. ⁶Instead, the viewer's attention is pulled to the interaction between they. ⁷The works bold, thick brushstrokes help raise the picture from the canvas. ⁸Neither the magical horse in Laurence Yep's folktale nor the horse in the painting seem quite real.

Helen Oji, *H.P.*, 1986

Answers: Exercise 9
Proofreading

This proofreading activity provides editing practice with (1) the current or previous units' skills, (2) the **Troubleshooter** errors, and (3) spelling errors. Students should be able to complete the exercise by referring to the units, the **Troubleshooter,** and a dictionary.

Error (Type of Error)
1. subjects (spelling)
2. is shown (subject-verb agreement)
   by her (object pronoun)
3. water, (comma in a series)
   are (subject-verb agreement)
4. characterize (subject-verb agreement)
5. are (subject-verb agreement)
6. between them (object pronoun)
7. work's (singular possessive)
8. seems (subject-verb agreement)

Viewing the Art

Helen Oji, H.P., 1986

H.P., an oil-on-canvas painting, measures 51 by 78 inches and hangs in a private collection. Have students discuss the painting, using the information in the paragraph above as a point of departure. Ask them to evaluate the writer's opinions. What opinions of their own would they add?

Answers: Exercise 10
Mixed Review

Answers will vary, but some suggestions are given below.

1. of
2. both, and
3. by
4. From
5. Yes
6. and
7. of
8. During
9. and
10. Both, and
11. in
12. Because of
13. in
14. through
15. Wow
16. but
17. during
18. Along with
19. through
20. in

Close

Ask students to write a short paragraph on a topic of their choice. Encourage them to use prepositions, conjunctions, and interjections to make their writing lively. Have students exchange papers with a partner. Partners should underline the prepositions, double underline the conjunctions, and circle the interjections in the paragraph. Have students share examples of these three parts of speech, using sentences from their writing.

Prepositions, Conjunctions, & Interjections

Review: Exercise 10

Mixed Review

In this exercise, you can practice what you have learned about prepositions, conjunctions, and interjections. Write each sentence, filling in the blank or blanks as directed.

1. One _____ the primitive American artists was Edward Hicks. (preposition)
2. Revere was _____ a silversmith _____ a patriot. (correlative conjunction)
3. Revere's portrait was painted _____ John Singleton Copley. (preposition)
4. _____ an early engraving, we can get an idea of how colonial Boston looked. (preposition)
5. _____, this painting is the only way we know what happened. (interjection)
6. Sometimes people who were not present at an event are shown in a painting, _____ some who were there are not shown. (coordinating conjunction)
7. That is a well-known painting _____ the Revolutionary War. (preposition)
8. _____ the early years of our Republic, George Washington was a favorite subject for painters. (preposition)
9. Native Americans were sometimes shown as heros _____ sometimes as victims of American growth. (coordinating conjunction)
10. _____ George Catlin _____ Alfred Miller visited Native American encampments and painted them. (correlative conjunction)
11. Catlin recorded Native American life _____ great detail. (preposition)
12. _____ Catlin, we have an idea of what Native American life was like in the early days. (compound preposition)
13. The works of Catlin and Bierstadt amazed and inspired Americans living _____ the East. (preposition)
14. Early Americans saw America's beauty only _____ art. (preposition)
15. In the *Last of the Buffalo* by Bierstadt, a Native American is shown bravely plunging his spear into a charging buffalo. _____! (interjection)
16. George Caleb Bingham depicted scenes of the frontier, _____ his paintings are reflective and quiet. (coordinating conjunction)
17. Mathew Brady was a photographer _____ the Civil War. (preposition)
18. _____ industrialization came many abuses. (compound preposition)
19. In the late nineteenth century, some writers and artists depicted injustice and cruelty _____ their works. (preposition)
20. Those works helped improve conditions _____ factories. (preposition)

Writing Application

Prepositions in Writing

Mary Q. Steele uses prepositions in this passage from *Journey Outside* to give readers a detailed understanding of the movements and actions in a boy's first encounter with a bird. Examine the passage, paying particular attention to the italicized prepositions and prepositional phrases.

He cried out abruptly. Something was coming *toward him in the air*, a little fish gliding *through the air*, helping itself along *with great fins* that stuck out *from its sides* and then folded tight *against them.* A wonder, a wonder! The fish stopped suddenly *in the top of one of the little trees*, put out little legs, . . . threw back its head, and opening its mouth made such sounds as Dilar had never heard before.

Techniques with Prepositions

Try to apply some of Mary Q. Steele's writing techniques when you experiment with drafting and revising your own work.

❶ Use prepositions to settle readers within a situation and to make your writing clearer and more detailed.

WITHOUT PREPOSITIONS Something was coming.

STEELE'S VERSION Something was coming *toward him in the air.*

❷ Make your writing more specific and engaging by adding prepositional phrases that tell readers how, when, and where an action is taking place. Compare the following:

GENERAL WORDS great fins that stuck out and then folded tight

STEELE'S VERSION great fins that stuck out *from its sides* and then folded tight *against them*

TIME

For more about the writing process, see **TIME Facing the Blank Page,** pp. 97–107.

Prepositions, Conjunctions, & Interjections

Prepositions in Writing

You may have students read the paragraph silently without interruption. Then go back and discuss the italicized prepositions and prepositional phrases with them. Discuss these choices in relation to the Techniques with Prepositions.

Techniques with Prepositions

Discuss the examples provided that show how using prepositional phrases can make writing more specific and clear. Have students refer to the earlier passage from *The Magical Horse* and identify prepositional phrases that clarify and enhance the writing.

Practice

The answers to this challenging and enriching activity will vary. Refer to Techniques with Prepositions as you evaluate student choices.

Sample:

It must be Tuesday. Sharon Urstand was pulling her little sister Gina to school in a red wagon. They rolled quickly along Main Street to Everett Street, stopping at the traffic light. Suddenly Gina climbed out of the wagon and began to jump up and down in distress. Gina's yells reached all the way to my window. "But I can't go to school without my homework!" she shouted. Sharon steered the wagon around and headed for home. Gina sat in the wagon, wearing a look of relief on her face as they climbed steadily up the hill.

Practice Practice these techniques by revising the following passage, using a separate sheet of paper. As you work, expand or clarify the passage's meaning by adding prepositional phrases in the places marked with carets (∧).

It must be Tuesday. Sharon Urstand was pulling her little sister Gina ∧. They rolled quickly ∧ to Everett Street, stopping at the traffic light. Suddenly Gina climbed out ∧ and began to jump up and down in distress. Gina's yells reached all the way ∧. "But I can't go to school ∧!" she shouted. Sharon, steered the wagon around and headed ∧. Gina sat ∧, wearing a look of relief ∧, as they climbed steadily ∧.

Writing Application **499**

✔ ASSESSMENT OPTIONS

📁 *Tests with Answer Key & Rubrics*
Unit 13 Mastery Test, pp. 55–56

💾 *Testmaker*
Unit 13 Mastery Test

You may wish to administer the Unit 13 Mastery Test at this point.

📼 *MindJogger Videoquizzes*

INTRODUCING

UNIT 14

Objectives

- To develop an understanding of simple, compound, and complex sentences
- To develop the ability to distinguish among adjective, adverb, and noun clauses
- To be able to write and punctuate properly simple, compound, and complex sentences

✔ ASSESSMENT OPTIONS

📁 *Tests with Answer Key and Rubrics*
Unit 14 Pretest, pp. 57–58
Unit 14 Mastery Test, pp. 59–60

💾 *Testmaker*
Unit 14 Pretest
Unit 14 Mastery Test

You may wish to administer the Unit 14 Pretest at this point.

Key to Ability Levels

L1 Level 1 activities are within the basic ability range of students.

L2 Level 2 activities are within the ability range of average students.

L3 Level 3 activities are more challenging activities.

UNIT 14 Clauses and Complex Sentences

Resource Manager

 **Planning Resources**
- *Lesson Plans*
- *Block Scheduling*

 Transparencies
- *Bellringer*
- *Daily Language Practice*

 **Other Print Resources**
- *Grammar and Composition Handbook*
- *Grammar Enrichment*
- *Grammar Practice*
- *Grammar Reteaching*
- *Grammar Workbook*
- *Sentence-Combining Practice*
- *Tests with Answer Key and Rubrics*

📹 **Video**
- *MindJogger Videoquizzes*

💾 **Software**
- *Interactive Grammar and Language Workbook*
- *Language Arts PASS*
- *Presentation Plus!*
- *Revising with Style*
- *Testmaker*

💻 **Web Sites**
- *writerschoice.glencoe.com*

A **sentence** is a group of words that has a subject and predicate and expresses a complete thought.

■ A **simple sentence** has one complete subject and one complete predicate.

The **complete subject** names whom or what the sentence is about. The **complete predicate** tells what the subject does or has. Sometimes it tells what the subject is or is like.

Complete Subject	Complete Predicate
Some people	travel.
Neither cars nor jets	are completely safe.
Trains and buses	carry passengers and transport luggage.
Freight trains	transport products to various cities.

■ A **compound sentence** is a sentence that contains two or more connected simple sentences. Each simple sentence in a compound sentence is called a main clause.

■ A **main clause** has a subject and a predicate and can stand alone as a sentence.

In the compound sentences below, each main clause is in black. The connecting elements are highlighted in red.

Millions of people live in cities, **but** many others reside in the suburbs.

Most people travel to work, **and** many of them use public transportation.

Commuters take trains, buses, and cars; some even fly.

Helicopters are often used to monitor traffic conditions, **but** computers can more accurately predict traveling time.

If the main clauses are connected by *and*, *but*, or *or*, a comma precedes the conjunction. If the main clauses are not joined by a conjunction, a semicolon can be used as the connector.

14.1 Sentences and Clauses **501**

Clauses and Complex Sentences

Focus

Lesson Overview

Objectives
- To identify and distinguish between simple and compound sentences
- To recognize main clauses
- To punctuate simple and compound sentences correctly
- To use main clauses appropriately in simple and compound sentences

 Bellringer
Daily Language Activity

When students enter the classroom, have this assignment on the board: *Underline each part of this sentence that could stand alone as a separate sentence. Don't underline connecting words.*

The loading of the wagons seemed to take forever, but at last the first driver cracked his whip, and the procession began.

—Zilpha Keatley Snyder
Song of the Gargoyle

See also *Daily Language Practice*

Motivating Activity

Discuss answers from the Bellringer activity. Ask students to identify the kind of sentence shown in the activity (compound). Have students monitor their understanding and seek clarification as needed.

Teach

☑ **Teaching Tip**

In grammar, the term *compound* indicates the joining of two or more elements of the same kind. A compound subject joins two or more subjects; a compound predicate joins two or more predicates; a compound sentence joins two or more simple sentences.

 **Resource Manager**

📂 **Planning Resources**
- *Lesson Plans*

🖥 **Transparencies**
- *Bellringer*
- *Daily Language Practice*

📂 **Other Print Resources**
- *Grammar and Composition Handbook*
- *Grammar Enrichment*, p. 31
- *Grammar Practice*, p. 31
- *Grammar Reteaching*, p. 32
- *Grammar Workbook*, Lesson 42

Practice and Assess

Answers: Exercise 1

1. simple	**6.** simple
2. simple	**7.** simple
3. compound	**8.** compound
4. compound	**9.** compound
5. compound	**10.** compound

Answers: Exercise 2

1. <u>Four . . . States</u>, and <u>problems . . . arise</u>.
2. <u>Accidents . . . delays</u>; <u>poor . . . jams</u>.
3. <u>Traffic . . . for drivers</u>, but <u>it . . . bypassed</u>.
4. <u>Radio . . . spots</u>.
5. <u>Drivers . . . time</u>, but <u>many . . . routes</u>.
6. <u>The . . . jam</u>; <u>it . . . conditions</u>.
7. <u>Roadways . . . use</u>.
8. <u>This . . . dangerous</u>, and <u>it . . . accidents</u>.
9. <u>Crews . . . repairs</u>; <u>the workers . . . roads</u>.
10. <u>Drivers . . . spots</u>.
11. <u>Detours . . . long</u>, and <u>they . . . travel</u>.
12. <u>Most . . . detours</u>, but <u>they . . . roads</u>.
13. <u>Travelers . . . detours</u>.
14. <u>Public . . . driving</u>, and <u>it . . . easier</u>.
15. <u>Subway . . . spaces</u>.
16. <u>Riding . . . free</u>, but <u>it . . . driving</u>.
17. <u>Drivers . . . gas</u>, and <u>they . . . highway</u>.
18. <u>There . . . transportation</u>.
19. <u>Passengers . . . freedoms</u>.
20. <u>A driver . . . car</u>; <u>she . . . train</u>.

Additional Resources

 *Grammar Practice,* p. 31
Grammar Reteaching, p. 32
Grammar Enrichment, p. 31

Grammar Workbook, Lesson 42

Close

Have each student write a letter to a partner about a trip he or she would like to take. Students should use both simple and compound sentences. Ask them to trade papers and write a return letter, using simple and compound sentences. Students should critique each other's sentences in constructive ways.

502

Clauses and Complex Sentences

Exercise 1   Identifying Simple and Compound Sentences

Identify each sentence as *simple* or *compound*.

1. Long-distance travel was difficult for early Americans.
2. In those days, people traveled in stagecoaches and covered wagons.
3. Long-distance travel was possible, but it was not very fast or comfortable.
4. Eventually railroads were built; tracks were laid across the country.
5. Distant cities were connected, and people could travel between them.
6. The growth of railroads changed the lives of many Americans.
7. Americans found trains a pleasant alternative to stagecoaches and wagons.
8. Railroads were popular for long journeys, and they made short trips easier, too.
9. Workers moved out of crowded cities, and commuters used trains.
10. Family members moved across the country, but trains reunited them.

Exercise 2   Punctuating Simple and Compound Sentences

Write each sentence, and underline each main clause. Add a comma or a semicolon if needed.

1. Four million miles of roadways exist in the United States and problems with them do arise.
2. Accidents cause delays poor road conditions often result in traffic jams.
3. Traffic can be annoying for drivers but it can often be bypassed.
4. Radio listeners hear traffic reports and can avoid trouble spots.
5. Drivers could allow more driving time but many decide to take alternate routes.
6. The problem may not be a traffic jam it might be poor road conditions.
7. Roadways can become damaged by time and use.
8. This damage could be dangerous and it can cause accidents.
9. Crews are sent to make repairs the workers and equipment can block the roads.
10. Drivers take detours around these trouble spots.
11. Detours are usually long and they can take more time to travel.
12. Most drivers dislike detours but they prefer not to travel on damaged roads.
13. Travelers on public transportation usually avoid delays and detours.
14. Public transportation is often faster than driving and it can be much easier.
15. Subway commuters never need to find parking spaces.
16. Riding the train is not free but it is often less expensive than driving.
17. Drivers must pay for gas and they often pay tolls on the highway.
18. There are many other advantages to public transportation.
19. Passengers on trains or buses have additional freedoms.
20. A driver can't read in her car she could read the newspaper on the train.

Exploring Language

Combining Sentences

To combine two simple sentences that have the same subject and to add interest to their writing, students can replace the second subject with a pronoun: *The bus stops here. The bus picks up passengers. The bus stops here, and it picks up passengers.* Have students review a recent writing assignment for sentences that would be more effective if combined.

14.2 Complex Sentences

A **main clause** has a subject and a predicate and can stand alone as a sentence.

Sometimes sentences have more than one clause, with only one of the clauses being a main clause. The other clause is called a subordinate clause.

■ A **subordinate clause** is a group of words that has a subject and a predicate but does not express a complete thought and cannot stand alone as a sentence. A subordinate clause is always combined with a main clause in a sentence.

■ A **complex sentence** is a sentence that has one main clause and one or more subordinate clauses.

In each complex sentence below, the main clause is in light type, and the subordinate clause is in dark type.

> **When the sun set,** the caravans stopped for the night.
> The dromedary has one hump, **which stores fat.**
> Most people know **that camels are stubborn.**

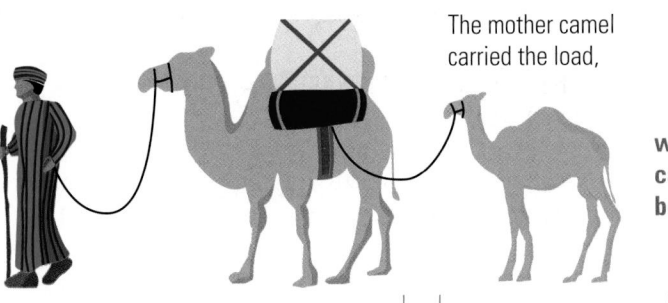

The mother camel carried the load,

while the baby camel walked behind.

MAIN CLAUSE   SUBORDINATE CLAUSE

14.2 Complex Sentences   **503**

Focus

Lesson Overview

Objectives
- To identify complex sentences and subordinate clauses
- To write more sophisticated sentences

Bellringer
Daily Language Activity

When students enter the classroom, have this assignment on the board: *Write three sentences using one of the following clauses in each:*

> *that candy is sweet*
> *which makes sense*
> *when the car stopped*

See also *Daily Language Practice*

Motivating Activity

Write examples of students' sentences on the board. Have them identify the part of each sentence that can stand alone (main clause) and the part that does not express a complete thought (subordinate clause). Ask students to monitor their understanding and to seek clarification as needed.

Teach

☑ Teaching Tip

To help students remember the distinction between compound and complex sentences, offer a mnemonic device. One way to keep the two terms straight is to associate the *x* in *complex* with the *x* in *mixed*: in a complex sentence there is a mixture of at least one main clause and one subordinate clause.

Clauses and Complex Sentences

Resource Manager

📂 Planning Resources
- *Lesson Plans*

🎵 Transparencies
- *Bellringer*
- *Daily Language Practice*

📂 Other Print Resources
- *Grammar and Composition Handbook*
- *Grammar Enrichment*, p. 32
- *Grammar Practice*, p. 32
- *Grammar Workbook*, Lesson 43

Practice and Assess

Answers: Exercise 3

1. The desert is a place <u>where most animals are not able to live or work</u>. (complex)
2. Camels are useful <u>because they cross the desert easily</u>. (complex)
3. Camels provide necessary transportation in the desert. (simple)
4. Long caravans of camels carry heavy loads across these dry, hot regions. (simple)
5. Camels have double eyelashes, <u>which protect their eyes from the blowing sand</u>. (complex)
6. Its eyelashes also help protect a camel's eyes from the strong glare of the sun. (simple)
7. Did you know <u>that a camel's hump contains fat and muscle?</u> (complex)
8. People usually ride dromedary camels, <u>which have only one hump</u>. (complex)
9. It is the Bactrian camel <u>that has two humps</u>. (complex)
10. People have found <u>that camels can survive sandstorms</u>. (complex)
11. <u>Until the sun sets</u>, camels maintain a 105-degree temperature. (complex)
12. We have learned <u>that the camel's temperature drops to 93 degrees at night</u>. (complex)
13. Camels survive desert life <u>because they can live with little water</u>. (complex)
14. Scientists have not always understood <u>how a camel could endure a lack of water</u>. (complex)
15. <u>Although people once believed camels store excess water in their humps</u>, this belief is a myth. (complex)
16. For short periods, both dromedaries and Bactrian camels can exist on fat from their humps. (simple)
17. <u>If a camel nourishes itself with the fat in its hump for several days</u>, the hump will sag and lean to one side. (complex)
18. <u>Because they can tolerate desert conditions so well</u>, camels were brought to America in the 1850s for use as pack animals in California and Nevada. (complex)
19. The camels annoyed stagecoach drivers, <u>whose teams of horses often became frightened at the sight of the camels</u>. (complex)
20. Camels were also brought to Australia as pack animals <u>since they could endure arid conditions better than horses</u>. (complex)
21. Many people do not know <u>that a Bactrian camel can swim for short distances</u>. (complex)
22. <u>Although a camel is relatively tall</u>, a rider can easily climb up onto the back of a kneeling camel. (complex)
23. Pads on its knees act as cushions <u>when the camel kneels in the sand</u>. (complex)
24. A baggage camel can carry a load of several hundred pounds. (simple)
25. Mehari camels are special camels <u>that are bred for warfare and racing</u>. (complex)

504

Clauses and Complex Sentences (sidebar)

Exercise 3   Identifying Complex Sentences

Write each sentence. Underline each main clause once and each subordinate clause twice. Then identify each sentence as *complex* or *simple*.

1. The desert is a place where most animals are not able to live or work.
2. Camels are useful because they cross the desert easily.
3. Camels provide necessary transportation in the desert.
4. Long caravans of camels carry heavy loads across these dry, hot regions.
5. Camels have double eyelashes, which protect their eyes from the blowing sand.
6. Its eyelashes also help protect a camel's eyes from the strong glare of the sun.
7. Did you know that a camel's hump contains fat and muscle?
8. People usually ride dromedary camels, which have only one hump.
9. It is the Bactrian camel that has two humps.
10. People have found that camels can survive sandstorms.
11. Until the sun sets, camels maintain a 105-degree temperature.
12. We have learned that the camel's temperature drops to 93 degrees at night.
13. Camels survive desert life because they can live with little water.
14. Scientists have not always understood how a camel could endure a lack of water.
15. Although people once believed camels store excess water in their humps, this belief is a myth.
16. For short periods, both dromedaries and Bactrian camels can exist on fat from their humps.
17. If a camel nourishes itself with the fat in its hump for several days, the hump will sag and lean to one side.
18. Because they can tolerate desert conditions so well, camels were brought to America in the 1850s for use as pack animals in California and Nevada.
19. The camels annoyed stagecoach drivers, whose teams of horses often became frightened at the sight of the camels.
20. Camels were also brought to Australia as pack animals since they could endure arid conditions better than horses.
21. Many people do not know that a Bactrian camel can swim for short distances.
22. Although a camel is relatively tall, a rider can easily climb up onto the back of a kneeling camel.
23. Pads on its knees act as cushions when the camel kneels in the sand.
24. A baggage camel can carry a load of several hundred pounds.
25. Mehari camels are special camels that are bred for warfare and racing.

Additional Resources

 Grammar Practice, p. 32
 Grammar Enrichment, p. 32

Grammar Workbook, Lesson 43

Close

Have students imagine they are traveling by camel in the desert. Have each write a brief description of the trip in which each subordinate clause is combined with a main clause.

14.3 Adjective Clauses

Sometimes a subordinate clause acts as an adjective. Each subordinate clause in dark type in the sentences below is an adjective clause. An adjective clause adds information about a noun or pronoun in the main clause.

Ed's bicycle, **which he bought on sale,** is a ten-speed.

He paid a price **that was incredibly low.**

■ An **adjective clause** is a subordinate clause that modifies, or describes, a noun or pronoun in the main clause of a complex sentence.

An adjective clause is usually introduced by a relative pronoun. Relative pronouns signal that a clause is a subordinate clause and cannot stand alone.

Relative Pronouns			
that	who	whose	what
which	whom	whoever	

A relative pronoun that begins an adjective clause is usually the subject of the clause.

Allene bought the ten-speed **that is the most popular.**

She is a person **who truly loves bicycling.**

In the first sentence above, *that* is the subject of the adjective clause. In the second sentence *who* is the subject of the adjective clause.

An adjective clause can also begin with *where* or *when*.

Allene likes trails **where she can see flowers.**

Clauses and Complex Sentences

Focus

Lesson Overview

Objectives
- To identify adjective clauses and the relative pronouns that usually introduce adjective clauses
- To use adjective clauses to make writing more detailed and interesting

Bellringer
Daily Language Activity

When students enter the classroom, have this assignment on the board: *Write a separate sentence for each of the following adjective clauses:*

that was told

who lives next door

where you can see the sign

See also *Daily Language Practice*

Motivating Activity

Have volunteers write their sentences on the board. Ask students to identify the noun or pronoun that each adjective clause describes. Explain that adjective clauses can make writing more interesting by providing more detail. Have students seek clarification as needed.

Teach

☑ **Teaching Tip**

The relative pronoun that usually begins an adjective clause must always have a noun as its antecedent. The relative pronoun frequently is next to the noun that the adjective clause modifies. Example: The car that he wants is an antique.

Resource Manager

📂 **Planning Resources**
- *Lesson Plans*

📂 **Transparencies**
- *Bellringer*
- *Daily Language Practice*

📂 **Other Print Resources**
- *Grammar and Composition Handbook*
- *Grammar Enrichment*, p. 33
- *Grammar Practice*, p. 33
- *Grammar Reteaching*, p. 33
- *Grammar Workbook*, Lesson 44

Practice and Assess

Answers: Exercise 4

1. <u>that many people enjoy</u>; (activity)
2. <u>that others obey</u>; (rules)
3. <u>who ride bicycles</u>; (athletes)
4. <u>who are extremely dedicated</u>; (amateurs)
5. <u>which took place in a park in Paris in 1838</u>; (race)
6. <u>who are devoted to the sport of bike racing</u>; (cyclists)
7. <u>which draws teams of riders from around the world</u>; (Tour de France)
8. <u>who take pleasure in bicycle riding</u>; (racers)
9. <u>who follow the simple rules of bicycle riding</u>; (People)
10. <u>that exist</u>; (rules)

Answers: Exercise 5

1. (that) could harm bike riders or anyone in their path
2. (that) are worn for protection against serious head injuries in accidents
3. (who) ride in cities
4. (who) may be in their path
5. (which) can alert drivers and pedestrians
6. that a (cyclist) will turn
7. (who) ride bicycles professionally
8. (who) ride for business purposes
9. (who) is on a bike
10. (who) travels through a city by bicycle

Additional Resources

 *Grammar Practice*, p. 33

📁 *Grammar Reteaching*, p. 33

📁 *Grammar Enrichment*, p. 33

📖 *Grammar Workbook*, Lesson 44

Close

Have students imagine they are riding their bikes through a city. Direct them to list the laws that they must obey and why they must obey them. Remind them to use adjective clauses in their writing. Ask students to critique one another's use of adjective clauses, responding in constructive ways.

Clauses and Complex Sentences

Exercise 4 Identifying Adjective Clauses

Write each sentence. Underline each adjective clause. Circle the noun that each adjective clause modifies.

1. Bicycle riding is an activity that many people enjoy.
2. Reckless bicyclists ignore the rules that others obey.
3. Some athletes who ride bicycles enjoy competing in races.
4. Many amateurs who are extremely dedicated decide to race professionally.
5. The first recorded bicycle race, which took place in a park near Paris in 1868, was slightly more than a mile long.
6. Some cyclists who are devoted to the sport of bike racing travel great distances to compete in races.
7. The most famous bike race is the Tour de France, which draws teams of riders from around the world.
8. It is not only professional racers who take pleasure from bicycle riding.
9. People who follow the simple rules of bicycle riding can benefit from this healthful and pleasant activity.
10. Rules that exist are for the protection of the bike riders and the people around them.

Exercise 5 Identifying Adjective Clauses and Relative Pronouns

Write each sentence. Underline each adjective clause. Circle the subject of the adjective clause.

1. Disregarding safety rules can result in accidents that could harm bike riders or anyone in their path.
2. All bicyclists should have helmets that are worn for protection against serious head injuries in accidents.
3. Those bicyclists who ride in cities should be especially cautious.
4. Bicycle riders should always be aware of pedestrians who may be in their path.
5. Careful riders also use arm signals, which can alert drivers and pedestrians.
6. Arm signals show the direction that a cyclist will turn.
7. Some people who ride bicycles professionally are not racers.
8. These are the people who ride for business purposes.
9. Packages can often be delivered faster by a messenger who is on a bike.
10. A messenger who travels through a city by bicycle follows the same laws as automobile drivers.

MEETING INDIVIDUAL NEEDS English Language Learners

Recognizing Adjective Clauses

Review with students the English words that introduce adjective clauses (relative pronouns) and those same words in the students' first language. Ask students to write the same sentence in both English and their first language and compare the two.

14.4 | Adverb Clauses

Sometimes a subordinate clause is an adverb clause. It may add information about the verb in the main clause. An adverb clause tells *how, when, where, why,* or *under what conditions* the action occurs.

Before Julia bought a bicycle, she compared models.

She likes ten-speeds **because they are versatile.**

In the first sentence, the adverb clause *Before Julia bought a bicycle* modifies the verb *compared.* The adverb clause tells *when* Julia compared bicycles. In the second sentence, the adverb clause *because they are versatile* modifies the verb *likes.* The adverb clause tells *why* she likes ten-speeds.

■ An **adverb clause** is a subordinate clause that modifies, or describes, the verb in the main clause of a complex sentence.

An adverb clause is introduced by a subordinating conjunction. Subordinating conjunctions signal that a clause is a subordinate clause and cannot stand alone. Some common subordinating conjunctions are listed below

Subordinating Conjunctions			
after	before	though	whenever
although	if	unless	where
as	since	until	whereas
because	than	when	wherever

You usually do not use a comma before an adverb clause that comes at the end of a sentence. When an adverb clause introduces a sentence, however, you do use a comma after the adverb clause.

Julia crossed the finish line . . .

before the other bicyclists arrived.

14.4 Adverb Clauses **507**

Clauses and Complex Sentences

Focus

Lesson Overview

Objectives
- To identify adverb clauses and subordinating conjunctions
- To use and punctuate adverb clauses appropriately

🔔 Bellringer
Daily Language Activity

When students enter the classroom, have this assignment on the board: *Write this sentence and underline the words that add information about the verb* rests.

Julia rests when she feels tired.

See also *Daily Language Practice*

Motivating Activity

Discuss the Bellringer activity with students. Explain that the adverb clause *when she feels tired* tells when Julia rests. Have students seek clarification as needed.

Teach

☑ Grammar Tip

Explain that when an adverb clause modifying a verb appears at the beginning or in the middle of a sentence, it must be set off with commas. If the clause appears at the end of the sentence, however, a comma is usually unnecessary.

⇄ Cross-Reference: Grammar

For instruction and practice with adverbs and their function, refer students to Lesson 12.6.

Resource Manager

📂 **Planning Resources**
- *Lesson Plans*

📖 **Transparencies**
- *Bellringer*
- *Daily Language Practice*

📂 **Other Print Resources**
- *Grammar and Composition Handbook*
- *Grammar Enrichment, p. 34*
- *Grammar Practice, p. 34*
- *Grammar Reteaching, p. 34*
- *Grammar Workbook, Lesson 45*

Practice and Assess

Answers: Exercise 6

1. <u>Before automobiles were available</u>; (rode)
2. <u>when they used this simple vehicle</u>; (covered)
3. <u>When people wanted company and exercise</u>; (rode)
4. <u>since they could ride it together</u>; (could enjoy)
5. <u>until the first one was built in 1839 by the Scottish inventor Kirkpatrick Macmillan</u>; (existed)
6. <u>because bicycles were first manufactured in the United States that year</u>; (purchased)
7. <u>since automobile travel was easier and faster</u>; (chose)
8. <u>When gasoline prices rose</u>; (used)
9. <u>when they speed</u>; (behave)
10. <u>before they proceed</u>; (reduce)

Answers: Exercise 7

1. (Although) it may have been less convenient than driving
2. (because) they disregard rules
3. (Unless) cyclists are careful
4. (If) a cyclist rides in the street
5. (Whenever) they ride their bicycles on the road
6. (Although) some riders ignore these rules
7. (After) they finish work
8. (when) they make local deliveries
9. (when) they are working
10. (whenever) you visit a large city

Additional Resources

 Grammar Practice, p. 34

Grammar Reteaching, p. 34

Grammar Enrichment, p. 34

Grammar Workbook, Lesson 45

Clauses and Complex Sentences

| Exercise 6 | Identifying Adverb Clauses |

Write each sentence. Underline each adverb clause. Circle the verb that each adverb clause modifies.

1. Before automobiles were available, some people rode bicycles.
2. Travelers covered miles easily when they used this simple vehicle.
3. When people wanted company and exercise, they rode tandem bicycles.
4. Two people could enjoy this type of bicycle, since they could ride it together.
5. No self-propelled bicycles existed until the first one was built in 1839 by the Scottish inventor Kirkpatrick Macmillan.
6. Many Americans probably purchased bicycles after 1878 because bicycles were first manufactured in the United States that year.
7. Eventually many people chose automobiles over bicycles, since automobile travel was easier and faster.
8. When gasoline prices rose, many people used bicycles.
9. Bicyclists behave dangerously when they speed.
10. At crosswalks cautious cyclists reduce speed before they proceed.

| Exercise 7 | Identifying Adverb Clauses and Subordinating Conjunctions |

Write each adverb clause. Circle the subordinating conjunction.

1. Although it may have been less convenient than driving, bicycle riding was more economical.
2. Some bicyclists are inconsiderate and unsafe because they disregard rules.
3. Unless cyclists are careful, they can cause injury to themselves and to others.
4. If a cyclist rides in the street, the bicycle is considered a motor vehicle.
5. Whenever they ride their bicycles on the road, cyclists must follow most motor vehicle rules.
6. Although some riders ignore these rules, cyclists should stop at red lights and use hand signals for turns.
7. After they finish work, many people commute by bicycle to their homes.
8. Many messengers use bicycles when they make local deliveries.
9. These messengers face heavy traffic when they are working.
10. Today you will see cycling messengers whenever you visit a large city.

Close

Have each student write a paragraph of promotional text for a favorite type of bicycle, using adjective and adverb clauses in their writing. Partners can exchange paragraphs and identify the adjective and adverb clauses

Cooperative Learning

Making a Chart

Help students learning English create a chart with these heads: *How? When? Why? Where? Under what conditions?* Students can work with English-proficient partners to identify in the exercises on this page the adverb clauses that answer each question. Students should provide constructive feedback.

14.5 Noun Clauses

A subordinate clause can be an adjective clause or an adverb clause.

Other subordinate clauses act as nouns. Notice how the noun in dark type in the sentence below can be replaced by a noun clause.

Bicyclists should wear a helmet.

Should **whoever rides a bike** wear a helmet?

In the second example above, the clause in dark type, like the noun it replaces, is the subject of the sentence. Since this kind of clause acts as a noun, it is called a noun clause.

■ A **noun clause** is a subordinate clause used as a noun.

You can use a noun clause in the same ways that you can use a noun—as a subject, a direct object, an object of a preposition, or a predicate noun.

How Noun Clauses Are Used	
Subject	**Whoever uses a bike** rides for fun or exercise.
Direct Object	Suki says **that she wants a ten-speed bike.**
Object of a Preposition	She is interested in looking at **whatever is on sale.**
Predicate Noun	The flea market is **where she can find a good deal.**

Some of the words that can introduce noun clauses are given in the chart below.

Words That Introduce Noun Clauses		
how, however	where	whose
that	which, whichever	why
what, whatever	who, whom	
when	whoever, whomever	

14.5 Noun Clauses **509**

Clauses and Complex Sentences

Focus

Lesson Overview

Objectives
- To identify noun clauses and the words that introduce them
- To understand how noun clauses are used and to use them appropriately

Bellringer
Daily Language Activity

When students enter the classroom, have this assignment on the board: *Copy the following sentence:*

Whoever crosses the line first is the winner.

Try to identify and circle the subject of the sentence. Hint: It's a subordinate clause.

See also *Daily Language Practice*

Motivating Activity

Discuss with students how the clause in the Bellringer activity sentence functions as the subject of the sentence. Explain that a clause that functions as a noun is called a noun clause. Have students seek clarification as needed.

Teach

☑ **Teaching Tip**

Tell students that noun clauses play roles that single nouns or pronouns can play—subject, object, object of a preposition, and predicate noun. They usually begin with *that* or with a *wh-* word: *when, which, who, whom.* Point out that, unlike adjective and adverb clauses, noun clauses cannot be deleted from a sentence—and they can rarely be moved—without changing the meaning of the sentence.

Resource Manager

📂 **Planning Resources**
- *Lesson Plans*

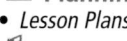 **Transparencies**
- *Bellringer*
- *Daily Language Practice*

📂 **Other Print Resources**
- *Grammar and Composition Handbook*
- *Grammar Enrichment*, p. 35
- *Grammar Practice*, p. 35
- *Grammar Reteaching*, p. 35
- *Grammar Workbook*, Lesson 46

Practice and Assess

Answers: Exercise 8

1. That bicycles . . . most countries
2. how the majority . . . travel.
3. what makes . . . for biking.
4. Where you will find many cyclists
5. that many people ride . . . work.
6. where most people . . . bike.
7. what equals one bike . . . people.
8. that the weather isn't always pleasant.
9. whoever rides a bicycle in traffic.
10. That bike lanes exist

Answers: Exercise 9

1. Where you ride, subj.
2. when bicycle . . . sport, pred. n.
3. that bicycle racing . . . 1896, DO
4. when the forty-nine mile . . . was added, DO
5. that this race . . . in 1984, DO
6. What many consider . . . each year, subj.
7. where some . . .are held, pred. n.
8. that outdoor . . . and tracks, DO
9. whichever . . . compete, obj. of prep.
10. that many cyclists . . . competitions, DO
11. what a race demands, pred. n.
12. how the participants . . . cycling, pred. n.
13. Whoever is eligible, subj.
14. Whoever races bicycles, subj.
15. what a cyclist shifts . . . uphill, pred. n.
16. Whoever keeps the best pace, subj.
17. where the next . . . held, DO
18. whoever fills . . . application, obj. of prep.
19. what a race requires, obj. of prep.
20. Which kind of equipment . . . uses, subj.

Additional Resources

 Grammar Practice, p. 35
Grammar Reteaching, p. 35
Grammar Enrichment, p. 35

Grammar Workbook, Lesson 46

Clauses and Complex Sentences

Exercise 8   Identifying Noun Clauses

Write each noun clause.

1. That bicycles outnumber cars in most countries may surprise you.
2. Bicycling is how the majority of people in Danish cities travel.
3. The flat terrain is what makes the Netherlands an ideal place for biking.
4. Where you will find many cyclists is along the many bridges of Amsterdam.
5. The fact is that many people ride bicycles to and from school and work.
6. Chongqing, China, is where most people travel locally by bike.
7. The people of Beijing own what equals one bike for every two people.
8. A drawback to commuting by bicycle is that the weather isn't always pleasant.
9. Many cities provide special lanes for whoever rides a bicycle in traffic.
10. That bike lanes exist does not guarantee a cyclist's safety on the streets.

Exercise 9   Identifying Noun Clauses

Write each noun clause. Then write *subject, direct object, object of a preposition*, or *predicate noun* to tell how it is used.

1. Where you ride is your choice.
2. The late 1800s was when bicycle racing became a popular spectator sport.
3. Did you know that bicycle racing has been an Olympic event since 1896?
4. Do you know when the forty-nine-mile women's bicycle race was added?
5. I know that this race became an Olympic event in 1984.
6. What many consider the most important race each year is the Tour de France.
7. A special indoor track is where some bicycle races are held.
8. This article says that outdoor races are held on roads, trails, and tracks.
9. Time trials are held for whichever racers wish to compete.
10. You know that many cyclists prefer team competitions.
11. Strength and endurance are what a race demands.
12. One consideration in the triathlon is how the participants should be judged in running, swimming, and cycling.
13. Whoever is eligible may compete at the Winterlude triathlon in Ottawa.
14. Whoever races bicycles must prepare for steep roads.
15. The bicycle gears are what a cyclist shifts for easier pedaling uphill.
16. Whoever keeps the best pace will win the race.
17. Bob knows where the next race will be held.
18. Most amateur races are open to whoever fills out an application.
19. Competitive riders must be ready for what a race requires.
20. Which kind of equipment a racer uses depends on the race.

Close

Have each student write a list of steps he or she would take to prepare for being in a bicycle race. Ask students to use complete sentences with noun clauses as subjects, direct objects, objects of prepositions, and predicate nouns. Have students trade papers and identify the function of the noun clause in each sentence, supporting their answers with examples from this lesson.

 **English Language Learners**

Using Noun Clauses

Ask each student to write a sentence containing a noun clause in both English and in his or her first language and then to compare the vocabulary and structure of the two sentences. Have students tell partners about any similarities.

Grammar Review

CLAUSES AND COMPLEX SENTENCES

John Steinbeck, a celebrated American author, won the Pulitzer Prize in 1940 for *The Grapes of Wrath*. In 1962 he won the Nobel Prize for Literature. The following passage is taken from *The Pearl*. Set on the coast of the Gulf of California, the novel is constructed around a young fisherman, Kino, who discovers an extraordinary pearl. In this passage, Kino and his wife, Juana, are preparing to paddle Kino's canoe out to the oyster beds. The passage has been annotated to show some of the kinds of clauses and sentences covered in this unit.

Clauses and Complex Sentences

Literature Model

from *The Pearl*

by John Steinbeck

Kino and Juana came slowly down to the beach and to Kino's canoe, which was the one thing of value he owned in the world. It was very old. Kino's grandfather had brought it from Nayarit, and he had given it to Kino's father, and so it had come to Kino. It was at once property and source of food, for a man with a boat can guarantee a woman that she will eat something. It is the bulwark against starvation. And every year Kino refinished his canoe with the hard shell-like plaster by the secret method that had also come to him from his father. Now he came to the canoe and touched the bow tenderly as he always did. He laid his diving rock and his basket and the two ropes in the sand by the canoe. And he folded his blanket and laid it in the bow.

- Adjective clause
- Compound sentence
- Complex sentence
- Adverb clause
- Simple sentence

Grammar Review **511**

Teach

About the Literature

Explain that the review contains a passage from *The Pearl*, a novel by John Steinbeck. It tells the story of a poor Mexican fisher whose discovery of a valuable pearl brings him misfortune. The passage is followed by exercises on related topics. After students have read the passage, discuss its characters, setting, and mood. Have students support their answers with details from the passage. Then ask students to identify different kinds of clauses and sentences in the passage. Encourage classmates to respond in constructive ways.

Linking Grammar and Literature

☑ **Teaching Tip**

Remind students that a simple sentence may contain a compound subject or a compound predicate. Ask students to identify the simple sentences that are not highlighted in the passage. Then see if they can identify the clauses that are not annotated, as well as the word that each adjective, adverb, and noun clause in the passage modifies. See *Grammar Reteaching*, page 2. Use of practice and enrichment pages may also be appropriate.

✔ ASSESSMENT OPTIONS

📁 *Tests with Answer Key and Rubrics*
Unit 14 Mastery Test, pp. 59–60

💾 *Testmaker*
Unit 14 Mastery Test

Resource Manager

📁 **Planning Resources**
- *Lesson Plans*

📁 **Other Print Resources**
- *Grammar and Composition Handbook*
- *Grammar Workbook,* Lessons 42–46; *Unit 7 Review; Cumulative Review: Units 1–7*

Practice and Assess

Answers: Exercise 1

1. simple
2. compound
3. simple
4. compound
5. compound
6. simple
7. compound
8. compound
9. simple
10. compound

Answers: Exercise 2

1. Pearl fisheries are on the gulf's western shore; the beds are on the eastern shore.
2. The formation of a pearl inside an oyster is actually an act of self-protection.
3. Oysters are a type of mollusk, and they have a shell like other mollusks.
4. A foreign substance may enter the oyster's shell and irritate the oyster.
5. The foreign substance can be a grain of sand, or it can be a harmful parasite.
6. An oyster will secrete nacre, and this secretion protects the oyster.
7. Oysters line the insides of their shells with thin layers of nacre.
8. Nacre is a substance oysters make, but they are not the only mollusks to make it.
9. The thin, smooth layers of nacre enclose a foreign body; this forms the pearl.
10. Nacre has the physical characteristics of the inside shell of the oyster.

Clauses and Complex Sentences

Review: Exercise 1   Identifying Simple and Compound Sentences

Write *simple* or *compound* to identify each sentence.

SAMPLE   Kino's grandfather came from Nayarit.
ANSWER   simple

1. The state of Nayarit lies on the western coast of Mexico.
2. The Santiago River flows through Nayarit; it empties into the Pacific Ocean.
3. Kino's grandfather moved north from Nayarit to a village near La Paz.
4. La Paz is in Baja, or Lower California, but this peninsula is part of Mexico.
5. Baja is divided into two states, and La Paz is the capital of the southern state.
6. The Gulf of California and the Pacific Ocean surround the Baja Peninsula.
7. La Paz is on the southeastern tip of Baja; this coast is on the Gulf of California.
8. Spanish explorers settled Baja in 1697, but Native Americans already inhabited the land.
9. In 1811 the city of La Paz was settled by the Spanish.
10. Pearls were found in oyster beds in area waters, and La Paz grew rapidly.

Review: Exercise 2   Punctuating Simple and Compound Sentences

Write each sentence and underline each main clause. Add a comma or a semicolon as needed.

SAMPLE   Pearls are found in oysters some oyster beds lie in the gulf.
ANSWER   Pearls are found in oysters; some oyster beds lie in the gulf.

1. Pearl fisheries are on the gulf's western shore the beds are on the eastern shore.
2. The formation of a pearl inside an oyster is actually an act of self-protection.
3. Oysters are a type of mollusk and they have a shell like other mollusks.
4. A foreign substance may enter the oyster's shell and irritate the oyster.
5. The foreign substance can be a grain of sand or it can be a harmful parasite.
6. An oyster will secrete nacre and this secretion protects the oyster.
7. Oysters line the insides of their shells with thin layers of nacre.
8. Nacre is a substance oysters make but they are not the only mollusks to make it.
9. The thin, smooth layers of nacre enclose a foreign body this forms the pearl.
10. Nacre has the physical characteristics of the inside shell of the oyster.

Review: Exercise 3 Distinguishing Between Simple and Complex Sentences

Write whether each sentence is *simple* or *complex*. If it is complex, write the subordinate clause.

SAMPLE The Gulf of California, which was explored by the Spanish explorer Hernando Cortez, was once called the Sea of Cortez.

ANSWER complex, which was explored by the Spanish explorer Hernando Cortez

1. John Steinbeck wrote a book that was titled *The Sea of Cortez*.
2. In this book, Steinbeck told about a story that he heard in Mexico.
3. The story, which was about a great pearl, gave Steinbeck the idea for *The Pearl*.
4. According to Steinbeck, the story may or may not be true.
5. An Indian boy found a pearl in the waters near La Paz.
6. The boy, who had never imagined a pearl of such size and worth, was excited.
7. This valuable pearl would surely bring him and many others happiness.
8. After he found the pearl, the boy had a series of terrible experiences.
9. He was almost killed by people who wished to steal the pearl.
10. Finally, he threw the pearl back into the sea.

Review: Exercise 4 Distinguishing Between Compound and Complex Sentences

Write *compound* or *complex* to identify each sentence. If it is complex, write the subordinate clause.

SAMPLE Steinbeck's story *The Pearl* is about a man and woman who are very poor.

ANSWER complex; who are very poor

1. The man's name is Kino, and his wife's name is Juana.
2. Kino, who earns a living as a pearl diver, is barely able to support his wife and their baby son Coyotito.
3. A crisis occurs when a scorpion bites the baby and injects him with its deadly poison.
4. The local doctor refuses to treat the baby because the couple is too poor to pay.
5. Juana prays that she and Kino will go out in the canoe and find a pearl.

Grammar Review **513**

Practice and Assess

Answers: Exercise 3

1. complex; that was titled *The Sea of Cortez*
2. complex; that he heard in Mexico
3. complex; which was about a great pearl
4. simple
5. simple
6. complex; who had never imagined a pearl of such size and worth
7. simple
8. complex; After he found the pearl
9. complex; who wished to steal the pearl
10. simple

Answers: Exercise 4

1. compound
2. complex; who earns a living as a pearl diver
3. complex; when a scorpion bites the baby and injects him with its deadly poison
4. complex; because the couple is too poor to pay
5. complex; that she and Kino will go out in the canoe and find a pearl

Practice and Assess

Answers: Exercise 5

1. <u>who</u> live near the sea; those
2. <u>which</u> people have done for thousands of years; Fishing
3. <u>which</u> is the main source of fish; sea
4. <u>which</u> is often unpredictable; weather
5. <u>that</u> is vital to a person's income; trip
6. <u>that</u> threaten the security of fishing families; problems
7. <u>that</u> were once bountiful with fish; areas
8. <u>whose</u> nets are empty; Fishers
9. <u>that</u> are vital to their livelihood; boats
10. <u>who</u> have always made a living from the sea; People

Answers: Exercise 6

1. <u>because</u> it is a good source of protein; eat
2. <u>Since</u> oysters provide nourishment; have become
3. <u>where</u> the water is quiet, calm, and shallow; are found
4. <u>When</u> they are twenty-four hours old; develop
5. <u>After</u> they grow for three to five years; are harvested.
6. <u>because</u> it consists of two parts, or valves; is called
7. <u>Unless</u> an enemy approaches; will keep
8. <u>whenever</u> it senses danger; snaps
9. <u>Because</u> they harvest millions of oysters each year; are
10. <u>before</u> it eats the oyster; will crush

Clauses and Complex Sentences

Review: Exercise 5   Identifying Adjective Clauses

Write each adjective clause. Underline each relative pronoun. Write the noun or pronoun that each adjective clause modifies.

SAMPLE   People who fish for a living face many difficulties.
ANSWER   <u>who</u> fish for a living, People

1. The fishing industry is important to those who live near the sea.
2. Fishing, which people have done for thousands of years, is the livelihood of millions of people.
3. Most commercial fishing occurs in the sea, which is the main source of fish.
4. The weather, which is often unpredictable, can be an enemy of fishers.
5. Rough, stormy seas can end a fishing trip that is vital to a person's income.
6. Today, there are other problems that threaten the security of fishing families.
7. Some areas, where fish were once bountiful, have been overfished.
8. Fishers whose nets are empty do not earn much money.
9. Families cannot pay bills or maintain the boats that are vital to their livelihood.
10. People who have always made a living from the sea must find other work.

Review: Exercise 6   Identifying Adverb Clauses

Write each adverb clause. Underline each subordinating conjunction. Write the verb or verb phrase that each adverb clause modifies.

1. People eat seafood because it is a good source of protein.
2. Since oysters provide nourishment, they have become a popular seafood.
3. Oysters are often found where the water is quiet, calm, and shallow.
4. When they are twenty-four hours old, oysters develop shells.
5. After being allowed to grow for three to five years, oysters are harvested.
6. An oyster is called a *bivalve* because it consists of two parts, or valves.
7. Unless an enemy approaches, the oyster will keep its two valves open.
8. The oyster snaps its valves shut tight whenever it senses danger.
9. Because they harvest millions of oysters each year, humans are the oyster's greatest enemy.
10. A crab will crush the tender shell of a young oyster before it eats the oyster.

Review: Exercise 7   Distinguishing Between Adjective and Adverb Clauses

Write each sentence. Underline each subordinate clause once and the word that the clause modifies twice. Then write whether the clause acts as an *adjective* or *adverb*.

SAMPLE   A canoe is very important to a simple man who fishes for a living.
ANSWER   A canoe is very important to a simple <u>man</u> <u>who fishes for a living</u>. (adjective)

1. Early canoes were made from tree trunks, which dwellers in the Caribbean islands hollowed out.
2. The North American peoples also used canoes, which they made from birchbark and wooden frames.
3. Birchbark canoes provided excellent transportation because they were light and relatively fast.
4. When they explored parts of North America, Marquette and Joliet traveled in birchbark canoes.
5. Today's canoes, which are used for recreation, are made from aluminum, canvas, fiberglass, or wood.

Review: Exercise 8   Identifying Noun Clauses

Write each noun clause, and label it *subject, direct object, object of a preposition,* or *predicate noun.*

SAMPLE   That canoeing is a popular outdoor sport is no surprise.
ANSWER   That canoeing is a popular outdoor sport—subject

1. Can you guess what makes canoeing so popular today?
2. That canoes are easy to use and affordable may help their popularity.
3. Another reason may be that they are easily transported from place to place.
4. Where you go canoeing adds to the pleasure.
5. Whoever has paddled a canoe down a quiet stream understands.
6. Instead of a noisy motor, a paddle is what propels a canoe.
7. People are delighted at how peaceful the world seems from a canoe.
8. Did you know that kayaks are popular with outdoor enthusiasts?
9. Whoever rides in a kayak must be prepared for an occasional dunking.
10. Kayakers know that kayaks can turn over and go under water.

Practice and Assess

Answers: Exercise 7

1. <u>trunks,</u> <u>which dwellers in the Caribbean islands hollowed out;</u> adjective
2. <u>canoes,</u> <u>which they made from birchbark and wooden frames;</u> adjective
3. <u>provided,</u> <u>because they were light and relatively fast;</u> adverb
4. <u>traveled,</u> <u>When they explored parts of North America;</u> adverb
5. <u>canoes,</u> <u>which are used for recreation;</u> adjective

Answers: Exercise 8

1. what makes canoeing so popular today; direct object
2. That canoes are easy to use and affordable; subject
3. that they are easily transported from place to place; predicate noun
4. Where you go canoeing; subject
5. Whoever has paddled a canoe down a quiet stream; subject
6. what propels a canoe; predicate noun
7. how peaceful the world seems from a canoe; object of a preposition
8. that kayaks are popular with outdoor enthusiasts; direct object
9. Whoever rides in a kayak; subject
10. that kayaks can turn over and go under water; direct object

Practice and Assess

Answers: Exercise 9

Answers will vary, but some suggestions are given below.

1. John Steinbeck, who wrote *The Pearl,* has written many novels.
2. Steinbeck was born and raised in northern California where many of his stories take place.
3. Because this area had fish canneries and farms, Steinbeck's stories are often about fish canning and farming.
4. Steinbeck worked at a series of temporary jobs while he attended Stanford University.
5. The characters in Steinbeck's novels were based on people whom he knew and respected.
6. After *Of Mice and Men* and *The Red Pony* were published in 1937, Steinbeck became a popular writer.
7. *The Grapes of Wrath,* which may be Steinbeck's best book, won the Pulitzer Prize in 1940.
8. The story is about the Joads, who are a poor farm family.
9. The family leaves Oklahoma and moves to California when they lose their farm during the Depression.
10. Although *The Grapes of Wrath* seems to be about the Great Depression of the 1930s, many people feel that this story is about human dignity.
11. If you enjoyed the book, you will enjoy *The Grapes of Wrath* movie.
12. During World War II, Steinbeck traveled to Italy and North Africa where he was a war correspondent.
13. After Steinbeck traveled to the Gulf of California, he wrote *The Pearl.*
14. He went with Ed Ricketts, who was a marine biologist.
15. *The Pearl,* which first appeared in a magazine, also became a film.
16. Steinbeck wrote the screenplay for the movie *Viva Zapata,* which is about a leader of the Indians during the Mexican Revolution.
17. John Steinbeck had a poodle whose name was Charley.

Clauses and Complex Sentences

Review: Exercise 9 **Writing Complex Sentences**

Combine each pair of sentences below, using the correct relative pronoun or subordinating conjunction in parentheses. You may have to delete some words.

1. John Steinbeck wrote *The Pearl*. He has written many novels. (who, which)
2. Steinbeck was born and raised in northern California. Many of his stories take place in northern California. (whatever, where)
3. This area had fish canneries and farms. Steinbeck's stories are often about fish canneries and farming. (because, until)
4. Steinbeck worked at a series of temporary jobs. He attended Stanford University. (while, as if)
5. The characters in Steinbeck's novels were based on people. He knew and respected these people. (whom, which)
6. *Of Mice and Men* and *The Red Pony* were published in 1937. Steinbeck became a popular writer. (wherever, after)
7. *The Grapes of Wrath* may be Steinbeck's best book. It won the Pulitzer Prize in 1940. (which, who)
8. The story is about a poor farm family. They are the Joads. (who, which)
9. The family leaves Oklahoma and moves to California. They lose their farm during the Depression. (when, than)
10. *The Grapes of Wrath* seems to be about the Great Depression of the 1930s. Many people feel that this story is about human dignity. (where, although)
11. You enjoyed the book. You will enjoy *The Grapes of Wrath* movie. (if, as)
12. During World War II, Steinbeck traveled to Italy and North Africa. He was a war correspondent in those places. (whom, where)
13. Steinbeck traveled to the Gulf of California. He wrote *The Pearl*. (until, after)
14. He went with Ed Ricketts. Ricketts was a marine biologist. (which, who)
15. *The Pearl* first appeared in a magazine. It also became a film. (which, who)
16. The movie *Viva Zapata* is about a leader of the Indians during the Mexican Revolution. Steinbeck wrote the screenplay for this film. (whereas, which)
17. John Steinbeck had a poodle. The dog's name was Charley. (which, whose)
18. *Travels with Charley* is a nonfiction book by Steinbeck. It is an account of his travels with his pet poodle. (whom, that)
19. John Steinbeck died in 1968. He received many awards, including the 1962 Nobel Prize for Literature. (because, before)
20. Steinbeck had a belief. He believed writers should celebrate the greatness of the human spirit. (which, that.)

18. *Travels with Charley* is a nonfiction book by Steinbeck that is an account of his travels with his pet poodle.
19. Before John Steinbeck died in 1968, he received many awards, including the 1962 Nobel Prize for Literature.
20. Steinbeck believed that writers should celebrate the greatness of the human spirit.

Review: Exercise 10

Proofreading

The following passage is about the artist Paul Sierra, whose painting *A Place in Time* appears below. Rewrite the passage, correcting the errors in spelling, capitalization, grammar, and usage. Add any missing punctuation. There are 10 errors.

Paul Sierra, *A Place in Time*, 1989

Clauses and Complex Sentences

Practice and Assess

Answers: Exercise 10
Proofreading

This proofreading activity provides editing practice with (1) the current or previous units' skills, (2) **Troubleshooter** errors, and (3) spelling errors. Students should be able to complete the exercise by referring to the units, the **Troubleshooter**, and a dictionary.

Error (Type of Error)
1. Cuban (capitalization)
2. received (verb form)
   encouragement, (introductory adverb clause)
3. sixteen, (introductory adverb clause)
   States, (compound sentence)
4. received (spelling)
5. works (verb form)
6. allows (verb form)
   himself, (compound sentence)
7. says, (direct quotation)

(continued)

Viewing the Art

Paul Sierra, *A Place in Time*, 1989
A boat is the central image in both *A Place in Time* and the passage from *The Pearl.* You may wish to discuss how the boat and the other images in this painting could illustrate Kino's relationship with his boat.

(Samples: *The freshly varnished boat could represent Kino's canoe after its annual refinishing. The sea could represent the fisher's livelihood.*) The oil painting measures forty-four by sixty-six inches and hangs in a private collection.

Practice and Assess

Answers: Exercise 11
Mixed Review

1. complex; That someone might find a precious pearl inside an oyster; noun clause
2. complex; Although it is possible to find a natural pearl in an edible oyster; adverb clause
3. compound
4. simple
5. complex; where natural pearls are scarce; adjective clause
6. complex; which looks deceptively like a natural pearl; adjective clause
7. complex; Unless you are gem expert; adverb clause
8. simple
9. compound
10. complex; who is sometimes called the Pearl King; adjective clause
11. complex; that are made into jewelry and sold today; adjective clause
12. complex; Whoever is interested in science and the habits of certain sea creatures; noun clause
13. complex; that oysters are still a very necessary and essential element in the production of a pearl; noun clause
14. simple
15. compound

Close

Have students reread the passage in the Mixed Review exercise. Discuss the effect of varied sentence structure on the writing. Then have students summarize their thoughts in their journals.

518

Clauses and Complex Sentences

Paul Sierra

¹Born in a cuban community in 1944, Paul Sierra was expected to enter a profession. ²Although he receive little encouragement he spent hours drawing in notebooks and reading books on painting. ³When he was sixteen Sierra moved to the united States, and he lived first in Miami and then in Chicago. ⁴The only formal art training Sierra recieved was three years at the Art Institute of Chicago, where he enrolled in 1963. ⁵Today Sierra work as the creative director of a small advertising agency. ⁶His job allow him the freedom to paint for himself and he can ignore the expectations of others. ⁷"I only hope," he says "to live long enough to make a good painting."

Review: Exercise 11

Mixed Review

Write whether the sentence is *simple*, *compound*, or *complex*. If a sentence is complex, write the subordinate clause. Then write whether the subordinate clause is an adverb clause, an adjective clause, or a noun clause.

¹That someone might find a precious pearl inside an oyster is intriguing and exciting. ²Although it is possible to find a natural pearl in an edible oyster, it isn't likely. ³Most natural pearls come from the Persian Gulf and Sri Lanka; the Red Sea and the Philippines are also a source of natural pearls. ⁴Pearls are valued for their color, shape, clarity, and weight. ⁵In areas where natural pearls are scarce, pearls are cultured. ⁶A cultured pearl, which looks deceptively like a natural pearl, has fewer and thicker layers of nacre inside. ⁷Unless you are a gem expert, you cannot see the difference between a natural and a cultured pearl. ⁸Only an X-ray of the pearl would reveal the truth. ⁹For centuries people had tried to culture pearls, but no one found commercial success until 1893. ¹⁰Then Kokichi Mikimoto, who is sometimes called the Pearl King, produced the first good cultured pearls in Japan. ¹¹Most pearls that are made into jewelry and sold today are cultured. ¹²Whoever is interested in science and the habits of certain sea creatures would be fascinated by the process of culturing pearls. ¹³The fact is that oysters are still a very necessary and essential element in the production of a pearl. ¹⁴The oysters just get a little assistance from humans. ¹⁵The process takes several years; it is part technology and part nature.

Writing Application

Sentence Variety in Writing

In this passage from *The Diary of Latoya Hunter*, the writer varies her sentence structure to capture the natural flow of her thoughts. Notice the underlined words.

It's hard to believe <u>but</u> people change as rapidly as the world does. <u>If I had kept you as a diary two years ago</u>, you would have heard about Jimmy. He was the first guy who I was close to and who was a real friend to me. I liked him <u>because</u> other boys always seemed to be in a popularity contest, and he didn't care about that stuff.

Techniques in Sentence Variety

Try to apply some of Latoya Hunter's writing techniques when you write and revise your own work.

❶ When appropriate in dialogue or personal writing, mix *simple*, *compound*, and *complex* sentences to help your writing sound lively and realistic.

FLAT SENTENCE PATTERN It's hard to believe. People change as rapidly as the world does.

HUNTER'S VERSION It's hard to believe *but people change as rapidly as the world does.*

❷ Make your writing more specific by using subordinate clauses to tell readers which ideas and information are the most important:

LESS SPECIFIC VERSION I liked him. Other boys always seemed to be in a popularity contest.

HUNTER'S VERSION I liked him *because other boys always seemed to be in a popularity contest.*

TIME

For more about the writing process, see **TIME Facing the Blank Page,** pp. 97–107.

Clauses and Complex Sentences

Practice

Practice these techniques as you revise the following passage. Identify the ideas that might be subordinated, and experiment with different sentence structures to create variety.

A strong wind tore across the fields. It rippled the wheat. Pieces scattered to the skies. Splinters of wheat struck the boy's face. Ernest struggled on toward the house. He could see Pa on the tractor in the far field. He hollered. His voice was lost on the wind. Slowly but steadily, Ernest inched his way against the gusts. He reached the house. His mother quickly opened the door. He plunged into the stillness.

Sentence Variety in Writing

Encourage students to read the passage on this page silently. Then ask them to find places where mixing different types of sentences helps make the writing more fluid and interesting. Discuss how the use of subordinate clauses helps to clarify details in the passage.

Techniques in Sentence Variety

Students can further examine techniques of varying sentence structure by reviewing the passage from *The Pearl* and discussing the clarity and dynamic nature of the piece.

Practice

The answers to this challenging and enriching activity will vary. Refer to Techniques in Sentence Variety as you evaluate student responses.

Sample:

A strong wind tore across the fields, rippling the wheat and scattering pieces to the skies. Splinters of wheat struck the boy's face, but Ernest struggled on toward the house. He could see Pa on the tractor in the far field. Though he hollered, his voice was lost on the wind. Slowly but steadily, Ernest inched his way against the gusts. When he reached the house, his mother quickly opened the door, and he plunged into the stillness.

✔ ASSESSMENT OPTIONS

📁 *Tests with Answer Key and Rubrics*
Unit 14 Mastery Test, pp. 59–60

💾 *Testmaker*
Unit 14 Mastery Test

You may wish to administer the Unit 14 Mastery Test at this point.

📼 *MindJogger Videoquizzes*

Objectives

- To develop an understanding of participals and participial phases, gerunds and gerund phrases, and infinitives and infinitive phrases
- To learn to use these three types of verbals and verbal phrases to express ideas

✔ ASSESSMENT OPTIONS

📁 *Tests with Answer Key and Rubrics*
Unit 15 Pretest, pp. 61–62
Unit 15 Mastery Test, pp. 63–64

💾 *Testmaker*
Unit 15 Pretest
Unit 15 Mastery Test

You may wish to administer the Unit 15 Pretest at this point.

Key to Ability Levels

L1 Level 1 activities are within the basic ability range of students.

L2 Level 2 activities are within the ability range of average students.

L3 Level 3 activities are more challenging activities.

UNIT
15 Verbals

Resource Manager

📁 **Planning Resources**
- *Lesson Plans*
- *Block Scheduling*

💻 **Transparencies**
- *Bellringer*
- *Daily Language Practice*

📁 **Other Print Resources**
- *Grammar and Composition Handbook*
- *Grammar Enrichment*

- *Grammar Practice*
- *Grammar Reteaching*
- *Grammar Workbook*
- *Tests with Answer Key and Rubrics*

📼 **Video**
- *MindJogger Videoquizzes*

💾 **Software**
- *Interactive Grammar and Language Workbook*
- *Language Arts PASS*

- *Presentation Plus!*
- *Testmaker*

🖥 **Web Sites**
- *writerschoice.glencoe.com*

15.1 Participles and Participial Phrases

A present participle is formed by adding *-ing* to a verb. A past participle is usually formed by adding *-ed* to a verb.

A participle can function as the main verb in a verb phrase or as an adjective to modify nouns or pronouns.

> The biplane was **soaring**. [verb]
> The flight had **astounded** skeptics. [verb]
> The **soaring** biplane flew 120 feet. [adjective]

In the first sentence above, the present participle *soaring* is the main verb, and *was* is the helping verb. In the second sentence, the past participle *astounded* is the main verb, and *had* is the helping verb. In the third sentence, the present participle *soaring* is used as an adjective to describe the noun *biplane*.

Sometimes a participle that is used as an adjective is part of a phrase called a participial phrase.

> **Sailing across the dunes,** the *Flyer* made history.

■ A **participial phrase** is a group of words that includes a participle and other words that complete its meaning.

A participial phrase that begins a sentence is always set off with a comma. Participial phrases in other places may or may not need commas. If the phrase is necessary to identify the modified word, it should not be set off with commas. If the phrase simply gives additional information about the modified word, it should be set off with commas.

> The biplane **displayed here** is a model of the *Flyer*.
> The model, **shaped with care,** attracts many visitors.

A participial phrase can appear before or after the word it describes. Place the phrase as close as possible to the modified word; otherwise, the meaning of the sentence may be unclear.

Verbals

15.1 Participles and Participial Phrases **521**

Focus

Lesson Overview

Objectives

- To identify and understand the function of present and past participles and participial phrases
- To punctuate participial phrases correctly

Bellringer
Daily Language Activity

When students enter the classroom, have this assignment on the board: *Write a sentence that contains the phrase* flying overhead.

See also *Daily Language Practice*

Motivating Activity

Invite volunteers to read aloud the sentences they wrote in the Bellringer activity. Write those sentences on the board. Guide other students to analyze each sentence, checking to make sure that the phrase *flying overhead* is positioned so as not to distort the writer's meaning. Have students respond in constructive ways.

Teach

☑ Grammar Tip

In grammar, a *verbal* is a verb form used as a noun, an adjective, or an adverb in a sentence. This unit presents participle, gerund, and infinitive forms of verbs that are used as adjectives or nouns.

⇄ Cross-Reference: Grammar

For instruction and practice with the principal parts of verbs, refer students to Lesson 10.6.

Resource Manager

📁 Planning Resources
- *Lesson Plans*

🎵 Transparencies
- *Bellringer*
- *Daily Language Practice*

📁 Other Print Resources
- *Grammar and Composition Handbook*
- *Grammar Enrichment*, p. 36
- *Grammar Practice*, p. 36
- *Grammar Reteaching*, p. 36
- *Grammar Workbook*, Lesson 47

Practice and Assess

Answers: Exercise 1

1. considered, part of verb phrase; flying, adjective
2. fascinated, part of verb phrase
3. pioneering, adjective
4. experimented, part of verb phrase
5. learned, part of verb phrase
6. experimenting, part of verb phrase
7. selected, part of verb phrase
8. lifting, adjective
9. advanced, adjective
10. working, adjective

Answers: Exercise 2

1. Witnessed by only a few,—flight
2. issued to the press—statement
3. committed to their work—inventors
4. Believing that airplanes eventually would transport passengers,—Wright brothers
5. , lasting up to five minutes each, —flights
6. Working hard,—Wrights
7. financing their invention—contract
8. demonstrating the brothers' new machine—flights
9. , used in airplanes even today, —principles
10. Piloted by bold aviators,—airplanes

Additional Resources

📁 *Grammar Practice*, p. 35
📁 *Grammar Reteaching*, p. 36
📁 *Grammar Enrichment*, p. 36

 Grammar Workbook, Lesson 47

Close

Tell students to imagine they are reporters covering the Wright brothers' first flight. Encourage them to use some participial phrases in their news stories. Have students read their stories aloud. Ask students to analyze the use of participles and participial phrases.

Verbals

Exercise 1 Identifying Participles

Write each participle, and write whether it is *part of a verb phrase* or is used as an *adjective*.

1. People throughout the world have considered the flying Wright brothers the first pilots.
2. Even as young children, the Wright brothers were fascinated by machines of all types.
3. Otto Lilienthal did pioneering work.
4. In the 1890s, he had experimented with gliders.
5. The Wrights had learned of his work.
6. Soon they were experimenting in North Carolina.
7. They had selected Kill Devil Hill near Kitty Hawk for their experiments.
8. Their first two models lacked enough lifting power.
9. In 1903 they built an advanced model.
10. This model became the world's first working airplane.

Exercise 2 Identifying Participial Phrases

Write each sentence and underline the participial phrase. Then draw two lines under the word that the phrase describes. Add commas as needed.

1. Witnessed by only a few the first successful flight gained little recognition for the Wright brothers.
2. A statement issued to the press about the Wright brothers' achievements received almost no attention.
3. The brothers, however, were inventors committed to their work.
4. Believing that airplanes eventually would transport passengers the Wright brothers perfected their invention.
5. Later flights lasting up to five minutes each attracted attention.
6. Working hard the Wrights built a wooden biplane.
7. By 1908 the Wright brothers had signed a government contract financing their invention.
8. Wilbur made many flights in the eastern United States demonstrating the brothers' new machine.
9. The Wright brothers' basic principles used in airplanes even today have stood the test of time.
10. Piloted by bold aviators airplanes still thrill the public.

MEETING INDIVIDUAL NEEDS

English Language Learners

Distinguishing Participles

Guide students learning English to understand the difference in meaning between present and past participles. If students intend to say *The movie made me bored,* make sure they don't write *The movie made me boring.*

Identifying Participial Phrases

To recognize participial phrases, reduce adjective clauses to present participial phrases. Have students identify the adjective clause in *I knew the man who was standing there.* Show how the clause can be reduced to a phrase: *I knew the man standing there.*

15.2 Gerunds and Gerund Phrases

The previous lesson explains that the present participle may be used as an adjective. A verb form ending in -*ing* may also serve as a noun, in which case it is called a *gerund*.

■ A **gerund** is a verb form that ends in -*ing* and is used as a noun.

Sometimes a gerund functions as the subject of the sentence.

> **Moving** involves a lot of work.

At other times, a gerund functions as the direct object of a verb. Remember, a direct object of a verb receives the action of the verb. It answers the question *whom?* or *what?* after an action verb.

> People enjoy **traveling.**

Do not confuse gerunds with other verb forms that end in -*ing*. You can tell them apart by distinguishing their functions in a sentence. A verb form ending in -*ing* may be the main verb in a verb phrase. It may be used as an adjective to describe a noun or pronoun. It also may function as a noun. Then it is called a gerund.

> Megan has been **packing.** [main verb in a verb phrase]
> She will take an **exciting** trip. [participle used as adjective]
> **Traveling** will be fast. [gerund]

In some sentences a gerund is part of a gerund phrase.

■ A **gerund phrase** is a group of words that includes a gerund and other words that complete its meaning.

> Many jobs require **long-distance traveling around the country.**
> **Choosing the best mode of travel** takes some consideration.

Verbals

Focus

Lesson Overview

Objectives
- To identify and understand the function of gerunds and gerund phrases
- To use gerunds and gerund phrases correctly

Bellringer
Daily Language Activity

When students enter the classroom, have this assignment on the board: *Read the sentence below. Write the* -ing *word. Then write how it functions in the sentence.*

> *We could hear the singing of the birds.*

See also *Daily Language Practice*

Motivating Activity

Have volunteers share their answers to the Bellringer activity (*singing;* direct object). Then invite students to brainstorm to develop a list of additional sentences in which an -*ing* word acts as a direct object. Have students monitor their understanding and seek clarification as needed.

Teach

☑ Teaching Tip

Students may have trouble shifting gears when they first encounter -*ing* verb forms used as nouns (gerunds). Review the role that nouns play in sentences: subject, object, predicate noun, object of preposition, and appositive. An -*ing* form playing any of these roles is a gerund. An -*ing* form playing the role of an adjective is a present participle.

Resource Manager

📁 Planning Resources
- *Lesson Plans*

📁 Transparencies
- *Bellringer*
- *Daily Language Practice*

📁 Other Print Resources
- *Grammar and Composition Handbook*
- *Grammar Enrichment,* p. 37
- *Grammar Practice,* p. 37
- *Grammar Reteaching,* p. 37
- *Grammar Workbook,* Lesson 48

Practice and Assess

Answers: Exercise 3

1. gerund	**6.** gerund
2. main verb	**7.** gerund
3. main verb	**8.** adjective
4. adjective	**9.** gerund
5. main verb	**10.** gerund

Answers: Exercise 4

1. Hauling . . . litters; subj.
2. using . . . litters; DO
3. floating . . . logs; DO
4. Transporting . . . vehicles; subj.
5. Steering these rafts; subj.
6. experimenting . . . design; DO
7. Adding . . . raft; subj.
8. Shipping goods; subj.
9. voyaging . . . Mediterranean; DO
10. Trading . . . goods; subj.
11. traveling . . . Britain; DO
12. Sailing the Mediterranean; subj.
13. building . . . world; DO
14. Finishing these roads; subj.
15. Exchanging goods; subj.
16. growing . . . routes; DO
17. Searching . . . Asia; subj.
18. acquiring . . . spices; DO
19. learning . . . explorers; DO
20. searching . . . Asia; DO

Additional Resources

 Grammar Practice, p. 37
Grammar Reteaching, p. 37
Grammar Enrichment, p. 37

Grammar Workbook, Lesson 48

Close

Invite students to imagine a new method of transportation and explain it in a letter to a friend. Tell them to use at least one gerund in their letters. Partners can identify each gerund and its function in a sentence.

Verbals

Exercise 3 — Identifying Verbs, Gerunds, and Participles

Write whether the underlined word is the *main verb in a verb phrase*, a *participle used as an adjective*, or a *gerund*.

1. Commerce requires <u>moving</u> goods between places.
2. For centuries people had <u>exchanged</u> one kind of goods for another.
3. People had been <u>transporting</u> objects long before the invention of the wheel.
4. Trade produced increased contact among <u>differing</u> groups of people.
5. In this way, new ideas were <u>carried</u> to many distant places.
6. <u>Trading</u> also presented problems.
7. For example, <u>traveling</u> could prove dangerous and expensive.
8. Ancient merchants depended on animals for their <u>growing</u> businesses.
9. Some merchants preferred <u>riding</u> in long caravans of people and animals.
10. People began <u>using</u> litters for heavy packages.

Exercise 4 — Identifying Gerund Phrases

Write each gerund phrase. Write whether it is used as a *subject* or a *direct object*.

1. Hauling packages on these litters simplified work.
2. Workers started using logs as rollers for litters.
3. Eventually people began floating crude rafts of logs.
4. Transporting various goods on these vehicles created new problems.
5. Steering these rafts was difficult.
6. Raft builders liked experimenting with the design.
7. Adding a wall of logs along each edge of the raft formed a boat.
8. Shipping goods became easier with the rafts.
9. The Phoenicians later began voyaging throughout the Mediterranean.
10. Trading raw materials and finished goods was the basis of their civilization.
11. They even started traveling as far away as Britain.
12. Sailing the Mediterranean was also important to the Greeks.
13. The Romans began building roads throughout the known world.
14. Finishing these roads took many years.
15. Exchanging goods also depended on rivers.
16. Large cities began growing along important trade routes.
17. Searching for new trade routes to Asia led to an age of exploration.
18. Europeans enjoyed acquiring Asian silks and spices.
19. They also liked learning about the East from explorers.
20. They began searching for a sea route to Asia.

Exploring Language

Recognizing Gerunds

Tell students that gerunds and gerund phrases can always be replaced by the pronoun *it*. (*Singing is fun. It is fun. Playing an instrument is fun. It is fun.*) Participles and participial phrases can never be replaced by *it*. (This substitution does not make sense: *The crowd was cheering. The crowd was it.*) Have students record this tip in their journals.

15.3 Infinitives and Infinitive Phrases

Verb forms that are used as adjectives and nouns are called *verbals*. Participles and gerunds are two kinds of verbals. Participles can act as adjectives. Gerunds act as nouns. A third kind of verbal is called an infinitive.

■ An **infinitive** is formed from the word *to* together with the base form of a verb. Infinitives are often used as nouns in sentences.

When the word *to* helps to form an infinitive, it is not a preposition. Remember, a preposition is a word that relates a noun or a pronoun to another word in the sentence. A prepositional phrase is a group of words that begins with a preposition and ends with a noun or pronoun as its object.

> Many children like **to skate.** [infinitive]
> Some adults skate **to their jobs.** [prepositional phrase]

In the first sentence, the words in dark type form an infinitive. In the second sentence, the words in dark type form a prepositional phrase.

Sometimes an infinitive functions as the subject of a sentence. It names *whom* or *what* the sentence is about. At other times, the infinitive may function as the direct object of a verb. The direct object receives the action of the verb. It answers the question *whom?* or *what?* after an action verb.

> **To stop** is sometimes difficult. [subject]
> Beginning skaters need **to practice.** [direct object]

Sometimes an infinitive is part of an infinitive phrase.

■ An **infinitive phrase** is a group of words that includes an infinitive and other words that complete its meaning.

> **To skate on cracked sidewalks** demands practice.

15.3 Infinitives and Infinitive Phrases **525**

Verbals

Focus

Lesson Overview

Objectives
- To identify infinitives and infinitive phrases used as nouns
- To distinguish infinitives from prepositional phrases that begin with *to*
- To use infinitives and infinitive phrases correctly

 Bellringer
Daily Language Activity

When students enter the classroom, have this assignment on the board: *Use the phrase* to write well *in three different sentences.*

See also *Daily Language Practice*

Motivating Activity

Have students share examples of their writing from the Bellringer activity. Using students' work, explain how the infinitive phrase is used in the examples offered. Have students monitor their understanding and seek clarification as needed.

Teach

☑ **Teaching Tip**

Although infinitives and infinitive phrases are often used as nouns, they can also function as adjectives and adverbs in sentences. *(He is to blame. He lives to eat.)*

⬌ **Cross-Reference: Grammar**

For instruction and practice in using prepositional phrases, refer students to Lesson 13.1.

Resource Manager

📂 **Planning Resources**
- *Lesson Plans*

📖 **Transparencies**
- *Bellringer*
- *Daily Language Practice*

📂 **Other Print Resources**
- *Grammar and Composition Handbook*
- *Grammar Enrichment*, p. 38
- *Grammar Practice*, p. 38
- *Grammar Reteaching*, p. 38
- *Grammar Workbook*, Lesson 49

Practice and Assess

Answers: Exercise 5

1. infinitive
2. prep. phrase
3. infinitive
4. infinitive
5. prep. phrase
6. infinitive
7. infinitive
8. infinitive
9. prep. phrase
10. prep. phrase

Answers: Exercise 6

1. To improve . . . design; subj.
2. To sit . . . traffic; subj.
3. to move . . . easily; DO
4. to speed; DO
5. To race; subj.
6. To compete . . . races; subj.
7. to work; DO
8. to perform . . . spins; DO
9. to perfect . . . moves; DO
10. to own . . . skates; DO
11. to make . . . metal; subj.
12. to use . . . skates; DO
13. to move . . . possible; DO
14. To glide . . . park; subj.
15. to spend . . . skating; DO
16. to move . . . fast; DO
17. To play . . . hockey; subj.
18. to score . . . team; DO
19. to rent . . . first; DO
20. To purchase . . . pads; subj.

Additional Resources

 Grammar Practice, p. 38
Grammar Reteaching, p. 38
Grammar Enrichment, p. 38

Grammar Workbook, Lesson 49

Close

Have each student write a paragraph about the first time he or she went roller skating or ice skating. Remind them to use infinitive phrases and prepositional phrases in their writing. Infinitive phrases will begin with the word *to* and will end with a verb. Have students exchange paragraphs and proofread one another's work in constructive ways.

Verbals

Exercise 5 · Distinguishing Infinitives from Prepositional Phrases

Write whether each underlined group of words is an *infinitive* or a *prepositional phrase*.

1. To wait in city traffic is difficult for people in a hurry.
2. Some people can walk to their jobs.
3. Others like to bicycle.
4. To skate is often the best choice of city transportation.
5. Skaters speed across town to their destinations.
6. They do not need to stop for slow traffic.
7. Some people want to learn this new skill.
8. Skaters must learn to keep their balance.
9. They often enjoy skating to music at indoor rinks.
10. The invention of the roller skate is attributed to Joseph Merlin.

Exercise 6 · Identifying Infinitive Phrases

Write each infinitive phrase and whether it is used as a *subject* or a *direct object*.

1. To improve on Merlin's design became the goal of James Plimpton.
2. To sit in a car amid traffic is a waste of time.
3. Experienced skaters have learned to move through crowds easily.
4. Some skaters like to speed.
5. To race professionally is the desire of others.
6. To compete in skating races seems quite a challenge.
7. Some skaters prefer to work in teams.
8. Free skaters learn to perform difficult jumps and spins.
9. The practice each day helps to perfect their moves.
10. Most people no longer want to own old-fashioned skates.
11. In the past, to make wheels of wood or metal was essential.
12. Many skaters prefer to use in-line skates.
13. Some skaters want to move as fast as possible.
14. To glide silently through the park is a skater's idea of a perfect afternoon.
15. Some people like to spend all of their free time skating.
16. The best skaters learn to move very fast.
17. To play roller hockey is the goal of some skaters.
18. Players like to score points against an opposing team.
19. Beginning skaters may want to rent their equipment at first.
20. To purchase skates and safety pads can be expensive.

Critical Thinking

Recognizing Infinitives

Help students recognize the difference between infinitives and prepositional phrases beginning with *to*. An infinitive ends with a verb, an action word (*to run*); a prepositional phrase ends with a noun or pronoun, a naming word (*to the park, for them*). Tell students there is a *v* in both *verb* and *infinitive*. Have students record this tip in the journals.

UNIT 15 Grammar Review

VERBALS

Amelia Earhart: First Lady of Flight, by Peggy Mann, is a biography of one of the world's most famous aviators. One of Earhart's greatest achievements occurred in 1932, when she became the first woman to successfully complete a solo flight across the Atlantic Ocean. The following excerpt from the book describes the early part of that historic flight. The passage has been annotated to show some of the types of verbals covered in this unit.

Literature Model

from *Amelia Earhart: First Lady of Flight*
by Peggy Mann

At first the flight seemed a dream coming true. The view was vast and lovely. As she looked about, she felt she was gulping beauty. The clouds were marvelous shapes in white, some trailing shimmering veils. In the distance the highest peaks of the fog mountains were tinted pink with the setting sun.

Gradually she flew into darkness, star-flecked, with moonlight shimmering through the endless skies.

Then, suddenly, the dream turned into nightmare. Something happened that had never occurred in all her twelve years of flying. The dials of the altimeter started to spin crazily. She could no longer tell how high she was above the sea. And she was flying through thick darkness—flying into a storm.

> Present participle as main verb

> Present participle as adjective

> Participial phrase

> Infinitive phrase

Verbals

Grammar Review **527**

Practice and Assess

Answers: Exercise 1

1. <u>Setting a record</u>, <u><u>Amelia Earhart</u></u>
2. <u>Working as a nurse's aide during World War I</u>, <u><u>she</u></u>
3. <u>Entered as a contestant in flying meets</u>, <u><u>aviator</u></u>
4. , <u>flying as a passenger</u>, <u><u>Earhart</u></u>
5. <u>Fascinated by machines</u>, <u><u>she</u></u>
6. <u>Soaring high above the clouds</u>, <u><u>planes</u></u>
7. <u>Interested in all types of flying</u>, <u><u>Earhart</u></u>
8. <u>welcoming her home</u> <u><u>Crowds</u></u>
9. <u>lasting many hours</u> <u><u>flights</u></u>
10. , <u>attempting to fly around the world</u>, <u><u>Earhart</u></u>

Answers: Exercise 2

1. She was awestruck by the breathtaking beauty.
2. The twinkling stars danced in the night sky.
3. Pink-tinted clouds glowed warmly in the sunset.
4. Traveling across the Atlantic, Earhart encountered some rough weather.
5. Flying through the storm, the pilot peered into the darkness.
6. She stared at the controls with spine-tingling dread.
7. Looking outside, Earhart could see nothing but black sky.
8. Frozen with fear, she sat rigidly.
9. Black-tipped clouds completely hid the earth from view.
10. This was only the beginning of Amelia Earhart's history-making journey.

Review: Exercise 1 **Identifying Participial Phrases**

Write each sentence, and underline each participial phrase. Then draw two lines under the word that the phrase describes. Add commas as needed.

1. Setting a record Amelia Earhart was the first woman to fly across the Atlantic alone.
2. Working as a nurse's aide during World War I she became interested in flying.
3. Entered as a contestant in flying meets the young aviator gained experience.
4. Earhart flying as a passenger was the first woman to cross the Atlantic by air.
5. Fascinated by machines she also worked on airplane engines.
6. Soaring high above the clouds her planes were small and fast.
7. Interested in all types of flying Earhart also performed stunts.
8. Crowds welcoming her home often greeted her safe return.
9. Some of Earhart's flights lasting many hours were exhausting.
10. Earhart attempting to fly around the world was lost in 1937.

Review: Exercise 2 **Using Participles and Participial Phrases**

Rewrite each sentence, inserting the participle or participial phrase in parentheses. Add commas as needed.

SAMPLE   Amelia Earhart watched the earth fade from view. (gazing down from the cockpit)

ANSWER   Gazing down from the cockpit, Amelia Earhart watched the earth fade from view.

1. She was awestruck by the beauty. (breathtaking)
2. The stars danced in the night sky. (twinkling)
3. Clouds glowed warmly in the sunset. (pink-tinted)
4. Earhart encountered some rough weather. (traveling across the Atlantic)
5. The pilot peered into the darkness. (flying through the storm)
6. She stared at the controls with dread. (spine-tingling)
7. Earhart could see nothing but black sky. (looking outside)
8. She sat rigidly. (frozen with fear)
9. Clouds completely hid the earth from view. (black-tipped)
10. This was only the beginning of Amelia Earhart's journey. (history-making)

Verbals

Review: Exercise 3 **Identifying Gerund Phrases**

Write each gerund phrase, and then write whether it is used as a *subject* or a *direct object*.

SAMPLE Achieving your goals can be very satisfying.
ANSWER Achieving your goals, subject

1. Receiving a pilot's license is an important achievement.
2. Being the first woman to cross the Atlantic made Amelia Earhart a hero.
3. Earhart disliked needing so many months for preparation.
4. Waiting eleven months made her restless.
5. She would try flying around the world at the equator.
6. Attempting such a feat would test her courage and endurance.
7. No man or woman had ever even tried piloting a plane that far.
8. After her announcement, she began making arrangements for her flight.
9. Flying across the Atlantic was the first real test of her ability.
10. Navigating by instinct was a necessary skill.

Review: Exercise 4 **Using Gerunds and Gerund Phrases**

Write a sentence that answers each question. Use the word or words in parentheses in your answer.

SAMPLE What was Amelia Earhart's biggest achievement? (pioneering aviation for women)
ANSWER Pioneering aviation for women was Amelia Earhart's biggest achievement.

1. What event filled Earhart with wonder in her youth? (seeing an airplane in the sky)
2. What was Earhart's first claim to fame? (flying across the Atlantic as a passenger in 1928)
3. What was Earhart's greatest passion? (flying faster, higher, and farther than anyone else had ever flown before)
4. What action gained Earhart renewed respect in 1935? (becoming the first person to successfully fly from Hawaii to California)
5. What was one of Earhart's major goals in her speeches? (promoting the rights of women)

Verbals

Answers: Exercise 3
1. Receiving a pilot's license, subj.
2. Being the first woman to cross the Atlantic, subj.
3. needing so many months for preparation, DO
4. Waiting eleven months, subj.
5. flying around the world at the equator, DO
6. Attempting such a feat, subj.
7. piloting a plane that far, DO
8. making arrangements for her flight, DO
9. Flying across the Atlantic, subj.
10. Navigating by instinct, subj.

Answers: Exercise 4
Answers will vary, but some suggestions are given below.
1. Seeing an airplane in the sky filled Earhart with wonder in her youth.
2. Earhart's first claim to fame was flying across the Atlantic as a passenger in 1928.
3. Earhart's greatest passion was flying faster, higher, and farther than anyone else had ever flown before.
4. Becoming the first person to fly successfully from Hawaii to California gained Earhart renewed respect in 1935.
5. One of Earhart's major goals in her speeches was promoting the rights of women.

Answers: Exercise 5

1. to prove herself, DO
2. to promote women's rights, subj.
3. to draft women into the armed services, DO
4. To earn money for flight lessons, subj.
5. To spend her life as a pilot, subj.
6. To make a nonstop, solo flight from . . . New Jersey, subj.
7. to earn a living as a pilot in her twenties, DO
8. to risk her life on a transatlantic flight, DO
9. to become a gifted speaker, DO
10. To pursue a dangerous goal, subj.

Answers: Exercise 6

1. Amelia Earhart started to fly around the world in 1937.
2. Fred Noonan's mission on the flight was to serve as her navigator.
3. Earhart and Noonan managed to complete two-thirds of their journey before they ran into trouble.
4. Ever since, searchers have failed to find a trace of Earhart.
5. Researchers continue to study Earhart's disappearance.

Verbals

Review: Exercise 5 Identifying Infinitive Phrases

Write each infinitive phrase, and then write whether it is used as a *subject* or a *direct object.*

SAMPLE Amelia Earhart loved to fly.
ANSWER to fly, direct object

1. Amelia Earhart wanted to prove herself.
2. Throughout her life, to promote women's rights was important for her.
3. Earhart even wanted to draft women into the armed services.
4. To earn money for flight lessons was the reason she worked as a file clerk, truck driver, and nurse's aide.
5. To spend her life as a pilot was her greatest dream.
6. To make a nonstop, solo flight from Mexico City into Newark, New Jersey, was a notable achievement.
7. She tried to earn a living as a pilot in her twenties.
8. She promised to risk her life on a transatlantic flight.
9. Despite her shyness, Earhart needed to become a forceful speaker.
10. To pursue a dangerous goal fascinated Earhart.

Review: Exercise 6 Using Infinitives and Infinitive Phrases

Write a sentence that answers each question, using the word or words in parentheses.

SAMPLE What did Amelia Earhart want? (to earn money for lessons)
ANSWER Amelia Earhart wanted to earn money for lessons.

1. What did Amelia Earhart start to do in 1937? (to fly around the world)
2. What was Fred Noonan's mission on the flight? (to serve as Earhart's navigator)
3. What did Earhart and Noonan manage to do before they ran into trouble? (to complete two-thirds of their journey)
4. What have searchers failed to do ever since? (to find a trace of Earhart)
5. What do researchers continue to do? (to study Earhart's disappearance)

Proofreading

The following passage is about Yvonne Jacquette, whose painting appears on the next page. Rewrite the passage, correcting the errors in spelling, capitalization, grammar, and usage. There are ten errors.

Yvonne Jacquette

¹Born in 1934 in Pittsburgh, Pennsylvania Yvonne Jacquette began her artistic career by painting landscapes. ²Later, she became facsinated with painting these scenes from a distance. ³Breaking with tradition she began painting landscapes from the vantage point of a single-engine plane.

⁴Flying high above the earth Jacquette selects particular views and makes sketches of they. ⁵Uses these drawings to help her make her paintings. ⁶In the painting on the next page, Jacquette has paint the view overlooking a stretch of rural landscape. ⁷Filled with cloud shapes the painting could illustrate what Amelia Earhart seen on her solo flight across the french countryside so long ago.

Mixed Review

Write each underlined word or phrase in the following paragraph. Tell whether each is a *participle*, a *gerund*, an *infinitive*, a *participial phrase*, a *gerund phrase*, an *infinitive phrase*, or a *main verb*.

Shortly before Amelia Earhart's <u>amazing</u> solo flight across the Atlantic, Charles A. Lindbergh had <u>accomplished</u> a similar feat. He managed <u>to become the first man</u> who flew across the Atlantic alone. <u>Flying such a mission</u> required <u>astonishing</u> endurance and bravery. Like Earhart, Lindbergh had <u>found</u> the <u>exciting</u> new field of aviation very attractive. He had left school <u>to perform</u> daredevil stunts in the air. <u>Gaining respect</u> as a careful pilot required time and practice. <u>Hoping for prize money</u>, Lindbergh took off from New York in May 1927. When he landed in Paris, he saw thousands of people. They <u>had gathered</u> to greet him. Soon the crowd started <u>calling his name</u>. They began <u>applauding</u> <u>wildly</u>. The spectators <u>organized</u> parades and celebrations in honor of the flight. As Amelia Earhart would five years later, Lindbergh had <u>become</u> a hero, <u>enjoying the admiration of people around the world</u>.

Verbals

This proofreading activity provides editing practice with (1) the current or previous units' skills, (2) **Troubleshooter** errors, and (3) spelling errors. Students should be able to complete the exercise by referring to the units, the **Troubleshooter,** and a dictionary.

Error (Type of Error)

1. Pennsylvania, (introductory participial phrase)
2. fascinated (spelling)
3. tradition, (introductory participial phrase)
4. earth, (introductory participial phrase) of them (object pronoun)
5. She uses (sentence fragment)
6. has painted (verb form)
7. shapes, (introductory participial phrase)
   saw (verb form)
   French (nationality)

Answers: Exercise 8
Mixed Review

1. amazing, participle
2. accomplished, main verb
3. to become the first man, infinitive phrase
4. Flying such a mission, gerund phrase
5. astonishing, participle
6. found, main verb
7. exciting, participle
8. to perform, infinitive
9. Gaining respect, gerund phrase
10. Hoping for prize money, participial phrase
11. had gathered, main verb
12. calling his name, gerund phrase
13. applauding wildly, gerund phrase
14. organized, main verb
15. become, main verb
16. enjoying the admiration of people around the world, participial phrase

Close

Ask students to turn back to the passage about Amelia Earhart. Have them offer their own substitutions for the underlined participial and infinitive phrases. Discuss how these phrases help make the writing clearer and more lively.

Verbals

Yvonne Jacquette, *Clouds over Farmland, Forked Tree Masses*, 1988

Viewing the Art

Yvonne Jacquette, *Clouds over Farmland, Forked Tree Masses*, 1988
Explain to students that Yvonne Jacquette's 1988 pastel drawing, *Clouds over Farmland, Forked Tree Masses,* portrays a country landscape as seen from an airplane. The drawing measures seventeen by fourteen inches and is in the collection of the Brooke Alexander Gallery in New York City.

Writing Application

Phrases in Writing

Minfong Ho uses gerund, infinitive, and participial phrases along with participles in this passage from *The Clay Marble* to add detailed imagery, as well as variety, to her sentences. Read the passage carefully, noting the italicized phrases.

> I closed my eyes now and tried *to imagine them all sitting around me:* Grandmother stroking me, Father and Sarun whittling on the steps, Mother stoking the embers of the cooking fire. It wasn't just the thick thatched roof that had sheltered me, I realized now. It was the feeling I had had then, of being part of a family as a gently *pulsing* whole, so natural it was *like the breathing of a sleeping baby.*

Techniques with Phrases

Try to apply some of Minfong Ho's writing techniques when you write and revise your own work.

❶ Use infinitive phrases when appropriate to expand meaning in your sentences. Compare the following:

GENERAL VERSION I closed my eyes now and thought.

HO'S VERSION I closed my eyes now and tried *to imagine them all sitting around me.*

❷ Create specific and vivid imagery by describing nouns with participles.

GENERAL VERSION part of a family as a whole

HO'S VERSION part of a family as a gently *pulsing* whole

TIME For more about the writing process, see **TIME Facing the Blank Page,** pp. 97–107.

Verbals

Practice Use a separate sheet of paper to practice these techniques as you revise the following passage. Choose places to insert infinitive and participial phrases, working to make the passage more specific and engaging. Let the underlined words be starting points for your changes.

"<u>This</u> will take at least a week," sighed Tabitha. Sandy's bike, <u>in a heap</u>, rested sadly against the wall of Tabitha's shop. "<u>If I work hard</u>, maybe I can do it in five days. Will that be fast enough?" she <u>said</u>. "Before I fix the frame, I need <u>help</u> with these. Hand me the wrench <u>over there</u>," Tabitha said, pointing to the opposite wall. "Don't worry. We'll get it done. I love <u>work</u>!"

Writing Application **533**

Phrases in Writing

Encourage students to read the passage from *The Clay Marble* silently and then discuss how the italicized infinitive and participial phrases affect the impact of the passage.

Techniques with Phrases

Have students create their own infinitive and participial phrases based on the general versions provided in the text and then share them with the class. Discuss in what ways the students' sentences are more effective than the samples.

Practice

The answers to this challenging and enriching activity will vary. Refer to Techniques with Phrases as you evaluate student choices.

Sample:

"To fix this bike will take at least a week," sighed Tabitha. Sandy's bike, crushed into a heap, rested sadly against the wall of Tabitha's shop. "Working hard, maybe I can do it in five days. Will that be fast enough?" she muttered under her breath. "Before I fix the frame, I need to remove the twisted pieces. Hand me the wrench hanging on that hook," Tabitha said, pointing to the opposite wall. "Don't worry. We'll get it done. I love to work under pressure!"

✔ ASSESSMENT OPTIONS

📁 *Tests with Answer Key & Rubrics*
Unit 15 Mastery Test, pp. 63–64

💾 *Testmaker*
Unit 15 Mastery Test

You may wish to administer the Unit 15 Pretest at this point.

📼 *MindJogger Videoquizzes*

Objectives

- To develop an understanding of subject-verb agreement
- To develop the ability to locate subjects, to determine number of collective nouns and other special subjects, and to choose verbs that agree with their subjects.
- To use sentences in speaking and writing in which subjects and verbs are in agreement

✔ ASSESSMENT OPTIONS

📁 *Tests with Answer Key and Rubrics*
Unit 16 Pretest, pp. 65–66
Unit 16 Mastery Test, pp. 67–68

💾 *Testmaker*
Unit 16 Pretest
Unit 16 Mastery Test

You may wish to administer the Unit 16 Pretest at this point.

Key to Ability Levels

L1 Level 1 activities are within the basic ability range of students.

L2 Level 2 activities are within the ability range of average students.

L3 Level 3 activities are more challenging activities.

534

UNIT
16

Subject-Verb Agreement

534

Resource Manager

📁 **Planning Resources**
- *Lesson Plans*
- *Block Scheduling*

 **Transparencies**
- *Bellringer*
- *Daily Language Practice*

📁 **Other Print Resources**
- *Grammar and Composition Handbook*
- *Grammar Enrichment*

- *Grammar Practice*
- *Grammar Reteaching*
- *Grammar Workbook*
- *Tests with Answer Key and Rubrics*

📼 **Video**
- *MindJogger Videoquizzes*

💾 **Software**
- *Interactive Grammar and Language Workbook*
- *Language Arts PASS*

- *Presentation Plus!*
- *Testmaker*

 **Web Sites**
- *writerschoice.glencoe.com*

16.1 Making Subjects and Verbs Agree

A subject and its verb are the basic parts of a sentence. A singular noun subject calls for a singular form of the verb. A plural noun subject calls for a plural form of the verb. The subject and its verb are said to agree in number. Read the sentences below. You can see that the subjects and verbs agree in number.

Notice that in the present tense the singular form of the verb usually ends in *-s* or *-es*.

Subject-Verb Agreement with Nouns as Subjects	
Singular	**Plural**
A **poet explores** beauty.	**Poets explore** beauty.
The **theme touches** readers.	The **themes touch** readers.
Robert Frost writes about farms.	**Frost and Robinson write** about farms.

Verbs and subject pronouns must also agree. Look at the chart below, and notice how the verb changes. In the present tense, the *-s* ending is used with the subject pronouns *it, he,* and *she.*

Subject-Verb Agreement with Pronouns as Subjects	
Singular	**Plural**
I **read.**	We **read.**
You **read.**	You **read.**
He, she, it **reads.**	They **read.**

The irregular verbs *be, do,* and *have* can be main verbs or helping verbs. They must agree with the subject, regardless of whether they are main verbs or helping verbs.

I **am** a poet. They **are** talking to a poet. He **is** a poet.
She **does** well. She **does** write poetry. They **do** write.
He **has** books. He **has** read poetry. They **have** written.

16.1 Making Subjects and Verbs Agree **535**

Focus

Lesson Overview

Objectives
- To recognize that verbs must agree with their subjects
- To use subjects and verbs that are in agreement in written sentences

Subject-Verb Agreement

 Bellringer
Daily Language Activity

When students enter the classroom, have this assignment on the board: *Write the subject and the verb from the sentence below.*

Are the subject and verb singular or plural?

> The poetic imagination produces poems, pictures, and cathedrals.
>
> —William Carlos Williams
> *Octavio Paz*

See also  *Daily Language Practice*

Motivating Activity

Discuss students' answers. Then have students work with the Bellringer sentence by changing the subject (*imagination*) and verb (*produces*). Have them use some plural subjects and then some first- and second-person subjects (*I, you, we*).

Teach

☑ **Grammar Tip**

Point out that in present-tense sentences, all verbs change form with a third-person singular subject. In the past tense, only the verb *be* changes form (*was/were*).

⮂ **Cross-Reference: Grammar**

For instruction and practice on singular and plural subject pronouns, refer students to Lesson 11.1.

Resource Manager

📂 **Planning Resources**
- *Lesson Plans*

📓 **Transparencies**
- *Bellringer*
- *Daily Language Practice*

📂 **Other Print Resources**
- *Grammar and Composition Handbook*
- *Grammar Enrichment,* p. 39
- *Grammar Practice,* p. 39
- *Grammar Reteaching,* p. 38
- *Grammar Workbook,* Lesson 50

Practice and Assess

Answers: Exercise 1

1. <u>poems</u> <u>appear</u>
2. <u>She</u> <u>was</u>, correct
3. <u>poetry</u> <u>has</u>
4. <u>She</u> <u>was</u>, correct
5. <u>people</u> <u>enjoy</u>
6. <u>spirit</u> <u>shines</u>, correct
7. <u>poems</u> <u>have</u>, correct
8. <u>Directness</u> <u>marks</u>
9. <u>house</u> and <u>library</u> <u>were destroyed</u>
10. <u>She</u> <u>discusses</u>, correct

Answers: Exercise 2

1. book contains	11. They have
2. Frost has	12. people think
3. Readers find	13. people do
4. He was	14. poetry does
5. libraries have	15. poems have
6. library does	16. poems are
7. Students talk	17. poetry focuses
8. poem is	18. students have
9. works share	19. book has
10. poems do	20. poetry continues

Additional Resources

📁 *Grammar Practice*, p. 39
📁 *Grammar Reteaching*, p. 38
📁 *Grammar Enrichment*, p. 39

 Grammar Workbook, Lesson 50

Close

Ask each student to write a paragraph telling why he or she enjoys a particular writer's work. Have students use in their writing subjects and verbs that agree in number. Direct students to exchange papers and critique one another's work in constructive ways as they check for subject-verb agreement.

Subject-Verb Agreement

Exercise 1   Identifying Subject and Verb Forms

Write the subject and verb of each sentence. Underline the subject once and its verb twice. If they agree, write *correct.* If they do not agree, change the verb.

1. Anne Bradstreet's poems appears first in this book.
2. She was an early American poet.
3. Her poetry have charm and wit.
4. She was a teenager in 1630.
5. Many people enjoys her poems today.
6. Her strong spirit shines through her work.
7. Her shorter poems have the most appeal.
8. Directness mark her style.
9. In 1666 her house and library was destroyed by fire.
10. She discusses the fire in a famous poem.

Exercise 2   Making Subject and Verb Forms Agree

For each sentence, write the subject and the correct form of the verb in parentheses.

1. This book (contain, contains) poems by Frost.
2. Frost (has, have) a great reputation as a lyric poet.
3. Readers (find, finds) his use of symbols interesting.
4. He (was, were) a teacher in his youth.
5. Most libraries (has, have) collections of Frost's work.
6. Certainly our local library (do, does).
7. Students (talk, talks) about Frost's poem "Fire and Ice."
8. This poem (is, are) rather bleak.
9. Several works (share, shares) common themes.
10. Robert Frost's poems (do, does) much for the American spirit.
11. They (have, has) meaning for us today.
12. Some people (think, thinks) his poems are cold.
13. Most people (do, does) admire his work, however.
14. Frost's poetry (do, does) require close study.
15. Even his short poems (have, has) hidden meanings.
16. Certain poems (is, are) apparently simple.
17. His poetry (focus, focuses) on ordinary people.
18. Most students (have, has) read some of his work.
19. His book *In the Clearing* (have, has) some of his most beautiful poems.
20. Frost's poetry (continue, continues) to be popular.

Exploring Language

Using Words That Must Agree

Many non-European languages have no subject-verb agreement. Some students may have trouble making sense out of subject-verb agreement. Assure them that many English-speaking students have similar difficulty grasping gender agreement in other languages.

Making Verbs and Subjects Agree

Write on the board a series of sentences with the subject *I* and a present-tense verb. Have one student read a sentence aloud, changing the *I* to a third-person noun or pronoun and making the verb form agree. Ask another student to change the written sentence. **L1**

16.2 Problems with Locating the Subject

Making a subject and its verb agree is easy when the verb directly follows the subject. Sometimes, however, a prepositional phrase comes between the subject and the verb.

> The **city,** in all its moods, **inspires** poets.
> The **cities** of the Midwest **inspire** poets.

In the first sentence above, *in all its moods* is a prepositional phrase. The singular verb *inspires* agrees with the subject of the sentence, *city,* and not with the plural noun *moods,* which is the object of the preposition. In the second sentence, *of the Midwest* is a prepositional phrase. The plural verb *inspire* agrees with the plural subject, *cities,* and not with the singular noun *Midwest,* which is the object of the preposition.

Some sentences begin with *here* or *there. Here* or *there* is never the subject of a sentence. Look for the subject after the verb.

> There **is** a great **poem** about Chicago.

To more easily identify the subject, rearrange the sentence so that the subject and verb are in their usual order.

> A great **poem** there **is** about Chicago.

In some interrogative sentences, a helping verb may come before the subject. The subject appears between the helping verb and the main verb.

> **Do** these **poems interest** you?

You can check the subject-verb agreement by making the sentence declarative.

> These **poems do interest** you.

16.2 Problems with Locating the Subject **537**

Resource Manager

Planning Resources
• *Lesson Plans*

Transparencies
• *Bellringer*
• *Daily Language Practice*

Other Print Resources
• *Grammar and Composition Handbook*
• *Grammar Enrichment,* p. 40
• *Grammar Practice,* p. 40
• *Grammar Reteaching,* p. 39
• *Grammar Workbook,* Lesson 51

Focus

Lesson Overview

Objectives

• To identify a subject when it is separated from a verb by a prepositional phrase, when the sentence begins with *here* or *there,* or when the subject appears between the helping verb and the main verb in a question

• To write using a verb form that agrees with a subject that does not immediately precede the verb

Subject-Verb Agreement

Bellringer
Daily Language Activity

When students enter the classroom, have this assignment on the board: *Read the following two sentences.* The girls who live down the street are at home. The girls who live down the street is at home. *Copy the sentence in which the subject and verb agree. Circle the subject and underline the verb.*

See also *Daily Language Practice*

Teach

Listening and Speaking

Ask students to listen for the subject, verb, and prepositional phrases as you read aloud the following passage.

> Yellow telephones
> in a row in the garden
> are ringing,
> shrill with light.
>
> —May Swenson
> "Daffodils"

Write the passage on the board and ask students to copy it. Have them circle the subject (telephones) and verb (are ringing) and underline the prepositional phrases that appear between the subject and the verb (in a row; in the garden).

537

Practice and Assess

Answers: Exercise 3

1. lines describe
2. phrase is correct
3. it Does introduce, correct
4. list is
5. Sandburg shows/showed
6. phrases are, correct
7. string appears
8. nickname is, correct
9. reputation comes
10. words echo

Answers: Exercise 4

1. writer, is
2. son, is
3. ideas, arise
4. days, inspire
5. man, Does succeed
6. Critics, praise
7. Poems, are
8. work, Does appear
9. idioms, mark
10. volumes, are
11. sights and sounds, interest
12. stories, appear
13. you, Do know
14. Nature, is
15. events, form
16. critics, Have changed
17. jobs, are
18. Poetry, was
19. sound, is
20. poem, is titled

Additional Resources

 Grammar Practice, p. 40
 Grammar Reteaching, p. 39
📁 *Grammar Enrichment*, p. 40

📖 *Grammar Workbook*, Lesson 51

Exercise 3 **Identifying the Subjects and Verbs**

Write the subject and verb for each sentence. Underline the subject once and its verb twice. If they agree, write *correct*. If they do not agree, correct the verb.

1. These lines of the poem describes the city of Chicago.
2. Here is the phrase "Hog butcher of the world."
3. Does it introduce a certain viewpoint?
4. A list of adjectives are in another line.
5. Sandburg, with a few words, show us the city.
6. There are longer phrases after the introduction.
7. A string of verbs appear among the long phrases.
8. Another nickname for Chicago is City of Big Shoulders.
9. Sandburg's reputation as the Chicago poet come from these lines.
10. The words of this poem echoes American popular speech.

Exercise 4 **Making the Subject and Verb Forms Agree**

For each sentence, write the subject and the correct form of the verb in parentheses.

1. The writer of these poems (is, are) Carl Sandburg.
2. This son of Swedish immigrants (is, are) famous.
3. Ideas for his work (arise, arises) from his travels.
4. His days in Puerto Rico (inspire, inspires) his earliest poems.
5. Does the young man (succeed, succeeds) in his career?
6. Critics around the world (praise, praises) his work.
7. Poems about modern industry (is, are) unusual.
8. (Do, Does) Sandburg's work appear in many collections?
9. The idioms of mid-American speech (marks, mark) his work.
10. The six volumes of his Lincoln biography (is, are) widely read.
11. The sights and sounds of the country also (interests, interest) Sandburg.
12. Bedtime stories for his family (appear, appears) in *Rootabaga Stories*.
13. (Do, Does) you know about Sandburg's school career?
14. Nature, especially in late summer and autumn, (is, are) a favorite subject.
15. The events of Lincoln's early life (forms, form) the basis of *The Prairie Years*.
16. (Has, Have) critics changed their view of Sandburg in recent years?
17. There (is, are) many jobs in Sandburg's past.
18. Poetry of other cultures (was, were) important to Sandburg's work.
19. Here (is, are) the sound of American speech as poetry.
20. A famous poem of his later years (is, are) titled "Timesweep."

Close

Ask each student to write a paragraph describing a place where he or she could write undisturbed. Remind students to be sure that subjects and verbs agree in their sentences. Direct students to exchange papers and proofread one another's work in constructive ways.

Cooperative Learning

Using Prepositional Phrases

Divide students into small groups that include students learning English and fluent English speakers. Write the following on the board: *Cats climb. Children play. The sun rises.* Ask groups to rewrite the sentences, adding prepositional phrases and other modifiers to expand the subject.

16.3 Collective Nouns and Other Special Subjects

It is difficult to tell whether certain special subjects are singular or plural. For example, collective nouns follow special agreement rules. A collective noun names a group. The noun has a singular meaning when used to tell about a group that acts as a unit. The noun has a plural meaning when used to describe members of the group acting as individuals.

The **audience sits** in silence. [one group, singular]

The **audience sit** on chairs and pillows. [individuals, plural]

Certain nouns, such as *mumps* and *mathematics*, end in -*s* but take a singular verb. Other nouns that name one thing, such as *pliers* and *binoculars*, end in -*s* but take a plural verb.

News is important to us all. [singular]

Scissors are useful and often attractive. [plural]

When the subject refers to an amount as a single unit, it is singular. When the subject refers to a number of individual units, it is plural.

Fifty years seems a long time. [single unit]

Fifty years pass quickly. [individual units]

Five dollars is the admission price. [single unit]

Five dollars are on the table. [individual units]

A title of a book or work of art is always singular even if a noun within the title is plural.

"The Victors" is a poem by Denise Levertov. [one poem]

***Collected Earlier Poems* was** published in 1979. [one book]

The class . . .

. . . **studies** modern poetry.

The class . . .

. . . **study** for their exams.

Subject-Verb Agreement

Resource Manager

📁 **Planning Resources**
- *Lesson Plans*

🎵 **Transparencies**
- *Bellringer*
- *Daily Language Practice*

📁 **Other Print Resources**
- *Grammar and Composition Handbook*
- *Grammar Enrichment*, p. 41
- *Grammar Practice*, p. 41
- *Grammar Reteaching*, p. 40
- *Grammar Workbook*, Lesson 52

Focus

Lesson Overview

Objectives
- To learn to determine number when using collective nouns, numbers, titles, and certain nouns ending in -*s* as subjects
- To use verbs that agree in number with special subjects in written sentences

🔔 **Bellringer**
Daily Language Activity

When students enter the classroom, have this assignment on the board: *Write in your journal a list of three to five steps to follow when deciding what form of a verb should follow a subject.*

See also 📖 *Daily Language Practice*

Motivating Activity

Explain that a number of nouns do not follow normal rules for agreement. Collective nouns and nouns that name amounts require an additional step to determine number for verb agreement.

Teach

☑ **Grammar Tip**

Explain to students that each time a collective noun or an amount is used, a writer must decide whether it refers to one group as a body (*it*) or to the individual members or parts of the group (*they*). Also, when a singular noun refers to many individuals, the verb is plural: *The majority of these poets create vivid images of nature.* Have students add this tip to their lists.

🔁 **Cross-Reference: Grammar**

For instruction and practice with collective nouns, refer students to Lesson 9.5.

Practice and Assess

Answers: Exercise 5

1. <u>work</u> <u><u>includes</u></u>
2. <u>class</u> <u><u>is studying</u></u>, correct
3. <u>*The Weary Blues*</u> <u><u>celebrates</u></u>, correct
4. <u>class</u> <u><u>have practiced</u></u>
5. <u>audience</u> <u><u>sits</u></u>, correct
6. <u>crowd</u> <u><u>look</u></u>
7. <u>band</u> <u><u>plans</u></u>, correct
8. <u>band</u> <u><u>take</u></u>, correct
9. <u>Binoculars</u> <u><u>help</u></u>, correct
10. <u>Two dollars</u> <u><u>is</u></u>

Answers: Exercise 6

1. crowd gathers
2. crowd look
3. Ten minutes seems
4. audience find
5. class attends
6. class is
7. class discuss
8. committee awards
9. committee accepts
10. thousand dollars is
11. audience includes
12. book wins
13. Two dollars is
14. club read
15. *Winter Trees* is
16. *Winter Trees* contains
17. News is
18. "Women" is
19. *Revolutionary Petunias* was
20. Twenty-five dollars is

Additional Resources

 Grammar Practice, p. 41
 Grammar Reteaching, p. 40
 Grammar Enrichment, p. 41

 Grammar Workbook, Lesson 52

Subject-Verb Agreement

Exercise 5 Identifying the Subject and Verb Forms

Write the subject and verb of each sentence. Underline the subject once and the verb twice. If they agree, write *correct.* If they do not agree, correct the verb.

1. Langston Hughes's work include more than fifty volumes.
2. The class is studying Hughes's poems for a performance.
3. *The Weary Blues* celebrates Harlem in the 1920s.
4. The class has practiced their poems for the performance.
5. The audience sits quietly, waiting for the curtain to rise.
6. The crowd looks at their programs to find the poem titles.
7. The band plans the blues pieces to be played.
8. The band take out their instruments.
9. Binoculars help those people in the back of the auditorium.
10. Two dollars are the admission price for the performance.

Exercise 6 Using the Correct Verb Form for Special Subjects

For each sentence, write the subject and the correct form of the verb in parentheses.

1. The crowd (gather, gathers) outside the room.
2. The crowd (look, looks) at their programs.
3. Ten minutes (seem, seems) like a long time.
4. The audience (find, finds) their seats.
5. The class (attend, attends) the poetry reading.
6. Our class (is, are) in the first row.
7. The class (discuss, discusses) the Pulitzer Prize among themselves.
8. A committee (award, awards) the prize each year.
9. The committee (accept, accepts) nominations of American poets.
10. A thousand dollars (is, are) the amount of the prize.
11. The audience (include, includes) the poet laureate of the United States.
12. His book *Promises* (win, wins) a prize for Robert Penn Warren.
13. Two dollars (is, are) the price of admission.
14. The poetry club (read, reads) their favorite poems.
15. *Winter Trees* (is, are) a book by Sylvia Plath.
16. *Winter Trees* (contain, contains) some of Plath's best poems.
17. News of other events (is, are) posted at the reading.
18. "Women" (is, are) a poem by Alice Walker.
19. Walker's *Revolutionary Petunias* (was, were) published in 1973.
20. Twenty-five dollars (is, are) the average price of a new book.

Close

Suggest that students imagine winning an award for great achievement in a field of their choice. Ask each of them to write a brief acceptance speech that includes collective nouns as subjects. Suggest that students use a computer to work through the steps of the writing process. Some may wish to give their speeches to the class.

Exploring Language

Using Special Nouns

It may be helpful for students to copy the following rules into their notebooks or computer files:

- Use a singular verb with a branch of learning and with a disease, even if the noun ends in *-s* (*physics, measles*).
- Use a plural verb with an article of clothing that has leg openings (*pants, shorts*) and with a tool that ends in *-s* (*scissors*).

In addition, students might wish to practice using these plural nouns that do not end in *-s*: *sheep, deer, police, the French.*

16.4 Indefinite Pronouns as Subjects

■ An **indefinite pronoun** is a pronoun that does not refer to a specific person, place, thing, or idea.

Some indefinite pronouns are singular. Others are plural. When they are used as subjects, the verb must agree in number with these indefinite pronouns. Study the indefinite pronouns in the chart below.

Indefinite Pronouns			
Singular			**Plural**
another	everybody	no one	both
anybody	everyone	nothing	few
anyone	everything	one	many
anything	much	somebody	others
each	neither	someone	several
either	nobody	something	

The indefinite pronouns *all, any, most, none,* and *some* may be singular or plural, depending on the phrase that follows. Notice how indefinite pronouns are used below.

> **Everyone admires** the poems of Emily Dickinson.[singular]
> **Many** of the poems **deal** with death and love. [plural]
> **Most** of her world **is** within four walls. [singular]
> **Most** of the poems **are** very short. [plural]

Often a prepositional phrase follows an indefinite pronoun that can be either singular or plural. To determine whether the pronoun is singular or plural, look at the object of the preposition.

For example, in the third sentence above, *most* refers to *world*. Because *world* is singular, *most* is singular. In the fourth sentence *most* refers to *poems*. Because *poems* is plural, *most* is plural.

16.4 Indefinite Pronouns as Subjects **541**

Focus

Lesson Overview

Objectives
* To identify singular and plural indefinite pronouns
* To use verbs that agree in number with indefinite pronoun subjects

 **Bellringer**
Daily Language Activity

When students enter the classroom, have this assignment on the board: *Copy this sentence. Underline the indefinite pronoun and circle the verb.*
Answers: *All, seems*

> All seems beautiful to me.
>
> —Walt Whitman
> *Song of the Open Road*

See also  *Daily Language Practice*

Motivating Activity

Have students share their answers. Explain that *All* is singular here because the indefinite pronoun refers to a single unit. In similar sentences, you might suggest that students try substituting *everything* for *all*. Have students monitor their understanding and seek clarification as needed.

Teach

☑ **Teaching Tip**
Since most indefinite pronouns are singular, students may want to memorize ten exceptions. *Both, few, many, others,* and *several* always take a plural verb. *All, any, most, none,* and *some* are variable.

Resource Manager

 **Planning Resources**
* *Lesson Plans*

 **Transparencies**
* *Bellringer*
* *Daily Language Practice*

📁 **Other Print Resources**
* *Grammar and Composition Handbook*
* *Grammar Enrichment,* p. 41
* *Grammar Practice,* p. 41
* *Grammar Reteaching,* p. 41
* *Grammar Workbook,* Lesson 53

Practice and Assess

Answers: Exercise 7

1. Anyone is
2. Most have
3. Others stand
4. Someone reads
5. Everyone listens
6. Few have
7. Several are
8. Everybody laughs
9. Most is
10. Several seem

Answers: Exercise 8

1. Much was
2. Few understand
3. Many study
4. Each learns
5. Everything inspires
6. One uses
7. Another is
8. Everyone knows
9. Someone prefers
10. Both are
11. Few use
12. No one appreciates
13. Many are
14. Few write
15. Most sounds
16. Each has
17. All reap
18. Both rely
19. Few were
20. Nobody uses

Additional Resources

 Grammar Practice, p. 41
Grammar Reteaching, p. 41
Grammar Enrichment, p. 41

Grammar Workbook, Lesson 53

Close

Have each student write a paragraph about someone who has influenced him or her, telling how and why. The influence may be as simple as the choice of a book to read, or it may be more significant, such as the choice of a school to attend. Students should be careful to select verbs that agree with their subjects.

Subject-Verb Agreement

Exercise 7   Identifying Subject and Verb Forms

For each sentence, write the indefinite pronoun and the correct form of the verb.

1. Anyone (is, are) invited to read poems at this poetry reading.
2. Most of the audience (has, have) found seats.
3. Others (stands, stand) in the back of the room.
4. Someone (reads, read) six recently written poems.
5. Everyone (listens, listen) with quiet attention to the poems.
6. Few of the poets (has, have) published their work yet.
7. Several of the poems (is, are) funny.
8. Everybody (laughs, laugh) at a poem about slippery foods.
9. Most of the work (is, are) more serious in tone.
10. Several of the poets (seems, seem) quite young.

Exercise 8   Using the Correct Verb Form for Indefinite Pronoun Subjects

For each sentence, write the subject and the correct form of the verb in parentheses.

1. Much of Emily Dickinson's life (was, were) solitary.
2. Few (understand, understands) her need for quiet.
3. Many (study, studies) her life and times.
4. Each (learn, learns) about her lonely adulthood.
5. Everything in nature (inspire, inspires) the poet.
6. One of the poems (use, uses) a spider as its focus.
7. Another in this tradition (is, are) Walt Whitman.
8. Everyone (know, knows) "O Captain! My Captain!"
9. Someone in class (prefer, prefers) "When Lilacs Last in the Dooryard Bloom'd."
10. Both of these poems (is, are) in memory of Abraham Lincoln.
11. Few (use, uses) rhythm in such a musical way.
12. No one (appreciate, appreciates) Whitman's poetry without effort.
13. Many of Dickinson's poems (is, are) not titled.
14. Few (write, writes) as sparely as Dickinson.
15. Most of Whitman's work (sound, sounds) powerful.
16. Each (have, has) an individual style.
17. All of us (reap, reaps) benefits from the study of these poets.
18. Both of the poets (rely, relies) heavily upon the use of symbolism.
19. Few of Dickinson's poems (was, were) published in her lifetime.
20. Nobody (use, uses) dashes in the same way as Dickinson.

English Language Learners

Using *Much, Many,* and *Any*

The indefinite pronouns *much, any,* and *many* are very difficult for students learning English to understand. *Much* is used to refer to mass or to "noncount" nouns: *Much of our homework is difficult. Many* is used with "count" nouns: *Many have finished their assignments.*

Any may refer to either "count" or "noncount" items. It is used often in questions and in sentences with negative meanings: *Have you eaten any of the apples? I haven't eaten any.*

16.5 Agreement with Compound Subjects

■ A **compound subject** contains two or more simple subjects that have the same verb. The way the subjects are joined determines whether the compound subject takes a singular or a plural verb. When two or more subjects are joined by *and* or by the correlative conjunction *both . . . and,* the plural form of the verb should be used.

> Chicago, Boston, **and** Paris **inspire** many poets.
> Maya Angelou **and** Nikki Giovanni **are** poets.
> **Both** Angelou **and** Giovanni **write** about their times.

All of these sentences refer to more than one person, place, thing, or idea.

Sometimes *and* is used to join two words that are part of one unit or refer to a single person or thing. In these cases, the subject is considered to be singular. In the example below, notice that *teacher* and *adviser* refer to the same person. Therefore, the singular form of the verb is used.

> Her teacher **and** adviser **is** a famous writer.

When two or more subjects are joined by *or, nor,* or the correlative conjunction *either . . . or* or *neither . . . nor,* the verb agrees with the subject that is closest to it.

> The listener **or** the reader **responds** to the rhythm.
> **Either** music **or** street sounds **inspire** urban poets.

In the first sentence, *responds* agrees in number with *reader,* which is the subject closer to it. The verb is singular because the subject is singular. In the second sentence, *inspire* agrees with *sounds,* which is the closer subject. The verb is plural because *sounds* is a plural subject.

16.5 Agreement with Compound Subjects **543**

Subject-Verb Agreement

Focus

Lesson Overview

Objectives

- To learn to determine whether a compound subject takes a singular or a plural verb
- To use the appropriate verb form with a compound subject

Bellringer
Daily Language Activity

When students enter the classroom, have this assignment on the board: *Copy the following sentence and explain why it is incorrect.*

A stove and refrigerator is provided in every kitchen.

See also *Daily Language Practice*

Motivating Activity

Have students share their answers to the Bellringer activity. Explain that such individual subjects name separate items and should not be treated as a single entity. If another article (*a, an, the*) is inserted before the second noun (*a stove and a refrigerator*), it is easier to tell that a plural verb is used. Have students monitor their understanding and seek clarification as needed.

Teach

Cross-Reference: Grammar

For instruction and practice of compound subjects, refer students to Lesson 8.5.

Resource Manager

Planning Resources
- *Lesson Plans*

Transparencies
- *Bellringer*
- *Daily Language Practice*

Other Print Resources
- *Grammar and Composition Handbook*
- *Grammar Enrichment,* p. 39
- *Grammar Practice,* p. 39
- *Grammar Workbook,* Lesson 54

Practice and Assess

Answers: Exercise 9

1. Countee Cullen and Langston Hughes
   write
2. Africa and the South are
3. Drums or pianos appear
4. Heritage and history form
5. W. S. Merwin and John Ashbery are
6. Merwin and Ashbery live
7. woods and gorges stir
8. cold nor snow keeps
9. Hughes and Cullen influence
10. Blues, jazz, or gospel music provides
11. concerns and hope drive
12. poet and novelist is
13. Children and adults enjoy
14. boy or girl appears
15. inspiration and subject is
16. Maya Angelou and Alice Walker are
17. Angelou nor Walker has
18. Africa or South is
19. novel and film were
20. mother and father were
21. verse and essays are
22. Levertov or Walker was
23. poets nor poets have
24. sound and meaning are
25. Poets and readers contribute

Additional Resources

 Grammar Practice, p. 39

 Grammar Enrichment, p. 39

Grammar Workbook, Lesson 54

Close

Ask students what music influences them. Have each of them describe that favorite music in a short paragraph, naming at least two characteristics of the music and describing the effects of those characteristics. Remind students to use some compound subjects in their writing. Have students trade papers to constructively critique verb agreement with compound subjects in their paragraphs.

| **Exercise 9** | Using the Correct Verb Form for Compound Subjects |

For each sentence, write the subject and the correct form of the verb in parentheses.

1. Countee Cullen and Langston Hughes (write, writes) of Africa.
2. Africa and the South (is, are) settings in Hughes's poems.
3. Drums or pianos (appear, appears) often in Hughes's poetry.
4. Heritage and history (form, forms) Cullen's main themes.
5. W. S. Merwin and John Ashbery (is, are) poets.
6. Both Merwin and Ashbery (live, lives) in New York state.
7. The woods and gorges there (stir, stirs) these poets' emotions.
8. Neither cold nor snow (keep, keeps) them from their work.
9. Both Hughes and Cullen (influence, influences) young poets.
10. Blues, jazz, or gospel music often (provide, provides) a background for a poem.
11. Personal concerns and hope for a better world (drive, drives) poet Maya Angelou's work.
12. A poet and novelist (is, are) scheduled to read from her work in the next month.
13. Children and adults (enjoys, enjoy) Angelou's poetry.
14. Either a boy or a girl (appears, appear) in many of these poems.
15. Her inspiration and her subject (is, are) African American life.
16. Maya Angelou and Alice Walker (is, are) African American women and poets.
17. Neither Angelou nor Walker (has, have) ignored the problems of real people.
18. Either Africa or the rural South (is, are) the setting for much of Walker's work.
19. Both the novel and the film of Walker's *The Color Purple* (was, were) very popular.
20. A Welsh mother and a Russian Jewish father (was, were) Denise Levertov's parents.
21. Both her verse and her essays (is, are) lively and precise.
22. Either Levertov or Walker (was, were) a member of the award panel.
23. Neither yesterday's poets nor today's poets (has, have) found all the possibilities of poetry.
24. Both the sound and the meaning of a poem (is, are) important.
25. Poets and readers of poetry (contributes, contribute) to the future of poetry.

Subject-Verb Agreement

Critical Thinking

Determining Singular and Plural Compound Subjects

Have students use the pronouns *he, she, it,* and *they* to replace the compound subjects in a series of sentences you provide. Examples: *Jay and Casey love to write poetry. Their friend and favorite poet meets with them weekly to discuss poetry. Their rhythm and choice of words have improved lately.*

SUBJECT-VERB AGREEMENT

In this passage from "Robert Frost: Visit to a Poet," Octavio Paz describes the wooded area near Robert Frost's cabin in Vermont. The passage has been annotated to show examples of subject-verb agreement.

Literature Model

from "Robert Frost: Visit to a Poet"

by Octavio Paz

translated from the Spanish by Michael Schmidt

In the air there was a scent of green, hot growth, thirsty. Not a tree, not a leaf stirred. A few clouds rested heavily, anchored in a blue, waveless gulf. A bird sang. I hesitated: "How much nicer it would be to stretch out under this elm! The sound of water is worth more than all the poets' words." I walked on for another ten minutes. . . . When I reached the top I could see the whole little valley; the blue mountains, the stream, the luminously green flatland, and, at the very bottom, the forest. The wind began to blow; everything swayed, almost cheerfully. All the leaves sang. I went toward the cabin. It was a little wooden shack, old, the paint flaked, grayed by the years. The windows were curtainless; I made a way through the underbrush and looked in. Inside, sitting in an easy chair, was an old man. Resting beside him was a woolly dog. When he saw me the man stood up and beckoned me to come around the other side. I did so and found him waiting for me at the door of his cabin.

> After the word *there*, a singular verb is followed by its singular noun subject.

> Agreement between a singular subject and verb that have a prepositional phrase between them

> Agreement between a singular pronoun subject and a singular verb

Subject-Verb Agreement

Teach

About the Literature

Explain that this review contains a passage from Octavio Paz's essay "Robert Frost: Visit to a Poet." It describes Paz's visit to Frost in June 1945, when the American poet was more than seventy years old. The passage appears in a book of essays by Paz entitled *On Poets and Others.* It is annotated to show examples of subject-verb agreement, followed by exercises on the same topic. After students have read the passage, have them examine the three sample sentences pointed out in the margin. Call on volunteers to explain, in their own words, subject-verb agreement in these sentences.

Linking Grammar and Literature

☑ **Teaching Tip**

Have students individually read through the paragraph and ask for help if they are unable to locate or determine the number of any subjects.

Listening and Speaking

Ask students to notice the different kinds of sentences as you read aloud the passage by Octavio Paz. Call on volunteers to locate the subjects in various sentences and identify them as singular or plural.

Critical Thinking

Have students identify and explain which subjects were hardest to locate and then those that were hardest to identify as singular or plural.

✔ ASSESSMENT OPTIONS

📁 *Tests with Answer Key and Rubrics*
Unit 16 Mastery Test, pp. 67–68

💾 *Testmaker*
Unit 16 Mastery Test

Resource Manager

📁 **Planning Resources**
• *Lesson Plans*

📁 **Other Print Resources**
• *Grammar and Composition Handbook*
• *Grammar Workbook,* Lessons 50–54; *Unit 16 Review; Cumulative Review:* Units 1–16

Grammar Review

Practice and Assess

Answers: Exercise 1

1. <u>He</u> listens
2. <u>Clouds</u> float
3. <u>bird</u> begins
4. <u>It</u> inspires
5. <u>flock</u> continue
6. <u>dog</u> lies
7. <u>Both</u> notice
8. <u>They</u> greet
9. <u>day</u> pleases
10. <u>mountains</u> appear

Answers: Exercise 2

1. air has
2. clouds are
3. bird has
4. mountains are
5. cabin is
6. It does
7. windows have
8. dog has
9. Paz and Frost have
10. men do

Subject-Verb Agreement

Review: Exercise 1   **Making Verbs Agree with Noun and Pronoun Subjects**

For each sentence, write the subject and the correct form of the verb in parentheses. Underline the subject.

SAMPLE Octavio Paz (walk, walks) toward Robert Frost's cabin.
ANSWER <u>Octavio Paz</u> walks

1. He (listen, listens) to the still air.
2. Clouds (float, floats) lazily in the sky above.
3. One bird (begin, begins) to sing a song.
4. It (inspire, inspires) other birds to sing as well.
5. The flock (continue, continues) to sing their songs all afternoon.
6. Beside Robert Frost (lie, lies) his dog.
7. Both (notice, notices) Paz's arrival.
8. They (greet, greets) him with pleasure.
9. The summer day (please, pleases) each of them.
10. The distant mountains (appear, appears) blue.

Review: Exercise 2   **Making Forms of *Be, Do,* and *Have* Agree with Subjects**

For each sentence, write the subject and the correct form of the verb in parentheses.

SAMPLE The pine needles (is, are) soft under foot.
ANSWER needles are

1. The air (has, have) the scent of hot, green growth.
2. The clouds (is, are) anchored in the blue, waveless gulf.
3. A bird (has, have) started to sing.
4. The mountains (is, are) blue in the distance.
5. Frost's cabin (is, are) old, with flaking grayed paint.
6. It (do, does) look like a good place for a poet to work.
7. The windows (has, have) no curtains.
8. The dog (have, has) a woolly coat.
9. Paz and Frost (has, have) arranged this visit in advance.
10. The two men (do, does) feel glad for the chance to talk.

Review: Exercise 3   Locating Subjects and Making Verbs Agree

Write each sentence and complete it with the correct form of the verb in parentheses. Then underline the subject once and the verb twice. If the verb consists of two words, underline both words.

1. There (is, are) a few clouds hanging heavily overhead.
2. Paz (wants, want) to talk with Frost.
3. There (is, are) the sound of water running in a small brook.
4. (Do, does) Paz enjoy the sound of the water?
5. The fields at the bottom of the valley (is, are) luminously green.
6. Here (is, are) Frost's cabin at the top of the hill.
7. (Do, Does) Frost's cabin seem remote?
8. Where (is, are) the woolly dog and his master?
9. There (is, are) signs of movement inside the cabin.
10. The windows (is, are) curtainless.

Review: Exercise 4   Making Verbs Agree with Collective Nouns and Other Special Subjects

For each sentence, write the subject and the correct form of the verb in parentheses.

1. Binoculars (offer, offers) a view of the valley.
2. The woods (is, are) home to many small animals.
3. A cluster of trees (provides, provide) a moment of coolness.
4. Frost's "Fire and Ice" (discusses, discuss) heat and cold.
5. Twenty minutes of walking (makes, make) Paz feel hot.
6. A few minutes under the elms (seems, seem) appealing.
7. In the sun, the audience (waves, wave) small fans to stay cool.
8. A flock of crows (moves, move) like many shadows in the blue sky.
9. The fleet of clouds (clumps, clump) together, darkening the hills.
10. Mathematics (was, were) not of much interest to the young Frost.

Answers: Exercise 3

1. <u>clouds</u> <u>are hanging</u>
2. <u>Paz</u> <u>wants</u>
3. <u>sound</u> <u>is</u>
4. <u>Paz</u> <u>does enjoy</u>
5. <u>fields</u> <u>are</u>
6. <u>cabin</u> <u>is</u>
7. <u>cabin</u> <u>does seem</u>
8. <u>dog and master</u> <u>are</u>
9. <u>signs</u> <u>are</u>
10. <u>windows</u> <u>are</u>

Answers: Exercise 4

1. Binoculars offer
2. woods are
3. cluster provides
4. "Fire and Ice" discusses
5. minutes makes
6. minutes seems
7. audience waves
8. flock moves
9. clouds clump
10. Mathematics was

Answers: Exercise 5

1. Most deals
2. Most use
3. Some remember
4. Anyone treasures
5. Everybody remembers
6. Nobody puts
7. Something makes
8. Few have
9. Most know
10. No one is

Answers: Exercise 6

1. Frost and Paz discuss
2. Vermont and Mexico do
3. fear or loneliness drives
4. failure or adventures await
5. Frost nor Paz trusts
6. poets nor professors are
7. fantasy nor science fiction appeals
8. work and work interest
9. Frost and Antonio Machado have
10. Frost nor Machado has

Subject-Verb Agreement

Review: Exercise 5 Making Verbs Agree with Indefinite Pronoun Subjects

For each sentence, write the subject and the correct form of the verb in parentheses.

1. Most of Robert Frost's poetry (deals, deal) with the landscape.
2. Most of his poems (uses, use) simple language.
3. Some of us (remembers, remember) his reading at Kennedy's inauguration.
4. Anyone present that day (treasures, treasure) the memory of Frost's reading.
5. Everybody (remembers, remember) Angelou's reading at Clinton's inauguration.
6. Nobody (puts, put) together a collection of American poetry without including Frost.
7. Something in his poems (makes, make) them touch our hearts.
8. Few (has, have) never read any of his works.
9. Most of us (knows, know) "Stopping by Woods on a Snowy Evening."
10. No one (is, are) likely to miss this poem's meaning.

Review: Exercise 6 Making Verbs Agree with Compound Subjects

For each sentence, write the subject and the correct form of the verb in parentheses.

1. Frost and Paz (discusses, discuss) their countries' landscapes.
2. Vermont and Mexico (does, do) not look much alike.
3. According to Frost, either fear or loneliness (drives, drive) people away from the countryside.
4. According to both men, failure or adventures (awaits, await) every poet.
5. Neither Frost nor Paz (trusts, trust) people who cannot laugh, especially at themselves.
6. According to Frost, neither solemn poets nor humorless professors (is, are) worthy of trust.
7. Neither fantasy nor science fiction (appeals, appeal) to Frost.
8. Both the work of young poets and the work of philosophers (interests, interest) him.
9. According to Paz, Frost and the Spaniard Antonio Machado (has, have) much in common.
10. Neither Frost nor Machado (has, have) any fondness for solemn topics.

Proofreading

The following passage is about French artist Pierre Bonnard, whose work appears below. Rewrite the passage, correcting the errors in spelling, capitalization, grammar, and usage. Add any missing punctuation. There are ten errors.

Pierre Bonnard

¹Pierre Bonnard (1867–1947) began his career as one of the french artists who rejected the more brighter colors and broken brush strokes of a popular style of art. ²Later Bonnard begun painting scenes of everyday life. ³Brighter colors and textured brush strokes marks his work.

⁴The painting below reflect Bonnard's change of style. ⁵Full of light and color, the painting capture the effect of sunlight streeming into a room. ⁶The view of the trees and woods are peaceful. ⁷The picture could show what Octavio Paz saw when he reached Robert Frosts cabin. ⁸The vivid blues and greens in the picture contrasts sharply with the deep red colors.

Pierre Bonnard, *Dining Room in the Country,* 1913

Answers: Exercise 7
Proofreading

This proofreading activity provides editing practice with (1) the current or previous units' skills, (2) **Troubleshooter** errors, and (3) spelling errors. Students should be able to complete the exercise by referring to the units, the **Troubleshooter,** and a dictionary.

Error (Type of Error)
1. French (capitalization)
   the brighter (double comparison)
2. began (verb form)
3. mark (subject-verb agreement)
4. reflects (subject-verb agreement)
5. captures (subject-verb agreement)
   streaming (spelling)
6. is (subject-verb agreement)
7. Frost's (singular possessive)
8. contrast (subject-verb agreement)

Viewing the Art

Pierre Bonnard, *Dining Room in the Country,* 1913

In *Dining Room in the Country,* Pierre Bonnard (1867–1947) presents a section of a room. This technique allows the artist to reveal the sunlit landscape that exists outside the dwelling. Presenting only a portion of the room also makes the scene seem casual, as if it had been captured in a snapshot. The woman at the window seems to have struck a pose for the camera. Bonnard's oil painting, which measures 64 1/2 by 80 inches, is in the Minneapolis Institute of Arts. Have students discuss the painting to expand on the ideas present in the passage above.

Answers: Exercise 8
Mixed Review

1. is
2. has
3. lives
4. includes
5. are
6. are
7. contains
8. shows
9. is
10. was
11. reflect
12. seems
13. influences
14. appeals
15. form
16. needs
17. are
18. was
19. are
20. were
21. serves
22. were
23. was
24. Have
25. was

Close

Have students listen to a variety of speakers on television, on radio, in person, or in everyday conversations. Have them record on paper any errors in subject-verb agreement. Collect papers, redistribute them, and have students correct the subject-verb agreement errors.

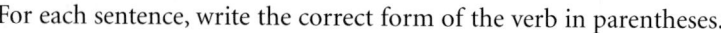

Review: Exercise 8

Mixed Review

For each sentence, write the correct form of the verb in parentheses.

Octavio Paz: Mexican Poet

1. Octavio Paz (is, are) a poet, an essayist, and a diplomat.
2. The Nobel Prize committee (has, have) awarded him its highest honor.
3. With his family, he (live, lives) in Mexico City.
4. His literary output (includes, include) poems, essays, and translations.
5. Most of his poems (is, are) written in Spanish.
6. His early poems (is, are) among his most powerful.
7. *On Poets and Others* (contains, contain) Paz's interview with Frost.
8. The poem "Renga" (shows, show) his grasp of languages.
9. Languages or literature (are, is) Paz's primary interest.
10. Mixcoac, one of Mexico City's suburbs, (was, were) his childhood home.
11. The colonial buildings of Mixcoac (reflects, reflect) a long heritage.
12. Paz's place in literary reference books (seems, seem) secure.
13. His six years as ambassador to India (influences, influence) his poetry.
14. The Eastern idea of *yin* and *yang* (appeals, appeal) to him.
15. The two sides of the Mexican coin (forms, form) an important image in Octavio Paz's work.
16. Anybody interested in literature (needs, need) to read Octavio Paz.
17. Many of his works (is, are) available in English.
18. *Selected Poems* (was, were) published in 1963.
19. Harvard and the University of Texas (is, are) important in Octavio Paz's educational career.
20. The United States, France, and Japan (was, were) early posts in his diplomatic career.
21. For younger writers, Paz (serves, serve) as a teacher and as a guide.
22. Both his father and his grandfather (was, were) involved in politics.
23. A lawyer and liberal reformer (was, were) Paz's grandfather Ireneo.
24. (Has, Have) Paz's writings become more available recently?
25. News of Octavio Paz's receiving the honor (was, were) no surprise to readers of his work.

Subject-Verb Agreement

Writing Application

Subject-Verb Agreement in Writing

As he discusses the earth's complex biology in this passage from *Living Treasure,* Laurence Pringle is careful not to distract his readers with unmatched subjects and verbs. Read the passage, focusing especially on the italicized words.

> *Scientists are* dazzled and puzzled by the diversity of life on earth. *No one knows* how many different *kinds* of plants, animals, and other organisms there *are.* But we do know that the *organisms* identified so far *are* only a small fraction of all living things. There are *millions*—perhaps many millions—that *await* discovery.

Techniques with Subject-Verb Agreement

Try to apply some of Laurence Pringle's writing techniques when you revise your own work.

❶ Watch carefully for phrases and unusual sentence structures that make the subject difficult to identify. Notice below how removing a phrase from the sentence or rearranging the sentence to place the subject at the beginning allows you to check for subject-verb agreement:

HARD TO CHECK The *study* of living things *is* called biology

EASIER TO CHECK The *study is* called biology

❷ Pay special attention to subject-verb agreement when the subject is an indefinite pronoun. You must determine whether the indefinite pronoun is singular or plural.

INCORRECT VERSION *No one know* how many different kinds . . . there are.

CORRECT VERSION *No one knows* how many different kinds . . . there are.

TIME
For more about the writing process, see **TIME Facing the Blank Page,** pp. 97–107.

Subject-Verb Agreement

Subject-Verb Agreement in Writing

Call on a volunteer to read the paragraph aloud. Then go back and discuss the italicized (subject-verb) choices. Discuss these choices in relation to the Techniques with Subject-Verb Agreement below.

Techniques with Subject-Verb Agreement

Discuss the two writing techniques described. Have students turn to page 549 and apply these techniques to the Proofreading exercise.

Practice

The answers to this challenging and enriching activity will vary. Refer to Techniques with Subject-Verb Agreement as you evaluate student choices. The following are sample answers:

1. annoy
2. sing
3. is
4. brings
5. do
6. are

✔ ASSESSMENT OPTIONS

📁 *Tests with Answer Key and Rubrics* Unit 16 Mastery Test, pp. 67–68

💾 *Testmaker* Unit 16 Mastery Test

You may wish to administer the Unit 16 Mastery Test at this point.

📼 *Mindjogger Videoquizzes*

Practice Practice these techniques by revising the following passage, using a separate sheet of paper. At each blank space, insert a verb that agrees with the sentence subject.

"The words of this song _____ me every time," complained Lucia. Look, both characters _____ throughout the song, yet she _____ never named. Still, the lovely melody _____ audiences to their feet every time. Very few songs _____ that. Here _____ some copies of the music. Let's give it a try." With that speech, Lucia signaled the beginning of our new school Chorus Club.

Objectives

- To develop an understanding of the difference between words that are often confused, misused, or misspelled
- To use these words correctly

☑ ASSESSMENT OPTIONS

📁 *Tests with Answer Key & Rubrics*
Unit 17 Pretest, pp. 69–70
Unit 17 Mastery Test, pp. 71–72

💾 *Testmaker*
Unit 17 Pretest
Unit 17 Mastery Test

You may wish to administer the Unit 17 Pretest at this point.

Key to Ability Levels

L1 Level 1 activities are within the basic ability range of students.

L2 Level 2 activities are within the ability range of average students.

L3 Level 3 activities are more challenging activities.

UNIT
17

Glossary of Special Usage Problems

552

Resource Manager

📁 **Planning Resources**
- *Lesson Plans*
- *Block Scheduling*

📠 **Transparencies**
- *Bellringer*
- *Daily Language Practice*

📁 **Other Print Resources**
- *Grammar and Composition Handbook*
- *Grammar Enrichment*

- *Grammar Practice*
- *Grammar Reteaching*
- *Grammar Workbook*
- *Tests with Answer Key and Rubrics*

📼 **Video**
- *MindJogger Videoquizzes*

💾 **Software**
- *Interactive Grammar and Language Workbook*
- *Language Arts PASS*

- *Presentation Plus!*
- *Testmaker*

 **Web Sites**
- *writerschoice.glencoe.com*

17.1 Using Troublesome Words I

Like all languages, English contains a number of confusing expressions. The following glossary will help you understand some of the more troublesome ones.

Word	Meaning	Example
accept	"to receive"	Most stores readily **accept** credit cards as well as cash.
except	"other than"	I have no money **except** a dollar.
all ready	"completely prepared"	I am **all ready** to go shopping.
already	"before" or "by this time"	I **already** spent all of my allowance for this week.
all together	"in a group"	We will shop **all together.**
altogether	"completely"	The shirts I liked were **altogether** too costly.
amount	"quantity of things thought of as a unit"	That **amount** of money will buy a large **number** of roses.
number	"quantity of things thought of as separate units"	
beside	"next to"	The shoe store is **beside** the bank.
besides	"in addition to"	**Besides** shoes it carries socks.
between	Use *between* for two people or things.	Choose **between** two styles.
among	Use *among* when talking about groups of three or more.	Distribute the suits **among** the seven stores.
bring	"to carry from a distant place to a closer one"	We **bring** goods into this country.
take	"to carry from a nearby place to a more distant one"	They **take** goods from this country to other lands.
choose	"to select" (present)	We **choose** items to import.
chose	"selected" (in the past)	Buyers **chose** silk last year.
in	"inside"	Factories are often **in** cities.
into	indicates movement from outside to a point within	Imports come **into** a country.

Focus

Lesson Overview

Objectives
- To understand the differences in meaning and usage between some commonly confused words
- To use these commonly confused words correctly

 Bellringer
Daily Language Activity

When students enter the classroom, have this assignment on the board: *Read the following excerpt and write why you think* between *is used in the first sentence and* among *is used in the second.*

> Between the rows of hanging carpets and tapestries were whole canoes, a few as long as forty feet. . . . Interspersed among these were carved and painted wood chests.
>
> —Virginia Hamilton
> *The House of Dies Drear*

See also  *Daily Language Practice*

Motivating Activity

Ask students to explain their responses to the Bellringer activity. (*Between* refers to two sets of things; *among* refers to a group.)

Teach

Vocabulary Link

The word *accept* always refers to taking something in or including something. *Except* is related to the word *exception.* The prefix *ex-* means "out." *Except* means "taking out" or "excluding."

Glossary of Special Usage Problems

Resource Manager

📁 **Planning Resources**
- *Lesson Plans*

🔖 **Transparencies**
- *Bellringer*
- *Daily Language Practice*

📁 **Other Print Resources**
- *Grammar and Composition Handbook*
- *Grammar Enrichment,* p. 42
- *Grammar Practice,* p. 42
- *Grammar Reteaching,* p. 42
- *Grammar Workbook,* Lessons 63–65

Practice and Assess

Answers: Exercise 1

1. accept
2. between
3. already
4. chose
5. Take
6. all together
7. into
8. except
9. Besides
10. many

Answers: Exercise 2

1. chose
2. beside
3. all ready
4. except
5. Besides
6. take
7. in
8. between
9. among
10. accepts
11. bring
12. all together
13. choose
14. already
15. into
16. except
17. beside
18. Take
19. chose
20. All together

Additional Resources

 Grammar Practice, p. 42

Grammar Reteaching, p. 42

Grammar Enrichment, p. 42

Grammar Workbook, Lessons 63–65

Close

Sample sentences can help students remember the proper usage of troublesome words. For example, both *all together* and *altogether* are adverbs. However, *all together* usually modifies a verb (*We shopped all together*), while *altogether* modifies an adjective or another adverb (*My mother was altogether delighted*). Encourage students to write in their own journals their own sentences for pairs of confusing words.

Glossary of Special Usage Problems

Exercise 1 · Choosing the Correct Word

Write each sentence, choosing the correct word or words in parentheses.

1. Most countries (accept, except) foreign goods.
2. Trade (between, among) China and the United States has grown.
3. Food distribution has (all ready, already) improved in China.
4. Jan (choose, chose) silk from Hong Kong.
5. (Bring, Take) enough money, or yuan, with you when you go to Guangzhou.
6. The buyers flew (all together, altogether) to Shanghai.
7. Exports go out of a country, whereas imports come (in, into) it.
8. Most countries export all goods (accept, except) those needed by their people.
9. (Beside, Besides) machinery, China imports grain, cotton, and fertilizers.
10. China trades with (many, a lot of) countries, including Japan.

Exercise 2 · Using the Correct Word

Write each sentence, using a word or words from the lesson. A definition of the word or a clue appears in parentheses.

1. Nigeria _____ to lower the price of oil. (selected)
2. Oil is loaded on tankers _____ the docks. (next to)
3. That tanker is _____ to sail to foreign lands. (completely prepared)
4. Nigeria produces most of its major foods _____ fish. (other than)
5. _____ oil, Nigeria exports rubber. (in addition to)
6. He will _____ our order to the mill. (carry to a distant place)
7. Many foreign companies operate oil wells _____ Nigeria. (inside)
8. Oil causes money to flow _____ Nigeria and the United States. (two places)
9. Farming, mining, and fishing are _____ their activities. (group of three)
10. Nigeria _____ foreign goods from trading partners. (receives)
11. Foreign ships _____ imports to Nigeria. (carry from a distant place)
12. The Nigerians stood on the dock _____, waiting for the ship. (in a group)
13. A person can _____ to be a farmer or a miner. (select)
14. When I arrived, the tanker was _____ at the dock. (by that time)
15. The oil was pumped _____ a tanker. (movement from outside to within)
16. That ship carried no goods _____ oil. (other than)
17. The captain and crew stood _____ their ship. (next to)
18. _____ this crop to the nearest market. (carry to a distant place)
19. Nigeria _____ to lease oil wells to foreign companies. (selected)
20. _____ Nigerian wells produce millions of barrels of oil daily. (in a group)

Cooperative Learning

Working with Word Pairs

Non-native English speakers may have trouble understanding the difference in meaning between such word pairs as *between, among; choose, chose;* and *in, into.* You might pair these students with native English speakers who can help them create simple phrases demonstrating each word's meaning (*between a rock and a hard place; among friends*). The students should write the sentences in a notebook or put them in a computer file to refer to as needed.

17.2 Using Troublesome Words II

Word	Meaning	Example
its	the possessive form of *it*	A country may limit **its** imports.
it's	the contraction of *it is*	**It's** vital to protect jobs.
lay	"to put" or "to place"	Vendors **lay** shoes in rows.
lie	"to recline" or "to be positioned"	Fish **lie** packed in ice.
learn	"to receive knowledge"	We **learn** about trade.
teach	"to give knowledge"	Economists **teach** in colleges.
leave	"to go away"	I will **leave** on a sales trip.
let	"to allow"	**Let** them buy our product.
loose	"not firmly attached"	A **loose** bolt damages a product's quality.
lose	"to misplace" or "to fail to win"	Buyers often **lose** trust in a product.
raise	"to cause to move upward" or "to grow"	We **raise** the nets. They **raise** corn.
rise	"to move upward"	Porpoises **rise** from the water.
set	"to place" or "to put"	They **set** products on display.
sit	"to place oneself in a seated position"	**Sit** here and take orders.
than	*Than* introduces the second part of a comparison.	My price is lower **than** hers.
then	"at that time"	If prices are low, **then** buy.
their	*Their* is the possessive form of *they.*	**Their** products are well made.
they're	*They're* is the contraction of *they are.*	**They're** taught to work carefully.
who's	*Who's* is the contraction of *who is.*	**Who's** a great economist?
whose	*Whose* is the possessive form of *who.*	She is a person **whose** views are valued.

Glossary of Special Usage Problems

Focus

Lesson Overview

Objectives

- To understand the difference in meaning and usage between some commonly confused words
- To use the troublesome words introduced in the lesson correctly

Bellringer
Daily Language Activity

When students enter the classroom, have this assignment on the board: *List ten words you commonly misspell or misuse.*

See also *Daily Language Practice*

Motivating Activity

Discuss with students their own troublesome words. Encourage them to keep personal lists of words that confuse them. Point out that many common troublesome words are homophones. Students may brainstorm to compile a list of common homophone mix-ups and review their meanings.

Teach

Technology Tip

Students with access to computers can use the "search and replace" function of their word-processing programs to search for troublesome words. Students can then check the usage of each word and replace it if they have not used it correctly.

Cross-Reference: Composition

For instruction and practice for editing and making final adjustments, refer students to Lesson 2.9.

Resource Manager

Planning Resources
- *Lesson Plans*

Transparencies
- *Bellringer*
- *Daily Language Practice*

Other Print Resources
- *Grammar and Composition Handbook*
- *Grammar Enrichment,* p. 42
- *Grammar Practice,* p. 42
- *Grammar Reteaching,* p. 42
- *Grammar Workbook,* Lessons 65–67

Practice and Assess

Answers: Exercise 3

1. their
2. than
3. it's
4. learn
5. then
6. lose
7. lie
8. whose
9. rise
10. sit

Answers: Exercise 4

1. lets	11. learn
2. lie	12. teach
3. loose	13. then
4. leave	14. whose
5. raise	15. lies (or sits)
6. lie	16. It's
7. its	17. their
8. than	18. lose
9. rise	19. They're
10. their	20. sit

Additional Resources

📁 *Grammar Practice*, p. 42
📁 *Grammar Reteaching*, p. 42
📁 *Grammar Enrichment*, p. 42

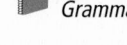 *Grammar Workbook*, Lessons 65–67

Close

Many troublesome words are exceptions to rules or are sound-alikes. Ask students to brainstorm to create a list of ways to remember differences in usage and meaning, such as linking a word to an image, exaggerating differences in pronunciation, and substituting near-synonyms for difficult words. Ask students to record the best memory devises in their journals.

Glossary of Special Usage Problems

Exercise 3 Choosing the Correct Word

Write each sentence, choosing the correct word in parentheses.

1. Italians are proud that (their, they're) country's products are in demand.
2. Italy produces more olives (than, then) any other country.
3. Tourists agree that (its, it's) a beautiful country.
4. Many Italian students (learn, teach) skills in industry.
5. We drove into Milan and (than, then) brought back fabrics.
6. We feared we would (loose, lose) our way.
7. The Alps (lay, lie) along Italy's northern border.
8. Italy looks like a boot (whose, who's) toe points toward Sicily.
9. Sardinia seems to (raise, rise) out of the Mediterranean Sea.
10. Many statues (sit, set) in the plazas of Italy's large cities.

Exercise 4 Using the Correct Word

Write each sentence, using a word from the lesson. A definition of the word or a clue appears in parentheses.

1. Britain _____ its trade with Europe expand. (allows)
2. North Sea oil rigs _____ on steel pilings. (are positioned on)
3. These oil rigs can become _____. (not firmly attached)
4. Workers on these rigs _____ their families for months. (go away from)
5. Visits home _____ the spirits of these workers. (cause to move upward)
6. They can then _____ down and rest. (recline)
7. Great Britain is proud of _____ oil wells. (possessive form of *it*)
8. Today oil production is better _____ in the past. (used in comparisons)
9. Now oil rigs _____ from the North Sea. (move upward)
10. Once the people had to import _____ oil. (possessive form of *they*)
11. The British had much to _____ about mining oil. (receive knowledge)
12. By the 1970s, they could _____ others about oil rigs. (give knowledge)
13. First they pumped the oil, and _____ they exported the surplus. (at that time)
14. Britain is a country _____ mines are well known. (possessive form of *who*)
15. Much of the country _____ above rich deposits of coal. (is positioned)
16. _____ a fact that coal output has declined lately. (contraction of *it is*)
17. Most people use gas or oil to heat _____ homes. (possessive form of *they*)
18. The British will _____ little export revenue. (fail to win)
19. _____ still mining coal and natural gas. (contraction of *they are*)
20. They _____ above other minerals. (place themselves in a seated position)

Viewing and Representing

Interpreting Visuals

Making a Collage of Meanings Some students may benefit from a visual presentation of the words listed on page 555. Ask the class to cut photos that illustrate the meanings of the words from newspapers and magazines. For example, a picture of a teacher speaking to a group of students could illustrate both *learn* and *teach*. Collect the pictures and label the words illustrated. Then use the pictures to make a collage. Post it on a class bulletin board so that students can learn to identify each word with a visual image.

Grammar Review

GLOSSARY OF SPECIAL USAGE PROBLEMS

The Clay Marble, by Minfong Ho, tells of a Cambodian family forced to flee when Vietnamese troops invaded Cambodia in 1980. In the following passage, the narrator, twelve-year-old Dara, and her friend Nea load rice seed onto a cart.

Literature Model

from *The Clay Marble*
by Minfong Ho

Half running and half stumbling with the sack of rice held between us, Nea and I headed for one of the oxcarts, probably looking very much like a crab scuttling across the sand. But we managed to reach the cart, and even to swing the sack neatly into it. Nea wiped the sweat off her forehead. "We did it," she said, sounding very surprised.

"I told you we could," I grinned, panting.

Again and again we did this, moving sack after sack from the shelter of the blue tarp and into the wagon. After a while there was a layer two-deep of the precious rice-seed bags on the bottom of the oxcart.

If we planted the rice seeds with care and if the weather was good, I knew that the seeds we brought home in the cart would be enough to supply half the village next year. I felt a deep satisfaction that these seeds, at least, would not be broken and crushed to feed the soldiers here.

> *Between* used with two people

> *Into* used to indicate movement from outside to within

> *Brought* used to mean "carried from a distant place to a closer one"

Grammar Review **557**

Teach

About the Literature

Explain that the review contains a passage from Minfong Ho's *The Clay Marble* that reflects Dara and Nea's determination to return home to Cambodia and rebuild their lives. The novel was inspired by the author's experiences as a volunteer working in a Thai refugee camp.

After students have read the passage, initiate a discussion about the characters and mood. Then ask students to determine which words are or are not essential to the meaning of the passage. Have students support their answers with evidence, elaboration, or examples.

Linking Grammar and Literature

☑ **Teaching Tip**

Ask students to focus on the highlighted words in the passage. Ask: *Would the meaning of the passage be as clear if the writer had used some of these words incorrectly?*

Critical Thinking

Have students discuss some of the mental images evoked by Minfong Ho's word choices in this passage.

Listening and Speaking

Have students make up their own sentences using the words *between, into,* and *brought* and then share the sentences with the class. Discuss any errors students may have in their sentences.

✓ ASSESSMENT OPTIONS

📁 *Tests with Answer Key and Rubrics*
Unit 17 Mastery Test, pp. 71–72

💾 *Testmaker*
Unit 17 Mastery Test

Resource Manager

📂 **Planning Resources**
• *Lesson Plans*

📂 **Other Print Resources**
• *Grammar and Composition Handbook*
• *Grammar Workbook,* Lessons 63–67; *Unit 11 Review; Cumulative Review: Units 1–11*

Practice and Assess

Answers: Exercise 1

1. take
2. raise
3. already
4. among
5. beside
6. all together
7. all ready
8. let
9. their
10. its
11. teach
12. loose
13. It's
14. its
15. learn
16. lie
17. they're
18. whose
19. leave
20. Then
21. chose
22. altogether
23. accept
24. rise
25. than

Grammar Review

Review: Exercise 1   **Making Usage Choices**

The following sentences were suggested by passages from *The Clay Marble*. Write the correct word in parentheses to complete each sentence.

SAMPLE   Carrying each sack of rice (between, among) them, the two girls loaded the cart.
ANSWER   between

1. Dara and Nea planned to (bring, take) the rice back to their home in Cambodia.
2. The countries of Asia (raise, rise) much rice.
3. They had (all ready, already) repaired the oxcart.
4. Oxcarts find much use (between, among) the people of Cambodia.
5. They placed the sacks (beside, besides) each other.
6. Dara hoped her family would be ready to plant the seeds (all together, altogether).
7. When the girls finished their work, the oxcart was (all ready, already) for the trip home.
8. Jantu (leave, let) Dara play with the clay toys.
9. Many poor people must make (their, they're) own toys.
10. Clay gets (its, it's) color from the materials in it.
11. Farmers (learn, teach) their children that too much clay is bad for crops.
12. One day Jantu gathered some (loose, lose) clay, rolled it into a perfect sphere, and gave it to Dara.
13. "(Its, It's) a magic marble," said Jantu.
14. Dara believed in (its, it's) magical powers.
15. The girl had to (learn, teach) that the magic was in her.
16. Thick layers of clay (lay, lie) under the rich, black soil.
17. Artists often use clay when (their, they're) sculpting a person or an animal.
18. Jantu, (who's, whose) brother was hurt, had to go to the hospital with him.
19. Dara was afraid to (leave, let) her friend.
20. (Than, Then) she remembered the magic marble.
21. Bravely the girl (choose, chose) to look for her family on her own.
22. Dara knew that it was (all together, altogether) possible for her to fail.
23. But she would not (accept, except) defeat.
24. Now her hopes of finding her family began to (raise, rise).
25. Dara's determination, rather (than, then) the marble, gave her courage.

Glossary of Special Usage Problems

Review: Exercise 2

Proofreading

The following passage is about the cultivation of tea in China, which is illustrated in the work below. Rewrite the passage, correcting the errors in spelling, grammar, and usage. Add any missing punctuation. There are ten errors.

Tea Cultivation in Ancient China

[1]By the ninth century into China, the cultivation of tea was subject to well-established procedures and traditions. [2]The seeds first had to be planted in sandy soil to leave them drain properly. [3]When the seeds sprouted, the farmers lightly watered the plants, using the same water in which the seeds had all ready been washed. [4]The figures in *Tea Cultivation* is watering the young tea plants and fertilizing them. [5]According to Lu Yü, who's essay on tea helped popularize tea cultivation, fertilizer made from the wastes of silkworms was prefered.

Artist unknown, China, *Tea Cultivation*, nineteenth century

(continued)

Answers: Exercise 2 Proofreading

This proofreading activity provides editing practice with (1) the current or previous units' skills, (2) **Troubleshooter** errors, and (3) spelling errors. Students should be able to complete the exercise by referring to the units, the **Troubleshooter,** and a dictionary.

Error (Type of Error)
1. in (word usage)
2. let (word usage)
3. already (word usage)
4. are (subject-verb agreement)
5. whose (word usage)
   preferred (spelling)

Viewing the Art

Artist unknown, *Tea Cultivation*, nineteenth century This silk print was created in the nineteenth century by an unknown Chinese artist. Have students discuss how the artist's choice of elements portrayed in *Tea Cultivation* helps to represent the meaning of the passage above.

Grammar Review

Answers: Exercise 2 (continued)

Error (Type of Error)

6. raised (word usage)
7. meant (verb form)
8. their (word usage)
9. Except (word usage)

Answers: Exercise 3
Mixed Review

1. their
2. it's
3. Except
4. many
5. among
6. It's
7. raise
8. besides
9. choose
10. rise
11. let
12. in
13. its
14. all together
15. lose
16. lie
17. accept
18. all ready
19. then
20. take

Close

List on the board several of the most troublesome words reviewed in this unit. Have students explain in their own words the rule for the correct usage of each word. Brainstorm with the class to write a sample sentence for each word, illustrating its proper usage. You may want to post the sentences on a bulletin board as a reminder to the class or have the students copy the sentences into their journals for future reference.

560

Glossary of Special Usage Problems

[6]Rice is another major crop rose in China and in many other Asian countries. [7]To Dara and her family in *The Clay Marble*, rice meaned life. [8]Planting the seeds enabled them to rebuild they're lives. [9]Accept for the rice, they might have starved.

> **Review: Exercise 3**

Mixed Review

In the following exercise, you will learn more about rice, which was so important to Dara and Nea. Write the correct word or words in parentheses to complete each sentence.

1. About half of the world's people eat rice as (their, they're) main food.
2. Although wheat is important here, (its, it's) rice that's important in Asia.
3. (Accept, Except) for rice, many Asians have little to eat.
4. In Asia (a lot of, many) people eat rice three times a day.
5. Rice plays a role in the religious life (between, among) people of India.
6. (Its, It's) thought that the throwing of rice at weddings came from India.
7. Many Asian farmers (raise, rise) rice on their land.
8. Cereal grains (beside, besides) rice include oats, rye, wheat, and barley.
9. Rice farmers must (choose, chose) to plant in areas that have much rain.
10. Mature rice plants (raise, rise) from two to six feet above the ground.
11. Rice farmers (leave, let) the grains in the head of each plant ripen.
12. A rice grain has a rough hull, or shell, (in, into) which the kernels are found.
13. Each kernel is surrounded by (its, it's) brown skins, called bran coats.
14. Kernel, bran coats, and hull are (all together, altogether) in the rice grain.
15. We usually (loose, lose) the bran coats when rice is milled.
16. Valuable vitamins and minerals (lay, lie) within the bran coats.
17. Rather than (accept, except) this loss, we add these ingredients back to milled rice.
18. When rice plants are (all ready, already) to harvest, their stalks are cut.
19. The stalks are (than, then) left in the sun to dry.
20. Some farmers (bring, take) their sun-dried stalks to a thresher.

Writing Application

Usage in Writing

A persuasive argument can be seriously weakened by a usage error. In Bel Kaufman's article about the value of public libraries, she avoided confusing certain similar words. Note the italicized words as you read this passage from "The Liberry."

It seems to me that especially now, when there are so many people in our city *whose* language is not English, *whose* homes are barren of books, who are daily seduced by clamorous offers of instant diversion, especially now we must hold on to something that will endure when the movie is over, the television set broken, the class dismissed for the last time.

For many, the public library is the only *quiet* place in an *unquiet* world; a refuge from the violence and ugliness outside; the only space available for privacy or thought.

Techniques with Usage

Try to apply some of Bel Kaufman's writing techniques when you write and revise your own work.

❶ Make your meaning clear by using *whose* correctly to indicate possession and *who's* when a contraction of *who* and *is* is appropriate:

INCORRECT USAGE *who's* language

KAUFMAN'S VERSION *whose* language

❷ Be alert to frequently confused word pairs, such as *quiet* and *quite*. Choose the correct word to help keep your writing accurate and precise.

INCORRECT USAGE the public library is the only *quite* place in an un*quite* world . . .

KAUFMAN'S VERSION the public library is the only *quiet* place in an un*quiet* world . . .

> **TIME**
>
> For more about the writing process, see **TIME Facing the Blank Page,** pp. 97–107.

Glossary of Special Usage Problems

Practice Gain practice distinguishing confusing pairs of words as you revise the passage below. Check each underlined word. If the word is correct, write *correct* on your paper. If the word is wrong, write the correct word.

"Be sure to <u>take</u> your costume when you come to dress rehearsal. <u>It's</u> our last chance to get everything <u>already</u> for the show." Mr. Oberg, <u>who's</u> voice filled the theater as he spoke to the cast, then <u>sat</u> each student's script on a pile <u>beside</u> the stairs to the stage. "Pick these up as you <u>leave</u>. <u>There</u> all marked with last-minute reminders and tips. And don't <u>loose</u> them," he implored, "or I won't <u>leave</u> you attend the cast party!"

Writing Application **561**

Usage in Writing

Encourage students to read silently the passage from "The Liberry." Discuss how the words in italics are used and identify the words with which they could be confused.

Techniques with Usage

Discuss the correct and incorrect usage of the words *whose, who's, quiet,* and *quite* as they are used in the Kaufman passage.

Practice

The answers to this challenging and enriching activity will vary. Refer to Techniques with Usage as you evaluate student choices.

Sample:

"Be sure to <u>bring</u> your costume when you come to dress rehearsal. <u>It's</u> our last chance to get everything <u>all ready</u> for the show." Mr. Oberg, <u>whose</u> voice filled the theater as he spoke to the cast, then <u>lay</u> (or set) each student's script on a pile <u>beside</u> the stairs to the stage. "Pick these up as you <u>leave.</u> <u>They're</u> all marked with last-minute reminders and tips. And don't <u>lose</u> them," he implored, "or I won't <u>let</u> you attend the cast party!"

✔ ASSESSMENT OPTIONS

📁 *Tests with Answer Key & Rubrics*
Unit 17 Mastery Test, pp. 71–72

💾 *Testmaker*
Unit 17 Mastery Test

You may wish to administer the Unit 17 Mastery Test at this point.

📼 *MindJogger Videoquizzes*

Objectives

- To develop an understanding of and the ability to identify various kinds of sentences and sentence parts
- To be able to represent sentences and sentence parts in sentence diagrams.

Key to Ability Levels

L1 Level 1 activities are within the basic ability range of students.

L2 Level 2 activities are within the ability range of average students.

L3 Level 3 activities are more challenging activities.

UNIT 18 Diagraming Sentences

562

Resource Manager

📁 **Planning Resources**
- *Lesson Plans*
- *Block Scheduling*

 Transparencies
- *Bellringer*

📁 **Other Print Resources**
- *Grammar and Composition Handbook*
- *Grammar Enrichment*
- *Grammar Practice*

- *Grammar Reteaching*
- *Grammar Workbook*
- *Tests with Answer Key and Rubrics*

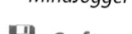 **Video**
- *MindJogger Videoquizzes*

💾 **Software**
- *Interactive Grammar and Language Workbook*
- *Language Arts PASS*
- *Presentation Plus!*

- *Sentence-Diagraming*
- *Testmaker*

 **Web Sites**
- *writerschoice.glencoe.com*

18.1 Diagraming Simple Subjects and Simple Predicates

Every sentence contains a subject and a predicate. To diagram a sentence, first draw a horizontal line. Then draw a vertical line that crosses the horizontal line.

To the left of the vertical line, write the simple subject. To the right of the vertical line, write the simple predicate. Use capital letters as they appear in the sentence, but do not use punctuation.

Apples grow.

| Apples | grow |

Be sure to write only the simple subject and the simple predicate in this part of the diagram. Remember that the simple predicate can include a helping verb.

Some **apples are falling** already.

| apples | are falling |

Exercise 1   **Diagraming Simple Subjects and Simple Predicates**

Diagram each simple subject and simple predicate.

1. Apples fell.
2. They have ripened.
3. Joan tastes one.
4. Workers pick the fruit.
5. Some people are resting.
6. The orchard is busy.
7. Many people are working.
8. We trimmed the tree.
9. Mom removed the old branches.
10. Birds fill the orchard.

Objective

- To identify simple subjects and simple predicates and to represent them in sentence diagrams

Teach

☑ **Teaching Tip**

Before they begin diagraming, advise students that the first word in a sentence keeps its capital letter.

Practice and Assess

Answers: Exercise 1

1. | Apples | fell
2. | They | have ripened
3. | Joan | tastes
4. | Workers | pick
5. | people | are resting
6. | orchard | is
7. | people | are working
8. | We | trimmed
9. | Mom | removed
10. | Birds | fill

Close

Students may want to diagram the simple subjects and simple predicates of sentences from text found in an early reader or on a product label. Have students share and discuss their sentences and diagrams. Revise the diagrams as needed.

Diagraming Sentences

Resource Manager

📂 **Planning Resources**
- *Lesson Plans*

📂 **Other Print Resources**
- *Grammar and Composition Handbook*
- *Grammar Workbook,* Lesson 55

Objective

• To diagram simple subjects and simple predicates in four kinds of sentences

Practice and Assess

Answers: Exercise 2

1. I | brought
2. you | Do like
3. (you) | Taste
4. pear | is
5. pear | is
6. Pears | are
7. you | Do eat
8. (you) | Try
9. you | Have eaten
10. (you) | Slice
11. trees | grow
12. trees | Do grow
13. Pears | have
14. trees | are
15. pears | came
16. pears | grow
17. pears | Are
18. pears | ripen
19. pears | are
20. (you) | Wash

Diagraming Sentences

18.2 Diagraming the Four Kinds of Sentences

The simple subject and simple predicate of the four kinds of sentences are diagramed below. Note that the location of the simple subject and simple predicate in a sentence diagram is always the same, regardless of the word order in the sentence.

DECLARATIVE

Many **people eat** pears.

people | eat

INTERROGATIVE

Do many **people eat** pears?

people | Do eat

IMPERATIVE

Eat a pear.

(you) | Eat

EXCLAMATORY

How many pears **people eat!**

people | eat

Note that in an interrogative sentence, the subject often comes between the two parts of a verb phrase. In an imperative sentence, the word *you* is understood to be the simple subject.

Exercise 2 **Diagraming Simple Subjects and Predicates**

Diagram the simple subject and the simple predicate of each sentence.

1. I brought a pear for lunch.
2. Do you like pears?
3. Taste this one.
4. This pear is delicious.
5. How delicious this pear is!
6. Pears are good in salads.
7. Do you eat pears often?
8. Try some pear juice.
9. Have you ever eaten pear pie?
10. Slice these pears.
11. Pear trees grow everywhere.
12. Do the trees grow high?
13. Pears have few calories.
14. How tall these trees are!
15. American pears came from France.
16. Many pears grow in California.
17. Are these pears ripe?
18. Most pears ripen in the fall.
19. How juicy these pears are!
20. Wash these pears.

564 Unit 18 Diagraming Sentences

Close

Ask students to write an exclamatory and an interrogative sentence about a favorite food. As they share their sentences, they can identify the subject and predicate of each. Have volunteers diagram the simple subjects and simple predicates on the board. Students should discuss corrections that are needed.

Resource Manager

📂 **Planning Resources**
• *Lesson Plans*

📂 **Other Print Resources**
• *Grammar and Composition Handbook*
• *Grammar Workbook,* Lesson 56

18.3 Diagraming Direct and Indirect Objects

In a sentence, a direct object usually comes after the verb. In a sentence diagram, place the direct object to the right of the action verb. Use a vertical line to separate the direct object from the verb. The vertical line does *not* extend below the horizontal line.

The Cruzes grow **apples.**

Cruzes	grow	apples

They have an **orchard.**

They	have	orchard

A sentence can also have an indirect object. In a sentence diagram, place an indirect object on a line below and to the right of the verb. Join it to the verb with a slanted line.

Rosa showed **us** the trees.

Rosa	showed	trees
	us	

Exercise 3 **Diagraming Sentences**

Diagram the simple subject, the simple predicate, and the direct object of each sentence. If there is an indirect object, diagram it also.

1. Our class was studying agriculture.
2. Mrs. Hong showed us some peaches.
3. She told the students many historical facts.
4. The ancient Chinese discovered peaches.
5. They gave the trees care.
6. Artists painted pictures of the lovely fruit.
7. People gave their friends this treat.
8. Travelers took Europeans some peaches.
9. Europe developed different varieties.
10. American colonists brought them to Virginia.

Objective

- To identify direct objects and indirect objects and to represent them in sentence diagrams

Teach

⇄ Cross-Reference: Grammar

For instruction and practice with transitive verbs and direct objects, refer students to Lesson 10.2. For help with indirect objects, see Lesson 10.3.

Practice and Assess

Answers: Exercise 3

1. | class | was studying | agriculture |

2. | Mrs. Hong | showed | peaches |
   | | us | |

3. | She | told | facts |
   | | students | |

4. | Chinese | discovered | peaches |

5. | They | gave | care |
   | | trees | |

6. | Artists | painted | pictures |

7. | People | gave | treat |
   | | friends | |

8. | Travelers | took | peaches |
   | | Europeans | |

9. | Europe | developed | varieties |

10. | colonists | brought | them |

Close

Ask students to create pairs of transitive verbs and related objects (example: *slam* and *door*). Have students trade lists with partners, write a simple sentence for each word pair, and diagram the subject, predicate, and direct object of each sentence. Partners should discuss each other's work.

Resource Manager

📂 **Planning Resources**
- *Lesson Plans*

📂 **Other Print Resources**
- *Grammar and Composition Handbook*
- *Grammar Workbook,* Lesson 57

Objective

• To identify adjectives and adverbs and to represent them in sentence diagrams

Practice and Assess

Answers: Exercise 4

1.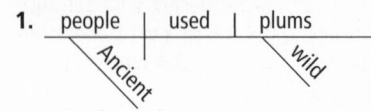

2.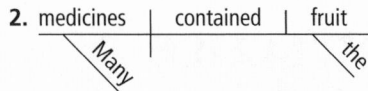

3.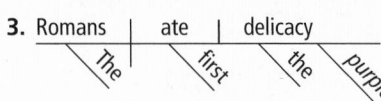

4.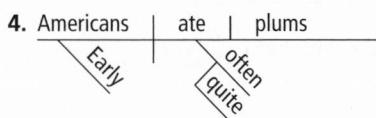

5.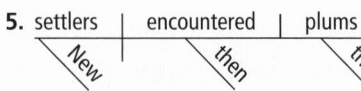

6.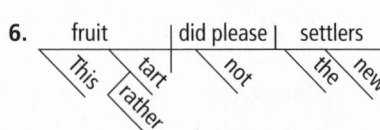

7.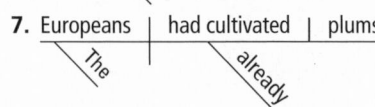

8.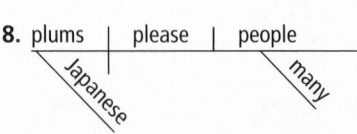

9.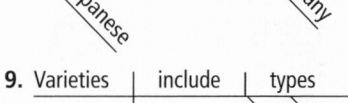

10.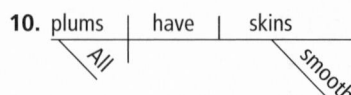

Diagraming Sentences

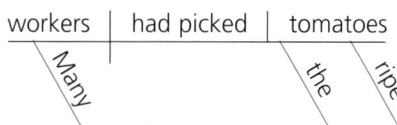

18.4 Diagraming Adjectives and Adverbs

An adjective modifies a noun or a pronoun. In a diagram, write the adjective on a slanted line beneath the noun or pronoun it modifies. Diagram the articles *a, an,* and *the* as you would diagram other adjectives.

Many workers had picked **the ripe** tomatoes.

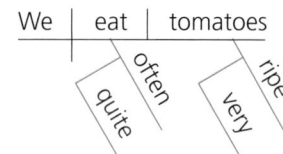

An adverb can modify a verb, an adjective, or another adverb. Note how adverbs are diagramed.

We eat **very ripe** tomatoes **quite often.**

Exercise 4 Diagraming Sentences

Diagram each sentence.

1. Ancient people used wild plums.
2. Many medicines contained the fruit.
3. The Romans first ate the purple delicacy.
4. Early Americans ate plums quite often.
5. New settlers then encountered the plums.
6. This rather tart fruit did not please the new settlers.
7. The Europeans had already cultivated plums.
8. Japanese plums please many people.
9. Varieties include many popular types.
10. All plums have smooth skins.

Close

Invite students to create lists of five adjectives and the adverbs that might describe them. Have them trade their lists with partners, write a sentence for each word pair, and diagram each sentence. Partners should check and discuss each other's work.

Resource Manager

📁 **Planning Resources**
• *Lesson Plans*

📁 **Other Print Resources**
• *Grammar and Composition Handbook*
• *Grammar Workbook,* Lesson 58

18.5 Diagraming Predicate Nouns and Predicate Adjectives

In a sentence diagram, a direct object follows the action verb.

We bought grapefruit.

| We | bought | grapefruit |

A predicate noun follows a linking verb in the complete predicate of a sentence. In a sentence diagram, place the predicate noun after the linking verb. Draw a slanted line to separate the linking verb from the predicate noun.

Grapefruits are tart **fruits.**

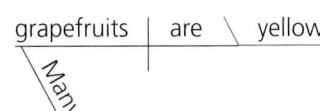

Diagram a predicate adjective as you would a predicate noun.

Many grapefruits are **yellow**

Exercise 5   Diagraming Sentences

Diagram each sentence.

1. Grapefruit is a healthful food.
2. Fruits are nutritious.
3. Some grapefruits are seedless.
4. They were popular.
5. Many grapefruits taste sour.
6. This can be an enjoyable taste.
7. Heavy grapefruits are juicy.
8. The grapefruit is a favorite breakfast food.
9. The fruit is a West Indian native.
10. It is popular lately.

Diagraming Sentences

Objective
• To identify predicate nouns and predicate adjectives and to represent them in sentence diagrams

Practice and Assess

Answers: Exercise 5

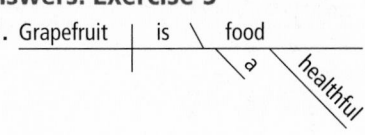

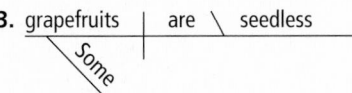

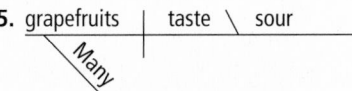

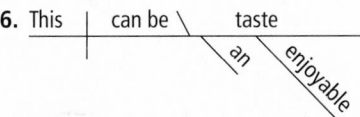

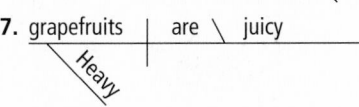

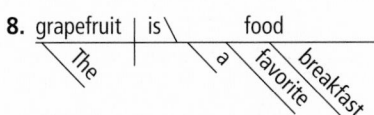

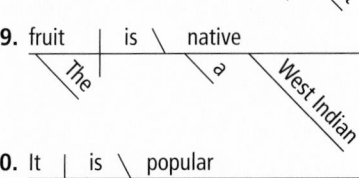

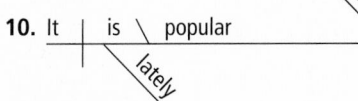

Resource Manager

☞ **Planning Resources**
• *Lesson Plans*

☞ **Other Print Resources**
• *Grammar and Composition Handbook*
• *Grammar Workbook*, Lesson 57

Close

Have students write sentences about a favorite food, using predicate nouns and predicate adjectives. Partners can exchange sentences and diagram them. Have students check each other's work and discuss needed revisions.

Objective

- To identify prepositional phrases and to represent them in sentence diagrams

Teach

☑ Grammar Tip

A prepositional phrase always functions as a modifier and thus is placed below the word it modifies.

Practice and Assess

Answers: Exercise 6

1.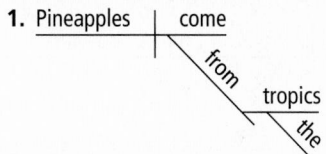
2.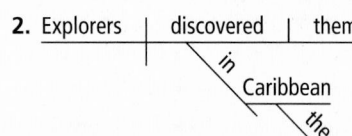
3.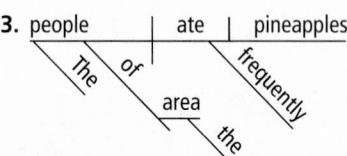
4.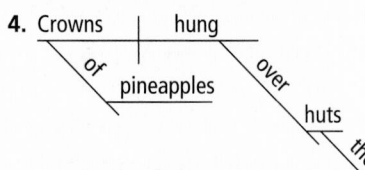
5.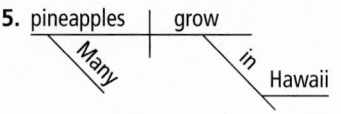

In a sentence diagram, connect modifiers to the words that they modify. If the modifier is a prepositional phrase, connect the phrase to the word that it modifies. The model below shows a prepositional phrase used as an adjective.

The berries **on those bushes** are ripe.

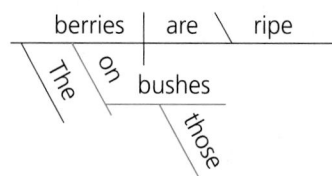

In this sentence, the prepositional phrase *on those bushes* modifies the noun *berries.*

The same phrase can be used as an adverb.

Raspberries grow **on those bushes.**

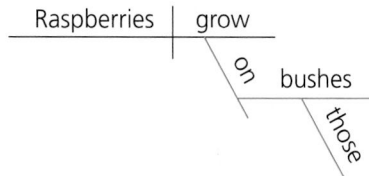

In this sentence, the adverb phrase modifies the verb *grow.*

Exercise 6   Diagraming Sentences

Diagram each sentence.

1. Pineapples come from the tropics.
2. Explorers discovered them in the Caribbean.
3. The people of the area ate pineapples frequently.
4. Crowns of pineapples hung over the huts.
5. Many pineapples grow in Hawaii.

Close

Have students work in small groups to write two simple sentences, each containing a prepositional phrase. Invite groups to exchange and diagram sentences. Groups should check each other's work and suggest changes as needed.

Resource Manager

📁 Planning Resources
- *Lesson Plans*

📁 Other Print Resources
- *Grammar and Composition Handbook*
- *Grammar Workbook,* Lesson 59

18.7 Diagraming Compound Sentence Parts

Coordinating conjunctions such as *and, but,* and *or* are used to join words, phrases, and sentences. To diagram compound parts of a sentence, place the second part of the compound below the first. Then write the coordinating conjunction on a dotted line connecting the two parts.

COMPOUND SUBJECT

Lemons or limes add flavor.

COMPOUND PREDICATE

Trees **grow and blossom.**

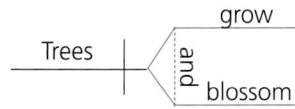

COMPOUND DIRECT OBJECT

Lemon trees produce **leaves and blossoms.**

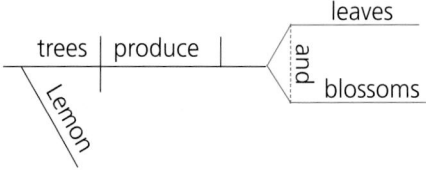

Exercise 7 **Diagraming Sentences**

Diagram each sentence.

1. Oranges and peaches came from China.
2. Traders bargained or bartered.
3. Traders sought fruit and spices.
4. Oranges provide flavor and color.
5. Oranges and peaches are sweet and flavorful.

Resource Manager

📂 **Planning Resources**
• *Lesson Plans*

📂 **Other Print Resources**
• *Grammar and Composition Handbook*
• *Grammar Workbook,* Lesson 60

Objective

• To learn how compound sentence parts function in simple sentences and how to represent them in sentence diagrams

Teach

☑ **Teaching Tip**

Advise students not to confuse the compound subject or compound predicate of a simple sentence with the clauses of a compound sentence.

Diagraming Sentences

Practice and Assess

Answers: Exercise 7

1.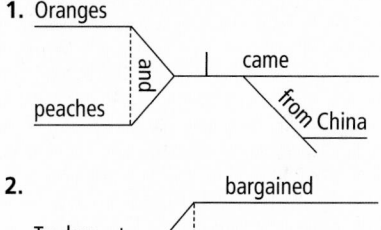

2.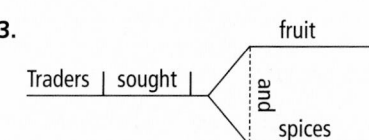

3.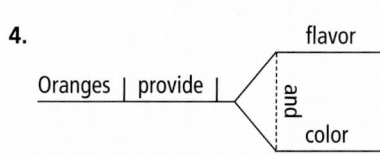

4.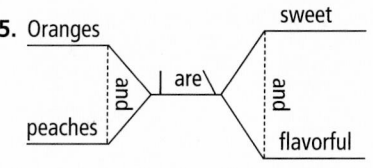

5.

Close

Invite pairs of students to find examples of compound subjects, predicates, and direct objects in a piece of literature. Partners can identify, discuss, and diagram the compound sentence parts. Partners should exchange papers with another pair, check diagrams, and work together to correct errors.

18.8 Diagraming Compound Sentences

Objective
• To identify compound sentences and to represent main clauses separately in sentence diagrams

Answers: Exercise 8

1.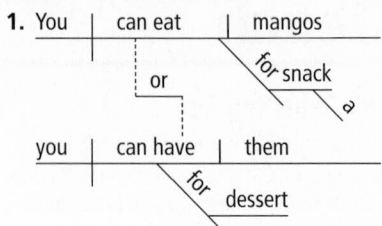

2.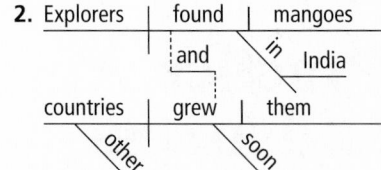

3.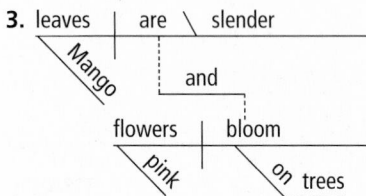

4.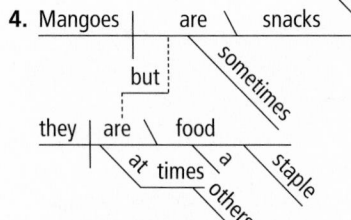

5.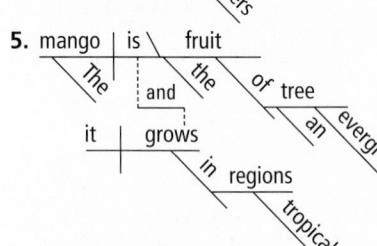

6.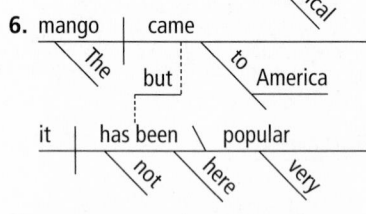

7.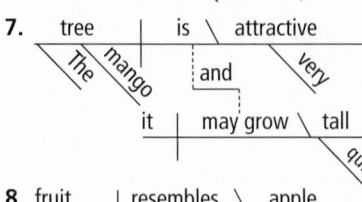

8.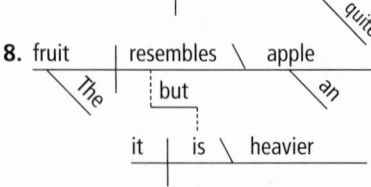

9.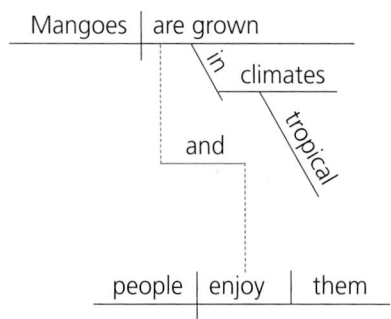

10.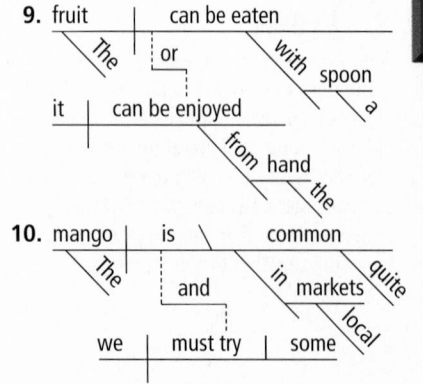

Diagraming Sentences

18.8 Diagraming Compound Sentences

To diagram compound sentences, diagram each main clause separately. If the main clauses are connected by a conjunction such as *and*, *but*, or *or*, place the conjunction on a solid horizontal line, and connect it to the verbs of each clause by vertical dotted lines. If the clauses are connected by a semicolon, use a vertical dotted line to connect the verbs of each clause.

Mangoes are grown in tropical climates, **and** people enjoy them.

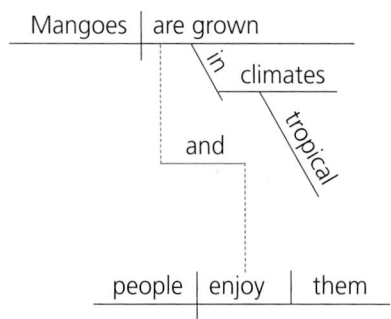

Exercise 8   Diagraming Sentences

Diagram each sentence.

1. You can eat mangoes for a snack, or you can have them for dessert.
2. Explorers found mangoes in India, and other countries soon grew them.
3. Mango leaves are slender, and pink flowers bloom on the trees.
4. Sometimes mangoes are snacks, but at other times, they are a staple food.
5. The mango is the fruit of an evergreen tree, and it grows in tropical regions.
6. The mango came to America, but it has not been very popular here.
7. The mango tree is very attractive, and it may grow quite tall.
8. The fruit resembles an apple, but it is heavier.
9. The fruit can be eaten with a spoon, or it can be enjoyed from the hand.
10. The mango is quite common in local markets, and we must try some.

18.9 Diagraming Complex Sentences with Adjective and Adverb Clauses

To diagram a complex sentence with an adjective clause, place the adjective clause below the main clause. Draw a dotted line between the relative pronoun of the adjective clause and the word it modifies in the main clause. Position the relative pronoun according to its function in the adjective clause.

ADJECTIVE CLAUSE

People **who grow fruit** work hard.

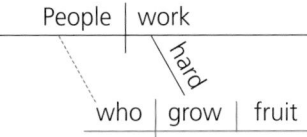

Similarly, diagram an adverb clause below the main clause. Draw a dotted line between the verb of the adverb clause and the verb in the main clause. Write the subordinating conjunction on the dotted line.

ADVERB CLAUSE

As a banana ripens, it turns yellow.

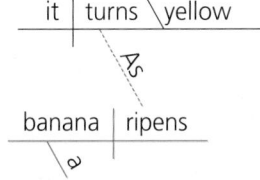

| Exercise 9 | **Diagraming Sentences** |

Diagram each sentence.

1. Bananas are green before they ripen.
2. A banana that is brownish is very ripe.
3. Bananas smell fragrant when they are ripe.
4. When a banana has turned yellow, its seeds have matured.
5. Bananas are shipped before they are ripe.

Objective
- To identify adjective and adverb clauses in complete sentences and to represent them in sentence diagrams

Practice and Assess

Answers: Exercise 9

1.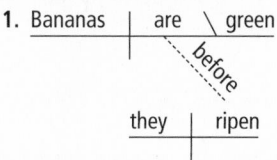

2.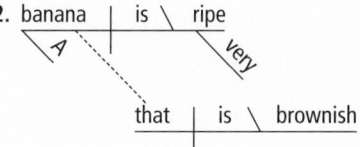

3.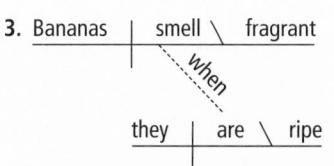

4.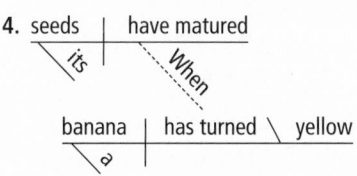

5.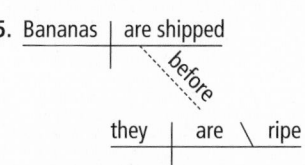

Close

Have students look through their own journal writing or other writing projects to find and discuss examples of adjective clauses and adverb clauses in complex sentences. Then they can diagram their examples, and partners can suggest necessary corrections.

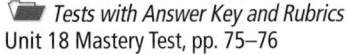

Resource Manager

Planning Resources
- Lesson Plans

Other Print Resources
- Grammar and Composition Handbook
- Grammar Workbook, Lesson 62; Unit 10 Review; Cumulative Review: Units 1–10

✔ ASSESSMENT OPTIONS

📂 *Tests with Answer Key and Rubrics*
Unit 18 Mastery Test, pp. 75–76

💾 *Testmaker*
Unit 18 Mastery Test

You may wish to administer the Unit 18 Mastery Test at this point.

📼 *Mindjogger Videoquizzes*

Objectives

- To develop an understanding of the rules for the capitalization of sentences, quotations, salutations, names and titles of people, names of places, and other proper nouns and adjectives
- To capitalize words correctly to clarify and enhance meaning

Key to Ability Levels

L1 Level 1 activities are within the basic ability range of students.

L2 Level 2 activities are within the ability range of average students.

L3 Level 3 activities are more challenging activities.

UNIT 19 Capitalization

572

Resource Manager

📁 **Planning Resources**
- *Lesson Plans*
- *Block Scheduling*

 Transparencies
- *Bellringer*
- *Daily Language Practice*

📁 **Other Print Resources**
- *Grammar and Composition Handbook*

- *Grammar Enrichment*
- *Grammar Practice*
- *Grammar Reteaching*
- *Grammar Workbook*
- *Tests with Answer Key and Rubrics*

📺 **Video**
- *MindJogger Videoquizzes*

💾 **Software**
- *Interactive Grammar and Language Workbook*
- *Language Arts PASS*
- *Presentation Plus!*
- *Testmaker*

🖥 **Web Sites**
- *writerschoice.glencoe.com*

19.1 Capitalizing Sentences, Quotations, and Letter Parts

A capital letter appears at the beginning of a sentence. A capital letter also marks the beginning of a direct quotation and the salutation and closing of a letter.

RULE 1:   Capitalize the first word of every sentence.

> **P**ioneers pushed the American frontier westward.

RULE 2:   Capitalize the first word of a direct quotation that is a complete sentence. A direct quotation gives a speaker's exact words.

> Tyrone said, "**T**he pioneers acted very bravely."

RULE 3:   When a quoted sentence is interrupted by explanatory words, such as *she said*, do not begin the second part of the sentence with a capital letter.

> "They left their homes," said Lee, "**s**o they could improve their lives."

When the second part of a quotation is a new sentence, put a period after the interrupting expression and begin the second part of the quotation with a capital letter.

> "Many pioneers went west for the rich farmland," said Maria. "**T**hey also wanted to build new homes."

RULE 4:   Do not capitalize an indirect quotation. An indirect quotation does not repeat a person's exact words and does not appear in quotation marks. It is often introduced by the word *that*.

> Tanya read **that m**any pioneers traveled in Conestoga wagons.

RULE 5:   Capitalize the first word in the salutation and closing of a letter. Capitalize the title and name of the person addressed.

> **D**ear **M**rs. Johnson,   **Y**ours truly,
> **D**ear friend,   **S**incerely,

19.1 Capitalizing Sentences, Quotations, and Letter Parts   **573**

Focus

Lesson Overview

Objectives
- To understand the rules for capitalizing sentences, quotations, and letter parts
- To capitalize sentences, quotations, and letter parts correctly

Bellringer
Daily Language Activity

When students enter the classroom, have this assignment on the board: *Write five sentences in which you repeat a conversation between yourself and a friend. Use no capital letters.*

See also   *Daily Language Practice*

Motivating Activity

Invite a volunteer to write his or her sentences on the board. Discuss with students what effect the lack of capital letters has on the reading of the sentences. Does it make it more confusing? Does it make any difference? Elicit from students where capital letters should be placed in the sentences.

Capitalization

Teach

☑ Teaching Tip

If students have difficulty distinguishing between direct and indirect quotations, remind them that the word *that* is often used to introduce an indirect quotation. The word *that* often follows a verb such as *say* or *state* to introduce an indirect quotation: *Tyrone said that the pioneers acted bravely.* *That* should not be used after such verbs to introduce a direct quotation. The correct form would be *Tyrone said, "The pioneers acted bravely."*

Resource Manager

📂 Planning Resources
- *Lesson Plans*

📦 Transparencies
- *Bellringer*
- *Daily Language Practice*

📂 Other Print Resources
- *Grammar and Composition Handbook*
- *Grammar Enrichment,* p. 43
- *Grammar Practice,* p. 43
- *Grammar Reteaching,* p. 43
- *Grammar Workbook,* Lesson 68

Practice and Assess

Answers: Exercise 1

1. We were preparing a report on . . .
2. Joan said, "The pioneers needed . . .
3. "They hunted," said Carlos, "and . . . "
4. Ann added, "Some pioneers . . . "
5. "They also had skill in building," she said. "Many pioneers . . . "
6. Joan said, "Most pioneers . . . "
7. "Can you imagine life without stores?" asked Ann. "Pioneers . . . "
8. We decided that pioneers had to . . .
9. "Most pioneers kept a cow for milk, butter, and cheese," said Carlos. "They also raised chickens . . . "
10. "Before the railroads," said Joan, "pioneers traveled . . . "
11. correct
12. He added, "A loaded wagon . . . "
13. Most families . . .
14. In one book, Ann read, "The . . . "
15. "The trip . . . ," said Joan. "It often . . . "
16. "One trail . . . ," Joan added, "which . . . "
17. "We followed . . . ," Lee told us. "In some . . . "
18. Pioneers wrote letters that began, "Dear loved ones."
19. They signed them, "With much . . . "
20. Pioneers and . . .
21. Joan asked, "Would you have . . . "
22. Carlos replied, "No, I would . . . "
23. "The railroad," said Ann, "opened . . . "
24. "Stagecoach company . . . ," Joan said. "The railroads . . . "
25. "They were . . . ,"Lee added, "and more . . . "

Additional Resources

 Grammar Practice, p. 43

Grammar Reteaching, p. 43

Grammar Enrichment, p. 43

Grammar Workbook, Lesson 68

Exercise 1   Capitalizing Sentences, Quotations, and Letter Parts

Write each sentence, using capital letters where needed. If an item contains no error, write *correct.*

1. we were preparing a report on westward expansion.
2. Joan said, "the pioneers needed many skills."
3. "they hunted," said Carlos, "and farmed."
4. Ann added, "some pioneers were trappers."
5. "they also had skill in building," she said. "many pioneers built their own homes."
6. Joan said, "most pioneers made their own clothing."
7. "can you imagine life without stores?" asked Ann. "pioneers had to take with them everything they couldn't make themselves."
8. we decided that pioneers had to be self-sufficient.
9. "most pioneers kept a cow for milk, butter, and cheese," said Carlos. "they also raised chickens for meat and eggs."
10. "before the railroads," said Joan, "pioneers traveled by wagon."
11. Carlos said that the wagons were pulled by oxen.
12. he added, "a loaded wagon might weigh a ton."
13. most families traveled in groups.
14. in one book, Ann read, "the normal speed for a wagon was two miles an hour."
15. "the trip from Missouri to California was long," said Joan. "it often took five months."
16. "one trail the pioneers followed was the Santa Fe trail," Joan added, "which went from Missouri to New Mexico."
17. "we followed part of that trail last summer," Lee told us. "in some places you can still see wagon ruts!"
18. pioneers wrote letters that began, "dear loved ones."
19. they signed them, "with much love."
20. pioneers and other travelers left their letters at the trading posts that dotted the trails.
21. Joan asked, "would you have gone west, Carlos?"
22. Carlos replied, "no, I would have stayed home."
23. "the railroad," said Ann, "opened the West."
24. "stagecoach company owners resented the railroads' competition," Joan said. "the railroads won in the end."
25. "they were faster than stagecoaches," Lee added, "and more comfortable too."

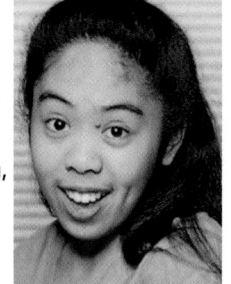

"Most of these people," said Mihn, "live in cities or towns."

Close

Ask students to imagine they are pioneers in the nineteenth century traveling west with a wagon train. Have students write a letter to a friend back east, describing a typical day on the trail. Ask students to carefully review the capitalization in their letters.

MEETING INDIVIDUAL NEEDS   Less-Proficient Readers

Capitalizing Direct Quotations

Directly quoted complete sentences do not change capitalization with the placement of words such as *she said.* For example: *"Many pioneers pursued wealth. Trappers sought furs."* No matter where *she said* might be placed, only *many* and *trappers* would be capitalized.

19.2 Capitalizing People's Names and Titles

A common noun is the general name of a person, place, thing, or idea. A common noun is not capitalized. A proper noun names a particular person, place, or thing and is capitalized.

RULE 1:   Capitalize the names of people and the initials that stand for their names.

> **M**eriwether **L**ewis   **S**usan **B. A**nthony   **J. F. C**ooper

RULE 2:   Capitalize a title or an abbreviation of a title when it comes before a person's name or when it is used instead of a name.

> **G**eneral Lee   **S**en. John Glenn   **M**rs. Adé
> Did **L**ieutenant Clark say, "Yes, **C**aptain, I'll go with you"?

Do not capitalize a title that follows a person's name or is used as a common noun.

> Clark himself was later promoted to **c**aptain.
> Thomas Jefferson, then **p**resident, planned the expedition.

RULE 3:   Capitalize the names and abbreviations of academic degrees that follow a person's name. Capitalize *Jr.* and *Sr.*

> M. Katayama, **M.D.**   Jan Rangel, **Ph.D.**   Robert Ayers **J**r.

RULE 4:   Capitalize words that show family relationships when used as titles or as substitutes for a person's name.

> In 1960 **F**ather retraced the steps of Lewis and Clark.
> He was accompanied by **U**ncle Bill.

Do not capitalize words that show family relationships when they follow a possessive noun or pronoun.

> Sharon's **a**unt Janet wrote an article about the trip.

RULE 5:   Always capitalize the pronoun *I*.

> Social studies is the subject **I** like most.

Resource Manager

📂 **Planning Resources**
- *Lesson Plans*

🖥 **Transparencies**
- *Bellringer*
- *Daily Language Practice*

📂 **Other Print Resources**
- *Grammar and Composition Handbook*
- *Grammar Enrichment,* p. 43
- *Grammar Practice,* p. 43
- *Grammar Reteaching,* p. 44
- *Grammar Workbook,* Lesson 69

Focus

Lesson Overview

Objectives
- To recognize correct capitalization of names and titles of people
- To use correct capitalization of names and titles of people

 Bellringer
Daily Language Activity

When students enter the classroom, have this assignment on the board: *List five first or last names that could belong to a person and could also be used as ordinary words, such as Rob and Baker.*

See also 🏴 *Daily Language Practice*

Motivating Activity

Invite students to share their lists of names with the class. (Other examples include Pat, Sandy, Bob, Dawn, Green, Miller, and Burns.) Ask a volunteer to choose one of the words and write two sentences on the board, one using the word as a name and one using it as a word. Discuss with students how readers can tell when a word refers to a person and when it refers to something else. Focus on context and capitalization.

Teach

☑ **Grammar Tip**

When the title of a family member is used after a possessive noun or pronoun, the title is a common noun and is not capitalized. When such a title is used to address someone directly, the title is a proper noun and is capitalized. Compare *My dad* (common noun) *works downtown* and *Are you going to work, Dad?* (proper noun).

Capitalization

Practice and Assess

Answers: Exercise 2

1. John C. Frémont
2. C. W. Peale
3. King George
4. Aunt Lena
5. Lynn Bader, M.D.
6. his uncle Ted
7. Dr. Chiang
8. Max Bond Jr.
9. General Ellen Jones
10. Ms. Amanda Swenson
11. President Thomas Jefferson
12. Cartier, an explorer
13. Grandma Shepard
14. Governor Barbara Roberts
15. Mr. William P. Scholz
16. Representative. Kasich
17. Uncle Morris
18. Susan Curtis, M.S.W.
19. Jedediah Strong Smith
20. Queen Elizabeth II

Answers: Exercise 3

1. Lewis, William Clark
2. Jefferson
3. Meriwether Lewis
4. Captain Lewis
5. I
6. Clark
7. Sacajawea
8. Toussaint Charbonneau
9. Cameahwait
10. Clark, Sacajawea's, I
11. Jean Baptiste
12. Captain
13. Jean Baptiste, Jefferson Clark
14. Jefferson's, Lewis, Clark
15. Captain Lewis
16. Fielding Lewis, General George Washington's
17. Charles
18. Lewis, Clark's
19. Mr. Nicholas Biddle
20. Patrick Gass, John Ordway, Biddle

Additional Resources

 *Grammar Practice*, p. 43
📁 *Grammar Reteaching*, p. 44
📁 *Grammar Enrichment*, p. 43

📖 *Grammar Workbook*, Lesson 69

Exercise 2 Capitalizing People's Names and Titles

Write each item, using capital letters where needed.

1. john c. frémont
2. c. w. peale
3. king george
4. aunt lena
5. lynn bader, m.d.
6. his uncle ted
7. dr. chiang
8. max bond jr.
9. general ellen jones
10. ms. amanda swenson
11. president thomas jefferson
12. cartier, an explorer
13. grandma shepard
14. governor barbara roberts
15. mr. william p. scholz
16. representative kasich
17. uncle morris
18. susan curtis, m.s.w.
19. jedediah strong smith
20. queen elizabeth II

Exercise 3 Using Capital Letters

Write each sentence, using capital letters where needed for names, titles, and abbreviations.

1. Meriwether lewis and william clark explored the Northwest all the way to the Pacific Ocean.
2. President jefferson sponsored their expedition.
3. The president had known meriwether lewis as a young boy.
4. He chose his former neighbor—now captain lewis—to lead the expedition.
5. Jefferson wrote, "i could have no hesitation in confiding the enterprise to him."
6. Lewis himself invited clark, his former company commander, to serve as coleader.
7. A Shoshone woman named sacajawea was one member of the expedition.
8. Sacajawea and her husband, toussaint charbonneau, served as interpreters.
9. Sacajawea's brother, cameahwait, a Shoshone chief, provided the expedition with pack horses.
10. Captain clark adored sacajawea's son, i believe.
11. Clark helped the boy, jean baptiste, with his schooling.
12. Can you imagine his saying, "Thank you, captain"?
13. Later jean baptiste led jefferson clark to the West Coast.
14. Of course, jefferson's father had helped lead the lewis and clark expedition.
15. In 1807 captain lewis became governor of Louisiana.
16. Lewis's uncle, fielding lewis, had married general george washington's sister.
17. His uncle charles was a patriot who fought in the Revolutionary War.
18. The story of lewis and clark's great adventure was published in 1814.
19. A magazine editor, mr. nicholas biddle, edited the book.
20. Journals kept by patrick gass and john ordway, two sergeants, helped biddle.

Capitalization

Close

Have students write a paragraph describing several friends or family members. Be sure they include names and tell some things they do together. Ask students to proofread their paragraphs, carefully checking capitalization.

 **English Language Learners**

Using Titles

Titles that are used as both common and proper nouns may confuse students learning English. Explain that titles such as *general* and *captain* are capitalized only for direct address or preceding a name. Help students understand how to correctly capitalize these examples of the use of the word *mother: my mother; Mother Hubbard; Mother, come here.*

19.3 Capitalizing Place Names

The names of specific places are proper nouns and are capitalized. Do not capitalize articles and prepositions that are part of geographical names, however.

RULE 1: Capitalize the names of cities, counties, states, countries, and continents.

> Houston   Orange County   Iowa   Japan

RULE 2: Capitalize the names of bodies of water and geographical features.

> Mediterranean Sea   Gulf of Mexico   Cape Ann
> Niagara Falls   Mojave Desert   Atlantic Ocean

RULE 3: Capitalize the names of sections of the country.

> New England   the Midwest   the Far West

RULE 4: Capitalize compass points when they refer to a specific section of the country.

> the West Coast   the Southeast   the North

Do not capitalize compass points when they indicate direction.

> Los Angeles is south of San Francisco.

Do not capitalize adjectives derived from words indicating direction.

> easterly wind   western Texas

RULE 5: Capitalize the names of streets and highways.

> Monroe Street   Route 66

RULE 6: Capitalize the names of buildings, bridges, and monuments.

> Chrysler Building   Brooklyn Bridge

RULE 7: Capitalize the names of celestial bodies.

> Pluto   North Star   the Milky Way

Focus

Lesson Overview

Objective
- To recognize and capitalize the names of specific places

 Bellringer
Daily Language Activity

When students enter the classroom, have this assignment on the board: *In one paragraph, tell what the difference is between going west and going to the West.*

See also *Daily Language Practice*

Motivating Activity

Ask students to list places that are west of where they are and places that are in the West. Repeat for *north* and *the North, east* and *the East, south* and *the South.* Ask students what pattern they see in their responses.

Teach

☑ **Teaching Tip**

Tell students that geographical terms such as *lake, mountain, river, island,* and *ocean* are capitalized if they are part of a name: *Silver* Lake, *Hawaiian* Islands, *Pacific* Ocean, *Nile* Delta, *Rocky* Mountains. However, when a geographical term is used descriptively rather than as part of a name, it is not capitalized: for example, *the California* desert, *the Texas* plains, *the Kansas* prairie.

Capitalization (vertical tab)

Resource Manager

 **Planning Resources**
- *Lesson Plans*

 **Transparencies**
- *Bellringer*
- *Daily Language Practice*

Other Print Resources
- *Grammar and Composition Handbook*
- *Grammar Enrichment,* p. 44
- *Grammar Practice,* p. 44
- *Grammar Reteaching,* p. 44
- *Grammar Workbook,* Lesson 70

Practice and Assess

Answers: Exercise 4

1. Europe
2. the Pacific Northwest
3. South Dakota
4. the East Coast
5. Omaha
6. Canada
7. Mojave Desert
8. Lexington Avenue
9. the Great Lakes
10. the Big Dipper
11. Sioux City
12. northern California
13. Montague Expressway
14. Mount Rushmore
15. Franklin County
16. Rocky Mountains
17. Empire State Building
18. West Virginia
19. Lincoln Memorial
20. Saturn

Answers: Exercise 5

1. Spain
2. Caribbean Sea, Mexico, Central America, South America
3. Americas
4. Mexico, Monterey
5. Mexico, Tenochtitlán.
6. Lake Texcoco
7. Florida
8. Caribbean Sea
9. Grand Canyon
10. Mount Potosí, Bolivia
11. Atlantic Ocean, Spain
12. Spain, Europe
13. Spain, Mexico, Peru, Central America, Florida
14. Southwest
15. Mississippi River
16. Pacific Coast, California
17. El Camino Réal
18. San José Mission, San Antonio, Texas
19. San Diego
20. North America

Additional Resources

 Grammar Practice, p. 44
 Grammar Reteaching, p. 44
Grammar Enrichment, p. 44

Grammar Workbook, Lesson 70

Capitalization

Exercise 4 Capitalizing Place Names

Write each word or group of words, using capital letters where needed.

1. europe
2. the pacific northwest
3. south dakota
4. the east coast
5. omaha
6. canada
7. mojave desert
8. lexington avenue
9. the great lakes
10. the big dipper
11. sioux city
12. northern california
13. montague expressway
14. mount rushmore
15. franklin county
16. rocky mountains
17. empire state building
18. west virginia
19. lincoln memorial
20. saturn

Exercise 5 Using Capital Letters

Write each sentence, using capital letters where needed for geographical names.

1. Adventurers from spain came to the New World in the early sixteenth century.
2. From island bases in the caribbean sea, they set sail to conquer mexico, central america, and south america.
3. Like Hernando Cortés, they came to the americas looking for gold.
4. These adventurers crossed the harsh, lonely deserts of mexico and reached monterey.
5. In mexico, Cortés conquered the Aztec capital city, tenochtitlán.
6. This great city was built on an island in lake texcoco.
7. Spanish explorers searched for the Fountain of Youth in florida.
8. They explored several islands in the caribbean sea.
9. These Spaniards encountered natural wonders, like the grand canyon, but they cared only for riches.
10. A mine on mount potosí in bolivia yielded tons of silver.
11. Spanish treasure ships sailed across the atlantic ocean to spain.
12. American gold and silver made spain the richest nation in europe.
13. By 1600 spain controlled mexico, peru, all of central america, and florida.
14. The Spaniards even explored what is now called the southwest.
15. One explorer reached the mississippi river in 1541.
16. Other explorers traveled up the pacific coast as far as northern california.
17. They established military posts and missions along a road called el camino réal.
18. Spanish heritage can be seen today in the san josé mission in san antonio, texas, and other missions.
19. Many United States cities have Spanish names, such as san diego.
20. Spain held its outposts in north america for more than two hundred years.

Close

Invite students to write a paragraph about a region that they have dreamed of visiting that includes directions to that location and identifies specific natural features to explore there. Have students check partners' work for correct capitalization.

Cooperative Learning

Capitalizing Geographical Names

Invite students to come to the board in turn, copy one geographical term from Exercise 4, read it, and capitalize where needed. Provide colored chalk for making corrections. Encourage all members of the group to help one another state the reasons for capitalization.

19.4 Capitalizing Other Proper Nouns and Adjectives

Many nouns besides the names of people and places are proper nouns. Adjectives that are formed from proper nouns are called proper adjectives. For example, the proper adjective *Egyptian* is formed from the proper noun *Egypt*.

RULE 1: Capitalize the names of clubs, organizations, businesses, institutions, and political parties.

    Data Corporation   Boy Scouts   Republican Party

RULE 2: Capitalize brand names but not the nouns following them.

    Cruncho peanut butter   Spiffy cleaning fluid

RULE 3: Capitalize the names of important historical events, periods of time, and documents.

    Battle of Yorktown   Bronze Age   Bill of Rights

RULE 4: Capitalize names of days of the week, months of the year, and holidays. Do not capitalize names of the seasons.

    Thursday   April   Memorial Day   summer

RULE 5: Capitalize the first word, the last word, and all important words in the title of a book, play, short story, poem, essay, article, film, television series, song, magazine, newspaper, and chapter of a book.

    A Wrinkle in Time   "The Raven"   *Washington Post*

RULE 6: Capitalize the names of ethnic groups, nationalities, and languages.

    Asian   German   Spanish

RULE 7: Capitalize proper adjectives that are formed from the names of ethnic groups and nationalities.

    Asian languages   Italian food

Capitalization

19.4

Focus

Lesson Overview

Objectives

- To identify correct capitalization of proper nouns and adjectives
- To use correct capitalization of proper nouns and adjectives

Bellringer
Daily Language Activity

When students enter the classroom, have this assignment on the board: *In a few sentences, tell why you think the word <u>Saturday</u> is capitalized but <u>today</u> is not.*

See also *Daily Language Practice*

Motivating Activity

Have students share their sentences from the Bellringer activity. Challenge students to identify other kinds of words or titles that are capitalized (other than the names of people or places).

Teach

☑ **Teaching Tip**

The names of philosophical, literary, musical, and other artistic movements, styles, and periods are often capitalized: *Baroque, Classical, Impressionism, Romantic*. Nonetheless, when words such as *realistic, romantic,* and *classical* are used as descriptions of style or approach rather than as names of movements, they are not capitalized.

Cross-Reference: Mechanics

For an alternative presentation of the material in Rule 5, refer students to Lesson 20.6.

Resource Manager

📁 **Planning Resources**
- *Lesson Plans*

📑 **Transparencies**
- *Bellringer*
- *Daily Language Practice*

📁 **Other Print Resources**
- *Grammar and Composition Handbook*
- *Grammar Enrichment,* p. 44
- *Grammar Practice,* p. 44
- *Grammar Reteaching,* p. 44
- *Grammar Workbook,* Lesson 71

Practice and Assess

Answers: Exercise 6

1. Sierra Club
2. Thanksgiving Day
3. Belgian waffles
4. *Los Angeles Times*
5. War of 1812
6. Halloween
7. the Middle Ages
8. Sneezo tissues
9. October
10. French horn
11. World War II
12. *National Geographic*
13. Chase Manhattan Bank
14. *Anne of Green Gables*
15. "Casey at the Bat"
16. Saturday
17. Presidents' Day
18. Girl Scouts
19. Associated Press
20. Best Friend dog food

Answers: Exercise 7

1. January
2. correct
3. Japanese, Chinese, European, American
4. "My Darling Clementine"
5. *California Monthly Magazine*
6. *The California Gold Rush*
7. *Three Weeks in the Gold Mines*
8. correct
9. *Rocky Mountain News*
10. Homestake Mine
11. Civil War
12. Scandinavian
13. Alaska Gold Mining Company
14. February
15. correct
16. War Production Board, World War II
17. correct
18. Middle Ages
19. Massachusetts Statehouse
20. Chinese

Additional Resources

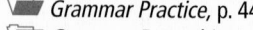 *Grammar Practice*, p. 44
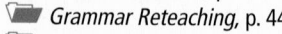 *Grammar Reteaching*, p. 44
Grammar Enrichment, p. 44

 *Grammar Workbook*, Lesson 71

580

Exercise 6 — Capitalizing Proper Nouns and Adjectives

Write the following items, using capital letters where needed.

1. sierra club
2. thanksgiving day
3. belgian waffles
4. *los angeles times*
5. war of 1812
6. halloween
7. the middle ages
8. sneezo tissues
9. october
10. french horn
11. world war II
12. *national geographic*
13. chase manhattan bank
14. *anne of green gables*
15. "casey at the bat"
16. saturday
17. presidents' day
18. girl scouts
19. associated press
20. best friend dog food

Exercise 7 — Using Capital Letters

Write each sentence, using capital letters where needed for proper nouns and adjectives. Write *correct* if the sentence has no errors.

1. James Marshall found gold in California on january 24, 1848.
2. In the spring, thousands of prospectors arrived at Sutter's Mill.
3. Hawaiian, japanese, chinese, european, and american fortune seekers joined the rush.
4. The song "my darling clementine" immortalized these miners as '49ers.
5. One woman's letters appeared in the *california monthly magazine.*
6. Have you read *the california gold rush?*
7. The book *three weeks in the gold mines* was popular.
8. A similar rush to Colorado took place in 1858.
9. In 1859 a newspaper called the *rocky mountain news* reported on the search for gold in Colorado.
10. In 1875 the homestake mine was the West's most productive gold mine.
11. Long after the civil war, gold was found in Alaska.
12. During autumn 1898, three scandinavian men found gold near Nome.
13. The alaska gold mining company tried to steal miners' claims.
14. Its owner was sentenced to jail on february 11, 1901.
15. In 1906 a federal mint opened in Denver.
16. In 1942 the war production board shut down gold mines until the end of world war II.
17. People have prized gold down through the ages.
18. Alchemists in the middle ages tried to create gold from other metals.
19. Gold covers the massachusetts statehouse dome.
20. Gold was even used as medicine by chinese doctors.

Close

Have students write paragraphs in which they tell their times and places of birth. Encourage students also to mention other important dates in their lives and to state the importance of the events.

MEETING INDIVIDUAL NEEDS — English Language Learners

Using Capital Letters

Students who are learning English may be confused about the treatment of titles and proper nouns. Ask students to find examples of names and titles in newspapers and magazines. They can highlight the examples and save them as reminders.

CAPITALIZATION

In "The Pomegranate Trees," a short story by William Saroyan, the narrator's uncle Melik attempts to grow pomegranates in the middle of a desert. In the following excerpt from the story, the narrator reflects on his uncle's dream of creating a garden on the land. The passage has been annotated to show some of the rules of capitalization covered in this unit.

Capitalization

Literature Model

from "The Pomegranate Trees"

by William Saroyan

My uncle Melik was just about the worst farmer that ever lived. He was too imaginative and poetic for his own good. What he wanted was beauty. He wanted to plant it and see it grow. I myself planted over one hundred pomegranate trees for my uncle one year back there in the good old days of poetry and youth in the world. I drove a John Deere tractor, too, and so did my uncle. It was all pure esthetics, not agriculture. My uncle just liked the idea of planting trees and watching them grow.

Only they wouldn't grow. It was on account of the soil. The soil was desert soil. It was dry. My uncle waved at the six hundred and eighty acres of desert he had bought and he said in the most poetic Armenian anybody ever heard, "Here in this awful desolation a garden shall flower, fountains of cold water shall bubble out of the earth, and all things of beauty shall come into being."

"Yes, sir," I said.

> Name of a person

> Brand name

> Name of a language

> First word of a direct quotation that is a complete sentence

> The pronoun *I*

Teach

About the Literature

Explain that the review contains a passage from William Saroyan's "The Pomegranate Trees" followed by exercises on related topics.

William Saroyan (1908–1981) was born in Fresno, California. His stories often emphasize the basic goodness in human beings and include portrayals of down-and-out characters whose energy and decency shine through. Saroyan won a Pulitzer Prize for his 1939 play *The Time of Your Life.*

After students have read the passage, discuss its characters, setting, and mood. Then ask students to determine why certain words are capitalized.

Linking Grammar and Literature

☑ Teaching Tip

Ask students to think about what kind of person Uncle Melik is as they read the passage from "The Pomegranate Trees." Promote discussion by asking how the narrator feels about his uncle. Ask students to focus on the capitalized words in the passage. Then ask *How would the meaning be different if the author had used improper capitalization?*

Critical Thinking

Have students find other examples of capitalized words in the passage and place them in categories, such as words in a title or the first word in a sentence.

Resource Manager

📁 **Planning Resources**
• *Lesson Plans*

📁 **Other Print Resources**
• *Grammar and Composition Handbook*
• *Grammar Workbook,* Lesson 68–71; *Unit 12 Review; Cumulative Review:* Units 1–12

✔ ASSESSMENT OPTIONS

📁 *Tests with Answer Key and Rubrics*
Unit 19 Mastery Test, pp. 79–80

💾 *Testmaker*
Unit 19 Mastery Test

Practice and Assess

Answers: Exercise 1

1. Uncle . . .
2. . . . he said, "why I . . ."
3. "You want . . . "
4. . . . thought that his uncle . . .
5. "Most farmers . . ."
6. "but they won't . . ."
7. He told . . .
8. His uncle . . .
9. . . . fountains of . . .
10. "Here in this . . ."

Answers: Exercise 2

1. "wrote about . . ."
2. "One story . . ."
3. . . . chance meetings . . .
4. "that Saroyan . . ."
5. "My favorite . . ."
6. "who drove a . . ."
7. "That was a . . ."
8. "Do you remember . . ."
9. "were held by . . ."
10. "made up funny . . ."

Review: Exercise 1   Capitalizing Sentences and Quotations

Find any errors in capitalization. Write the words correctly.

1. uncle Melik wanted to bring beauty to the desert.
2. "I think you understand," he said, "Why I bought this land."
3. "Yes," I said. "you want to plant a garden here."
4. The narrator thought that His Uncle was a poet.
5. "most farmers don't try to grow pomegranate trees on dry desert land," explained the narrator.
6. "I'll help you plant the trees," the narrator said, "But they won't grow in this soil."
7. he told his uncle that the soil was too dry.
8. his uncle was convinced that beauty would grow on his land.
9. He said that Fountains of fresh, cold water would bubble out of the ground.
10. Uncle Melik said, "here in this awful desolation a garden shall flower.

Review: Exercise 2   Capitalizing Direct Quotations

Find any errors in capitalization. Write the words correctly.

1. "William Saroyan," said Marge, "Wrote about people he met."
2. She added, "one story was about a Parisian shoemaker with a pet owl."
3. Saroyan said that Chance meetings are sometimes the most memorable.
4. "I read," said Jorge, "That Saroyan cherished most meeting his newborn son and daughter."
5. "He met a lot of characters!" said Nicki. "my favorite is Aram Joseph."
6. "Joseph was a wrestler," Marge put in, "Who drove a car backward at sixty miles per hour."
7. "Yes," Nicki said. "that was a funny story."
8. Jorge asked, "do you remember the story about Saroyan's job at the cemetery in San Francisco?"
9. "All the best jobs," he reminded us, "Were held by men named Johnson."
10. "One of them," added Nicki, "Made up funny slogans."

Capitalization

Review: Exercise 3   **Capitalizing People's Names and Titles**

Find any errors in capitalization. Write the words correctly.

1. William saroyan wrote about strange jobs he had had.
2. For a few days, he worked for mr. papulius, who published *The Macaroni Review*.
3. A man and a woman named mr. and mrs. Goostenhouse shared the office with Papulius.
4. Papulius called his dentist, dr. john r. skouras, d.d.s., while Saroyan was in the office.
5. Saroyan had a job helping his Uncle Melik plant pomegranate trees.
6. Saroyan wrote a short story about uncle melik.
7. Saroyan also worked at a cemetery owned by the johnson family.
8. The man Saroyan remembers best was vice president, mr. Johnson.
9. Among other things, the Vice President wrote slogans for the cemetery.
10. "When i quit after a month, he was terribly disappointed," Saroyan wrote.

Review: Exercise 4   **Capitalizing Place Names**

Find any errors in capitalization. Write the words correctly.

1. Armenia is an ancient kingdom of western asia.
2. Today its land is divided among iran, turkey, and the republic of Armenia.
3. Armenia is located Southeast of the black sea and southwest of the caspian sea.
4. A mountainous region, it reaches 13,418 feet at mount aragats.
5. The euphrates river and the araks river have their sources there.
6. A few Armenians were invited to the americas by the early Colonists.
7. Fleeing from Turkish oppression between the 1890s and the 1920s, many Armenians went to other countries, such as greece, russia, bulgaria, france, england, and the balkans.
8. Because of trouble in the middle east, another wave of immigration started in 1975.
9. New York, massachusetts, and rhode island attracted the most Armenians.
10. Many Armenian farmers settled in the san joaquin valley of california.

Capitalization

Answers: Exercise 3

1. Saroyan
2. Mr. Papulius
3. Mr., Mrs.
4. Dr. John R. Skouras, D.D.S
5. uncle
6. Uncle Melik
7. Johnson
8. Mr.
9. vice president
10. I

Answers: Exercise 4

1. Asia
2. Iran, Turkey, Republic
3. southeast, Black Sea, Caspian Sea
4. Mount Aragats
5. Euphrates River, Araks River
6. Americas, colonists
7. Greece, Russia, Bulgaria, France, England, Balkans
8. Middle East
9. Massachusetts, Rhode Island
10. San Joaquin Valley, California

Answers: Exercise 5

1. August
2. World War
3. Armenians
4. Russians, Turks
5. Russo-Turkish Treaty
6. Armenian American
7. *My Name Is Aram*
8. *The Time of Your Life*
9. Columbia University
10. "The Daring Young Man on the Flying Trapeze."

Answers: Exercise 6

1. Chinese people
2. Roman ruins
3. Spanish olives
4. Indian subcontinent
5. Alaskan sled dogs
6. Mexican food
7. French fashions
8. Swiss cheese
9. Greek dances
10. Hawaiian volcanoes
11. African nations
12. Russian winters
13. Polish sausages
14. English countryside
15. Brazilian coffee
16. Egyptian pyramids
17. Italian movies
18. Vietnamese jungles
19. Cuban government
20. Japanese cars

Capitalization

Review: Exercise 5   **Capitalizing Other Proper Nouns**

Find any errors in capitalization. Write the words correctly.

1. William Saroyan was born in the summer, on august 31, 1908.
2. That was before the beginning of world war I.
3. His parents were armenians who came to the United States.
4. Armenia's fight for independence was opposed by the russians and the turks.
5. The russo-Turkish treaty of 1921 divided the country.
6. Saroyan's autobiography described his life as an armenian american.
7. Its title is *my name is aram.*
8. Saroyan was awarded the Pulitzer Prize for his play *the time of your life.*
9. In Joseph Pulitzer's will, he gave money to columbia university so that annual awards for journalism, the Pulitzer Prizes, could be awarded.
10. Saroyan also wrote short stories such as "the daring young man on the flying trapeze."

Review: Exercise 6   **Capitalizing Proper Adjectives**

Write each of the following phrases correctly.

SAMPLE   armenian language
ANSWER   Armenian language

1. chinese people
2. roman ruins
3. spanish olives
4. indian subcontinent
5. alaskan sled dogs
6. mexican food
7. french fashions
8. swiss cheese
9. greek dances
10. hawaiian volcanoes
11. african nations
12. russian winters
13. polish sausages
14. english countryside
15. brazilian coffee
16. egyptian pyramids
17. italian movies
18. vietnamese jungles
19. cuban government
20. japanese cars

Proofreading

The following passage is about artist Rudy Fernandez, whose work appears below. Rewrite the passage, correcting the errors in spelling, capitalization, grammar, and usage. Add any missing punctuation. There are ten errors.

Rudy Fernandez, *Hot and Cold: Cold,* 1987

(continued)

Capitalization

Answers: Exercise 7
Proofreading

This proofreading activity provides editing practice with (1) the current or previous units' skills, (2) **Troubleshooter** errors, and (3) spelling errors. Students should be able to complete the exercise by referring to the units, the **Troubleshooter,** and a dictionary.

Error (Type of Error)
1. Fernandez (person's name)
   Southwest (section of the country)
2. Mexican (nationality)
3. New Mexico (state)
4. Fernandez's (singular possessive)
5. desert (spelling)
6. The (first word of a sentence)
7. Uncle (family relationship)
   Trees (title of short story)
8. have (subject-verb agreement)

Viewing the Art

Rudy Fernandez, *Hot and Cold: Cold,* 1987
This work by Rudy Fernandez combines an almost-abstract image of a cactus and other images rendered in great detail within a carved frame. While much of his work reflects his interest in the landscape of the Southwest, Fernandez's work also evidences the influence of his religious upbringing and his Chicano heritage.
Hot and Cold: Cold measures 62 by 53 by 6 inches and is rendered in mixed media. Invite students to evaluate Fernandez's painting and to share their opinions of the artist's work.

585

Answers: Exercise 8
Mixed Review

1. uncle, Armenia
2. West
3. California
4. uncle, "The
5. Sierra
6. tractor
7. why
8. "He, I
9. "and
10. Armenian
11. "It's
12. Saroyan, uncle
13. summer
14. American
15. Mr.
16. western

Close

Have students write a paragraph on a topic of their choice. The paragraph should have at least one example of each capitalization rule reviewed (quotations, direct quotations, sentences, names and titles, place names, proper nouns, and proper adjectives). Have students check one another's work.

Capitalization

Rudy Fernandez

[1]Rudy fernandez was born in 1948 and grew up in the southwest. [2]The mexican American artist feels an intense affection for the area's landscape. [3]He especially loves the high deserts of new mexico. [4]Many of Fernandez paintings capture the beauty of the desert landscape.

[5]Fernandez celebrates the dessert by using abstract images of a flowering cactus in his picture. [6]the simply-drawn cactus glows warmly against the blue background. [7]Like uncle Melik in "The Pomegranate trees," Fernandez believes that beauty can survive in the desert. [8]The plants and flowers of the desert has their own beauty.

Review: Exercise 8

Mixed Review

The following passage contains twenty errors in capitalization. Find them, and write the words correctly.

[1]William Saroyan's Uncle Melik had come from armenia to the West with the dream of creating beauty out of desolation. [2]He wanted to create a garden on the west Coast. [3]Along with many others, Melik settled in california. [4]The author wrote about his Uncle in a story titled "the Pomegranate Trees."

[5]Saroyan's uncle purchased 680 acres of land at the foot of the sierra Nevada. [6]Melik hired workers to clear the land and bought a John Deere Tractor. [7]The author asked his uncle Why he wanted to plant pomegranate trees. [8]Saroyan said, "he knew i would understand the impulse that was driving him to ruin." [9]"I like the idea of planting trees," Melik told his nephew, "And watching them grow." [10]In the armenian language, Uncle Melik spoke like a poet. [11]"But this is desert soil," the author told his uncle. "it's too dry." [12]However, saroyan helped his Uncle Melik plant hundreds of pomegranate trees. [13]The hot Summer sun baked the young trees, and they failed to thrive in the desert soil. [14]When Melik finally raised a crop, the pomegranates didn't sell because the american people didn't know what they were.

[15]Eventually Melik had to give the land back to mr. Griffith, the man who had sold it to him. [16]At the end of the story, the pomegranate trees had died, and cactus had returned to the Western desert land.

Writing Application

Capitalization in Writing

Correct capitalization makes your writing clearer. Mistakes in capitalization can distract readers from the substance of your writing. As you read the passage below from "A Huge Black Umbrella," notice how author Marjorie Agosín uses capitalization to identify proper nouns. Notice the italicized words.

> Mario went traveling abroad and I decided to spend my honeymoon on *Easter Island,* that remote *island* in the middle of *the Pacific Ocean,* six hours by plane from *Chile.* It is a place full of mysterious, gigantic statues called Moais. Ever since I was a child, I had been fascinated by those eerie statues, their enormous figures seeming to spring from *the earth,* just as *Delfina Nahuenhual* and her huge black umbrella did when she first came to my house.

Techniques with Capitalization

Try to apply Agosín's writing techniques when you write and revise your own work.

❶ Be alert to the difference between a word used within a proper noun to identify a specific place and the same word used as a common noun to identify a general place.

INCORRECT VERSION on *Easter Island,* that remote *Island* in the middle

AGOSÍN'S VERSION on *Easter Island,* that remote *island* in the middle

❷ Except when beginning a new sentence, remember to capitalize only the main words in a proper noun that names a geographical place:

INCORRECT VERSION The *Pacific Ocean,* six hours by plane

AGOSÍN'S VERSION the *Pacific Ocean,* six hours by plane

TIME

For more about the writing process, see **TIME Facing the Blank Page,** pp. 97–107.

Capitalization

Practice Practice these capitalization techniques as you revise the following passage, using a separate piece of paper.

the bus came to a halt at the head of the road leading to treetop farm. as clarice headed down to the dusty road to the farm, she tossed a quick farewell to the driver, "see ya, frank. i've got to run and finish my chores. i want to ride into town to the library before dark." clarice hurried through her chores, wishing she lived at the hortense place, where hired staff did the farm chores. within an hour, she was entering the river view park town square, pedaling full speed towards the pearson memorial library.

Writing Application **587**

Capitalization in Writing

You may have students read the paragraph silently to themselves. Ask them to look for examples of the italicized capitalization choices. Discuss these choices in relation to Techniques with Capitalization below.

Techniques with Capitalization

Suggest that students revisit the passage in the proofreading exercise. What examples can they find of place names that are proper names?

Practice

The answers to this challenging and enriching activity will vary. Refer to Techniques with Capitalization as you evaluate student choices.

Sample answer:

The bus came to a halt at the head of the road leading to Treetop Farm. As Clarice headed down the dusty road to the farm, she tossed a quick farewell to the driver, "See ya, Frank. I've got to run and finish my chores. I want to ride into town to the library before dark." Clarice hurried through her chores, wishing she lived at the Hortense place, where hired staff did the farm chores. Within an hour, she was entering the River View Park town square, pedaling full speed towards the Pearson Memorial Library.

Objectives

- To develop an understanding of the common forms of punctuation
- To use correct punctuation to clarify and enhance meaning

✔ ASSESSMENT OPTIONS

📁 *Tests with Answer Key and Rubrics*
Unit 20 Pretest, pp. 81–82
Unit 20 Mastery Test, pp. 83–84

💾 *Testmaker*
Unit 20 Pretest
Unit 20 Mastery Test

You may wish to administer the Unit 20 Pretest at this point.

Key to Ability Levels

L1 Level 1 activities are within the basic ability range of students.

L2 Level 2 activities are within the ability range of average students.

L3 Level 3 activities are more challenging activities.

UNIT
20 Punctuation

588

Resource Manager

📁 **Planning Resources**
- *Lesson Plans*
- *Block Scheduling*

📋 **Transparencies**
- *Bellringer*
- *Daily Language Practice*

📁 **Other Print Resources**
- *Grammar and Composition Handbook*
- *Grammar Enrichment*
- *Grammar Practice*
- *Grammar Reteaching*
- *Grammar Workbook*
- *Tests with Answer Key and Rubrics*

**Video**
- *MindJogger Videoquizzes*

💾 **Software**
- *Interactive Grammar and Language Workbook*
- *Language Arts PASS*
- *Presentation Plus!*
- *Testmaker*

💻 **Web Sites**
- *writerschoice.glencoe.com*

20.1 Using the Period and Other End Marks

Three punctuation marks signal the end of sentences. The period is used for declarative and imperative sentences. The question mark is used for interrogative sentences. The exclamation point is used for exclamatory sentences and interjections.

RULE 1: Use a period at the end of a declarative sentence. A declarative sentence makes a statement.

> I enjoy traveling by train.
> Almost every country in the world has at least one major railroad line.

RULE 2: Use a period at the end of an imperative sentence. An imperative sentence gives a command or makes a request.

> Read about Russia's long rail system. [command]
> Please explain the meaning of the word *railroad*. [request]

RULE 3: Use a question mark at the end of an interrogative sentence. An interrogative sentence asks a question.

> Do we still use steam trains in this country?
> Why are diesel engines used now?

RULE 4: Use an exclamation point at the end of an exclamatory sentence. An exclamatory sentence expresses strong feeling.

> What a high-speed train this is!
> How fast it moves!

RULE 5: Use an exclamation point at the end of an interjection. An interjection is a word or group of words that expresses strong emotion.

My!	Alas!	Oops!
Well!	Whew!	Sh!
Wow!	Gee!	Ouch! Oh, no!

20.1 Using the Period and Other End Marks   **589**

Focus

Lesson Overview

Objectives

- To develop an understanding of end marks
- To use periods at the end of declarative and imperative sentences, question marks at the end of interrogative sentences, and exclamation points at the end of exclamatory sentences and after interjections

Punctuation

🔔 **Bellringer**
Daily Language Activity

When students enter the classroom, have this assignment on the board: *Copy the following sentence. Add the end mark (period, question mark, or exclamation point) that you think is correct.*

Is it time for lunch yet

See also 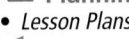 *Daily Language Practice*

Motivating Activity

Use students' answers to the Bellringer activity to introduce the question mark. Then introduce the exclamation point by having a volunteer come to the board and supply an end mark for the sentence *Help*.

Teach

Listening and Speaking

Have students compose sample declarative, imperative, interrogative, and exclamatory sentences. When volunteers read their sentences aloud, see if classmates can tell from the speaker's voice what end mark is needed.

Resource Manager

📁 **Planning Resources**
- *Lesson Plans*

🎵 **Transparencies**
- *Bellringer*
- *Daily Language Practice*

📁 **Other Print Resources**
- *Grammar and Composition Handbook*
- *Grammar Enrichment*, p. 45
- *Grammar Practice*, p. 45
- *Grammar Reteaching*, p. 45
- *Grammar Workbook*, Lesson 72

Practice and Assess

Answers: Exercise 1

1. transportation. (dec.)
2. railroads? (int.)
3. invented? (int.)
4. locomotive. (dec.)
5. locomotion? (int.)
6. book. (imp.)
7. locomotive. (dec.)
8. Tom Thumb. (imp.)
9. was! (excl.)
10. Tom Thumb. (dec.)
11. lost. (dec.)
12. slipped. (dec.)
13. Cooper! (excl.)
14. century. (dec.)
15. Mountains. (dec.)
16. Sierra Nevada. (dec.)
17. mountains? (int.)
18. railroad. (dec.)
19. Utah! (excl.)
20. railroad. (imp.)
21. rates? (int.)
22. railroads. (dec.)
23. brake. (imp.)
24. was! (excl.)
25. country? (int.)

Additional Resources

📂 *Grammar Practice,* p. 45
📂 *Grammar Reteaching,* p. 45
📂 *Grammar Enrichment,* p. 45

 Grammar Workbook, Lesson 72

Close

Tell students to imagine they are riding across the country by rail in 1870. Have them write a paragraph describing their trip. Remind students to use different kinds of sentences with appropriate end marks. Have students trade papers and check for correct end punctuation.

590

Exercise 1 — Using End Marks

Write the correct end mark for each sentence. Then write whether the sentence is *declarative, imperative, interrogative,* or *exclamatory.*

1. Railroads provide an important means of transportation
2. Are we going to learn about the history of railroads
3. When was the first steam locomotive invented
4. Wood was shoveled into a firebox attached to the boiler that makes steam for the locomotive
5. What do you think were the dangers of this means of locomotion
6. Read about railroads in your book
7. An English inventor named Richard Trevithick built the world's first steam locomotive
8. Please tell me about the race between a horse and the tiny steam locomotive called the *Tom Thumb*
9. What an exciting race that was
10. In 1830 Peter Cooper built the *Tom Thumb*
11. This small locomotive raced against a horse but lost
12. The *Tom Thumb* led until an engine belt slipped
13. What a disappointment for Peter Cooper
14. Railroads grew rapidly in the mid-nineteenth century
15. The Union Pacific Railway company built track westward from eastern Nebraska toward the Rocky Mountains
16. The Central Pacific Railroad company laid track eastward from the coast of California across the Sierra Nevada
17. How were the railroads able to find enough workers to build the railroad across California's high mountains
18. More than five thousand Chinese workers were brought to California from China to work on the railroad
19. What excitement when the tracks met in Utah
20. Picture the scene when spikes made of gold and silver were hammered into the last section of track for the transcontinental railroad
21. Did these early railroads have high accident rates
22. As a safety measure, George Westinghouse developed an air brake for railroads
23. Explain the difference between an air brake and a hand brake
24. What a wonderful invention the air brake was
25. Isn't rail travel still a wonderful way to see the country

Punctuation

MEETING INDIVIDUAL NEEDS

English Language Learners

Listening and Writing

Students who are learning English may be accustomed to expressing and punctuating sentences, questions, commands, and interjections in ways different from English. Other languages may use changes in intonation or word order or different punctuation rules to signal sentence type. Choose a paragraph that has several types of end punctuation. Read the paragraph straight through aloud. Then reread it, stopping after each sentence to discuss the sentence type. Ask students to discuss what sentence clues might help them guess the correct end punctuation for each sentence.

20.2 Using Commas I

Commas make sentences easier to understand by signaling a pause or separation between parts of a sentence.

RULE 1: Use commas to separate three or more words, phrases, or clauses in a series.

> Columbus commanded the *Niña, the Pinta,* and the *Santa Maria.*

RULE 2: Use a comma after two or more introductory prepositional phrases, after a long introductory phrase, or when a comma is needed to make the meaning clear.

> For thousands of years, shipbuilders constructed large ships. [two prepositional phrases—*For thousands* and *of years*]
>
> For many years people crossed the ocean in ships. [one prepositional phrase—*For many years.* A comma could be used, but it is not needed.]

RULE 3: Use a comma after introductory participles and introductory participial phrases.

> Daydreaming, I found myself on an ancient ship.
> Traveling the Mediterranean, the Minoans became seafarers.

RULE 4: Use commas to set off words that interrupt the flow of thought in a sentence.

> Ships, you might imagine, were invented thousands of years ago.

RULE 5: Use commas to set off an appositive if it is not essential to the meaning of the sentence.

> The Egyptians, the inventors of sails, built barges from planks of wood. [The appositive, *the inventors of sails,* is not essential.]

RULE 6: Use commas to show a pause after an introductory word and to set off names used in direct address.

> Ms. Mar, did the Romans have a large fleet?
> Yes, that was one of the reasons for their power.

Focus

Lesson Overview

Objectives
- To develop an understanding of how commas are used to clarify and enhance meaning
- To use commas in a series
- To use commas to set off introductory and interrupting words and phrases

 Bellringer
Daily Language Activity

When students enter the classroom, have this assignment on the board: *List three different examples of the use of commas in writing.*

See also *Daily Language Practice*

Motivating Activity

Ask students to share their answers to the Bellringer activity. You may want to point out which of the six rules for commas their answers exemplify. Students should monitor their understanding and seek clarification as needed.

Teach

☑ Teaching Tip

Remind students that commas are used to separate three or more items in a series. Give an example showing that, if all the items are joined by *and,* no commas are necessary: *Weary travelers around the country boarded the trains and boats and planes.*

Punctuation

Resource Manager

📁 **Planning Resources**
- *Lesson Plans*

📑 **Transparencies**
- *Bellringer*
- *Daily Language Practice*

📁 **Other Print Resources**
- *Grammar and Composition Handbook*
- *Grammar Enrichment,* p. 46
- *Grammar Practice,* p. 46
- *Grammar Reteaching,* p. 46
- *Grammar Workbook,* Lesson 73

Practice and Assess

Answers: Exercise 2

1. Packet ships, clipper ships,
2. century, trade
3. time, . . . reports,
4. ships, you might imagine,
5. ship, a ship . . . feet,
6. prospectors, miners,
7. clipper ships, . . . ships,
8. speed,
9. correct
10. tea, spices,
11. huge, *swift,*
12. *Titanic,* a British liner,
13. furnished,
14. Atlantic,
15. had, as it turned out,
16. men, women,
17. twentieth century,
18. *Queen Mary,* the *Queen Elizabeth,*
19. late 1940s,
20. correct
21. Yes,
22. Juanita,
23. Yes, Peter,
24. sunshine,
25. sailing,

Additional Resources

 Grammar Practice, p. 46

 Grammar Reteaching, p. 46

 Grammar Enrichment, p. 46

Grammar Workbook, Lesson 73

Close

Have students in small groups discuss ways that commas make writing easier to understand. What would it be like to read long sentences without commas? Would they enjoy reading as much? Why or why not?

Punctuation

Exercise 2 · Using Commas

Write the following sentences, adding any needed commas. Write *correct* if a sentence needs no changes.

1. Packet ships clipper ships and ocean liners are three kinds of ships.
2. By the early part of the nineteenth century trade between the United States and Europe had grown.
3. At that time according to newspaper reports American shipowners built packet ships for carrying cargo and passengers.
4. Packet ships you might imagine were not comfortable.
5. The first packet ship a ship that measured about one hundred feet did not travel very fast.
6. Clipper ships carried prospectors miners and traders to Gold Rush country.
7. In the 1850s clipper ships the most beautiful of all sailing ships provided speed and comfort.
8. Driving at top speed the captain of a clipper could cut through the water at twenty knots.
9. Merchants and sailors in America lost interest in the speedy clipper ships after a while.
10. The British sailed the fast clipper ships to China for tea, spices, and silk.
11. The age of the huge swift and luxurious ocean liner began in the early 1900s.
12. The *Titanic* a British liner began her maiden voyage in April 1912.
13. Luxuriously furnished the ship carried many wealthy and important people.
14. Racing across the Atlantic the *Titanic* hit an iceberg and sank.
15. The boat's builders had as it turned out claimed the ship was unsinkable.
16. More than fifteen hundred men women and children died in that tragic disaster.
17. For the first half of the twentieth century the only way to cross the Atlantic was by ship.
18. Among the famous luxury liners were the *Queen Mary* the *Queen Elizabeth* and the *United States.*
19. Beginning in the late 1940s airplanes attracted passengers.
20. Most ocean liners could not compete with airplanes.
21. Yes in the 1960s some European shipping companies tried to compete with jet planes.
22. Juanita do you enjoy sailing?
23. Yes Peter I love to go sailing.
24. It is more fun to sail in the sunshine you must admit.
25. After an hour of sailing we will need to head back to the boathouse.

Cooperative Learning

Listening for Pauses

Pair students learning English with students who are proficient in English. Have the English-proficient students read the sentences in Exercise 2 without commas, then with commas. Encourage students learning English to notice how the sentences read with commas are easier to understand—the sense is clearer.

20.3 Using Commas II

Commas clarify meaning in sentences with more than one clause. A clause is a group of words that has a subject and a predicate and is used as part of a sentence. A main clause can stand alone as a sentence.

Two or more main clauses can be joined by a comma plus the conjunction *and, or,* or *but.*

RULE 7: Use a comma before *and, or,* or *but* when they join main clauses.

> Camels can travel great distances, and their strength enables them to carry heavy loads.
> Camels can live alone, but most travel in small herds.
> Camel's hair is used for making blankets, or it is woven into cloth for suits and coats.

Subordinate clauses cannot stand alone as sentences. They are always joined with a main clause to make a complex sentence. One common kind of subordinate clause is an adverb clause which tells how, when, why, or where an action takes place. Some adverb clauses are separated from the main clause by commas.

RULE 8: Use a comma after an adverb clause that introduces a sentence. Adverb clauses begin with subordinating conjunctions, such as *after, although, as, because, before, considering (that), if, in order that, since, so that, though, unless, until, when, whenever, where, wherever, whether,* or *while.*

> Since camels are the main means of transportation in many dry areas, they are called ships of the desert.

Usually commas are not used with adverb clauses that come at the end of sentences.

> Nomads value their camels because these animals are vital to desert life.

20.3 Using Commas II **593**

Focus

Lesson Overview

Objectives
- To recognize the appropriate use of commas in compound sentences and after introductory adverb clauses
- To use commas correctly in compound sentences and after introductory adverb clauses

Bellringer
Daily Language Activity

When students enter the classroom, have this assignment on the board: *Copy the following sentences, adding commas where necessary.*

The caravan was packed and the families began their desert journey. After the caravan was packed the families began their desert journey.

See also *Daily Language Practice*

Motivating Activity

Call on volunteers to explain their responses in the Bellringer activity. Use the responses and explanations to introduce and discuss Rules 7 and 8 on this page. Invite students to ask questions to clarify their understanding.

Teach

Critical Thinking

In the passage below, have students identify the adverb clause (*As we walked past each caravan,*) and the subordinating conjunction (*as*).

> As we walked past each caravan, we called out greetings to the families, asking where they were headed.
>
> —Minfong Ho
> *The Clay Marble*

Punctuation

Resource Manager

Planning Resources
- *Lesson Plans*

 **Transparencies**
- *Bellringer*
- *Daily Language Practice*

 **Other Print Resources**
- *Grammar and Composition Handbook*
- *Grammar Enrichment,* p. 47
- *Grammar Practice,* p. 47
- *Grammar Reteaching,* p. 47
- *Grammar Workbook,* Lesson 74

Practice and Assess

Answers: Exercise 3

1. trading, camels
2. speed, and
3. stupid, malicious
4. evil, and
5. needs, millions
6. plows, or
7. roads, camels
8. soft sand, and
9. travel, they
10. water, people
11. fat, and
12. correct
13. easily, they
14. environment, and
15. sandstorms, their
16. transportation, nomads
17. correct
18. camel, the
19. moving, it
20. walking, it
21. willingly, they
22. upset, they
23. annoyed, they
24. correct
25. teeth, and

Additional Resources

 Grammar Practice, p. 47
 Grammar Reteaching, p. 47
 Grammar Enrichment, p. 47

Grammar Workbook, Lesson 74

Close

Ask students whether they would prefer to travel across the desert by camel or by car. Have them describe their imagined journey in a paragraph that uses a compound sentence and a complex sentence. Students should check their paragraphs for correct usage of commas.

Exercise 3   **Using Commas with Clauses**

Write each sentence. Add a comma or commas where needed. For a sentence that needs no commas, write *correct*.

1. Ever since ancient people began trading camels have been used as beasts of burden.
2. Some camels were bred for speed and they were then used in warfare.
3. Because camels were considered stupid malicious stories told about them were not very complimentary.
4. Camels were linked with evil and some people considered them unclean.
5. Since camels supply so many needs millions of people depend on them.
6. In the desert, camels pull plows or they turn water wheels.
7. Because they carry nomads to places without roads camels are highly valued in the desert.
8. These animals walk easily on soft sand and they go where trucks cannot pass.
9. When camels travel they go without water for days.
10. Because camels can go without water people thought they stored water in their humps.
11. The humps are actually fat and camels store food as fat in their humps.
12. A camel's hump gets smaller when the animal goes without food for a while.
13. Since camels do not sweat easily they retain their bodily fluids.
14. Camels are well adapted to their environment and they can live where other animals could not survive.
15. If camels pass through sandstorms their nostrils shut.
16. Because camels provide such a practical means of transportation nomads use them regularly.
17. Camels may seem strange to us because they are not native to our country.
18. When a person gets on a camel the beast usually whines.
19. Until a camel begins moving it grunts and groans.
20. After a camel starts walking it carries its load quietly.
21. Since camels do not work willingly they never learn obedience.
22. If camels become upset they may bite.
23. Because camels are easily annoyed they often kick with their hind legs or bite.
24. Camels may look larger than they are because they are covered with very thick, woolly fur.
25. Camels have very strong, sharp teeth and they will eat almost anything put in front of them.

MEETING INDIVIDUAL NEEDS   **Less-Proficient Readers**

Recognizing Introductory Clauses

Some students may need to be reminded that a clause has a subject (who or what) and a predicate (what the subject does or is). A phrase does not have a subject and a predicate. Tell students that introductory clauses are followed by commas. Then give examples of sentences with introductory clauses. Have students provide appropriate commas, working with partners proficient in English.

20.4 Using Commas III

Several rules for using commas—including those for punctuating dates and addresses, titles, direct quotations, and salutations—are a matter of standard usage

> **RULE 9:** Use commas before and after the year when it is used with both the month and the day. Do not use a comma if only the month and the year are given.
>
> > The bus trip began on July 5, 2001, and lasted four weeks.
> > The journey ended in August 2001.
>
> **RULE 10:** Use commas before and after the name of a state or a country when it is used with the name of a city. Do not use a comma after the state if it is used with a ZIP code.
>
> > People came from as far away as Buffalo, New York, to travel with the tour.
> > The address on the envelope was as follows:
> > 136 East Main St., Huntington, NY 11743.
>
> **RULE 11:** Use a comma or pair of commas to set off an abbreviated title or degree following a person's name.
>
> > Carol Warren, M.D., studied the effects of motion sickness.
>
> **RULE 12:** Use a comma or commas to set off *too* when *too* means "also."
>
> > Dr. Warren, too, rode on the bus with us.
>
> **RULE 13:** Use a comma or pair of commas to set off a direct quotation.
>
> > Kerry said, "Buses are more efficient than cars."
> > "Train travel," Sarah said, "is pleasant and safe."
>
> **RULE 14:** Use a comma after the salutation of a friendly letter and after the closing of both a friendly and a business letter.
>
> > Dear Dad,   Your pal,   Yours truly,
>
> **RULE 15:** Use a comma to prevent misreading.
>
> > Instead of two, five teachers made the trip.

20.4 Using Commas III **595**

Focus

Lesson Overview

Objective
- To recognize special conventions for comma use, including commas with dates, titles, direct quotations, salutations, and closings
- To use commas appropriately

 Bellringer
Daily Language Activity

When students enter the classroom, have this assignment on the board: *List the situations in which you use commas when you write. Time limit: one minute.*

See also Daily Language Practice

Motivating Activity

Incorporating students' answers from the Bellringer activity, compile on the board a list of when to use commas correctly in writing.

Teach

Listening and Speaking

Explain to students that commas sometimes indicate pauses, but pauses do not always call for commas. For example, we might pause at the end of a long subject: *Basketball, soccer, swimming, and tennis* (pause) *are a few of my favorite sports.* Point out that if a comma is placed where this pause occurs, it would separate the subject from the verb. Remind students that sentences should be punctuated by structure, not solely by ear. Read aloud other examples and have students determine if commas are needed.

Resource Manager

📁 **Planning Resources**
- *Lesson Plans*

📁 **Transparencies**
- *Bellringer*
- *Daily Language Practice*

📁 **Other Print Resources**
- *Grammar and Composition Handbook*
- *Grammar Enrichment,* 48
- *Grammar Practice,* p. 48
- *Grammar Reteaching,* p. 48
- *Grammar Workbook,* Lessons 75–76

Practice and Assess

Answers: Exercise 4

1. New York, arrived
2. said, "I'm
3. hope," said Nora, "that
4. Quebec City, Canada, and
5. Chin, M.A., will
6. said, "I have
7. asked, too, if
8. "Tomorrow," Alan said, ". . . John Cage, M.D., to
9. Burlington, Vermont," Patty
10. in Montreal, Canada, on July 15,
11. Quebec City, Montreal
12. Montreal," Alan explained,
13. Montreal, too,
14. Montreal, Canada,
15. City, too, is
16. July 24,
17. "Jean LeGrand, Ph.D., will be our guide in Quebec,"
18. Patty, Maria
19. September 14, 1759.
20. Albany, New York.

Answers: Exercise 5

1. no comma
2. Somers, New York 10589
3. August 8, 2001
4. Dear Keith,
5. no comma
6. Troy, New York, to Quebec City, Canada.
7. no comma
8. Carlos Espinoza, Ph.D.
9. hours, four
10. Your friend,

Additional Resources

 *Grammar Practice,* p. 48

📁 *Grammar Reteaching,* p. 48

📁 *Grammar Enrichment,* p. 48

📖 *Grammar Workbook,* Lessons 75–76

Exercise 4   Using Commas

Write each sentence. Add a comma or commas where needed.

1. A letter from Troy, New York arrived in May 2001.
2. Alan said "I'm planning a tour of Canada."
3. "I hope" said Nora "that we can go in July."
4. The bus will go from New York to Quebec City Canada and then back.
5. Pamela Chin M.A. will lead the tour.
6. Nora said "I have always wanted to visit Quebec City."
7. Patty and Jennifer asked too if they could go.
8. "Tomorrow" Alan said "we will ask John Cage M.D. to accompany us."
9. "I hope we go through Burlington Vermont" Patty said.
10. The tour stops in Montreal Canada on July 15 2001.
11. Like Quebec City Montreal has many interesting sights.
12. "In Montreal" Alan explained "French and English are both used."
13. Montreal too is an important seaport.
14. Montreal Canada was the site of the World's Fair in August 1967.
15. Quebec City too is on the St. Lawrence River.
16. The group will be in the city from July 20 to July 24 2001.
17. "Jean LeGrand Ph.D. will be our guide in Quebec" Pamela announced.
18. Instead of Patty Maria will be my roommate.
19. The British took Quebec City from the French on September 14 1759.
20. The group will tour the State Capitol in Albany New York.

Exercise 5   Using Commas

Add commas if needed to the following numbered items.

> [1]98 Heritage Road
> [2]Somers New York 10589
> [3]August 8 2001

[4]Dear Keith

[5]I have just returned from a terrific bus trip. [6]We went from Troy New York to Quebec City Canada. [7]Mike went too. [8]On the bus, I read a great book about Quebec by Carlos Espinoza Ph.D. [9] Instead of three hours four hours were allotted for our meals.

> [10]Your friend
> *Ahmad*

Close

Display the following: Rules 10, 13; Rules 11, 14; Rules 12, 15, 16. Assign a set of rules to student pairs. Ask pairs to write an example for each rule number assigned to them. Have partners explain their work to the class. Remind classmates to respond to one another's work in constructive ways.

Real World Connection

Locating Commas in Newspapers

Pair English language learners with English-proficient students and have them find examples, in magazines or newspapers, of commas used correctly to punctuate dates, addresses, and titles or degrees. Ask pairs to share their examples with the class.

20.5 | Using Semicolons and Colons

The semicolon and the colon are punctuation marks that separate parts of a sentence that might otherwise be confused.

RULE 1: Use a semicolon to join parts of a compound sentence when a conjunction, such as *and*, *but*, or *or*, is not used.

> In the 1890s the electric car became the most popular car in America; people liked electric cars because they ran quietly and cleanly.

RULE 2: Use a semicolon to join parts of a compound sentence when the main clauses are long and are subdivided by commas. Use a semicolon even if the clauses are joined by a coordinating conjunction such as *and*, *but*, or *or*.

> Before the invention of the automobile, people rode horses, bicycles, or streetcars for short distances; and they took horse-drawn carriages, trains, or boats for longer trips.

RULE 3: Use a colon to introduce a list of items that ends a sentence. Use a phrase such as *these*, *the following*, or *as follows* to signal that a list is coming.

> A few years ago you could order a car only **in the following** colors: black, white, blue, and brown.

Do not use a colon immediately after a verb or a preposition. Either leave out the colon or reword the sentence.

> Large automobile companies **sell** cars, trucks, and vans.
>
> Most of the world's cars are built **in** the United States, Japan, or Europe.

RULE 4: Use a colon to separate the hour and the minute when you write the time of day.

> Ms. Cole starts her car at 7:15 A.M. each day.

RULE 5: Use a colon after the salutation of a business letter.

> Dear Sir or Madam: Dear Ms. Delgado:

Tasha drove downtown at rush hour

she found a parking space in front of the library.

Punctuation

20.5 Using Semicolons and Colons **597**

Focus

Lesson Overview

Objectives
- To develop an understanding of semicolons and colons
- To use semicolons to separate main clauses and series that contain commas
- To use colons to introduce lists, to separate hour and minute, and to end salutations in business letters

🔔 **Bellringer**
Daily Language Activity

When students enter the classroom, have this assignment on the board: *On your paper, copy the run-on sentence below. Then punctuate it to correct the problems.*

> *We arrived late, and it was dark at our campsite the first things we unpacked were the following flashlights, lanterns, and candles.*

See also 📖 *Daily Language Practice*

Motivating Activity

Discuss how the first two clauses of the Bellringer activity could be separated by replacing *and* with either a period or a semicolon. The third clause introduces a list, which should be preceded by a colon.

Teach

Listening and Speaking

Tell students that the words *the following* or *as follows* usually indicate that a speaker is about to recite a list. They signal listeners to pay extra attention to what comes next. Point out that in writing, these phrases are followed by colons.

Practice and Assess

Answers: Exercise 6

1. travelers; these
2. month; it
3. items: a road
4. 5:30
5. items: a flashlight,
6. correct
7. destination; I plan
8. safely; but
9. following: a bathing suit,
10. 8:30 . . . 8:00

Answers: Exercise 7

1. Madam:
2. correct
3. cities: Richmond
4. following: a road map
5. 8:00

Additional Resources

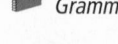 *Grammar Practice,* p. 49

Grammar Reteaching, p. 49

Grammar Enrichment, p. 49

Grammar Workbook, Lesson 78

Close

After reviewing the exercises, have students draw up a fantasy itinerary for a trip they would like to take. They should use colons and semicolons correctly in their timetables, lists, and sentences. Invite students to check one another's work.

Exercise 6 Using Semicolons and Colons

Write each sentence, adding semicolons or colons as needed. Write *correct* if the sentence needs no changes.

1. Large automobile clubs aid travelers these travelers often write to the clubs for information.
2. I wrote to one of these organizations last month it promised to send me a packet of information.
3. Within a week, the organization sent me the following items a road map, a guidebook, and a car manual.
4. I plan to leave next Saturday at 530 A.M.
5. For possible emergencies, I am taking these items a flashlight, a first-aid kit, and a spare tire.
6. I also have a set of flares with instructions in case I have an accident.
7. It will take approximately nine hours for me to reach my destination I plan to stop every two hours to rest during the trip.
8. When you drive long distances, it's important to stay awake, stay alert, and drive safely but it's easy to get tired and bored on long trips.
9. I have taken everything I need in my suitcase, including the following a bathing suit, a pair of sunglasses, and a good book.
10. On the return trip, I will leave at 830 A.M. and expect to be home by 800 P.M.

Exercise 7 Using Semicolons and Colons in a Letter

Add semicolons or colons, if needed, to punctuate the following numbered items.

¹Dear Sir or Madam

²I am planning a trip. I am, therefore, seeking information about Virginia, Tennessee, and North Carolina. ³I would like to visit the following cities Richmond, Raleigh, and Atlanta. ⁴Please send the following a road map and a guidebook and hotel information. ⁵ If I leave my home in Baltimore, Maryland, at 800 A.M., at what time will I arrive in Richmond?

Sincerely,
An-Mei Cho

MEETING INDIVIDUAL NEEDS **Listening and Speaking**

Punctuating for Meaning

Have student pairs read to each other the unpunctuated Exercise 6 sentences that require a semicolon. Partners can work together to figure out where semicolons should be used when one thought ends and another thought begins in a sentence.

20.6 Using Quotation Marks and Italics

Quotation marks signal a person's exact words, as well as the titles of some works. Italic type—a special slanted type that is used in printing—identifies titles of other works. You can show italics on a typewriter or in handwriting by underlining.

> **RULE 1:** Use quotation marks before and after the exact words in a direct quotation.
>
> "For centuries people dreamed of flying," Iris said.
>
> **RULE 2:** Use quotation marks with both parts of a divided quotation.
>
> "Leonardo da Vinci," said Ray, "drew plans of flying machines."
>
> **RULE 3:** Use a comma or commas to separate a phrase such as *he said* from the quotation itself. Place the comma inside closing quotation marks.
>
> Chan said, "Orville and Wilbur Wright invented the airplane."
>
> "It was a great advance for civilization," Lou said.
>
> **RULE 4:** Place a period inside closing quotation marks.
>
> Ed said, "An Air Force captain made the first supersonic flight."
>
> **RULE 5:** Place a question mark or an exclamation point inside the quotation marks when it is part of the quotation.
>
> Amy asked, "When did jumbo jets begin carrying passengers?"
>
> **RULE 6:** Place a question mark or an exclamation point outside the quotation marks when it is part of the entire sentence.
>
> Did I really hear Sam say, "Jumbo jets are just big airplanes"?
>
> **RULE 7:** Use quotation marks around the title of a short story, essay, poem, song, magazine or newspaper article, or book chapter.
>
> "Araby" [short story]   "Trees" [poem]
>
> **RULE 8:** Use italics (underlining) for the title of a book, play, film, television series, magazine, newspaper, or work of art.
>
> The Pearl [book]   Seventeen [magazine]

20.6 Using Quotation Marks and Italics **599**

Punctuation

Focus

Lesson Overview

Objectives
- To develop an understanding of quotation marks and italics
- To use quotation marks and punctuation correctly with direct quotations and titles of short works
- To use italics (or underlining) appropriately

 Bellringer
Daily Language Activity

When students enter the classroom, have this assignment on the board: *Copy the following sentence. Circle the punctuation that tells you that Kim's exact words are being quoted.*

> *"I'm beat," said Kim. "Can we take a break?"*

See also *Daily Language Practice*

Motivating Activity

Elicit from students the answer to the Bellringer activity. Point out that since the quoted sentence is itself a question, the end punctuation goes inside the quotation marks. (A quoted exclamatory sentence follows the same rule.) Then elicit from students or explain how the punctuation would be different if the sentence read *Kim said she was beat and asked if we could take a break.* Invite students to seek clarification as needed.

Teach

Cross-Reference: Mechanics
For instruction and practice in capitalizing titles of works, see Lesson 19.4.

Resource Manager

 **Planning Resources**
- Lesson Plans

 **Transparencies**
- Bellringer
- Daily Language Practice

Other Print Resources
- Grammar and Composition Handbook
- Grammar Enrichment, p. 50
- Grammar Practice, p. 50
- Grammar Reteaching, p. 50
- Grammar Workbook, Lessons 79–81

Practice and Assess

Answers: Exercise 8

1. "Through the Tunnel"
2. <u>Denver Post</u>
3. "Dream Variations"
4. <u>Much Ado About Nothing</u>
5. "Kilimanjaro"
6. <u>Nova</u>
7. <u>Hook</u>
8. <u>Newsweek</u>
9. "Stardust"
10. "The Budget Amendment Riddle"

Answers: Exercise 9

1. said, "Supersonic . . . speeds."
2. "Only spacecraft," added Randy, "travel . . . airplanes."
3. "Is it true . . . hours?" asked
4. Dolores shouted, "What an . . . be!"
5. Randy asked, "Is that plane . . . transport?"
6. Ms. Chu answered, "Yes, . . . the film <u>Airport.</u>"
7. "Isn't that . . . Concorde?"
8. "Yes," said Ms. Chu. "It . . . Paris."
9. "How fast . . . travel?" asked Randy.
10. <u>The World Book Encyclopedia.</u>
11. <u>Time</u> . . . plane.
12. Roberto, . . . say, "That surprises me"?
13. "Some countries," Ms. Chu continued, "have . . . trains."
14. The article "Japan's Bullet Trains" talks . . . Japan.
15. exclaimed, "Riding . . . terrific!"
16. "The ride . . . bullet train,"
17. . . . Ms. Chu said, "I . . . train."
18. "Have . . . trains?"
19. asked, "Do . . . popular?"
20. states, "Most . . . plane."

Additional Resources

 Grammar Practice, p. 50

 Grammar Reteaching, p. 50

 Grammar Enrichment, p. 50

Grammar Workbook, Lessons 79–81

Exercise 8   Using Quotation Marks and Underlining for Titles

Write each item, adding quotation marks or underlining for italics where needed.

1. Through the Tunnel (short story)
2. Denver Post (newspaper)
3. Dream Variations (poem)
4. Much Ado About Nothing (play)
5. Kilimanjaro (essay)
6. Nova (television series)
7. Hook (film)
8. Newsweek (magazine)
9. Stardust (song)
10. The Budget Amendment Riddle (article)

Exercise 9   Using Punctuation Marks

Write each sentence, adding quotation marks, italics, and other punctuation marks where needed.

1. Dolores said Supersonic planes travel at great speeds
2. Only spacecraft added Randy travel faster than these airplanes
3. Is it true supersonic transports cross the Atlantic in three hours asked Ms. Chu.
4. Dolores shouted What an exciting ride that must be
5. Randy asked Is that plane a supersonic transport
6. Ms. Chu answered Yes a supersonic transport appeared in the film Airport
7. Isn't that plane called the Concorde asked Akira.
8. Yes said Ms. Chu it flies between New York and Paris
9. How fast does the Concorde travel asked Randy.
10. Dolores looked up the information in The World Book Encyclopedia
11. The article in Time explained why no American company built such a plane
12. Roberto did you say That surprises me
13. Some countries Ms. Chu continued have very fast trains
14. The article Japan's Bullet Trains talks about the fast trains in Japan
15. Randy exclaimed Riding on a train like that sounds terrific
16. The ride is very quiet and smooth on the bullet train Ms. Chu said.
17. Then Ms. Chu said I have been on such a train
18. Have you ever been on France's fast trains Dolores asked.
19. Peter asked Do you know why train travel in America is not popular
20. The article states Most Americans seem to prefer traveling by plane

---

Close

Have students discuss how italics, quotation marks, and other marks of punctuation make written material easier to understand. Elicit examples.

Cooperative Learning

Punctuating Quotations

Divide a piece of paper in half. On the left, write words to introduce quotations, such as *Simon says.* On the right, write unpunctuated quotations, such as *Jump in the lake.* Have partners pair items to form sentences, inserting all necessary punctuation.

20.7 Using Apostrophes

An apostrophe can show possession. It can indicate that letters are missing within a contraction. It can also signal the plurals of letters, numbers, or words when they refer to themselves

> **RULE 1:** Use an apostrophe and an *s* *('s)* to form the possessive of a singular noun.
>
> James + **'s** = James**'s**   nation + **'s** = nation**'s**
>
> **RULE 2:** Use an apostrophe and an *s* *('s)* to form the possessive of a plural noun that does not end in *s*.
>
> men + **'s** = men**'s**   geese + **'s** = geese**'s**
>
> **RULE 3:** Use an apostrophe alone to form the possessive of a plural noun that ends in *s*.
>
> boys + **'** = boys**'**   Thompsons + **'** = Thompsons**'**
>
> **RULE 4:** Use an apostrophe and an s *('s)* to form the possessive of an indefinite pronoun, such as *everyone, everybody, anyone, no one,* and *nobody.*
>
> anybody + **'s** = anybody**'s**   someone + **'s** = someone**'s**
>
> Do not use an apostrophe in a possessive pronoun, such as *mine, its, yours, his, hers, ours,* and *theirs.*
>
> That car is **ours**.   Is that cat **yours**?
>
> The bird flapped **its** wings.   This cassette is **hers**.
>
> **RULE 5:** Use an apostrophe to replace letters that have been omitted in a contraction.
>
> it + is = it**'s**   I + will = I**'ll**
> we + are = we**'re**   is + not = isn**'t**
>
> **RULE 6:** Use an apostrophe to form the plurals of the names of letters, figures, and words. Underline the name to show its special use. Do not underline the *'s.*
>
> three <u>b</u>**'s**   five <u>4</u>**'s**   <u>if</u>**'s**, <u>and</u>**'s**, or <u>but</u>**'s**

Focus

Lesson Overview

Objectives
- To develop an understanding of how apostrophes are used
- To use apostrophes with contractions, special plurals, and possessives

 Bellringer
Daily Language Activity

When students enter the classroom, have this assignment on the board: *Write three examples of the different uses of apostrophes.*

See also *Daily Language Practice*

Motivating Activity

Have volunteers write their examples from the Bellringer activity on the board. Point out which of the six rules each sample reflects.

Teach

Cross-Reference: Grammar

For instruction in and practice with plural and possessive nouns and contractions, refer students to Lesson 9.4.

Punctuation

 **Resource Manager**

Planning Resources
- *Lesson Plans*

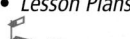 **Transparencies**
- *Bellringer*
- *Daily Language Practice*

Other Print Resources
- *Grammar and Composition Handbook*
- *Grammar Enrichment,* p. 51
- *Grammar Practice,* p. 51
- *Grammar Reteaching,* p. 51
- *Grammar Workbook,* Lesson 82

Practice and Assess

Answers: Exercise 10

1. teacher's	14. dessert's
2. teachers'	15. friends'
3. Ms. Sandoval's	16. dress's
4. adults'	17. islands'
5. deer's	18. mice's
6. man's	19. Thomas's
7. country's	20. wind's
8. countries'	21. tents'
9. dog's	22. people's
10. Celia's	23. youth's
11. women's	24. teeth's
12. heroes'	25. teams'
13. Gladys's	

Answers: Exercise 11

1. friends'
2. she's
3. I'm
4. We're
5. correct
6. correct
7. *T*'s
8. It's anyone's
9. correct
10. correct
11. There's
12. *ABC*'s
13. it's
14. ticket's
15. *J*'s
16. correct
17. it's
18. It's
19. Claudia's
20. *p*'s and *q*'s

Additional Resources

 Grammar Practice, p. 51

 Grammar Reteaching, p. 51

 Grammar Enrichment, p. 51

Grammar Workbook, Lesson 82

Punctuation

Exercise 10 **Using Apostrophes in Possessive Forms**

Write the possessive form of each word or group of words below. Use an apostrophe and an *-s ('s)* or an apostrophe alone (').

1. teacher	7. country	13. Gladys	19. Thomas
2. teachers	8. countries	14. dessert	20. wind
3. Ms. Sandoval	9. dog	15. friends	21. tents
4. adults	10. Celia	16. dress	22. people
5. deer	11. women	17. islands	23. youth
6. man	12. heroes	18. mice	24. teeth
			25. teams

Exercise 11 **Using Apostrophe Items**

For each sentence, write any words that require apostrophes. Insert apostrophes where needed. Write *correct* if the sentence needs no changes.

1. The friends bicycles are ready for the long trip.
2. Ada has made sure shes prepared.
3. "Im ready to start,"Ada said.
4. "Were ready when you are," replied Jess and Kim.
5. "Is the bicycle with the basket yours?" asked Kim.
6. The friends stopped cycling to watch two soccer games.
7. "Why do all the shirts have *T*s on them?" asked Isamu.
8. "Its anyones guess," said Inez.
9. That shirt is hers.
10. A train went by with its horn blaring.
11. Theres more food for everyone in the kitchen.
12. The picture book on sale in the store next door is perfect for teaching your cousin her ABCs.
13. "We should take umbrellas with us," Jack said, "since it looks as if its raining outside."
14. The tickets date seems to be incorrect.
15. The jackets all had large *J*s on the back.
16. The coach gave rings to the girls.
17. According to Jon, its yours.
18. Its clear that the people in charge of the event planned carefully.
19. Claudias watch broke when she fell off her bicycle.
20. His parents told him to watch his *p*s and *q*s.

Critical Thinking

Distinguishing Between Possessive Pronouns and Contractions

Students may have difficulty distinguishing between possessive pronouns, such as *its*, which do not have apostrophes, and contractions like *it's*, which do. As a test, students can expand the term into an uncontracted form. If it makes sense, the original term has an apostrophe.

20.8 Using Hyphens, Dashes, and Parentheses

RULE 1: Use a hyphen to show the division of a word at the end of a line. Always divide the word between its syllables.

Astronauts operate spacecraft and conduct engi-neering, medical, and scientific experiments in space.

RULE 2: Use a hyphen in compound numbers from twenty-one through ninety-nine.

seventy-six   twenty-three

RULE 3: Use a hyphen to spell out a fraction.

Some astronauts receive **one-half** pay upon retirement. [modifier]

One-half of all astronauts have a master's degree. [noun]

RULE 4: Use a hyphen or hyphens in certain compound nouns. Check the dictionary to see which ones need hyphens.

great-grandmother   sister-in-law   attorney-at-law

RULE 5: Use a hyphen in a compound modifier when it precedes the word it modifies.

She is a **well-trained** astronaut.   She is **well trained**.

RULE 6: Use a dash to show a sudden break or change in thought or speech. If the sentence continues, use a second dash to mark the end of the interruption.

Dr. Owens—he lives nearby—teaches astronomy.

RULE 7: Use parentheses to set off words that define, or helpfully explain, a word in the sentence.

Flight training for the space program consists of training in simulators **(**devices that reproduce the conditions of space flight**)** and in other special equipment.

Punctuation

Focus

Lesson Overview

Objectives
- To recognize the correct use of hyphens, dashes, and parentheses
- To use hyphens, dashes, and parentheses correctly

 Bellringer
Daily Language Activity

When students enter the classroom, have this assignment on the board: *Write an example of how a hyphen, a dash, and parentheses are used.*

See also  *Daily Language Practice*

Motivating Activity

Write the seven rules for hyphens, dashes, and parentheses on the board. Have students offer an example from their Bellringer activity and identify the corresponding rule.

Teach

☑ **Teaching Tip**

Share with students the following rules for dividing words at the end of a line of writing: (a) divide only between syllables, (b) do not divide after a one-letter syllable, (c) do not carry just two letters over to the next line, (d) avoid dividing personal names, (e) use a dictionary.

Resource Manager

📁 **Planning Resources**
- *Lesson Plans*

📇 **Transparencies**
- *Bellringer*
- *Daily Language Practice*

📁 **Other Print Resources**
- *Grammar and Composition Handbook*
- *Grammar Enrichment,* p. 51
- *Grammar Practice,* p. 51
- *Grammar Reteaching,* p. 51
- *Grammar Workbook,* Lesson 83

Practice and Assess

Answers: Exercise 12

1. one-half interest
2. correct
3. thirty-five
4. Anglo-Saxon
5. well-liked leader
6. merry-go-round
7. thirty-two missions
8. three-fourths majority
9. forty-two
10. high-powered speaker
11. correct
12. forty-minute class
13. English-speaking actor
14. ninety-five
15. red-haired girl
16. twenty-story building
17. soft-boiled egg
18. sight-seeing
19. two-thirds vote
20. five-mile walk

Answers: Exercise 13

1. six-month
2. pilots—they
3. (only military men were selected).
4. women—both scientists and other professionals—can
5. low-fat diet
6. Apollo-Soyuz Test Project
7. with—but you know that.
8. correct
9. Dr. Ilych—he is a fine teacher—led
10. correct
11. two-thirds
12. four-week
13. trips—these are space shuttle flights—are
14. correct
15. much-improved technology
16. astronauts (they can . . . too).
17. stars (some in other galaxies).
18. income-producing inventions.
19. accident—a very tragic one—has occurred
20. one-half hour

Exercise 12 Using Hyphens

Write the items below, using a hyphen or hyphens where needed. Write *correct* if an item needs no changes.

1. one half interest
2. great uncle
3. thirty five
4. Anglo Saxon
5. well liked leader
6. merry go round
7. thirty two missions
8. three fourths majority
9. forty two
10. high powered speaker
11. first lady
12. forty minute class
13. English speaking actor
14. ninety five
15. red haired girl
16. twenty story building
17. soft boiled egg
18. sight seeing
19. two thirds vote
20. five mile walk

Exercise 13 Using Hyphens, Dashes, and Parentheses

Write each sentence, adding hyphens, dashes, and parentheses where needed. Write *correct* if a sentence needs no changes.

1. Astronauts undergo a six month training course.
2. Most astronauts are pilots they already know about flying.
3. At first no civilians could be astronauts only military men were selected.
4. Now men and women both scientists and other professionals can fly into space.
5. Astronauts must follow a low fat diet as part of their training.
6. The astronauts and cosmonauts in the Apollo Soyuz Test Project visited each other's countries.
7. The astronauts familiarized themselves with the equipment, with the flight plan, with but you know that.
8. The space travelers participated in joint rehearsals of the mission.
9. Dr. Ilych he is a fine teacher led the sessions.
10. As a scientist, Dr. Ilych is well regarded in Russia.
11. He trained two thirds of the participants.
12. Russian scientists sometimes schedule four week missions.
13. American space trips these are space shuttle flights are fairly short.
14. The crew is well trained to carry out scientific experiments.
15. Thanks to much improved technology, we can watch them on television.
16. It's possible to speak directly to the astronauts they can answer directly too.
17. Astronauts study distant stars some in other galaxies.
18. Space flights have resulted in income producing inventions.
19. Only one accident a very tragic one has occurred with the space shuttle.
20. The shuttle lifted off one half hour late.

Punctuation

Additional Resources

 Grammar Practice, p. 51

 Grammar Reteaching, p. 51

 Grammar Enrichment, p. 51

Grammar Workbook, Lesson 83

Close

Ask students to imagine that they are astronauts working with cosmonauts. Have them write a journal entry about the experience. They should use hyphens, dashes, and parentheses.

 **Cultural Connections**

British English

Students who have learned British English may have a special problem with word division because British English divides words by derivation rather than by syllables (*demo-cracy* rather than *democ-racy, know-ledge* instead of *knowl-edge*).

20.9 Using Abbreviations

RULE 1: Use the abbreviations *Mr., Mrs., Ms.,* and *Dr.* before names. Abbreviate professional or academic titles that follow names.

> **Mr.** Carl Baird **Jr.**   Vivian Huang, **M.D.**   Ana Elias, **Ph.D.**
> **Ms.** Leona Wilson, **M.A.**   James Nichols, **R.N.**

RULE 2: Use all capitals and no periods for abbreviations that are pronounced letter by letter or as words. Two exceptions are *U.S.* and *Washington, D.C.*, which do use periods.

> **NHS** National Honor Society   **PDT** Pacific daylight time
> **NATO** North Atlantic Treaty Organization
> **PIN** personal identification number

RULE 3: With exact times use *A.M.* (*ante meridiem,* "before noon") and *P.M.* (*post meridiem,* "after noon"). For years use *B.C.* (before Christ) and, sometimes, *A.D.* (*anno Domini,* "in the year of the Lord," after Christ).

> 8:45 A.M.   6:30 P.M.   30 B.C.   A.D. 476

RULE 4: Abbreviate days and months only in charts and lists.

> **Mon. Tues. Wed.   Apr. Aug. Sept. Oct. Nov. Dec.**

RULE 5: In scientific writing, abbreviate units of measure. Use periods with abbreviations of English units but not of metric units.

> inch(es) **in.**   pound(s) **lb.**   gallon(s) **gal.**
> centimeter(s) **cm**   gram(s) **g**   liter(s) **l**

RULE 6: On envelopes, abbreviate words such as *Street, Avenue, Road, Boulevard, Court, Drive,* and *Circle.* Spell out these words everywhere else.

> **St.   Ave.   Rd.   Blvd.   Ct.   Dr.   Cir.**
> Let's meet at the corner of First **Avenue** and Elm **Street**.

RULE 7: On envelopes, use the U.S. Postal Service two-letter abbreviations for state names.

> **AL** Alabama   **MO** Missouri   **WA** Washington
> **KY** Kentucky   **ME** Maine   **MA** Massachusetts

Focus

Lesson Overview

Objectives
- To recognize the correct form of abbreviations
- To use abbreviations correctly

Bellringer
Daily Language Activity

When students enter the classroom, have this assignment on the board: *Copy the abbreviations Mr., M.D., and Ph.D. Write what each abbreviation stands for.* (Answers: Mister, Doctor of Medicine, Doctor of Philosophy)

See also *Daily Language Practice*

Motivating Activity

Have students address each other aloud, using the appropriate social titles. Challenge students to spell the titles aloud. Point out that the courtesy titles *Mr., Mrs.,* and *Ms.* are used with periods. *Miss* is not followed by a period.

Teach

Vocabulary Link

The term *abbreviation* stems from a Latin verb *abbreviare,* meaning "to shorten." Words such as *abridge* and *brief* can also be traced to the same Latin verb.

Punctuation

Resource Manager

Planning Resources
- *Lesson Plans*

Transparencies
- *Bellringer*
- *Daily Language Practice*

Other Print Resources
- *Grammar and Composition Handbook*
- *Grammar Enrichment,* p. 52
- *Grammar Practice,* p. 52
- *Grammar Reteaching,* p. 52
- *Grammar Workbook,* Lesson 84

Practice and Assess

Answers: Exercise 14

1. A.D.		**14.**	B.C.
2. Mr.		**15.**	I
3. Ave.		**16.**	Apr.
4. Jr.		**17.**	in.
5. Wed.		**18.**	UN
6. in.		**19.**	Ph.D.
7. GA		**20.**	Rd.
8. KY		**21.**	Oct.
9. M.D.		**22.**	Jan.
10. IRS		**23.**	MO
11. Dr.		**24.**	WA
12. ft.		**25.**	ME
13. Nov.			

Answers: Exercise 15

1. correct	**11.** correct
2. R.N.	**12.** correct
3. A.M., P.M.	**13.** correct; P.M.
4. correct	**14.** correct
5. Dr.	**15.** A.D.
6. M.A.	**16.** OSU *or* correct
7. EPA *or* correct	**17.** CIA's *or* correct
8. correct	**18.** Dr.
9. correct	**19.** Dr.
10. FBI *or* correct	**20.** MO

Additional Resources

 *Grammar Practice,* p. 52

Grammar Reteaching, p. 52

Grammar Enrichment, p. 52

Grammar Workbook, Lesson 84

Close

Have students write a letter inviting a friend to a party. Remind them to include all the necessary information and tell them to use some of the abbreviations covered in this lesson. Have them review their writing for legibility.

Exercise 14   Using Abbreviations

Write the correct abbreviation for each underlined item.

1. <u>after Christ</u> 1000
2. <u>Mister</u> Roosevelt
3. 76 Melrose <u>Avenue</u>
4. Don Newell <u>Junior</u>
5. <u>Wednesday</u>
6. 1 <u>inch</u>
7. Atlanta, <u>Georgia</u>
8. Lexington, <u>Kentucky</u>
9. Tat Lam, <u>Medical Doctor</u>
10. <u>Internal Revenue Service</u>
11. 42 Bradford <u>Drive</u>
12. 32 <u>feet</u>
13. <u>November</u> 23
14. 1100 <u>before Christ</u>
15. 15 <u>liters</u>
16. <u>April</u> 23
17. 7 <u>inches</u>
18. <u>United Nations</u>
19. Fred Jackson, <u>Doctor of Philosophy</u>
20. Blake <u>Road</u>
21. <u>October</u> 24
22. <u>January</u> 15
23. Kansas City, <u>Missouri</u>
24. Seattle, <u>Washington</u>
25. Portland, <u>Maine</u>

Exercise 15   Using Abbreviations

Write the abbreviation for each underlined item. Write *correct* if no abbreviation should be used.

1. Our new house is at 14 Laurel <u>Street</u>.
2. The letter from Gail R. Momaday, <u>Registered Nurse,</u> contained information about the public-health seminar.
3. It stated that a meeting will be held from 11:30 <u>in the morning</u> until 4:45 <u>in the afternoon</u>.
4. The meeting will be held on <u>Monday</u>, <u>August</u> 17.
5. Scheduled speakers include <u>Doctor</u> Hilario Reyes.
6. Carol McQuaid, <u>Master of Arts</u>, plans to speak on art therapy.
7. Write to the <u>Environmental Protection Agency</u>.
8. The nearest office is in Boston, <u>Massachusetts</u>.
9. That office is twenty <u>kilometers</u> from my house.
10. That large building houses the <u>Federal Bureau of Investigation</u>.
11. The mall is full of shoppers on <u>Saturday</u> and <u>Sunday</u>.
12. Our tour begins on <u>August</u> 13 and ends on <u>September</u> 4.
13. The bus leaves from Newark, <u>New Jersey</u>, at 8:30 <u>at night</u>.
14. On <u>Tuesday</u> we will be in Baltimore, <u>Maryland</u>.
15. That cathedral is a copy of one built in <u>after Christ</u> 1000.
16. The students from <u>Ohio State University</u> toured with us.
17. The <u>Central Intelligence Agency's</u> headquarters are not open to the public.
18. [on an envelope]   <u>Doctor</u> Amy Salazar
19.   6758 Bradley <u>Drive</u>
20.   Jackson, <u>Missouri</u> 63755

Punctuation

Cultural Connections

Using British Abbreviations

Students may be interested to know that British English draws a distinction between an abbreviation, in which the end of the word is dropped off (*Vol.* for *Volume*), and a contraction, in which the middle of the word is dropped (*Mr.* for *Mister*). In British English, periods are used with abbreviations but not with contractions. In British English, no period is used with *Dept, Mr, Jr,* and *Sr.*

20.10 Writing Numbers

In charts and tables, you always write numbers as figures. However, in an ordinary sentence you sometimes spell out numbers and sometimes write them as numerals

---

RULE 1: Spell out numbers that you can write in one or two words.

In the early nineteenth century, stagecoaches traveled at a speed of less than **twenty-five** miles per hour.

RULE 2: Use numerals for numbers of more than two words.

The first coaches traveled a distance of **392** miles.

RULE 3: Spell out any number that begins a sentence, or reword the sentence so that it does not begin with a number.

Three thousand one hundred coaches existed in England by 1836.

RULE 4: Write a very large number as a numeral followed by the word million or billion.

Did these coaches carry more than **25 million** passengers?

RULE 5: If related numbers appear in the same sentence, use all numerals.

For a trip of **390** miles, drivers changed horses every **20** miles.

RULE 6: Spell out ordinal numbers (such as *first* or *second*).

In America, Wells, Fargo & Company ranked **first** for its coach service.

RULE 7: Use words to express the time of day unless you are writing the exact time or using the abbreviation A.M. or P.M.

The journey began at **six o'clock** in the morning. It ended at **9:15** P.M.

RULE 8: Use numerals to express dates, house and street numbers, apartment and room numbers, telephone numbers, page numbers, amounts of money of more than two words, and percentages. Write out the word *percent*.

 July **19, 1832** 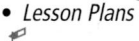 **15** Summit Road  Apartment **6E**   **40 percent**

Punctuation

Focus

Lesson Overview

Objectives
- To recognize the correct use of numbers and numerals
- To write numbers and numerals correctly

Bellringer
Daily Language Activity

When students enter the classroom, have this assignment on the board: *Write five places where you might find numbers included in reading material.*
(Sample answers: newspapers, magazines, advertisements, brochures, and mail envelopes)

See also *Daily Language Practice*

Motivating Activity

Have students look through a newspaper or magazine and circle numerals and spelled-out numbers in the text. On the board, write examples students offer and point out which of the eight rules for writing numbers are exemplified.

Teach

Vocabulary Link

Tell students that in technical, scientific, and other types of writing involving many numbers, numerals may be used instead of numbers. For example, the ages of subjects in a scientific study would be written in numerals. Figures are used to save space and to make the information easier to compare.

Resource Manager

Planning Resources
- *Lesson Plans*

Transparencies
- *Bellringer*
- *Daily Language Practice*

Other Print Resources
- *Grammar and Composition Handbook*
- *Grammar Enrichment,* p. 52
- *Grammar Practice,* p. 52
- *Grammar Reteaching,* p. 52
- *Grammar Workbook,* Lesson 85

Practice and Assess

Answers: Exercise 16

1. 1670
2. 651
3. 55 million
4. Two hundred
5. correct; correct; 20
6. 6:30
7. first; 1756
8. correct
9. correct
10. 1875
11. first
12. correct
13. correct; 1873
14. second
15. twentieth
16. correct; 100,000
17. 1910
18. correct; 1930s
19. $1.25 (Exact sums of money should be written in numerals.)
20. 40

Additional Resources

📁 *Grammar Practice*, p. 52
📁 *Grammar Reteaching*, p. 52
📁 *Grammar Enrichment*, p. 52

 Grammar Workbook, Lesson 85

Close

Have students imagine they are visiting Colorado and taking a stagecoach ride. Students should write a paragraph describing the ride. Encourage students to use at least four of the rules for writing numbers. (Sample: *The road has been used only three times since 1850. The second hill, which is the steepest, rises 620 feet above sea level.*) Ask students to constructively evaluate one another's use of numbers.

Punctuation

Exercise 16   Writing Numbers

Write the correct form for the underlined numbers in the following sentences. Write *correct* if a sentence needs no changes.

1. The first stage line came into existence in England in about <u>sixteen hundred seventy</u>.
2. This stage line covered a distance of <u>six hundred and fifty-one</u> kilometers.
3. Did coaches in England travel at least <u>fifty-five million</u> miles before the rail-ways replaced them?
4. <u>200</u> years ago the United States Congress began mail service by stagecoach.
5. For a trip of <u>360</u> miles, <u>eighteen</u> drivers each traveled about <u>twenty</u> miles.
6. Some trips from Philadelphia to Ohio began at <u>six-thirty</u> a.m.
7. The <u>1st</u> stagecoach lines were established in colonial America in <u>seventeen hundred fifty-six</u>.
8. Horse-drawn coaches rode along at <u>ten</u> miles per hour.
9. Now Americans can fly to London in the Concorde jet at nearly <u>fourteen hundred</u> miles per hour.
10. Before <u>eighteen hundred seventy-five</u> the streetcar (or tram) had replaced the horse-drawn coach.
11. The <u>1st</u> streetcars were called horsecars because teams of horses pulled the wooden cars.
12. <u>Four</u> horses were needed to haul the cars up the steep hills of San Francisco, California.
13. The <u>first</u> trolley line in San Francisco was opened in <u>eighteen hundred seventy-three</u>.
14. A trolley line in Portland, Oregon, was the <u>2nd</u> steepest ever built in the United States.
15. Most of the trolley lines in San Francisco had been abandoned by the beginning of the <u>20th</u> century.
16. American cities were growing quickly—<u>fifty</u> cities had more than <u>one hundred thousand</u> inhabitants.
17. By <u>nineteen hundred and ten</u> electric streetcars had replaced horsecars.
18. In the <u>1920s</u> and <u>nineteen thirties,</u> car travel made streetcars obsolete.
19. It costs <u>one dollar and twenty-five cents</u> to buy one token for the bus or subway.
20. The new subway system built recently in the city carries <u>forty</u> percent of all commuters.

Cooperative Learning

Practicing Writing Numbers

Have students learning English tell about the rules for writing numbers in their first language. They can work with English-proficient partners to figure out the similarities and differences in English.

Spelling Out Numbers

Have students review the general rules for spelling out numbers. (One- and two-digit numbers are spelled out. Large numbers ending in hundred, thousand, million, and billion are also spelled out. With million and billion, the figure is not spelled out: 1 million.) Invite them to discuss reasons why these rules may have developed.

Grammar Review

PUNCTUATION

Time travel is one of Jack Finney's favorite subjects. In the story "The Third Level," Finney's narrator believes there are three levels at Grand Central Station, the monumental railroad station located in the heart of Manhattan. Finney writes, however, that "the presidents of the New York Central and the New York, New Haven and Hartford railroads will swear on a stack of timetables that there are only two." The passage has been annotated to show some of the rules of punctuation covered in this unit.

Literature Model

from "The Third Level"
by Jack Finney

I turned into Grand Central from Vanderbilt Avenue, and went down the steps to the first level, where you take trains like the Twentieth Century. Then I walked down another flight to the second level, where the suburban trains leave from, ducked into an arched doorway heading for the subway—and got lost. That's easy to do. I've been in and out of Grand Central hundreds of times, but I'm always bumping into new doorways and stairs and corridors. Once I got into a tunnel about a mile long and came out in the lobby of the Roosevelt Hotel. Another time I came up in an office building on Forty-sixth Street, three blocks away.

Sometimes I think Grand Central is growing like a tree, pushing out new corridors and staircases like roots. There's probably a long tunnel that nobody knows about feeling its way under the city right now, on its way to Times Square, and maybe another to Central Park.

> **Period at the end of a declarative sentence**

> **Comma before** *but* **that is joining main clauses**

> **Hyphen in a compound number**

> **Apostrophe in a contraction**

(continued)

Punctuation

Grammar Review **609**

Grammar Review

Practice and Assess

Answers: Exercise 1

1. Station. declarative
2. idea! exclamatory
3. him. declarative
4. him? interrogative
5. you. imperative
6. Japan. declarative
7. street! exclamatory
8. station? interrogative
9. train. imperative
10. system? interrogative

Answers: Exercise 2

1. Station, unbelievably, is
2. underground transport system, a bus system, and streetcars.
3. Public transportation, as you can tell, is
4. Los Angeles, two large cities, have
5. know, Dr. McFarlan, that

Punctuation

> **Dashes to show an interruption in thought**
>
> And maybe — because for so many people through the years Grand Central has been an exit, a way of escape — maybe that's how the tunnel I got into . . . But I never told my psychiatrist friend about that idea.

Review: Exercise 1   Using End Marks

Write the correct end mark for each sentence. Then write whether the sentence is *declarative, imperative, interrogative,* or *exclamatory.*

1. The narrator, a young man named Charley, claimed that there were three levels at Grand Central Station
2. What a crazy idea
3. His friends didn't believe him
4. Would you believe him
5. Think of when your friends didn't believe you
6. If you think Grand Central Station is complicated, you should see the train stations in Tokyo, Japan
7. Some stations have as many as twenty-five exits to the street
8. Did you know that you can do all your shopping—from groceries to shoes—in the train station
9. Buy your ticket before you get on the train
10. Do you need a map of the transit system

Review: Exercise 2   Using Commas

Write each sentence, adding commas where needed.

1. The main waiting room at Grand Central Station unbelievably is large enough to hold a football field.
2. Many large cities have an underground transport system a bus system and streetcars.
3. Public transportation as you can tell is often ignored and not well funded.
4. Washington and Los Angeles two large cities have just built public transit systems to make commuting easier.
5. Did you know Dr. McFarlan that France and Japan have trains that operate much faster than ours?

Review: Exercise 3 | **Using Commas with Introductory Words and Phrases**

Write each sentence, adding commas where needed. Write *correct* if a sentence needs no changes.

1. For centuries people have dreamed about space travel.
2. On October 4, 1957, the first artificial satellite was placed in orbit.
3. For the Russians in the 1950s the launch of *Sputnik* was a major achievement.
4. Staying in orbit for twenty-three days Sputnik relayed information to Earth.
5. At the age of twenty-seven Yuri Gagarin became the first person in space.
6. At first unfortunately many of America's rocket tests were unsuccessful.
7. Blasting off in May 1961 Alan Shepard became America's first astronaut.
8. America was finally able to claim it had entered the space age.
9. Orbiting the Earth three times John Glenn found the view magnificent.
10. Unfortunately accidents have marred the American space program.

Review: Exercise 4 | **Using Commas in Compound Sentences**

Write each compound sentence, adding commas where needed. If a sentence needs no commas, write *correct*.

1. Some ferries just carry people and some transport people and vehicles.
2. Oil tankers load oil in one port and pump it out at its destination.
3. Oil tankers are very efficient for oil but they cannot transport other cargoes.
4. Tugs help push big ships into position and turn ships around.
5. A cruise can be very relaxing and many cruise lines offer a wide variety of trips for vacationers.
6. Most cruise ships offer several restaurants and provide a range of activities.
7. The ship can dock at a deep-water port or passengers can be ferried ashore in small boats.
8. You can cruise for a few days or sail for up to a month.
9. Iron ships played a role in the Civil War but they were soon replaced with ships built of steel.
10. Outdated warships are mothballed or they are sold for scrap.

Punctuation

Answers: Exercise 3
1. correct
2. correct
3. in the 1950s,
4. for twenty-three days, Sputnik
5. of twenty-seven, Yuri Gagarin
6. first, unfortunately, many
7. in May 1961, Alan Shepard
8. correct
9. three times, John Glenn
10. Unfortunately, accidents

Answers: Exercise 4
1. people, and some
2. correct
3. for oil, but they
4. correct
5. very relaxing, and many
6. correct
7. deep-water port, or passengers
8. correct
9. Civil War, but they
10. mothballed, or they

Answers: Exercise 5

1. correct
2. founded, mail
3. in California, everyone
4. correct
5. was used, the trip
6. proposed, the Pony Express
7. correct
8. correct
9. be riders, only eighty
10. was completed, the riders

Answers: Exercise 6

1. Stanford, California, at
2. correct
3. Roy Williams, M.D., travel
4. March 4, 2005, at
5. 231 North Ridge Road, Palo Alto, CA 94301.
6. correct
7. Along with shoes, shirts
8. on March 10, 2005, will
9. Sacramento, California, and Reno, Nevada, will
10. of rings, scholarships

Punctuation

Review: Exercise 5   Using Commas with Introductory Adverb Clauses

Write each sentence, adding commas where needed. If a sentence needs no commas, write *correct*. Remember that an adverb clause is a subordinate clause that tells *how, when why,* or *where* an action takes place.

1. The Pony Express is very famous even though it lasted just eighteen months.
2. Before it was founded mail was transported to California by ship.
3. When a ship docked in California everyone rushed to hear the latest news and pick up mail.
4. Delivering mail overland was difficult because winter weather was harsh.
5. Even when a southern route was used the trip across the country by stagecoach took more than three weeks.
6. When it was proposed the Pony Express promised a ten-day crossing.
7. The Pony Express used stagecoach stations wherever it was possible.
8. Other stations were built so that riders could get fresh horses.
9. Although hundreds applied to be riders only eighty were chosen.
10. When the first run was completed the riders were hailed as heroes.

Review: Exercise 6   Using Commas

Write each sentence, adding commas where needed. If a sentence needs no commas, write *correct*.

1. The game will be played in Stanford California at Maples Pavilion.
2. The last time the team won was February 1991.
3. Will Roy Williams M.D. travel with the team?
4. The date of the championship game is March 4 2005 at eight o'clock.
5. Address the ticket request to 231 North Ridge Road Palo Alto CA 94301.
6. Parents will be traveling with the team too.
7. Along with shoes shirts and jackets were donated by the booster group.
8. The award ceremony on March 10 2005 will be held in San Francisco.
9. Bands from Sacramento California and Reno Nevada will be playing.
10. Instead of rings scholarships will be given to the winners.

Review: Exercise 7 **Using Commas with Direct Quotations**

Write each sentence, adding commas where needed.

1. "The first around-the-world nonstop flight took place in 1986" Mark said.
2. "The pilots" Jessica stated proudly "were Dick Rutan and Jeanna Yeager."
3. "In order to make the trip without refueling" Mark explained "the plane had to carry its own fuel supply."
4. "The plane's long, narrow wings" he said "were designed to carry fuel."
5. "The trip took nine days" Jessica added.
6. "This was so different from Charles Lindbergh's flight across the Atlantic" Mark said.
7. "Lindbergh's flight" Jessica stated "took thirty-three hours."
8. "His plane was called the *Spirit of St. Louis*" she said.
9. "Lindbergh was hailed as a hero when he landed in France" stated Mark.
10. "He was revered in America" Jessica added.

Review: Exercise 8 **Using Commas and End Marks in Direct Quotations**

Write each sentence, adding commas and end marks where needed.

SAMPLE "When did man first step on the moon" Jamie asked.
ANSWER "When did man first step on the moon?" Jamie asked.

1. "How long did the astronauts train for their mission" Sam asked.
2. "Three astronauts were on the *Apollo 11* flight to the moon" Jamie explained.
3. "Neil Armstrong, you know" Mark announced "was not a military man"
4. Jamie exclaimed, "I found Neil Armstrong's words so inspiring"
5. Sam asked "What exactly did he say when he stepped on the moon"
6. "I wonder" Sam said "what he expected to find on the moon's surface"
7. Peter asked "Does anyone remember the name of the second man to walk on the moon"
8. Who heard Armstrong say "*The Eagle* has landed"
9. Sam said "Millions of Americans watched the landing on television"
10. Jamie asked "What happened to the rock samples they brought back"

Answers: Exercise 7

1. in 1986," Mark said.
2. "The pilots," Jessica stated proudly, "were
3. refueling," Mark explained, "the plane
4. wings," he said, "were
5. days," Jessica added.
6. the Atlantic," Mark said.
7. flight," Jessica stated, "took
8. *Spirit of St. Louis*," she said.
9. France," stated Mark.
10. America," Jessica added.

Answers: Exercise 8

1. mission?" Sam asked.
2. to the moon, " Jamie explained.
3. you know," Mark announced, "was not a military man."
4. Jamie exclaimed, "I found Neil Armstrong's words so inspiring!"
5. Sam asked, "What exactly did he say when he stepped on the moon?"
6. "I wonder," Sam said, "what he expected to find on the moon's surface."
7. Peter asked, "Does anyone remember the name of the second man to walk on the moon?"
8. Who heard Armstrong say, "The Eagle has landed"?
9. Sam said, "Millions of Americans watched the landing on television."
10. Jamie asked, "What happened to the rock samples they brought back?"

Punctuation

Grammar Review

Answers: Exercise 9

1. Juan asked, "How many interstates are there in the United States?"
2. Theresa explained, "The major roads are all numbered."
3. "With interstates," she said, "the highways that go east-west across the country are given even numbers."
4. "The interstates that go north-south," she continued, "are given odd numbers."
5. Todd asked, "Is Interstate 90 in the north or the south of the United States?"
6. "Interstate 90," Juan answered, "runs from Massachusetts to Seattle."
7. "Where is Interstate 5?" Theresa asked.
8. Juan exclaimed, "That's one of the newest roads in the country!"
9. "Did I hear you say that it's easy to find your way around Boston?" asked Juan.
10. "I like to navigate when my parents drive," Theresa said, "as long as I have a good map to follow."

Answers: Exercise 10

1. What's
2. correct
3. World's
4. correct
5. It's
6. correct
7. women's
8. *A*'s and *B*'s
9. someone's
10. Adams's

Punctuation

Review: Exercise 9 — Punctuating Direct Quotations

Write each sentence, adding quotation marks, commas, and end marks where needed.

1. Juan asked How many interstates are there in the United States
2. Theresa explained The major roads are all numbered
3. With interstates she said the highways that go east-west across the country are given even numbers
4. The interstates that go north-south she continued are given odd numbers
5. Todd asked Is Interstate 90 in the north or the south of the United States
6. Interstate 90 Juan answered runs from Massachusetts to Seattle
7. Where is Interstate 5 Theresa asked
8. Juan exclaimed That's one of the newest roads in the country
9. Did I hear you say that it's easy to find your way around Boston asked Juan.
10. I like to navigate when my parents drive Theresa said as long as I have a good map to follow

Review: Exercise 10 — Using Apostrophes

For each sentence, write any words that require apostrophes. Insert apostrophes where needed. Write *correct* if a sentence needs no apostrophes.

SAMPLE   Its snowing hard right now.
ANSWER   It's

1. Whats it like to ride on a monorail?
2. Some monorails hang down from a single rail.
3. In Disney Worlds monorail system, the car straddles the track.
4. Is their system like yours in Seattle?
5. Its a transportation system that has not been very popular in America.
6. My seat is here, but theirs is on the other side of the car.
7. The womens packages were accidentally left on the train.
8. Only tickets marked with *A*s and *B*s are accepted for the ride.
9. The conductor said that it was someones seat.
10. Dr. Adamss invention will make train travel more comfortable.

Review: Exercise 11

Proofreading

The following passage is about Russian artist Simon Faibisovich, whose work appears on the next page. Rewrite the passage, correcting the errors in spelling, capitalization, grammar, and usage. Add any missing punctuation. There are ten errors.

Simon Faibisovich

¹Simon Faibisovich a russian painter who lives in Moscow. ²Trained as an architect he teached himself to paint. ³His work was never shown publically before American gallery owner Phyllis Kind discovered him in 1987. ⁴There have been several shows of his work in New York, New York since then.

⁵Mister Faibisovich paints large pictures of ordinary people doing ordinary things, such as standing at a bus stop or waiting in line for food. ⁶His portraits are more better than snapshots. ⁷The faces of the people he paints reflects a yearning for something else in their lifes. ⁸Just as Charley views a train station as an opportunity to escape the boy in the painting on the next page is clearly longing for something besides a bus ride.

Review: Exercise 12

Mixed Review

Write correctly the sentences with spelling and punctuation errors. There are twenty errors in all. If the sentence contains no errors, write *correct*.

¹When a person lives in a big city with a large population its easy to feel lonely sometimes. ²Trucks and buses speed by on the roads and crowds jam the sidewalks. ³Are you ever afraid of just crossing the street ⁴Getting away may mean going to the country or it may mean taking a walk in a big park.

⁵In Central Park in New York City you can forget that youre in the middle of one of Americas biggest cities. ⁶The parks trees shade people on summer days you can take long walks on a five mile path through the woods. ⁷You can even go boating if you want. ⁸On Sundays people arent allowed to drive their cars through the park.

⁹Imagine what an escape a space trip must be ¹⁰Looking down on

(continued)

Answers: Exercise 11
Proofreading

This proofreading activity provides editing practice with (1) the current or previous units' skills, (2) the **Troubleshooter** errors, and (3) spelling errors. Students should be able to complete the exercise by referring to the units, the **Troubleshooter,** and a dictionary.

Error (Type of Error)

1. Faibisovich is (sentence fragment) Russian (capitalization)
2. architect, (introductory participial phrase)
   taught (verb form)
3. publicly (spelling)
4. New York, New York, (name of a state with name of a city)
5. Mr. (abbreviation) This is an optional correction.
6. are better (double comparison)
7. reflect (subject-verb agreement) lives (spelling)
8. escape, (introductory adverb clause)

Answers: Exercise 12
Mixed Review

1. population, it's
2. roads,
3. street?
4. country, or
5. City, . . . you're . . . America's
6. park's . . . days; . . . five-mile
7. correct
8. aren't
9. be!
10. spaceship, you
11. It's . . . space—no one
12. moon, he . . . said, "Beautiful . . . desolation."

Punctuation

Grammar Review

Close

Ask students to work in groups to write brief comedic skits. Encourage students to create two lines of dialog with incorrect punctuation. The dialog might create a mis-understanding or just sound funny. Have each group perform its skit. Following each performance, the audience members can attempt to remedy the punctuation and the situation.

Punctuation

Earth from a spaceship you would have the most magnificent view. [11]Its so quiet out in space no one would bother you. [12]When Buzz Aldrin landed on the moon he looked around and said Beautiful, beautiful, beautiful—a magnificent desolation.

Simon Faibisovich, *Boy*, 1984

Viewing the Art

Simon Faibisovich, *Boy*, 1984

Simon Faibisovich is a Russian artist. Born in Moscow in 1949, he still lives in that city. Faibisovich paints scenes of people carrying out everyday activities. However, the people in his paintings clearly dream of a more exciting life. The young man in *Boy*, for example, is physically present at the bus stop, but his mind is far away, perhaps engaged in an adventurous fantasy. The painting, *Boy*, is in oil on masonite board, measuring 50 1/2 by 39 inches. The work is in a private collection.

Writing Application

TIME
For more about the writing process, see **TIME Facing the Blank Page,** pp. 97–107.

Quotation Marks in Writing

In this passage from *The Gathering*, Virginia Hamilton brings her characters to life by presenting their exact words. She uses quotation marks and commas to clearly identify where those words, known as dialogue, begin and end. Note the punctuation marks.

> "Wow! Magic!" said Dorian. Celester hummed a comic toning, entertaining them with the light.
> "Whatever it was, it got hot," Thomas said. He eyed Celester suspiciously.
> "A property of light is heat," toned Celester. "He who puts hand in fire will singe his fingertips."
> "I get the message," Thomas muttered.
> "Celester, you have powerful gifts," Justice said.

Techniques with Quotation Marks

Try to apply some of Virginia Hamilton's writing techniques as you write and revise your own work.

❶ Make your characters vivid by capturing their exact words. Use quotation marks before and after each direct quotation. Compare the following:

BLAND VERSION Dorian was surprised.

HAMILTON'S VERSION "Wow! Magic!" said Dorian.

❷ Keep your dialogue clear by using commas to signal the shift from a quoted sentence to surrounding text.

INCORRECT VERSION "A property of light is heat" toned Celester.

HAMILTON'S VERSION "A property of light is heat," toned Celester.

Punctuation

Practice Try out these techniques by revising the following passage, using a separate piece of paper. Decide which information might be better presented as dialogue in quotation marks. Use commas as necessary to separate that dialogue from other text.

> Nan's toes felt frozen. She looked around in wonder at all the snow. Seeing her dismay, her father told her about the Blizzard of 1888. He explained that cities had been buried under several feet of snow. People were stranded on trains and at work. Nan suggested that it might have been interesting to see that much snow. It might help her feel happier about living in Tucson where it never snows. Her father laughed at her suggestion and headed back inside.

Writing Application **617**

Quotation Marks in Writing

You may have students read the dialogue silently, without interruption. Then go back and discuss how the writer uses quotation marks and commas to show where the dialogue begins and ends. Discuss this punctuating technique in relation to the Techniques with Quotation Marks activity on this page.

Techniques with Quotation Marks

Discuss with students the techniques explained on this page. Then have students apply the techniques in the proofreading exercise on page 615.

Practice

The answers to this challenging and enriching activity will vary. Refer to Techniques with Quotation Marks as you evaluate student choices. A sample answer follows:

"I think my toes are frozen," complained Nan. "I wanted snow, but I wasn't looking for a blizzard."

"This is nothing," replied her father. "Have you ever heard of the Blizzard of 1888? Cities were buried under several feet of snow. People were stranded on trains and at work. It was incredible!"

"Wow! I almost wish I could have been there," said Nan. "Maybe then I'd get snow out of my system and be happy living in sunny Tucson."

"That'll be the day," laughed her father as he headed back inside.

✔ ASSESSMENT OPTIONS

📁 *Tests with Answer Key & Rubrics* Unit 20 Mastery Test, pp. 83–84

💾 *Testmaker* Unit 20 Mastery Test

You may wish to administer the Unit 20 Mastery Test at this point.

📼 *MindJogger Videoquizzes*

Objectives

- To develop an understanding of how to combine groups of short sentences into longer sentences
- To use sentence combining to exhibit greater clarity of thought, conciseness of style, and variety of expression

✓ ASSESSMENT OPTIONS

📁 *Tests with Answer Key & Rubrics*
Unit 21 Pretest, pp. 85–86
Unit 21 Mastery Test, pp. 87–88

💾 *Testmaker*
Unit 21 Pretest
Unit 21 Mastery Test

You may wish to administer the Unit 21 Pretest at this point.

Key to Ability Levels

L1 Level 1 activities are within the basic ability range of students.

L2 Level 2 activities are within the ability range of average students.

L3 Level 3 activities are more challenging activities.

UNIT
21 Grammar Through Sentence Combining

618

Resource Manager

📁 **Planning Resources**
- *Lesson Plans*
- *Block Scheduling*

📠 **Transparencies**
- *Bellringer*

📁 **Other Print Resources**
- *Grammar and Composition Handbook*
- *Grammar Enrichment*
- *Grammar Practice*

- *Grammar Reteaching*
- *Grammar Workbook*
- *Sentence-Combining Practice*
- *Tests with Answer Key and Rubrics*

📹 **Video**
- *MindJogger Videoquizzes*

💾 **Software**
- *Interactive Grammar and Language Workbook*

- *Language Arts PASS*
- *Presentation Plus!*
- *Revising With Style*
- *Testmaker*

🖥 **Web Sites**
- *writerschoice.glencoe.com*

21.1 Prepositional Phrases

Prepositional phrases are useful in sentence combining. Like adjectives and adverbs, prepositional phrases enable you to give more information about nouns and verbs. Because prepositional phrases show relationships, they often express complex ideas effectively.

> EXAMPLE **a.** Latoya Hunter faithfully kept a diary.
> **b.** Latoya's home was **New York City. [from]**
> **c.** She wrote the diary **in seventh grade.**

Latoya Hunter **from New York City** faithfully kept a diary **in seventh grade.**

The new information (in dark type) in sentences *b* and *c* takes the form of prepositional phrases when added to sentence *a*. In the new sentence, the phrase *from New York City* modifies the noun *Latoya Hunter*. The phrase *in seventh grade* modifies the verb *kept*. Prepositional phrases that modify nouns follow the nouns they modify. Prepositional phrases that modify verbs come before or after the verbs they modify. (For a list of common prepositions see page 479.)

■ A **prepositional phrase** is a group of words that begins with a preposition and ends with a noun or pronoun. Prepositional phrases modify nouns, pronouns, and verbs.

| Exercise 1 | Combining Sentences with Prepositional Phrases |

The following sentences are based on passages from *The Diary of Latoya Hunter,* which you can find on pages 32–37. Combine each group of sentences, turning the new information into a prepositional phrase. In the first few items, the new information is in dark type.

1. **a.** Latoya missed her old social life.
   b. She was **attending her new school. [at]**
2. **a.** Latoya envied her diary.
   b. She envied the diary **for its detachment.**

Focus

Lesson Overview

Objectives
- To recognize prepositional phrases
- To use prepositional phrases correctly

 Bellringer
Daily Language Activity

When students enter the classroom, have this assignment on the board: *Rewrite the sentence "Elizabeth had a dream" to include the prepositional phrases* of hiking *and* in the Himalayas.

Motivating Activity

Have students read aloud the original sentence in the Bellringer activity. Have them write and read aloud variations containing one and then two of the prepositional phrases. Ask students which of the three sentences is most interesting. Point out that combining sentences provides sentence variety and improves the flow of the writing.

Teach

⇄ Cross-Reference: Grammar

For instruction and practice on prepositional phrases and how they function in sentences, refer students to Lessons 13.1 and 13.3.

Grammar Through Sentence Combining

Resource Manager

📂 **Planning Resources**
- *Lesson Plans*

🖥 **Transparencies**
- *Bellringer*

📂 **Other Print Resources**
- *Grammar and Composition Handbook*
- *Grammar Workbook,* Lesson 38
- *Sentence-Combining Practice,* p. 5

Practice and Assess

Answers: Exercise 1

1. At her new school, Latoya missed her old social life.
2. Latoya envied her diary for its detachment.
3. Latoya's best friend had moved away during the spring.
4. Latoya's progress toward greater maturity is revealed in her diary.
5. Each new entry in her diary is like a snapshot of the writer's mind.
6. Latoya's diary traces her development from an unhappy girl into a self-confident young woman.
7. Latoya named her diary Janice after her best friend in Jamaica.
8. One Sunday Latoya got in trouble at home with both parents.
9. Latoya was feeling desperate about her situation in school.
10. A book editor wanted the diary of a teenager in distress.

Answers: Exercise 2

Answers will vary, but a suggested beginning is given below.

Latoya devoted one entry in her diary to a former teacher. Her words about Mr. Pelka create a wonderful picture of a warm and caring man. From Mr. Pelka, the class learned to empathize with other people. One day Latoya learned the moving story of a Jewish girl in the time of the Holocaust. According to Latoya, Mr. Pelka should go down in history.

Additional Resources

📁 *Sentence-Combining Practice,* p. 5

📕 *Grammar Workbook,* Lesson 38

3. a. Latoya's best friend had moved away.
   b. She moved **during the spring.**
4. a. Latoya's progress is revealed in her diary.
   b. Her progress was toward greater maturity.
5. a. Each new entry is like a snapshot.
   b. The entry is in her diary.
   c. The snapshot is of the writer's mind.
6. a. Latoya's diary traces her development.
   b. Her development was from an unhappy girl.
   c. Her development was into a self-confident young woman.
7. a. Latoya named her diary Janice.
   b. She named it after her best friend.
   c. Janice was her friend in Jamaica.
8. a. One Sunday Latoya got in trouble.
   b. There was trouble at home.
   c. She was in trouble with both parents.
9. a. Latoya was feeling desperate.
   b. She wrote about her situation.
   c. Her main concern was how she felt in school.
10. a. A book editor wanted the diary.
    b. She wanted the diary of a teenager.
    c. The teenager had been in distress.

Exercise 2   Combining Sentences

Rewrite the paragraphs below, using prepositional phrases to combine sentences. Make any other changes in wording that you feel are necessary.

Latoya devoted one entry to a former teacher. The entry is in her diary. Her words create a wonderful picture. The words are about Mr. Pelka. The picture is of a warm and caring man. The class learned to empathize with other people. They learned this from Mr. Pelka. One day Latoya learned the moving story of a Jewish girl. This girl lived in the time of the Holocaust. Mr. Pelka should go down in history. This is according to Latoya.

Mr. Pelka made history come alive. He did that for all his students. He made them understand that history is like a story. It's like a story from a movie. History is about major events. It's also about people. It's about people like us. Latoya learned to understand major events through her reading. She read about real people. Those stories helped her understand herself better. Now she knew more. Now she knew something about other people's feelings.

Close

Invite students to consider the advantages and disadvantages of writing diaries of their own. Have students write a paragraph explaining whether the idea appeals to them. Make sure they use prepositional phrases in their writing.

MEETING INDIVIDUAL NEEDS Less-Proficient Readers

Distinguishing Prepositional Phrases from Infinitive Phrases

To help students distinguish infinitive phrases from prepositional phrases with *to,* point out that an infinitive phrase has *to* plus an action word (verb); a prepositional phrase has *to* plus a naming word (noun or pronoun). **L1**

21.2 Appositives

You can use appositives to combine sentences in a compact and informative way. Single word appositives and appositive phrases identify or tell something new about a noun or a pronoun.

EXAMPLE **a.** Mars is too cold to support life.
b. Mars is **Earth's neighbor.**

Mars, **Earth's neighbor,** is too cold to support life.

The appositive phrase *Earth's neighbor* tells us more about the noun *Mars*. Note that the appositive phrase is set off with commas because it gives extra information about Mars. If an appositive supplies information that is essential for identifying a noun, it is not set off with commas. (For more information about appositives, see pages 389–390.)

■ An **appositive** is a noun placed next to another noun to identify it or give additional information about it. An **appositive phrase** includes an appositive and other words that describe it.

Grammar Through Sentence Combining

| Exercise 3 | Combining Sentences with Appositives |

The sentences below are based on an excerpt from *Living Treasure* by Laurence Pringle, which you can find on pages 248–253. Combine each group of sentences so that the new information is turned into an appositive or an appositive phrase. In the first few items, the new information is in dark type. The information in brackets indicates that you should add a comma or commas to the new sentence.

1. **a.** Earth lies between icy Mars and hot Venus.
   b. Earth is **our home planet.** [, + ,]
2. **a.** Because of its climate, our own planet is an oasis.
   b. The planet is **Earth.** [, + ,]
3. **a.** According to the writer, scientists are astounded by the great diversity of life forms on Earth.
   b. The writer is **Laurence Pringle.**

21.2 Appositives **621**

Focus

Lesson Overview

Objectives

- To recognize and use appositives and appositive phrases
- To use appositives and appositive phrases correctly

Bellringer
Daily Language Activity

When students enter the classroom, have this assignment on the board: *Combine the three sentences below into one.*

My brother is a mechanic.

My brother is a classic-car mechanic.

He is working on a 1930 Rolls-Royce.

(My brother, a classic-car mechanic, is working on a 1930 Rolls-Royce.)

Motivating Activity

Write the word *appositive* on the board. Explain that it comes from a Latin word *appositus,* meaning "placed near." Point out that the phrase *a classic-car mechanic* placed beside the noun *brother* tells something new about the brother. Explain that this phrase is called an appositive phrase.

Teach

☑ **Teaching Tip**

An appositive that gives information essential for identifying a noun is an essential, or restrictive, appositive. An appositive that gives nonessential information is a nonessential, or nonrestrictive, appositive.

Resource Manager

📂 **Planning Resources**
- *Lesson Plans*

📑 **Transparencies**
- *Bellringer*

📂 **Other Print Resources**
- *Grammar and Composition Handbook*
- *Grammar Enrichment,* p. 52
- *Grammar Practice,* p. 52
- *Grammar Reteaching,* p. 52
- *Grammar Workbook,* Lesson 11
- *Sentence-Combining Practice,* pp. 7–8

Practice and Assess

Answers: Exercise 3

1. Earth, our home planet, lies between icy Mars and hot Venus.
2. Because of its climate, our own planet, Earth, is an oasis.
3. According to one writer, Laurence Pringle, scientists are astounded by the great diversity of life forms on Earth.
4. The Swedish botanist Carl von Linné developed the Linnaean system, the modern means of classifying plants and animals.
5. One threat to humanity is the loss of biodiversity, the variety of life on Earth.
6. The tropical rain forest, the heart of Earth's biodiversity, is valuable to all of us, the inhabitants of this planet.
7. New species, undescribed organisms, may have the ocean floor as a habitat, a place where plants and animals naturally grow or live.
8. Terry Erwin, an entomologist, collected insects in Panama for the Smithsonian.
9. Edward O. Wilson, a Harvard University biologist, found forty-three kinds of ants from one habitat, a single tropical tree.
10. Some scientists specialize in biology, the study of living things.

Answers: Exercise 4

A sample beginning is given below.

Funding for tropical research increased in the 1980s, a period of discovery of the rain forest. From one tree in Peru, an entomologist collected many ants. Upon examining them, a biologist at Harvard University discovered as many ant species as have been identified in all of Canada or Great Britain. The Earth's biodiversity is probably unique in the solar system.

Additional Resources

📁 *Sentence-Combining Practice*, pp. 7–8
📁 *Grammar Practice*, p. 52
📁 *Grammar Reteaching*, p. 52
📁 *Grammar Enrichment*, p. 52

📖 *Grammar Workbook*, Lesson 11

Grammar Through Sentence Combining

4. a. The Swedish botanist developed the Linnaean system.
   b. The botanist was **Carl von Linné.**
   c. The Linnaean system is **the modern means of classifying plants and animals.** [,]
5. a. One threat to humanity is the loss of biodiversity.
   b. Biodiversity is the variety of life on Earth.
6. a. The tropical rain forest is valuable to all of us.
   b. The rain forest is the heart of Earth's biodiversity.
   c. All of us are the inhabitants of this planet.
7. a. New species may have the ocean floor as a habitat.
   b. New species are undescribed organisms.
   c. A habitat is a place where plants and animals naturally grow or live.
8. a. Terry Erwin collected insects in Panama for the Smithsonian.
   b. Terry Erwin is an entomologist.
9. a. Edward O. Wilson found forty-three kinds of ants from one habitat.
   b. Wilson is a Harvard University biologist.
   c. The habitat was a single tropical tree.
10. a. Some scientists specialize in biology.
    b. Biology is the study of living things.

Exercise 4 — Combining Sentences

Rewrite the following paragraphs. Use appositives and appositive phrases to combine sentences. Make any changes in wording that you feel are necessary.

Funding for tropical research increased in the 1980s. These years were a period of discovery of the rain forest. From one tree in Peru, for example, an entomologist collected many ants. The entomologist was Terry Erwin. His ants were examined by Edward O. Wilson. Wilson was a biologist at Harvard University. In that one tree, Wilson discovered as many ant species as have been identified in all of Canada or Great Britain. These countries are areas far to the north of the rain forest. The biodiversity of the planet is probably unique in the solar system. The planet is Earth.

These entomologists made their discoveries in the rain forest. The entomologists are experts in the branch of biology that deals with insects. The rain forest has also led to new discoveries in botany. Botany is the branch of biology dealing with plant life. Terry Erwin and these other biologists are especially interested in studying the rain forest's canopy. Terry Erwin has called the canopy "the heart" of Earth's biodiversity.

Close

Have students explain in their own words how using appositives makes their writing more varied and clear. Ask them to provide some examples from actual written work.

Critical Thinking

Differentiating Appositives

Show students a picture of several people. Point to one and say *my cousin Tony.* This phrase is essential because Tony is one of several cousins. Show a picture of one person and say *my cousin, Sally.* This phrase is nonessential because Sally is the only cousin.

21.3 Adjective Clauses

Adjective clauses are useful in sentence combining. When two sentences share information, one of them can often be made into an adjective clause modifying a word or phrase in the other.

EXAMPLE   **a.** Dara and Jantu had both lost part of their families
         b. Dara and Jantu **were good friends. [, who . . . ,]**

Dara and Jantu, **who were good friends,** had both lost part of their families.

The new information (in dark type) in sentence *b* becomes an adjective clause modifying *Dara and Jantu. Who* now connects the clauses. Notice the commas in the new sentence. Adjective clauses that add nonessential information require commas. Those that add essential information do not. (For more information see pages 505–506.)

■ An **adjective clause** is a subordinate clause that modifies a noun or pronoun in the main clause. The relative pronouns *who, whom, whose, which,* and *that* are used to tie the adjective clause to the main clause.

| Exercise 5 | **Combining Sentences with Adjective Clauses** |

The following sentences are based on an excerpt from *The Clay Marble* by Minfong Ho, which you can find on pages 90–94. Combine each numbered group of sentences so that the new information is turned into an adjective clause. In the first few items, the new information is in dark type; the information in brackets indicates the relative pronoun to use and that a comma or commas are needed.

1. **a.** Jantu spent afternoons under the stone beam.
   b. Jantu **loved to play with clay. [, who . . . ,]**
2. **a.** Palm fronds shaded one end of the beam.
   b. The beam **became a cavelike shelter. [, which]**

21.3 Adjective Clauses   **623**

Grammar Through Sentence Combining

Focus

Lesson Overview

Objectives
- To recognize adjective clauses
- To use adjective clauses correctly in combining sentences

Bellringer
Daily Language Activity

When students enter the classroom, have this assignment on the board: *Copy the passage below. Underline the essential adjective clause.*

> From the dark spruce he heard an owl call—once, and again—and the questions that had been rising all day long reached the door of his mind and opened it.
>
> —Margaret Craven
> *I Heard the Owl Call My Name*

Teach

Critical Thinking

Challenge students to compare and contrast clauses and phrases. (Sample response: *Both clauses and phrases can modify adjectives. A clause has a subject and predicate, but a phrase does not.*) Then have students think of examples of clauses and phrases on the theme of friends. (Clauses: *who was my best friend, whom she never liked, whose friendship he valued;* Phrases: *on the friend's porch, to her friend, for their friends*)

Resource Manager

📁 **Planning Resources**
- *Lesson Plans*

🖥 **Transparencies**
- *Bellringer*

📁 **Other Print Resources**
- *Grammar and Composition Handbook*
- *Grammar Workbook,* Lesson 44
- *Sentence-Combining Practice,* pp. 14–15

Practice and Assess

Answers: Exercise 5

Answers may vary.

1. Jantu, who loved to play with clay, spent afternoons under the stone beam.
2. Palm fronds shaded one end of the beam, which became a cavelike shelter.
3. Jantu . . . from clay that she had scooped from a mud puddle.
4. Dara, who would hold Jantu's baby brother, watched Jantu.
5. The girls talked of family members whom they had lost.
6. Continuity in her life was important to Dara, who hated change.
7. The war that had broken Jantu's family made many people suffer.
8. Jantu described a real family as a loving group that grows with new members all the time.
9. Dara's memories, which were a great comfort to her, helped her feel her family around her.
10. The rain on the roof was like the soft touch of Dara's grandmother, who would massage the girl's head.

Answers: Exercise 6

Answers will vary, but a sample beginning is given below.

Jantu created a thatched shelter that was like a leafy cave. Dara would sit in the shelter holding Jantu's baby brother and watch Jantu, who was sculpting clay figures. Dara wished aloud that everything would stay the same, which—of course—couldn't happen. Jantu understood her friend, who had endured so much change already. Jantu and Dara had both once had whole families, which were just fragments now. Jantu spoke of their families as leftovers that were like pieces from a broken bowl. Both girls wanted to be part of a real family, one that was growing and not shrinking. Jantu hoped to surprise Dara with the gift she was making.

Additional Resources

📁 *Sentence-Combining*, pp. 14–15

📙 *Grammar Workbook*, Lesson 44

Grammar Through Sentence Combining

3. **a.** Jantu made delicate figures from clay.
   b. **She had scooped** this clay **from a mud puddle.** [that]
4. **a.** Dara watched Jantu.
   b. Dara **would hold Jantu's baby brother.** [, who . . . ,]
5. **a.** The girls talked of family members.
   b. **They had lost** family members. [whom]
6. **a.** Continuity in her life was important to Dara.
   b. Dara hated change.
7. **a.** The war made many people suffer.
   b. The war had broken Jantu's family.
8. **a.** Jantu described a real family as a loving group.
   b. This group grows with new members all the time.
9. **a.** Dara's memories helped her feel her family around her.
   b. Those memories were a great comfort to her.
10. **a.** The rain on the roof was like the soft touch of Dara's grandmother.
    b. Her grandmother would massage the girl's head.

Exercise 6   Combining Sentences

Rewrite the paragraphs below, using adjective clauses to combine sentences. Make any changes in wording and punctuation you feel necessary. If any sentence doesn't make sense when trying to combine it, leave it as is.

Jantu created a thatched shelter. The shelter was like a leafy cave. Dara would sit in the shelter holding Jantu's baby brother and watch Jantu. Jantu was sculpting clay figures. Dara wished aloud. She wished that everything would stay the same. This of course couldn't happen. But Jantu understood her friend. Her friend had endured so much change already. Jantu and Dara had both once had whole families. The families were just bits and pieces of ones now. Jantu spoke of their families as leftovers. The leftovers were like fragments from a broken bowl. Both girls wanted to be part of a real family. A real family was one that was growing and not shrinking. Jantu hoped to make her friend feel better with a surprise. She had been working on the surprise.

Jantu showed Dara some clay figures. Jantu wanted to comfort her. The girls were interrupted by a rainfall. The rainfall reminded Dara of long-lost rainy afternoons with her family. Dara imagined her family as a soft blanket. The blanket sheltered her. Jantu invited Dara to play with the family of dolls. Jantu was remembering her own lost family. In the clay figures, Dara recognized her own family members, as well as members of Jantu's family. Jantu had made their broken families whole again. Jantu had the skill and the imagination of an artist.

Close

Have each student write a brief paragraph describing a friend, using specific incidents that illustrate the friend's qualities. Direct students to use adjective clauses in their writing. Ask them to review their paragraphs and evaluate the effectiveness of the phrases in their writing.

MEETING INDIVIDUAL NEEDS   Less-Proficient Readers

Combining Sentences

Break down the process of sentence combining into steps, progressing only as steps are understood. For example, for item one in exercise 5, first make sure students understand that the common element in the two sentences is *Jantu*. **L1**

21.4 Adverb Clauses

You can use adverb clauses to combine sentences. Adverb clauses are especially effective in establishing clear relationships between two or more actions. For example, adverb clauses can indicate that one action follows another or causes another.

> **EXAMPLE** **a.** Bel Kaufman read a great deal a a girl.
>   **b.** She was trying to master the English language.
>   **[because]**
>
> Bel Kaufman read a great deal as a girl **because she was trying to master the English language.**

In the new sentence, the adverb clause *because she was trying to master the English language* modifies the verb *read*. The adverb clause tells why Bel Kaufman was reading so much. Note that the subordinating conjunction *because* makes the relationship between the action and its reason very clear. An adverb clause may occupy different positions within a sentence. If it begins the sentence, it is followed by a comma. (For more information about adverb clauses, see pages 507–508.)

■ An **adverb clause** is a subordinate clause that modifies the verb in the main clause. Adverb clauses are introduced by subordinating conjunctions, such as *after, although, because, before, since, when, whenever, if,* and *while.*

Exercise 7   **Combining Sentences with Adverb Clauses**

The following sentences are based on "The Liberry" by Bel Kaufman, which can be found on pages 298–301. Use adverb clauses to combine each group of sentences. Vary the position of the adverb clause and vary the subordinating conjunction too. In the first few items, the information in brackets signals the subordinating conjunction and the punctuation you should use.

1. **a.** Bel Kaufman came to New York City at the age of twelve. [**Before . . . ,**]
   b. She had lived in Russia.

Focus

Lesson Overview

Objectives
- To recognize adverb clauses
- To use adverb clauses correctly in combining sentences

Bellringer
Daily Language Activity

When students enter the classroom, have this assignment on the board: *Copy the following sentence. Circle the main clause, which describes a particular action. Underline the subordinate clause, which explains why the action occurred.*

Rafael went to the library because he wanted to learn about the pyramids of ancient Egypt.

Motivating Activity

Call on volunteers to identify and explain the clauses they circled and underlined in the Bellringer activity. Use students' responses to introduce the term *adverb clause.* Ask students to monitor their comprehension and ask for clarification if needed.

Teach

Vocabulary Link

Subordinating conjunctions introduce clauses that cannot stand alone and must be connected to a main clause. Some other subordinating conjunctions are *as, so that, than, unless, until,* and *whether.*

Grammar Through Sentence Combining

Resource Manager

📁 **Planning Resources**
- *Lesson Plans*

🖼 **Transparencies**
- *Bellringer*

📁 **Other Print Resources**
- *Grammar and Composition Handbook*
- *Grammar Workbook,* Lesson 45
- *Sentence-Combining Practice,* pp. 18–20

Practice and Assess

Answers: Exercise 7

Answers will vary. Samples:

1. Before Bel Kaufman came to New York City at the age of twelve, she had lived in Russia.
2. She never felt the need to use the library's card catalog because she went through the bookshelves alphabetically.
3. Whenever she found a book with dog-eared pages and many dates on its card, she recognized a book that she would probably want to read.
4. When Kaufman glanced through a book's pages, she enjoyed reading comments scribbled in the margins although she knew it was wrong to mark up a library book.
5. One reader might write "How true!" in a book's margins, whereas another reader would write "This book stinks."
6. Kaufman wrote an essay about the importance of libraries because she was very concerned about cuts in funds for libraries.
7. People are . . . reading skills, while public libraries are closing their doors.
8. When people have less leisure time, they are less inclined to read.
9. In a library, . . . a book because you are surrounded by large numbers of books and readers.
10. Because it has . . . works, the public library . . . people when they need . . . project.

Answers: Exercise 8

Answers will vary, but a sample is given below.

What needs do libraries fill? According to Bel Kaufman, libraries offer us a quiet refuge whenever we seek peace and privacy. Libraries also give people a chance to read if they have no other access to free books.

Bel Kaufman is very distressed about library closings because she remembers libraries so fondly. When she taught high school English in New York City, she required her students

to bring a library card to class. If they actually had a card, they might go to the library. One student brought in his aunt's card because he did not have one of his own. Nevertheless, some of her students did use their cards because the cards were there. Some people still go to the library because the library is still there. According to Kaufman, the city will suffer if everyone's neighborhood library is forced to close.

2. **a.** She never felt the need to use the library's card catalog.
   b. She went through the bookshelves alphabetically. [**because**]
3. **a.** She found a book with dog-eared pages and many dates on its card. [**Whenever . . . ,**]
   b. She recognized a book that she would probably want to read.
4. **a.** Kaufman enjoyed reading comments scribbled in the margins.
   b. Kaufman glanced through a book's pages. [**When . . . ,**]
   c. She knew it was wrong to mark up a library book. [**although**]
5. **a.** One reader might write "How true!" in a book's margins.
   b. Another reader would write "This book stinks." [**, whereas**]
6. **a.** Kaufman wrote an essay about the importance of libraries.
   b. She was very concerned about cuts in funds for libraries.
7. **a.** People are increasingly troubled about children's reading skills.
   b. Public libraries are closing their doors.
8. **a.** People have less leisure time.
   b. They are less inclined to read.
9. **a.** In a library, it is hard to avoid sitting down and reading a book.
   b. You are surrounded by large numbers of books and readers.
10. **a.** It has a vast selection of reference works.
    b. They need information on a special assignment or project.
    c. The public library is also invaluable for many people.

Exercise 8   Combining Sentences

Rewrite the following paragraphs, using adverb clauses to combine sentences. Make any other changes in punctuation or wording that you feel are necessary.

What needs do libraries fill? According to Bel Kaufman, libraries offer us a quiet refuge. We seek peace and privacy. Libraries also give people a chance to read. They have no other access to free books.

Bel Kaufman is very distressed about library closings. She remembers libraries so fondly. She taught high school English in New York City. She required her students to bring a library card to class. They actually had a card. They might go to the library. One student brought in his aunt's card. He did not have one of his own. Nevertheless, some of her students did use their cards. The cards were there. Some people still go to the library. The library is still there. According to Kaufman, the city will suffer. Everyone's neighborhood library is forced to close.

MEETING INDIVIDUAL NEEDS   English Language Learners

Seeing Connections

Encourage students learning English to make connections in their own words between the sentences in Exercises 7 and 8. Then work with students to combine the sentences using adverb clauses.

Grammar Through Sentence Combining

Review: Exercise 9

Mixed Review

The following sentences are based on "A Huge Black Umbrella" by Marjorie Agosín, which you can find on pages 188–191. Combine each group of sentences so that the new information is turned into the kind of phrase or clause indicated in dark type. Any necessary pronouns or punctuation are also indicated.

1. **a.** She was covered by a huge black umbrella.
   b. Delfina Nahuenhual arrived at their house. [**adverb clause; When . . . ,**]
   c. The umbrella was ripped in many places. [**adjective clause; that**]
2. **a.** The umbrella was useless in the rain.
   b. It had many holes. [**adjective clause; ,which . . . ,**]
   c. It let the rainwater fall on her. [**adverb clause; because**]
3. **a.** Delfina explained to Mother that she always traveled with the umbrella.
   b. Mother welcomed her. [**adjective clause; ,who . . . ,**]
   c. The umbrella protected her from the sun, elves, and little girls. [**adjective clause; ,which**]
4. **a.** Delfina Nahuenhual was a survivor.
   b. We called her by her full name. [**adjective clause; ,whom . . . ,**]
   c. She was a survivor of a Chilean earthquake. [**prepositional phrase**]
5. **a.** Mother was really a friend of Delfina.
   b. Mother was the lady of the house. [**appositive phrase; , . . . ,**]
   c. Delfina was my mother's servant. [**appositive phrase; ,**]
6. **a.** Delfina Nahuenhual told us many stories.
   b. The stories were about tormented souls and frogs. [**prepositional phrase**]
   c. The frogs became princes. [**adjective clause; that**]
7. **a.** Delfina Nahuenhual would write long letters.
   b. The letters she would number and wrap up. [**adjective clause; that**]
   c. She would wrap them up in newspaper. [**prepositional phrase**]
8. **a.** She kept the letters in an old pot filled with lemon rind, garlic, and cumin.
   b. Cumin is a kind of spice. [**appositive phrase; ,**]
9. **a.** Cynthia and her sister tried to read those letters.
   b. Delfina was busy in the kitchen. [**adverb clause; Whenever,**]
10. **a.** After Mario was born, Delfina Nahuenhual said she was tired and wanted to go back to Chile.
    b. Mario was the spoiled one of the family. [**appositive phrase; , . . . ,**]

Answers: Exercise 9
Mixed Review

Answers will vary. Samples:
1. When Delfina Nahuenhual arrived at their house, she was covered by a huge black umbrella that was ripped in many places.
2. The umbrella, which had many holes, was useless in the rain because it let the rainwater fall on her.
3. Delfina explained to Mother, who welcomed her, that she always traveled with the umbrella, which protected her from the sun, elves, and little girls.
4. Delfina Nahuenhual, whom we called by her full name, was a survivor of a Chilean earthquake.
5. Mother, the lady of the house, was really a friend of Delfina, the servant.
6. Delfina Nahuenhual told us many stories about tormented souls and frogs that became princes.
7. Delfina Nahuenhual would write long letters that she would number and wrap up in newspaper.
8. She kept the letters in an old pot filled with lemon rind, garlic, and cumin, a kind of spice.
9. Whenever Delfina was busy in the kitchen, Cynthia and her sister tried to read those letters.
10. After Mario, the spoiled one of the family, was born, Delfina Nahuenhual said she was tired and wanted to go back to Chile.

Additional Resources

📁 *Sentence-Combining Practice,* pp. 18–20

📗 *Grammar Workbook,* Lesson 45

Close

Have students explain how adverb clauses establish clear relationships between two or more actions; give examples.

Less-Proficient Readers

Punctuating Adverb Clauses

Explain to students that an adverb clause may occupy several positions within a sentence. When an adverb clause appears at the beginning of a sentence, it is followed by a comma. (*When you finish your homework, you may play the video game.*) When an adverb clause appears at the end of a sentence, it is not preceded by a comma. (*You may play the video game when you finish your homework.*) **L1**

✔ ASSESSMENT OPTIONS

📁 *Tests with Answer Key & Rubrics*
Unit 21 Mastery Test, pp. 87–88

💾 *Testmaker*
Unit 21 Mastery Test
You may wish to administer the Unit 21 Mastery Test at this point.

📼 *MindJogger Videoquizzes*

Resources and Skills

Objectives

The goal of the units in Part 3 is to help students, through example and instruction,

- to understand and use the features of a library and the services it provides for research
- to understand the influence of other cultures and languages on the spelling of English words
- to use context clues, word analysis, and other resources to determine the meanings of unfamiliar words
- to spell derivatives correctly by applying the spellings of bases and affixes
- to identify and understand synonyms, antonyms, homonyms, homophones, and homographs, and use them to enhance writing
- to develop skills for finding information and studying
- to develop effective test-taking skills
- to listen effectively and to evaluate spoken messages
- to refine the ability to speak informally and to prepare and deliver formal speeches
- to interpret, analyze, and produce media messages
- to understand the features of the Internet and other electronic resources and to use them to find information and communicate

"In the old days it was not unusual to find several generations living together in one home."

—Rudolfo Anaya

628

Resource Manager

 **Planning Resources**
- *Lesson Plans*
- *Block Scheduling*

 **Transparencies**
- *Bellringer*
- *Daily Language Practice*
- *Two-Minute Skill Drill*

Other Print Resources
- *Dinah Zike's Foldables™ for Writer's Choice*
- *Guide to Using the Internet and Other Electronic Resources*
- *inTime*
- *ITBS® Preparation and Practice Workbook*
- *Listening and Speaking Activities*
- *SAT-9 Preparation and Practice*
- *Spelling Power*

PART 3

Resources and Skills

Egon Schiele
Houses with Drying Laundry
1917

629

Viewing the Art

Houses with Drying Laundry is from the brush of the Austrian expressionist painter and draftsman Egon Schiele (1890-1918). Expressionism, which began in 1905, is characterized by symbolic colors and exaggerated imagery that reflect an artist's state of mind and inner convictions rather than the reality of the external world. Expressionists often used an image of the modern city with distorted shapes and colors to convey the idea of a lonely, hostile world. Schiele was at odds with art critics and society for most of his brief life, which ended with his sudden death at 28 of influenza. His independent, aggressive style features dark colors, harsh, jagged outlines, and linear effects.

Interpret and Analyze Use the following questions for discussion:

- What mood does Schiele's use of color produce?
- What techniques does Schiele use to show how he feels about his subject?
- Why do you think he felt as he did about the world?

Discussing the Quotation

Suggest that students read or reread "The Boy and His Grandfather." Ask them to consider in what way living arrangements today are different from the way they were in the story? How do today's living arrangements make things better or worse for the elderly? for those who care for the elderly?

Writing Prompt Ask students to study the painting and imagine the inhabitants of Schiele's houses. Remind them to let the lines and colors as well as the images of the painting aid their imaginations. Have each of them write a paragraph in which they relate the quotation to Schiele's painting.

- *Taking Standardized Tests*
- *TerraNova Preparation and Practice*
- *Tests with Answer Key and Rubrics*
- *Thinking and Study Skills*
- *Viewing and Representing Activities*
- *Vocabulary and Spelling Strategies and Practice*
- *Vocabulary Power*

▥ Video
- *MindJogger Videoquizzes*

▤ Software
- *Presentation Plus!*
- *Testmaker*
- *Vocabulary Power Puzzlemaker*

▤ Web Sites
- *writerschoice.glencoe.com*

Objectives

- To develop an understanding of how a library is arranged and how to find materials using a card catalogue or a computer catalogue
- To learn how to find information in reference sources
- To understand how to use a dictionary and a thesaurus

✔ ASSESSMENT OPTIONS

📁 *Tests with Answer Key and Rubrics*
Unit 22 Pretest, pp. 89–90

💾 *Testmaker*
Unit 22 Pretest

You may wish to administer the Unit 22 Pretest at this point.

Key to Ability Levels

L1 Level 1 activities are within the basic ability range of students.

L2 Level 2 activities are within the ability range of average students.

L3 Level 3 activities are more challenging activities.

UNIT 22

Library and Reference Resources

630

Resource Manager

📁 **Planning Resources**
- *Lesson Plans*
- *Block Scheduling*

 **Transparencies**
- *Bellringer*
- *Daily Language Practice*

📁 **Other Print Resources**
- *Guide to Using the Internet and Other Electronic Resources*
- *Tests with Answer Key and Rubrics*
- *Thinking and Study Skills*
- *Vocabulary and Spelling Strategies and Practice*

**Video**
- *MindJogger Videoquizzes*

 **Software**
- *Presentation Plus!*
- *Testmaker*

 **Web Sites**
- *writerschoice.glencoe.com*

22.1 The Arrangement of a Library

The library is a good place to satisfy your curiosity about anything from aardvarks to Zuñis. It also offers a wealth of information you can use for school assignments and projects.

A trip to the library can be eye opening even when you don't have a purpose in mind. Just browsing, you might find a new magazine that's all about your favorite hobby. You might spot a video of a movie you've been wanting to see. You might find a book you'd like to read or a Web site where you can take notes about a place you've always wanted to visit.

You can expect to make discoveries at a library. You can also expect most libraries to be arranged in roughly the same way. Turn the page to learn more about what you can find at a library.

22.1 The Arrangement of a Library **631**

Focus

Lesson Overview

Objectives
- To become familiar with the arrangement of a library
- To learn the common features and services of community libraries in preparation for doing research

Skills
- identifying common library resources

Critical Thinking
- analyzing

Listening and Speaking
- discussing

Bellringer
Daily Language Activity

When students enter the classroom, have this assignment on the board: *List five resources you would expect to find in any library.*

See also *Daily Language Practice*

Motivating Activity

Ask students to describe the efforts and difficulties involved in finding information for a research report they wrote. Did they find all the information they needed? How much time did they spend researching their topics? Explain that in this lesson students will learn to use the library more effectively so that the next time they do a report, they will be able to find more information and find it more quickly.

Resource Manager

📂 Planning Resources
- *Lesson Plans*

📖 Transparencies
- *Bellringer*
- *Daily Language Practice*

📂 Other Print Resources
- *Thinking and Study Skills,* pp. 28–29
- *Vocabulary and Spelling Strategies and Practice,* pp. 35–40

Teach

Finding Materials

Many students need extra encouragement when using the library. Reassure them that if they have trouble finding materials, the librarian is there to help. Review the types of materials to be found in each part of the library.

Making a Chart

Ask students where they would go in the library to find a copy of a book on tape. Then have each student make a chart with columns labeled *Young Adult and Children's Section, Stacks, Audio-Visual Area,* and so on. Work with students to recall titles of books they have read, and help them place those titles in the correct categories.

Library and Reference Resources

No two libraries are alike, but most of them share the same characteristics and have similar resources.

Librarian   A librarian can be the most important resource of all. He or she can help you use the library wisely by directing you to different resources, showing you how to use them, and giving you advice when needed. You might want to prepare your questions for the librarian ahead of time. Be sure to ask your questions clearly but quietly. Do not disturb others in the library.

Young Adult and Children's Section
Young readers can find books written for them in a separate area of the library. Sometimes reference materials for students are also shelved here, along with periodicals and audiovisual materials.

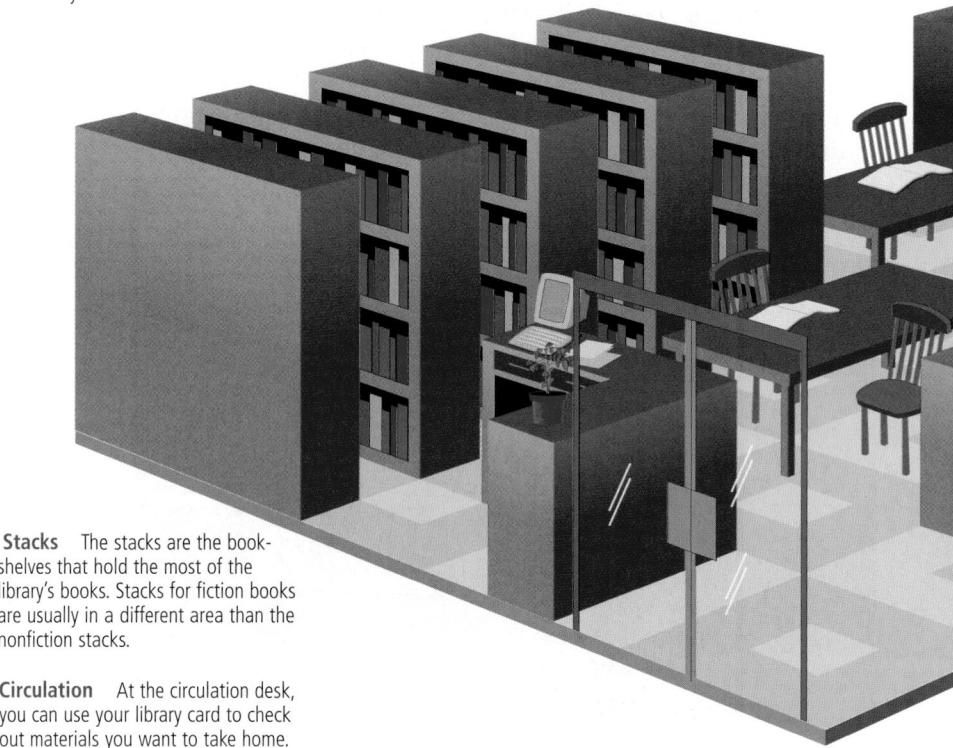

Stacks   The stacks are the bookshelves that hold the most of the library's books. Stacks for fiction books are usually in a different area than the nonfiction stacks.

Circulation   At the circulation desk, you can use your library card to check out materials you want to take home.

Periodicals   You can find current issues of periodicals—newspapers, magazines, and journals—in a general reading area. Here you can read local newspapers as well as newspapers from around the world. Periodicals are arranged alphabetically and by date. Older issues may be available in the stacks or on microfilm or microfiche. Use the computer catalog to locate them or ask a librarian to help you. Some libraries allow you to check out the older issues of periodicals.

Enrichment and Extension

Ancient Libraries

The oldest known libraries date from about five thousand years ago. Libraries were established by the ancient Sumerians, who lived in what is now southern Iraq. Their books were clay tablets. The principal purpose of these books was to record commercial transactions. However, the uses gradually expanded. Ancient Sumerian libraries have been excavated and found to contain tablets that tell of the earliest schools, social reform, philosophy, and politics. They also contain literature that is a thousand years older than Homer's *Iliad.*

Reference The reference area holds dictionaries, encyclopedias, atlases, and other reference works. Usually you are not allowed to check out these materials. They are kept in the library so that everyone may have access to them. Computer databases are also part of the reference area. These systems allow you to search for facts or articles from periodicals. For example, InfoTrac provides complete articles and article summaries from more than one thousand newspapers and magazines. Some computer databases allow you to search for particular types of information, such as history or art.

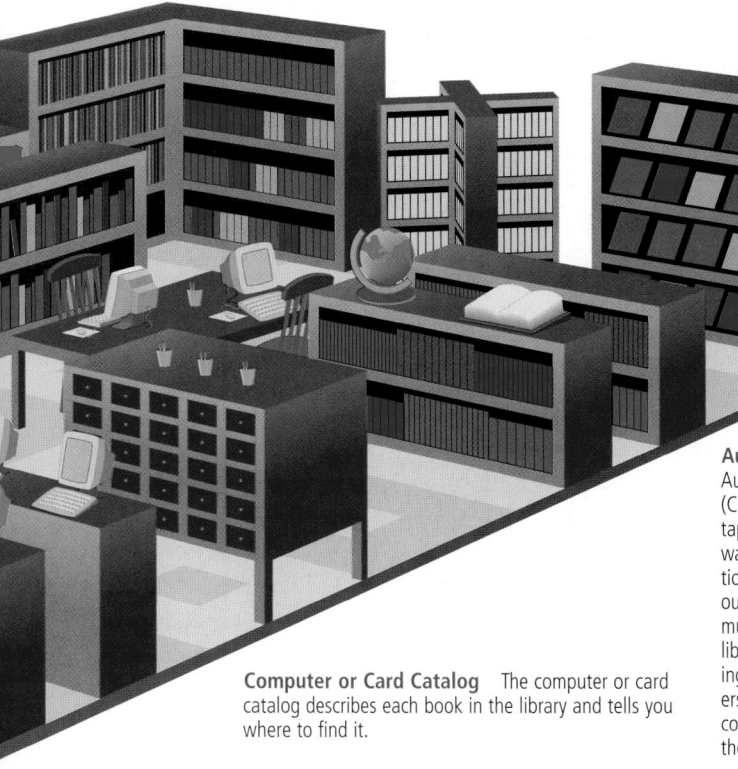

Computer or Card Catalog The computer or card catalog describes each book in the library and tells you where to find it.

Audiovisual Materials Audiocassettes, compact discs (CDs), videotapes, digital video-tapes (DVDs), and computer software are in the audiovisual section. In this section, you can check out a movie, a CD of your favorite music, or a book on tape. Some libraries have listening and viewing areas with audiocassette players, videocassette players, and computers to allow you to review the materials while at the library.

Exercise 1

In which section of the library might you find each of the following items?

1. A video of the film *Across Five Aprils*
2. *The Times Atlas of World Exploration*
3. This week's issue of *Sports Illustrated*
4. *Dictionary of the Middle Ages*
5. *A Wrinkle in Time* (a fantasy novel for young readers)

22.1 The Arrangement of a Library   **633**

Practice and Assess

Answers: Exercise 1

1. audiovisual area
2. reference area
3. periodicals area
4. reference area
5. fiction stacks

Additional Resources

Thinking and Study Skills, pp. 28–29
Vocabulary and Spelling Strategies and Practice, pp. 35–40

Close

Ask students to describe library resources they have used. What books have they used in the reference section? What audio-visual materials have they used? What are the procedures for checking out books? Have students use their knowledge to generalize about information and services available at public libraries.

Viewing and Representing

Interpreting Visuals

Making Library Diagrams Point out that the diagram shows standard sections of a library and how they might be organized. Have each student make a diagram of the school or community library. Ask students to locate on the diagrams each resource section shown in this textbook. Have them add to their diagrams any additional resource or reference sections they find in their libraries.

Focus

Lesson Overview

Objectives

- To understand how books in libraries are categorized
- To learn to use the Dewey decimal system

Skills

- locating books within the Dewey decimal system; using alphabetical order to locate fiction books by author

Critical Thinking

- analyzing; categorizing

Listening and Speaking

- discussing

 Bellringer

Daily Language Activity

When students enter the classroom, have this assignment on the board: *List five topics you would expect to find in the science section of a library.*

See also *Daily Language Practice*

Motivating Activity

Have students share the science topics they listed in the Bellringer activity. Make a composite list of all the topics and have students suggest ways books on these topics are, or could be, organized in a library.

Library and Reference Resources

22.2 ## The Dewey Decimal System

Suppose a library had no system for organizing its books. You'd have to search every shelf to find a book you wanted. Many public libraries use the Dewey decimal system of classification to organize their books. This system groups books into ten broad categories of knowledge, as shown on the chart below. As you search for a book, begin by asking yourself in what group it might be classified.

Dewey Decimal System			
Category Numbers	**Major Category**	**Example of a Subcategory**	**Sample Book Title**
000–099	General works	Encyclopedias	*World Book Encyclopedia*
100–199	Philosophy	The senses	*The Amazing Five Senses*
200–299	Religion	Mythology	*Greek Mythology*
300–399	Social sciences	Law	*We, the People*
400–499	Language	Chinese language	*Speaking Chinese*
500–599	Science	Astronomy	*The Night Sky Book*
600–699	Technology	Medicine	*Sports Medicine*
700–799	The arts	Dance	*Ballet Basics*
800–899	Literature	Plays	*Our Town*
900–999	History	Mexican history	*The Ancient Maya*

Books in each major category are labeled with a similar number. For example, all books about science have a number in the 500s. Books about the arts—for example, painting, sculpture, photography, dance, theater—have numbers in the 700s.

Each major category is broken up into smaller categories. Each added digit, or single numeral, in the Dewey decimal number narrows the category further. A book about photography would have a number in the 770s. Look at the Dewey decimal number on the following page for *Mountains of Fire*. This book by Robert W. Decker is about volcanoes. Notice how each digit in the number further narrows down the topic.

 **Resource Manager**

📂 **Planning Resources**
- *Lesson Plans*

 **Transparencies**
- *Bellringer*
- *Daily Language Practice*

📂 **Other Print Resources**
- *Thinking and Study Skills,* pp. 28–29
- *Vocabulary and Spelling Strategies and Practice,* pp. 35–40

500	**Science**	A book about science is listed in the 500s.
550	**Earth Sciences**	This book is about a subcategory of science.
551	**Geology**	Geology is a subcategory of earth sciences.
551.21	**Volcanoes**	The numbers after the decimal narrow down the topic even further.

Books are shelved in order according to the Dewey decimal number and then alphabetically by author's last name. For example, among all the books with number 551.21, a book by Robert W. Decker would come before a book by Margaret Poynter.

A fiction book is not usually given a Dewey decimal number. Instead, the first line of the call number is either an *F* or *FIC*, for *fiction*. The second line almost always shows the first three letters of the author's name. Fiction books are arranged on the shelves by the author's last name. Books by the same author are further alphabetized by title.

Exercise 2

Go to the nonfiction stacks in your school or neighborhood library. Find a book that looks interesting in each category listed below. Write down the book's Dewey decimal number, author, title, and topic.

1. 000–099
2. 100–199
3. 300–399
4. 600–699
5. 700–799

22.2 The Dewey Decimal System **635**

Teach

Using the Dewey Decimal System

Send students on a treasure hunt through the school library stacks. Choose actual call numbers from each of the Dewey decimal categories. The numbers should clearly indicate the subject matter. Have students find the books without looking in the card catalog for author or title information and then have them write down the titles. **L2**

Practice and Assess

Evaluation Rubrics: Exercise 2

Answers will vary. They should include a title, a complete call number, and an inference about the book's topic based on its Dewey decimal number and title. The books should represent the following categories:

1. General works
2. Philosophy
3. Social sciences
4. Technology
5. The arts

Additional Resources

Thinking and Study Skills, pp. 28–29
Vocabulary and Spelling Strategies and Practice, pp. 35–40

Close

Ask each student to write a paragraph explaining the difference between books shelved under the 800s as literature and books shelved in the fiction stacks. Have students describe how fiction titles are organized.

Cultural Connections

Classifying Books

Book classification systems have long been a thorn in the side of librarians. Because individual books cover a wide range of subjects, precise classification is nearly impossible. Most systems have been based on classifying books either by subject matter or author's name. In medieval colleges, classification was based on subject and book size. In colonial America, books were organized by subject and location, such as *alcove 4, shelf C, book 8*. The Dewey decimal system, developed in 1872 by Melvil Dewey, is now the most commonly used system.

Focus

Lesson Overview

Objectives
- To understand how computer catalogs and card catalogs are set up
- To learn to use computer catalogs and card catalogs to find information in the library

Skills
- identifying features of computer catalog and card catalog entries; using call numbers to find books

Critical Thinking
- analyzing; categorizing

Listening and Speaking
- discussing; questioning

Bellringer
Daily Language Activity

When students enter the classroom, have this assignment on the board: *List three topics you would like to research for a classroom assignment.*

See also *Daily Language Practice*

Motivating Activity

Point out that computer catalogs and card catalogs give listings only for major subjects covered by a book. Ask students to brainstorm to develop a list of related topics for the three topics they listed in the Bellringer activity. These related topics might help them find additional information for their main topics.

22.3 Using a Library Catalog

How do you find the book you want in a library filled with books? The library catalog is the best place to start. Your library may have a computer catalog, a card catalog, or both. Either catalog can tell you which books the library owns.

Using a Computer Catalog

The computer catalog lists all the books, periodicals, and audio-visual materials in the library. You can search for these materials by title, author, subject, or keyword. A **keyword** is a word or phrase that describes a topic. If you type an author's name, you can view a list of all the books written by that author. Typing a subject enables you to view all the books about that particular topic. The computer catalog tells you the title, author, and call number of each book, and whether it is available for checkout. Be sure to take notes or print out the information to help you find the book.

For example, suppose you are looking for books about career guidance for young actors. Your computer search might proceed as follows:

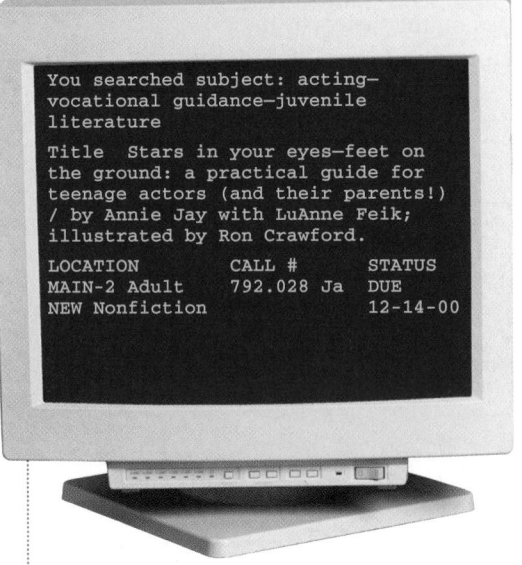

You searched subject: acting—vocational guidance—juvenile literature

Title Stars in your eyes—feet on the ground: a practical guide for teenage actors (and their parents!) / by Annie Jay with LuAnne Feik; illustrated by Ron Crawford.

LOCATION   CALL #   STATUS
MAIN-2 Adult   792.028 Ja   DUE
NEW Nonfiction   12-14-00

Library and Reference Resources

1. Type in the subject, *acting—vocational guidance*.
2. The computer will show a list of all the books in the library on this subject. Each item is numbered.
3. Now, for more detailed information on an item, type in its number.
4. You will then see a screen, like the one shown here, with detailed information about the book.

The way the computer catalog works may differ slightly from library to library. Follow the on-screen directions to use any

---

Resource Manager

📂 **Planning Resources**
- *Lesson Plans*

📠 **Transparencies**
- *Bellringer*
- *Daily Language Practice*

📂 **Other Print Resources**
- *Thinking and Study Skills*, pp. 28–29
- *Vocabulary and Spelling Strategies and Practice*, pp. 35–40

computer catalog. If you have trouble with your search, ask a librarian for help.

Using a Card Catalog

The card catalog, a cabinet of long, narrow drawers, holds cards describing each book in the library. The cards are arranged in alphabetical order. The book's Dewey decimal number, or call number, is usually printed in the upper-left corner of the card. This number also appears on the spine of the book.

Most fiction books have two cards: an author card and a title card. Nonfiction books usually have three catalog cards: an author card, a title card, and a subject card. In some libraries, subject cards are grouped separately from author and title cards.

You may also see cross-reference cards in the catalog. These cards direct you to other ways a subject is listed in the catalog.

Teach

Creating Catalog Cards

Bring a nonfiction book from the library to class. Work with students to create an author card, a title card, and subject cards for the nonfiction book. Discuss the book's general subject matter by referring to the table of contents. Help students determine what subject cards should be made for the book. Have them create subject cards individually. Show students that the same information appears on the author, title, and subject cards, but the order of presentation is slightly different. Have students create an author card and a title card.

Investigating a Computer Catalog

If your school library has a computer catalog, have students talk with the librarian and become familiar with the operating procedures and any special features of the computer program. Then have volunteers develop a step-by-step guide that can be shared with other members of the class. **L3**

Library and Reference Resources

22.3 Using a Library Catalog **637**

Real-World Connections

Exploring the Stacks

Many libraries place biographies and autobiographies, science fiction, and westerns on separate sets of shelves. They may also separate oversized books and rare books. You may want to investigate separate shelving used by your school library and then call these stacks to the students' attention.

Practice and Assess

Additional Resources

📂 *Thinking and Study Skills*, pp. 28–29
📂 *Vocabulary and Spelling Strategies and Practice*, pp. 35–40

Close

Have students share experiences they may have had using computers in the library. Emphasize that the computers are simple to use and have prompts on the screen that will guide them through the process. Encourage students to seek help from the librarian if they have any problems.

Finding a Book

When you have located a book you want in the catalog, write down its call number. In the stacks locate the shelf that holds books with numbers close to your call number. For example, if your number is 862.12, first find the 800s section. Then look for the 860s. If several books have the same call number, they will be shelved alphabetically by author.

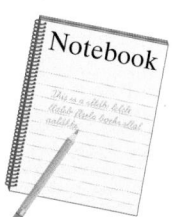

Identify the book by the specific author, title, or subject.

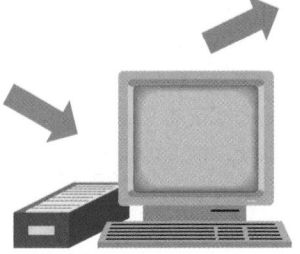

Look up the book in the computer catalog or the card catalog.

Find the book in the stacks or in the reference section.

Check out the book at the circulation desk unless it must be used only in the library.

Exercise 3

Use the catalog to find a book for each of the following topics. List the author, title, and call number of each book you find.

1. Types of sailing ships
2. Rocks and minerals
3. Japan's economy
4. Castles
5. Egyptian mythology
6. Poems by Myra Cohn Livingston
7. Geometry
8. African masks
9. Guide dogs
10. Olmec civilization

Library and Reference Resources

Cooperative Learning

Researching in a Group

Allow students to work in small groups to complete Exercise 3. For each topic, students should list one or two headings under which books might be found. Each student should then find books for two or three topics. Have students meet again to combine their work for the exercise.

22.4 Basic Reference Sources

The next time you want to satisfy your curiosity about the world, try the library's reference section. The reference section contains many general information sources, both in print and online. These sources are useful when you are doing research or working on a class assignment. They're useful any time you need an answer to a question. The chart below gives some examples of the kinds of questions basic references can answer.

Using Basic Reference Books to Answer Questions

Question	Where to Look	Examples of Sources
When did Elizabeth I rule England?	**Encyclopedias** include general information on a variety of topics.	• *The World Book Encyclopedia* • *Grolier Encyclopedia* • *Encyclopaedia Britannica*
What is the average temperature in Lagos, Nigeria?	**Atlases** are collections of maps. They often include special maps on climate, population, and other topics.	• *Hammond Contemporary World Atlas* • *The Rand McNally Atlas of World Exploration*
Who won the Nobel Prize for literature in 1999?	**Almanacs** provide lists, statistics, and detailed information on recent events.	• *Information Please Almanac* • *World Almanac and Book of Facts*

Encyclopedias

You have probably used encyclopedias for research papers and class projects. These basic reference books may be contained in a single volume or in many volumes. General encyclopedias have articles on a wide variety of topics. Some examples are countries, animals, noteworthy people, historical events, and scientific ideas. Whatever you're looking for, you'll probably find something about it in an encyclopedia.

An encyclopedia is a good place to start a research project. An encyclopedia article will give you an overview of the topic. It may provide a list of books for further research.

In addition to general encyclopedias, most libraries have some specialized encyclopedias. These provide more detailed

Focus

Lesson Overview

Objectives
• To become familiar with the kinds of information basic reference books contain
• To use encyclopedias, atlases, and almanacs to answer questions

Skills
• differentiating among encyclopedias, almanacs, and atlases; identifying specialized types of encyclopedias, atlases, and almanacs

Critical Thinking
• categorizing

Listening and Speaking
• discussing

Bellringer
Daily Language Activity

When students enter the classroom, have this assignment on the board: *You need to quickly find information about Puerto Rico for a report. Name three library sources you would go to first.*

See also *Daily Language Practice*

Motivating Activity

Ask students to name specific library reference materials they have used. What kinds of information did they find in these sources? Why did they use these references instead of some other library resources? Encourage students to keep a list of resources and to note the kinds of assignments for which each reference might be used.

Library and Reference Resources

Resource Manager

📂 **Planning Resources**
• *Lesson Plans*

🖼 **Transparencies**
• *Bellringer*
• *Daily Language Practice*

📂 **Other Print Resources**
• *Thinking and Study Skills,* pp. 28–29
• *Vocabulary and Spelling Strategies and Practice,* pp. 35–40

Teach

Making a Chart

Because some students become easily confused by the vast number of materials in a library, the reference area is a good place for them to begin learning about libraries. Help them become comfortable with the wide range of resources available by having them make up a checklist of questions they can use while researching a particular topic.

Suggest such questions as the following:

- Is it in a general encyclopedia?
- What does the encyclopedia index tell me?
- On what page can I find the information?
- What is the guide word at the top of the page?
- Where can I find more information? **L1**

⇄ Cross-Reference: Writing

For more information on how library references can be useful when doing research for a report, refer students to Lesson 5.7.

information on a specific subject. Two examples are the *The Everything You Want to Know About Sports Encyclopedia* and *Sciences of the Earth: An Encyclopedia of Events, People and Phenomena.*

Articles in an encyclopedia are arranged alphabetically. To find out if an encyclopedia has information on your topic, look up the topic in the index. The index may be contained in a separate volume. The index will tell you the volume and page numbers on which the information appears. Below is a sample encyclopedia page. Do you think the photographs on the page below help communicate important information? Explain.

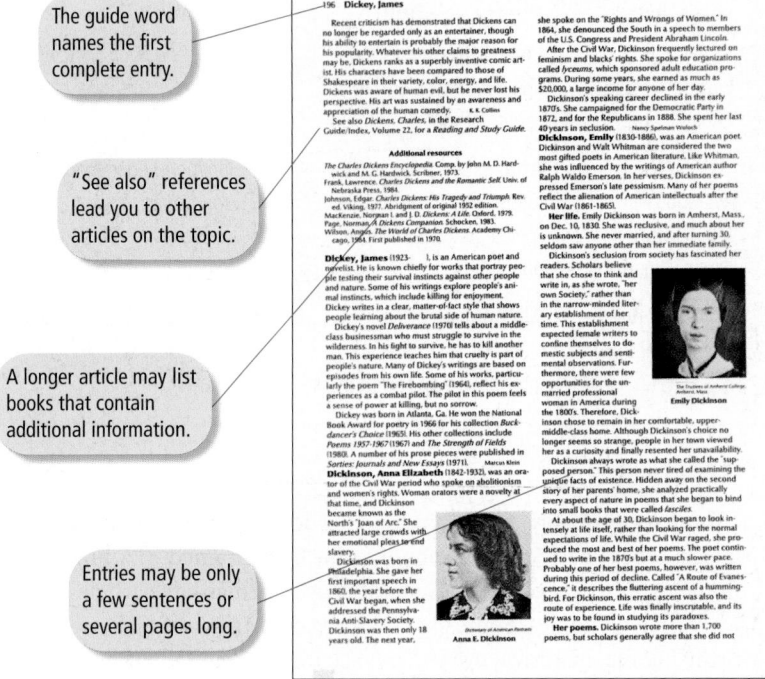

The guide word names the first complete entry.

"See also" references lead you to other articles on the topic.

A longer article may list books that contain additional information.

Entries may be only a few sentences or several pages long.

Atlases

An atlas is a collection of maps. Some atlases contain maps of all the countries in the world. The *Times Atlas of the World* is an example of a large general atlas. Other atlases may focus on one continent or one country. An atlas of the United States, for example, generally includes one or more maps of each state.

MEETING INDIVIDUAL NEEDS — English Language Learners

Using an Almanac

Have students open an almanac and guide them in understanding its function. Model terminology with specific references for these open sentences.

The biggest _____ in the world is _____.
The oldest _____ in the United States is _____.

The state with the largest _____ is _____.
The first _____ to win the _____ was _____.
Students acquiring English can use this open sentence format to communicate additional information from the almanac.

The maps in an atlas show various land and water areas—mountains, plateaus, oceans, lakes, and rivers. These are called natural, or physical, features. Maps also show cities, towns, roads, countries, and boundaries between places. These are called cultural features because they were made by people. Many atlases have special maps showing climate, population, natural resources, and other special information.

Almanacs

Who first ran a mile in less than four minutes? What's the population of Bolivia? When is the next eclipse of the sun? What is the world's highest mountain? largest ocean? longest river? deepest lake? coldest place? The answers to these and thousands of other questions are in an almanac.

An almanac is a book of up-to-date general information. Almanacs are usually published once a year. They contain the most recent information for the preceding year. An almanac includes lists of important people and events and facts about governments, history, geography, and weather. It gives figures on population, industry, farm production, and much more.

22.4 Basic Reference Sources **641**

Teach

Researching Atlases

Ask students to work as a group to become familiar with all the atlases in the school library collection. Have students compile a list of the atlases along with their copyright dates and publishers. Then ask them to write a very brief description of the contents of each book. Help them look for ways in which each atlas is different from the others, either in content or in the way information is presented. Have students compile their results and pass out their reports to classmates. **L3**

Enrichment and Extension

Exploring Reference Works

Have students explore the reference section of the school library and find an almanac, a specialized encyclopedia, an atlas, or another reference work previously unfamiliar to them. Tell them to examine it carefully so that they can give a report about it to the class. Ask them to explain in their reports what kind of information the reference work contains, how current the information is, how the information is organized, and how students can locate information in the work.

Practice and Assess

Answers: Exercise 4

1. encyclopedia (almanac and atlas are also acceptable); Mozambique
2. encyclopedia; the first woman to run for president of the U.S.
3. almanac; Mildred D. Taylor
4. encyclopedia or atlas; forest
5. encyclopedia; a bird found in Australia and New Guinea
6. encyclopedia; the burning of fossil fuels such as coal, gasoline, and oil by cars, factories, and power plants
7. almanac; West Germany
8. atlas or encyclopedia; Pacific Ocean
9. atlas; Nigeria, Niger, Chad, Cameroon
10. almanac; *Shakespeare in Love*

Additional Resources

📁 *Thinking and Study Skills,* pp. 28–29
📁 *Vocabulary and Spelling Strategies and Practice,* pp. 35–40

Close

Have each student write a list of specific current or past assignments for which an encyclopedia, atlas, or almanac would be useful.

Library and Reference Resources

Because an almanac presents a huge amount of information in very concise form, you can locate a specific fact very quickly. To look up a specific fact, use the index. An almanac's index is often placed at the front of the book rather than at the back.

Exercise 4

Which would be the best resource to answer each of the following questions—an encyclopedia, an atlas, or an almanac? Find the answer to each question.

1. Of what country is Maputo the capital?
2. Who was Victoria Woodhull?
3. Who was the winner of the Newbery Medal in 1977?
4. Is Thailand primarily forest or crop land?
5. What is a kookaburra, and where does it live?
6. What is the major cause of acid rain?
7. Who won the World Cup in soccer in 1990?
8. In what ocean are the Cook Islands located?
9. What countries border Lake Chad in Africa?
10. What film won the Academy Award for best picture of 1998?

642 Unit 22 Library and Reference Resources

Technology Tip

Discovering Reference CDs

Many reference resources, including encyclopedias, dictionaries, thesauruses, and atlases, are currently available on compact discs (CDs) that are linked to computers. You may want to have students investigate this new technology and report back to the class. They might start by interviewing the school librarian. If your school or local libraries have computer reference programs, have students work with them to see how easy they are to use and how useful the information is.

22.5 Other Library Resources

When you think about a library's resources, you probably think of books. However, most modern libraries offer much more than books. Some libraries are now called resource centers or media centers to show that they include resources other than books.

Internet Access

Computers at your public library also provide access to the Internet, a valuable source of information. The Internet—also known as *The Net*, *Cyberspace*, or *The Information Highway*—is the largest computer network in the world. The World Wide Web is the part of the Internet that provides information in various formats, including print, sound, graphics, and video.

Because there are so many Internet sites, the best way to find worthwhile information on the Net is by using a *search engine*. Search engines work by sending out software agents called *spiders*. Spiders search every Internet link they can find. If you do not get any useful results with one search engine, try several others. They each search the Internet differently.

All Internet sources are not equally reliable, however. Always check any site for accuracy and timeliness. Check to see when it was last updated. Check for errors and omissions. Check to see what agency sponsors the site. Many libraries now provide a collection of recommended Web sites.

Online Libraries   Online libraries on the Internet are important reference sources. These sites are available 24 hours a day. You can connect from home if you have access to a computer and a modem. Examples of excellent online reference sites include *The Internet Public Library*, sponsored by the School of Information at the University of Michigan, and *Thor: The Virtual Reference Desk +*, the online resource site of Purdue University Library.

Other Nonprint Resources

Nonprint resources can take many different forms. Microforms, audiotapes, compact discs, and videotapes are some of the nonprint resources you can find in libraries.

Focus

Lesson Overview

Objectives
- To become familiar with print (other than books) and nonprint library resources
- To use library resources other than books

Skills
- identifying a variety of print (other than books) and nonprint library resources; using appropriate library resources

Critical Thinking
- analyzing; classifying

Listening and Speaking
- discussing

Bellringer
Daily Language Activity

When students enter the classroom, have this assignment on the board: *List five information resources, other than books, found in the library.*

See also *Daily Language Practice*

Motivating Activity

Survey students' responses to the Bellringer activity. Ask students where, other than in books, they would look to find information on a current political campaign or on the destruction of the rain forest. (a local newspaper; national newspapers or magazines; films)

Library and Reference Resources

Resource Manager

Planning Resources
- *Lesson Plans*

 **Transparencies**
- *Bellringer*
- *Daily Language Practice*

Other Print Resources
- *Thinking and Study Skills,* pp. 28–29
- *Vocabulary and Spelling Strategies and Practice,* pp. 35–40

Teach

Discussing Print and Nonprint Library Resources

Discuss with students print materials (other than books) found in libraries (newspapers, magazines). Then work with students to create a list of nonprint resources found in libraries, such as videos, films, audiotapes, and compact discs. Ask students to name various resources they have used in the library and tell what information they learned from them. **L2**

Practice and Assess

Answers: Exercise 5

1. microform of magazine or newspaper
2. videotape, audiotape, CD
3. magazine
4. newspaper
5. audiotape, CD

Additional Resources

📁 *Thinking and Study Skills,* pp. 28–29
📁 *Vocabulary and Spelling Strategies and Practice,* pp. 35–40

Close

List on the board types of library resources discussed in the lesson. Have each student write a paragraph explaining the kinds of information found in the various resources.

Microforms   Libraries often store old issues of magazines and newspapers on microforms. Microforms are reduced images on either rolls of film (microfilm) or small film cards (microfiche). An entire issue of a magazine can be stored on a three-by-five-inch or four-by-six-inch microfiche. Microforms save space and are less likely to be damaged by use.

Special viewing machines enlarge the photographs for viewing. Some viewing machines can also produce copies of the enlarged image. Such machines are usually located in the newspaper and magazine section.

Sound Recordings   If you want to listen to music, a poetry reading, or a drama reading, try your library's collection of audiotapes and compact discs (CDs). The library may have players for each of these sound resources in the audio-visual section. You can check these recordings out to take home.

Video Recordings   Most libraries with audio-visual sections have a collection of videotapes. There you may find tapes of films, documentaries, how-to videos, and travelogues. Videos, like sound recordings, are usually listed in a special catalog in the audio-visual section and may be checked out.

Exercise 5

In what library resource would you expect to find each of the following? (Resources include the Internet, microform of periodicals, audiotape, CD, and videotape.) More than one answer may be possible in some cases.

1. The results of a political poll taken just before the presidential election of 2000
2. The musical *Into the Woods* by Stephen Sondheim
3. An issue of *Sports Illustrated* describing an auto race held last month
4. An article about a new bridge now being built in your community
5. Information on a hurricane currently approaching the east coast

Library and Reference Resources

Technology Tip

Finding Newspaper Articles

Most libraries preserve back issues of some local and some major newspapers on microfilm. Larger newspapers, such as the *New York Times,* prepare indexes for finding articles in past issues. You may wish to have students investigate the newspaper holdings of their school and community libraries and report their findings to the class.

22.6 | Searching for Periodicals

Suppose you wanted to find information on the latest developments in computer technology. How would you find magazine articles on your topic?

Until the early 1990s, most searching for periodicals articles was done with printed indexes and then by searching either bound periodicals or microforms (copies of magazines and newspapers stored on film). Today you can do periodicals searches electronically on the Internet and on various databases. A database is a collection of electronic files that are easily retrieved by a computer.

If you are searching for older publications, however, such as a magazine from about 1980 or before, you still need to search the older way. Scan for your topic in a bound copy of *The Readers' Guide to Periodical Literature* and then follow your citation to the correct issue of the magazine in the periodical section.

But often you will search online. Most libraries provide two types of electronic databases: general periodical ones, and ones specific to a subject. *The Electric Library,* which searches newspapers, general magazines, maps, and TV and radio transcripts, is an example of a general periodical database. *Social Issues Resource* is an example of a database that is focused on one main subject area, sociology and current social problems.

All databases share common features. Most offer the option to do a basic search or a more advanced search. Each has a query screen. On it you key in the search term(s)—either one word or a search phrase. Many databases allow you to use natural language. In other words, you ask the question the way you would ask it of a friend.

Sample Periodical Search

This search was done on a database called *MasterFILE Premier,* which searches current magazines and newspapers.

Focus

Lesson Overview

Objectives

- To become familiar with the electronic resources that libraries provide for periodical searches
- To learn to use libraries' print and electronic resources to find information in magazines

Skills

- exploring magazines to find information; using the *Readers' Guide* to find magazine articles; searching for periodicals online

Critical Thinking

- using criteria; classifying

Listening and Speaking

- discussing

 Bellringer
Daily Language Activity

When students enter the classroom, have this assignment on the board: *Write a description of a research assignment for which you had to find current information.*

See also *Daily Language Practice*

Motivating Activity

Have volunteers share their responses to the Bellringer activity. Ask students why the most current information possible was desirable. Were nonfiction books useful for finding this information? Why or why not?

Resource Manager

Planning Resources
- *Lesson Plans*

Transparencies
- *Bellringer*
- *Daily Language Practice*

Other Print Resources
- *Thinking and Study Skills,* pp. 28–29
- *Vocabulary and Spelling Strategies and Practice,* pp. 35–40

Teach

Finding Current Information

Explain that because of the time it takes to publish a book, even the most recent books may include out-of-date information. Make available a copy of the *Readers' Guide*. Then ask students to name some current topics they might expect to learn about from magazines. Have students work in pairs to look up a topic in the *Readers' Guide* and name one source of information they find for the topic. **L2**

Practice and Assess

Answers: Exercise 6

1. The first article
2. *Forbes*; it would have more space and attention devoted to it and would probably be more detailed
3. Three—the first two articles and the last article

Additional Resources

📁 *Thinking and Study Skills*, pp. 28–29
📁 *Vocabulary and Spelling Strategies and Practice*, pp. 35–40

Close

Copy several entries from the *Readers' Guide* onto the board. Ask students to interpret the citations, using the sample entries in their textbooks as a guide.

Library and Reference Resources

Screen One The researcher here is looking for information on connections between the Internet and radio. The search has been limited by date.

Screen Two Examine the first five references that came up for this search. An *X* indicates *Full Text*; that is, the entire text of the article is available.

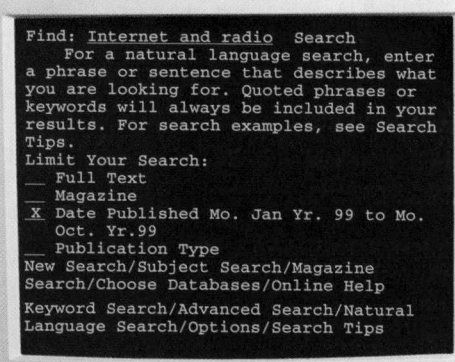

```
Find: Internet and radio   Search
     For a natural language search, enter
a phrase or sentence that describes what
you are looking for. Quoted phrases or
keywords will always be included in your
results. For search examples, see Search
Tips.
Limit Your Search:
__ Full Text
__ Magazine
_X Date Published Mo. Jan Yr. 99 to Mo.
     Oct. Yr.99
__ Publication Type
New Search/Subject Search/Magazine
Search/Choose Databases/Online Help

Keyword Search/Advanced Search/Natural
Language Search/Options/Search Tips
```

```
Examine the first five references that came up
for this search. An X indicates Full Text; that
is, the entire text of the article is available.
Records (1 to 5) of 349
Mark Full Text  Select Result for More Detail
X How CBS Is Bartering Its Way Into the Dot.com
   World.; By: Kover, Amy., Fortune, 09/27/99,
   Vol. 140 Issue 6, p312, 2p, 1c Full Page Image
X Web key in CBS, Viacom merger.; By: Garrity,
   Brian., Billboard, 09/18/99, Vol. 111 Issue 38,
   p5, 2p
   Old Media Get a Web Windfall.; By: Hwang, Suein
   L., Wall Street Journal -- Eastern Edition,
   09/17/99, Vol. 234 Issue 55, pB1, 0p, 1bw
   MTV Networks Unit Sues Imagine Radio Founders.,
   Wall Street Journal -- Eastern Edition,
   09/15/99, Vol. 234 Issue 53, pB9, 0p
X Fun. (cover story); By: Pappas, Ben. and
   Schifrin, Matthew. and Berentson, Ben. and
   Solan, Joshua. and Manzo, Emily and Nathan,
   Adit. and Leitzes, Adam., Forbes, 09/13/99,
   Vol. 164 Issue 6, p105, 1p, 2c
   (1 to 5) of 349 Refine Search Print/ Email/ Save
```

Look over your display results carefully. The display screen gives you important information about each article. It includes the titles, the author, the source, the date of the article, its length, and availability of photographs or other graphics. The symbols *c* and *bw* stand for *color* or *black and white* photos.

Exercise 6

Look at the sample screens and answer these questions.

1. Which of these articles has a full page image?
2. Which of these periodicals did a cover story on this topic? Why might a cover story be more valuable than just any story?
3. How many of these articles have full text available?

MEETING INDIVIDUAL NEEDS **English Language Learners**

Using Abbreviations

Many students with limited English skills have difficulty using the *Readers' Guide* due to the abbreviations it contains, or simply because they are not familiar with many of the periodicals it lists. Review with students the abbreviations of the more commonly known magazines listed at the front of the guide. You may also wish to have available some examples of the magazines cited.

22.7 | The Dictionary and the Thesaurus

A dictionary and a thesaurus can help put more words on the tip of your tongue and at the tip of your pencil. Both references are essential tools for writers. Both can be found in print, on CD-ROM, and online.

The Dictionary

A dictionary contains entries in alphabetical order. An entry is a single term, or word, along with its pronunciation, definition, and other information. Some characteristics of three types of dictionaries are summarized below.

Types of Dictionaries		
	Characteristics	**Examples**
Unabridged Dictionaries	• Detailed word histories • Detailed definitions • Found mostly in libraries	• *Random House Unabridged Dictionary* • *Webster's Third New International Dictionary*
College Dictionaries	• Detailed enough to answer most questions on spelling or definition • Widely used in schools, homes, and businesses • 130,000–250,000 entries	• *Random House Dictionary* • *The American Heritage Dictionary* • *Webster's New World Dictionary*
School Dictionaries	• Definitions suitable for students' grade levels • Emphasizes common words • 90,000 or fewer entries	• *Macmillan Dictionary* • *Webster's School Dictionary*

Library and Reference Resources

Focus

Lesson Overview

Objectives
• To learn the characteristics of three types of dictionaries and a thesaurus
• To use dictionaries and a thesaurus to make writing vivid and precise

Skills
• using a dictionary; using a thesaurus

Critical Thinking
• categorizing; comparing

Listening and Speaking
• discussing

Bellringer
Daily Language Activity

When students enter the classroom, have this assignment on the board: *Write one sentence telling about a time you used a dictionary and another sentence telling about a time you used a thesaurus.*

See also *Daily Language Practice*

Motivating Activity

Provide dictionaries from each category shown on the chart for students to examine. Ask students in which category each dictionary belongs. Then ask students how a thesaurus could be useful in their writing. (It could make their writing more precise and vivid.) Point out that a thesaurus is a dictionary of synonyms (words with similar meanings).

Resource Manager

📂 **Planning Resources**
• *Lesson Plans*

📑 **Transparencies**
• *Bellringer*
• *Daily Language Practice*

📂 **Other Print Resources**
• *Thinking and Study Skills,* pp. 28–29
• *Vocabulary and Spelling Strategies and Practice,* pp. 35–40

Teach

Choosing a Synonym

Point out that synonyms listed in a thesaurus seldom have exactly the same meaning. Write the following headline on the board: *Pirates Beat the Mets!* Have students use their thesauruses to find synonyms for the word *beat* and write them on the board. Ask volunteers to read the headline aloud, choosing a synonym to substitute for *beat*. Discuss whether the synonyms change the overall meaning of the headline. **L2**

Finding Words in a Dictionary

One of students' most common problems with using dictionaries is how to look up words they can't spell. Suggest that they use a thesaurus in these situations. Tell them to think of a synonym they *can* spell and then look for the word they can't spell in the entry for the synonym. Choose a difficult word and guide them through this process. **L1**

Each page of a dictionary has guide words along the top of the page. Guide words indicate the first and last entries on the page. Using the guide words will help you locate an entry much more quickly than browsing will.

Every page or every two-page spread has a pronunciation key at the bottom. The pronunciation key shows you how to use the special pronunciation symbols found in the dictionary.

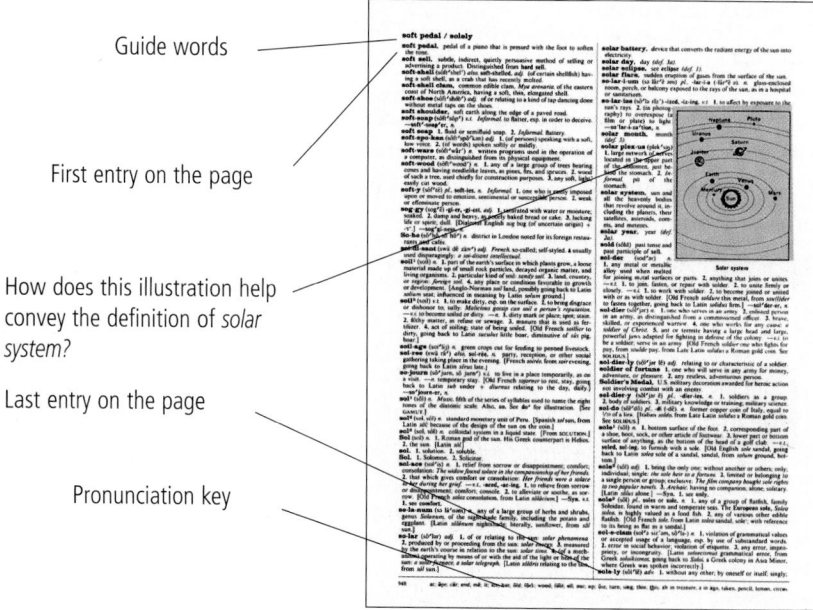

Guide words

First entry on the page

How does this illustration help convey the definition of *solar system?*

Last entry on the page

Pronunciation key

The Thesaurus

A thesaurus is a special type of dictionary that lists synonyms, or words with similar meanings. If you do word processing, your computer software may even include a thesaurus. You probably most often use a dictionary to find the meaning of a particular word. When you use a thesaurus, you already know the meaning you want to convey. However, you need to find the word that best expresses that meaning. For example, you want to write that you were tired. But how tired were you? A thesaurus would give you *drained, exhausted, fatigued, tired, wearied, worn-out,* and more such words.

Technology Tip

Using a Thesaurus

Many dictionaries have become available in software versions for computers. The *Oxford English Dictionary*, for example, is available in CD-ROM (compact disc–read-only memory) format. Some computer programs combine a thesaurus and dictionary, which can be even more useful.

In a thesaurus entry, each definition is followed by several synonyms. The entry may also include a cross-reference to one or more other major entries. If you look up a cross-reference entry, you will find more synonyms for the word listed. Following is an example of a thesaurus entry.

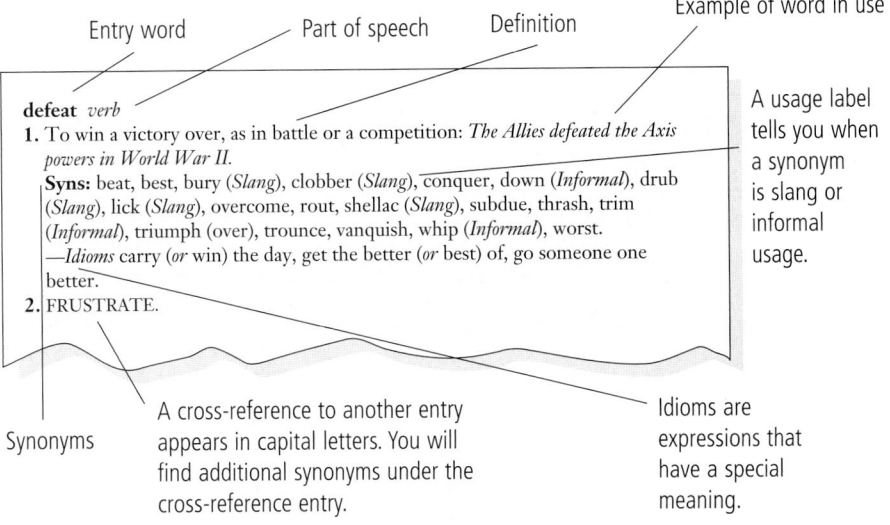

Entry word   Part of speech   Definition   Example of word in use

defeat *verb*
1. To win a victory over, as in battle or a competition: *The Allies defeated the Axis powers in World War II.*
Syns: beat, best, bury (*Slang*), clobber (*Slang*), conquer, down (*Informal*), drub (*Slang*), lick (*Slang*), overcome, rout, shellac (*Slang*), subdue, thrash, trim (*Informal*), triumph (over), trounce, vanquish, whip (*Informal*), worst.
—*Idioms* carry (*or* win) the day, get the better (*or* best) of, go someone one better.
2. FRUSTRATE.

A usage label tells you when a synonym is slang or informal usage.

Synonyms

A cross-reference to another entry appears in capital letters. You will find additional synonyms under the cross-reference entry.

Idioms are expressions that have a special meaning.

Exercise 7

Use a dictionary or a dictionary-style thesaurus to answer these questions.

1. What guide words are on the dictionary page that contains each of the following words?
   a. crackle   **c.** municipal
   b. groan   **d.** solarize
2. Other than at the bottoms of pages, where can you find a guide to pronunciation in a dictionary? Tell which dictionary you used to answer the question.
3. Does the word *deign* rhyme with *mine, mean,* or *main*?
4. What synonyms for *friendly* are listed in the thesaurus? Give at least three.
5. What are six synonyms for *sad*?

Practice and Assess

Answers: Exercise 7

1. Guide words will depend on the dictionary used. The following examples are from the *Macmillan Dictionary,* a school dictionary:
   a. coyote/cradle
   b. gristle/grotesque
   c. mullion/muralist
   d. soft pedal/solely
2. Examples: inside front (and/or back) cover; guide to the dictionary pages in the front part of the book
3. main
4. Examples (any 3): amiable, amicable, chummy, congenial, convivial, neighborly, sympathetic, warmhearted
5. Examples (any 6): depressing, dismal, blue, dejected, downcast, gloomy, joyless, low, melancholy, depressed, mournful, spiritless

Additional Resources

📁 *Thinking and Study Skills,* pp. 28–29
📁 *Vocabulary and Spelling Strategies and Practice,* pp. 35–40

Close

Have each student write a paragraph explaining how using a dictionary or a thesaurus would produce a better final product for current writing assignments.

Cultural Connections

Using Pronunciation Guides

Students will be most familiar with standard dictionaries offering pronunciations and definitions of English words. Foreign-language dictionaries also can be found in many libraries and homes. Have small groups of students examine dictionaries of various languages. Ask why the pronunciation guides in these dictionaries are especially helpful.

Focus

Lesson Overview

Objectives

• To become familiar with common dictionary entries
• To use dictionary entries to find informaton about words

Skills

• using dictionary entries; using a dictionary to find synonyms

Critical Thinking

• analyzing; synthesizing

Listening and Speaking

• discussing

 Bellringer
Daily Language Activity

When students enter the classroom, have this assignment on the board: *List the kinds of information you would expect to find about a word in a dictionary.*

See also 📖 *Daily Language Practice*

Motivating Activity

Ask students to locate the definition, usage labels, synonyms, and other parts of a word entry in the dictionary. You may wish to have several different dictionaries available to show students. Discuss the various ways these dictionaries present similar information.

22.8 Using a Dictionary Entry

The dictionary offers much more than the definitions of words. In a dictionary, you can find out how to divide a word into syllables. You can get information about a word's spelling and pronunciation, its part of speech, and its history. Many dictionaries have entries for places (like cities, countries, and rivers) and famous people.

Entry Word and Pronunciation

A dictionary entry begins with the entry word. The word appears in bold type so that it stands out. In addition, the entry word is broken into syllables. In your writing, you may need to hyphenate a word at the end of a line. You should break up a word only between syllables. The entry word in a dictionary will show you how to hyphenate a word.

The guide to a word's pronunciation follows the entry word. A special set of sound symbols shows how the word is pronounced. Simple words in the pronunciation key at the bottom of the page help you pronounce each symbol. Some of the vowel sounds might be shown in the pronunciation key like this:

fat, āpe, cär; ten, ēven; is, bīte, gō, hôrn, fo͞ol, ūse

You also can find a complete pronunciation key at the front of the dictionary. Try using the sound symbols to pronounce the following word:

in•noc•u•ous (i nok′ ū əs)

> Note that the last syllable has the schwa (ə) sound, which sounds like the *a* in ago.

Part of Speech

Dictionaries also indicate a word's part of speech. In the entry on the following page, for example, *partition* is first defined as a noun (*n.*) and then as a transitive verb (*v.t.*). You'll find a complete list of abbreviations used for the parts of speech at the front of the dictionary. The example shows the word's meanings for both parts of speech.

Resource Manager

📁 **Planning Resources**
• Lesson Plans

🗂 **Transparencies**
• *Bellringer*
• *Daily Language Practice*

📁 **Other Print Resources**
• *Thinking and Study Skills,* pp. 28–29
• *Vocabulary and Spelling Strategies and Practice,* pp. 35–40

par·ti·tion (pär tish´ən) *n.* **1.** a dividing or being divided into shares or distinct parts; division or distribution of portions: *the partition of territory between rival states.* **2.** section or part into which a thing is divided. **3.** that which divides, as an interior wall separating parts of a room.–*v.t.* **1.** to divide into shares or distinct parts: *to partition land for sale, to partition office space into small cubicles.* **2.** to separate by a partition (with *off*): *to partition off a space for storage.* [Latin *partītiō* division.]

> Note that *partition* as a noun means "a division." *Partition* as a verb means "to divide something into parts."

> The dictionary provides examples illustrating many of the word's definitions.

Definition

Many words have more than one meaning. Some words, in fact, have more than a dozen different meanings. Each definition in an entry is numbered, as shown above. In most school dictionaries, definitions are arranged from the most common to the least common.

Word Origins

Most dictionaries indicate a word's origin and history at the beginning or end of an entry. This brief account tells how the word entered the English language. Sometimes the entry traces the word back through several stages. It shows how the word changed as it passed from language to language.

bom·bard (bom bärd´) *v.t.* **1.** to attack with artillery or bombs. **2.** to subject to a vigorous or persistent attack: *He bombarded her with questions.* **3.** Physics. to subject (atomic nuclei) to a stream of high-speed subatomic particles. [French *bombarder*, from *bombarde* cannon, from Medieval Latin *bombarda* weapon for hurling stones, from Latin *bombus*. See BOMB.]

> This word is traced back first to French, the language from which it was borrowed into English. Then the word is traced back to its Latin origin.

Dictionaries often use abbreviations, such as *L.* for *Latin* or *Fr.* for *French*, to show a word's language of origin. You can find a list of these abbreviations at the front of the dictionary. The chart on the next page shows the origins of some English words.

Library and Reference Resources

Teach

Understanding Symbols and Abbreviations

Review the form for word origins used in the classroom dictionary. Make sure that students understand any symbols or abbreviations used and that they can interpret word histories correctly. **L2**

Using a Thesaurus

Ask each student to write a short paragraph and exchange it with a classmate who will rewrite the work, using synonyms from a dictionary or thesaurus. Discuss shades of difference in meaning. **L3**

Cross-Reference: Grammar, Usage, and Mechanics

For more information on forms of plural nouns, refer students to Lesson 9.4.

MEETING INDIVIDUAL NEEDS **Less-Proficient Readers**

Becoming Familiar with a Pronunciation Key

Give students several familiar words and help them write and pronounce the words using the sound symbols located in the pronunciation key in their classroom dictionaries. If students need more assistance, you may want to make a tape of the pronunciation key with sample words in the front of the dictionary. Students can replay the tape while looking at the pronunciation key.

Practice and Assess

Answers: Exercise 8
1. pe•cu•li•ar•i•ty
2. Algonquian (Native American)
3. age, epoch, period
4. adjective

Additional Resources

📁 *Thinking and Study Skills*, pp. 28–29
📁 *Vocabulary and Spelling Strategies and Practice*, pp. 35–40

Close

Ask students to name at least five things that can be found in a dictionary word entry. Have them identify those elements that are most common in all dictionaries. Compare their responses to those on their Bellringer activity lists.

✓ ASSESSMENT OPTIONS

📁 *Tests with Answer Key and Rubrics*
Unit 22 Mastery Test, pp. 91–92

💾 *Testmaker*
Unit 22 Mastery Test

📼 *MindJogger Videoquizzes*

You may wish to administer the Unit 22 Mastery Test at this point.

Library and Reference Sources

The Origins of Some English Words		
English Word	**Origin**	**Word of Origin**
cookie	Dutch	*koeje*, meaning "small cake"
gumbo	Bantu	*gumbo*, referring to okra, the vegetable
judo	Japanese	*ju*, meaning "gentle" + *do*, meaning "way"
thesaurus	Greek	*thesauros*, meaning "treasure" or "storehouse"

Synonyms

A thesaurus is one place to look for synonyms. A dictionary may also offer a list of synonyms for some words. Some dictionaries give definitions to help you understand the differences in meaning among synonyms. Following is an example.

> **Syn. Excessive, immoderate, inordinate, intemperate, exorbitant** mean going beyond what is normal or proper. **Excessive** suggests an amount or quantity too great for what is required: *The summer rains were excessive and flooded the fields.* **Immoderate** implies going beyond bounds, esp. in emotional matters: *His speech was received by the opposition with immoderate laughter.* **Inordinate** suggests lack of judgment or regulation: *They asked an inordinate price for the house.* **Intemperate** implies lack of control: *His talk turned out to be an intemperate attack on bankers.* **Exorbitant** suggests a rather sharp divergence from the normal: *The new job made exorbitant demands on his time.*

An example sentence helps you understand the meaning of each synonym.

Exercise 8

Use a dictionary to answer the following questions.

1. How is the word *peculiarity* divided into syllables?
2. From what language did the word *pecan* come?
3. What synonyms are given for *era*? List at least three.
4. What part of speech is the word *obstreperous*?

Viewing and Representing

Library Settings in Films

Discuss why some movie scenes are set in a library. Cite (and, if possible, show scenes from) movies such as *Ghostbusters*, *Indiana Jones and the Last Crusade*, and *War Games*. Ask students to decide what mood is evoked by a library's hushed atmosphere.

UNIT 23 Vocabulary and Spelling

Objectives

- To develop an understanding of how roots, prefixes, and suffixes are used and how they affect the meaning of a word
- To learn about the relationship between synonyms and antonyms
- To use various rules to spell commonly misspelled words correctly

✔ ASSESSMENT OPTIONS

📁 *Tests with Answer Key and Rubrics*
Unit 23 Pretest, pp. 93–94

💾 *Testmaker*
Unit 23 Pretest

You may wish to administer the Unit 23 Pretest at this point.

Key to Ability Levels

L1 Level 1 activities are within the basic ability range of students.

L2 Level 2 activities are within the ability range of average students.

L3 Level 3 activities are more challenging activities.

653

Resource Manager

📁 **Planning Resources**
- *Lesson Plans*
- *Block Scheduling*

 **Transparencies**
- *Bellringer*
- *Daily Language Practice*

📁 **Other Print Resources**
- *Tests with Answer Key and Rubrics*
- *Thinking and Study Skills*
- *Spelling Power*
- *Vocabulary and Spelling Strategies and Practice*
- *Vocabulary Power*

**Video**
- *MindJogger Videoquizzes*

💾 **Software**
- *Presentation Plus!*
- *Testmaker*
- *Vocabulary Power Puzzlemaker*

🖥 **Web Sites**
- *writerschoice.glencoe.com*

Focus

Lesson Overview

Objectives

- To become familiar with borrowed words
- To use and correctly spell words borrowed from other languages

Skills

- using the dictionary to research word origins; exploring how historical movements shape language

Critical Thinking

- analyzing; synthesizing; relating

Listening and Speaking

- discussing

 Bellringer
Daily Language Activity

When students enter the classroom, have this assignment on the board: *Write a list of ten English words whose origins you are curious to know.*

See also *Daily Language Practice*

Motivating Activity

Explain that many English words were borrowed from other languages. Ask students to speculate about the roles of immigration and trade in the entry of foreign words into English. Ask how technology, transportation, and communication would accelerate this process. Have students give examples of words borrowed from other cultures. Guide them to name, for example, ethnic foods, music, and imports (*tortilla, pita, croissant, rumba,* and so on).

Vocabulary and Spelling

23.1 **Borrowed Words**

How do languages grow and change? One way is through borrowing words from other languages. When people interact with each other, they're likely to borrow some of one another's words. This can happen even when they speak different languages. This kind of word borrowing into English began when the language was still young.

Early Word Borrowings

In the middle of the fifth century A.D., Germanic tribes from northwestern Europe settled in England. Today we refer to these people as Anglo-Saxons. Their language, now called Old English, was the earliest form of English.

In the late 500s, Christian missionaries came to England from Rome. They began to convert the Anglo-Saxons to Christianity. These missionaries brought to England not only their religion, but also their language—Latin. Many words still in use today were borrowed into Old English from Latin. Some examples are *candle, altar, temple,* and *school.*

Detail from Bayeux Tapestry, *William of Normandy's Ship Before Pevensey Shore,* c. 1066

A few hundred years later, in A.D. 1066, English came under another important influence.

In that year the French-speaking Normans invaded England and conquered the Anglo-Saxons. Over the next few hundred years, many French words came into the English language. The chart on the following page shows some words borrowed from early French.

Resource Manager

 **Planning Resources**
- *Lesson Plans*

 **Transparencies**
- *Bellringer*
- *Daily Language Practice*

Other Print Resources
- *Thinking and Study Skills,* pp. 9, 25–27
- *Vocabulary and Spelling Strategies and Practice,* pp. 13, 21–26

English Borrowings from French	
Government and Law	city, authority, tax, prison, crime, suit, jury, bail
The Military	army, navy, soldier, sergeant, lieutenant, captain, assault
Dining and Food	dinner, table, fork, plate, roast, sausage, veal, pork
The Arts	music, art, beauty, color, design, theater, poem
Trades	barber, butcher, grocer, painter, tailor, carpenter
Religion	saint, grace, mercy, salvation, clergy, preach

Words from Many Lands

Not long after the Norman invasion, European traders began traveling regularly to the Middle East. Arab traders there sold them silk, spices, and other goods from Asia. Often, the Arabic words for these goods were passed on as well. Some English words that came from Arabic include *alcohol, cotton, mattress, orange, sugar,* and *syrup.*

In the late 1400s, European traders and explorers began traveling even farther. They found new sea routes, explored new lands, and brought back new products— and new words. Portuguese sailors set up trade routes to Africa and Asia. Other Europeans—explorers, sailors, soldiers, missionaries, and colonists—traveled to the Americas. They brought back foods new to Europeans, such as chocolate, potatoes, turkeys, and maize (corn). The words for these foods were added to the English language.

Vocabulary and Spelling

Teach

Using Borrowed Words

Have students form small groups and create an advertisement listing sale items for a store that sells housewares, groceries, clothing, or other specialty items. Students should list only sale items that have names borrowed from other languages. Examples include *pasta, poncho, sarong, hammock, canoe,* and *futon.* They can use a dictionary to check word origins. Initiate a discussion about the role commerce has played in the entry of words into English. **L2**

Using a Dictionary

Some students may need help pronouncing and comprehending the words in the charts. Read the words aloud. Call on volunteers to define any words they know and identify unfamiliar words. Help students use a dictionary to look up uncommon words, such as *musk, rattan,* and *taboo.* Point out that the word origin is listed in these entries. **L1**

Cultural Connections

French Influence

One reason so many French words were incorporated into English after the Norman Conquest (1066) was that during this time, the ruling class spoke French. Many Norman kings spoke no English at all. French remained the official language of England until the 1400s when Henry V became the first English king since the Norman Conquest to use English in official documents. In spite of the French influence, however, the grammatical structure of English remained Germanic.

Practice and Assess

Answers: Exercise 1

1. Dutch
2. German
3. Tibetan
4. Hindi
5. Italian
6. Spanish

Evaluation Rubrics: Exercise 2

Answers will vary depending on the explorers or traders chosen. A large store of words came into English from various Native American languages during the centuries of exploration and expansion.

Additional Resources

📂 *Thinking and Study Skills*, pp. 9, 25–27
📂 *Vocabulary and Spelling Strategies and Practice*, pp. 13, 21–26

Close

Point out the difference between knowing the meaning of a word and actually using the word in context. Have students role-play a scene at a restaurant, museum, or shopping mall using words from the lesson.

Vocabulary and Spelling

The chart below shows some words that were borrowed from cultures around the world. A few of these words came directly into English. Most were borrowed by other European languages first and then borrowed into English. For example, *banana* began as an African word. The word was picked up in West Africa by traders from Portugal. Later, it was borrowed from Portuguese into Spanish. Then, after bananas were brought into England, the English started using the word. It became part of the English language.

English Words Borrowed from Other Lands	
Africa	banana, chimpanzee, gorilla, okra, zebra
Australia & New Zealand	boomerang, kangaroo, kiwi, koala
India	bandanna, cot, ginger, jungle, loot, pepper, shampoo
Malaya & Polynesia	bamboo, ketchup, paddy, rattan, taboo, tattoo
Mexico & Caribbean	canoe, chocolate, cocoa, coyote, hammock, tomato
Persia (now Iran)	caravan, musk, pajamas, scarlet, shawl

Exercise 1

Look up each of the following words in a dictionary. Tell what language each word was borrowed from.

1. boss
2. zinc
3. yak
4. bungalow
5. spaghetti
6. hurricane

Exercise 2

Work with a partner or a small group. Do some research on European traders or explorers active between the 1100s and the 1800s. Find two new products they brought back to Europe. In a dictionary look up the words that name those products. Tell what language or languages each word came from.

Exploring Language

Borrowed Words

Draw on bilingualism as a valuable resource by encouraging students to list English words borrowed from languages they have studied or that they grew up speaking. If they need guidance, ask for names of foods or imported items. You might also ask whether, in studying a second language, they have recognized any words that are similar in both languages.

Wordworks

FAMILY RESEMBLANCES

Perhaps you've been told that you have your grandmother's eyes, your father's voice, or your aunt's kind nature. Similarities in appearance and personality often show up in families.

Languages belong to families, too. English is part of the language family called Indo-European. Most European languages plus many languages spoken in India belong to this family.

Words from different languages in the same family sometimes have family resemblances. These words, which look similar and often have the same meaning, are called cognates. But don't confuse them with borrowed words. Cognates are words that have descended from the same older language. For example, the English word *mother* has cognates in German (*mutter*), Latin (*mater*), Swedish and Danish (*moder*), French (*mère*), and Italian (*madre*).

Because they often began in very early languages, cognates usually refer to something basic about human relations or culture. Many cognates refer to body parts, family relationships, and plants and animals. The numbers one to ten in most Indo-European languages are cognates. For example, English *ten* has cognates in Latin (*decem*), Greek (*deka*), Spanish (*diez*), Welsh (*deg*), and Dutch (*tien*).

FATHER
Latin–Pater
Greek–Patér
Spanish–Padre
German–Vater
French–Père
Dutch–Vader

Challenge

Can you figure out the English words for the cognates in this sentence?

The vind blew snø against the Haus.

ACTIVITY

Pick A Number

Following are the numbers one through five in different languages. Which word in each item is not a cognate?

1. en, uno, yksi, een
2. två, dos, due, dva
3. tres, kolme, tri, tre
4. fire, vier, ctyri, four
5. cinq, cinco, cinque, fem

Vocabulary and Spelling

WordWorks 657

Writing in the Real World

Mathematics/Science

Cognates Medical and research scientists and mathematicians often need to communicate internationally for their work. Fortunately, there are many cognates across languages for scientific and numeric terms. As new concepts, procedures, or specimens are discovered and added to a language, they are commonly shared in several languages with little or no translation.

Lesson Overview

Objective
• To become familiar with cognates and word families

Skills
• using the dictionary; exploring patterns and word parts across languages

Critical Thinking
• analyzing

Listening and Speaking
• discussing

Teach

Discussion

Have students read Wordworks on this page and discuss the following questions: How might a word have a grandmother? How might a word be related to a word from another century? How might a word in English be a cousin of a word in German, Greek, or Cherokee?

Making a Word Family Tree

Help students look up Indo-European roots in a dictionary. Have each researcher select one Indo-European root word and create a "family tree" tracing the root's evolution in Hindi, or Latin, and several modern languages. As an example, draw a tree for one of the words in the lesson, such as *mother* or *ten*. **L3**

Practice and Assess

Answers: Challenge
wind, snow, house

Answers: Pick a Number
1. yksi   4. ctyri
2. två   5. fem
3. kolme

Close

Spark a discussion of when cognates might be helpful, such as in learning a foreign language.

Focus

Lesson Overview

Objectives
- To become familiar with specific types of context clues
- To use context clues to help determine the meanings of unknown words

Skills
- identifying definition, example, comparison, contrast, and general context clues in reading passages

Critical Thinking
- analyzing; inferring; synthesizing

Listening and Speaking
- discussing

 Bellringer
Daily Language Activity

When students enter the classroom, have this assignment on the board: *List three possible definitions of the nonsense word* prizzed *from its context in this sentence: Esperanza's leg prizzed, and she scratched it until the skin was red.*

See also Daily Language Practice

Motivating Activity

Encourage students to share their responses from the Bellringer activity. Then have them work with partners to create context sentences for their own nonsense words. They can exchange sentences with other pairs and infer definitions.

Vocabulary and Spelling

23.2 Using Context Clues

Imagine this. You're reading a book and doing fine until you come across the word *exobiologist*. You have no idea what *exobiologist* means, and you don't have a dictionary handy. What do you do? One thing you could do is look for clues in the words and the sentences that surround the unfamiliar word. When you use those surrounding clues, you are using context.

Context Clues

Writers often give clues to the meaning of an unfamiliar word. Sometimes they even tell you what the word means. In the paragraph above, for example, you are told what the word *context* means. The chart below shows some types of context clues.

Interpreting Clue Words		
Type of Context Clue	**Clue Words**	**Examples**
Definition The meaning of the word is given in the sentence.	that is in other words or which means	Janet put the wet clay pot in the *kiln,* **or** oven, to harden.
Example The unfamiliar word is explained through familiar examples.	like such as for example for instance	The new program has been *beneficial* for the school; **for example,** test scores are up and absences are down.
Comparison The unfamiliar word is compared to a familiar word or phrase.	too also likewise similarly resembling	Maria thought the dress was *gaudy.* Lisa, **too,** thought it was excessively flashy.
Contrast The unfamiliar word is contrasted to a familiar word or phrase.	but on the other hand unlike however	Robins are *migratory* birds, **unlike** sparrows, which live in the same region all year round.

 **Resource Manager**

📂 **Planning Resources**
- *Lesson Plans*

📑 **Transparencies**
- *Bellringer*
- *Daily Language Practice*

📂 **Other Print Resources**
- *Thinking and Study Skills,* pp. 9, 25–27
- *Vocabulary and Spelling Strategies and Practice,* pp. 13, 21–26

Using the General Context

Sometimes you'll have to look for less specific clues in the context. The surrounding sentences may give you subtle clues to the meaning of the unfamiliar word. Look at the passage below. Notice the clues in the general context that help you figure out the meaning of *exobiologist.*

> Maryann was determined to become an <u>exobiologist.</u> She knew that there was no proof that any <u>forms of life existed on other planets.</u> However, she knew it was possible that life *could* have developed beyond our planet. Maryann had been interested in <u>space exploration</u> ever since her childhood. She felt that the <u>study of exobiology</u> was an exciting new <u>field,</u> and she wanted to be part of it.

You can tell from the sentence structure that exobiologist is a noun that names a person.

These clues show that it has something to do with life on other planets.

These clues show that exobiology, a word related to exobiologist, is a field of study.

You know from the other clues that the word has to do with life on other planets. You can figure out that an exobiologist studies life on other planets.

Exercise 3

Use context clues to figure out the meaning of the italicized word in each passage. Write the meaning of the word. Then tell what context clue or clues you used.

1. Their pet dog, Topper, had been like a member of the family for more than ten years. It was no surprise, then, that Jeff's whole family *lamented* Topper's death.
2. Nikolai is *conscientious* about cleaning his room. Andrew, on the other hand, must be reminded again and again to clean up his room.
3. Julie, a straight-A student, is *exempt* from final exams. Carlos, another straight-A student, is also excused from taking the exams.
4. The film must be completely *immersed,* or covered with fluid.
5. The little boy was *naive.* For instance, he believed the stories older boys told him about space aliens.

Vocabulary and Spelling

23.2

Teach

Understanding Unfamiliar Words

Help students understand how to use what they already know to figure out the meanings of unfamiliar words. Present this sentence: *Meiko thought the hike was arduous; Steven also thought it was difficult.* Elicit from students that *also* in the second part of the sentence is a clue that *arduous* means the same thing as *difficult.* **L2**

Practice and Assess

Answers: Exercise 3

1. grieved about—general
2. careful or thorough—contrast
3. free from a requirement—comparison
4. completely covered in a liquid—definition
5. simpleminded; tending to believe too readily; lacking worldly wisdom—example

Additional Resources

📂 *Thinking and Study Skills,* pp. 9, 25–27
📂 *Vocabulary and Spelling Strategies and Practice,* pp. 13, 21–26

Close

Have students identify three different context clue strategies they could use to help unlock the meaning of a word they do not know.

MEETING INDIVIDUAL NEEDS
Less-Proficient Readers

Thinking Aloud

You may demonstrate the following think-aloud strategy for the second passage in Exercise 3: The first sentence says *Nikolai is conscientious about cleaning his room.* The phrase *on the other hand* tells me that Andrew is different from Nikolai, and this sentence says Andrew needs reminders to clean his room. *Conscientious* must mean the opposite of needing to be reminded, or *careful* and *thorough.*

Lesson Overview

Objective
• To understand pictographic writing

Skills
• creating pictographs and rebuses

Critical Thinking
• visualizing; analyzing

Listening and Speaking
• explaining a process

Teach

Discussion

Have students read Wordworks on this page and discuss the following questions: *Which classes of words would be easiest to encode in pictographic writing? Which would be the most difficult?* Guide them to the conclusion that words for concrete objects and actions would lend themselves better to pictographic writing than would words for abstract concepts.

Creating Pictographs

Have students use headlines from the newspaper to create pictographs. Provide an opportunity for the pictographs to be shared with the class. Point out that prior knowledge of the news helped students to read the pictographs more easily. **L3**

Practice and Assess

Answers: Challenge

The rebus translates as *Can you write in pictures?*

Evaluation Rubrics: Pictoplay

Students should make a creative attempt to use symbols and pictures for as many words and syllables as possible.

Close

Ask students to name at least three advantages and three disadvantages of communicating with pictographics and with words.

Wordworks

DOES THIS MAKE ¢¢¢ 2 U?

Have you ever played the picture game in which you draw a picture to represent a word? Your teammates must guess the word by looking at your drawing. The game is fun because not all words are easy to draw or guess.

What if you always had to use pictures when writing? You'd have something in common with people living about 5,500 years ago, when writing systems were first developing. Pictographic writing was one of the earliest forms of writing—before any alphabet was developed. In pictographic writing, a picture of a tree would mean "tree" and a picture of the sun would mean "sun." There are limitations to pictographic writing, though. Try creating a simple picture to mean "hungry" or "thinking" or "dizzy." You'll soon find that a picture isn't always worth a thousand words.

As pictographic writing developed further, people used pictures to represent the sounds of words. For example, if you used pictographs today, a picture of the sun could mean "sun" or "son."

A picture could also be used in place of just one syllable of a word. Using a picture of a key to stand for the second part of *lucky* would be one example.

A picture that represents a part of a word or phrase is called a *rebus.* The use of rebuses was a big step toward the development of modern writing systems. The rebus is now popular in games and puzzles.

> ### Challenge
> *Figure out the question in the rebus below.*

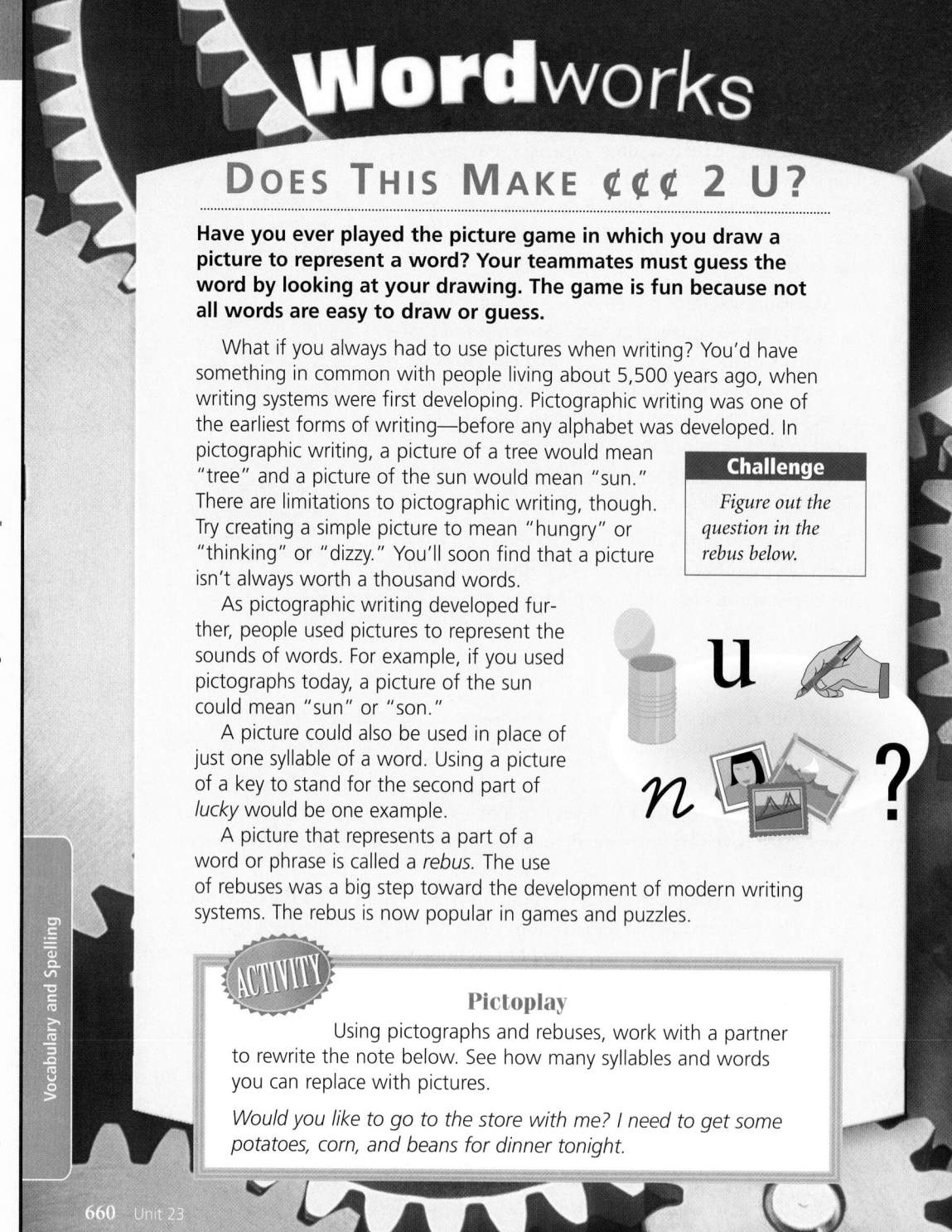

Vocabulary and Spelling

ACTIVITY

Pictoplay
Using pictographs and rebuses, work with a partner to rewrite the note below. See how many syllables and words you can replace with pictures.

Would you like to go to the store with me? I need to get some potatoes, corn, and beans for dinner tonight.

23.3 Roots, Prefixes, and Suffixes

Like pieces of a puzzle, parts of words can be fitted together to make a whole word. Unlike a puzzle, however, the same word piece can be put together with many other pieces. Thus, a few word parts can make many different words.

The main part of a word is the root. Prefixes and suffixes are other pieces that can be attached to a root to change its meaning. The diagram below shows how prefixes, roots, and suffixes fit together to make new words.

Re	**align**	**ment**
prefix	root	suffix
again	to arrange in a line	the action or process of

Roots

The **root** of a word carries the main meaning. Some roots, like the word *align*, above, can stand alone. Other roots must have other parts attached to make a complete word. For example, the root *ject* ("throw") is useless by itself. But combined with a prefix it can become *reject, project,* or *inject.* Add a suffix and you get *rejection, projection,* or *injection.*

Knowing the meanings of common roots can help you figure out the meanings of unfamiliar words. The following chart shows two more helpful roots. Can you think of some other words that contain these roots?

ROOTS	WORDS AND MEANINGS	
script means "writing"	*scripture*	sacred writing
	transcript	a written record
phon means "sound" or "voice"	*telephone*	instrument for sending voices
	phonics	the study or science of sounds

Focus

Lesson Overview

Objective
- To become familiar with roots, prefixes, and suffixes

Skills
- combining word parts; using the meanings of common word roots, prefixes, and suffixes

Critical Thinking
- analyzing; identifying characteristics

Listening and Speaking
- discussing

Bellringer
Daily Language Activity

When students enter the classroom, have this assignment on the board: *Write a definition for the made-up word* preparty. *Then use it in a sentence.*

See also *Daily Language Practice*

Motivating Activity

Ask students what might be on a host's preparty checklist. Call on volunteers to read their invented definitions for *preparty.* Then write *refigure* on the chalkboard. Read aloud: *We invited extra guests, so refigure the amount of food.* Ask students for definitions of *refigure.*

Resource Manager

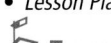

Planning Resources
- *Lesson Plans*

Transparencies
- *Bellringer*
- *Daily Language Practice*

Other Print Resources
- *Thinking and Study Skills,* pp. 9, 25–27
- *Vocabulary and Spelling Strategies and Practice,* pp. 13, 21–26

Teach

Brainstorming with Prefixes, Suffixes, and Roots

Divide the class into small groups. Ask each group to choose a recorder and a reporter. Assign each group a different prefix, and give each group two minutes to list as many words as possible that contain the prefix. Repeat the process with roots and with suffixes. Group reporters can then share their lists aloud with the class. **L2**

Combining Word Parts

To help students visualize and manipulate word parts, make a set of flash cards. On separate cards, write the prefixes *un-* and *dis-*, the suffix *-ful*, and the word roots *help, thank, truth, trust, skill,* and *event*. Use the cards to demonstrate how to join a prefix and/or a suffix with a word root to form a new word, such as *untruthful, distrustful, unskillful,* and *uneventful*. Encourage students to make their own cards containing some basic word roots and the prefixes and suffixes presented in this lesson. **L1**

Prefixes

Prefixes are syllables attached before a root. Prefixes can change, or even reverse, the meaning of a word. Two or more prefixes may have the same, or nearly the same, meaning. A single prefix may have more than one meaning. The chart below shows the meanings of some common prefixes. For example, *un-* (as in *unknown*) and *il-* (as in *illegal*) both can mean "not" or "the opposite of."

Prefixes			
	Prefixes	**Words**	**Meanings**
Prefixes that reverse meaning	*un-* means "not" or "the opposite of"	unnatural unhappy	not natural not happy
	il- means "not" or "the opposite of"	illegal illogical	not legal not logical
Prefixes that show relations	*re-* means "again"	rebuild reconsider	to build again to consider again
	super- means "beyond, above, or more"	superfine superhuman	extra fine more than human
Prefixes that show judgment	*pro-* means "in favor of" or "on the side of"	progovernment	in favor of the government
	anti- means "against" or "opposite"	antiaircraft	against aircraft (as in "antiaircraft gun")
Prefixes that show number	*semi-* means "half" or "partial"	semiyearly semisweet	twice a year somewhat sweet
	uni- means "one"	unicycle unilateral	one-wheeled vehicle one-sided
	bi- means "two"	biweekly bicycle	every two weeks cycle with two wheels
	tri- means "three"	triangle tripod	having three angles three-legged stand
	deci- means "ten"	decade decimal system	period of ten years system based on tens

Cultural Connections

Building Meaning in Different Ways

Although some languages do not use affixes at all, others use affixes much more heavily and for more purposes than English does. For example, some Native American languages, such as the Nootka language, do not use sentences made of separate words. Instead, prefixes and suffixes attach to a syllable to build one word that has a meaning equivalent to a full sentence in English.

Suffixes

A **suffix** is a syllable added to the end of a root that changes the meaning of the root. Many suffixes also change the part of speech of a root word. Learning the meanings and uses of suffixes can help you build your vocabulary. As with prefixes, two or more suffixes can have the same or a similar meaning.

> A single root or word can have a variety of suffixes added to it. Each one gives the word a slightly different meaning.

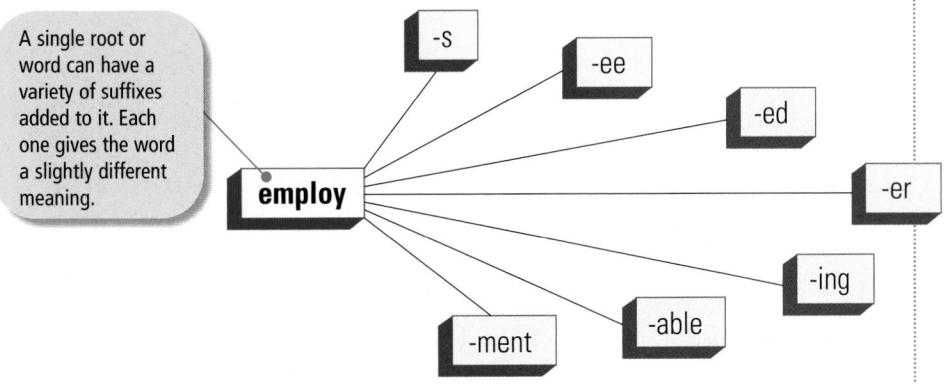

-s
-ee
-ed
-er
-ing
-able
-ment

employ

Suffixes			
	Suffixes	**Words**	**Meanings**
Suffixes that show state of being	*-ship* means "state or condition of"	leadership friendship	state of being a leader state of being a friend
	-hood means "state or condition of"	childhood nationhood	condition of being a child condition of being a nation
Suffixes that mean "one who"	*-ist* means "one who"	archaeologist physicist	one who studies archaeology one who studies physics
	-ian means "belonging to" or "characteristic of"	librarian Bostonian	worker in a library person who lives in Boston
Suffixes that mean "related to"	*-ish* means "relating to" or "like"	childish boyish	like a child like a boy
	-al means "relating to"	global tropical	relating to the globe relating to the tropics

Teach

Using Latin and Greek Roots

Many of the most frequently used English word roots have been taken from Latin and Greek. A root, which carries the main meaning of a word, is combined with a prefix or a suffix or both to form a new word. You may wish to provide students with a list of common roots and their meanings. Below are examples of Latin and Greek roots and their meanings.

Latin
dict	say
flect or *flex*	bend
miss or *mit*	send
port	carry
spec or *spect*	look
vid or *vis*	see

Greek
chron	time
graph	write
phon	sound
poly	many
tele	distant
therm	heat

Have students list as many words as they can containing a Latin or Greek root. Select volunteers to define the meaning of selected words.

⮂ Cross-Reference: Spelling

For a discussion of spelling rules that apply when adding prefixes or suffixes to words, refer students to Lesson 23.6.

Additional Resources

📁 *Thinking and Study Skills,* pp. 9, 25–27
📁 *Vocabulary and Spelling Strategies and Practice,* pp. 13, 21–26

Vocabulary and Spelling

MEETING INDIVIDUAL NEEDS **English Language Learners**

Finding Affixed Words

Some students may speak a first language in which prefixes and suffixes are not used. In Chinese languages, for example, all words have one syllable. Semitic languages, such as Arabic and Ethiopian, do not use suffixes and prefixes. Work with students to find examples of affixed words in the English language in books, magazines, and newspapers. Encourage students to keep a list of the words they find to use for future reference.

Practice and Assess

Answers: Exercise 4

1. script; "writing"; formula written by a doctor for the preparation and use of a medicine or remedy
2. ject; "throw"; cause or reason for opposing, disliking, or disapproving of something
3. phon; "sound"; relating to the sounds of speech
4. script; "writing"; a typewritten or handwritten article or book
5. phon; "voice"; a person who studies languages by their speech sounds
6. phon; "sound"; an instrument used in recording and transmitting sound

Answers: Exercise 5

Answers will vary. Some samples are given.
1. illegible—unreadable
2. unnatural—artificial, fake, or phony
3. reform—to form again; to make better
4. antiwar—against war
5. undone—reversed or unfastened
6. superhighway—expressway or divided highway
7. biweekly—once every two weeks
8. refresh—to make fresh again; to replenish
9. bicycle—a two-wheeled vehicle
10. violinist—a person who plays the violin

Close

Have each student write a brief paragraph about something that he or she did recently. Tell students to use as many affixed words as they can in their writing. When paragraphs are finished, pair students and have partners share and revise their work discussing the meanings of any affixed words they used.

Notice that sometimes the spelling of a word is changed when a suffix is added to it. For example, the ending of *library* is changed to make the word *librarian*. Look at pages 673, 674, and 677 to learn more about spelling words with suffixes.

Words seldom have more than a single prefix added to them. However, more than one suffix can be added to the same word. Each added suffix can change the word's part of speech as well as its meaning. The following examples show how suffixes can change a single root word.

peace (noun)
peace + -ful = peaceful (adjective)
peace + -ful + -ly = peacefully (adverb)
peace + -able = peaceable (adjective)
peace + -able + -ly = peaceably (adverb)

Exercise 4

Identify and write the meaning of the root in each of the following words. Then write the definition of each word. Use your dictionary for help if necessary.

1. prescription
2. objection
3. phonetic
4. manuscript
5. phonetician
6. microphone

Exercise 5

Add a prefix, a suffix, or both to each of the following words. Use prefixes and suffixes from the charts in this lesson. Then write the definition of the new word. Use a dictionary to check your definitions.

1. legible
2. nature
3. form
4. war
5. done
6. highway
7. weekly
8. fresh
9. cycle
10. violin

Vocabulary and Spelling

Enrichment and Extension

Creating Aphorisms

Students may enjoy making up sayings that contrast standard English words with unconventional uses of prefixes, suffixes, and roots. Write these examples on the board for students to follow: *You can quicken your pace, but you can't slowen it* and *You can be childish, but not adultish.* Encourage students to make up their own aphorisms and create classroom posters of the sayings to remind them of various affixes.

Wordworks

"MAN TURNS INTO SEA MONSTER"

The newspaper headline "Man eating lobster wrecks restaurant" probably wouldn't worry you. But "Man-eating lobster wrecks restaurant" might send you into a panic. The two headlines look similar, but their meanings are obviously very different. Why is that?

Like all other languages, English has the capacity to grow, or add new words. One way to add words is through compounding, or joining words to make new words. The compound *man-eating* comes from joining *man* and *eating.*

Often the meanings of the words that make up a compound give a clue to its meaning. For example, *doghouse* means "a house for a dog."

Sometimes, though, the meaning of the compound is more than the sum of its parts. The word *underdog,* for instance, doesn't refer to something under a dog but to a predicted loser in a competition.

Words that form compounds can be spelled closed (*troublemaker*), open (*high school*), or hyphenated (*man-eating*). Compounds can be made with most parts of speech—noun plus noun (*fire drill*), verb plus verb (*blow-dry*), adjective plus noun (*fast food*), and so on. The compounds themselves can be almost any part of speech.

Challenge

Pronounce hothouse *and* hot house. *Do you pronounce them differently? Try other similar compounds. How do we indicate compounds in speech?*

ACTIVITY

Get It Together

See how many compounds you can form by joining words from opposite columns.

bird	blue
over	house
light	dog
air	night
watch	flow

Vocabulary and Spelling

Wordworks **665**

Real-World Connection

Classifying Compounds

To help students become familiar with which words are open compounds, closed compounds, or hyphenated compounds, ask them to look through magazines, newspapers, catalogs, or circulars at home. Have them circle or highlight any compounds they encounter and classify them as open, closed, or hyphenated compounds. Encourage them to bring in the examples and share them with the class. They may wish to post them on a class bulletin board.

Close

Write a class poem, using compound words to describe an event in nature such as a sunrise or an earthquake.

Lesson Overview

Objective
• To become familiar with compound words

Skills
• identifying word parts; using precise vocabulary

Critical Thinking
• analyzing

Listening and Speaking
• discussing

Teach

Discussion

Have students read Wordworks on this page and discuss the following question: *What things in this room can be named or described with a compound word?* (Possible answers: *classroom, chalkboard, ballpoint*)

Making New Words

Encourage students to develop a list of compound words, such as *motorcycle* and *bookkeeper.* Then invite them to create new compound words, such as *motorcruiser* or *keykeeper.* Demonstrate how compound words are functional words, created as needed to describe new ideas. **L2**

Practice and Assess

Answers: Challenge
In pronouncing compound words, most people accent the first word.

Answers: Get It Together
bluebird, birdhouse, bird dog, overnight, overflow, lighthouse, nightlight, airflow, watchdog

Focus

Lesson Overview

Objectives
- To become familiar with synonyms and antonyms
- To use synonyms and antonyms to enhance writing

Skills
- expanding vocabulary by using synonyms and antonyms; forming antonyms by adding prefixes

Critical Thinking
- analyzing; comparing

Listening and Speaking
- discussing

Bellringer
Daily Language Activity

When students enter the classroom, have this assignment on the board: *Write the word* big *on a piece of paper. Using the classroom clock as a timer, take 60 seconds to write as many words as you can that have almost the same meaning as* big. *Then take another 60 seconds and write words that mean the opposite of* big.

See also  *Daily Language Practice*

Teach

Writing Interesting Sentences

Point out that using a thesaurus is one way to avoid relying on overused, general words when writing. List on the chalkboard the words *nice, old,* and *intelligent.* Ask students to write sentences that use each of these words. Then have them find the words in a thesaurus and rewrite the sentences using replacement words. Which sentences sound more interesting? **L2**

23.4 | **Synonyms and Antonyms**

As a writer, you want to present your ideas as clearly as possible. You also want your writing to be interesting and lively. A knowledge of synonyms and antonyms can improve your vocabulary and your writing.

The trouble began on a sizzling *August day.*

Synonyms

Synonyms are words that have the same, or nearly the same, meaning. Synonyms can make your writing more colorful. When you describe something, you want to make your readers "see" what you describe. One way to do that is to avoid dull, overused words. For example, suppose you're describing a tired old dog walking across the street. You could simply write "The tired old dog walked across the street." Or you could write "The worn-out, ancient mutt hobbled across the street." Choosing the right synonyms for overused words can make your writing livelier.

A dictionary gives synonyms for some words. However, the best place to find synonyms is in a dictionary of synonyms. Such a book is also called a thesaurus. (See pages 647–649 for more information about using a thesaurus.) Remember that synonyms rarely mean exactly the same thing. For example, *weary, worn-out, drained,* and *exhausted* are all synonyms for *tired.* However, each word has a slightly different meaning. Check the meanings of synonyms to make sure the one you choose is the right one.

sizzling
blistering
scalding
sultry
torrid
scorching
red-hot
boiling

Antonyms

Antonyms are words with opposite, or nearly opposite, meanings. *Up* and *down,* and *tall* and *short* are examples of antonyms. While many English words have synonyms, antonyms are less common.

Vocabulary and Spelling

Resource Manager

📁 Planning Resources
- *Lesson Plans*

📑 Transparencies
- *Bellringer*
- *Daily Language Practice*

📁 Other Print Resources
- *Thinking and Study Skills,* pp. 9, 25–27
- *Vocabulary and Spelling Strategies and Practice,* pp. 13, 21–26

Antonyms are often formed by adding a prefix meaning "not." *Un-*, *il-*, *dis-*, *in-*, and *non-* are all prefixes that can reverse meaning to form antonyms. For example, you can easily form antonyms for the words *happy, legal, comfort, complete,* and *fattening.* Just add the prefixes above in the order listed.

When adding a prefix to make an antonym, make sure you know the exact meaning of the new word. For example, you can add the prefix *dis-* to the word *ease.* However, the word formed, *disease,* is no longer an antonym for *ease,* as it was formerly.

Exercise 6

In each of the following sentences, replace the underlined word with a synonym. Use a thesaurus if you wish. Hint: When checking a verb in the thesaurus, look for the present-tense form.

1. The horse <u>ran</u> around the track.
2. The flower was a <u>pretty</u> color.
3. Carla stood at the <u>top</u> of the mountain.
4. Jake waxed and <u>polished</u> his new car.
5. Rochelle <u>looked</u> out the window.
6. It was a <u>hard</u> test.
7. The meal was <u>tasty</u>.
8. We picked some of the <u>good</u> peaches.
9. Leon listened to the two men <u>talking</u>.
10. <u>Grab</u> the other end of the rope.

Exercise 7

Think of an antonym for each of the following words. Then write a sentence, using the antonym. Underline the antonym in the sentence. Remember that many antonyms can be made by adding prefixes that reverse meaning.

1. cruel
2. friendly
3. dull
4. common
5. cheerful

Practice and Assess

Answers: Exercise 6
Answers will vary. Accept other valid synonyms.
1. galloped
2. lovely, beautiful
3. peak, crest
4. buffed
5. stared, peered
6. difficult
7. delicious
8. excellent
9. conversing, chatting
10. grasp, seize

Answers: Exercise 7
Answers will vary. Accept other valid antonyms. Students should use the chosen word correctly in a complete sentence.
1. kind
2. unfriendly, hostile
3. bright, sharp
4. uncommon, rare
5. cheerless, sad

Additional Resources
📁 *Thinking and Study Skills,* pp. 9, 25–27
📁 *Vocabulary and Spelling Strategies and Practice,* pp. 13, 21–26

Close

Ask students whether they agree or disagree with the following statements: *Using synonyms makes my writing more interesting. Knowing antonyms expands my vocabulary.* Have them explain their ideas.

Vocabulary and Spelling

Listening and Speaking

Discussing Connotations of Synonyms

On the chalkboard, write the following sentence: *I felt good.* Ask students to suggest words that could be used instead of *good,* such as *pleasant, marvelous, super, terrific, wonderful,* and *fine.* List their suggestions on the chalkboard. Then ask students to cite situations in which they might use these synonyms. Have them discuss the shades of meaning of the various synonyms and tell how the various synonyms affect the meaning of the sentence.

Wordworks

THE CAT WANTS HIS PAJAMAS BACK

"Those red sleepers are the cat's pajamas." Suppose a father said this to his young daughter about what she wanted to wear to bed one night. Should she try to scrounge up something else to wear so that she won't upset the cat? Or should she accept the compliment? It might help to know that at one time, *the cat's pajamas* meant "something good or desirable."

Challenge

The passage below uses 1960s slang. What do the underlined slang words mean? What slang words would you use instead?

Get with it, and go to the dance. It'll be a blast! I really dig school dances. They're boss.

The *cat's pajamas* is an example of slang, the informal vocabulary of a group of people. Slang usually begins with a small group of people, who use it almost as a code for group identity. Over time more and more people may use it.

Slang goes in and out of style. Have you heard *rat fink,* meaning "someone who gives information behind another's back"? Does *swinging,* meaning "lively and up-to-date," ring a bell? These two phrases were popular in the 1950s and 1960s but aren't used now.

Some words begin as slang and later become accepted into the language. *Hot dog* and *fan* both began as slang. Other slang words simply remain so. One current example of a slang expression is " I'm out of here," meaning "I'm leaving."

What's the Word

Put your ears on "slang alert" for a day. Listen for examples of slang that you, your friends, or even characters on TV use. Take notes as you listen. Create an American "Slanglish-English" dictionary. Write each word and its "translation," as in a foreign-language dictionary.

Vocabulary and Spelling

23.5 Homonyms

Did you ever play the *bass* or catch a *bass* in the lake? Did you ever shed a *tear* when you found a *tear* in your favorite shirt? Pairs (not *pears*) of words that sound alike or are spelled alike are called homonyms. Homonyms can be divided into two groups. One group contains words called homographs.

Homographs

The word *homograph* is made up of two roots: *homo* (same) and *graph* (writing). Homographs are words that are spelled alike. However, the words have different meanings and may have different pronunciations. *Bass* (pronounced to rhyme with *face*) is a musical instrument or type of voice. (He sang in the *bass* section of the chorus.) *Bass* (pronounced to rhyme with *lass*) is a kind of fish. (I caught an eight-pound striped *bass*.) The chart shows some more examples of homographs.

Homographs		
Word	**Meaning**	**Example**
object (ob′ jekt)	a thing	What is that strange *object?*
object (əb jekt′)	to oppose	"I *object!*" the lawyer shouted.
sow (sō)	to plant	Farmers *sow* their crops.
sow (sou)	a female pig	The *sow* has five piglets.
lead (lēd)	to go in advance	Will you *lead* the way?
lead (led)	a kind of metal	This pipe is made of *lead.*
dove (duv)	a type of bird	The *dove* is a symbol of peace.
dove (dōv)	past tense of *dive*	He *dove* into the lake.
bow (bō)	a knot with two loops	The child learned to tie a *bow.*
bow (bou)	to bend at the waist	She refused to *bow* to the king.
wind (wind)	air that moves	Listen to the *wind* in the trees.
wind (wīnd)	to wrap around	Help me *wind* up this ball of string.
wound (woond)	an injury	Cover the *wound* with gauze.
wound (wound)	past tense of *wind*	He *wound* the gauze around his hand.

23.5 Homonyms **669**

Vocabulary and Spelling

Focus

Lesson Overview

Objective
• To become familiar with homonyms

Skills
• reading and writing homonyms; using context to determine word meanings

Critical Thinking
• analyzing; categorizing; identifying characteristics

Listening and Speaking
• discussing; listening well

Bellringer
Daily Language Activity

When students enter the classroom, have this assignment on the board: *Copy this sentence: If you haven't read* The Red Pony, *you should read it. Circle words that are spelled differently but sound the same. Underline words that are spelled the same but sound different.*

See also 🖳 *Daily Language Practice*

Teach

Inventing Homophone Riddles

Read aloud this homonym riddle: *Why were the dark ages so dark?* Ask students to guess the answer. (because there were so many knights) Write the word *knights* on the chalkboard and ask a volunteer to write a homophone for this word. Then invite students to make up their own riddles based on homophones. Point out that the homophone will be in the answer of the riddle, so it may help to start there. **L2**

Practice and Assess

Answers: Exercise 8

1. to, two, too; see, sea; sun, son
2. sail, sale; for, four; new, knew, gnu
3. I, eye; need, knead; to, two, too; buy, by; pair, pear, pare
4. wait, weight; in, inn; here, hear; there, their, they're
5. would, wood; you, ewe; four, for

Additional Resources

📁 *Thinking and Studying Skills,* pp. 9, 25–27

📁 *Vocabulary and Spelling Strategies and Practice,* pp. 13, 21–26

Close

Ask students to brainstorm to develop a list of misused homophones or homographs, such as *dove* (the bird) *in the water* or *pleased to meat you.* Have them share their examples with the class and have volunteers make corrections.

Vocabulary and Spelling

Homophones

Homophones are a second type of homonym. Homophones are words that sound alike. *Bass* (the instrument) sounds the same as *base* (as in *first base*). *Pair, pare,* and *pear* are another group of homophones.

Homophones sound alike but have different spellings and different meanings. That's why they're often confused. Always check a dictionary if you're unsure about which homophone to use. The chart below shows some common homophones. Can you think of any additional examples?

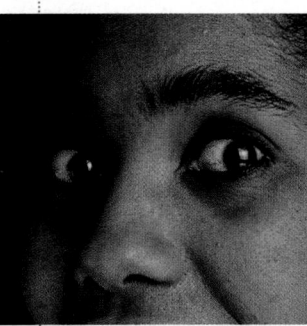
See

HOMOPHONES
to, too, two
meat, meet
here, hear
there, their, they're
deer, dear
sail, sale
for, four

Sea

Exercise 8

In each sentence below, find as many words as you can that have homophones. Write each word you find. Then write its homophone or homophones.

1. Angela sat on the shore, waiting to see the sun come up over the horizon.
2. How much will the sail for the new boat cost?
3. I need to buy a necktie and a pair of shoes.
4. The boys will wait in here, and the girls will wait over there.
5. Would you like four more of those?

Writing in the Real World

Spelling and Legibility

Using a Spell Checker If students use word-processing features to check spelling, caution them that these programs will ignore misused homophones. After the computer check, they must examine the manuscript carefully for mistaken substitutions such as *too* for *two.* Encourage students to look up an individual word in a dictionary if they are confused about which homophone is correct.

Wordworks

CAN YOU PICK A FLOUR?

"How is bread made?"

"I know that!" Alice cried eagerly. "You take some flour—"

"Where do you pick the flower?" the White Queen asked. "In a garden, or in the hedges?"

"Well, it isn't picked at all," Alice explained: "it's ground—"

"How many acres of ground?" said the White Queen.

In this passage from *Through the Looking Glass,* Lewis Carroll plays with homophones, words having the same sounds but different meanings.

Most of today's homophones didn't always sound alike. *Bear* and *bare* began as English words with the same meanings as today—a *bear* was an animal, and *bare* meant "uncovered." However, hundreds of years ago *bear* and *bare* didn't sound the same at all. The word *bear,* spelled *bera,* had two syllables. The word *bare,* spelled *bær,* had the vowel sound of the *a* in *bat.* Gradually, the pronunciations grew closer until the words became homophones.

Grate, which was borrowed from French originally had the same meaning as it does today, "a metal lattice to cover a window or fire." The English word *great,* which originally meant "thick" or "coarse," had two syllables. Later, the second syllable was lost, so that today we have another pair of homophones .

Challenge

"Cinderella opened a photo shop and waited for her prints to come." Think of another silly joke that depends upon homophones. Better yet, make one up.

Get It Together

Give the homophones for each pair of clues.

1. a story; what a dog wags
2. it stops your bike; a crack in a vase
3. bread before baking; female deer
4. a dark time; a medieval warrior
5. animal feet; a short rest

Wordworks **671**

Vocabulary and Spelling

Writing in the Real World

Writers and Writing

Finding Slogans Advertisers and campaign managers often use homonyms in slogans and promotional messages. Point out that a play on words helps the words jump out at a reader or listener. Ask students to write down examples of word play with homonyms that they may encounter in print or on television. Encourage them to bring their examples into class for further discussion.

Lesson Overview

Objective
- To understand playful uses of homonyms

Skills
- reading and writing homonyms; using context to determine word meanings

Critical Thinking
- using metaphors

Listening and Speaking
- discussing

Teach

Discussion

Have students read Wordworks on this page. Point out that several words that are homonyms appear in the dialogue between Alice and the White Queen. Work with students to list these homonym pairs on the board.

Writing Dialogue

Encourage students to write their own scenes in which one character is confused by the homonyms in the speech of another character. **L3**

Practice and Assess

Answers: Challenge

Answers will vary. Example: *The colt was not afraid of Sally, because Sally was a little hoarse too.*

Answers: Get It Together

1. tale, tail
2. brake, break
3. dough, doe
4. night, knight
5. paws, pause

Close

Have partners write new dialogue for Alice and the Queen. Tell them to include other homonym pairs in their writing. Invite partners to read aloud their new scenes for the class.

23.6

Focus

Lesson Overview

Objective
- To become familiar with spelling rules

Skills
- applying spelling rules to real reading and writing applications

Critical Thinking
- recalling; patterning; analyzing

Listening and Speaking
- discussing; formal speaking

Bellringer
Daily Language Activity

When students enter the classroom, have this assignment on the board: *List five words you consistently have trouble spelling.*

See also *Daily Language Practice*

Motivating Activity

Invite students to offer some of their troublesome spelling words and list them on the board. Then ask students to share mnemonic (memory) devices they use to help them remember how to spell difficult words. List each phrase next to the troublesome word. If a word does not have a mnemonic device listed next to it, ask students to make one up.

Vocabulary and Spelling

23.6 Spelling Rules I

What would you think of a letter or an essay full of misspelled words? You might think that the writer was careless. You might even have trouble understanding the writer's ideas. Good writing includes careful attention to details such as spelling.

Do you have trouble with spelling? One reason for the problem may be that the spelling of English words doesn't always make sense. For example, pronounce the words *through, dough, ought, bough, cough,* and *rough.* Did you notice that the letters ough are pronounced differently in each word? Worse yet, the same sound can be spelled several ways. For example, pronounce oh. Some other ways to spell the same sound are *oe (doe), ou (soul), ew (sew),* and *oa (road).*

The best way to avoid spelling errors is to check your spelling against a dictionary. However, you won't always have a dictionary handy. Learning a few spelling rules will help you master the spelling of thousands of words.

Spelling *ie* and *ei*

The letters *ie* and *ei* are contained in many English words. They often cause confusion. The following rhyme can help you remember how to spell words with these letter combinations. There are so few exceptions to this rule that you can easily memorize all the important ones.

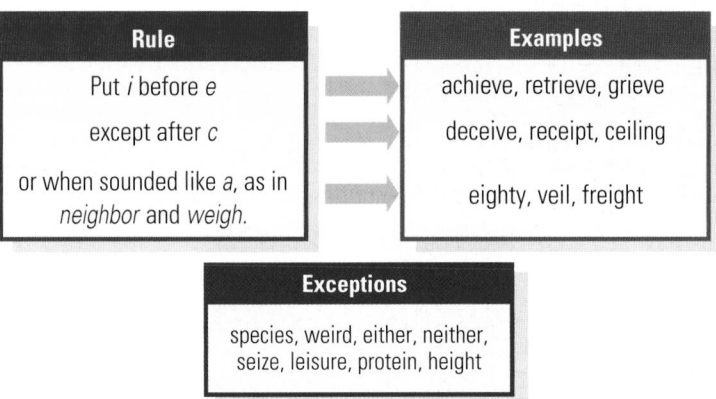

Rule		Examples
Put *i* before *e*		achieve, retrieve, grieve
except after *c*		deceive, receipt, ceiling
or when sounded like *a*, as in *neighbor* and *weigh.*		eighty, veil, freight

Exceptions
species, weird, either, neither, seize, leisure, protein, height

Resource Manager

 Planning Resources
- *Lesson Plans*

Transparencies
- *Bellringer*
- *Daily Language Practice*

Other Print Resources
- *Thinking and Study Skills,* pp. 9, 25–27
- *Vocabulary and Spelling Strategies and Practice,* pp. 13, 21–26

Spelling Unstressed Vowels

English is full of words with an unstressed vowel sound. In dictionaries this sound is represented by a special symbol called a schwa (ə). Say the word *about* aloud, listening to the sound of the vowel in the first syllable. This unstressed vowel always *sounds* the same (*uh*), but it can be spelled *a, e, i, o, u,* or more than a dozen other ways. Listen for the sounds of the underlined letters in the words *c<u>a</u>nal, angel, penc<u>i</u>l, pers<u>o</u>n, circ<u>us</u>, mount<u>ai</u>n,* and *serge<u>a</u>nt.* All these words have the same unstressed vowel sound.

As you can see, words with this vowel sound can cause spelling problems. You can't just "spell it the way it sounds." Sometimes, however, you can get around the difficulty. Think of a related word in which the vowel is stressed. When the vowel is stressed, it may not be as great a spelling problem. For example, you may not be sure whether *legal* or *legel* is the correct spelling. However, you may know the related word *legality* (notice the stress). You can see that the vowel letter you want is *a.* The chart below shows some additional examples of how you can use this strategy.

Spelling Unstressed Vowels		
Unknown Letter	**Related Word**	**Correct Spelling**
opp_site	opp<u>o</u>se	opposite
rid_cule	rid<u>i</u>culous	ridicule
phot_graph	phot<u>o</u>graphy	photograph
observ_nt	observ<u>a</u>tion	observant
inform_tive	inform<u>a</u>tion	informative

Suffixes and the Silent e

Many English words end with a silent letter *e.* When you add a suffix to words that end in a silent *e,* the *e* is often dropped. However, sometimes the silent *e* is kept. The following chart shows the rules for suffixes and the silent *e.*

Vocabulary and Spelling

23.6

Teach

Finding Examples of Spelling Rules

Have students look through newspapers or magazines and find at least one example of each of the spelling rules in this lesson. Encourage students to share their words with the class. Guide volunteers to tell what spelling rule each word exemplifies. **L2**

MEETING INDIVIDUAL NEEDS **English Language Learners**

Practicing Spelling Rules

Some students may have difficulty spelling words with unstressed vowel sounds. Guide students through the strategy on the chart, helping them think of related examples. Provide additional words they may use to practice the strategy, such as *evident/evidently, substance/substantially, strategy/strategic, combination/combine.*

Teach

📁 **Cross-Reference: Vocabulary and Spelling**

For more information on words containing suffixes, refer students to Lesson 23.3.

Vocabulary and Spelling

Adding Suffixes to Words That End with Silent *e*	
Rule	**Example**
When adding a suffix that begins with a consonant to a word that ends with a silent *e*, keep the *e*.	safe + -ly = safely hope + -ful = hopeful **Common exceptions** awe + -ful = awful judge + -ment = judgment
When adding *-ly* to a word that ends with an *l* plus a silent *e*, always drop the *e* and one *l*.	incredible + -ly = incredibly laughable + -ly = laughably
When adding a suffix that begins with a vowel or *y* to a word that ends with a silent *e*, usually drop the *e*.	shape + -ing = shaping rose + -y = rosy **Common exceptions** dye + -ing = dyeing mile + -age = mileage
Sometimes the *e* is kept to avoid changing the sound or confusing the meaning of the original word.	
When adding a suffix that begins with *a* or *o* to a word that ends with *ce* or *ge*, keep the *e* so that the word will keep the soft *c* or *g* sound.	trace + -able = traceable change + -able = changeable
When adding a suffix that begins with a vowel to a word that ends in *ee* or *oe*, keep the *e*.	agree + -able = agreeable canoe + -ing = canoeing

Suffixes and the Final *y*

Adding suffixes to words that end in *y* can often cause spelling problems. Follow these rules for adding suffixes to such words.

- When a word ends in a vowel + *y*, keep the *y*.

  play + -ful = playful   pray + -ing = praying
  enjoy + -ment = enjoyment

- When a word ends in a consonant + *y*, change the *y* to *i*.

  fry + -ed = fried   try + -ed = tried
  happy + -ness = happiness

- BUT if the suffix begins with an *i*, keep the *y* so that two *i*'s don't come together.

  fry + -ing = frying   carry + -ing = carrying

Enrichment and Extension

Writing Rhyming Poems

Students may enjoy writing poems whose lines end in rhyming words that have unlike spellings, such as *stuff* and *rough,* or *shade* and *played.* Invite students to think of similar rhyming words and to make up rhyming lines. You may wish to use these lines from the second stanza of "With Rue My Heart Is Laden," by A. E. Housman, as a model.

By brooks too broad for leaping
The lightfoot boys are laid;
The rose-lipped girls are sleeping
In fields where roses fade.

Adding Prefixes

The addition of a prefix doesn't change the spelling of a word. This is a rule you can remember easily.

- When you add a prefix to a word, do not change the spelling of the word or the prefix.

pre- + pay = prepay	re- + act = react
dis- + able = disable	im- + possible = impossible
un- + natural = unnatural	de- + odorize = deodorize
il- + legal = illegal	co- + operate = cooperate

Exercise 9

There is one misspelled word in each of the following sentences. Find the word, and write its correct spelling.

1. Luckily, our tickets were exchangable for a performance on another night.
2. Winning the trophy for the third straight year was a tremendous acheivment for our team.
3. The two friends were inseparible when they were children.
4. Attending the play was an agreable experience.
5. Jack tryed canoeing through white water, but he regretted it.

Exercise 10

Look at each set of words below. Find the one misspelled word in each set, and write it correctly.

1. shoeing, changable, freeing
2. judgeing, safely, wholly
3. ilogical, immediate, correspond
4. relieve, deceive, hieght
5. grading, rosey, dyeing.

Practice and Assess

Answers: Exercise 9

1. exchangeable
2. achievement
3. inseparable
4. agreeable
5. tried

Answers: Exercise 10

1. changeable
2. judging
3. illogical
4. height
5. rosy

Additional Resources

📁 *Thinking and Study Skills*, pp. 9, 25–27
📁 *Vocabulary and Spelling Strategies and Practice*, pp. 13, 21–26

Close

Review the class list of problem words and identify those that relate to the spelling rules discussed in this lesson. Encourage students to use either a rule or a mnemonic device to spell their problem words correctly.

Vocabulary and Spelling

Listening and Speaking

Playing Spelling Baseball

Divide the class into two teams to play spelling baseball. Members of the fielding team take turns pitching words that exemplify the spelling rules in this lesson. Members of the scoring team take turns at bat. The player at bat must spell the word correctly and identify the rule that applies. A player advances one base for a correct spelling and one base for stating a rule. A player who can neither spell the word nor state the rule is out. A player walks one base if the pitcher pitches a word that does not fit one of the rules. The umpire is the student who checks spellings in the dictionary.

Lesson Overview

Objective
- To become familiar with the origins of silent letters in words

Skills
- understanding that languages develop and change over time

Critical Thinking
- analyzing

Listening and Speaking
- discussing

Teach

Discussion

Have students read Wordworks on this page. Ask students, *How would you pronounce* tight *if you were sounding it out? What problems have you had with silent letters in words?*

Keeping a Notebook

Encourage students to keep notebooks in which they group similar words. For example, they could list *light, knight, sight, bright, night, fight, plight, might, slight, tight,* and *right* . **L1**

Practice and Assess

Answers: Challenge

Benjamin Franklin and Noah Webster proposed simpler spelling systems based on phonology. If spelling followed a predictable sound-symbol correspondence, it would be easier to read and spell. However, people resist giving up familiar spellings. Spelling also gives clues to meaning and origin, and some of this would be lost if traditional spelling were modified.

Evaluation Rubrics: Can You Speak Old English?

Every letter should be pronounced. Items 4–6 should be consistent with the specified vowel sounds.

Wordworks

LEFTOVER LETTERS

English spelling can seem strange. Why, for example, is there a *w* in *two* and *answer*? What is *gh* doing in *thought* and *though*? Where did we get all those silent *e*'s?

The answers lie in the history of English. Like all languages, English has changed over time, and one major change has occurred in its pronunciation. Until about five hundred years ago, most of today's leftover letters stood for sounds.

Consider an old friend, silent *e*. Originally the final *e* in words like *bake* and *time* wasn't silent. It stood for an unstressed sound much like the final sound in *Rita*. The pronunciation changed, but not the spelling.

Silent *gh* is harder to explain since the sound it once stood for no longer exists in English. The letters *gh* spelled a rough, throat-clearing *k* sound. That sound is gone, but not the spelling.

You may wonder why all these leftover letters didn't disappear once pronunciations changed. The printing press, invented in 1440, was one reason. By then pronunciation had begun to change, but spelling had not. Printers used the familiar spellings, which became standard as more and more people read books. Thus, printing helped to freeze many early spellings of English words.

Challenge

Some people have wanted to simplify the English spelling system, changing though *to* tho, *for example. What pro and con arguments can you think of for this proposal?*

sign	signal
bomb	bombard
hymn	hymnal

Can You Speak Old English?

Imitate early pronunciations of English words. Try to make each consonant letter stand for a sound.

1. folk
2. gnat
3. answer
4. two (long *o*)
5. light (short *i*)
6. knight (short *i*)

Vocabulary and Spelling

Close

Together with students, create a list of words commonly seen in advertisements and product names that reflect phonetic rather than correct spelling. (Examples: thru, kleen, quik, and lite.)

23.7 Spelling Rules II

The rules in the last lesson and in this one will help you improve your spelling skills. You probably won't memorize all these rules right away. However, reviewing them from time to time should help you improve your spelling.

Doubling the Final Consonant

Adding suffixes to words that end in a consonant can be confusing. In some cases you double the final consonant when adding the suffix. In other cases you don't double it. The following rules can help you avoid many spelling errors.

Double the final consonant when a word ends in a single consonant following one vowel and

- the word is one syllable

  run + -ing = running   ship + -ing = shipping
  mad + -er = madder   top + -ed = topped

- the word has an accent on the last syllable and the accent stays there after the suffix is added

  regret + -ed = regretted   prefer + -ed = preferred
  forget + -able = forgettable commit + -ing = committing

Do not double the final consonant when

- the accent is not on the last syllable

  number + -ed = numbered   differ + -ed = differed

- the accent moves when the suffix is added

  prefer + -ence = preference   fatal + -ity = fatality

- the word ends in two consonants

  hang + -er = hanger   haunt + -ed = haunted

- the suffix begins with a consonant

  light + -ness = lightness   real + -ly = really

Special case: When a word ends in *ll*, and the suffix *-ly* is added, drop one *l*.

  full + -ly = fully   dull + -ly = dully

Vocabulary and Spelling

Focus

Lesson Overview

Objectives
- To become familiar with spelling rules
- To spell plurals, compound words, and words with suffixes correctly

Skills
- knowing when to double the final consonant when adding suffixes; creating plurals and compound words

Critical Thinking
- classifying; recalling patterns

Listening and Speaking
- discussing

 Bellringer
Daily Language Activity

When students enter the classroom, have this assignment on the board: *Write three questions you have about making words plural.*

See also  *Daily Language Practice*

Motivating Activity

Ask students to name plural nouns for you to list on the chalkboard. With student guidance, group words according to the way the plural is formed. For example, *lice, mice, men,* and *feet* would belong in one group; *cats, boys,* and *skates* in another; and *dishes, matches,* and *foxes* in another.

Teach

 **Cross Reference: Usage**

For more information on suffixes, refer students to Lesson 23.3.

Resource Manager

📁 **Planning Resources**
- *Lesson Plans*

 Transparencies
- *Bellringer*
- *Daily Language Practice*

📁 **Other Print Resources**
- *Thinking and Study Skills,* pp. 9, 25–27
- *Vocabulary and Spelling Strategies and Practice,* pp. 13, 21–26

Teach

Listing Additional Examples

Encourage students to list more examples for each rule on this page. You may wish to have them list examples of common exceptions as well. For additional practice with proper names, provide time for students to take turns writing the plural forms of their classmates' names. **L2**

◼ Cross Reference: Usage

For additional information and instruction on plural nouns, refer students to Lesson 9.4.

Forming Plurals

The usual way to form plurals in English is to add *-s* or *-es*. However, there are other ways to form plurals. The following chart shows the general rules for plurals.

General Rules for Plurals		
If the Noun Ends in	**Then Generally**	**Examples**
s, sh, ch, x, or z	add -es	bus → buses rush → rushes match → matches tax → taxes buzz → buzzes
a consonant + y	change y to i and add -es	buddy → buddies candy → candies
a vowel + y	add -s	boy → boys way → ways
a vowel + o	add -s	stereo → stereos studio → studios
a consonant + o	generally add -s **Common exceptions** but sometimes add -es	solo → solos photo → photos cargo → cargoes hero → heroes tomato → tomatoes
f or ff	add -s **Common exceptions** change f to v and add -es	roof → roofs cuff → cuffs thief → thieves hoof → hooves wolf → wolves
lf	change f to v and add -es	shelf → shelves calf → calves
fe	change f to v and add -s	wife → wives knife → knives

MEETING INDIVIDUAL NEEDS — English Language Learners

Creating Plural Nouns

Some students' first language may make it difficult to grasp the concept of plural nouns and, therefore, to develop the habit of changing singular nouns to the plural form. Some Asian languages, for example, do not have plural forms of nouns. Provide additional practice for students who need it. You may wish to team them with peers who can dictate sentences.

Some nouns don't follow the general rules in the chart on page 678. They form plurals in a special way. Most of these special rules are easy to remember. Some of them resemble the general rules. The following chart includes examples of each rule.

Special Rules for Plurals	
Special Case	**Example**
To form the plurals of most proper names, add -s. But add -es if the name ends in s, ch, sh, x, or z.	Troy → Troys Smith → Smiths James → Jameses Thatch → Thatches Rush → Rushes Marx → Marxes Jiminez → Jiminezes
To form the plural of one-word compound nouns, follow the general rules for plurals.	pocketknife → pocketknives gooseberry → gooseberries schoolbag → schoolbags pickax → pickaxes
To form the plural of hyphenated compound nouns or compound nouns of more than one word, make the most important word plural.	sister-in-law → sisters-in-law head of state → heads of state court-martial → courts-martial
Some nouns have irregular plural forms and do not follow any rules. You simply have to remember these plural forms.	goose → geese mouse → mice child → children woman → women
Some nouns have the same singular and plural forms.	fish → fish moose → moose dozen → dozen Sioux → Sioux

Forming Compound Words

The rule for spelling compound words is simple. Keep the original spelling of both words, no matter how the words begin or end.

Listing Additional Examples

Encourage students to list additional examples of each rule. You may have them list exceptions as well. **L2**

Vocabulary and Spelling

Cooperative Learning

Writing Irregulars in Context

Ask students to work in groups of four to brainstorm to develop a list of words that highlight irregularities in plural formation. (*We found mice in all the houses, not hice. I saw a bunch of men driving blue vans, not ven. The doll has hands but no feet, not foots.*) Ask each group to create a chart of irregular plurals to help classmates remember them.

Practice and Assess

Answers: Exercise 11

1. granddaughter
2. calves
3. leaves
4. chiefs of staff
5. geese

Answers: Exercise 12

1. elves
2. bookkeeping
3. mice
4. permitted
5. realism

Additional Resources

📁 *Thinking and Study Skills,* pp. 9, 25–27

📁 *Vocabulary and Spelling Strategies and Practice,* pp. 13, 21–26

Close

Refer students to the three spelling questions they wrote in the Bellringer activity on page 677. Check to see if the questions have been answered. Discuss any additional questions students may have.

---

surf + board = surfboard
green + house = greenhouse
easy + going = easygoing
side + walk = sidewalk

night + time = nighttime
inn + keeper = innkeeper
house + boat = houseboat
home + made = homemade

horse   shoe   horseshoe

Exercise 11

Find the one misspelled word in each of the following sentences, and write its correct spelling.

1. Mrs. Hart's grandaughter will perform two solos.
2. The calfs were injured when the barn ceiling collapsed.
3. The autumn leafs dropped slowly as gentle breezes shook the branches.
4. Two of the chief of staffs met with the president.
5. The truckload of noisy cattle frightened the gooses, which ran about the barnyard in a panic.

Exercise 12

Look at each set of words below. Find the one misspelled word in each set, and write it correctly.

1. halves, puffs, elfs
2. fully, bookeeping, brothers-in-law
3. deer, mouses, children
4. permited, hopped, preferred
5. reelism, houseboat, observant

Viewing and Representing

Creating Picture Equations

Students may wish to create their own picture equations similar to the one shown on this page. They should leave the equations open so that they may exchange them. Each student can solve another's equation by putting the words together and creating a final picture. This will help students practice creating compound words that do not follow the typical spelling rules for doubling final consonants and dropping final *e*'s.

23.8 Spelling Problem Words

Do you often forget whether *tomorrow* has one *m* or two? Is the correct spelling *advertise* or *advertize*? Most people have trouble spelling certain words. But there are ways in which you can learn to spell even the most difficult words.

Improving Spelling Skills

Here is a spelling strategy that will help you master the spelling of new or difficult words. As you write, note words that you have trouble spelling. When reading, note unfamiliar words or words that look hard to spell. Then use the following steps to learn to spell them.

Say It	Visualize It	Write It	Check It
Look at the printed word, and say it out loud. Say it a second time, pronouncing each syllable clearly.	Without looking at the word, imagine seeing it printed or written. Try to picture the word spelled correctly.	Look at the printed word, and write it two or three times. Then write it without looking at the printed word.	Check what you have written against the printed word. Did you spell the word correctly? If not, try the process again.

Remember also that your dictionary can be an important tool for improving your spelling. You might say, "How can I look up a word if I can't spell it?" You probably can spell enough of a word's beginning to locate it in your dictionary. Look up one spelling, and if you don't find the word, consider alternative letter combinations that could make the sounds you hear, and try again. Once you've located the word, use the four-step spelling method to learn it.

Another way to learn difficult words is to use memory devices, or tricks for remembering. Rhymes, such as *i before e except after c,* are good memory devices. You also can think up clues about how to spell a certain word. For example, if you have trouble remembering that *mathematics* has an *e,* remind yourself that there is *them* in ma<u>them</u>atics.

23.8 Spelling Problem Words **681**

Vocabulary and Spelling

Focus

Lesson Overview

Objective
- To become familiar with strategies for spelling problem words

Skills
- learning to spell problem words; distinguishing between commonly misspelled words

Critical Thinking
- analyzing; visualizing; comparing

Listening and Speaking
- discussing

 Bellringer
Daily Language Activity

When students enter the classroom, have this assignment on the board: *List three words that you have difficulty spelling. After you have written the words, check their spellings in a dictionary.*

See also *Daily Language Practice*

Motivating Activity

From the lists students developed in the Bellringer activity, compile a class list of words that are difficult to spell. As you add students' words to the list, ask them why they think they have problems spelling these particular words.

Resource Manager

📂 **Planning Resources**
- *Lesson Plans*

📑 **Transparencies**
- *Bellringer*
- *Daily Language Practice*

📂 **Other Print Resources**
- *Thinking and Study Skills,* pp. 9, 25–27
- *Vocabulary and Spelling Strategies and Practice,* pp. 13, 21–26

Teach

Spelling Commonly Misspelled Words

Display on the chalkboard several words from the "Words Often Misspelled" box on page 683. Model for students how to use the four steps to improving spelling skills listed on page 681. Provide time for volunteers to demonstrate using the steps for learning to spell problem words. **L2**

Using Pronunciation Guides

Silent letters and other spelling irregularities may create pronunciation difficulties for some students. Encourage these students to rely on pronunciation guides in dictionaries. If the phonetic keys are unfamiliar to them, review the phonetic samples, using words to illustrate each sound. Then guide students through the phonetic respellings in several dictionary entries to demonstrate their use as aids to pronunciation. **L1**

Vocabulary and Spelling

Try to think of other tricks, sentences, or rhymes that help you remember how to spell the hard parts of troublesome words.

Keeping a personal word list of difficult words is another way to improve your spelling. You should keep your list up-to-date, adding new words as you come across them. Delete words from the list once you have mastered them. Study the words a few at a time, using the four-step spelling method.

Easily Confused Words

Certain words sound alike or nearly alike but have different spellings and meanings. Look at the following example:

affect   "to bring a change in"
        How does acid rain affect *the forests?*

effect   "a result"
        This test will have a bad effect *on my final grade.*

If you don't know the difference between the two words, you're likely to use the wrong word and therefore the wrong spelling. Some of these easily confused words are listed below.

Words Often Confused	
accept, except	loose, lose
affect, effect	than, then
all ready, already	their, there, they're
all together, altogether	to, too, two
choose, chose	whose, who's
its, it's	your, you're

Frequently Misspelled Words

The following words are often misspelled. Look for your "problem" words on this list. What other words would you add to the list?

Cooperative Learning

Creating Homophone Charts

Ask students to work in pairs. Instruct partners to make a list of homophones and then to choose three homophone pairs to feature on a chart. The chart should contain two sentences for each homophone pair selected, with each sentence illustrating a different meaning. Partners will divide responsibility for composing and writing the sentences. Display the charts as aids to the spelling and meaning of homophones.

Words Often Misspelled			
absence	convenient	jewelry	receipt
accidentally	definite	laboratory	recognize
accommodate	disease	leisure	recommend
adviser	dissatisfied	library	restaurant
all right	embarrass	license	rhythm
analyze	environment	misspell	schedule
answer	essential	molasses	separate
beautiful	February	muscle	sincerely
beginning	foreign	necessary	succeed
blaze	forty	neighborhood	technology
business	funeral	niece	theory
cafeteria	genius	noticeable	tomorrow
canceled	government	nuisance	traffic
canoe	grammar	occasion	truly
cemetery	guarantee	original	usually
choir	height	parallel	vacuum
commercial	humorous	permanent	variety
colonel	immediate	physician	Wednesday

Exercise 13

On a separate piece of paper, write the word in the parentheses that correctly completes each sentence.

1. The team was (all together, altogether) satisfied with the outcome of the game.
2. Is this (your, you're) glove?
3. Do you think that Janet will (except, accept) the gift?
4. The car needs to have (its, it's) brakes replaced.
5. If it's not Kim's, then (whose, who's) is it?
6. How will this loss (effect, affect) the playoffs?
7. We can't afford to (lose, loose) the next game.
8. I think dogs are smarter (then, than) cats.
9. We (choose, chose) to see the movie last night.
10. The farmers harvested (their, there, they're) crops.

Practice and Assess

Answers: Exercise 13

1. altogether
2. your
3. accept
4. its
5. whose
6. affect
7. lose
8. than
9. chose
10. their

Additional Resources

📁 *Thinking and Study Skills,* pp. 9, 25–27
📁 *Vocabulary and Spelling Strategies and Practice,* pp. 13, 21–26

Close

Encourage students to share with their classmates the strategies they use to spell problem words correctly.

✔ ASSESSMENT OPTIONS

📁 *Tests with Answer Key and Rubrics*
Unit 23 Mastery Test, pp. 95–96

💾 *Testmaker*
Unit 23 Mastery Test

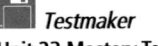 *MindJogger Videoquizzes*

You may wish to administer the Unit 23 Mastery Test at this point.

Vocabulary and Spelling

MEETING INDIVIDUAL NEEDS — Less-Proficient Readers

Spelling Words That Are Easily Confused

Some students may have difficulty completing Exercise 13. Encourage them to use dictionaries to verify meanings of both words in each pair. Review the sentences with these students to make sure they understand the meanings of the other words in the sentence before they attempt to choose the correct spelling.

Objectives

- To develop useful reading, writing, and organizing strategies for studying
- To learn about the SQ3R Method
- To learn how to read, understand, and produce graphic information such as charts and maps

✔ ASSESSMENT OPTIONS

📁 *Tests with Answer Key and Rubrics*
Unit 24 Pretest, pp. 97–98

💾 *Testmaker*
Unit 24 Pretest

You may wish to administer the Unit 24 Pretest at this point.

Key to Ability Levels

L1 Level 1 activities are within the basic ability range of students.

L2 Level 2 activities are within the ability range of average students.

L3 Level 3 activities are more challenging activities.

684

Resource Manager

📁 **Planning Resources**
- *Lesson Plans*
- *Block Scheduling*

 **Transparencies**
- *Bellringer*
- *Daily Language Practice*

📁 **Other Print Resources**
- *Listening and Speaking Activities*
- *Tests with Answer Key and Rubrics*
- *Thinking and Study Skills*

 **Video**
- *MindJogger Videoquizzes*

💾 **Software**
- *Presentation Plus!*
- *Testmaker*

🖥 **Web Sites**
- *writerschoice.glencoe.com*

24.1 The Parts of a Book

When doing research, you may find more books on your topic than you can read. How do you decide which books will be the most useful? How do you find out if a book has the information you need? Certain pages in the front and the back of a book can help you. These pages can give you clues about whether the information in the book is up-to-date and reliable.

In the Front of the Book

The pages shown below are found in the front part of the book, before the main text. They can help you see whether the book contains what you need.

The **title page** gives the title of the book. It also names the book's author, authors, or editor.

The **contents** lists the names of the book's parts, chapters, sections, and so on. It tells you the page on which each one begins.

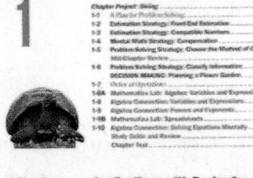

The date on the **copyright page** tells you when the book was published.

Study Skills

Resource Manager

📁 **Planning Resources**
• *Lesson Plans*

📘 **Transparencies**
• *Bellringer*
• *Daily Language Practice*

📁 **Other Print Resources**
• *Listening and Speaking Activities,* pp. 10–11
• *Thinking and Study Skills,* pp. 2–4, 8, 18, 30–32, 34–36, 39–40

Focus

Lesson Overview

Objectives
• To become familiar with standard parts of a book
• To use parts of a book to find information

Skills
• using a title page; using a table of contents; using a copyright page; using an index; using a glossary

Critical Thinking
• analyzing; recalling; relating

Listening and Speaking
• discussing

🔔 **Bellringer**
Daily Language Activity

When students enter the classroom, have this assignment on the board: *List five topics you would expect to be covered in a book entitled* Endangered Wildlife.

See also 📖 *Daily Language Practice*

Teach

Using Parts of a Book

Divide the class into pairs, giving each pair a nonfiction book to preview. First ask students to discuss the cover and title. What information do they expect to find in the book? Then have students take five minutes to examine features of the book, such as the table of contents, index, glossary, and bibliography. Ask them how these features can help them find information about a topic. Have partners summarize what they found out about their book and indicate one topic they might research using that book. **L2**

Practice and Assess

Answers: Exercise 1

1. pages 661–665
2. photo, publisher's name and locations
3. Unit 19
4. glossary
5. copyright page

Additional Resources

📁 *Listening and Speaking Activities,* pp. 10–11

📁 *Thinking and Study Skills,* pp. 2–4, 8, 18, 30–32, 34–36, 39–40

Close

Discuss the table of contents as a feature of a book. Have students write a paragraph to share their ideas about a table of contents' usefulness when they are trying to select appropriate books for research on a specific topic.

In the Back of the Book

The glossary and the index are found in the back of a book. Glossaries are found especially in books that use many specialized or technical terms. You often find glossaries in books on science or technology and in some textbooks.

The **index** contains an alphabetical list of topics in the book, including important people, places, events, and terms. Page numbers are given for each entry.

The **glossary** is an alphabetical list of special or unfamiliar terms in the book. Each term is defined.

Exercise 1

Use this textbook as needed to answer the questions. Tell where you found each answer.

1. On what page or pages are prefixes discussed in *Writer's Choice?*
2. What information besides the title can you find on the title page of *Writer's Choice?*
3. What unit in this book discusses capitalization?
4. Suppose you had a book called *An Introduction to Computers* and wanted to find a definition of *system disk.* Where would you look first to find it?
5. Where would you look to discover whether the book *An Introduction to Computers* was up-to-date?

Enrichment and Extension

Science

The word *appendix* originally was a Latin word meaning *appendage,* from *appendere, to weigh* or *to hang.* Appendixes primarily appear in science books and articles and may contain a variety of reference materials that add to a subject or make it easier to understand. A science book might have appendixes such as metric conversion charts, time lines, tables, or bibliographies.

24.2 Reading Strategies

Suppose you needed information about the structure of a plant cell or the events leading up to the Crusades. What would you do? Chances are you would read something. Reading is your most important tool for gaining information. However, there are different ways of reading. Using the best reading strategy for your purpose can save you time.

Skimming

When you skim a piece of writing, you glance over the text rapidly to get a general overview of the material presented. In skimming a textbook, for example, you might look at all the headings and illustrations and any words that are highlighted in bold type. You might also read the first sentence of each paragraph.

You can use skimming to preview material before beginning to read or to study for a test. You can also skim to find out if a book contains information you need.

Scanning

When you scan, your eyes move over the text rapidly, looking for particular information. For example, you may be looking for a name, a date, a figure, or a definition. You might scan to review key terms or main ideas for a test. You often scan to see if a book has any information on a specific topic. Keeping your topic in mind, you would look for words that relate to it. While scanning, you're interested only in finding out if a topic is covered. You'll learn what the book or article actually says about the topic during your careful reading.

Careful Reading

Careful reading means reading the text slowly and carefully to make sure you fully understand the information presented. You need to read carefully when learning material for the first time. Studying a new chapter in one of your textbooks would require careful reading.

Study Skills

Resource Manager

📂 Planning Resources
- *Lesson Plans*

📓 Transparencies
- *Bellringer*
- *Daily Language Practice*

📂 Other Print Resources
- *Listening and Speaking Activities,* pp. 10–11
- *Thinking and Study Skills,* pp. 2–4, 8, 18, 30–32, 34–36, 39–40

Focus

Lesson Overview

Objectives
- To become familiar with different strategies for reading
- To use skimming, scanning and careful reading appropriately

Skills
- skimming to find overall content; scanning to find specific information; reading carefully

Critical Thinking
- classifying; identifying main idea; evaluating; summarizing; predicting

Listening and Speaking
- discussing

 Bellringer
Daily Language Activity

When students enter the classroom, have this assignment on the board: *Read the headline*

"Work Stopped at National Snacks. Call for Safety Key Issue."

List some information you would expect to find in this article.

See also *Daily Language Practice*

Teach

Skimming Materials

On an overhead projector, place a textbook page or two containing several headings, captions to illustrations or photos, and bold-faced words. Tell students to skim the material, taking notes as they read.

Turn off the projector after students have had a chance to briefly skim the information. Then ask volunteers to discuss information they have gathered from their quick look at the material and to briefly predict what they think they will learn from a careful reading. **L2**

Practice and Assess

Evaluation Rubrics: Exercise 2

Answers will vary. Responses should reflect an understanding of skimming, scanning, and careful reading. The reading style chosen for each assignment should be appropriate to the chosen material.

Additional Resources

📁 *Thinking and Study Skills,* pp. 2–4, 8, 18, 30–32, 34–36, 39–40

📁 *Listening and Speaking Activities,* pp. 10–11

Close

Encourage students to discuss some of their own purposes for reading. What do they tend to read most often? Which reading strategies would be most appropriate for these types of reading?

Careful reading requires that you pay attention to whether you understand the material. You may need to read difficult passages more than once. For example, you need to read technical or scientific material very slowly and carefully to make sure you understand the ideas. If the material contains unfamiliar or technical terms, be sure to define and clarify those words or phrases. If the book has no glossary, keep a dictionary handy to look up unfamiliar terms.

Three Strategies for Reading

Strategy	Purpose	Examples of Purpose
Skimming	Looking over a piece of writing fairly quickly to get an overall view of its content	Will I like this book of short stories? What is this article about? What are the main ideas of this chapter? How is this unit organized? What will I learn from this lesson?
Scanning	Looking rapidly over a piece of writing to find a particular piece or type of information	Does this book tell about the Trail of Tears? What are the characteristics of a sonnet? What key terms will I need to know to understand this chapter? Will I learn anything from this book about African Americans in the Civil War?
Careful Reading	Slowly and carefully reading a piece of writing in order to fully understand its content	What is the purpose of this article? What happens to the characters in this novel? What is this writer trying to say about changes in the English language? What can I learn about computers from this book?

Exercise 2

List some of the reading you have done, both for classes and for yourself, in the past several weeks. Next to each assignment write which of the three reading strategies listed above you would use, and tell why. Meet with a small group of your classmates to compare and discuss your lists.

Study Skills

Viewing and Representing

Evaluating Visual Formats

As students look at the chart on this page, ask them if they think this visual format makes it easier to understand the meanings of the three terms. Discuss with students how the columns of the chart lead their eyes from left to right for each term, enabling them to find the connecting information. Tell them to write one paragraph recording the information from the chart. Which is easier to read and understand—the chart or the paragraph? Suggest that students work in groups to construct a similar chart on another topic.

24.3 Writing Summaries

Have you ever told a friend about a movie you saw or a book you read? Have you ever explained to a classmate what was covered in a class he or she missed? Summarizing—telling the main ideas of something—saves time. Imagine trying to tell someone every single detail about a movie. It could take longer than the movie itself.

Summarizing in your own words also helps you to organize and remember ideas. After preparing a written summary of something, you'll find that you understand it better.

When to Summarize

Summarizing can help you almost anytime you need to understand and remember ideas or facts. The following chart shows some situations in which you might need to prepare a written summary of some sort.

Summarizing	
SITUATION	**KINDS OF SUMMARIES**
Preparing a written or oral research report	Brief restatements of the important facts and ideas from the various sources you used
Listening to lectures, speeches, or discussions	Notes on the main ideas from the lecture, speech, or discussion
Viewing a film or video documentary	Notes on the main ideas or techniques of the documentary
Reading textbook material	A restatement of the most important information in the textbook

How to Summarize

When you summarize a movie for a friend, you include all the important ideas or events. However, you leave out most of the details. In the same way, a good written summary includes only the main ideas. It leaves out examples and other supporting details.

24.3 Writing Summaries   **689**

Study Skills

Lesson Overview

Objectives
- To understand the elements of a good summary
- To write effective summaries

Skills
- understanding when written summaries are helpful; knowing how to write summaries

Critical Thinking
- summarizing; identifying main ideas; categorizing

Listening and Speaking
- discussing; taking notes

Bellringer
Daily Language Activity

When students enter the classroom, have this assignment on the board: *On a piece of paper, write the name of a movie or TV show you enjoyed recently. Then write one or two sentences that tell what the movie or show was about.*

See also *Daily Language Practice*

Teach

Practicing Summarizing

Select a self-contained passage of several paragraphs from a textbook or a magazine article. Read it aloud to the students, suggesting that they take notes as you read. Afterward, ask them to suggest ways of summing up the passage succinctly without leaving out any of the main ideas. Discuss their summaries. Remind students that summarizing involves distinguishing essential information from non-essential information.
L2

Resource Manager

 **Planning Resources**
- *Lesson Plans*

 **Transparencies**
- *Bellringer*
- *Daily Language Practice*

📂 **Other Print Resources**
- *Listening and Speaking Activities,* pp. 10–11
- *Thinking and Study Skills,* pp. 2–4, 8, 18, 30–32, 34–36, 39–40

Practice and Assess

Evaluation Rubrics: Exercise 3

Answers will vary. Summaries should reflect the main ideas of the articles selected. They should be comprehensible to someone who has not read the full article.

Additional Resources

📁 *Thinking and Study Skills,* pp. 2–4, 8, 18, 30–32, 34–36, 39–40
📁 *Listening and Speaking Activities,* pp. 10–11

Close

Ask students to reread the opening paragraph of this lesson and the paragraphs about when and how to summarize. Suggest that they take notes as they read. Have them use their notes to summarize for a classmate what they learned in Lesson 24.3.

When you write a summary, you should put the ideas in your own words. Using the author's words is quoting directly, not summarizing. Occasionally you may wish to quote a sentence or a phrase from the author. If you do so, be sure to use quotation marks around the author's words.

Compare the student summary below with the original text shown. Notice how the summary shortens the original but still includes the most important information.

Ferdinand Magellan (1480?–152... ...mmanded the first European voyage to sai... around the world, Magellan wa... his expedition was backed by t... monarch Charles I. What Ma... find for Spain was a westwar...

The Spice Islands (the Mo... lured Magellan on his histo... thought he could reach the... sailing west across the Atl...

The voyage began in 1... three years later in 1522... crew members and one... the voyage and returned to Spain. Mag... himself was killed in the Philippines in April 1521. Nevertheless, he is remembered as a great navigator and the first to command an around-the-world voyage.

> Portuguese navigator Ferdinand Magellan commanded a 1519–1522 Spanish voyage to the Spice Islands. Magellan did not live to complete the voyage. However, he is remembered for being the first to show that it was possible to sail around the world.

Exercise 3

Find a short, interesting article in an encyclopedia or some other written source. If you wish, you can select about three or four paragraphs from a longer article. Write a brief summary of the selection you choose. Remember to use your own words.

Study Skills

Viewing and Representing

Making a Chart

After students have looked at the chart of situations and kinds of summaries on page 689, ask them to make a chart of their own, showing the best kinds of summaries for each of the following situations:
• watching a TV documentary on healthful eating

• reading a magazine article that will furnish material for a classroom report on Peru
• listening to a speaker talk about the importance of exercise
• watching a film on photosynthesis in science class

24.4 Making a Study Plan

Imagine having extra time each week to do what you want without losing study time. One way to gain additional free time is by learning efficient study habits. To get the most out of your study time, try making a study plan.

Setting Goals

Music, art, or physical education classes might not require much work outside the classroom. On the other hand, you could have daily homework in math or many pages to read weekly in social studies. Begin by making a chart of all your classes that require some study time. Next to each class, write any assignments you have received. Then set your goals for each class.

A goal is an objective you want to achieve. Learning to play the piano is a goal. Understanding the rules of grammar is another goal. Simply completing any school assignment, such as reading twenty pages of a textbook, can be a goal.

Get in the habit of always studying in the same place. That will help you concentrate when you sit down to study.

Always check a calendar that shows assignment due dates and the dates on which you will complete your goals.

Keep your study supplies—pencils, notebooks, dictionary—at your study place so you don't waste time looking for them.

Study Skills

Focus

Lesson Overview

Objectives
- To develop an understanding of study plans
- To learn how to make an effective study plan

Skills
- identifying long- and short-term goals; creating a study-plan calendar

Critical Thinking
- analyzing; defining and clarifying; decision making; visualizing

Listening and Speaking
- discussing

Bellringer
Daily Language Activity

When students enter the classroom, have this assignment on the board: *Draw a picture or a diagram of your idea of the perfect place for studying. Use your imagination and show as many details as possible.*

See also *Daily Language Practice*

Motivating Activity

Have students imagine they must write a report on a continent. With class participation, make a flow chart on the chalkboard using student examples for short-term and long-term goals. The flow chart should show main goals and due dates, then a breakdown of smaller goals and due dates.

Resource Manager

📁 **Planning Resources**
- *Lesson Plans*

📁 **Transparencies**
- *Bellringer*
- *Daily Language Practice*

📁 **Other Print Resources**
- *Listening and Speaking Activities,* pp. 10–11
- *Thinking and Study Skills,* pp. 2–4, 8, 18, 30–32, 34–36, 39–40

Teach

Learning to Identify Goals

Remind students that a goal is something they want to make happen, such as earning money for new clothes or achieving a personal best in sports. Help them picture short-term goals as a series of small steps; with each step they can get closer to a larger, long-term goal. An example might be saving a little money each week from a job in order to ultimately buy something important. Have students use the same technique to identify a long- or short-term study goal for a particular subject. **L1**

Analyzing Interests

Help students analyze their interests and predict their future professional goals. Students might research jobs at the library and write brief job descriptions to share with the class. **L3**

Study Skills

Divide school assignments into short-term goals and long-term goals. Short-term goals are those that can be completed in one study session. Learning ten new spelling words or reading a few pages in a textbook are short-term goals. A long-term goal might be completing a research report, reading a novel, or preparing for a unit test.

Long-term goals can be broken down into smaller tasks. For example, studying for a unit test might require reviewing one chapter per study session. Completing a research report would include many short-term tasks. Looking for resources, gathering information, listing and outlining ideas, and writing a rough draft are some examples. Be realistic about what you can do in a study session of one or two hours. For instance, you probably can't read a novel or plan and write a report in one session.

Scheduling Study Time

Setting goals is important, but just as important is setting deadlines to reach your goals. The tool that will help you reach your goals is a study-plan calendar. After you have listed your goals, write each one on your calendar. For long-term goals, first write the final due date. For example, if you have a unit test on the nineteenth, write that on your calendar. Then work backward from the final due date and write each short-term goal on the date that you will work on it. You might want to set goals of reviewing, say, one chapter each day for a week.

You may have a test in science and an oral report in English both due on Monday. If so, you need to carefully balance your study time for both so that you are not overwhelmed. Also, remember to write your goals on your study calendar as soon as you receive your assignments. You don't want to remember some night as you go to bed that you have an English test the following morning!

Be sure to write other important activities, such as sports, music lessons, or school club meetings, on your calendar as well. You probably wouldn't want to schedule writing a draft of a report on the same day that you have a band recital. The calendar on the next page shows a student's study calendar. You can use it as a model for one of your own.

Technology Tip

Using Electronic Calendars

Inform students that some computer programs contain weekly or monthly appointment calendars that can be adapted to list goals. When students complete, change, or add a goal, they can update their lists easily. If they use a computer at home, they might find it helpful to consult, or even print a copy of their schedules of goals before beginning each study session.

Monthly Planner Month October

Sunday	Monday	Tuesday	Wednesday	Thursday	Friday	Saturday
				1	**2**	**3**
4	**5** Study for social studies quiz	**6** Social studies quiz Read the story "To Build a Fire"	**7** Library research for science report	**8** Study new vocabulary words, English Complete exercise 12, math	**9** Do outline of science report English quiz on vocabulary words Hand in exercise 12, math	**10**
11	**12** start rough draft of science report	**13** write rough draft of science report	**14** Read chapter 26, social studies	**15** Revise rough draft, science report	**16** Learn new vocabulary words, English Complete exercise 13, math	**17**
18 Type finished science report English quiz on vocabulary words Hand in exercise 13, math	**19** Proofread science report	**20** Hand in science report	**21**	**22**	**23**	**24**
25	**26**	**27**	**28**	**29**	**30**	**31**

Top Priority List

Important Phone Calls

Messages – Reminders

No. HT-1502 – Monthly

Visual Organizers, Inc. – 1987

Practice and Assess

Evaluation Rubrics: Exercise 4

Answers will vary. Assignment calendars should demonstrate good judgment and effective use of time. Goals should be clearly written and appropriately entered.

Additional Resources

📁 *Thinking and Study Skills,* pp. 2–4, 8, 18, 30–32, 34–36, 39–40

📁 *Listening and Speaking Activities,* pp. 10–11

Close

Have students choose a particular subject area and then write out the steps they will take to develop a study plan for a week of assignments in that class.

Exercise 4

Work with a classmate to make a list of your classes and the assignments due in each class. Discuss what special activities, such as sports or music lessons, you should include. Discuss with each other ways of breaking down long-term goals into several short-term goals. Discuss what amount of time should be given to each goal. Then prepare an assignment calendar for one month, based on the list you develop.

Study Skills

24.4 Making a Study Plan **693**

Cultural Connections

Egyptian Calendars

The Egyptians were probably the first people to adopt a predominantly solar, rather than lunar, calendar. They noticed that the Dog Star, Sirius, was not visible in the sky for several months and then would suddenly appear. Shortly afterward, the Nile river always flooded. The

Egyptians used this knowledge to plan a calendar of twelve 30-day months that added up to a 365-day year, with five days added at the end. However, they did not allow for the extra fourth of a day, which the modern calendar accommodates by having a leap year every four years.

24.5

Focus

Lesson Overview

Objectives
- To become familiar with the SQ3R Method
- To learn how to apply the SQ3R Method to classroom assignments

Skills
- skimming text; developing questions; reading to answer questions; recording answers; checking answers

Critical Thinking
- analyzing; defining and clarifying; recalling; summarizing

Listening and Speaking
- discussing; taking notes

 Bellringer
Daily Language Activity

When students enter the classroom, have this assignment on the board: *Write a list of the steps you take when you read a class assignment.*

See also *Daily Language Practice*

Teach

Using the Five *W's* and *H*

Write the words *who, what, when, where, why,* and *how* on the chalkboard. Have volunteers read headings from a chapter in a social studies or science text. With help from the class, write a question that begins with any of the five *W's* or *H* for each heading. Explain that when students read the chapter on their own, they will be able to answer these questions. **L1**

24.5 Using the SQ3R Method

Good study habits involve working efficiently and using an appropriate study strategy. The SQ3R study method will make your study time more productive. The SQ3R method is based on five steps: Survey, Question, Read, Record, Review.

You can use the SQ3R method with any subject. Once you have learned the method and use it regularly, it will become a habit. Using the method, you will remember more of what you read and will understand it better. You will also be better prepared to participate in class.

You **survey** by skimming the text quickly. (See pages 687–688 for hints on skimming.) Remember, look for the main ideas in the material. Pay attention to any sentences or terms that are highlighted. Also look at all photographs, graphs, maps, and other illustrations. Think about how the graphic material is related to the main ideas.

The next step is to **question.** Write out a list of questions that you want to have answered when you read the material. For example, suppose you are studying a section on Ferdinand Magellan in your social studies text. You might write such questions as, Who was Ferdinand Magellan? What was Magellan looking for on his voyage? Why was his voyage important? If you are studying a textbook that has its own review questions, add those to your list. Having a list of questions before you begin reading will help you focus on important ideas in the material.

Read through the material slowly and carefully. As you read, take notes about the main ideas and look for answers to your questions. Also, as you read, you may add questions to your list. Make sure you understand each paragraph or passage.

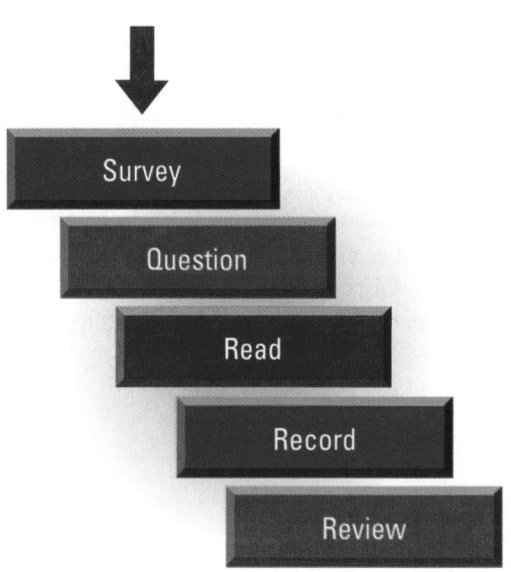

Resource Manager

Planning Resources
- *Lesson Plans*

Transparencies
- *Bellringer*
- *Daily Language Practice*

Other Print Resources
- *Listening and Speaking Activities,* pp. 10–11
- *Thinking and Study Skills,* pp. 2–4, 8, 18, 30–32, 34–36, 39–40

After you have carefully read the material, **record** the answers to your questions. Don't look in the book. Rely on your memory of what you have read to answer the questions. In this way, you will test whether you have really learned the material. If you have to struggle to answer the questions, you may need to reread the material.

After answering the questions, check your answers against the material you have read. If you have missed any answers, **review** that section again. Following your review, rephrase your questions, or write new ones that cover the same material. Continue rewriting questions and reviewing the material until you are able to answer all questions correctly. Keep your review questions and answers in your notebook. You can use this material later to study or to review for tests.

Exercise 5

Choose from history a famous person who interests you. Read an encyclopedia article about that person, using the SQ3R method. Be sure you take notes, and prepare and answer your review questions carefully. After you have studied the material using the SQ3R method, answer the following questions. Try to do so without referring to your notes.

1. What was the full name of the person you read about?
2. What accomplishment is this person most noted for?
3. What inspired this person to achieve?
4. When did this person live, and when did this person achieve something notable?
5. Where was this person born, or where did this person live most of his or her life?
6. Where did this person make his or her most important accomplishment?
7. Why is this person important in history?
8. How, if at all, is your life different because of this person?

Practice and Assess

Evaluation Rubrics: Exercise 5

Answers will vary. Responses should reflect a good grasp of the key facts about the chosen person's life and importance.

Additional Resources

📂 *Thinking and Study Skills,* pp. 2–4, 8, 18, 30–32, 34–36, 39–40

📂 *Listening and Speaking Activities,* pp.10–11

Close

Have students explain, either in discussion or in a brief writing assignment, how to use each of the steps in the SQ3R Method.

Study Skills

Enrichment and Extension

Science

Have students determine the extent to which they can rely on their memories to answer questions after reading a scientific or technical article in an encyclopedia. They might quiz each other to test their understanding about topics that contain detailed descriptions, such as how an internal combustion engine works. Then discuss how graphic organizers help readers better understand and remember material that contains new or difficult concepts.

Focus

Lesson Overview

Objectives
- To become familiar with taking notes while listening and reading
- To organize notes into outline form

Skills
- outlining; taking notes

Critical Thinking
- identifying main ideas; classifying; summarizing

Listening and Speaking
- taking notes; discussing

Bellringer
Daily Language Activity

When students enter the classroom, have this assignment on the board: *List three situations in which you might need to take notes. Why?*

See also *Daily Language Practice*

Motivating Activity

Play an audio tape of a famous speech, such as Martin Luther King Jr.'s "I Have a Dream" speech. Tell students to note what they think is important. After they have finished, have them exchange papers with a classmate who will circle key words in the notes. (Key words from King's speech might include *dream, equal, freedom,* and *justice.*) Have partners compare notes. They can ask each other what ideas and statements might be listed under each of the key words if they were to make an outline together.

Study Skills

24.6 Taking Notes and Outlining

Suppose someone asked you to go to the grocery store to pick up ten different items. What would you do to be sure you remembered all the items? Write them down, of course! Most people don't remember *everything* they read or hear, or even *most* of what they read or hear. That's why taking notes is important.

Taking Notes

As a student, you will need to remember many things. What was said in a classroom discussion? What main ideas were presented in a video documentary shown in class? What important ideas did you find when researching a topic for a report?

While Listening Taking notes during classroom lectures or discussions or while viewing films will help you remember what you hear. You can't write down every word that is said. Instead, listen for ideas the speaker emphasizes. Write the key words of those main ideas. Then write the key words for each supporting detail or example the speaker gives to support a main idea.

Highlight or star major ideas or categories of information. Underline important ideas or examples.

Don't try to write notes in complete sentences. Use numbers, dashes, abbreviations, and symbols to save time.

☆ *Water pollution*
   1. *oil spills—tankers*
   2. *chemical wastes—industry*
☆ *Air pollution*
   1. *exhaust fumes—autos*
   2. *carbon dioxide—factories, forest fires*
☆ *Land pollution*
   1. *garbage—landfills*
   2. *industrial waste—dumping*

Resource Manager

📂 **Planning Resources**
- *Lesson Plans*

📁 **Transparencies**
- *Bellringer*
- *Daily Language Practice*

📂 **Other Print Resources**
- *Listening and Speaking Activities,* pp. 10–11
- *Thinking and Study Skills,* pp. 2–4, 8, 18, 30–32, 34–36, 39–40

While Reading Naturally, you don't want to copy down everything you read when doing research for a report. Have a specific topic or theme in mind when you begin your research. Take notes on just the information you think is important to your topic. Summarize that information in your own words, using as few words as possible.

Write your notes on 3 x 5 note cards. Use a new card for each source or each bit of information you read. At the top of the card write the name of your source, its author, and the page numbers where you found the information. You will need this information for your report. You may also need to go back to a source to look for further information.

Avoid copying long direct quotations. When using a quotation, make sure you copy the words exactly as they appear in the source. Enclose them in quotation marks, and include the name of the person being quoted.

Michael Wyeth, The Story of Romulus and Remus, pp.127–140.
According to legend they were twin boys brought up by a fe[r]
decided to build a n[ew]
Tiber River. Romul[us]
argument. Then he

> Always record the source of your information, that is, the title, author, and page numbers of the book or article.

Janet Harper, The City of Rome, pp. 23--25.
Rome has been an important city for more than 2,000 years. According to legend it was founded by twin brothers Romulus and Remus, 753 B.C. Rome began as a small village built on seven hills along the Tiber River in Italy.

> Summarize the information in your own words. Write only the main ideas and important supporting details.

Study Skills

Teach

Unscrambling Outlines

Demonstrate how an outline serves to organize and present important main ideas and details. Prepare some index cards with main topics that focus on one subject, such as *Coyotes.* (Topics might include *hunting, environment,* and *role in legends.*) Then prepare several subtopic cards, such as *Navajo legends* or *desert environment.* Finally, prepare several fact cards with phrases or sentences, such as *clever trickster* or *they hunt rodents.* Students can work cooperatively to lay out the cards as they would wish to present them in an outline. Explain that the outline is like a puzzle. The completed outline should form a picture of the subject. Students should check that the outline proceeds from big ideas to smaller facts. **L2**

Cooperative Learning

Taking notes in a Study Group

Use the Think-Pair-Share technique to have students take notes on 3 x 5 note cards. Provide each group with a non-fiction book and three note cards. Ask each group to choose one chapter from the book and use the SQ3R study method. Have pairs skim, scan, and question each other.

Then have the pairs choose a page from the chapter to take notes on and compare their notes with those taken by other pairs on the same page. Students should share with the class their note-taking experiences and any facts they learned.

Practice and Assess

Evaluation Rubrics: Exercise 6

Answers will vary. The group-prepared outlines should reflect an understanding of outline form and demonstrate a coherent structure of main ideas, subtopics, and divisions of subtopics.

Additional Resources

📁 *Thinking and Study Skills,*
   pp. 2–4, 8, 18, 30–32, 34–36, 39–40
📁 *Listening and Speaking Activities,*
   pp. 10–11

Close

Suggest that students apply their note-taking and outlining skills in one of their classes. Have them report back to the class in the next several days about their experiences.

Outlining

After you finish your research, organize the information on your note cards. Examine the information on each card, and group cards with similar ideas together. Each group can be a main topic. Within each group, separate cards into subgroups. These will become subtopics in your outline.

You might try several ways of organizing your cards to see which works best. The order you use will depend on your topic. A history of early Rome would probably require chronological order, or the order in which events happened. A science paper on pollution could be ordered by cause and effect, showing how one thing causes another.

Following is an example of the start of an outline.

Use Roman numerals to number your main topics. Main topics are the "big ideas."

Indent and use letters and numbers for subtopics and their divisions. If a main topic has subtopics, there must be at least two of them.

If you divide a subtopic, there must be at least two divisions.

The Eternal City
I. The Founding of Rome
  A. The Myth of Romulus and Remus
    1. Twins cared for by wolf
    2. Romulus kills Remus and builds Rome
  B. Began as small village built on seven hills
II. Rome Becomes Powerful
  A. Romans defeat Etruscans
  B. Conquer neighbors in Italy

Study Skills

Exercise 6

Work with a small group of classmates. Brainstorm to make a list of topics for a report. As a group, choose one of the topics. Then have group members read and take notes about the topic from a variety of resources. Look over the group's notes and decide on a method of organization for the material. Then, as a group, prepare an outline for a report on the topic.

698   Unit 24 Study Skills

MEETING INDIVIDUAL NEEDS   Less-Proficient Readers

Using Note Cards

Using note cards before writing the outline can help students organize information. Help students place the main topic note card at the top of their desks, and then group together the subtopic cards. Have students do the same for the division cards, grouping and arranging them below the appropriate subtopics. When students feel their information is organized, they can begin to write their outlines.

24.7 Understanding Graphic Information

Have you ever read so many facts at once that you had trouble grasping them? A paragraph containing many numbers, for example, could leave you wondering what the main point is. Tables, graphs, and other graphic aids often do a better job of organizing information for you than text.

Tables

Tables organize information by putting it into categories arranged into columns and rows. You can read a table from top to bottom in columns or from left to right across rows. Look at the table below. Suppose you need information about immigration in the 1980s. Find the heading 1981–1990 at the top of the table and read down that column. To see how Asian immigration changed from the 1960s through the 1980s, read across the row labeled Asia.

Immigration to the United States by Region (Numbers in 1,000s)

REGIONS	1961–1970	1971–1980	1981–1990
Europe	1,238.6	801.3	705.6
Asia	445.3	1,633.8	2,817.4
The Americas	1,582.3	1,929.4	3,580.9
Africa	39.3	91.5	192.3
All Other	19.1	37.3	41.9

The title tells you what kind of information the table contains.

Headings along the top and labels at the left side help you locate the information you need.

Note that numbers are given in 1,000s. The number 705.6, therefore, means 705,600 immigrants.

Graphs

Graphs are used to show groups of numbers. The numbers in a table, in fact, can often be turned into a graph. Two types of graphs you will see often in your schoolwork are bar graphs and circle graphs. Examples of both types of graphs are shown on the following page.

Study Skills

24.7 Understanding Graphic Information **699**

Focus

Lesson Overview

Objective
- To become familiar with graphic information

Skills
- reading tables; understanding bar and circle graphs; reading maps; understanding diagrams

Critical Thinking
- visualizing; contrasting; comparing; summarizing

Listening and Speaking
- discussing

Bellringer
Daily Language Activity

When students enter the classroom, have this assignment on the board: *List school subjects in which maps, graphs, tables, or diagrams could help you understand information. Then write a sentence explaining why graphic aids are useful learning tools.*

See also *Daily Language Practice*

Motivating Activity

Discuss with students why viewing complex data in graphic aids can make the data easier to understand and remember.

Resource Manager

📁 **Planning Resources**
- *Lesson Plans*

🖥 **Transparencies**
- *Bellringer*
- *Daily Language Practice*

📁 **Other Print Resources**
- *Listening and Speaking Activities*, pp. 10–11
- *Thinking and Study Skills*, pp. 2–4, 8, 18, 30–32, 34–36, 39–40

Teach

Making a Bar Graph

Draw a table on the chalkboard with the following data:

Star	Distance in Light Years	Temperature (°C)
Pollux	40	4900
Canopus	100	7200
Antares	400	3500

Work with the class to create two bar graphs showing the same information presented in the table. Discuss how the table differs from the bar graphs. Ask which type of graphic aid works better and why. **L2**

Answers: Bar Graph Callout

Asian immigration has increased the most.

Answers: Circle Graph Callout

Africa and "all others" are closest.

Bar Graphs   Each number in a bar graph is represented by a bar. The graph can have horizontal (left to right) or vertical (bottom to top) bars. The length or height of the bar indicates the size of the number. The bar graph below shows some of the same information that the table on page 699 shows. Notice how the heights of the bars allow you to compare the numbers easily.

The scale at the left tells what the numbers mean. It also allows you to measure how much or how many of something each bar stands for.

You can quickly see how immigration has changed since the 1960s. From what region has the number of immigrants increased the most since the 1960s?

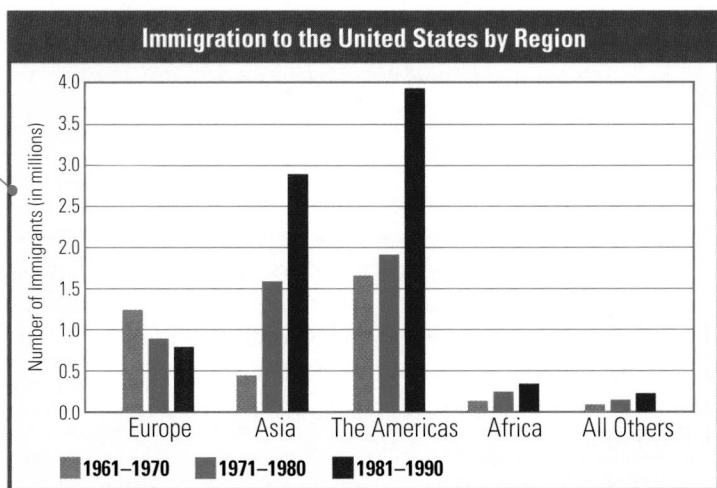

Circle Graphs   In a circle graph, information is presented as slices of a "pie." (Circle graphs are sometimes called pie charts.) The graph begins with a circle that stands for the whole of something. For example, the whole circle could represent the world population. Each slice of the circle shows a part of the whole. If the whole circle is the world's immigrant population, each slice could show the immigrant population of one region.

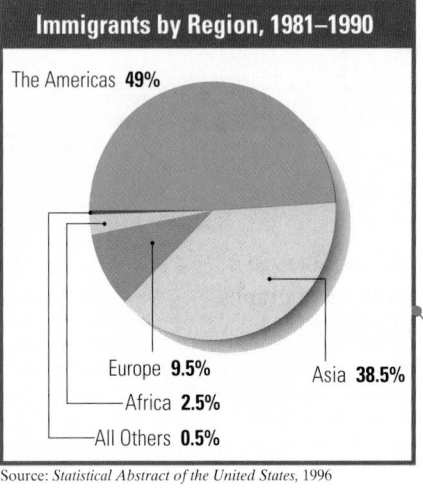

Source: *Statistical Abstract of the United States*, 1996

Notice how easy it is to compare the sizes of the slices. Which two regions come closest in numbers of immigrants?

Study Skills

700   Unit 24 Study Skills

English Language Learners

MEETING INDIVIDUAL NEEDS

Exploring Graphic Aids

Often students acquiring English can understand information more easily when it is presented graphically than when the same information is given in text. Graphs can communicate considerable information in few words, using clear symbols and numbers that are widely understood. Encourage students to study the graphs on this page and to explain to a partner their interpretation of the data.

Since a circle graph shows parts of a whole, the slices are often marked as percentages. The whole circle is 100 percent—or *all*. The percentages of all the slices add up to 100 percent. The circle graph on the previous page shows information taken from the table on page 699.

Maps

Maps show a portion of the earth's surface. Maps can show a variety of information. Physical maps show natural features of the earth's surface, such as rivers and mountains. Political maps show the boundaries of countries, states, and other political divisions, as well as cities. Physical and political features are often combined on a single map. Historical maps may show areas held by particular groups during a certain period in history. They may show changes in boundaries over time or other historical information.

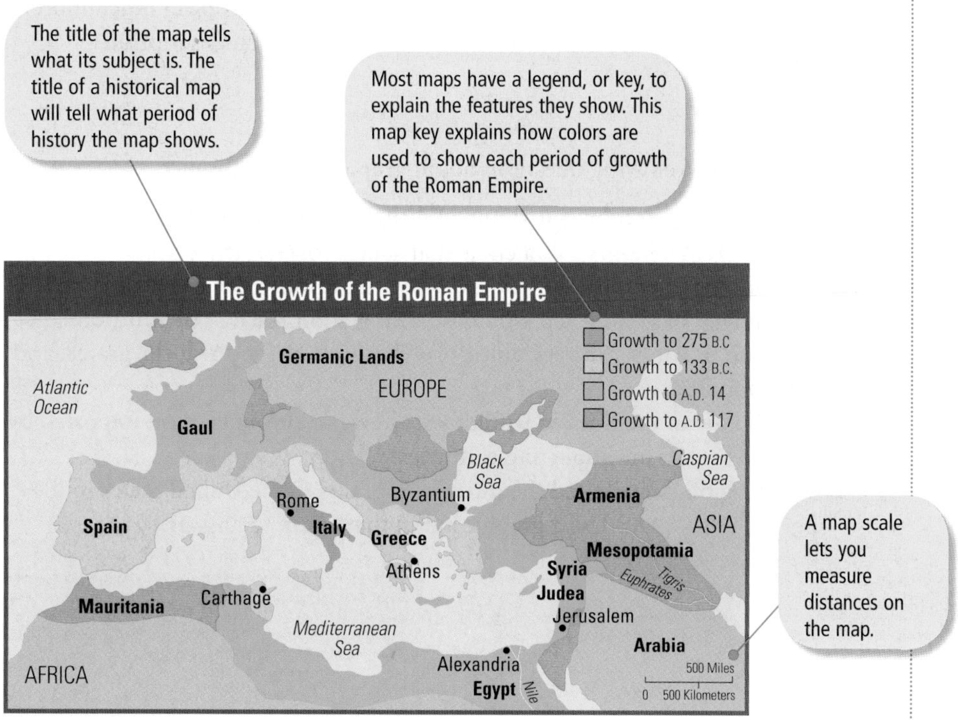

The title of the map tells what its subject is. The title of a historical map will tell what period of history the map shows.

Most maps have a legend, or key, to explain the features they show. This map key explains how colors are used to show each period of growth of the Roman Empire.

The Growth of the Roman Empire

Growth to 275 B.C
Growth to 133 B.C.
Growth to A.D. 14
Growth to A.D. 117

Atlantic Ocean · Germanic Lands · EUROPE · Gaul · Black Sea · Caspian Sea · Byzantium · Armenia · ASIA · Rome · Italy · Greece · Spain · Mesopotamia · Athens · Syria · Euphrates · Tigris · Judea · Mauritania · Carthage · Mediterranean Sea · Jerusalem · Arabia · AFRICA · Alexandria · Egypt · Nile

A map scale lets you measure distances on the map.

500 Miles
0   500 Kilometers

24.7 Understanding Graphic Information   **701**

Study Skills

Teach

Making a Table

Give students social studies books, and ask them to locate information that does not appear as a table—for example, population statistics, the characteristics of the three branches of government, and so on. Tell students to organize the information into a table to present to the class. As they make their presentations, have students tell the difference between reading information in sentence form and reading information in a table. **L3**

Viewing and Representing

Reading a Map

Use transparencies of maps showing rainfall, population density, and land forms to help students understand the importance of map-reading skills. Ask students to answer questions such as the following:

- What is the purpose of the map?
- What kind of information does the map key give?
- What color shows the heaviest population?
- What color shows the least rainfall?

Practice and Assess

Answers: Exercise 7

1. map
2. diagram
3. circle graph
4. bar graph or table
5. the Americas

Additional Resources

📁 *Thinking and Study Skills,*
pp. 2–4, 8, 18, 30–32, 34–36, 39–40

📁 *Listening and Speaking Activities,*
pp. 10–11

Close

Discuss the following questions with students: Which type of graphic aid do you find most helpful? Which kind is easiest for you to understand? Why? Which type confuses you most? Why?

Study Skills

Diagrams

Has someone ever tried to describe an unfamiliar object or process to you? Perhaps you had trouble understanding it until he or she drew a picture. Being able to picture the parts of an object or to picture how the object works can help you understand it. That's why we use diagrams.

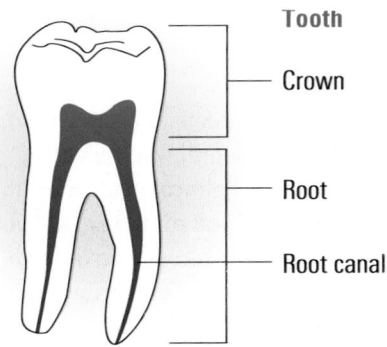

Many diagrams are cutaways that show the inside of something you would not normally see.

Diagrams are pictures that show a process or show relationships among parts of an object. In some diagrams, each part of an object is labeled. A label may include an explanation of what that part does or how it relates to the whole. Diagrams help you understand an object much more easily than if you had a written or spoken description.

Exercise 7

Answer the following questions about graphic information.

1. Which type of graphic aid would best show the areas controlled by Egypt in 1800 B.C.?
2. Which type of graphic aid would best show how the space shuttle works?
3. Which type of graphic aid would best show what portion of your total diet is made up of fruits and vegetables, protein foods, dairy products, grains, and other foods?
4. Which type of graphic aid would best show the amounts of oil imported by the five biggest oil-importing countries?
5. What region contributed the most immigrants to the United States in the period 1981–1990? Use a graphic aid in this lesson to answer.

702 Unit 24 Study Skills

Enrichment and Extension

Constructing a Diagram

Encourage students to use the diagram on this page as a model to draw a cross-section diagram of some familiar object that contains different layers, such as an apple (skin, fruit, core, seeds) or a candy bar (e.g., chocolate, caramel, fruit, or nuts). Tell them to label the parts.

24.8 Using Memory

Think of the trouble you'd have multiplying 1,634 x 391 if you didn't know the multiplication tables. (You may not always have a pocket calculator handy.) Memorizing certain information helps you in your schoolwork. It saves you the time of looking up the same facts over and over.

How to Memorize

The most often-used memory technique is repetition—just repeating something over and over. Putting a group of items in some order can make them easier to remember. Alphabetical order, smallest to largest, and nearest to farthest are some possible ways of ordering items.

Writing out what you want to memorize is a good technique. Writing out poems, sayings, or long lists and saying them aloud as you write will help you memorize them.

Tricks for Remembering

Another way of remembering material is by using tricks such as sayings or rhymes. The chart shows a few examples.

Tricks for Remembering	
Purpose	**Memory Aid**
To remember the year Columbus sailed to the Americas	In fourteen hundred and ninety-two, Columbus sailed the ocean blue.
To remember that the order of the planets from the Sun is <u>M</u>ercury, <u>V</u>enus, <u>E</u>arth, <u>M</u>ars, <u>J</u>upiter, <u>S</u>aturn, <u>U</u>ranus, <u>N</u>eptune, and <u>P</u>luto	<u>M</u>y <u>v</u>ery <u>e</u>xcellent <u>m</u>other <u>j</u>ust <u>s</u>erved <u>u</u>s <u>n</u>ine <u>p</u>izzas.
To remember that the order of colors in a rainbow is <u>r</u>ed, <u>o</u>range, <u>y</u>ellow, <u>g</u>reen, <u>b</u>lue, <u>i</u>ndigo, and <u>v</u>iolet	Roy G. Biv
To remember that the person who runs a school is a princip<u>al</u>, not a princip<u>le</u>	The princip<u>al</u> is my p<u>al</u>.

24.8

Focus

Lesson Overview

Objectives
- To become familiar with different ways of memorizing
- To use various mnemonic devices and strategies for memorizing

Skills
- memorizing; creating memory aids; recalling facts

Critical Thinking
- comparing; relating; using criteria; visualizing

Listening and Speaking
- discussing; listening for clues

 Bellringer
Daily Language Activity

When students enter the classroom, have this assignment on the board: *Recall a song or rhyme you know. List the factors that helped you memorize the words.*

See also *Daily Language Practice*

Teach

Study Skills

Using Mental Pictures

Tell students that while rhythm, rhyme, and repetition can help them memorize information, it is also helpful to create a vivid mental picture to accompany the words. Ask students to choose an item from the chart and form a mental image to go with it. Explain that making their images vivid, startling, and appealing will aid their understanding and their recall. For example, Roy G. Biv must be a very colorful character. How might he be dressed? What would his business card look like? To link planets with a saying about pizzas, students might imagine a night sky full of nine orbiting pizzas.
L1

Resource Manager

📂 **Planning Resources**
- *Lesson Plans*

📖 **Transparencies**
- *Bellringer*
- *Daily Language Practice*

📂 **Other Print Resources**
- *Listening and Speaking Activities,* pp. 10–11
- *Thinking and Study Skills,* pp. 2–4, 8, 18, 30–32, 34–36, 39–40

Practice and Assess

Evaluation Rubrics: Exercise 8

Answers will vary. Responses should contain easy tricks for memorizing the information, such as the following:

<u>O</u>ur <u>e</u>xhibit <u>h</u>ad <u>m</u>any <u>s</u>nakes.
<u>O</u>ne <u>e</u>ager <u>h</u>elper <u>m</u>ade <u>s</u>andwiches.

If order were not a priority, the word HOMES could help in remembering the lakes' names.

Exercise 9

Answers will vary. Responses should reflect an understanding of how mnemonic devices are used.

Additional Resources

📁 *Thinking and Study Skills*, pp. 2–4, 8, 18, 30–32, 34–36, 39–40
📁 *Listening and Speaking*, pp. 10–11

Close

Encourage students to work in small groups to develop a mnemonic device for remembering all of the countries in South America, Africa, Europe, or Asia.

✔ ASSESSMENT OPTIONS

📁 *Tests with Answer Key and Rubrics*
Unit 24 Mastery Test, pp. 99–100

💾 *Testmaker*
Unit 24 Mastery Test

📺 *MindJogger Videoquizzes*

You may wish to administer the Unit 24 Mastery Test at this point.

The memory aids in the chart are just a few of the common ones. You can make up your own tricks to help you remember information. For example, you may need to memorize the scientific classifications of living things: kingdom, phylum, class, order, family, genus, and species. You could make up a sentence in which the first letter of each word is the same as the first letter of each category. Try to use the names of familiar people or places. Using familiar names will make it easier to remember your sentence.

Rhymes are especially effective memory tricks. Poetry can be easier to remember than prose. Another effective trick is to see if the first letters of the items in a list spell a word or a name. For example, atoms contain <u>p</u>rotons, <u>e</u>lectrons, and a <u>n</u>ucleus. Think of a <u>pen</u> to remember that fact. The name Roy G. Biv in the chart on page 703 is another example. It's even easier if the items do not have to be memorized in order.

Experiment with these techniques the next time you need to memorize information. Try tricks of your own as well. You may find just the right techniques for your own use.

Exercise 8

Work with one or two classmates. Develop a memory trick to remember the names of the five Great Lakes from east to west: Ontario, Erie, Huron, Michigan, and Superior. Experiment with several of the techniques you learned in this lesson.

Exercise 9

With one or two classmates brainstorm some item of information that should be memorized, such as members of the animal kingdom or the names of important navigators during the Age of Exploration. Decide on the best technique for memorizing the information. Then develop a memory trick to remember it.

Study Skills

Cultural Connections

Remembering Mnemon

The word *mnemonic* comes from the Greek mythological figure, Mnemon. Achilles had been warned that he would die by Apollo's hand if he ever killed a son of the gods. It was the sole duty of Mnemon, one of his servants, to remind Achilles of this fact. While the Greeks were on their way to Troy, Mnemon failed to remind Achilles, who killed Thenedos, a son of Apollo. Mnemon was put to death for this dereliction of duty. During the Trojan War, Apollo guided Paris's arrow to Achilles' heel, the only vulnerable part of his body.

UNIT
25 Taking Tests

Objectives

- To learn about test-taking strategies and to use them effectively
- To identify various types of test items and to respond to them effectively
- To become familiar with standardized test questions and to develop useful methods for approaching them
- To gain an understanding of standardized tests and to practice taking them

✔ ASSESSMENT OPTIONS

📁 *Tests with Answer Key & Rubrics*
Unit 25 Pretest, pp. 101–102

💾 *Testmaker*
Unit 25 Pretest

You may wish to administer the Unit 25 Pretest at this point.

Key to Ability Levels

L1 Level 1 activities are within the basic ability range of students.

L2 Level 2 activities are within the ability range of average students.

L3 Level 3 activities are more challenging activities.

705

Resource Manager

📁 **Planning Resources**
- *Lesson Plans*
- *Block Scheduling*

📠 **Transparencies**
- *Bellringer*
- *Daily Language Practice*

📁 **Other Print Resources**
- *SAT-9 Preparation and Practice*
- *Taking Standardized Tests*
- *Tests with Answer Key and Rubrics*
- *Thinking and Study Skills*

📼 **Video**
- *MindJogger Videoquizzes*

💾 **Software**
- *Presentation Plus!*
- *Testmaker*

🖥 **Web Sites**
- *writerschoice.glencoe.com*

Focus

Lesson Overview

Objectives
- To learn how to prepare for a test and how to take one effectively
- To implement strategies for studying and test-taking

Skills
- reviewing notes; making a study plan; managing time

Critical Thinking
- generating questions; establishing criteria

Listening and Speaking
- meeting as a group; taking notes; listening accurately

Bellringer
Daily Language Activity

When students enter the classroom, have this assignment on the board: *List three things you normally do to prepare for a test.*

See also 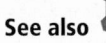 *Daily Language Practice*

Motivating Activity

Ask students to share their answers to the Bellringer activity. Tell students to take notes on any new tips they might want to incorporate into their test-taking strategies. Have students monitor their understanding and seek clarification as needed.

Teach

Preparing with a Group

Ask students how they feel about taking tests. Do they usually feel relaxed and confident during a test, or does the experience make them nervous? How does the way they prepare for a test affect their feelings while taking it? Point out that by preparing with a small study group, students can pretest each other and make use of each

other's knowledge about a subject. Divide the class into small study groups and ask each group to brainstorm a list of study questions that would help them prepare for a test on Unit 24 of this book. Encourage them to generate sample test questions and practice answering them. **L2**

25.1 Test-Taking Strategies

Your teacher has just announced you will have an English test in two weeks. How will you get ready for it? Careful attention to daily classroom assignments and discussions is the best way to be prepared. However, you can also get ready by learning how to take a test. Effective test-taking involves budgeting your time wisely both before and during the test.

Preparing for a Test

You can prepare for a test as soon as it is announced. First, note when the test will be given, and find out what it will cover. Then make a study plan that allows you to organize your time effectively. For suggestions on making a study plan, see pages 691–693.

Once you've decided how to budget your study time, start reviewing the material. Look over your textbook, class notes, homework assignments, and quizzes. Write a list of study questions as you review. If possible, get together with other students and work in a study group. Quiz one another with the questions each of you has prepared.

Taking a Test

The day of the test has arrived. You've prepared wisely, and your hard work should pay off. Keep in mind, however, that tests usually last one class period or less. Since the time is limited, you will need to use your time efficiently during the test. The following page has some tips that will help you.

Taking Tests

Resource Manager

📂 **Planning Resources**
- *Lesson Plans*

🎵 **Transparencies**
- *Bellringer*
- *Daily Language Practice*

📂 **Other Print Resources**
- *Taking Standardized Tests*
- *Thinking and Study Skills*, pp. 41–42

Tips on Managing Your Time During a Test

1. Read the directions carefully before you begin. Understanding the directions will help you answer items correctly.

2. Answer all the items you are sure of first. Skipping hard items will give you time to answer all of the items you know.

3. After you have finished the easier items, go back and try the items you skipped. Give the best answers you can.

4. Allow time to check your answers before you turn in your test. This review will decrease your chances of making simple errors.

Exercise 1

Choose the response that best completes each of the following statements:

1. A good way to prepare for a test is to make a _____.
   a. class schedule   c. study plan
   b. study break   d. summary

2. It's a good idea to review your _____.
   a. homework   c. quizzes
   b. textbook   d. all of the above

3. When a test is announced, one of the first things to find out is _____.
   a. whether you will need a pencil or a pen
   b. what the test will cover
   c. the teacher's name
   d. how the test will be graded

4. When taking a test, it is a good idea to skip the _____ until you have completed the other items.
   a. first few items   c. easy items
   b. even-numbered items d. difficult items

5. Allow time to _____ your answers before you turn in your test.
   a. remove   c. rearrange
   b. check   d. none of the above

25.1 Test-taking Strategies **707**

Practice and Assess

Answers: Exercise 1
1. c
2. d
3. b
4. d
5. b

Additional Resources
📁 *Taking Standardized Tests*
📁 *Thinking and Study Skills,* pp. 41–42

Close

Ask students to think of times when they did less well on a test than they thought they should have. Was it because they didn't organize their time? Students may realize that they answered test items incorrectly because they failed to read the directions carefully. Maybe they tried to answer all the difficult questions first and then ran out of time while answering the easy ones. Ask how the tips in the chart can help them improve their performance on tests.

Taking Tests

Cooperative Learning

Listening and Speaking

Point out that while the general strategies of time management and cooperative studying can be helpful to all learners, individual students will find strategies that work best for them. Encourage students to try to determine whether it is easier to remember information they have reviewed on a printed page or information they have heard. Pair students and ask them to read first silently and then aloud to each other the four items on time management in the yellow box on this page. Ask them which method was the most helpful.

Focus

Lesson Overview

Objective
- To become familiar with types of test items and to respond to them effectively

Skills
- reading thoroughly; responding to test items; choosing a strategy

Critical Thinking
- establishing and evaluating criteria

Listening and Speaking
- discussing; taking notes; listening accurately

Bellringer
Daily Language Activity

When students enter the classroom, have this assignment on the board: *Write which type of test you prefer, multiple-choice or short-answer. List reasons for your choice.*

See also *Daily Language Practice*

Motivating Activity

Ask students to share their answers to the Bellringer activity. Which types of test items do students feel most comfortable with? Which types are the most troublesome? Why? If some students say they dislike fill-in and short-answer items, is it because they have to supply their own answers rather than choose from various given responses? Students who have difficulty in choosing among alternatives may prefer fill-in and short-answer items because they can use their own words. Why is guessing more difficult with fill-in and short-answer items than with true-false, multiple-choice, and matching items? Emphasize the importance of using the strategies discussed in this lesson for dealing with each type of test item.

Taking Tests

25.2 Types of Test Items

Your teacher has just informed the class of an upcoming test. It will contain true-false, multiple-choice, matching, fill-in, and short-answer items. Don't panic. There are strategies you can learn that will help you answer each of these types of test items.

True-False Items

A true-false item asks you to decide whether a statement is true or false. A single true-false statement may contain some information that is true and some that is false. However, the item should be marked true only if the *entire* statement is true. If *any* part of the statement is false, you should mark it false. Look at the following example.

> The first part of this sentence is true, but the second part is not. Columbus landed in what is now the Bahamas. The statement is false.

> Columbus sailed westward from Spain in 1492 and landed at the site of present-day New York City on October 12.

Multiple-Choice Items

Multiple-choice test items are the kind you will encounter most often. Each item includes an incomplete sentence or a question and several responses. You must choose the response that best completes the sentence or answers the question. Read all of the responses before writing your answer. Eliminate those you know are incorrect. This method will help you zero in on the correct response.

Be careful about choosing responses that contain absolute words, such as *always, never, all,* or *none.* Since most statements have exceptions, absolute statements are often incorrect.

The following multiple-choice item might appear on an English test. As you read it, decide how you would select the correct answer.

Resource Manager

📂 **Planning Resources**
- *Lesson Plans*

📖 **Transparencies**
- *Bellringer*
- *Daily Language Practice*

📂 **Other Print Resources**
- *Taking Standardized Tests*
- *Thinking and Study Skills,* pp. 41–42

Which statement concerning the book *Julie of the Wolves* is accurate?

a. It was written by Jean Craighead George.
b. It takes place in North America.
c. It is the story of a girl and wild animals.
d. all of the above

> You probably know that response *a* is correct. However, read all of the responses before answering.

> Select this response only if you are sure that at least two of the responses are correct. In this case, *d* is correct.

Matching Items

In a matching activity you are given two lists of items. You must match items in the first list with items from the second list. Before you begin, notice whether each list contains the same number of items. Often the second column will contain more items than the first column. When that is so, some items in column 2 will not be used.

If each item is to be used only once, make a note of each item as you use it. (If you are permitted to write on the test, cross it out.) Complete the easy matches first. Then there will be fewer items to choose from when you try the more difficult matches.

Match each city with the name of its state.

___ 1. Chicago   a. Alaska
___ 2. Dallas   b. Florida
___ 3. Miami   c. Georgia
___ 4. Atlanta   d. Illinois
___ 5. Fairbanks   e. Texas
                 f. Wisconsin

> On your test paper or answer sheet you must write the correct letter from column 2 for each item in column 1.

> Column 2 has one more item than column 1. One item in column 2 will not be used.

Teach

Reading Test Questions

Emphasize the importance of reading test items carefully and completely before attempting to answer them. Ask students to discuss the types of test items named in the section heads of this lesson. Ask if they understand why they should read all the responses to a multiple-choice question before answering it. Why is it necessary to read an entire true-false statement before answering? How much of a matching test item should be read before deciding on an answer? **L2**

Answers: Matching Items

1. d
2. e
3. b
4. c
5. a

Taking Tests

Enrichment and Extension

Reading Further

Jean Craighead George has written a number of books besides *Julie of the Wolves* that are appropriate for seventh graders. These include *My Side of the Mountain, Spring Comes to the Ocean, The Talking Earth, Who Really Killed Cock Robin?, Cry of the Crow,* and *Shark Beneath the Reef.* In both her fiction and nonfiction works, George writes authoritatively about the natural world.

Teach

Describing Test-taking Strategies

Ask students to review the test items on pp. 708–710. Divide the class into small groups and instruct each group to list and then describe the different types of test items. Have students identify the test-taking strategies for each type of question. Then have each group select a student to present its findings to the class.

Cross-Reference: Study Skills

For more information on how the SQ3R method can be used in preparing study questions, refer students to Lesson 24.5.

Fill-in Items

Fill-in items usually consist of a sentence with one or more blanks for you to fill in. The number of blanks usually shows how many words will be needed for the response. Your answer should make the statement both true and grammatically correct. Check your choice by rereading the sentence with your answer included. Try answering the following fill-in item.

> Notice that four names are needed. The correct fill-in answers are *George Washington, Thomas Jefferson, Abraham Lincoln,* and *Theodore Roosevelt.*

> The United States presidents carved on Mount Rushmore are _____, _____, _____, and _____.

Short-Answer Items

Short-answer questions ask you for specific information. Always read the question carefully to be sure you understand what is being asked. Unless you are told not to, answer each question with a complete sentence. Look at the following question, which might appear on a social studies test.

> First, think out your answer. You can compose the sentence in your head before you begin writing.

> Why did the early colonists risk the dangerous voyage across the Atlantic Ocean to settle in America?

> Be sure you understand the question before you begin your answer. In this case, you will need to give the reasons early colonists came to America.

> Rephrase the question to answer with a complete sentence. For example: *The early colonists settled in America to gain religious and political freedom and economic opportunity.*

Taking Tests

MEETING INDIVIDUAL NEEDS — Gifted and Talented

Developing Comprehensive Test Items

Students can benefit from carrying out independent and in-depth studies of historical figures from a period they are studying currently. Working in teams, students can conduct research, write an essay about the person they selected, and compose a test based on the essay. The test should include at least one item of each type described in this lesson. Teams should exchange essays and tests. They should read the essays, then try to take the tests, and then come together to discuss them.

Practice the test-taking skills you covered in this lesson. Read the passage below. Then answer the test items that follow the passage.

Although he never sailed himself, Prince Henry of Portugal (1394–1460) was an important influence on early exploration. Prince Henry's crews sailed the oceans more than five hundred years ago. They used their knowledge of water currents, winds, and the sun and stars to get them to their destinations.

These sailors also used instruments. Henry, often called the Navigator, set up a school of navigation in Portugal. He brought together experts who worked to improve the compass and the astrolabe. A compass shows directions. With an astrolabe, sailors can tell latitude, or distance from the equator. Led by Henry, the Portuguese developed a fast, maneuverable ship called a caravel. In addition, sailors kept careful records of all they saw. These records added to the information map makers needed and sailors used for later voyages.

1. True or False: Portuguese sailors depended on experience, not on instruments.
2. Why was Prince Henry called the Navigator?
   a. He sailed on many overseas voyages.
   b. He was the king of Portugal.
   c. He encouraged improvements in navigation.
   d. all of the above
3. Match each item with the correct description.
   1. astrolabe   a. indicates direction
   2. caravel   b. shows latitude
   3. compass   c. fast, maneuverable ship
4. Fill in the blanks: Map makers used information from _____ kept by Portuguese _____.
5. Write a short answer: How did Portugal contribute to future world exploration by Europeans?

Practice and Assess

Answers: Exercise 2
1. False
2. c
3. 1 b
   2 c
   3 a
4. records; sailors
5. The Portuguese developed a fast ship, kept careful records, and developed new instruments.

Additional Resources
📁 *Taking Standardized Tests*
📁 *Thinking and Studying Skills,* pp. 41–42.

Close

Ask students to think of times when they failed to read directions carefully on a test. Have each of them write a paragraph comparing "careless mistakes" in a math quiz with mistakes on a fill-in, true-false, or short-answer English test.

Taking Tests

MEETING INDIVIDUAL NEEDS   Less-Proficient Readers

Asking Questions

Once students have read the directions and test questions in Exercise 2, ask them to think about anything that doesn't seem clear. You may wish to read the test aloud as students follow it silently. Students may be reluctant to speak up about their confusion. Point out that individual questions may be useful to everyone. Prompt them to form questions such as, *Is it okay to choose more than one letter for a multiple-choice answer?*

Focus

Lesson Overview

Objective

- To identify various types of standardized test questions and to respond to them appropriately

Skills

- applying specific strategies to be more effective in responding to questions on standardized tests

Critical Thinking

- synthesizing; recalling; relating; defining and clarifying

Listening and Speaking

- discussing, explaining process

Bellringer

Daily Language Activity

When students enter the classroom, have this assignment on the board: *List the ways in which you prepare yourself to take a standardized test.*

See also *Daily Language Practice*

Motivating Activity

Discuss students' answers to the Bellringer activity. Ask students if they answer reading-comprehension questions while doing their regular classwork. Explain that they are preparing for standardized reading tests any time they read material and answer questions about it.

Taking Tests

25.3 Standardized Tests

You have probably taken standardized tests, which are given to groups of students throughout the country. In order to do your best, you need to be familiar with the types of test items on these exams. Learning how to answer standardized test items will make you feel more relaxed and confident.

Reading Comprehension

Reading comprehension test items measure how well you understand what you read. These items usually include a passage about a specific topic followed by questions. The questions may ask you to identify main ideas or to recognize supporting details. The questions may also ask you to draw conclusions based on the passage. The following is an example of an item from a reading-comprehension test.

> The titles in *a* and *b* describe only supporting details. Item *d* is not specific enough. Item *c* focuses on the passage's specific topic and is the correct choice.

> Women artists have long been respected in Native American culture. Women in the Great Plains nations have created beautiful ceremonial robes and pottery. In traditional Navaho culture women artists wove magnificent rugs with bold designs and patterns. Cheyenne women developed the art of sewing porcupine and bird quills into elaborate symbols and designs. Some of these women even formed an organization called the Sacred Quillworker's Guild. Members of the organization teach the art to other Cheyenne women.
>
> What would be the best title for this passage?
> a. The Sacred Quillworker's Guild
> b. Basketry, Weaving, and Design
> c. Native American Women Artists
> d. Native American Artists

Resource Manager

📁 **Planning Resources**
- *Lesson Plans*

📁 **Other Print Resources**
- *Taking Standardized Tests*
- *Thinking and Study Skills,* pp. 41–42

Vocabulary

Standardized tests often include vocabulary items. One type of vocabulary item asks you to complete a sentence with one of several multiple-choice items. To complete the sentence correctly, you need to know the meaning of a particular word.

Sometimes you can use your knowledge of word parts to identify a word's meaning. See if you can analyze the parts of *preface* to complete the item below.

> 1. A book's preface appears _____ .
>
>   a. at the end of the book
>   b. at the beginning of the book
>   c. in the middle of the book
>   d. just before the book's index

Notice that *preface* contains the prefix *pre-*, which means "before." You can use this knowledge to determine that the correct answer is *b*.

In another type of vocabulary item, you show that you understand a word's meaning by choosing a synonym for it. In the following example you must choose the word closest in meaning to the underlined word in the sentence.

By trying each choice in the sentence, you can eliminate *worry, attack,* and probably *ignore.* The best synonym for *expunge* is *remove.*

> In delivering his speech, the senator decided to <u>expunge</u> the part that attacked the vice president.
>
> a. ignore   b. remove   c. worry   d. attack

Taking Tests

Teach

Searching for Key Words

Suggest that students approach a test item by searching for key words in the test sentence. Guide them in figuring out the most important word in the first sample question. Is part of the word *preface* already familiar?

Understanding that *speech, senator, attacked,* and *vice president* are key words in the second example should help students select an answer. Why might a senator *expunge,* or *remove,* attacks on a vice president? **L1**

Cross-Reference: Vocabulary and Spelling

For instruction and practice on roots, refer students to Lesson 23.3.

Cross-Reference: Vocabulary and Spelling

For instruction and practice on synonyms, refer students to Lesson 23.4.

Enrichment and Extension

Reviewing Vocabulary Questions

Vocabulary items may present difficulties for students. Go through the strategies suggested in the text, emphasizing that context clues can alert students to a word's unsuitability for a given sentence. Using the words in sentences is one way to determine their suitability. Be certain students understand that they should read through the choices given and find the word that fits the best.

Teach

Reviewing Analogies

Go through the strategies on pp. 714–715. Emphasize that the first step in completing an analogy is to decide how the first pair of words is related. Be certain students understand that they should read through the choices given and find another pair of words with a similar relationship.

Practicing Analogies

Give students additional practice on determining the relationships between things by having them complete the items below.

Texas: United States
a. Quebec: Canada (correct)
b. Canada: World
c. North America: Canada
d. Paris: Europe

Analogies

Analogy items test your understanding of relationships between things or ideas. For example, think about the relationship between *strong* and *weak*. The words are antonyms—words that have opposite meanings. A test item may begin with a pair, such as *strong* and *weak*. You must then choose another pair of words with a similar relationship. Since *strong* and *weak* are opposites, the second pair of words should also be opposites.

> *Big* and *large* have the same meaning. *Red* is not the opposite of *pink* nor is *athletic* the opposite of *musical*. Only *young* and *old*, choice *c*, are antonyms.

```
Strong is to weak as

a. big is to large        c. young is to old
b. red is to pink         d. athletic is to musical
```

Sometimes colons are used to shorten analogies. A single colon separates the words in each pair, and a double colon separates the two pairs. For example, "strong is to weak as young is to old" is shown as "strong : weak :: young : old." What is the relationship in the item below?

> Remember, you read the single colon as though it said "is to" and the double colon as "as." This item begins "Kitten is to cat as . . ."

```
kitten : cat ::

a. book : play            c. horse : donkey
b. computer : calculator  d. calf : cow
```

Taking Tests

Cooperative Learning

Writing Analogies

Divide students into small groups. Each group should write several analogy items such as the examples shown on this page. Once the groups have finished writing, have volunteers from each group read an analogy item aloud, or write it on the board, and call on students from another group for the answer.

If the relationship is unclear, try making up a sentence that describes the relationship between the first pair of words. For instance, in the example above you might say, "A kitten is a baby cat." Then try substituting each pair of words in that sentence. After trying each pair of words in the example above, you should find that *d* makes the most sense.

Grammar, Usage, and Mechanics

Standardized tests often include sections that test your knowledge of grammar, usage, and mechanics. These items often present a sentence divided into several underlined sections. Each section is marked with a letter. You must tell which of the underlined sections contains an error. You can also indicate that there is no error.

Another type of item gives a sentence with only one section underlined. The sentence is followed by several possible corrections. One of the choices may be the same as the underlined part. Examples of both types are shown on the following page.

1. Each of the girls checked their own book
   a   b   c

   out of the library. no error
   d   e

2. Aaron is the biggest of the two boys.

   a. the biggest   c. the more bigger
   b. the bigger   d. the most biggest

In this item you must decide if the sentence contains an error. If it does, you must indicate which underlined section contains the error. In this example, section *c* contains the error.

In this type of item, you choose the response that best replaces the underlined part. One of the choices may be the same as the underlined part. The correct choice here is *b*.

Taking Tests

Listening for Common Errors

Point out to students that when they practice answering grammar test items, reading the sentences aloud sometimes makes it easier to find the errors. Point out that even though they cannot read aloud during a test, practice in listening for errors will help them "listen" to themselves as they read test items silently.

Cross-Reference: Usage

For instruction and practice on troublesome words, refer students to Lessons 17.1 and 17.2.

Practice and Assess

Additional Resources

📁 *Taking Standardized Tests*
📁 *Thinking and Study Skills*, pp. 41–42

Close

Have students discuss the situations in which they could apply the test-taking strategies discussed in this lesson.

Taking Tests

Exercise 3

Use the test-taking strategies described in this lesson to complete the following items.

1. A transparent piece of glass is one that _____.
   a. cannot be seen through   c. is easily broken
   b. is clear   d. is very thick
2. dentist : teeth :: _____
   a. mechanic : engines   c. dog : bone
   b. doctor : nurse   d. student : pencil
3. Choose the letter of the underlined section that needs to be corrected in the following sentence. Choose *e* if no correction is needed.

   The captain past the ball to another member of
        a   b   c
   the basketball team. no error
            d   e
4. Decide whether the underlined section in the following sentence needs correction. Then choose the best correction from the choices listed.

   Meg has taken the dog out for a run in the park.
   a. has taken   c. has took
   b. take   d. taking

Enrichment and Extension

Taking Tests On Computers
Students can use the computer to practice their test-taking skills. Create several files containing sample tests with the types of items covered in this unit. Students can work directly on the computer as they complete the tests, or they can print out one or more files and mark their answers on the hard copy.

25.4 | Standardized Test Practice

Introduction

The following pages of exercises have been designed to familiarize you with the standardized writing tests that you may take during the school year. These exercises are very similar to the actual tests in how they look and what they ask you to do. Completing these exercises will not only provide you with practice, but also will make you aware of areas you might need to work on.

These writing exercises—just like the actual standardized writing tests—are divided into three sections.

Sentence Structure   In this section, pages 718 to 725, you will be given a short passage in which some of the sentences are underlined. Each underlined sentence is numbered. After you finish reading the passage, you will be asked questions about the underlined sections. The underlined sections will be either incomplete sentences, run-on sentences, correctly written sentences that should be combined, or correctly written sentences that do not need to be rewritten. You will need to select which is best from the four choices provided.

Usage   In this section, pages 726 to 733, you will also be asked to read a short passage. However, in these exercises, a word or words in the passage will be omitted and a numbered blank space will be in their place. After reading the passage, you will need to determine which of the four provided words or groups of words best belongs in each numbered space.

Mechanics   Finally, in the third section, pages 734 to 741, the short passages will have parts that are underlined. You will need to determine if, in the underlined sections, there is a spelling error, capitalization error, punctuation error, or no error at all.

Writing well is a skill that you will use the rest of your life. You will be able to write more accurate letters to your friends and family, better papers in school, and more interesting stories. You will be able to express yourself and your ideas more clearly and in a way that is interesting and engaging. These exercises should help to improve your writing and to make you comfortable with the format and types of questions you will see on standardized writing tests.

One way you may wish to use this section of *Writer's Choice* is to have students complete an exercise or a series of exercises in an environment that resembles a testing environment. Students should be encouraged to work slowly and carefully. After students have completed the assigned exercises, you may want to go over the answers with students. You can explain the correct answers and review the grammar skills being tested.

Not covered in these test practices is the section in many standardized test situations that requires students to write a composition based on a provided topic. In this section, students are tested on their ability to write clear, concise and persuasive compositions. You may want to assign topics to your students and have them write one or two page compositions so that they get practice for this section. When assigning a topic, choose subjects that require the student to have an opinion and to write convincingly as to why their opinion is valid. When advising students on how to prepare for the composition section, tell students that the following abilities may earn not only a higher grade on the test, but may also result in good writing skills: use specific examples to illustrate your point, organize your argument in a logical manner, carefully choose words that effectively and descriptively state your thoughts and opinion, be consistent in style and purpose throughout the composition. These are some of the ways that students can create interesting, persuasive and clearly written compositions.

Students are often anxious about taking standardized tests. Part of a teacher's responsibility is to provide support and instruction and to assure students that thorough preparation will enable them to meet the challenges of the test.

Resource Manager

📂 **Planning Resources**
- *Lesson Plans*

📂 **Other Print Resources**
- *Taking Standardized Tests*
- *Thinking and Study Skills,* pp. 41–42

Standardized Test Practice

Read each passage. Some sections are underlined. The underlined sections may be one of the following:

- Incomplete sentences
- Run-on sentences
- Correctly written sentences that should be combined
- Correctly written sentences that do not need to be rewritten

Choose the best way to write each underlined section and mark the letter for your answer. If the underlined section needs no change, mark the choice "Correct as is" on your paper.

> "Genius is two per cent inspiration and ninety-eight per cent perspiration." Thomas Alva Edison, the most famous American inventor, said this in relation to his own work. <u>Edison invented the electric lightbulb. He did this in 1879.</u> (1) He seemed to have limitless patience and energy. <u>He worked in his laboratory. For as long as nineteen hours a day without stopping.</u> (2) His hard work paid off in many important inventions, including the phonograph, the motion picture projector, and the alkaline battery. <u>By the time of his death in 1931, he had patented 1,093 inventions.</u> (3)

Answers and Analyses

1. A Explain to students that these two sentences are complete and grammatically correct, but will have a clearer meaning and read more smoothly if combined. The correct answer places the date in the beginning of the sentence and removes the redundant pronouns and verb *(He did this)*.

2. H The underlined section consists of a complete sentence and a sentence fragment. Students should recognize that the second sentence is a subordinate clause, dependent on the first part of the sentence for its meaning. The correct answer combines the two into one complete sentence by removing the period.

3. D The sentence is correct as it appears in the selection.

---

1 A In 1879 Edison invented the electric lightbulb.

B In 1879 Edison invented the electric lightbulb, and that's when he invented it.

C Edison invented in 1879 the electric lightbulb.

D Edison invented the electric lightbulb since 1879.

2 F He worked in his laboratory for as long as nineteen hours a day. Without stopping.

G He worked in his laboratory, he worked for as long as nineteen hours a day without stopping.

H He worked in his laboratory for as long as nineteen hours a day without stopping.

J Correct as is

3 A By the time of his death, in 1931, patenting 1,093 inventions.

B By the time of his death it was in 1931, he had patented 1,093 inventions.

C By the time of his death in 1931. He had patented 1,093 inventions.

D Correct as is

Test-Taking Tip

Suggest to students that they first try to identify the error in each sentence. Is it a run-on sentence? A sentence fragment? Or are the sentences correct, but better if combined?

Standardized Test Practice

In 1849, <u>Harriet Tubman was an enslaved person on a plantation in the South. When she decided to</u>
<u>escape to the North.</u> To avoid capture, she traveled only by night. <u>She was assisted by the Underground</u>
<u>Railroad. It was a secret system of people who helped enslaved people escape to the northern states and</u>
<u>Canada.</u> In 1850, Harriet made the first of nineteen courageous trips back to the South to help other
enslaved people. <u>She led her parents, most of her brothers and sisters, and hundreds of other enslaved people</u>
<u>to freedom.</u> Harriet Tubman was never captured.

(1)

(2)

(3)

1 A In 1849, Harriet Tubman was an enslaved
person on a plantation, then she decided to
escape to the North.

B In 1849, Harriet Tubman being an enslaved
person on a plantation when she decided
to escape to the North.

C In 1849, Harriet Tubman was an enslaved
person on a plantation when she decided
to escape to the North.

D Correct as is

2 F She and the Underground Railroad were
assisted by a secret system of people who
helped enslaved people escape to the
northern states and Canada.

G She was a secret system of people who
helped enslaved people escape to the
northern states and Canada, assisted by
the Underground Railroad.

H She was assisted by the Underground
Railroad, a secret system of people who
helped enslaved people escape to the
northern states and Canada.

J She was assisted by the Underground
Railroad, it being a secret system of people
who helped enslaved people escape to the
northern states and Canada.

3 A She leading her parents, most of her brothers and sisters, and hundreds of other
enslaved people to freedom.

B She led her parents, most of her brothers
and sisters, and hundreds of other enslaved
people. To freedom.

C She led her parents, and she also led most
of her brothers and sisters, and hundreds
of other enslaved people to freedom.

D Correct as is

STOP

25.4 Standardized Test Practice **719**

Answers and Analyses

1. C   The underlined selection consists of a
complete sentence and a sentence fragment. The fragment or subordinate
clause, starting with *when*, tells us more
information about the first independent
clause. It can not stand on its own. The
correct answer combines the two into
one complete sentence by removing the
period.

2. H   Students should recognize that the
two sentences are complete and grammatically correct, but read better when
combined. The correct answer creates
one sentence by eliminating the unnecessary pronoun and verb (*it was*). The
second clause is separated from the first
with a comma and serves to modify–or
give further information–about the
Underground Railroad.

3. D   Explain to students that this is a
complete sentence because it consists of
a subject and verb and states a complete
thought.

Test-Taking Tip

Students should have a solid understanding of the meaning of a clause. A
clause has a subject and a verb. Clauses
are either dependent or independent. An
independent clause has a subject and a
verb and can stand on its own. A
dependent (or subordinate clause) cannot stand on its own. It is dependent on
the rest of the sentence to complete its
meaning.

Tested Objective

- To recognize appropriate English usage and sentence structure within the context of a written passage

Answers and Analyses

1. C Students should recognize that the underlined selection consists of a complete sentence and a sentence fragment. The fragment, or dependent clause, makes no sense without the first, independent clause. The correct answer combines the two into one complete sentence simply by removing the period.

2. G This is a run-on sentence because it consists of two complete sentences linked only by a comma. The correct answer turns the run-on sentence into a complete sentence by adding the conjunction *and*.

3. B Explain to students that the underlined section consists of two complete sentences that will read more smoothly if combined. The correct answer removes the repeated second subject (*some audience members*) and replaces it with a conjunction (*while*) and pronoun (*others*).

Test-Taking Tip

Make sure that students can identify a run-on sentence. A run-on sentence is two complete sentences put together without punctuation or with only a comma. Encourage students to read some sample run-on sentences out loud. Is it hard to read the entire sentence without taking a breath?

Test-Taking Tip

Encourage students to come up with ways to correct run-on sentences by either making them into two complete sentences, or by removing some words to shorten the sentence.

720

Standardized Test Practice

Read each passage. Some sections are underlined. The underlined sections may be one of the following:

- Incomplete sentences
- Run-on sentences
- Correctly written sentences that should be combined
- Correctly written sentences that do not need to be rewritten

Choose the best way to write each underlined section and mark the letter for your answer.
If the underlined section needs no change, mark the choice "Correct as is" on your paper.

> Can you imagine cowboys of the Old West quoting Shakespeare? It sounds strange, but it was not uncommon. <u>Throughout the nineteenth century, theater companies from the East headed West with</u> <u>Shakespeare's plays. To perform them for the people of the frontier.</u> ⁽¹⁾ These plays were performed in a variety of settings and were quite popular. <u>Western audiences, however, were not used to watching plays, they didn't</u> <u>like to sit quietly.</u> ⁽²⁾ They would often yell suggestions to the actors in the middle of the show. <u>Some audience</u> <u>members threw money at good performers. Some audience members threw fruit and vegetables at</u> ⁽³⁾ <u>bad performers.</u>

1 A Throughout the nineteenth century, theater companies from the East headed West with Shakespeare's plays, they wanted to perform them for the people of the frontier.
 B Throughout the nineteenth century, theater companies from the East headed West with Shakespeare's plays to perform them. For the people of the frontier.
 C Throughout the nineteenth century, theater companies from the East headed West with Shakespeare's plays to perform them for the people of the frontier.
 D Correct as is

2 F Western audiences, however, were not used to watching plays. And didn't like to sit quietly.
 G Western audiences, however, were not used to watching plays and didn't like to sit quietly.
 H Western audiences, however, not used to watching plays. They didn't like to sit quietly to watch the plays.
 J Correct as is

3 A Some audience members threw money, or other audience members threw fruit and vegetables at bad performers.
 B Some audience members threw money at good performers, while others threw fruit and vegetables at bad performers.
 C Some audience members and others threw money or fruit and vegetables.
 D Some audience members threw money at good performers, because others threw fruit and vegetables at bad performers.

Mrs. Rosenberg, the eighth-grade French teacher, took papers out of her bag and set them down they
were on her desk. She told her students to stop talking because she had something to discuss with them.

(1)

It was just after the midterm. The students were nervous and worried.

(2)

"I want to talk about your midterm exams," Mrs. Rosenberg said.

Finally, she broke into a huge smile and told the class what was on her mind. She explained that the test
scores had been especially good and she wanted to reward them. With French cookies that she had baked.

(3)

The students congratulated each other. They ate the whole plate of cookies, which were delicious.

1 A Mrs. Rosenberg, the eighth-grade French
teacher, took papers out of her bag and set
them down on her desk.

B Mrs. Rosenberg, the eighth-grade French
teacher. She took papers out of her bag and
set them down on her desk.

C Mrs. Rosenberg, the eighth-grade French
teacher, took papers out of her bag and set
them down. On her desk.

D Correct as is

2 F Just after the midterm the students were
nervous and worried.

G It was just after the midterm, and they
were nervous and worried, and it was the
students.

H It was just after the midterm, and the
students were nervous and worried.

J It was just after the midterm because the
students were nervous and worried.

3 A She explained that the test scores especially
good, and she wanted to reward them with
French cookies that she had baked for
them.

B She explained that the test scores had been
especially good, and she wanted to reward
them with French cookies that she had
baked for them.

C She explained that the test scores wanted to
reward them with French cookies that she
had baked for them especially good.

D Correct as is

1. A Students should understand that this
is a run-on sentence because it is two
sentences that are not separated by any
punctuation. The correct answer removes
the second subject (*they*), which is
unnecessary because it is repeated, and
the verb (*were*). Now the sentence has a
clearer meaning.

2. H These two sentences are complete
and grammatically correct, but will flow
better if combined. The correct answer
joins the sentence with a coordinating
conjunction (*and*).

3. B Explain to students that the underlined section consists of an independent,
main clause and a dependent clause
beginning with the preposition *with*. Can
this second clause stand on its own? No.
Therefore, it must be dependent. The correct answer joins the two clauses by
removing the period.

Remind students that one important way
in which sentences can be linked is with
conjunctions. The coordinating conjunction connects equal parts of sentences.
Encourage students to make a list of
coordinating conjunctions: *and, but, for,
nor, so, yet.*

Standardized Test Practice

Tested Objective

- To recognize appropriate English usage and sentence structure within the context of a written passage

Answers and Analyses

1. **C** Explain to students that this is a run-on sentence because it consists of two complete sentences that are not separated by punctuation. The correct answer turns the run-on sentence into one complete sentence by removing the comma and redundant subject (*they*) and verb (*are made*).

2. **J** This is a complete sentence, consisting of two independent clauses that are joined with a conjunction (*and*).

3. **B** Explain to students that the underlined portion consists of a sentence fragment followed by a complete sentence, or independent clause. Students should be able to recognize the fragment because it does not make sense on its own. The correct answer combines the two by replacing the period with a comma.

4. **F** Explain to students that these are two complete sentences, but that they will read more smoothly when combined. Notice how the two sentences begin with the same subject. The correct answer removes the second, repeated subject and verb (*they are baked*) to combine the sentences.

Read each passage. Some sections are underlined. The underlined sections may be one of the following:

- Incomplete sentences
- Run-on sentences
- Correctly written sentences that should be combined
- Correctly written sentences that do not need to be rewritten

Choose the best way to write each underlined section and mark the letter for your answer. If the underlined section needs no change, mark the choice "Correct as is" on your paper.

For thousands of years, people in desert regions have made adobe buildings, they made them out of mud. (1) Adobe, or sun-dried clay, is formed into bricks to create dwellings. First, sandy clay is mixed with water and then bits of straw or grass are added. (2) The straw or grass helps the mud to stick together. To create the bricks. The mixture is set into wooden forms and left to solidify. (3) It may take several days for the bricks to cure, or harden. The hardened bricks are then baked in the sun. They are baked in the sun for about two weeks. (4) In the desert, there is little rain or freezing weather to melt or crack the hardened mud houses.

---

1 A For thousands of years, people in desert regions have made adobe buildings. They made them out of mud.

B For thousands of years, people in desert regions have made adobe buildings. Out of mud.

C For thousands of years, people in desert regions have made adobe buildings out of mud.

D Correct as is

2 F First, sandy clay is mixed with water and then bits of straw or grass added.

G First, sandy clay is mixed with water. And then bits of straw or grass are added.

H First, sandy clay is mixed with water, added then are bits of straw or grass.

J Correct as is

3 A To create the bricks the mixture is set. Into wooden forms and left to solidify.

B To create the bricks, the mixture is set into wooden forms and left to solidify.

C To create the bricks, the mixture is set it goes into wooden forms and is left to solidify.

D Correct as is

4 F The hardened bricks are then baked in the sun for about two weeks.

G The hardened bricks are then baked in the sun, and the sun bakes them for about two weeks.

H The hardened bricks are then in the sun for about two weeks baked.

J The hardened bricks are then baked in the sun that is for about two weeks.

Test-Taking Tip

Remind students of the correlative conjunction. These conjunctions connect clauses or phrases (like coordinating conjunctions) but they are really two conjunctions (both-and, either-or, neither-nor, not-only-but, also).

Test-Taking Tip

Make sure that students can identify and use the conjunction known as the subordinating conjunction. Subordinating conjunctions connect independent and dependent clauses. Encourage students to make a list of subordinate conjunctions: after, because, *except that, when, before, until, while, since, as.*

What is the most popular team sport in the world? If you guessed soccer, you are almost right. <u>Officially, football is the most popular sport. Because what Americans call soccer is called football in the rest of the world.</u> ₍₁₎ Soccer is played almost everywhere. There are records of soccer-type sports played in China and other countries over 2,000 years ago. <u>By creating uniform rules for play in 1863. England became the birthplace of soccer as we know it today.</u> ₍₂₎ More than 140 nations are members of the international soccer community. <u>There are more soccer players throughout the world than people who play basketball, baseball, or golf.</u> ₍₃₎

1 A Officially, football is the most popular sport, so what Americans call soccer is called football. In the rest of the world.

 B Officially, football is the most popular sport because what Americans call soccer is called football in the rest of the world.

 C Officially, football is the most popular sport, this is because what Americans call soccer is called football in the rest of the world.

 D Correct as is

2 F By creating uniform rules for play in 1863, England became the birthplace of soccer as we know it today.

 G By creating uniform rules for play in 1863, England it is becoming, the birthplace of soccer as we know it today.

 H By creating uniform rules for play in 1863, England became. The birthplace of soccer as we know it today.

 J Correct as is

3 A There are more soccer players throughout the world than people who basketball, baseball, or golf.

 B There are more soccer players throughout the world. They play basketball, baseball, or golf.

 C There are more soccer players throughout the world than people who play basketball, there are also more than play baseball, or golf.

 D Correct as is

Answers and Analyses

1. B Explain to students that the underlined portion consists of a complete sentence and a sentence fragment, or dependent clause. Students can identify the dependent clause because it begins with a conjunction (*because*). The correct answer combines the two clauses by simply removing the period.

2. F The underlined selection consists of a sentence fragment, a dependent clause. The dependent clause, beginning with *by*, does not make sense on its own. The correct answer combines the two into one complete sentence by replacing the period with a comma.

3. D Students should recognize that this is a complete and grammatically correct sentence.

Test-Taking Tip

Make sure that students know that a complete sentence has a subject and verb and states a complete thought.

Standardized Test Practice

Tested Objective

- To recognize appropriate English usage and sentence structure within the context of a written passage

Answers and Analyses

1. **D** Students should recognize that this is a complete sentence, consisting of a subject and verb, and that it states a complete thought.

2. **H** Explain to students that this is a run-on sentence because it consists of two complete sentences separated only by a comma. The correct answer turns the run-on sentence into a complete sentence by adding the preposition *in* and the relative pronoun *which*.

3. **B** Students should be able to recognize that the underlined portion consists of two complete sentences. As two sentences, they are choppy and repetitious. The second sentence adds to the information stated in the first sentence, but is repetitive. The correct answer removes the repeated information (*she also said that people in wheelchairs*) and adds a conjunction (*and*).

Test-Taking Tip

Suggest to students that when they read the answer choices, they make sure that the meaning of the original sentence or sentences is retained.

Read each passage. Some sections are underlined. The underlined sections may be one of the following:

- Incomplete sentences
- Run-on sentences
- Correctly written sentences that should be combined
- Correctly written sentences that do not need to be rewritten

Choose the best way to write each underlined section and mark the letter for your answer. If the underlined section needs no change, mark the choice "Correct as is" on your paper.

Tim and Lily were walking to school when a man sped by them in a wheelchair.
(1)
"What was that?" asked Tim, in amazement.

Lily explained that the man was using a wheelchair especially designed for handicapped athletes. Lily said that her uncle had a wheelchair like that, he used it to play tennis. These new wheelchairs are lighter
(2)
than traditional ones, so they can move more quickly. Lily said that people in wheelchairs can play basket-
(3)
ball today. She also said that people in wheelchairs can enter marathons. Lily and Tim decided to watch the marathon on television because there would be several wheelchair athletes competing.

---

1 A Tim and Lily were walking to school. When a man sped by them in a wheelchair.
  B Tim and Lily were walking to school, a man sped by them in a wheelchair.
  C Tim and Lily were walking to school when a man sped by them. In a wheelchair.
  D Correct as is

2 F Lily saying that her uncle had a wheelchair like that. He used to play tennis.
  G Lily said that her uncle had a wheelchair like that. Which he used to play tennis.
  H Lily said that her uncle had a wheelchair like that, in which he used to play tennis.
  J Correct as is

3 A Lily said that people in wheelchairs, who can play basketball, can also enter marathons today.
  B Lily said that people in wheelchairs can play basketball and enter marathons today.
  C Lily said that people in wheelchairs can play basketball today, and she also said that people in wheelchairs can enter marathons.
  D Lily said that people in wheelchairs can play basketball today and marathons.

Standardized Test Practice

Karen had planned what she would wear. She was going to wear her favorite blue shirt and a blue skirt
that matched. It was the first eighth-grade dance of the year, and Karen had every detail thought out. At
eight o'clock, Karen's father dropped her off at the school gym, her friends were standing outside waiting
for her. As they went inside, they talked about how much fun the seventh-grade dances had been. The music
had been great and lots of kids had danced. They hoped this dance would be the same as the seventh-grade
dances. The only difference would be that now they were the older kids.

(1) (2) (3)

---

1 **A** Karen had planned what she would wear
that it was her favorite blue shirt and a
blue skirt that matched

 B Karen had planned what she would wear,
and she was going to wear her favorite blue
shirt and a blue skirt that matched.

 C Karen had planned to wear her favorite
blue shirt and a blue skirt that matched.

 D Karen had planned to wear what matched
and was going to wear her favorite blue
shirt and a blue skirt that matched

2 **F** At eight o'clock, Karen's father dropped her
off at the school gym. Where her friends
were standing outside waiting for her.

 G At eight o'clock, Karen's father dropped her
off at the school gym. Her friends standing
outside waiting for her.

 H At eight o'clock, Karen's father dropped her
off at the school gym where her friends
were standing outside waiting for her.

 J Correct as is

3 **A** They hoped this dance. Would be the same
as the seventh-grade dances.

 B They hoped this dance would be the same.
As the seventh-grade dances.

 C They hoped this dance the same as the
seventh-grade dances.

 D Correct as is

Answers and Analyses

1. C Students should understand that the
underlined portion contains two grammatically correct, complete sentences
that will sound better when combined.
The object of the first sentence (*what she
would wear*) is changed to the infinitive
(*to wear*) and the repeated subject and
verb of the second sentence (*she was
going to wear*) is removed.

2. H Students should recognize that this
is a run-on sentence because it contains
two complete sentences linked only by a
comma. The correct answer turns the
run-on sentence into a complete sentence by adding the linking conjunction
where.

3. D Students should note that the
answer is correct as is because it is a
complete sentence with a subject, verb,
and object.

Test-Taking Tip

Point out to students that with questions
in which the sentences are correct but
could be improved if combined into one,
there is never a *Correct as is* option. Why
is this? Because the sentences are, in
fact, grammatically correct. However,
they will read better and more smoothly
if combined.

Tested Objective

- To recognize appropriate English usage within the context of a written passage

Answers and Analyses

1. D Explain to students that the sentence requires a superlative adjective. The superlative, describing the best or most of something, is created using the word *most* or by adding *-est* to the adjective. *Enormous* is used here to compare the Great Wall of China to every other construction project ever attempted. Since the Wall is the largest, or *most enormous,* the superlative form should be used.

2. F Students should recognize that the sentence requires a verb in the singular past tense. The subject of the verb is *the work,* which is singular. The past tense is used because it describes something that happened and was completed in the past (*between 221 and 206 B.C.*).

3. D The sentence is completed with a verb in the past tense because it should match the tense of the other verb in the sentence (*was unified*). The verb should be plural because it refers to *the existing segments.*

4. F Students should recognize that this answer requires an adverb. The blank space describes how the wall *is.*

Encourage students to review adverbs. Adverbs modify verbs, adjectives, or other adverbs. Adverbs often end in *-ly.* Adverbs often tell *when, where,* or *how.*

Standardized Test Practice

Read each passage and choose the word or group of words that belongs in each space. Mark the letter for your answer on your paper.

What is the ___(1)___ engineering and construction project ever tackled? The honor belongs to the Great Wall of China. The Wall reaches about 1,500 miles across China and is made of dirt, brick, and stone.

Segments of the Wall date from the fourth century B.C., but the majority of the work ___(2)___ in the Ch'in Dynasty, between 221 and 206 B.C. China was unified in 214 B.C. and the existing segments of wall ___(3)___ to form one long wall. The Wall was designed to act as fortification against attacking nomads, or roving tribes. The Great Wall no longer serves as protection, but it still exists and is ___(4)___ the largest tourist attraction in China.

1 A enormousest
  B more enormous
  C enormous
  D most enormous

2 F happened
  G happens
  H has happened
  J will happen

3 A has been connected
  B is connected
  C was connected
  D were connected

4 F certainly
  G more certainly
  H certain
  J most certain

Have you ever eaten a durian? Chances are that you would remember if you had. The durian is a fruit that has a terrible odor, but a delicious flavor. They have a custardy texture and many people prize ___(1)___ as exotic delicacies.

Durians ___(2)___ in Southeast Asia on trees. These trees can ___(3)___ 130 feet tall. They are expensive because they ripen quickly and are only ripe for a very short time before they are inedible. The only way to know whether or not they are ripe is to smell them. A horrible smell means that the durian is ___(4)___ ripe!

1 A its
  B our
  C them
  D they

2 F have been grown
  G is grown
  H are grown
  J were grown

3 A reach
  B reached
  C had reached
  D will reach

4 F perfectly
  G perfect
  H more perfect
  J most perfect

STOP

UNIT 25

Answers and Analyses

1. **C** Students should recognize that the sentence requires a plural objective pronoun. The sentence contains two pronouns that both refer to the same antecedent, *the durians.* The first is *they,* a subject pronoun. The second—and the correct answer—is an object pronoun (*them*) because it has something done to it (*people prizing them*).

2. **H** The sentence requires a verb in the plural present tense. What is performing the action? The *durians,* which is a plural noun. When did the action happen? It's happening now. The durians are still growing. The correct answer uses the plural present form of the verb *to grow* (*are grown*).

3. **A** This sentence also requires the present tense to correspond with the tense of the passage. The antecedent is *trees,* so the correct answer is in the plural present form, *reach.*

4. **F** Students should understand that this answer has to be an adverb because it modifies how the durian *is ripe* (the verb).

Test-Taking Tip

Encourage students to review the basic parts of speech used in sentences, such as the pronoun. Pronouns stand in for nouns. Which pronoun to use depends on the noun the pronoun is replacing and what function it has in the sentence. If the noun is the subject of the sentence, use a personal pronoun (*I, you, he, she, it, we,* and *they*). One way to identify subjects is to ask, "Is the word doing something or performing an action?" If the answer is yes, the word is the subject of the sentence.

Tested Objective

- To recognize appropriate English usage within the context of a written passage

Answers and Analyses

1. B This answer requires a verb in the past tense to correspond with the verb tense in the previous sentence (*was*). The simple past tense is formed by adding *-ed* to the infinitive.
2. G Students should understand that a verb in the past tense is required. Note the tense of the other verb in the sentence (*was*). The verb tenses in the same sentence should be the same.
3. C The blank space is modifying *rookie year*, which is a noun. Words that modify nouns are adjectives. The only adjective in the answer choices is *remarkable*.
4. G Students should recognize that out of all the answer choices, only *will probably never* is not a double negative.

Test-Taking Tip

Remind students that a double negative is two negative words used to convey a single negative idea. In English, only one negative word is needed to make an idea negative. Make sure that students can identify negative words like *never, hardly, scarcely, not*, etc.

Standardized Test Practice

Read each passage and choose the word or group of words that belongs in each space. Mark the letter for your answer on your paper.

> Nancy Lopez was more than just a good golfer, she __(1)__ better than any other female golfer in the history of the sport. Before turning professional, she won the New Mexico Women's Amateur when she was just 12 years old. She also won the U.S. Junior Girls and Western Junior titles three years in a row. In addition, she __(2)__ for second place in the U.S. Women's Open when she was still an amateur.
>
> When Nancy turned professional in 1978, she had a __(3)__ rookie year. She won rookie of the year, player of the year, and a trophy for the best scoring average. The world of women's golf __(4)__ see a player as successful as Nancy Lopez for a long time.

1 A plays
  B played
  C is playing
  D was playing

2 F has tied
  G tied
  H is tying
  J was tying

3 A remarked
  B remarkability
  C remarkable
  D remarkably

4 F will scarcely never
  G will probably never
  H will hardly never
  J will not never

Three years ago, Julia Kramer noticed a vacant lot down the street from her apartment building. It was full of garbage. Julia was an avid gardener, but since she lived in the city, she didn't have many opportunities to garden. She __(1)__ that the empty lot might be a great spot for a garden.

Julia organized a meeting of __(2)__ neighbors to talk about creating a garden. The project became a cooperative community undertaking as local schools and organizations chipped in to help clean up the lot and plant the garden. A local plant shop even __(3)__ trees and plants. Due to the efforts __(4)__ put in, the people of Julia's neighborhood are now able to sit and play in a beautiful garden.

1 A thought
   B think
   C is thinking
   D has thought

2 F his
   G your
   H her
   J us

3 A donated
   B donate
   C had donated
   D are donating

4 F their
   G they
   H theirs
   J them

STOP

Answers and Analyses

1. A   Students should recognize that the passage describes something that happened in the past. Remind them to look at other verbs in the passage (*noticed, was, lived*). The antecedent is *she*, which is singular. The correct answer is a verb in the singular past tense: *thought*. Students should note that *to think* is an irregular verb, and therefore the answer is *thought*, not *thinked*.

2. H   Point out to students that a pronoun is required. It is a pronoun that refers to ownership. Whose neighbors? Julia's. Since the noun *Julia* is singular and feminine, the answer is *her*.

3. A   The sentence is not complete without an action, or verb. What did the *shop* do? It *donated trees and plants*. The past tense is used because the passage is in the past tense. A clue is provided by the surrounding verb tenses.

4. G   The sentence requires a pronoun. Point out to students that in this case, the noun it replaces comes later in the sentence. The pronoun replaces *the people of Julia's neighborhood*. The pronoun functions as a subject in the sentence *they put in the effort*.

Test-Taking Tip

Review verbs with students. Verbs express action (*run, jump*) or a state of being (*am, will be, seems*). The tense of a verb depends on the point in time the action is taking place. Students should understand that on writing tests like these, the tense of verbs within a particular passage or sentence should be uniform.

Test-Taking Tip

Students should be able to identify when to use the different forms of verbs. Regular verbs are conjugated (or changed into their different forms) by adding suffixes (for example, *-ed* for the past tense). Irregular verbs do not follow the same rules. Encourage your students to make a list of irregular verbs (*to be, to dive, to hang*).

Tested Objective

- To recognize appropriate English usage within the context of a written passage

Answers and Analyses

1. **B** Students should recognize that the sentence requires a verb. The performer of the action is *she,* a third person, singular noun. The past tense is used because Emily Dickinson was born in the 1800's and also because the other verbs in the passage are in the past tense (*were discovered, was*).

2. **G** Explain to students that all the answer choices, except G, *almost never,* contain double negatives, or two negative words.

3. **C** Students should recognize that the blank space requires an adjective because the word is modifying Emily Dickinson's language. The only adjective in the answer choices is *simple.*

4. **F** The answer is a singular verb in the past tense. The passage is written in the past tense. Have students point out the other verbs in the sentence.

Test-Taking Tip

Encourage students to review subject-verb agreement. In a sentence, the form of the verb needs to agree with the subject. This means that if the sentence has a singular subject (*I, the man*) it should also have a singular verb (*I ran, the man climbed the stairs*). If the subject is plural, the verb must agree with it.

Standardized Test Practice

Read each passage and choose the word or group of words that belongs in each space. Mark the letter for your answer on your paper.

Emily Dickinson was born in 1830 in Amherst, Massachusetts. She was one of the most productive poets in all of American literature. She ___(1)___ nearly 1,800 poems, many of which were only discovered after her death in 1886.

Dickinson ___(2)___ traveled or even left her house. She didn't even like to leave her room to greet visitors. She used ___(3)___ language and generally wrote poems that are composed of brief four-line stanzas. Her poems, although short, explored large issues like the search for knowledge, the concept of time, and the meaning of life. Through her poetry, Emily Dickinson ___(4)___ in affecting the world outside of her little house in Amherst.

1 A writes
  B wrote
  C had written
  D was writing

2 F barely never
  G almost never
  H not never
  J hardly never

3 A simplify
  B simpleness
  C simple
  D simply

4 F succeeded
  G will succeed
  H succeed
  J are succeeding

Red lined cleaning shrimp are among the most peculiar and helpful creatures in the sea. The strange thing about them is how they gather ___(1)___ food. They get food by cleaning ___(2)___ organisms off fishes' bodies. The fish depend upon the shrimp to free them of parasites. The shrimp wave their antennae to call to any fish in need of a cleaning. When an interested fish comes along, the shrimp ___(3)___ any stray parasites from the fish's skin. When the fish is clean, it will swim away. The shrimp sleep at night, and clean and eat all day. It is ___(4)___ a strange but practical way to live.

1 A their
  B his
  C our
  D its

2 F tiny
  G tiniest
  H most tiny
  J more tiny

3 A was eating
  B ate
  C eat
  D had eaten

4 F definitely
  G most definiter
  H more definite
  J definite

Answers and Analyses

1. A The answer is a possessive pronoun. Whose food? *Their* food. The sentence contains a total of three pronouns. They all refer to the same antecedent, the *shrimp.*

2. F Students should recognize that the answer is an adjective that modifies the *organisms.* Note that the other answer choices are all comparative adjectives, that are not needed because no comparison is being made.

3. C Students should be able to determine that the answer is a verb in the singular present tense. The subject of the action is *the shrimp,* which is singular. *Eat* matches the tense of the other verb in the sentence (*comes*).

4. F The answer is an adverb because it is a word that modifies *to live.* All of the other answer choices are adjectives except for *definitely.*

Test-Taking Tip

Assure students that on writing tests like these, the names of the tenses of verbs or the parts of speech are not tested. What is being tested, and what they should review, is how words function in a sentence and why.

Tested Objective

- To recognize appropriate English usage within the context of a written passage

Answers and Analyses

1. **B** Students should recognize that the answer is a noun. The word is preceded by a possessive pronoun, *their*. Their what? *Their irritation*. All of the other answer choices are verbs. Remind students that states of emotions, such as happiness, anger, and irritation, are nouns.

2. **H** The answer is a verb in the singular present tense because the subject of the sentence—and what is doing the action—is *that stream*, which is singular. The surrounding verbs (*do, said*) are in the present tense.

3. **A** Explain to students that a comparative adjective is required. The comparison is between waiting until others clean up the stream, or cleaning up the stream themselves. For a one-syllable word such as *fast,* a comparative adjective is formed by adding *-er* to the adjective.

4. **H** The answer is a verb in the past tense. The verb must agree with *the trash,* which is singular. The second verb in the sentence (*looked*) is in the past tense, and this verb must agree with that tense, so the answer is *had been removed.*

Test-Taking Tip

Encourage your students to review the superlative adjective and comparative adjective. Superlatives describe the most or best of something. The superlative is created with the word *most + the adjective* or, for one- syllable words, by adding *-est* to the adjective. The comparative adjective compares two things with each other. For one-syllable words such as *fast,* a comparative adjective is formed by adding *-er* to the adjective (*faster*).

Standardized Test Practice

Read each passage and choose the word or group of words that belongs in each space. Mark the letter for your answer on your paper.

Kevin and Marco sat in their classroom before school and talked about their __(1)__ with the pollution in the stream where they liked to fish. Kevin said, "That stream __(2)__ by the whole town. Why doesn't anyone do anything about it?"

"It's easy to put responsibility onto others," said Mr. Leery, their teacher. "But you'll get results __(3)__ if you take it upon yourselves to improve things."

Kevin and Marco explained the situation to the other students in the class. Everyone volunteered to help clean the stream. By the end of the day, the trash __(4)__ from the stream and it looked a lot better.

1 A irritate
 B irritation
 C irritating
 D irritated

2 F are owned
 G have been owned
 H is owned
 J were owned

3 A faster
 B more fast
 C fastly
 D most fast

4 F has been removed
 G is being removed
 H had been removed
 J will be removed

"You grew up in the city?" Ellen said with amazement as she looked at the boyhood pictures of her father in the photo album.

Her father replied, "Of course I did. I was a real city boy. I __(1)__ a tree until I was eight years old."

"But, Dad," Ellen exclaimed, "There are parks in every city in the country. There must have been one where you lived."

"You're right, Ellen, I was just teasing you about the tree," answered Dad. "We used to go to the park every afternoon after school to play baseball. We liked to think of it as __(2)__ private park." Dad continued nostalgically, "I loved playing baseball with my friends. We __(3)__ quite a good team and would play other neighborhood teams. It was the __(4)__ time of my life.

1 A had never seen
   B hadn't never seen
   C hadn't barely seen
   D hadn't never hardly seen

2 F his
   G our
   H your
   J their

3 A assembles
   B assembling
   C assembled
   D assembler

4 F most exciting
   G exciting
   H more exciting
   J excitingest

Answers and Analyses

1. **A** The answer is a verb in the past that is made negative. Students should be able to recognize double negatives, which are always incorrect. All of the other answer choices contain double negatives.
2. **G** The answer is a possessive pronoun. Whose private park? *Our* private park because the antecedent is *we*.
3. **C** Students should understand that the answer is a verb in the past tense. The verb in the previous sentence (*loved*) is in the past tense and this verb must agree in tense. Choices A and B are verbs, but they are in the present tense. Choice D is a noun.
4. **F** Students should recognize that a superlative adjective is required. The *the* before the blank space is a hint. Superlative adjectives start with *most,* so the answer is *most exciting.*

Test-Taking Tip

Point out to students that on writing tests like these, made up words, or words that don't really exist, are often provided as answer choices. They can be easily eliminated.

Tested Objective

- To proofread for spelling, punctuation, and capitalization errors within the context of a written passage

Answers and Analyses

1. **B** The error is one of capitalization. *Post* should be capitalized because it is part of the proper noun *Saturday Evening Post.*

2. **H** Students should recognize a punctuation error. An apostrophe is missing after *newspaper* because it is possessive. Whose top draftsperson was he? *The newspaper's.*

3. **A** The error is in spelling. *Illustration* requires two *l*s.

4. **H** There should be commas before and after the word *Massachusetts.*

5. **D** There is no error in the underlined sentence. Note that the correct apostrophe and *s* is used to show possession: whose art is it? *Rockwell's.*

6. **H** The error is in punctuation. Students should recognize that a comma is required to separate *carriage* and *a new,* because commas are used to separate items in a list.

Encourage students to review the basic rules governing the use of the comma. 1) Commas are used to separate two independent clauses that are separated by *and, but, or, nor, for.* 2) Commas are used to separate elements in a list or series. 3) Use a comma if a series of adjectives could also be separated by *and.* 4) Commas separate introductory phrases and clauses from the independent, or main clause. 5) Use commas to separate phrases or clauses that interrupt the flow of a sentence.

734

Standardized Test Practice

Read each passage and decide which type of error, if any, appears in each underlined section. Mark the letter for your answer on your paper.

Norman Rockwell is one of the most popular artists of the 20th century. Rockwell began working at the Saturday Evening post in 1916. He soon became the newspapers top draftsman. Over the next 47 years, he
(1)   (2)
illustrated 322 covers for the newspaper. Rockwell also ilustrated advertisements for popular products like
(3)
Crest and Jell-O.

Rockwell lived in Stockbridge Massachusetts with his wife. He died in 1978. Stockbridge is the home of
(4)
the Rockwell Museum.

Rockwell's art depicts small town America. His subjects are ordinary people in everyday situations. Some
(5)
examples of the scenes he illustrated are a woman taking her daughter for a ride in a horse-drawn carriage a
new television antenna being installed on the roof of a Victorian house, and a mom and dad driving
(6)
grandma and the kids to their summer vacation.

Rockwell brought great joy to many people over his long career as an artist.

1 A Spelling error
  B Capitalization error
  C Punctuation error
  D No error

2 F Spelling error
  G Capitalization error
  H Punctuation error
  J No error

3 A Spelling error
  B Capitalization error
  C Punctuation error
  D No error

4 F Spelling error
  G Capitalization error
  H Punctuation error
  J No error

5 A Spelling error
  B Capitalization error
  C Punctuation error
  D No error

6 F Spelling error
  G Capitalization error
  H Punctuation error
  J No error

Standardized Test Practice

The Olympic Games began in greece in the year 776 B.C. The first Olympics had only one event: a 200-
    (1)
yard dash. Later, other events such as longer races, wrestling discus throwing, javelin throwing, boxing, and
                                                              (2)
chariot races were added.

Political problems between the Greeks and Romans caused the Olympics to be abolished in A.D. 394.
                    (3)
However, they were revived in the late nineteenth century, and the first modern summer Olympics opened
                                                                                                (4)
in Athens, Greece on Sunday March 24, 1896.

The Olympics are now held every four years and feature the best athletes from almost every country in
                                              (5)
the world. The goals of the Olympic Games are to encourage physical fitness and to promote good will
                              (6)
among the Nations of the world.

1 A Spelling error
   B Capitalization error
   C Punctuation error
   D No error

2 F Spelling error
   G Capitalization error
   H Punctuation error
   J No error

3 A Spelling error
   B Capitalization error
   C Punctuation error
   D No error

4 F Spelling error
   G Capitalization error
   H Punctuation error
   J No error

5 A Spelling error
   B Capitalization error
   C Punctuation error
   D No error

6 F Spelling error
   G Capitalization error
   H Punctuation error
   J No error

25.4 Standardized Test Practice **735**

Answers and Analyses

1. B The error is in capitalization because the names of countries, such as *Greece*, need to be capitalized.
2. H Students should recognize that the error is one of punctuation. There should be a comma between the words *wrestling* and *discus throwing* because items in a list should be separated by commas.
3. A The error is in spelling. *Problems* is misspelled.
4. H The error is in punctuation. There should be a comma after the word *Sunday* because, when writing a date, a comma comes after the day and before the month. There should also be a comma after *Greece*.
5. D Students should recognize that there are no errors in the underlined sentence.
6. G The underlined sentence contains a capitalization error. *Nations* should not be capitalized because it is not a proper noun.

Test-Taking Tip

Students should know that proper nouns must be capitalized. Examples of proper nouns are: names and titles of people; titles of magazines, books etc.; days of the week, months of the year, seasons and holidays; adjectives derived from proper nouns, such as Italian bread or Mexican music; geographical names, such as Peru or the Alps, and names of streets, buildings, parks, etc.

Tested Objective

- To proofread for spelling, punctuation, and capitalization errors within the context of a written passage

Answers and Analyses

1. **B** Students should be aware that there is an error in capitalization. *France* should be capitalized because it is the name of a country, and names of countries are proper nouns.
2. **J** There is no error in the underlined portion.
3. **D** The error is in punctuation because an apostrophe is required after *Louis* to show ownership. It is *Louis's goal.*
4. **G** The error is in capitalization because *Barbier* is a proper name, and therefore should be capitalized.
5. **A** Students should recognize that *using* is misspelled.
6. **H** The error is in punctuation because a comma is required to separate the introductory dependent clause starting with *By the time* from the main, independent clause starting with *he had.*

Test-Taking Tip

Point out to students that on writing tests like these, they should not assume that just because an underlined portion consists of punctuation, it does not mean that it is incorrect.

736

Standardized Test Practice

Read each passage and decide which type of error, if any, appears in each underlined section. Mark the letter for your answer on your paper.

Louis Braille was born in france in 1809. At the age of three, he was accidentally blinded and his parents (1) arranged for him to go to a special school for blind children. (2) When he was older, Louis goal was to create an (3) alphabet that would allow blind people to read and write more easily. He had heard about Charles barbier, a (4) French army captain, who had developed a way of writing that involved useing raised dots to permit (5) soldiers to communicate at night without light.

Louis worked with the method ceaselessly. By the time he was fifteen years old he had developed the six- (6) dot and standard spelling method that is used by millions of blind people today. The method is called Braille, after Louis.

1 **A** Spelling error
   B Capitalization error
   C Punctuation error
   D No error

2 **F** Spelling error
   G Capitalization error
   H Punctuation error
   J No error

3 **A** Spelling error
   B Capitalization error
   C Punctuation error
   D No error

4 **F** Spelling error
   G Capitalization error
   H Punctuation error
   J No error

5 **A** Spelling error
   B Capitalization error
   C Punctuation error
   D No error

6 **F** Spelling error
   G Capitalization error
   H Punctuation error
   J No error

Standardized Test Practice

Michael was staring at the ceiling. "Shouldn't you be doing your homework?" his grandmother asked.

"I am doing my homework, Grandma." Michael replied.
<u>(1)</u>

His grandmother put down her crossword <u>puzzle "You are just staring at the ceiling. I have</u> never heard
<u>(2)</u>

of homework like that. Are you sure you're following your teacher's instructions?"

"I promise that I am doing exactly what my Teacher asked me to do, Grandma."
<u>(3)</u>

"I beleive you, but that's the strangest way of studying I've ever seen!"
<u>(4)</u>

<u>Michael smiled as he reveeled his secret.</u> "I am supposed to think about what <u>I will do over Winter</u>
<u>(5)</u>   <u>(6)</u>

<u>vacation</u> and then write about it. I'm doing the thinking part now!"

1 **A** Spelling error
   B Capitalization error
   C Punctuation error
   D No error

2 **F** Spelling error
   G Capitalization error
   H Punctuation error
   J No error

3 **A** Spelling error
   B Capitalization error
   C Punctuation error
   D No error

4 **F** Spelling error
   G Capitalization error
   H Punctuation error
   J No error

5 **A** Spelling error
   B Capitalization error
   C Punctuation error
   D No error

6 **F** Spelling error
   G Capitalization error
   H Punctuation error
   J No error

Answers and Analyses

1. **D** Students should recognize that there are no errors in the underlined section.

2. **H** The error is in punctuation. Commas are required after an introductory sentence and before a direct quotation. There should be a period after *puzzle.*

3. **B** There is an error in capitalization. *Teacher* is not used as a proper name, and therefore should not be capitalized.

4. **F** The error is a spelling error because *believe* is spelled incorrectly.

5. **A** *Revealed* is spelled incorrectly.

6. **G** There is an error in capitalization because *winter* should not be capitalized.

Test-Taking Tip

Review the basic rules of spelling with students. For example, the letter *i* comes before *e* except after *c* (as in *believe*) or when sounding like long *a*, (as in *neighbor* and *weigh*).

Test-Taking Tip

Explain to your students that words with double consonants are often misspelled in these types of writing tests. Try to come up with a short list of words that fit this description (examples: *disappear, arrival, roommate*).

Standardized Test Practice

Tested Objective

- To proofread for spelling, punctuation, and capitalization errors within the context of a written passage

Answers and Analyses

1. **B** Students should recognize that the error is in capitalization because *George Washington High School* is the name of a place and needs to be capitalized. Students should know that names are proper nouns, and that proper nouns must be capitalized.
2. **J** There are no errors in the underlined section.
3. **A** Students should recognize that *becoming* is spelled incorrectly.
4. **H** The error is in punctuation. A comma is required after the conjunction *but,* which separates two independent clauses.
5. **A** The error is in spelling. *Disease* is spelled incorrectly.
6. **G** Students should recognize that *Career* is incorrectly capitalized. It is not a proper noun, and therefore does not need to be capitalized.

Test-Taking Tip

It might be useful to review the rules for using quotation marks with students. Quotation marks should be placed around direct quotations. Quotation marks always come in pairs. Make sure your students find opening and closing quotation marks when someone is speaking in the text. A comma is used to separate the quote from explanatory words that precede or follow. (For example, "I like chocolate cake," said Francis.) Commas do not appear if the quotation ends with an exclamation point or a question mark and the explanatory words follow the quotation. (For example, "Would you like to be my partner?" she asked.)

Read each passage and decide which type of error, if any, appears in each underlined section. Mark the letter for your answer on your paper.

One day Darryl began to think about what he might like to do with his future. First, of course, <u>he had to graduate from george Washington High School</u> and then he had to pick a college to attend. <u>He thought he might study medicine.</u>
(1)
(2)
<u>Darryl had often considered becomming a doctor.</u> It would mean many <u>more years of school, studying,</u> and hard work but <u>Darryl thought it would</u> be worth it. He would be able to help sick people get better, <u>and maybe even find a cure for a diseaze.</u> Darryl <u>could not think of a better Career.</u>
(3)
(4)
(5)
(6)

1 **A** Spelling error
  B Capitalization error
  C Punctuation error
  D No error

2 **F** Spelling error
  G Capitalization error
  H Punctuation error
  J No error

3 **A** Spelling error
  B Capitalization error
  C Punctuation error
  D No error

4 **F** Spelling error
  G Capitalization error
  H Punctuation error
  J No error

5 **A** Spelling error
  B Capitalization error
  C Punctuation error
  D No error

6 **F** Spelling error
  G Capitalization error
  H Punctuation error
  J No error

Standardized Test Practice

An almanac is an annual publication that includes information <u>such as weather forecasts tide tables, and</u>
<u>astronomical information.</u> The most famous almanac is *The Old Farmer's Almanac.* It was first published in
   (1)
1792. The almanac provided reliable <u>weather forcasts that were said to be eighty-percent acurate.</u>
                                     (2)

The emphasis of the book was changed 1861. <u>The editor at that time, Charles l. Flint, encouraged more</u>
<u>articles on farming.</u> By 1900, general features about modern life and nature replaced many of the
   (3)
agriculture articles.

During <u>World war II, a German spy was captured by the FBI. He had</u> landed on the coast of Long
        (4)
Island, New York. <u>What was suprising was that the spy had a copy of the almanac in his coat pocket! The</u>
                                                   (5)
government guessed that the Germans were using the book's weather predictions.

<u>The almanac is still published each year in Dublin, New hampshire.</u> *The Old Farmer's Almanac* has not
                                           (6)
missed a publication for over two hundred years.

---

1 A Spelling error
  B Capitalization error
  C Punctuation error
  D No error

2 F Spelling error
  G Capitalization error
  H Punctuation error
  J No error

3 A Spelling error
  B Capitalization error
  C Punctuation error
  D No error

4 F Spelling error
  G Capitalization error
  H Punctuation error
  J No error

5 A Spelling error
  B Capitalization error
  C Punctuation error
  D No error

6 F Spelling error
  G Capitalization error
  H Punctuation error
  J No error

25.4 Standardized Test Practice **739**

Answers and Analyses

1. C   The error is a punctuation error. There should be a comma after *forecasts* because they are items in a series.

2. F   The error is a spelling error because *forecasts* and *accurate* are misspelled.

3. B   Students should recognize that since *L* is the middle initial of *Charles Flint,* it should also be capitalized. Names are proper nouns and should always be capitalized.

4. G   Students should recognize that the word *war* should be capitalized because it is part of the name of an historical event. Historical events are proper nouns.

5. A   There is a spelling error in the underlined portion. *Surprising* is misspelled.

6. G   *Hampshire* should be capitalized because it is part of the name of a state, and state names are proper nouns.

Test-Taking Tip

Remind students that compass headings—north, south, east, west, etc.—are capitalized only when they indicate specific regions. The rule is capitalize locations, but not directions.

Standardized Test Practice

Tested Objective

- To proofread for spelling, punctuation, and capitalization errors within the context of a written passage

Answers and Analyses

1. **C** Students should recognize that there is an error in punctuation in the underlined portion. The name *Claudia* requires an apostrophe and an *s* to show possession. Whose father is it? It is *Claudia's father.*

2. **F** *Excited* is misspelled.

3. **C** Point out to students that there must be a comma before the word *but* to separate the sentence fragment, beginning with *never,* from the main clause, beginning with *She had.*

4. **G** The error is one of capitalization because *father* is not used as a proper noun in this case and therefore should not be capitalized.

5. **D** There is no error in the underlined portion. This is a grammatically correct, complete sentence, that needs no correction.

6. **G** There is an error in capitalization. *O'Hare* is a proper noun because it is the name of a place and should be capitalized.

Test-Taking Tip

Students should be aware that possession is indicated by adding apostrophe + *s* (*'s*). Make a list with students of some examples (*Laura has an umbrella. It is Laura's umbrella. The hat of Sharon. Sharon's hat.*)

Read each passage and decide which type of error, if any, appears in each underlined section. Mark the letter for your answer on your paper.

Claudias father told her that they were going to fly to Chicago to visit his sister Carol. Claudia was exited
(1)
because she had never been on an airplane before. She had been on several car trips but never a trip so far
(2)   (3)
away that she had to take a plane. She could not wait for the day of the trip to arrive.

On the day of the trip, Claudia and her Father took a taxi to the airport. When they got to the gate, she
(4)
looked out the window and became mesmerized by the aircraft. The captain smiled at her as she boarded
(5)
the plane. At that moment, Claudia decided that she wanted to be a captain and she spent the rest of the
flight dreaming about flying. The plane landed at o'hare International Airport. Aunt Carol was waiting at
(6)
the gate for them.

1 A Spelling error
   B Capitalization error
   C Punctuation error
   D No error

2 F Spelling error
   G Capitalization error
   H Punctuation error
   J No error

3 A Spelling error
   B Capitalization error
   C Punctuation error
   D No error

4 F Spelling error
   G Capitalization error
   H Punctuation error
   J No error

5 A Spelling error
   B Capitalization error
   C Punctuation error
   D No error

6 F Spelling error
   G Capitalization error
   H Punctuation error
   J No error

In the spring, <u>twenty eighth-graders took a trip to see the Statue of Liberty in New York City New York.</u>
                                                                                              (1)
It was their first time in New York and they were excited to see the statue. Their teacher, <u>Mrs. costas, led</u>

<u>them up the 142 steps of the spiral staircase</u> and told them about the history of the statue.
                     (2)

She explained that <u>the statue had been given to the United States by france</u> to commemorate the hun-
                                                                        (3)
dredth anniversary of the signing of <u>the Declaration of Independence. She also told them</u> that the statue is
                                                          (4)
over 151 feet and weighs 204 tons. <u>"We will climb to the crown, she said.</u> "There is an observation deck."
                                                          (5)
<u>From the deck, they would have a breathtaking view of New York.</u>
                                    (6)

1 **A** Spelling error
   B Capitalization error
   C Punctuation error
   D No error

2 **F** Spelling error
   G Capitalization error
   H Punctuation error
   J No error

3 **A** Spelling error
   B Capitalization error
   C Punctuation error
   D No error

4 **F** Spelling error
   G Capitalization error
   H Punctuation error
   J No error

5 **A** Spelling error
   B Capitalization error
   C Punctuation error
   D No error

6 **F** Spelling error
   G Capitalization error
   H Punctuation error
   J No error

25.4 Standardized Test Practice **741**

Answers and Analyses

1. **C** Students should recognize that there is an error in punctuation because a comma needs to separate *New York City* from *New York*. Cities and the states in which they are located, when put together, should be separated by a comma.

2. **G** There is an error in capitalization. *Mrs. Costas* is the name of a person, a proper name, and should therefore be capitalized.

3. **B** Students should know that *France* is the name of a country and therefore a proper noun, which should be capitalized.

4. **F** The error is one of spelling because *Independence* is misspelled.

5. **C** There is a punctuation error. There should be quotation marks after *crown*.

6. **J** There is no error in the underlined portion.

Test-Taking Tip

Remind students that a colon is a punctuation mark that means *as follows.* Use colons when making lists. For example, I learned three important lessons on my last job: meet deadlines, work hard, and retain a sense of humor.

✔ ASSESSMENT OPTIONS

📁 *Tests with Answer Key and Rubrics*
Unit 25 Mastery Test, pp. 103–104

💾 *Testmaker*
Unit 25 Mastery Test

You may wish to administer the Unit 25 Mastery Test at this point.

📼 *MindJogger Videoquizzes*

Objectives

- To learn to listen effectively and to evaluate spoken messages
- To improve the ability to speak informally
- To prepare, deliver, and evaluate formal speeches

✔ ASSESSMENT OPTIONS

📁 *Tests with Answer Key and Rubrics*
Unit 26 Pretest, pp. 105–106

💾 *Testmaker*
Unit 26 Pretest

You may wish to administer the Unit 26 Pretest at this point.

Key to Ability Levels

L1 Level 1 activities are within the basic ability range of students.

L2 Level 2 activities are within the ability range of average students.

L3 Level 3 activities are more challenging activities.

UNIT 26 Listening and Speaking

742

Resource Manager

📁 **Planning Resources**
- *Lesson Plans*
- *Block Scheduling*

 **Transparencies**
- *Bellringer*
- *Daily Language Practice*

📁 **Other Print Resources**
- *Listening and Speaking Activities*
- *Tests with Answer Key and Rubrics*
- *Thinking and Study Skills*

📼 **Video**
- *MindJogger Videoquizzes*

💾 **Software**
- *Presentation Plus!*
- *Testmaker*

🖥 **Web Sites**
- *writerschoice.glencoe.com*

26.1 | How to Listen

As you turn on the radio to listen to your favorite station, you run into a problem. You're ready to listen to music, but all you hear is static. When there's interference, it's difficult to enjoy or understand what you're listening to.

You may face forms of mental "interference" every day. Ignoring the static, though, will help you listen.

Listening in Class

Does your mind ever wander during school? Maybe you can't stop thinking about your bad morning. Maybe the sun is shining, and you'd like to be outside. You have to get your thoughts back on track. You know you need to listen if you're going to learn. These tips will help you get started.

Tips for Effective Listening

1. Sort out any interference, such as classroom noise or wandering thoughts. Focus your attention completely on the speaker.

2. Determine your purpose for listening. Are you trying to obtain information? Are you trying to solve a problem? Are you listening for enjoyment?

3. Identify main ideas as you listen. Then write them down in your own words. These are the most important points to remember.

4. Put a star or check mark next to any ideas that your teacher tells you are especially important or that might appear on a test.

5. Review your notes after class. Do you have any questions? Clear them up right away to avoid confusion later.

Interpreting Special Clues   Gestures and tone of voice often indicate which information is important. Sometimes your teacher may speak certain words or phrases more loudly than others. Write those down. Hand and body movements also tell you to pay special attention to what's being said.

26.1 How to Listen   **743**

Focus

Lesson Overview

Objectives
- To learn to listen effectively
- To evaluate spoken messages

Skills
- listening effectively; recognizing persuasive language; evaluating commercials

Critical Thinking
- analyzing; classifying; evaluating

Listening and Speaking
- listening to a persuasive speech; evaluating

Bellringer
Daily Language Activity

When students enter the classroom, have this assignment on the board: *Make a list of noises you hear in the classroom that sometimes make it difficult for you to pay attention to the teacher.*

See also Daily Language Practice

Motivating Activity

Prior to class, ask a few students to be disrupters. These students should provide sound interference by tapping pencils, conversing, coughing, and so on. Ask the class to listen while you read aloud a passage. Tell them to concentrate on your voice but to jot down any other noises they hear as you read. After you finish reading the passage, ask students whether other noises in the classroom distracted them or whether they were able to concentrate on your words and block out the interference. Discuss how students could eliminate these obstacles to effective listening.

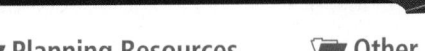

Resource Manager

📂 **Planning Resources**
- *Lesson Plans*

🎵 **Transparencies**
- *Bellringer*
- *Daily Language Practice*

📂 **Other Print Resources**
- *Listening and Speaking Activities*, pp. 6–8, 12–13, 16–24
- *Thinking and Study Skills*, pp. 33–34

Teach

Listening for Emotional Words, Opinions, and Facts

Record a five-minute segment of a news broadcast and play it in class. Have students write down every emotional word they hear. Encourage them to pay attention to the speaker's tone of voice to signal possible opinionated statements. Stop the tape frequently to discuss whether the speakers stay with facts or interject opinions in their statements. **L2**

Writing Facts and Opinions

Ask students to write factual statements about themselves, such as "I have brown eyes." Then ask them to change the fact into an opinion, such as "Brown eyes are the best!" As students share their statements, have them explain why one is a fact and the other is an opinion. **L1**

⬛ Cross-Reference: Usage

For more information on adjectives and adverbs, refer students to Unit 12.

Listening and Speaking

Listening to Persuasive Speech

Television commercials, political speeches, and editorials on the evening news all have one thing in common. Each speaker wants to convince you that what you're hearing is the truth. Don't listen without thinking, though. You must decide if the speaker is saying something you can believe.

Fact Versus Opinion Identifying the speaker's attitude is very important. Do you know when you're hearing facts and when you're hearing opinions? A fact is something that can be proven. An opinion is what someone *believes* to be true. In the following examples try to separate the facts from the opinions.

Evaluating News Statements	
Heard on the Evening News	**Questions to Ask Yourself**
Today when both candidates met, Smith grudgingly shook hands with his opponent.	What one word tells me how the news reporter thinks the candidate feels? Is this necessarily true?
Twenty-seven boy scouts camped in the mountains last weekend.	Does this story introduction try to convince me of anything?
Last night a ferocious dog attacked a gas station attendant.	Would I feel differently if the dog were described as frightened rather than ferocious?
Local high school girls are taking a stand against their new band uniforms.	Does this statement try to persuade me of something, or does it just give me information?

Persuasive Speeches Speakers often try to sway you to their point of view. They use emotional words and actions to make you feel strongly about what they're saying. The emotional words they use are often adjectives and adverbs. Would you feel good about something described in such terms as *dreary, rotten, foul-smelling, eerie, dingy?* Probably not. Now think about these: *golden, shiny, energetic, wonderful, pure.* These words would probably make you feel good.

MEETING INDIVIDUAL NEEDS

Less-Proficient Readers

Separating Opinions from Facts

To help students separate opinions from facts in persuasive speeches, have them brainstorm to develop a list of words that show or cause emotion. Point out that emotional words, particularly adjectives and adverbs, not only modify verbs and nouns but also can modify the truth.

Arrange students in groups and give them a written news statement. Tell students to identify emotional words in the news statement and to add these to their lists of "emotional" words. Have students identify *why* each word is emotional.

Speakers often use actions to accompany their emotional words. In these cases, you need to "listen" with your eyes. They might make eye contact with you and smile. They could nod their heads or move their arms or hands.

Emotional words and actions are good to use, but you need to think through what's being said. Speakers might be sincere, or they might be trying to force their messages on you. It's up to you to decide what their intentions are.

Listening to Commercials Commercials bombard us every day. Though they sometimes give information, their main function is to boost sales. They do this by delivering two messages—one is obvious, and the other is hidden. The obvious message is *what* you hear or see. The hidden message comes through in *how* the information is presented.

Have you ever heard a commercial declare that its product is new and improved? To know exactly what this means, you need to know what it was like before the improvement. If the product was poor to begin with, it may still be poor. Beware of words like *more, better, whiter, brighter, longer-lasting,* and so on.

Teach

Analyzing Words Used in Commercials

Ask students whether they can recall any current television commercials that use comparative words, such as *more, better,* and *brighter.* Why do advertisers use words like these? Do they help sell products? Tell students to note that when they hear comparative words they should ask themselves what is really being said. **L2**

⮀ Cross-Reference: Writing

For more information on using emotional words effectively in writing, refer students to Lesson 3.3.

Listening and Speaking

Listening and Speaking

Performing Skills

Have pairs of students prepare skits in which they role-play persuasive encounters, such as a child trying to persuade a parent to let her go somewhere, a teen trying to persuade a friend to do something, a parent trying to persuade a small child to eat his dinner, a salesperson trying to persuade a customer to buy an item, and so on. Partners can present their skits in small groups. Remind students to speak clearly. Ask listeners to identify the main idea and supporting evidence of the persuasive message. Groups can then discuss the emotional words and actions that were used in the skits.

745

Teach

Finding Hidden Messages

Explain that although television commercials convey information that is often only partially true, they are very effective and persuasive. Many people's ideas are influenced by commercials. As students keep track of hidden messages, they should discuss any messages that seem to overgeneralize or stereotype. What in these messages do they find insulting or offensive and why? **L2**

Listening and Speaking

Commercials also may give information that only *sounds* true. Your dog may eat the dog food advertised. But that doesn't mean that your dog will look as healthy as the dog in the commercial. That's what you're supposed to believe, though. Can you catch the faulty reasoning in the sample commercials in the chart below?

Rush right out, and pick up a tube of the new, improved Skinscrub. Those ugly skin blemishes will vanish in hours as the miracle ingredient X-34 goes to work.

Advertising: Believe it or Not

Advertisement	Think It Through
A girl wearing the advertiser's product sits among a group of friends, laughing and talking.	What is the hidden message here? If you wear this product, you will be as popular as the girl in the commercial. Is this true?
You are told that the bike advertised is the best in its class.	What class is the advertiser talking about? Maybe you do not need that kind of bike. Maybe it is not worth the money.
A famous actor tells you that the car in the television commercial is simply the best.	An actor may know about performing, but does that make him an expert on a car's performance? Should you believe him?
A group of athletes are shown celebrating a win while drinking a particular soft drink.	What idea are you being asked to accept? You are supposed to believe that if you drink the same soft drink, you will be a winner.

Critical Thinking

Viewing Critically

Encourage students who are skilled at visual learning to identify ways in which television commercials use pictures to persuade viewers to buy their products. For example, in the television commercial illustration on this page, what message are viewers supposed to believe? (If they use Skinscrub, their skin will be as beautiful as the model's.) Ask students to describe and discuss faulty reasoning in some current television ads.

Evaluating What You Hear Faulty reasoning can exist in any form of persuasion. You may hear it in editorials on the news. You may hear it from your friends. At times you may even hear it from your own mouth. Look at the examples in the following chart. Do you recognize the faulty reasoning in each example? Where might you hear each form?

Recognizing Forms of Faulty Thinking	
Testimonial	Fred Jackson, a famous water polo player, says, "After I get out of the pool, I dry my hair with an All Hot Air hair dryer."
Bandwagon	"Hot Fish Lips is the hottest band to come to town," the D.J. says. "The concert will be a sellout. Get your tickets now."
Name Calling	"The other candidate is a total loser. If he gets elected, it won't be long until he messes up our country."
Faulty Cause and Effect	"Mom didn't buy me new basketball shoes. I didn't make the team. I'd be a starter, though, if she'd bought me the shoes."
Generalization	"Six out of ten people chose Brighty Bright toothpaste over Brand X. Brighty Bright is the best toothpaste you can buy."

Exercise 1

Listen carefully to any radio or television advertising, television editorials, and conversations you hear this week. Try to determine what is really being said. Can you sort out the facts and opinions? Which ones use faulty reasoning to persuade the listener? Find at least two examples of the forms of faulty reasoning listed in the chart above. Compare your responses with those of your classmates, and discuss why you believe or do not believe the messages.

Listening and Speaking

Practice and Assess

Evaluation Rubrics: Exercise 1

Answers will vary. Students should focus on unearthing both the obvious and the hidden messages in the commercials, editorials, and conversations they hear. For example, if they describe a car commercial, they might note that the low sticker price would be a selling point, but the attractive people standing next to the car would convey a hidden sales message.

Additional Resources
📁 *Listening and Speaking Activities*, pp. 6–8, 12–13, 16–24
📁 *Thinking and Study Skills*, pp. 33–34

Close

Have students tell why effective listening, recognition of persuasive language, and being able to distinguish between fact and opinion can help increase their enjoyment and understanding of what they hear and read.

Cooperative Learning

Creating a Commercial
Invite pairs of students to write their own commercials for a fictitious product. Tell them to use different kinds of faulty reasoning in their scripts. When they have finished, partners can perform their commercials for the class. Ask students to identify the faulty thinking in each of the commercials.

Focus

Lesson Overview

Objectives
- To understand the function of an interview
- To prepare for and conduct interviews

Skills
- choosing a subject for an interview; preparing for an interview; conducting an interview; recording an interview

Critical Thinking
- formulating questions; establishing and evaluating criteria

Listening and Speaking
- using telephone communication; listening accurately; interviewing

Bellringer
Daily Language Activity

When students enter the classroom, have this assignment on the board: *If you could interview anyone in the world, whom would you choose? Write three questions you would ask.*

See also *Daily Language Practice*

Motivating Activity

Ask volunteers to name occupations in which interviewing is used, such as talk show host, reporter, market researcher, doctor, lawyer, and writer. Ask students these questions: What are some purposes of an interview? What are the most important things an interviewer should do? What problems are likely to interfere with effective listening during an interview?

Interviewing a person is a good way to get information. Information from an interview can add life to a paper or speech. It also makes research more fun. By talking with someone, you may find useful information that you wouldn't find in a book. If you improve your interviewing skills, you may never have trouble finding information again.

When to Interview

Not every topic lends itself to interviewing. For example, let's say your oral report is on Christopher Columbus. Finding someone who sailed on the *Santa María* might be difficult. The library or museum is the place to go for that kind of report. Often, though, there are experts in the field you're researching, and they're right under your nose. You just have to look for them.

Let's say you're researching basketball rules. You might find information by asking the physical education teacher or the basketball coach. Or maybe you know someone who is a referee. When thinking about resources, don't overlook the people in your family, your school, or your community. Look at the chart below for examples of topics and possible sources of information about them.

Subjects for Interviews	
Topic	**Resources**
The history of your town	Mayor's office; local historian; oldest resident
How ice cream is made	Ice cream shop owner; parents; restaurant manager
Fly-cast fishing	Family and friends; local bait-and-tackle store owner; fly-cast fisher
Laws about children	Lawyer or judge at juvenile court; law department professor at local university; social worker
Dog breeding	Local kennel; dog breeder; veterinarian

Listening and Speaking

Resource Manager

 **Planning Resources**
- *Lesson Plans*

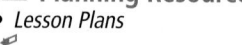 **Transparencies**
- *Bellringer*
- *Daily Language Practice*

Other Print Resources
- *Listening and Speaking Activities;* pp. 6–8, 12–13, 16–24
- *Thinking and Study Skills,* pp. 33–34

When you interview someone, you become a reporter. Keep in mind the six favorite words of every good reporter: *who, what, where, when, why,* and *how.* These words are like the signs along a road. You need them if you want to get where you want to go. Otherwise you might get lost in your interview.

Preparing to Interview

When you find someone to interview, write or call that person to request a meeting. Introduce yourself and your topic, and ask if there's a time you can meet. When you decide on a time, write it down and get ready.

Before you interview someone, find out all you can about your topic. Use encyclopedias, books, newspapers, and magazines to find basic background information. If you know something about your topic before the interview, you can focus the purpose of your interview and ask more relevant questions.

Write out those questions. Then review them before you meet with your subject. You want to make sure you haven't left out anything important.

Some materials you may need for the interview include the following:

- a tape recorder (ask if it's OK to use it)
- a notebook (tape recorders don't always work)
- a couple of pens or pencils

26.2 Interviewing **749**

Listening and Speaking

Teach
Practicing Interviewing

To help students practice interviewing in a nonthreatening situation, arrange the class in pairs for an interview exercise in which each student interviews another. First ask partners to think of an outlandish topic. Then tell them to work individually to prepare questions about the topic. When each partner has prepared a set of questions, have one of them begin to address direct questions to his or her partner. The interviewee will use imagination to respond, but the answers should make sense in the context of the made-up topic. After a few minutes, tell partners to switch roles. When both interviews are finished, ask pairs to share with the class what they considered easy or difficult about the interviews. **L1**

Cross-Reference: Writing

For information on pinpointing appropriate topics, refer students to Lesson 2.2.

Cross-Reference: Writing

For more information on interviewing, refer students to Lesson 5.8

Technology Tip

Using a Tape Recorder

Tape recorders can enable an interviewer to relax and concentrate on the flow of conversation. Later, by playing the tape back a little at a time, a reporter can write the exact language of the interview. Students should make sure that
- the interviewee approves of being recorded
- the interviewee speaks clearly and loudly enough to be recorded on tape

- the batteries or power source works
- the microphone is close enough and strong enough to pick up words clearly
- the interview will fit on the tape
- the tape cassette is labeled with the date and the subject of the interview

Teach

Choosing Subjects

After students have discussed the chart on page 748, hold a class brainstorming session to think of interesting subjects and people who could be interviewed to find out more about each subject. **L1**

The more prepared and professional you are in your interview, the better it will go.

For a helpful interview, you need to ask good questions. For example, if you interviewed a firefighter in your town, here are some questions you might ask.

List of Sample Questions to Ask a Firefighter

1. What were you like as a child? Was it your childhood dream to be a firefighter?

2. When did you decide to be a firefighter?

3. Where did you attend school to learn to fight fires? What was the training like?

4. What is the scariest thing about fighting fires? Have you ever been close to losing your life?

5. What was the worst fire you ever fought? How long did it take to put it out?

6. What tasks do you have to perform when you're not fighting fires?

Conducting an Interview

Check the questions from your notes, and take them to the interview. Then listen closely, take good notes, and ask follow-up questions. Also, be sure to relax. If you're at ease, chances are the person you're interviewing will be relaxed, too.

Ask Open-ended Questions   Open-ended questions can't be answered with a simple yes or no. The point of an interview is to get your subject to talk freely. Ask, "What's it like to ride a bronco?" rather than, "Is it frightening to ride a bronco?" The first question will encourage your subject to describe how bronco riding feels. You will get more information with questions like that. You'll also find more questions to ask as you go along.

Avoid Saying Too Much   Don't start a conversation with the person you're interviewing. You're there to listen. Don't get sidetracked into giving your own opinions about the topic. Just ask your

English Language Learners

Conducting Bilingual Interviews

Language barriers may make interviewing difficult for some students. Help students write clear questions and pronounce words properly. Some students may consider using a bilingual translator in their interviews. Students who speak two languages might volunteer to act as interpreters. Some students will benefit from recording their interviews so they can take their time interpreting an interviewee's responses.

questions, and then listen. Look at the following list of interviewing tips. Keep these in mind as you plan and conduct your interview.

Interviewing Tips
1. Have a general idea of the information you want to gain from the interview. Review your questions. Make sure they flow in a logical order.
2. Eliminate distractions that might impede your ability to listen and your subject's ability to speak.
3. Start with the most important questions. Be friendly, but stick to business. Keep the interview going in the right direction. Remain in charge, and stay focused.
4. If you do not understand something, ask for clarification. If you want additional information about something that was said, ask a follow-up question.
5. Pay attention as you take notes. Jot down important points, but do not get overly involved in note-taking. Eye contact is a must. You can fill in the blanks later.
6. Thank the person when the interview is over. Ask whether you may phone if you think of additional questions. You may also want to send a thank-you note.

Exercise 2

Choose several careers that interest you, and list local people in those fields. Find out the *who, what, where, when,* and *why* of each person on your list.

Begin by writing down the names of people who might provide information. Call them to see whether you could interview them. Then find as much background information as you can. Use the library or any family files for your research. Next, write out questions you can ask each person.

Conduct your interviews, using the guidelines in this lesson. Write a short biography of each person you interviewed, and add a summary telling which careers you might pursue and why. Present your results to the class.

Listening and Speaking

Practice and Assess

Evaluation Rubrics: Exercise 2

Answers will vary. Written biographies should include a person's name, what he or she did or does for a living, why he or she chose that particular career, and where and when the person was born. A strong biography will be a reflection of a strong interview. Biographies should accurately represent each person interviewed as well as each career represented. Make sure students explain why they would choose a particular career.

Additional Resources
📁 *Listening and Speaking Activities,* pp. 6–8, 12–13, 16–24
📁 *Thinking and Study Skills,* pp. 33–34

Close

Challenge students to think of specific instances in which an interview would provide better information than written sources. Then reverse the question—when would it be better to rely on written sources?

Real-World Connection

Viewing Professional Interviews
Videotape a professional interviewer at work and show the video in class or encourage students to watch an interview on a television program, such as *60 Minutes, Meet the Press,* or *Nightline.* Ask students to evaluate how well the interviewer followed the tips in the chart on this page. Invite students to share any other interviewing tips they learned from the professional.

Focus

Lesson Overview

Objectives
- To appreciate the role that informal speech plays in everyday life
- To refine the ability to speak informally

Skills
- listening accurately; speaking informally

Critical Thinking
- setting goals; formulating questions

Listening and Speaking
- speaking informally; making introductions; discussing; explaining a process; making brief announcements

Bellringer
Daily Language Activity

When students enter the classroom, have this assignment on the board: *List all the situations in which you have used spoken language today.*

See also *Daily Language Practice*

Motivating Activity

Ask students to think about any speaking they did in the past twenty-four hours. What were they talking about? To whom were they speaking? Why were they talking? Then direct students' attention to the chart. Which of these types of informal speaking did they use?

Listening and Speaking (sidebar)

26.3 Speaking Informally

You engage in informal speaking many times every day. You talk with your friends in the lunchroom or at your locker. You speak to your parents or your neighbors. These are all examples of informal speech. The tone is casual, and everyone involved usually joins in. Here are some tips on speaking informally.

Tips on Speaking Informally		
Type	**Description**	**Hint**
Conversation	This is the most informal type of speech. Each person is free to listen and speak spontaneously.	Courtesy is very important. Do not interrupt another speaker. Listen until he or she has finished.
Discussion	A discussion generally concerns one topic. One person may be chosen to act as discussion leader. The leader's job is to keep the group focused on the topic.	Letting each person speak in turn will help the group fully develop its ideas about the topic.
Announcement	Announcements are descriptions of upcoming events or activities. They should be brief but should provide all the important information.	After your announcement ask if there are questions. You want to be sure that everyone understands what you have announced.
Demonstration	The speaker explains how a process works or how something is made.	Demonstrate the steps of a process in the correct order. Number the steps so that your audience can follow the process.
Storytelling	Stories are usually meant to entertain, to teach a moral, or to make a point. You could tell a story about almost anything.	Let your enthusiasm for your story show in how you tell it. Act out the parts. Re-create the story. Draw your audience in.

Resource Manager

 Planning Resources
- *Lesson Plans*

 Transparencies
- *Bellringer*
- *Daily Language Practice*

📁 **Other Print Resources**
- *Listening and Speaking Activities,* pp. 6–8, 12–13, 16–24
- *Thinking and Study Skills,* pp. 33–34

Participating in a Discussion

You probably take part in discussions of some kind every day. You may have them in classes, on sports teams, in choir, and so on. You probably also have discussions with your family or among friends.

Often in discussions groups try to make decisions. Discussion leaders are needed then, because people don't always agree. Leaders aren't the only people who help discussions run smoothly, though. It's the job of everyone involved. Here are some tips for taking part in an informal discussion.

Tips for Participating in a Discussion

1. Let everyone take turns speaking. Do not interrupt when someone else is talking.

2. Pay attention to the discussion leader. If it is time to move on or quiet down, be cooperative.

3. Listen to what everyone says. Jot down notes on points you want to remember.

4. When it is your turn to talk, look at everyone around you. If you state an opinion, clarify and support it with evidence or examples.

5. If something is unclear to you, ask a question.

6. Help the group stick to the topic under discussion. Make sure your comments relate directly to it.

Explaining a Process

Building a model airplane and making blueberry muffins may not seem to have anything in common, but they do. Both are processes that require step-by-step directions.

When giving directions, explain the process in a simple and clear way, and in the correct order. If you don't give good directions, your blueberry muffins may end up tasting like the model airplane. On the next page you'll find step-by-step directions for explaining things.

Listening and Speaking

26.3 Speaking Informally **753**

Teach

Practicing Speaking in a Group

Suggest a topic and ask four or five volunteers to participate in a demonstration discussion. Invite the group to the front of the classroom and guide them through a practice discussion about the selected topic. After the model discussion, ask other students for constructive comments about how the various participants contributed to the discussion as a whole. **L2**

Pacing Conversation

Point out that sometimes students may be so accustomed to "carrying the ball" in class discussions that they unintentionally monopolize group discussions. Have the class brainstorm to develop a list of ways to encourage the participation of less vocal students. To prompt their thinking, provide examples such as the following:

- Ask questions to draw others into the conversation.
- Resist the impulse to interrupt others who may respond or speak more slowly.
- Listen attentively and allow pauses in dialogue. **L3**

Technology Tip

Drafting and Revising

If possible, students should draft and revise their process explanations on a personal computer. The editing features in word processing software make it easy to experiment with the order of steps and the proper wording of directions. Students could also print out more than one form of the process and ask others to comment on which is easiest to follow.

Teach

Working Through a Process

Students may have a difficult time putting the steps of a process into the proper order. Advise them to physically work through the process, writing down the steps as they complete them. Encourage them to express their ideas in visual aids, such as models or diagrams, to help them present information about the process. **L1**

Cross-Reference: Writing

For instruction and practice on ordering and explaining a process, refer students to Lesson 5.4.

How to Give Step-By-Step Directions

1. Determine your audience and the information they will need to understand the process.

2. Write out the process on a piece of paper. Make a diagram to use as a visual aid if you think that will help make the process clear.

3. Go back and fill in any steps you have forgotten.

4. Review the steps, and rearrange any that are out of order.

5. Reword each step so that it is simply and clearly stated.

Making Announcements

If you had to make an announcement to your class about an upcoming event, would you know what to do? Making a good announcement requires you to consider three things. First of all, you must understand your audience. What do they need to hear? Second, consider the announcement itself. What are the facts? How can you make sure you state all the facts clearly and briefly? Finally, you need to decide how you can strengthen the persuasiveness of your announcement. How can you make people *want* to hear what you say?

Tips for Making Announcements

1. Write down the most important points. The name of the event and the date, time, and place are necessary, so include them.

2. If you can, add a little life to what you have written. Think of your audience—what would make them want to attend the event?

3. Make sure everyone is quiet before you begin speaking. Look over your audience to get everyone's attention.

4. While speaking, look at your audience to convey your message.

5. Speak slowly and in a normal voice. Be sure that everyone has heard the entire message.

6. When you have finished, ask if there are any questions.

Listening and Speaking

754 Unit 26 Listening and Speaking

Enrichment and Extension

Making Announcements

Suggest that interested students volunteer to write an announcement of upcoming events and present it over the school's public address system. Students could gather information from the school newspaper, teachers, coaches, club sponsors or members, and student council officers. Tell students to avoid talking softly or too quickly when speaking into the microphone. Make sure they secure the principal's permission to make an announcement.

Exercise 3

Imagine that the following announcement came over your school's public address system. Meet with a small group to discuss the announcement. Have one group member read it aloud to judge its effectiveness. What is good about the announcement? What is not so good about it? Has anything been left out? Working as a group, rewrite the announcement so that it is as effective as you can make it.

A dance will be held in the gym this Friday after the basketball game. If you attend the game, you get into the dance free. Our basketball team's record so far this season is 4–0. It's our school's best start in ten years. We're playing our biggest rival. Tip-off is at seven o'clock. The dance will follow immediately and go until midnight. The bleachers will be pushed back, and music will be played through the gym's sound system. If you want to come, you must have a permission slip filled out by a parent or guardian.

Exercise 4

Break into small groups to make a list of events that would require announcements. The events can be real or imaginary. Allow each member to choose one event and work independently. Make a list, including as much information about your event as you can. Don't actually write the announcement. Just list the information.

When your list is complete, fold your paper and put it into a container. Each group member should pick a list from the container and write a short announcement for it. Read the announcements aloud in your group, and discuss their effectiveness.

Practice and Assess

Evaluation Rubrics: Exercise 3

Answers will vary. Monitor the groups during their discussions. In their groups, students should determine which information can be discarded (such as the detail about bleachers being pushed back) and what information needs to be added (such as the cost of dance tickets for those who do not attend the game). Groups should attempt a lively, engaging tone in their announcements.

Evaluation Rubrics: Exercise 4

Answers will vary. Announcements should contain pertinent information, such as what the event is, when it will be held, where it will be located, who should attend, and how much (if anything) it costs. They should also include an interesting hook to catch the audience's attention. Students should read their announcements clearly, making eye contact with their audience.

Additional Resources

📁 *Listening and Speaking Activities,* pp. 6–8, 12–13, 16–24
📁 *Thinking and Study Skills,* pp. 33–34

Close

Ask students to review ways to get an audience's attention before or during the delivery of an announcement. What are ways to get a listener's attention in conversation? What are sure-fire ways to put an audience to sleep?

Listening and Speaking

Speaking Formally

Focus

Lesson Overview

Objectives

- To appreciate the role that speaking formally plays in everyday life
- To prepare and deliver formal speeches

Skills

- identifying main idea; summarizing; defining and clarifying

Critical Thinking

- analyzing; classifying; evaluating

Listening and Speaking

- taking notes; formal speaking

 Bellringer
Daily Language Activity

When students enter the classroom, have this assignment on the board: *Write a sentence giving a reason why you or someone else might have to or want to give a speech before an audience.*

See also *Daily Language Practice*

Motivating Activity

Ask students if they have ever given a speech in front of a group of classmates or a larger audience. What was their speech about? How did they prepare for it? Were they nervous, or did they enjoy speaking before people? Would they like the opportunity to give another speech? What would they do the same? differently?

Listening and Speaking

Writing a formal speech is similar to writing a research paper, but it can be more satisfying. When you write a paper for a class, your teacher is probably the only one who reads it. But if you give a speech on the same topic, your whole class gets to hear it. Speeches are great opportunities to share with others what you've learned and what you believe in. You'll find that speeches are easy to give if you use the three steps of preparation, practice, and delivery. These steps all lead to a well-researched, well-organized, and successful presentation.

Preparing a Speech

Preparation is the most important part of writing a speech. It's the foundation on which everything is built. A weak foundation almost always makes for a weak house. The same is true of speeches. Put a lot of time and effort into the preparation of your speech. Make it as strong as you can. If you do, you'll be able to write and deliver a strong speech.

Prewriting You first need to consider the purpose of your speech. What are you attempting to do? Inform? Persuade? Then think of your audience. What do they already know about your topic? What don't they know? Use this information to help you adapt your language to your audience and purpose.

Next, narrow the topic. A subject such as "Dogs of the World" is too broad. Maybe selecting one breed would be wise. You might further narrow the topic to either the characteristics or the history of the dog.

Drafting Once you feel comfortable with your topic, audience, and purpose, it's time to move on. Write out your main point in one sentence. This is your thesis statement. It summarizes the entire speech. Your thesis statement might read, "Cocker spaniels are good pets for children." Everything in your speech should then support this statement.

With your thesis statement written, start drafting. Like a research paper, a formal speech usually contains three main parts. The introduction is first; it sets up the speech. Next comes the body, containing your main ideas and supporting details. Last, the conclusion wraps up everything. There are two ways to compose your speech. You can write it out exactly as you'll say it, or you can use note cards. Outlining your main points and supporting details on note cards usually works better.

Resource Manager

📁 **Planning Resources**
- *Lesson Plans*

🗂 **Transparencies**
- *Bellringer*
- *Daily Language Practice*

📁 **Other Print Resources**
- *Listening and Speaking Activities,* pp. 6–8, 12–13, 16–24
- *Thinking and Study Skills,* pp. 33–34

You can refer to what you need to say without having to read your speech word for word.

Revising At this point you want to take an X-ray of your speech. Look at its skeleton—the structure you've built out of words. Do your words support the ideas you want to get across? Does your speech flow logically from one idea to the next? Do all your ideas lead toward a conclusion? If you find areas where the structure breaks down, rework them. Don't be surprised if you go back and forth between drafting and revising. It takes time to fine-tune a speech.

Also, use strong transitions. You don't want to lose your audience when you move to the next thought. For example, you could begin another main point with, "*Another* way in which the cocker spaniel is a good pet . . ."

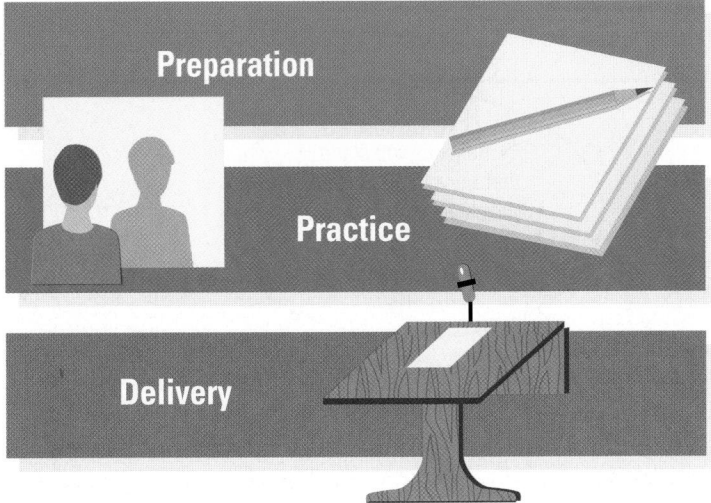

As you prepare your oral report, use the diagram on the next page to help you structure it. Notice the writing stages shown in the box between Prewriting and Presenting. You'll spend most of your time in the Drafting, Revising, and Practicing stages. Move back and forth among these until you're ready to present your report.

Practicing a Speech

Once you write your speech, practice it as much as you can. If your speech is supposed to be a certain length, time yourself. This will help you speed it up or slow it down. Also, practice delivering your speech

Teach

Preparing a Speech

Write a general subject on the board, such as *Unusual Hobbies, Protecting the Environment,* or *Space Exploration.* Have students brainstorm to develop a list of related, narrower speech topics. As a class, write a thesis statement for each topic. Ask students where they would begin looking if they were preparing a speech from the list. Who might they be able to interview in their research? In what ways could they make this speech unique? **L2**

⊠ Cross-Reference: Writing

For more instruction and practice on sentence revising strategies, refer students to Lesson 2.8.

Listening and Speaking

MEETING INDIVIDUAL NEEDS **Less-Proficient Readers**

Using Transitions in Speeches

Encourage students to write out different transitions on individual note cards. (Some verbal transitions might be *another, also, on the other hand, however, next, so far, again,* and *in summary.*) Tell students to keep the cards in front of them as they practice to remind them to use transitions as oral road signs that help the audience follow a speech.

Teach

Identifying the Differences Between Oral and Written Reports

After the class has studied the stages in the diagram, ask students to identify some differences between oral and written reports (see Unit 5). How do the stages differ? Which stages are emphasized more in oral reports? How will content and organization be different in an oral report than in a written one? Discuss the advantages and disadvantages of oral reports and written reports. **L2**

📇 Cross-Reference: Writing

For more information about determining a topic, a purpose, and an audience, refer students to Lesson 2.2.

📇 Cross-Reference: Writing

For more information about writing stages, refer students to Lesson 2.1.

Prewriting
- Determine your purpose and audience.
- Decide on a topic and narrow it.

Drafting
- Make an outline of the important points.
- Fill in the supporting details.
- Write out what you want to say.

Revising
- Review your report. Does it flow logically from one point to the next?
- Reword unclear statements.
- Write an outline on note cards to make practicing easier.

Practicing
- Practice your report out loud and alone, then again in front of a friend or family member.
- Ask for advice and accept it to improve your report.
- Time the report if it needs to be a certain length.

Presenting
- Relax as you stand before your audience.
- Make eye contact with the audience at all times.
- Speak up and speak clearly.

in front of a mirror. Look for unnatural gestures or exaggerated movements. If you can, practice giving your speech into a tape recorder. Listen to your voice. Are you emphasizing important words and ideas? Are you speaking too slowly or too quickly? Are you pronouncing words clearly and distinctly?

Rehearse your speech in front of a few friends or relatives. Ask for comments on what is strong and what needs work. Don't be afraid of criticism. Consider the changes they suggest, and make the changes if you feel comfortable doing so.

If you can, practice your speech at the site where you'll later give it. That way, the surroundings will be familiar, and you'll feel comfortable when you deliver the speech.

Listening and Speaking

Listening and Speaking

Recording Speeches and Noticing Patterns

A tape recorder is a valuable tool for any speaker. Suggest that students who have access to a tape recorder record their practice runs. They can use the recording to analyze the speed, volume, tone, and flow of their voices.

Use your notes to remind yourself of the main points. Your note cards shouldn't serve as script, though. If you just read your speech, your audience may lose interest.

Delivering a Speech

You've prepared and practiced your speech. Now it's important that you remember to relax. Be yourself in front of the audience. It's the best way to capture and hold people's attention. If you enjoy giving your speech, your audience will enjoy listening.

If you're a bit nervous, don't worry. Use that uneasiness to your advantage. Athletes, stage actors, and singers all know how to use "butterflies" to make their performance more energetic and full of life. You can do the same thing.

Before the Speech   At the last minute, just before you deliver your speech, you may be tempted to make changes. That could be a bad idea, though. You've drafted, revised, and rehearsed your speech. Changes might upset the careful preparation you've just completed. Change only what positively needs improvement in your speech.

Tips for Relating to Your Audience		
Audience Signals	**Interpretation**	**Speaker Response**
People in your audience are moving around in their chairs or staring off into space.	You may have lost their attention.	You may recapture their interest by raising and lowering your voice or adding gestures. Perhaps you need to speed up your delivery.
Your audience seems puzzled. Some are talking with a neighbor.	They may not have understood something you said.	You may need to back up and explain a portion of your speech again. Briefly review your main ideas before continuing.
You notice some people trying to get closer to you. A few are leaning forward in their chairs.	They may be unable to hear you.	Speak up. Maybe some other noises are preventing people from hearing. Ask the audience if you need to repeat anything.
Your audience is listening attentively and nodding.	You have their full attention.	You are doing well. Do not change a thing. Keep up the good work.

Teach

Using Notes or Scripts

If students have trouble with vocabulary or grammar or with focusing on their audience, suggest that they use note cards or a script (handwritten, typed, or done on a computer) when presenting their speeches. Help them mark their scripts for pronunciation of difficult words. Suggest also that they put notes or symbols in the margins to remind them to look up or to use body gestures. If students tend to lose their places during their speeches, tell them to use their fingers to follow line by line down the margins of their scripts. **L1**

Listening and Speaking

Listening and Speaking

Learning from Contrast

To help students learn how delivery affects a speech, have them take turns giving a one-minute "nervous" speech. Tell students to use unsatisfactory speaking habits (talk too quietly or loudly, or too slowly or quickly; fail to make eye contact with anyone; let thoughts wander). When students have finished, ask volunteers to give the same speeches, this time with effective delivery. Have your students contrast speeches. Finally, ask them to make inferences on the basis of what they have heard.

Teach

Learning from Accomplished Speakers

Show a video of an accomplished orator giving a speech. (Check your local public library for a video of a speech by Martin Luther King Jr., or John F. Kennedy.) Afterward, ask students to discuss their observations and responses. Was the speech persuasive? Why or why not? What words, phrases, or body gestures made the speech powerful? **L3**

Just before you speak, take a moment to look at your audience. You created your speech just for them. Keeping that in mind will help you deliver your speech confidently.

During the Speech   As you begin speaking, remember to make eye contact with your audience. Try talking to each person in turn. As you focus on each member of the audience, tell yourself that you're speaking directly to that person. Think about what you're saying and to whom you're saying it. When you take your mind off yourself, you become more relaxed.

Keep an eye out, too, for audience signals. No matter how well you plan, something unexpected can always occur. Think about what went wrong and how you can make it right. Above all, don't panic if something goes wrong. Below are some tips that will help you identify possible problems.

Deliver your speech with all the gestures and voice variations you've practiced. You can also respond to your audience. If they smile, smile back. Whatever happens, though, don't allow yourself to be distracted. Use your note cards, and keep up the rhythm and flow of your speech. Stay focused on what you're saying, and you'll deliver a successful speech. Following are a few more tips for speaking effectively.

Tips for Speaking Effectively

1. After you make an important point, pause a moment. A pause allows your audience to think about what you have said. It also creates a dramatic break that will capture people's attention.

2. Look around the room as you speak, making eye contact with each person in the audience. Think of your own experience. You probably dislike it when a speaker talks at you rather than to you.

3. Use your arms and hands while speaking. If you just stand there stiffly, your voice may also turn flat. Avoid going overboard. You do not want your gestures to be unnatural, but you do want them to strengthen your words.

4. To make sure you are speaking loudly enough, start out by speaking directly to someone in the last row of your audience.

Cooperative Learning

Responding to Audience Signals

Have small groups of students review the Tips for Relating to Your Audience chart on this page. Ask groups to compile a list of other signals from an audience that speech makers should be alerted to. Have groups suggest ways that a speaker might respond when he or she notices these signals from the audience.

Exercise 5

Choose a partner to work with throughout this exercise. Together choose a topic for a formal speech. Pick one from the list below, or use another of your choice.

- the history of the trombone (or of another instrument)
- the extinct mammoth
- sign language: the language of the deaf
- the northern lights
- what you should know about cars
- the joy of computers

After you have narrowed and researched the topic together, you should each write and practice your own speech. Your speech can either inform or persuade. When you are finished, deliver them to each other. Express your ideas fluently, using Standard American English. Discuss how your speeches are alike and different. What are the strong points and weak points? Make suggestions to each other for improving your speeches.

Practice and Assess

Evaluation Rubrics: Exercise 5

Answers will vary. Evaluate the student responses to this exercise not only on the basis of how well each student wrote and delivered a speech but also on how effectively students worked together to offer each other suggestions for improving their speeches and their performances.

Additional Resources

📂 *Listening and Speaking Activities,* pp. 6–8, 12–13, 16–24
📂 *Thinking and Study Skills,* pp. 33–34

Close

List the following topics from Lesson 26.4 on the chalkboard:

- How to Prepare for a Speech
- Practicing a Speech
- Delivering a Speech
- Tips for Relating to Your Audience
- Tips for Speaking Effectively

Ask students to prepare and make a brief speech about one of the topics, using what they have learned in Lesson 26.4. After each speech, have students identify the speaker's main ideas. Then ask them to evaluate the speaker's presentation, using the tips found on page 760.

Listening and Speaking

26.4 Speaking Formally **761**

Listening and Speaking

Practicing a Speech in Front of a Video Camera

Videotaping a practice speech is a valuable exercise. Tell students that friends may tell them about some of their bad speaking habits, but seeing those habits on screen for themselves will have a greater impact. Encourage students to include a visual aid or prop as a part of their practice speech. If students or their friends do not have a video camera, tell them to check with the library to see if it has any video equipment.

Focus

Lesson Overview

Objective
• To prepare and present a dramatic interpretation of a poem

Skills
• selecting and analyzing a poem; researching and rehearsing for an oral presentation

Critical Thinking
• establishing and evaluating criteria; defining and clarifying

Listening and Speaking
• formal speaking

Bellringer
Daily Language Activity

When students enter the classroom, have this assignment on the board: *You have been selected to give a poetry reading. List five things you would do to prepare for your presentation.*

See also *Daily Language Practice*

Motivating Activity

Encourage students to express their concerns about speaking in front of a group. Ask them to suggest ways to overcome these fears. Guide them in thinking about an occasion when they gave or heard an oral presentation of a poem. Did they or the speaker speak with confidence? Based on their experiences, what do they think are the most important things to keep in mind when preparing and presenting a dramatic interpretation of a poem?

26.5 Presenting a Dramatic Interpretation

The impulse to tell a story, whether in the form of a poem, a song, a myth, or an epic, has always been a part of human culture. Such stories, often passed from one generation to the next, tell the hopes, the sorrows, and the history of a culture. In ancient Greece and Rome, bards, or traveling poets, presented their works at public festivals. At festivals today, poets and storytellers continue to entertain and delight their audiences.

The art of reciting or reading poetry aloud is not limited to poets; anyone can prepare and deliver an oral interpretation of a favorite poem. Choose a poem and follow these steps as you prepare to present a poem to your class.

Preparing a Poetry Reading

1. Think about who the speaker might be. Whose "voice" do you hear? What is the speaker's tone, or attitude, toward the subject? How might you use your voice to convey that tone?
2. Read through the poem again, this time focusing on your own reaction to it. What emotions do you feel? What ideas and questions come to mind? Jot down your responses to the poem, and look up any unfamiliar words. Make notes about how the poet's choice of language and imagery helps convey the intended meaning. Which words, phrases, or sentences will you emphasize in your oral interpretation?
3. Notice sound devices such as rhyme, rhythm, and repetition. Consider how you will emphasize sound devices as you recite or read the poem aloud.
4. Decide where you will pause to take a breath. Pause at the end of a line only if there is a punctuation mark or a natural pause. Otherwise, read through the ends of lines—even rhyming lines—until you reach a good place to pause.
5. Experiment with volume and speed to convey feeling.

Resource Manager

📂 Planning Resources
• *Lesson Plans*

Transparencies
• *Bellringer*
• *Daily Language Practice*

📂 Other Print Resources
• *Listening and Speaking Activities,* pp. 6–8, 12–13, 16–24
• *Thinking and Study Skills,* pp. 33–34

Giving a Poetry Reading

Think of your presentation as an opportunity to give yourself, as well as your classmates, a better understanding and greater appreciation of the poem.

1. Eliminate any distractions that might disrupt the flow of your reading or your classmates' ability to concentrate.
2. The way you present your poem will depend on how you have interpreted it. However, you should always speak clearly and loudly enough so that all of your classmates can hear you.
3. Make eye contact with your audience to help them feel involved in your performance.
4. After you share your oral interpretation with your class, ask for questions or comments. Compare your understanding of the poem with your audience's interpretation.
5. Remember that poetry is open to many interpretations. Insights from your classmates may even help to expand your understanding of the poem further.

Exercise 6

In groups of three, generate criteria for evaluating poetry readings. Think about tone, rate of speaking, rhythm, volume, and pitch. How might these factors affect the presentation of the poem's meaning? Then, as a group, choose a poem to use for a poetry reading. Individually, prepare your own reading of the poem and tape record it. Regroup and listen to each reading of the same poem. How are they the same? Different? Discuss the similarities and differences and the reasons for them. Use your list of criteria to judge the effectiveness of each reading.

Exercise 7

Think about reasons why poetry has often been used to carry on oral traditions in many cultures. What purpose do you think poetry might have served in these cultures? Then think about the role of poetry in your culture. What purposes might it serve? Share your ideas with a group.

Listening and Speaking

Practice and Assess

Evaluation Rubrics: Exercise 6

Students should be given an appropriate amount of time to complete this exercise. Students may suggest the following criteria to evaluate a poetry reading:

- Poem is appropriate for the audience
- Speaker uses effective rate, volume, pitch, and tone for the audience and setting
- Speaker emphasizes sound devices to convey the mood and message of the poem
- Speaker uses appropriate posture and makes eye contact with the audience
- Speaker uses effective gestures and facial expressions
- Delivery is smooth and well rehearsed

Answers: Exercise 7

Students may say that poetry is more vivid and condensed than prose. The rhythm, rhymes, images, colorful language, and sounds of the words in poetry make it possible to remember poems even after many years. For this reason, in many cultures poetry was used as a repository for history as well as for entertainment.

Additional Resources

📁 *Listening and Speaking Activities,* pp. 6–8, 12–13, 16–24
📁 *Thinking and Study Skills,* pp. 33–34

✔ ASSESSMENT OPTIONS

📁 *Tests with Answer Key and Rubrics*
Unit 26 Mastery, pp. 107–108

💾 *Testmaker*
Unit 26 Mastery Test

📼 *MindJogger Videoquizzes*

You may wish to administer the Unit 26 Mastery Test at this point.

Cooperative Learning

Preparing a Presentation

Make it possible for students who are learning English to work with English-proficient students to prepare their poetry readings. Together partners can work on selecting a poem, understanding its lines, pronouncing difficult words, and rehearsing its delivery.

Close

Discuss with the class what strategies would help them to prepare for and give a poetry reading. Have students identify what skills or strategies they need to continue to work on.

Objectives

- To develop skills for interpreting visual messages and for identifying the techniques that are used to emphasize them
- To learn to analyze and evaluate media messages
- To produce media messages

✔ ASSESSMENT OPTIONS

📁 *Tests with Answer Key and Rubrics*
Unit 27 Pretest, pp. 109–110

💾 *Testmaker*
Unit 27 Pretest

You may wish to administer the Unit 27 Pretest at this point.

Key to Ability Levels

L1 Level 1 activities are within the basic ability range of students.

L2 Level 2 activities are within the ability range of average students.

L3 Level 3 activities are more challenging activities.

UNIT
27 Viewing and Representing

764

Resource Manager

 **Planning Resources**
- *Lesson Plans*
- *Block Scheduling*

 **Other Print Resources**
- *Tests with Answer Key and Rubrics*
- *Viewing and Representing Activities*

 **Video**
- *MindJogger Videoquizzes*

 **Software**
- *Presentation Plus!*
- *Testmaker*

 **Web Sites**
- *writerschoice.glencoe.com*

Studies show that young people spend an average of one thousand hours a year watching television. That's almost three hours every day. Added to that are the many hours they spend watching movies, playing video games, reading magazines, listening to CDs and the radio, and surfing the Web. For better or worse, young people, far more than their parents and grandparents, have become very attached to **mass media.**

The term *mass media* means "a form of communication that is widely available to many people." Examples include newspapers, magazines, television, radio, movies, videos, and the Internet. Most of such forms of mass media also contain advertisements, messages that have only one purpose: to persuade readers or viewers to buy a certain product.

The various forms of mass media will have a great influence on your life. The influences can bring both positive and negative messages and results. Some forms of the media will enable you to learn new skills and explore new ideas and opportunities. Others will bring you inspiring or exciting entertainment. However, some forms of the media, if you are not careful, can mislead you, confuse you, and even endanger you.

The media often present difficult challenges. How can readers and viewers decide which media messages are valuable and truthful, and which messages are harmful, unfair, or just plain junk? Knowledge is power! Learning how to interpret, analyze, and evaluate the many messages that are sent to you—by the press, the radio and television, the movie and video game industry, the advertisers, and the Web— will give you the power and the skills to enjoy the media's benefits and discard the media junk. This unit will help.

27 Introduction **765**

Visual Literacy

Explain to students that *literacy* refers to the ability to read and write, that is, to understand the meaning of something written and to use letters or symbols to convey a message. Remind them that in these days of television, movies, the Internet, and advertising, it is not enough to be literate only in regard to the printed word. Society must be visually literate as well. People living in a global environment must be able to understand the meaning of images and the ways in which they are presented. Emphasize to students that only as consumers who are visually literate will they be able to make rational choices about what to buy or to believe.

Viewing and Representing

Focus

Lesson Overview

Objectives

- To develop effective skills for identifying, understanding, and interpreting visual images and messages sent by various forms of mass media
- To create and produce mass media messages

Skills

- identifying and analyzing visual elements; understanding visual design; using charts, graphics, film, and video segments

Critical Thinking

- interpreting; drawing conclusions; classifying; speculating; comparing and contrasting

Listening and Speaking

- discussing; asking and answering questions; informal speaking; interpreting and explaining various visual techniques

 Bellringer
Daily Language Activity

When students enter the classroom have this assignment on the board: *Write a definition of the term* mass media.

Motivating Activity

Discuss the meaning of **mass media**—"a form of communication that is widely available to many people." Call on volunteers to name types of mass media that contain pictures, citing specific examples, such as newspapers with cartoons, graphs, and photos, or a specific television program or movie. Ask students to describe what types of visual messages the pictures send. Then display advertisements for products students will consider familiar. Call on volunteers to suggest how these advertisements persuade readers and viewers to buy a certain product. Explain that in this lesson students will learn more about visual messages sent by the mass media and that they will develop an understanding of how to interpret those messages.

Viewing and Representing

27.1 Interpreting Visual Messages

Radio is the only example of mass media that does not contain pictures. Just like written text, pictures carry messages. Every photograph, painting, cartoon, drawing, advertisement, and computer graphic is created carefully to send a distinct visual message. If you understand how artists and photographers craft pictures to send messages, you will be able to "read" each message and evaluate its value and truthfulness.

Understanding Visual Design

The colors, shapes, and various types of lines make up the **visual design** of a picture. The arrangement of features in a picture is called **composition.** The following chart lists some basic elements in the visual design and composition of a picture. It also describes how the artist or photographer can manipulate, or work with, these elements to send different visual messages that convey distinct thoughts, feelings, and moods.

Elements of Visual Design and Composition

Element	Possible Effect
Lines	
Heavy, thick lines	Suggest boldness or power
Thin or broken lines	Suggest weakness or lightness
Straight lines	Point in a direction, or lead the eye, to something else
Curved lines	Suggest motion, warmth
Vertical lines	Suggest power, status
Horizontal lines	Suggest peace, stillness
Diagonal lines	Suggest tension, action, energy
Shapes	
Round	Suggest wholeness, happiness
Square	Suggest firmness, stability
Colors	
Cool colors (blue, green, gray)	Convey a sense of calm and coldness
Warm colors (orange, yellow, red)	Convey a sense of energy and vibrancy
Bright colors	Create a sense of warmth and joyfulness
Subdued or pastel colors	Suggest innocence or softness
Repetition of color	Can suggest a pattern or assign a value to what is portrayed

 **Resource Manager**

Planning Resources
- *Lesson Plans*

Other Print Resources
- *Viewing and Representing Activities*

Elements of Visual Design and Composition *continued*	
Element	**Possible Effect**
Position of subjects	
Center of picture	Suggests strength, dominance; draws attention to the subject
Top of picture	Suggests power, importance
Bottom of picture	Suggests weakness, lack of power
Space	
Large space around subject	Draws attention to subject; can suggest loneliness, vastness
Small amount of space around subject	Makes subject seem very powerful

Study this photograph. The bright, warm colors suggest energy and joyfulness. The girl is positioned in the center top of the picture. Your eye is drawn immediately to her face, and her facial expression matches the message sent by the design and composition: She is having fun! Note also that the round snow tube and its shadow take up almost all the space in the photograph. This makes the subject seem very powerful. So does the head-on shot. You relate to the girl's feelings because she is looking right into your eyes. How might the visual message, or mood of this picture be different if the photographer had taken it from the sidelines as the girl raced by?

Exercise 1

Use the Elements of Visual Design and Composition chart to help you interpret the visual message contained in the photograph to the left. Explain how shapes and position, as well as colors and facial expression, work together to send that message.

Many artists and photographers choose to work in black and white rather than in color. The absence of color lets them emphasize dark and light. Study the chart on the next page to understand how light and shadow often send visual messages.

Viewing and Representing

27.1 Interpreting Visual Messages   **767**

Teach

Using the Chart

Help students use the Elements of Visual Design and Composition chart to interpret the first photograph on this page. Discuss how the photographer uses shapes, colors, space, and position of the subject to create a visual message. Lead students to understand that if the picture had been taken from the side, the viewer would not have had such a strong sense of identification with the girl on the snow tube, and the vibrant power of the oncoming motion might have been lost. **L2**

Interpreting Music Videos

Show students a music video with the sound turned off. Have them analyze the visual impressions they experience, using the elements from the chart on pp. 766–767. Then replay the video with the sound. Ask students if the video and the song lyrics tell the same story. Does the video add meaning to the song? Discuss whether analyzing the visual elements before listening to the music increased students' enjoyment of the video. **L2**

Interpreting a Visual Message

Have students work with partners to interpret the messages in the photograph on the bottom of page 767. Encourage students to refer to the Elements of Visual Design and Composition chart on pages 766–767 and ask them to determine how position, space, and color work together with the child's facial expression to send a message. Have students present their ideas in a class discussion. **L2**

Enrichment and Extension

Interpreting School Messages

Have students apply the information in the Elements of Visual Design and Composition chart to interpret messages incorporated into posters, photographs, cartoons, and other visual images displayed in their school building. Ask them to write several paragraphs evaluating these messages and then share those evaluations with the class. **L3**

Teach

Exploring Light and Shadow

Discuss the Visual Messages of Light and Shadow chart on this page. Help students understand the various effects that are possible with black-and-white film. Then direct students' attention to the Lewis Hine photograph on this page. Ask them to speculate about what message the photographer intended by placing the child's face in the light, while plunging the rest of her body and the heavy machinery into darkness. **L2**

Evaluation Rubrics: Exercise 2

Following class discussion, students should work independently to complete Exercise 2 as a written activity. Advise them to write two paragraphs—first, to identify the visual message and to explain how the photographer used various elements of visual design and composition to send it; and second, to compare and contrast the design and message of this photograph with the two photographs already discussed.

Use these criteria when evaluating the written assignment:

- Does the first paragraph include details concerning the photographer's use of lines, position, and space to stress or extend his visual message?
- Does the second paragraph effectively compare and contrast this photograph, and its message, to the two photographs discussed previously?

Viewing and Representing

Visual Messages of Light and Shadow	
Use of Light	**Possible Effect**
Brightly lit areas	Draw the eye to them; create a cheerful mood
Dimly lit areas or shadows	Give a sense of mystery, sadness, or doom

Study this photograph. It was taken in 1909. At that time, many children worked in factories and mills. Laws to protect them had not yet been passed. Lewis Hine took this photograph of a young mill worker. He used it to illustrate a report he wrote that urged lawmakers to pass protective child-labor laws. Note that the objects shown in the top of the photograph are brightly lit, while the objects in the lower half of the photograph are dark and heavy. The photographer purposely used this contrast of light and dark. He wanted to draw the viewer's attention to the child's face. He also used the sunlight on her face to represent youth and innocence. Then he plunged most of the child's body, and the heavy machinery surrounding her, into darkness.

Exercise 2

Think about the photographer's use of light and darkness in this photograph. Summarize in your own words the visual message that he wanted to send. Then refer to the Elements of Visual Design and Composition chart. Explain how the photographer used lines, position, and space to stress or extend his visual message.

Finally, compare and contrast the visual design of this photograph with one of the others used in this section. How did both photographers manipulate the elements of visual design and composition to send entirely different messages?

Understanding Film Techniques

Like a short story or novel, a movie or television show tells a story. Also like written literature, films use dialogue to tell much of the story. However, films also use a variety of techniques that go beyond

Viewing and Representing

About the Photographer

This photograph, entitled "Little Spinner in Carolina Cotton Mill, " was taken by Lewis Hine (1874–1940) and appeared in his book *Child Labor in the Carolinas,* published in 1909. Educated and trained as a sociologist, Hine used his photographic talents to document the often horrible conditions endured by American factory workers and miners. His work contributed to the passage of several reform bills.

Many of Hine's photographs can be viewed at major museums, including the National Archives in Washington, D.C.

what can be done on the written page. Think back to stories that you have both read and seen performed in a film or television version. How did the two versions compare? What, if anything, did the film techniques add to your understanding or enjoyment of the story?

The following chart lists some of the special visual techniques that directors of movies and television shows use to extend or emphasize the mood or message of the film.

Film Techniques for Sending Visual Messages	
Technique	**Possible Effect**
Camera angles	
High (looking down on subjects)	Often makes subject seem smaller, less important, or more at risk
Low (looking up at subject)	Emphasizes subject's importance or power
Straight-on (eye level)	Puts viewer on equal level with subject; can make viewer identify with subject
Camera shots	
Close-up (picture of subject's face)	Emphasizes character's facial expressions; leads viewer to identify with him or her
Long shot (wide view, showing character within larger setting)	Shows relationship between character and setting
Lighting	
High, bright lighting	Creates cheerful, optimistic tone
Low, shadowy lighting	Creates gloomy, mysterious tone
Lit from above	Makes subject seem to glow with power or strength
Lit from below	Often creates tone of tension or fear
Editing	
Quick transitions between frames	Speed up pace; increase suspense or excitement
Slow dissolve or fade out	Often shows that a change in time has taken place
Special effects	
Slow motion	Emphasizes movement and builds drama
Blurred motion	Suggests speed or confusion
Background music	Arouses audience's emotional response

27.1 Interpreting Visual Messages **769**

Viewing and Representing

Thinking Critically

Display examples of the dramatic black-and-white nature photographs by Ansel Adams. Additionally, display some full-color nature photographs from such publications as *National Geographic*. Challenge students to use the Elements of Visual Design and Composition chart on pages 766–767 and the Visual Messages of Light and Shadow chart on page 768 to interpret the messages in each photograph. Then have students compare and contrast the effects of full-color photography with the effects of black-and-white photos. **L3**

Using the Internet

Direct students to the Web sites of daily newspapers and television network news departments. Explain that such news organizations use dramatic photographs to draw visitors to their sites. Have students interpret the visual messages of the photographs they find and evaluate the strength and effectiveness of each photograph.

Interpreting a Movie Still

Work with students to use the Film Techniques for Sending Visual Messages chart to interpret the movie still from *Rio Bravo* on page 770. Allow time for students to offer suggestions about the types of background music they would choose for this scene. Accept all reasonable suggestions; part of the creative filmmaking process of combining dialogue, pictures, and music involves experimenting with various techniques until the desired result is reached. Commend creative answers, using them to point out the ways in which each choice might represent or extend the visual messages in the scene. **L2**

Exploring Language

Thinking About Dialogue

Remind students that along with music, filmmakers have two major tools that still photographers do not have—movement and dialogue. Ask students who are familiar with the work of John Wayne to describe his voice, explaining, if necessary, that it was deep and powerful. How might that voice contribute to the visual message of the scene from which the still photo on page 770 is taken? Then have students explore what Wayne might have said during this scene. What is happening? What is suggested by his stance, position, and props? What language would emphasize or extend the visual message?

As a historical note, you might also point out that when talking movies replaced silent films, many established stars did not make the transition. Although their facial expressions, physical appearances, and movements had been effective for emphasizing or extending the visual images on the screen during the silent era, their voices were judged to be inappropriately high or low for speaking parts.

769

Practice and Assess

Evaluation Rubrics: Exercise 3

Have students work independently to write answers to Exercise 3. Urge them to use the Elements of Visual Design and Composition chart and the Film Techniques for Sending Visual Messages chart.

Use these criteria when evaluating the written assignment:

• Do the answers include details concerning the animator's use of lines, color, lighting, camera angle, and camera shot?

• Do the answers indicate an accurate interpretation of the director's intended visual message?

• Does the choice of background music support that interpretation?

Close

Call on volunteers to identify specific visual techniques used by still photographers and film directors. Which techniques do students feel are particularly effective in getting across verbal messages? Why is it helpful to be aware of these techniques?

Throughout his long film career, actor John Wayne continually played the strong, no-nonsense hero—characteristically in Westerns and in war movies. Study the movie still at left from the 1959 classic John Wayne Western, *Rio Bravo.* Note that the director, Howard Hawks, used a low camera angle, shooting up at Wayne. This gives the character added height, and emphasizes his power and strength. Note also that Wayne is lit from above; the bright sun emphasizes the whiteness of his hat, leading viewers to perceive him as the "good guy." Then note elements in the Elements of Visual Design and Composition chart that Hawks used. He has probably instructed Wayne to stand as straight as possible, using the vertical line of that stance to emphasize the character's power and status.

What message do you think the director sends through Wayne's facial expression? At what pace do you think Wayne is walking? If you were on the creative staff of this movie, what type of background music would you choose for this scene?

Exercise 3

Study this movie still from *The Lion King.* Use the Film Techniques for Sending Visual Messages chart, as well as the Elements of Visual Design and Composition chart on pages 766–767, to describe the visual messages that the animator and director aim to send to viewers. In your answer, include such features as lines, shapes, color, lighting, camera angle, and camera shot. Then describe the type of background music you imagine in this scene. Explain your choice.

Viewing and Representing

27.2 Analyzing Media Messages

Photographs, movies, and television programs often seem "true to life." In other words, they show scenes and actions that seem realistic. However, all media messages are constructed carefully to emphasize a particular point of view. Even a factual film documentary or a public service message on such topics as the environment or personal health uses carefully chosen colors, lines, and camera angles to present information from a certain perspective.

The artist, photographer, or director makes many decisions about what pictures and information to include, what camera angles will prove most effective, and what information should not be included because it might support another point of view. Every time you view an example of mass communications, analyze it carefully. Begin by using these steps.

Key Questions to Ask Yourself About Media Messages

To analyze a media message, ask yourself these Key Questions:

- What message is this visual (photo, drawing, cartoon, television program, video) trying to send to viewers?
- What techniques were used to present the information from a particular viewpoint?
- What do I already know about this subject?
- How can I use what I already know to judge whether this message is
  —fair or unfair?
  —based on reality or fantasy?
  —based on facts or opinions?
- What additional sources might I use to find other viewpoints that I can trust on this subject?
  —parent, teacher, or other trustworthy adult
  —reliable books or other reference sources

Then, on the basis of your answers to the questions and of other trusted viewpoints that you find, make a decision about the visual message. Make sure that you can support that decision with well-thought-out reasons.
  —I agree with the visual message because . . . .
  —I disagree with the visual message because . . . .

27.2 Analyzing Media Messages **771**

Resource Manager

📂 **Planning Resources**
- *Lesson Plans*

📂 **Other Print Resources**
- *Viewing and Representing Activities*

Focus

Lesson Overview

Objectives
- To develop an understanding of how to analyze and critique visual images, messages, and meanings
- To effectively analyze media messages

Skills
- interpreting ideas; evaluating purposes and effects of varying media; evaluating how media forms influence and inform; analyzing techniques used in mass media; comparing and contrasting film with print version of a story

Critical Thinking
- interpreting; analyzing; evaluating; drawing conclusions; classifying; speculating; comparing and contrasting

Listening and Speaking
- discussing; asking and answering questions; informal speaking; interpreting, analyzing, and evaluating

🔔 **Bellringer**
Daily Language Activity

When students enter the classroom, have this assignment on the board: *On a piece of paper, describe your favorite advertisement.*

Motivating Activity

Have students share their descriptions from the Bellringer activity and invite them to explain why they made their selections. Discuss how visual and verbal messages are carefully created to support a particular point of view. Explain that facts and opinions are carefully blended, particularly in persuasive writing and advertising materials, to persuade readers and viewers to agree with a specific point of view. Then explain to students that in this lesson they will learn how to analyze and evaluate visual and verbal messages sent by various forms of mass media.

Viewing and Representing

Teach

Introducing the Key Questions

Use a photograph or other realistic visual image with a clear point of view to lead students through their first use of the Key Questions. Help them practice the Key Questions as they read and discuss the text related to the photograph and caption on page 771. **L1**

Analyzing Messages

For partners working to complete Exercise 4, provide source materials, such as newspapers and newsmagazines containing public service announcements or paid political messages. Following each presentation, encourage other class members to offer constructive ideas and comments. Use the discussion to emphasize the importance and usefulness of careful analysis and evaluation of media messages. **L2**

Viewing and Representing

> **If our population growth continues, we'll have drastic shortages of water, land, roads, and housing.**

Practice using the **Key Questions** by examining this photograph and its caption.

- **WHAT THE MESSAGE IS:** The writer of the article in which this photograph appears wants the viewer to accept the point of view that the United States faces serious shortages brought about by population growth.

- **WHAT TECHNIQUES WERE USED:** The photograph is almost totally filled with trash at a landfill. The low camera angle emphasizes the amount of trash. The use of black-and-white rather than color photography emphasizes the drabness and ugliness of trash. In addition, the use of a landfill as the focus of the message plays right into the public's knowledge about the problems of trash disposal. In other words, the writer is selling a point of view by tying it to a point of view the public has already accepted.

- **WHAT YOU KNOW:** You know that trash is a problem, but you also know that the problem isn't related only to population growth.

- **HOW YOU CAN USE WHAT YOU KNOW:** You can question the fairness of this picture and this line of reasoning. You can decide to learn more before accepting the writer's point of view.

- **OTHER SOURCES YOU MIGHT USE TO FIND OTHER VIEWPOINTS THAT YOU CAN TRUST:** Ask a parent or other trusted adult to give his or her point of view. Use reference materials to find facts that support—or *don't* support—the visual message. In addition, use reference sources to help you learn about the writer. Find out whether you can trust the writer to deliver fair and truthful messages.

Decision time! Now you can make a well-thought-out decision, based on your analysis, to agree or disagree with the writer's visual message. Your decision will be valuable because *it is backed up by careful analysis.*

Exercise 4

Working with a partner, find a public-service announcement or paid political message in a current newspaper or newsmagazine. With your partner, use the Key Questions to help you analyze the fairness of the message. Present your findings to the class.

MEETING INDIVIDUAL NEEDS

Less-Proficient Readers

Skimming

Some students may benefit from a reminder that as they review newspaper articles and news magazines for public service announcements or for paid political messages, they will want to use an appropriate reading strategy. Tell them that in reviewing large amounts of text for a specific purpose, it is often necessary to locate information at a glance.

Distribute copies of a newspaper story and explain or review skimming. Help students list all the relevant information by reading the article quickly, looking for words or phrases that will give them an overview of the whole piece. **L1**

Analyzing Movies, Music, and Television Shows

You can use the Key Questions to help you analyze and evaluate a variety of different types of mass-media messages. In this section, use the Key Questions to help you analyze the messages that the producers of movies, music videos, and television shows send viewers.

Actors in movies and television shows play fictional characters. Some characters in music videos exist only in fantasy settings. What visual messages do such characters and settings send viewers, and are these messages valuable and fair? Use the Key Questions to help you decide.

Exercise 5

Watch carefully as your teacher plays a scene or two from a popular movie or television show. Then work together as a class to use the Key Questions to help you analyze and evaluate the visual messages you received.

Key Questions to Ask Yourself About Media Evaluation

To analyze a variety of media, ask yourself these Key Questions:

- How does this particular medium present messages to viewers?
- What techniques were used to persuade viewers to agree with that message?
- What do I already know about this subject?
- How can I use what I already know to judge whether this message is
  —fair or unfair?
  —based on reality or fantasy?
  —based on facts or opinions?
- What additional sources might I use to find other viewpoints that I can trust on this subject?
  —parent, teacher, or other trustworthy adult
  —reliable books or other reference sources

Then, on the basis of your answers to the questions and of trusted viewpoints that you find, make a decision about the visual message. Make sure that you can support that decision with strong facts and reasons.
  —I agree with the visual message because . . . .
  —I disagree with the visual message because . . . .

Teach

Analyzing Characters and Situations

Ask students to think about specific movies, television shows, or videos they've seen, and invite volunteers to identify ways in which people are stereotyped. Point out that using the Key Questions About Media Evaluation can help viewers analyze and evaluate the messages that such characters and situations send. **L1**

Analyzing Film and Television

Show students several thought-provoking scenes from popular movies or television programs. Then work together with the class to apply the Key Questions About Media Evaluation, and draw conclusions about the messages presented in the scenes. Invite discussion about the value of those messages. **L2**

Comparing Original Texts with Film Adaptations

Select a videotape of the film version of a book that students have read and enjoyed, such as *Robin Hood, Treasure Island,* or *The Yearling.* Depending on the time available, play the entire video or one or more pivotal scenes. Discuss how the original print version and the film adaptation differ. Stress that the film version is often a simplified version of the original work. Characters and scenes are often dropped or combined. Discuss how readers often have a deeper, more satisfying experience than film viewers, since they are empowered to create their own mental images of characters and settings, rather than relying on the images chosen by the film director. **L2**

Viewing and Representing

Analyzing Print Advertisements

Have students discuss why certain advertising strategies are popular and which strategies appeal to particular groups of people. Have students work in small groups to find three advertisements from newspapers and news magazines. Students should analyze each ad by recording answers to the following questions:

- What does this ad show?
- If there is text in the ad, what message do the words communicate?
- What advertising strategies does the advertiser use?
- How does the advertiser want us to feel when we see this ad?
- What is the general message of the ad? **L2**

Using the Internet

Challenge students to use the Internet to locate two sources of information on the same subject, such as influenza information from the Center for Disease Control and influenza information from a pharmaceutical company. Have students use the Key Questions About Media Evaluation to analyze and evaluate each source separately. Then ask them to compare their findings and draw conclusions regarding the credibility of the information they found. Discuss their results, emphasizing that not all Internet Web sites are reliable sources of information. **L3**

Evaluating Advertising Techniques

Ask students these questions:

- Do you think it is fair for actors to pretend they are doctors recommending a certain medicine to the public? Why or why not?
- Several people feel that programs directed at young children should not contain advertisements. Do you agree? Why or why not? What advice about television advertisements would you give to a young child?

Invite students to share their thoughts in a class discussion. **L2**

Viewing and Representing

Exercise 6

Choose a favorite movie, television show, music video, or video game. Use the Key Questions to analyze and evaluate its visual messages. Write a brief report on your findings and conclusions.

Analyzing Advertisements and Commercials

You can also use the Key Questions to help you analyze and evaluate the media messages appearing in advertisements, in newspapers and magazines, on computer Web sites, and in television commercials.

More than any other form of media, advertisements and commercials have one and *only* one goal: *to persuade the viewer to buy the product being advertised.* To accomplish that goal, advertisers often use techniques included in the Elements of Visual Design and Composition listed on pages 766–767 and the Film Techniques for Sending Visual Messages listed on page 769. In addition, they often use one or more of the following advertising techniques.

Common Advertising Techniques		
Technique	**Description**	**Example**
Bandwagon: "Jump on the bandwagon and join in the fun!"	showing through visual images or carefully chosen words that everybody, especially "every popular, attractive, well-liked person," uses this product	an advertisement for a certain soft drink, showing attractive, smiling people enjoying each other's company as they drink it
Testimonial: "Be like your favorite celebrity!"	showing a popular star of movies or television, a famous athlete, or a leading musical performer using the product	an advertisement for a car, showing a popular television or movie star driving it
Partial truth: "Use this for incredible results!"	using oils, dyes, and other substances to make the results of using the product seem "too good to be true"	an advertisement for a certain facial cosmetic, showing an attractive teenager with perfect skin who claims to have used the product
Card stacking: "Leading experts are convinced that you should use this product."	using actors to pretend that they are doctors, dentists, and other experts to present only what supports the advertiser's opinion	an advertisement for a certain medicine, in which an actor portrays a doctor who recommends using it

774 Unit 27 Viewing and Representing

MEETING INDIVIDUAL NEEDS — English Language Learners

Understanding Main Ideas in Dialogue

Students learning English may have difficulty understanding the dialogue in films and other video presentations. Pair English Language Learners with helpful partners during classroom video presentations and encourage the paired students to discuss the dialogue and then summarize main ideas and events at the conclusion of the presentation.

Common Advertising Techniques		
Technique	**Description**	**Example**
Name calling or appeal to guilt: "Do you still use those paper towels that are harming the beauty of our countryside?"	manipulating scientific terms, statistics, or other data to convince viewers that using another product would be foolish or wasteful	an advertisement for paper products that claims that using any other brand of paper product will be harmful to the environment

Although commercials and advertisements often include a few convincing facts, those facts are surrounded by persuasive words and often unrealistic claims. Remember: Knowledge is power! Viewers can use a version of the Key Questions to help them "cut through" the glossy language and promises of advertisements and commercials. Then viewers can make informed, wise decisions about which products to buy. As an example, examine the following model of an advertisement.

27.2 Analyzing Media Messages **775**

775

Teach

Analyzing Advertising Materials

Remind students that all media messages are carefully crafted to present and support a particular point of view. Emphasize that this is particularly true of advertisements, which blend facts and opinions—expressed in persuasive language—to get the viewer or reader to buy a product. Ask students to consider why consumers should analyze and evaluate an advertisement before deciding whether they really want or need the product being advertised.

Display several advertisements for products that are of interest to the students. Ask them to consider the message or messages conveyed in each instance. Point out that analyzing and evaluating commercial messages can help develop effective consumer skills. **L2**

Using the Chart

Discuss each entry on the Common Advertising Techniques chart. Call on volunteers to suggest further examples of each technique. Lead students to understand how each technique represents a clever method for persuading viewers or readers to buy a product. **L2**

Viewing and Representing

Teach

Analyzing the Advertisement

Have students refer to the Common Advertising Techniques chart on pages 774–775 to identify the advertising techniques used in the Starz ad on page 775. Ask students to discuss how specific techniques from the chart were used in the ad. **L2**

Evaluating the Advertisement

Have students work with partners or in small groups to use the Key Questions to evaluate the Starz advertisement. Provide time for them to present and discuss their findings with the class. **L2**

Assess

Evaluation Rubrics

Use these criteria when evaluating students' analyses of commercial messages:
- Do the answers indicate careful analysis of film and advertising techniques?
- Do the answers indicate fair evaluations, based on the Key Questions?
- Has the student analyzed and evaluated both verbal messages and visual messages?

Close

Identify and discuss specific techniques used to persuade viewers and readers to accept a particular point of view or buy a particular product. Which techniques are particularly effective? Why is it important for readers and viewers to be aware of these techniques and to analyze and evaluate media messages carefully before deciding to accept or reject the messages?

Exercise 7

Use the Key Questions that follow to help you analyze and evaluate this advertisement. Discuss your findings with classmates.

Key Questions to Ask Yourself About Commercial Messages

To analyze a commercial message, ask yourself these Key Questions:

- What message is this commercial trying to send to readers or viewers?
- What visual techniques were used to extend the written message and persuade readers or viewers to agree?
- What do I already know about this subject?
- How can I use what I already know to judge whether this message is
  —fair or unfair?
  —based on reality or fantasy?
  —based on facts or opinions?
- What additional sources might I use to find other viewpoints that I can trust on this subject?
  —parent, teacher, or other trustworthy adult, such as an expert in the field
  —reference sources, including magazines such as *Consumer Reports* and *Consumer's Digest*

Then, on the basis of your answers to the questions and of trusted viewpoints that you find, make a decision about the visual message. Make sure that you can support that decision with strong facts and reasons.
  —I agree with the visual message because . . . .
  —I disagree with the visual message because . . . .

Exercise 8

Watch carefully as your teacher plays a video clip of one or more television commercials. Then work as a class to use the Key Questions to identify, analyze, and evaluate the messages that the commercials convey.

Viewing and Representing

Real World Connection

Targeting Audiences

Explain that advertisers use marketing surveys and statistics on buying trends to decide which specific group of consumers will be most likely to buy their product. Then they create advertisements specifically geared toward this "target audience." Using the model advertisement in the student edition, as well as samples of real advertisements and taped television commercials, ask students such questions as: Which types of people might be particularly attracted by this ad? How could the advertisers change the ad so that it might appeal to a different audience?

27.3 Producing Media Messages

Another way to increase your understanding of media messages is to apply the techniques that artists, filmmakers, and advertisers use. Produce your own media messages! This section will help you to create two of them: a printed public service announcement and a television commercial.

Creating a Public Service Announcement

What changes would you like to see in your community or among your peers? Newspapers and magazines often contain public service announcements, or PSAs. There are two kinds of PSAs:

- **free advertisements** created by government agencies, charities, or community groups to convey useful information to the community and urge viewers to take action

Example: The United States Department of Education might place a full-page announcement in a family-oriented magazine, using written text and one or more photographs to convey why it is important for young children to learn to read. The purpose would be to urge parents to set aside time every day to read to their young children.

- **Paid advertisements** sponsored by a business, political party, or political action committee to convey useful information to the community and urge viewers to take action. Such ads also subtly mention the name of the sponsor to encourage viewers to form a good opinion of it.

Example: A fast-food restaurant chain might place a full-page announcement in a young people's magazine, with text that provides information about the tragic state of the nation's homeless. It would then urge readers to sign up for a road race to benefit the homeless. A photograph might include a group of healthy, attractive teenagers running in a model race, wearing T-shirts with the restaurant's familiar logo.

Follow these tips to plan and create a PSA of your own.

Viewing and Representing

Focus

Lesson Overview

Objectives
- To develop an understanding of media messages
- To learn to produce media messages

Skills
- selecting, organizing, and producing visuals; using media to produce communications; assessing language, medium, and presentation techniques

Critical Thinking
- establishing goals; considering audience and purpose; organizing; drawing conclusions; classifying; adapting techniques and concepts

Listening and Speaking
- discussing; asking and answering questions; informal speaking; interpreting, analyzing, and evaluating visual techniques; presenting work to others; listening to others' presentations

Bellringer
Daily Language Activity

When students come into the classroom, have this assignment on the board: *What one change would you like to see in your community? Write a brief paragraph that identifies the change and explains why you think it is needed.*

Motivating Activity

Ask volunteers to review techniques used by photographers, film makers, television producers, and advertisers to create effective visual messages. Then ask students which techniques seem particularly interesting and effective. Point out that in this lesson they will use what they have learned to produce their own visual messages.

Resource Manager

📂 **Planning Resources**
- *Lesson Plans*

📂 **Other Print Resources**
- *Viewing and Representing Activities*

Teach

Introducing the PSA Project

List the various issues that students wrote about in the Bellringer activity as possible topics for public service announcements. Then display several examples of the two types of public service announcements. Work with students to use what they have learned in the first lessons of this unit to interpret, analyze, and evaluate each announcement. Have students identify the techniques that they feel are most effective in representing, complementing, and extending messages. Encourage students to keep these techniques in mind as they plan their own public service announcements. **L1**

Guiding the PSA Project

Encourage students to use the basic steps of the Writing Process (Prewriting, Drafting, Revising, Editing/Proofreading, and Publishing/Presenting) as they plan, create, and present their PSAs. Encourage students to refer to the Elements of Visual Design and Composition chart on page 766 for ideas.

Discuss with students the Tips for Creating a Public Service Announcement. Make sure that they understand each step. Provide assistance as necessary. Plan ahead to secure a place for students to display and share their finished work. **L1**

Viewing and Representing

Tips for Creating a PSA for a Newspaper or Magazine

1. **BEGIN BY BRAINSTORMING.** Think about causes that you support or concerns that you have about such issues as the environment, education, or health. Jot down several ideas and then pick one to develop into a public service announcement.

2. **IDENTIFY YOUR PURPOSE AND MESSAGE.** What underlying message do you want your PSA to send to your readers? What action would you like your readers to take, once they understand and agree with your point of view? On notebook paper, write a sentence that states your purpose. Then write another sentence that states your message. Keep both in mind as you decide what facts you will include in your message.

3. **LIST YOUR FACTS.** List the facts that you plan to include in your PSA. Be sure to check reference sources to make sure your facts are accurate and up-to-date. Note the sources of your facts. Your PSA may carry greater weight if you quote experts or provide supportive statistics from reliable sources. Once your list is complete, examine each fact carefully. Decide which facts strongly support your point of view and which ones do not. Cross out any that seem weak.

4. **DECIDE ON THE VISUAL IMAGES.** Art is very important because it will catch the reader's attention and will extend and emphasize the message you want to send. On scrap paper, draw sketches of the art you might include or look through magazines for photographs you might use. Refer to the Elements of Visual Design and Composition chart on page 766 for ideas about use of lines, colors, and positions of your subjects. Experiment with different elements and techniques, always keeping your purpose and message in mind.

5. **DRAFT AND REVISE YOUR TEXT.** Turn your list of facts into full sentences, catchy slogans, and persuasive language that sends your message clearly. Reread your text several times to make sure your language is strong. You might ask a friend to read it and offer suggestions too.

6. **DECIDE ON A LAYOUT.** Sketch various page designs—experimenting with the position of the art and text. Select a page design that will draw the readers in and will encourage them to read and understand your message.

Real World Connection

The Right Stuff

Advertisers know how to use language and images to catch the attention of consumers and sell a product. They use words and visuals that tap into market trends and have special connotations. Have students study food packaging—words, images, and lists of ingredients. Ask them to list words such as *natural*, *lite*, and *fat-free* that "sell" the product. The lists can be shared with the class for use in writing commercials.

7. **MAKE YOUR FINAL COPY.** When you are satisfied with your art choice, your text, and your page layout, make a final copy of your public service announcement.

8. **PUBLISH YOUR PUBLIC SERVICE ANNOUNCEMENT.** Share your PSA with viewers—friends, members of the school community, neighbors, and family members. You might publish it in the school newspaper, hang it as a poster in the school, or post it on a community bulletin board. Ask for comments and suggestions. Find out whether your viewers understood and agreed with your message.

Exercise 9

Use the tips to create your own public service announcement.

Creating a Television Commercial

What product would you like to convince viewers to buy? How can you most effectively combine visual images, persuasive language, background music, and such film techniques as camera angles, camera shots, and lighting to make viewers understand and agree with your media message? Follow these tips to create an effective television commercial.

Tips for Creating a Television Commercial

1. **BUILD A PRODUCTION TEAM.** The creation of a filmed message requires the skills and cooperative effort of a group of people. Each member of the production team is responsible for one or more of the following jobs, based on his or her skills and interests.

   - **Director**—leads the group, overseeing the work of all team members and supervising the filming.
   - **Scriptwriter**—writes and revises the facts, opinions, and persuasive language included in the spoken message.
   - **Organizer and layout expert**—creates a series of simple sketches, showing each scene in the commercial and outlines the format of the commercial, from beginning to end. He or she creates a plan for the director, actors, camera operator, and music arranger to follow during the filming.

27.3 Producing Media Messages **779**

Viewing and Representing

 **Special Needs**

Working Collaboratively

Some students may have difficulty taking on ambitious roles on their production teams. Two or three students could work together on a given task and be called, for example, "lighting specialists" to emphasize their collaboration in creating and producing their commercial messages.

779

Practice and Assess

Evaluation Rubrics: Exercise 9

Use the following criteria to evaluate the students' public service announcements. Make sure students' work reflects:

- comprehension and inclusion of elements from the Elements of Visual Design and Composition chart
- comprehension and application of the Tips listed on page 778 of the student edition

Exercise 10

Use these criteria to evaluate the students' television commercials. Make sure that the commercials

- reflect the comprehension and inclusion of elements from the Elements of Visual Design and Composition chart and the Film Techniques for Sending Visual Messages chart
- reflect the comprehension and application of Common Advertising Techniques
- are persuasive
- follow the Tips listed on page 779–780
- are the result of team cooperation with members contributing equally

Close

Discuss the results of both media projects. Invite students to share their ideas about the steps they followed and the results they achieved in both instances. Invite them to reflect on how learning to analyze and evaluate mass media messages might help them as readers, viewers, consumers, and responsible citizens.

Viewing and Representing

- **On- and off-camera actor(s)**—appear in the commercial. The on-camera actor or actors might speak the script, or they may act out a scene while an off-camera actor does a "voice-over," narrating the scene and delivering the spoken commercial message.
- **Lighting expert**—follows the director's plan for creating the proper lighting during the filming
- **Video operator**—videotapes the commercial
- **Music arranger**—works with the director to choose any background music that may be used and follows the director's cue to start the music at the appropriate time during the filming

2. **BEGIN BY THINKING ABOUT, OR VIEWING, OTHER COMMERCIALS.** Work with your group to view and discuss existing television commercials. Evaluate the techniques, agreeing on those that seem particularly interesting and effective in persuading viewers to buy the advertised product.

3. **BRAINSTORM.** Jot down everyone's ideas about products that you would enjoy promoting. The group's enthusiasm for the product will help you to write and produce a convincing commercial. Select one product.

4. **WORK COOPERATIVELY TO PLAN THE COMMERCIAL.** Work together to decide upon persuasive language, visual images, the roles that actors might play, and other issues. For guidance in your planning, refer to the charts on pages 766, 769, and 774. Then work independently to plan and prepare your assigned part. Come together to review and revise ideas until everyone is satisfied.

5. **REHEARSE.** Do several run-throughs of the commercial before actually taping it. At this point, the director should be in charge, planning the camera shots and angles, the lighting, the movements and positions of the actors, and the voice and music cues.

6. **SHOOT!** Create your commercial, following the plan that you perfected during rehearsals.

7. **PRESENT YOUR COMMERCIAL.** Play the commercial for classmates and friends. Invite members of the audience to comment and make suggestions on your message and your techniques.

Exercise 10

Use the tips to create an effective television commercial.

✔ ASSESSMENT OPTIONS

📁 *Tests with Answer Key and Rubrics*
Unit 27 Mastery Test, pp. 111–112

💾 *Testmaker*
Unit 27 Mastery Test

📼 *MindJogger Videoquizzes*

You may wish to administer the Unit 27 Mastery Test at this point.

Enrichment and Extension

Expanding on an Idea

Point out to students that many products are advertised on radio spots, in printed media, and on the Internet, as well as on television. Challenge interested students to expand their television commercials into full-fledged advertising campaigns that include messages in a variety of media forms. Ask students to present their expanded campaigns to the class. Have them evaluate the effectiveness of one another's persuasive techniques. **L3**

UNIT 28

Electronic Resources

Objectives

- To become familiar with the Internet and learn how to access Web sites
- To evaluate the accuracy of information presented on a Web site
- To learn how to send and edit e-mail messages
- To identify and use other electronic resources, such as CD-ROMs and DVDs

 **ASSESSMENT OPTIONS**

> *Tests with Answer Key and Rubrics*
Unit 28 Pretest, pp. 113–114

Testmaker
Unit 28 Pretest

You may wish to administer the Unit 28 Pretest at this point.

Key to Ability Levels

L1 Level 1 activities are within the basic ability range of students.

L2 Level 2 activities are within the ability range of average students.

L3 Level 3 activities are more challenging activities.

781

 **Resource Manager**

Planning Resources
- *Lesson Plans*
- *Block Scheduling*

Other Print Resources
- *Guide to Using the Internet and Other Electronic Resources*
- *Tests with Answer Key and Rubrics*

**Video**
- *MindJogger Videoquizzes*

 **Software**
- *Presentation Plus!*
- *Testmaker*

Web Sites
- *writerschoice.glencoe.com*

Focus

Lesson Overview

Objectives
- To become familiar with the Internet
- To listen and to organize ideas in order to gain information
- To evaluate the influence of a medium
- To assess how language contributes to a message

Skills
- using the Internet

Critical Thinking
- recalling; comparing and contrasting; predicting

Listening and Speaking
- discussing

 Bellringer
Daily Language Activity

When students enter the classroom, have these questions on the board: *When was the last time you used the Internet or World Wide Web? Did you use it for a school project? personal interests? to order merchandise?*

Motivating Activity

Ask students to make a chart or graph on the board to record the information elicited in the Bellringer. What have they named as the most common reasons for using the Internet? the least?

Teach

Getting Online

Divide the class into small groups and allow each group to spend one class period learning how to access the Internet. Ask each group to create a list of the steps they took to get online and have them share those steps with the other groups. **L2**

Electronic Resources

28.1 The Internet

The **Internet** is an electronic connection to a world of information and services that you can tap into with a computer. It uses telephone lines, cable lines, and satellites to link your computer to computers all over the world. Until recently, the Internet was something that many people knew little about. Today, the Internet is for many people a common resource for research, up-to-the-minute news, shopping, and entertainment.

The Internet, often referred to simply as the Net, is a collaborative enterprise. No one organization or company owns it. A few organizations work together to set standards and keep the Internet running smoothly.

The first Internet was established with Department of Defense funding in 1969 for research, educational, and government purposes. It linked computers at four university sites, three of them in California. Most of the users were computer experts, scientists, and engineers. Commands had to be given in difficult computer language.

From this limited beginning, the Internet expanded in response to the need for information. In less than two decades, most universities and government offices were using the Internet for communication and research. By that time, inexpensive desktop computers had been developed and were finding their way into average American homes. By the early 1990s, after the introduction of user-friendly browsers, the Internet became a widely used avenue of knowledge for the average person.

When most people speak of the Internet, they mean that part of the Internet called the World Wide Web. The **World Wide Web** makes it easy to connect to millions of different Web sites that may include video, graphics, animation, and sound as well as text.

The Internet has revolutionized not only research but also business and social communication, shopping, and even recreation. Here are a few of the ways in which people use the Internet.

- **NEWS REPORTS:** A user can have access to the latest news within minutes of its being reported. Most major newspapers and several television news departments have Web sites.
- **SHOPPING:** Books, games, computer equipment, clothing, and even groceries can be ordered online.
- **WORK:** Many people can work at home, receiving assignments from the work site and sending in completed work. Businesses

---

 **Resource Manager**

📂 **Planning Resources**
- *Lesson Plans*

📂 **Other Print Resources**
- *Guide to Using the Internet and Other Electronic Resources*

can communicate with other businesses, clients, or customers almost instantly via e-mail.

- **CLASS WORK:** College students can access lectures and lecture notes and even take open-book tests without leaving their homes or dormitories. Numerous middle schools and high schools have established their own student-operated Web sites.
- **SOCIAL LIFE:** People can make new friends, keep in touch with old ones, and share thoughts and ideas with others through e-mail and chat rooms.
- **ENTERTAINMENT:** Besides listening to music and reading news and reviews of movies, plays, concerts, and other performances, Internet users can play games with opponents who are miles, or even continents, away.

Exercise 1

Work with a small group to make an Internet time line that shows the history of the Internet. Use Internet, classroom, and library resources to help create the time line. Combine your group's time line with those of other groups to create a classroom "Internet Time Line." You might use e-mail to share information about the project with other students your age. Display the time line in your classroom or in one of the common areas of the school.

28.2 Using the Internet

How can you access the Internet? Besides the computer itself, you need a modem, an Internet service provider, and a browser.

- A **modem** (derived from MOdulation plus DEModulation) is a device that allows a computer to communicate and share information with another computer over telephone or cable lines. Most computers now come with a built-in modem.
- An **Internet service provider**, or ISP, provides a service (for a fee) that allows your computer to dial into the Internet by way of

Practice and Assess

Evaluation Rubrics: Exercise 1

Student timelines should begin with the first Internet connection in 1969. They should also include key developments such as the advent of the personal computer in the late 1970s, the invention of the World Wide Web in 1990, and the growing numbers of Internet users over the years.

Close

Ask students to describe ways in which the World Wide Web might be helpful in completing school assignments. Have them discuss why they think the Web has become so popular.

28.2

Focus

Lesson Overview

Objectives
- To learn how to use Web site addresses to access Web sites
- To compare and contrast the significance of various media images

Skills
- accessing and using the World Wide Web

Critical Thinking
- observing; synthesizing

Listening and Speaking
- discussing; explaining a process

Electronic Resources

Resource Manager

📂 **Planning Resources**
- *Lesson Plans*

📂 **Other Print Resources**
- *Guide to Using the Internet and Other Electronic Resources*

Bellringer
Daily Language Activity

When students enter the classroom, have this assignment on the board: *List four topics that you might want to investigate on the Internet.*

Motivating Activity

Ask volunteers to share their answers to the Bellringer activity. Have students identify where they would expect to find the four subjects they named in the Bellringer.

Teach

Compare and Contrast

Ask students what different ISPs and online services they've used. Have them discuss what features these services have in common. What features are unique to each service? Do they prefer to use an ISP or an online service? Why? **L2**

---

existing telephone lines. Newer service methods, already in place in some locations, use TV cable lines or wireless transmission for the signals. Instead of an ISP, online services, such as America Online or Microsoft Network, will let you access the Internet as well as their own private services. For example, America Online users can use private chat rooms and message boards where members can exchange messages.

- To display the contents of a Web site, your computer must have a browser. A **browser** is a software program that displays Web pages that can include text, graphics, pictures, and video on your computer. The best-known browsers are Netscape Navigator and Microsoft Internet Explorer. A browser enables you to get around the Web. With a browser, you can also use plug-ins. These software programs extend the abilities of your browser—for example, to play sounds or display movies from an Internet site.

Even if you don't have your own computer, you can probably access the Internet at your school or in a public library. Most libraries now have Internet terminals that their patrons can use.

Searching the Internet

When writing a report, doing research, or just using the Internet for amusement, you may want to find specific information. The fastest way to find the Web sites you are looking for is to use a search engine. A **search engine** lets you look for information on the Web by searching for keywords. A **keyword** is a word or phrase that describes your topic.

If you haven't narrowed your search to a specific topic, you can start with a subject directory. A **subject directory** lists general topics, such as arts and humanities, science, education, entertainment, sports, and health. After you select a broad topic, the directory will offer a list of possible subtopics from which to choose. Several search engines and subject directories, such as Yahoo!, Alta Vista, and Excite, are available on the Internet. A **metasearch engine,** such as Dogpile or Metafind, will let you search several search engines at the same time.

You can do a more precise search by using the **Boolean search** method. The following chart will help you to use this technique.

Electronic Resources

Real World Connection

Using Cyberspeak

Do you like to *surf the Net,* explore *cyberspace,* or play *virtual reality* games? These terms are relatively new to our vocabulary, but each has its origin in old terms. *Surfing the Net* comes from the phrase *channel surfing*—which in turn comes from the activity of *surfing,* riding an ocean wave. The word *cyberspace* was first used by William Gibson in his 1984 science fiction novel *Neuromancer.* The term comes from the word part *cyber-,* which refers to computers. *Virtual* is an old term that refers to anything that does not physically exist. *Virtual reality,* however, is a new term, referring to a computer world that does not exist in the physical world.

SEARCH TIP

TIPS FOR DOING A BOOLEAN SEARCH

A Boolean search uses the operators AND, OR, and NOT between keywords to further limit the terms of a search.

AND Link two keywords with AND to find only Web sites that contain both words (galaxy AND Jupiter). You will get fewer matches, but most of them will relate to your topic. Some programs use a plus sign instead of AND (galaxy + Jupiter).

OR The command OR tells the search engine to look for Web pages that use one term *or* the other (Mars OR Jupiter). You will get hits for every site that uses either word.

NOT If there is information that you do not want, use NOT between the two keywords (planets NOT Jupiter). You will get information about other planets but not about the planet Jupiter. Some programs use a minus sign instead of NOT (planets – Jupiter).

Addresses

If you use a search engine or a subject directory, your list of hits will include hyperlinks to each site. All you need to do to reach a site is to click on its hyperlink. Otherwise, to get to a particular Web site you need to know its address. Every Web site on the Internet has a unique address or URL. **URL** stands for Uniform Resource Locator. No two Web sites can have the same URL.

As an Internet user, you may want to keep track of some Web sites that you visit. You can keep a record of them by using your browser's **bookmark** (in Navigator) or **favorites** (in Internet Explorer) option. This option lets you keep a file of your favorite sites. Instead of typing the address each time you want to view a Web site, you simply go to the bookmark or favorites menu on your browser and click on the site's name.

28.2 Using the Internet   **785**

Electronic Resources

Teach

URL Components

Give pairs of students a list of five URLs. Have students break down each part of the URL and name each component. **L1**

The *Writer's Choice* Web site can be found at **writerschoice.glencoe.com**. Recommend this site as one that students may wish to explore.

Internet Connection

Using Keywords

Ask students to generate keywords for the following searches. Students can then "try out" these keywords and evaluate their search results.
1. Search for a recipe for chocolate cake. (*recipes, desserts, chocolate*)
2. Search for a map of your community, city, or state (*maps, name of city, name of state*)

Teach

Identifying Clues

Write the following URL on the board:

http://www.spaceflight.nasa.gov/mars/missions/

Ask students to predict what they will find when they go to the address. Have them identify the clues that help them make their prediction. Students should infer that NASA owns the site and that the specific page is about NASA's missions to Mars. **L2**

Using a Dictionary

Suggest that students find the etymology of the word "hyperlink." Ask them to search for other words containing one of the word parts and to discuss ways in which these words are and are not related.

Electronic Resources

URL COMPONENTS

Following is a typical URL. Notice that it is typed with no spaces between its parts and usually (but not always) is in all lowercase letters.

http://www.domainname.com/path/filename

http://—stands for hypertext transfer protocol, the rules for moving text over the Net. This protocol allows your computer to get information from any other computer hooked to the Web.

domain name—identifies the Net site. The part before the dot names the site owner. After the dot comes a suffix identifying the type of domain (see list of domain types below).

path—identifies the path within the site that leads to a specific document

file name—names the specific file that you are looking for

Domain Types

The following suffixes found in domain names identify the type of domain.

.com	for-profit company
.edu	educational institution
.gov	government body
.mil	military site
.net	network or internet service provider
.org	nonprofit organization

Hyperlinks

You may notice as you begin to investigate various Web sites that some words or phrases are underlined or are in a different color from the rest of the text (or both). These words or phrases are hyperlinks. **Hyperlinks** are text or graphics (often buttons) that, when clicked on, take you to a specific page of a Web site or to a related Web site. Sometimes it may be difficult to find a hyperlink on a Web page. It may be a word or an illustration rather than a button. If you are not sure whether a part of the text or graphics contains a hyperlink, drag the arrow cursor over it. If your arrow changes to a pointing finger, you've found a hyperlink.

Enrichment and Extension

Designing a Web Site

Have students break into groups and sketch designs for their own Web sites. Students should create an address and illustrate a home page with different path options. Ask volunteers to present their Web sites to the class. Students can then suggest improvements that would make these Web sites easier to use. **L3**

Exercise 2

On a sheet of paper, create a four-column chart. In each column, write one of the headings *Animals, History, Sports,* and *Art.* If you used any of these general words as keywords you would get far too many hits to be useful. Under each heading, write more-specific keywords you could use to search for information within that topic. Write at least five terms in each column. Then compare lists with your group or the class.

Exercise 3

Use a search engine to find Web sites that provide information about the nine known planets in the solar system. Write down the URLs of each Web site that you visit and record information that you learn about the planets on note cards. After you have information about all nine planets, present your findings to the class.

28.3 Using E-mail

One of the most popular and useful features of the Internet is the ability to send and receive **e-mail**, or electronic mail. With the click of a button, you can send a message to anyone in the world. You can also attach other computer files to your e-mail message. You can send pictures of yourself to your family, send a sound clip of your favorite song to a friend, or send a story you have written to one of your teachers.

For many people, e-mail has replaced regular mail or telephone as the preferred medium of communication for personal and business use. It reaches its destination, no matter how far, in a matter of seconds. When used to transmit complex data, it is less likely to be misunderstood than a voice-mail message and can be printed out for reference.

To send e-mail, you need a unique e-mail address. Your Internet service provider will provide you with one. You can also use another service, such as Yahoo!, to provide you with an e-mail account.

A typical e-mail address has four parts. The first part is the user name. This is the name that you choose or that is assigned to you by your

28.3 Using E-mail **787**

Resource Manager

📁 **Planning Resources**
• *Lesson Plans*

📁 **Other Print Resources**
• *Guide to Using the Internet and Other Electronic Resources*

Electronic Resources

Practice and Assess

Evaluation Rubrics: Exercise 2

Students' answers will vary. Possible keywords might be:
Animals: *dog, pet,* or *breeding*
History: *British, military,* or *Lincoln*
Sports: *school, rugby,* or *extreme*
Art: *painting, renaissance,* or *performance*

Exercise 3

After the students have presented their findings, discuss with the class what conclusions they have come to. Ask them if they have found a significant difference in the quality, usefulness, or relevance among the sites they have found.

Close

Have students discuss how search engines can help them find the information they might need for reports, research papers, or presentations.

Focus

Lesson Overview

Objectives
• To learn how to use e-mail
• To understand and appreciate e-mail etiquette
• To edit e-mail drafts

Skills
• using the Internet and exploring its features

Critical Thinking
• categorizing; analyzing; identifying types of information

Listening and Speaking
• discussing; explaining ideas

Bellringer
Daily Language Activity

When students enter the classroom, have this assignment on the board: *What do these abbreviations stand for: FAQ, IMHO, BTW, FYI, LOL, ROFL, GMTA?* (see chart on p. 790).

Motivating Activity

Point out that e-mail has become a popular form of communication. Ask students how e-mail is used for informal communication (among friends and relatives) as well as formal communication (among businesses and customers).

Teach

Internet Dictionary

Have students add terms to the "Internet Dictionary" they made at the beginning of the Unit using terms from this lesson. Each word in the dictionary should include a definition, an example, and, when possible, an illustration. **L1**

Internet service provider. The second part is the @ symbol, which stands for "at." This symbol separates the user name from the rest of the e-mail address. The third part is the domain name, which is the name of your ISP's computer or the service that hosts your e-mail account. The last part of an e-mail address is the suffix, usually *.net* if you use an ISP. The suffix indicates the type of organization that provides your e-mail service.

With many e-mail programs, you can store frequently used e-mail addresses in an address book. When you want to send a message to a person whose address is in your address book, you simply double-click on his or her name. You can also store additional information, such as the person's street address, birthday, and phone number in your address book.

Just as you can send an e-mail message to any address in the world, anyone in the world can send an e-mail message to you. Sometimes you will receive junk e-mail, or **spam**. Spam is similar to the junk mail you receive at home. Advertisements are the main form of spam, and sometimes this kind of e-mail can be annoying, or even offensive. If you receive an e-mail from someone whose e-mail address you don't recognize, show it to an adult, and do not write back unless the adult gives you permission. Some people send links to Web sites through e-mail. If you receive a message with a link to a Web site, show it to an adult before clicking on the link.

E-mail Pen Pals

You've probably worked with partners or small groups many times in school. E-mail allows you to collaborate with people who are not in the same room, the same school, or even the same country. Imagine comparing descriptions of your school day with a student from Australia. How about having your class collaborate on a project with a class from South Africa? With e-mail, the whole world can be at your fingertips.

The International Registry of Schools Online (http://web66.unm.edu/schools.html) will help you locate middle schools all over the United States and in countries around the world. Talk to your teacher about finding a class in a "sister school" you can work with or seek e-mail pen pals from.

E-mail Etiquette

When sending e-mail, follow the Internet "rules of the road," called Netiquette.

- Use the subject line wisely. Be as brief as you can, but let the person to whom you are sending e-mail know what your message is about.

Electronic Resources

Internet Connection

Choosing an E-mail Provider
Point out to students that there are many free e-mail providers. Some of these providers have their own programs for accessing e-mail. Encourage students to try out a few different e-mail providers to see which program they like best.

- When responding to a long message, don't include the entire message in your response. Quote just enough of it to let your correspondent know what you are responding to.

- Keep messages short and to the point.

- Use appropriate capitalization. Using all capital letters is considered SHOUTING.

- Avoid sending unfriendly e-mail. Sending an unfriendly e-mail message is called "flaming."

- It is important to use correct spelling.

- Always include your e-mail address at the bottom of any message you send.

- Be careful when using humor or sarcasm. It is difficult to convey some emotions in print. Use "smileys" if you want to show emotion (see next page).

- Remember that good behavior on the Internet is no different from good behavior in face-to-face situations. Treat others as you would like them to treat you.

Mailing Lists

If there is a particular subject that you need to research, you might want to consider subscribing to a mailing list. A **mailing list** is like a bulletin board on which you exchange information through e-mail. Use a search engine to find a mailing list that discusses your topic of interest. Type either *listserv* or *majordomo*, the names of two mailing-list servers, into a search engine. Choose a catalog from the search results and find a mailing list that interests you.

Before joining a mailing list, read the FAQ (Frequently Asked Questions). The FAQ should provide you with enough information to know whether the mailing list is what you are looking for. If it is, just follow the directions to subscribe.

Once you subscribe to a mailing list, you will receive e-mail messages from people discussing your subject of interest. Before you post your own messages on the mailing list, read the postings already there until you are familiar with the type of discussion the group is having. Post a message only when you have something new to say, and remember to keep your posts brief and to the point. Be sure to follow the rules of Netiquette. You can cancel your subscription to a mailing list at any time.

28.3 Using E-mail **789**

Electronic Resources

Global Communication

Obtain the e-mail addresses of people you know who live in several geographic areas. Have students work together to write e-mail messages to each person, asking questions about the climate and geography of the place where he or she lives. Proofread the messages on the board or overhead projector before sending them. As people respond to the class, print their responses and post them on a map. **L2**

Enrichment and Extension

Internet Safety Rules

Invite a small group of students to work together to list what they have learned about Internet safety. Have them use this list to create a computer-generated poster or banner listing their Internet safety rules. Encourage students to think carefully about design elements, such as color schemes, layout, and typefaces, so that the text of the poster is attractive, engaging, and easy to read from a distance. **L2**

Practice and Assess

Evaluation Rubrics: Exercise 4

Results will vary. The students' logs may include summaries of each message they received through their mailing list, or they may include printouts of the messages themselves. Students may indicate that they now have a stronger sense of the global community of people who share the students' interests.

Exercise 5

Encourage students to contact students from other states and/or countries, so that they can receive messages from those areas. If there are areas on the map where no e-mail is coming from, suggest to students that they try to contact one of those areas.

Close

Have students discuss how they can use e-mail for fun and for getting information.

Electronic Resources

"SMILEYS" AND ACRONYMS

"Smileys," or emoticons (icons that show emotion), can be used to give expression to the e-mail messages that you send. They are created with the characters on your computer keyboard. Tilt your head to the left to see the "smileys."

:-)	smile
;-)	wink
:-(	frown/unhappy
:-D	laughing
:-o	wow!
:*)	clowning around
:-P	tongue out
:-/	confused
0:-)	angel (with halo)

Acronyms are words formed from the first letters of other words. Many people use special acronyms to save typing time and space in their e-mail. These are a few of the most commonly used ones.

BTW	By the way
FAQ	Frequently asked questions
FYI	For your information
GMTA	Great minds think alike
IMHO	In my humble opinion
LOL	Laugh out loud
ROFL	Rolling on the floor laughing
TYVM	Thank you very much

Exercise 4

Using a search engine, find and subscribe to a mailing list that discusses a topic of interest to you. Create a mailing-list log to keep track of the correspondence that the mailing list generates. Keep the log for a week and then share what you've learned with the class.

Exercise 5

Working with the class, create a United States map or a world map to show all the places from which you and your classmates have received e-mail. Use colored thumbtacks to show where the e-mail originated. Keep track of incoming e-mail for the next month and update the maps as necessary.

Viewing and Representing

Inventing "Smileys"

Invite the class to work on the computer and experiment with different symbols to invent their own "smileys". e.g.: %O (yelling), i I (robot), :-# (can't talk). **L2**

28.4 Selecting and Evaluating Internet Sources

Before you even begin searching the Internet, you need to decide what kinds of information you are looking for. Is it personal information, such as learning more about a hobby, or is it related to your school work? These types of information can overlap, of course, but having a particular goal in mind will help you in the search process.

Personal Information

Whatever your interest, there is probably a Web site—more likely several of them—devoted to it. Do you have a favorite computer game? You can probably find a few sites and discussion groups devoted to it. On these sites, you can chat with other players, learn new strategies, find out about upgrades or when a new version of the game will be released, and perhaps even find people to play the game with on the Net.

Think of a hobby, one you currently have or one you're just considering. Try a keyword search and see how many sites you can find devoted to that hobby. You may be surprised, possibly even bowled over, by the results.

Are you interested in music, movies, books, sports? The number of sites for any of these topics is overwhelming. Your only challenge will be finding the site or sites that best suit your needs.

Would you like information about teen-related topics, such as getting along in school, dating, or *your* music, clothing, and values? Hundred of teen sites are available for your special interests. Check with your teacher, librarian, or computer lab head for suggestions.

School Work

Suppose you need to find information for a research project. You may use print resources, such as books, magazines, and newspapers, or you may decide to access the wealth of information available to you on the Web. Two general categories of sites can give you the help you need. One group consists of the millions of sites devoted to particular topics. To find these, you'll need to use a search engine or subject directory. The second group includes the many sites devoted to general reference sources, such as dictionaries, encyclopedias, and electronic "handbooks."

Focus

Lesson Overview

Objectives
- To learn how to determine the accuracy of Internet information
- To assess how presentation contributes to a message

Skills
- using the Internet; verifying and recording information

Critical Thinking
- analyzing and evaluating reference sources; identifying fact and opinion

Listening and Speaking
- discussing

Bellringer
Daily Language Activity

When students enter the classroom, have this assignment on the board: *Answer this question on a sheet of paper: How do you know if information on the Internet is accurate?*

Motivating Activity

Make a list of five facts on the board. Ask students how they would verify each of the facts.

Electronic Resources

Resource Manager

📂 **Planning Resources**
- *Lesson Plans*

📂 **Other Print Resources**
- *Guide to Using the Internet and Other Electronic Resources*

Practice and Assess

Evaluation Rubrics: Exercise 6

Results will vary. Ask students to indicate if the original site led them to other links. Have them comment on how easy or difficult the search was. How many links did they have to follow to get their information?

Exercise 7

Results will vary. Ask the student if he or she had any instincts about the reliability of that Web site, and if so, what gave him or her that feeling.

Teach

Reliable Web Sites

Have students explain what elements make a Web site reliable. Ask students to search the Internet and provide at least two examples of Web sites that they believe are reliable and give reasons why they selected these Web sites. **L2**

Fact and Opinion

Put the headings *Fact* and *Opinion* on the board. Select a Web site that contains both facts and opinions (any site where something is reviewed). Have students read through the Web site and point out each statement to the students. Work with students to decide if the statement is a fact or an opinion. **L1**

Close

Engage students in a discussion of what they have learned about evaluating Web sites. Could these same evaluation techniques be applied to books, magazines, or newspapers?

For a start, look for a Web site that contains links to a variety of other reference sources. One example of such a site is B. J. Pinchbeck's Homework Helper (www.bjpinchbeck.com). It contains links to dozens of good reference sources, including several dictionary and encyclopedia sites, sites for converting currencies or units of measure, directories of various kinds, and sources of statistics. Many of these links contain still more useful links. Another useful site is the Internet Public Library (www.ipl.org). Try the reference section of its teen division. When you find a site that you know will be useful for your school work, bookmark it.

Exercise 6

Think of three questions that have short answers but would require some research to answer. (For example: How many acres are there in a mile? What's the meaning of *xenophobic*? Who was Akira Kurosawa?) Write your questions on a piece of paper. Then exchange questions with a partner. Use one of the Internet sites mentioned above for help in finding the answers to your partner's questions.

Evaluation

Whether you use print or electronic sources, you are responsible for verifying the accuracy of the information you gather. One way to check the reliability of a Web site is to find out who owns it or who created it. For instance, if you are looking for the average snowfall in Boston during December, you can probably rely on the National Weather Service Web site to be accurate. However, if you find the information on a site created by a student in California, you might need to verify it in another source.

Criteria for Evaluation In evaluating any information source, ask the following questions.

1. What person, organization, or company created the information? Is that source well known? Is it considered reliable? Generally (but not always), you can expect a government or university site to be more accurate than an individual's site. If the source is not given, you have reason to question the authenticity of the material.
2. How current is the information you have found? If it is important for the information to be current, look for the date of publication. If you are researching a topic in medicine, science, or technology, it is important that you use up-to-date information. In areas such

Electronic Resources

MEETING INDIVIDUAL NEEDS — English Language Learners

Recognizing Opinions

Some students whose first language is not English might have difficulty distinguishing between facts and opinions. Share the following phrases with students. Explain to them that these phrases usually indicate that an opinion is being expressed.

I believe that . . .
I really like . . .
I really hate . . .
. . . is beautiful (or ugly)

as literature and history, older material may be as good as current data.

3. What is the purpose of the information? If it is obvious that the purpose of the information is to entertain or persuade or if it was provided by a group with a particular bias, you may want to be cautious in how you use the information.

4. Has the material been reviewed? It is often relatively easy to find a review of printed material, but it is more difficult to determine whether there is any review process for material on a Web site. It is probably safe to assume that material from a government or university site has undergone some form of review.

5. Is the material suitable for your purpose? Be sure that the information you use is written in a way that you (or your intended audience) can understand. If it contains difficult-to-understand ideas or vocabulary, consider looking for another source.

Exercise 7

Choose a famous current or historical event and find a Web site that provides information about the event. Record the URL and five to ten facts that you learned about the event on the Web site. Check the accuracy of the facts in another source, such as an encyclopedia. Then report to the class on the accuracy of the Web site.

28.5 CD-ROMs and Other Electronic Resources

Besides the resources available to you on the Internet, a computer can help you access a wide variety of information from CD-ROMs, DVDs, diskettes, and magnetic tape. These items can be viewed at and sometimes borrowed from a library. The number and variety of topics covered in them is constantly growing. If your family is considering

Focus

Lesson Overview

Objectives
- To identify electronic resources, other than the Internet, that provide useful information
- To evaluate sources of information
- To frame questions to direct research

Skills
- understanding the value of electronic resources; using a CD-ROM

Critical Thinking
- evaluating reference resources

Listening and Speaking
- discussing

Bellringer
Daily Language Activity

When students enter the classroom, have this assignment on the board: *What other resources, besides the Internet and books, can you use to find information?*

Motivating Activity

Have students discuss their answers to the Bellringer activity. Ask students for examples of the types of things that can be found on CD-ROMs. Ask volunteers who have educational CD-ROMs at home to bring them in to share with the class.

Resource Manager

📁 **Planning Resources**
- *Lesson Plans*

📁 **Other Print Resources**
- *Guide to Using the Internet and Other Electronic Resources*

Teach

Extrapolation

Ask students to imagine what libraries of the future may be like when all information is on CD-ROM. Discuss with them what some of the pros and cons would be to having information on a CD-ROM rather than in book form.

the purchase of a new computer, be sure that the computer can accommodate these informational items, some of which are relatively recent developments.

CD-ROMs

A **CD-ROM**, or Compact Disc–Read-Only Memory, looks like an audio compact disc, but it can store more than just audio information. **Read-only memory** is computer memory on which data has been prerecorded. Once data has been written onto a CD-ROM, it

cannot be removed and can only be read. A CD-ROM can store text, sounds, graphics, and video files. Because CD-ROMs can store large amounts of information, many dictionaries, encyclopedias, and other reference works are stored on them. In fact, one CD-ROM can store as much information as hundreds of floppy diskettes. You can use CD-ROMs to read text and look at pictures. You can also use them to view video and hear audio files of historic events.

To use a CD-ROM, your computer must have a CD-ROM drive. CD-ROM drives are standard on most new computers. Some CD-ROM drives are able to record information, just as you might record music on an audiocassette.

DVDs

A **DVD**, or Digital VideoDisc, can store up to six times the data of a CD-ROM on the same surface area. Similar in size and shape to a CD-ROM, a DVD can hold enough information for a full-length movie. Like a VCR, a DVD player can be used to watch movies, and like a CD-ROM, a DVD requires a special drive on a computer. Although a DVD drive can play CD-ROMs, a CD-ROM drive cannot play DVDs.

Removable Storage

Your computer uses a built-in hard drive that stores information. All computers also include a drive for removable discs that can increase your storage capacity. You can insert a removable disc into another computer and transfer files to it. These removable discs can also be used to send information to someone else or to store files as a backup in case your hard drive crashes and you lose the information there.

Electronic Resources

Cooperative Learning

Planning a CD-ROM

Have students break into small groups and plan a CD-ROM. Each group should choose a topic of interest that is narrow enough to present to the class. Students should sketch at least three "pages," including both text and illustrations. Have students present their plans to the class. **L2**

Diskettes, also called floppy disks, have been commonly used for years to store text documents. The average computer user still uses diskettes to store information, although most software is now being distributed on a CD-ROM. The use of diskettes, however, may be coming to an end. Many computers now come with Zip drives, and some have abandoned diskette drives altogether. A Zip disc can hold as much information as almost one hundred diskettes. Certainly, as more people get involved in multimedia, they will need storage devices that can hold the larger multimedia files.

Digital Magnetic tape for a computer is similar to tape for an audiocassette player. The tape stores information on a magnetically coated strip of plastic. The tape can store large amounts of information, but it is not as convenient to use as a CD-ROM or a diskette. It is more difficult to access information from a magnetic tape. If you need to view information that is at the end of a tape, you must sort through all of the information on the tape until you find it. CD-ROMs and diskettes let you choose the information you wish to view with the click of a button. Magnetic tape is used mostly for backing up information or storing large quantities of information that do not have to be accessed quickly.

Exercise 8

Find a book and a CD-ROM on the same subject at your neighborhood or school library. If you were writing a report on this subject, which source would be the most helpful? Create a chart listing the advantages and disadvantages of each.

Troubleshooting Guide

As you work on the Web, you may need help in dealing with possible problems. Here are some error messages that you might see as you spend time on the Web. They are followed by their possible causes and some suggestions for eliminating the errors.

Message: Unable to connect to server. The server may be down. Try connecting again later.
Possible Causes: The server is having technical problems. The site is being updated or is not communicating properly with your browser.
Suggestion: It usually helps if you try again in a few minutes; however, it could be a few days before the server is working properly.

Electronic Resources

Practice and Assess

Evaluation Rubrics: Exercise 8
Results will vary. Whichever resource a student finds more useful, the charts should demonstrate a serious consideration of both resources.

Enrichment and Extension

Keeping perspective

In the late 1970s, using magnetic tape was a common way of storing information electronically. In the 1980s, floppy disks became more popular as they became able to store more and more information. Today we are amazed at how much information can be stored on a CD-ROM or a Zip disk. Remind the class that this technology is constantly changing, and that in just a few years our current storage abilities may seem as outdated as magnetic tape seems now.

Close

Ask students to look up two or three of the same subjects in different resources to see how information differs. Have students discuss the differences they find. Suggest that they use books, film, and Internet sources to compare information, reviews, and styles of presentation.

✔ ASSESSMENT OPTIONS

📁 *Tests with Answer Key and Rubrics*
Unit 28 Mastery Test, pp. 115–116

💾 *Testmaker*
Unit 28 Mastery Test

📼 *MindJogger Videoquizzes*

You may wish to administer the Unit 28 Mastery Test at this point.

Electronic Resources

Message: Unable to locate the server: www.server.com. The server does not have a DNS (Domain Name System) entry. Check the server name in the URL and try again.

Possible Causes: You have typed in the URL incorrectly, or the site no longer exists.

Suggestion: Be sure you have entered the URL correctly—check for proper capitalization and punctuation. If you have entered it correctly, try using a search engine to find the site. Keep in mind, though, the possibility that the site may have been abandoned.

Message: File Not Found: The requested URL was not found on this server.

Possible Causes: You have reached the server, but that particular file no longer exists or you have entered the path or file name incorrectly.

Suggestion: Check the URL again. If you have entered it correctly, try searching for the page from the server's home page.

Message: Network connection refused by the server. There was no response.

Possible Causes: You have reached the server, but it is too busy (too many other people are trying to access it) or temporarily shut down.

Suggestion: Try to access the site later.

Message: Connection timed out.

Possible Causes: Your browser attempted to contact the host, but the host took too long to reply.

Suggestion: Try to access the site later.

Message: Access denied. You do not have permission to open this item.

Possible Causes: The URL has moved, the Webmaster no longer allows public access to the site, or you have been denied access to the site.

Suggestion: Contact the Webmaster to verify the URL or try the site again in a few days. Sometimes there is nothing you can do if access has been denied. Many colleges, for example, allow access to parts of their sites only to faculty and registered students.

Technology Tip

Troubleshooting for Software

Have students search for troubleshooting Web sites for specific computer software, such as a word processing program. Students should use the keyword *troubleshooting* plus the name of the software to search for possible Web sites. Ask volunteers to present their search results to the class.

WRITING AND LANGUAGE
GLOSSARY

This glossary will help you quickly find definitions used in writing and grammar.

Adjective. A word that modifies, or describes, a noun or a pronoun. An adjective may tell *what kind, which one, how many,* or *how much.*

The **comparative degree** of an adjective compares two people, places, things, or ideas. (*worse, sadder*)

The **superlative degree** of an adjective compares more than two people, places, things, or ideas. (*worst, saddest*)

A **possessive adjective** is a possessive pronoun used before a noun.

A **predicate adjective** always follows a linking verb. It modifies the subject of the sentence.

A **proper adjective** is formed from a proper noun. It always begins with a capital letter.

A **demonstrative adjective** is the word *this, that, these,* or *those* used before a noun.

Adjective clause. A dependent clause that modifies a noun or pronoun.

Adverb. A word that modifies a verb, an adjective, or another adverb. Adverbs may tell *how, when, where, in what manner,* and *how often.* Some adverbs have different forms to indicate **comparative** and **superlative degrees.** (*loud, louder, loudest; sweetly, more sweetly, most sweetly*)

Adverb clause. A dependent clause that modifies a verb, an adjective, or an adverb.

Allusion. A reference in a piece of writing to a well-known character, place, or situation from a work of literature, music, or art or from history.

Analysis. The act of breaking down a subject into separate parts to determine its meaning.

Anecdote. A short story or incident usually presented as part of a longer narrative.

Antecedent. *See* Pronoun.

Appositive. A noun placed next to another noun to identify it or add information about it. (My basketball coach, *Ms. Lopes,* called for a time out.)

Argument. A statement, reason, or fact for or against a point; a piece of writing intended to persuade.

Article. The adjectives *a, an,* and *the. A* and *an* are **indefinite articles.** They refer to any one item of a group. *The* is a **definite article.** It indicates that the noun it precedes is a specific person, place or thing.

Audience. The person(s) who reads or listens to what the writer or speaker says.

Base form. *See* Verb tense.

Bias. A tendency to think a certain way. Bias may affect the way a writer or speaker presents his or her ideas.

Bibliography. A list of the books, articles, and other sources used as reference sources in a research paper.

Body. The central part of a composition that communicates and explains the main idea identified in the introduction.

Bookmarks/favorites. The feature on many Web browsers that allows the user to save addresses of Internet sites so that the sites can be accessed quickly.

Brainstorming. A group activity in which people generate as many ideas as possible without stopping to judge them.

C

Case. The form of a noun or pronoun that is determined by its use in a sentence. A noun or pronoun is in the **nominative** case when it is used as a subject, in the **objective** case when it is used as an object, and in the **possessive** case when it is used to show possession.

Cause-and-effect chain. A series of events in which one cause leads to an effect that in turn leads to another effect, and so on.

Characterization. The methods a writer uses to develop the personality of the character. A writer may make direct statements about a character's personality or reveal it through the character's words and actions or through what other characters think and say about the character.

Chronological order. The arrangement of details according to when events or actions take place.

Clarity. The quality of a piece of writing that makes it easy to understand.

Clause. A group of words that has a subject and a predicate and that is used as part of a sentence.

An **independent clause,** also called a **main clause,** has a subject and a predicate and can stand alone as a sentence.

A **dependent clause,** also called a **subordinate clause,** has a subject and a predicate, but it makes sense only when attached to a main clause.

Cliché. An overused expression. *(white as snow)*

Clustering. The grouping together of related items as a way of organizing information.

Coherence. A quality of logical connection between the parts of a paragraph or composition.

Cohesive writing. A type of writing in which sentences and paragraphs are logically connected to one another.

Collaboration. The process of working with others on writing or other projects.

Colloquialism. A casual, colorful expression used in everyday conversation.

Comparative degree. *See* Adjective; Adverb.

Comparison-and-contrast organization. A way of organizing ideas by illustrating their similarities and differences.

Complement. A word or phrase that completes the meaning of a verb. Three kinds of complements are **direct objects, indirect objects,** and **subject complements.**

Conceptual map. A graphic device that develops a central concept by surrounding it with examples or related ideas in a weblike arrangement.

Conclusion. A restatement or summing up of the ideas in a composition that brings it to a definite close.

Conflict. The struggle between two opposing forces that lies at the center of the plot in a story or drama.

Conjunction. A word that joins single words or groups of words.

A **coordinating conjunction** (*and, but, or, nor, for, yet*) joins words or groups of words that are equal in grammatical importance. **Correlative conjunctions** (*both . . . and, just as . . . so, not only . . . but also, either . . . or, neither . . . nor*) are pairs of words used to connect words or phrases in a sentence.

Connotation. The thoughts and feelings associated with a word, rather than its dictionary definition.

Constructive criticism. Comments on another person's writing made with the intention of helping the writer improve a particular draft.

Context. The words and sentences that come before and after a specific word and help to explain its meaning.

Conventions. Correct spelling, grammar, usage, and mechanics.

Coordinating conjunction. *See* Conjunction.

Correlative conjunction. *See* Conjunction.

Credibility. The quality of a speaker or writer that makes that person's words believable.

Declarative sentence. A sentence that makes a statement.

Deductive reasoning. A way of thinking or explaining that begins with a general statement or principle and applies that principle to specific instances.

Definite article. *See* Article.

Demonstrative adjective. *See* Adjective.

Denotation. The dictionary definition of a word.

Dependent clause. *See* Clause.

Descriptive writing. Writing that uses sensory detail to convey a dominant impression of, for example, a setting, a person, an animal, and so on.

Desktop publishing. The use of computer programs to format and produce a document that may include written text, graphics, and/or images.

Dialect. A variation of a language spoken by a particular group of people. A dialect may be regional (based on location) or ethnic (based on cultural heritage).

Dialogue. The conversation between characters in a written work.

Diction. A writer's choice of words and the arrangement of those words in phrases, sentences, or lines of a poem.

Direct object. *See* Complement.

Documentation. Identification of the sources used in writing research or other informative papers; usually in the form of endnotes or footnotes, or using parenthetical documentation.

Drafting. One of the steps in the writing process; the transforming of thoughts, words, and phrases into sentences and paragraphs.

Editing. One of the steps in the writing process in which a revised draft is checked for standard usage, varied sentence structure, and appropriate word choice.

Editorial. An article in a newspaper or other form of media that expresses an opinion about a topic of general interest.

Elaboration. The support or development of a main idea with facts, statistics, sensory details, incidents, anecdotes, examples, or quotations.

Ellipsis. A mark of punctuation, consisting of three spaced periods, that shows the omission of a word or words.

Writing and Language Glossary **799**

E-mail. Short for electronic mail. Messages, usually text, sent from one person to another by way of computer.

Evaluating. Making a judgment about the strengths and weaknesses of a draft in content, organization, and style.

Evidence. Facts or examples from reliable sources that can be used to support statements made in speaking or writing.

Exclamatory sentence. A sentence that expresses strong or sudden emotion.

Explanatory writing. *See* Expository writing.

Expository writing. A kind of writing that aims at informing and explaining. Examples of expository writing are news articles, how-to instructions, and research papers.

Expressive writing. Writing that emphasizes and conveys the writer's feelings.

Fact. A piece of information that can be verified.

Feedback. The response a listener or reader gives to a speaker or writer about his or her work.

Figurative language. Words used for descriptive effect that express some truth beyond the literal level. Figures of speech such as similes, metaphors, or personification are examples of figurative language.

Formal language. Language that uses correct grammar and omits slang expressions and contractions. It is especially common in nonfiction writing that is not personal.

Fragment. An incomplete sentence punctuated as if it were complete.

Freewriting. A way of finding ideas by writing freely, without stopping or limiting the flow of ideas, often for a specific length of time.

Future tense. *See* Verb tense.

Generalization. A statement that presents a conclusion about a subject without going into details or specifics.

Genre. A division of literature. The main literary genres are prose, poetry, and drama. Each of these is further divided into subgenres.

Gerund. A verb form ending in *–ing* that is used as a noun.

Graphic organizer. A visual way of organizing information; types of graphic organizers are charts, graphs, clusters, and idea trees.

Home page. The location on a Web site by which a user normally enters the site. A typical home page may explain the site, summarize the content, and provide links to other sites.

Hyperlink. Highlighted or underlined phrases or words on a Web page that, when clicked, move the user to another part of the page or to another Web page.

Hypertext. Links in some electronic text that take the user to another document or to a different section in the same document.

I

Ideas. In writing, the message or theme and the details that elaborate upon that message or theme.

Idiom. A word or phrase that has a special meaning different from its standard or dictionary meaning. (*Burning the midnight oil* is an idiom that means "staying up late.")

Imagery. Language that emphasizes sensory impressions that can help the reader of a literary work to see, hear, feel, smell, and taste the scenes described in the work.

Imperative sentence. A sentence that makes a request or gives a command.

Indefinite article. *See* Article.

Indefinite pronoun. *See* Pronoun.

Independent clause. *See* Clause.

Inductive reasoning. A way of thinking or explaining that begins with a series of examples and uses them to arrive at a general statement.

Infinitive. A verbal made up of the word *to* and the base form of a word. An infinitive often functions as a noun in a sentence.

Informative writing. A kind of writing that explains something, such as a process or an idea. *See also* Expository writing.

Intensifier. An adverb that emphasizes an adjective or another adverb. (*very* important; *quite* easily)

Interjection. A word or phrase that expresses strong feeling. An interjection has no grammatical connection to other words in the sentence.

Internet. A worldwide computer network that allows users to link to any computer on the network electronically for social, commercial, research, and other purposes.

Interpretation. An explanation of the meaning of a piece of writing, a visual representation, or any other type of communication.

Interview. A question-and-answer dialogue that has the specific purpose of gathering up-to-date or expert information.

Intransitive verb. *See* Verb.

Introduction. The beginning part of a piece of writing, in which a writer identifies the subject and gives a general idea of what the body of the composition will contain.

Inverted order. The placement of a predicate before the subject in a sentence. In most sentences in English, the subject comes before the predicate.

Irregular verb. *See* Verb tense.

 J

Jargon. Special words and phrases used by a particular trade, profession, or other group of people.

Journal. A personal notebook in which a person can freewrite, collect ideas, and record thoughts and experiences.

L–M

Learning log. A journal used for clarifying ideas about concepts covered in various classes.

Lexicon. A wordbook or dictionary.

Listing. A technique for finding ideas for writing.

Literary analysis. The act of examining the different elements of a piece of literature in order to evaluate it.

Logical fallacy. An error in reasoning often found in advertising or persuasive writing. Either-or reasoning and glittering generalities are types of logical fallacies.

Main clause. *See* Clause.

Main idea. *See* Thesis statement.

Main verb. The most important word in a verb phrase.

Media. The forms of communication used to reach an audience; forms such as newspapers, radio, TV, and the Internet reach large audiences and so are known as mass media.

Memoir. A type of narrative nonfiction that presents an account of an event or period in history, emphasizing the narrator's personal experience.

Metaphor. A figure of speech that compares seemingly unlike things without using words such as *like* or *as*. (*He is a rock.*)

Mood. The feeling or atmosphere of a piece of writing.

Multimedia presentation. The use of a variety of media, such as video, sound, written text, and visual art to present ideas or information.

N

Narrative writing. A type of writing that tells about events or actions as they change over a period of time and often includes story elements such as character, setting, and plot.

Nonfiction. Prose writing about real people, places, and events.

Noun. A word that names a person, a place, a thing, an idea, a quality, or a characteristic.

Noun clause. A dependent clause used as a noun.

Number. The form of a noun, pronoun, or verb that indicates whether it refers to one (**singular**) or more than one (**plural**).

O

Object. *See* Complement.

Onomatopoeia. The use of a word or phrase that imitates or suggests the sound of what it describes. (*rattle, boom*)

Opinion. A belief or attitude that cannot be proven true or false.

Oral tradition. Literature that passes by word of mouth from one generation to the next. The oral tradition of a culture may reflect the cultural values of the people.

Order of importance. A way of arranging details in a paragraph or other piece of writing according to their importance.

Organization. The arrangement of main points and supporting details in a piece of writing.

Outline. A systematic arrangement of main and supporting ideas, using Roman numerals, letters, and numbers, for a written or an oral presentation.

P

Paragraph. A unit of writing that consists of related sentences.

Parallel construction. The use of a series of words, phrases, or sentences that have similar grammatical form.

Paraphrase. A restatement of someone's ideas in words that are different from the original passage but retain its ideas, tone, and general length.

Parenthetical documentation. A specific reference to the source of a piece of information, placed in parenthesis directly after the information appears in a piece of writing.

Participle. A verb form that can function as an adjective. Present participles always end in -*ing.* Although past participles often end in -*ed,* they can take other forms as well.

Peer response. The suggestions and comments provided by peers, or classmates, about a piece of writing or another type of presentation.

Personal pronoun. *See* Pronoun.

Personal writing. Writing that expresses the writer's own thoughts and feelings.

Personification. A figure of speech that gives human qualities to an animal, object, or idea.

Perspective. *See* Point of view.

Persuasion. A type of writing that aims at convincing people to think or act in a certain way.

Phrase. A group of words that acts in a sentence as a single part of speech.
   A **prepositional phrase** begins with a preposition and ends with a noun or a pronoun.

A **verb phrase** consists of one or more auxiliary verbs followed by a main verb.

Plagiarism. The dishonest presentation of another's words or ideas as one's own.

Plot. The series of events that follow one another in a story, novel, or play.

Plural. *See* Number.

Poetry. A form of literary expression that emphasizes the line as the unit of composition. Traditional poetry contains emotional, imaginative language and a regular rhythm.

Point of view. The angle, or perspective, from which a story is told, such as first- or third-person.

Portfolio. A collection of various pieces of writing, which may include finished pieces and works in progress.

Predicate. The verb or verb phrase and any of its modifiers that make an essential statement about the subject of a sentence.

Predicate adjective. *See* Adjective.

Preposition. A word that shows the relationship of a noun or pronoun to some other word in the sentence.

Prepositional phrase. *See* Phrase.

Presentation. The way words and design elements look on the page.

Presenting/Publishing. The last step in the writing process; involves sharing the final writing product with others in some way.

Present tense. *See* Verb tense.

Prewriting. The first stage in the writing process; includes deciding what to write about, collecting ideas and details, and making an outline or a plan. Prewriting strategies include brainstorming and using graphic organizers, notes, and logs.

Prior knowledge. The facts, ideas, and experiences that a writer, reader, or viewer brings to a new activity.

Progressive form. *See* Verb tense.

Pronoun. A word that takes the place of a noun, a group of words acting as a noun, or another pronoun. The word or group of words that a pronoun refers to is called its **antecedent**.

A **personal pronoun** refers to a specific person or thing.

Pronoun case. *See* Case.

Proofreading. The final part of the editing process that involves checking work to discover typographical and other errors.

Propaganda. Information aimed at influencing thoughts and actions; it is usually of a political nature and may contain distortions of truth.

Proper adjective. *See* Adjective.

Prose. Writing that is similar to everyday speech and written language, as opposed to poetry and drama.

Publishing. The preparation of a finished piece of writing often involving available technology, so that it can be presented to a larger audience.

Purpose. The aim of writing, which may be to express, discover, record, develop, reflect on ideas, problem solve, entertain, influence, inform, or describe.

Regular verb. *See* Verb tense.

Representation. A way in which information or ideas are presented to an audience.

Research. The search for information on a topic.

Review. The analysis and interpretation of a subject, often presented through the mass media.

Revising. The stage of the writing process in which a writer goes over a draft, making changes in its content, organization, and style in order to improve it. Revision techniques include adding, elaborating, deleting, combining, and rearranging text.

Root. The part of a word that carries the main meaning.

Run-on sentence. Two or more sentences or clauses run together without appropriate punctuation.

Sensory details. Language that appeals to the senses; sensory details are important elements of descriptive writing, especially of poetry.

Sentence. A group of words expressing a complete thought. Every sentence has a **subject** and a **predicate**. *See also* Subject; Predicate; Clause.

A **simple sentence** has only one main clause and no subordinate clauses.

A **compound sentence** has two or more main clauses. Each main clause of a compound sentence has its own subject and predicate, and these main clauses are usually joined by a comma and a coordinating conjunction. A semicolon can also be used to join the main clauses in a compound sentence.

A **complex sentence** has one main clause and one or more subordinate clauses.

Sentence fluency. The smooth rhythm and flow of sentences that vary in length and style.

Sentence variety. The use of different types of sentences to add interest to writing.

Setting. The time and place in which the events of a story, novel, or play takes place.

Simile. A figure of speech that compares two basically unlike things, using words such as *like* or *as.*

Simple sentence. *See* Sentence.

Spatial order. A way of presenting the details of a setting according to their location—for example, from left to right or from top to bottom.

Standard English. The most widely used and accepted form of the English language

Style. The writer's choice and arrangement of words and sentences.

Subject. The noun or pronoun that tells who or what the sentence is about.

Subordinate clause. *See* Clause.

Summary. A brief statement of the main idea of a composition.

Supporting evidence. *See* Evidence.

Suspense. A literary device that creates growing interest and excitement leading up to the climax and resolution of a story. A writer creates suspense by providing clues to the resolution without revealing too much information.

Symbol. An object, a person, a place, or an experience that represents something else, usually something abstract.

Tense. *See* Verb tense.

Theme. The main idea or message of a piece of writing.

Thesis statement. A one- or two-sentence statement of the main idea or purpose of a piece of writing.

Time order. The arrangement of details in a piece of writing based on when they occurred.

Tone. A reflection of a writer's or speaker's attitude toward a subject.

Topic sentence. A sentence that expresses the main idea of a paragraph.

Transition. A connecting word or phrase that clarifies relationships between details, sentences, or paragraphs.

U–V

Unity. A quality of oneness in a paragraph or composition that exists when all the sentences or paragraphs work together to express or support one main idea.

URL. The standard form of an Internet address; stands for Uniform Resource Locator.

Venn diagram. A graphic organizer consisting of two overlapping circles; used to compare two items that have both similar and different traits.

Verb. A word that expresses an action or a state of being and is necessary to make a statement.

Verbal. A verb form that functions in a sentence as a noun, an adjective, or an adverb. The three kinds of verbals are participles, gerunds, and infinitives. *See also* Gerund; Infinitive; Participle.

Verb phrase. *See* Phrase.

Verb tense. The form a verb takes to show when an action takes place. The **present tense** names an action that happens regularly. The **past tense** names an action that has happened, and the **future tense** names an action that will take place in the future. All the verb tenses are formed from the four principal parts of a verb: a **base form** (*freeze*), a **present participle** (*freezing*), a **simple past** form (*froze*) and a **past participle** (*frozen*). A **regular verb** forms its simple past and past participle by adding -*ed* to the base form. Verbs that form their past and past participle in some other way are called **irregular verbs**.

In addition to present, past, and future tense, there are three perfect tenses—present perfect, past perfect, and future perfect. Each of the six tenses has a **progressive** form that expresses a continuing action.

Voice. A writer's unique way of using tone and style to communicate with the audience.

W

Web site. A location on the World Wide Web that can be reached through links or by accessing a Web address, or URL. *See* URL.

Word choice. The vocabulary a writer chooses to convey meaning.

Word Processing. The use of a computer for the writing and editing of written text.

World Wide Web. A global system that uses the Internet and allows users to create, link, and access fields of information. *See* Internet.

Writing process. The series of stages or steps that a writer goes through to develop ideas and to communicate them.

GLOSARIO
DE ESCRITURA Y LENGUAJE

Este glosario permite encontrar fácilmente definiciones de gramática inglesa y términos que usan los escritores.

 A

Adjective/Adjetivo. Palabra que modifica, o describe, un nombre (*noun*) o pronombre (*pronoun*). Un adjetivo *indica qué tipo, cuál, cuántos o cuánto.*

> **Comparative degree/Grado comparativo.** Adjetivo que compara a dos personas, lugares, cosas o ideas (*worse, sadder;* en español: *peor, más triste*).

> **Superlative degree/Grado superlativo.** Adjetivo que compara más de dos personas, lugares, cosas o ideas (*worst, saddest;* en español: *el peor, la más triste*).

> **Possessive adjective/Adjetivo posesivo.** Pronombre posesivo que va antes del nombre.

> **Predicative adjective/Adjetivo predicativo.** Siempre va después de un verbo copulativo y modifica al sujeto de la oración.

> **Proper adjective/Adjetivo propio*.** Adjetivo que se deriva de un nombre propio; en inglés siempre se escribe con mayúscula.

> **Demonstrative adjective/Adjetivo demostrativo.** Se usa antes del nombre: *this, that, these, those (este, ese, aquel, estos, esos, aquellos).*

Adjective clause/Proposición adjetiva. Proposición dependiente que modifica un nombre o un pronombre.

Adverb/Adverbio. Palabra que modifica a un verbo, adjetivo u otro adverbio. Los adverbios indican *cómo, cuándo, dónde, de qué manera* y *qué tan seguido* sucede algo. Algunos adverbios tienen diferentes formas para indicar los grados **comparativo** (*comparative*) y **superlativo** (*superlative*) (*loud, louder, loudest; sweetly, more sweetly, most sweetly;* en español: *fuerte, más fuerte, lo más fuerte; dulcemente, más dulcemente, lo más dulcemente*).

Adverb clause/Proposición adverbial. Proposición dependiente que modifica un verbo, un adjetivo o un adverbio.

Allusion/Alusión. Referencia en un texto escrito a un personaje, lugar o situación muy conocidos de una obra literaria, musical, artística o histórica.

Analysis/Análisis. Acción de descomponer un tema o escrito en distintas partes para encontrar su significado.

Anecdote/Anécdota. Narración breve o incidente que se presenta como parte de una narrativa más larga.

Antecedent/Antecedente. *Ver Pronoun.*

Appositive/Apositivo. Nombre colocado junto a otro para identificarlo o agregar información sobre él. (Mi entrenadora de baloncesto, *Ms. Lopes,* pidió tiempo fuera.)

Argument/Argumento. Afirmación, razón o hecho en favor o en contra de algún comentario; texto escrito que trata de persuadir.

Article/Artículo. Nombre dado a las palabras *a*, *an* y *the* (en español: *un, uno/a, el, la*). *A* y *an* son artículos **indefinidos** (*indefinite articles*), que se refieren a cualquier cosa de un grupo. *The* es un artículo **definido** (*definite article*); indica que el nombre al que precede es una persona, lugar o cosa específicos.

Audience/Público. Persona (o personas) que lee o escucha lo que dicen un escritor o un hablante.

B

Base form/Base derivativa. *Ver Verb tense.*

Bias/Tendencia. Inclinación a pensar de cierta manera. La tendencia influye en la manera en que un escritor o hablante presenta sus ideas.

Bibliography/Bibliografía. Lista de los libros, artículos y otras fuentes que se utilizan como referencia en una investigación.

Body/Cuerpo. Parte central de una composición que comunica la idea principal identificada en la introducción.

Bookmarks/favorites/Marcadores/favoritos. Característica de muchos buscadores de red que permiten guardar direcciones de Internet para entrar a ellas rápidamente.

Brainstorming/Lluvia de ideas. Actividad de grupo en que se generan tantas ideas como sea posible sin detenerse a analizarlas.

C

Case/Caso. Forma de un nombre o pronombre que está determinado por su uso en la oración. El nombre o pronombre está en caso **nominativo** (*nominative case*) cuando se utiliza como sujeto; en caso **acusativo** y **dativo** (*objective case*) cuando recibe la acción del verbo, y en caso **posesivo** * (*possessive case*) cuando se utiliza para indicar posesión o propiedad.

Cause-and-effect chain/Cadena de causa y efecto. Serie de acontecimientos en que una causa lleva a un efecto que, a su vez, lleva a otro efecto, y así sucesivamente.

Characterization/Caracterización. Métodos que utiliza un escritor para crear sus personajes. Puede ser describiendo directamente su personalidad, o revelándola con sus palabras y acciones, o bien a partir de lo que otros personajes piensan y dicen de él.

Chronological order/Orden cronológico. Organización de detalles de acuerdo con el tiempo en que sucedieron los acontecimientos o acciones.

Clarity/Claridad. Cualidad de un escrito que lo hace fácil de entender.

Clause/Proposición. Grupo de palabras que consta de sujeto y predicado, y que se usa como parte de una oración compuesta.

Independent clause/Proposición independiente. También llamada **proposición principal** (*main clause*); tiene sujeto y predicado y hace sentido por sí misma.

Dependent clause/Proposición dependiente. También llamada **proposición subordinada** (*subordinate clause*); tiene sujeto y predicado pero depende de la proposición principal.

Cliché/Cliché. Expresión usada con demasiada frecuencia (*blanco como la nieve*).

Clustering/Agrupamiento. Reunión de temas relacionados para organizar la información.

Coherence/Coherencia. Relación lógica entre las partes de un párrafo o composición.

Cohesive writing/Escritura coherente. Tipo de escritura en que las oraciones y párrafos están lógicamente relacionados entre sí.

Collaboration/Colaboración. Proceso de trabajar en equipo para escribir un texto o realizar un proyecto.

Colloquialism/Expresión coloquial. Expresión informal y pintoresca que se utiliza en la conversación diaria.

Comparative degree/Grado comparativo. *Ver Adjective; Adverb.*

Comparison-and-contrast/Comparación y contraste. Manera de organizar ideas, señalando sus similitudes y diferencias.

Complement/Complemento (u objeto). Palabra o frase que complementa el significado de un verbo. Tres complementos son: **directo** (*direct object*), **indirecto** (*indirect object*) y **predicativo** (**atributo**) (*subject complement*).

Conceptual map/Mapa conceptual. Recurso gráfico que desarrolla un concepto central rodeándolo con ejemplos o ideas relacionadas a manera de red.

Conclusion/Conclusión. Afirmación que resume las ideas de una composición, antes de ponerle punto final.

Conflict/Conflicto. Lucha entre dos fuerzas opuestas que constituye el elemento central de la trama en un cuento u obra de teatro.

Conjunction/Conjunción. Palabra que une palabras o grupos de palabras.

> **Coordinating conjunction/Conjunción coordinante.** Las palabras *and, but, or, nor, for, yet* (*y, pero, o, no, para, aun*) unen palabras o grupos de palabras que tienen igual importancia gramatical.
>
> **Correlative conjunction/Conjunción correlativa*.** Las palabras *both . . . and, just as . . . so, not only . . . but also, either . . . or, neither . . . nor* (*tanto . . . como, así como, no sólo . . . sino, o . . . o*) son palabras en pares que vinculan palabras o frases en una oración.

Connotation/Connotación. Pensamientos y sentimientos relacionados con una palabra, más que con su definición de diccionario.

Constructive criticism/Crítica constructiva. Comentario sobre lo que escribe otra persona, con la intención de ayudar a que mejore el borrador.

Context/Contexto. Palabras y oraciones que vienen antes y después de una palabra y ayudan a explicar su significado.

Conventions/Reglas de escritura. Normas que regulan la ortografía, la gramática, el uso y la puntuación de un escrito.

Coordinating conjunction/Conjunción coordinante. *Ver Conjunction.*

Correlative conjunction/Conjunción correlativa*. *Ver Conjunction.*

Credibility/Credibilidad. Cualidad de un hablante o escritor que hace creer sus palabras.

Declarative sentence/Oración afirmativa. Oración que declara algo.

Deductive reasoning/Razonamiento deductivo. Pensamiento o explicación que parte de una afirmación o principio generales y los aplica a casos específicos.

Definite article/Artículo definido. *Ver Article.*

Demonstrative adjective/Adjetivo demostrativo. *Ver Adjective.*

Denotation/Denotación. Definición de una palabra que da el diccionario.

Dependent clause/Proposición dependiente. *Ver Clause.*

Descriptive writing/Escritura descriptiva. Tipo de escritura que ofrece detalles sensoriales para comunicar la impresión de un escenario, persona, animal, etcétera.

Desktop publishing/Edición por computadora. Uso de programas de computadora para formar un documento con texto escrito, gráficas y/o imágenes.

Dialect/Dialecto. Variedad de lenguaje hablado que usa un grupo particular. Un dialecto puede ser regional (de un lugar) o étnico (de un grupo cultural).

Dialogue/Diálogo. Conversación entre personajes en un escrito.

Diction/Dicción. Palabras que escoge un escritor y cómo las utiliza en frases, oraciones o versos.

Direct object/Complemento directo. *Ver Complement.*

Documentation/Documentación. Identificación de las fuentes que se emplean para escribir un artículo u otros textos informativos; generalmente se ponen como notas al pie, al final del texto o entre paréntesis.

Drafting/Borrador. Paso del proceso de escritura; transformación de ideas, palabras y frases a oraciones y párrafos.

E

Editing/Edición. Paso del proceso de escritura en que se revisa que el borrador corregido tenga un lenguaje estándar, una estructura sintáctica variada y la elección adecuada de palabras.

Editorial/Editorial. Artículo en un periódico u otro medio que expresa una opinión sobre un tema de interés general.

Elaboration/Elaboración. Sustento o desarrollo de una idea principal con hechos, estadísticas, detalles sensoriales, incidentes, anécdotas, ejemplos o citas.

Ellipsis/Puntos suspensivos. Signo de puntuación que consiste en dejar tres puntos para indicar que se están suprimiendo una o varias palabras.

E-mail/Correo electrónico. Mensajes, generalmente textos, que se envían por computadora.

Evaluating/Evaluación. Juicio sobre las fallas y aciertos de un borrador en cuanto a contenido, organización y estilo.

Evidence/Evidencia. Datos o ejemplos de fuentes confiables que sirven para sustentar afirmaciones escritas o habladas.

Exclamatory sentence/Oración exclamativa. Oración que expresa una emoción fuerte o repentina.

Explanatory writing/Texto explicativo. *Ver Descriptive text.*

Expository writing/Texto descriptivo. Tipo de escritura que informa o explica, como artículos periodísticos, instrucciones y artículos de investigación.

Expressive writing/Texto expresivo. Texto que realza y transmite los sentimientos del escritor.

F

Fact/Hecho. Información que puede comprobarse.

Feedback/Retroalimentación. Respuesta del escucha o lector al mensaje de un hablante o escritor.

Figurative language/Lenguaje figurado. Palabras usadas con un efecto descriptivo que expresa una verdad más allá del nivel literal. Los tropos, como el símil, la metáfora y la personificación, son ejemplos de lenguaje figurado.

Formal language/Lenguaje formal. Lenguaje que utiliza una gramática correcta y omite contracciones y expresiones coloquiales. Es común en textos de no ficción, que no son de carácter personal.

Fragment/Fragmento. Oración incompleta con puntuación de oración completa.

Freewriting/Escritura libre. Búsqueda de ideas escribiendo durante un tiempo determinado, sin detenerse ni limitar el flujo de ideas.

Future tense/Tiempo futuro. *Ver Verb tense.*

Generalization/Generalización. Afirmación que presenta una conclusión sobre un tema sin dar detalles específicos.

Genre/Género. Clasificación literaria o de otro medio. Los principales géneros literarios son la prosa, la poesía y el drama. Cada uno se divide en subgéneros.

Gerund/Gerundio. Verboide que termina en *–ing* y se usa como nombre (en inglés).

Graphic organizer/Organizador gráfico. Manera visual de organizar la información, como las tablas, las gráficas, las redes y los árboles de ideas.

Home page/Página principal. Página por medio de la cual un usuario entra normalmente a un sitio de Web. Por lo general, explica el sitio, resume el contenido y proporciona vínculos con otros sitios.

Hyperlink/Hipervínculo. Oraciones o palabras sombreadas o subrayadas en una página en red que al activarse con un clic conectan con otra parte de la página o con otra página de la red.

Hypertext/Hipertexto. Vínculos en textos electrónicos que llevan a otro documento o a una sección distinta del mismo documento.

Ideas/Ideas. En composición, el mensaje o tema y los detalles que lo elaboran.

Idiom/Modismo. Palabra o frase cuyo significado es diferente del significado estándar o de diccionario. (*Se le pegaron las sábanas* es un modismo que significa "se levantó muy tarde").

Imagery/Imaginería. Lenguaje que describe impresiones sensoriales para que el lector de un texto literario pueda ver, oír, sentir, oler y gustar las escenas descritas.

Imperative sentence/Oración imperativa. Oración que exige u ordena algo.

Indefinite article/Artículo indefinido. *Ver Article.*

Indefinite pronoun/Pronombre indefinido. *Ver Pronoun.*

Independent clause/Proposición independiente. *Ver Clause.*

Inductive reasoning/Razonamiento inductivo. Pensamiento o explicación que parte de varios ejemplos para llegar a una afirmación general.

Infinitive/Infinitivo. Verboide que consta de la palabra *to* y la base del verbo (en español terminan en *-ar, -er* o *-ir*). Se usa como sustantivo en la oración.

Informative writing/Texto informativo. Texto que explica un proceso o una idea. *Ver también Descriptive text.*

Intensifier/Intensificador. Adverbio que refuerza un adjetivo u otro adverbio (*very* important, *quite* easily; *muy* importante, *bastante* fácil).

Interjection/Interjección. Palabra o frase que expresa un sentimiento muy fuerte. La interjección no tiene relación gramatical con las demás palabras de la oración.

Internet/Internet. Red mundial computarizada que permite comunicarse electrónicamente con cualquier computadora de la red para buscar información social, comercial, de investigación y de otro tipo.

Interpretation/Interpretación. Explicación del significado de un texto, de una representación visual o de cualquier otro tipo de comunicación.

Interview/Entrevista. Diálogo a base de preguntas y respuestas cuyo propósito es obtener información actualizada o de expertos.

Intransitive Verb/Verbo intransitivo. *Ver Verb.*

Introduction/Introducción. Sección inicial de un texto en la que el escritor identifica el tema y da la idea general de lo que contendrá el cuerpo del mismo.

Inverted order/Orden invertido. Colocación del predicado antes del sujeto. En la mayoría de las oraciones en inglés, el sujeto va antes del predicado.

Irregular verb/Verbo irregular. *Ver Verb tense.*

Jargon/Jerga. Palabras y frases que usa un determinado grupo.

Journal/Diario. Libreta personal en la que con toda libertad se anotan ideas, pensamientos y experiencias.

Learning log/Registro de aprendizaje. Diario para aclarar ideas sobre conceptos tratados en varias clases.

Lexicon/Léxico. Diccionario.

Listing/Lista. Técnica para generar ideas a partir de las cuales se escribe un texto.

Literary analysis/Análisis literario. Examen de las diferentes partes de una obra literaria a fin de evaluarla.

Logical fallacy/Falacia lógica. Error de razonamiento que se encuentra con frecuencia en publicidad o en escritos persuasivos, como razonamientos con dos alternativas opuestas o generalidades muy llamativas.

Main clause/Proposición principal. *Ver Clause.*

Main idea/Idea principal. *Ver Thesis statement.*

Main verb/Verbo principal. La palabra más importante de una frase verbal.

Media/Medios. Formas de comunicación usadas para llegar a un público. Los periódicos, la radio, la televisión y la Internet llegan a públicos muy grandes, por lo que se conocen como medios de comunicación masiva.

Memoir/Memoria. Tipo de narrativa de no ficción que presenta el relato de un hecho o período de la historia, resaltando la experiencia personal del narrador.

Metaphor/Metáfora. Tropo que compara dos cosas aparentemente distintas sin usar las palabra *like* o *as (como). (Él es una roca.)*

Mood/Atmósfera. Sentimiento o ambiente de un texto escrito.

Multimedia presentation/Presentación multimedia. Uso de una variedad de medios como video, sonido, texto escrito y artes visuales para presentar ideas e información.

Narrative writing/Narrativa. Tipo de escritura que narra sucesos o acciones que cambian con el paso del tiempo; por lo general tiene personajes, escenario y trama.

Nonfiction/No ficción. Texto en prosa acerca de personas, lugares y sucesos reales.

Noun/Nombre (o sustantivo). Palabra que nombra a una persona, lugar, cosa, o a una idea, cualidad o característica.

Noun clause/Proposición nominal. Proposición dependiente que se usa como nombre.

Number/Número. Forma del nombre, pronombre o verbo que indica si se refiere a uno (**singular**) o a más de uno (**plural**).

Object/Objeto. *Ver Complement.*

Onomatopoeia/Onomatopeya. Palabra o frase que imita o sugiere el sonido que describe (*rattle, boom;* en español: *pum, zas*).

Opinion/Opinión. Creencia o actitud; no puede comprobarse si es falsa o verdadera.

Oral tradition/Tradición oral. Literatura que se transmite de boca en boca de una generación a otra. Puede representar los valores culturales de un pueblo.

Order of importance/Orden de importancia. Forma de acomodar los detalles en un párrafo o en otro texto escrito según su importancia.

Organization/Organización. La disposición y el orden de los puntos principales y los detalles de apoyo en un escrito.

Outline/Esquema. Organización sistemática de ideas principales y secundarias con números romanos, letras y números arábigos para una presentación oral o escrita.

Paragraph/Párrafo. Una unidad de un texto que consta de oraciones relacionadas.

Parallel construction/Construcción paralela. Serie de palabras, frases y oraciones que tienen una forma gramatical similar.

Paraphrase/Parafrasear. Repetir las ideas de otro con palabras diferentes del original pero conservando las ideas, el tono y la longitud general.

Parenthetical documentation/Documentación parentética. Referencia específica a la fuente de la información que se pone entre paréntesis directamente después de ésta.

Participle/Participio. Verboide que se usa como adjetivo. El participio presente siempre termina en –*ing* y el participio pasado por lo general termina en –*ed.*

Peer response/Respuesta de compañeros. Sugerencias y comentarios que dan los compañeros de clase sobre un texto escrito u otro tipo de presentación.

Personal pronoun/Pronombre personal. *Ver Pronoun.*

Personal writing/Escritura personal. Texto que expresa los pensamientos y sentimientos del autor.

Personification/Personificación. Tropo que da cualidades humanas a un animal, objeto o idea.

Perspective/Perspectiva. *Ver Point of view.*

Persuasion/Persuasión. Tipo de escritura encaminado a convencer a pensar o actuar de cierta manera.

Phrase/Frase. Grupo de palabras que forma una unidad en una oración.

> **Prepositional phrase/Frase preposicional.** Comienza con una preposición y termina con un nombre o un pronombre.
>
> **Verb phrase/Frase verbal.** Consta de uno o más **verbos auxiliares** (*auxiliary verbs*) seguidos del verbo principal.

Plagiarism/Plagio. Presentación deshonesta de palabras o ideas ajenas como si fueran propias.

Plot/Trama. Serie de sucesos en secuencia en un cuento, novela u obra de teatro.

Plural/Plural. *Ver Number.*

Poetry/Poesía. Forma de expresión literaria compuesta por versos. La poesía tradicional contiene un lenguaje emotivo e imaginativo y un ritmo regular.

Point of view/Punto de vista. Ángulo o perspectiva desde el cual se cuenta una historia; por ejemplo, primera o tercera persona.

Portfolio/Portafolio. Colección de varias obras escritas de un estudiante, que puede tener obras terminadas y otras en proceso.

Predicate/Predicado. Verbo o frase verbal y sus modificadores que hacen una afirmación esencial sobre el sujeto de la oración.

Predicate adjective/Adjetivo predicativo. *Ver Adjective.*

Preposition/Preposición. Palabra que muestra la relación de un nombre o pronombre con otra palabra en la oración.

Prepositional phrase/Frase preposicional. *Ver Phrase.*

Presentación. La forma en que se ven en una página las palabras y los elementos de diseño.

Presenting/Publishing/Presentación/ Publicacíon. Último paso del proceso de escritura que implica compartir con otros lo que se ha escrito.

Present tense/Tiempo presente. *Ver Verb tense.*

Prewriting/Preescritura. Primer paso del proceso de escritura: decidir sobre qué se va a escribir, reunir ideas y detalles, y elaborar un plan para presentar las ideas; usa estrategias como lluvia de ideas, organizadores gráficos, notas y registros.

Prior knowledge/Conocimiento previo. Hechos, ideas y experiencias que un escritor, lector u observador lleva a una nueva actividad.

Progressive form/Durativo. *Ver Verb tense.*

Pronoun/Pronombre. Palabra que va en lugar del nombre; grupo de palabras que funcionan como un nombre u otro pronombre. La palabra o grupo de palabras a que se refiere un pronombre se llama **antecedente** (*antecedent*).

> **Personal pronoun/Pronombre personal.** Se refiere a una persona o cosa específica.

Pronoun case/Caso del pronombre. *Ver Case.*

Proofreading/Corrección de pruebas. Último paso del proceso editorial en que se revisa el texto en busca de errores tipográficos y de otra naturaleza.

Propaganda/Propaganda. Información encaminada a influir en los pensamientos o acciones; en general es de naturaleza política y puede distorsionar la verdad.

Proper adjective/Adjetivo propio*. *Ver Adjective.*

Prose/Prosa. Escritura similar al lenguaje cotidiano tanto oral como escrito, a diferencia de la poesía y el teatro.

Publishing/Publicación. Presentación de una obra escrita terminada mediante el uso de la tecnología, para darla a conocer a un público amplio.

Purpose/Finalidad. Objetivo de la escritura: expresar, descubrir, registrar, desarrollar o reflexionar sobre ideas, resolver problemas, entretener, influir, informar o describir.

Regular verb/Verbo regular. *Ver Verb tense.*

Representation/Representación. Forma en que se presenta información o ideas al público.

Research/Investigación. Proceso de localizar información sobre un tema.

Review/Reseña. Análisis e interpretación de un tema presentado por lo general a través de los medios de comunicación masiva.

Revising/Revisión. Paso del proceso de escritura en que el autor repasa el borrador, cambia el contenido, la organización y el estilo para mejorar el texto. Las técnicas de revisión son agregar, elaborar, eliminar, combinar y reacomodar el texto.

Root/Raíz. Parte de una palabra que contiene el significado principal.

Run-on sentence/Oración mal puntuada. Dos o más oraciones o proposiciones seguidas, cuyo significado es confuso debido a su inadecuada puntuación.

S

Sensory details/Detalles sensoriales. Lenguaje que apela a los sentidos; los detalles sensoriales son elementos importantes de la escritura descriptiva, sobre todo en la poesía.

Sentence/Oración. Grupo de palabras que expresa un pensamiento completo. Cada oración tiene **sujeto** (*subject*) y **predicado** (*predicate*). *Ver también Subject; Predicate; Clause.*

> **Simple sentence/Oración simple.** Consta de una proposición principal y no tiene proposiciones subordinadas.
> **Compound sentence/Oración compuesta.** Tiene dos o más proposiciones principales, cada una con su propio sujeto y predicado; por lo general van unidas por una coma y una conjunción coordinante, o por un punto y coma.
> **Complex sentence/Oración compleja.** Tiene una proposición principal y una o más proposiciones subordinadas.

Sentence Fluency/Fluidez oracional. El vitmo suave y suelto de las oraciones que varían en longitud y estilo.

Sentence variety/Variedad de oraciones. Uso de diferentes tipos de oraciones para agregar interés al texto.

Setting/Escenario. Tiempo y lugar en que ocurren los sucesos de un cuento, novela u obra de teatro.

Simile/Símil. Tropo que compara dos cosas esencialmente distintas, usando las palabras *like* o *as* (*como*). (*Su pelo era como hilo de seda.*)

Simple predicate/Predicado simple. *Ver Predicate; Sentence; Subject.*

Simple sentence/Oración simple. *Ver Sentence.*

Spatial order/Orden espacial. Forma de presentar los detalles de un escenario según su ubicación: de izquierda a derecha o de arriba hacia abajo.

Standard English/Inglés estándar. La forma más ampliamente usada y aceptada del idioma inglés.

Style/Estilo. Forma en que un escritor elige y organiza las palabras y oraciones.

Subject/Sujeto. Nombre o pronombre principal que informa sobre quién o sobre qué trata la oración.

Subordinate clause/Proposición subordinada. *Ver Clause.*

Summary/Resumen. Breve explicación de la idea principal de una composición.

Supporting evidence/Sustento. *Ver Evidence.*

Suspense/Suspenso. Recurso literario que genera interés y emoción para llegar al clímax o desenlace de una historia. Un escritor crea suspenso al proporcionar pistas sobre el desenlace pero sin revelar demasiada información.

Symbol/Símbolo. Objeto, persona, lugar o experiencia que representa algo más, por lo general, abstracto.

Tense/Tiempo. *Ver Verb tense.*

Theme/Tema. Idea o mensaje principal de una obra escrita.

Thesis statement/Exposición de tesis. Exposición de la **idea principal** o finalidad de una obra en una o dos oraciones.

Time order/Orden temporal. Organización de detalles en un texto escrito según el momento en que ocurrieron.

Tone/Tono. Reflejo de la actitud del escritor o hablante hacia un sujeto.

Topic sentence/Oración temática. Oración que expresa la idea principal de un párrafo.

Transition/Transición. Palabra o frase de enlace que aclara las relaciones entre los detalles, oraciones o párrafos.

U-V

Unity/Unidad. Integridad de un párrafo o composición; coherencia entre todas las oraciones o párrafos para expresar o sustentar una idea principal.

URL/URL. Forma estándar de una dirección de Internet. (Son iniciales de *Uniform Resource Locator.*)

Venn diagram/Diagrama de Venn. Organizador gráfico que consta de dos círculos que se traslapan, usado para comparar dos cosas con características comunes y diferentes.

Verb/Verbo. Palabra que expresa acción o estado y que es necesaria para hacer una afirmación.

Verbal/Verboide. Forma del verbo que funciona como nombre, adjetivo o adverbio en la oración. Los verboides son: participio *(participles)*, gerundio *(gerunds)* e infinitivo *(infinitives)*.

Verb phrase/Frase verbal. *Ver Phrase.*

Verb tense/Tiempo verbal. El tiempo de un verbo indica cuándo ocurre la acción.

> **Present tense/Presente.** Indica una acción que sucede regularmente.
> **Past tense/Pasado.** Indica una acción que ya sucedió.
> **Future tense/Futuro.** Indica una acción que va a suceder.
> En inglés todos los tiempos verbales están formados por las cuatro partes principales del verbo: **base derivativa** *(base form)* *(freeze, congelar)*, **participio presente** *(present participle) (freezing, congelando)*, **pretérito simple** *(simple past form) (froze, congeló)* y **participio pasado** *(past participle) (frozen, congelado)*.
> Un **verbo regular** *(regular verb)* forma su pretérito simple y su participio pasado agregando la terminación *ed* al infinitivo. Los verbos que forman su pretérito y participio pasado de otra forma se llaman **verbos irregulares** *(irregular verbs)*.
> Además de los tiempos presente, pasado y futuro hay tres tiempos perfectos: **presente perfecto** *(present perfect)*, **pretérito perfecto** *(past perfect)* y **futuro perfecto** *(future perfect)*.
> Cada uno de los seis tiempos tiene una forma **durativa** *(progressive form)* que expresa acción continua.

Voice/Voz. La forma única que tiene un escritor o escritora de usar el tono y el estilo para comunicarse con los lectores.

Web site/Sitio Web. Sitio de World Wide Web que puede ser alcanzado mediante vínculos o una dirección Web o URL. *Ver también URL; World Wide Web.*

Word Choice/Léxico. El vocabulario que selecciona una escritora o escritor para presentar un significado.

Word processing/Procesador de palabras. Programa de computadora para escribir y editar un texto.

World Wide Web/World Wide Web. Sistema global que usa Internet y permite a los usuarios crear, vincularse y entrar a campos de información. *Ver también Internet.*

Writing process/Proceso de escritura. Serie de pasos o etapas por los que atraviesa un escritor para desarrollar sus ideas y comunicarlas.

*Este término o explicación solamente se aplica a la gramática inglesa.

*W*hat are the basic tools for building strong sentences, paragraphs, compositions, and research papers? You'll find them in this handbook—an easy-to-use "tool kit" for writers like you. Check out the helpful explanations, examples, and tips as you complete your writing assignments.

Writing Good Sentences

A sentence is a group of words that expresses a complete thought. Every sentence has a subject and a predicate.

Using Various Types of Sentences

How you craft a sentence—as a statement, question, command, or exclamation—depends on the job you want the sentence to do.

Type	Job It Does	Ways to Use It
Declarative	Makes a statement	Report information *October is National Pizza Month.*
Interrogative	Asks a question	Make your readers curious *Why is pizza so popular?*
Imperative	Gives a command or makes a request	Tell how to do something *Spread the toppings on the pizza dough.*
Exclamatory	Expresses strong feeling	Emphasize a startling fact *Every second, Americans eat about 350 slices of pizza!*

Varying Sentence Structure and Length

Many sentences in a row that look and sound alike can be boring. Vary your sentence openers to make your writing interesting.

- **Start a sentence with an adjective or an adverb.**
  Suddenly the sky turned dark.

- **Start a sentence with a phrase.**
  Like a fireworks show, lightning streaked across the sky.

- **Start a sentence with a clause.**
  As the thunderstorm began, people ran for cover.

✓ Check It Out

For more about how to vary sentence length and structure, review Unit 21, Sentence Combining, pages 618–627.

Many short sentences in a row make writing sound choppy and dull. To make your writing sound pleasing, vary the sentence length.

- **Combine short sentences into longer ones.**

   Tornadoes are also called twisters. They are spinning clouds. The clouds are funnel shaped.

   Tornadoes, also called twisters, are spinning funnel-shaped clouds.

- **Alternate shorter sentences with longer sentences.**

   Tornado winds are powerful. They can hurl cows into the air, tear trees from their roots, and turn cars upside down.

Using Parallelism

Parallelism is the use of a pair or a series of words, phrases, or sentences that have the same grammatical structure. Use parallelism to call attention to the items in the series and to create unity in writing.

Not Parallel   Gymnasts are strong, flexible, and move gracefully.
Parallel   Gymnasts are strong, flexible, and graceful.

Not Parallel   Do warm-up exercises to prevent sports injuries and for stretching your muscles.
Parallel   Do warm-up exercises to prevent sports injuries and to stretch your muscles.

Not Parallel   Stand on one leg, bend the other leg, and you should pull your heel.
Parallel   Stand on one leg, bend the other leg, and pull your heel.

Revising Wordy Sentences

Revise wordy sentences to make every word count.

- **Cut needless words.**

   Wordy   We need to have bike lanes in streets due to the fact that people like to ride their bikes to work and school, and it's not safe otherwise.
   Concise   We need bike lanes in streets so that people can safely ride to work and school.

- **Rewrite sentences opening with the word *there*.**

   Wordy   There are many kids riding their bikes in the street.
   Concise   Many kids ride their bikes in the street.

- **Change verbs in passive voice to active voice.**

   Wordy   Bikes are also ridden by grown-ups who want to keep fit.
   Concise   Grown-ups who want to keep fit also ride bikes.

TRY IT OUT

Write four sentences, one of each type—declarative, interrogative, imperative, and exclamatory—about food, sports, or another topic that interests you.

Writing Good Paragraphs

A paragraph is a group of sentences that relate to one main idea. A good paragraph develops a single idea and brings that idea into sharp focus. All the sentences flow smoothly from the beginning to the end of the paragraph.

Writing Unified Paragraphs

A paragraph has **unity** when the sentences belong together and center on a single main idea. One way to build a unified paragraph is to state the main idea in a topic sentence and then add related details.

Writing Topic Sentences A **topic sentence** gives your readers the "big picture"—a clear view of the most important idea you want them to know. Many effective expository paragraphs (paragraphs that convey information) start with a topic sentence that tells the key point right away.

Elaborating Topic Sentences Elaboration gives your readers a specific, more detailed picture of the main idea stated in your topic sentence. Elaboration is a technique you can use to include details that develop, support, or explain the main idea. The following chart shows various kinds of elaboration you might try.

Revising Tip

To make a paragraph unified, leave out details that do not relate to the topic sentence.

Topic Sentence: The state of Florida is known for its alligators.	
Descriptions	Alligators look like dinosaurs from millions of years ago.
Facts and statistics	Alligators can weigh as much as six hundred pounds.
Examples	Alligators eat a wide variety of foods, such as fish, insects, turtles, frogs, and small mammals.
Anecdotes (brief stories)	Silvia almost fainted when she came home to find an alligator paddling around in her swimming pool.
Reasons	Face-to-face encounters with alligators are now common because people have built golf courses over the animals' habitat.

Writing Coherent Paragraphs

A paragraph has **coherence** when all the sentences flow smoothly and logically from one to the next. All the sentences in a paragraph *cohere,* or "stick together," in a way that makes sense. To be sure your writing is coherent, choose a pattern of organization that fits your topic and use transition words and phrases to link ideas.

Organizing Paragraphs A few basic patterns of organization are listed below. Choose the pattern that helps you meet your specific writing goal.

- Use **chronological order,** or time order, to tell a story or to explain the steps in a process.
- Use **spatial order** to order your description of places, people, and things. You might describe the details in the order you see them— for example, from top to bottom or from near to far.
- Use **order of importance** to show how you rank opinions, facts, or details from the most to least important or the reverse.

Using Transitions Linking words and phrases, called **transitions,** act like bridges between sentences or between paragraphs. Transitions, such as the ones shown below, can make the organization of your paragraphs stronger by showing how ideas are logically related.

To show time order or sequence
after, at the beginning, finally, first, last year, later, meanwhile, next, now, second, sometimes, soon, yesterday

To show spatial relationships
above, ahead, around, at the top, below, beyond, down, here, inside, near, on top of, opposite, outside, over, there, under, within

To show importance or degree
above all, first, furthermore, in addition, mainly, most important, second

✓ Check It Out

For more about transitions, see page 72.

TRY IT OUT

Copy the following paragraph on your paper. Underline the topic sentence. Cross out the sentence that is unrelated to the topic sentence. Add a transition to make a clear connection between two of the sentences.

A local artist creates weird and funny sculptures from fruits and vegetables. First he uses a sharp knife to carve faces that look like animals, such as bears and pigs. He glues on tiny beans to make eyes. Finally he uses beet juice to paint the mouth. Although the process sounds easy, it requires great imagination. The octopus sculpted from a banana is the silliest work of art I've ever seen.

Writing Good Compositions

A composition is a short paper made up of several paragraphs, with a clear introduction, body, and conclusion. A good composition presents a clear, complete message about a specific topic. Ideas flow logically from one sentence to the next and from one paragraph to the next.

Making a Plan

The suggestions in the chart below can help you shape the information in each part of your composition to suit your writing purpose.

Introductory Paragraph

Your introduction should interest readers in your topic and capture their attention. You may

- give background
- use a quotation
- ask a question
- tell an anecdote, or brief story

Include a **thesis statement,** a sentence or two stating the main idea you will develop in the composition.

Body Paragraphs

Elaborate on your thesis statement in the body paragraphs. You may

- offer proof
- give examples
- explain ideas

Stay focused and keep your body paragraphs on track. Remember to

- develop a single idea in each body paragraph
- arrange the paragraphs in a logical order
- use transitions to link one paragraph to the next

Concluding Paragraph

Your conclusion should bring your composition to a satisfying close. You may

- sum up main points
- tie the ending to the beginning by restating the main idea or thesis in different words
- make a call to action if your goal is to persuade readers

Drafting Tip

You may need two paragraphs to introduce your topic. The first can tell an anecdote; the second can include your thesis statement. See page 831 for an example.

Drafting Tip

A good conclusion follows logically from the rest of the piece of writing and leaves the reader with something to think about. Make sure that you do not introduce new or unrelated material in a conclusion.

Using the 6+1 Trait® Model

What are some basic terms you can use to discuss your writing with your teacher or classmates? What should you focus on as you revise and edit your compositions? Check out the following seven terms, or traits, that describe the qualities of strong writing. Learn the meaning of each trait and find out how using the traits can improve your writing.

Ideas The message or the theme and the details that develop it

Writing is clear when readers can grasp the meaning of your ideas right away. Check to see whether you're getting your message across.

✔ Does the title suggest the theme of the composition?

✔ Does the composition focus on a single narrow topic?

✔ Is the thesis, or main idea, clearly stated?

✔ Do well-chosen details elaborate the main idea?

Organization The arrangement of main points and supporting details

A good plan of organization steers your readers in the right direction and guides them easily through your composition—from start to finish. Find a structure, or order, that best suits your topic and writing purpose. Check to see whether you've ordered your key ideas and details in a way that keeps your readers on track.

✔ Are the beginning, middle, and end clearly linked?

✔ Is the order of ideas easy to follow?

✔ Does the introduction capture your readers' attention?

✔ Do sentences and paragraphs flow from one to the next in a way that makes sense?

✔ Does the conclusion wrap up the composition?

Voice A writer's unique way of using tone and style

Your writing voice comes through when your readers sense that a real person is communicating with them. Readers will respond to the **tone,** or the attitude, that you express toward a topic and to the **style,** the way that you use language and write sentences. Read your work aloud to see whether your writing voice comes through.

✔ Does your writing sound interesting when you read it aloud?

✔ Does your writing show what you think about your topic?

✔ Does your writing sound like you—or does it sound like you're imitating someone else?

Revising Tip

Use the cut-and-paste features of your word processing program to experiment with the structure—the arrangement of sentences or paragraphs. Choose the clearest, most logical order for your final draft.

6+1 Trait® is a registered trademark of Northwest Regional Educational Laboratory, which does not endorse this product.

Word Choice The vocabulary a writer uses to convey meaning

Words work hard. They carry the weight of your meaning, so make sure you choose them carefully. Check to see whether the words you choose are doing their jobs well.

✔ Do you use lively verbs to show action?

✔ Do you use vivid words to create word pictures in your readers' minds?

✔ Do you use precise words to explain your ideas simply and clearly?

Sentence Fluency The smooth rhythm and flow of sentences that vary in length and style

The best writing is made up of sentences that flow smoothly from one sentence to the next. Writing that is graceful also sounds musical—rhythmical rather than choppy. Check for sentence fluency by reading your writing aloud.

✔ Do your sentences vary in length and structure?

✔ Do transition words and phrases show connections between ideas and sentences?

✔ Does parallelism help balance and unify related ideas?

Conventions Correct spelling, grammar, usage, and mechanics

A composition free of errors makes a good impression on your readers. Mistakes can be distracting, and they can blur your message. Try working with a partner to spot errors and correct them. Use this checklist to help you.

✔ Are all words spelled correctly?

✔ Are all proper nouns—as well as the first word of every sentence—capitalized?

✔ Is your composition free of sentence fragments?

✔ Is your composition free of run-on sentences?

✔ Are punctuation marks—such as apostrophes, commas, and end marks—inserted in the right places?

Presentation The way words and design elements look on a page

Appearance matters, so make your compositions inviting to read. Handwritten papers should be neat and legible. If you're using a word processor, double-space the lines of text and choose a readable font. Other design elements—such as boldfaced headings, bulleted lists, pictures, and charts—can help you present information effectively as well as make your papers look good.

Revising Tip

Listen carefully to the way your sentences sound when someone else reads them aloud. If you don't like what you hear, revise for sentence fluency. You might try adding variety to your sentence openers or combining sentences to make them sound less choppy.

✔ **Check It Out**

See the Troubleshooter, pages 304–327, for help in correcting common errors in your writing.

Evaluating a Composition Read this sample composition, which has been evaluated using the 6+1 Trait® model.

Ideas The focus is clear from the start. The thesis statement suggests the organizational structure of the composition.

Sentence Fluency A variety of sentence types helps the writing flow smoothly.

Conventions The composition is free of errors in spelling, grammar, usage, and mechanics.

Word Choice Notice the use of strong, vivid verbs, such as *persevered, diagnosed,* and *defied.*

Organization Paragraphs follow the order suggested in the introduction. The repetition of key words links ideas from one paragraph to the next.

Voice The writer's values and attitude toward the topic are clearly expressed.

True Courage

Are you courageous? According to *Webster's Dictionary,* if you have the "mental or moral strength to venture, persevere, and withstand danger, fear, or difficulty," you are. Three people who have shown mental or moral strength are Stacy Allison, Lou Gehrig, and Rosa Parks. Although the challenges they faced were different, their responses were similar. Their actions define what courage truly is.

For Stacy Allison, courage came one step at a time. In 1987 she tried to climb Mount Everest, the tallest mountain in the world. She and three other experienced climbers had spent two years carefully planning the climb. However, they couldn't have planned on a heavy snowstorm, which forced them down the mountain. After such a disappointing defeat, most people would have given up their dream, but Allison was not like most people. The following year, she returned to Everest, and despite the dangers and difficulties, she persevered. Her courage paid off, and she became the first woman from the United States to reach the summit of Mount Everest.

Baseball great Lou Gehrig had another kind of mountain to climb. Gehrig began playing first base for the New York Yankees in 1925. In the years that followed, he set many records, some of which stood until the 1990s. He left baseball in 1939 when he was diagnosed with a deadly disease called ALS. But he didn't leave life then. He bravely battled his disease and even gave a speech at Yankee Stadium, though he was too weak to stand without support. Less than two years later he was gone, but his courage is still remembered.

Rosa Parks's courage is also unforgettable. To me, she is the most courageous person of all. On December 1, 1955, Parks defied Alabama law and refused to give up her seat on a bus to a white person. She was arrested, but she took her case all the way to the Supreme Court. The Court later ruled that segregated buses were unconstitutional. Unlike Allison, Parks did not plan to make history. Unlike Gehrig, she was not already famous and admired. She was just an ordinary working woman who found the moral strength to challenge an unfair law. She stands as an everlasting example of what courage can do.

Stacy Allison, Lou Gehrig, and Rosa Parks had the mental and moral strength to persevere. Instead of giving in to difficulty or fear, they managed to overcome their challenges with dignity. Do you have what it takes to be courageous? If you follow their examples, you might find that you do.

Writing Good Research Papers

A research paper reports facts and ideas gathered from various sources about a specific topic. A good research paper blends information from reliable sources with the writer's original thoughts and ideas. The final draft follows a standard format for presenting information and citing sources.

Exploring a Variety of Sources

Once you've narrowed the topic of your research paper, you'll need to hunt for the best information. You might start by reading an encyclopedia article on your topic to learn some basic information. Then widen your search to include both primary and secondary sources.

- **Primary sources** are records of events by the people who witnessed them. Examples include diaries, letters, speeches, photos, posters, interviews, and radio and TV news broadcasts that include eyewitness interviews.
- **Secondary sources** contain information that is often based on primary sources. The creators of secondary sources conduct original research and then report their findings. Examples include encyclopedias, textbooks, biographies, magazine articles, Web site articles, and educational films.

When you find a secondary source that you can use for your report, check to see whether the author has given credit to his or her sources of information in **footnotes, endnotes,** or a **bibliography.** Tracking down such sources can lead you to more information you can use.

If you're exploring your topic on the Internet, look for Web sites that are sponsored by government institutions, famous museums, and reliable organizations. If you find a helpful site, check to see whether it contains links to other Web sites you can use.

Evaluating Sources

As you conduct your research, do a little detective work and investigate the sources you find. Begin by asking some key questions so you can decide whether you've tracked down reliable resources that are suitable for your purpose. Some important questions to ask about your sources are listed in the box on the next page.

Research Tip

Look for footnotes at the bottom of a page. Look for endnotes at the end of a chapter or a book. Look for a bibliography at the end of a book.

Ask Questions About Your Sources

✔ **Is the information useful?**
Find sources that are closely related to your research topic.

✔ **Is the information easy to understand?**
Look for sources that are geared toward readers your age.

✔ **Is the information new enough?**
Look for sources that were recently published if you need the most current facts and figures.

✔ **Is the information trustworthy and true?**
Check to see whether the author documents the source of facts and supports opinions with reasons and evidence. Also check out the background of the authors. They should be well-known experts on the topic that you're researching.

✔ **Is the information balanced and fair?**
Read with a critical eye. Does the source try to persuade readers with a one-sided presentation of information? Or is the source balanced, approaching a topic from various perspectives? Be on the lookout for **propaganda** and for sources that reflect an author's **bias,** or prejudice. Make sure that you learn about a topic from more than one angle by reviewing several sources of information.

Giving Credit Where Credit Is Due

When you write a research paper, you support your own ideas with information that you've gleaned from your primary and secondary sources. But presenting someone else's ideas as if they were your own is **plagiarism,** a form of cheating. You can avoid plagiarism by citing, or identifying, the sources of your information within the text of your paper. The chart below tells what kinds of information you do and don't need to cite in your paper.

DO credit the source of . . .	DON'T credit the source of . . .
• direct quotations	• information that can be found in many places—dates, facts, ideas, and concepts that are considered common knowledge
• summaries and paraphrases, or restatements, of someone else's viewpoints, original ideas, and conclusions	
• photos, art, charts, and other visuals	• your own unique ideas
• little-known facts or statistics	

Citing Sources Within Your Paper The most common method of crediting sources is with parenthetical documentation within the text. Generally a reference to the source and page number is included in parentheses at the end of each quotation, paraphrase, or summary of information borrowed from a source. An in-text citation points readers to a corresponding entry in your **works-cited list**—a list of all your sources, complete with publication information, that will appear as the final page of your paper. The Modern Language Association (MLA) recommends the following guidelines for crediting sources in text.

✓ **Check It Out**

Study the sample research paper on pages 831–832 to see the relationship between parenthetical documentation and a works-cited list.

- **Put in parentheses the author's last name and the page number where you found the information.**

  All too often the injury becomes infected, and then the manatee dies (Clark 35).

- **If the author's name is mentioned in the sentence, put only the page number in parentheses.**

  Margaret G. Clark says that it's common for manatees to die from infected injuries (35).

- **If no author is listed, put the title or a shortened version of the title in parentheses. Include a page number if you have one.**

  Accidents involving floodgates and canal locks are the second leading cause of manatee deaths ("Manatee Mortality").

Preparing the Final Draft

Ask your teacher how to format the final draft. Most English teachers will ask you to follow the MLA guidelines listed below.

- Put a heading in the upper left-hand corner of the first page with your name, your teacher's name, and the date on separate lines.
- Center the title on the line below the heading.
- Number the pages one-half inch from the top in the right-hand corner. After page one, put your last name before the page number.
- Set one-inch margins on all sides of every page; double-space the lines of text.
- Include an alphabetized, double-spaced works-cited list as the last page of your final draft. All sources noted in parenthetical citations in the paper must be listed.

On the next three pages, you'll find sample style sheets that can help you prepare the list of sources—the final page of the research paper. Use the one your teacher prefers.

MLA Style

MLA style is most often used in English and social studies classes. Center the title *Works Cited* at the top of your list.

Source	Style
Book with one author	Price-Groff, Claire. *The Manatee.* Farmington Hills: Lucent, 1999.
Book with two or three authors	Tennant, Alan, Gerard T. Salmon, and Richard B. King. *Snakes of North America.* Lanham: Lone Star Books, 2003. [If a book has more than three authors, name only the first author and then write "et al." (Latin abbreviation for "and others").]
Book with an editor	Follett, C. B., ed. *Grrrrr: A Collection of Poems About Bears.* Sausalito: Arctos, 2000.
Book with organization or group as author or editor	National Air and Space Museum. *The Official Guide to the Smithsonian Air and Space Museum.* Washington: Smithsonian Institution Press, 2002.
Work from an anthology	Soto, Gary. "To Be a Man." *Hispanic American Literature: An Anthology.* Ed. Rodolfo Cortina. Lincolnwood: NTC, 1998. 340–341.
Introduction in a published book	Weintraub, Stanley. Introduction. *Great Expectations.* By Charles Dickens. New York: Signet, 1998. v–xii.
Encyclopedia article	"Whales." *World Book Encyclopedia.* 2003.
Weekly magazine article	Trillin, Calvin. "Newshound." *New Yorker* 29 Sept. 2003: 70–81.
Monthly magazine article	Knott, Cheryl. "Code Red." *National Geographic* Oct. 2003: 76–81.
Online magazine article	Rauch, Jonathan. "Will Frankenfood Save the Planet?" *Atlantic Online* 292.3 (Oct. 2003). 15 Dec. 2003 <http://www.theatlantic.com/issues/2003/10/rauch.htm>.
Newspaper article	Bertram, Jeffrey. "African Bees: Fact or Myth?" *Orlando Sentinel* 18 Aug. 1999: D2.
Unsigned article	"Party-Line Snoops." *Washington Post* 24 Sept. 2003: A28.
Internet	"Manatees." *SeaWorld/Busch Gardens Animal Information Database.* 2002. Busch Entertainment Corp. 3 Oct. 2003 <http://www.seaworld.org/infobooks/Manatee/home.html>.
Radio or TV program	"Orcas." *Champions of the Wild.* Animal Planet. Discovery Channel. 21 Oct. 2003.
Videotape or DVD	*Living with Tigers.* DVD. Discovery, 2003. [For a videotape (VHS) version, replace "DVD" with "Videocassette."]
Interview	Salinas, Antonia. E-mail interview. 23–24 Oct. 2003. [If an interview takes place in person, replace "E-mail" with "Personal"; if it takes place on the telephone, use "Telephone."]

CMS Style

CMS style was created by the University of Chicago Press to meet its publishing needs. This style, which is detailed in *The Chicago Manual of Style* (CMS), is used in a number of subject areas. Center the title *Bibliography* at the top of your list.

Writing & Research Handbook

Source	Style
Book with one author	Price-Groff, Claire. *The Manatee.* Farmington Hills, MI: Lucent, 1999.
Book with multiple authors	Tennant, Alan, Gerard T. Salmon, and Richard B. King. *Snakes of North America.* Lanham, TX: Lone Star Books, 2003. [For a book with more than ten authors, name only the first seven authors and then write "et al." (Latin abbreviation for "and others").]
Book with an editor	Follett, C. B., ed. *Grrrrr: A Collection of Poems About Bears.* Sausalito, CA: Arctos, 2000.
Book with organization or group as author or editor	National Air and Space Museum. *The Official Guide to the Smithsonian Air and Space Museum.* Washington, DC: Smithsonian Institution Press, 2002.
Work from an anthology	Soto, Gary. "To Be a Man." *Hispanic American Literature: An Anthology,* edited by Rodolfo Cortina, 340–341. Lincolnwood, IL: NTC, 1998.
Introduction in a published book	Dickens, Charles. *Great Expectations.* New introduction by Stanley Weintraub. New York: Signet, 1998.
Encyclopedia article	[Credit for encyclopedia articles goes in your text, not in your bibliography.]
Weekly magazine article	Trillin, Calvin. "Newshound." *New Yorker,* September 29, 2003, 70–81.
Monthly magazine article	Knott, Cheryl. "Code Red." *National Geographic,* October 2003, 76–81.
Online magazine article	Rauch, Jonathan. "Will Frankenfood Save the Planet?" *Atlantic Online* 292, no. 3 (October 2003). http://www.theatlantic.com/issues/2003/10/rauch.htm.
Newspaper article	[Credit for newspaper articles goes in your text, not in your bibliography.]
Unsigned article	[Credit for unsigned newspaper articles goes in your text, not in your bibliography.]
Internet	Busch Entertainment Corp. "Manatees." *SeaWorld/Busch Gardens Animal Information Database.* http://www.seaworld.org/infobooks/Manatee/home.html.
Radio or TV program	[Credit for radio and TV programs goes in your text, not in your bibliography.]
Videotape or DVD	*Living with Tigers.* Discovery, 2003. DVD. [For a videotape (VHS) version, replace "DVD" with "Videocassette."]
Interview	[Credit for interviews goes in your text, not in your bibliography.]

APA Style

The American Psychological Association (APA) style is commonly used in the sciences. Center the title *References* at the top of your list.

Source	Style
Book with one author	Price-Groff, Claire. (1999). *The manatee.* Farmington Hills, MI: Lucent.
Book with multiple authors	Tennant, A., Salmon, G. T., & King, R. B. (2003). *Snakes of North America.* Lanham, TX: Lone Star Books. [For a book with more than six authors, name only the first six authors and then write "et al." (Latin abbreviation for "and others").]
Book with an editor	Follett, C. B. (Ed.). (2000). *Grrrrr: A collection of poems about bears.* Sausalito, CA: Arctos.
Book with organization or group as author or editor	National Air and Space Museum. (2002). *The official guide to the Smithsonian Air and Space Museum.* Washington, DC: Smithsonian Institution Press.
Work from an anthology	Soto, G. (1998). To be a man. In R. Cortina (Ed.), *Hispanic American literature: An anthology* (pp. 340–341). Lincolnwood, IL: NTC.
Introduction in a published book	[Credit for introductions goes in your text, not in your references.]
Encyclopedia article	Whales. (2003). In *World Book encyclopedia.* Chicago: World Book.
Weekly magazine article	Trillin, C. (2003, September 29). Newshound. *The New Yorker,* 70–81.
Monthly magazine article	Knott, C. (2003, October). Code red. *National Geographic, 204,* 76–81.
Online magazine article	Rauch, J. (2003, October). Will Frankenfood save the planet? *Atlantic Online, 292.* Retrieved from http://www.theatlantic.com/issues/2003/10/rauch.htm
Newspaper article	Bertram, J. (1999, August 18). African bees: Fact or myth? *The Orlando Sentinel,* p. D2.
Unsigned article	Party-line snoops. (2003, September 24). *The Washington Post,* p. A28.
Internet	Busch Entertainment Corp. (2003). Manatees. In *SeaWorld/Busch Gardens animal information database.* Retrieved October 3, 2003, from http://www.seaworld.org/infobooks/Manatee/home.html
Radio or TV program	Orcas. (2003, October 21). *Champions of the wild* [Television series episode]. Animal Planet. Silver Spring, MD: Discovery Channel.
Videotape or DVD	*Living with tigers.* (2003). [DVD]. Discovery. [For a videotape (VHS) version, replace "DVD" with "Videocassette."]
Interview	[Credit for interviews goes in your text, not in your references.]

Evaluating a Research Paper Read this sample research paper, which has been evaluated using the 6+1 Trait® model.

The Endangered Manatee

When Christopher Columbus sailed to the New World, he thought he saw mermaids, but they didn't look like the ones he'd seen in paintings. In his journal, he wrote that these mermaids were "not so beautiful as they are painted, since in some ways they have a face like a man" (Ellis 88). Columbus was most likely describing West Indian manatees. These gentle gray-brown sea mammals have hairy snouts, and they weigh about a thousand pounds.

Manatees still live in Florida's warm waters, but possibly not for much longer. The number of manatees in the region has been declining. As of July 2000, only about twenty-four hundred manatees remained (Sawicki 6). The manatees are still dying off, even though environmental laws have been passed to help them survive. What is responsible for the decline of this gentle giant? Sadly, the answer is people. The development of Florida's coastal areas spelled trouble for manatees. Boats, canal locks, and pollution are the top three causes of manatee injuries and deaths.

Boating is fun for people, but it can be harmful to manatees. In fact, the chief cause of manatee deaths in recent years has been collisions with boats ("Manatee Mortality"). Manatees eat plants that grow deep in the water, but like seals and other water mammals, they must rise to the surface to breathe. As they rise to the surface, they sometimes swim into the path of an oncoming motorboat or another water craft. Because manatees are slow swimmers, they cannot get out of the way. And even if they could, they might not know which direction they should swim. Scientists believe that manatees cannot hear low-frequency sounds, such as the hum of a motorboat. As a result, manatees are often hit and killed by boats. Not every accident is deadly: The Mote Marine Laboratory in Sarasota, Florida, estimates that 80 percent of Florida's manatees have been hit at least once by marine craft (Koeppel 68).

Accidents involving floodgates and canal locks are the second leading cause of manatee deaths ("Manatee Mortality"). To understand why these accidents occur, picture what floodgates and canal locks look like and what they do. Try to imagine large underwater walls that can be raised and lowered or opened and closed to control water levels. When those walls are opened, the rushing water creates a strong current. That current is strong enough to pull in just about anything around it, including slow-moving manatees. Some manatees drown when they are pulled in by the current and cannot get to the surface of the water to breathe. Others caught between the gates are crushed or trapped and drowned (Clark 37).

(continued)

Organization The opening paragraph captures readers' attention with an interesting anecdote.

Ideas The thesis statement clearly states the main point or central idea.

Organization The body paragraphs follow the order suggested in the thesis statement.

Ideas Carefully chosen details support the paragraph's main idea. The writer uses parenthetical citations (MLA style) to document the sources of information.

Conventions The composition is free of errors in grammar, usage, spelling, and mechanics.

Sentence Fluency Sentence openings vary, and the writing flows smoothly from one idea to the next.

Objects that people put in the water also cause problems that can result in injury or death of manatees. For example, fishermen set small floating objects called buoys at the water's surface to warn boaters of the crab traps below. The fishermen attach the traps to the buoys with wires or strong plastic lines that can tangle around a manatee's flippers. When the manatee struggles to free itself, it can be injured. All too often the injury becomes infected, and then the manatee dies (Clark 35). Manatees have also been known to choke to death on fishhooks and on garbage that people have thrown into the water.

Sentence Fluency The use of parallelism effectively ties together related ideas.

Environmental laws are supposed to protect the manatee from all these dangers. But according to Judith Valle of Save the Manatee Club, a group that works to protect manatees, enforcement of those laws is currently "pathetic" (Sawicki 6). What can we do to save the manatee? We can begin by putting an end to water pollution that kills manatees and other organisms, large and small. We can avoid boating in areas where manatees commonly swim. And we can invest in new technologies that will help keep manatees safe. For example, scientists are working on warning devices that could be attached to boats and canal locks that would keep manatees away. These devices send out high-frequency sounds that manatees can hear (Eliot). If people are responsible for the decline of manatees, then we must also be responsible for their ultimate survival.

Voice The writer's attitude toward the topic shines through.

Works Cited

Clark, Margaret Goff. *The Vanishing Manatee.* New York: Cobblehill, 1990.

Eliot, John L. "Deaf to Danger: Manatees Can't Hear Boats." *National Geographic* Feb. 2000: Earth Almanac section.

Ellis, Richard. *Monsters of the Sea.* New York: Knopf, 1994.

Koeppel, Dan. "Kiss of the Manatee." *Travel Holiday* Feb. 1999: 66–69.

"Manatee Mortality." *Save the Manatee Club.* Save the Manatee Club, Inc. 31 Oct. 2003 <http://www.savethemanatee.org/mort.htm>.

Sawicki, Stephen. "Manatee Protectors Turn to the Courts." *Animals* July 2000: 6.

Presentation A properly formatted works-cited list is part of every good research report. This one follows MLA style (see page 828). Remember to double-space your entire report and to put your works-cited list on a separate sheet of paper.

INDEX

paper
Inside address, of business
    letter, 287
Institutions, capitalizing names
    of, 579
Instructions
    giving, 753–754
    listening to, 743
Intensifiers, 463, 801
Intensive pronouns, 439
Interjections, 487, 589, 801
    exclamation point after,
        487, 589
    list of common, 487
Internet, 223, 643, 782–793, 801
    acronyms, 790
    Boolean search, 784–785
    bookmarks/favorites, 785, 798
    browser, 784
    e-mail, 27, 69, 787–789, 800
    etiquette, 788–789
    evaluating sources, 791
    keyword, 784
    mailing list, 789
    metasearch engine, 784
    online library, 643
    search engine, 784
    smileys, 790
    spam, 788
    subject directory, 784
    URL, 785–786
    World Wide Web, 782, 805
Interpretations, 801
Interrogative pronouns, 441
Interrogative sentences, 357, 441,
    589, 817
    diagraming, 564
Interrupters, comma with, 591
Intervening expressions,
    commas to set off, 591
Interviews, 341–344, 801
    conducting, 341, 343, 750–751
    preparing for, 749–750
    for research reports,
        228–231
    subjects for, 748–749
    tips for, 751
Into, in, 553
Intransitive verbs, 401
Introduction, 801, 821
    to a presentation, 756
    report, 233, 234
Irregular comparative forms, 455,

465
Irregular verbs, 415, 417, 805
Italics, for titles of works, 599
Items in a series, 591
Its, it's, 324, 555

Jargon, 801
Journal, 8, 801
Journal writing, 9, 13, 17, 21, 23,
    25, 29, 31, 47, 51, 55, 59, 63,
    67, 71, 75, 79, 83, 89, 115,
    119, 123, 127, 131, 135, 141,
    157, 161, 165, 167, 169, 173,
    177, 179, 181, 187, 201, 205,
    209, 213, 217, 221, 225, 229,
    233, 237, 241, 247, 263, 267,
    271, 275, 279, 283, 287, 291,
    297
    computer entries for, 13
    in learning log, 14
    tips for, 13

Languages
    capitalizing names of, 579
    See Vocabulary; Words
Lay, lie, 555
Learn, teach, 555
Learning log, 14, 15, 801
Legibility, 78, 82
Letters
    of complaint, 286–289, 330
    personal, 11, 18, 27, 211
    See also Business letters;
        Business writing
Letters of the alphabet apostrophe
    to form plural of, 601
Lexicon, 801
Library
    arrangement of, 631–633
    audiovisual materials, 633
    card catalog, 633, 637
    computer catalog, 633, 636–637
    Dewey decimal system in,
        634–635
    finding books in, 632, 638
    getting information from, 225
    library catalog in, 633, 636–637
    nonprint resources in, 643–644
    periodicals in, 632, 645–646

Reader's Guide to Periodical
    Literature in, 645
    reference books in, 633,
        639–642, 647–652
Library catalog, 633, 636–637
Lie, lay, 555
Linking verb, 405
    defined, 405
    list of, 405
    predicate adjective after, 405,
        451, 455
    predicate nominative after,
        405
Listening
    active, 743–746, 750, 753
    in class, 743
    to commercials, 745–746
    critical, 743–747
    focused, 743
    for information, 743
    interpreting special clues, 743
    in interview, 230
    note taking while, 696
    to persuasive speech, 744–747
    tips for effective, 743
    See also Speaking; Speech
Listening and speaking, 11, 19, 27,
    81, 117, 125, 137, 159, 163,
    171, 175, 203, 211, 215, 219,
    223, 227, 231, 235, 239, 243,
    269, 273, 277, 285, 289, 293
Listing, 9, 21, 25, 60, 137, 159,
    161, 165, 175, 201, 205, 213,
    223, 261, 801
Literary analysis, 801
Literature. For a complete listing
    of the literature in this book,
    see p. xxv.
Literature, responding to, 38, 95,
    148, 192, 254, 302
    See also Writing about
        literature
Logical fallacy, 801
Logical organization, 127
Logical thinking, 276
Loose, lose, 555

Magazine writing, 97–107
Magazines. See Periodicals
Main clauses, 501, 593
Main idea

ACKNOWLEDGMENTS

Text

UNIT ONE From *The Diary of Latoya Hunter*. Copyright © 1992 by Latoya Hunter. Reprinted by permission of Crown Publishers, a division of Random House, Inc.

UNIT TWO From "Smart, Cool and on the Air" by Maisha Maurant, reprinted by permission of the Detroit Free Press and Copyright Clearance Center.

From *The Clay Marble* by Minfong Ho. Copyright © 1991 by Minfong Ho. Reprinted by permission of Farrar Straus Giroux.

From "Ode to la Tortilla" by Gary Soto, from *Neighborhood Odes: Poems by Gary Soto*. Copyright © 1992 by Gary Soto. Reprinted by permission of Harcourt, Inc.

UNIT THREE From *Song of the Gargoyle,* by Zilpha Keatley Snyder. Copyright © 1991 by Zilpha Keatley Snyder. Used by permission of Dell Publishing, a division of Random House, Inc.

From *The Gathering* by Virginia Hamilton. Copyright © 1981 by Virginia Hamilton. By permission of Greenwillow Books, a division of HarperCollins Publishers, Inc.

UNIT FOUR "User Friendly" by T. Ernesto Bethancourt, copyright © 1989 by T. Ernesto Bethancourt, from *Connections: Short Stories* by Donald R. Gallo, Editor. Used by permission of Delacorte Press, a division of Random House, Inc.

"A Huge Black Umbrella" by Marjorie Agosin. Reprinted by permission.

UNIT FIVE From *Living Treasure* by Laurence Pringle. Copyright © 1991 by Laurence Pringle. By permission of Morrow Junior Books, a division of HarperCollins Publishers, Inc.

UNIT SIX Taken from *Gifted Hands* by Ben Carson. Copyright © 1990 by Review & Herald Publishing Association. Used by permission of Zondervan Publishing House.

"The Liberry" by Bel Kaufman. Reprinted by permission of the author.

Photo

Cover, KS Studio; **vi vii** Ralph J. Brunke; **viii** © Time, Inc; **ix** Laura Derichs; **x** NASA; **xi** (t)Bettmann/CORBIS, (b)Focus on Sports; **xii** *Circus Parade*, 1979. Kathy Jakobsen. Oil on canvas, 24" x 36". Museum of American Folk Art, New York, NY, gift of Robert Bishop 1979.11.1; **xv** Allan Landau; **xvi** Courtesy R.H. Love Gallery; **xvii** Pete Saloutos/Photographic Resources; **xix** Courtesy Phyllis Kind Gallery, Chicago/New York; **xxi** Courtesy Brooke Alexander Gallery; **xxii** Hirshhorn Museum and Sculpture Garden, Smithsonian Institution, gift of the Joseph H. Hirshhorn Foundation, 1974. Photograph by Lee Stalsworth; **xxiii** Allan Landau, *Altas of the Living World* by David Attenborough. ©1989 by Marshall Editions Ltd. Reprinted by permission of Houghton Mifflin Co. All rights reserved; **xxiv** Giraudon/Art Resource, NY, with special authorization of the City of Bayeux; **xxv** Ralph J. Brunke; **xxvii** SEF/Art Resource; **xxviii** Gilson Ribeiro; **xxix** Giraudon/Art Resource, NY; **xxxii-1** Roger Winter; **2-3** Kevin Stillman/TXDOT; **4** Allan Landau; **5** Art Wise; **8 through 14** Ralph J. Brunke; **16** (t)David Woo/Stock Boston, (b)Ralph J. Brunke; **17 18** Ralph J. Brunke; **20** Tom Walker/Stock Boston; **21** Ralph J. Brunke; **23** Gilson Ribeiro; **24** Selection reprinted by permission of HarperColllins Publishers. Photo by Ralph J. Brunke; **26** Ralph J. Brunke; **28** Bob Daemmrich/The Image Works; **31** Richard Hutchings/PhotoEdit; **35** Giraudon/Art Resource, NY; **36** file photo; **39** Kevin Stillman/TXDOT; **40-41** Chris Shinn/Tony Stone Images; **42** William Jordan; **46 50** Allan Landau; **53** Picnic in Washington Park, Pat Thomas, Milwaukee, WI, Acrylic over oil on masonite. Dated 1975. 20 1/2 x 27 1/2". Collection of the Museum of American Folk Art, New York City; Gift of Rose Winters; **56 58 59** Allan Landau; **61** © 1992 Succession H. Matisse/ARS, New York/ Giraudon/Art Resource, NY; **62 63 64** Allan Landau; **65** National Museum of American Art, Washington, DC/Art Resource, NY; **66 70 74 75** Allan Landau; **77** Hirshhorn Museum and Sculpture Garden, Smithsonian Institution, Gift of the Joseph H. Hirshhorn Foundation, 1974. Photograph by Lee Stalsworth; **78 82 83** Allan Landau; **86** Bob Daemmrich/Stock Boston; **92** The Phillips Collection, Washington, DC; **94** Courtesy Bernice Steinbaum Gallery; **96** Chris Shinn/Tony Stone Images; **108-109** David Myers/Tony Stone Images; **112 113** Ralph J. Brunke; **114** Charles Seaborn/Odyssey Productions, Chicago; **116** Ralph J. Brunke; **118** *Fruit of the Spirit*, Martin Charlot © 1983; **122** John Elk III/Stock Boston; **124** (l)Robert Brenner/PhotoEdit, (r)Debby Davis/ PhotoEdit; **126** Pete Saloutos/Photographic Resources; **128** Gayna Hoffman/Stock Boston; **130** Laura Derichs; **131** (t)Laura Derichs, (b)Ralph J. Brunke; **132** (t)Laura Derichs, (b)Ralph J. Brunke; **134 135** Ralph J. Brunke; **138** Amy Etra/PhotoEdit; **143** Scala/Art Resource, NY; **144** Peter Blume. "Light of the World," 1932. Oil on composition board. 18 x 20 1/4 inches. (45.7 cm x 51.4 cm). Collection of the Whitney Museum of American Art. Purchase 33.5; **149** David Myers/Tony Stone Images; **150-151** Karl Weatherly/CORBIS; **152** (l)Tom Tondee, (r)Laura Derichs; **153 154** Laura Derichs; **156** Photofest; **160** Florence H. J. Ward; **168** From Alice's Adventures in Wonderland by Lewis Carroll, illustration, S. Michelle Wiggins. Copyright ©1983 by Armand Eisen. Reprinted by permission of Alfred A. Knopf, Inc; **172** Calvin and Hobbes © 1986 Watterson. Reprinted with permission of Universal Press Syndicate. All rights reserved; **176** NASA; **179** Boston Athenaeum; **181** Nathaniel Bruns; **184** Tony Freeman/PhotoEdit; **191** Bridgeman/Art Resource, NY; **193** Karl Weatherly/CORBIS; **194-195** Charles Doswell III/Tony Stone Images; **196** (t)Courtesy Monterey Bay Aquarium, (b)Charles Seaborn/Odyssey Productions, Chicago; **198 199** Ralph J. Brunke; **208** (l)Carl Roessler/Animals Animals, (r)Richard Kolar/Animals Animals; **212** Courtesy the Estate of Rube Goldberg; **216** Maresa Pryor/Earth Scenes; **220 222 226** Allan Landau; **228** Bob Daemmrich/Stock Boston; **230 232** Allan Landau; **236** Ralph J. Brunke; **241** (l)BET, (r)Focus on Sports; **244** Robert Brenner/PhotoEdit; **247** Lawrence Migdale/Stock Boston; **249** Courtesy of Patricia Gonzalez; **251** Courtesy of Kathryn Stewart; **254** Art Wise; **255** Charles Doswell III/Tony Stone Images; **256-257** Peter & Stef Lamberti/Tony Stone Images; **258** Christine Armstrong. © Review & Herald; **259** (t)Ralph J. Brunke, (b)William DeKay/ Detroit Free Press; **260** Ralph J. Brunke; **261** Art Wise; **262** James D. Watt/Animals Animals; **270** Allan Landau; **273** Courtesy John Weber Gallery; **274 278 290** Allan Landau; **294** Bob Daemmrich/ Tony Stone Images; **300** National Museum of American Art, Washington D.C./Art Resource, NY; **303** Peter & Stef Lamberti/Tony Stone Images; **304-305** CORBIS; **325** Ralph J. Brunke; **354-355**

Christie's Images/SuperStock; **357** (t)Mark Burnett/Stock Boston, (bl)Greenlar/The Image Works, (bc)John Cancalosi/Natural Selection, (br)Neal Mishler/Natural Selection; **375** American Museum of Natural History #4587 (2). Photo by Lynton Gardiner; **387** Bob Daemmrich; **395** Courtesy of Robert McCall; **399** Ralph J. Brunke; **426** Courtesy R.H. Love Gallery; **447** Michael Holford; **463** Malcolm S. Kirk/Peter Arnold, Inc; **475** © 1992 Charles Simonds, ARS, New York; **487** Robert Frerck/Tony Stone Worldwide; **489** SEF/Art Resource; **497** © 1986, Helen Oji. Collection of Doris and Jack Weintraub, New York, NY; **507** Focus on Sports; **517** Courtesy Phyllis Kind Gallery, New York/Chicago; **532** Courtesy Brooke Alexander Gallery; **539** (t)Bob Daemmrich, (b)Tony Freeman/PhotoEdit; **549** Giraudon/Art Resource, NY; **559** Scala/Art Resource, NY; **574** Tony Freeman/PhotoEdit; **585** Courtesy Elaine Horwitch Galleries, Scottsdale, Arizona; **589** Tony Freeman/PhotoEdit; **616** Phyllis Kind Gallery, New York/Chicago; **628-629** Burstein Collection/CORBIS; **631** Bill Bachman/ Photographic Resources; **640** From The World Book Encyclopedia © 1992 World Book, Inc. By permission of World Book, Inc; **641** Allan Landau, Atlas of the Living World by David Attenborough. © 1989 by Marshall Editions Ltd. Reprinted by permission of Houghton Mifflin Co. All rights reserved; **642** Aaron Haupt; **647** Ralph J. Brunke; **648** Courtesy of Macmillan Publishing; **654** Giraudon/Art Resource, NY, with special authorization of the city of Bayeux; **655** Art Resource, NY; **657 through 676** (gears)VCG/ FPG; **666** Tony Stone Images; **668** Tony Griff; **670** (l)Willie L. Hill, Jr./The Image Works, (r)Thomas R. Fletcher/Stock Boston; **685 through 749** Ralph J. Brunke; **765** (tl)Ian Howarth, (tc)The Kobal Collection, (tr)George Eastman House, (bl)Nick Vedros/Tony Stone Images, (br)D. Young-Wolff/Photo Edit; **767** (t)Ian Howarth, (b)D. Young-Wolff/Photo Edit; **768** George Eastman House; **770** (t)The Kobal Collection, (b)Photofest; **772** Nick Vedros/Tony Stone Images; **775** Tom & DeeAnn McCarthy/The Stock Market; **784** file photo; **794** Aaron Haupt.